DEVELOPMENT AND APPLICATIONS

OF

ATM

Selected Readings

Edited By

Mehmet Toy
Lucent Technologies
Bell Laboratories
Red Bank, New Jersey

Printed in the United States of America.

Editor - Mehmet Toy and Barbara Coburn
Typography/Layout - Jill R. Cals

Published by the Institute of Electrical and Electronics Engineers, Inc.
445 Hoes Lane, PO Box 1331, Piscataway, NJ 08855-1331

Library of Congress Cataloging-in-Publication Data available upon request

http://www.ieee.org/eab/

CONTENTS

IV.   ROUTING

V.   Performance/Delay Analysis

VI. EFFECTIVE BANDWIDTH MANAGMENT

VII. ATM NETWORK MANAGEMENT

VIII. APPLICATIONS

PREFACE

The book provides tutorial papers and an overview of ATM theory and applications, and probes deeper into details with more focused papers. It is intended to be useful for practicing researchers, system and development engineers as well as a reference for instructors and students.

Asynchronous Transfer Mode (ATM) is a revolutionary technology based on fixed-length cells. It is a switching and transmission technology that can support LAN and WAN, as well as voice, data and video traffic. Currently, switching and transmission technologies for LAN and WAN are quite different from those used for voice, data and video traffic. ATM has the potential to be the technology for the next-generation infrastructure for public and private networks. With ATM, there will be one type of network which will carry all types of traffic.

LAN access needs high bandwidth and low delay over long distances. Everyone knows that accessing a Web Site on the Internet can become a nightmare with the existing infrastructure. ATM, with its high bandwidth and fine degree of granularity and dynamic bandwidth allocation will be able to provide the bandwidth needed and use it efficiently. That, in turn, will improve service quality substantially.

The control and maintenance of the networks are crucial to service providers and users. Currently each network type has its own operating systems. Integrating various types of operating systems and training administrators on their use is very costly. With ATM, there will be one type of operating system, thus, integration of these systems that deal with different applications will be much easier.

However, managing ATM networks is challenging. Everything happens very quickly with large volumes in ATM. As the demand for a higher bandwidth grows, ATM switching technology will move from electrical to optical. The complexity of ATM network management systems will increase even more.

Despite ATM's slow start, it is fast becoming the cornerstone for future visual and multimedia applications. Research and standard contributions for offering voice, data, and video traffic over ATM, as well as the use of ATM for satellite and wireless applications are phenomenal. These are addressed here.

This book is organized into eight chapters. Chapter I explains the fundamentals of ATM. Chapter II discusses ATM switching architectures and implementation issues. Chapters III through VI address ATM traffic and congestion control, routing, ATM switching system and network performance analysis, and effective bandwidth management. Chapter VII focuses on network management issues of ATM networks. Finally, Chapter VIII discusses various ATM applications.

I would like to gratefully acknowledge the authors and publishers for their permission to reprint their work in this collection. Thanks are due to Barbara Coburn and Jill Cals for doing a fine job in this project. Finally I would like to dedicate this book to my parents Halit and Hatice Toy.

Mehmet Toy
Lucent Technologies
Bell Laboratories
Red Bank, New Jersey
July 5, 1996

Chapter 1

Concept

This chapter provides tutorials on ATM concept, ATM's benefits and shortcomings.

Computer Networks and ISDN Systems 24 (1992) 279–309
North-Holland

The Asynchronous Transfer Mode: a tutorial

Jean-Yves Le Boudec

IBM Research Division, Zürich Research Laboratory, Säumerstrasse 4, 8803 Rüschlikon, Switzerland

Abstract

Le Boudec, J.-Y., The Asynchronous Transfer Mode: a tutorial, Computer Networks and ISDN Systems 24 (1992) 279–309.

The Asynchronous Transfer Mode (ATM) is the switching and multiplexing technique chosen by CCITT for the broadband access to the ISDN. The user-network interface offers one physical channel over which connections are multiplexed using short, fixed length packets (called cells). The ATM layer in the network performs relaying functions, with every cell carrying a label used for switching.

This report is a tutorial. It aims at providing the reader with the background information that is necessary to understand the debate about potential virtues and shortcomings of the ATM.

Keywords: ATM, CCITT, SMDS, ISDN.

Contents

Correspondence to: Dr. J-Y. Le Boudec, IBM Research Division, Zürich Research Laboratory, Säumerstrasse 4, 8803 Rüschlikon, Switzerland. Fax +41(1) 710 3608.

1. Introduction

The Broadband User–Network Interface (UNI) being considered by CCITT [1,2] for the Integrated Services Digital Network (ISDN) offers a single physical channel over which all traffic is sent in short, fixed length packets (called cells). Cells are switched in the network based on the routing information contained in their headers. The associated multiplexing and switching technique is called the Asynchronous Transfer Mode (ATM). This differs significantly from the Narrow-band User–Network Interface, where several digital channels are offered, that are circuit switched in the network.

We use the terms Broadband ISDN (B-ISDN) and Narrowband IDSN (N-ISDN) to designate the part of the ISDN that uses the ATM, even though the CCITT view is that there is a single ISDN with both narrowband and broadband accesses.

In the B-ISDN, the *ATM layer* is in charge of transporting cells to their destinations. We present the details of it in Section 2. The ATM cells are carried by a transmission system, which builds the *physical layer*. This is described in Section 3. The ATM is intended to transport all services with the same format. Switching fabrics need not be aware of the services being transported. In

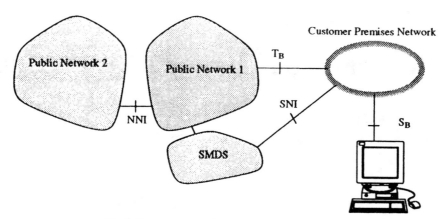

Fig. 1. The reference points or interfaces in this report.

Section 4, we discuss how various kinds of information (voice, data, animated images and multimedia) can make use of the ATM.

The ATM also underlies the Switched Multi-Megabit Data Service (SMDS) proposed by Bellcore as a future service of the Regional Bell Operating Companies. The SMDS is presented as a Metropolitan Area Network (MAN) service, that can evolve into a country-wide service. The relation between ATM and SMDS is described in Section 4.2.3.

The ATM is the subject of a heated debate among various players in the telecommunications arena. In Section 5, we introduce the reader to some of the technical issues that are at the heart of the debate.

The ATM can be used at bit rates below those of the B-ISDN; however, except when explicitly mentioned, "ATM" refers to the corresponding CCITT layer.

The T reference point is the boundary between a public network and private equipment;

(the T_B interfaces are thus defined at the T reference point; subscript "B" stands for 'Broadband"); the S point is the boundary between terminal equipment and private networks (see Fig. 1). The descriptions in this report relative to the UNI apply primarily to the T reference point.

The S_B interface definitions should be quite similar, if not identical. The Network–Node Interface is between public networks that participate in the B-ISDN. The Subscriber–Network Interface (SNI) (NNI) is defined for SMDS.

Abbreviations and acronyms are listed at the end.

2. The ATM layer

2.1. Label switching

With the ATM, information is carried in *fixed size* packets, called *cells* (Fig. 2).

Jean-Yves Le Boudec was born in France in 1958. He graduated from "Ecole Normale Supérieure de Saint-Cloud" (Paris, France), where he obtained the "Agrégation" in mathematics in 1980. He received his doctorate in 1984 from the University of Rennes, France. He then was assistant professor at INSA/IRISA, Rennes. In 1987 and 1988 he was with Bell Northern Research, Ottawa, Canada, as a Member of Scientific Staff in the Network and Product Traffic Design department. In 1988 he joined the IBM Zurich Research Laboratory at Rüschlikon, Switzerland. He is currently chairman of the technical committee of a RACE project. His interests are in the performance and architecture of communication systems, queuing systems and queuing theory.

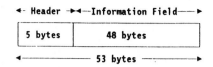

Fig. 2. Cell information field and header sizes.

The cell routing information contained in the header is a *label*, not an explicit address. One of the reasons for this is that explicit addressing is not possible because of the short, fixed cell size. Switching is performed as follows (Fig. 3): whenever a switching unit (switch, multiplexer) reads an incoming cell with routing label m on an input port i, it consults the switch *routing table* in order to determine an output port j and a label n. The cell is written on the output port j with the new label n. The new label will be used by the next switching unit encountered by the cell. The routing tables have to be set up in advance; they can be either pre-defined or dynamically allocated. In all cases, transporting cells requires a connection.

The full header format is described in Fig. 4. The label, or routing field, is the concatenation of VPI and VCI fields.

2.2. ATM connections

ATM cell transport requires a connection because of the lookup tables required by switching and multiplexing units. Connection setup is similar to 64 kbit/s connection setup in the narrowband ISDN, namely, it can be executed at subscription time or dynamically. In the latter case, a signaling protocol (extending Q.931 [3]) will be used.

Connections can be point-to-point, or point-to-multipoint. It is not yet decided whether ATM connections are unidirectional or not. If they are, then a reverse connection has to be used for two-way communication. Even in that case, the reverse direction might be used for management purposes.

ATM connections always guarantee delivery of cells in sequence.

Two levels of ATM connections are defined by CCITT: *virtual channel connections* and *virtual path connections*.

2.2.1. Virtual channel (VC) connections

This is the basic type of connection [4]. A *virtual channel* **link** exists between two switching points; it is defined by the value of the routing information contained in the ATM header. Here, the routing information is given by the concatenation of the VCI and VPI fields shown in Fig. 4. A *virtual channel* **connection** is the concatenation of virtual channel links defined by the lookup tables in the switching points. It is an end-to-end connection, as illustrated in Fig. 5.

Assume for example that A and B are end-user terminals (e.g., video-telephones). When A requests a connection to B, the network indicates the value a that will be used by A to write outgoing information, and the value z that will be used by B to read the incoming traffic. At the same time, lookup tables are setup in the network. A similar process holds for the reverse direction if the communication is both ways (not shown on the figure). [1]

A virtual channel connection is not only a purely logical association used for routing. As discussed in Section 2.4, *traffic usage* parameters are associated with the connection, as well as some quality of service objectives, for instance relative to the cell loss rate over the connection. In the above example, the virtual channel connection from A to B could have an attribute specifying a peak rate of 34 Mbit/s. The reverse connection may have different attributes.

The association of entries in lookup tables would impose a large amount of processing at connection setup, if this had to be done for every connection at every ATM switching point. This is particularly true if a node carries a large amount of low-speed connections, such as voice. This is alleviated by the use of *virtual path connections*, as described in the next section.

2.2.2. Virtual path (VP) connection

Virtual path connections are meant to contain bundles of virtual channel connections that are switched together as one unit. More precisely, Virtual Path *Links* and Virtual Path *Connections* are defined in a similar way as for virtual chan-

---

[1] 1 In such a case, the value of the label used by A to read incoming information could in general be different from a, the outgoing connection label, if connections are unidirectional.

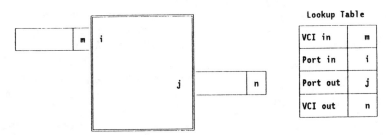

Fig. 3. Label switching.

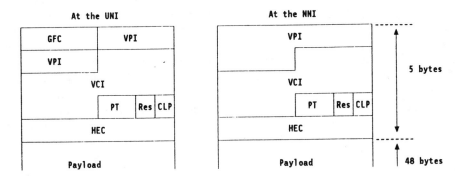

Fig. 4. Header of the ATM cell. The header formats differ at the User–Network Interface (UNI) and at the Network–Node Interface (NNI). GFC: Generic Flow Control (Section 2.4.4), VPI: Virtual Path Identifier (Section 2.2), VCI: Virtual Channel Identifier (Section 2.2), PT: Payload Information Type (is used to indicate network internal information, not passed to the user ATM layer; see also Section 3), Res: Reserved for futere usage (Section 2.4.4), CLP: Cell Loss Priority (Section 2.4.2), HEC: Header Error Control (Section 2.4.3, Section 3).

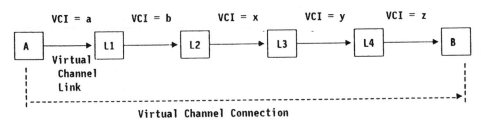

Fig. 5. Virtual channel connection.

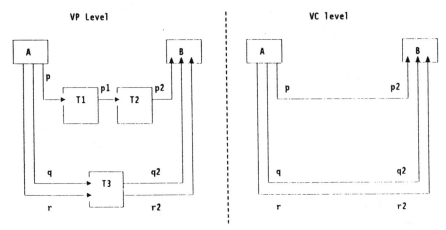

Fig. 6. Virtual paths connections.

nels above, except that the *routing* field used for switching is restricted to the VPI part of the cell header. Since the VPI field is a subset of the routing field used for a virtual *channel*, another way of viewing this is to consider that two layers of ATM connections exist: the virtual connection layer on top of the virtual path layer. The switching elements of the lower layer (*virtual path switches*) examine only the VPI part of the header, whereas the switching elements of the upper layer (*virtual channel switches*) examine the whole routing field, VPI + VCI. At a VP switch, all virtual channel connections with the same VPI are switched together.

Examine as an example the network illustrated in Fig. 6. Three virtual path connections exist from A to B. They are seen by A as corresponding to the values p, q, r of the VPI field, and by B as corresponding to the values $p2$, $q2$, $r2$. Whenever A wants to send some information to B on the VP connection seen as p, it writes the value p in the VPI field of the cell. The VP switches $T1$, $T2$ and $T3$ swap the VPI labels according to the lookup tables. The VCI field is not changed by the VP switches, so it can be used by A to multiplex several virtual *channel* connections on any one of the three VP connections. Therefore, at the VC level, A has at its disposal three direct links to B.

The inter-working of VP and VC switches is illustrated in Fig. 7. In the example there exist virtual path connections between A and T on one hand, between T and B on the other hand. Assume now that A wants to setup a VC connection to B using those two VP connections. The network has to provide a VCI value, say $a1$, for the A to T link, and a VCI value, say $a2$, for the T to B link. The VC connection from A to B is thus made of two VC links only. At switching points $D1$ through $D4$, only the VPI field is swapped. At the switching point T, both VPI and VCI fields are swapped, as seen in Section 2.2.1. The situation is thus similar to that where A and B would be access nodes in a circuit switched network, T would be a transit node, and $D1$ through $D4$ would be cross-connects.

A main feature illustrated in the above examples is that the VCI value is transported unchanged through the entire virtual path connection. Virtual path connections can thus be used as an alternative to leased lines for interconnecting nodes in private networks. A private node can use any VCI value on VP connections, with the exception of a few predefined ones. Note that several virtual path links can share a physical channel with each other. A single user–network interface is thus able to carry several VP connections.

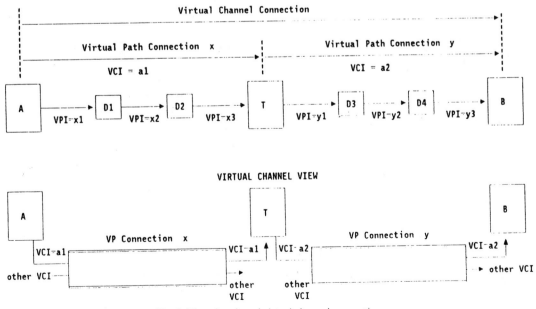

Fig. 7. Virtual path and virtual channel connections.

Virtual path connections are not defined solely at the user–network interface, but also at the network–node interfaces. This can be used to provide direct connections through entire networks.

A similar concept can be used *within* the network run by one single operator (by nature, the CCITT recommendations apply to UNI and NNI only). In that case, virtual path connections might be used as a way of reducing the processing associated with the establishment and releasing of individual virtual channel connections. Consider again Fig. 7, and assume now that A and B are access nodes located in areas served by different operators whereas T, $D3$ is a pair of interconnected inter-area gateways. Setting up a connection from A to B requires processing (including lookup table updates) at nodes A, B and T only. This allows a reduction of size in lookup tables at nodes that act as VP switches, and also a faster connection setup and release since fewer nodes are involved.

Note that, at least in theory, the functions of VP switches and VC switches can both be performed by the same node.

Virtual path connections can also be used to provide pre-defined paths to overlay functions, such as connectionless servers, as discussed in Section 4.2.

Apart from the transport of the VCI value (and the resulting potential uses), virtual path connections do not differ from virtual channel connections. They can be set up permanently or by using ad-hoc signalling (extension of Q.931). Like VC connections, they are also associated with traffic usage and quality of service attributes. Of course, the attributes of VC connection have to be compatible with those of an underlying VP connection, if any.

In summary for this section, the splitting of the routing field into VCI and VPI allows a two-level hierarchy for ATM connections.

2.3. Signalling, metasignalling

The establishment and release of connections is performed using a specific ATM connection called the *Signalling Virtual Channel Connection* (SVCC). The SVCC is a point-to-point connection between a terminal and the connection handling function (in the NT2 or in the central

office). This is similar to using the D-channel in the N-ISDN, but with the difference that every terminal has its own SVCC.

The allocation of a SVCC to a terminal is not permanent. It is performed during the *metasignalling* phase that can take place for instance at terminal activation. Communication during the metasignalling phase uses a predefined virtual channel connection called the *Metasignalling VCC* (MVCC). The MVCC is a broadcast connection that is accessed in contention mode.

The functions related to signaling are part of the *control plane*, as described in Section 2.5.

Signalling protocols are not yet fully defined by CCITT.

2.4. Connection flow control

2.4.1. Connection usage monitoring

The ATM is a packet mode and the physical channel rate (over which the ATM is transported) may be much higher than the connection rates. Therefore there is a need to control the flow of information within all connections at the access to the network.

Existing packet networks use some kind of window flow control [5], either between communicating ends, or between the user and the edge of the network. In contrast, the ATM layer uses rate *control*, between user and network access. Rate control is implemented by the network.

- Every connection (VPC or VCC) is associated with a traffic contract, negotiated between user and network. The terms of the contract can be *related* to such characteristics as mean and peak bit rates, and duration at which the peak rate can be sustained.
- The network monitors all connections for possible contract violations. In the case of a violation, the network can either discard cells, or mark the cells with a low priority for loss.

The main considerations that led to the choice of rate control are the following:

- Window flow control is not feasible for services that have real time constraints (voice, video) and there is no provision in CCITT works to apply distinct flow control schemes to different types of upper layer traffic. [2]

---

[2] This is not to be confused with the Cell Loss Priority mentioned below.

bly process. An indicative target value found in [10] is that, with probability less than 10^{-8}, the delay difference between any two cells in one connection crossing 30 ATM buffers is less than 1 s. Bounds on the maximum delays depend on the type of connection; they are of the order of 30 ms for terrestrial links less than 1000 km.

Other parameters concern the residual bit error rates in the ATM payload.

For connections that use the CLP bits, different targets values apply to the low and high-priority cells. In [11], target values for the cell loss rates over entire ATM connections are 10^{-4} for high-priority cells and 10^{-4} for low-priority cells, but more stringent values can be found.

Lastly, we mention again that ATM connections guarantee in sequence delivery of information.

2.4.4. Generic flow control

There is a four-bit-field in the cell header at the UNI for *generic flow control* (GFC). Its use is not yet fully specified. It is meant to be used by access mechanisms (like DQDB) that implement different level of priorities. It can be used either by the Customer Premises Network (NT2), or at

the access to the network, in the case where several UNIs would share a common resource (shared medium such as DQDB or remote multiplexer). The GFC field values is not transported across the network; it does not appear at network–node interfaces (NNIs).

2.5. The protocol reference model

The ATM layer uses the service of the Physical Layer (PL) in order to transport cells. The ATM layer delivers cell payloads to the upper layers. In most cases, it is necessary to perform some adaptation functions, for instance to transform a sequence of cells into the byte stream used to transport digitalized signals. This is performed by the ATM Adaptation Layer (AAL), as illustrated in Fig. 9. The physical layer is described in Section 3; the AAL is described in Section 4.

The AAL provides a variety of services; as a result, it has several service access points (SAPs), as explained in Section 4.1.

The CCITT protocol reference model (PRM) also incorporates the notion of control plane and user plane. The control plane is used for connection control (like setting up and releasing connections). An example is illustrated in Fig. 10. There,

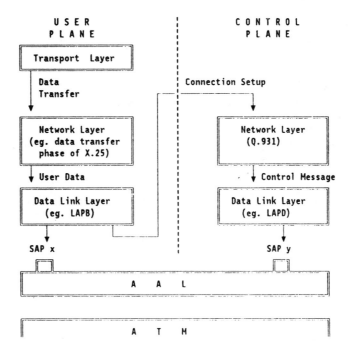

Fig. 10. An example of utilization of user and control planes for data transfer.

the transport protocol uses the control plane to set up a network connection, using a control plane network layer service (Q.931). The network layer function in turn uses lower layers to transmit the control messages: in particular a data link function on the signalling link between the terminal and the connection control function in the *central office* (for instance), and an AAL function to transmit the resulting frames in ATM cells. Once connections are established, the user data are transmitted using possibly different protocols, in the user plane. The layers up to AAL are common to both planes. The CCITT PRM [12] also indicates how management functions relate to the user and control planes.

3. The physical layer

The Physical Layer (PL) offers to the ATM layer the following service:
1. Transport of valid cells
2. Delivery of timing information, made available to upper layer services such as *circuit emulation* (Section 4.4).

Right from the early days of the ATM standardization, two different views appeared (Fig. 11).

(1) *Cell-based*: The *frames* used by the transmission system match exactly the ATM cells. In other words, the transmission system provides a bit stream over which ATM cells are directly transmitted. Different links in such a system can

operate in plesiochronous mode (with free running clocks), as described below.

(2) *SDH-based*: The cells are written on the byte stream provided by a underlying transmission system. The transmission system is the Synchronous Digital Hierarchy (SDH) defined by CCITT [13–15]. SDH is derived from SONET, with different names and rates starting at 155.52 Mbit/s. All timing and synchronization functions are performed by the SDH system. One drawback is the addition of overhead, as discussed in Section 5. The advantage is that SDH products are already in operation in the transport network of some telecommunication operating companies [16].

It should be noted, however, that the ATM can be used equally well (but with a different line rate) on any transmission system, and in particular on the plesiochronous digital hierarchy. In some countries like France, this might be the initial offering at the UNI [76].

The service offered by both transmission systems are different: the former delivers cells, whereas the latter delivers a byte stream (possibly organized in channels). CCITT allows the use of both systems, but the PL layer definition is such that a unique service is offered to the ATM layer. This is achieved by further dividing the PL into two sublayers: the Transmission Convergence (TC) and the Physical Media (PM) sublayers (Fig. 9). The flow of information between sublayers is illustrated in Fig. 12. More details of the layer functions at the UNI are given below. Specifications for the NNI are not yet available, but should not differ significantly.

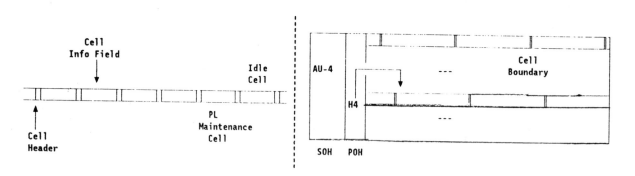

CELL BASED TRANSMISSION   SDH BASED TRANSMISSION

Fig. 11. The two transmission systems for ATM.

3.1. The physical media sublayer

This sublayer provides bit transmission and physical access to the media. Two access rates are defined. The rates apply to both cell based and SDH based transmission.

(a) *Access at 155.520 Mbit / s*: This rate is the line rate for STM-1 rate (or equivalently, the SONET OC-3 rate). The access in this case is symmetric (same rate in both directions).

(b) *Access at 622.080 Mbit / s*: This rate is the line rate for STM-3 rate (or equivalently, the SONET OC-12 rate). The access in this case could be symmetric, or, in contrast, be 622.020 Mbit/s in one direction and 155.020 in the other direction. The asymmetric interface would be useful in case where television programs would be distributed across the interface (with the higher rate from the network to end user).

3.2. The transmission convergence sublayer

The TC sublayer receives cells from the ATM layer and packs them into the appropriate formats for transmission over the PM sublayer (cell or SDH based). In so doing it needs to insert idle cells in order to provide a continuous flow of cells ("rate decoupling", Section 3.2.1). Idle cells are not passed to the ATM layer. They are identified by a specific header value (where the place of the ATM "payload type" field is the discriminator) (Fig. 4). On the receiving side, the TC extracts cells from the bit or byte stream received from the PM sublayer, verifies cell headers, and delivers valid cells to the ATM layer (Section 3.2.2).

3.2.1. Transmission frame adaptation

For cell-based transmission. With this scheme, the transmission frame contains exactly one cell. Framing is performed by the cell delineation function, described below. The TC also uses some idle cells to transmit PL information, in management cells (Fig. 11). Such cells are not passed to the ATM layer. They are identified by a specified header value which is not allowed for ATM cells. Local timing is provided by the PM sublayer. With this transmission method, different links need not be bit synchronized.

For SDH-based transmission. The SDH frame payload is not a multiple of the cell size. Therefore, the cell boundaries do not have a fixed position in the transmission frame (Fig. 11). Cell boundary are determined by the cell delineation function described it, the next section [15].

The TC also uses some path overhead to communicate management information [17,18].

3.2.2. Cell delineation and header verification

The TC has to delineate cells within the bit or byte stream received from the PM sublayer ("cell

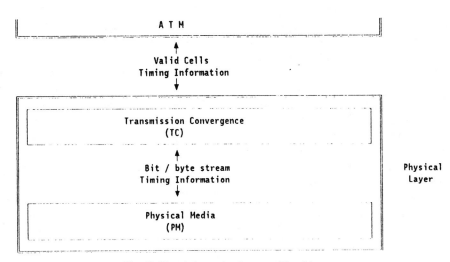

Fig. 12. Flow information between PL sublayers.

synchronization"). This is performed by using the cell Header Error Control (HEC) field already mentioned in Section 2.

The algorithm used to establish cell synchronization is as follows [17]. Initially, the receiver is in the HUNT-state. From there, it monitors the incoming bit stream bit by bit, searching for 5-byte words that belong to the code defined for the cell header (namely, 5-byte words for which the CRC check is correct). Once a match is obtained, the receiver moves to the PRESYNC state; from there, if δ consecutive matches are obtained, then synchronization is considered to be confirmed and the receiver moves to the SYNC state; any single mismatch from the PRESYNC state returns the receiver to the HUNT state. Similarly, while in the SYNC state, synchronization is assumed to be lost only after α consecutive mismatches occur. Suggested values are currently $\delta = 6$ and $\alpha = 7$.

There is always a risk that the ATM payload exhibits a pattern that would be recognized as a valid header. The use of the PRESYNC state reduces the implications of such mismatches. Additional protection is offered by scrambling the ATM payload before putting it into the bit stream. As an additional trick, the HEC is offset by a fixed pattern before transmission in order to better detect cell headers that are full of 0s, such as idle cells [17].

For SDH based transmission, an alternative to this method would be to use a pointer in the Path Overhead (POH). The POH is a part of the SDH frame which is transmitted end-to-end and is designed to transmit overhead information. One of these pointers (the $H4$ pointer) is used to determine the offset between itself and the next cell boundary (Fig. 11) However, CCITT allows this only as a way to verify synchronization, but not to establish it.

The HEC field is also used for single bit error correction in the cell header, when the receiver is in the SYNC state. The SYNC state is thus subdivided in two substates CORRECTION MODE and DETECTION MODE. When in CORRECTION MODE, the HEC can correct a detected single bit error, and discards cells with multiple errors. The corrected cells or cells without errors are considered *valid* cells. Any detected error triggers a transition to the DETECTION MODE, in which all cells in error are discarded. This method allows isolated errors to be corrected, while reducing the risk of

delivering errored cells in the presence of bursts of errors.

4. Services above the ATM layer

4.1. The ATM adaptation layer (AAL)

The AAL provides a variety of services. A complete list of service access points does not yet exist. However, four classes of services are defined in [19].

Class A: Circuit emulation (Section 4.4).

Class B: Variable bit rate service with time synchronization between sender and receiver(s) (Section 4.5).

Class C: Connection oriented data service (Section 4.3).

Class D: Connectionless data service (Section 4.2).

A number of AAL *protocols* are being defined by CCITT defined as type 1 to type 4. The Service Access Points (SAPs) to the adaptation layer are classified accordingly as SAPs 1 to 4. So far, the correspondence is straightforward: SAP 1 offers a service of class A, SAP 2 of class B, etc. In addition, signalling uses SAP 3. This is illustrated in Fig. 9, where SAPs 1, 2, 3 and 4 are defined. However, this relationship is not mandatory, and a service of a certain class can use an AAL SAP of another type

The AAL is further divided into two sublayers, as illustrated in Fig. 9.

(1) The *Segmentation And Reassembly* (SAR) sublayer processes the data units (bytes bit streams, variable length frames) so that they can fit into cells (segmentation) and conversely, reconstructs data units from information contained in cells (reassembly).

(2) The *Convergence Sublayer* (CS) performs additional functions like multiplexing, cell loss detection, timing recovery, as explained in the rest of this section.

The division of the AAL is internal, namely, the sublayers cannot directly be accessed. Function allocation to SAR and CS is also discussed in "Functions of CS and SAR", Section 4.3.1. The CS sublayer is currently being itself split into a service specific convergence sublayer, and a common convergence sublayer [77].

4.2. Connectionless data service

A connectionless data service accepts units of information (called *frames* in this section) that contain sufficient addressing information so that they can be delivered without prior association of sender and recipients. In the CCITT model, such a service is offered by the AAL, at a Service Access Point (SAP) of class D (currently at the SAP corresponding to type 4). The connectionless data service is also the main service offered by the SMDS proposal. In both cases, the main feature is that it requires no associated signalling. The provision of such a service is triggered by the need to interconnect Local Area Networks (LANs) more economically than with leased lines. The connectionless data service can be viewed as one of the first services that will be deployed using the ATM. The absence of signaling is certainly central in facilitating an early introduction.

We describe the *service* as can be best guessed from the current status of the CCITT recommendations. The main features of possible implementations of the CCITT proposal are described (*broadcast connections* and *connectionless servers*). Then the positioning of SMDS is discussed.

4.2.1. The CCITT connectionless data service

The CCITT connectionless data service solutions are based on the use of an *overlay switching level*. Predefined ATM connections are used, over which connectionless frames are sent in sequences of cells as described below. The use of datagram cells is not considered by CCITT, mainly because of the small cell size which prevents the full destination address to be put in every cell of a message [21,22].

The current status of the CCITT recommendations mainly describes formats and some aspects of the functions. The following description is therefore a *likely* solution.

Assume a frame is passed to the AAL for transmission. The CS part of the AAL adds proper header and trailer to the frame, which is needed to support the segmentation process described below. The overhead has the following fields (Fig. 13):

- a CS-PDU sequence number (modulo 256, called Begin–End tag), placed in the header and repeated in the trailer. It is used to detect losses or insertions in the lower layers (SAR and ATM) that span several CS-PDUs;

- a Buffer Allocation (BA) size estimation, placed in the header to assist the receiving AAL in allocating memory. It is at least equal to the CS-PDU size;
- a length field, placed in the trailer. It contains the actual size of the CS-PDU payload. It is used to help the re-assembly process detect losses or insertions;
- a Common Part Indicator (CPI), used to indicate the specific convergence sublayer protocol (if any).
- In addition, the CS "pad" is added to make the CS payload a multiple of 4 bytes. The "AL" byte is a dummy byte to make the trailer size equal to 4 bytes.

The resulting CS-PDU is split by the SAR into fixed size parts that fit in ATM cell payloads. In order for the receiver to be able to reconstruct the frame, the SAR adds its own Protocol Control Information. The resulting AAL-PDU, here called *segment* is passed to the ATM layer to be transported on an ATM connection reserved for the connectionless service. The segments contain fields for

- sequence Number (SN, see Fig. 13)
- indication of whether a segment is the first one of message, the last one, a continuation of message, or a single segment message (Segment Type, ST)
- indication of the meaningful part of the segment for partly filled cells (Length Indication, LI)
- Multiplex Identification (MID).

The first two fields allow the receiving end to handle segment losses properly. The third field is justified by the fixed size of ATM cells; it replaces flagging mechanisms that are not suitable here.

The last field (MID) is the *glue* that is used to recognize different segments as belonging to one frame. It is needed because a single AAL entity may concurrently receive frames from different sources (and also if a source is allowed to interleave the segments of several frames). More details are given in Section 4.2.2.

No re-sequencing is needed because the ATM service preserves sequence.

The destination identification information could be carried in the ATM overhead; this is possible only if this connection is a virtual path connection; in that case, the addressing informa-

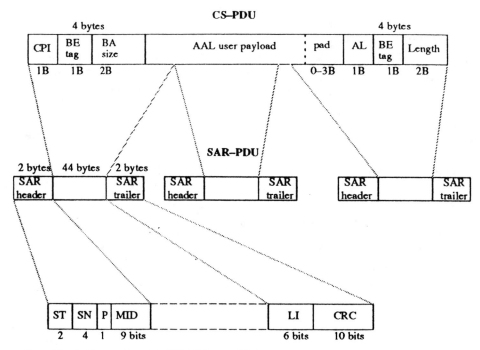

Fig. 13. Common format for AAL types 3 and 4. CPI: CS Protocol Information, BE tag: Begin-End tag, BA size: Buffer Allocation size, AL: ALignment byte, Length: CS-PDU lenght, ST: Segment Type, SN: Sequence Number, P: Priority, MID: Multiplex IDentifier, LI: Length Indication.

tion could be in the VCI field. Although such a scenario is possible for limited user domains, we do not describe it further here. In contrast, with the CCITT (and SMDS) solution, the address would be conveyed in the information field of the *first* segment of a frame. Subsequent segments do not contain any addressing information; they can be related to a specific frame by means of the MID field.

The receiving function of the AAL in such a case is performed as follows.

- The AAL permanently monitors the ATM connection used for the connectionless data service.
- When a segment is indicated as a beginning of message or single segment message, the AAL checks the destination address field; in case of a match with the station address, the station *initiates* a new frame and stores the corresponding MID (and the segment).
- When the segment is a continuation or end of message, the AAL checks whether the MID corresponds to an already initiated frame. If so, the segment is appended where necessary.

End of message segments trigger the delivery of the frame at the AAL interface.

Detailed field formats as defined by CCITT are given in Fig. 13. On top of the fields seen above, the CCITT recommendation adds a Cyclic Redundancy Code (CRC) for error detection, covering the whole segment. Whether this is really necessary is not clear, since AAL users are all likely to perform error detection on every frame.

4.2.2. Features of possible implementations .

As already mentioned, the connectionless data service requires some overlay switching on top of the ATM. One important issue in order to provide the service concerns the routing of the cells carrying the different segments of a message. This is because the destination address is contained in the first segment of a message only. Two methods can be used: *broadcast connections* and *connectionless servers*.

Broadcast connection

This section describes how the connectionless data service can make use of a shared broadcast virtual connection (VPC or VCC). An access protocol to the shared connection has to be implemented; it is not discussed here. Such a scenario is naturally supported by some physical configurations such as buses or rings, but can be also supported by central switches.

The AAL monitors the ATM shared connection and reads *all* segments (Fig. 14).

- When a begin-of-message or single-message segment is received, the AAL reads the destination address. In case of a match with the station address, the segment is stored and a frame is initiated. The corresponding MID value is written in the appropriate table as *pending*. Otherwise, the segment is further ignored.
- For other types of segments, the AAL reads the MID and checks whether it is in the table of pending MIDs. If so, the segment is appended to the proper initiated frame, otherwise it is ignored.

With this scheme, all MID values have to be unique for different frames sent on the shared connection.

This scheme is used by the MAC layer in IEEE 802.6. In that case, the shared connection is defined by the physical link; other ATM connections do not share the medium (see also Section 4.2.3).

The drawback of this scheme is the complex operation of the AAL: depending on the nature of the segment, the fields that trigger acceptance is in the ATM header or in the AAL PCI. Furthermore, the AAL receives all cells originated by all the connectionless service users on the broadcast connection, and no advantage is taken of switching at the ATM level.

Connectionless servers. With this scheme, the predefined ATM connection used by the AAL

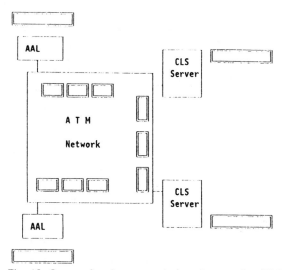

Fig. 15. Servers for the connectionless data service (CLS servers) as an overlay of the ATM network.

accesses a ConnectionLess Server (CLS). The CLS routes the frame to the destination or to another CLS, using ATM connections. The CLSs thus build the overlay *frame* switching network (Fig. 15). CLSs are peers to the AAL.

The operation of the CLS can be sketched as follows.

- On reception of a cell with a *begin of message* indication, the server takes a routing decision, resulting in the choice of an outgoing ATM connection. All subsequent cells belonging to the frame will be placed on this connection.
- The server also has to decide on a MID value for all outgoing cells belonging to the frame. It is not possible to assume that the incoming MID value is kept unchanged in all cases, because it cannot be guaranteed that all stations in the network have distinct MID values. In contrast, the MID need be unambiguous on only one ATM connection.

The server thus performs *MID swapping*, as illustrated in Fig. 16. The swapping tables are updated for every frame.

Many functions are not described here. In particular, routing and bandwidth allocation on the ATM connections have to be solved. A critical issue is also the buffering. The above description does not preclude that the CLS buffers the entire frames before sending them out, but pipelining has definite advantages regarding buffer utilization.

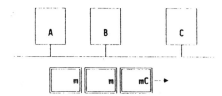

Fig. 14. Frame destined to station *C*. The first station has the full address *C* and the MID value *m*. Subsequent cells have only the MID value *m*.

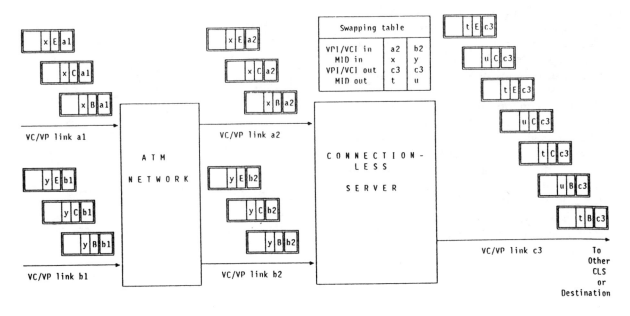

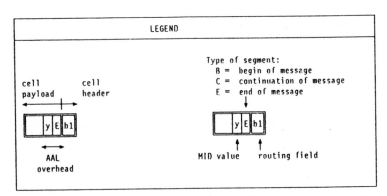

Fig. 16. MID swapping. Two frames are transmitted by the ATM network to a connectionless server (CLS). The original MID values (x and y) may be equal. The MID label is updated for every frame, based on the address contained in the firts segment. The CLS swaps MID based on identification and connection (ATM routing field) and incoming MID values. The cells of both frames are forwarded interleaved on the same ATM connection to a CLS or to the destination.

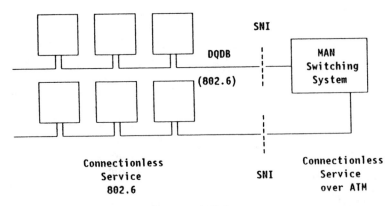

Fig. 17. SMDS.

16

4.2.3. SMDS

The Switched Multi-Megabit Data Service (SMDS) is planned to offer a connectionless data service, whose basic part is identical to the AAL connectionless data service described above. The access configuration is described in Fig. 17.

The main features are as follows [23].

– The user–network interface (called Subscriber Network Interface, SNI) uses a protocol (Subscriber Interface Protocol, SIP) containing three levels, very roughly corresponding to the levels up to AAL of CCITT (Fig. 18). The part of the CCITT connectionless data service that is defined so far is practically a subset of the service at level 3 of SIP.

– The level 1 of SIP uses DS-1 or DS-3 transmission.

– The flow of traffic through the SNI is *policed* using the equivalent of a leaky bucket (*ingress access control*).

– At the level 2 of SIP, the SMDS uses *one single predefined ATM connection*. There is no signalling; the connection characteristics can be modified by the network management system only.

– The SNI is based on the IEEE 802.6 (Distributed Queue Dual Bus, DQDB) MAC protocol. However, the DQDB access is not shared among different subscribers. It can be used, though, for the interconnection of user equipment (multidrop configuration). In that case,

the access DQDB is such that all traffic crosses the interface at level 2, including the traffic whose source and destination are both on the user side of the SNI. The network is not allowed to access this internal traffic.

– On the network part of the SNI, the network implements a SMDS Switching System (SSS). The SSS operates the SIP, and switches the frames that cross the interface to their destination or to another SSS. The SSS may be distributed (using a DQDB system, for instance), or not.

The SSS has to transport frames. Therefore, *it need not be based on ATM*. It can use any fast packet switching system, like the PARIS architecture [24]. If the ATM solution is chosen, then the SMDS would be a forerunner of the B-ISDN. In that case, the network supporting SMDS would use broadcast media and connectionless servers, interconnected by ATM switches (called here ATM cross connects) (Fig. 19 and section "Broadcast connection").

The SMDS differs from B-ISDN services by the use of the access DQDB within the user side of the user–network interface. Besides, the SMDS protocol differs in some minor ways from the B-ISDN protocol reference model. The function placement within the protocol stack is sometimes different: for instance policing is performed in the SIP at level 3 (for every frame), whereas for CCITT it is an ATM function (performed for

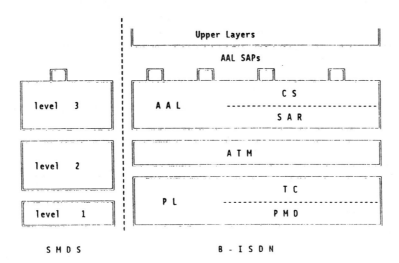

Fig. 18. Three levels of SIP and CCITT Reference Model.

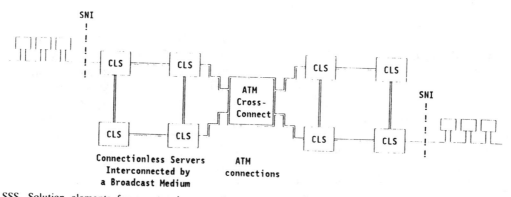

Fig. 19. SSS. Solution elements for a network supporting the SMDS based on ATM. The connectionless servers can be interconnected by broadcast connections or by ATM cross-connects.

every cell); the physical layer of CCITT contains some cell header verification functions that belong to the level 2 of the SIP.

At the SIP level 2, the VCI/VPI field is not used by SMDS (only the *all 1*'s value is allowed). This is actually not a divergence from CCITT, since SMDS uses only one single predefined ATM connection. The cell formats are almost identical, with a difference in the first byte (generic flow control). The SIP level 3 and CCITT AAL formats match one another.

The target loss rate for SMDS frames (level 3-PDUs) is 10^{-4} for frames with an average length of 1200 bytes (see Section 5.2.2 for a discussion).

In conclusion for this section, for the relation between SMDS and ATM, it is necessary to consider two distinct parts:

1. *At the access*, the SMDS uses a broadcast connection (IEEE 802.6) that has similarities with an ATM connection. The connection is predefined and no signalling is required.

2. *Internally*, the SMDS uses a datagram transport system, which can be supported by ATM connections or not. In the former case, datagram switching is performed by an overlay network of connectionless servers.

4.3. Connection-oriented data service

4.3.1. Service definition

The ATM can be used to build a data transfer service with connection. Such services belong to class C (Section 2.5). CCITT has started defining one such protocol as AAL type 3.

In order to use the service, it is first necessary to establish an ATM connection, using the network layer in the control plane. Connections can be point to point or point to multipoint. Then, the data transfer phase uses the AAL at the appropriate class C SAP.

One main difference with the connectionless service concerns addressing. Since a connection is used, it is not necessary that the AAL includes a destination address in every CS-PDU. In contrast, only a multiplexing identifier is necessary if several AAL connections are multiplexed on one single ATM connection.

The nature of the service offered at a class C SAP can vary depending on the degree of integration of the surrounding layers with the ATM. The CCITT defines two attributes qualifying the service. They are as follows.

1. *Assured / Non-assured*: The assured service guarantees error free delivery of all AAL-SDUs. Flow control is provided. In contrast, the non-assured service may lose some AAL-SDU or deliver corrupted AAL-SDUs to the destination.

2. *Message / Streaming mode*: The streaming mode accepts only fixed size AAL-SDUs and delivers them as distinct SDUs to the receiving ends. The message mode accepts AAL-SDUs of variable size.

Scenarios for functions. Three service scenarios are described in Table 1 (see also Fig. 9). The scenarios are not part of CCITT recommendations, but are possible scenarios constructed for this report with the intention of illustrating the key concepts of this section.

(a) *Scenario 1* is extracted from [25]. This set of functions was originally introduced in support of signaling connections, but it can also be used to support the frame relay service [26]. With this

Table 1
Possible sets of functions for the AAL offering connection oriented data transfer service

	Scenario 1 (Minimal Interworking)	Scenario 2 (HDLC-like Service)	Scenario 3 (Streamlined for ATM)
Attributes of service	Non-assured, message mode	Assured, message mode	Assured, streaming mode
CS functions		Flow Control Error Recovery Cell Loss Detection and Recovery	Flow control Bit error detection and recovery Cell loss detection and recovery Multiplexing
SAR functions	Segmentation and Reassembly Segment type identification Handling partly filled cells Cell Loss detection	Segmentation and Segment type identification Handling partly filled cells Bit error detection within one segment Multiplexing on one ATM connection	Handling partly filled cells

scenario, the AAL transmits frames (AAL-SDUs) in one or more cells. The size of the frame does not have to match the size of the ATM payload. The AAL service is used by a data link level that performs all flow control and error recovery functions. Multiplexing is left to the link level and the ATM level (using ATM routing fields). The function of the AAL is reduced to the minimal set necessary to handle the transport of a frame in one or more cells. The selection of an ATM connection is performed in the control plane and is not a function of the AAL. This scenario can be used to support existing data link level operation with minimal modification. The main modification for the upper layer is that the AAL provides a frame delineation mechanism using the ATM service, the segment type identification and the partly filled cell indication. The AAL adds up to two byte of overhead per segment.

(b) *Scenario 2* utilizes the same formats as for the connectionless service (Fig. 13). As scenario 1, it is able to support existing data link level operation, but adds error handling and multiplexing functions. The CS adds 8 bytes of overhead per CS-SDU and the SAR layer adds 4 bytes of overhead per SAR-SDU.

(c) *Scenario 3* speculates on maximum integration of the upper layers (especially transport protocols) with the ATM. It assumes that the network layer directly uses the AAL service. The

AAL-SDU is assumed to fit in one segment, therefore no segmentation is necessary. The AAL functions are then similar to those of LAP-D. In particular, an addressing field is used to allow multiplexing on ATM connections. The usual windowing mechanism is able to handle cell losses. The resulting overhead is of 6 bytes per AAL-SDU: 1 byte for the multiplexing field, 2 bytes for sequence number, 2 bytes for error detection code (CRC), and one byte for length indication. AAL-SDUs are assumed to be of constant size, therefore the AAL does not have to indicate partly filled cells. The SAR function is thus empty. This scenario fits with transport protocol that are designed to operate with the ATM as in [27]. It avoids the superposition of overheads.

The discussion of the three scenarios above reveals a point of concern for the AAL, namely the superposition of layers that perform similar functions. This is discussed in Section 5.

The service with connection allows for resource reservation in the ATM layer. This may result in high qualities of connections. Target cell loss rates for the ATM layer can be of the order of 10^{-8} [11]. This is to compare with the target frame loss rates for the connectionless service of SMDS in Section 4.2.

An issue is the ability of the ATM layer to statistically multiplex the variable rate traffic generated by the AAL (see Section 5.2.2).

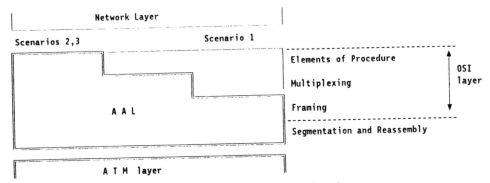

Fig. 20. AAL function and the OSI layer 2.

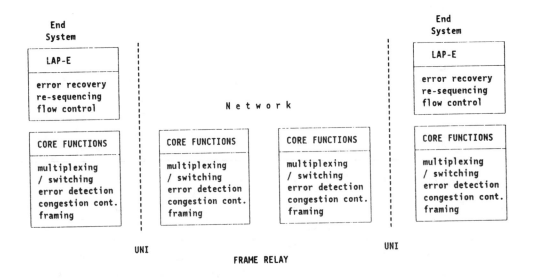

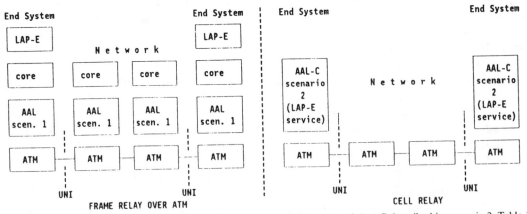

Fig. 21. Frame relay and ATM. "AAL-C scenario 2" refers to the AAL service of class C described in scenario 2, Table 1.

Other scenarios are possible. Data services can also be supported using circuit emulation (Section 4.4) and existing bit or byte oriented protocols.

Functions of CS and SAR. The scenarios above illustrate the need for multiple service definition for connection oriented data transfer (class C AAL service). The objective of CCITT is to provide a set of core functions in a sublayer, called AAL-L (for "Low") that can be used by all class C services. This sublayer could match the SAR or not.

The scenarios also illustrate that the AAL may actually perform data link level functions. The AAL service boundary depends on the type of service (Fig. 20).

1. For scenario 1, the AAL provides the framing service for the upper parts of layer 2. Framing is not performed using the HDLC flags, but rather uses the Segment Type (ST) and Length Indication (LI) fields.
2. For scenarios 2 and 3, it provides a full HDLC service.

The functions are described in the previous section. Framing is different from "normal" HDLC. No flag and bit stuffing is necessary. Frame delineation is provided by the combination of the ATM layer service (providing individual segments), the segment type identification (ST) and partly filled cell indication (LI).

The data unit *formats* for the CS for connection oriented data services are not yet specified. For the SAR, they are similar to the connectionless case (Fig. 13), with the only difference that the MID field is replaced by a "reserved" field.

4.3.2. Frame relay and the AAL service

Frame relay. The frame relay bearer service is being standardized by CCITT and ANSI [28] as part of the ISDN. In the USA, the long distance carriers have announced support of the Frame Relay service (US SPRINT in 1991; AT&T on Integrated Access Cross Connect Systems, IACS) [29].

The frame relay service offers two parts: connection control and HDLC connectivity.

(1) *Connection control* handles connections across the network, over which data are transferred. Connection control uses the ISDN signal-

ing protocol and is similar to the ATM connection control.

(2) Once a connection is established, the end-systems communicate using data link level service of the HDLC type, for instance LAP-E: this is the *layer 2 connectivity.* LAP-E is an extension of LAP-D that is compatible with LLC, the corresponding service standardized by IEEE for LANs. The network routes frames to their destination, performing only error detection and discarding frames in error (this forms the set of *core* functions). No error recovery or window flow control is performed by the network. They are performed by the end systems only (Fig. 21). The core functions may also include some congestion control functions, such as marking the appropriate field in the LAP-E protocol header to indicate congestion. At the network access, multiplexing is performed using the DLCI (data link connection identifier) field. This allows all end-to-end LAP-E connections to share one single physical channel in the N-ISDN.

The frame relay service has analogy to the X.25 service but it differs mainly by the fact that the full data link protocol is performed only end-to-end. Because of that, it can be used to provide much higher throughputs.

Although it is connection oriented, frame relay can be used to interconnect LANs [30]. Frame Relay is intended to be offered at link speeds of up to 2 Mbit/s, but it has the potential to work at higher speeds.

Frame relay and ATM. We examine here how a network using the ATM can offer a service to end users similar to frame relay. We do not address the interworking between the existing frame relay bearer service and ATM based services. Several cases can be envisioned, as follows (Fig. 21).

1. The first case (FRAME RELAY OVER ATM) simply uses the AAL to provide an underlying connectivity [26]. The ATM network just provides channels for the frame relay service. Frame relay servers are necessary in the network to perform the core functions. Adaptation layer functions could be as in *scenario 1* (Table 1). They are necessary at the terminals and at every frame relay server:
   – Segmentation and reassembly are needed because the size of the frame for frame relay can be up to 1600 bytes.

- No multiplexing is necessary within the AAL because it can use *predefined* ATM connections to get to access the frame relay servers.
- Within the network, the frame relay server switch frames using DLCI routing tables setup at connection establishment time.

2. In the second case (CELL RELAY), the frame relay service is directly provided by the AAL. The core functions of frame relay are performed by the ATM network. Adaptation layer functions are necessary at the end systems only, where functions as in *scenario 2* can be used. Multiplexing can be implemented or not, since every DLCI value can be mapped to one ATM routing field (VPI/VCI).

The network nodes perform only the switching function using ATM labels. Error detection is not performed in the network.

The advantage of the second solution is the integration with the ATM and the resulting performance advantages. The service uses the ATM in native mode, with no overlay structure inside the network. However, several issues arise:

- The AAL service definition has to be such that it allows interworking with end systems not using the ATM [26].
- Flame relay uses some fields in the frame relay overhead to report network congestion. The ATM layer has no provision for similar functions. In contrast, ATM flow control relies entirely on source rate control, as described in Section 2.4.

In *conclusion* for Section 4.3, the adaptation layer service for connection oriented data can be used

- either to support an overlay frame relay network,
- or to provide a full HDLC-like end-to-end service.

The frame relay service has the potential to be fully integrated with the ATM. This contrasts with the connectionless services such as SMDS that need overlay structures.

4.4. Circuit emulation

This is probably one of the first services (with the connectionless data service) that will have to be provided by ATM networks [31]. The AAL receives and delivers bit streams at a service access point of class A (at a SAP of type 1). The bit stream can have any rate, from a few kbit/s to tens of Mbit/s.

The AAL has to hide two non-desired effects of the packetized nature of the ATM: cell losses and transfer delay variation [32].

- In order to detect cell losses, the AAL adds a sequence number into the ATM payload. This sequence number steals one byte from the ATM payload. Once detected, cell losses may in some cases be corrected by adding a dummy cell into the received cell stream. More sophisticated schemes can be used, like sending the original data stream into interleaved cells in order to spread the effect of a single cell loss over a larger time period [33]. In [34], it is assumed that the sequence number field is protected against single bit errors (4 bit integer coded over 8 bits), and that the rest of the ATM payload is not protected against bit errors by the AAL.
- Transfer delay variation is compensated by a *playout buffer*. At the beginning of the connection, the first cells are buffered until a predefined threshold is reached (counted in time or in buffer fill). Then, if the delay variation is within specified requirements, the buffer is able to deliver a continuous, periodic stream. Excessive delay variations cause buffer starvation (no cell to deliver) or buffer overflow. In the former case, the AAL outputs dummy information (stuffing); in the latter case, some cells are lost (slipping). According to [10], the buffer size that is sufficient to guarantee starvations or overflow are as rare as otherwise caused cell losses is of the order of:
  - 2 cells for connection rates of 64 kbit/s;
  - 100 cells for connection rates of approximately 40–50 Mbit/s, this speed range being the worst case for link speeds of 155 Mbit/s.

These figures were obtained by estimating the cell delay variation over connections traversing up to 30 ATM switching matrices.

The AAL also has to handle the packetization (segmentation) of the original data stream. This contributes to the end-to-end transfer delay. The combined effect of packetization, reassembly and playout buffer contributes to about 10 ms for connections at 64 kbit/s; in that case the packetization delay is the most significant part (5.75 ms). For higher speed connections, the delay is less important (about 1 ms for connections at several Mbit/s).

The AAL service also provides synchronization between the different *end-systems*. In theory, the sender and receiver(s) could use independent clocks with frequencies that are nominally equal. The slight difference in frequencies would be compensated by the playout buffer, resulting in information stuffing or slipping, as mentioned above for the handling of delay variation. The resulting performance (impairments due to slip and stuffing) depends on the accuracy of the clocks. The performance objectives for digital circuits in G.822 require (in the best case) an accuracy of 0.9×10^{-7}, which would result in expensive clock circuitry [35]. The solution to this is to allow a receiver to recover the clock used by the sender to transmit the signal. Several methods are possible; solutions depend on whether the physical layer provides a synchronous network. Three main solutions are being envisioned.

1. *Terminal synchronized with the transmission network*: Both sender and receiver get their clocks from the physical layer (transmission network). This solution is conceptually simple; it also has advantages in the case of multipoint connections with several senders such as in a videoconference. It is, however, not applicable if one of the terminals is connected via a customer premises network that may not (necessarily) be synchronized with the public network.

2. *ATM clocking cells*: It is possible to synchronize two terminals without using any network clock. The basic scheme is to fine-tune the receiver clock (used to read the playout buffer) based on the filling level of the buffer. When the buffer shows an upward trend, then the receiver clock is accelerated; in the opposite case, it is slowed down. This scheme alone results in excessive jitter for the delivered bit stream, due to the variations in the frequency of the reading clock. Therefore, it is complemented by the use of periodic ATM clocking cells [36]. The clocking provided by these cells information has a low frequency; it is thus less sensitive to cell delay variation and results in better jitter performance for the delivered bitstream. It can be implemented with free running terminals, even on a customer premises network not synchronized with the public network. It is interesting for low-cost consumer products.

3. *Synchronous frequency encoding*: The Synchronous Frequency Encoding Technique (SFET) [37] is an alternative to the "clocking cells" scheme. It uses the network clock to recover the sender clock at the receiver without requiring that the original bitstream be synchronized with the network. It works as follows. The network clock is used to encode a low frequency signal, the frequency encoding signal (FES), at the adaptation layer at the sender. The received FES is read at the receiver with the network clock; the result is used to adjust to the original signal clock. The delivered bitstream at the receiver is synchronized with the original bitstream at the sender, but none of them is synchronized with the network. Indications are that the performance of the SFET is similar to that of the "clocking cells" scheme [77]. It requires that the network timing reference is available at the points where ATM adaptation is performed.

Assuming a one byte AAL overhead (protected sequence number), the maximum circuit bit rate that can be offered at a UNI using SDH at 155.52 Mbit/s is 132.4 Mbit/s. This can be less if additional overhead is used for synchronization.

4.5. Variable bit rate services

It is envisioned that the B-ISDN would transport real time services such as voice and video over variable bit rate connections. The main reason for that is to take advantage of the statistical multiplexing capability of the ATM.

Most video codecs produce a variable output, namely, the code word corresponding to one frame does not always have the same size. It is possible to use a constant bit rate connection (for example a circuit). This is done by buffering the codec output before sending it on the circuit, which impacts the quality when the buffer becomes congested. An alternative is to use a variable bit rate connection, as is possible with ATM. This can guarantee a better quality [38] provided that cell loss priority is used. Cell loss priority can be implemented with the use of the CLP bit as described in Section 2.4.2. In the absence of cell loss priority, the ATM is not able to offer significant statistical multiplexing to high bit rate connections [9,39]. The service can also be used to transport packetized voice or high quality sound.

The functions of the AAL are similar to the case of circuit emulation, except for the handling of synchronization that is more complex. The cells that carry the part of the signal used for end-to-end synchronization can be protected against overflows by the use of the CLP bit.

4.6. Multimedia services

AAL functions are not defined by CCITT for multimedia services. A multimedia service is likely to use several AAL services. At the ATM level, one or several connections can be used.

- In the first case, information is serialized and transported on a single VC connection [40].
- An alternative is to use multiple connections for the different information components. Synchronization between the components can be imbedded in every connections. Synchronization requirements are not as tight as for transmission systems [41].

The multicast capability of ATM connections can be used to build multimedia videoconferencing connections [42].

5. The debate about ATM

The concept of ATM can be related back to two different ancestor technologies. The first one is implemented in some multiplexors which dynamically allocate every bit within the DS-1 frame [43]. The second one is packet switching, as implemented in wide- or local-area networks. Experimental networks used to transport all services in a packet format have evolved from a variable length packets to fixed size as in ATM [44]. For ATM, packet switching was chosen because of its flexibility and the fixed format mainly because it allows higher hardware performance. The actual cell size is a compromise between short and long cells ($48 = (32 + 64)/2$) and $5 = (4 + 6)/2$). Short cells reduce the transfer delay for services like voice (Section 4.4), whereas longer cells reduce the ratio of overhead.

The implication of these choices on the building of broadband networks raises some issues (see [45] for a list). We highlight some of them in this section, based on the descriptions in the previous parts. It is not the intent of this report to give opinions on those issues.

5.1. Physical layer and circuit emulation

Although ATM cells can be transported on any transmission system, the SDH is very likely to be the main realizations of the B-ISDN physical layer in many countries (but we might see the UNI over the Plesiochronous Digital Hierarchy in some countries, see Section 3). However, according to CCITT, multiplexing at the UNI is offered only at the ATM level. Intelligent, flexible transmission networks can be built using VP connections. A possible scenario for a flexible transport network is [46] to use two layers:

- The ATM VP layer switches bit rates that can be used at the UNI (up to approximately 140 Mbit/s);
- Another, SDH based layer is used to switch higher bit rates for the internal needs of the public operator's network (Gbit/s scale).

Although the ATM is mainly pushed by the telecommunication operating companies, it can also be used by private networks to better utilize the bandwidth rented from a carrier. This can be done using a private network consisting of VP connections.

This raises several issues when comparing the CCITT defined B-ISDN access to alternatives such as SDH or hybrid access; we first list negative arguments (seen from the side of ATM proponents).

- SDH provides many maintenance functions that are thus not made available at the UNI. Besides, the operators networks comprise two distinct transport systems, one ATM VP based, one SDH based. The interworking of the maintenance systems for both systems adds a level of complexity that would not be present if only SDH were used [47].
- The superposed overheads reduce the available bandwidth. At the 155.52 Mbit/s UNI, the SDH offers a 149.8 Mbit/s payload, but due to ATM and AAL overhead, the maximum circuit bit rate that can be transported is at best 132.4 Mbit/s (Section 4.4).
- The all ATM interface prevents the use of hybrid access. Hybrid access would be composed of several channels, one of them supporting ATM [48].
- The SDH interface can be used to build private networks using their own technology, which need not be ATM. This can be variable

length packet transport [24], or hybrid transmission frames built by the private multiplexors.

On the other hand, the following positive arguments can be considered.

- The VP connections provide more flexibility for bandwidth management than SDH. This can result in a better bandwidth utilization. This may be used by a public network operator to provide cost effective bandwidth and thus bypass private multiplexors. It can also be used in private networks to provide high bandwidth multiplexors. The ATM can be viewed as a cross-connect technology for backbone networks.
- The unique interface is an advantage for end users. Private heterogeneous networks can be built on VP connections using a single technology. In contrast, the hybrid solutions favour short term proprietary solutions that best exploit the bandwidth rented from the carriers.
- Evolution to and interworking with cell based transmission systems requires the single interface.

5.2. Data services

5.2.1. Connectionless

The connectionless data service is not really provided by the ATM; it requires an overlay network of connectionless servers. In contrast, variable length fast packet switching networks are able to provide datagram services in native mode [24].

The transport of datagrams over ATM connections requires segmentation and reassembly. The segmentation process imposes additional overhead, as described in Section 4.2. Besides, the fixed cell size adds an additional padding cost. When compared to a variable length scheme such as in [24], the ATM solution costs 22% more overhead (i.e., it takes 122 bytes instead of 100 in the average). However, the segmentation process causes a better buffer utilization which may offset the additional overhead. Overhead directly impacts the link throughputs, measured in user traffic.

Another related issue concerns the segmentation and reassembly at InterWorking Units (IWUs), interfacing between an ATM based service and a LAN. The IWU handles interleaved

frames split into cells. When a cell arrives, it has to be buffered until the complete frame reaches the IWU; in the interim, other cells belonging to other frames have to be stored. Cells belonging to frames that will not complete (due to cell losses) have to be managed. All these functions have to be performed at very high speed. This is why some very high speed LANs use contiguous time slots to transmit data frames, thus avoiding segmentation [49–51]. The same discussion applies to *servers* with direct ATM access.

The frame loss rate of a network offering the connectionless data service depends on both the ATM level (if any) and the connectionless servers. The resulting performance is far from the loss rates that could be expected for a pure ATM network. Target cell loss rates for ATM connections are of the order of 10^{-8} (Section 2.4.3). Assuming that cell losses are independent (here a worst case assumption), this leads to a frame loss rate due to ATM cell losses of 0.3×10^{-6} for frames with a length of 1200 bytes. [4] This is much better than similar target rates announced for SMDS, namely 10^{-4} for the same frame sizes. This seems to indicate that most losses are expected to be due to the overlay connectionless servers. Of course, it still remains to be seen whether such ATM cell loss rates can be achieved for variable rate services.

5.2.2. Connection oriented

The connection oriented data services have the potential to be an evolution of the frame relay bearer service (Section 4.3), without overlay switching. However, small ATM buffers are not able to handle such traffic efficiently [52], whereas other services require small buffers because of their delay constraints. This can be solved by giving data traffic a smaller delay priority, and assigning larger buffers in front of ATM switching matrices for cells with low *delay priority* [53]. This is part of the ATM network, but increases the complexity of bandwidth management.

The same *overhead* argument holds for connectionless data, in particular concerning the link utilization. However, the problems due to seg-

---

[4] The frame loss rate is approximately equal to $10^{-8} \times 1200/44$. The AAL segment payload is 44 bytes (Section 4.2) and the frame size 1200 bytes as in [23].

mentation and reassembly are not present if the terminals are using directly the ATM service.

The definition of the AAL functions will have to be very careful (Section 4.3) in order to reduce function duplication, resolve addressing and congestion control differences [54].

In conclusion for this section, the use of the ATM to support a connectionless data service implies some complexity and performance cost. This is true to a lesser extend for connection oriented data services; in contrast, they can use ATM in native mode and offer higher performance.

5.3. Real time services

For the transfer of animated images, one concern is that a new synchronization procedure is needed when using ATM connection rather than circuits, thus leading to a larger development effort.

For the telephony service, the packetization, reassembly adds a 6 ms [5] delay to the end to end transfer time. For very long distance connections, the resulting round trip delay becomes important (more than 30 ms [55]), thus imposing echo cancellation. This could have been avoided using smaller cell sizes, but then the ATM overhead ratio would also have been larger.

On the positive side, the ATM offers full flexibility for the definition of bit rates. It would be difficult to define a channelized structure at the UNI, because the choice of a specific bit rate mix is difficult [48]. As a comparison, the choice of two 64 kbit/s channels at the narrowband UNI is not optimal now, given that voice can be transported using the ADPCM standard at 32 kbit/s. This issue is important for future multimedia services, that have complex, variable bit rate requirements during one connection. This flexibility is also important for switching and multiplexing technology, as mentioned in Section 5.5.

5.4. Traffic control

This is the main issue conditioning the availability of ATM services.

---

[5] For a 64 kbit/s emulated circuit, the time to fill a 47-byte segment is $47 \times 125 \mu s = 5.75$ ms.

5.4.1. Flow enforcement

There are doubts about the effectiveness of flow enforcement schemes using rate control such as the leaky bucket (Section 2.4) [56,57]. Rate control schemes have to be tuned in order to minimize the following two problems.

1. Cells may be discarded even though the traffic contract was not violated. This occurs because the rate control is enforced by the network at a point distant from the source. Between the source and the rate control point, cells incur variable transfer delays.
2. Cells may be accepted although the contract is violated. This occurs because some safety margin is allowed by the rate control scheme due to point 1 above.

Although it was initially believed that these two risks can be minimized, more accurate studies tend to show that protecting against risk 1 requires such large safety margins that rate control is not effective (no protection against risk 2).

Alternatives have been proposed. A first one is to use more sophisticated rate control algorithms than a single leaky bucket [7]. Another one is to replace cell discarding by cell tagging: violating cells are given a low priority for loss [56]. This allows the use of a smaller safety margin since tagged cells are likely to be still transmitted. Some authors propose to add buffering capabilities to the leaky bucket [58,59]. Another original method proposed in [60] is the Spacer Controller (SC). The SC is used for both shaping and policing traffic *peak rate*. A connection with a peak rate of c cells per second is filtered by the SC in such a way that at the output, the interval between cells is at least $1/c$ s. Early cells are buffered in the SC in order to enforce the spacing required by peak rate enforcement. This is able to minimize the two risks 1 and 2 above, for peak rate policing only.

The use of a single congestion control method (source policing and call acceptance) is challenged in [61]. There, it is argued that additional schemes should be considered as well, for instance window flow control should not be totally excluded. The control of variable rate connections such as data connections and variable rate real time services might need such extra congestion control schemes [62]. A few potential candidates are given below.
- Explicit congestion notification as for Frame

Relay is carried by the network to the access points in order to reduce the bandwidth allocated to sources [63]. One difficulty is that ATM connections are unidirectional.

- For sporadic sources, bandwidth is allocated on a burst basis, using the Fast Reservation Protocol (FRP). With the FRP, connection setup is separated from bandwidth allocation. Data bursts always use the same route within one connection, but have to request bandwidth individually.
- Variable bit rate video and sound connections could be handled without policing, using the fact that few codec types will be in use. Codec authentication could be used instead.

5.4.2. Bandwidth allocation

On top of congestion control as mentioned above, the ATM network has to find solutions to bandwidth allocation. There are two distinct parts to this problem; they are discussed below. In the following discussion, we assume that connection types are classified by classes $1, \ldots, K$. All connections within one class have identical traffic parameters (such as peak and average rates, for instance, or relate to the same codec, see above) and identical Quality of Service requirements.

The first part is specific to ATM. It can be formulated as follows.

Link capacity criterion: Given that $N_1, \ldots, N_K$ connections of classes $1, \ldots, K$ are offered to a link of bit rate B, can the link carry them simultaneously so that the Quality of Service requirements are satisfied for all classes.

With *channelized systems* (using Synchronous Transfer Mode), the criterion is

$$\sum_{k=1}^{K} B_k N_k \leqslant B,$$

where B_k is the rate required for connections of class k. Note that this criterion leads in practice to policies that never achieve a 100% fill because of the lack of flexibility of the channelized structure.

With an ATM system, the criterion is more complex, and only sufficient (conservative) solu-

tions can be found. The *peak rate* allocation is one of them. It can be written as:

$$\sum_{k=1}^{K} B_k N_k \leqslant B \rho_{\max}$$

In the formula, B_k is also the rate required for connections of class k, but $\rho_{\max}$ is the maximum bit rate that can be sustained in order to meet the most stringent cell loss rate requirements among all classes.

Of course, one might think of better policies than peak rate allocation. However, it should be noted that the ATM introduces a total flexibility with regard to the rate of a connection within a multiplex. This alone allows a better bandwidth utilization in a multirate environment than channelized systems.

Solutions to go beyond peak rate allocation are emerging [64–67], but even in the case of one single class the solution to this problem is not easy if the sources are bursty [68].

One way to settle the problem is to segregate different traffic classes, at least in a first phase. A proposal in [63] is to handle separately the following families of traffic:
- SMDS,
- Television on fixed bit rate channels (H4 channels),
- Low bandwidth circuits,
- Low bandwidth variable rate connections.

The link capacity criterion may have a dynamic form, whereby the observed traffic is the basis for determining the capacity. This is particularly relevant if the link is carrying virtual paths used to multiplex many connections, or connectionless traffic [69].

Once rules are available to determine the capacity of links, there remains the following problem:

Connection acceptance criterion: "Given that $N_1, \ldots, N_K$ of classes $1, \ldots, K$ are present on a link of bit rate B, should a new call of class k be accepted or not, given that connection blocking requirements have to be met for all classes?"

Of course, a necessary condition to accept a connection is that the link can support it, namely, that the link capacity criterion is satisfied. This is however not sufficient, because accepting all connections as they are offered might cause a greater blocking probability for the connections requesting large bandwidth.

This problem is not specific to ATM. In contrast, it is found in all multiple bit rate networks where it is referred to as "multiservice blocking." Solutions exist, but complete analysis is difficult even for one single link with several classes [70].

In addition to bandwidth allocation, the traditional issues of routing and connection setup across a network have to be solved, taking into account the variety of requirements of different connection classes [71]. Here too, the segregation of traffic mentioned above simplifies the problem.

The previous points show the complexity of bandwidth management in ATM networks. On the other hand, the use of virtual path connections inside a network simplify the bandwidth allocation problem [72]. However, no complete solution to the whole problem is available today.

5.4.3. Correlated traffic

A specific problem related to the rate control is that of correlated traffic. Correlated traffic occurs when several variable rate connections sharing a single link have correlated burst occurrences. Several scenarios may be imagined [57], among the most likely are the following.

– One connection is split by the user (outside the network) into several connections with smaller bandwidth.

– A multimedia service is carried over several distinct connections.

When a link supports several variable rate connections that are correlated, then its *capacity* (Section 5.4.2) is decreased. This problem occurs only if the bandwidth allocation is not based on the peak rate, and if the connection rates are high relative to the link rate [73]. The early introduction strategy mentioned in [63] would circumvent the problem.

5.5. Switches

The use of packet switching is a solution to two requirements for modern high speed switches.

1. *Capability to switch different bit rates*: The multiplexor market is based on the capability to switch and multiplex any bit rate, including bit rates below 64 kbit/s. The introduction of the narrow band ISDN, and especially inexpensive primary rate access [29] increases the need for such a function. The new services based on multimedia connections will accelerate the trend.

2. *Integration of packet and circuit switching*: Although the integration is not mandatory, it is a strategic option that reduces development costs for the equipment manufacturer, and maintenance costs for the operator. The evolution of integrated switches is illustrated in Fig. 22. A switching matrix integrating packet and circuit modes can be used in multiplexors, data

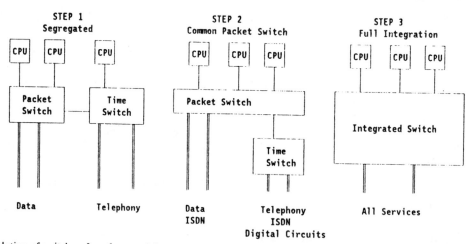

Fig. 22. Evolution of switches. Interface modules are not shown. Steps 1 and 2 are implemented in products. Step 3 is enabled by ATM switches. **Step 1**: Voice and data switches are separate. **Step 2**: The packet switch is used to integrate switching for data services and the messaging inside the installation. Servers can appear on the platform. Separate paths are used for packet-switched and circuit-switched data. **Step 3**: One single integrated switch is used for switching all services and for internal communication.

switches, cross connects, PBXs, and central office ISDN switches [74].

These two requirements can be met by Packet Switching in general; *fixed size* packet switching is well adapted to very high speed [53].

The issue here is not whether ATM switches are the best solution to these requirements, but whether the ATM should expand beyond the switch, or be limited to it. In the latter case, ATM switch fabrics are used to build powerful circuit and packet switches.

Virtually every equipment manufacturer has plans to deliver products based on ATM switches. The technology to produce ATM switches with very high throughput (in the order of 10^6 Mbit/s) is already available [75].

6. Conclusion

The ATM is the foundation for the future broadband ISDN. Sections 2 to 4 of this report have given a overview of the main concepts associated with it. The ATM is intended to support all services.

- Circuit emulation takes advantage of the flexibility for bit rate definition. Flexible transport networks can be built using virtual path connections.
- The SMDS offers a connectionless data service on top of ATM. At the user network interface, a predefined ATM connection is used. Inside the network, a datagram transport service is used; it can be implemented over ATM connections or not. In the former case, it requires an overlay network of connectionless servers. The service can be implemented without ATM signalling.
- Connection oriented data services require signaling and adaptation layer protocols that are still to be specified. Such services can provide full HDLC-like connections like frame relay.
- In a later phase, variable rate connections can support real time services (sound and animated images) and take full advantage of ATM multiplexing.

The cell format is now stable and the technology to build ATM *switches* is already available. In contrast, this is not yet true for networks that offer an ATM access. Protocols for signalling and adaptation layer remain to be fully specified.

Fundamental issues still to be solved concern traffic control and connection usage enforcement.

ATM is a universal technology, with the associated benefits and drawbacks. On the negative side, service adaptation introduces additional overhead and complexity when compared to ad-hoc solutions such as variable length packet switching for data applications or circuit switching for television distribution. On the positive side, the use of a universal, standard technology has long-term benefits for service providers and users.

Abbreviations and acronyms

AAL	ATM Adaption Layer
ATM	Asynchronous Transfer Mode
B-ISDN	Broadband ISDN
CLP	Cell Loss Priority
CLS	ConnectionLess Server
CS	Convergence Sublayer
DQDB	Distributed Queue Dual Bus
FES	Frequency Encoding Signal
Frame	AAL-SDU for data services (class C or D)
GFC	Generic Flow Control
HEC	Header Error Control
IWU	InterWorking Unit
LI	Length Indication
MID	multiplex identification
N-ISDN	Narrowband ISDN
NNI	Network–Node Interface
PCI	Protocol Control Information
PL	Physical Layer
PM	Physical Media sublayer
PT	Payload Type
S	Broadband S Reference Point
SAP	Service Access Point
SAR	Segmentation And Reassembly
SDU	Service Data Unit (unit of information crossing a SAP)
SFET	Synchronous Frequency Encoding Technique
SIP	Subscriber Interface Protocol
SMDS	Switched Multi-Megabit Data Service
SN	Segment Number
SNI	Subscriber–Network Interface
SSS	SMDS Switching System
ST	Segment Type
T	Broadband T Reference Point

TC	Transmission Convergence sublayer
UNI	User–Network Interface
VC	Virtual Channel
VCI	Virtual Channel Identifier
VP	Virtual Path
VPI	Virtual Path Identifier

Acknowledgements

The author is indebted to his colleagues at IBM, in the Race and in the COST Programs for their invaluable help and comments. Special thanks to the referees for their careful reading of the manuscript and their many constructive comments.

References

[1] Recommendations drafted by Working Party XVIII/8 (General B-ISDN aspects) to be approved in 1991, CCITT Report R45, November 1990.

[2] Draft Recommendation I.121: Broadband Aspects of ISDN, CCITT SG XVIII, Report R34, June 1990.

[3] CCITT Recommendation I.451 (Q.931), ISDN User Network Interface Layer 3 Specification for Basic Call Control, CCITT Blue Book, 1988.

[4] Draft Recommendation I.150, B-ISDN ATM Functional Characteristics, CCITT SG XVIII, Report R34, June 1990.

[5] C.A. Sunshine, ed., Computer Network Architectures and Protocols (Plenum, New York, NY 1989).

[6] F. Denissen et al., The policing function in an ATM network, International Zürich Seminar on Digital Communications, 1990.

[7] E.P. Rathgeb, Comparison of policing mechanisms for ATM Networks. Race 1022 Workshop, Paris, October 1989, CNET.

[8] G. Hebuterne and A. Gravey, A space-priority queueing mechanism for multiplexing ATM channels, ITC Specialist Seminar, Adelaide, September 1989.

[9] J.-Y. Le Boudec, An efficient solution method for Markov models of ATM links with loss priorities, Research Report RZ 2001, IBM, July 1990.

[10] P. Boyer et al., Modelling the ATD transfer technique, CNET Research Report, LAA/SLC/EVP, 1987.

[11] P. Boyer, R1022/TG8, Bearer capabilities in ATM networks, Race 1022 Workshop, Paris, October 1989, CNET, Lannion.

[12] Draft Recommendation I.321, B-ISDN Protocol Reference Model and its application, CCITT SG XVIII, Report R34, June 1990.

[13] Revised Draft Recommendation G.707, CCITT SG XVIII, Report R33, June 1990.

[14] Revised Draft Recommendation G.708, CCITT SG XVIII, Report R33, June 1990.

[15] Revised Draft Recommendation G.709, CCITT SG XVIII, Report R33, June 1990.

[16] World News Today, December 17, 1990, Contel Company of Virginia Installs Northern Telecom SONET Transport System.

[17] Draft Recommendation I.432, B-ISDN User Network Interface Specifications, CCITT SG XVIII, Report R34, June 1990.

[18] Draft Recommendation I.610, OAM Principles of B-ISDN Access, CCITT SG XVIII, Report R34, June 1990.

[19] Draft Recommendation I.362, B-ISDN AAL Functional Description, CCITT SG XVIII, Report R34, June 1990.

[20] Draft Recommendation I.363,: B-ISDN AAL Specification, CCITT SG XVIII, Report R34, June 1990.

[21] Contribution from Japan (D368) CCITT SG XVIII, Addressing and routing schemes for ATM connectionless service, 1989.

[22] Contribution from Japan (D369) CCITT SG XVIII, Cell transport method for ATM connectionless data service, 1989.

[23] Generic System Requirements in Support of Switched Multimegabit Data Service, Bellcore Technical Advisory TA-TSY-000772, Issue 3, October 1989.

[24] I. Cidon, I. Gopal and H. Meleis, Paris: an approach to integrated private networks. IEEE ICC Conference, 1986, pp. 48.2.1–48.2.4.

[25] G.I. Stassinopoulos and I.S. Venieris, ATM adaptation layer protocols for signalling, Comput. Networks ISDN Systems 23 (4) (1992) 287–304.

[26] A. Vanderwel, R. Kositpaiboon and M. Wernik, Networking requirements for interworking of frame relay and ATM, ITC Specialist Seminar, NJ, October 1990.

[27] A. Lespagnol and T. Houdouin, A high speed transport protocol on an atm network, EFOC/LAN, pp. 152–155, 1989.

[28] Wai Sum Lai, Packet mode services: from x.25 to frame relaying. Comput. Comm. 12 (1) (1989) 10–16.

[29] Communications Week, 11/12/90, p. 64, Robin Gareiss.

[30] D. Jaepel and E. Port, LAN/ISDN interconnect via frame relay, in: IEEE Globecom, 1988.

[31] J.-P. Coudreuse, ATM: domains of short term applications, ITC Specialist Seminar, NJ, October 1990.

[32] C.K. Kim, S.H. Lee and L.T. Wu, Circuit emulation. IJDACS 1 (1988) 245–256.

[33] H. Hessenmuller and S. Nunes, High quality audio and video signal transmission in a B-ISDN based on ATD—the problem of cell loss, SBT/IEEE ITS'90 (1990) 87–91.

[34] P. Pirat, Synchronization and error recovery in video terminal adapters in an ATM environment, Race 1022 Workshop, Paris, October 1989, CNET.

[35] Contribution from France (D294) CCITT SG XVIII, Timing for CBO services, 1989.

[36] Contribution from the UK (D359) CCITT SG XVIII, Timing for CBO services, 1989.

[37] Contribution from the USA CCITT SG XVIII, Timing recovery for CBO services in an ATM based network, 1989.

[38] B. Maglaris et al., Performance models of statistical multiplexing in packet video communication. IEEE Tech. Comm. 36 (7) (1988) 834–844.

[39] G. Ramamurthy and B. Sengupta, Modelling and analysis

of variable bit rate video multiplexor, ITC Specialist Seminar, NJ, October 1990.

[40] C. Nicolaou, An architecture for real time multimedia communication systems, *IEEE J. Selected Areas Comm.* **8** (3) (1990) 391–400.

[41] W.H. Leung et al., A software architecture for workstations supporting multimedia conferencing in packet switching networks, *IEEE J. Selected Areas Comm.* **8** (3) (1990).

[42] D. Thomas, C. Little and A. Ghafoor, Network considerations for distributed multimedia object composition and communication, *IEEE Network* (November 1990) 32–49.

[43] K.L. Moran, Fast packet switching—a breakthrough technology, *Telecomunications* **54** (1990) 62.

[44] J.P. Coudreuse, Les Réseaux Temporels Asynchrones: du transfert de donnéees a l'image animée, *l'Echo des Recherches* (**112**) (1982) 33–48.

[45] M. Décina, Open issues regarding the universal application of ATM for multiplexing and switching in the B-ISDN. ICC'90, 1990.

[46] P.A. Probst and S. Rao, Transport network evolution strategies for ATM based B-ISDN, ICC 90, 1990, 1469–1472.

[47] J.-P. Coudreuse, ATM: a contribution to the debate on broadband ISDN, *IJDACS* **1** (1988) 213–221.

[48] R. Haendel, Evolution of ISDN towards broadband ISDN, *IEEE Network* (January 1989) 7–13.

[49] P. Heinzmann, H.R. Muller, D. Pitt and H.R van As, Buffer-insertion Cell Synchronized Multiple Access (BCMA) on a slotted ring. IBM Research Report RZ 2063, December 1990.

[50] P. Zafiropulo, On LANs and MANs: an evolution from mbit/s to gbit/s, EFOC-LAN (1990) 15–22, 1990.

[51] M. Nassehi, Cyclic reservation multiple access scheme for Gbit/s LANs and MANs, EFOC-LAN, (1990) 246–251.

[52] S. Fuhrmann and J.-Y. Le Boudec, Burst and cell level models for ATM buffers, IBM Research Report RZ 2014, August 1990.

[53] H. Ahmadi, et al., A high performance switch fabric for integrated circuit and packet switching. IEEE Infocom 88, New Orleans, LA, 27–31 March, 1988.

[54] J.P. Hurault, Le Point Sur le Relayage de Trame, DNAC '90, 1990, Paris, France.

[55] P. Adam, Echo subjective tests and switching delays, Workshop on Hybrid and ATM Topics, 1988.

[56] A.E. Eckbert, D.T. Luan and D.M. Lucantoni, An approach to controlling congestion in ATM networks, *IJDACS* **3** (2) (1990) 199–209.

[57] KOS TUTUFOR (European Project COST 224), On admission control and policing in ATM networks, ITC Specialist Seminar, NJ, October 1990.

[58] H. Ahmadi, R. Guérin and M. Naghshineh, Analysis of rate based access control mechanisms for high speed networks. IBM Research Report RC 15831, May 1990.

[59] M.C. Chuah and R.L. Cruz, Approximate analysis of average performance of $\alpha - \rho$ regulators. Infocom '90, (1990) 874–880.

[60] P. Boyer, A congestion control for the ATM, 7th ITC Seminar, 1990.

[61] R. Jain, Myths about congestion control in high speed networks, ITC Specialist Seminar, NJ, October 1990.

[62] A. Gersht and K.J. Lee, A congestion control framework for ATM networks, Infocom '89 (1989) 701–710.

[63] C.A. Cooper and K.I. Parks, A reasonable solution to the broadband congestion problem, *IJDACS* **3** (2) (1990) 103–115.

[64] H. Ahmadi and R. Guérin, Bandwidth allocation in high speed networks based on the concept of equivalent capacity, ITC Specialist Seminar, NJ, October, 1990.

[65] Z. Dziong et al., Admission control and routing in atm networks, ITC Specialist Seminar, Adelaide, 1989.

[66] M. Decina and T. Toniatti, On bandwidth allocation to bursty virtual connections in ATM networks, ICC '90, 1990.

[67] G. Gallassi, G. Rigolio and L. Fratta, ATM: bandwidth assignment and bandwidth enforcement policies, Globecom '89, 1989.

[68] J.A.S. Monteiro, M. Gerla and L. Fratta, Statistical multiplexing in ATM networks, *Performance Evaluation* **12** (3) (1991) 157–167.

[69] P. Crocetti, G. Gallassi and M. Gerla, Internetworking of MANS and ATM, ITC Specialist Seminar, NJ, October 1990.

[70] B. Dines Larsen, Performance evaluation and quality of service in telecommunication networks, Research Report 3/1990, IMSOR, August 1990.

[71] D. Ferrari and D.C. Verma, A scheme for real time channel establishment in wide area networks, *IEEE J. Selected Areas Comm.* **8** (3) (1990) 368–379.

[72] W. Kleinöder, P. Lebouc, P.E. Stern and M. Tielemann, Constraint logic programming for a virtual path bandwidth manager. 4th TMN Workshop, Dublin, November 1990.

[73] J.-Y. Le Boudec, Monitoring cell losses due to buffer overflow. 3rd TMN Workshop, London, November 1990.

[74] Bell-Northern Research, DMS SuperNode: Architecture and Technology, Miscellany (1988) 5.

[75] T.T. Lee, A modular architecture for very large packet switches, Globecom, 1989.

[76] Anonymous referee's comment.

[77] CCITT WG XVIII/8, Report of Working Party XVIII/8; General B-ISDN Aspects, TD 22 (Plen), June 1991.

CHAPTER II

SWITCHING

This chapter provides a survey of ATM switching architectures, and then includes in-depth treatment of switching implementations.

An Analysis of Universal Multimedia Switching Architectures

Radhika R. Roy

Ashok K. Kuthyar

Vanita Katkar

Distributed multimedia applications impose stringent and complex requirements on the switching and transport architectures of a network. An analysis shows that both synchronous transfer mode (STM) and asynchronous transfer mode (ATM) can meet the bandwidth and performance requirements of the emerging multimedia applications. ATM becomes the technology of choice, however, since it can:

- Transfer multimedia traffic efficiently, via its channel sharing capability,

- Employ statistical multiplexing using cell-switching to obtain high channel utilization, and

- Support connectivity eficiently in many-to-one, one-to-many, and many-to-many communications environments.

Introduction: A Confluence of Technologies

High-level cell-switching technology is becoming more cost-effective than traditional packet-switching, due to the:
- Integration of more functions into the hardware, and
- Falling price of hardware.[1]

The present high-speed technologies permit bandwidth-intensive distributed multimedia applications to be switched cost-effectively and efficiently. For example, large-capacity storage disks and high-speed fiber-optic networks are making it possible to integrate diverse media, such as audio, video, and data.[2] This paper defines data to include text, still images, and graphics.

Most of us have seen the AT&T "You Will" television commercial in which a man on a tropical beach communicates via a portable workstation with his less fortunate peers back in their office. His workstation screen shows a two-way video capability, text and graphics areas, and a collaborative work area where changes made in a document by one participant are visible on all other participants' workstations.

Although apparently a very simple application from the user's point of view, the combining of audio, video, and data (called a multimedia application) places very stringent performance requirements on the network.

This is especially so if, as in the commercial, the applications involve real-time interactions between senders and receivers. These performance requirements include:
- Limits on voice and video signal delays, so that they are not perceptible to users;
- Synchronization of intramedia and intermedia signal streams;
- Low bit-error-rates (BER) to accommodate requirements, especially for data; and
- Very low probabilities of losing cells during transmission.

In this paper, emphasis is on how multimedia applications affect the network by presenting data streams with varying characteristics, and not on how the user interfaces with the applications.

Let's return to the commercial for an example. The video communications between the beach comber and his office mates would involve video encoders in each workstation. These encoders, which use bit compression techniques to reduce the bandwidth necessary to transmit a video signal, introduce a certain amount of intrinsic processing delay that would exceed any delay in a typical voice signal. Yet, the voice signals might also be encoded to compress the bit rate, introducing their own delay. Thus, the voice and video signals, each with different amounts of pro-

dous challenges for system engineers to design an optimal, yet cost-effective, global switching system. To list but a few of these challenges, the hardware architecture must provide high processing power to handle multimedia applications. A multimedia operating system must support multimedia data types, real-time scheduling of calls, and fast-interrupt processing, when a computer's central processing unit has to execute complex functions of multimedia applications. Storage and memory requirements include very high-capacity, fast access times, and high transfer rates. The high bandwidth, low latency, and low jitter required for multimedia applications also will necessitate new networking and protocol architectures.

Requirements for Multimedia Applications

To understand the basic switching requirements for multimedia networking, these applications can be categorized based on:
- Whether the delivery of media signals is real-time or non-real-time among the communicating entities, or participants;
- The types of connections between endpoints; and
- The symmetry of the traffic flow.

The major categories of multimedia applications are:
- Multimedia collaboration (MMC), where multiple participants located at different locations can work collaboratively;
- Multimedia information services (MIS), where individuals can access network-based or third-party databases;
- Video-on-demand (VOD), where subscribers can access any video presentation;
- Multimedia mail (MMM), where subscribers can send and receive enhanced versions of electronic mail that include video and audio storage capabilities.

All four categories are expected to be used by both business and residential customers.

The key attributes that differentiate each type of application are shown in Table I. These attributes will have a major impact on determining the appropriate multimedia networking architecture. It is clear that most MMC, MIS, and VOD will be real-time applications, while MMM, a form of electronic mail, will usually be a non-real-time application.

Multimedia Collaboration (MMC). Multimedia collaboration enables a number of participants to use vari-

cessing delay, have to be synchronized by the network before they are presented to the other participants.

Delay is also involved in any collaborative work in which electronic files have to be accessed by the workstations, formatted, and transmitted to all other participants. A certain amount of file search and processing delay is expected in this operation, but not so much that the natural rhythm of the conference would be adversely affected by delays.

Interactive data traffic, in which the participants react to each other in real time, also requires very fast response times. This is made all the more complicated for network management because the bandwidth for these applications vary between a few kilobits per second (Kbits/s), for terminal-to-terminal communication, to multi-gigabits per second (Gbits/s) for, say, video conferencing that involves collaborative work on text and high-resolution graphics.

The functional requirements for distributed multimedia applications also are very complex. For example, a simple point-to-point voice call can evolve, at the users' discretion, to become a multimedia call, or a multipoint multimedia call if additional participants are added on. Or a call may, in the extreme, exist without any connections. That is, since audio, video, and data connections can be established, then dropped and re-established without a new call setup being required, it is possible that a call can exist but be without any connections.

The requirements imposed by multimedia applications on the network are enormous, and pose tremen-

Table I. Attributes for differentiating multimedia applications

Multimedia application category	Media [audio, video, data (text, still images)] delivery		Connectivity			Traffic flow characteristic	
	Real time	Non-real time	One-to-many	Many-to-one	Many-to-many	Symmetric	Asymmetric
Multimedia collaboration	Yes		Yes		Yes	Yes	
Multimedia information service	Yes		Yes				Yes
Video on demand	Yes		Yes				Yes
Multimedia messaging		Yes	Yes	Yes		Yes	Yes

ous media in either real-time or non-real-time, while located at multiple sites.[3] Multipoint communications can be one-to-many, called multicast; many-to-one; or many-to-many. Each participant will be able to send and receive audio, video, and data signals, and perform certain collaborative activities with other participants by using a multimedia workstation and other devices equipped with a built-in or attached video camera and audio capabilities. The multimedia workstation uses the concept of a virtual work space that, given the current level of terminal sophistication, consists of a space, or window, on a screen for the participants' video images; a collaborative information window for reference materials, such as text, still images, graphics, and other video applications; other function-specific or general-use windows; plus, of course, the audio signals.

This basic, though not particularly simple concept of a virtual work space is expected to become even more complex as computer technology continues to advance. Thus, any network plans being made today must take into account that multimedia applications are in their infancy, and are guaranteed to become more complex.

MMC is primarily used for real-time communications, but collaborative activities also can be done on a non-real-time basis. A real-time application would be a user adding or deleting multiple parties, or media, as desired during a call, or actively editing a file. An example of a non-real-time application could be a chess game carried on via e-mail, with participants viewing, whenever they desired, the stored video signals of their opponents making each move.

Real-time multimedia also will have to support audio and video conferences in much the same manner that people participate in person-to-person conferences today. In addition to expected features, such as a graceful way to interrupt a speaker, the technology will have to support such ancillary interactions as 'break outs' or sub-conferencing, 'whispering' or side conversations during the main conference, and e-mail note passing. In addition, conference recording storage capabilities will be required for MMC, including those features commonly found today on a VCR, including playback, pause, rewind, random access, slow-motion, and fast-forward.

Real-time multimedia collaboration also has to provide acceptable real-time responses between participants. The biggest performance challenge in MMC occurs when conference participants continuously transmit audio and video data streams. Whereas a face-to-face conference has a chairperson to moderate the participants, some sort of network protocol will have to be developed to act as a 'traffic cop' for the multiple data streams in a multimedia conference.

Other issues are being studied to ensure optimal communications architectures for multimedia collaboration, including such functions as the mixing of audio and video streams to provide both intramedia and intermedia synchronization continuously, and sharing applications between multiple users at different sites while still providing consistent views of all meeting places.

Multimedia Information Service (MIS). Multimedia information service gives end-users access to multimedia information. Like MMC, multimedia workstations or other devices are used to interact with multimedia servers and navigate through a wide variety of information. A wide range of electronic information services could include such obvious examples as electronically accessible print news from newspapers, magazines, and journals; stored images of television news, medical information, real-estate services, and sales catalogues; ecological information and library services. Once multimedia capabilities are commonplace in the network, MIS will electronically bring together information seekers and content providers in as yet undreamed of applications.

Communications between an MIS end-user and the service application server is usually point-to-point, although with multiple end users accessing the service, it will appear to be point-to-multipoint from the server's perspective. In some situations, multiple servers will be involved for a given transaction if all the information is not available on a single server. The outputs of these servers, therefore, have to be coordinated to provide an integrated response to the end-user. The downstream bandwidth (from the server to the user) usually is much higher than that of the upstream bandwidth (from the user to the server). This on-demand interactive application can be characterized as point-to-point and multipoint, bi-directional, asymmetric service.

The MIS system must provide a number of functions, such as call and connection setup and control, a client-server architecture, the dynamic allocation of network and multimedia database resources, media synchronization, fast retrieval times, error-free transmission of textual data, graceful degradation under fault conditions, and, of course, the multimedia information databases.

Video-on-Demand (VOD). Video-on-demand is an interactive service that lets the user access a large selection of movies or video programs via a point-to-point connection. This connection gives the user individual and instantaneous control of the storage medium, in terms of program start, fast-forward, pause, slow motion, random access, and rewind actions. Indeed, the service should have at least all the features offered by a VCR today.

The set-up movie device attached to the set, along with the television monitor and the remote control, lets viewers connect to the video server and browse through a selection of movies or other contents, such as news stories, documentaries, software, do-it-yourself programs, or games. Multimedia workstations, high definition televisions, or other devices could be used for this application.

The primary characteristics of this service are:

- Retrieving the program content from the video server at the user's request;
- A very fast completion rate of the user's request;
- High-quality transmission for all media;
- The degree of interactivity being determined by the user, such as interactive VOD with a choice of instantaneous or delayed access;
- Instantaneous control of the video program by the user, including start, fast-forward, pause, random access, and rewind actions; and
- A very high quality of service, including a very low bit-error-rate (BER), very low jitter rate, and the maintenance of intramedia and intermedia synchronization.

This on-demand, bi-directional, asymmetrical service will require a very high bandwidth for downstream transmission from the server to the user, compared to that of the upstream transmission from the user to the server. Although the bandwidth required for the individual user to access and control the service may not be significant, the total volume of bandwidth generated by all users could be substantial to the network.

Multimedia Messaging (MMM). Multimedia messaging, or electronic mail, is a non-real-time messaging service that transfers multimedia information in a store-and-forward mode. The end-to-end communication characteristics of MMM can be point-to-point or multipoint, and bi-directional, asymmetric or unidirectional.

MMM is considered to be an extension of existing electronic messaging systems, with the addition of audio or video features in the body of the message. Although the use of MMM is in its infancy, it is expected that this application will be popular with both business and residential customers alike.

The performance requirements for multimedia mail are not stringent, compared to those for real-time multimedia communication, because MMM is a non-real-time, store-and-forward, communication system. The service should, however, support a unified mailbox, in which messages incorporating a variety of media can be stored, controlled, and accessed.

Summary of Multimedia Requirements. The key requirements for multimedia communications that should be supported by the underlying switching and transport systems can be summarized as follows:

- Bandwidth allocation for each medium;
- Performance parameters appropriate to each media, such as delay, BER/cell loss rate, and synchronization; and

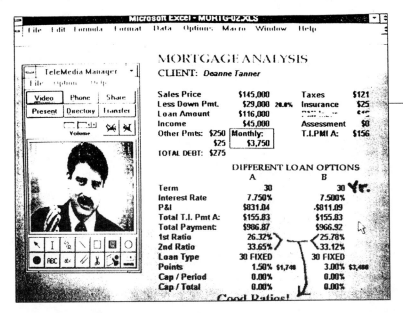

Figure 1. Multimedia applications involve two-way, real-time voice, data, and video data streams, including collaborative work areas where changes made by one conference participant can be viewed in real time by all others. Such applications place very stringent performance requirements on the network.

- Functional features, including call and connection control, routing, congestion control, quality of service (QOS) parameter control, and media bridging.

These multimedia applications have many more functional requirements than we have discussed, such as conference management, multimedia databases, multimedia storage, video server technology, user directories, security issue, and others. While important, these requirements have relatively minor influence on the selection of switching or transport architectures. As such, they are not addressed in this paper.

Multimedia and Switching Requirements

Multimedia collaboration imposes complex requirements for transferring real-time traffic within acceptable response times for point-to-point or multipoint, and multipoint-to-multipoint communications. There is a tremendous challenge to designing an optimal switching communication architecture that guarantees performance for all media. Although MIS, VOD, and MMM have certain unique characteristics, the requirements of these applications can be met by any switching systems that fulfill the requirements of multimedia collaboration.

It is reasonable to assume that the common characteristics of these applications constitute the fundamental requirements that must be met by any switching system. The switching system must be capable of handling a wide range of different bit rates and traffic parameters, as well as any functional requirements, in flexible and cost-effective ways. The requirements that have the greatest influence on the design of the switching characteristics are addressed in this section.

Bandwidth Requirements. The range of bandwidth requirements for an individual medium can be summarized[3] as follows:
- Audio bandwidth - Uncompressed at 64 Kbits/s to

1.536 Mbits/s; compressed at 16 to 384 Kbits/s; burstiness (peak/average) at 1-3.
- Video bandwidth - Uncompressed at 3 to 166 Mbits/s (high definition TV not included); compressed at 56 Kbits/s to 35 Mbits/s (HDTV not included); burstiness (peak/average) at 1-10.
- Data (text, still images, graphics) - Uncompressed at 155 bits/s to 12 Gbits/s; compressed at 800 Kbps to 1.2 Gbits/s; burstiness (peak/average) at 3 to 1000.

The bandwidth of any multimedia application depends on a combination of media, and the total traffic may vary between a few Kbits/s and multi-Gbits/s. Thus, any switching system must support this wide range of different bit rates and traffic parameters.

Traffic Characteristics. The switching system of a network must be informed of the expected traffic characteristics of a call, when a connection is requested, in order to optimize the switch's resources and accurately predict its ability to maintain a certain level of performance.

The burstiness of traffic depends on two parameters: *peak* and *average* traffic. In addition to the burstiness of traffic from multimedia applications, *burst length* and the *variance of traffic* are also useful parameters. Statistical multiplexing is less effective with longer lengths of bursts[4] and, thus, fewer active users can be supported for a given amount of bandwidth. Therefore, a set of traffic descriptors should be used within the network switch to accurately characterize the traffic parameters for each medium. Algorithms may have to be used to calculate the composite bandwidth required for a given multimedia call, based on the peak bit rate, peak-to-average bit rate ratio, variance of the bit rate, and the burst length of each medium.

From the amount of traffic that a switch must handle in order to establish a multimedia call, it becomes apparent that a switching system needs to employ sophisticated control mechanisms to enforce bandwidth for the bursty sources.[5, 6]

Performance Requirements. The performance characteristics of real-time multimedia collaboration are usually more stringent than for any other applications, such as MIS, VOD, and MMM. As noted, MMM is primarily a non-real-time application, and its performance requirements are the least stringent. If a switching system meets the requirements for real-time multimedia traffic, therefore, it can be expected that it will meet the requirements of non-real-time traffic, as well. This section describes the general characteristics for performance *parameters*[3] that must be satisfied by the switching system.

Delay. The delay requirements of multimedia applications are the most important parameters to consider in designing the fundamental constraints of the switching architecture. Many delay constraints are required to be maintained.

For example, a *one-way, end-to-end* delay for a real-time isochronous medium, such as audio or video, should be between 100 and 150 milliseconds, including propagation, network, and equipment delay.

End-to-end delay jitter should be very low, less than 250 microseconds in some cases, but a precise limit has yet to be determined.

The *differential delay* between audio and video transmission should be no more than -20 milliseconds to +40 milliseconds.

The *response time* for retrieving an object, such as a file, should be between one and two seconds, with a 0.5-second delay or less for document browsing.

The *recovery* of data traffic from errors through retransmissions should be done before the time-outs of the higher-layer protocols.

The *combination* of multiple video streams into a single composite video stream (for display in a single video window) should be done with negligible delay—if all originating video sources are synchronized to the same video clock. Otherwise, combining the signals should not take more than one video frame time.

The *frequency* of call setup, tear down, and redirection for audio and video should be less than that of a mouse click or keyboard stroke.

Bit-Error-Rate and Cell Loss. *Bit-error-rates* (BER) should be very low, such as one cell in error for every

hour of transmission in the case of a cell-switching network. The precise value required, however, has yet to be determined.

Recovery from bit errors for data traffic, such as text, still images, and graphics, should be done through retransmissions, with the help of higher-layer protocols.

Synchronization. Multimedia applications include multiple sources of various media, separated either *spatially* or *temporally*, to create integrated composite multimedia objects. The switching system should have the capabilities to ensure both intramedia and intermedia synchronization:

Intramedia synchronization is required to determine the rate at which events must occur within a single medium stream. The limit of delay jitter has to be maintained by the given media stream.

Intermedia synchronization determines the relative schedule of separate synchronization streams, such as the intermedia synchronization between audio and video streams. The limits of differential delay have to be maintained between the different media streams.

Functional Requirements. Multimedia applications have many complex functional requirements, and the switching system should be flexible enough to support those functions in order to optimize the performance of multimedia communications.

The *call control* and *connection control* are two such important functions that must be supported. Call control involves establishing the parameters of the call, such as the characteristics of the call and the types of end points to be connected. Connection control, applied after the completion of the call control stage, includes such functions as routing, congestion control, QOS parameter control, and media bridging.

Call and Connection Setup/Control. Distributed networked multimedia applications, especially MMC, require call setup modifications as required, call execution, and call release for communications between different users. It is clear from the characteristics of these applications that a call can no longer be viewed as a monolithic object, that is, a static point-to-point connection. Rather, it has to be managed as a complex interaction of multipoint communications that may change even *after* the call is set up.

The components of a composite multimedia call must be handled individually and dynamically. It becomes a prerequisite, therefore, to separate call and connection functions for controlling the various combina-

tions of connectivity and interactivity of a multimedia communications. Such combinations can include:
- Setup and release of a call, involving virtual circuits, that has no connection;
- Setup and release of a call and its connection(s) simultaneously;
- Modification of existing calls to add or drop connections, add or drop parties, or change the QOS parameters and bandwidth for heterogeneous communication between parties; and
- Context or persistency maintenance before, during, and after the communication session of a call.

Separating call and connection functions:
- Frees the switching resources from being tied up during call negotiation when the call is being established,
- Allows for independent routing connections in order to globally optimize the use of networking resources, and
- Permits flexible choices for providing switching resources.

Call control is viewed as a preparation to initiate a communication between the parties involved, setting the stage prior to the connection being established. The requirements for call control to support multimedia, multi-user applications can be summarized as follows:
- A call will have phases to establish, modify, execute, and terminate communications between different entities. All requests and negotiations for resources supporting the individual connections by a call can be done dynamically. It also may be necessary that a call be established or released with no connections, or that a call and its connections be established or released simultaneously.
- A call involves multiple media and multiple parties or entities, along with their specific characteristics and requirements. Therefore, the coordination functions for connections between parties or entities will be required in a call.
- A call contains relationships between users, media, and system resources, and their capabilities and compatibilities must be expressed to the network for a successful communication. A call between parties or entities also can be established in a heterogeneous communications environment. Either way, the use of these capabilities can also be augmented, modified, or deleted dynamically during a call.
- Each user can control the information of a medium individually for an existing call.
- Intermedia relationships can exist in a multimedia, multi-user application call.
- Parties or entities can be added and removed dynamically at any time during a call. Parties will be notified of any changes.
- Different permissions to modify the call can be given to individual parties through authentication procedures. These permissions can be changed dynamically during the call to maintain ownership and call control rights. Services can be screened between the parties.
- A call will allow negotiations between different entities for system resources.

Connection control comes after the completion of all preparations of the call control stage. In the connection control stage, a real connection links the parties or entities. In brief, the functions of the connection control are:
- Establishing, modifying, executing, and releasing connections between parties or entities;
- Supervising the quality-of-service parameters;
- Providing flow control, congestion control, routing, and reservation, allocation, negotiation, and renegotiation of resources;
- Notifying the network of party or entity changes; and
- Managing ownership and control rights.

From the point of view of the switching architecture, it also may be necessary to guarantee end-to-end QOS parameters within and across networks for a given call, and connection control will be required to translate these requirements in real-time to establish and manage connections.

Routing. The switching system should be fast enough to select the routing strategy that maximizes the long-term network throughput and provide the lowest possible end-to-end delay. Connection management will select paths between the source and destination points that will meet these objectives to optimize the use of network resources.

Many routing algorithms that provide optimal dynamic routing, such as load balancing, shortest path, and load balancing with modified shortest path, are discussed in the literature.[7, 8] These studies primarily consider, however, a single medium for a given call. Routing algorithms now must be developed to consider multimedia traffic containing audio, video, and data, and the criteria for selecting a path should include the traffic parameters of each medium to calculate the load for each connection. Therefore, switching systems must employ more complex routing algorithms than they use today to optimize network capacity.

Congestion Control. Congestion control is a primary concern of cell-switching networks, where the multimedia traffic will be switched in the form of cells. In general, the cell-switching network will provide neither link-by-link error control through retransmissions, nor link-by-link flow control. Instead, it will use end-to-end error control, internal virtual circuits, and hardware switching to:
- Avoid large delays due to cell processing and queuing time within the switching nodes, and
- Minimize the variable delays between the cells.[9]

From a switching point of view, a multimedia connection can be considered as a connection that carries several media. Each medium has its own characteristics and QOS requirements, and should be treated separately. Audio and video traffic, for example, cannot be retransmitted to recover from errors, but data traffic must be recovered from errors through retransmissions.

In high-speed switching networks—where propagation delays across the network typically dominate switching, and buffering delays and the traditional feedback from the network to control congestion are outdated—any action the source that is generating the traffic takes is too late to resolve buffering or switching congestion. This situation becomes worse if the network has to handle real-time audio or video traffic. Therefore, high-speed networks will have to provide preventive congestion control schemes to handle bandwidth-intensive multimedia applications.

Quality-of-Service Parameter Control. In cell-switching networks, the primary QOS parameters include cell delays, cell-delay variations, and cell-loss probability. In addition, BER, differential delay between audio and video, and end-to-end delay also are important performance parameters.

A call will be accepted based on the QOS parameters negotiated at the time of call setup. The network, before accepting a call, will examine the current load and decide whether the switching system can maintain the required performance levels. Congestion can occur when the system accepts too many calls, which will deteriorate the QOS. Thus, congestion control schemes that are used by the switching systems are very critical to maintaining the promised QOS and preventing congestion.

Media Bridging. Media bridging provides the capability to communicate from any given point to any other end points, in the same or different networks, for audio, video, or data. In other words, bridging provides point-to-multipoint or multicast communications.

Multicasting is an important requirement for many multimedia applications, especially for MMC. In a circuit-switched environment, a point-to-multipoint dedicated connection is established for a call. Because these circuits are dedicated, not shared, for the duration of the call, they are costly propositions, especially for variable bit rate traffic, because of the low utilization of trunk bandwidth. In a cell or packet switching mode, however, multiple virtual connections can be set up for multicast connections. The bandwidth of each circuit path can be shared logically among different calls. This provides economies of scale by taking advantage of the bursty characteristics of multimedia communications.

Shared medium LANs, such as AT&T's StarLAN network or Ethernet,* have the unique property of providing multipoint connectivity by broadcasting in a limited local environment. But the same cannot be applied in a wide area network environment, because of the increased probability of packet collisions. Recently, however, a multicast protocol has been developed for multimedia traffic across wide area networks.[10]

Many algorithms also are available to implement broadcasting or multicasting to a group of connected entities. A limited implementation could be achieved by placing a multicast server in each switching system, but a much more efficient approach is to support multicast operation directly within the switch.[11]

The idea of supporting multimedia bridging within the switch is an active research subject, made all the more complex by the fact that the requirements for bridging each medium may differ to some extent. For example, audio bridging requires the summation of all (or the loudest) audio incoming signals, and it then delivers only the sum to each endpoint. This summation has to be performed before the multicasting of the audio signals. In addition, if the endpoints use different coding standards, the conversion between the different types of speech coding techniques used may also be required.

In simple video bridging, a single video signal is sent to multiple destinations. In the case of multimedia collaboration, the video signal that is to be multicast may have to be transmitted based on some agreed upon principles. For example, a voice control scheme may be based on audio intensity and, therefore, multicasts of the video will be associated with the highest audio intensity.

If a pre-designated chairperson controls the selection of the video source, the video bridge will multicast that video source, based on the chairperson's selection. In some instances, each viewer also might choose an individual video for multicasting. Therefore, video multicasting, which may change several times during the course of the conference, has to be coordinated with audio bridging. This inter-relationship between audio and video is the fundamental cornerstone for multimedia applications, especially for MMC.

Data bridging is required when more than one entity is allowed to send data. The ordering of data can be performed in accordance with some predefined procedures. For example, a simple multicast function can be performed when a single source has to transmit data to multiple destinations. In more complex interactions, however, a data bridge might receive data units from different sources. It then must send all data units to all destinations as they are received, without performing any ordering of the data units.

In another situation, the data bridge may be required to multicast data units received from multiple sources in a strict order. In all, there may be many more variations of these data bridging functions, depending upon user needs.

The performance objectives of media bridging is very stringent for multimedia applications. For example, lip-synchronization of audio and video signals and the fast processing of all required bridging functions, to name but two applications, present tremendous challenges to the switching systems. Needless to say, media bridging also is an active topic for research for the engineering community.

Switching Technique Alternatives

The switching systems that carry multimedia applications should have certain basic properties to satisfy the performance requirements of real-time audio and video, as well as data traffic.

Cell-switching networks should provide fixed, low end-to-end delay with little or no variation, and little or no variation in cell delay. In this respect, asynchronous transfer mode (ATM), synchronous transfer mode (STM, also called circuit switching), frame relay (FR), and Switched Multimegabit Data Service* 802.6 (SMDS) switching techniques are four candidates for comparison. This section compares the properties of these different switching techniques.

The traditional packet-switching technologies using software switching and variable packet size have not been considered here, because these systems cannot guarantee the performance of real-time audio and video traffic. Most of these traditional switching technologies use link-by-link error and flow control, and some of them use connectionless routing. Consequently, these systems have large end-to-end delays, with significant variability and considerable packet delay jitter. Moreover, if these large traditional systems happen to transfer multimedia traffic, they can develop serious bottlenecks, even though they use sophisticated adaptive routing and congestion control algorithms.

Table II shows a high-level comparison between ATM, STM, SMDS, and FR. SMDS uses fixed cell size and connectionless routing, while FR uses variable packet size and connection-oriented routing. ATM uses fixed cell size and connection-oriented routing. STM circuit-switching uses connection-oriented routing and transfers information bit streams to maintain that order. Connectionless routing does not incur any call setup delay, since cells are transferred without prior establishment of the routing path.

Connectionless routing schemes, as noted, do not guarantee to maintain the order of the cells, and resequencing of the cells is usually required at the destination point. In addition, more processing is needed for connectionless traffic, since routing has to be performed on a per-cell or per-packet basis.

Both connectionless routing and variable packet size will cause relatively large variable cell and packet delays, and may not guarantee the delay performance parameters required for real-time audio and video traffic.

Performance: STM is the best technology to guarantee performance for both real-time audio, video, and data, although ATM also can guarantee that performance parameters are met for all multimedia traffic. Both SMDS and FR will be able to guarantee the performance for data, but it is not clear whether these switching technologies will guarantee delay performance for real-time audio and video traffic.

Bandwidth: STM and ATM will provide multi-

Gigabits per seconds bit rates; SMDS and FR are currently defined at 45 and 1.5 Mbits/s, respectively, although it is claimed that FR can also transfer efficiently up to45 Mbits/s.

Synchronization: STM and ATM technology will guarantee both intra- and inter-media synchronization of audio and video traffic, because of negligible or no delay jitter, low fixed end-to-end delay, and little or no variation in cell delay.

Connectivity: ATM, SMDS, and FR can provide flexible connectivity for one-to-many, many-to-one, and many-to-many communications environments. STM can provide one-to-many and many-to-one connectivity in a limited way, but it does not offer efficient many-to-many communications, as compared to cell- and packet-switching technology.

Support of Multimedia Traffic: Both ATM and STM can carry audio, video, and data traffic, but STM is not intended to transfer variable-bit rate (VBR) audio and video traffic efficiently. SMDS and FR have been standardized to carry data only.

Channel Sharing and Trunk Utilization: ATM, FR, and SMDS can both exploit the bursty characteristics of multimedia traffic and share channels through statistical multiplexing. As noted, however, STM cannot share a channel using statistical multiplexing. Consequently, trunk bandwidth utilization remains very low for STM, while ATM, SMDS, or FR technology supports very high utilization of the trunk bandwidth.

Congestion Control: One advantage of STM is that, with its dedicated channel for a call, it does not need to have a congestion control scheme after call setup, whereas ATM, SMDS, and FR require elaborate congestion control to guarantee the required QOS parameters negotiated at the time of the call setup. The success of these cell and packet-switching technologies to carry multimedia traffic will depend on the effectiveness of their congestion control schemes.

Summary of Comparisons. By this comparison, it is clear that ATM is the only

Table II. Comparison of switching technologies multimedia traffic

Parameters			Technology alternatives			
			ATM	STM (Circuit switching)	SMDS (802.6)	Frame Relay
Support of multimedia traffic transfer	Data		Yes	Yes	Yes	Yes
	Audio	CBR	Yes	Yes		
		VBR	Yes			
	Video	CBR	Yes	Yes		
		VBR	Yes			
Connectivity	One-to-many		Yes	Limited	Yes	Yes
	Many-to-one		Yes	Limited	Yes	Yes
	Many-to-many		Yes		Yes	Yes
Performance guarantee	Delay for audio/video		Yes	Yes		
	Packet loss for data		Yes	Not applicable	Yes	Yes
Bandwidth			1.5 Mbits/s to multi Gbits/s	Few bits/s to multi Gbits/s	1.5 Mbits/s to 45 Mbits/s	56 kbits/s to 1.5 (claim 45) Mbits/s
Guarantee of media synchronization			Yes	Yes		
Round trip delay			Low	Lower than ATM	Higher than ATM	Higher than ATM
Channel/trunk sharing capabilities			Yes	No	Yes	Yes
Channel/trunk utilization			High	Low	High	High
Congestion control			Required	Not required	Required	Required

ATM - Asynchronous transfer mode
CBR - Constant bit rate
SMDS - Switched Multi-megabit Data Service
STM - Synchronous transfer mode
VBR - Variable bit rate

switching technology of choice that has the promise to carry multimedia signals efficiently by sharing channels through statistical multiplexing. In addition, ATM can guarantee the performance for multimedia traffic, including the synchronization for each medium. STM technology also will guarantee superior performance for multimedia traffic, but it lacks the capability of efficient trunk utilization. Moreover, there is no cost-effective scheme that can compete with ATM, on a multiparty variable-bit rate call, to transfer multimedia signals. Furthermore, ATM also can support circuit connections through synchronous-to-ATM conversion (SAC).

Therefore, ATM will support both circuit- and cell/packet-switching traffic and has the ability to be the core switching technology.

Conclusions

The key parameters of multimedia applications that most influence the criteria for switching architecture are:
- Media, such as audio, video, and data;
- Bandwidth, from a few Kbits/s to multi-Gbits/s;
- Traffic characteristics, including burstiness, burst length, and variance of bandwidth;
- Performance, including end-to-end delay, delay jitter, differential delay (primarily between audio and video), response time, cell and packet switching time and retransmission delay (for data traffic), bit-error-rate and cell loss rate, and intra- and intermedia synchronization; and
- Functional requirements, including call control and connection control, connectivity, routing, congestion control, QOS parameters control, and media bridging.

The bandwidth requirements, traffic characteristics, and performance criteria are the fundamental parameters that should determine the basic switching technology. Multimedia applications have diverse, but stringent, requirements for audio, video, and data. The complex functional requirements of multimedia applications impose additional burdens on the switching system.

A given switching architecture is required to meet the stringent requirements in a cost-effective way to provide an optimized solution for multimedia networking. The comparison between switching techniques reveals that both STM and ATM can meet both performance and bandwidth requirements for the emerging multimedia applications. ATM needs to employ sophisti-

cated congestion control to guarantee the required QOS parameters. But STM appears to be incapable of providing an efficient solution in many-to-many communications. This technology also does not have channel sharing capability, which provides for the high utilization of the channel bandwidth by taking advantage of the burstiness of multimedia traffic.

ATM can provide statistical multiplexing for bursty multimedia traffic, thus yielding a high utilization of the trunk bandwidth. ATM also can support circuit connections. Therefore, ATM can become the core switching technique to support both circuit, cell, and packet switching applications.

The efficient support of additional functionalities, such as media bridging within the switching architecture, is a significant challenge because of the complexities involved. Routing algorithms used for switching also must be optimized to meet the diverse requirements of multiple media. The separation of call control and connection control is a fundamental requirement, in a distributed networked multimedia environment, to:
- Optimize the use of the network resources, and
- Maintain flexibility for the complex interaction between different networking entities.

The ATM switching system[12] appears to be flexible enough to support these functions, and to optimize the execution of multimedia communications.

* Ethernet is a registered trademark of Xerox Corporation;
Switched Multi-megabit Data Service is a registered trademark of Bellcore

References

1. J. McQuillan, "From Packet to Cell: Better Performance," *Business Communications Review* (BCR), May 1994.
2. S. Ramanatham and P. Venkat Rangan, "Architecture for Personalized Media," *IEEE Multimedia*, Vol. 1, No. 1, Spring 1994.
3. R. Roy, "Networking Constraints in Multimedia Conferencing and the Role of ATM Networks," *AT&T Technical Journal*, Vol. 73, No. 4, July-August, 1994.
4. L. Dittmann and S. B. Jacobsen, "Statistical Multiplexing of Independent Bursty Sources in ATM Network," *Proceedings*, IEEE GLOBECOM 1988.
5. A. E. Eckberg, Jr., D. T. Luan, and D. M. Lucantoni, "Meeting the Challenge: Congestion and Flow Control Strategies for Broadband Information Transport," *Proceedings*, IEEE GLOBECOM, 1989.
6. M. Sidi, W. Z. Liu, I. Cidon, and I. Gopal, "Congestion Control Through Input Rate Regulation," *Proceedings*, IEEE GLOBECOM, 1989.
7. M. Schwartz, "Telecommunication Networks: Protocols, Modeling and Analysis," Addision-Wesley Publishing Company, 1987.

45

8. I. Cidon, I. Gopal and R. Guerin, "Bandwidth Management and Congestion Control in plaNET," *IEEE Communication Magazine*, Vol. 29, No. 10, October, 1991.
9. W. Stallings, "ISDN and Broadband ISDN," McMillan Publishing Company, 1992.
10. S. Casner, "Are You on the MBone?," *IEEE Multimedia*, Vol. 1, No. 2, Summer 1994.
11. P. Newman, "ATM Technology for Corporate Networks," *IEEE Communications Magazine*, Vol. 30, No. 4, April 1992.
12. T. M. Chen and S. S. Liu, "Management and Control Functions in ATM Switching Systems," *IEEE Network, the Magazine of Computer Communications*, Vol. 8, No. 4, July/August 1994.

(Manuscript approved August 1994)

Radhika R. Roy *is a member of technical staff in the Interactive Information Services Architecture Department of AT&T Bell Laboratoires in Holmdel, New Jersey. He works on the development of multimedia services, multimedia network design, and technology assessment. He has a B.S.E.E. degree from the University of Engineering and Technology in Dhaka, Bangladesh, an M.S.E.E. degree from Northeastern University, Boston, Massachusetts, and a Ph.D. in electrical engineering from the City University of New York. He joined AT&T in 1990.*

Ashok K. Kuthyar *is head of the Interactive Information Services Architecture Department in AT&T Bell Laboratories in Holmdel, New Jersey. His group is responsible for developing new multimedia and image product and service concepts, providing a technology transfer from research to the business units, defining end-to-end architectures and requirements, and developing prototypes. He has a B.S.E.E degree from Bangalore University, in Bangalore, India, and an M.S.E.E. degree from Kansas State University in Manhattan, Kansas. He joined the company in 1986.*

Vanita Katkar *is a technical manager in the Next Generation Network Architecture Department at AT&T Bell Laboratories in Holmdel, New Jersey. Her group is responsible for developing the multimedia services creation architecture. She joined AT&T in 1980. She has a B.S. degree and an M.S. degree in mathematics from the University of Poona in Poona, India.*

Reprinted from Computer Networks and ISDN Systems 27 (1995), pp. 1567-1613 with kind permission from Elsevier Science - NL, Sara Burgerhartstraat 25, 1055 KV Amsterdam, The Netherlands.

ELSEVIER

Computer Networks and ISDN Systems 27 (1995) 1567–1613

COMPUTER
NETWORKS
and
ISDN SYSTEMS

Survey of ATM switch architectures ☆

Ra'ed Y. Awdeh [a], H.T. Mouftah [b,*]

[a] *Bell-Northern Research, P.O. Box 3511, Station C, Ottawa, Ontario, Canada K1Y 4H7*
[b] *Department of Electrical and Computer Engineering, Queen's University, Kingston, Ontario, Canada K7L 3N6*

Accepted 21 July 1994

Abstract

For reasons of economy and flexibility, BISDN (*Broadband Integrated Services Digital Network*) is expected to replace existing application-oriented communication networks. ATM (*Asynchronous Transfer Mode*) is a high-speed packet-switching technique that has emerged as the most promising technology for BISDN. Since early 1980s, a large number of architectures have been proposed for ATM switching. In this paper, we present a descriptive survey of ATM switch architectures, with emphasis on electronic space-division point-to-point switches.

Keywords: ATM switching; Buffering strategies; Fast packet switching; Switch architectures

1. Introduction

Currently, heavy research is being carried out to design an integrated network that supports all services, existing and emerging, in a unified fashion [20], [25], [56], [67], [68], [107], [161], [187], [213]. Flexibility to accommodate volatile changes in service mixes, ease of installation and maintenance, better user access, and more efficient resource utilization, are among the reasons for such a drive. The advances in fiber optics technology have made available huge amounts of transmission bandwidth, and have resulted in the emergence of new applications, specially real-time services, which require much higher bandwidth than

possible in existing networks. Fiber is already widely deployed in both public and private networks, which served to reduce its cost dramatically. Also, as the geometries of various VLSI components continue to shrink, both higher speeds and higher levels of circuit integration are made possible [25]. However, the design of a network that can support very high bandwidth services remains a challenge. *Broadband Integrated Services Digital Networks* (BISDNs) are expected to provide diverse services with diverse performance requirements. Three issues are to be satisfactorily resolved before BISDN becomes a reality [181].

· The development of a network protocol capable of supporting the diversity of services expected by BISDN.
· The design of switching nodes which are within the implementation capability of current VLSI technology.
· The development of a control strategy that

☆ This work was performed while the first author was at Queen's University. The views expressed in this paper do not necessarily represent those of BNR.
* Corresponding author. Tel (613) 545-2925, Fax (613) 545-6615, Email mouftahh@qucdn.queensu.ca

guarantees for every user the required quality of service regardless of the network traffic conditions.

The third issue is still an open and even an unclear problem. In BISDN, the performance bottleneck of the network, which was once the channel transmission speed, is shifted to the processing speed at the switching nodes and the propagation delay of the channel [20]. Many flow/congestion control strategies for BISDN have been proposed [20], [108]. Regarding the first issue, ATM (*Asynchronous Transfer Mode*) has been selected as the multiplexing and switching technique for BISDN, and is currently receiving much standardization activity [20], [32], [68], [187]. With regard to the second issue, a large number of ATM switch architectures have been proposed [2], [8], [115], [157], [168], [173], [213], and it has been shown that many of them can be implemented using current technology. Berthold [25] has shown that currently-available digital VLSI technology is more than adequate to the ATM switching needs. Rooholamini et al. [190] and Steffora [200] describe several already commercially-available ATM switches. It is our intention in this paper to survey the different ATM switch proposals. Our survey paper differs from existing surveys in the following points:

· It focuses on *both* the buffering strategy and internal structure of ATM switches in a *clear* and *comprehensive* manner.
· It includes for the first time some recently-proposed categories of ATM switches.
· It covers in detail many more ATM switch proposals (some of which have been proposed only recently) than any existing survey.

2. Definitions

This section provides some background and describes some assumptions related to this survey.

2.1. Broadband Integrated Services Digital Network (BISDN) [20], [25], [56], [67], [68], [107], [161], [184], [187], [213]

A major step that has already been accomplished towards BISDN is Narrowband (N) ISDN

or simply ISDN. ISDN is a concept that was developed during the 1970s with the advent of digital telephone systems. It has been deployed in many countries in the world, where *digital* communications at the aggregate rate of 144 Kbps (two 64 Kbps circuit switched channels for voice or data, and one 16 Kbps packet switched signalling channel) is made available to the public. Besides extending digital transmission capabilities to existing twisted wire pairs, another new aspect of ISDN is the use of an out-of-band common channel for signalling, which insures the transparency of the information channels. Unfortunately, ISDN has many shortcomings including the following. The number of simultaneous connections to a subscriber is determined by the number of physical channels installed to the subscribers premises, which makes ISDN inflexible with regard to future or even some existing services. Moreover, there is no provision either for a range of services with different bit rates or for services with variable-bit rates. Even for the limited range of narrowband services it offers, ISDN is not really integrated as there are still two different bearer services resulting in two overlay networks.

The main concept of BISDN is the support of a wide range of existing and emerging voice, video, and data applications within the same network. It will provide an integrated access for its users in a flexible and cost-effective manner. The network will include support for: interactive and distributive services, broadband and narrowband rates, bursty and continuous traffic, connection-oriented and connectionless services, and point-to-point and multipoint communications. The general goal of BISDN is to define a user interface and a network that will meet the required quality of service of each of these applications.

2.2. Synchronous Transfer Mode (STM) [20], [25], [33], [60], [68], [105], [161], [184], [216]

STM was the first switching and multiplexing technique to be considered for BISDN due to its compatibility with most existing systems, and the desire to preserve the investment in existing equipments while *evolving* to a more flexible network. In the multiplexing system (multiplexing refers to the arbitration of access to a link and should be distinguished from switching), time slots within a periodic structure called *frame*, are allocated to a service for the duration of a connection. This is usually referred to as *time-division multiplexing*. An STM channel is identified by the position of its time slot in a frame. STM provides fixed throughput and constant delay, and thus it is suitable for fixed-rate services. STM switching is known as *circuit switching*, and is widely used in voice telephone networks. The switching function in circuit switches is performed continuously for the duration of the connection. Circuit switching can be performed in space, in time, or in a combination of both.

Rigidly-structured STM is very inefficient in handling the different and variable-bit rates required by the diversity of services which are expected to be supported by BISDN. Even in complex multirate STM which allows the allocation of bandwidths equal to integer multiples of some basic rate, the choice of this basic rate is an uneasy engineering design decision. In general, as the number of channels increases, STM-based approaches grow cumbersome.

2.3. Packet switching [21], [26], [67], [68], [184], [213], [216]

Baran [21] was the first to propose the concept of packet switching in 1964. In packet switching networks, user information is organized into packets (usually of variable length) which contain additional information used inside the network for routing, error detection and correction, flow control, etc. Packets are transmitted from a source to a destination through multiple switches in a store-and-forward manner. Sources transmit their packets as soon as they are available, which is referred to as *statistical-multiplexing*. Switching of packets is done by computers running communication processes. In contrast to circuit switching, the switching function here needs to be performed only when packets are present at the inputs of the switch.

Packet switching networks, such as those based on X.25, were designed at the time only poor-to-medium transmission links were available. In or-der to offer an acceptable end-to-end performance, complex protocols were therefore necessary to perform flow and error control (e.g., packet re-transmission) on each link of the network. Also, because packets have variable lengths, complex buffer management was required inside the network. All of the above result in large delay and large jitter (the variance of the delay) on this delay, making conventional packet switching unsuitable for high-speed integrated services networks.

2.4. Asynchronous Transfer Mode (ATM) [20], [25], [32], [56], [67], [68], [86], [161], [187], [216]

ATM has been chosen as the transfer mode for BISDN since it overcomes the problems of STM and conventional packet switching altogether. In short, ATM is a high-speed connection-oriented packet-switching technique with minimal functionality in the network. This is why ATM is also known as *fast packet switching*. Turner [216] was among the first who noticed that the disadvantages usually attributed to packet switching are not due to any inherent properties, but are side effects of the conventional implementations. ATM differs from conventional packet switching in many aspects. First, high-level protocol functions such as error control are performed on an end-to-end and not link-by-link basis. This is possible because of the high-quality links which are going to be used in BISDN. Furthermore, ATM uses short fixed-length packets called cells (this is why ATM is also known as *cell switching*). Each cell consists of 53 bytes or octets; 48 for the payload and 5 for the header or label. This choice simplifies the design of switching nodes, and reduces delay and jitter especially for delay-sensitive services such as voice and video. (Also, is was argued that this results in controlled or "fair" handling of multiple traffic streams [187].)

ATM is a connection-oriented transfer mode. In a connection, three phases can be distinguished: set-up, information transfer, and teardown. This paper deals with the second phase only. The first and third phases have to do with

ATM signalling standards [32], [187], and are out of the scope of the current work. We conclude this subsection by pointing out that the term "Asynchronous" in ATM does not necessarily imply asynchronous transmission or switching systems. Rather, it implies aperiodicity; i.e., no source shall own a time slot on a periodic basis. In ATM, the association of a cell with a connection is made explicit through the label of that cell.

2.5. ATM switch

An ATM switch of size N can be regarded as a box with N input ports and N output ports, that routes cells arriving at its input ports to their desired output ports (destinations). For the sake of simplicity, in this paper it is assumed that cells arrive at the input ports in a time-slotted fashion, and that all input lines are synchronized. (In reality, arriving cells at different input ports need to be aligned and synchronized to the local clock.) The minimum slot size is equal to the transmission time of a single cell. Input and output lines are assumed to operate at the same speed. Each arriving cell carries two fields: the ATM header, and the payload (the actual information to be transmitted). Prior to entering the switching fabric, each cell is provided with a local switching header that is used within the switch. A local header may include the following two fields:

· An activity bit (a) to indicate the presence of a cell when $a = 1$.
· An address field which contains the address of the local destination port. Usually, N is assumed to be a power of two, and in this case the address field will be in a binary form $d_1 d_2 ... d_n$, where $n = \log_2 N$ and d_1 is the most significant bit (MSB).

ATM switching fabrics can be classified into time-division fabrics and space-division fabrics [213]. In the former, all cells flow through a single resource that is shared by all input and output ports. This resource may be either a common memory, or a shared medium such as a ring or a bus. The capacity of the entire switching fabric is limited by the bandwidth of this shared resource. Thus, this class of switches do not scale well to large sizes. Another factor that usually limits the

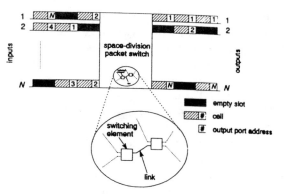

Fig. 1. A generic space-division ATM switch.

maximum size of a common memory architecture, is the centralized control requirement. On the other hand, in a space-division switch multiple of concurrent paths can be established between input and output ports, so that many cells may simultaneously be transmitted across the switching fabric. Space-division ATM switches are usually constructed from identical basic switching blocks, called *switching elements* (SEs), which are interconnected in a specific topology by *links*. The switch directs incoming cells to their destinations, as specified by the information contained in their local headers (see Fig. 1). A problem arises when it is impossible for all required paths to be simultaneously established. This is called *blocking*, and it negatively affects the throughput performance of the particular space-division switch.

With a multiplicity of paths in a space-division switching fabric, a routing function is now required to select a path to the requested output port for each incoming cell. The routing can be centralized or distributed. With the former, a central unit examines the destination addresses of all incoming cells, and sets up the required paths in the switching fabric accordingly. In this case, the capacity of the central processor establishes a physical limit to the performance and scalability of the switch. Distributed-routing, better known as *self-routing*, switches avoid central control bottlenecks by distributing the routing function among several smaller processors. Here, each SE in the fabric makes a very fast local routing decision, simply by examining the destination addresses (or part of them) of the cells at its inlets. In all cases, each cell arrives at its desired destination regardless of its port of entry.

Many ATM switch architectures have been proposed within the past fifteen years or so [2], [8], [115], [157], [168], [173], [199], [213]. Most of the proposed architectures are based on highly-parallel structures, are characterized by distributed control, and perform switching at the hardware level. Since most of the proposed ATM switches are of the space-division type, time-division architectures are not covered by this survey. Interested readers are referred to [213] in which both an excellent discussion and a survey of time-division fast packet switches are given. Before discussing the different approaches of classifying space-division ATM switches, we give some important definitions which are relevant to any space-division packet switch:

· *Internal blocking*. Occurs when two or more cells, destined to different output ports, contend over the same internal link. A switch that does not suffer from internal blocking is called nonblocking. (A nonblocking packet switch is not necessarily nonblocking as a circuit switch.)

· *Output blocking*. Occurs when more than one cell request the same output port within the same time slot. A blocking switch suffers from both internal and output blocking. Nonblocking switches can be further classified into output-blocking and output-nonblocking architectures. An output-nonblocking switch is able to clear all incoming cells in any given time slot to the buffers of the requested output ports before the next time slot.

Cell-sequencing. A switch is said to preserve cell-sequencing if, for each input-output pair, it delivers incoming cells in the order by which they have arrived at the switch.

Speed-up. Speeding-up an ATM switching fabric is sometimes necessary to improve the performance and/or compensate for processing overheads. The speed-up can be implemented in time or in space. In the former, the switch is said to have a speed-up factor of S if the internal switching fabric operates S times faster than the external lines. In the latter implementation, S concurrent paths are provided to each output port.

· *Multicast connections*. BISDN must support multipoint communications in which more than two users are participating in a connection. At the switch level, a multicast or point-to-multipoint connection refers to the situation where an incoming connection requests K output ports ($1 \leq K \leq N$). When $K = 1$, we are back to point-to-point (unicast) connections, while $K = N$ refers to broadcasting.

· *Performance measures*. The performance of an ATM switch is usually evaluated based on three measures: throughput, delay, and cell loss probability. Throughput (TP) is defined as the average number of cells which are successfully delivered by the switch per time slot per input line. Maximum throughput (TP_{max}) is the value of TP under maximum-load conditions. While TP_{max} is an important performance measure, it will not be directly felt by network users. On the other hand, the end-to-end delay, which includes the delay of individual switching nodes, will be experienced by network users. Switch delay (D) is defined as the average time (in time slots) a cell spends from the time it arrives at an input port, till the time it is successfully delivered on its requested output line. D includes the time spent in any input, internal, and/or output buffers. Cell loss probability (P_{loss}) is defined as the fraction of cells lost within the switch. Cell loss might occur as a result of blocking and/or buffer overflows. Because cell re-transmission takes place on an end-to-end basis in ATM networks, and because of the high speeds involved in these networks, P_{loss} is considered as a very important performance measure. Typically, an ATM switch is required to support a high throughput, a small delay, and an extremely low cell loss probability. Finally, an important performance measure that is often ignored in most switch proposals is the jitter, which should be very small.

Space-division ATM switch architectures can be classified according to many different criteria. Some typical classifications are the following:

· *Single-stage versus multistage* [157]. Input and output ports are interconnected through one stage only in single-stage switches; thus, a cell is switched in a single phase. On the other hand, in multistage switches, switching is performed by SEs in consecutive stages.

· *Single-path versus multipath* [168]. In a single path switch, only one path exists for any input-output pair, while in a multipath switch there are more than one path for each input-output pair.

· *Blocking versus nonblocking* [46], [173]. As has been explained in the above definitions.

· *Unicast versus multicast.* As has been explained in the above definitions. While some of the architectures to be surveyed in this paper do support multicasting, the emphasis is on unicast switching.

· *Buffering based classifications* [168], [173], [181]. Based on the location of buffers, ATM switches can be input-buffered, internally-buffered, output-buffered, or any combinations of these. Also, based on the memory sharing policy, ATM switches can have dedicated buffers, shared buffers, or a mixture of both.

· *Structure based classification* [2], [8], [213]. According to their internal structures, ATM switches can be possibly classified into crossbar based, disjoint-path based, and banyan based.

In this paper, while keeping in mind all the above classifications, we first review the buffering based classifications, then we classify ATM switches into the following categories:
· Crossbar based switches.
· Disjoint-path based switches.
   · Paths are disjoint in space.
   · Paths are disjoint in time.
· Banyan based switches.
   · Internal node buffering.
   · Multiple banyans.
   · Dilation.
   · Sorting.
   · Deflection-routing.
   · Load-sharing.
   · Expansion.

2.6. Traffic model

Here, we refer to the traffic as seen by the input ports of the switch. The traffic model is described by two random processes. The first is the process that governs the arrival of cells in each time slot. The second process describes the distribution by which arriving cells choose their destination ports. It is clear that input traffic can follow an infinite number of models. In the following, we describe three of the most frequently-used traffic models for the performance evaluation of ATM switches.

Uniform traffic

In this model, cells arrive at the input ports of the switch according to independent and identically distributed Bernoulli processes, each with parameter p $(0 < p \le 1)$. In other words, at an input port in a given time slot, a cell arrives with probability p, and there is no arriving cell with probability $1 - p$. Thus, p represents the input load or the arrival rate to each input port of the switch. An incoming cell chooses its destination uniformly among all N output ports, and independently from all other requests; i.e., it chooses a particular output port with probability $1/N$. This traffic model is sometimes referred to as the independent uniform traffic model [213], or simply the random traffic model. Asserting the assumption of uniformity for real-life situations may lead to optimistic evaluation of performance measures. However, a large number of studies on the performance evaluation of ATM switches assume uniform traffic. The main reasons behind this trend are as follows:

· This assumption makes the analytical evaluation of the switch more tractable, specially if the switch is of the blocking type and/or employs a complex buffering strategy.

· A distribution/randomization network can be used at the front end of the switch to randomize incoming traffic.

· It was observed that the traffic arriving at the switching nodes is less bursty than the traffic arriving at user access nodes, due to the inherent smoothing that takes place when bursty cell streams are queued and then released at a given rate (the link service rate) to the network [87]. Furthermore, it was shown that subsequent stages of switching cause the traffic to become even less bursty [69], [87], making the uniform traffic assumption closer to reality.

By definition, any traffic model that is not uniform is called a nonuniform traffic model. In this paper, unless otherwise specified, we assume the traffic to be uniform.

Bursty traffic

Future BISDN is expected to support virtually all existing and emerging services including voice, video and data. Strong correlation may exist among cells originating from the same source, giving rise to bursty traffic. A bursty source generates cells at a peak or a near-peak rate for very short durations, and remains almost inactive in between. Several models have been proposed to describe such *bursty* sources [20], [198]. One popular and simple model is the On/Off model, where the source alternates between a busy (also called on, active, or burst) period, and an idle (also called off or silent) period. The length of the active period (in time slots) is geometrically distributed with parameter a. The probability that the active period lasts for a duration of i time slots is given by

$$B(i) = a(1-a)^{i-1}, i \geq 1. \tag{1}$$

In the above equation, it is assumed that a burst contains at least one time slot. The average length of a burst is given by

$$A = \sum_{i=1}^{\infty} iB(i) = \frac{1}{a}. \tag{2}$$

Similarly, the length of the idle period (in time slots) is geometrically distributed with parameter s. Thus, the probability that the idle period lasts for a duration of i time slots is given by

$$I(i) = s(1-s)^{i}, i \geq 0. \tag{3}$$

The average idle period length is obtained by

$$B = \sum_{i=0}^{\infty} iI(i) = \frac{1-s}{s}. \tag{4}$$

Cells are continuously generated during the active period. Thus, the offered load to an input port is obtained by

$$p = \frac{A}{A+B}. \tag{5}$$

All cells belonging to the *same* burst address the same output port which is chosen uniformly among all N output ports, independently from all other bursts. Finally, uniform traffic results when $A = 1$; in this case, $p = s$.

Hot-spot traffic

Hot-spot traffic refers to a situation where many input ports prefer to communicate with one output port (the hot-spot). This kind of traffic may arise in many real-life applications [231]. It occurs, for example, when many callers compete to call a popular location in a telephone network. Another example is a local area network consisting of many diskless computer systems and a single file server. In the model introduced in [186], a single hot-spot of higher access rate is superimposed on a background of uniform traffic. The cell arrival process is the same as for the uniform traffic case. If we let h be the fraction of cells directed at the hot-spot, then p, the arrival rate to an input port, can be expressed as $p = ph + p(1-h)$. In other words, hp cells are directed at the hot-spot, and $p(1-h)$ cells are uniformly distributed over all output ports. Also, the average number of cells which request the hot-spot per time slot is $phN + p(1-h)$.

3. Buffering strategies

Due to the statistical nature of the traffic, buffering in any packet switch is unavoidable. This is true because even with an output-non-blocking switch (which can clear all incoming cells to the output side of the switch before a new time slot begins), two or more cells may address the same output port within the same time slot. In such a situation, given the assumption that input and output lines operate at the same speed, each output line can serve only one cell per time slot; other cells must be buffered. This is called *output buffering* since the buffers will be physically located at the output side of the switch.

With a switch that is able to deliver a maximum of one cell to each output port in any given time slot, output buffering is not needed. In such switches, buffers can be placed at the input ports (called *input buffering*), within the switching fabric at possible points of contention (called *internal buffering*), or both (called *input-internal buffering*). On the other hand, if the switch can deliver more than one cell (but not all possible cells) to each output port simultaneously, then it also needs output buffering. This yields *input-output buffering*, *internal-output buffering*, or *input-internal-output buffering*. Finally, some switches while being blocking require only output buffering because they employ certain methods to significantly reduce blocking while offering multiple paths to each output port. Such switches can be engineered to make cell loss probability within the switching fabric extremely small.

In this section, we consider a generic nonblocking space-division packet switch, without regard to its internal structure except for the assumption that it has no internal buffers. First, we review and compare two extreme strategies of external buffering, namely, input buffering and output buffering. Then, we review various methods for improving the performance of input buffering switches. Where applicable, we assume that the size of each input buffer is B_{in} cells, and the size of each output buffer is B_{out} cells. Since internal buffering is architecture-dependent, we defer its discussion to the following sections. However, it is noteworthy that generally speaking, internal buffering is not desirable for one or more of the following reasons [139]:

· In multipath architectures, cells may be delivered out-of-sequence.
· It complicates the internal design of the SEs.
· It complicates fault-diagnosis testing if a cut-through mechanism [122] is implemented (this

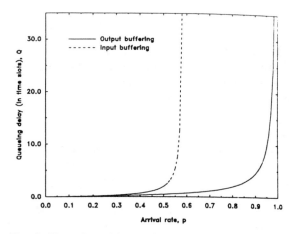

Fig. 3. Throughput-delay performance of pure input and output buffering for nonblocking switches.

mechanism will be explained later in this paper).
· It limits the maximum length of packets which can use the switch to the maximum internal buffer size.

Finally, unless otherwise specified, the numerical results presented in this section are for the case where both the switch and buffer sizes are infinite.

3.1. Output buffering

Here, we assume an output-nonblocking switch (Fig. 2) where all arriving cells in a given time slot are cleared to the output side (i.e., are switched) before the beginning of the next time slot, even if all N inputs have cells destined to the same output port. This can be achieved by, for example, speeding-up any switching fabric by a factor of N. However, only one cell can be served by an output line in each time slot and other cells with the same output request have to buffered, if space is available. The system is stable, since the average utilization of an output line is the same as that of an input line. The average queueing delay Q when $N = \infty$ and $B_{out} = \infty$ is the same as that of an M/D/1 queue [75], [101], [120]:

$$Q = \frac{p}{2(1 - P)}; \quad 0 \le p < 1. \tag{6}$$

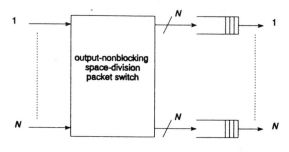

Fig. 2. A generic nonblocking output buffering switch.

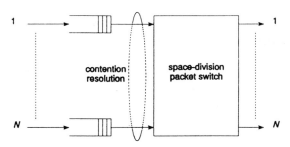

Fig. 4. A generic input buffering switch.

The above equation is plotted in Fig. 3. Studies concerning the performance evaluation of nonblocking output buffering switches under nonuniform traffic models include [31], [48], [76], [153], and [228].

3.2. Input buffering

With an input buffering switch (Fig. 4), an arriving cell enters a *first-in first-out* (FIFO) buffer located at its port of entry, if space is available. In each time slot, the switch resolves contentions prior to switching. If all *head-of-line* (HOL) cells are destined to distinct output ports, then all of them are admitted and switched to their desired output lines. However, if K HOL cells ($1 < K \leq N$) are destined to a particular output port, only one cell is chosen, according to some selection policy, to be switched and other cells wait to participate in the next time slot selection process.

Several selection policies (also called contention resolution mechanisms or HOL arbitration schemes) have been proposed and studied in the literature including the following:
· *Random* selection [14], [42], [65], [97], [101], [104], [118], [120], [149], [150], [151].
· *HOL FIFO* (or *oldest HOL*) selection [17], [18], [34], [42], [65], [85], [97], [112], [154], [182].
· *HOL LIFO* (last-in first-out) selection [42].
· *Global FIFO* (or *earliest arrival*) selection [17].
· *Longest queue* selection [17], [18], [85], [120].
· *Oldest queue* selection [17], [85] where age is defined as the length of time a non-empty queue has been unserved.

· *Cyclic* (or *round-robin*) selection and its variations [16], [17], [30], [99], [153], [155].
· *HOL blocking based* selection [97]: to select a cell that is causing HOL blocking (defined below).
· *Prediction based* selection [99].
It should be emphasized here that while the selection policy among contending HOL cells can be non-FIFO, the service discipline within each input buffer is still assumed to be FIFO.

Input buffering switches with FIFO queueing suffer from the so-called *HOL blocking* [101], [104], [120], [185]: in any given time slot while a cell is waiting its turn for access to an output port, other cells may be blocked behind it despite the fact that their destination ports are possibly idle. As a consequence, the maximum throughput is limited to $(2-\sqrt{2}) \approx 0.586$ [101], [104], [120], regardless of the specific selection policy used. This figure also represents the saturation value of p, above which steady state queue sizes grow without limit, and cells experience infinite waiting times. The following equation [104] describes the relationship between the average queueing delay Q and the arrival rate p (for $N = \infty$, $B_{in} = \infty$, and random selection):

$$Q = \frac{(2-p)(1-p)}{(2-\sqrt{2}-p)(2+\sqrt{2}-p)} - 1;$$

$$0 \leq p < 2 - \sqrt{2}. \tag{7}$$

The above equation is plotted in Fig. 3.

It is noteworthy that a maximum throughput of $(1 - e^{-1}) \approx 0.632$ can be achieved by eliminating the input buffers and dropping cells upon contention [120], [176]. In general, the throughput with this blocked-loss scheme is given by the following equation [120], [176] (was derived in [202] for $p = 1.0$):

$$TP = 1 - \left(1 - \frac{p}{N}\right)^N; \quad 0 \leq p \leq 1. \tag{8}$$

Unfortunately, the above maximum throughput of 63.2% (compared to 58.6% for FIFO input buffering) is achieved at the expense of high cell loss probabilities which are unacceptable for ATM switches. For example, at $p = 0.50$ and

$N = \infty$, 21.3% of all incoming cells are dropped, compared to P_{loss} of 10^{-6} for FIFO input buffering with $B_{in} = 20$ and random selection [104].

Despite the fact that with FIFO queueing, the maximum throughput of an input buffering switch is 58.6% regardless of the selection policy, other performance measures are affected by the specific selection policy used when operating below the saturation level (i.e., when $p < 0.586$). For example, the longest queue selection policy results in less queueing delay, compared to the random selection policy [120], and to the HOL FIFO selection policy [18], [154]. Also, both the global FIFO and the longest queue selection policies have better cell loss performance, compared to the oldest queue or the HOL FIFO policies [17], [18]. Priority schemes [114] insure the delivery of delay-sensitive cells by giving them higher priority. Needless to say that the different selection policies have different implementation complexities. Finally, the performance of nonblocking input buffering switches was evaluated under nonuniform traffic models in [149] [150], [151], [153], and [155].

3.3. Comparison

It can be easily seen from Fig. 3 that output buffering significantly outperforms input buffering with regard to the throughput-delay performance under uniform traffic. (Although output buffering has significantly better throughput-delay performance than input buffering under uniform traffic for all switch dimensions, the advantage of output buffering over input buffering decreases as the switch dimensions become more and more asymmetric [154], [155].) Also, output buffering switches lend themselves naturally to multicast and broadcast functionalities. Despite the above, output buffering switches are usually more complex. In addition to the complexity of the switching fabric itself, which must transfer all incoming cells in any given time slot to the output side of the switch before the beginning of the next time slot, output memories are not easy to implement. Each output memory must have a minimum bandwidth of $(N + 1)\nu$ bps (where ν is the speed of the external lines), corresponding to

a maximum of N write and a single read operations [213]. Reduction in the memory speed is possible by using a bit-sliced organization of the memory [213], or by using output port concentration [230]. On the other hand, memory speed does not constitute a major concern for input buffering switches.

The superiority of output buffering over input buffering is valid under any traffic model, assuming infinite-size buffers. However, in reality buffer sizes are finite. It was shown that for the same values of N, p (uniform traffic), and target P_{loss}, an output buffering switch requires less amount of buffers [68], [153]. However, in an interesting simulation study [153], it has been concluded that it is *not* true that output buffering has better performance than input buffering in all situations. In particular, under bursty traffic, output buffering could have higher P_{loss} than input buffering, for the same buffer size. This has been explained as a result of inherent buffer sharing effects of input buffering under bursty traffic: although buffers are not actually shared, simultaneous cell arrivals with a common destination are automatically distributed across several buffers in input buffering. In the same study, it was also concluded that TP_{max} is not a good performance metric for input buffering under bursty traffic, since it is necessary to operate the switch at loads much lower than TP_{max} in order to obtain small P_{loss}. In general, bursty traffic requires much larger amounts of buffers, compared to uniform traffic, to achieve the same cell loss probability, for any buffering strategy [48], [153], [175], [203].

While complicating the design of a switch, using a shared-memory implementation of the buffers significantly reduces the amount of memory needed to achieve a certain cell loss performance, for any buffering strategy under uniform traffic [75], [78], [101], [110], [111], [160], [175], [181], [213]. In general, this is true under any balanced traffic model [78], [111] in which the overall input load is uniformly distributed across all input ports (input balance) and the destination requests are uniformly distributed across all output ports (output balance). This definition includes besides uniform traffic, the bursty traffic model as defined previously. As an example [175], for an output buffering switch of size (8×8), total buffer of 8000 cells, a 10^{-10} target P_{loss}, and an average burst length of 5 cells, the shared buffering technique allows up to 88% load compared to 45% allowed with dedicated buffering. Unfortunately, the advantage of buffer sharing diminishes under imbalanced traffic [78], such as hot-spot traffic [186]. This is because *favored* ports monopolize the use of the shared buffer, causing performance degradation for the whole switch [101], [213]. Therefore, the appropriate buffer sharing policy must lie somewhere between total separation and full sharing. Several buffer sharing policies have been proposed to avoid performance degradation of a shared buffer under imbalanced load, such as sharing with minimum and/or maximum allocation constraints [44], [78], [119], [160].

3.4. Improved input buffering

The problem of "ordinary" input buffering is HOL blocking resulting from FIFO queueing in each input buffer. Thus, the throughput performance of an input buffering switch is expected to be improved by allowing non-FIFO service. With the w-window mechanism [101], input ports which are not selected to transmit their HOL cells, contend again with their second cells for access to any of the remaining idle output ports, and so on up to w times, in each time slot ($w = 1$ corresponds to FIFO input buffering). This mechanism is sometimes referred to as *bypass queueing* or *look-ahead contention resolution*. Also, the window size w is sometimes called the *scanning range* or the *number of bypass offers*. TP_{max} improves as w increases for a given N. As an example, using simulation it was shown that for $N = 128$ and $w = 8$, $TP_{max} = 88\%$. In the same reference, it was concluded that input buffering even with an infinite window size does not attain the optimal throughput-delay performance of output buffering. However, approximate analytical models show that $TP_{max} = 100\%$ can be achieved using $w = \infty$ [142], [181]. Thomas and Man [212] noticed that the original windowing mechanism of [101] strives to minimize the number of input buffers which are not served at all.

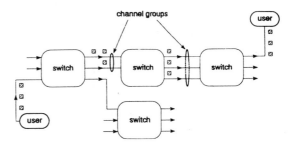

Fig. 5. The concept of channel grouping.

The same reference proposed an alternative approach where the goal is to maximize the number of assigned output ports in each time slot, even by allowing multiple selections from the same input buffer. For $N = 128$ and $w = 8$, a TP_{max} of 94% results. In general, more significant improvements over the basic windowing mechanism is achieved for smaller w and larger N. A similar improved windowing mechanism was also suggested in [218] and [219] in the context of internally-buffered multistage interconnection networks, under the name *parallel bypass queueing*. Window mechanisms were also studied in [35], [142], [192], [193], and [195].

In a network, it is possible to have multiple links interconnecting adjacent switching nodes, and these links can provide cells with multiple paths to a number of downstream switches as shown in Fig. 5. This results in the concept of *output channel grouping* [177], in which the output ports of a switch are partitioned into disjoint sets, with each port in a set offering the same service as the other members of the set. This technique can be used to more efficiently utilize the huge bandwidth of fiber optics, while avoiding the need for ultra-fast electronic switches, and to provide higher reliability by offering alternative paths. It was shown that output channel grouping also results in improving the throughput performance of an input buffering switch as the size of each group grows. As an example, TP_{max} increases from 58.6% to 87.8% for groups of 16 output ports, and to 91.2% for groups of 32 output ports [154], [155], [181]. However, Liew and Lu [154] have shown that with a group size of 1024, a TP_{max} of 98.4% results, which suggests that increasing the output group size above a certain value does not result in any more significant improvements. Studies dealing with output channel grouping have also been reported for cases involving non-uniform partitioning of the output ports [47], [136], and nonuniform traffic models [47], [129], [136], [152], [154], [155], [172]. Output channel grouping is also known as *multichannel bandwidth allocation, output trunk grouping, multiservice switching, output pooling*, or *output link group routing*. In [152], the concept of *input channel grouping* was examined, where the input ports are partitioned into disjoint sets each with a demultiplexer and each demultiplexer skips those input links with full buffers; an incoming cell is lost only if all input buffers within the same input channel group are full. Notice that the above is an implementation of partially-shared input buffering. While output channel grouping relieves traffic output contentions, input channel grouping prevents individual input links from overloading [152]. It has been shown that both techniques have significant impact in improving the performance of an input buffering nonblocking switch, especially in a highly nonuniform traffic environment [152].

Output conflicts and consequently HOL blocking can be reduced by switch expansion [153], [154], [155], [181]; i.e., by having the number of output ports O greater than the number of input ports I. The ratio $E = O/I$ is called the expansion factor, and as it increases, the throughput performance of an input buffering switch improves. As an example, for $E = 8$, the maximum throughput is 93.8%, compared to 58.6% for $E = 1$ [154], [155], [181]. For $E = \infty$, a 100% maximum throughput is achieved [181]. Finally, despite the "similarity" between output channel grouping and switch expansion, the concepts behind them are different. However, these two approaches can be used together; e.g., for $E = 2$ and an output channel group size of 2, $TP_{max} = 96.6\%$ [154], [155].

Using independent output port schedulers has been investigated in [170]. The scheduling algorithm has two phases: request and arbitration. In the request phase, each input buffer sends a request to the appropriate output port scheduler. While these schedulers are located in a centralized contention control unit, each schedules its own transmissions independently of the others. In the arbitration phase, each output port scheduler passes consecutive assigned slot times to requesting input ports. Each acknowledged input port checks its sending table: if the assigned time slot has already been reserved, the cell must participate in the request phase again in the next time slot. $TP_{max} = 65\%$ can be achieved with this algorithm (82% if input ports are organized into groups of 4, where all members of a group coordinate their requests; or if each input queue runs 4 times the speed of the input ports [171]). This scheduling algorithm can be improved further by re-using those time slots which inputs cannot use due to earlier assignments [121]. The modified algorithm achieves a TP_{max} of 92% (95% with 4-member input groups). Matsunaga and Uematsu [158] proposed a similar algorithm but in which there exists full coordination between the outputs in the scheduling process. It has been shown that $TP_{max} = 94\%$ can be achieved. Another scheduling algorithm that resolves conflicts and optimizes performance by maximizing throughput was proposed in [90].

Ali and Youssefi [3] considered having a separate queue for each output port at each input port; i.e., a total of N^2 input queues for an $(N \times N)$ switch. In each time slot, HOL cells in all N input queues corresponding to a particular output link contend for routing. Winners are chosen in such a way as to maximize the throughput of the switch. A neural network implementation of the controller has been suggested to overcome the high complexity required by the optimal selection process. A similar approach was previously suggested in [85], but using a heuristic selection scheme with a number of operations of $O(N)$ in time. Del Re and Fantacci [65] examined the same structure under two other selection policies: random and HOL FIFO. In all cases, the throughput-delay performance approaches that of pure output buffering at the expense of large buffer requirements. Chen and Guerin [41] considered only two queues per input port; one for high-priority traffic, and the other for low-priority traffic. For each input port, the high-priority queue is served first, and upon contention between different input ports, high-priority cells win. The maximum throughput achieved by this approach is 60.6%. Multiple queues per input port were also studied in [220] in the context of internally-buffered multistage interconnection networks.

3.5. Combined input-output buffering

In order to achieve an acceptable performance level while avoiding the complexities associated with pure output buffering, many switch designs employ a combined input-output buffering strategy. This can be achieved by speeding-up a nonblocking switch by a factor (S) greater than 1. By doing so, up to S cells can be switched to each output port in every time slot, which necessitates the use of output buffers. In input-output buffering switches, one of two possible mechanisms can be used: queue loss [42], [182], or backpressure [17], [18], [19], [34], [96], [109], [111], [112], [118], [182], [194]. In the queue loss mechanism, cells can be lost after being switched as a result of output buffer overflows. However, with the backpressure mechanism, cell flow from the input buffers to the output buffers is limited by the current free space in each output buffer jointly with the speed-up factor.

Within the past three years, great interest has been shown in input-output buffering switches built around nonblocking fabrics. An analytical model of such switches has been developed in [182] for $N = \infty$, arbitrary values of B_{in}, B_{out}, and S, and both queue loss and backpressure. The analysis of [118] makes the above assumptions but considers backpressure only. In [194], an approximate model that allows N to be finite for the backpressure mechanism has been reported. The analysis of [42] assumes Poisson arrivals of variable-length packets, $N = \infty$, $B_{in} = \infty$, $B_{out} = \infty$, and arbitrary S. It also estimates the packet loss rate resulting from finite input and output buffers, with queue loss. Assuming that $S = B_{out}$, $N = \infty$, $B_{in} = \infty$, Poisson arrivals, fixed or variable-length packets, and synchronous or asynchronous switch operation, an input-output buffering switch with backpressure has been analyzed in [112]. The packet loss rate resulting from finite B_{in} has also been estimated. Other studies dealing with input-output buffering nonblocking switches under uniform traffic include [34], [96], [109], [110], [142], [174], and [180]. Also, the performance of these switches under nonuniform traffic models has been examined in [18], [42], [99], [111], and [180].

Some of the main observations about input-output buffering nonblocking switches include the following:

· Given a fixed total buffer budget, there exists an optimal placement of buffers among input and output ports to minimize P_{loss}. This is true for the queue loss mechanism [42], [182], as well as for the backpressure mechanism [182].

· The backpressure mechanism requires less $B_{in} + B_{out}$ to achieve a given P_{loss} under a very wide range of load values [182]. Also, the queue loss mechanism requires in general larger B_{out} to achieve a target P_{loss} given a fixed $B_{in} + B_{out}$ [182].

· With backpressure, the effect of B_{out} is more dominant on the performance than that of B_{in} [118].

· Assuming infinite size buffers at input and output ports, fixed-length packets, and $N = \infty$, $TP_{max} = 88.5\%$, 97.6%, and 99.6%, when $S = 2$, 3, and 4, respectively [96], [174]. Buffering cells at the input ports results in a significant reduction in the value of S needed to attain a given P_{loss} at a given load value [174]. Assuming $B_{out} = \infty$, $p = 0.90$, and target $P_{loss} = 10^{-6}$, we need $S = 8$, 4, and 3, if $B_{in} = 0$, 1 (with priority scheme), and 9, respectively [174].

· With $S = B_{out}$, fixed-length packets, Poisson arrivals, and backpressure, TP_{max} is the same for both synchronous and asynchronous modes of switch operation [112]. However, for a given load, asynchronous operation results in a slightly better performance in terms of delay and packet loss probability [112]. On the other hand, if the synchronous mode assumes Bernoulli arrivals, it achieves better delay performance compared to asynchronous operation with Poisson arrivals [109].

· Under Poisson arrivals, a higher TP_{max} is achieved with fixed-length packets compared to that achieved with packets having exponentially-distributed lengths [42]. For the latter

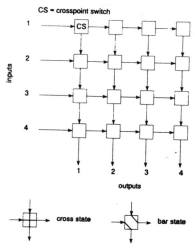

Fig. 6. The crossbar switch.

case, TP_{max} = 50.0%, 82.8%, 96.1%, and 99.3%, when S = 1, 2, 3, and 4, respectively [42].

4. Crossbar based switches

The term "crossbar" derives from a particular design of a single-stage single-path nonblocking switching fabric, originally developed for circuit switching [25], [33], [55], [184], [213]. Later on, crossbar switches were considered for interconnecting processors and memory modules in multiprocessor systems [27], [84], [159], [176]. Currently, many ATM switch proposals are based on the crossbar switch, or use it as the basic building block. A crossbar switch is schematically shown in Fig. 6 for $N = 4$, where horizontal lines represent the inputs to the switch, and vertical lines represent the outputs. Basically, an $(N \times N)$ crossbar switch consists of a square array of N^2 individually-operated crosspoints, one for each input-output pair. In general, crosspoints could be electromechanical relays or semiconductor switches (transistors, SCRs, or logic gates) [25]. (Clearly, the first option is not suitable for a high-speed packet switching environment.) Each crosspoint has 2 possible states: cross (default) and bar. A connection between input port i and output port

j is established by setting the (i, j)th crosspoint switch to the bar state.

Crossbar switches have always been attractive to switch designers because they are nonblocking, simple in architecture, and modular. However, they have the following two main drawbacks [213]:
· Square growth of complexity (i.e., the number of crosspoints is of O(N^2)).
· Different input-output pairs may have different transit delays.

Because of the first problem, crossbar switches do not scale well to large sizes. The second drawback introduces a fairness problem when the switch operates in a self-routing mode, and can be solved using artificial time delays.

Despite being nonblocking, crossbar switches suffer from output blocking. Therefore, as in any packet switch, buffers are necessary to reduce cell losses. In the following, we review crossbar based switches by classifying them according to their buffering strategies.

4.1. Input buffering

In this case (Fig. 7), a contention resolution mechanism is needed to select one cell only out of those requesting the same output port. This can be done in one of two ways: centralized or distributed. The former approach requires a central controller that resolves output contentions in a slot-by-slot basis. Such an approach keeps the

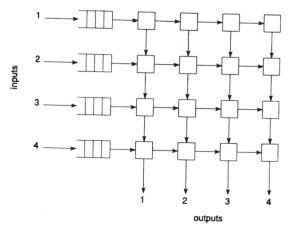

Fig. 7. An input-buffered crossbar switch.

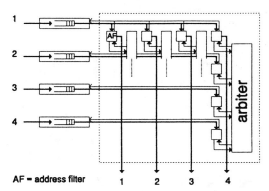

AF = address filter

Fig. 8. The arbiter implementation of an input-buffered crossbar switch.

switching fabric itself as simple and as economical as possible. However, the centralized control becomes a major bottleneck and constitutes a second limiting factor (besides the square growth of complexity) to the scalability of the switch. The other approach is to distribute the control over all output ports; i.e., each output port has its own controller, called *arbiter* [2], [213], as shown in Fig. 8. Each arbiter sees all cells which are destined to the corresponding output port, selects one of them according to some rule, and blocks all others by a means of a backpressure signal. Only a single bus is needed per input port to broadcast the cell and its destination port address, and only a single reverse control line is required per input port.

Input-buffered crossbar switches suffer from HOL blocking, and the various methods which have been discussed earlier to improve the performance of an input-buffered nonblocking switch can be used here. In particular, Del Re and Fantacci [64], [65] showed that the arbiter implementation (Fig. 8) can be modified to significantly improve the performance. This is done by splitting each input buffer into N separate queues, one for each output port, and having these N queues share the same input memory. Routing requests jointly with memory locations of new arriving cells are broadcast over the input buses to all arbiters, and each arbiter maintains its own destination queue. A cell is transmitted when its

routing request is selected by the arbiter of the desired output port. Interestingly, it was shown that the above approach achieves a smaller P_{loss} for a given load value and switch size, compared to classical output buffering [64], [65].

4.2. Internal or crosspoint buffering

Buffers can be placed within the switching fabric at possible locations of contention. For example, in the *Bus Matrix switch* [169], each crosspoint switch is replaced by an address filter (AF) and a FIFO buffer, as shown in Fig. 9 for $N = 4$. While an incoming cell is broadcast to all attached AFs, it can pass only through the one whose address matches its destination address. An arbitration mechanism determines which of the HOL cells in the N buffers connected to an output bus, may have access to the corresponding output line. This architecture has a throughput-delay performance which approaches that of output buffering switches, for large enough buffer sizes [3], [65]. However, the total memory required to achieve a certain performance level is larger than that needed by output buffering, since each output buffer is now distributed over N separate buffers [213]. Also, it is always desirable, from an implementation point of view, to separate buffering and switching functions [213]. A crossbar switch with FIFO buffers at each crosspoint has also been discussed in [189] under the name of the *Butterfly switch*.

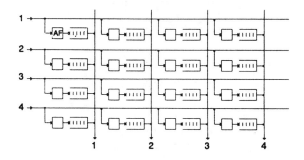

AF = address filter

Fig. 9. A crosspoint-buffered crossbar switch.

4.3. Input-internal buffering

To reduce the complexity of crosspoint-buffered crossbar switches [169], [189], which resulted in limiting an actual implementation to a (2×2) matrix [169], and at the same time to improve the performance of pure input buffering, the *Limited Intermediate Buffer* switch (LIB) has been proposed in [97]. Here, a single buffer (called an intermediate buffer) is provided at each crosspoint resulting in a total internal buffer size of N^2 cells, in addition to the FIFO buffers at the input ports (Fig. 10). An HOL cell can advance to the intermediate buffer connected to its desired destination port, only if that buffer is empty. Several policies for selecting a cell to be forwarded to an output line from the corresponding N intermediate buffers were examined, and it was found that the choice of the selection policy significantly influences the performance of the switch. A maximum throughput of 87.5% can be achieved for a (16×16) switch, compared to 60% for pure input buffering [101]. Surprisingly, it was found that the LIB switch has a maximum throughput that increases as the switch size increases. The explanation given in [97] was that the positive effect of the intermediate buffers becomes more dominant than the negative effect of the HOL blocking as N increases. Evaluating

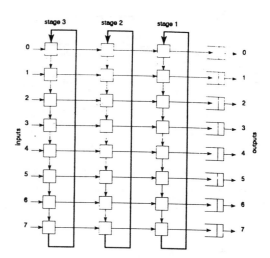

Fig. 11. An (8×8) input-to-output address-difference-driven switch.

the performance of the LIB switch under two-priority traffic classes has been reported in [98].

5. Disjoint-path based switches

In this section, we review some switching fabrics with the capability of disjointly establishing all possible N^2 paths. Thus, no blocking of any type can occur within the switching fabric itself, even among cells destined to the same output port. However, buffering at the output ports is needed to cope with the possibility of multiple cell arrivals. Being pure output-buffered, these architectures have the best possible throughput-delay performance. It can be seen that the Bus-Matrix [169] and Butterfly [189] switches which have been described previously, also lie under the current category. In disjoint-path based switches, paths can be disjoint either in time or in space; in the following we adopt this classification.

5.1. Paths disjoint in time

Speeding-up *any* switching fabric by a factor of N makes it a disjoint-path based switch in which paths are disjoint in time. A multistage self-routing switch, in which each stage is sped-up

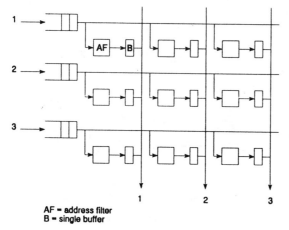

AF = address filter
B = single buffer

Fig. 10. The Limited Intermediate Buffer switch.

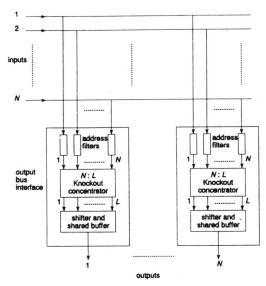

Fig. 12. The Knockout switch.

5.2. Paths disjoint in space

The most well-known example of this category is the *Knockout switch* [230] shown in Fig. 12. It exploits a key observation: in any practical switching system, cell loss within the network is unavoidable. This architecture uses a fully-interconnected topology to passively broadcast all incoming cells to all outputs. Each output port has a bus interface that performs several functions: filtering (to discard cells not intended to that particular port), concentration (only L out of N cells which may be destined to that port in a given time slot are admitted and the rest are dropped), and finally buffering (using a FIFO buffer that is shared among all L lines in a clever arrangement). A concentration cell loss probability smaller than 10^{-6} at a load of 0.90 can be achieved with $L = 8$ for an arbitrary large value of N. Larger values of L are required under

by a factor of N was proposed in [113]. This switch (Fig. 11) uses the difference between the input and output addresses of a cell as it routing tag. It consists of $n = \log_2 N$ stages, each with N (2×2) SEs. Let Y be the output port number and X be the input port number of an incoming cell, then the difference $F = (Y - X) \bmod N = f_n f_{n-1} ... f_1$ is used as the routing header (where f_n is the MSB). If the stages of the switch are numbered from 1 to n starting from the output side, then an SE in stage k examines f_k of an incoming cell: if $f_k = 1$, the cell is shifted by 2^{k-1} downward in the same switching stage and then transferred to the following stage; if $f_k = 0$, the cell is transferred directly to the following stage. Cell loss may occur only as a result of output buffer overflows. This switch is capable of handling multicast connections, in addition to unicast connections. Unfortunately, the requirement to run each stage N times faster than the external lines places a limit on the maximum size of the switch. Also, each output buffer must be capable of receiving up to N cells within a single time slot.

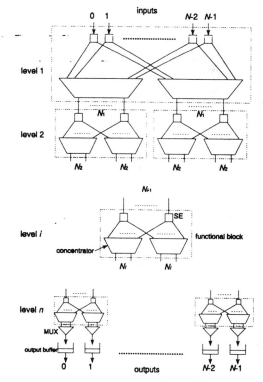

Fig. 13. The Christmas-Tree switch.

imbalanced traffic models [231]. Extending the function of the Knockout switch to variable-length packets was carried out in [79], and to multicasting in [80]. A Knockout switch employing priority-based concentration was studied in [82].

Despite its excellent performance, the Knockout switch is complex for large switch sizes. It requires N^2 distinct physical paths, N^2 address filters, and $N(N \times L)$ Knockout concentrators. Efforts to reduce the complexity of the Knockout switch include the following. The use of a single repeat contention resolution scheme was shown to reduce the required L by a factor of 2 [81]. In [126], it was suggested to build a large switch modularly from smaller Knockout switches in a multistage manner. In [221], it was observed that the high complexity of the Knockout switch is a result of the separation of the distribution and concentration functions. The same reference proposed the *Christmas-Tree switch* (Fig. 13), which is a self-routing output buffering switch architecture that interleaves the distribution and concentration functions in such a way as to achieve high performance with fewer than N^2 paths. While cell filtering and concentration (or contention resolution) functions are performed *centrally* at each output port in the Knockout switch [230], these functions are distributed in small switching

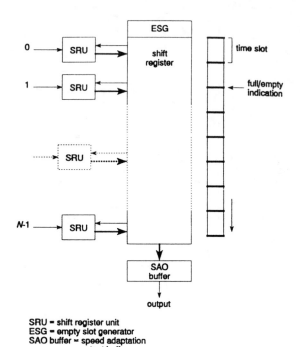

SRU = shift register unit
ESG = empty slot generator
SAO buffer = speed adaptation
　　　　　　output buffer

Fig. 15. An output bus interface of the GAUSS switch.

elements (SWEs) located at the intersections of the crossbar lines (Fig. 14) in the *distributed Knockout switch* [39]. The SWEs examine incoming cells from horizontal lines and route them to one of the L vertical lines of each output port. The number of vertical lines is reduced from N^2 to LN, and concentration within each output bus interface is no longer needed, however, at the expense of LN^2 SWEs. It was pointed out in [39] that this switch design has a regular and uniform structure, is modular, and with relaxed synchronization requirements. Several methods for reducing L were also discussed. It should be noted that both the multistage-based Knockout switch [126] and the Christmas-Tree switch [221] do not belong to the disjoint-path based class of switches; they are mentioned here because of their relation to the Knockout switch.

Several disjoint-path switch designs which differ from the Knockout switch in the structure and operation of the output bus interfaces were also proposed, such as the *GAUSS switch* [70], and the *Cylinder switch* [162]. The GAUSS (Grab Any

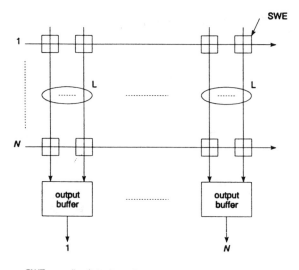

SWE = small switch element

Fig. 14. The distributed Knockout switch.

UnuSed Slot) switch was introduced in [70] and analyzed in [1]. In addition to the knockout principle, it also exploits also the observation that the probability of two cells originating from the same input port and heading for the same output port in successive time slots, gets smaller as N increases. (Notice that this observation may not be valid under bursty traffic.) An output bus interface is called here a GAUSS module and is shown in Fig. 15. It consists of a parallel shift register, shift register units (SRUs) and a speed adaptation output buffer (SAO-buffer). Each input of a GAUSS module has an SRU connected to the parallel shift register. This shift register is used to convey cells arriving at the SRUs to the SAO-buffer. Empty slots are inserted at the top of the shift register and can be filled along their way through the shift register. The speed at which the slots are shifted is higher than the cell arrival rate at the inputs. Each SRU uses an address filter to detect whether a received cell is destined for that output. If so, the SRU seizes an empty slot by means of 'grab any' mechanism. A small buffer is needed in the SRU to take care of the speed difference between the inputs and the shift register. A buffer is also necessary since an SRU may have to wait before it can access the shift register. A cell that arrives at an SRU with a busy buffer is lost. At the end of the shift register the SAO-buffer receives the emitted cells from the SRUs. The ratio of the speed of the shift register to the speed at the inputs is called the speed-up factor L, and is determined by the amount of tolerable cell loss probability. It has been shown that the GAUSS switch has better average cell loss performance compared to the Knockout switch for the same N, L, and load value, which is a result of using buffers in each SRU [1]. However, the GAUSS switch is unfair, since upper input lines are favored over lower ones.

The Cylinder switch [162] solves a basic problem with the Knockout switch, namely the possibility of discarding a cell at a concentrator (i.e., after it has been switched), even though a space is available in the corresponding output buffer. Each output bus interface (called here a ring buffer multiplexer) consists of a buffer ring that is connected to all input lines by input elements

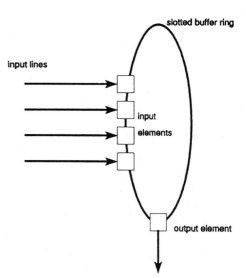

Fig. 16. An output bus interface of the Cylinder switch.

which perform the filtering function, and to the corresponding output line by an output element (Fig. 16). A buffer ring is a set of cell-width parallel shift registers arranged to form a ring (or a cylinder) that is shared between all input lines. Cells rotate in the buffer ring till they are read out by the corresponding output element, one in each time slot. The capacity of the ring is designed to be much greater than that of the input or output lines. Besides the above speed requirement, the switch requires a minimum of N shift registers in each of the N buffer rings.

6. Banyan based switches

The concept of multistage interconnection networks (MINs) was first introduced in the context of circuit switching [24], [33], [46], [55], [84], [159]. The aim was to design a nonblocking switch with less complexity than the crossbar switch. In 1953, Clos [55] showed that the use of a MIN of three or more stages built from relatively small crossbar switches, can significantly reduce the number of crosspoints required for building a large size switch. A 3-stage ($N \times N$) Clos network is shown in Fig. 17. This network is nonblocking if $m \geq 2s - 1$ [55], where m and s are as defined in

Fig. 17. (Notice that *m* paths exist for each input-output pair.) Such a network results in crosspoint savings compared to the crossbar switch for all $N \geq 36$ [159]. Despite the above, Clos network requires complex computations to find a connection path compared to the crossbar switch which can establish a connection without path search.

At this point, it is worth mentioning that the definition of the blocking property in a circuit switch is different from that in a packet switch. In the former [33], [46], [84], [105], [159], if any point-to-point connection between unused input-output ports:

· can be established without any disturbance to the existing connections, then the switch is *nonblocking* (or *strictly nonblocking*);

· can be established without any disturbance to the existing connections, provided that the existing connections were set-up according to some routing algorithm, then the switch is *wide-sense nonblocking*;

· can be established if one or more existing connections are rearranged, then the switch is *rearrangeably nonblocking*;

· cannot be established at all, then the switch is *blocking*.

A switch that is nonblocking in a packet switching environment is not necessarily nonblocking as a circuit switch. On the other hand, a circuit switch that is even rearrangeably nonblocking is nonblocking as a packet switch. One known MIN that

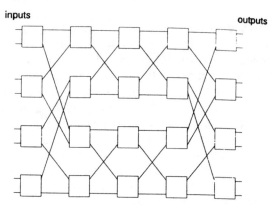

Fig. 18. An (8×8) Benes network.

is rearrangeably nonblocking as a circuit switch is Benes network [24], shown in Fig. 18. As a packet switch, it is nonblocking with the least known crosspoint complexity. However, as for the Clos network, its drawback is the time required for setting-up the paths [46], [105].

As the interest in large scale processing systems grew, many MINs were proposed and studied for the purpose of interconnecting processors and processors, and processors and memory modules in multiprocessor systems [27], [46], [72], [73], [84], [105], [159]. Among these are the networks which belong to the delta class, defined by Patel [176] as the class of MINs which possess two properties: unique path for each input-output pair, and digit-controlled routing. The latter property, known as *self-routing*, makes delta networks very attractive to high-speed packet switch designers. However, it comes at the expense of internal blocking as discussed below. Many well-known MINs belong to the delta class, such as Banyan [94], Baseline [226], Reverse Baseline [226], Omega [137], Modified Data Manipulator [226], Indirect Binary *n*-Cube [183], and Generalized Cube [197] networks. These networks were shown to be topologically equivalent [197], [226]. Currently, most ATM switching researchers tend to freely interchange their names; something that is usually justified by the fact that they have the same performance in under uniform traffic [73]. Some of these networks are shown in Fig. 19 for $N = 8$ (the most frequently-used names are

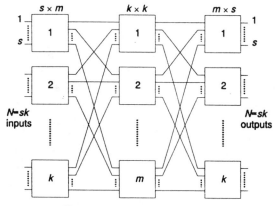

Fig. 17. A three-stage Clos network.

shown). In general, a rectangular $(N \times N)$ delta-b network is constructed using unbuffered $(b \times b)$ SEs (crossbars), organized in n stages, where $N = b^n$ $(n = 1, 2,...)$ and each stage has N/b SEs. In this survey, unless otherwise specified, we consider delta networks constructed with (2×2) SEs. Furthermore, we use the terms "delta" and "banyan" interchangeably when referring to any self-routing single-path $\log_2 N$ MIN.

A large number of ATM switch proposals is based on banyan networks due to their desirable features [2], [8], [46], [157], [173], [213]. Besides the self-routing property, banyan networks are modular, have the same latency for all input-output pairs, support synchronous and asynchronous modes of operation, are suitable for VLSI implementation because of their regular structure, and have a complexity of $O(N \log_2 N)$ compared to $O(N^2)$ for the crossbar switch. However, while path-uniqueness results in (the ease of) preserving cell-sequencing, it also results in banyan networks being internally blocking. This can be explained by the example shown in Fig. 20, which also illustrates the self-routing mechanism: an SE in stage i routes an incoming cell to the upper outlet if $d_i = 0$, or to the lower outlet if $d_i = 1$, where the stages of a banyan network are numbered from 1 to n $(= \log_2 N)$ starting from the input side. Internal blocking arises when two cells destined to different output ports request the same outlet of an SE; in such a situation, one cell is selected according to some policy, and the

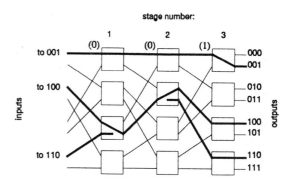

Fig. 20. Internal blocking and self-routing in banyan networks.

other cell is dropped. Furthermore, conflicts do occur among cells having the same destination.

As has been explained so far, the reduction of the crosspoint count from N^2 to $2N \log_2 N$, results in internal blocking. Patel [176] analyzed banyan networks with a random selection blocked-loss policy in the SEs, and derived the following recurrence relation $(1 \leq i \leq n)$:

$$p_i = 1 - \left(1 - \frac{p_{i-1}}{b}\right)^b, \qquad (9)$$

where $p_0 = p$ (cell arrival rate), p_i is the probability that an output link of stage i carries a cell, and $(b \times b)$ is the size of each SE. The throughput is simply $TP = p_n$. Kruskal and Snir [130] derived the following approximate closed-form solution for the throughput of a banyan network:

$$TP = \frac{2b}{(b-1)n + 2\frac{b}{p}}. \qquad (10)$$

Also, tight upper and lower bounds on TP were derived in [132]. TP is plotted (using Eq. (9)) as a function of $\log_2 N$ for $p = 1.0$ and $b = 2$ in Fig. 21. For the sake of comparison, the throughput of a crossbar switch with blocked-loss policy is also shown (using Eq. (8)). From the figure, it is clear that both the crossbar switch and banyan network have a performance that degrades as the switch size increases. However, the degradation is more significant for banyan networks. This is because the crossbar switch suffers only from output blocking, while banyan

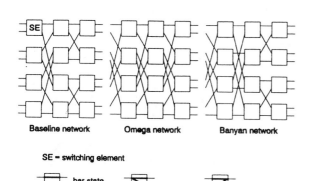

Baseline network   Omega network   Banyan network

SE = switching element

bar state   broadcast states   blocking states

cross state

Fig. 19. Three different topologies of banyan networks.

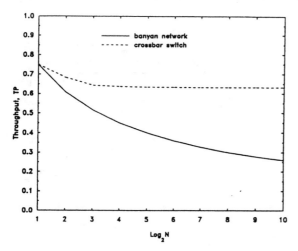

Fig. 21. **Maximum** throughput of banyan networks and crossbar switches as a function of the size.

networks suffer from both output and internal blocking and the latter increases with the number of stages of a banyan network. In particular, as N goes to infinity, TP_{max} (crossbar) = 0.632 and TP_{max} (banyan) = 0. From Eqs. (9) and (10), it can be seen that using SEs of sizes greater than (2×2) improves the throughput [176], [206], [207]. Increasing b reduces internal blocking by reducing the number of stages. Internal blocking is completely eliminated for $b = N$ (i.e., the crossbar switch). Switch architectures which are based on banyan networks use different methods to overcome blocking, and thus to improve the throughput performance. In the following, we classify banyan based switches according to these methods.

6.1. Internal node buffering

The most straightforward solution to the blocking problem in banyan networks (besides dropping blocked cells) is to place buffers within each SE, so that upon conflicts, blocked cells remain in their current buffers instead of being dropped. Typically, a buffered banyan network (BBN) is assumed to operate in a time-slotted fashion with cells advancing from a stage to the next synchronously. One of three possible modes of operation can be used: queue loss (QL), local

backpressure (LB), and global backpressure (GB). With QL, a cell that arrives at a full buffer is simply dropped. With LB, a cell can advance to the next stage only if the next buffer along its path is currently not full. On the other hand, with GB a cell can advance to the next stage even if the next buffer along its path is currently full as long as it is not going to be full upon the arrival of the cell under consideration. Intuitively speaking, QL results in the worst performance and GB results in the best; the situation is reversed with regard to complexity. Notice that with either LB or GB, cell loss can happen only at the buffers of the first stage, or at the external input buffers if used.

Buffers can be placed at the inlets of each SE yielding input-BBNs. This is the simplest and most researched type of buffered banyan networks [5], [35], [45], [71], [74], [88], [89], [95], [117], [124], [131], [143], [144], [148], [189], [191], [193], [195], [205], [211], [216], [217], [218], [219], [220], [227], [232]. An (8×8) input-BBN with external input buffers is shown in Fig. 22. Alternatively, buffers can be placed at each SE outlet (output-BBNs) [77], [83], [95], [127], [130], [134], [186], [189], [205], [229]; at the crosspoints of each SE (crosspoint-BBNs) [95], [102], [131], [133], [189]; within each SE shared among all its inlets and outlets (shared-BBNs) [29], [95], [163], [218], [219]; or at both the inlets and outlets of each SE (input-output-BBNs) [164], [205]. The performance of a BBN is a function of the performance of its individual SEs: the better the performance of each SE (which depends on the strategy/size of its buffers) is, the better is the performance of

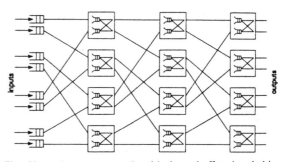

Fig. 22. A banyan network with input-buffered switching elements.

the whole network. With the assumption of infinite size buffers, output-BBNs [95], [127], [130], crosspoint-BBNs [95], and shared-BBNs [95], all achieve a 100% maximum throughput, while input-BBNs achieve only a 75% maximum throughput [71], [95], [205], for any value of N. The non-unity figure for input-BBNs is a result of HOL blocking within each SE, which in turn limits the maximum throughput of the whole structure to that of a single (2×2) SE [101].

For a 10-stage network with a single buffer at each SE inlet and GB, $TP_{max} = 0.32$ (according to simulation results [205], [211]; however, most analytical models give the optimistic figure of 0.45 [117], [191], [205], [232]). This is compared to 0.26 for an unbuffered banyan network of the same size [176]. It is clear that this improvement may not justify the added complexity. Increasing the buffer size improves the throughput performance. For example, with $N = 1024$, $TP_{max} = 0.43$ or 0.50 when 2 or 3 buffers, respectively, are used per SE inlet. Increasing the size of each SE in a BBN with single-input-buffered SEs also improves the throughput performance [35], [157], [218], [219], [232], as it is the case with unbuffered banyan networks [176]. However, with multiple buffers at each SE inlet, the throughput performance degrades as the size of the SE increases [35], [157], [218], [219], [232]. Bubenik and Turner [35] explained this by the increased negative effect of HOL blocking (which does not exist in a single-input-buffered SE) as the size of each SE increases [101]. A second reasoning [218], [219] is that the number of stages for a given N decreases as the size of the SEs increases, resulting in less buffering overall. The above suggests that it is better first to relax the FIFO queueing assumption at each SE inlet buffer (e.g., use bypass queueing [101]), and then to use SEs of sizes larger than (2×2) [35], [218], [219]. (Since the number of stages decreases with increasing the SE size, this also reduces the delay.) Adopting bypass queueing in input-BBNs built with (2×2) SEs also improves the performance [193], [195]. A cut-through mechanism [122], [216], [217] can be used to improve both the delay and throughput of a BBN [35], [157], [224]. With cut-through, a cell that arrives at an empty buffer and finds out that

the desired output link is free, advances directly without first being fully received and buffered. Widjaja et al. [224] showed that the effect of cut-through switching on the delay is most significant when the load is moderate. It was also shown that the effect of this mechanism on the performance diminishes as the SE buffer size increases, since a buffer takes a longer time to become empty and hence less opportunity for cells to cut-through. The above results have been shown to be true for both input and output-BBNs. Splitting each SE inlet buffer into two parallel queues was shown to improve the throughput performance of an input-BBN [74], [220]. In [89], a change was suggested to the VLSI implementation of an n-stage input-BBN that would result in achieving the throughput performance of an ($n - 1$)-stage network. Speeding-up the internal fabric of a BBN has also been suggested [35], [95], [189], [216], [217] to improve its performance.

Szymanski and Shaikh [205] showed that BBNs built with SEs containing a combination of single input buffers and output queues outperform BBNs built with SEs containing only input queues or only output queues, given a fixed finite total amount of memory. Also, it was shown [218], [219] that while a shared-BBN offers clearly superior performance for a given amount of buffering, a parallel bypass queueing input-BBN performs impressively as well. Based on $N = 64$ and an SE storage capacity of 16 cells, Goli and Kumar [95] showed that a shared-BBN outperforms input, output, and crosspoint-BBNs, while a crosspoint-BBN provides a performance comparable to output and shared-BBNs for loads below 80%. It was argued that a crosspoint-BBN is a very good choice if both performance and complexity [133] are considered.

BBNs are known to have a performance that is very sensitive to traffic nonuniformities, regardless of the buffering strategy of the SEs. Nonuniform traffic performance evaluation was carried out for input-BBNs [5], [35], [45], [74], [88], [124], [143], [220], [227]; for output-BBNs [77], [134], [186], [229]; for crosspoint-BBNs [95], [102]; and for input-output-BBNs [164]. In general, the degradation in performance is due to the so-called *tree-saturation* effect [186], which occurs when the buffers of a last stage SE become full, and then the buffers of its two predecessors are completely filled, and so on all the way back to the input ports. Several solutions have been suggested to overcome this problem [5], [35], [45], [134], [220]. Atiquzzaman and Akhtar [5] have studied the performance of both buffered and unbuffered banyan networks under hot-spot traffic and found that the latter can have better performance.

6.2. Multiple banyans

Many ATM switch architectures are based on the use of more than one banyan network. Among these switches, three types can be identified depending on the concept behind the switch operation. In the following, we review the different types of multiple-banyan switches.

Parallel loading

Here, it is noticed that blocking in a banyan network increases with the applied load. Thus, a possible solution is to use multiple banyan networks, and to distribute the load (according to some mechanism) among them. The best example of this type of switches is the *replicated delta network* [130], [132]. It uses K banyan networks in parallel, as shown in Fig. 23 for $N = 8$ and $K = 2$. The ith input port of the switch is connected to the ith input of each banyan through a $1:K$ demultiplexer, while the ith output of each banyan is connected to one of the inputs of the ith $K:1$ multiplexer.

An incoming cell randomly chooses one of the K banyan networks [130], [132] (other distribution policies have also been examined in [57], [132], and [147]). One of two possible mechanisms can be used at the output ports: single acceptance (SA) or multiple acceptance (MA). With SA, only one cell out of K cells which may reach an output port is accepted [10], [11], [130], [132]. On the other hand, with MA all cells which reach an output port are accepted [11], [57], [147], [214], which necessitates the use of output buffering. (Input buffering must be used with both policies in an ATM environment for reasonable values of K.) With $N = 1024$ and a target $TP_{max} = 0.60$, 20 or 4 banyan networks are needed when SA [130],

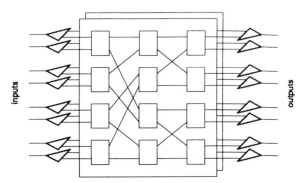

Fig. 23. An (8×8) replicated banyan network with $K = 2$.

[132] or MA [213], [214], respectively, is used. Finally, cell-sequencing may be disturbed if internal buffers are used, unless cells belonging to the same connection are forced to use the same banyan network.

Sequential loading

In sequential loading multiple-banyan switches, the traffic is offered to the first banyan network, then that part of the traffic that is blocked by the first banyan is offered to the second banyan network, and so on till the last (Kth) banyan network. The traffic that remains after that is either dropped [214], [222], re-offered to one of the banyan networks along with new incoming traffic [214], or buffered at the input ports [53], [192], [225]. In all cases, output buffering is required to cope with the possibility of multiple arrivals at each output port.

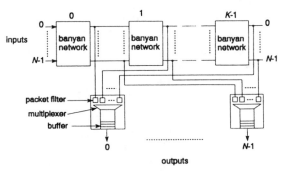

Fig. 24. The tandem-banyan switch.

The *tandem-banyan switch* [214] consists of K banyan networks in series (Fig. 24). Each output of every banyan network is connected to both the same-number input of the following banyan, and the corresponding output buffer (except for the last banyan which is connected only to the output buffers). A cell that loses contention in banyan network i ($0 \le i \le K - 2$) is misrouted after being marked, so as not to compete with properly routed cells in the following stages of the same banyan network. Marked cells out of network i are fed into network $i + 1$ with their marks removed, while unmarked cells are extracted by the output ports. Marked cells at the outputs of the last network are lost. While the performance of delta networks is the same under uniform traffic regardless of their topology [73], when cascaded in the form of the tandem-banyan switch, their performance differs significantly [196], [214]. As an example, for $N = 1024$ and $P_{loss} = 10^{-6}$, 10 Modified Data Manipulator networks or 14 Baseline networks are required. Even better performance can be achieved if Omega networks are used [196]. Re-injecting cells that exit the last banyan network into the routing fabric for further processing, reduces the number of networks needed to achieve a given P_{loss}. In [223], it has been shown that using 2-dilated banyan networks (to be described later) reduces the number of networks needed to achieve a given P_{loss} by a factor of two or more. Finally, the tandem-banyan switch may deliver cells out-of-sequence for large values of N unless artificial delays are used.

In [53], the authors of the tandem-banyan switch [214] give an interesting discussion of the practical limitations they faced in implementing their switch. The limitation on the size of the switch comes primarily from the complexity of the function of each SE (which must, in the case of the tandem-banyan switch, examine the conflict bits in addition to the destination bits, of both cells at its inlets). Also, the arrangement of banyan networks in series renders the chip-to-chip synchronization difficult. Based on these limitations, it has been concluded that placing banyan networks in parallel rather than in series while preserving the concept of operation is a better choice. A switch architecture based on parallel banyan networks along with input and output buffering was then proposed under the name the *Memory / Space-division / Memory* (MSM) *switch*. In the MSM switch, the input controllers (one for each input port) maximizes the utilization of each banyan network by dispatching the cells to the banyan networks in sequence; thus offering the maximum load to each banyan network. This is accomplished through a two-phase operation: route set-up phase, and cell transmission phase. Cell loss can occur at both the input and output buffers. Since any individual banyan network can be accessed directly, the MSM switch can support circuit switching besides packet switching. Also, it can support multicasting.

A switch design that is similar to the MSM switch is the *Double Phase Packet Switch* (DPPS) [222]. The DPPS uses K Baseline networks in parallel with pure output buffering. Arriving cells are offered to each Baseline network sequentially, and unsuccessful cells are lost. As for the MSM switch, the DPPS is a successful pipeline application, with a two-phase pipeline that allows some requests to be issued when some cells are being transmitted; thereby increasing the average throughput of a cycle. It was shown that no more than $\log_2 N$ Baseline networks are needed to achieve a cell loss probability of 10^{-6} (under full load). In both the MSM switch and the DPPS, the state of the SEs are set prior to the actual transmission of the cells (i.e., during the first phase); thus, simplifying the design and operation of the SEs.

Another switch that is based on a parallel banyan structure is the *Pipeline Banyan* [225]. It consists of a single control plane and a number of data planes, together with input and output buffering. Cell headers are routed via the control plane to set their routing paths in the data planes. At the control plane, time is divided into slots for reservation; in each reservation slot, a data plane is selected on a round-robin basis. The SEs of the data planes are not required to perform any processing, which results in simplifying their design. However, connections are required between control plane SEs and the corresponding SEs of the data planes. Cells which cannot establish conflict-free paths, or are destined to output ports with full buffers, remain in their current input buffers. It was shown that this switch achieves a better performance compared to the tandem banyan switch [214] for the same number of banyan networks.

A switch architecture that *can* use banyan networks in parallel was proposed in [192]. It consists of parallel planes in conjunction with input and output buffering. Besides pipelining, the key feature in this switch is the use of bypass queueing in the input buffers. Bypass queueing was shown to significantly improve the throughput performance given a particular number of planes. It was shown that using a banyan network in each plane is more cost-effective than using a nonblocking architecture, given a target performance level.

Double banyan

This type is based on cascading two banyan networks, as shown in Fig. 25. (Notice the resemblance to the previously mentioned Benes network [24].) The first network is called a randomization or distribution network, depending on the particular architecture. The second network is the usual self-routing banyan network and is responsible for the delivery of cells coming out of the first network to their desired output ports. The operation of the first network affects the performance of the whole switch and is different in different switch designs. In general, the reason behind using the first network is reduce the effect of incoming traffic imbalances on the performance of the routing (i.e., second) network.

In [166], both networks are internally-unbuffered with the first one acting as a cell-basis randomization network, in which each SE sets its

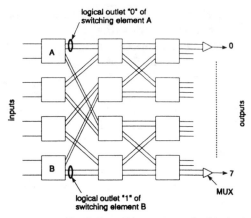

Fig. 26. An (8×8) dilated banyan network with $d = 2$.

state randomly and not based on the destination bits of incoming cells. In [217], two buffered banyan networks were used with the first one being called a distribution network. The SEs of the distribution network ignore the destination addresses of incoming cells and route them alternately to each of their outlets; if one or both outlets are busy, the first outlet to become available is used. Unfortunately, out-of-sequence cell delivery may occur in this switch because cells belonging to the same connection may follow different paths and suffer different queueing delays. A solution to this problem could be to randomize or distribute the traffic on a connection-basis rather than on a cell-basis [66]. In this case, cells belonging to the same connection are forced to follow the same path. In [4], different connection-based path selection algorithms were suggested.

6.3. Dilation

The throughput performance of a banyan network can be improved by replacing each internal link by d links as shown in Fig. 26 for $d = 2$. The resulting structure is known as the *dilated banyan network* [130], [132]. The SEs of a dilated banyan network are $(2d \times 2d)$ switches with 2 output addresses. The routing algorithm here is the same as without dilation, except that internal blocking occurs only when $d + 1$ or more cells all select the same logical outlet of an SE. In such a

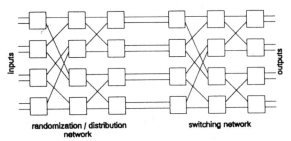

Fig. 25. A cascade of two banyan networks.

situation, d cells are randomly chosen and the others are dropped. One possible implementation of the SEs was given in [132], and is shown in Fig. 27 for $d = 4$. In this implementation, each SE consists of $2d$ 1:d demultiplexers, $2d$ d:1 multiplexers, and d ($d \times d$) sorters. Each ($d \times d$) sorter can be built using $d\log_2 d(\log_2 d + 1)/4$ binary comparators organized in $\log_2 d(\log_2 d + 1)/2$ stages [22].

As with the replicated banyan network, one of two acceptance policies can be used at the output side of a dilated banyan network: SA or MA. With SA, a maximum of one cell can be accepted at each output port every time slot [10], [11], [130], [132], [204], while with MA all successful cells (up to d cells) are accepted [11], [37], [91], [147], [205], [215], [223], [233]. Thus, output buffering is required only with MA. In an ATM environment, input buffering must be used with SA, while it can be ignored with MA if d is large enough to guarantee an acceptable cell loss probability within the interconnection network. It has been shown that with $d = 4$ and SA, the dilated banyan network is almost nonblocking. It becomes nonblocking when $d = 2^{\lceil n/2 \rceil}$, where $n = \log_2 N$.

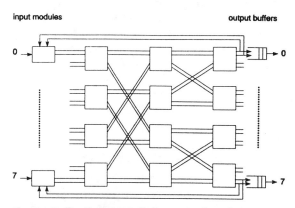

Fig. 28. An (8×8) dilated banyan network ($d = 2$) with deflection routing and recirculation.

The throughput performance of a dilated banyan network can be improved further with the MA policy. Ghosh and Daly [91] studied a dilated banyan network with pure output buffering, and showed that a TP_{max} exceeding 90% can be achieved with $d = 3$ and $B_{out} = 20$. Szymanski and Shaikh [205] showed that a dilation factor between 4 and 8 is sufficient to reduce the fraction of cells lost within the interconnection network to values between 10^{-3} and 10^{-6} under full-load conditions. Even with d as small as 3, a near-unity maximum throughput can be achieved using single output-buffered SEs [205]. However, cell-sequencing may be disturbed by this approach since it uses internal buffering in a multi-path architecture. A near-unity TP_{max} can also be achieved by misrouting (i.e., deflecting) losing cells instead of dropping them, and then re-injecting them into the network through the input ports [233]. The architecture of a switch adopting this approach is shown in Fig. 28 for $N = 8$ and $d = 2$. It should be noted, however, that this approach too does not preserve cell-sequencing. Finally, assuming an internally-unbuffered network, Lee and Liew [147] addressed an important issue, namely "how does the switch complexity grow as a function of the switch size for a given loss probability requirement?" for a number of switch architectures. Using analysis, it was shown that for a given target of P_{loss}, the dilated banyan network has a lower order of complexity than the

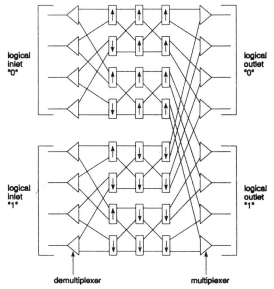

Fig. 27. A (2×2) switching element of a dilated banyan network with $d = 4$.

tandem-banyan switch or the replicated banyan network (with MA). It was concluded that dilation is a powerful design technique for improving performance and reducing complexity in a large switch.

6.4. Sorting

Some of banyan networks have an interesting property: a Banyan or an Omega network becomes nonblocking if incoming cells are ordered according to their output port addresses (in either an ascending or a descending order), and concentrated (i.e., compact with no gaps between active inputs), provided that output conflicts do not exist [105], [141], [165]. This is the basic idea behind all sort banyan based ATM switches. A well-known architecture that can perform the sorting function in a distributed and parallel manner is the Batcher network [22]. The operation of the Batcher network is based on the bitonic sorting principle that was introduced in the same reference. An $(N \times N)$ Batcher network can be built using $\log_2 N(\log_2 N + 1)/2$ stages, each with $N/2$ binary comparators or sorting elements. The Batcher network can sort an arbitrary set of active cells based on their output port addresses (and/or any other information contained in cell headers; this is useful when supporting prioritized traffic), and group them consecutively at the bottom or the top of its output ports. Thus, the combination of a Batcher network and a Banyan (or Omega) network solves the problem of internal blocking and renders this

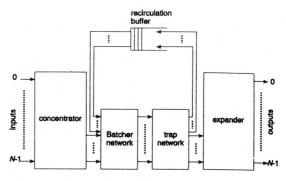

Fig. 30. The Starlite switch.

combination as effective as the crossbar switch, provided that multiple cells with the same output port address are prevented from entering the Batcher-Banyan (BB) network. The particular approach used for resolving output conflicts in a BB based switch is strongly related to the buffering strategy that the switch adopts, as will become clear below. An (8×8) BB network is shown in Fig. 29.

Although the BB network is nonblocking with less complexity than the crossbar switch, it can not be easily partitioned into integrated circuits, and maintaining synchronization across the entire structure (a total of $\log_2 N + \log_2 N(\log_2 N + 1)/2$ stages) becomes difficult as N increases [168]. The same reference noticed that most of the interest in the BB switching fabric came from the research community rather than from the industry. Some physical issues, concerning the scalability of BB networks to architectures suitable for large broadband central offices, were examined in [92].

Internal buffering

The *Starlite* switch [103] was the first sort banyan based switching fabric to be proposed in the literature. (Also, demultiplexing input traffic to cope with the very high speeds of fiber links was suggested for the first time in the same reference.) The structure of the Starlite switch is shown in Fig. 30, and it basically consists of a cascade of a concentrator, a sorting network, a trap network, and an expander. The concentrator (built from running sum adders followed by a

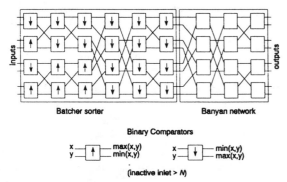

Fig. 29. The Batcher-Banyan network.

reverse Omega network, which is the mirror image of an Omega network) is used to reduce the size of the following networks, assuming that it is likely to have a significant number of idle input ports. The outputs of the sorting (Batcher) network are fed into a trap network (built from a single stage of comparators followed by an Omega network) so that only one cell per each set of cells destined to the same output port is admitted to the expander (an Omega network), while all others are recycled back into the sorting network. Two points should be noted. The first is that cell-sequencing is not preserved by this recycling approach, but out-of-sequence cell delivery can be avoided by aging cells. Also, a buffering stage must be provided for recycled cells (i.e., internal buffering). To reduce cell loss within the recirculation buffers, a substantial fraction of the input ports must be dedicated for recirculators, which under-utilizes the switch capacity. However, sharing buffers and smoothing bursty traffic both can be achieved by this recirculation mechanism. Finally, this switch can support a special type of multicasting.

Internal-output buffering

The *Sunshine* switch [93], shown in Fig. 31, achieves high performance by utilizing both internal and output buffering. It basically combines a Batcher network with parallel Banyan networks. Incoming cells enter a Batcher network, where they are sorted according to their output port addresses and priority levels. A trap network then

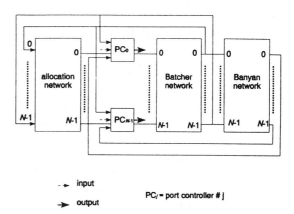

Fig. 32. The 3-phase Batcher-Banyan switch.

resolves output conflicts by selecting the K highest priority cells present for each output port address within a common time slot. Cells which exceed K for a single address must be recirculated. A concentrator (another Batcher network) separates cells to be recirculated from those to be routed, and the selector directs cells either to the recirculators for queueing, or to the Banyan networks for routing. Thus, K cells per output port address may be always switched within a given time slot, one through a different Banyan network. It was shown that this architecture can achieve the extremely low cell loss probabilities necessary for circuit emulation [93], and is robust in a bursty environment for a large enough number of Banyan networks [69]. The switch can also support output channel grouping which further improves its performance particularly under extremely bursty traffic. Finally, it is interesting to notice that when $K = 1$, the Starlite switch [103] results.

Input buffering

Perhaps the most straightforward approach to operate the BB network is to use FIFO input buffers and to resolve conflicts prior to switching. However, this approach has two drawbacks. First, the need for a contention resolution mechanism suitable for the BB network. Also, the maximum throughput is significantly less than unity due to HOL blocking [101], [104], [120]. The first pro-

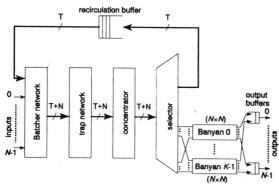

Fig. 31. The Sunshine switch.

posal for contention resolution in an input-buffered BB network was given in [104] under the name *3-phase algorithm*, and the resulting switch was called the *BB switch*. The block diagram of the BB switch is shown in Fig. 32 [181]. Notice that same-number input and output port controllers are located in the same module PC_i ($i = 0,..., N-1$) that interfaces both input port i and output port i of the switch. In phase 1 of the algorithm, request packets formed from the destination and the source addresses of each HOL cell are sorted by the Batcher network according to the destination addresses. At the outputs of the Batcher network, adjacent cells with the same destinations are purged (by the allocation network). In phase 2, winning requests are fed into the inputs of the Batcher network, and routed through the BB network using this time the source addresses, so that they acknowledge their originating input ports. Selected input ports admit their cells to the fabric in phase 3. Fig. 33 shows an example of the operation of the first two phases of this algorithm. Prioritized traffic can be easily supported by the BB switch by sorting request packets (in phase 1) according to both the destination addresses and the priority levels.

A reservation-based contention resolution mechanism for the BB network was proposed in [30]. Here, the input ports are interconnected via a ring which is used to reserve access to the output ports. Arriving cells are buffered till they can participate in the reservation process. At the beginning of each time slot, an N-bit token is circulated around the ring, where each bit corresponds to a particular output port and indicates whether that port is available or has already been reserved. When the token passes by, the HOL cell in each input buffer tries to make a reservation. When an output is successfully reserved, the corresponding HOL cell is admitted to the BB network at the beginning of the next cycle. To insure fairness, the ring is shifted one revolution plus one more position in each time slot.

Both the 3-phase algorithm [104] and the ring-reservation mechanism [30] suffer from drawbacks. The 3-phase algorithm requires significantly large processing overhead (e.g., 33% for $N = 1024$ and an ATM cell size) [104], and suffers from a fairness problem since either lower or higher address input ports are given priority in the allocation of the switching bandwidth when contending for the same output port [178]. On the other hand, while the ring-reservation mechanism is simpler than the 3-phase algorithm, the need to run the ring N times the speed of the external lines, to be able to poll all N input ports within each time slot, constitutes a major limitation on the scalability of the switch. Furthermore, extending the function of this mechanism to prioritized traffic does not seem to be straightforward.

To overcome the above problems, Awdeh and Mouftah [14] have recently proposed a 2-phase contention resolution algorithm that has been shown to be fair, to require less processing overhead than that required by the 3-phase algorithm [104], and to easily support prioritized traffic. The basic idea in this algorithm is to let the binary comparators of the Batcher network explicitly participate in the arbitration process. Phase 1 starts at the beginning of each time slot by forming request packets (RPs), each from a HOL cell destination address (DA) and a flag bit (FB) that is initially set to 1. RPs are then sorted by the Batcher network according to the DAs, but with the following two modifications. First, the binary sorting elements hold their settings after the RPs pass through them. Also, if a binary sorter finds out that both RPs at its inputs have the same destination address (i.e., $DA_0 = DA_1$), then it examines their FBs:

· if $FB_0 = FB_1 = 1$ (i.e., both unmarked), it *randomly* selects one of the contending RPs and marks it by resetting its FB to 0, and it treats

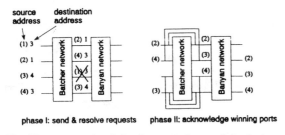

phase I: send & resolve requests   **phase II: acknowledge winning ports**

Fig. 33. An example of the first two phases of the 3-phase algorithm for the Batcher-Banyan switch.

the marked RP as the one having the largest DA;

· if $FB_0 \neq FB_1$ (i.e., one is marked and the other is unmarked), it treats the marked RP as the one having the largest DA.

In all other cases, the routing decisions are entirely based on the DAs, without altering or being affected by the FBs. This includes the case where $DA_0 \neq DA_1$. An RP wins if it remains unmarked after being processed by a last stage sorting element. ACKs are formed from the current FBs and sent back to the originating input ports through the paths that have just been set. In phase 2, input ports which receive ACKs of 1, send their full HOL cells through the BB network to self-route to their desired destination ports.

With any of the above mechanisms, the maximum throughput is 58.6% due to HOL blocking. Pattavina [177] tried to solve this problem by modifying the operation of the 3-phase BB switch [104] to support output channel grouping. In phase 1 of the modified algorithm, requests are sorted according to the desired group numbers. The channel allocation network of Fig. 32 (now consists of $\lceil \log_2 R \rceil$ stages of hardware adders, where R is the group size) computes an index for each request that identifies a specific output port in a group. Requests which cannot be accommodated in a channel group are given an incorrect index. In phase 2, an acknowledgement packet with the assigned index is sent back to the requested port, and each active port controller determines if it is a winner based on the received index. It is important to notice that an incoming cell stream (belonging to the same connection) may be divided and switched through different output ports, since the allocation of the connec-

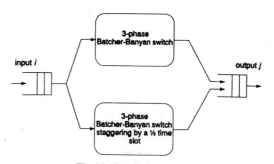

Fig. 35. The duplex switch.

tion was made to a channel group rather than a specific output port. This may affect the connection end-to-end cell sequence integrity (however, this switch still delivers cells in sequence within itself).

In [135], it was noticed that the BB switch [104] has shortcomings in its ability to share buffers, its large buffer requirement to insure a small cell loss probability, and its poor performance under imbalanced traffic. In the same reference, a buffer subsystem which attempts to solve these problems was proposed. Fig. 34 shows the block diagram of the resulting switch, which consists of a cascade of an $(N \times N)$ distribution network, N physically-separate buffers, a second $(N \times N)$ distribution network, and finally an $(N \times N)$ BB switch. The first distribution network routes incoming cells to the buffers of lower occupancy, while the second distribution network routes cells from buffers of higher occupancy to the idle input ports of the BB switch. (Clearly, this design does not preserve cell-sequencing.) Each distribution network is constructed from a Batcher sorter with feedback paths, together with a connection algorithm to perform the path set-up. Significant buffer savings were shown to be achieved by this architecture. As an example, for a switch of size 32 loaded at 90% of capacity, a total buffer size of about 30 cells is required to achieve a cell loss probability of 10^{-10}, compared to 1600 for the BB switch. Also, the adverse effect of imbalanced traffic on performance is eliminated. Despite the above, the switch still suffers from a poor throughput performance. The operation of the switch has been modified to support output chan-

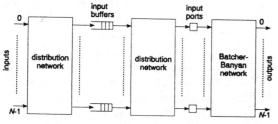

Fig. 34. A buffer subsystem for the Batcher-Banyan switch.

nel grouping in [136], where any partition of the output ports is allowed.

Input-output buffering

The *duplex switch* [104], shown in Fig. 35, consists of two BB switch planes in parallel, with the second plane staggering by a half time slot behind the first plane. HOL cells present themselves to the first switch plane for contention resolution. At the end of phase 2, winning cells are admitted to the first plane and an updated set of contending HOL cells present themselves to the second switch plane, and so on. This process alternates between the two switch planes. Output buffering is needed to cope with the possibility of simultaneous arrivals from the two switch planes at the same output port. In general, for S BB switch planes in parallel, with adjacent planes staggered by a period of time longer than that required by phases 1 and 2 of the 3-phase algorithm [104], the capacity is equal to S times the single BB switch capacity. Furthermore, this configuration ($S > 1$) provides redundancy for enhancing system reliability.

A modular architecture for very large packet switches has been proposed by Lee [142], and its block structure is shown in Fig. 36. The inputs to the switch are partitioned into K equal subsets, with each subset being interfaced to a switch

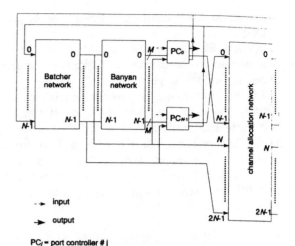

PC$_j$ = port controller # j

Fig. 37. Pattavina's input-output buffering switch.

module of size $(M \times N)$, where $M = N/K$. Each switch module is a cascade of an $(M \times M)$ Batcher sorter, a stack of M binary trees, and K parallel $(M \times M)$ Banyan networks. Each subset of input cells is sorted by a Batcher sorter, then partitioned into finer sub-subsets by the binary trees. In each module, the ordered cells of these sub-subsets are routed concurrently to the output buffers by K Banyan networks. Each switch module adopts a ring-reservation contention resolution mechanism [30], together with a w-windowing scheme [101]. This architecture can be considered as a result of a unification of the BB network (obtained when $K = 1$) and the Knockout switch [230] (obtained when $K = N$). Since the switch modules are interconnected only at the outputs, relaxed synchronization requirements, easy operation and maintenance, and higher reliability are achieved. It was shown that a TP_{max} greater than 90% can be achieved with $w = 2$ for $K \geq 2$. Finally, the parallel Banyan networks can be replaced with a dilated banyan network without sacrificing the nonblocking property [147]. This also applies to the Sunshine switch [93] that was described earlier.

The above described input-output buffering switches provide no means to prevent buffer overflows at the output ports. On the other hand, the switch architecture described in [179] and

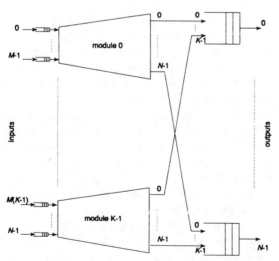

Fig. 36. Lee's modular switch architecture.

[180] uses mixed input-output buffering with a backpressure mechanism. Fig. 37 shows the block structure of this switch. The switch is able to transfer up to M cells per time slot to a given output port. It is constructed using a Batcher network, a Banyan network, and a channel allocation network. The channel allocation network consists of 3 different networks: a $(2N \times 2N)$ merge network (of $n + 1$ stages of (2×2) SEs), a $(2N \times 2N)$ path allocation network (of $L = \lceil \log_2 M \rceil$ stages of adders), and a $(2N \times 2N)$ concentration network (of $n + 1$ stages of (2×2) SEs). The size of the Banyan network is $(N2^L \times N2^L)$ where N inputs only are used. A probe-ack contention resolution algorithm is employed to set up conflict-free paths for the cells through the interconnection network, and at the same time to insure that cell losses do not occur as a result of output buffer overflows. This makes it possible to jointly optimize the cell storage capacity at input and output buffers, and easier to define congestion control procedures. It was shown that for M as small as 3 or 4, the HOL blocking effect is significantly reduced. Also, it was shown that bursty traffic requires much more buffer capacity at the outputs to give throughputs comparable to those achieved under uniform traffic.

Output buffering

In [52], it was observed that the high complexity of the Knockout switch [230] is mainly due to the need of each bus driver to drive N loads, and also to having a separate concentrator in each of its N output bus interfaces. The same reference proposed the *Shared Concentration Output Queueing* (SCOQ) *switch*, shown in Fig. 38. The switch is composed of an $(N \times N)$ Batcher network, followed by L switching modules (SMs), each of size $(N \times K)$, where $K = N/L$. The basic idea here is that each SM concentrates and routes cells corresponding to its K outputs. Therefore, concentration is now shared among the K output ports of each SM. Also, each output of the Batcher network needs to drive only L loads. Besides the output buffers, each SM consists from a bank of address filters and L $(K \times K)$ Banyan networks. If more than L cells are destined to the same output port at the same time, at most L

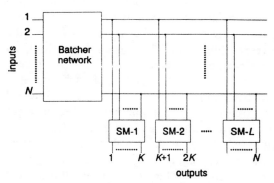

SM: switching module

Fig. 38. The Shared Concentration Output Queueing switch.

of them will be successfully routed and the remaining cells are lost due to contentions within the Banyan networks. The SCOQ switch has been shown to compare well with the Knockout switch [230], the Sunshine switch [93], and Lee's modular switch [142], in terms of complexity.

6.5. Deflection-routing

Instead of dropping or internally buffering a losing cell in a multistage interconnection network, a third approach is to route that cell the *wrong* way (i.e., to misroute or to deflect it). A cell that has been deflected can get involved in the routing process again at a later stage. It should be noticed that both the tandem-banyan switch [214] and the dilated banyan network with recirculation [233] (which have been described earlier) are based on the deflection-routing principle.

Folded Shuffle switch

This is an input-output buffering switch architecture that adopts a cylindrical (i.e., the outputs of the last stage are connected to the inputs of the first) interconnection network [38]. An $(N \times N)$ switch is constructed using $n = \log_2 N$ stages, each with N unbuffered (3×3) SEs, where successive stages are interconnected through the perfect shuffle pattern [201]. In this architecture, a switch input and a switch output are associated with all SEs in each row of the network, as shown in Fig. 39 for $N = 8$. An input buffer can access any SE in the corresponding row, and an output buffer receives successful cells from any SE in the corresponding row. Thus, each input (output) buffer must be able to send (receive) up to n cells per time slot. At the beginning of each time slot, each SE computes for the cells at its internal inlets (see Fig. 39) the minimum number of stages remained to the required destinations (called cell distances). A cell with zero distance is admitted to the corresponding output buffer through the external outlet; otherwise, it is transmitted through an internal outlet according to the shortest path algorithm. Conflicts arising when more than one cell request the external outlet (leading to an output buffer) or the same internal outlet (leading to the next stage) of an SE, are resolved by deflecting a *randomly* selected cell through an internal outlet. If at least one of the internal outlets is idle, the corresponding SE allows the reception of a new cell through the external inlet (assuming that a newly received cell has no immediate access to the external outlet of the SE). Thus, cell loss is avoided between the interconnection network and the input buffers. It was shown that small input buffer sizes and considerably large output buffer sizes are needed to achieve a very small cell loss probability at rea-

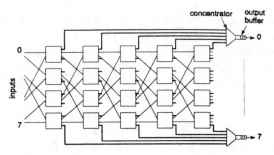

Fig. 40. An (8×8) Shuffleout switch with $K = 5$.

sonable loads. Finally, this design does not preserve cell-sequencing.

Shuffleout switch

Another switch architecture, in which successive stages are interconnected through the perfect shuffle pattern [201], and routing is performed according to the shortest path algorithm with deflection, has been proposed in [62] under the name the Shuffleout switch (Fig. 40). It is constructed using $K (\geq n = \log_2 N)$ stages, each with $N/2$ unbuffered (2×4) SEs, where the two outer outlets, called local outlets, are connected to the corresponding output ports. The number of buses entering an output port is equal to K; thus, concentration is required to reduce system complexity. Each SE attempts to route each received cell along its shortest path measured in remaining number of stages to destination. In case of contention, the cell *closest* to its destination wins, and the other cell is deflected through a remote outlet; if both have the same output distance, a random selection is performed. An SE computes the output distance of each incoming cell by comparing the binary address of the row in which it is located, with the $n - 1$ least significant bits of the destination address of the cell. Cells which do not reach their destinations by stage K are lost. It was shown that the Shuffleout switch is robust against nonuniform traffic at the expense of few more stages compared to uniform traffic [23]. This switch architecture may deliver cells out-of-sequence, unless an additional fixed delay of ($K - s)\tau$ (where τ is the SE latency) is imposed on each cell exiting the network from stage s ($1 \leq s$

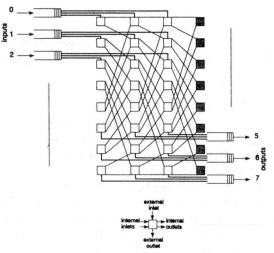

Fig. 39. An (8×8) Folded Shuffle switch.

$\leq K$). Also, the Shuffleout switch is unfair since cells addressing central output ports are better served by the network than cells addressing peripheral output ports [23]. The function of the Shuffleout switch has been extended to support variable-length packets in [63].

Instead of dropping cells which do not reach their destinations after crossing the whole interconnection network, these cells are recirculated for further processing in the *closed-loop* Shuffleout switch [61]. Two different implementations have been considered: buffered and expanded. In the former, each input of the first stage is shared between an input line and a link connected to an outlet of an SE in the last stage. Input buffers are needed to cope with the possibility of two concurrent arrivals at the same input port. Priority is always given to recirculated cells. In the expanded closed-loop Shuffleout switch, recirculated cells are fed into dedicated switch inputs. Thus, an expansion of the network size is required in order to concurrently feed into the network both new and recirculated cells. A concentration stage can be used for the recirculation links before feeding them into the network inputs. In general, the expanded version requires a smaller number of stages for a given cell loss probability, compared to the buffered version at the expense of network expansion. Compared to the original switch (called the *open-loop* Shuffleout), both implementations require less number of stages for the same cell loss probability. However, they both require resequencing mechanisms

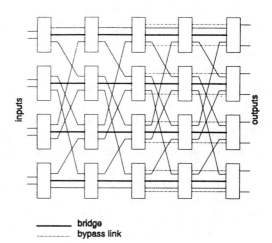

bridge
bypass link

Fig. 42. An (8×8) Bridged Shuffle-Exchange Network with $K = 5$.

in the output buffers to avoid out-of-sequence cell delivery.

Dual Shuffle-Exchange Network

A Dual Shuffle-Exchange switching network (DSN) constructed by interleaving a shuffle-exchange (SN) network and an unshuffle-exchange (USN) network, has been described in [156]. (Having two complementary shuffle networks together was previously suggested in [208], although in a different context.) A DSN consists of K ($\geq n = \log_2 N$) stages, each having $N/2$ (4×4) SEs, as shown in Fig. 41 for $N = 8$ and $K = 5$. The upper (lower) half outlets of each SE are connected to the next stage according to an unshuffling (a shuffling) pattern. Routing bits used in successive stages proceed from the least significant bit (LSB) to the most significant bit (MSB) in the USN, and from the MSB to the LSB in the SN. A routing algorithm for the DSN was described in the above reference. Basically, the SN links are used for normal routing of cells, while any error caused by deflection in the SN is corrected in the USN in a single step, so that the corresponding cell can return to its normal path in the SN again after one stage. Bypass links (not shown in the above figure) are used to collect and multiplex cells which reach their destinations. Cells which do not reach their destinations by stage K are lost. It was shown that the DSN

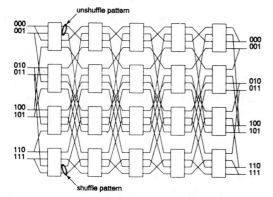

Fig. 41. An (8×8) Dual Shuffle-Exchange Network with $K = 5$.

achieves the $N \log_2 N$ lower bound on switch complexity for an arbitrary small cell loss probability. Finally, the cell-sequencing problem has not been addressed in [156].

Bridged Shuffle-Exchange Network

Zarour and Mouftah [234] noticed that the DSN [156] uses (4×4) SEs and requires a relatively complicated routing scheme. In the same reference, the Bridged Shuffle-Exchange Network (Fig. 42) was proposed and shown to achieve the $N \log_2 N$ order of complexity for an arbitrary small cell loss probability. In this architecture, a losing cell is passed without changing its status to the same-position SE in the next stage through a "bridge". Thus, the routing error is prevented and the cell can resume its routing from the following stage. However, it is possible that all arriving cells at the three inlets of an SE request the same outlet; in such a case, one cell must be deflected. Using 2 bridges from each SE to two different SEs in the following stage belonging to the same "group" (as defined in the next section) has also been considered. In both cases, cells which do not reach their destinations by the last stage are lost. A closed-loop version of the switch, analogous to the buffered closed-loop Shuffleout switch [61], was proposed in [235], and shown to require less number of stages to achieve a given cell loss probability, compared to several other deflection-routing switches. In the closed-loop design, a resequencing mechanism for the output buffers has been suggested to preserve the cell sequence integrity.

Multi Single-Stage-Shuffling switch

Up to now, we described switches which use SEs of size larger than (2×2) and require considerable amount of processing in the SEs. A deflection-routing switch architecture based on unbuffered (2×2) SEs has been proposed [7], [12], [13] under the name the Multi Single-Stage-Shuffling Switch (MS4). As with the last three described switches, the MS4 consists of K ($\geq n = \log_2 N$) stages, each with $N/2$ SEs (Fig. 43). Successive stages are interconnected through the perfect shuffle pattern [201]. The routing algorithm here is a simple extension of that in a

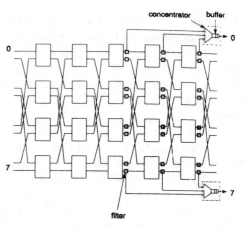

Fig. 43. An (8×8) Multi Single-Stage-Shuffling switch with $K = 5$.

banyan network. Each cell carries a counter field (C) of $\lceil \log_2 n \rceil$ bits that is initially set to n. C acts as a pointer to the particular bit (d_{n-C+1}) that an SE must examine in the destination tag of the corresponding cell. Each time a cell is correctly routed, C is decremented by one, and each time it is deflected, C is reset to n. In any conflict, the cell closest to its destination wins. A cell reaches it destination when C becomes zero. At the outputs of the last stage, cells with $C \neq 0$ are lost. It has been shown that the MS4 can achieve an arbitrary small cell loss probability with complexity of $O(N \log_2 N)$. Furthermore, the MS4 preserves cell-sequencing without using artificial delays even for strict cell loss requirements and large switch sizes. The MS4 has been shown to be robust against nonuniform traffic [7], [13]. Finally, an interesting result has been reported in [13]: for the same switch size, output concentration ratio, and output buffer size, the MS4 (with large enough K) could have better overall cell loss performance, compared to the Knockout switch [230]. This has been explained by the positive effect of presenting the traffic in an imbalanced fashion to the inputs of each output concentrator in the MS4.

Statistical Data Fork

The Statistical Data Fork (SDF) [58] is (to the best of our knowledge) the only deflection-routing switch architecture that supports output channel grouping. The switching platform of the SDF is the Omega network [137] with unbuffered (2 × 2) SEs. The output ports of the SDF are partitioned into groups and each group is assigned a codeword (a binary string). Different groups may have different priority levels in different SEs. In a similar fashion to self-routing in a banyan network, an SE in the SDF uses the codeword carried by each cell to determine its proper routing. A contention within an SE is resolved according to the priority rule associated with that SE; otherwise, random selection is used. A losing cell is deflected, and thus it *may* exit on the wrong output channel group. If a cell does not encounter too many contentions within the network, it can still exit on the correct output group. The partition of the output ports into channel groups can be done in such a way as to minimize the probability of a routing error. Filters are inserted at the outputs of the interconnection network to destroy misrouted cells. To make the SDF robust against general traffic models, a Benes network [24] can be placed at the front end of the SDF to randomize incoming traffic. Also, misrouted cells or a subset of them, can be fed back (into the randomization network) in order to increase efficiency.

6.6. Load-sharing

The concept of load-sharing in a banyan network was first introduced in [138]. It is based on

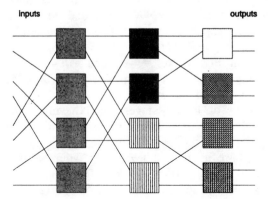

Fig. 44. Switching elements with the same type of shading belong to the same group.

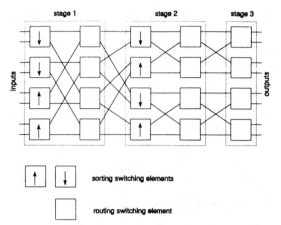

Fig. 45. A possible implementation of the load-sharing banyan network ($N = 8$).

the following observation. The SEs of any given stage of a banyan network can be organized into a number of groups in such a way that the proper routing function is not disturbed by sharing the input traffic of any two SEs in the same group. This is illustrated in Fig. 44; notice that all SEs in the first stage are in the same group, while all SEs in the last stage are in different groups. A cell can be sent to any SE in a group, and still be correctly routed to its destination. This can be useful in handling imbalanced traffic: if an SE is congested, other SEs in the same group can be used to handle incoming traffic. In the load-sharing banyan network, the idea is to allow *two* SEs in the same group to share their input traffic, which provides cells with multiple paths. SEs can be paired in such a way as to achieve the maximum possible number of alternate paths. The resulting network has higher throughput compared to banyan networks (e.g., for $N = 1024$ the load-sharing banyan network achieves at least $TP_{max} = 0.39$ compared to 0.26 achieved by a banyan network), can tolerate multiple faults, and can be diagnosed as easily as banyan networks. Finally, the concept of load-sharing is applicable to both unbuffered and buffered banyan networks. However, it might cause a cell-sequencing problem in the latter.

A self-routing implementation of the load-sharing banyan network has been reported in

[145], and is shown in Fig. 45. It is constructed by inserting sorting SEs before regular routing SEs in each stage of a banyan network, except the last stage. For an n-stage network, routing SEs in each stage, except the last one, are partitioned into 2^{n-2} groups, each of two members. Two routing SEs belonging to the same group receive cells from the same two sorting elements; thus, they share their load. Blocking occurs only when more than two cells received by any group are to be simultaneously routed to the upper or the lower output links. Both uniform and nonuniform traffic models have been considered for both unbuffered and internally-buffered routing SEs.

A self-routing ATM switch that is based on the load-sharing principle was proposed in [123], and its block diagram is shown in Fig. 46. Here, an $(N \times N)$ switch is constructed using n stages of (2×2) SEs, and $n-1$ stages of distributors. If a stage is defined to be a column of SEs and the following distributors, then stage i ($1 \leq i \leq n$; starting from the left-most stage) consists of $N/2$ SEs and 2^i distributors of size $(2^{n-i} \times 2^{n-i})$. The switch requires a speed-up factor of two. A distributor distributes the cells at its inputs evenly across its outputs which are connected to SEs belonging to the same group. Thus, *all* SEs of a group (except those in the first stage) share their traffic load, in contrast to the designs of [138] and [145] in which only *two* SEs in any group share their load. A distributor basically consists of a reverse Banyan network [128] with output buffers. With large enough buffers, the maximum

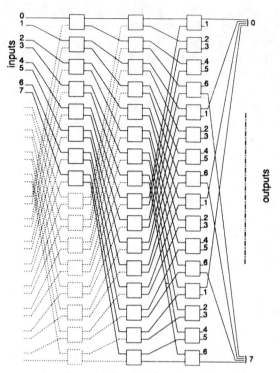

Fig. 47. An (8×8) expanded delta network with $EF = 4$.

throughput of this switch approaches 100%. Unfortunately, cell-sequencing is not preserved.

6.7. Expansion

An approach that overcomes both internal and output blocking of a banyan network while preserving self-routing and path-uniqueness has been proposed in [9] under the name the *expanded delta network*. An $(N \times N)$ expanded delta network with expansion factor EF is constructed by interleaving EF $(N \times N)$ delta networks, as shown in Fig. 47 for $N = 8$ and $EF = 4$. The resulting network can be regarded as an $(M \times M)$ interconnection network (where $M = N \times EF$) consisting of $\log_2 N$ stages, each having $M/2$ SEs. Only N input links are used, while each output port is connected to EF of the output links. If we assume that $EF = 2^k$ where k is a positive integer, then blocking-free routing is guaranteed till stage k, inclusive. Also, $N(2^{k-1} - 1)$ SEs in the first $k - 1$ stages are jobless and can be removed. Increasing EF has two joint effects:

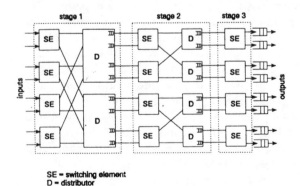

SE = switching element
D = distributor

Fig. 46. Kim's self-routing multistage switch.

reducing internal blocking and increasing the number of cells (up to EF cells) which may be simultaneously switched to the same output port. This results in improving the throughput performance.

At the output side of the network, either single acceptance (SA) [10], [11], or multiple acceptance (MA) [9], [11] can be used. Assuming MA, it has been shown that for a switch of size 1024 and $EF = 16$, above 90% maximum throughput can be achieved [9], compared to 26% achieved by a banyan network. Also, with either SA or MA, the expanded delta network requires the least number of crosspoints (almost always) to achieve a given target of TP_{max}, compared to the replicated and dilated delta networks [10], [11]. With MA and $1 < EF < N$, both input and output buffers are needed to reduce cell loss to an acceptable level. An ATM switch that is built around the expanded delta network has been proposed and studied in [9] under the name the *Expanded Delta Fast Packet Switch* (EDFPS). It has been shown that preventing output buffers from overflowing by a means of backpressure signals, can reduce the overall memory size needed to achieve a given P_{loss}. This can be achieved while keeping the switch operation completely distributed. The EDFPS has also been shown to be robust against bursty traffic.

An internally-buffered version of the EDFPS has been studied in [15]. This design was motivated by the fact that cell-sequencing is not disturbed by the introduction of internal buffers, since the expanded delta network is a single-path structure. It has been shown (using both analysis and simulation) that above 95% maximum throughput can be achieved for a very large switch size using single-input-buffered SEs and expansion factor as small as 4. In general, having both the expansion factor and SE buffer size/strategy as design parameters makes it easier to jointly optimize both performance and complexity.

7. Concluding remarks

This paper has presented a survey of space-division ATM switch architectures. It has given a descriptive overview of these architectures by classifying them according to the basic structure, into three categories: crossbar based, disjoint-path based, and banyan based. A considerable portion of this paper has been devoted to reviewing some necessary background, as well as discussing the various buffering strategies employed by ATM switches. While we do not claim that our survey covers *all* ATM switches proposed to-date, we hope that this paper would serve as a good starting point for those who are entering this interesting area of research. Furthermore, it should provide an ATM switching researcher with an overview of the work that has been done by other researchers in the field.

This paper has focused on electronic point-to-point switch architectures, and their performance under uniform traffic. First, despite the fact that transmission technology in broadband networks is based on fiber optics due to their enormous bandwidth, both the lack of efficient optical buffer memories and the requirement of processing cell headers, have resulted in mostly electronic solutions for switching [116]. Nevertheless, heavy research is being carried out to design fully-photonic ATM switches. Second, although some of the surveyed architectures can support multicast/broadcast connections, the extension of the function of any unicast switch to multicasting/broadcasting can be achieved by placing a copy network at the front end of the unicast switch, to replicate incoming multicast cells; each copy is then forwarded to the following unicast switch for routing. Interested readers are referred to [6], [28], [35], [36], [40], [43], [49], [50], [51], [54], [59], [80], [100], [106], [125], [140], [141], [146], [167], [188], [209], [210], [217], and [237]. Third, more research is required to evaluate and compare the different switch architectures against integrated services traffic environment, since asserting the assumption of uniformity for real-life situations may lead to optimistic evaluation of performance measures. Of course, this would require first the development of suitable traffic models [198]. Finally, it is important to extend the comparison beyond performance, and consider other factors such as implementation complexity and cost [236], fault tolerance and reliability.

References

[1] E. Aanen, J.L. van den Berg, and R.J.F. De Vries, Cell loss performance of the GAUSS ATM switch, *Proc. IEEE INFOCOM'92*, Florence, Italy, pp. 717–726, May 1992.

[2] H. Ahmadi, and W.E. Denzel, A survey of modern high-performance switching techniques, *IEEE J. Selected Areas Commun.*, Vol. 7, No. 7, pp. 1091–1103, Sep. 1989.

[3] M.K.M. Ali, and M. Youssefi, The performance of an input access scheme in a high-speed packet switch, *Proc. IEEE INFOCOM'91*, Miami, FL, pp. 454–461, Apr. 1991.

[4] G.J. Anido, and A.W. Seeto, Multipath interconnection: a technique for reducing congestion with fast packet switching fabrics, *IEEE J. Selected Areas Commun.*, Vol. 6, No. 9, pp. 1480–1488, Dec. 1988.

[5] M. Atiquzzaman, and M.S. Akhtar, Effect of nonuniform traffic on the performance of multistage interconnection networks, *IEE Proc. – Comput. Digit. Tech.*, Vol. 141, No. 3, pp. 169–176, May 1994.

[6] R.Y. Awdeh, and H.T. Mouftah, A non-typical approach for the design of multicast ATM switch architectures, *Proc. 2nd ISCA / ACM SIGCOMM Int. Conf. Computer Commun. and Networks (IC³N)*, San Diego, CA, pp. 399–404, June 1993.

[7] R.Y. Awdeh, and H.T. Mouftah, Multi single-stage-shuffling for fast packet switching, *Proc. 36th IEEE Midwest Symp. Circuits and Systems*, Detroit, MI, pp. 1136–1139, Aug. 1993.

[8] R.Y. Awdeh, and H.T. Mouftah, Broadband packet switch architectures, *Proc. Photonics'93: 3rd IEEE Int. Workshop on Photonic Networks, Components, and Applications*, Atlanta, GA, pp. 183–188, Sep. 1993.

[9] R.Y. Awdeh, and H.T. Mouftah, The Expanded Delta Fast Packet Switch, *Proc. IEEE SUPERCOMM / ICC'94*, New Orleans, LA, pp. 397–401, May 1994.

[10] R.Y. Awdeh, and H.T. Mouftah, Approach for comparing delta-based networks with the crossbar switch, *Electronics Letters*, Vol. 30, No. 3, pp. 201–202, Feb. 1994.

[11] R.Y. Awdeh, and H.T. Mouftah, A comparative study of unbuffered interconnection networks based on cross-point complexity, *Proc. 6th IEEE Int. Conf. Computing and Information (ICCI'94)*, Peterborough, ON, pp. 604–621, May 1994; also *CD-ROM J. Computing and Information*, to appear.

[12] R.Y. Awdeh, and H.T. Mouftah, Design and performance analysis of an output-buffering switch with complexity of $O(N \log_2 N)$, *Proc. IEEE SUPERCOMM / ICC'94*, New Orleans, LA, pp. 420–424, May 1994.

[13] R.Y. Awdeh, and H.T. Mouftah, MS4 – A high performance output buffering ATM Switch, *Computer Commun.*, to appear.

[14] R.Y. Awdeh, and H.T. Mouftah, A contention resolution algorithm for input-buffered Batcher-Banyan networks, *Int. J. Commun. Systems*, Vol. 7, No. 1, pp. 33–38, Jan.–Mar. 1994.

[15] R.Y. Awdeh, and H.T. Mouftah, Analysis and simulation of the Buffered-Expanded Delta Fast Packet Switch, *Proc. IEEE GLOBECOM'94*, San Francisco, CA, Nov. 1994.

[16] H.F. Badran, and H.T. Mouftah, Fairness for broadband integrated switch architectures under backpressure mechanisms, *Proc. IEEE ICC'91*, Denver, CO, pp. 1033–1037, June 1991.

[17] H.F. Badran, and H.T. Mouftah, Head of line arbitration in ATM switches with input-output buffering and backpressure control, *Proc. IEEE GLOBECOM'91*, Phoenix, AZ, pp. 347–351, Dec. 1991.

[18] H.F. Badran, and H.T. Mouftah, Input-output-buffered broad-band packet-switch architectures with correlated input traffic, *Canadian J. Electrical and Computer Engineering*, Vol. 18, No. 3, pp. 133–139, 1993.

[19] H.F. Badran, and H.T. Mouftah, Input-output-buffered ATM switches with delayed backpressure mechanisms, *Proc. Canadian Conf. Electrical and Computer Engineering*, pp. 771–774, 1993.

[20] J.J. Bae, and T. Suda, Survey of traffic control schemes and protocols in ATM networks, *Proc. IEEE*, Vol. 79, No. 2, pp. 170–189, Feb. 1991.

[21] P. Baran, On distributed communication networks, *IEEE Trans. Commun.*, Vol. 12, pp. 1–9, March 1964.

[22] K.E. Batcher, Sorting networks and their applications, *Proc. AFIPS Spring Joint Comp. Conf.*, Vol. 32, pp. 307–314, 1968.

[23] S. Bassi, M. Decina, and A. Pattavina, Performance analysis of the ATM Shuffleout switching architecture under nonuniform traffic patterns, *Proc. IEEE INFOCOM'92*, Florence, Italy, pp. 734–742, May 1992.

[24] V.E. Benes, Optimal rearrangeable multistage connecting networks, *Bell Syst. Tech. J.*, Vol. 43, pp. 1641–1656, July 1964.

[25] J.E. Berthold, High speed integrated electronics for communications systems, *Proc. IEEE*, Vol. 78, No. 3, pp. 486–511, Mar. 1990.

[26] D. Bertsekas, and R. Gallager, *Data Networks*, Prentice-Hall, Englewood Cliffs, NJ, 2nd ed., 1992.

[27] L.N. Bhuyan, Q. Yang, and D.P. Agrawal, Performance of multiprocessor interconnection networks, *IEEE Computer*, Vol. 22, No. 2, pp. 25–37, Feb. 1989.

[28] R.P. Bianchini Jr., and H.S. Kim, Design of a nonblocking shared memory copy network for ATM, *Proc. IEEE INFOCOM'92*, Florence, Italy, pp. 876–885, May 1992.

[29] G. Bianchi, and J.S. Turner, Improved queueing analysis of shared buffer switching networks, *IEEE / ACM Trans. Networking*, Vol. 1, No. 4, pp. 482–490, Aug. 1993.

[30] B. Bingham, and H. Bussey, Reservation-based contention resolution mechanism for Batcher-Banyan networks, *Electronics Letters*, Vol. 24, No. 13, pp. 772–773, June 1988.

[31] F. Bonomi, S. Montagna, and R. Pagkino, Busy period analysis for an ATM switching element output line, *Proc. IEEE INFOCOM'92*, Florence, Italy, pp. 544–551, May 1992.

[32] J.-Y.L. Boudec, The Asynchronous Transfer Mode: a tutorial, *Computer Networks and ISDN Systems*, Vol. 24, pp. 279–309, 1992.

[33] G. Broomell, and J.R. Heath, Classification categories and historical development of circuit switching topologies, *Computing Surveys*, Vol. 15, No. 2, pp. 95–133, June 1983.

[34] G. Bruzzi, and A. Pattavina, Performance evaluation of an input-queued switch with internal speed-up and finite output queues, *Proc. IEEE GLOBECOM'90*, San Diego, CA, pp. 1455–1459, Dec. 1990.

[35] R.S. Bubenik, and J.S. Turner, Performance of a broadcast packet switch, *IEEE Trans. Commun.*, Vol. 37, No. 1, pp. 60–69, Jan. 1989.

[36] R. Bubenik, J. Dettart, and M. Gaddis, Multipoint connection management in high speed networks, *Proc. IEEE INFOCOM'91*, Miami, FL, pp. 59–68, Apr. 1991.

[37] E.T. Bushnell, and J.S. Meditch, Dilated multistage interconnection networks for fast packet switching, *Proc. IEEE INFOCOM'91*, Miami, FL, pp. 1264–1273, Apr. 1991.

[38] P. Campoli, and A. Pattavina, An ATM switch with folded shuffle-topology and distributed access, *Proc. IEEE ICC'91*, Denver, CO, pp. 1021–1027, June 1991.

[39] H.J. Chao, A distributed modular tera-bit/sec ATM switch, *Proc. IEEE GLOBECOM'90*, San Diego, CA, pp. 1594–1601, Dec. 1990.

[40] C.-J. Chang, and C.-J. Ling, Overflow controller in copy network of broadband packet switch, *Electronics Letters*, Vol. 27, No. 11, May 1991.

[41] J.S.-C. Chen, and R. Guerin, Input queueing of internally nonblocking packet switch with two priority classes, *Proc. IEEE INFOCOM'89*, pp. 529–537, 1989.

[42] J.S.-C Chen, and T.E. Stern, Throughput analysis, optimal buffer allocation, and traffic imbalance study of a generic nonblocking packet switch, *IEEE J. Selected Areas Commun.*, Vol. 9, No. 3, pp. 439–449, Apr. 1991.

[43] X. Chen, J.F. Hayes, and M.K.M. Ali, Performance analysis of cyclic-priority input access method for a multicast switch, *Proc. IEEE INFOCOM'91*, Miami, FL, pp. 1189–1195, Apr. 1991.

[44] X. Chen, and J.F. Hayes, A shared buffer memory switch with maximum queue and minimum allocation, *Proc. Canadian Conf. Electrical and Computer Engineering*, paper 7.1, 1991.

[45] W.-S.E. Chen, Y.M. Kim, K.L. Lee, and M.T. Liu, A distributed congestion-prevention scheme for ATM switching fabrics based on buffered delta networks, *Proc. IEEE INFOCOM'91*, Miami, FL, pp. 304–313, Apr. 1991.

[46] X. Chen, A survey of multistage interconnection networks for fast packet switches, *Int. J. Digital and Analog Commun. Systems*, Vol. 4, pp. 33–59, 1991.

[47] T.H. Cheng, and D.G. Smith, Queueing analysis of a multichannel ATM switch with input buffering, *Proc. IEEE ICC'91*, Denver, CO, pp. 1028–1032, June 1991.

[48] D.X. Chen, and J.W. Mark, Performance analysis of output buffered fast packet switches with bursty traffic loading, *Proc. IEEE GLOBECOM'91*, Phoenix, AZ, pp. 455–459, Dec. 1991.

[49] X. Chen, and J.F. Hayes, Call scheduling in multicasting packet switching, *Proc. IEEE ICC'92*, pp. 895–899, 1992.

[50] X. Chen, I. Lambadris, and J.F. Hayes, A general unified model for performance analysis of multicast switching, *Proc. IEEE GLOBECOM'92*, Orlando, FL, pp. 1498–1502, Dec. 1992.

[51] W.-T. Chen, Y.-R. Chang, and C.-F. Huang, A low-cost self-routing multicast network, *Proc. IEEE ICC'93*, Geneva, Switzerland, pp. 1691–1695, May 1993.

[52] D.X. Chen, and J.W. Mark, SCOQ: a fast packet switch with shared concentration and output queueing, *IEEE/ACM Trans. Networking*, Vol. 1, No. 1, pp. 142–151, Feb. 1993.

[53] F.M. Chiussi, and F.A. Tobagi, A hybrid shared-memory/space-division architecture for large fast packet switches, *Proc. IEEE ICC'92*, pp. 904–911, 1992.

[54] J.S. Choi, C.K. Un, and B.C. Shin, Design of cascade ring multicast switch, *Electron. Lett.*, Vol. 28, No. 14, July 1992.

[55] C. Clos, A study of nonblocking switching network, *Bell Syst. Tech. J.*, Vol. 32, pp. 406–424, Mar. 1953.

[56] C.S. Cooper, High-speed networks: the emergence of technologies for multiservice support, *Computer Commun.*, Vol. 14, No. 1, pp. 27–43, Jan./Feb. 1991.

[57] G. Corazzi, and C. Raffaelli, Performance evaluation of input-buffered replicated banyan networks, *IEEE Trans. Commun.*, Vol. 41, No. 6, pp. 841–845, June 1993.

[58] R.L. Cruz, The Statistical Data Fork: a class of broadband multichannel switches, *IEEE Trans. Commun.*, Vol. 40, No. 10, pp. 1625–1634, Oct. 1992.

[59] R. Cusani, and F. Sestini, A recursive multistage structure for multicast ATM switching, *Proc. IEEE INFOCOM'91*, Miami, FL, pp. 1289–1295, Apr. 1991.

[60] G.E. Daddis Jr., and H.C. Torng, A taxonomy of broadband integrated switching architectures, *IEEE Commun. Mag.*, No. 5, pp. 32–42, May 1989.

[61] M. Decina, P. Giacomazzi, A. Pattavina, and E. Tombolini, Shuffle interconnection networks with deflection routing for ATM switching: the Closed-Loop Shuffleout, *Proc. IEEE INFOCOM'91*, Miami, FL, pp. 1256–1263, Apr. 1991.

[62] M. Decina, P. Giacomazzi, A. Pattavina, and E. Tombolini, Shuffle interconnection networks with deflection routing for ATM switching: the Open-Loop Shuffleout, *Proc. ITC-13*, pp. 27–34, 1991.

[63] M. Decina, P. Giacomazzi, and A. Pattavina, Connectionless switching by the Asynchronous Shuffleout Network, *Proc. IEEE ICC'93*, Geneva, Switzerland, pp. 701–707, May 1993.

[64] E. Del Re, and R. Fantacci, An efficient high-speed packet switching with shared input buffers, *Proc. IEEE GLOBECOM'92*, Orlando, FL, pp. 1472–1476, Dec. 1992.

[65] E. Del Re, and R. Fantacci, Performance evaluation of

input and output queueing techniques in ATM switching systems, *IEEE Trans. Commun.*, Vol. 41, No. 10, pp. 1565–1575, Oct. 1993.

[66] M. De Prycker, and M. De Somer, Performance of a service-independent switching network with distributed control, *IEEE J. Selected Areas Commun.*, Vol. 5, No. 10, pp. 1293–1301, Oct. 1987.

[67] M. De Prycker, Evolution from ISDN to BISDN: a logical step towards ATM, *Computer Commun.*, Vol. 12, No. 3, pp. 141–146, June 1989.

[68] M. De Prycker, *Asynchronous Transfer Mode: Solution For Broadband ISDN*, Ellis Horwood, Chichester, 1991.

[69] A. Descloux, Stochastic models for ATM switching networks, *IEEE J. Selected Areas Commun.*, Vol. 9, No. 3, pp. 450–457, Apr. 1991.

[70] R.J.F. De Vries, GAUSS: a single-stage ATM switch with output buffering, *Proc. IEE Int. Conf. Integrated Broadband Services and Networks*, pp. 248–252, 1990.

[71] D.M. Dias, and J.R. Jump, Analysis and simulation of buffered delta networks, *IEEE Trans. Computers*, Vol. 30, No. 4, pp. 273–282, April 1981.

[72] D.M. Dias, and J.R. Jump, Packet switching interconnection networks for modular systems, *IEEE Computer*, Vol. 14, No. 12, pp. 43–53, Dec. 1981.

[73] D.M. Dias, and M. Kumar, Packet switching in NlogN multistage networks, *Proc. IEEE GLOBECOM'84*, Atlanta, GA, pp. 114–120, Nov. 1984.

[74] J. Ding, Nonuniform traffic analysis of multistage interconnection networks with split buffers, *Proc. IEEE ICC'93*, Geneva, Switzerland, pp. 58–62, May 1993.

[75] A. Eckberg, and T.-C. Hou, Effects of output buffer sharing on buffer requirements in an ATDM packet switch, *Proc. IEEE INFOCOM'88*, New Orleans, LA, pp. 459–566, Mar. 1988.

[76] T.E. Eliazov, V. Ramaswami, W. Willinger, and G. Latouche, Performance of an ATM switch: simulation study, *Proc. IEEE INFOCOM'90*, San Fransisco, CA, pp. 644–659, June 1990.

[77] A.I. Elwalid, and I. Widjaja, Efficient analysis of buffered multistage switching networks under bursty traffic, *Proc. IEEE GLOBECOM'93*, pp. 1072–1078, 1993.

[78] N. Endo, T. Kozaki, T. Ohuchi, H. Kuwahara, and S. Gohara, Shared Buffer Memory switch for an ATM exchange, *IEEE Trans. Commun.*, Vol. 41, No. 1, pp. 237–245, Jan. 93.

[79] K.Y. Eng, M.G. Hluchyj, and Y.S. Yeh, A Knockout switch for variable length packets, *Proc. IEEE ICC'87*, Seattle, WA, pp. 794–799, June 1987.

[80] K.Y. Eng, M.G. Hluchyj, and Y.S. Yeh, Multicast and broadcast services in a Knockout packet switch, *Proc. IEEE INFOCOM'88*, New Orleans, LA, pp. 29–34, Mar. 1988.

[81] K.Y. Eng, A photonic Knockout switch for high-speed packet networks, *IEEE J. Selected Areas Commun.*, Vol. 6, No. 7, pp. 1107–1115, Aug. 1988.

[82] J. Evans, E. Duron, and Y. Wang, Analysis and imple-

mentation of a priority knockout switch, *Proc. IEEE INFOCOM'93*, pp. 1099–1106, 1993.

[83] Y. Fan, J. Wang, and C. Wang, Performance analysis of banyan network based ATM switches, *Proc. IEEE ICC'92*, pp. 1609–1613, 1992.

[84] T.-Y. Feng, A survey of interconnection networks, *IEEE Computer*, Vol. 14, No. 12, pp. 12–27, Dec. 1981.

[85] G.J. Fitzpatrick, and E.A. Munter, Input-buffered ATM switch traffic performance, *Proc. Multimedia'89*, paper 4.2, 1989.

[86] A. Fraser, Early experiments with Asynchronous Time Division networks, *IEEE Network*, Vol. 7, No. 1, pp. 12–26, Jan. 1993.

[87] V.J. Friesen, and J.W. Wong, The effect of multiplexing, switching and other factors on the performance of broadband networks, *Proc. IEEE INFOCOM'93*, pp. 1194–1203, 1993.

[88] U. Garg, and Y.-P. Huang, Decomposing banyan networks for performance evaluation, *IEEE Trans. Computers*, Vol. 37, No. 3, pp. 371–376, March 1988.

[89] U. Garg, and Y.-P. Huang, Improving the performance of banyan networks, *Computers and Electrical Engineering*, Vol. 14, No. 1/2, pp. 29–33, 1988.

[90] D.P. Gerakoulis, J. Mathew, and T.N. Saadawi, Performance analysis of a packet switch with channel assignment capabilities, *Proc. IEEE ICC'91*, Denver, CO, pp. 1527–1531, June 1991.

[91] D. Ghosh, and J.C. Daly, Delta networks with multiple links and shared output buffers: a high performance architecture for packet switching, *Proc. IEEE GLOBECOM'91*, Phoenix, AZ, pp. 949–953, Dec. 1991.

[92] J.N. Giacopelli, T.T. Lee, and W.E. Stephens, Scalability study of self-routing packet switch fabrics for very large scale broadband ISDN central offices, *Proc. IEEE GLOBECOM'90*, San Diego, CA, pp. 1609–1614, Dec. 1990.

[93] J.N. Giacopelli, J.J. Hickey, W.S. Marcus, W.D. Sincoskie, and M. Littlewood, Sunshine: a high-performance self-routing broadband packet switch architecture, *IEEE J. Selected Areas Commun.*, Vol. 9, No. 8, pp. 1289–1298, Oct. 1991.

[94] L.R. Goke, and G.J. Lipovski, Banyan networks for partitioning processor systems, *Proc. 1st Annual Symp. Computer Architecture*, pp. 21–28, Dec. 1973.

[95] P. Goli, and V. Kumar, Performance of a crosspoint buffered ATM switch fabric, *Proc. IEEE INFOCOM'92*, Florence, Italy, pp. 426–431, May 1992.

[96] A.K. Gupta, and N.D. Georganas, Analysis of a packet switch with input and output buffers and speed constraints, *Proc. IEEE INFOCOM'91*, Miami, FL, pp. 694–700, Apr. 1991.

[97] A.K. Gupta, L.O. Barbosa, and N.D. Georganas, A 16×16 limited intermediate buffer switch module for ATM networks, *Proc. IEEE GLOBECOM'91*, Phoenix, AZ, pp. 939–943, Dec. 1991.

[98] A.K. Gupta, L.O. Barbosa, and N.D. Georganas, Limited intermediate buffer switch modules and their inter-

connection networks for BISDN, *Proc. IEEE ICC'92*, pp. 1646–1650, 1992.

[99] J.G. Haro, C.C. Pastor, J.P. Aspas, and H.T. Mouftah, Evaluation study of several head-of-line selection schemes for high-performance non-blocking ATM switches, *Proc. IEEE Pacific Rim*, pp. 327–332, 1993.

[100] J.F. Hayes, R. Breault, and M.K.M. Ali, Performance analysis of a multicast switch, *IEEE Trans. Commun.*, Vol. 39, No. 4, pp. 581–587, Apr. 1991.

[101] M.G. Hluchyj, and M.J. Karol, Queueing in high-performance packet switching, *IEEE J. Selected Areas Commun.*, Vol. 6, No. 9, pp. 1587–1597, Dec. 1988.

[102] T.-C. Hou, and M. Sarraf, Internal traffic characterization of a multi-stage ATM switch, *Proc. ISCA / ACM SIGCOMM 2nd Int. Conf. Computer Commun. and Networks (IC³N)*, San Diego, CA, pp. 391–398, June 1993.

[103] A. Huang, and S. Knauer, Starlite: a wideband digital switch, *Proc. IEEE GLOBECOM'84*, Atlanta, GA, pp. 121–125, Nov. 1984.

[104] J.Y. Hui, and E. Arthurs, A broadband packet switch for integrated transport, *IEEE J. Selected Areas Commun.*, Vol. 5, No. 8, pp. 264–273, Oct. 1987.

[105] J.Y. Hui, *Switching and Traffic Theory for Integrated Broadband Network*, Kluwer Academic Publishers, Boston, 1990.

[106] J.Y. Hui, and T. Renner, Queueing strategies for multicast packet switching, *Proc. IEEE GLOBECOM'90*, San Diego, CA, pp. 1431–1437, Dec. 1990.

[107] *IEEE Commun. Mag.*, Vol. 30, No. 8, whole issue, Aug. 1992.

[108] *IEEE Network*, Vol. 6, No. 5, whole issue, Sep. 1992.

[109] I. Iliadis, and W.E. Denzel, Performance of packet switches with input and output queueing, *Proc. IEEE ICC'90*, Atlanta, GA, pp. 747–753, Apr. 1990.

[110] I. Iliadis, Performance of a packet switch with shared buffer and input queueing, *Proc. ITC-13*, pp. 911–916, 1991.

[111] I. Iliadis, Performance of a packet switch with input and output queueing under unbalanced traffic, *Proc. IEEE INFOCOM'92*, Florence, Italy, pp. 743–752, May 1992.

[112] I. Iliadis, Synchronous versus asynchronous operation of a packet switch with combined input and output buffering, *Performance Evaluation*, Vol. 16, pp. 241–250, 1992.

[113] H. Imagawa, S. Urushidani, and K. Hagishima, A new self-routing switch driven with input-to-output address difference, *Proc. IEEE GLOBECOM'88*, Hollywood, FL, pp. 1607–1611, Nov. 1988.

[114] A. Iyengar, and M. El Zarki, Switching prioritized packets, *Proc. IEEE GLOBECOM'89*, Dallas, TX, pp. 1181–1186, Nov. 1989.

[115] A.R. Jacob, A survey of fast packet switches, *Computer Commun. Review*, Vol. 20, No. 1, pp. 54–64, Jan. 1990.

[116] A. Jajszczyk, and H.T. Mouftah, Photonic fast packet switching, *IEEE Commun. Mag.*, No. 2, pp. 58–65, Feb. 1993.

[117] Y.-C. Jeng, Performance analysis of a packet switch based on single buffered banyan networks, *IEEE J.*

[118] Y.C. Jung, and C.K. Un, Analysis of backpressuring-type packet switches with input and output buffering, *IEE Proceedings-I*, Vol. 140, No. 4, pp. 277–284, Aug. 1993.

[119] F. Kamoun, and L. Kleinrock, Analysis of shared finite storage in a computer network node environment under general traffic conditions, *IEEE Trans. Commun.*, Vol. 28, No. 7, pp. 992–1003, July 1980.

[120] M.J. Karol, M.G. Hluchyj, and S.P. Morgan, Input versus output queueing on a space-division packet switch, *IEEE Trans. Commun.*, Vol. 35, No. 12, pp. 1347–1356, Dec. 1987.

[121] M.J. Karol, K.Y. Eng, and H. Obara, Improving the performance of input-queued ATM packet switches, *Proc. IEEE INFOCOM'92*, Florence, Italy, pp. 110–115, May 1992.

[122] P. Kermani, and L. Kleinrock, Virtual cut-through: a new computer communication switching technique, *Computer Networks*, pp. 267–286, 1979.

[123] H.S. Kim, and A. Leon-Garcia, A self-routing multistage interconnection network for broadband ISDN, *IEEE J. Selected Areas Commun.*, Vol. 8, No. 3, pp. 459–466, April 1990.

[124] H.S. Kim, and A. Leon-Garcia, Performance of buffered banyan networks under nonuniform traffic patterns, *IEEE Trans. Commun.*, Vol. 38, No. 5, pp. 648–658, May 1990.

[125] C.-K. Kim, and T. Lee, Performance of call splitting algorithms for multicast traffic, *Proc. IEEE INFOCOM'90*, San Fransisco, CA, pp. 348–356, June 1990.

[126] Y.M. Kim, and K.Y. Lee, KSMINs: Knockout switch based multistage interconnection networks for high-speed packet switching, *Proc. IEEE GLOBECOM'90*, San Diego, CA, pp. 218–223, Dec. 1990.

[127] H.S. Kim, I. Widjaja, and A. Leon-Garcia, Performance of output buffered banyan networks with arbitrary buffer sizes, *Proc. IEEE INFOCOM'91*, Miami, FL, pp. 701–710, Apr. 1991.

[128] H.S. Kim, and A. Leon-Garcia, Nonblocking property of Reverse Banyan networks, *IEEE Trans. Commun.*, Vol. 40, No. 3, pp. 472–476, Mar. 1992.

[129] H.S. Kim, Multichannel ATM switch with preserved packet sequence, *Proc. IEEE ICC'92*, pp. 1634–1638, 1992.

[130] C.P. Kruskal, and M. Snir, The performance of multistage interconnection networks for multiprocessors, *IEEE Trans. Computers*, Vol. 32, No. 12, pp. 1091–1098, Dec. 1983.

[131] M. Kumar, and J.R. Jump, Performance enhancement in buffered delta networks using crossbar switches and multiple links, *J. Parallel and Distributed Computing*, Vol. 1, pp. 81–103, 1984.

[132] M. Kumar, and J.R. Jump, Performance of unbuffered shuffle-exchange networks, *IEEE Trans. Computers*, Vol. 35, No. 6, pp. 573–577, June 1986.

[133] V.P. Kumar, J.G. Kneuer, D. Pal, and B. Brunner,

PHOENIX: a building block for fault tolerant broadband packet switches, *Proc. IEEE GLOBECOM'91*, Phoenix, AZ, pp. 228–233, Dec. 1991.

[134] T. Lang, and L. Kurisaki, Nonuniform traffic spots (NUTS) in multistage interconnection networks, *J. Parallel and Distributed Computing*, Vol. 10, pp. 55–67, 1990.

[135] P.S.Y. Lau, and A. Leon-Garcia, Design and performance analysis of a buffer subsystem for the Batcher-Banyan switch, *Proc. IEEE GLOBECOM'90*, San Diego, CA, pp. 1926–1930, Dec. 1990.

[136] P.S.Y. Lau, and A. Leon-Garcia, Design and analysis of a multilink access subsystem based on the Batcher-Banyan network architecture, *IEEE Trans. Commun.*, Vol. 40, No. 11, pp. 1757, Nov. 1992.

[137] D. Lawrie, Access and alignment of data in an array processor, *IEEE Trans. Computers*, Vol. 24, No. 12, pp. 1145–1155, Dec. 1975.

[138] C.-T.A. Lea, The load-sharing banyan network, *IEEE Trans. Computers*, Vol. 35, No. 12, pp. 1025–1034, Dec. 1986.

[139] C.-L. Lea, Design and performance evaluation of un-buffered self-routing networks for wideband packet switching, *Proc. IEEE INFOCOM'90*, San Fransisco, CA, pp. 148–156, June 1990.

[140] T.T. Lee, R. Boorstyn, and E. Arthurs, The architecture of a multicast broadband packet switch, *Proc. IEEE INFOCOM'88*, New Orleans, LA, pp. 1–8, Mar. 1988.

[141] T.T. Lee, Nonblocking copy networks for multicast packet switching, *IEEE J. Selected Areas Commun.*, Vol. 6, No. 9, pp. 1455–1467, Dec. 1988.

[142] T.T. Lee, A modular architecture for very large packet switches, *IEEE Trans. Commun.*, Vol. 38, No. 7, pp. 1097–1106, July 1990.

[143] T.-H. Lee, Analytic models for performance evaluation of single-buffered banyan networks under nonuniform traffic, *IEE Proc.-E*, Vol. 138, No. 1, pp. 41–47, Jan 1991.

[144] T.H. Lee, and S.J. Liu, Banyan network nonblocking with respect to cyclic shifts, *Electronics Letters*, Vol. 27, No. 16, pp. 1474–1476, Aug. 1991.

[145] T.-H. Lee, Design and analysis of a new self-routing network, *IEEE Trans. Commun.*, Vol. 40, No. 1, pp. 171–177, Jan. 1992.

[146] T.-H. Lee, and S.-J. Liu, A fair high-speed copy network for multicast packet switch, *Proc. IEEE INFOCOM'92*, Florence, Italy, pp. 886–894, May 1992.

[147] T.T. Lee, and S.C. Liew, Broadband packet switches based on dilated interconnection networks, *Proc. IEEE ICC'92*, pp. 255–261, 1992.

[148] K.Y. Lee, H. Yoon, and M.T. Liu, Performance evaluation of multipath packet switching interconnection networks, *J. Parallel and Distributed Computing*, Vol. 17, pp. 353–359, 1993.

[149] S.-Q. Li, and M.J. Lee, A study of traffic imbalances in a fast packet switch, *Proc. IEEE INFOCOM'89*, pp. 538–547, 1989.

[150] S.-Q. Li, Performance of a nonblocking space-division packet switch with correlated input traffic, *Proc. IEEE GLOBECOM'89*, Dallas, TX, pp. 1754–1763, Nov. 1989.

[151] S.-Q. Li, Nonuniform traffic analysis on a nonblocking space-division packet switch, *IEEE Trans. Commun.*, Vol. 38, No. 7, pp. 1085–1096, July 1990.

[152] S.-Q. Li, Performance of trunk grouping in packet switch design, *Proc. IEEE INFOCOM'91*, Miami, FL, pp. 688–693, Apr. 1991.

[153] S.C. Liew, Performance of input-buffered and output-buffered ATM switches under bursty traffic: simulation study, *Proc. IEEE GLOBECOM'90*, San Diego, CA, pp. 1919–1925, Dec. 1990.

[154] S.C. Liew, and K.W. Lu, Performance analysis of asymmetric packet switch modules with channel grouping, *Proc. IEEE INFOCOM'90*, San Fransisco, CA, pp. 668–676, June 1990.

[155] S.C. Liew, and K.W. Lu, Comparison of buffering strategies for asymmetric packet switch modules, *IEEE J. Selected Areas Commun.*, Vol. 9, No. 3, pp. 428–437, Apr. 1991.

[156] S.C. Liew, and T.T. Lee, NlogN dual shuffle-exchange network with error correcting routing, *Proc. IEEE ICC'92*, pp. 262–268, 1992.

[157] M. Listanti, and A. Roveri, Switching structures for ATM, *Computer Commun.*, Vol. 12, No. 6, pp. 349–358, Dec. 1989.

[158] H. Matsunaga, and H. Uematsu, A 1.5 Gb/s 8×8 cross-connect switch using a time-reservation algorithm, *IEEE J. Selected Areas Commun.*, Vol. 9, No. 8, pp. 1308–1317, Oct. 1991.

[159] R.J. McMillen, A survey of interconnection networks, *Proc. IEEE GLOBECOM'84*, Atlanta, GA, pp. 105–113, Nov. 1984.

[160] J.F. Meyer, S. Montagna, R. Paglino, Dimensioning of an ATM switch with shared buffer and threshold priority, *Computer Networks and ISDN Systems*, Vol. 26, pp. 95–108, 1993.

[161] S.E. Minzer, Broadband ISDN and Asynchronous Transfer Mode (ATM), *IEEE Commun. Mag.*, Vol. 27, No. 9, pp. 17–24, Sep. 1989.

[162] B. Monderer, G. Pacifici, and C. Zukowski, The cylinder switch: an architecture for a manageable VLSI giga-cell switch, *Proc. IEEE ICC'90*, Atlanta, GA, pp. 567–571, Apr. 1990.

[163] A. Monterosso, and A. Pattavina, Performance analysis of multistage interconnection network with shared-buffered switching elements for ATM switching, *Proc. IEEE INFOCOM'92*, Florence, Italy, pp. 124–131, May 1992.

[164] T.D. Morris, and H.G. Perros, Performance modelling of a multi-buffered banyan switch under bursty traffic, *Proc. IEEE INFOCOM'92*, Florence, Italy, pp. 436–445, May 1992.

[165] M. Narasimha, The Batcher-Banyan self-routing network: universality and simplification, *IEEE Trans. Commun.*, Vol. 36, No. 10, pp. 1175–1171, Oct. 1988.

[166] P. Newman, A fast packet switch for the integrated services backbone network, *IEEE J. Selected Areas Commun.*, Vol. 6, No. 9, pp. 1468–1479, Dec. 1988.

[167] P. Newman, and M. Doar, The slotted ring copy fabric for a multicast packet switch, *Proc. Int. Switching Symp.*, Stockholm, Sweden, Session C8, Paper 6, June 1990.

[168] P. Newman, ATM technology for corporate networks, *IEEE Commun. Mag.*, pp. 90–101, Apr. 1992.

[169] S. Nojima, E. Tsutsui, H. Fukuda, and M. Hashimoto, Integrated services packet network using bus-matrix switch, *IEEE J. Selected Areas Commun.*, Vol. 5, No. 10, pp. 1284–1292, Oct. 1987.

[170] H. Obara, and T. Yasushi, An efficient contention resolution algorithm for input queueing ATM cross-connect switches, *Int. J. Digital and Analog Cabled Systems*, Vol. 2, No. 4, pp. 261–267, Oct.–Dec. 1989.

[171] H. Obara, Optimum architecture for input queueing ATM switches, *Electronics Letters*, Vol. 27, No. 7, pp. 555–557, Mar. 1991.

[172] K. Ohtsuki, K. Takemura, J.F. Kurose, H. Okada, and Y. Tezuka, A high-speed packet switch architecture with a multichannel bandwidth allocation, *Proc. IEEE INFOCOM'91*, Miami, FL, pp. 155–162, Apr. 1991.

[173] Y. Oie, T. Suda, M. Murata, and H. Hiyashara, Survey of switching techniques in high-speed networks and their performance, *Int. J. Satellite Commun.*, Vol. 9, pp. 285–303, 1991.

[174] Y. Oie, M. Murata, K. Kubota, and H. Hiyashara, Performance analysis of nonblocking packet switch with input and output buffers, *IEEE Trans. Commun.*, Vol. 40, No. 8, pp. 1294–1297, Aug. 1992.

[175] M.A. Pashan, M.D. Soneru, and G.D. Martin, Technologies for broadband switching, *AT&T Tech. J.*, pp. 39–47, Nov./Dec. 1993.

[176] J.H. Patel, Performance of processor-memory interconnections for multiprocessors, *IEEE Trans. Computers*, Vol. 30, No. 10, pp. 771–780, Oct. 1981.

[177] A. Pattavina, Multichannel bandwidth allocation in a broadband packet switch, *IEEE J. Selected Areas Commun.*, Vol. 6, No. 9, pp. 1489–1499, Dec. 1988.

[178] A. Pattavina, Fairness in a broadband packet switch, *Proc. IEEE ICC'89*, Boston, MA, pp. 404–409, June 1989.

[179] A. Pattavina, A broadband packet switch with input and output queueing, *Proc. Int. Switching Symp.*, Stockholm, Sweden, pp. 11–16, June 1990.

[180] A. Pattavina, Design and performance evaluation of a packet switch for broadband central offices, *Proc. IEEE INFOCOM'90*, San Fransisco, CA, pp. 1252–1259, June 1990.

[181] A. Pattavina, Nonblocking architectures for ATM switching, *IEEE Commun. Mag.*, No. 2, pp. 38–48, Feb. 1993.

[182] A. Pattavina, and G. Bruzzi, Analysis of input and output queueing for nonblocking ATM switches, *IEEE / ACM Trans. Networking*, Vol. 1, No. 3, pp. 314–328, June 1993.

[183] M.C. Pease, The Indirect Binary n-Cube multiprocessor array, *IEEE Trans. Computers*, Vol. 26, No. 5, pp. 458–473, May 1977.

[184] S.D. Personick, and W.O. Fleckenstein, Communications switching – from operators to photonics, *Proc. IEEE*, Vol. 75, No. 10, pp. 1380–1403, Oct. 1987.

[185] J. Peterson, Throughput limitation by head-of-line blocking, *Proc. ITC-13*, pp. 659–663, 1991.

[186] G.F. Pfister, and V.A. Norton, 'Hot spot' contention and combining in multistage interconnection Networks, *IEEE Trans. Computers*, Vol. 34, No. 10, pp. 943–948, Oct. 1985.

[187] P.K. Prasanna, R. Levy, and J. Swenson, Principles and standards for Broadband ISDN, *AT&T Tech. J.*, pp. 9–14, Nov./Dec. 1993.

[188] M. Rahnema, The fast packet ring switch: a high-performance efficient architecture with multicast capability, *IEEE Trans. Commun.*, Vol. 38, No. 4, pp. 539–545, Apr. 1990.

[189] E.P. Rathgeb, T.H. Theimer, and M.N. Huber, Buffering concepts for ATM switching networks, *Proc. IEEE GLOBECOM'88*, Hollywood, FL, pp. 1277–1281, Nov. 1988.

[190] R. Rooholamini, V. Cherkassky, and M. Garver, Finding the right ATM switch for the market, *IEEE Computer*, Vol. 27, No. 4, pp. 16–28, Apr. 1994.

[191] A. Saha, and M.D. Wagh, Performance analysis of banyan networks based on buffers of various sizes, *Proc. IEEE INFOCOM'90*, San Fransisco, CA, pp. 157–164, June 1990.

[192] K.W. Sarkies, The bypass queue in fast packet switching, *IEEE Trans. Commun.*, Vol. 39, No. 5, pp. 766–774, May 1991.

[193] K. Shiomoto, M. Murata, Y. Oie, and H. Miyahara, Performance evaluation of cell bypass queueing discipline for buffered banyan ATM switches, *Proc. IEEE INFOCOM'90*, San Fransisco, CA, pp. 677–685, June 1990.

[194] H. Shi, and O. Wing, Design of a combined input/output buffered ATM switches with arbitrary switch size, buffer size, and speed-up factor, *Proc. ISCA / ACM SIGCOMM 2nd Int. Conf. Computer Commun. and Networks (IC³N)*, San Diego, CA, pp. 377–382, June 1993.

[195] Y. Shobatake, and T. Kodama, A cell switching algorithm for the buffered banyan network, *Proc. IEEE ICC'90*, Atlanta, GA, pp. 754–760, Apr. 1990.

[196] S. Sibal, and J. Zhang, On a class of banyan networks and tandem banyan switching fabrics, *Proc. IEEE INFOCOM'93*, pp. 481–488, 1993.

[197] H.J. Siegel, *Interconnection Networks for Large-Scale Parallel Processing: Theory and Case Studies*. D.C. Health and Company, Lexington, 1985.

[198] G.D. Stamoulis, M.E. Anagnostou, and A.D. Georgantas, Traffic models for ATM networks: a survey, *Computer Commun.*, Vol 17, No. 6, pp. 428–438, June 1994.

[199] W.E. Stephens, M. DePrycker, F.A. Tobagi, and T. Yamaguchi, Guest editorial: large-scale ATM switching

91

systems for B-ISDN, *IEEE J. Selected Areas Commun.*, Vol. 9, No. 8, pp. 1157–1158, Oct. 1991.

[200] A. Steffora, ATM: the year of the trial, *IEEE Computer*, Vol. 27, No. 4. pp. 8–10, Apr. 1994.

[201] H.S. Stone, Parallel processing with the perfect shuffle, *IEEE Trans. Computers*, Vol. 20, No. 2, pp. 153–161, Feb. 1971.

[202] W. Strecker, Analysis of the instruction execution rate in certain computer structures, Ph.D. dissertation, Carnegie-Mellon Univ., 1970.

[203] H. Suzuki, H. Nagano, T. Suzuki, T. Takeuchi, and S. Iwasaki, Output buffer switch architecture for asynchronous transfer mode, *Proc. IEEE ICC'89*, Boston, MA, pp. 99–103, June 1989.

[204] T.H. Szymanski, and V.C. Hamacher, On the universality of multipath multistage interconnection networks, *J. Parallel and Distributed Computing*, Vol. 7, pp. 541–569, 1989.

[205] T. Szymanski, and S. Shaikh, Markov chain analysis of packet-switched banyans with arbitrary switch sizes, queue sizes, link multiplicities and speedup, *Proc. IEEE INFOCOM'89*, pp. 960–971, 1989.

[206] Q. Ta, and J.S. Meditch, A high-speed integrated services switch based on 4×4 switching elements, *Proc. IEEE INFOCOM'90*, San Fransisco, CA, pp. 1164–1171, June 1990.

[207] Q. Ta, and J.S. Meditch, A high-speed integrated services switch based on 4×4 switching elements, *Computers and Electrical Engineering*, Vol. 19, No. 5, pp. 387–397, 1993.

[208] X.-N. Tan, and K.C. Sevcik, Reduced distance routing in single-stage shuffle-exchange interconnection networks, *Performance Evaluation Review*, Vol. 15, No. 1, pp. 95–110, May 1987.

[209] C.-L. Tarng, and J.S. Meditch, A high-performance copy network for B-ISDN, *Proc. IEEE INFOCOM'91*, Miami, FL, pp. 171–181, Apr. 1991.

[210] C.-L. Tarng, J.S. Meditch, and A.K. Somani, Fairness and priority implementation in nonblocking copy networks, *Proc. IEEE ICC'91*, Denver, CO, pp. 1002–1006, June 1991.

[211] T.H. Theimer, E.P. Rathgeb, and M.N. Huber, Performance analysis of buffered banyan networks, *IEEE Trans. Commun.*, Vol. 39, No. 2, pp. 269–277, Feb. 1991.

[212] G. Thomas, and J. Man, Improved windowing rule for input buffered packet switches, *Electronics Letters*, Vol. 29, No. 4, pp. 393–395, Feb. 1993.

[213] F.A. Tobagi, Fast packet switch architectures for broadband integrated services digital networks, *Proc. IEEE*, Vol. 78, No. 1, pp. 133–166, Jan. 1990.

[214] F.A. Tobagi, T. Kwok, and F.M. Chiussi, Architecture, performance, and implementation of the tandem-banyan fast packet switch, *IEEE J. Selected Areas Commun.*, Vol. 9, No. 8, pp. 1173–1193, Oct. 1991.

[215] S. Tridandapassi, and J.S. Meditch, Priority performance of banyan based broadband ISDN switches, *Proc.*

[216] J.S. Turner, Design of an integrated services packet network, *IEEE J. Selected Areas Commun.*, Vol. 4, No. 8, pp. 1373–1380, Nov. 1986.

[217] J.S. Turner, Design of a broadcast packet switching network, *IEEE Trans. Commun.*, Vol. 36, No. 6, pp. 734–743, June 1988.

[218] J.S. Turner, Queueing analysis of buffered switching networks, *Proc. ITC-13*, pp. 35–40, 1991.

[219] J.S. Turner, Queueing analysis of buffered switching networks, *IEEE Trans. Commun.*, Vol. 41, No. 2, pp. 412–420, Feb. 1993.

[220] N.-F. Tzeng, Alleviating the impact of tree saturation on multistage interconnection network performance, *J. Parallel and Distributed Computing*, Vol. 12, pp. 107–117, 1991.

[221] W. Wang, and F.A. Tobagi, The Christmas-Tree switch: an output queuing space-division fast packet switch based on interleaving distribution and concentration functions, *Proc. IEEE INFOCOM'91*, Miami, FL, pp. 163–170, Apr. 1991.

[222] C.-M. Weng, and J.-J. Li, Solution for packet switching of broadband ISDN, *IEE Proc.-I*, Vol. 138, No. 5, pp. 384–400, Oct. 1991.

[223] I. Widjaja, Tandem-banyan switching fabric with dilation, *Electronics Letters*, Vol. 27, No. 19, pp. 1770–1772, Sep. 1991.

[224] I. Widjaja, A. Leon-Garcia, and H.T. Mouftah, The effect of cut-through switching on the performance of buffered banyan networks, *Computer Networks and ISDN Systems*, Vol. 26, pp. 139–159, 1993.

[225] P.C. Wong, and M.S. Yeung, Pipeline Banyan – a parallel fast packet switch architecture, *Proc. IEEE ICC'92*, pp. 882–887, 1992.

[226] C.-L. Wu, and T.-Y. Feng, On a class of multistage interconnection networks, *IEEE Trans. Computers*, Vol. 29, No. 8, pp. 694–702, Aug. 1980.

[227] L.T. Wu, Mixing traffic in a buffered banyan network, *Proc. ACM 9th Symp. Data Commun.*, pp. 134–139, 1985.

[228] Y. Xiong, and H. Bruneel, Approximate analytic performance study of an ATM switching element with train arrivals, *Proc. IEEE ICC'92*, pp. 1614–1620, 1992.

[229] Y. Xiong, H. Bruneel, and G. Petit, On the performance evaluation of an ATM self-routing multistage switch with bursty and uniform traffic, *Proc. IEEE ICC'93*, Geneva, Switzerland, pp. 1391–1397, May 1993.

[230] Y.S. Yeh, M.G. Hluchyj, and A.S. Acampora, The Knockout switch: a simple, modular, architecture for high-performance packet switching, *IEEE J. Selected Areas Commun.*, Vol. 5, No. 8, pp. 1274–1283, Oct. 1987.

[231] H. Yoon, M.T. Liu, and K.Y. Lee, The Knockout switch under nonuniform traffic, *Proc. IEEE GLOBECOM'88*, Hollywood, FL, pp. 1628–1634, Nov. 1988.

[232] H. Yoon, K.Y. Lee, and M.T. Liu, Performance analysis

of multibuffered packet-switching networks in multiprocessor systems, *IEEE Trans. Computers*, Vol. 39, No. 3, pp. 319–327, Mar. 1990.

[233] Y.S. Youn, and C.K. Un, Performance of dilated banyan network with recirculation, *Electronics Letters*, Vol. 29, No. 1, pp. 62–63, Jan. 1993.

[234] R. Zarour, and H.T. Mouftah, Bridged Shuffle-Exchange Network: a high performance self-routing ATM switch, *Proc. IEEE ICC'93*, Geneva, Switzerland, pp. 696–700, May 1993.

[235] R. Zarour, and H.T. Mouftah, The Closed-Loop Bridged Shuffle-Exchange Network: a high performance self-routing ATM switch, *Proc. IEEE GLOBECOM'93*, pp. 1164–1168, 1993.

[236] E. Zegura, Architectures for ATM switching systems, *IEEE Commun. Mag.*, No. 2, pp. 28–37, Feb. 1993.

[237] W. Zhong, Y. Onozato, and K. Kaniyil, A copy network with shared buffers for large scale multicast ATM switching, *IEEE/ACM Trans. Networking*, Vol. 1, No. 2, pp. 157–165, Apr. 1993.

Ra'ed Y. Awdeh received the B.Sc. degree (distinction with honor) from Kuwait University, Kuwait, in 1987, the M.Sc. degree from the University of Colorado at Boulder, USA, in 1988, and the Ph.D. degree from Queen's University, Ontario, Canada, in 1994, all in electrical engineering. He was the recipient of the 1994 CATA (Canadian Advanced Technology Association) Annual Scholarship in the Telecommunications area.

From 1988 to 1990 he was a Lab Engineer and Teaching Assistant at the Department of Electrical and Computer Engineering, Kuwait University, and from 1991 to 1994 he was Research and Teaching Assistant at the Department of Electrical and Computer Engineering, Queen's University. In August 1994 he joined Bell Northern Research (BNR), Ottawa, Canada, as a Member of Scientific Staff in the Broadband Systems Design group, where he is currently working on various projects on ATM and is actively participating in the ATM Forum Traffic Management SWG.

Dr. Awdeh's current research interests include the design, modeling and performance evaluation of various aspects of ATM networks such as switching routing and trafficmanagement. He is a member of the IEEE (ComSoc) and the ACM (SIGCOMM). E-mail: raed@bnr.ca

H.T. Mouftah received the B.Sc. degree in Electrical Engineering, and the M.Sc. degree in Computer Science from the University of Alexandria, Alexandria, Egypt, in 1969 and 1972, respectively; and the Ph.D. degree in Electrical Engineering from Laval University, Quebec, Canada, in 1975.

From 1969 to 1972 he was an instructor at the University of Alexandria, Research and Teaching Assistance at Laval University from 1973 to 1975, Postdoctoral Fellow for the year 1975/76 at the University of Toronto, and Senior Digital Systems Engineer and then Chief Engineer at Adaptive Microelectronics Ltd., Thornhill, Ontario from 1976 to 1977. From 1977 to 1979 he worked with the Data System Planning Department at Bell Northern Research, Ottawa. In 1979 he joined the Department of Electrical Engineering, Queen's University at Kingston, Ontario, Canada, where he is presently at Full Professor. He spent his sabbatical years (1986/87 and 1993/94) with Bell Northern Research of Ottawa, working in the area of High Speed Networks, Routing, Traffic Management and Performance Evaluation. Since 1989 he is a Principal Investigator for the Telecommunications Research Institute of Ontario, a government Centre of Excellence in Communications, responsible for a project on Broadband Packet Switching Networks. He has been a Project leader with the Canadian Institute for Telecommunications Research, a government Network of Centres of Excellence in Communications, responsible for the project On-Board Satellite Switching Systems (1992–93). He has consulted for government and industry in the areas of Computer Networks, Digital Systems, and Fault Tolerant Computing. He holds a number of patents and published a large numbr of technical articles in the areas of Computer Networks, Digital Systems, and Systems Reliability. He is the author of "Microprocessors and Microcomputers, Principles, Design and Applications", Jackson Press, Second Edition 1985. He is the recipient of the 1989 Engineering Medal for Research and Development of the Association of Professional Engineers of Ontario (APEO).

Dr. Mouftah is a Fellow of the IEEE and Member of the APEO, the Canadian Society for Electrical Engineering and the Canadian Association of University Teachers.

Technologies for Broadband Switching

Mark A. Pashan
Marius D. Soneru
Gary D. Martin

For an asynchronous transfer mode (ATM) network to provide a wide range of services, high-capacity and low-cost network elements are needed. The capacity and cost of these elements are determined by the costs of the underlying hardware and software devices necessary to build them: ATM line cards, switching fabrics, and control structures. These devices, in turn, are built upon the advanced technologies of digital devices, optics, algorithms, and architectures. In this paper, we explore the applications of these technologies to develop ATM line cards, ATM switching fabrics, and ATM control structures.

Introduction

Advances in the fields of integrated circuits and fiber optics have led to the possibility of people communicating and being entertained as never before. Fax machines, mobile phones, laptop computers, supercomputers, wide area networks, videophones, and video distribution systems are common in the marketplace. Now, the worldwide telecommunications network must change to provide the flexible, multi-service, high-capacity, and low-cost communications these products will require. One important change in the telecommunications network is the introduction of asynchronous transfer mode (ATM) technologies and systems.

ATM is the basis of the broadband integrated services digital network (BISDN), the international standard for the next generation telecommunications network. Unlike time-slotted circuit-switched systems, such as the 4 ESS® and 5ESS® switches, which also are called synchronous transport mode (STM) systems, ATM systems are based upon a fixed-length packet or cell technique. BISDN promises flexibility, service integration, and high bandwidth. ATM technology is a flexible platform that can quickly implement new BISDN services, while providing significant operations, administration, and maintenance (OA&M) savings due to service integration. The vision of voice, data, and video services provided via a single network is possible with ATM.

To implement this vision, an ATM system should support a wide range of traffic types. The system should be capable of supporting:
- The low-jitter restriction of high-bandwidth, constant bit rate (CBR) traffic, such as clear-channel leased lines and video connections,
- The high burst rates of high-speed data connections, which could generate bursts of hundreds of cells, yet generate low cell-loss rates, and
- High use for the most important types of traffic mixes in a network, to keep the overall cost per service low.

To satisfy the needs of the telecommunications network, the ATM system should be highly reliable, easily maintainable, gracefully expandable, and cost-effectively evolvable.

AT&T has been working on high-bandwidth statistical communications for a long time, and was the first telecommunications equipment vendor to demonstrate high-bandwidth packet communications, with live customer traffic, in a wideband packet field experiment. That work, and its later laboratory extensions, were among the first steps toward ATM.[1,2] AT&T's broadband efforts are continuing to pursue a set of ATM technologies designed to meet emerging customer needs.

The ATM technologies for cell transport are the ATM line cards, the ATM switching fabric, and the ATM control structure, as shown in Figure 1.

94

- The *line cards* are based on high-speed VLSI technology and optics to implement the ATM processing functions.
- The *switching fabric* uses a cell-expansion network, followed by a shared-memory switching fabric, that allows the AT&T system to handle a wide range of traffic types.
- The *control structure* allows for modular growth and increasing service functionality.

The first product based upon AT&T's ATM technology is the GCNS-2000, developed by the Operations Systems Data Business Unit.

System Principles

AT&T's design philosophy is to meet the long-term, broadband service traffic needs with an expandable and modular architecture that also meets the highest performance standards. The various ATM line cards (such as those interfacing DS-3, STM-1, STS-3c, OC-3, etc., data streams) are plug compatible, which means various input/output configurations can be mixed and matched in one switching-unit shelf, using standard line-card slots for a variety of line-card terminations. This flexibility will meet the wide range of services and network configurations proposed for ATM systems.

The ATM switch fabric architecture provides a way to modularly construct large ATM fabrics out of ideal performance memory modules, that is, modules in which no input or output can block any other input or output to affect overall delay/throughput performance. The architecture consists of a bufferless front-end cell expansion into an array of shared-memory ATM modules, where optimal buffering can be achieved. The overall architectural design is based on several key features:

- Increased *processing power* of the ATM line cards,
- A front-end *expansion/concentration network* that provides self-routing, near-optimal and conflict-free distribution of cells to the shared-memory switching fabric, which eliminates internal congestion,
- A *shared-memory switching fabric* that requires minimal RAM buffering to route traffic to the appropriate output ports, and
- *Buffered output port queuing* that yields the best delay/throughput performance.

These features are discussed in this paper.

The ATM control structure is based upon distributed processing for modularity and growth. The three-level hierarchy of distributed processors map into the ATM Protocol Reference Model. (For a description of the ATM Protocol Reference Model, see "Network Aspects of Broadband ISDN" in this issue). The overall architecture is duplicated for reliability, and unique cell processing algorithms allow hitless, or errorless, switching between active and inactive units with minimal overhead. Finally, the modularity of the architecture allows for the components to independently evolve.

ATM Line Cards

Line cards provide the interface between the physical media used to transport ATM cells and the ATM switch fabric. The physical media may be either electrical or optical, and there are many possible data rates and signal formats (such as DS-3, STS-1, STM-1, OC-3, etc). Many types of line cards are needed to accommodate the wide range of transport options.

Except for very high-rate signals, line cards generally contain multiple port interfaces per card, supporting multiple access or egress lines. Advances in device, optics, and packaging technology are allowing more functions and more ports to be packaged onto each line card. Line cards are usually bi-directional, but there are applications, such as one-way video on demand, in which the source of a line card input is different from the destination of its output.

Figure 2 depicts some of the signal-processing functions that could be performed by a quad, or four-port, STM-1 line card. The functions for a generic line card are described below.

Ingress Functions. For cells coming into the network switch, ATM line card hardware first synchronizes the various received signals with an associated recovered clock. Then, the line card will locate the transmission frame pattern, such as a DS-3 or STM-1, and then strip the transmission overhead from the signal. Next, the actual ATM cell boundaries are located from the information in the header error control (HEC) field. The HEC field also is used to correct errors in the header or, if the errors are too severe, the errored cells may be dropped entirely. The ATM cell payload then is descrambled, meaning the pseudo-random signals, inserted in the data stream for clock recovery (also called 1's density), are removed.

Cells are presented to the ATM switch fabric before they are synchronized to the system cell clock. This is done by passing the cells through an elastic store, or expandable buffer, and inserting or deleting idle cells as needed. Once cells from different input ports are synchronized to a common clock, they can be interleaved to form a higher-rate cell stream.

Several ATM processing functions also are performed by line cards. For each virtual path (VP), that is, a logical path through the network that can be changed in real time, and for each virtual channel (VC) in a virtual path, the received cells are counted, and the bandwidth "policed" for excessive user throughput. This policing is

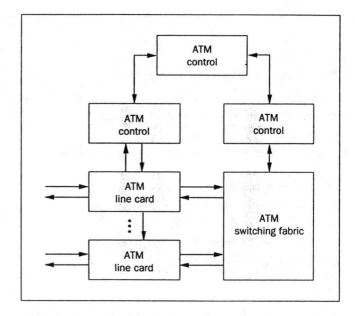

Figure 1. Three key elements in AT&T's ATM switching products are the ATM line cards, the ATM switch fabric, and the ATM control structure. *Line cards* were developed to interface a variety of electrical and optical media at a variety of rates. The cards also provide the "low-level" control functions of the three-level control structure. The *switch fabric* uses cell-expansion and concentration modules and a shared-memory switching fabric to handle a variety of traffic types with minimal buffering, providing low delay and optimal throughput. The *control structure* includes line card software, and two other levels of control, that are mapped to the control functions required in each level and plane in the ATM Protocol Reference Model.

done by matching the customer's input to the allocated virtual path or virtual channel data rate, as determined by the customer when the service was provisioned. If the cell rate exceeds the provisioned rate, the cells either can be dropped or they can be marked for possible elimination later, if they encounter congestion in the network.

Line cards also translate the incoming VP/VC identifier (VPI/VCI) fields in each cell from the incoming value, or address, to the outgoing value. The incoming VPI/VC identifier is used to access, or index, a routing table, which contains the destination-port code for the cell. This destination-port code is then attached, or prepended, to the cell for routing by the switching fabric. ATM operation, administration, and maintenance (OA&M)

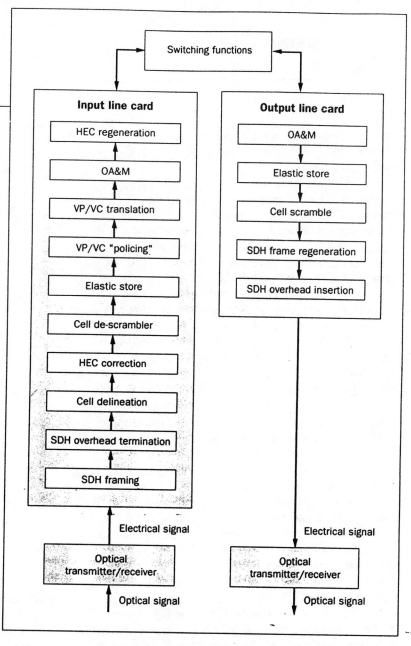

Figure 2. The line cards in AT&T's ATM systems provide a number of functions made possible in recent years due to advances in device, optics, and packaging technology. Some of the key features provided by this example, for an STM-1 line card, include operations, administration, and maintenance (OA&M) functions, elastic store, cell scrambling and descrambling, synchronous digital hierarchy (SDH) frame generation and overhead insertion, and virtual path/virtual channel (VP/VC) translation and policing.

functions, such as generating virtual path and virtual channel alarm indication signals (AISs), also are done by line cards. Finally, the head error-control field is recalculated for all cells whose headers are modified by the line cards.

Egress Functions. After cells are routed by the switch fabric, which will be discussed below, they are returned to output-line cards for further processing. If an output-line card supports multiple output ports, cells arriving from the switch fabric are demultiplexed to their appropriate ports. OA&M functions also are performed, such as generating a VP/VC far-end receive failure (FERF) message, which informs the switch to discontinue sending data when a line failure is detected. Any non-standard ATM cell bits (such as prepended destination-code bits) are removed, and the cell rate is adapted to the available line rate by passing the cells through an elastic store and

adding or deleting idle cells when necessary.

The cells are then scrambled, that is, pseudo-random signals are inserted in the data stream for clock recovery, and are packed into the payload signal of the transmission format generated by the line card. The resulting data stream is then converted into the line electrical, or optical, signal for transmission to the next ATM switch in the network, or to the end user.

ATM Switching Fabric

Broadband ATM cell switching has been extensively studied at AT&T Bell Laboratories, where significant contributions have been made in fundamental theory, as well as innovative fabric designs.[2-6] Throughout these research efforts, the critical issues of self-routing interconnect, destination conflict resolution, queuing arrangement, delay and throughput performance, and switch complexity were studied carefully and now are well understood.

Although various switches can, on paper, be designed to large dimensions, technological and physical constraints often impose a practical limit on their maximum size, say $M \times M$. If we want a larger switch system, say $2M \times 2M$, then multiple $M \times M$ switches have to be interconnected. A conventional way to do so is to employ three columns of $M \times M$ modules. This is an effective and proven technique in circuit-switched systems, but a hardware-expensive solution, nonetheless. Although each individual switching module can be constructed as the *ideal* cell switch, with optimum throughput, the complete multiple-column switch fabric no longer reflects the optimal design conceived for its individual switch modules. A principal disadvantage in such multistage-buffered approaches is the performance degradation due to internal congestion, usually arising from non-uniform traffic loads. Therefore, it was our architectural goal to achieve the same high performance expected of an ideal module for the *entire* switch fabric, regardless of traffic conditions.

The switch fabric architecture is depicted in Figure 3. The ATM switch fabric contains two stages, the cell expansion and concentration network, and the shared-memory switching fabrics. The expansion and concentration network routes cells to the appropriate shared-memory fabrics. The shared-memory fabrics provide the last stage of switching, and most of the queuing, required for the ATM traffic.

Cell-Expansion Module. When the input cell arrives at the shared-memory module, it is first processed by the cell-expansion module. The cell-expansion network is memoryless, that is, buffering is not used in this module. Instead, all the input cells are cleared out in each time slot in the next clock cycle, and there is no internal congestion. Because the input cell is self-routing, due to the prepended destination-port code, path conflicts are automatically resolved without the need for a centralized controller. The function of the cell-expansion network, therefore, is merely to transport cells to each concentration module in every slot.

It should be noted that address discrimination can be performed at both the cell-expansion module and the concentration module. Studies indicate that for small switching systems, address discrimination is more efficient at the concentration module; for large systems,

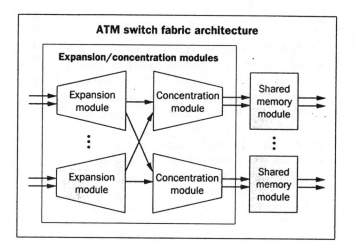

Figure 3. The expansion and concentration modules route cells to the appropriate shared-memory switching fabric. The expansion module is memoryless, and routes the cells to the concentration module. This module, in turn, requires a small amount of buffering, since it provides 32 inputs and eight outputs to the shared-memory switch fabric.

it is more efficient at the cell-expansion module. We describe the former situation here.

The cell-expansion module copies an incoming cell to all of the output ports leading to the concentration modules. For example, if the module is 4×4 (four inputs and four outputs), a single input would be written to all four outputs, that is, transported to all four concentration modules connected to the cell-expansion module.

Concentration Module. The concentration module, in turn, funnels the cells into an associated shared-memory switch fabric. Unlike the cell-expansion module, which is connected to multiple concentration modules, each concentration module is connected to only one shared-memory module (excluding redundancy for reliability). Since the expansion module broadcasts the cell to multiple concentration modules, each concentration module first must determine the address of the cell, and drop any cell not destined to its shared-memory module. The appropriately addressed cell is then routed to the shared-memory fabric. A small amount of buffering is required in the concentration modules, since the module accepts 32 inputs, but delivers only eight outputs in one cell time, or clock cycle. The 32×8 concentration is possible due to the statistical nature of data transmission, wherein not all of the inputs will be active at the same

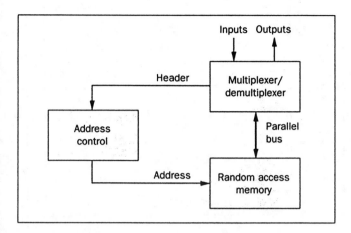

Inputs   Outputs

Header   Multiplexer/
demultiplexer

Address
control   Parallel
                          bus

Address   Random access
          memory

Figure 4. AT&T's ATM shared-memory module architecture is shown in this illustration. Input cells are routed to the multiplexer/demultiplexer, and header information is routed to the address control, while the user data is stored in RAM until processing is completed. Then the user data is read from RAM to the multiplexer/demultiplexer for transmission.

time. Therefore, since the chance of contention is statistically small, only a small amount of buffering is required. The control consists of a single queue with up to 32 'writes' and eight 'reads' to the queue in one cell time.

There are three basic approaches for providing the queuing in an ATM switch: at the input port, throughout the fabric, or at the output port. It has been shown that the best possible delay/throughput performance for an ATM switch is achieved by output queuing,[7] that is, by providing any queuing *after* the switching functions are performed. This approach has been taken by AT&T. Most cell buffering in the ATM switch is done at the shared-memory modules, and the optimal output-queuing design of the shared-memory modules ensures the best delay/throughput performance for the entire switch.

Therefore, the input cell arrival rate to the switching fabric has no effect on the design of either the cell-expansion network or the cell-concentration network. This is because the input cells are cleared into the concentration modules on a slot-by-slot basis. The only effect is on the sizing of the buffer space, inside the concentration module, to handle the statistically small amount of contention expected at this 32×8 stage, and the buffer space required for the shared-memory module.

Shared Memory Module. The general architecture of the 20-Gbits/s shared-memory module is shown in

Figure 4. The ATM fabric cells (53-byte ATM link cell enveloped in a larger fabric cell) arrive at and leave from each module synchronously. The shared-memory module writes arriving cells into, and reads leaving cells out of, a single, large random-access memory (RAM). It should be emphasized that there is no buffer-specific RAM—thus the name, shared memory. Indeed, the entire RAM in the shared-memory module could be used for buffering, if necessary. The high-bandwidth RAM is accessed via a wide parallel bus. By controlling the addresses for the RAM read and write operations, logical output buffers for each of the module outputs can be created, as required, within the single physical RAM.

The data path is composed of a multiplexer/demultiplexer (mux/dmux), a wide data bus, and the large RAM. The mux/demux multiplexes the incoming and outgoing cell streams onto the wide data bus. The data bus also is connected to the RAM data inputs—which could, as noted, be as wide as an entire fabric cell—to achieve the high RAM access bandwidth. The address control block uses copies of the switch fabric headers as input to generate the RAM address information. The operations of each module are pipelined, that is, an operation is divided into subprocesses that are processed simultaneously.

In each cell time, the 8×8 (for eight inputs and eight outputs) shared-memory module performs eight write operations (one for each arriving cell) and eight read operations (one for each leaving cell). In general, the address control logically contains an output control queue associated with each module output. Each output control queue holds the RAM addresses of all the cells stored in the RAM destined for a particular module output. The process of possibly dropping cells that exceed the customer's contract is controlled by the terms of the provisioning process, the size of the RAM, and, of course, by ever-changing network conditions. If conditions are favorable, the customer's cells will not be dropped.

Output Queuing. When multiple cells arrive simultaneously, for the same output port in the 8×8 switch, they have to be buffered. The output can only serve one cell at a time. As previously noted, it has been shown that the best possible delay/throughput performance is achieved by buffering, or queuing, at the output port. That is, all cells in each time slot are swept through the switch fabric to their destinations such that, if several cells arrive at the same time at the same output, they can be buffered in respective output queues. They are not delayed by, nor do they delay, cells destined for other outputs. The comparison between delay-throughput performance for input queuing, versus output queuing, is shown in Figure 5.

Consequently, the shared-memory fabric is a 20-Gb/s ATM output-buffered switch module. If the switch is expanded later, the concentration modules and the shared-memory modules can be reused.

ATM Control Structures

The control structure is based on the mapping of the control functions—required by each layer and plane in the ATM Protocol Reference Model—into a three-level hierarchy of distributed control processors. The mapping takes into account the characteristics of the control functions, such as the required response time, processing needs, and expected reliability. It also identifies corresponding control processors with the associated execution environments.

First, the *low-level* control functions in the three-level control hierarchy are associated with the ATM layer, and are performed by processors residing on the ATM line cards. As previously described, the control functions performed here include source policing, VPI/VCI routing, traffic and performance measurements, and error detection and reporting. A powerful microprocessor with a real-time execution environment and a fast scheduling and dispatching algorithm implements these functions on each line card. The line card-based microprocessors communicate with the higher-level processors using a functional, message-based interface that hides many of the hardware-specific characteristics of the line cards from the higher levels.

The *middle level* of control in the hierarchy provides operational and administrative control for the ATM fabric and the line cards, including basic connection management, measurements collection, and event reporting. It also is responsible for the reliable operation of the ATM fabric and line cards, providing fault recovery and diagnostics.

The reliability requirements on public switching systems have led to duplexed (side 0/side 1) architectures. This is also true for ATM systems. In the event of an error in one side, the other side can take over instantly, since both sides normally operate in lock step.

For the duplex hardware, when fault recovery detects a fault in the active side, it switches to the standby side, initializes the newly active side, and returns the

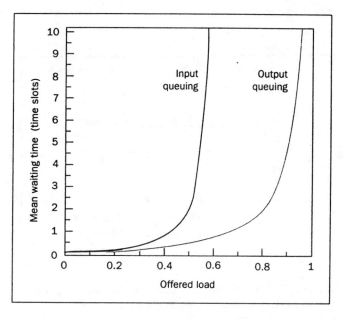

Figure 5. This figure shows the delay/throughput for input versus output queuing. If input queuing is employed, the waiting time increases significantly with an offered load of 0.5. With output queuing, a similar waiting time is not reached until an offered load of 0.8 is experienced. Thus, AT&T's ATM technology uses output queuing based on statistical probability.

unit to service. Then fault recovery initiates a diagnosis of the faulty unit. This procedure leads to a high level of availability for the transport hardware. These functions are implemented by a highly reliable, fully duplicated processor, with a real-time execution environment that is capable of continuous operation and fast response time.

Operating practices often result in occasional side switches, so that each side can be routinely tested. This is known as routine exercises. In the event that an active side detects a fault while the inactive side is completing its testing procedures, the unloaded inactive side takes over the switching operation from the loaded active side in a short period of time. The GCNS-2000, for example, handles this feature with a fast synchronization procedure.

The control software is designed for reliable operation by using a number of fault-tolerant techniques: data is continuously validated by background audit programs and software execution errors are detected, leading to corresponding recovery actions, including the automatic escalation to progressively higher levels of initialization. The communication between the middle-level control processor and the processors at the next higher level is performed by a functional message-base interface using the Abstract Syntax Notation 1 (ASN.1).

The *high-level* control in the control hierarchy provides several functions corresponding to the higher layers in the ATM Protocol Reference Model. One function is the operations and administration of one or several ATM nodes. This includes configuration and provisioning control, measurements, event reporting, database access, and customer network management (CNM). The control is implemented, on one or more UNIX-based processors, with BaseWorX software, a standard interface for application packages, and a graphical user interface (GUI) on a computer workstation. Another function at this level is to provide the control needed for switched services, including signal processing and call control. This is implemented by several highly reliable processors with real-time execution environments.

The different processors in the control hierarchy have different characteristics that match the needs of the functions they perform. They provide real-time or time-sharing environments, depending on the response time desired. They can provide open interfaces for programming customer-specific applications; reliable operation with high-availability, for example, call processing; and reliable transaction operation, such as operations and administration. The distribution of control among processors, and the well-defined interfaces between the three levels of processors in the hierarchy, lead to a modular and flexible control architecture that can evolve with the ATM network.

Cell Transport Performance

ATM cells are of fixed length. Cell traffic will have certain performance characteristics, due to the switch's incoming and outgoing link bandwidth restrictions (such as whether they are DS-3, STS-1 etc.) and the resulting traffic queuing. Unlike input-buffered fabrics that can suffer from head-of-line, or input-side, blocking, and Banyan fabrics that have internal link contention, output-buffered fabrics allow the incoming traffic to flow to the outgoing buffer/link without contention. In such a system, buffers are only required for those cases when traffic from multiple inputs are simultaneously destined for a single output, such as if there is output contention.

The size of the output buffer needed is dependent on the allowed cell-loss rate, incoming link utilization, the characteristics of incoming traffic, and the buffering technique. A 10^{-9} cell-loss rate and 80 percent incoming link load, for example, requires 45 cell buffers at each output port of a dedicated output-buffer system for random traffic. If the incident traffic is not random, but is instead bursty, such as when long packets are broken into a series of cells, then holding the output-buffer size fixed, and holding the cell-loss probability constant, results in a decreased system throughput. In fact, burst size, link utilization, and cell-loss probability are interrelated. For a given cell buffer size and technique, increasing the incident-burst size, or increasing the link utilization, or decreasing the cell-loss probability, will degrade one or both of the remaining parameters.

The only way to avoid this situation in dedicated output buffering systems is to increase the output buffer size. In other words, larger output buffers are required to carry increasingly bursty traffic at high-utilization and low cell-loss rates. In fact, the output queue size scales almost linearly with burst size, given the same cell-loss rates and link utilizations.

For example, if a switch routinely experiences burst rates of 10 cells in a row, and there is a high probability of multiple bursts, the switch might require, say, 50 output buffers. In a linear fashion, then, a switch experiencing bursts of 100 cells would require a linear increase to 500 output buffers, which greatly increases the hardware cost of the switch.

Another method to handle the problem of bursty traffic, and the one used by AT&T to reduce the linearity problem, is that of sharing the output buffers between the outputs. In other words, use one shared buffer for all of the outputs, such that space unused by one output can be reused by another output. The impact of such a technique is shown in Table I for a traffic type consisting of a mean-burst length of five cells, a 10^{-10} cell-loss rate, a fabric size of 8×8, and total buffer of 8000 cells. The shared-buffering technique allows almost twice the link

Table I. Utilization Comparisons

Fabric Type	Dedicated Buffering	Shared Buffering
Allowed Link Utilization	45%	88%

utilization as the dedicated buffering technique for this traffic type. Consequently, systems designed with a shared-buffering technique are better able to support a wide range of services with a minimal amount of buffering and, consequently, with minimal switch cost.

Due to these theoretical findings, the AT&T system uses memory-based modules that implement shared-output buffering. These architectures provide ideal delay/throughput performance characteristics and use a minimum of buffering for any traffic type or mix, such as constant bit rate and variable bit rate (VBR). Additionally, the AT&T system will incorporate delay and loss priorities to segregate traffic types and provide another level of congestion control.

Summary

AT&T's ATM technology has been designed to provide a wide range of services in an efficient and cost effective manner. The ATM line cards can be interchanged on a single shelf, providing flexible configurations. The ATM switch fabric has ideal output-buffering performance for up to 20 Gbits/s, and near ideal performance for systems larger than 20 Gbits/s. The fabric has the ability to carry random and bursty traffic at high-load and low cell-loss rates as appropriate. No fabric rearrangement or central processor routing is required. The ATM control structure is modular and extensible. The system is duplexed for reliability and fault tolerance. These technologies provide the basis of AT&T's ATM-based products, such as the GCNS-2000, the ATM Cross-connect, and the Broadband Switching System-2000.

References

1. R. W. Muise, T. J. Schonfeld, G. H. Zimmerman, "Experiments in Wideband Packet Technology," 1986 International Zurich Seminar on Digital Communications, March 11–13, 1986.
2. A. K. Vaidya and M. A. Pashan, "Technology Advances in Wideband Packet Switching," Globecom 1988, Hollywood Florida, Nov. 28–Dec. 1, 1988.
3. A. Huang and S. Knauer, "STARLITE: A Wideband Digital Switch," Globecom '84 Conference Record, Nov. 1984, pp. 5.3.1–5.3.5.
4. Y. S. Yeh, M. G. Hluchyj and A. S. Acompora, "The Knockout Switch: A simple Architecture for High Performance Packet Switching," IEEE JSAC, Vol. SAC-5, No. 8, Oct. 1987, pp. 1274–1283.
5. K. Y. Eng, M. J. Karol and Y. S. Yeh, "A Growable Packet (ATM) Switch Architecture: Design Principles and Applications," IEEE Globecom 1989, Nov. 27–30, pp. 1159–1165.
6. M. J. Karol and C. L. I, "Performance Analysis of a Growable Packet Architecture For Broadband Packet (ATM) Switching," IEEE Globecom 1989, Nov. 27–30, pp. 1173–1180.
7. M. J. Karol, M. G. Hluchyj and S. P. Morgan, "Input Versus Output Queuing on a Space-Division Packet Switch," IEEE Transactions on Communications., Vol. COM-35, No. 12, Dec. 1987, pp. 1347–1356.

(Manuscript approved November 1993)

Mark A. Pashan is a technical manager in the ATM Platform Division at AT&T Bell Laboratories, Naperville, Illinois. He joined AT&T 1982 and manages ATM cell switching fabric design for AT&T's ATM products. He has a B.S. in engineering science from Iowa State University, Ames, Iowa, a M.S.E.E from Stanford University, Palo Alto, California, and a M.B.A. from the University of Chicago, Chicago, Illinois.

Marius D. Soneru is a technical manager in the Switching ATM Platform Department at AT&T Bell Laboratories in Naperville, Illinois. His group designs and develops software for the ATM platform infrastructure, inter-processor communications, initialization, and measurement. He joined AT&T in 1973 and holds a M.S.E.E. degree from Polytechnic Institute of Bucharest, Hungary, an M.S. degree in computer science from the University of California at Los Angeles, and a Ph.D. in computer science from the Illinois Institute of Technology in Chicago.

Gary D. Martin is a technical manager in the ATM Core Hardware Department at AT&T Bell Laboratories, North Andover, Massachusetts. He joined AT&T in 1978 and currently supervises a group that designs VLSI devices. He has a B.S.M.E. and M.S.M.E. from Oklahoma State University in Stillwater, and an M.S. and Ph.D. in electrical engineering from Stanford University, Palo Alto, California.

A Distributed Control Architecture
of High-Speed Networks

Israel Cidon, *Senior Member, IEEE*, Inder Gopal, *Fellow, IEEE*, Marc A. Kaplan, and Shay Kutten, *Member, IEEE*

Abstract— A control architecture for a high-speed packet-switched network is described. The architecture was designed and implemented as part of the PARIS (subsequently plaNET and BBNS) networking project at IBM. This high bandwidth network for integrated communication (data, voice, video) is currently operational as a laboratory prototype. It will also be deployed within the AURORA Testbed that is part of the NSF/DARPA gigabit networking program.

The high bandwidth dictates the need for specialized hardware to support faster packet handling for both point-to-point and multicast connections. A faster and more efficient network control is also required in order to support the increased number of connections and their changing requirements with time. The new network control architecture presented exploits specialized hardware, thereby enabling tasks to be performed faster and with less computation overhead. In particular, since control information can be distributed quickly using hardware packet handling mechanisms, decisions can be made based upon more complete and accurate information. In some respects, this has the effect of having the benefits of centralized control (e.g., easier bandwidth resource allocation to connections), while retaining the fault tolerance and scalability of a distributed architecture.

I. INTRODUCTION

PACKET SWITCHING networks have changed considerably in recent years. One factor has been the dramatic increase in the capacity of the communication links. The advent of fiber optic media has pushed the transmission speed of communication links to more than a gigabit per second, representing an increase of several orders of magnitude over typical links in most packet switching networks [19] that are still in use today. Increases in link speeds have not been matched by proportionate increases in the processing speeds of communication nodes. This implies that switching of information cannot be performed using traditional software store-and-forward functions.

Another factor is the changed nature of traffic carried by these networks. As opposed to pure data networks, or pure voice networks, it is now accepted that packet-switching networks (or variants of packet switching networks like ATM

Paper approved by A. A. Lazar, the Editor for Voice/Data Networks of the IEEE Communications Society. Manuscript received June 8, 1990; revised February 15, 1993. This paper was presented in part at the 9th Annual ACM Symposium on Principles of Distributed Computing, P.Q., Canada, August 1990. The work of I. Cidon was done while he was at IBM T. J. Watson Research Center.

The authors are with IBM T. J. Watson Research Center, Yorktown Heights, NY 10598 USA.

I. Cidon is with Sun Microsystems Labs, Mount View, CA 94043 USA, and with the Department of Electrical Engineering, Technion, Haifa 32000, Israel.

IEEE Log Number 9406234.

[6]) will form the basis for multimedia high-speed networks that will carry voice, data, and video through a common set of nodes and links. Real time traffic (e.g., voice and video) requires that the route selection function be capable of guaranteeing for a long period the availability of adequate network resources along the chosen path for a particular traffic stream. These streams typically require that a minimal amount of bandwidth be available to them as long as the stream is active. On the other hand, nonreal-time services (such as traditional data services) are much less predictable and must be supported on a demand basis. Such nonreal-time services can be slowed down or be postponed for a later time when the network is heavily loaded but require quick and prompt setup if resources are available. The increased number and the heterogeneous characteristics of users (or calls) makes traditional network control schemes functionally inadequate and inefficient.

Both of the preceding factors have a significant impact on the design of the protocols and control procedures for the network. The disparity between communication and processing speeds suggests that processing may become the main bottleneck in future networks. A common partial solution to this problem is to introduce high-speed switching hardware which off-loads the routine packet handling and routing functions from the processing elements [12]. This issue has been heavily investigated in the literature and several high-speed hardware switches have been described [22]. A second issue, the need for enhancing the performance and the functionally of the network control layer, is much less explored.

In this paper we explore this second issue, specifically focusing on the lessons that we have learned during the design and implementation of the PARIS network [8]. We believe that most of our conclusions are general and can be applied to any high-speed packet network.

The early stage of PARIS was described in [8]. A subsequent paper [10] describes a successor to PARIS called plaNET. (For clarity, we only refer to PARIS though plaNET is largely similar as far as distributed control is concerned.) Both works also include some initial ideas regarding distributed control. In the current paper we describe for the first time the distributed control functions and the way they fit into the complete network. We elaborate on the way in which network control performance can be gained by exploiting specialized hardware features. In particular, we introduce new multicast features implemented in hardware and exploit them in performing fast and computation efficient information distribution for different network control tasks. We also describe some new algorithmic ideas that save computation overheads associated with previous network control solutions. Our performance measures are stated in terms of worst case time and processing costs associated with the distributed procedures used for network control.

Let us now describe the problems solved by the distributed control architecture presented in this paper. The control procedures of the PARIS network facilitate virtual circuit routing. Thus we have the notion of a "connection" or "call" being established between a source and a destination (a call can carry either real-time or nonreal-time traffic). For each call, all the traffic of that call (in one direction) traverses the same path through the network. The control process is as follows. Requests for "calls" arrive at nodes asynchronously. Each call has associated with it some parameters such as average packet rate, burstiness, tolerance for packet loss, etc. Calls are either denied access to the network ("blocked") or accepted into the network. If accepted, a call is provided with a route that has adequate capacity to handle the request. The mechanisms used by each node to perform these functions (accept/deny calls, provide a route, and guarantee/reserve bandwidth) are referred to as the control procedures of the network. In a similar way, existing calls might request for additional network resources along the established call path (or release some of the resources not used any more).

Traditional data networks typically employ distributed control but do not guarantee availability of bandwidth to calls. They are usually too slow to be extended to perform fast setup and takedown of calls or bandwidth reservations. Their distribution of routing information is usually computational inefficient because of an extensive use of a software based hop-by-hop information flood mechanism. Control procedures in common carrier networks (circuit switched networks) deal with capacity allocation but are typically more centralized, rely on the availability of significant computing power and support rigid types of reservations which do not change in time. A key contribution of PARIS is showing that by employing hardware speedups and new algorithmic techniques in the control flow it is possible to provide performance guarantees and considerable speedup of the reservation operation while preserving the fault tolerance and growth capabilities of a distributed control architecture. In particular, we develop a new topology and utilization information update algorithm which employs a hardware based broadcast over a tree replacing the traditional hop-by-hop software flooding employed in previous architectures such as ARPANET [20] and APPN [5]. The advantages of the new approach are much faster distribution of the topology/utilization information and a major reduction in the processing involved. We develop fault-recovery and load balancing mechanisms to insure its operation under topological changes and rapid changes of network load. In addition, we develop a new call setup/takedown procedure which employs another hardware multicast mechanism and accelerates the bandwidth reservation/release process compared to previously developed hop-by-hop software procedures such as the one in APPN [5]. We also incorporate additional mechanisms to efficiently handle large number of calls, failures over the call's path, and graceful recovery of nodes.

The work presented in this paper is more than a "paper study." Considerable prototype implementation has been done and much more is planned. A prototype PARIS network, operating at switching speeds of over 1 Gb/s, has been built and tested within a laboratory environment. More realistic deployments are underway. For example, a PARIS network is being installed in the AURORA testbed. Many of the mechanisms described in this paper will be implemented and experimentally validated as part of that project. The AURORA project is part of the NSF/DARPA gigabit networking program, under the auspices of the Corporation for National Research Initiatives. It will involve the construction of a gigabit/second network that will link together four research centers in the Northeastern United States (MIT, University of Pennsylvania, IBM, and Bellcore). Other field trials include a trial with Rogers Cable Services in Toronto and a Trial with Bell South Services in Tennessee. It is likely that the results of this trials will provide considerable experience and understanding of how distributed control algorithms will operate in future networks.

The overall PARIS architecture is described in [8] and its followup plaNET is described in [10]. Briefly, PARIS is a high-speed packet-switching system for integrated voice, video, and data communications. The system uses simplified network protocols in order to achieve the low packet delay and high nodal throughput necessary for the transport of real time traffic. The packet handling functions are implemented mainly in dedicated high-speed hardware, with only some low-speed control functions requiring software implementation. PARIS uses variable sized packets with automatic network routing. Automatic network routing (ANR) is a form of source routing where each packet contains an ANR header composed of a concatenation of link identifiers. It also supports (in hardware) a rich set of alternative routing schemes which include tree multicast, label swapping (including ATM VC/VP formats), copy mechanisms, and more. We later elaborate on the specific routing schemes which are exploited by the network control procedures. Details on all the routing schemes including the ones which are not described in this paper can be found in [10].

Note that the paper deals with distributed control algorithms. Therefore, we mainly present performance results from a worst case complexity perspective, typical in the algorithmic literature. Average case results are very difficult to obtain analytically and are very rare and limited in the algorithmic literature. Past and current lab prototypes as well as simulation studies are very limited (3–4 nodes) for a performance study of the network control software and are used mainly for validity and correctness test. Therefore, we believe that comprehensive performance results will only come when the network is actually used in a production environment.

The rest of the paper is organized as the following. In Section II we describe the model of the communication subsystem assumed for the operation of the network control algorithms. In particular, we discuss the hardware supported functions that can be exploited for faster control. In Section III we describe the overall structure of the network control architecture. We explain the notion of the "bandwidth reservation cycle." In this section we list and motivate the distributed algo-

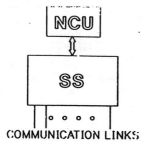

Fig. 1. Node structure.

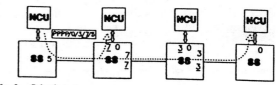

Fig. 3. Selective copy.

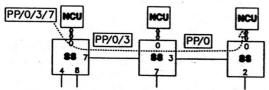

Fig. 2. Automatic network routing.

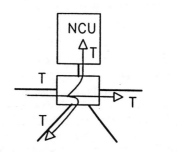

Fig. 4. Multicast.

rithms that are used for the network control. Next we address the different components of the network control. Section IV briefly summarizes the route computation procedure assuming a correct topology database is available. Section V describes the distributed procedures used to assemble and update the topology database at every node. (Details of the algorithms are described in the Appendix.) We also address new aspects such as the load balancing of update messages. Section VI addresses call setup, maintenance, and takedown. We describe the distributed algorithm used and the method of tracking, updating, and recovering local load parameters. We summarize the paper in a short conclusion section.

II. NETWORK MODEL

Each PARIS node consists of two components, a fast hardware switching component (the switching subsystem (SS)) and a slower controller (network control unit (NCU)) (see Fig. 1). The switching subsystem performs the packet routing functions while the NCU performs the more complex control functions. Bidirectional transmission links are attached directly to the switching subsystem. The NCU is also attached to the switching subsystem by a bidirectional link. We assume that each link has a finite, nonempty, set of identities (ID's). The hardware permits each link's ID set to be configured dynamically under software control. In this paper we assume that the various ID sets are defined in order to perform the following functions.[1]

1) *Automatic Network Routing (ANR*; see Fig. 2): This requires every link to own an ID that is unique within its switching subsystem. If a certain node (where no ambiguity exists, we say "node" instead of "the NCU in a node") wishes to send a packet to a certain destination node and if it has knowledge of a path to that destination node, it can send the

[1] The following intermediate routing functions are only a subset (used by the control algorithms of this paper) of the set of routing functions (or modes) implemented by plaNET. The interested reader is referred to [10] for more details.

message by prefixing the data with a string that is composed of the concatenation of all the link ID's along the computed path. Used ID's are stripped off before the packet is forwarded.

2) *Selective copy* (see Fig. 3): Assume that for each link attachment (excepting the NCU's attachment) we define a "copy ID" that is identical to the (primary) link ID except for its most significant bit (MSB). For each link, both the copy and the primary link ID's are configured as members of the ID set. By also assigning all of the copy ID's to the ID set of the NCU's attachment, it is possible to achieve a selective copy function. A packet may be copied by several preselected nodes along a path by substituting the copy ID for the normal ID for these preselected nodes, e.g., if MSB = 1 a copy will be received by the NCU of that particular node; if MSB = 0 no copy will be delivered. In Fig. 3, MSB = 1 is marked by an underscore of the respected link ID.

3) *Multicast* (see Fig. 4): If more than one link recognizes the same ID (marked as "T" in Fig. 4), it is possible to perform a multicast within the node. This feature is exploited in the tree broadcast procedure used for topology/utilization update (see Section V.A for more details). We denote this scheme also as *tree multicast* as it is correctly operated if a tree of links is labeled with no loops. We replace the term multicast by broadcast in case the multicast covers the complete network.

Note that these routing mechanisms are currently parts of the PARIS/plaNET architecture. However, other architectures such as ATM or frame relay can implement them (possibly in hardware) just above the cell or the frame layer.

As previously mentioned, the basic unit of traffic is a "call" or a "connection." From the viewpoint of the control procedures, a call is defined to be a stream of packets from some external source with a specified average rate, variance, service requirement, etc. The duration of a call can be either long (more than minutes for a phone call or video connection) or short (for the duration of a fast file transfer). We enforce that each source restricts itself to the specified parameters through an input rate regulation scheme [8]. The "leaky bucket" scheme proposed in [22] and the credit manager scheme used in SMDS A [21] are examples of input rate regulation schemes. The PARIS rate-control mechanism is a buffered version of previously suggested leaky bucket scheme with additional components (e.g., a spacer) as is described and analyzed in [4], [21], and [15]. In general, the scheme guarantees that the long term average rate does not exceed the prespecified rate of the connection. Over shorter periods, it permits bursts at a much higher rate which is constrained by the maximum speed of the communication links in the path.

III. CONTROL CYCLE

The PARIS approach to connection control is a decentralized one. This design choice is motivated by the fact that PARIS is aimed at private networks rather than public carrier networks. For fault tolerance and performance reasons, it is well accepted that for such networks decentralized control is preferable to reliance upon one or more central controller(s) [5]. Thus, in the PARIS system, every backbone node participates in a set of distributed algorithms which collectively comprise the connection control of the system.

While distributed control mechanisms are commonly used in most of today's data networks [5], [20], they do not deal with traffic that requires service guarantees. In particular, they use hop-by-hop software based "flooding" algorithm to distribute the local states and loads. While this is acceptable in the environment of relatively slow data networks, in the environment of high-speed networks (high rate of new calls and rapid change of network load) such schemes will result in excessive overhead and high information latency. Similarly, they use hop-by-hop call setup and takedown procedures with similar consequences.

As mentioned in Section II, an input rate regulation is used to regulate the traffic rate and it is assumed that all traffic that passes through the throttle is guaranteed a certain level of service. Thus, before admitting a call into the network, some guarantee must be provided that the communication capacity required by the call is available. If not, the call must be denied access into the network or "blocked."

In PARIS, we use a distributed route selection mechanism based on a replicated routing topology database similar to the one in ARPANET [20] and APPN [5]. Basically, each node maintains a complete routing topology database with link weights reflecting the traffic over each link (utilization). When link weights change substantially updates flow to every node using a broadcast algorithm.[2]

At the call setup time, the source node obtains the parameters associated with the new call. These parameters define the type of call, the destination, and the parameters of the

input throttle that is associated with this connection (specifying either directly or indirectly the average capacity of the connection and the level of burstiness). Typically, these traffic parameters are based on traffic type (e.g., a voice call requires a steady 64 kb/s) and may be changed dynamically during the operation of the connection. The source node then computes a path based on its local topology database and generates the ANR field from source to destination and back. The source node uses the information in the local topology database to ensure that the chosen route is capable of carrying the traffic and providing the level of service required by the traffic type. The computed information is then sent to the adaptor that actually interfaces with the source of traffic. The call setup procedure is then initiated. As part of the procedure, an end-to-end call setup packet flows over the path and is copied by the intermediate nodes along the path. Based on the bandwidth information in the call setup packet, each of these nodes updates its database of the bandwidth utilization on its link attachments. This updated information may change the link weights and trigger an update broadcast.

If no suitable path can be found between source and destination, the call will be blocked. The scheme provides control of the path at the source and obtains relatively efficient paths. However, because the information about remote link utilization takes a nonzero time to propagate through the network, there is a possibility of some unnecessary blocking caused by temporarily inaccurate information in the routing topology database. To minimize this inaccuracy, in PARIS, we employ an efficient way for performing the topology and utilization update both in term of speed and processing overhead. A fast tree broadcast function is employed which permits a direct broadcast of information to all network nodes with no software involvement at the intermediate nodes. Using the speed of the network hardware, this fast broadcast reduces the problem of transient inconsistencies in the routing topology databases. This new feature also reduces the message processing overhead by restricting the broadcast to deliver only a single copy of the information to every node. Therefore, a considerable amount of overhead is saved compared to traditional "flooding" mechanisms which may deliver multiple messages to each node and require software processing to ensure that duplicates are not forwarded [5], [20]. (See Section V.)

The process of connection control can be captured in the form of a "control cycle" shown in Fig. 5. The cycle represents the flow of information in the system. The cycle starts with a request for a new connection. This request contains the call parameters. The information used to compute a route for the call comes from the local topology database which also contains link weights including link utilizations. This information is obtained through the topology and utilization broadcast/update algorithm. The trigger for the utilization update comes from the local link weight computation of each node. These weights are computed from the knowledge of the call parameters for each of the calls that traverse the links, knowledge that is gained during the call setup process. The initial source of the parameters is the connection request. This closes the cycle.

---

[2] Note that in PARIS, only network nodes (which are the set of gigabit/second switches) are presented in the routing topology database. Furthermore, only network nodes are required to participate in the maintenance of the routing topology database. Therefore in the PARIS environment (a private network) the routing topology database is typically limited to less than a hundred nodes. Similarly, the topology database consists of the collection of backbone links (gigabit/second links) whose number is also not too large. However, similarly to the ARPANET case and using the algorithmic improvements we describe later on, we don't view the size of the database or the amount and rate of database updates to be a practical limiting factor in a public high-speed work.

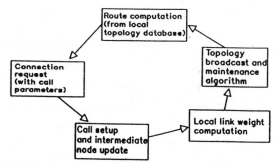

Fig. 5. Control cycle.

Note that two components of the cycle involve interactions among several nodes. These are the call setup process and the topology/utilization update. We use the fast copy and the fast broadcast capabilities of the switching subsystem hardware to speed up the operation of these two critical components of the control cycle. We also employ novel algorithmic ideas in order to reduce to processing load required for these two tasks. In the rest of this paper, we discuss briefly the various components of the cycle. Note that as the task of utilization update is a subset of the the topology update task we focus in the rest of the paper mainly on the latter.

IV. ROUTE COMPUTATION

Recall that since the full topology and link utilizations are known at each network (NCU) node, this is essentially a local operation. This procedure also determines whether or not a given call is permitted access to the network. While the scheme is basically a collection of heuristics, the underlying "optimality" criterion or long-term objective is to maximize network throughput subject to the maximum loss probability allowed by each packet. (Packet loss increases with throughput.) Unlike the case in traditional networks, minimizing delay is not an objective, since in a fast network a packet sent and not lost will arrive within the delay conditions of even very time sensitive applications.

We use several "rules of thumb" to guide us in the development of the route computation scheme. For example, the route computation method should attempt to find a path with the minimum number of hops as this minimizes the overall use of network capacity. Thus, calls with excessive capacity demands should be denied access to the network. We define "excessive" by comparing the number of hops in the current route with the "minimum hop" route. This criterion is particularly important under high load conditions and for calls with large holding times.

The resulting scheme is sketched as follows. Based on the characteristics of the call the first step is to identify the set of links that can accommodate the call. (It is assumed that a computational procedure is known whereby given the characteristics of the call, and link weights in the topology database, it is possible to compute the expected packet loss—the primary parameter in determining acceptability of a link.) Among the subset of acceptable links, a minimum hop path is then chosen. If the length of the chosen path is within a permitted

multiple ("stretch factor") of the minimum possible path length the call is admitted into the network. (The "stretch factor" is determined by the current load conditions and input call parameters). Otherwise, the call is blocked. (This may require some calls to be blocked even though resources are available, in anticipation of future calls which are expected to make better use of the resources.) Further investigation of this idea is being conducted [1].

V. INFORMATION UPDATE

A. Overview

Each local node is responsible for determining the bandwidth utilization of its adjacent links, for determining when to inform remote nodes of changes in utilization, and for distributing this information to remote nodes. Distributing this information is called a utilization broadcast/update. A similar task is the topology update where the information about the active and inactive state of the links is distributed. In fact, the state of the link in the routing topology database and in the topology/utilization update messages includes several fields in addition to link activity state and link utilization. These fields include indication whether the link is a part of the hardware multicast tree and additional link weight characteristics to be later discussed.

For both updates it is possible to use a conventional flooding based mechanism as in ARPANET [20]. However, the ARPANET algorithm has some deficiencies that make it suboptimal for this purpose. First, it delivers a copy of every message over every link (which can be translated to $O(|E|)$ overhead per topology item change, where E is the set of links). This means that each node has to process a large amount of redundant packets. (It is enough that each node receives only one copy of each message.) This considerably limits the effective size of the distributed database and the rate at which database changes can be processed. Second, this algorithm is hard to implement in fast hardware. (Remembering which message has been received before is a task that hardware switches currently cannot perform fast and cheaply. Thus the relatively slow NCU in each node must decide whether to forward a received message, or to discard it as a copy.) The propagation of the update messages hop-by-hop through the software layers makes the algorithm too slow to operate in a rapidly changing traffic environments (this can be translated to $O(|V|)$ delay where V is the set of nodes).

The selective copy mechanism can be used to perform a multicast or broadcast (e.g., through a path that traverses a depth first search. See, e.g., [14].) This, however, has drawbacks in that it results in very long paths (and consequently long message headers) and it requires that the sender must know a route that reaches all the recipients of the message. When topology information itself is delivered by this process such a route may not be available. Variations of this approach are discussed in [12] and found to be inefficient.

The method used in PARIS employs a hardware multicast mechanism which delivers messages directly from the source to all potential recipients with no software involvement in the transfer. Moreover, only a single copy of each message is delivered to the endpoints. Hence, the processing cost is only $O(|V|)$ and the delay is only a function of the hardware switching and the propagation delays in the network.

The *multicast* message mode was introduced mainly for this purpose. Recall from Section II that a link may have multiple ID's (labels) and that these ID's can be changed dynamically by the local NCU. Suppose that some link adaptors, in various nodes, have (among other labels) the label T. Assume further that the collection of the T labeled links forms a tree. This tree is used for a fast hardware broadcast as follows. When a node wishes to perform a broadcast, it generates a multicast type message, using label T. When this message arrives to the switching subsystem, it is forwarded over all links labeled T of that switch except the link over which it was received. Note that this broadcast will reach every node on the tree, and will terminate.

Topology updates are triggered whenever a node senses the failure or recovery of an adjacent link. Utilization updates are triggered whenever the node senses that the utilization of an adjacent link has changed substantially [1] from the time of the previous update. Utilization updates are also sent periodically (as described below) to guarantee reliability.

The multicast type messages as defined above have no built-in error recovery mechanism. There is some finite (very small) probability that a multicast message sent on the tree will not arrive at some of its destinations. In both the topology and the utilization update tasks we make use of a "backup" periodic broadcast of utilization updates to achieve reliability. The periodic approach is suitable for such tasks because it is important to receive only the most recent link information (previous updates becomes obsolete once a new one is received). (Note that a link utilization message is also implicitly a link topology message; a link that is utilized must be active). The periodic broadcast is achieved by having each node maintain a timeout period and performing a "periodic" broadcast if no event driven utilization broadcast has occurred within this time period. Note that we expect utilization updates to be very frequent and do not expect this periodic mechanism to be triggered very often.

As we would like to use a hardware tree broadcast for the topology update protocol, we need a mechanism to enable the nodes to label their adjacent links as tree links or nontree links correctly and consistently. Since every node maintains a local network topology database, it seems that it could have computed a tree according to some procedure that is consistent among all nodes (e.g., a minimum spanning tree) and thereby know how to label its adjacent links (either a tree link or a nontree link). This simple approach does not work in a dynamically changing network as it may result in transient loops in the tree labeled links. This will cause looping of messages through the hardware and excessive traffic in the network. Thus, we introduce a tree maintenance procedure that uses network topology but imposes careful coordination between the nodes in order to ensure that transient loops do not occur.

Thus our complete information update protocol is composed of two modules. The first module, topology update protocol

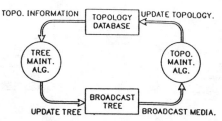

Fig. 6. Relations of topology update and tree maintenance routines.

(together with the utilization update) broadcasts over the tree computed by the second module, the tree maintenance protocol. On the other hand, the tree maintenance module uses the topology knowledge in order to maintain the tree (see Fig. 6). That is, when the tree is disconnected the replicated topology database is used to locate the edges that will reconnect the tree. The topology update and the tree maintenance algorithms are described in Appendix A.

Let us comment that a somewhat similar tree maintenance protocol appears in [2]. However this protocol cannot make use of a hardware broadcast, since it assumes reliable delivery of messages (that our basic broadcast does not provide). Also, the protocol of [2] is more complex than required since it does not permit the use of sequence numbers (used here). While sequence numbers may lead to theoretically unbounded message length, for practical purposes, 64 bits of sequence numbering is more than enough. The use of sequence numbers simplifies the tree maintenance and topology/utilization update protocols and the data structure of the topology database.

The topology knowledge also enables us to adjust the tree easily to be a minimum spanning tree (rather than any spanning tree). It also helps us to achieve a stabilization of the tree even in the presence of some less reliable links (their weights will be increased to reflect their instability).

B. Load Balancing

In a high-speed environment where links are very reliable and of very high bandwidth, we expect utilization information to change at a rate which is several orders of magnitude faster than the link topology information (seconds versus hours or days). Therefore, the utilization update messages dominate the total update traffic and are the main concern of this section.

A key issue to ensure avoidance of congestion in the process of utilization update is that of load-balancing. If every node is permitted to send utilization updates at any time we may run into potential problems. It is possible that even if the processing rate at a node is on average adequate to cope with the total rate of updates, there might be periods in which the number of concurrent updates exceeds the processing speed causing the update message queue to become congested. Adding to this problem is the fact that utilization updates at different nodes might be correlated. The reason for that is the introduction (setup) of high-bandwidth calls through a long path of nodes. Since the call setup is almost instantaneous at all these intermediate nodes they may issue a utilization update at almost the same time. Another scenario is a failure of a high bandwidth link which causes rerouting of a large number of calls all within a short period. This means that even though our broadcast media is not a collision type we would prefer to spread updates over time in order to guarantee load-balancing.

We employ a scheduling mechanism (BRAM) that is usually used for scheduling transmissions in a shared media network (radio or coax) in order to avoid collisions see [7]. In such a scheme the scheduling is done by ordering the transmission of nodes in a round robin fashion. Nodes that have nothing to transmit are skipped dynamically by detecting the absence of their transmission.

The implementation of the BRAM algorithm in the PARIS network is straightforward. The ordering of the transmission can be done locally by each node using its replica of the topology database and the topology of the broadcast tree. The node can also estimate the propagation delay through each link and in particular the tree links. Inconsistencies between the replicated topology databases can be ignored since the network can tolerate "collisions." The BRAM algorithm works better if the sum of the propagation delays between consecutive nodes of the round-robin schedule is minimized. If the broadcast is performed on a general network this would pose a difficult graph problem. (It is NP Complete [17].) However, since the broadcast is accomplished over the hardware based tree this problem is solved using a simple depth-first-search procedure. Since our broadcast mechanism is collision free and the delays are only estimated, the BRAM algorithm is only approximated.

VI. CALL SETUP, MAINTENANCE, AND TAKEDOWN

Traditionally, in virtual circuit based networks, (i.e., TYM-NET, X.25 etc.) call setup and termination procedures are used for two different tasks. First, the intermediate nodes must update their label swapping tables in order to activate the intermediate switching operation for a specific call. Second, the two end-points must establish an end-to-end connection and exchange session parameters (i.e., window size, packet size etc.).

In the PARIS system, since we use ANR routing, there is no need for any table update to allow the physical communication. The endpoints are able to communicate once the routes have been computed. However, for bandwidth management reasons we use the call setup/takedown procedure as the mechanism to inform the intermediate nodes about the amount of bandwidth that is allocated to the new call. (Recall (Section V) that the nodes track the amount of reserved capacity for each of their local links and broadcast a utilization update if some significant change has been identified.)

Another task of the setup procedure is to reconfirm the availability of the reserved bandwidth for the new call. This task is necessary sometimes because of the potential latency in the operation of the bandwidth control cycle. Calls which are concurrently routed from different sources may allocate capacity from some link without being aware of each other. Typically, this will cause no harm if the call bandwidths are small compared with the residual available capacity. However, for congested links or high bandwidth calls (such as high quality video calls) this might cause an overutilization and hence excessive packet loss.

We introduce the concept of a call maintenance procedure in order to satisfy the following requirements:

1) to track in real time the bandwidth being reserved and released in order to pass significant load changes to the topology/utilization update mechanism;
2) to notify the endpoints of a call about failures along the call's path that require a call drop or a switchover to an alternate path;
3) to release the reserved capacity of explicitly terminated calls (with explicit take-down messages);
4) to release eventually the reserved capacity of implicitly terminated calls. The absence of an explicit take-down message can be caused by

   a) failure of the endpoints before the normal termination of the call;
   b) link/node failures that isolate the intermediate node from the endpoints of the call.

In addition to the above we use the call maintenance procedure to enhance the fault-tolerant operation of the network. Since the switching subsystem is a stand alone hardware module, independent of the NCU, the failure of the NCU does not necessarily impact the flow of steady-state traffic of existing calls. (This failure, however, will prevent the setup of new calls through this node). Thus, a recovering NCU (or a backup NCU) may not "know" the reserved bandwidth and the actual capacity used in its links. We introduce a mechanism by which such a processor can first regain the reservation information and then rejoin the call setup process.

A. Setup/Takedown

The call setup procedure is composed of two complementary phases. They are described in detail in [13]. In the first phase the source of the call notifies the destination and the intermediate nodes along the path of the new call and its characteristics. This phase is accomplished by the source sending a direct message to the destination which is also copied by the intermediate nodes (using the selective copy mechanism).

The second phase includes a call confirmation process in which a confirmation message is transferred through the intermediate nodes back to the source. Each node checks whether the reserved capacity is indeed available. Otherwise it will convert the confirmation message into an abort message. The confirmation phase is optional in the sense that in most cases the source does not wait for the confirmation message before end-to-end communication is enabled. However, the reception of an abort message will cause the session to be aborted immediately. (The confirmation process can be accelerated by having the nodes on the way send confirmations in parallel using ANR; alternatively, some nodes along the way may accumulate some downstream confirmations, and send a single consolidated confirmation [13].)

The same procedure of call setup is also used for changing the required bandwidth during the connection active period. It can also be used to poll the nodes over the path regarding the amount of bandwidth available over the path. Such use of the same setup mechanism is described in [10].

The call takedown is very similar to the call setup without the confirmation phase. The reserved capacity is released. Since the call might be terminated by external events such as failures along the path we must have other ways to takedown the call and to release the reserved capacity in such events. These mechanisms are discussed in the following.

B. Call Maintenance

In the call maintenance procedure each source send periodically refresh messages which include the call parameters. These messages are acknowledged immediately by similar messages from the destination. These acknowledgment messages are also copied by intermediate nodes. The basic assumption of this scheme is that in the absence of failures, the packet loss probability for control messages is very small and thus the probability that some fixed small number of such consecutive messages (K in the range of 2–5) will be lost is practically negligible [11].

The periodic message exchange is used in several ways. First, it serves as a path integrity check for the endpoints of the session. The absence of a refresh message indicates to the endpoints a failure along the path or the failure of the other endpoint. Second, these messages allow the intermediate nodes to track the existence of calls and the amount of bandwidth reserved for these calls. (This will be further explained later on). This requires the copy of the refresh messages by the NCU. The time requirements for this second task are less strict than for the first one. Therefore, only a certain subset of the refresh messages should be marked as messages to be copied. Third, this periodic transmission of the call parameters allows nodes to refresh their reservation knowledge or automatically recover it after a NCU crash just by processing the copied refresh messages for some period of time.

Tracking Bandwidth Reservation: There are two basic approaches to the reservation refresh procedure: 1) explicit; and 2) implicit. In the explicit refresh the NCU maintains a call table in which each call ID has an explicit entry that describes the amount of capacity reserved. A timeout period is maintained for each entry. After the reception of a refresh message for a specific call ID the timer for that entry is reset. If after some predetermined number of refresh periods (considerably larger than the above K) no refresh is received, the call is considered terminated and its entry is removed from the table. We assume that a similar but shorter timeout period is used by the end-points so they will drop the call before the intermediate nodes. This ensures that actual transmission ceases before the call capacity is released.

The drawback of the explicit refresh is that a large amount of memory and processing is required. A typical high-speed link (say SONET STS48 which is approximately 2.4 Gb/s) may carry over 40 000 64kb/s phone calls. The duration of a voice call is usually around 200 s which leads to a refresh time for the reserved capacity of about 1–10 s. This results in 4000–40 000 such operations (which include finding the entry in the table, resetting the timeout flag, and other overheads) per second per link and a table size of 40 000 entries per link.

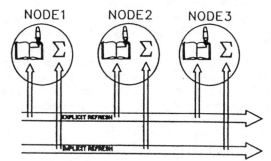

Fig. 7. Explicit and implicit update.

Thus, we would like to avoid the use of explicit refresh for calls that use only a small fraction of the link capacity. For this majority of calls we employ an alternative implicit approach which is less exact but also less computationally expensive. The idea is that over some sufficiently large "window" of time (which will depend on the maximal difference in the delay between consecutive packets) the number of refresh packets that will be received is fairly constant. (In our example the window can be set to 10 refresh periods; using the law of large numbers, for 40 000 calls the number of refresh messages received in a window will be very close to $10 \times 40\,000$ with very high probability). Here, we do not have to maintain an individual table entry per call but simply need to keep the sums of the reserved capacity for the last window. A weighted sum of these short term estimations serves as the node estimate for the link utilization.

A potential problem exists since some calls may be of a very high capacity and therefore the total implicit sum will depend much more on their refresh messages than on the messages of the other calls. This causes the law of large numbers not to hold for the sum (it will still hold for the total number of refresh messages). In PARIS, we make such calls use the explicit refresh procedure and these refresh messages are not taken into account for the implicit summation. A typical rule is that if a call requires more than $x\%$ of the total link capacity (say 1%), then this call will be explicitly maintained in the reservation table and will not be part of the implicit summation. Thus, we have a strict upper bound on the number of calls we maintain explicitly (say 100). The resulting hybrid scheme is illustrated in Fig. 7. A different approach would be to break the large capacity calls into smaller pieces and instead of sending a single message per refresh period to send a multiplicity of refresh messages each carrying a fraction of the total call capacity.

A further way of reducing the computational burden of the NCU is to introduce additional hardware associated with each link. Since the processing is trivial, the refresh messages can be processed on-the-fly by some special purpose module which will be part of the link adaptor hardware. Only sums will be reported to the NCU.

VII. CONCLUSION

We have described the basic components of the control layer of the PARIS Gb/s experimental network. The main conclusion is that in the new environment of high-speed integrated network fast links and switches are not enough to provide a satisfactory solution for the heterogeneous traffic demands. New methods and mechanisms should be developed to cope with the increased demand for fast call setup, reservation, and changes of call parameters. The PARIS solution consists of a set of distributed procedures which exploits the hardware routing mechanisms and algorithmic methods which accelerate the call control process and avoid excessive processing as much as possible. In particular, we have described efficient methods for updating distributed topology and utilization databases and for setup and maintenance of calls by the intermediate nodes.

Such schemes can also be employed by other high-speed networks such as ATM-based systems.

ACKNOWLEDGMENT

The authors would like to thank B. Awerbuch for helpful discussions.

APPENDIX
TOPOLOGY UPDATE ALGORITHM

In subsection A we describe the tree maintenance module assuming that the topology maintenance module ensures that nodes on a tree know eventually the topology of their tree, and neighboring edges. In subsection B we explain how this assumption is realized.

We use the graph representation of the network and refer to the actions of the NCU as being actions of nodes.

A. Tree Maintenance

For any link (v, u) the only node that can put it into the tree is its endpoint node v. (Node u does similarly for edge (u, v), so each edge has two entries in the tree description.) This is done by 1) updating the local topology map to show that this is a tree link; 2) putting the tree's label on the adaptor, in the switch (SS), so that the switch will know to forward update messages over it; and 3) notifying the other nodes so that they too can update the status of the link (to be "tree") in their local topology map. Tasks 2) and 3) are performed by generating a topology change (i.e., the edge changes from nontree status to tree status) which will be handled by the topology update protocol. A node w that gets a notification from the topology update protocol about an edge (u, v) becoming a tree edge updates its topology map. Similarly a topology update may be either the failure or the recovery of a link, or the fact that it has stopped being a tree link.

Note that when the tree is temporarily disconnected (e.g., due to a failure) it is actually a forest of node-disjoint trees, rather than a single tree. The protocol strives to make this forest into one tree that spans the whole (connected component of the) network.

The algorithm maintains each tree a rooted directed tree. Each node remembers which of its tree edges leads to its Parent (the parent is the neighbor node in the direction toward the root). The protocol keeps the values of these Parent variables

(in different nodes) consistent in the sense that if node v is the Parent of node u, then u is not the Parent of v. (The one exception is the time that a message from u is on its way to v to transfer the parenthood from u to v.) Each tree has a single node with no Parent. This node (whose Parent = nil) is the tree *root*. It coordinates the effort of the tree to merge with another tree. This merging is repeated whenever possible. Thus, if the network is stable for a reasonable amount of time all the trees in a connected component of it merge into one tree. (It has been estimated that in very large SNA networks, of few thousands nodes, a topological change will take place about every 1 hour.)

Using the forest description in its own database, a root r knows which nodes belong to its own tree. Using the topology database map root r can also find whether there is an edge connecting a node in its own tree to a node which is not a member of the same tree. Furthermore, we assume that each edge has a unique weight, known to both its endpoints. This can be achieved by using concatenation of the names of its endpoint nodes as the least significant part of the edge's name (a tie breaker in case that all other field are equal). The description of the more significant parts of the weight is deferred to Section A.1.1.

Let (k, j) be the edge with the lowest weight among those edges connecting root r's tree to a node not in this tree. (Call it the minimum *outgoing* edge.) If $k \neq r$, then the "rootship" (the state of being the root) is transferred to k hop-by-hop by sending root-change messages and changing the values of the Parent variables (the edge which leads to the root) in the nodes on the way from r to k. Note that during this transfer the minimum outgoing edge may change (by the failure of edge (k, j), or by the recovery of another edge). This is detected by the current root that transfers the rootship to the endpoint node of the new minimum edge.

When the root is the endpoint of the minimum outgoing edge (according to its local database), it negotiates merging with the tree on the other endpoint of the edge. For the merging it is required (similar to [16]) that both endpoints will be the roots of their trees, and that both will agree on the merging. (This is introduced in order to prevent entering cycles into the tree.) The root with the lower identity suggests the merging, and waits until the other endpoint agrees.

Similar to [2] this suggestion is canceled in the case that the edge fails. It may also be canceled when a lower weight edge recovers. In this case the suggesting root must first ask the other root whether the suggestion has already been accepted. If the other root has already agreed to the suggestion, then it is not canceled. Otherwise the suggestion is withdrawn, and the suggesting root is free to suggest a merge over another edge.

When both sides agree to the merge the topology update protocol is invoked (to exchange topology information between the nodes, and to notify about the new edge). Finally the trees are connected by having both sides put the edge in the forest as described above. The side with the higher identity (say j) remains a root, while the other, k, sets its Parent Variable to point at j.

Links Weights: Finally, let us say a few words on the weights of the links. A field in the weight that is more significant than the nodes names (according to a lexicographical order in which the link weights are compared) is the link's speed (faster links are assigned lower weights) in order to prefer fast links in the tree construction. Consider a node u that is an endpoint of a "heavy weight" link (u, v) (e.g., a T1 [19] or slower link) that learns (from the topology update) about the existence of a lower weight link that should replace link (u, v) in the tree. (We expect that the tree links will usually be SONET OC3 [3] and above.) Node u removes link (u, v) from the tree. This is a topology change. Thus the tree root learns about it (from the topology update protocol) and moves to mend the tree. Note that the better link will be put in the tree this time. In order to prevent excessive changes to the tree node u removes link (u, v) from the tree only if the difference between the weights of link (u, v) and the new link is above some predefined value.

Note that a link that goes up and down frequently will usually not disrupt the operation of the tree maintenance algorithm unless it is a candidate for a tree link. This may happen if the unstable link has a very small weight and therefore each time it recovers it is the best tree candidate. Such a phenomena can make the protocol repeat the same step again and again ignoring the failure of other links. (This is a case of *starvation*.) This is an unlikely case, since the detection of a link failure is rather slow [18]. Still it is prevented by including the reliability of the link as the most significant field in its weight. Each failure of a link increases its weight. Note that this weight may now not be consistent in the endpoints of the link as long as the link is disconnected. However, for our protocol only the weight of links that are *up* (not disconnected) matters. (When the link is brought up, its two endpoints, and hence their trees, agree on the weight. This is considered a topology change, and hence triggers a broadcast).

B. Topology Update

First let us assume that no messages are lost by the fast broadcast.

Each node v has a single counter (initially zero) Seq-No (nodal *sequence number*). Whenever v notices a topological change in one of v's edges (v, w) the value of Seq-No is incremented by 1. The topology update item generated includes the new description of the edge (up, down, tree...), and the new value of Seq-No. This item is broadcast over the tree that includes v.

Recall (subsection *A*) that when two trees merge their roots invoke the topology update protocol to exchange topology information. To reduce the traffic, they first exchange their Seq-No vectors. This vector contains the sequence number of the last topology (or utilization) update received from each node in the network including nodes which are not at that tree. Its value is updated with the reception of each update. Next, each side of the merged tree sends the other the utilization information the other missed. This is detected as follows. Assume one side has a value x as the last sequence number received from k and in the other side the value of the last sequence number received from k is y. Assume further that x is larger than y. The root of the first side will send to the root

of the second side all the utilization updates generated from node k with sequence numbers greater than y (up to x). The root of the second side will then broadcasts this information on its side of the new tree.

The hardware tree broadcast is much faster than the transfer of the rootship. Therefore, if a node receives a hardware broadcast and then is disconnected from a certain tree and later it is reconnected, the broadcast is already terminated and the node will not get the same message again. The sequence numbers exchange at the time of tree merging also cost at most one item exchange per each topology change.

Let us now consider the case that messages may be lost (because of congestion or link errors) during the hardware broadcast. We employ a backup mechanism that is "piggybacked" on the transmission of utilization updates (Section V-B). These updates also carry topological information. However, in order to guarantee prompt delivery with high probability, we need that such messages will be triggered at some minimum rate. It is very unlikely that a node will not have new utilization information to send about its link for a long time. (See Section V-B.) However, if this does happen, the node will send an update if a certain time has elapsed since its previous update. This guarantees a minimum periodic transmission rate.

So far we have ignored the possibility that a node fails and its Seq-No counter is erased. Since we use a nonvolatile memory for the sequence number counter this event is unlikely. However, in case it does happen, we have added a random number 64 bits field to the node's name. When a node recovers from a failure it chooses the value of this field at random. This will differ from the previous name with an overwhelming probability. Thus the new topology updates sent by this node will not be discarded by other nodes, even though they have small sequence numbers. A name that is no longer used will disappear, due to a slow time driven backup update and garbage collection protocol. This backup is used anyhow to let a node "forget" about another node from which it becomes disconnected forever. Similarly, a node that has not heard a utilization update of some edge for a long time, assumes that this edge is disconnected. (This backup protocol will actually recover also from the extremely unlikely case that the chosen node name is the same as the previous one.)

REFERENCES

[1] H. Ahmadi, J. S.-C. Chen, and R. Guerin, "Dynamic routing and call control in high-speed integrated networks," in *Proc. ITC-13 Workshop* Copenhagen, Denmark, June 1991, pp. 379–403.
[2] B. Awerbuch, I. Cidon, and S. Kutten, "Communication-optimal maintenance of replicated information," in *Proc. 31st Annu. Symp. Found. Comput. Sci.* St. Louis, MO, Oct. 1990, pp. 492–502.
[3] R. Ballart and Yau-Chau Ching, "Sonet: Now it's the standard optical network, *IEEE Commun. Mag.*, vol. 27, no. 3, pp. 8–15, Mar. 1989.
[4] K. Bala, I. Cidon, and K. Sohraby, "Congestion control for high-speed packet switched networks," in *Proc. INFOCOM'90*, June 1990.
[5] A. E. Baratz, J. P. Gray, P. E. Green Jr., J. M. Jaffe, and D. P. Pozefsky, "Sna networks of small systems," *IEEE J. Select. Areas Commun.*, vol. SAC-3, pp. 416–426, 1985.
[6] J. Le Boudec, "The asynchronous transfer mode: A tutorial," *Comput. Networks ISDN Syst.*, no. 24, pp. 279–309, 1992.
[7] I. Chlamtac, W. Franta, and K.D. Levin, "Bram: The broadcast recognizing access method," *IEEE Trans. Commun.*, vol. COM-27, pp. 1183–1190, 1979.

IEEE TRANSACTIONS ON COMMUNICATIONS, VOL. 43, NO. 5, MAY 1995

[8] I. Cidon and I. S. Gopal, "Paris: An approach to integrated high-speed private networks," *Int. J. Digital Analog Cabled Syst.*, vol. 1, no. 2, pp. 77–86, Apr.–June 1988.

[9] ——, "Control mechanisms in high speed networks," in *Proc. of ICC'90*, 1990.

[10] I. Cidon *et al.*, "The plaNET/ORBIT high-speed network," *J. High Speed Networks*, vol. 2, no. 3, pp. 171–208, 1993.

[11] I. Cidon, I. Gopal, G. Grover, and M. Sidi, "Real-time packet switching: A performance analysis," *IEEE J. Select. Areas Commun.*, vol. 6, pp. 1576–1586, Dec. 1988.

[12] I. Cidon, I. Gopal, and S. Kutten, "New models and algorithms for future networks," in *Proc. 7th ACM Symp. Princip. Distrib. Comput.*, Aug. 1988, pp. 74–89.

[13] I. Cidon, I. Gopal, and A. Segall, "Connection establishment in high speed networks," *IEEE/ACM Trans. Net.*, vol. 1, pp. 469–481, Aug. 1993.

[14] S. Even, *Graph Algorithms*. Rockville, MD: Computer Science, 1979.

[15] I. Gopal and R. Guerin, "Network transparency: The plaNET approach," *IEEE/ACM Trans. Net.*, vol. 2, pp. 226–239, June 1994.

[16] R. G. Gallager, P. A. Humblet, and P. M. Spira, "A distributed algorithm for minimum-weight spanning trees," *ACM Trans. Programming Lang. Syst.*, vol. 5, no. 1, Jan. 1983, pp. 66–77.

[17] M. R. Garey and D. S. Johnson, *Computers and Intractability*. New York: Freeman, 1979.

[18] A. Herzberg and S. Kutten, "Fast isolation of arbitrary forwarding-faults," in *Proc. 8th ACM PODC*, Aug. 1989.

[19] P. Kaiser, J. Midwinter, and S. Shimada, "Status and future trends in terrestrial opical fiber systems in North America, Europe, and Japan," *IEEE Commun. Mag.*, vol. 25, Oct. 1987.

[20] J. McQuillan, I. Richer, and E. Rosen, "The new routing algorithm for the arpanet," *IEEE Trans. Commun.*, vol. 28, pp. 711–719, May 1980.

[21] M. Sidi, W. Z. Liu, I. Cidon, and I. Gopal, "Congestion control through input rate regulation," *IEEE Trans. Commun.*, vol. 41, no. 3, pp. 471–476, March 1993.

[22] J. Turner, "New directions in communications, or which way to the information age?" *IEEE Commun. Mag.*, vol. 24, Oct. 1986.

Inder Gopal (S'81–M'82–SM'88–F'91) received the B.A. degree in engineering science from Oxford University, Oxford, England, in 1977, and the M.S. and Ph.D. degrees in electrical engineering from Columbia University, NY in 1978 and 1982, respectively.

Since 1982, he has been with the IBM Corporation serving in various technical and management positions. Currently, he is Division Director of Architecture in the Networked Applications Solutions Division. Previously, he was Manager of the Advanced Networking Lab at the T. J. Watson Research Center. In that capacity he was involved in the NSF/DARPA sponsored AURORA Gigabit testbed, and in several other research projects in the area of high-speed networking. His other research interests are in distributed algorithms, communication protocols, network security, high-speed packet switches, and multimedia communications. He has published extensively in these areas. He is an editor for the *Journal on High Speed Networking* and has previously served as an area editor for *Algorithmica*, guest editor for IEEE JOURNAL ON SELECTED AREAS IN COMMUNICATIONS, editor for Network Protocols for the IEEE TRANSACTIONS ON COMMUNICATIONS, and technical editor for *IEEE Communications Magazine*. He has served on several program committees for conferences and workshops.

Dr. Gopal has received an Outstanding Innovation Award from IBM for his work on the PARIS high-speed network.

Israel Cidon (M'85–SM'90) received the B.Sc. (summa cum laude) and the D.Sc. degrees from the Technion–Israel Institute of Technology in 1980 and 1984, respectively, both in electrical engineering. From 1984 to 1985, he was on the Faculty with the Electrical Engineering Department at the Technion. In 1985 he joined the IBM T. J. Watson Research Center, NY, where he was a Research Staff Member and a Manager of the Network Architectures and Algorithms group involved in various broadband networking projects. Recently, he joined Sun Microsystems Labs in Mountain View, CA, as Manager of High-Speed Networking working on various ATM projects including Openet—an open ATM network control platform. Since 1990 he is also with the Department of Electrical Engineering at the Technion. He currently serves as an editor for the IEEE/ACM TRANSACTIONS ON NETWORKS. Previously he served as the Editor for Network Algorithms for the IEEE TRANSACTIONS ON COMMUNICATIONS and as a guest editor for *Algorithmica*. In 1989 and 1993 he received the IBM Outstanding Innovation Award for his work on the PARIS high-speed network and topology update algorithms respectively. His research interests include high-speed wide and local area networks, distributed network algorithms, network performance and wireless networks.

Marc A. Kaplan received the B.A. degree from Cornell University in 1974, and the Ph.D. degree in electrical engineering and computer science from Princeton University in 1978.

He has held various Staff positions at the T. J. Watson Research Center since the summer of 1978, where he has designed and programmed file and security subsystems, operating system kernels, and communications systems. He architected, coded, and managed the software for the Paris/2-Planet-Orbit project. Currently, he is a Program Manager with IBM Networked Applications Services.

Shay Kutten (M'90) received the Master's degree (on scheduling of Radio Broadcasts) and the Ph.D. degree (on distributed algorithms) in computer science from the Technion, Israel in 1984 and 1987, respectively.

Since 1982 he has been with IBM T. J. Watson Research Center, as a Postdoctoral Fellow, as a Research Staff Member, and as the Manager of the Network Architecture and Algorithms Group. He has developed algorithms for network control, network security, and distributed processing control. He is also an editor in wireless networks and served on several program committees for conferences and workshops.

Dr. Kutten received an Outstanding Innovation Award in 1992, and a Supplemental Outstanding Innovation Award from IBM for his work on IBM BBNS high-speed network; an Outstanding Innovation Award (in 1994) from IBM for his work on NETSP Network Security Server, and an IBM Research Division Award for his work on IBM Samba Wireless LAN.

Real-Time Processing For Virtual Circuits In ATM Switching

C. Woodworth, S. Paul, and M. J. Karol

AT&T Bell Laboratories, Room 4F-503, 101 Crawfords Corner Rd., Holmdel, NJ 07733

clark@research.att.com, tel: 908-949-6362, fax: 908-949-9118

August 9, 1995

Abstract

In this paper, we propose adding real-time hardware primitives to packet switches, ATM in particular, to provide efficient support for inward multicasting similar to some of today's switches that support real-time multicast in the switch hardware. To implement this, we propose extending the lookup table used for routing by adding additional opcode and operand fields (or pointers to those fileds) into the routing table and by including ALU circuitry to process these fields and corresponding fields in the arriving cells. With the rapid capacity growth of todays RAM and the modest gate count required for ALUs, memory word widths can be extended with minimal additional chip count and the ALU can be a small addition in a header processing VLSI, thereby giving only a modest increase in complexity.

The benefit of including real-time processing in the switch is that it is now possible to solve the ACK implosion problem associated with high-speed reliable multicasting transport protocols. By keeping the primitives as general as possible, other applications can benefit from these real-time primitives.

1 Introduction

ATM switches can be classified into three categories: dumb switches, smart switches, and intelligent switches. Dumb switches perform basic switching functions and sometimes operate in the hundreds of Gb/s throughput region with multi-Gb/s port rates. However, they cannot support multicast or other special functions. Most commercially available ATM switches fall into this category. At the other extreme, intelligent switches have the complete programmability found in software-defined microprocessor-based switches. However, due to technological limitations, intelligent switches today cannot operate in real time, except for lower-throughput switches. Routers, most of which operate below 100 Mb/s, are one example of intelligent switches. In the smart switch category are the ATM switches that support multicast and broadcast. These switches can operate in the tens of Gb/s throughput region with port rates in the hundreds of Mb/s.

Today, there is a transition from dumb ATM switches toward smarter switches that support multicast[1], and a transition from intelligent router-like switches toward faster ATM switches that can support new high-bandwidth applications with quality-of-service requirements. Further, new TV distribution services are likely to accelerate the transition to smart switches [2]. In this paper, we extend and generalize smart switches to provide capabilities near that of intelligent switches with minimal throughput penalty. The limiting factor will be the maximum port speed. Specifically, we propose the addition of real-time state and combinatorial logic to the ATM-layer hardware, so that ATM switches provide general-purpose primitives to support efficiently a variety of applications including signaling, maintenance, wireless, games, software distribution, synchronization, telemetry, and computing. To make this more concrete, we briefly give one example, efficient multicast transport, of how a logic primitive can be used to support an important higher-level capability. This example will be covered in more detail in a later section.

Typically, on multicasting switches, hardware integral to the switch efficiently duplicates packets at several destination ports and, for some switches, even on different VCIs on the same port. Unfortunately, the promise of multicast cannot be fully and efficiently realized for many traditional computer-based applications until the "acknowledgment (ACK) problem" is solved. Achieving reliable delivery (which is a fundamental requirement for many applications) in a multicasting environment typically requires the source to process the ACKs for a potentially large number of destinations, resulting in "ACK implosion" and inefficiency [3].

Protocols have been proposed at higher layers, including transport [Concast] through application levels, that provide processing to support a "combine function" in which ACKs, for example, are combined logically before being passed to the source application. Typically, the combine would be located at the branches along the multicast tree so that the source would not be inundated with messages.

We propose bringing the logical combine function down to the ATM hardware level and placing it within the switch VLSIs. By associating the combine function within the multicasting switches, it can be applied at the branches of the multicast tree where it will be most effective. Implementation in hardware allows high throughput and low delay by processing the cells in real time. Depending on the design, the cost is table lookup memory, to hold the state, plus some combinatorial logic.

While combine functions have their roots in higher-layer protocols and multicast has its roots in the ATM-layer hardware, we bring these complementary ideas together in ATM-layer hardware. We also generalize the functions into a set of simple primitives that can be implemented in real-time. Although the penalty for working at the ATM layer is no cell-loss protection and the cell-length and hardware technology limitations, the big benefit is efficiency.

In the next section, we show how to implement the primitives in hardware, and how to resolve issues including cell synchronization, cell loss and cell duplication, and we show some hardware design options that trade off speed with memory requirements. The next section details a proposed instruction set and some options. To show the utility of these primitives, we show a reliable multicasting transport layer can be supported, and then we close with a summary.

Reprinted from IEEE Globecom Conference Proceedings, 1995, pp. 1712-1718.

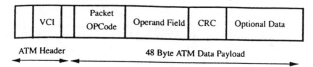

ATM Switch-Instruction Cell Format

	VCI	Packet OPCode	Operand Field	CRC	Optional Data

ATM Header ◄──────► 48 Byte ATM Data Payload ◄──────────────────►

Figure 1: Cell Format

2 Cell-Based ALU Computational Hardware

In order to access switch primitives, we assume higher-layer protocols in the end system have access to the raw ATM layer. The cells using these primitive services in the switch will have the special format given in Figure 1. The data portion of the cell contains an opcode field, an operand field, a CRC field, and an optional data (comment) field. The opcode specifies the operation to be performed while the operand field may contain one or more pieces of data that may enter the computation. The CRC is provided because there is no error protection at the ATM level. A simple CRC calculation is performed over the opcode and operand before completing the calculation. The function is aborted with no change when a CRC error is detected. Cell losses are handled at a higher level and will be discussed later.

Figure 2 shows the high-level hardware architecture. The CRC hardware is not shown in the figure. Based on the control word (described in more detail shortly), the state stored in the lookup table, and the operand field of the packet, a computation is performed and zero, one or both the state table and the operand field in the outgoing packet is updated with the result. In addition, the ALU sets flags based on the results of the computation, and depending on the flag control word, the exiting cell may be deleted or updated with the result and the result can also be saved in the operand portion of the state table. Typical functions include counting, addition, AND, OR, and other specialized functions detailed further in the section on instructions.

The opcode can come from two sources: the opcode portion of the lookup table or the opcode field of the received cell. Signaling software is used to update the opcode in the lookup table while the virtual-channel user inserts the cell opcode. The opcode control circuitry uses the lookup table opcode or additional permission bits from the lookup table to select which opcodes will be accepted from the cell or whether only the opcodes from the lookup table will be used. Once the opcode source has been selected, it generates the control word that selects the ALU operation and flag control function. VCI information may also used to modify the opcode function and the arrival state bits as described in a later subsection.

The Routing and Quality of Service (QoS) fields of the lookup table are used in the traditional fashion in the ATM switch to route and schedule the cell at the appropriate output port of the switch. The translation of the VCI field occurs in the output section of the line card of the switch.

2.1 Unary VCI Combine Functions

The hardware described above can be used to compute functions over cells in a single VCI stream or over cells from multiple VCI streams. In this section, we describe functions computed over a single VCI. Multiple VCIs will be covered in the next section.

When doing unary VCI functions, the operands from one or more

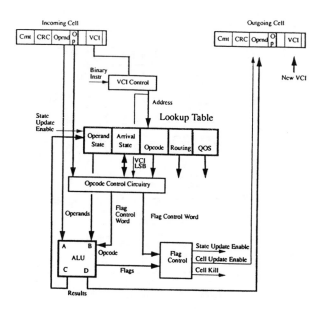

Figure 2: Hardware Architecture

cells are used to compute a result. Although some steps can be combined or eliminated, typically there are three steps: initialization, computation, and retrieving the result. The initialization can be performed at call setup by the signaling software or through cell opcodes, and the initialization is usually a copy of the operand field of the cell to the operand field in the lookup table so that it is set to a known value.

Next, the computation is performed by sending one or more cells to the switch with suitable opcodes and operands. The results of the operations are accumulated in the operand field of the lookup table. Finally, the result accumulated in the operand field of the state table can be copied to the output cell and sent to its destination. Alternatively, the result of each intermediate and the final calculation can be forwarded to the destination during each computation, thereby eliminating the last step.

For example, suppose there are a dozen nodes that must perform maintenance functions (e.g., distribution of table or software updates) under the control of a network manager. The manager establishes VCI A from each node to a switch and continues the inverse multicast connection from the switch to itself. It also establishes a connection from itself to the switch on VCI A, which it uses to initialize the operand state to 0. On a separate VCI it multicasts the command to have the nodes perform the first maintenance step of the function. On completion, the nodes send a cell on VCI A with the OR opcode and with an operand containing a unary representation of their station id (e.g. station zero sets bit zero, station one sets bit one). After a suitable time period, the manager sends an opcode on VCI A to copy the result to the output cell, which it then receives and uses to verify that all stations have completed the maintenance function. It can then take action for any stations that failed to respond, and it can then continue with the next maintenance function.

2.2 Binary VCI Combine Functions

The hardware described above can also be used to compute functions over multiple VCI streams. We begin describing computation over binary streams in this subsection. Multiple combines can also be

1713

115

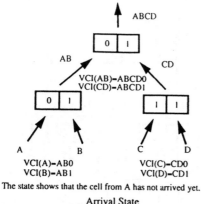

The state shows that the cell from A has not arrived yet.

Arrival State

Key to boxes	Set If VCI LSB Is 0	Set If VCI LSB Is 1

Figure 3: Hierarchical Combine

handled directly in hardware wiht only a modest increase in complexity.

2.2.1 Hierarchical Combine Functions

To support arbitrary numbers of VCIs in a combine function, it is sufficient to support computation over two streams since larger numbers of streams can be combined using computations on pairs of VCIs and then combined in a hierarchical fashion as shown in Figure 3. Cells from stations A and B are combined to form cell stream AB, cells from stations C and D are combined to form cell stream CD, and cells AB and CD are combined to form cell stream ABCD. We let the symbols A, AB, etc, refer to either the stations or the combined results or to the VCI of the stream, depending on context.

2.2.2 Obtaining Uniqueness Over Multiple VCIs

To compute a function over more than one VCI, exactly one cell from each VCI is needed. While cells from both A and B are needed to compute the result AB, A and B will arrive sequentially either A, B or B, A. As a result, the first arrival must be stored in the state memory and the cell deleted from the output, pending the second arrival. On the second arrival, the logic function can be computed from both the state table and the operand field of the second cell and the result copied back into the outgoing cell.

Care must be taken to prevent an A, A arrival from triggering the outgoing cell. Instead of simply counting, we use a technique to ensure uniqueness (one cell from each station). We assume that VCI A + 1 = VCI B and that during call setup, the ALU is enabled for these two VCIs. The ALU operation causes both the A and the B lookup to access the same state table by ignoring the VCI LSB. The LSB instead is used to update a separate two-bit state field on an arrival. Either *neither* cell has arrived 0,0, *one* cell has arrived from A 1,0 or from B 0,1, or *both* cells have arrived 1,1. When both cells have arrived, the system either disables itself staying in state 1,1 after issuing the combined result, or it issues the result and clears itself to state 0,0 waiting for the next operation. If the system disables itself in the 1,1 state, a separate instruction must be issued (multicast if a hierarchy) to reset the state to 0,0 for the next operation.

If assigning adjacent VCIs is impossible for the call-setup software, common VCIs can be used and a separate bit in the data field used as the least significant VCI bit described next. Alternatively, a level of indirection can be added to the operand field, eliminating any special requirements on the VCI relationship (at perhaps a speed penalty).

2.2.3 Handling Duplicate And Lost Cells

Potentially, we can get two As before the first B cell arrives. Either we can replace the stored A state with the new A' cell information or we can drop the cell. The correct choice depends on the application.

Lost cells must be handled through proper design at higher layers and must be considered since the ATM layer does not guarantee cell delivery. In the earlier maintenance-function example, the application could recover gracefully through timeouts in the network manager. Note that while it would be fairly difficult to add timeouts that would spark a cell transmission from the ALU switch hardware, any source in the connection can easily send probe or timeout cells to achieve a similar result.

3 General Computational Instruction Set

In this section, we will list a proposed instruction set for a smart switch. The instruction operations and a summary of their actions are listed in table 1. The notation S is the contents of the state operand field stored for this VCI. The notation I is the contents of the immediate operand field following the instruction opcode in the cell. The destination of these operations will be discussed shortly. All arithmetic operations set flag bits that can participate in conditional operations. The SOP opcode specifies that the opcode inserted into the opcode portion of the state table be used instead of a cell-based opcode. The operands can be either integer (int) or unsigned integer (uint).

The arithmetic operations above can be used to combine the contents of two cells from different VCIs to form a result. This is called BINARY mode. BINARY mode operation requires that the information from each cell arrive at the same time and be combined. It is nearly impossible to synchronize two sources so that their cells arrive at the switch at the same time. Thus, to accomplish synchronization, the state from the cell that arrives first is stored in S while the second arrival causes the computation using the stored value S and the immediate value I from the operand field of the cell. There are state bits that track the arrival state of the connections. These states are listed in table 2.

In the BINARY mode, the opcode functions can be modified by control bits (These can be part of the opcode in the incoming cell or can be saved into part of the state register by the signaling software or by a CPY instruction.) One bit determines the disposition of a second cell arrival on one input when the second input has not received a cell yet (e.g., state A_ARRIVED or B_ARRIVED). The duplicate cell can either update S or it can be dropped.

Second, on the arrival of the cell for each input, the arrival state can automatically switch from the BOTH_ARRIVED state to NEITHER state allowing the next round of BINARY combination to occur or it can stay in the BOTH_ARRIVED state until a RSTAS instruction is received and the arrival states are reset. This allows for end-point synchronization. The modifications are shown in table 3.

When the ALU is not used in BINARY mode, the result of the operation can be specified to either update or not update the state table. This specification could also be carried as part of the opcode field. In

1714

116

Opcode	Comments
CPYS	Copy State (S)
CPYI	Copy Immediate (I)
AND	Bitwise binary AND (uint S & uint I)
OR	Bitwise binary OR (uint S | uint I)
XOR	Bitwise binary XOR (uint S ^ uint I)
MINU	Minimum of unsigned (MIN(unit S, uint I)
MINS	Minimum of signed (MIN(int S, int I)
MAXU	Maximum of unsigned (MAX(unit S, uint I)
MAXS	Maximum of signed (MAX(int S, int I)
WAND	Windowed AND
WOR	Windowed OR
RSTAS	Reset arrival state
CPYAS	Set arrival state and copy arrival state to output if both arrived
ADDS	Signed 2s complement add (int S + int I)
ADDU	Unsigned add (uint S + uint I)
SUBS	Signed 2s complement subtract (int S - int I)
SUBU	Unsigned subtract (uint S - uint I)
MULU	Unsigned multiply (uint S * uint I)
MULS	Signed multiply (int S * int I)
DIVU	Unsigned divide (uint S / uint I)
DIVS	Signed divide (int S / int I)
SOP	Use default state opcode
INC	Increment state (uint S <- uint S + 1)
CPYSP	Copy permissions and status

Table 1: Instruction Set

Binary Arrival States	Comments
NEITHER	No cells have arrived on either input VCI
A_ARRIVED	A cell has arrived on the first VCI but not the second
B_ARRIVED	A cell has arrived on the second VCI but not the first
BOTH_ARRIVED	Both input cells have arrived

Table 2: Arrival States In Binary Mode

Binary Mode Opcode Variations	Comments
DROP_DUP	Drop duplicate cells after first arrival
ACCEPT_DUP	Latter arrivals update state
AUTOCLR	Automatically clear arrival state on second input arrival
MANUALCLR	Manually reset (RSTAS) arrival state for next binary operation

Table 3: Binary Duplicate And Auto Clear Modes

State Table Update Mode	Comments
UPDATE	Result is copied to State Table (S)
NOUPDATE	State Table Maintains Previous Value
BINARY	First Input Loads State Table (Selected by output cell mode)

Table 4: State Table Control Modes

Output Cell Mode	Comments
UPDATE	Result is copied to the output cell(S)
BINARY	Second input cell and state update output cell
DELETE	No cell is output
DEL_ZERO	Delete cell if result is zero else update and send
DEL_NZ	Delete cell if result is non-zero
DEL_NEG	Delete cell if result is negative
DEL_NOVF	Delete cell if no overflow
DEL_POS	Delete cell if result positive

Table 5: Output Cell Control Modes

BINARY mode, the state table must be loaded on the first arrival and will be overwritten in later rounds. BINARY mode is selected by the output mode, thus only a single bit is needed to encode the update modes listed in the table 4.

Additional bits in the opcode field can specify whether the operation is in the BINARY mode and determine whether an output cell is generated. Based on the result of flags from arithmetic operations, an output cell can be conditionally generated with the result. These modes are specified in table refOutputControl.

For security reasons, it may be important to limit the use of arbitrary opcodes and allow only cell operand data to be supplied. In this case, the signaling channel can store an opcode into the state memory. The security state can be set through the signaling channel as in table 6. When packet opcodes are permitted, the state opcode instruction (SOP) selects the default opcode. When packet opcodes are not allowed, the opcode field is ignored and the opcode stored in the state table is always used. For the INC instruction, none of the fields of the cell are used if packet opcodes are disabled. Thus, it can be used as a packet counter that could be useful for billing by deleting the output cell except on overflow.

At this point, it is not known whether all of the opcodes or modes be given above will be useful or whether other additional opcodes or modes will prove critical to certain applications. Only experience and time can provide these answers. Several additions under consideration include instructions for (1) Other conditional operations, (2) Logical and arithmetic shift instructions, (3) Floating point support, (4) Billing support instructions, (5) A binary mode instruction that concatenates subfields of the two operands.

Permissions	Comments
ALLOWPACKETOPS	Packets opcodes are enabled
NOPACKETOPS	Packet opcodes are disabled and only signaling opcodes allowed

Table 6: Permissions

4 Applications of the ALU Technique

We will further clarify the idea of cell-based ALU computation by way of an examples drawn from the transport protocol area. Protocols are as natural a use of the cell-based computation as number crunching has been to mainframes. But, much as mainframes support databases, games, graphics and interactive computing (though this was not recognized initially), we believe that these network ALU units may prove to be of very general utility as hinted at by the example in section 2.1. We believe that one of the most important initial applications of these primitives will be in the support of reliable multicasting protocols, and we examine this in detail next.

4.1 Reliable Multicast Transport Protocol Example

Providing efficient and reliable transport in a high-speed multicast environment will be a challenge in emerging networks, and several promising techniques have been proposed. [5] [6] The combination of selective retransmission and periodic transmission of the receiver state has been proposed as a high-speed transport-layer protocol [7], and this work has been extended to the multicast environment. [8] To solve the ACK implosion problem, a hierarchy of local processing nodes perform the combine function. In one scenario in the reference, the switch provides the combine function. Here we extend that idea by providing real-time switch-level primitives to complement the combine function and to avoid the need to go up and back down the protocol stack at the intermediate combining switch centers. We use the protocol referenced above as our example.

A hierarchical combine tree is established at call setup time to transmit the ACKs from the receivers to the switch ALU units where they are combined pairwise using a binary combine function (section 2.2.1) until eventually a single summary cell is available for transmission to the source.

4.1.1 ACK Tree Setup And Duplicate Cells

We begin by addressing the issue of uniqueness and duplicate cells over the pair of VCIs. In other words, how do we handle multiple cells from a single VCI and synchronize their pairwise combination? One feature of this protocol is that the ACK state information is transmitted independently and periodically by each of the multicast receivers. As a result of the independence, no special synchronization is needed between the ACK streams and we can use the self-clearing binary mode (section 2.2.2) where the ALU resets itself for the next cell from each input VCI as soon as it has computed and sent the current result from the two most recent pairs. This allows us to keep the pipeline full and avoid the need to reset the state of the tree after each ACK. Because the transmissions of state information from each source are independent but at nominally the same rate, we update the stored state with the more recent state whenever duplicate cells arrive on a given input port. (Section 2.2.3). This enters the most current status of the ACK state into the computation.

4.1.2 Handling Lost Cells

In addition to handling duplicate cells, there is the possibility that one of the cells from a source is lost because of a bit error or, more likely, because of congestion. This must be handled at a higher level. In this case, the combined result never gets transmitted to the source until the next period when the periodic status from the missing cell finally

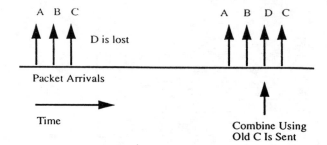

Figure 4: Cell Skew On Loss

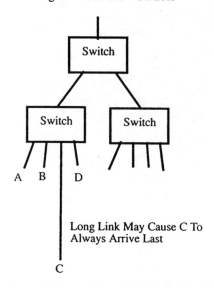

Figure 5: Example Of A Long Fixed Delay

gets retransmitted completing the arguments for the combine function. This will cause a time skew in the combined status information to the source (see Figure 4). If A, B, and C arrive and D is lost, no combined cell is generated. Later, if the cells from the subsequent periodic transmission arrive in the sequence A, B, D, C, then the result ABCD will be generated following the arrival of D using the *old* status of C. This means that the *new* status from C will not be looked at until the next combine function. Further, if C is always last, perhaps because it has the longest path, as in Figure 5, then its status will always be late by one periodic status interval.

In this protocol, this is acceptable since there are many periodic status transmissions in one round-trip window and since duplicate arrivals from the same station simply update the state. In this protocol, each receiver periodically transmits its state based on its own clock. Therefore, although periodic transmissions may all occur at a nominal rate, they are not synchronized and the phases of their transmissions will slide through each other. Thus, any skews built up as a result of a lost cell as outlined above will quickly dissipate and status updates will remain within a few periodic transmission intervals of each other.

4.1.3 Synchronization and Lost Detection

Other protocols may prefer to detect missing cells from a combine function. A source can initiate, with a multicast, the transition from the disabled 1,1 state to the enabled 0,0 state while notifying each

1716

118

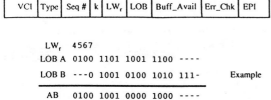

VCI	Type	Seq #	k	LW_r	LOB	Buff_Avail	Err_Chk	EPI

```
LW_r   4567
LOB A  0100 1101 1001 1100 ----
LOB B  ---0 1001 0100 1010 111-      Example
------------------------------------------------
AB     0100 1001 0000 1000 ----
```

Figure 6: Status Packet Format From Reference [7]

VCI	Type	Seq #	k	Win#	LOB	Buff_Avail	Err_Chk	EPI

```
Win#    1    2    3    4
LOB A 0100 1101 1001 1100 ----
LOB B 1110 1001 0100 1010 111-       Example
------------------------------------------------
AB    0100 1001 0000 1000 ----
```

Figure 7: Modified Status Packet Showing Window Number

station with the comment field of the same cell to transmit their status. The source station can quickly detect cell loss when the combine packet doesn't arrive in a specified period of time. As previously mentioned, only limited pipelining can be achieved using this method making its use with long round trip delays slower than the method outlined above.

4.1.4 High-Speed Protocol Background

Continuing with our protocol example, Figure 6 shows the format of the status packet that is periodically broadcast from each multicast destination. We next focus on and describe only the Buff_Avail field, the LOB field, and the LW_r field, and how they are used. The other fields can be treated as comments with respect to the computation and combine functions in the ATM switches. The Buff_Avail field is transmitted by each destination. (Here, the destination refers to the destination of the original data packet, and these multicast destinations are actually the source of the status packets to be combined and sent to the source of the original data packet.) The source needs the minimum of this field over all destinations so that it can prevent buffer overrun. The LOB field is a bitmap of the data blocks successfully received at the destination sending this status cell, while LW_r gives the block number of the LSB of the LOB field. In other words, it anchors the bitmap and gives the first block number not yet successfully received. The source uses this information to determine which blocks to selectively retransmit and to adjust its transmission rate. The multicast branches must combine the LOB bitmaps so that it has the AND (assuming 0 represents "not received" and 1 represents "received") of each of the LOBs properly shifted so that the bit maps are aligned so that the first bit of each LOB has the same block number. Variations on the protocol use the OR function instead.

4.1.5 Implementing The Status Packet Combine Using Hardware Primitives

Since an ATM cell is small and the operand field that can participate in the combine function is only a few bytes, we separate each field that is independent into separate streams. Since the Buff_Avail field is logically independent of the LOB combine function, Buff_Avail cells travel on a VCI separate from the LOB combine function. (In other protocol examples where suitable coordination in time exists, this can be relaxed and the same VCIs can be used for multiple combines.) The LOB field is not independent of the LW_r and we will discuss how to handle this case shortly.

4.1.6 Buff_Avail Field Combine Function Using ATM Primitives

The ALU hardware described earlier can be used to compute the *min* function over all status cells from the destinations. Using the hierar-

chical tree discussed above, each destination transmits its Buff_Avail field as an operand. The first arrival of each pair gets stored in the switch state table while the second packet causes the minimum of the stored and received operand to be transmitted to the next level in the tree. The source will receive the minimum over all destinations.

4.1.7 Combining LOB and LW_r Over All Destinations

As mentioned above, the LW_r and LOB fields are not independent and must be transmitted together. In fact, LW_r indicates the starting position of the list of outstanding blocks (LOB). For example, if LW_r is 123 and LOB = 01011100, it means that blocks 123, 125, 129 and 130 have not been received, where the bitmap in LOB corresponds to increasing block numbers from left to right. Thus, if there are two status messages (with different LW_rs), the LOBs need to be aligned by shifting one of them as many positions to the left (or right if the LOBs need to be ORed) as the difference between the LW_rs. This functionality of *combining* the LOBs can be achieved in hardware as follows. First of all, the ALU operand fields and opcodes need to be extended to handle large multi-field operands. The opcode function needed to handle this *combine* function would require subtracting the two LW_r fields and shifting the LOB fields until they match. Then, the LOB fields would have to be ANDed.[1] The result of ANDing would be sent along with the smaller of the two LW_r fields. But this could become too hardware intensive. In order to reduce the hardware complexity, we propose a simple modification of the combine function of the protocol without affecting its correct operation.

As is obvious from the above description of the combine function, the LOBs must be *aligned* before ANDing in order that the corresponding bits in the two LOBs refer to the status of the same block. We align the LOBs in a different way as described in Figure 7. We divide the LOB into smaller chunks of equal size, which we call *windows*. For example, if the LOB is 64 bits and a window is 4 bits, there are 16 windows. We denote by Win#, the first window in a LOB. Thus, LW_r is effectively replaced with the window number, Win#. Using Win# results in an integer representation requiring less bits than LW_r. Now, instead of transmitting LW_r and LOBs starting from the LW_r, we transmit Win# and LOB blocks with fixed boundaries. Note that two status messages can have the same Win# but not necessarily the same LW_r. In fact, if the window size is Δ, the LW_rs in the two status messages may vary by as much as Δ - 1 but still have the same Win#. Thus, if there are two status messages with the same Win# (but different LW_rs), the LOBs can be *directly* ANDed *without any shifting*, which would be necessary if the alignment were done based on LW_rs as in the original protocol. The detailed *combine* function under this new scheme is described next. Each destination is expected to transmit the Win# and the bitmap of the corresponding window in each cell. When

---

[1] We consider the case of ANDing to keep the description simple, although similar description holds true for ORing as well.

one window on the LOB bitmap is completed (all 1s), the destination advances to and transmits the next window. The *combine opcode* first compares the Win#s and the LOB of the smaller one is copied to the result cell. If the Win#s are equal, then the Win# and the AND of the two LOBs are copied to the result cell. A simple example will clarify the above ideas. Suppose the size of LOB is 16, the size of a window is 4, LW_rs for two destinations A and B are 4 and 7, respectively, and the LOBs for A and B are, respectively, 0100 1101 1001 1100 and 0 1001 0100 1010 111. In short, A gives the LOB for blocks between 4 and 19 and B gives the LOB for blocks between 7 and 22. If we combine them using the *original protocol*, LOB of B would be aligned with that of A by shifting its LOB 3 bits to the right and then ANDed to produce 0100 1001 0000 1000 and the combined LW_r would be 4 (minimum of the two LW_rs). In our *new* scheme, Win# for both A and B is 1 (since Win# 0 extends from 0 - 3 and Win# 1 corresponds to blocks 4 - 7) and the LOB transmitted would be 0100 1101 1001 1100 and 1110 1001 0100 1010, respectively (notice that the three left-most bits of the LOB of B are 1s, indicating that B has received blocks 4, 5, and 6). Since the Win# is the same, the combine function will simply AND the bitmaps, resulting in 0100 1001 0000 1000, which is exactly the same as in the original protocol. The combined Win# will be 1 (same as the combined LW_r, which is 4). However, the *new* scheme will produce slightly worse results if the LW_rs of A and B belong to different windows. For example, if the LW_rs of A and B are 7 (Win# = 1) and 9 (Win# = 2), respectively, then the original protocol will produce a combined LOB starting from combined LW_r = 7 (the minimum of the two LW_rs), while the new scheme will produce a combined LOB starting from Win# = 1 (minimum of the two Win#s). However, Win# = 1 corresponds to LW_r = 4 and thus the combined LOB obtained by the new scheme contains some stale results.

4.2 Other Protocols and Timeouts

In the previous section, we showed how hardware ALU functions could support a high-performance, high-speed, multicast transport-layer protocol. This protocol required the support of a special opcode to handle the dependency of the Win# and LOB fileds. In general, many protocols can be handled by general-purpose primitives like MAX, MIN, OR, AND, SUM, INC, etc. The Buff_Avail example given above is a prime example. Standard go-back-N protocols are easily implemented using the MIN function on the last-received packet number. Retransmissions among local destinations as described in the extensions above also apply to go-back-N protocols in addition to selective repeat.

Other protocols sometimes require synchronization or timeouts. Timeouts can be implemented at the source station. After a predefined time, the source can transmit a packet to flush the state of a combine up to that time. In other words, we push the timing function back onto a host connected to the network. This is because it may not be practical to maintain timers for each VCI at the switch and to invoke operations including packet transmissions upon expiration of the timer.[2] Instead, the host at the root of a multicast tree can maintain a timer and trigger events in the switch by sending a cell with a suitable opcode and VCI to the switch to flush the state by causing the switch to issue a cell computed from the saved state. This is useful for counting the packet arrivals in an interval, for example.

---

[2] Although it is possible to have, for example, a state machine cycle through all of the state memory space testing or decrementing locations marked as timed. In some architectures it may not be unreasonable to queue a cell for transmission. However, the ALU or other logic would have to generate the CRC and pad out the cell while handling all current traffic.

5 Summary

We have proposed extending the memory in the VCI lookup table and adding arithmetic logic unit (ALU) functionality to the header processing circuitry to support an ATM instruction set. We have shown how this can be used to support a high-speed reliable multicast transport protocol. Based on additional work beyond the scope of this document, we believe that the general purpose instruction set can also support applications and services including: (1) The combine function to complement multicast, (2) Synchronization, (3) Efficient cell-based billing, (4) OA&M, (5) Computation.

We proposed a set of instructions that we believe are useful for these applications and are reasonable to implement. There is a tradeoff of the instruction complexity and the need to compute the result in real time to preserve the advantages of hardware implementation. Thus, instruction set complexity must be considered carefully.

Although hardware implementation at the ATM layer has the disadvantage of needing to handle cell loss (payloads are protected with a CRC and discarded if bad) at a higher layer, we have shown how applications can gracefully handle cell losses without significant penalties. Also, from the applications, we found that synchronization is a key consideration and must be considered in the instruction set. The BINARY or extended N-ARY instruction mode provides this capability for multiple cell streams by synchronizing operands and computing functions over multiple virtual circuit streams.

Finally, although discussed in the context of ATM, these techniques are equally suitable for implementation on many non-ATM packet switches.

References

[1] Session 3a Multicast Switch Architecture and Session 7a Network Multicast Routing, proceedings from IEEE INFOCOM '94, Toronto, Ontario, Canada, June 12-16 1994, pp 290, 840.

[2] Fred A. Joyce, "Telephone and Cable TV: Two Industries or One?", Convergence 93, Chilton Publications, 600 South Cherry Street, Suite 400, Devner, CO 80222, pp 30.

[3] Bala Rajagopalan, "Reliability and Scaling Issues in Multicast Communication," Proceedings of the ACM SIGCOMM, August 1992, pp. 188-198.

[4] B. Rajagopalan, A Mechanism for Scalable Concast Communication, 51352-921119-01TM

[5] W. Doeringer, D, Dykeman, M. Kaiserswerth, B. Meister, H. Rudin and R. Williamson, "A Survey of light-weight transport protocols for high-speed networks," IEEE Transactions on Communication, Nov. 1990.

[6] T. F. La Porta and M. Schwartz, "Architectures, Features and Implementation of High Speed Transport Protocols," IEEE Network magazine, May 1991.

[7] A. N. Netravali, W. D. Roome and K. K. Sabnani, "Design and Implementation of a High Speed Transport Protocol," IEEE Transactions on Communications, Vol.38. No.11, November 1990.

[8] S. Paul, K. K. Sabnani and D. M. Kristol, "Multicast Transport Protocols for High Speed Networks," proceedings of International Conference on Network Protocols, Boston, Massachusetts. October 25-28, 1994, pp. 4-14.

Design and Analysis of a Large-Scale Multicast Output Buffered ATM Switch

H. Jonathan Chao, *Member, IEEE*, and Byeong-Seog Choe

Abstract—We propose and analyze a recursive modular architecture for implementing a large-scale multicast output buffered ATM switch (MOBAS). A multicast knockout principle, an extension of the generalized knockout principle, is applied in constructing the MOBAS in order to reduce the hardware complexity (e.g., the number of switch elements and interconnection wires) by almost one order of magnitude. In our proposed switch architecture, four major functions of designing a multicast switch: cell replication, cell routing, cell contention resolution, and cell addressing, are all performed distributively so that a large switch size is achievable. The architecture of the MOBAS has a regular and uniform structure and, thus, has the advantages of: 1) easy expansion due to the modular structure, 2) high integration density for VLSI implementation, 3) relaxed synchronization for data and clock signals, and 4) building the center switch fabric (i.e., the multicast grouping network) with a single type of chip. A two-stage structure of the multicast output buffered ATM switch (MOBAS) is described. The performance of the switch fabric in cell loss probability is analyzed, and the numerical results are shown. We show that a switch designed to meet the performance requirement for unicast calls will also satisfy multicast calls' performance. A 16×16 ATM crosspoint switch chip based on the proposed architecture has been implemented using CMOS 2-μm technology and tested to operate correctly.

I. INTRODUCTION

BROADBAND INTEGRATED SERVICES digital networks (B-ISDN's) are expected to provide efficient and reliable end-to-end transport for various services. The asynchronous transfer mode (ATM) technique [1] has been standardized and widely accepted as a basis for transporting and switching user's traffic in emerging broadband networks, where user's information is packetized and carried in fixed length *cells* (53 bytes). Recently, many ATM switch architectures have been proposed for point-to-point and/or multicast switching [2], [3].

In the point-to-point switch design, cell-routing and output port contention resolution are the two major issues for implementing a fast packet switch fabric. Preferably, both functions should be performed in a distributed way so that no centralized cell processing will cause a bottleneck to limit the switch size. The output port contention can be resolved by placing buffers at input ports, internal stages, or output ports of the switch.

Manuscript received August 17, 1994; revised November 14, 1994; approved by IEEE/ACM TRANSACTIONS ON NETWORKING Editor J. Turner. This work was supported by NSF under Grant NCR-9216287. This paper was presented in part at the IEEE Proc. GLOBECOM'93 and INFOCOM'94.

H. J. Chao is with Polytechnic University, Brooklyn, NY 11201 USA (e-mail: chao@antioch.poly.edu).

B.-S. Choe is with Myong-Ji University, Yong-In, Korea (e-mail: bchoe@wh.myongji.ac.kr).

IEEE Log Number 9409110.

For the multicast switch design, three more issues need to be considered: 1) how to replicate cells, 2) how to address the multicast cells, and 3) how to reduce the translation table complexity.

Among these three issues, multicast addressing is a fundamental and challenging problem since there are 2^N multicast patterns for N destinations, while there are only N unicast patterns for point-to-point communication. In order to distinguish multicast patterns, at least $N(= \log_2 2^N)$ bits information is needed, while for unicasting the required routing information is $\log_2 N$ b long. There are three possible schemes for multicast addressing. The first one is to carry the addresses of all output ports in the cell header. The second one is to carry a multicast pattern that is a bit map of all output ports; each bit indicates if the cell is to be accepted at the associated output port. The third scheme often applied to a nonself-routing network uses indirect addressing via a multicast identification that is translated into a bit map of output ports involved in the multicast. The first scheme results in a variable-length header and is not desirable for implementing an ATM switch because of high hardware complexity. All three schemes have a potential problem of having a long cell header for a large switch size, resulting in a higher operation speed required in the switch fabric.

The architectures that have been proposed for multicast ATM switches can be classified into two categories based on their cell-replication methods: 1) multicast tree type [4]–[7], and 2) broadcast type [8]–[13] as shown in Fig. 1(a) and (b), respectively. The switches in the first type create a multicast tree in a binary network, such as a banyan or omega network, to replicate cells. They consist of a multicast tree network (often called a copy network) and a routing network, solving the multicast addressing problem by separating cell-replication function from cell-routing function. The copy network uses $O(\log_2 N)$ bits information (copy request number [4], [7] or address intervals [6]) for cell-replication, and the routing network uses $O(\log_2 N)$ bits information (destination address) for routing each copy of multicast cells.

A bit map addressing scheme can be employed for the multicast switches that use a broadcast medium for cell-replication. If a multiple-stage structure is applied to implement the broadcast-typed multicast switches, the number of addressing bits is reduced from $O(N)$ to $O(\sqrt[n]{N})$, where n is the number of stages.

The architectures proposed in [4], [5] use internal buffers at every stage to resolve internal blocking caused by the contention among replicated cells and thus tends to have a

Reprinted from IEEE/ACM Transactions on Networking, Vol. 3, No. 2, April 1995, pp. 126-138.

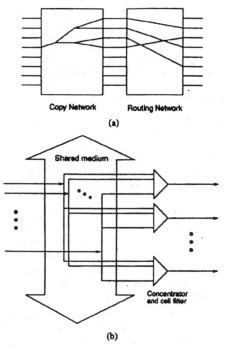

Fig. 1. (a) Multicast tree type switch architecture. (b) Broadcast type switch architecture.

higher queueing delay and smaller system throughput. The copy network in [6] employs a running adder, dummy address encoders, and a concentrator to eliminate internal blocking of the copy network. The one in [7] uses a feedback acknowledge mechanism to avoid internal blocking. However, this feedback scheme may be inefficient for certain input request patterns because requesting calls may be rejected while there are still idle routing paths in the copy network. This scheme may even cause a deadlock problem for certain multicast tree patterns where none of the cells can be replicated in the copy network. The multicast switches in [6], [7] have high hardware complexity for translation tables. This is because cells of either unicast or multicast calls may appear randomly at the outputs of the copy network. Thus, information such as routing address and new virtual channel identifier (VCI) for every call (unicast and multicast) must be stored in each translation table, increasing the table complexity dramatically.

The second category of multicast switches is the broadcast type, where incoming cells are broadcast to all output ports through a time-division shared medium (bus or ring) [8]–[11] or a space-division network [12], [13]. The switches that use a time-division bus or ring usually have a size limitation caused by the speed constraint of a centralized processor for address matching and table look up, or by the memory. The multicast switch in [12] has a centralized multicast unit to replicate cells and broadcast them over a fully-connected network. Due to the centralized processing, the number of multicast calls and the switch size are limited. The Gauss switch in [13] has a large delay difference between input ports in a large-scale switch because cells from an upper input port have to pass through all cell processing units of the input ports that are below it.

We have proposed a large-scale multicast output buffered ATM switch (MOBAS) that utilizes a recursive structure [14], [15] to achieve a large switch size. The new switch architecture was modified from the one proposed in [16] to cope with the multicast capability. The proposed multicast switch belongs to the second category, broadcast type. It employs: 1) multicast knockout principle, extending the generalized knockout principle to incorporate the multicast function, 2) output queuing with cell duplication capability to achieve the best possible delay/throughput performance [17], 3) distributed processing for cell replication, cell filtering, and cell contention, and 4) multiple stages to overcome the multicast addressing problem. The cell replication is achieved by broadcasting incoming cells to multiple switch modules, each of which consists of a two-dimensional array of switch elements (SWE's). The cell filtering and contention resolution functions are performed distributively by switch elements. In the MOBAS, the output ports are partitioned into a number of groups by switch modules. A routing-link sharing concept (known as channel grouping in [18], [19]) is applied to construct the entire switch, reducing hardware complexity (e.g., number of SWE's and interconnection wires) by almost one order of magnitude while compared to a switch without sharing the routing links.

Section II describes an architecture of a two-stage MOBAS. Section III presents the multicast knockout principle and the switch performance analysis. Section IV shows the effectiveness of a cell duplicator at the output port. Section V shows the MOBAS to be "quasifair" by calculating cell loss rates of all input ports. Section VI presents our conclusions.

II. MULTICAST SWITCH ARCHITECTURE

A. Two-Stage Configuration

Fig. 2 shows a two-stage structure of the multicast output buffered ATM switch (MOBAS), which consists of input port controllers (IPC1, IPC2), multicast grouping networks (MGN1, MGN2), and output port controllers (OPC). The IPC's terminate arrived cells, look up necessary information in translation tables, and attach routing information (e.g., multicast patterns and priority bits) to the front of the cells such that cells can be routed properly in the MGN's. The MGN's replicate multicast cells based on their multicast patterns and send one copy to each output group. The OPC's temporarily store multiple arriving cells destined for that output port in an output buffer, generate multiple copies for multicast cells with a cell duplicator (CD), assign a new VCI obtained from a translation table to each copy, convert the internal cell format to the standardized ATM cell format, and finally send the cells to the next switching node or the final destination. Section II-C contains a detailed description of the translation tables and cell routing formats in the MGN's.

To simplify the explanation of how the MOBAS functions, let us first consider a unicast case and then a multicast case. The key concept used to implement the unicast switch in [16] is the combination of the knockout principle [20] and channel sharing, or the so-called generalized knockout principle [21]. Multiple output ports are bundled in a group so that cells

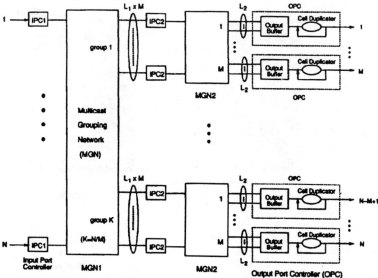

Fig. 2. The architecture of the multicast output buffered ATM switch (MOBAS).

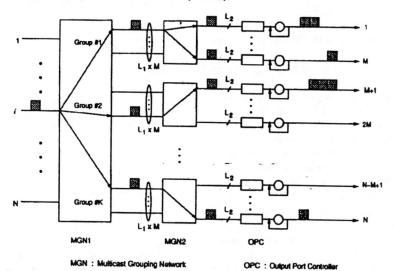

MGN : Multicast Grouping Network   OPC : Output Port Controller

Fig. 3. An example of replicating multiple cells for a multicast call in the MOBAS.

destined for these output ports can share the routing links in a switch fabric. Therefore, the complexity of interconnection wires and building elements can be reduced significantly, e.g., almost one order of magnitude [16].

As shown in Fig. 2, every M output ports are bundled in a group, and there are a total of K groups (K = N/M) for a switch size of N inputs and N outputs. $L_1 \times M$ routing links are provided to each group of M output ports, due to cell contention. If there are more than $L_1 \times M$ cells in one cell time slot destined for the same output group, the excess cells will be discarded and lost. However, we can engineer L_1 (or called group expansion ratio) such that the probability of cell loss due to the competition for $L_1 \times M$ links is lower than that due to the buffer overflow at the output port or bit errors occurring in the cell header. Performance study shows that the larger the M is, the smaller L_1 needs to be to achieve the

same cell loss probability. For instance, for a group size of one output port, which is the case in the second stage (MGN2), L_2 needs to be at least 12 to have a cell loss probability of 10^{-10}. But for a group size of 32 output ports, which is the case in the first stage (MGN1), L_1 just needs to be 2 to have the same cell loss probability. Cells from input ports are properly routed in MGN1 to one of the K groups; they are then further routed to a proper output port through MGN2. Up to L_2 cells can arrive simultaneously at each output port. An output buffer is used to store these cells and send out one cell at each cell time slot. Cells that originate from the same traffic source can be arbitrarily routed to any of the $L_1 \times M$ routing links. Chao presented a solution in [16] to preserve cell sequence.

Now let us consider a multicast situation where a cell is replicated into multiple copies in MGN1, MGN2, or both, and these copies are sent to multiple outputs. Fig. 3 shows an

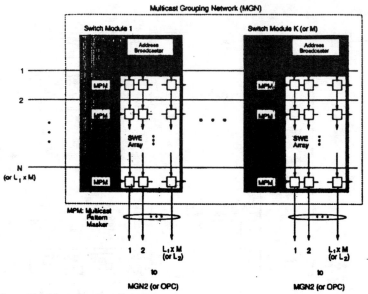

Fig. 4. The architecture of the multicast grouping network (MGN).

example to illustrate how a cell is replicated in the MGN's and duplicated in the CD. Suppose a cell arrives at an input port i and is to be multicast to four output ports: #1, #M, #(M+1), and #N. The cell is first broadcast to all K groups in MGN1, but only groups, #1, #2, and #K accept the cell. Note that only one copy of the cell appears in each group, and the replicated cell can appear at any one of the $L_1 \times M$ links. The copy of the cell at the output of group #1 is again replicated into two copies at MGN2. There are in total four replicated cells created after MGN2. When each replicated cell arrives at the OPC, it can be further duplicated into multiple copies by the CD as needed. Each duplicated copy at the OPC is updated with a new VCI obtained from a translation table at the OPC before it is sent to the network. For instance, two copies are generated at output port #1 and three copies at output port #(M+1). The reason for using the CD is to reduce the output port buffer size by storing only one copy of the multicast cell at each output port instead of storing multiple copies that originate from a traffic source and are multicast to multiple virtual circuits at an output port. Also note that since there are no buffers in both MGN1 and MGN2, the replicated cells from either MGN are aligned in time. But, the final duplicated cells at the output ports can be unaligned in time because they may have different queueing delays in the output buffers.

B. Multicast Grouping Network (MGN)

Fig. 4 shows a modular structure for the MGN at the first or the second stage. The MGN consists of K switch modules for the first stage or M for the second stage. Each switch module contains a switch element (SWE) array, a number of multicast pattern maskers (MPM), and an address broadcaster (AB). Since the structure and the operations for MGN1 and MGN2 are identical, we will only give the explanation for MGN1.

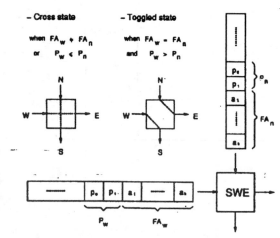

Fig. 5. Switching condition of the switch element (SWE).

Each switch module in MGN1 has N horizontal input lines and $L_1 \times M$ ($M = N/K$) vertical routing links. These routing links are shared by the cells that are destined for the same output group of a switch module. Each input line is connected to all switch modules, meaning that cells from each input line are broadcast to all K switch modules.

The routing information carried in front of each arriving cell is a multicast pattern, which is a bit map of all the outputs in the MGN. Each bit indicates if the cell is to be sent to the associated output group. For instance, let us consider a multicast switch with 1024 inputs and 1024 outputs and the number of groups in MGN1 and MGN2, K and M, are both chosen to be 32. Thus, the multicast pattern in both MGN1 and MGN2 has 32 bits. For a unicast cell, the multicast pattern is basically a flattened output address (i.e., a decoded output address) in which only one bit is set to "1" and all other 31 bits are set to "0." For a multicast cell, there are more than

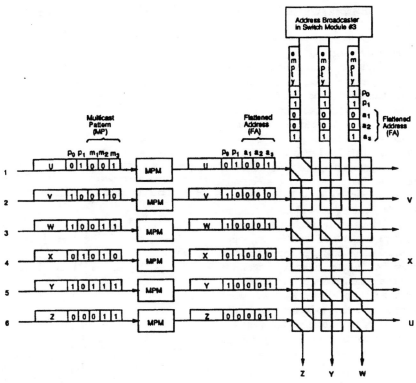

Fig. 6. An example of routing cells in a switch module.

one bit in the multicast pattern set to "1." For instance, if a cell, X, is multicast to switch modules i and j, the ith and jth bit in the multicast pattern are set to "1."

The MPM performs a logic AND function for the multicast pattern with a fixed 32 b pattern in which only the ith bit, corresponding to switch module i, is set to "1" and all other 31 bits are set to "0." So, after cell X passes through the MPM in switch module i, its multicast pattern becomes a flattened output address where only the ith bit is set to "1."

Each empty cell that is transmitted from the address broadcaster (AB) is attached, in the front, a flattened output address with only one bit set to "1." For example, empty cells from the AB in switch module i have only the ith bit set to "1" in their flattened address. Cells from horizontal inputs will be properly routed to different switch modules based on the result of comparing their multicast patterns with empty cells' flattened addresses. For cell X, since its ith and jth bit in the multicast pattern are both set to "1," it matches with the flattened addresses of empty cells from the AB's in switch modules i and j. Thus, cell X will be routed to the outputs of these two switch modules.

The SWE has two states, cross state and toggled state, as shown in Fig. 5. The state of the SWE depends on the comparison result of the flattened addresses and the priority fields in cell headers. The priority is used for cell contention resolution. The SWE is at cross state initially, i.e., cells from the north side are routed to the south side, and cells from the west side are routed to the east side. When the flattened address of a cell from the west (FA_w) is matched with the flattened

address of a cell from the north (FA_n), and when the west's priority level (P_w) is higher than the north's (P_n), the SWE's state is toggled; the cell from the west side is routed to the south side, and the cell from the north is routed to the east. In other words, any unmatched or lower-priority (including the same priority) cells are always routed to the east side. Each SWE introduces a 1 b delay as the cell passes it in either direction. The cells from MPM's and AB are skewed by 1 b before they are sent to each SWE array, due to the timing alignment requirement [16].

Fig. 6 shows an example of how cells are routed in a switch module. Cells U, V, W, X, Y, and Z arrive at inputs 1 to 6, respectively, and are to be routed in switch module #3. In the cell header, there is a 3 b multicast pattern (m_3 m_2 m_1) and a 2 b priority filed (p_1 p_0). If a cell is to be sent to an output of this switch module, its m_3 b will be set to "1." Among these six cells, cells U, V, and X are for unicast, where only one bit in the multicast pattern is set to "1." The other three cells are for multicast, more than one bit in the multicast pattern set to "1." We assume a smaller priority value has a higher priority level. For instance, cell Z has the highest priority level ("00") and empty cells transmitted from the address broadcaster have the lowest priority level ("11"). The MPM performs a logic AND function for each cell's multicast pattern with a fixed pattern of "100". For instance, after cell W passes through the MPM, its multicast pattern ("110") becomes "100" (a_3 a_2 a_1), which has only one bit set to "1" and is denoted as a flattened address. When cells are routed in the SWE array, their routing paths are determined by the state of SWE's, which are controlled according to the rules in Fig. 5. Since cells V and X are not destined for this group, the SWE's they pass remain in a cross state. Consequently, they are routed to the right side of the module and are discarded. Since there are only three routing links in this example, while there are four cells destined to this switch module, the one with the lowest priority (i.e., cell U) loses the contention with the other three and is discarded.

Since the crossbar structure inherits the characteristics of identical and short connection wires between switch elements, the timing alignment for the signals at each SWE is much easier than that of other types of interconnection network, such as the binary network, the Clos network, and so on. The unequal length of the interconnection wires increases the difficulty of synchronizing data signals, and, consequently limits the switch fabric's size, such as in the Batcher-banyan network. The SWE's in the grouping networks only communicate locally with their neighbors, so as the chips that contain the SWE's. Therefore, chips do not need to drive long wires to others on the same printed circuit board. To ensure that data signals are aligned at the SWE's at the following stages, the interconnection wires between the SWE's in each column or in each row should have the same lengths. However, wires between columns and rows do not have to be the same length. Furthermore, the requirement of synchronizing data signals at each SWE is confined in each switch module instead of in the entire switch fabric.

C. IPC and OPC Translation Tables

The translation tables in the IPC1, IPC2, and OPC contain necessary information for properly routing cells in the switch modules, MGN1 and MGN2, and for translating old VCI values into new VCI values. As mentioned above, cells routed in the MGN's depend on the multicast pattern and priority values. To reduce the translation table's complexity, the table contents and the information attached to the front of cells are different for the unicast and multicast calls.

In a point-to-point ATM switch, an arrived cell's VCI at an input line can be identical with other cells' VCI's on other input lines. Since the VCI translation table is associated with the IPC at each input line, the same VCI values can be repeatedly used for different virtual circuits at different input lines without causing any ambiguity. But cells that are from different virtual circuits and destined for the same output port must have different translated VCI's.

In a multicast switch, since a cell is replicated into multiple copies that are likely to be transmitted on the same routing links inside a switch fabric, the switch must use another identifier, BCN, to uniquely identify each multicast call. In other words, the BCN of a multicast call at an input line has to be different from that of other multicast calls at different input lines, which is unlike the VCI in the point-to-point switch, where a VCI value can be repeatedly used for different calls at different input lines.

For the unicast situation, upon a cell's arrival, its VCI value is used as an index to access the necessary information in the IPC1's translation table, such as the output addresses in MGN1 and MGN2, a contention priority value, and a new VCI, as

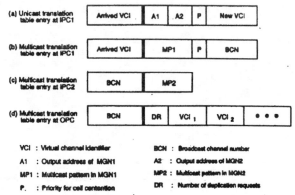

Fig. 7. Translation tables in IPC and OPC.

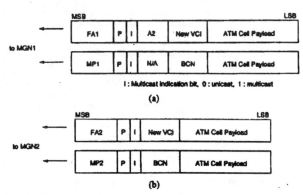

Fig. 8. (a) Unicast and multicast cell formats in MGN1. (b) Unicast and multicast cell formats in MGN2.

shown in Fig. 7(a). The output address of MGN1, A1, is first decoded into a flattened address, which has K bits and is put into the MP1 field in the cell header, as shown in Fig. 8(a). The MP1 and P are used for routing cells in the MGN1, and A2 is used for routing cells in the MGN2. The "I" bit is the multicast indication bit, which is set to "0" for unicast and "1" for multicast. When a unicast cell arrives at IPC2, the A2 field is simply decoded into a flattened address and put into the MP2 field as the routing information in MGN2. Thus, no translation table in IPC2 is required for unicast cells. Note that A2 is not decoded into a flattened address until it arrives at IPC2. This saves some bits in the cell header (e.g., this saves 27 bits for the above example of a 1024×1024 switch) and thus reduces the required operation speed in the switch fabric. The unicast cell routing format in MGN2 is shown in Fig. 8(b).

For the multicast situation, besides the routing information of MP1, MP2, and P, an important piece of information, so-called broadcast channel number (BCN), is used to identify cells that are routed to the same output group of a switch module. Similar to the unicast case, an arrived cell's VCI is first extracted to look up the information in the translation table in IPC1, as shown in Fig. 7(b). After a cell has been routed through MGN1, the MP1 is no longer used. The BCN is used to look up the next routing information, MP2, in the IPC2's translation table, as shown in Fig. 7(c). The cell formats for a multicast call in MGN1 and MGN2 are shown in Fig. 8(a) and

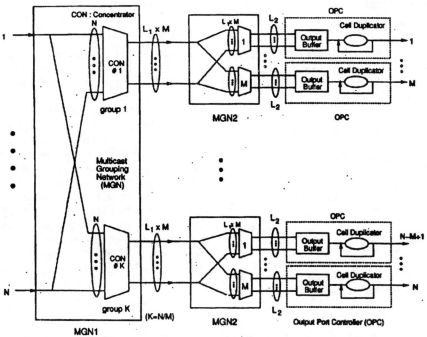

Fig. 9. Logical connection of the multicast output buffered ATM switch (MOBAS).

(b). The BCN is further used at the OPC to obtain a new VCI for each duplicated copy that is generated by a cell duplicator at the OPC. The entry for the multicast translation table in OPC is shown in Fig. 7(d).

Note that the translation tables in IPC2's that are connected to the same MGN2 contain identical information because the copy of a multicast cell can appear randomly at any one of $L_1 \times M$ output links to the MGN2. However, while comparing to those in [6], [7], the translation table size in IPC2 is much smaller. This is because the copy of a multicast cell can appear at any of $L_1 \times M$ output links in our case versus appear at any of N links in [6], [7] ($L_1 \times M << N$). Thus the table entries required in IPC2 is much less. In addition, since the VCI values of replicated copies are not stored in IPC2's translation table, the content of each table entry in IPC2 is also less.

III. MULTICAST KNOCKOUT PRINCIPLE

A new multicast knockout principle, an extension of the generalized knockout principle, has been applied to our two-stage multicast output buffered ATM switch (MOBAS) to cope with the multicasting capability. We will show the cell loss performance of the MOBAS and the numerical results for the first and the second stages (MGN1, MGN2). In order to analyze the performance of MOBAS, we redraw Fig. 2 to show its logical connections. In Fig. 9 each trapezoid corresponds to each switch module (SM) in the MGN. Since the SM performs a concentration function (e.g., N to $L_1 \times M$), it is also called a concentrator in this paper. Each concentrator has N input lines, because every incoming cell is broadcast to all concentrators. The concentrator has $L_1 \times M$ outputs, meaning that up to $L_1 \times M$ cells can be accepted in each concentrator.

A. Cell Loss Rate in MGN1

In the analysis, we assume that the traffic at each input port of the MOBAS is independent of the other inputs' and replicated cells are uniformly delivered to all output groups. The average cell arrival rate, ρ, is the probability that a cell arrives at an input port in a given cell time slot. We assume that the average cell-replication in MGN1 is $E[F_1]$, the average cell-replication in MGN2 is $E[F_2]$, the average cell-duplication in OPC is $E[D]$, and that these random variables, F_1, F_2, and D, are independent of each other.

Every incoming cell is broadcast to all concentrators (SM's), and is properly filtered at each concentrator according to the multicast pattern in the cell header. The average cell arriving rate, p, at each input of a concentrator is considered as

$$p = \frac{\rho E[F_1]}{K}$$

where $K(= N/M)$ is the number of concentrators in MGN1. The probability (A_k) that k cells are destined for a specific concentrator of MGN1 in a given time slot is

$$A_k = \binom{N}{k} p^k (1-p)^{N-k}$$
$$= \binom{N}{k} \left(\frac{\rho E[F_1] \cdot M}{N}\right)^k \left(1 - \frac{\rho E[F_1] \cdot M}{N}\right)^{N-k}$$
$$0 \le k \le N \tag{1}$$

where $\frac{\rho E[F_1] \cdot M}{N}$ is the probability of a cell arriving at an input of a specific concentrator in MGN1.

As $N \to \infty$, (1) becomes

$$A_k = e^{-\rho E[F_1] \cdot M} \cdot \frac{(\rho E[F_1] \cdot M)^k}{k!} \tag{2}$$

where ρ should satisfy the following condition for a stable system.

$$\rho \cdot E[F_1] \cdot E[F_2] \cdot E[D] < 1.$$

Since there are only $L_1 \times M$ routing links available for each output group, if more than $L_1 \times M$ cells are destined for this output group in a cell time slot, excess cells will be discarded and lost. The cell loss rate in MGN1, P_1, is

$$P_1 = \frac{\sum_{k=L_1 \times M+1}^{N} (k - L_1 \times M) \cdot A_k \cdot E[F_2]E[D]}{N \cdot p \cdot E[F_2]E[D]} \quad (3)$$

$$= \frac{1}{\rho E[F_1] \cdot M} \sum_{k=L_1 \times M+1}^{N} (k - L_1 \times M)$$

$$\times \binom{N}{k} \left(\frac{\rho E[F_1] \cdot M}{N} \right)^k \left(1 - \frac{\rho E[F_1] \cdot M}{N} \right)^{N-k}. \quad (4)$$

The denominator in (3), $N \cdot p \cdot E[F_2]E[D]$, is the average number of cells effectively arriving at a specific concentrator during one cell time, and the numerator in (3), $\sum_{k=L_1 \times M+1}^{N}(k - L_1 \times M) \cdot A_k \cdot E[F_2]E[D]$, is the average number of cells effectively lost in the specific concentrator. Both the denominator and the numerator in (3) include the term $E[F_2]E[D]$ to cope with the cell replication in MGN2 and OPC.

As $N \rightarrow \infty$, (4) becomes (5) shown at the bottom of this page.

Note that (5) is similar to the one in the generalized knockout principle [21], except that the parameters in the two equations are slightly different due to the cell replication in MGN1 and MGN2, and the cell duplication in the OPC.

Fig. 10(a) shows the plots of the cell loss probability at the MGN1 versus different L_1 and fanout values for an offered load ($= \rho \cdot E[F_1] \cdot E[F_2] \cdot E[D]$) of 0.9 at each output port. We notice from these plots that as M increases (i.e., more outputs are sharing their routing links), the required L_1 value decreases for a given cell loss rate. The switch design parameters M and L_1 are more stringent to the unicast case than to the multicast. Since the load on MGN1 decreases as the product of the average fanouts in MGN2 and OPC increases, the cell loss rate of MGN1 under the multicast case is lower than that of the unicast case. The replicated cells from a multicast call will never contend with each other for the same output group (concentrator) since the MOBAS replicates at most one cell for each output group. In other words, MGN1 that is designed

to meet the performance requirement for unicast calls will also satisfy multicast calls' performance requirement.

B. Cell Loss Rate in MGN2

Special attention is required when analyzing the cell loss rate in MGN2 because the cell arriving pattern at the inputs of MGN2 is determined by the number of cells passing through the corresponding concentrator in MGN1. If there are l ($l \leq L_1 \times M$) cells arriving at MGN2, these cells will appear at the upper l consecutive inputs of MGN2. If more than $L_1 \times M$ cells are destined for MGN2, only $L_1 \times M$ cells will arrive at MGN2's inputs (one cell per each input port), while excessive cells are discarded in MGN1.

We assume the cell loss rate of a concentrator in MGN2 to be P_2, and the probability that l cells arrive at a specific concentrator in MGN2 to be B_l. Both P_2 and B_l depend on the average number of cells arriving at the inputs of MGN2 (i.e., the number of cells passing through the corresponding concentrator in MGN1). This implies that P_2 is a function of A_k in (1). In order to calculate P_2, the probability of j cells arriving at MGN2, denoted as I_j, is

$$I_j = \begin{cases} A_j & \text{for } j < L_1 \times M \\ \sum_{k=L_1 \times M}^{N} A_k & \text{for } j = L_1 \times M. \end{cases}$$

If j ($j \leq L_1 \times M$) cells arrive at MGN2, they will appear at the upper j consecutive inputs of MGN2. Since how and where the cells appear at the MGN2's inputs does not affect the cell loss performance, we will simplify our performance analysis by assuming that a cell can appear at any input of the MGN2.

Let us denote the probability that l cells arrive at the inputs of a specific concentrator in MGN2 for given j cells arrived at MGN2 to be $B_{l|j}$.

Then,

$$B_{l|j} = \binom{j}{l} q^l (1-q)^{j-l} \quad 0 \leq j \leq L_1 \times M, \quad 0 \leq l \leq j$$

where q is equal to $\frac{E[F_2]}{M}$ under the assumption that replicated cells are uniformly delivered to M concentrators in MGN2.

If less than or equal to L_2 cells arrive at MGN2 ($0 \leq j \leq L_2$), no cell-discarding will occur in MGN2, because each concentrator can accept up to L_2 cells during one cell time slot. If more than L_2 cells arrive at MGN2 ($L_2 \leq j \leq L_1 \times M$),

$$P_1 = \left[1 - \frac{L_1 \times M}{N \times p} \right] \left[1 - \sum_{k=0}^{L_1 \times M} \frac{(N \times p)^k e^{-N \times p}}{k!} \right] + \frac{(N \times p)^{L_1 \times M} e^{-N \times p}}{(L_1 \times M)!}$$

$$= \left[1 - \frac{L_1 \times M}{\rho E[F_1] \times M} \right] \left[1 - \sum_{k=0}^{L_1 \times M} \frac{(\rho E[F_1] \cdot M)^k e^{-\rho E[F_1] \cdot M}}{k!} \right]$$

$$+ \frac{(\rho E[F_1] \cdot M)^{L_1 \times M} e^{-\rho E[F_1] \cdot M}}{(L_1 \times M)!}. \quad (5)$$

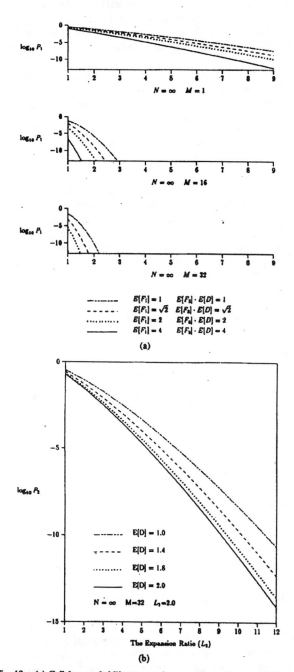

Fig. 10. (a) Cell loss probability versus the group expansion ratio ($L1$) in MGN1. (b) Cell loss probability versus the expansion ratio ($L2$) in MGN2.

cell loss will occur in a specific concentrator with a certain probability.

Since replicated cells are assumed to be uniformly distributed to all M outputs in MGN2, the probability that l cells are destined for a specific output port of MGN2 in a cell time slot, B_l, is

$$B_l = \sum_{j=l}^{L_1 \times M} B_{l|j} \cdot I_j.$$

The cell loss rate in MGN2, P_2, is

$$P_2 = \frac{\displaystyle\sum_{l=L_2+1}^{L_1 \times M} (l - L_2) \cdot B_l \cdot E[D]}{\dfrac{N \cdot \dfrac{\rho E[F_1]}{K} \cdot (1 - P_1) \cdot E[F_2]}{M} \cdot E[D]} \tag{6}$$

$$= \frac{\displaystyle\sum_{l=L_2+1}^{L_1 \times M} (l - L_2) \cdot B_l}{\rho E[F_1] \cdot (1 - P_1) \cdot E[F_2]}.$$

$N \cdot \frac{\rho E[F_1]}{K}$ is the average number of cells destined for a specific concentrator in MGN1 from the inputs of the MOBAS. $N \cdot \frac{\rho E[F_1]}{K} \cdot (1 - P_1)$ is the average number of cells that have survived in this concentrator, which in turn becomes the average number of cells arriving at the corresponding MGN2. Thus, the denominator in (6), $\left[N \cdot \frac{\rho E[F_1]}{K} \cdot (1 - P_1) \cdot E[F_2] \cdot E[D] \right]/M$, is the average number of cells effectively arriving at a specific output port. The numerator in (6), $\sum_{l=L_2+1}^{L_1 \times M}(l - L_2) \cdot B_l \cdot E[D]$, is the average number of cells effectively lost in a specific concentrator in MGN2 because the lost cell can be a cell that would be duplicated in the OPC.

Fig. 10(b) shows the plots of the cell loss probability at MGN2 versus different L_2 values and average duplication values for an effective offered load ($= \rho \cdot E[F_1] \cdot E[F_2] \cdot E[D]$) of 0.9. The average fanout on MGN1 is assumed to be 1.0 ($E[F_1] = 1.0$), the group size to be 32 ($M = 32$), and the group expansion ratio to be 2.0 ($L_1 = 2.0$). Since the traffic load on MGN2 reduces as the average cell duplication ($E[D]$) increases, the cell loss rate in MGN2 decreases as $E[D]$ increases. Therefore, the switch design parameter, L_2, is more stringent to the unicast case than to the multicast. Consequently, if MGN2 is designed to meet the performance requirement for unicast calls, it will also satisfy multicast calls' performance requirement.

C. Total Cell Loss Rate in MOBAS

Total cell loss rate in MOBAS is shown in (7) at the bottom of the next page. The first term of numerator in (7), $\frac{N}{M} \sum_{k=L_1 \times M+1}^{N} (k - L_1 \times M) \cdot A_k \cdot E[F_2] E[D]$, is the average number of cells effectively lost in MGN1. The second term of numerator in (7), $N \sum_{l=L_2+1}^{L_1 \times M} (l - L_2) \cdot B_l \cdot E[D]$, is the average number of cells effectively lost in all of MGN2's. The denominator in (7), $N \cdot \rho E[F_1] E[F_2] E[D]$, is the average number of cells effectively offered to the MOBAS.

In (7) L_1 and L_2 should be in a certain range to guarantee the required cell loss performance in the MOBAS. For example, in order to have the cell loss rate of 10^{-10} in the MOBAS with a very large size ($N \geq 1024$) and a group size of M ($=32$), L_1 and L_2 should be greater than 2 and 12, respectively. If any one of them is less than the required number, the total cell loss rate in the MOBAS cannot be guaranteed since the term of the numerator of (7), which is a function of the smaller number, dominates the total cell loss rate in the MOBAS.

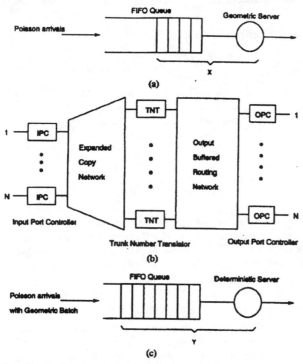

Fig. 11. (a) Queueing model of the OPC in MOBAS (Model I). (b) A multicast switch with an expanded copy network. (c) Queueing model of the OPC in Fig. 11(b) (Model II).

We conclude in this section that a switch that is designed to meet the performance requirement for unicast calls will also satisfy multicast calls' performance requirement because the switch design parameters such as M, L_1, and L_2 are more stringent to the unicast case than to the multicast. The design parameters, M, L_1 and L_2, should be in a certain range to guarantee the required cell loss performance in the the MOBAS.

IV. EFFECTIVENESS OF THE CELL DUPLICATOR

This section discusses the effectiveness of the cell duplicator (CD). Two models for the cell duplication are considered here. Fig. 11(a) shows the model for the OPC in MOBAS, denoted as Model I. Fig. 11(b) shows a multicast switch that consists of input port controllers (IPC's), an expanded copy network, trunk number translators (TNT's), and an output-buffered point-to-point switch. The expanded copy network is similar to the one proposed in [22]. Fig. 11(c) shows the model for the OPC in the multicast switch with an expanded copy network, denoted as Model II.

The mean queue lengths of Model I and Model II are calculated and compared. It is shown that Model I has a smaller queue length than Model II does for the same traffic distributions, and that both models have the same queueing delay.

In this study, the duplication request in Model I is assumed to be a geometric distribution. Based on the analysis of the cell loss rate in the previous section, Model I can be considered as Poisson/Geom./1 [23]. The Poisson arrival assumption is reasonable because we have assumed that traffic at each input port of the MOBAS is independent of the other ports and that the expansion ratios L_1 and L_2 are sufficiently large to have a negligible cell loss rate in the switch fabric. Model II can be considered as discrete Batch Poisson/D/1 [24]. Here, the batch size of Model II has the same distribution as the service time of Model I. These assumptions are reasonable because the cell duplication that is performed inside the expanded copy network in Fig. 11(b) is performed in the OPC of the MOBAS.

Thus, the number of arriving cells at Model I has a Poisson distribution with a rate of λ (i.e., number of cells/one cell time slot),

$$P_r\{k \text{ cells arrive during a cell time slot}\} = e^{-\lambda}\frac{\lambda^k}{k!}$$

where

$$\lambda = \rho E[F_1]E[F_2].$$

The service time has a geometric distribution with an average of $1/q \ (= E[D])$ cell times,

$$P_r\{\text{service time} = k \text{ cell time slots}\} = (1-q)^{k-1}q,$$
$$k = 1, 2, \cdots.$$

The number of arriving cell batches at Model II has a Poisson distribution with a rate of λ (i.e., number of cell batches/one cell time slot),

$$P_r\{k \text{ batches arrive during a cell time slot}\} = e^{-\lambda}\frac{\lambda^k}{k!}.$$

The batch size has a geometric distribution with an average of $1/q$ cells,

$$P_r\{\text{batch size} = b \text{ cells}\} = (1-q)^{b-1}q, \qquad b = 1, 2, \cdots.$$

The distribution of the number of arriving cells at Model I and that of the number of arriving cell batches at Model II are the same. The service time of Model I (the time needed to complete cell duplications and transmissions) has the same distribution as the batch size in Model II (i.e., a geometric distribution).

$$P_T = \frac{\text{Avg. \# of cells effectively lost in both MGN1 and MGN2's}}{\text{Avg. \# of cells effectively offered to MOBAS}}$$

$$= \frac{\frac{N}{M}\sum_{k=L_1 \times M+1}^{N}(k - L_1 \times M) \cdot A_k \cdot E[F_2]E[D] + N\sum_{l=L_2+1}^{L_1 \times M}(l - L_2) \cdot B_l \cdot E[D]}{N \cdot \rho E[F_1]E[F_2]E[D]}. \tag{7}$$

Let us define X and Y be random variables for the number of cells in the buffer in Model I and Model II, at the beginning of a cell time slot, respectively. And let us define D_I and D_{II} be random variables for the delays experienced by cells in the buffer in Model I and Model II, respectively. From [23] and [24], we can find the average queue lengths of Model I and Model II as follows:

$$E[X]_{M/\text{Geom.}/1} = \frac{\frac{\lambda}{q}(2-\lambda)}{2(1-\frac{\lambda}{q})}.$$

$$E[Y]_{M^{[B]}/D/1} = \frac{\lambda}{2q} + \frac{\frac{\lambda}{q}(2-q)}{2(1-\frac{\lambda}{q})}$$

$$= \frac{1}{q}\left[\frac{\frac{\lambda}{q}(2-\lambda)}{2(1-\frac{\lambda}{q})}\right]$$

$$= \frac{1}{q}\left[E[X]_{M/\text{Geom.}/1}\right].$$

Note that the mean queue length of Model I is smaller than that of Model II by a factor of the mean batch size, $E[B]$ (=1/q). Using Little's formula [25], the average delays of Model I and Model II are as follows and found to be equal.

$$E[D_I]_{M/\text{Geom.}/1} = \frac{E[X]_{M/\text{Geom.}/1}}{\lambda}$$

$$= \frac{\frac{1}{q}(2-\lambda)}{2(1-\frac{\lambda}{q})}.$$

$$E[D_{II}]_{M^{[B]}/D/1} = \frac{E[Y]_{M^{[B]}/D/1}}{\lambda/q}$$

$$= \frac{1}{q}\left[\frac{(2-\lambda)}{2(1-\frac{\lambda}{q})}\right]$$

$$= E[D_I]_{M/\text{Geom.}/1}.$$

From the above, the delays experienced by multicast cells are the same in these two models, but the queue length occupied by the multicast cells in the MOBAS is smaller than that in the cascaded type output-buffered multicast switch by a factor of the average cell duplication request in the OPC of the MOBAS, which is equal to the mean batch size in

Model II. It implies that for a finite output buffer, the cell loss rates in the MOBAS's output buffer are smaller than those in the cascaded type multicast switch for any arrival process and any duplication request distribution. The effectiveness of the CD will be more profound when congestion occurs at the output buffer due to bursty arrivals of multicast calls with large number of duplication requests.

V. QUASIFAIRNESS OF MOBAS

In this section, we show that the MOBAS is quasifair by calculating the cell loss rates of all input ports. We conclude that unfairness among the input ports can be neglected by properly choosing switch parameters (e.g., expansion ratios), based on multicast knockout principle, such that the cell loss rate of every input port is less than 10^{-10}.

Fig. 12 depicts an example of unfairness (different cell loss rates) among the input ports. The operation of the SWE (switch element) and how the cells are routed in the SWE array can be found in Section II. In this example, 5 cells, U, V, W, X, and Y are destined for an output port, e.g., #3. Since only four routing links are available in this SWE array, one cell will be discarded. Cells arriving at upper input ports have better service preference than those that have the same priority level but arrive at lower input ports. As shown in Fig. 12, cell Y is discarded because it arrives at the bottom input port.

Let us assume only one priority level exists, the switch has N inputs and N outputs, and L routing links are available per output port. P_k is defined to be the cell loss rate of the kth input port. The cell loss rates of L uppermost input ports is zero, meaning that cells from these input ports are delivered in loss free.

$$P_k = 0 \qquad 1 \leq k \leq L$$

Now let us consider the cell loss rate of the remaining input ports, from the $(L+1)$th to the Nth (shown at the bottom of this page).

Fig. 13 shows the cell loss rate of each input port for a single stage 64×64 MOBAS. For $L = 12$, the cell loss rate for the bottom input port (the worst case) is less than 10^{-10}, which meets the cell loss rate requirement for existing services.

VI. CONCLUSION

We proposed a recursive modular architecture to implement a large-scale multicast output buffered ATM switch (MOBAS).

$$P_k = P_r\left\{\begin{array}{l} \text{more than or equal to } L \text{ input} \\ \text{ports, located above} \\ \text{the } k\text{th input port,} \\ \text{have active cells} \end{array} \middle| \begin{array}{l} \text{the } k\text{th input port} \\ \text{has an active cell} \end{array}\right\}$$

$$= P_r\{\text{more than or equal to } L \text{ active cells arriving at input ports 1 to } (k-1)\}$$

$$= \sum_{i=L}^{k-1}\binom{k-1}{i}\left(\frac{\rho}{N}\right)^i\left(1-\frac{\rho}{N}\right)^{k-1-i}$$

$$= 1 - \sum_{i=0}^{L-1}\binom{k-1}{i}\left(\frac{\rho}{N}\right)^i\left(1-\frac{\rho}{N}\right)^{k-1-i} \qquad L+1 \leq k \leq N.$$

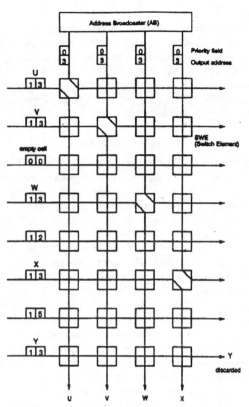

Fig. 12. An example of unfairness among input ports.

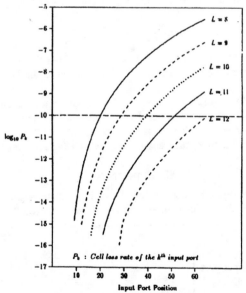

Fig. 13. Cell loss rate of each input port of a 64 × 64 MOBAS.

3) distributed processing for cell replication, cell filtering, and cell contention, and 4) multiple stages to reduce routing address overhead.

Cell replication is achieved by broadcasting incoming cells to multiple switch modules, which consists of a two-dimensional array, of switch elements. In the MOBAS, the output ports are partitioned into a number of groups by the switch modules. The routing-link sharing concept is applied to construct the entire switch, which reduces the hardware complexity (number of switch elements and interconnection wires) by almost one order of magnitude. The routing address used in the MOBAS is a bit map of all the outputs in the first and second stage routing networks. In order to reduce translation table complexity, the contents stored in the tables, including routing addresses, priority levels, and new VCI values, are different for unicast and multicast calls.

Through the analysis based on the multicast knockout principle, we conclude that for a two-stage MOBAS, the switch design parameters, such as routing link expansion ratios at the first and the second stage networks, are more stringent to the unicast case than to the multicast case. This implies that if a switch is designed to meet the performance requirements for unicast calls, it will also satisfy multicast calls' performance requirement.

The effectiveness of the cell duplicator (CD) has been shown by comparing the mean queue lengths of the output buffer of two models: 1) Model I, the OPC in the MOBAS, and 2) Model II, a multicast switch consisting of an expanded copy network, trunk number translators (TNT's), and an output-buffered point-to-point switch. The delays experienced by multicast cells are the same in these two models, but the queue length occupied by the multicast cells in the MOBAS is smaller than that in the cascaded type output-buffered multicast switch by a factor of the average cell duplication request in the OPC of the MOBAS. It implies that the cell loss rates in the MOBAS's output buffer are smaller than those in the cascaded type multicast switch for any arrival process and any duplication request distribution under a finite output buffer condition.

The architecture of the MOBAS has been proven to be quasifair through the calculation of the cell loss rates of all input ports. By properly engineering design parameters (e.g., routing link expansion ratios), the cell loss rate of each input port can be arbitrarily small (e.g., 10^{-10}) to meet the performance requirement of all broadband services. Thus, there is no need to be concerned about the unfairness issue in the MOBAS.

An ATM crosspoint switch chip with 16 × 16 switch elements has been implemented using CMOS 2-μm technology. The chip has been tested and functions correctly at about 50 Mb/s (limited by test equipment's speed); it was simulated to operate properly at 100 Mb/s. The chip's photograph is shown in Fig. 14.

ACKNOWLEDGMENT

The authors would like to thank Dr. N. Uzun for laying out and testing the switch chip. They are also grateful to

It employs: 1) multicast knockout principle, extending the generalized knockout principle to incorporate the multicast capability, 2) output queuing with cell duplication capability to achieve the best possible delay/throughput performance,

Fig. 14.   The photograph of the ATM crosspoint switch chip.

anonymous reviewers' comments that improved the quality of this paper.

REFERENCES

[1] CCITT SG XVIII Draft Recommendation I.150: "B-ISDN ATM functional characteristics," Geneva, May 1990.

[2] H. Ahmadi and W. E. Denzel, "A survey of modern high-performance switching techniques," *IEEE J. Select. Areas Commun.*, vol. 7, pp. 1091–1103, Sept. 1989.

[3] W. E. Stevens, M. DePrycker, F. A. Tobagi, and T. Yamaguchi, Special issue on "Large-scale ATM switching systems for B-ISDN," *IEEE J. Select. Areas Commun.*, vol. 9, Oct. 1991.

[4] J. S. Turner, "Design of a broadcast packet switching network," *IEEE Trans. Commun.*, vol. 36, June 1988.

[5] H. S. Kim and A. Leon-Garcia, "A self-routing multistage switching network for broadband ISDN," *IEEE J. Select. Areas Commun.*, vol. 8, Apr. 1990.

[6] T. T. Lee, "Non-blocking copy networks for multicast packet switching," *IEEE J. Select. Areas Commun.*, vol. 6, pp. 1455–1467, Dec. 1988.

[7] C. L. Tarng and J. S. Meditch, "A high performance copy network for B-ISDN," in *Proc. INFOCOM '91*, Apr. 7–11, 1991, pp. 171–180.

[8] H. Suzuki, H. Nagano, T. Suzuki, T. Takeuchi, and S. Iwasaki, "Output-buffer switch architecture for asynchronous transfer mode," in *Proc. ICC '89*, Boston, MA, 1989, pp. 99–103.

[9] T. Kozaki, N. Endo, Y. Sakurai, O. Matsubara, M. Mizukami, and K. Asano, "32 × 32 shared buffer type ATM switch VLSI's for B-ISDN's," *IEEE J. Select. Areas Commun.*, vol. 9, Oct. 1991.

[10] M. Rahnema, "The fast packet ring switch: A high-performance efficient architecture with multicast capability," *IEEE Trans. Commun.*, vol. 38, Apr. 1990.

[11] J. S. Choi and B. C. Shin, "Design of cascade ring multicast switch," *Electron. Lett.*, vol. 28, no. 14, pp. 1330–1332, July 1992.

[12] K. Y. Eng, M. G. Hluchyj, and Y. S. Yeh, "Multicast and broadcast services in a knockout packet switch," in *Proc. INFOCOM '88*, Mar. 27–31, 1988, pp. 29–34.

[13] Rein J. F. de Vries, "ATM Multicast connections using the Gauss switch," in *Proc. GLOBECOM '90*, pp. 211–217.

[14] N. Pippenger, "The complexity theory of switching networks," Ph.D. dissertation, Mass. Inst. Tech., 1973.

[15] J. Y. Hui, *Switching and Traffic Theory for Integrated Broadband Networks.*   Norwell, MA: Kluwer, 1990.

[16] H. J. Chao, "A recursive modular Terabit/sec ATM switch," *IEEE J. Select. Areas Commun.*, vol. 9, pp. 1161–1172, Oct. 1991.

[17] M. J. Karol, M. G. Hluchyj, and S. P. Morgan, "Input versus output queueing on a space-division packet switch," *IEEE Trans. Commun.*, vol. 35, pp. 1347–1356, Dec. 1987.

[18] A. Pattavina, "Multichannel bandwidth allocation in a broadband packet switch," *IEEE J. Select. Areas Commun.*, vol. 6, pp. 1489–1499, Dec. 1988.

[19] H. Saidi, P. S. Min, and M. V. Hedge, "Non-blocking multi-channel switching," presented at *Proc. Annu. Allerton Conf. Commun., Contr., Comput.*, Univ. Illinois, Oct. 1993.

[20] Y. S. Yeh, M. G. Hluchyj, and A. S. Acampora, "The knockout switch: a simple architecture for high-performance packet switching," *IEEE J. Select. Areas Commun.*, vol. 5, pp. 1274–1283, Oct. 1987.

[21] K. Y. Eng, M. J. Karol, and Y. S. Yeh, "A growable packet (ATM) switch architecture: Design principles and applications," *IEEE Trans. Commun.*, vol. 40, Feb. 1992.

[22] J. S. Turner, "A practical version of Lee's multicast switch architecture," WUCS-91-46, Aug. 26, 1991.

[23] J. Hsu, "Buffer behavior with Poisson arrival and geometric output processes," *IEEE Trans. Commun.*, pp. 1940–1941, Dec. 1974.

[24] W. W. Chu, "Buffer behavior for batch poisson arrivals and single constant output," *IEEE Trans. Commun.*, vol. 18, pp. 613–618, Oct. 1970.

[25] J. D. C. Little, "A proof for the queueing formula $L = \lambda W$," *Oper. Res.*, vol. 9, pp. 383–387, 1961.

H. Jonathan Chao (S'82–M'85) received the B.S.E.E. and M.S.E.E. degrees from National Chiao Tung University, Taiwan, in 1977 and 1980, respectively, and the Ph.D. degree in electrical engineering from The Ohio State University, NY, in 1985.

He is an Associate Professor of Electrical Engineering at Polytechnic University, New York, which he joined in January 1992. His areas of research include large-scale multicast ATM switches, photonic ATM switches, high-speed computer communications, and congestion/flow control in ATM networks. He holds 14 patents and has published over 40 journal and conference papers in the above areas. From 1985 to 1991, he was a Member of Technical Staff at Bellcore, NJ, where he has implemented several high-speed VLSI chips for SONET/ATM-based broadband networks. He has also proposed various architectures, along with their performance studies, for B-ISDN applications. These architectures include an optical customer premises network, a large-scale multicast ATM switch, traffic shaper, and priority queue manager for ATM network congestion control. He played a key role in designing a HIPPI-to-SONET/ATM network interface for the Nectar Gigabit Testbed, one of the five gigabit network testbeds in the US. From 1977 to 1981, he worked at Taiwan Telecommunication Laboratories, where he was engaged in the development of a digital switching system.

Byeong-Seog Choe was born in Seoul, Korea in 1957. He received the B.S.E.E. degree from Seoul National University in 1985, and the M.S.E.E degree from Fairleigh Dickinson University, NJ, in 1987. He received the M.S. and Ph.D. degrees in electrical engineering from Polytechnic University, NY, in 1993 and 1994, respectively.

From 1992 to 1993, he was a Research Fellow in the Center for Advanced Technology in Telecommunications of Polytechnic University. He was involved in the design and performance analysis of ATM switches. Since March 1994, he has been on the faculty of the Department of Electronics Engineering at Myongji University, Korea, where he is an Assistant Professor. His current research interests include congestion control in BISDN and photonic ATM switches.

The Tera Project: A Hybrid Queueing ATM Switch Architecture for LAN

Ronald P. Bianchini, *Member, IEEE*, and Hyong S. Kim, *Member, IEEE*

Abstract—The Tera ATM LAN project at Carnegie Mellon University addresses the interconnection of hundreds of workstations in the Electrical and Computer Engineering Department via an ATM-based network. The Tera network architecture consists of switched Ethernet clusters that are interconnected using an ATM network. This paper presents the Tera network architecture, including an Ethernet/ATM network interface, the Tera ATM switch, and its performance analysis. The Tera switch architecture for asynchronous transfer mode (ATM) local area networks (LAN's) incorporates a scalable nonblocking switching element with hybrid queueing discipline. The hybrid queueing strategy includes a global first-in first-out (FIFO) queue that is shared by all switch inputs and dedicated output queues with small speedup. Due to hybrid queueing, switch performance is comparable to output queueing switches. The shared input queue design is scalable since it is based on a Banyan network and N FIFO memories. The Tera switch incorporates an optimal throughput multicast stage that is also based on a Banyan network. Switch performance is evaluated using queueing analysis and simulation under various traffic patterns.

I. INTRODUCTION

ASYNCHRONOUS transfer mode (ATM) provides flexible bandwidth allocation, dynamic reconfiguration of calls, service independency, and efficient multiplexing of bursty traffic. Although initially proposed for public networks, ATM networks have gained acceptance in high-speed local area networks (LAN's). ATM is an attractive option for high-speed LAN's due to its ability to handle heterogeneous traffic and its seamless connectivity to public networks.

This paper presents the Carnegie Mellon University Tera Project, which is an ATM LAN trial in the Electrical and Computer Engineering Department. The Tera network architecture consists of hundreds of workstations, currently utilizing Ethernet network connections, an ATM switch backbone, and an Ethernet/ATM network interface. Each workstation is connected to an Ethernet port of a network interface. Ideally, only a single workstation is connected to each Ethernet port, yielding a dedicated 10 Mb/s communication channel to the workstation. The network interface consists of a cluster of 16 Ethernet ports and a single ATM port and performs Ethernet switching and switches Ethernet packets between local Ethernets and the ATM network.

The Tera switch architecture consists of a novel nonblocking shared memory switch developed for the ATM LAN environment. The switch architecture incorporates a hybrid

Manuscript received March 4, 1994; revised September 12, 1994.
The authors are with the Department of Electrical and Computer Engineering, Carnegie Mellon University, Pittsburgh, PA 15213.
IEEE Log Number 9407071.

queueing structure, consisting of a globally shared input queue and discrete output queues. The shared input queue allows the switch input ports to share a common buffer, permitting the queueing of bursty traffic without significant cell loss. Cells are not dropped by the switch unless all input buffer locations are filled. The shared input queue, in combination with discrete output queues yields high cell throughput, with performance comparable to nonblocking output queueing switches. Nonblocking access is provided to all inputs ports of the shared-memory input queue using a Banyan network and N interleaved banks of memory, for an N input switch. Typically, higher complexity networks are required for this function, due to internal blocking present in Banyan networks. A novel nonblocking property [17] of the Banyan network in combination with consecutively addressed interleaved memory is utilized to guarantee that internal blocking does not occur. This feature is exploited to perform cell input, feedback and multicast in the three Banyan networks of the switch architecture. In this work, output queues are proposed to improve switch throughput beyond the 58% limit typically found in input queueing switches due to head-of-line (HOL) blocking. A low speedup factor (i.e., 2) is shown to be sufficient to achieve adequate performance in terms of throughput, delay and cell loss probability.

The hierarchical network structure is proposed to accommodate existing workstations with Ethernet cards. The network interface transparently multiplexes 16 Ethernets to a single 155 Mb/s ATM channel. Communication within the network interface group is switched locally in the interface. Communication among workstations in different groups are carried through the ATM network. The network architecture allows significant increases in network throughput without upgrading workstation hardware nor software. Initially the Tera network will be deployed within a small group of workstations within the Electrical and Computer Engineering Department. As deployed, workstations with native ATM capability can be added directly to a network ATM port and can coexist with Ethernet workstations. Native ATM workstations will be able to take full advantage of the 155 Mb/s dedicated ATM channels.

The remainder of this paper is organized as follows. The network architecture, including the switch and interface specifications, is described in Section II. Performance of the Tera switch is analyzed through queueing analysis and simulations under various traffic patterns in Section III. Concluding remarks are given in Section IV.

0733–8716/95$04.00 © 1995 IEEE

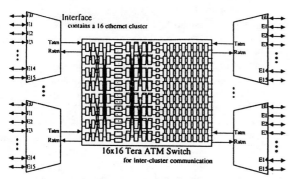

Fig. 1. Network architecture.

II. NETWORK ARCHITECTURE

The proposed network architecture consists of "Ethernet clusters" of 16 separate Ethernet networks that are interconnected via a **Network Interface** supporting switched Ethernet. Inter-cluster communication is facilitated by a central **ATM Switching Network**. See Fig. 1. Each Ethernet is expected to contain a single port of a Network Interface and a single workstation, but may contain multiple workstations. A workstation communicates on its local Ethernet, as before, without modification to its hardware, or operating system software. The Network Interface receives all packets and routes them to their appropriate destinations. The goal of this work is to provide as many workstations as possible with dedicated 10 Mb/s of communication bandwidth. The initially deployed system will consist of a single Tera 16 port ATM switch and sixteen network interfaces that support switched Ethernet to ATM communication.

Within the Ethernet cluster, the Network Interface performs the function of an intelligent bridge. Ethernet packets are routed between the Ethernet networks by maintaining a routing table based on Ethernet hardware addresses. Packets are routed between clusters via the ATM Switching Network. The Network Interface segments an Ethernet packet into ATM cells using ATM adaptation layer 5 (AAL5). The segmented cells are routed through the ATM switching network to the appropriate Network Interface and are reassembled. See Fig. 2. All Ethernet functions are performed transparently to the workstations, i.e., messages are only routed to their destination Ethernet and reconstructed to appear as transmitted. Ethernet broadcast messages are routed locally to all other Ethernet networks and are broadcasted by the ATM switching network to all other interfaces and reconstructed as if all Ethernet networks received the initial broadcast. If a message is received by a network interface whose destination is not in its current routing table, by default it is broadcasted to all local Ethernet networks and to all other network interfaces to ensure that it reaches its proper destination.

The proposed network architecture is to be deployed in the CMU-ECE network, consisting of approximately 500 networked workstations located in three buildings. See Fig. 3. All campus buildings are wired with IBM token ring type I cabling (IEEE 802.5) in a star configuration. As currently configured, the Ethernet connection of most workstations are

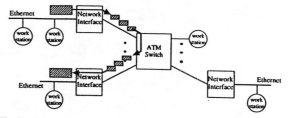

Fig. 2. Ethernet packet segmentation and reassembly.

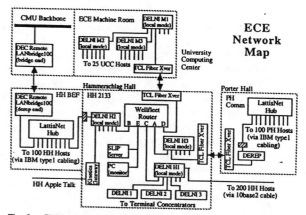

Fig. 3. CMU-ECE network map.

wired directly to a wiring closet which contains a LattisNet Hub that implements a single bussed Ethernet. Thus, no modifications to the workstations or building wiring are required to facilitate deployment of the Tera LAN. The ATM Switch and Network Interfaces are located in the wiring closet. Each workstation will be disconnected from its current Hub and uniquely connected to one port of a Network Interface. In the new configuration, each workstation is contained on its own Ethernet with one port of a Network Interface, supporting a dedicated 10 Mb/s for each workstation. The initial deployment is located in Porter Hall and will contain approximately 100 workstations.

A detailed architectural description of the Tera Switch as modified for LAN traffic is given in Section II-A. The original architectural description of the Tera Switch is given in [4], modifications for scanning ahead in the input queue and for switching multiple priorities is given in [18]. The architecture of the Network Interface is given in Section II-B.

A. Tera Switch Architecture

An overview of the switch architecture with $N = 8$ inputs and eight outputs is given in Fig. 4. The architecture consists of three Banyan networks, an interleaved shared input queue containing all blocked input cells, an output network and a dedicated output queue for each switch output. A detailed description of the Tera switch implementation for LAN's is given in [12]. The Banyan networks transfer cells between the input ports, the shared memory, the output network and temporary feedback registers. The output network transfers cells from the feedback and copy networks to the output

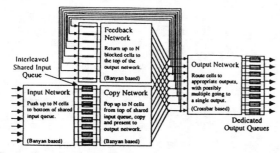

Fig. 4. Tera switch architecture.

queues. A typical input cell arrives at an input port, is temporarily stored in the shared input queue and then routed through the multicast Banyan and output network.

The first three switching networks of the architecture are Banyan networks with $O(N \log_2 N)$ 2×2 switching elements. The output network could be any switching network such as a crossbar or a Batcher-Banyan network [5], [14]. A crossbar network is feasible for small numbers of inputs, of approximately $N = 32$ or less. For larger switches either a batcher-banyan network or a blocking network with lower complexity can be utilized. Nonblocking output networks result in higher switch throughput than blocking output networks, although either can be utilized in the architecture. For the LAN environment, with the potential overlap of long cell bursts to a single output, the output network must be able to send multiple cells to a single output. This can be performed with either multiple parallel output networks, or with a single output network operating faster than the input data rate. The later scheme is termed an output network with "speedup."

The shared input queue consist of N interleaved banks of FIFO memory. Each memory bank is connected to a single input and output port of two of the Banyan networks. A queue is implemented in memory with a top and a bottom pointer. The top and bottom pointers contain the addresses of the top and bottom elements in the queue. Intermediate queue elements are located at consecutive addresses between the top and bottom pointers. Since memories are interleaved with N banks, any N sequential queue elements are located in unique and consecutive memory banks. This feature is exploited in the switch operation to input cells to and output cells from the queue simultaneously, without blocking. An interleaved memory with eight banks is illustrated in Fig. 5.

Shaded elements in the memory banks correspond to valid data cells in the queue. In this example the top cell in the queue is located at address 1 and the bottom cell in the queue is located at address 12. Note that up to eight consecutive cells can be input to (output from) the queue simultaneously on eight unique input (output) banks of the memory.

Typical operation of the switch architecture is illustrated in Fig. 6. In the example, three cells are received at the switch inputs and routed to the bottom of the shared input queue. Four cells are removed from the top of the shared input queue and copied, as required. Eight cells are presented to the output network to be considered for output queueing and transmission. Of the eight cells to be considered for output,

seven are stored in their appropriate output queues. Five cells are transmitted out of the switch, one is fed-back due to a conflict in the output switching network and two are sent to output ports that are already transmitting a cell and queued. In general, operation of the switch requires the following four functions: input, copy, feedback, and output.

Cell input is performed in the first, or input Banyan network of the switch. Cells arrive at the input ports of the switch and are simultaneously routed to the bottom of the input cell queue. It is shown in Section II-A1), that these cells can be simultaneously routed under distributed control by utilizing *combining fetch-and-add* operations in the Banyan network and an interleaved shared-memory. The algorithm is proven to require nonblocking paths in the Banyan network. Thus, cells are inserted into the shared-memory input queue simultaneously, without blocking. Cells are removed from the top of the input queue to be considered for copying.

Cell copying is performed in the second Banyan network of the switch. To copy cells, each cell in the input queue is replicated to multiple cells in the second Banyan network, one for each output of a multicast connection. For example, if a cell is multicasted to three output ports, then that cell requires one location in the input queue and is replicated to three cells in the copy Banyan. An algorithm that is an enhancement of Lee's [20] is presented in Section II-A2) that simultaneously copies cells in the Banyan network. As with cell input, cell copying permits simultaneous operation and is performed under distributed control. The greatest number of cells are removed from the input queue and are copied, such that the number of feedback cells plus the newly replicated cells does not exceed the number of output ports of the Banyan network. Cells from the second Banyan network (and feedback networks) are considered for output by the output network.

Cell output is performed by the output network of the switch, as discussed in Section II-A4). Cells are received from the copy and feedback Banyans, in FIFO order, with the first cell to be considered for output arriving on port 0. For each cell to be considered for output, if the cell's output queue is not over-allocated to other cells, the cell is accepted by the output network. If the number of cells that require the same output port exceeds the speedup of the output network, then the cells arriving on the lower numbered ports are accepted for output and the others will feedback.

Cell feedback is performed in the last Banyan network. Cells that cannot be routed to their desired output queue in the output network are transferred to feedback registers. At the beginning of the next switch cycle, the feedback Banyan inserts the feedback cells on the lower-numbered inputs ports of the output network. The blocked cells are simultaneously routed to the lowered numbered ports, to preserve overall cell sequence in the switch. The algorithm required to perform cell feedback is similar to that required for cell input and is discussed in Section II-A3).

1) Cell Input: The cell input network performs the simultaneous insertion of up to N received cells to the input queue. Queue insertion requires two steps, address generation and simultaneous queue access. Each cell requiring input to the queue must receive a unique address in the shared-

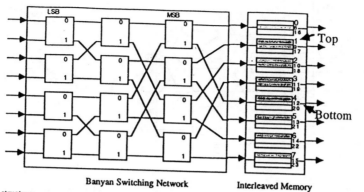

Fig. 5. Interleaved memory structure.

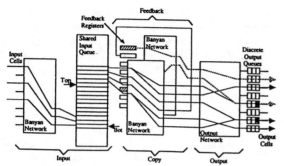

Fig. 6. Switch operation.

memory. Addresses must be sequential to guarantee proper queue structure. After address generation, simultaneous access of the queue is required and is provided by the input Banyan network. For N inputs and N outputs, addressed 0 to $N-1$, the Banyan contains $\log_2 N$ stages of 2×2 switching elements. It is proven in [17] that simultaneous, non blocking, access is provided in a reverse Banyan network, a mirror image of the Banyan network, if the inputs are ordered and the outputs are sequential in modulo N as shown in Fig. 7. Since the queue is sequential, simultaneous access can occur if address generation provides ordered addresses. An address generation scheme is required to generate proper addresses at the input ports. The example of Fig. 7 illustrates six cells arriving on ports 0, 1, 2, 4, 5 and 7. The cells are to be routed to the next six consecutive queue addresses in the input queue: 43, 44, 45, 46, 47 and 48, which are located in memory banks 3, 4, 5, 6, 7 and 0, respectively, of the input queue. Simultaneous access is permitted in the Banyan network since the consecutive queue addresses (located at consecutive outputs of the Banyan network) are allocated to the arriving cells in order from input port 0 to input port 7.

A scheme for address generation is given in [1] that yields unique, sequential addresses in the Banyan network. The scheme utilizes a *fetch-and-add* memory operation. A fetch-and-add operation in a uniprocessor occurs in a single memory cycle, reads a memory location and simultaneously stores the previous value plus an offset to the same location. A fetch-and-add of 6, written fetch-and-add (6), on a memory

location that contains value 43 returns 43 and writes 49 $(43 + 6)$ to the memory. The fetch-and-add operation can be utilized to generate unique addresses in a sequential fashion. Consider six input ports that require the addresses of the next available elements in the queue. These addresses can be determined by the ports sequentially executing fetch-and-add (1) on the bottom pointer. Although this procedure provides correct operation, the address generation is sequential and is thus a bottleneck.

Simultaneous fetch-and-add access of a memory location is provided in [9] by combining fetch-and-add operations at each stage of a Banyan network. Examine Fig. 8. Ports 0, 1, 2, 4, 5 and 7 attempt simultaneous fetch-and-add (1) operations on the bottom pointer. The upper-left 2×2 switching element of the Banyan network combines the fetch-and-add operations into a fetch-and-add (2) and records a 1, corresponding to the upper-most fetch-and-add input. Similar combining occurs at other 2×2 switching elements, resulting in a fetch-and-add (6) at the lower right 2×2 switching element. As a result of the fetch-and-add operation, six is added to the bottom pointer and 43 (shown in bold) is returned to the lower right 2×2 switching element. The 2×2 switching element decomposes the fetch-and-add (6) by returning 43 on its upper return path and adding 43 to its stored 3 and returning 46 on its lower return path. The same decomposition occurs at the other 2×2 switching elements, resulting in simultaneous generation of ordered addresses 43 through 48. Order is maintained at the input ports since each 2×2 switching element directs the lower of the two address values to the numerically lower input port address.

Input cells are inserted in the buffer using simultaneous fetch-and-add address generation and then simultaneous memory access. Input cell addresses are generated by accessing the bottom pointer with fetch-and-add (1) at each input port receiving as cell. Simultaneous access of the memory without blocking in the reverse Banyan network is guaranteed due to ordered inputs and sequential outputs.

An example of the routing procedure utilized in the input Banyan is illustrated in Fig. 7. Routing is accomplished for a cell entering any input by utilizing the least significant $\log_2 N$ b of the input queue address generated by the fetch-and-add instruction. Each stage of the reverse Banyan network utilizes

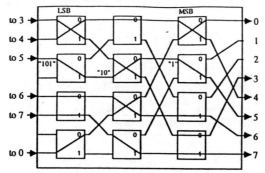

Fig. 7. Banyan nonblocking property.

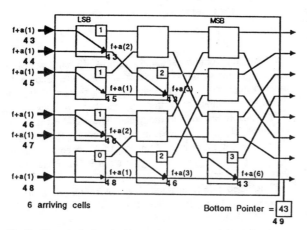

6 arriving cells
Bottom Pointer = 43
49

Fig. 8. Example fetch and add operation.

a single bit of the input queue address to route the cell. The input queue address of the cell is presented to a 2 × 2 switching element of the first stage. The least significant bit of the address is removed and the remaining address bits are forwarded to the 2 × 2 switching element output corresponding to the removed address bit. For example, in Fig. 7 a cell destined for input queue memory bank 5 enters input 2. Address "101" is transferred to the 2 × 2 switch connected to input 2. That switch removes the least significant bit, "1" and forwards address "10" to its "1" output. This procedure is repeated by the switching elements in subsequent stages of the reverse Banyan network until the cell arrives at its destination. Using this routing scheme, the cell will correctly arrive at memory bank 5 from any input of the reverse Banyan network.

2) Cell Copying: Cell copying is performed in the second Banyan network of the switch. The top elements of the input queue are removed, replicated for each multicast output and forwarded to sequential input ports of the output network. The copy Banyan transfers entries from the top of the input queue to sequential ports of the output network. The combination of the copy and feedback Banyans put the oldest cell contained in the switch on port 0 of the output network, with subsequently aged cells routed to subsequent ports.

Due to the memory interleaving of the input queue, the top N cells are stored in different and consecutive memory banks

and can be simultaneously forwarded to the copy Banyan. To facilitate multicast routing, a single input cell of the copy Banyan can be transferred to multiple output cells. In general, multicasting a single input cell to multiple outputs of a Banyan network is a difficult problem. In this architecture, the general multicast problem is simplified into two phases. In the first phase, cells are multicast in the copy Banyan from consecutive single inputs to multiple consecutive outputs only. In the second phase, the output network switches the replicated cells to the appropriate output ports.

As with cell input, cell copying requires address generation and cell routing. Every cell to be considered for copying must be assigned an address, or a range of addresses, that identify output ports of the copy Banyan. Since the range identifies consecutive addresses, it is specified by its upper and lower address bounds. As with cell input, address calculation occurs in a distributed fashion, utilizing combining fetch-and-add operations. For each cell to be copied, a fetch-and-add is initiated with the intended copy number of the cell. For example, if a cell in the input queue is to be replicated to three cells in the multicast queue, a fetch-and-add (3) is initiated. The value returned by the combining fetch-and-add operation is the lower address of the range. The upper address is easily calculated by adding the copy number to the lower address. Using this procedure, the address ranges for the top N cells of the input queue are generated simultaneously.

The simplified multicast routing problem of copying a single input to multiple consecutive outputs is solved with minor enhancements to the Banyan network. A multicast input is transferred to a range of consecutive output addresses, specified by **upper** and **lower**, the upper and lower address bounds of the range, respectively. Note that **lower** is always less than **upper** since there is no wrap at the output of the copy Banyan. The new routing procedure is similar to the standard Banyan network routing procedure, except that instead of manipulating a single output address, the address pair, [**lower**, **upper**], is manipulated. A 2 × 2 switching element receives the address pair and removes the most significant bit of each. If the removed bits are the same, the remaining bits of upper and lower are forwarded as before, to the 2 × 2 switching element output corresponding to value of the removed address bits. If the removed bits differ, then the most significant bit of lower is "0" and the most significant bit of upper is "1". In

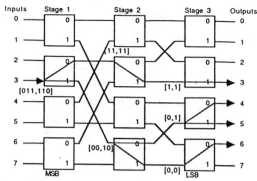

Fig. 9. Banyan network multicast routing.

this case, some part of the range of output addresses must be routed to the 2×2 switching element output "0" and the remaining range must be routed to output "1". The cell will be forwarded to both outputs. To facilitate correct routing the address pairs [lower, $11 \cdots 1$] and [$00 \cdots 0$, upper] are generated and forwarded to ports "0" and "1" respectively. Using this routing scheme, the cell will be correctly routed to all consecutive output addresses from lower to upper.

An example of the multicast routing procedure is illustrated in Fig. 9. A single cell arrives at input 3, to be copied to outputs 3 through 6. The address pair "[011, 110]" is transferred to the 2×2 switch connected to input 3. That switch removes the most significant bits "0" and "1" from upper and lower. Since the most significant bits differ the switching element transfers the incoming cell to both of its outputs. Address pair "[11, 11]" ([lower, 11]) is forwarded to output "0" and "[00, 10]" ([00, upper]) is forwarded to output "1". Examine the second switching element of Stage 2. The element receives the address pair "[11, 11]". Since the most significant bits of the address pair are the same, the remaining address pair, "[1, 1]", is forwarded to its "1" output. At completion of the routing procedure, input 3 is correctly routed to consecutive outputs 3 through 6. This routing procedure can be utilized for the standard (unicast) Banyan network with a single destination by setting upper = lower.

The presented copying procedure facilitates the routing of a single input of the Banyan network to multiple consecutive outputs. The routing procedure permits several consecutive inputs to each be simultaneously routed to multiple consecutive outputs. The paths required for one of the inputs will not block, or interfere with the paths of the other inputs. To maintain high switch throughput, cell copying is performed on as many elements of the input queue as possible such that at most N cells, including feedback cells, are routed to the output network. If only partial copying of an input cell is possible, the initial cells are expanded up to the limit of the copy network and the remaining are expanded on the subsequent switch cycle.

3) Cell Feedback: The feedback Banyan routes any cells that can not be routed to switch outputs by the output network back to the inputs of the output network. Initially, all cells that are sent to the output network are also stored in feedback registers. The registered cells are forwarded through the

feedback Banyan if they were blocked in the output network on the previous switch cycle. To maintain global cell order, cells must be routed to the top ports of the output network in the order that they previously appeared at the output network. Feedback cells are transmitted through the feedback Banyan network in a similar manner to that of the input cells through the input Banyan network. As with the input Banyan, address generation is distributed and simultaneous access is provided in the Banyan network.

4) Cell Output: Cell output is performed in the output switching network. Cells that are removed from the top of the shared input queue by the copy Banyan and in combination with the feedback Banyan are placed in order on the inputs of the output network. All cells that can be routed to output ports without internal or external conflicts are routed through the output network. The remaining cells are marked for feedback by the feedback Banyan. The output network is assumed to be able to route multiple cells to a single output queue. Routing multiple cells to a single output is facilitated by either speeding up the output network to operate multiple times during a single switch cycle, or by operating multiple parallel output networks. Any network can be used for the output network in the switch architecture. A nonblocking network [14], [5], [6] yields higher throughput than a blocking network. The prototype contains two parallel crossbar networks yielding a speedup of 2 in the output network.

Routing of the output network is simplified, since fair-access is not required at its inputs. In typical switch designs, the output network must fairly provide access to all inputs that desire a single output. In this architecture, access to an output port is always granted to the cells that enter the output network on lower numbered input ports. A lower numbered port will always contain an "older" cell than a higher numbered port.

For LAN applications, output queues are utilized to absorb messages that contain long cell bursts and can overlap with other messages directed to the same output port. The output queues operate in strict FIFO order, accept multiple cells and always outputting one cell during each switch cycle if the queue contains any cells.

5) Cell Dropping Discipline: Under abnormally high loads, the switch will not be able to effectively handle all inputted cells. The mechanism utilized to drop cells significantly affects overall switch performance. Two cell dropping disciplines are considered that are shown to yield significantly different performance bounds in Section III. Under both dropping disciplines, the oldest cells presented to the output network, or those at the head-of-line (HOL), are dropped. The difference between the two schemes is the determination of when to drop the cells at the HOL.

In the first discipline, called *HOL dropping*, cells are dropped at the HOL if the output queue for a particular port is full. Consider the Tera architecture with a speedup factor $S = 2$ in the output network. Using HOL dropping, two cells are always removed from the output of the copy/feedback Banyans for each output port to be stored in the output queue for that port. If two queue locations are available in the output queue, both are stored. If not, then one cell is stored (1 location must always be available, since 1 cell must be transmitted on

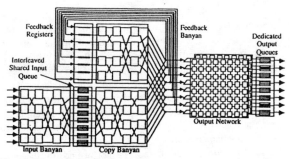

Fig. 10. Detailed switch architecture.

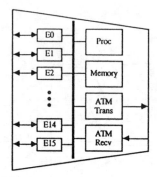

Fig. 11. Network interface architecture.

each switch cycle) and the other cell is dropped. In the second dropping discipline, called *HOL dropping with backpressure*, the second cell is only dropped if the shared input queue is also full. If it is not full, the second cell is fed back in the feedback Banyan to be considered for output on subsequent switch cycles. Using backpressure, a full output queue forces the feedback registers and subsequently the input queue to store cells that can not be stored in an output queue.

6) Detailed Tera LAN Switch Architecture: A detailed illustration of the Tera switch architecture for LAN's with eight inputs and outputs is given in Fig. 10. The 8-ported input Banyan network is connected to the input ports of the switch. The shared memory consists of eight FIFO memory chips, connected to the input and copy Banyans. The copy Banyan is 8-ported, receives cells from the input queue and in combination with the feedback Banyan sends cells to the output network. All cells that are sent to the output network are also stored in feedback registers and are forwarded through the feedback Banyan if they were blocked in the output network on the previous switch cycle. The output network consists of two 8-ported Crossbar Networks.

Note that the final stages of the input Banyan and initial stages of the copy Banyan require "shuffled connections" of the input and output ports. A VLSI layout for switch implementation is simplified by removing those "shuffled connections" and addressing the interleaved input queue memories in shuffled order.

B. Network Interface Architecture

The ATM to Ethernet network interface consists of a high performance RISC microprocessor, a high-speed bus, ATM transmitter and receiver cards and multiple Ethernet cards. See Fig. 11. A detailed description of the Network Interface is given in [11]. The Network Interface implements output queueing for each of the connected devices using time division multiplexing of a central bus. The bus is 32-b wide, with a throughput of over three times the ATM line rate of 155 Mb/s, supporting the ATM transmitter, the ATM receiver and 16 Ethernet channels, each operating at capacity.

All packets are stored in a centralized processor memory in Ethernet message format. A centralized memory is utilized so that Ethernet broadcast messages (e.g., ARP's) can be handled efficiently. A FIFO queue of packet pointers is maintained for each transmitter. When a transmitter completes a previously

transmitted packet, it returns a packet pointer to the processor that is returned to a free list. The pointer at the top of its queue is forwarded to the transmitter for subsequent transmission. Received packet pointers are appended to the transmit queue(s) of all packet destinations. If the destination address is not found at routing time, the packet is broadcasted to the ATM and all Ethernets ports. Currently, the interface does not source address resolution protocol (ARP) packets, but does monitor workstation ARP's and ARP responses to update its routing table.

The Ethernet card of the Network Interface operates as follows. When a packet arrives at an Ethernet receiver, the receiver requests a packet address from the microprocessor. The microprocessor allocates a packet buffer for a maximum size Ethernet packet and returns a pointer to the receiver. The receiver stores the packet to packet memory via DMA. At completion, the Ethernet check-sum is calculated by the Ethernet card. If valid, the packet address is returned to the processor with the packet length and the processor begins processing the packet. If not valid, the address is returned to the processor with a packet length of zero. An on-board FIFO memory is utilized to buffer the beginning of a partially received Ethernet packet that is received prior to the processor returning a packet address. For Ethernet transmission, the processor loads a packet starting address and length to the Ethernet card. The transmitter DMA's the packet from memory, recalculates the check-sum and transmits the message.

The Network Interface ATM cards operate in a similar fashion to the Ethernet card. However, since the packets are stored in memory in Ethernet format, the ATM interface also performs segmentation and reassembly (SAR). ATM adaptation layer 5 (AAL5) is utilized [2]. The transmitter is given a packet address and ATM header information (VPI/VCI). The transmitter reads 48 bytes at a time from packet memory and generates an ATM cell. At the final cell, the pad and AAL5 check-sum fields are calculated and transmitted with an appropriately modified ATM header. At completion, the packet address is returned to the processor.

The ATM receiver is the most complicated part of the interface. It maintains multiple open packet buffers in memory, one for each partially received Ethernet packet. Each Ethernet packet consists of multiple ATM cells, that can be received interleaved with ATM cells of other Ethernet packets. On

Fig. 12. Sixteen input, sixteen output switch prototype 2.

receipt of a cell, the receiver must identify the cell as part of a currently received Ethernet packet, or the start of a new packet. If it is part of a currently received packet, it is appended to the packet in memory. If it is new, a buffer address is requested from the processor. Some FIFO buffering is required locally on the ATM receiver card, due to processor latency.

C. Network Prototypes

A direct implementation of the switch architecture with 16 inputs and 16 outputs is shown in Fig. 12. Prototype 2 consists of a printed circuit board of approximately 16×18 inches using standard "off-the-shelf" integrated components. Packets are assumed to arrive at the input ports of the switch at a fixed frequency that is determined by the maximum transmission rate. The shortest interarrival time is identified as a switch cycle. The switch performs all of the operations identified in Section II-A within a single switch cycle. Internal datapaths of the switch are 8-b wide. Fifty-four clock periods occur within a switch cycle to facilitate the switching of 53 bytes of ATM data and 1 byte of control data. The ATM data rate of 155 Mb/s is maintained at each port, yielding a 50 ns clock period and an aggregate switch throughput of 2.48 Gb/s.

Cells arriving at the switch are received asynchronously in serial ATM format and are transferred to 8-b wide data paths by a standard ATM interface [2] using AMD Taxi transceivers. The interface includes 50 two-element synchronization buffers that delay incoming cells if necessary to begin transmission into the switch at the beginning of a switch cell cycle. Synchronous FIFO memories [15] are utilized for the memory banks of the shared input queue. Xilinx XC3090s field programmable gate arrays (FPGA) [26] are utilized for the Banyan networks. Since a 16×16, 8-b wide Banyan network will not fit into a single XC3090 due to pin restrictions, the Banyan networks are bit-sliced. Four bits of the input and feedback Banyans fit into a single Xilinx part. Due to intensive pipelining, the Xilinx parts operate within the required 50 ns clock period. The prototype was successfully implemented and operational as of December 1994. It is currently undergoing extensive experimentation under load to verify simulation studies. It is expected that multiple priorities as given in [18] will be handled in future prototypes to support other ATM services.

The Network Interface prototype consists of a VME-sized double width, single height backplane. The processor is an AMD 29030 RISC microprocessor running at 25 MHz. A custom-designed TDM bus is utilized to support high bandwidth to packet memory. The Ethernet card consists of the AMD MACE chip and a simple DMA controller. The MACE chip includes two FIFO buffers, to queue a portion of received and transmitted packets and check-sum hardware to validate received Ethernet packets. The ATM interface consists of the AMD Taxi twisted pair transport chips and a number of Xilinx and MACH PLD's. The Network Interface prototype is expected to be operational by late 1994.

III. PERFORMANCE ANALYSIS

To determine the expected performance of the Tera switch embedded in an ATM-based LAN, an analytical and simulation model of a 64×64 switch is constructed. Point-to-point traffic is modeled as bursty arrival processes and multicast traffic is modeled with an average copy number and a truncated geometric distribution.

A. Traffic Model

Bursty traffic is generated by alternating between an active state in which cells are generated consecutively and an idle state in which no cells are generated. The duration of the active and idle states are geometrically distributed. Cell bursts are "heterogeneous" if the destination of each cell in a burst is assumed to be uniformly distributed for all output ports and "homogeneous" if all cells in a burst have the same destination address. Heterogeneous traffic models multiple low data rate sources, such as voice channels, that are multiplexed to form an ATM rate data link [10], [21].

Multicast traffic is modeled using a geometric interarrival distribution for the multicast copy number described by a truncated geometric distribution. The traffic load of the network is assumed to be uniform such that an incoming cell is equally likely to go to any of the output ports. Let ρ be the offered load and $q(Y_j = y)$ be the probability that the number of copies requested by an incoming cell is y. Let $p(X_j = x)$ be the probability that the number of copies generated is x. Then

$$p(k) = \Pr\left(X_i = k\right) = \begin{cases} 1 - \rho, & \text{for } k = 0 \\ \rho q(k), & \text{for } k = 1, 2, \cdots \end{cases} \quad (1)$$

$$P(s) = E\left[e^{sX_i}\right] = (1 - \rho) + \rho Q(s) \quad (2)$$

Thus

$$\text{effective offered load} = \rho E(Y_i) \quad (3)$$

Assuming that Y_j is distributed according to the truncated geometric distribution with the parameter q, then

$$q(k) = \Pr[Y_i = k] = \frac{(1 - q)q^{k-1}}{1 - q^N} \text{ for } 1 \le k \le N \quad (4)$$

where N is the maximum allowable number of copies, since an incoming cell will multicast to, at most, all of the switch

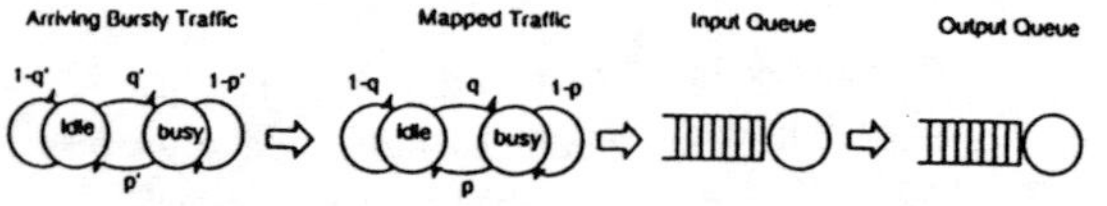

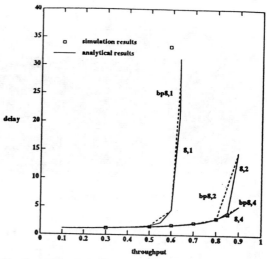

Fig. 13. Switch queueing model with heterogeneous bursty traffic.

outputs. The average number of copies per incoming packet is

$$E[Y_i] = \frac{1}{1-q} - \frac{Nq^N}{1-q^N}. \tag{5}$$

B. Heterogeneous Bursty Traffic Performance

The queueing behavior of the switch with bursty arrivals is modeled exactly as a discrete Markov process. The state of the system is defined as the occupancy of each input queue and the state of each source (active or idle). For an N input switch and with a queue depth of Q, the total number of states in the system is $(2(Q+1))^N$. Such a model quickly becomes unmanageable. To reduce the number of states in the model, the following assumptions are made: the destination addresses of the cells within a burst is assumed to be uniformly distributed (Heterogeneous); and traffic load to the input ports is balanced and the load to the output ports is uniformly distributed. Due to the above assumptions, each FIFO queue is identically and independently distributed. Since each input queue has identical arrival and service distributions and since service is fair such that each queue has equal access to the switch fabric, a single input queue is analyzed.

Assuming that cell arrivals to the queues are synchronized on cell boundaries and that the arriving traffic is bursty in nature, then each of the N cell sources behave independently with geometrically distributed active and idle times. An active source produces a cell every cycle and an idle source produces no cells. Fig. 13 presents the state transition diagram for each source. The active duration is geometrically distributed with parameter p' and the idle duration with parameter q'. The probability that the active state lasts for a duration of i time slots is

$$\text{Prob(active duration} = i) = B(i) = p'(1-p')^{i-1}. \tag{6}$$

The average burst length therefore is

$$\overline{B(i)} = \sum_{i=1}^{\infty} iB(i) = \frac{1}{p'}. \tag{7}$$

Similarly, the idle duration average is $1/q'$. The offered load λ clearly is

$$\lambda = \frac{q'}{q'+p'}. \tag{8}$$

Cell contention for the switch fabric is resolved randomly. If there are x cells in HOL positions with the same destination, the probability that any one of those cells will be allowed into the switch fabric is $1/x$. Since the output network operates with a speedup factor S, S times faster than the input and output channels, each output can accommodate up to S cells each cycle.

The shared queue is modeled with a one to one mapping of the input traffic model to the traffic arriving at a single FIFO

queue. Assuming a two-state Markov process model for bursty incoming traffic, the bursty traffic arriving at a single FIFO is modeled as a two-state Markov process with new bursty parameters obtained through analyzing the function of the input banyan network. To determine if a cell is transmitted that is contending for entry into the output network, the destinations of the HOL cells of the other queues must be determined. Thus, to solve for a single queue, the states of all other queues must be known to determine the service distribution of the tagged queue. Using this scheme, the Markov state space is reduced to only $O(Q)$ states. The analysis is an iterative approach: solve for the distribution of a tagged queue; apply that distribution to all other queues; then use that distribution to recalculate the tagged queues distribution. The procedure is repeated until the analysis converges to a single distribution. From the input FIFO queueing model, the arriving traffic model for the output queues are obtained. Fig. 13 summarizes the queueing model of the switch. Details of the analysis can be found in [16].

1) Numerical Results: The accuracy of the analytical model is verified using simulation results given in Fig. 14. The figure illustrates the delay versus throughput of the switch calculated using analysis and simulation results. The switch model is for a 64-port Tera switch with 20 cell buffers per port in the input and output queues, yielding a total of 40 cell buffers per port. The figure notation "bp, x, y" denotes the switch supporting backpressure and a speedup factor of y with an average burst length of x assumed for the input traffic. Notation "x, y" denotes the switch without the backpressure mechanism. The analytical results are slightly optimistic in terms of delay. The results match in the expected switch region of operation and differ at saturation.

Fig. 15 illustrates the delay versus throughput curves with average traffic burst length 16 and switch speedup factor from 1 to 5. There is a slight increase in cell delay for the switch utilizing the backpressure mechanism but the distinction becomes negligible as the speedup factor increases. The figure shows that a speedup factor of 2 is sufficient to achieve

Fig. 14. Comparison of analytical and simulation results.

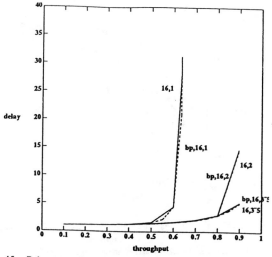

Fig. 15. Delay versus throughput with heterogenous burst length 16.

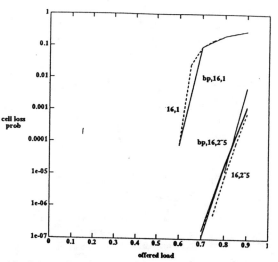

Fig. 16. Cell loss probability versus offered load with heterogeneous bursty traffic.

high throughput comparable to output queueing switches. Although not illustrated, the switch performs similarly under heterogeneous bursty traffic with an average burst length of 8. The input queue of the switch effectively reduces the effects of increased burst lengths of incoming heterogeneous traffic by spreading the bursts across the shared memory space.

Fig. 15 illustrates cell loss probability versus switch offered load. The switch with backpressure mechanism has slightly lower cell loss probability under heterogeneous traffic. Again, the figure indicates that a speedup factor of 2 is sufficient to achieve low cell loss probability. Further increase in speedup does not improve the cell loss performance which is limited by the size of the output queues. Fig. 15 illustrates throughput versus offered load using the same parameters to illustrate maximum switch throughput.

C. Homogeneous Bursty Traffic Performance

Due to the analytical model complexity of homogeneous bursty traffic, switch performance under homogeneous traffic is given using only Monte Carlo simulation [19]. Figs. 15 and 19 illustrate switch delay versus throughput for various speedup factors and average burst lengths of 8 and 16, respectively. The dotted curves represent switch performance without the backpressure mechanism. Unlike heterogeneous traffic, switch performance degrades as the average burst length of the homogeneous traffic increases. The dropping mechanism utilized by the switch significantly affects its performance. Using the backpressure mechanism, switch delay increases with throughput to a peak, whose value depends on the specific load (i.e., 0.3 for bp. 8.1), and then decreases. Delay decreases are due to dropped cells, as cells are dropped at the HOL to accommodate newly arriving cells. The HOL dropping scheme drops the oldest cells in the switch which are typically causing the congestion and throughput degradation. The figures illustrate that the backpressure dropping mechanism increases switch delay since cells can be delayed in both the input and output queues if the output queues begin to fill. Thus,

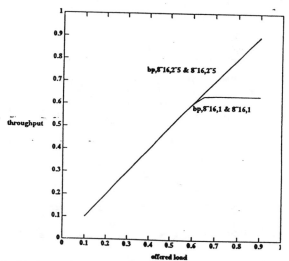

Fig. 17. Throughput versus offered load with heterogeneous bursty traffic.

the buffer space available to an output queue is effectively increased to the combination of the shared input and output queues.

Although increasing delay, the backpressure mechanism significantly improves cell loss performance as shown in Fig. 20. These results indicate that the speedup factor of 2~3 is sufficient to operate with reasonable delay, throughput and cell loss performance. Fig. 21 illustrates switch throughput versus offered load for various speedup factors and burst lengths, verifying that a speedup factor of 2 appears adequate to achieve acceptable throughput performance.

After the analysis, it is apparent that the Tera switch attains better performance under heterogeneous bursty traffic than homogeneous bursts. For the ATM LAN network proposed, the heterogeneous burst model is appropriate since the network interface multiplexes various traffic sources on to a single

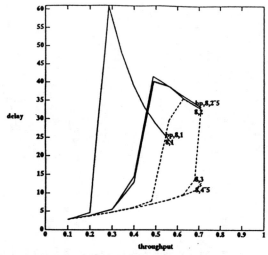

Fig. 18. Delay versus throughput with homogenous burst length 8.

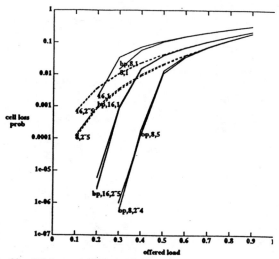

Fig. 20. Cell loss probability versus offered load.

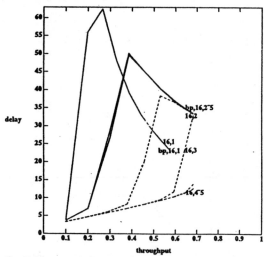

Fig. 19. Delay versus throughput with homogenous burst length 16.

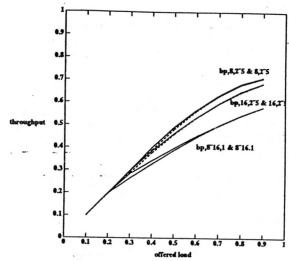

Fig. 21. Throughput versus offered load with homogeneous bursty traffic.

ATM channel. The statistical multiplexing of the traffic sources yields heterogeneous traffic bursts.

D. Multicast Traffic Performance

Figs. 22 and 23 illustrate the switch performance under multicast traffic, using the model described in Section III-A. Fig. 22 shows delay versus throughput curves for multicast traffic with an average copy number of 2, 5, and 7 as obtained from a truncated geometric distribution. Fig. 23 illustrates switch throughput versus offered load with the same parameters. With a speedup of 2, the Tera switch achieves throughput performance comparable to that of output queueing switches. The delay is close to minimum up to the switches maximum throughput. Traffic with higher average copy numbers typically have lower delay and higher throughput, since the offered load remains constant and the increased number of copies results in a reduced arrival rate of the multicast traffic with less conflicts

in the output network. There seems to be a negligible cell loss probability for the switch with speedup of 2 or higher. In fact, the simulation experiments did not produce any loss when four batches of 10 000 000 cells were generated during computer simulation of the Tera switch with speedup of 2 or higher at the offered load of 0.9. We extrapolate from these experiments that the cell loss probability should be less than 10^{-6} at the offered load of 0.9 with 40 buffers/port at the input and output combined.

IV. CONCLUSION

This paper presents the CMU Tera Project. Tera is a high-speed LAN network based on a novel ATM switch architecture with hybrid queueing. The Tera switch is based on the Banyan network and takes advantage of a globally shared input queue and dedicated output queues. Performance analysis of the Tera

684 IEEE JOURNAL ON SELECTED AREAS IN COMMUNICATIONS, VOL. 13, NO. 4, MAY 1995

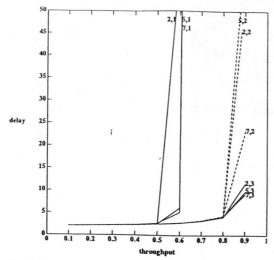

Fig. 22.   Delay versus throughput with 2, 5, and 7 copies.

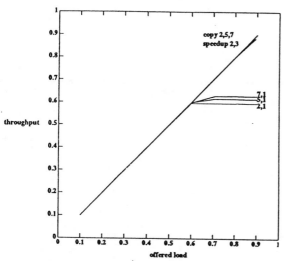

Fig. 23.   Throughput versus offered load with 2, 5, and 7 copies.

switch indicates that output network speedup of 2 is sufficient to achieve high performance in terms of throughput, delay and cell loss probability. The impact of LAN traffic on switch performance is also discussed. As expected, heterogeneous bursty traffic yields better performance than homogeneous bursty traffic. The Ethernet/ATM network interface design can significantly affect switch performance and it is critical to realize its performance impact of the interface design. A report on experimental data measured in the Tera ATM LAN is expected after deployment.

ACKNOWLEDGMENT

The authors would like to acknowledge the following people for the efforts: B. Collier for his numerical computation in the performance analysis; E. Helmsen for his efforts in design and implementation of the Network Interface; J. Helmsen for the redesign and M. Lepper for the implementation of the LAN-optimized 16×16 Tera printed circuit board; D. Anderson for overall system design and implementation; and W. Snider and T. Knaus for their support in installing the prototype network in the CMU-ECE LAN environment.

REFERENCES

[1] G. Almasi and A. Gottlieb, *Highly Parallel Computing.* Redwood City, CA: Benjamin/Cummings, 1989.
[2] "ATM user-network interface specification," version 3.0, *The ATM Forum*, Englewood Cliffs, NJ: Prentice-Hall.
[3] K. E. Batcher, "Sorting networks and their applications," in *Proc. AFIPS Sprint Joint Comput. Conf.*, 1968, pp. 307–314.
[4] R. P. Bianchini Jr. and H. S. Kim, "Design of a nonblocking shared-memory copy network for ATM," in *Proc. Infocom '92*, May 1992.
[5] B. Bingham and H. Bussey, "Reservation-based contention resolution mechanism for Batcher-banyan packet switches," *Electron. Lett.*, vol. 23, no. 13, pp. 772–773, June 1988.
[6] J. J. Degan, G. W. J. Luderer, and A. K. Vaidya, "Fast packet technology for future switches," *AT&T Tech. J.*, vol. 68, no. 2, pp. 36–51, Mar./Apr. 1989.
[7] A. E. Eckberg and T. C. Hou, "Effects of output buffer sharing on buffer requirements in an ATDM packet switch," in *Proc. INFOCOM '88* (New Orleans, LA), Mar. 1988, pp. 459–466.
[8] K. Y. Eng, M. G. Hluchyj, and Y. S. Yeh, "Multicast and broadcast services in a knockout packet switch," in *Proc. INFOCOM'88*, (New Orleans, LA), Mar. 1988, pp. 29–34.
[9] A. Gottliebet *et al.*, "The NYU ultracomputer-designing an MIMD shared memory parallel computer," *IEEE Trans. Comput.*, pp. 175–189, Feb. 1983.
[10] H. Heffes and D. M. Lucantoni, "A Markov modulated characterization of packetized voice and data traffic and related statistical multiplexer performance," *IEEE J. Select. Areas Commun.* vol. 4, pp. 856–868, Sept. 1986.
[11] "E. Helmsen, "Design and implementation of the MATER ATM to ethernet router," Master's Thesis, Carnegie Mellon Univ., Pittsburgh, PA, May 1994.
[12] J. Helmsen, "Printed circuit board implementation of the Tera 16×16 ATM Switch," Master's Thesis, Carnegie Mellon Univ., Pittsburgh, PA, May 1994.
[13] M. G. Hluchyj and M. J. Karol, "Queueing in high-performance packet switching," *IEEE J. Select. Areas Commun.*, vol. 6, pp. 1587–1597, Dec. 1988.
[14] J. Hui and E. Arthurs, "A broadband packet switch for integrated transport," *IEEE J. Select. Areas Commun.*, vol. 5, pp. 1264–1273, Oct. 1987.
[15] *The IDT Specialized Memories Data Book*, Integrated Devices Technology Inc., Santa Clara, CA, 1990.
[16] H. S. Kim and B. Collier, "Performance analysis of input queueing switches with correlated arrival processes," Center for Comput. Syst., Carnegie Mellon Univ., Pittsburgh, PA, Tech. Rep. 93-10, Sept. 1993.
[17] H. S. Kim and A. Leon-Garcia, "Non-blocking property of reverse Banyan network," *IEEE Trans. Commun.*, vol. 40, pp. 472–476, Mar. 1992.
[18] H. S. Kim and R. P. Bianchini Jr., "Design and performance of a scalable shared input queue ATM switch," submitted to *Int. J. Commun. Syst.*, Oct. 1993.
[19] A. M. Law and W. D. Kelton, *Simulation Modeling and Analysis.* New York: McGraw-Hill, 1982.
[20] T. T. Lee, "Nonblocking copy networks for multicast packet switching," *IEEE J. Select. Areas Commun.*, vol. 6, pp. 1455–1467, Dec. 1988.
[21] K. Q. Liao and L. G. Mason, "A discrete-time single server queue with a two-level modulated input and its applications," in *Proc. IEEE Globecom '89*, pp. 26.1.1–26.1.6.
[22] K. A. Lutz, "Considerations on ATM switching techniques," *Int. J. Digital, Analog Cabled Syst.* vol. 1, pp. 237–243, 1988.
[23] K. Shiomoto, M. Murata, Y. Oie, and H. Miyahara, "Performance evaluation of cell bypass queueing discipline for buffered Banyan type ATM switches," in *IEEE Proc. INFOCOM' 90*, June 1990, pp. 677–685.
[24] J. S. Turner, "Design of a broadcast packet switching network," in *IEEE Proc. INFOCOM' 86*, Mar. 1986, pp. 667–675.
[25] C. L. Wu and T. Y. Feng, "On a class of multistage interconnection networks," *IEEE Trans. Comput.*, vol. 29, pp. 694–704, Aug. 1980.
[26] *The Programmable Gate Array Data Book.* San Jose, CA: Xilinx, 1991.

Ronald P. Bianchini (S'86–M'86) was born in Brooklyn, NY, on April 29, 1962. He received the B.S. degree in electrical engineering from th Massachusetts Institute of Technology in 1983 and the M.S. and Ph.D. degrees in electrical and computer engineering from Carnegie Mellon University in 1985 and 1989, respectively.

He aided the New York University Ultracomputer project during the sumer of 1983 in the area of wireability. He consulted for AT&T Bell Laboratories during the summers of 1990 and 1991, in the application of a fault diagnosis system to AT&T reserach networks. Currently, he is an Associate Professor in the Electrical and Computer Engineering Department at Carnegie Mellon Unviersity. He directs research groups in the study of fault diagnosis in distributed systems and the design of telecommunication switching architectures. His research interests include system-level diagnosis, distributed computer systems, telecommunication switching and computer architecture.

Dr. Bianchini is a member of the IEEE Computer Society, the Association for Computing Machinery and was nominated to the Eta Kappa Nu Honor Society in 1983.

Hyong S. Kim (S'84–M'90) received the B.E. (Honours) degree in electrical engineering from McGill University in 1984, and the Master of Applied Science and Ph.D. degrees in electrical engineering from the University of Toronto in 1987, and 1990, respectively.

Currently, he is an Associate Professor in the Department of Electrical and Computer Engineering, Carnegie Mellon University. He was a lecturer for the Network Engineering Program at Northern Telecom in 1990. He worked as a research consultant addressing issues in the system modeling and performance analysis. He has been working in high-speed networks since 1984, and his Tera ATM switch architecture co-invented with Dr. Bianchini has recently been licensed to AMD for commercialization.

A High-Capacity ATM Switch Based on Advanced Electronic and Optical Technologies

As the number of ATM broadband subscribers grows, the construction of an efficient access and tandem network will require very large ATM switches. The authors propose an architectural approach based on a concept of satellite switches of moderate capacity, loosely coupled over very high-speed links through a cross-connect core.

Ernst Munter, James Parker, and Paul Kirkby

ERNST MUNTER is principal scientist advanced systems and technology at Bell-Northern Research.

JAMES PARKER is a manager at Bell-Northern Research.

PAUL KIRKBY is the Technical Strategy Manager for Access and Network Evolution at Bell-Northern Research.

As the number of asynchronous transfer mode (ATM) broadband subscribers grows and the traffic volume increases, the construction of an efficient access and tandem network will require very large ATM switches, with aggregate capacities in the 100s of gigabits per second (Gb/s).

An architectural approach is proposed which, together with a set of technologies, will make the design of such large switches practical. It is based on a concept of satellite switches of moderate capacity, loosely coupled over very high-speed links through a cross connect core.

The separation of functions permits optimal use of the technology: common memory fabrics in the satellites use high-speed RAM to achieve a throughput of 10 to 40 Gb/s per satellite; and a relatively simple space switch based on very high-speed serial electronic and optical technologies provides a large cross-connect capacity of up to 1000 Gb/s and more.

This article describes the architecture and the technology of a prototype switch designed at BNR to verify this approach experimentally. The switch contains a 16-by-16 cross-connect switch for optical links running at 10 Gb/s and the control algorithm and protocol to exchange ATM traffic efficiently.

Broadband access systems will be based on systems such as fiber to the home, fiber to the curb, coaxial cable, or wireless, and will serve to connect subscribers to local access nodes.

In the transit network, high-capacity fiber transmission already provides the technical means to move very large amounts of data from node to node at a reasonable cost.

To make full use of this bandwidth in the form of a worldwide broadband backbone network, switches of adequate capacity are required.

Innovations in network architecture may lead to a more distributed network of a larger number of smaller nodes. But the geographic clustering of traffic in cities and communities, the shrinking cost of collecting a large bandwidth over ring, tree, or star access networks, and the operational economics of fewer, larger, sites is likely to continue to favor the concentration of traffic into exchanges serving 10,000 to 100,000 subscribers.

Similarly, fewer but larger tandem switches will be more economical than a fully meshed network of smaller tandem switches or of access switches alone. These economics will be driven by the availability of high-capacity transmission links of 10 gb/s or more.

Several access technologies and topologies are possible for a broadband network, including fiber, coax, twisted pair, and even wireless.

Figure 1 is an example of a hypothetical broadband network, containing tandem and local exchanges, servers, and a broadband access network based on fiber distribution, and coax or twisted pair drops.

Given certain assumptions of service bit rates, we could estimate that a gross switching capacity of one Terabit/s would be required to handle the aggregate broadband traffic of a switch serving 100,000 subscribers.

Similarly, a nonhierarchical interexchange network of 5 to 20 fully meshed tandem switches of one Terabit/s capacity each, might provide the long distance network for 100 million subscribers, depending on traffic assumptions.

These may be futuristic scenarios, and many factors are likely to affect the ultimate architecture of the public broadband network, not just technology and economics.

In this article the authors are focusing on the goal of understanding what some of the technical solutions are.

We describe technological research being

Reprinted from IEEE Communications Magazine, Nov. 1995, pp. 64-71.

undertaken at BNR which is aimed at harnessing very high-speed electronic and optical technology for use in the core of a high-capacity ATM switch.

Switch Architecture

In a modular architecture, the switch is divided into a number of modules, in several groups or subsystems. Traditionally, we would find a control subsystem, a switching core, and a set of peripheral interface modules which connect to the outside world, in the form of SONET or SDH fiber links.

Here, we concentrate on the switch core component of a large ATM switch. The overall switch architecture is based loosely on a space switch cross point with input and output buffers.

The main components of a complete ATM switch are a switching core, peripheral units with transmission interfaces, and a software control structure running on embedded and/or external CPUs. We expand this architecture by inserting independent buffered satellite switches between groups of lower speed access peripherals and the switch core. Figure 2 illustrates this principle.

Another way of looking at this architecture would be to consider each buffered switch as a stand-alone switch. The large switch is created by tying together a cluster of smaller switches using very high-speed (10 Gb/s) trunks. However, that view would not be entirely correct since we expect the satellite switches to share control of the space switch core.

Similarly, a high-speed trunk peripheral with transmission interfaces of the same order as the space switch ports could assume a dual function, that of transmission interface and ATM processing, as well as input/output buffering for the core.

The link speed of 10 Gb/s was chosen because ATM buffers of this capacity are readily built and can be multiplexed to this serial speed. It is also possible today to build a simple non-blocking space switch crosspoint, using either electro-optical or all-optical technologies, to handle serial signals of this speed. The actual design described here corresponds to the first experimental implementation of a switch of an aggregate capacity of 160 Gb/s.

Principle of Operation

The purpose of the switch is to carry ATM cells from the input buffers to the appropriate output buffers through the core. Since there are no cell

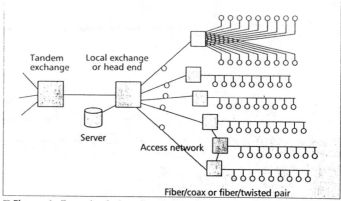
■ **Figure 1.** *Example of a broadband network.*

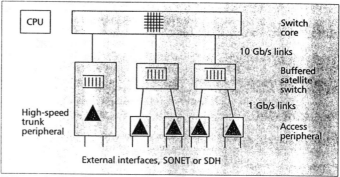
■ **Figure 2.** *High throughput AT switch architecture.*

buffers in the core, transmission into the core from the individual buffer modules must be coordinated in such a way that cells do not collide at the outputs. This is achieved by using a common hardware control circuit which receives status information from the buffers. It sets up space switch connections and sends control information back to the buffers to schedule the transmission of cells from the buffers to coincide with the crosspoint setup. Figure 3 shows the basic switch control architecture.

In the input buffer module, all arriving input cells are tagged according to the destination core output port and stored in the common memory buffer.

The buffer control circuit has two main functions: an input (write) and an output (read) scheduling function. Each cell that arrives as

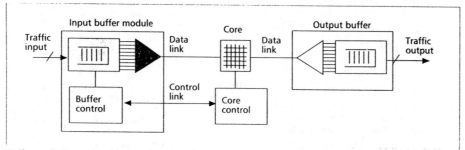
■ **Figure 3.** *Control architecture based on the separation of data and control.*

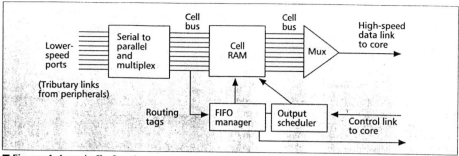

■ **Figure 4.** *Input buffer functions.*

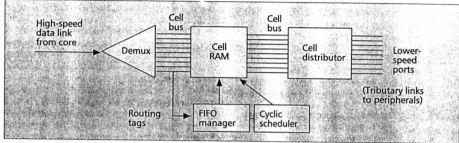

■ **Figure 5.** *Output buffer functions.*

The switch architecture is based on the premise that the optimum cost point for a large switch is achieved by selecting a simple topology, using the highest speed components available at a reasonable cost.

traffic input is written into a free buffer location, and core control is notified over the control link, in the form of a connection request message. Figure 4 illustrates the input buffer functions in more detail.

In response to each grant message received from the core control, cells are read out from memory and transmitted to the core over the data link. Although combined in the original ATM cell format, we separate the routing information from the payload and create a distinct control path for the high-speed core. The high-speed data paths carry cells transparently from buffer to buffer through the core, and the core does not need to inspect cell headers for routing.

The core control algorithm receives all request messages, arbitrates between them, and returns grant messages when the appropriate connection is about to be set up.

The output scheduler of the buffer control circuit in the input buffer module will receive a corresponding grant some time after the first request was sent; in the meantime, additional ATM cells for the same port destination may have arrived, and additional requests for the same connection would have been sent to the core. Thus, when the grant message arrives, several ATM cells can be sent in a single burst over the connection.

In essence, given a large enough RAM, the core control can be arbitrarily slow in processing requests and granting connections for the transmission of bursts. This simply results in longer bursts and longer waiting times. The algorithm must, of course, run fast enough to meet the delay, and delay variation performance expected for an ATM switch. Buffer space in the Cell RAMs must also be dimensioned appropriately to hold the waiting cells without overflowing.

The separation of control and data paths also requires synchronization between them: this would be difficult to achieve if space switch connections were changed after every ATM cell cycle. In our design, this has become easier as a result of the burst mode of switching in which we set up connections for a duration much longer than one cell period. In this way, it is possible and economical to provide a long guard time between cell bursts, of the order of one or two cell periods.

Bursts of ATM cells are then transmitted through the core to output buffers where the high-speed cell stream is stored in RAM and switched to the lower speed ports, in the same way as in a shared memory switch

Figure 5 is a block diagram of the output buffer. In reality, both input and output buffer functions are very similar and can be combined in a single shared memory module.

Selection of Technology

The switch architecture is based on the premise that the optimum cost point for a large switch is achieved by selecting a simple topology, and using the highest-speed components available at a reasonable cost.

Figure 6 illustrates this idea: to construct a switch of a given capacity, we can use fewer parts if we select a higher-speed technology. The exact shapes of the curves depend on the architecture, and they will also shift with time. However, we can generalize that over a large range, cost is less than proportional with speed, while for most switch architectures, the number of components drops more than proportionally with their speed. For example, an N-port space switch uses N-squared cross points; only one quarter as many crosspoints are needed to achieve the same traffic throughput if the port speed is doubled.

The high-speed technologies available to construct the prototype switch core included HBT GaAs ICs, direct drive FP and DFB lasers, optical splitters, and detector arrays with multi-fiber alignment. The control path (100 to 200 Mb/s per link) can be built from widely available components such as fiber channel or high-speed "Taxi" links, while the control logic could use silicon CMOS, BiCMOS, or even field programmable logic devices.

System Components

The Core

The core is a single rack unit, containing a passive 256 x 256 optical shuffle interconnect and sixteen port cards with the active switching components. The common controller circuit is shown as a single unit but is actually distributed among the port cards in the prototype. The overall switch core connectivity is shown in Fig. 7.

The set of port cards, each with a 1:16 splitter and a 16:1 selector, together provides a 16 x 16 crosspoint. The optical data path inputs are each split (replicated optically) 16 ways so that each selector receives all data path inputs. Each selector has 16 optical inputs, one optical output, and an electronic control input. Under the control of the control circuit, it selects one of the 16 input streams, regenerates it, and sends the optical data to the output buffer connected to that port.

Figure 8 shows the various technology components that make up a complete switch core, with one port card shown in detail.

The core control consists of the control link terminations associated with each port, and a control circuit made up of 16 port control circuits which communicate over a common control bus. We can trace the path of a switched serial

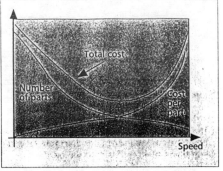

■ **Figure 6.** *Switch architecture economics.*

data connection through a number of high-speed components, referenced in Fig. 8 by circled numbers, as follows:

The signal originates in the input buffer, with a GaAs-HBT laser driver (1) and a direct drive laser (2).

The optical input to the port card is replicated in a passive optical splitter on silicon substrate (3).

The resulting 16 optical signals are connected through a pair of eight-way multifiber connectors (W) to the 256 by 256 passive optical shuffle network (4).

One of the signals from this port card, together with 15 signals from the other port cards returns from the shuffle through another pair of connectors (X), to illuminate an 8 + 8 PIN diode detector array (5), which is directly bonded to a 16:1 GaAs-HBT selector chip with integrated pre-amplifiers (6).

The electrical output from the selector is regenerated in a clock and data recovery circuit (7), and passed to a laser driver (8). The optical connection back to the output buffer is through

The high-speed data paths carry cells transparently from buffer to buffer through the core, and the core does not need to inspect cell headers for routing.

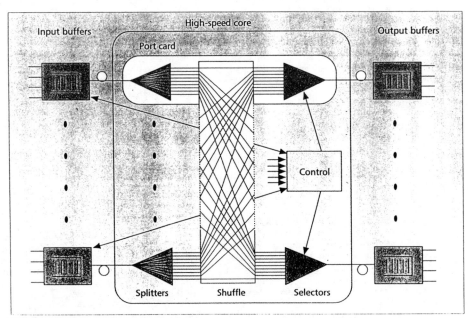

■ **Figure 7.** *High-speed core connectivity.*

a direct drive 10 Gb/s laser (9), a singlemode fiber, into a single PIN detector and preamplifier (10), and another clock and data recovery circuit (11). These components are described in more detail in the following sections.

Passive Optical Network

The passive optical network (components 3 and 4) consists of 16 planar 1:16 splitters, which convert the single fiber inputs into parallel ribbons of 16 fibers. This set of 256 fibers is then twisted through a shuffle pattern and reterminated in 16 ribbon fibers that feed back to the port cards.

The idea of using passive optics in a switch application is attractive because it provides the necessary shuffle and crossover of the entire switch bandwidth efficiently and compactly. We thus take advantage both of the high-speed of the optical signal to keep the number of signal paths low, and of the ability to route densely packed optical paths without mutual interference.

Electro-Optical Selector

The electro-optical selector (components 5-9) is a hybrid assembly on a silicon substrate with 16 optical inputs, one optical output, and a 4-bit electronic control input. The optical fibers are physically attached in grooves etched into the silicon which provide accurate alignment to a PIN diode array. The diodes are bonded across to the HBT GaAs device which contains amplifiers and selection circuitry, driven by a 4-bit control input. The output signal from the selector chip is regenerated digitally before driving the output laser.

For practical reasons, the devices to regenerate the selected signal (components 7-9) were mounted separately in the prototype, interconnected with semi-rigid coax.

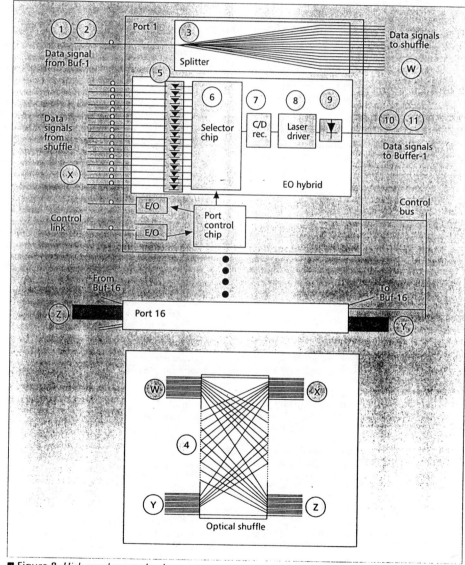

■ **Figure 8.** *High-speed core technology components.*

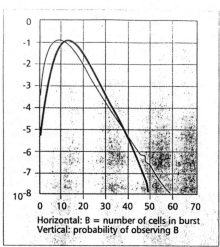

■ **Figure 9.** *Burst size distribution for 80 percent loading.*

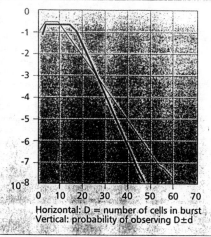

■ **Figure 10.** *Cell delay distribution for 80 percent loading.*

PIN-Diode Array

Standard high-speed PIN diodes (component 5) were fabricated as arrays on 250 micrometer spacing to match the spacing of the ribbon fibers.

Laser

Two types of laser (component 9), developed and manufactured at BNR, appeared suitable for use in this project. To reduce cost and complexity, we planned on driving the lasers with the 10 Gb/s digital signal directly rather than relying on the more conventional arrangement of CW laser plus modulator, since chirp and pulse dispersion is not a problem with the short fibers in the switch.

Ideally, we would also eliminate coolers and use a low cost FP laser which can operate over a wide temperature range. At present, however, a multiquantum well DFB ridge laser mounted on a cooler gives the best performance, combining fast switching with high power which is needed to overcome the 15 to 18 dB loss of the splitters and connectors.

Laser Drivers

The laser drivers (component 8), and clock and data recovery circuits were fabricated using the same GaAs HBT process as the selector device. With the exception of the PIN diode input, all high-speed electronic signals are differential.

Control

The purpose of the core control is to receive connection requests from the satellite switches and set the space switch connection configuration accordingly; it also sends the connection information back to the satellites as grant messages to trigger the transmission of the ATM bursts that will match the connection setup. Control is achieved by a set of port control circuits that cooperate over the common control bus to arbitrate connections.

A single connection generally involves two different ports: an input which received the request and an output port which controls the data selector to make a single connection.

The port control chip of the input port receives requests and issues grants by means of the associated control link. Each request message identifies the number of outstanding requests (cell counts in the input buffer) for each space switch port. This count later determines the size of the burst granted to the input buffer. A connection can only be made when both input and output ports are free. The control bus is used to allow each free input port to broadcast its outstanding requests, and each free output port to return grants to the input port circuits.

A control frame which lasts 16 cell periods is used to allow all inputs to match up with all outputs. In each of the control time slots, all 16 inputs communicate each with a different output circuit. If a match is found (free input, free output, and outstanding request), the corresponding connection is made for the duration indicated by the accumulated count, corresponding to the number of cells queued for this connection: the control circuit on the output port sets the 4-bit address of the data selector and the control circuit on the input port transmits a grant message to the input buffer.

At the high data rate of 10 Gb/s, the transmission delay of the links between buffers and the core may be of the order of several cell periods. To compensate for the link delay, connections are computed and scheduled ahead of time so that the new bursts arrive at the core, just as the connection is made.

A connection is released when the granted number of cells have passed through it. To improve efficiency, a waiting period is imposed before the same connection can be established again. During high load, this prevents the frequent set up of connections for very short bursts, and forces the input buffers to accumulate longer bursts, hence the ratio of guard time (two cells per burst) to traffic cells is reduced. Simulations have shown that a forced wait of 100 to 200 cell periods increases the average delay slightly, but reduces the cell delay variation and the maximum delay significantly.

The frequency distribution charts (Figs. 9 and

■ Figure 11. *Prototype port card.*

■ Figure 12. *Prototype switch core rack.*

10) illustrate the simulated behavior of this algorithm for the case of 80 percent occupancy of all links and random (Poisson) traffic, with two idle cells forced inserted after every burst.

The connection algorithm is dynamic, controlled by traffic pressure from the input buffers. The simulation shows the behavior for two different settings of the "forced wait" parameter. Increasing the "forced wait" value (bold curves) increases the average delay and burst length, but reduces the statistical worst case values.

It should be noted that the "bursts" observed in this model are bursts of cells traveling from one input buffer to one output buffer. These bursts are generally composed of cells belonging to different virtual connections (VCI) which may themselves contain bursts. However, the time scales are quite different.

Physical Implementation

*T*o demonstrate the practicality of both the architecture and the components, a demonstration switch is under construction in two phases: phase 1, a partial realization of the 160 Gb/s switch using simulated buffers and the electro-optic switch described above, is complete. In phase 2, the simulated buffers will be replaced with real ATM multiplexers and fully optical switching (as described below) will be introduced.

The buffers are simulated, in the first instance, by personal computers (PCs) with integral transmit and receive cards. These transform

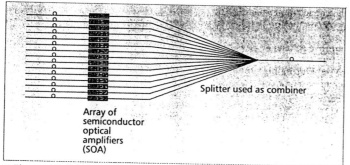

■ Figure 13. *Selector function with optical path.*

the source data from the memory busses into the format used on the 10 Gb/s links. They multiplex the low data rate streams to the 10 Gb/s line rate and perform the addressing and control functions, including, for example, start of burst detection.

The optoelectronic components for the terminals are housed on a separate board outside the PC Chassis. Single mode fibers link each simulator to a separate port card in the core rack.

Each port card (Fig. 11) contains all core components associated with the corresponding buffer port. This modularity is an important feature of the design that will simplify assembly and allow economical part-provisioned systems to be realized.

The ribbon fiber connectors on the rear edge of the board provide the interface to the optical shuffle, which is housed in a 3-unit high rack above the selector cards (Fig. 12).

Optical Switch

The photodiode array, HBT selector chip, and laser retransmitter were judged to be the most readily implementable 16:1 ATM packet selector, using presently available technology. However, this subsystem performs the function of an optical switch overall, and is a good candidate for replacement by a more advanced optical technology.

Progress on the integration of semiconductor optical amplifier switches and passive wave guides suggests that an optical switch similar to that shown in Fig. 13 will be practical.

Embedded in the architecture, a switch capacity of 1 Terabit/s appears to be well within reach, for example, as a combination of an optical cross-connect switch with twenty-five 40 Gb/s common memory satellite switches. Wavelength division multiplexing (WDM) could be used to transmit and switch the 40 Gb/s signals through the optical core, without requiring electronic speeds in excess of 10 Gb/s.

Conclusion

*T*here are many detailed studies, experiments, and comparisons with alternative technologies to be made, but from our present state of knowledge, this architecture appears most attractive for a Terabit ATM switch at about the turn of the century for the following reasons:

- It makes use of emerging high-speed electro-optical technology to drastically reduce switch complexity, compared to fully electronic solutions.
- It avoids the need for electronics operating above 10 Gb/s with its attendant high power consumption.
- It makes use of peripheral buffers that are based on smaller capacity ATM switches, which are already developed for earlier application.

There is a clear path forward from present electronic low-capacity ATM switches via an opto-electronic evolution stage, to an all-optical core of Terabit/s capacity.

References

[1] B. Gadher *et al.*, "A Distributed Metropolitan Network for Residential Multimedia Applications," *Proc. ISS '95*, April 1995, vol. 2, p. 190.
[2] R. Mauger and S. Brueckheimer, "The Role of ATM in 64 kb/s Switching and Transmission Networks," *Proc. ISS '95*, April 1995, vol. 2, p. 87.
[3] P. J. Dyke, "Fibre Access Penetration to Provide Broadband Services," *Proc. 6th Int'l Workshop on Optical Access Networks*, Kyoto, Oct. 1994.
[4] T. Lester *et al.*, "A Manufacturable Process for HBT Circuits," *Proc. Int'l Symposium of GaAs and Related Compounds*, Freiburg, Germany, 1993.
[5] E. Munter and I. Perryman, "Method and Apparatus for Input Buffered Asynchronous Transfer Mode Switch," USA patent 5,126,999, 1992.

Biographies

ERNST MUNTER was graduated from Munich Technical University in 1964, came to Canada in 1966, and has worked at Bell-Northern Research in Ottawa since 1974. A pioneer in the development of narrowband digital switching, he has been involved in ATM and broadband switching since 1987. As principal scientist for advanced systems and technology, his main interest today is to guide the choice of system architectures and appropriate technologies for future products.

JAMES PARKER was graduated from Cambridge University, England, with a degree in physics in 1981. After receiving his degree, he joined BNR where he worked on a variety of fiber-optic and guided wave devices and subsystems. In 1991, he assumed responsibility for developing advanced opto-hybrid packaging technology for low-cost, high-functionality optoelectronic modules and also managed a number of European and U.K. collaborative programs in this area. He was appointed manager of the Terabit Switch project in February 1994. He has published more than 20 papers and is a Chartered member of the Institution of Electrical Engineers.

PAUL KIRKBY is technical strategy manager for access and network evolution at BNR's Laboratory at Harlow, United Kingdom. During his career he progressed from work on optical components such as Semiconductor Lasers to systems work on high-capacity optical transmission. He received a B.Sc. in electronics and a Ph.D. in Lasers from Southampton University in 1971 and 1978, respectively. He is a Fellow of the IEE and a visiting professor in the Electrical Engineering Department at University College London.

There is a clear path from present electronic low-capacity ATM switch-es to an all-optical core of Terabit/s capacity.

CHAPTER III

TRAFFIC AND
CONGESTION CONTROL

This chapter identifies traffic management issues in ATM, and provides detailed treatment of congestion control in ATM networks.

Performance Management Issues in ATM Networks: Traffic and Congestion Control

Dominique Gaïti and Guy Pujolle, *Senior Member, IEEE*

Abstract—The goal of this paper is first to introduce performance monitoring aspects of asynchronous transfer mode (ATM) networks and then to focus on traffic and congestion control schemes. To deal with this performance monitoring management, a framework for defining a generic intelligent and integrated model for network management is described. As an example of the efficiency of this intelligent management architecture, we measure the performance of a new congestion control scheme. This scheme uses the cell loss priority (CLP) bit, the explicit forward congestion indicator and the explicit backward congestion indicator. The intelligent management uses different parameters and builds a complex but efficient control scheme. We show that this new control scheme allows performance to be increased by an order of magnitude.

I. INTRODUCTION

ASYNCHRONOUS Transfer Mode (ATM) was adopted by the International Telecommunications Union-Telecommunication Standardization Sector (ITU-T) as the transport method for the broadband integrated services digital networks (B-ISDN) ([12]–[14], [16], [18]). It is a packet-like switching and a multiplexing technique in which the packets are fixed-size cells of 53 bytes each. Cells are then multiplexed on the links to obtain the flexibility necessary to support all-purpose services.

ATM is both a packet-oriented transfer mode that uses an asynchronous time division multiplexing technique, and a connection-oriented technique. Connection identifiers are assigned to each link of a connection when required and released when no longer needed. The connection-oriented mode involves a virtual channel connection (VCC) that preserves sequencing of cells. Inside the cell header, two fields are of interest for our purpose:

- The payload-type (PT) field that contains 3 b. As far as congestion control is concerned, user data are transmitted by the end point through the field payload-type identifier (PTI), with PTI = 000 and PTI = 001 depending on the congestion at this point. Any congested network element, upon receiving a user data cell, modifies the PTI as follows:

  - when received with 000 or 010, cell is transmitted with 010;

Manuscript received March 21, 1994; revised November 25, 1994; approved by IEEE/ACM TRANSACTIONS ON NETWORKING Editor I. Cidon.

D. Gaïti is with Columbia University, Center for Telecommunications Research, New York, NY 10027-6699 USA.

G. Pujolle is with the University of Versailles, Laboratoire PRiSM-CNRS, 78035 Versailles Cedex, France.

Publisher Item Identifier S 1063-6692(96)02723-9.

  - when received with 001 or 011, cell is transmitted with 011.

  PTI = 100 or 101 will be used by operation and management (OAM) cells. PTI = 110 is reserved for resource management use.

- The cell loss priority (CLP) field is set to one when the cell is subject to discard, depending on network conditions. When the CLP bit is set to zero, the cell has a higher priority and should not be discarded by the network.

One of the main difficulties in ATM networks is to monitor the performance. Specifically, for traffic and congestion control purposes, the main problem is to tune the values of the parameters. We need an intelligent management platform providing distributed control capable of optimizing the performance of the system by efficiently tuning the parameters [8].

The goal of this paper is to introduce such a framework through the proposal of a generic intelligent and integrated model for network management. As an example of the efficiency of this intelligent management architecture, we will compare the performance of a new congestion control scheme with and without this intelligent management platform. This new congestion control scheme uses the CLP bit, the explicit forward congestion indicator and the explicit backward congestion indicator.

This paper is organized as follows. Section II describes the quality of service and performance monitoring aspects of ATM networks. Section III is devoted to the traffic and congestion control in ATM networks. The intelligent architecture to handle the requirements of the performance management is introduced in Section IV. Section V presents the entire network performance management architecture. Section VI develops an example through a new congestion control scheme to show the efficiency of the intelligent architecture. Finally, in Section VII, we discuss future issues in the area of intelligent agents and performance management.

II. PERFORMANCE MANAGEMENT IN ATM NETWORKS

The Main contribution to the control and management of an ATM network is considered in [18]. This recommendation covers both the user network interface (UNI) and network node interface (NNI), OAM, and thus provides transport and access network operation, maintenance principles, functions for the physical layer and ATM layer in a B-ISDN. Five areas have been specified: performance monitoring, defect and

Reprinted from IEEE/ACM Transactions on Networking, Vol. 4, No. 2, April 1996, pp. 249-257.

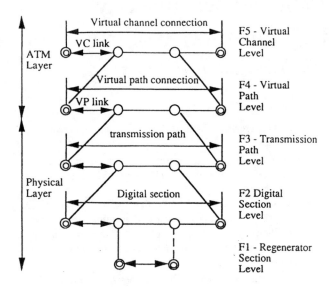

○ Endpoint of the corresponding level

○ Connecting point of the corresponding level

Fig. 1.   The OAM flows.

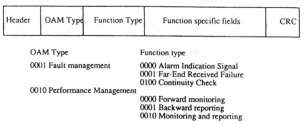

Fig. 2.   OAM cell format, OAM type, and function type.

failure detection, system protection, failure or performance information, and fault localization.

OAM functions in the network are performed on five OAM hierarchical levels associated with the ATM and physical layer of the ITU-T reference model. The functions result in corresponding bi-directional information flows F1–F5, referred to as OAM flows (Fig. 1):

F1) Regenerator section level.
F2) Digital section level.
F3) Transmission path level.
F4) Virtual path level.
F5) Virtual channel level.

Management operations require the exchange of management information between various nodes in the network. Peer ATM-layer management entities in each node will need to communicate to support virtual path connection/virtual channel connection (VPC/VCC) management. Specifically, the mechanisms at the virtual path (VP) and virtual channel (VC) levels are F4 and F5 flows, respectively.

The F5 flow is concerned with the virtual channel level. OAM cells for the F5 flow have the same VCI/VPI values as the user cells and are identified by the PTI in the header. The OAM cells for both directions of the F5 flow must follow the same physical route so that any connecting points supporting that connection can correlate the fault and performance information from both directions. These OAM cells can be inserted, monitored, or extracted at the VCC end points as well as any of the connecting points in that VCC.

The F4 flow deals with the VP level and allows control of the VPC. The F4 flow is bidirectional as the F5 flow and is identified by one or more preassigned VCI values. The characteristics of the F4 flow and F5 flow are quite identical. However, the F5 OAM cell is identified by a reserved PTI value.

The format of both F4 and F5 OAM cells is reported in Fig. 2.

The performance information of the ATM network can be monitored continuously and transferred by OAM monitoring cells periodically [2], [18]. Each VCC and VPC can have operations channels through which the OAM cells can be transferred. Based on the monitored performance information, the flow/congestion control schemes can adjust their control parameters (input rate, thresholds, etc.). We pointed out that the ITU-T has designed two PTI's (010 and 011) for indicating instantaneous congestion status in switching nodes. Relatively long term overload situations might be reported through OAM channels (statistic of input traffics, buffer occupancy, cell loss, etc.) to the telecommunication management network (TMN) center. TMN is defined by ITU-T as the computer-based system that supports all the operations of network management in a telecommunication environment.

The overloaded period duration is a critical parameter. The average of this period could be estimated by the network management center or by the destination node. Each overload period can be measured in a node and transferred to the management center and/or to the destination node. For example, as an estimator of this period, the loss information on N (128, 256, 512, 1024) cell blocks can be reported through F5 flow, periodically. The performance monitoring cell is inserted at the first free cell location after the monitoring cell insertion request is initiated. By checking the time between the first and the last cell that has been marked in the congestion indication field, the destination node can indirectly measure the overload periods. If the information is available, the modification of the mean can be performed by using a first-order recursive estimation.

A major point in performance management is quality of service (QoS), defined in the ITU-T recommendation E.800 as "collective effect of service performances which determine the degree of satisfaction of a user of the service." This definition is a wide one encompassing many areas of work, including subjective customer satisfaction. Within this recommendation, however, the aspects of QoS are restricted to the identification of parameters that can be directly observed and measured at the point at which service is accessed by the user.

Network performance (NP) is measured in terms of parameters that are meaningful to the network provider and are used for system design, configuration, operation, and maintenance. NP is defined independently of terminal performance and user actions.

As pointed out through [15], network providers should maintain the QoS of bearer services provided to users within acceptable limits. The QoS perceived by users should not be perceptibly degraded by network evolution.

For defining the QoS parameters of ATM networks, we have to understand traffic and congestion control aspects. These aspects are considered by standard bodies and are presented in the next section.

III. ATM TRAFFIC AND CONGESTION CONTROL

Traffic control refers to the set of actions taken by the network to avoid congested conditions. Congestion control refers to the set of actions taken by the network to minimize the intensity, spread, and duration of congestion. Congestion can be caused by unpredictable statistical fluctuations of traffic flows and fault conditions within the network. To meet these objectives, the following functions provide a framework for managing and controlling traffic and congestion in ATM networks [17].

Network resource management (NRM) provisioning may be used to allocate network resources to separate traffic flows according to service characteristics.

Connection admission control (CAC) is defined as the set of actions taken by the network during the call setup phase to establish whether a VC/VP connection request can be accepted or rejected.

Feedback controls are defined as the set of actions taken by the network and by the users to regulate the traffic submitted on ATM connections according to the state of the network.

Usage parameter control/network parameter control (UPC/NPC) is defined as the set of actions taken by the network to monitor and control traffic in terms of traffic offered and validity of the ATM connection, at the user access and the network access, respectively. Their main purpose is to protect network resources from malicious as well as unintentional misbehavior that can affect the QoS of other already established connections by detecting violations of negotiated parameters.

Priority control allows the user to generate different priority traffic flows by using the CLP bit. A congested network element may selectively discard cells with low priority to protect as far as possible the NP for cells with high priority.

Layered coding technique allows to adjust the rate depending on the available resources.

Traffic shaping is a mechanism that alters the traffic characteristics of a stream on a VCC or a VPC to achieve a desired modification of those traffic characteristics.

Fast resource management operates on the time scale of the round-trip propagation delay of the ATM connection.

CAC schemes would prevent average link loads from approaching maximum link capacity and UPC would throttle the peak rate into reasonable rate when the network is overloaded. These schemes allow each user to maintain a minimum throughput. The priority scheduling in a node can increase the utilization significantly if the delay requirements range from 1 ms to a few tenths of ms per node [11]. In this case,

the delay-tolerant services would use longer buffers than the delay-intolerant services.

Feedback control and UPC/NPC schemes may be performed through a leaky bucket mechanism [1], [3] or a spacer mechanism like the virtual scheduling algorithm (VSA). These mechanisms enforce the average bandwidth and the burst factor of a source. A possible implementation of a leaky bucket is to control the traffic flow by means of tokens: an arriving cell first enters a queue. If the queue is full, cells are simply discarded. To enter the network, a cell must first obtain a token from a token-pool. If there is no token, the cell must wait in the queue until a new token is generated. Tokens are generated at a fixed rate corresponding to the average rate of the connection. If the number of tokens in the token-pool exceeds some predefined threshold value, the process of token generation stops. This threshold value corresponds to the burstiness of the transmission.

The two extreme cases are without any input buffer and with an infinite input buffer. In the first case, a large number of cells may be discarded. In the second case, cells may suffer a long waiting time, not allowed to recover an isochronous flow. By choosing an appropriate input queue size, the trade-off between these two extremes can be found. A large number of possible implementations are available in the literature (see [20] and [23]). Moreover, violating cells may enter the network with the CLP bit set to one.

One of the most important factors to performing an efficient congestion control scheme is the duration of the congestion. In [27], it is reported that the average congestion period, for the case of telephone calls, ranges from about one hundred to several hundred ms. For the case of video, the peak rate may last several seconds [26], [27], but these measurements were performed without considering congestion/flow control schemes. The results of reactive congestion control schemes, such as CAC and UPC, on the internal congestion should be further studied. In fact, as it is indicated in [27], if the congestion period is less than the round trip delay, a reactive flow control has no meaning. On the other hand, very long congestion situation should be controlled by CAC and UPC cooperating with OAM functions to guarantee a minimum QoS.

For the realization of a traffic control scheme, the capability to detect congestion situations in switching elements and adjust transmission rate of the source node is required. Congestion states should be detected in time. As a congestion detection mechanism, the explicit forward congestion indication scheme and the explicit backward congestion indication scheme (EFCI/EBCI) are included in the recommendation [17]. A switching element in a congested state can modify the value of the field PTI in a cell header to indicate the congestion. But the use of the congestion information is up to the user. Performance on cell loss/insertion and cells in error can also be carried through OAM channels [2], [18], but, it might be difficult to use the monitored performance data for adjusting flow control parameters dynamically. The only channel through which the overload status can be transferred to the destination node immediately is the PTI field. The destination node can feedback the information to the source node through the reverse OAM channel or specially designed cells. The influence of OAM flows on congestion states may be non-negligible and these flows can involve a higher degradation of performance. That is the reason why in the traffic and congestion control scheme we propose in the sequel, the agents may work in isolation when an overloaded period begins. Nevertheless, the OAM cell traffic should be reduced by just indicating changes in the congestion states.

Cell loopback is a capability introduced in [18]. Loopback capability allows for operations information to be inserted at one location along a virtual (path/channel) connection and returned at a different location, without disrupting service. This capability [7] is performed by inserting an OAM cell at any accessible point along the virtual connection with instructions in the OAM cell payload for the cell to be looped back at one or two other identifiable points along the connection.

The cell loopback mechanism is used for traffic and congestion management functions. For example, during periods of excessive congestion, detected through this mechanism, a switch could begin selectively discarding ATM cells with the intent of maximizing delivery of high priority traffic. During congested periods, ATM switches also could transmit ATM layer congestion notification in both the forward and backward directions of VPC/VCC transmission. Upon reception of a congestion notification, the different nodes of the network could take measures to alleviate network congestion. Our congestion control proposal is supporting this principle by discarding cells with the CLP bit to one.

The layered coding technique and its variants are proposed for video and voice services [25]. They allow to adjust coding rate depending on the available resources. The principal concept of the layered coding is to divide the video or voice data into a number of layers. The layers contain hierarchical information such as a low resolution, a medium resolution, and a high resolution data. The adequate layer can be selected at call setup considering the available bandwidth, and the layers can be added or removed during a connection lifetime.

As a summary, traffic and congestion controls are provided by a set of mechanisms that could be associated with leaky bucket functions. The ATM-level control structure has three basic control capabilities [6] that have been pointed out:

1) A capability for selectively shedding load under congestion conditions through the CLP indicator belonging to the ATM cell header. If this indicator is set to one, this signifies that the cell may be discarded in any network element. For that, it is sufficient that a local congestion parameter be above a threshold.

2) A capability for forward notification of encountered congestion conditions along a path. This is implemented by way of the EFCI situated in the ATM cell header.

3) A capability for backward notification of encountered congestion conditions along a path. This is implemented by way of OAM cells as shown in Section II. This refers to the EBCI possibility.

The main difficulty found in monitoring performance and, specifically, when controlling traffic and congestion, is to tune the parameters. We need an intelligent platform capable of managing the system efficiently [22].

IV. INTELLIGENT DISTRIBUTED NETWORK MANAGEMENT

TMN should be used for managing ATM networks. The results of the monitoring functions have to be sent in an operation, administration and maintenance centre (OAMC). As the protocols used for maintenance in the TMN are specified through Q interfaces, a complete ATM architecture for the operation and maintenance will include $Q2$ and $Q3$ interfaces to send management information to the OAMC.

In this paper, we are mainly interested in the introduction of an intelligent architecture and in the transport of the control and management information. Therefore, we do not investigate the TMN approach.

A general principle stated in [18] is that each layer of the ITU-T reference model, as well as each network level, has its own independent management process. This means that each network level is equipped with its own OAM mechanisms. For performance monitoring, each level, by itself, is required to provide performance measurements. All the mechanisms that we have described in the previous section are quite simple and flexible at the origin. The problem is how to control the values of the parameters and how to optimize the performance of the control schemes described in the previous section. Due to the complexity of the control in ATM networks, we investigate a way to handle this complexity. An intelligent distributed mechanism seems to be the solution to handle the problem of performance monitoring and, more specifically, to control traffic and congestion schemes.

First, let us define a generic network management architecture supporting the framework of our proposal. This architecture is based on a distributed multi-agent system.

A multi-agent system can be defined as a system in which several agents interact [19]. An agent is considered as a physical or an abstract entity capable of acting on itself and on its environment, to manipulate a partial representation of its environment, and to communicate with other agents. The agent behavior is a consequence of its perception, knowledge, and interactions with other agents.

Several issues have emerged in research related to the study of multi-agents:

- Agents can be considered as autonomous entities that have perception and communication capabilities, as well as decision capabilities. They can act on their environment in an autonomous way. This approach corresponds to the paradigm of "autonomous agents" or of "a robot acting in a multi-robot environment."

- At the other extreme, agents can be considered as specialized modules interacting together according to a specific architecture. Each agent can be represented by a knowledge base or a specialized procedure. This approach corresponds to the "multiexpert system" paradigm based on the distributed artificial intelligence (DAI) field [10], [24].

- Between these two extreme cases, where we are working either with a unique system or with independent systems, there are the semi-autonomous multi-agent systems. In this case, the agents operate asynchronously and concurrently on different tasks, with several other agents and an incomplete knowledge of the global environment.

For traffic control purposes, we could not use any of the three directions listed above. We assume that each user interface and each cell switch contain an agent in charge of the control scheme. The first definition will assume that each agent works with its own knowledge. The advantage of such a method is to avoid all communication problems between the agents. This results in a simplified scheme and no overhead traffic occurs inside the network. With the second definition, all the agents are coordinated and only a global view of the network could lead to a decision. This is not possible in an ATM environment where the propagation delay of cells should be approximately on the same order of magnitude as the signal propagation delay.

This implies that the best choice is semi-autonomous agents so that local decisions may be made instantaneously when agents have enough knowledge for that. When the network is not too loaded, it is possible to exchange information on the life of the network to update and improve the knowledge of the agents. This considers that the agents are able to make better decisions using historical data. This partly corresponds to a learning process.

In this paper, the DAI organization [9] is implemented according to the principle of the blackboard architecture [5]. The blackboard incorporates three components:

- A structured knowledge base called "blackboard" that contains the current state of the solution for a given problem. This shared data area is analogous to the working memory accessed by many production rules in a rule-based system. But this area is divided into separate areas of semantic abstraction called levels.
- A collection of independent agents (or knowledge sources) which may read and write one or several levels. They can be seen as a collection of independent processes capable of cooperating to solve a problem.
- A control system that insures the supervision of the actions of the different knowledge sources. This system is also a collection of integrated control–knowledge sources.

This organization is not sufficient to realize a real multi-agent system. We need to describe an architecture for the agent itself. We decided to organize the agent following the principles of the blackboard architecture (Fig. 3) with three components:

- A knowledge module that deals with all the usual data and the knowledge of the domain.
- A control module that defines the problem solving strategy and the control mechanism to determine the next actions to perform.
- A communication module that models the other agents in the environment. This module also provides an interpreter of messages and a logic for communications with the other agents.

Each agent may be seen as an independent software processor with its own resources. The agents communicate by

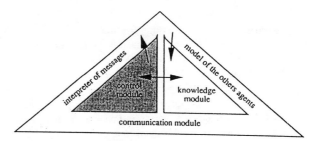

Fig. 3. The architecture of the agent.

sharing the information if we look at a high level, i.e., at the entire multi-agent system level. They communicate through a general blackboard that contains, at the beginning, the facts of a given problem. The agents read the information in the blackboard and write in it to reach a solution step by step.

In our ATM network we assume that an agent is attached to each node and may work in isolation when necessary. Moreover, information coming from outside is added to the knowledge module. We simulated a multi-agent system assuming that all the knowledge of the network is instantaneously provided in the information bases of all the agents (we do not take into account the propagation delay). This constraint could be discarded by the fact that the global state of the network can be predictable through the knowledge of the agents coming from the learning capability using the past.

V. NETWORK PERFORMANCE MANAGEMENT ARCHITECTURE

We use the previous architecture to realize the performance management of ATM networks. The information used by the agents is routed through the OAM flows.

For efficiency purposes, it is interesting to group resources according to one or several criteria. These sets will be named domains. Indeed, it is a way to introduce three levels in the distributed problem solving. The first level is concerned with the resolution performed by the agent alone. The second level is concerned with the resolution inside a domain if the problem is larger than the capabilities of the agent, and the third level occurs when more than one domain is involved. As an example, we describe a management architecture within a network composed of ATM subnetworks in Fig. 4. The bold line shows a domain situated on two subnetworks including only the machines of the manufacturer X. These machines may also belong to other domains through different views of these resources.

The domain is managed by one or several agents that can be situated in any node of the network belonging to the domain. These agents work in a coordinated manner on a common data structure: the blackboard. The blackboard is situated in the manager where all the management functions are provided. The agents may work in group on a given problem (in the blackboard) or may work alone or with some other agents of their environment to solve punctual problems when they have the appropriate knowledge.

As it was described in Section II, performance monitoring schemes have been developed and normalized. These performance monitoring schemes are made possible by OAM cell generation and processing functions performed by the agents along the ATM virtual connection being monitored. One advantage of using OAM cells to communicate performance indication from any point of the connection is that the report may be read at intermediate points all along the connection. This information is captured by the agents. Another attractive feature of OAM far-end reports is that they enable network management agents to collect end-to-end performance data for both directions of the connection.

Various performance parameters may be measured using the results of the aforementioned performance monitoring schemes. The parameters used to monitor the ATM layer QoS are defined in [15]:

- Cell loss ratio;
- Cell misinsertion rate;
- Cell error ratio;
- Severely erred cell block ratio;
- Cell transfer delay;
- Mean cell transfer delay;
- Cell delay variation.

As noted by [7], these performance monitoring schemes are flexible enough so that other ratio-based and even time-based performance parameters be taken into account (e.g., erred seconds, severely erred seconds, and coding violation).

All this performance information is captured by the agents of our architecture and leads to an optimization of the values of the parameters though the intelligent capabilities of these agents.

VI. PROPOSAL FOR A NEW TRAFFIC AND CONGESTION CONTROL SCHEME

In this section, we want to show the efficiency of the intelligent architecture we have just introduced through a performance study of a new traffic and congestion control scheme. In this scheme, we want to use the different notification capabilities explained in previous sections. A cell with the CLP bit set to one could be discarded by any intermediate node even if this node is not congested. This could happen when a node along the virtual circuit is congested. This information is provided through the EFCI or EBCI notification. Indeed, discarding cells with CLP = 1 as soon as possible, may have a large benefit for the cells with the indicator CLP = 0.

A model could be as follows: Several thresholds have to be defined depending on the status of the node. These thresholds determine the values of the EFCI and EBCI indications routed along the VP and VC.

We define thresholds determining several types of actions. The thresholds may depend on the number of busy buffers in the node and/or on a given throughput on a link and/or on any other performance measure.

We have chosen to work with thresholds that depend on the number of busy buffers. For each threshold, two levels are defined. Up to the first level, nothing happens. Above the first congestion threshold, and up to the second level, cells marked with the CLP = 1 are discarded. Finally, above the second level, cells with CLP = 1 are still discarded and explicit forward and backward congestion notifications are sent

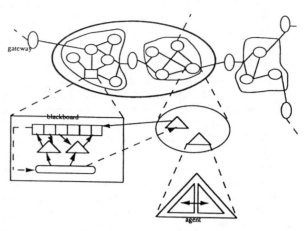

Fig. 4.   Example of the management architecture.

through ATM cells and OAM cells. The ITU-T proposal is to send an OAM cell each 128, 256, 512, and 1024 user cells. In our model, we assume that OAM cells are sent as soon as possible. The OAM cells are treated in the nodes with a "head of line" priority.

In our model, the CLP bit is set to one randomly when cells are entering the network with a probability α. We shall assume that $\alpha = 0.1$.

Let us assume that the network is composed of N nodes and let us define the following thresholds for node i, for $0 \leq i \leq N$:

$T1_{ij}$) If the number of buffers occupied in node i by cells leaving node i by the output port j is greater than $T1_{ij}$, then cells on route j with the CLP bit set to one are discarded.

$T2_i$) If the total number of buffers occupied in node i is greater than $T2_i$, then cells with the CLP bit set to one are discarded.

$T3_{ij}$) If the number of buffers occupied in node i by cells leaving the node i by the output port j is greater than $T3_{ij}$, then cells on route j with the CLP bit set to one are discarded. Moreover, explicit forward and backward congestion notifications are sent on the virtual circuits going through the output port j.

$T4_i$) If the total number of buffers occupied in node i is greater than $T4_i$, then cells with the CLP bit set to one are discarded. Moreover, explicit forward and backward congestion notifications are sent on all the virtual circuits passing through node i.

When a node receives an EBCI notification of one, the node automatically discards cells with CLP = 1 on the congested routes. The EBCI notification indicates the virtual circuits where congestion takes place. As soon as an EBCI notification comes back to zero, the process of discarding cells stops.

The choice of the values of the different thresholds is crucial for the performance of the system. In the simplest case, these values are fixed and independent on the number of VP's and independent on the congestion observed. With our distributed intelligent system, the values of the thresholds may vary according to the knowledge of the agents.

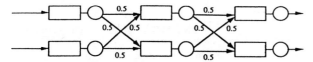

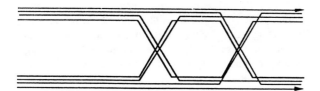

Fig. 5. The network under study.

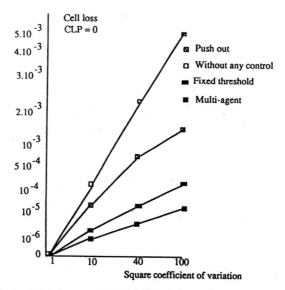

Fig. 7. Cell loss rate versus the square coefficient of variation for $\rho = 0.7$.

Fig. 6. Routing scheme.

A. Results for Fixed Thresholds

Measurements on simple models using simulation techniques show that if the thresholds are well chosen, the cell loss probability for the cells with the bit CLP = 0 is definitely improved. We are going to present some of these measurement results.

We adopt the queueing system shown in Fig. 5.

Eight routes are available with an equal probability to be used. These routes are described in Fig. 6. Let λ be the arrival rate in the input queues of the model. That means that each route supports an average rate of $\lambda/4$.

We limit the number of buffers to 20 (one cell per buffer) except for the input queues that are assumed infinite. The unit of time corresponds to the transmission of a cell. The cells are produced at a rate $\lambda = 0.7, 0.8,$ and 0.9. The arrival process is assumed hyperexponentially distributed with a square coefficient of variation of one (Poisson), 10, 40, and 100. This hyperexponential input process is modeled with just two exponential servers in parallel. Finally, we assume that a cell entering the system is tagged randomly (i.e., its CLP is set equal to one) with the probability $\alpha = 0.1$.

We show in Table I and Figs. 7–9, cell loss probabilities for cells with the bit CLP set to zero as a function of the square coefficient of variation (SCV) for different traffic rates r and for different flow control strategies.

B. Results for Dynamic Threshold Controlled by a Multi-agent System

Multi-agent systems are capable of evaluating at each instant, the values of the different thresholds depending on the state of the system. We assume that in a certain limit, the traffic in ATM networks is predictable. The traffic characterization could be predictable in many situations. The most predictable traffic is the telephone traffic that is a constant bit rate (CBR) flow. The length of the conversation is an estimated value (between 4 and 5 min according to France Telecom) but the traffic rate is well known (one byte every 125 μs). The traffic characteristics of VBR video can be extremely complex, generally depending on two main factors: scene content and coding algorithm [21]. While the image complexity is an important factor because it can vary significantly between sequences, the basic traffic characteristics

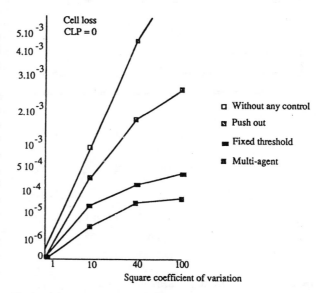

Fig. 8. Cell loss rate versus the square coefficient of variation for $\rho = 0.8$.

are primarily determined by the coding algorithm utilized by the video coder. Again, a certain prediction of the traffic is available through the learning of the previous sequences. Finally, the less predictable flows come from data streams. But again, for some applications, like a file transfer, a prediction is quite easy to get. A learning system that can know the user and the application profile is capable of giving a good approximation of the arriving flows in the immediate future. These predictions are a part of the knowledge of the agents and are used to determine the thresholds in a dynamic way.

To get the results reported in this section, we have chosen a multi-agent system composed of six agents, one in each queue. Each agent was structured as described in Section IV. At the beginning of the simulation, the knowledge of an

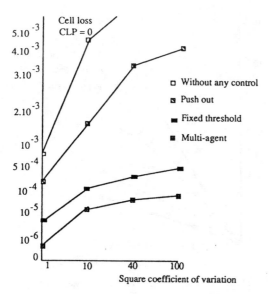

Fig. 9. Cell loss rate versus the square coefficient of variation for $\rho = 0.9$.

TABLE I
SIMULATION RESULTS

	SCV	cell loss without any control	cell loss fixed threshold	cell loss multi-agent	cell loss push out
$\rho = 0.7$	1	0	0	0	0
	10	$1.74 \ 10^{-4}$	$3.26 \ 10^{-6}$	$7.83 \ 10^{-7}$	$4.50 \ 10^{-5}$
	40	$1.93 \ 10^{-3}$	$5.43 \ 10^{-5}$	$5.87 \ 10^{-6}$	$7.17 \ 10^{-4}$
	100	$4.85 \ 10^{-3}$	$1.08 \ 10^{-4}$	$2.32 \ 10^{-5}$	$1.47 \ 10^{-3}$
$\rho = 0.8$	1	$8.47 \ 10^{-6}$	$3.92 \ 10^{-7}$	0	$9.81 \ 10^{-7}$
	10	$1.04 \ 10^{-3}$	$2.26 \ 10^{-5}$	$4.70 \ 10^{-6}$	$2.98 \ 10^{-4}$
	40	$4.56 \ 10^{-3}$	$1.14 \ 10^{-4}$	$2.08 \ 10^{-5}$	$1.68 \ 10^{-3}$
	100	$8.75 \ 10^{-3}$	$1.68 \ 10^{-4}$	$3.32 \ 10^{-5}$	$2.53 \ 10^{-3}$
$\rho = 0.9$	1	$7.37 \ 10^{-4}$	$6.80 \ 10^{-6}$	$5.42 \ 10^{-7}$	$1.97 \ 10^{-4}$
	10	$5.33 \ 10^{-3}$	$1.04 \ 10^{-4}$	$1.70 \ 10^{-5}$	$1.57 \ 10^{-3}$
	40	$1.06 \ 10^{-2}$	$2.07 \ 10^{-4}$	$3.27 \ 10^{-5}$	$3.43 \ 10^{-3}$
	100	$1.40 \ 10^{-2}$	$3.09 \ 10^{-4}$	$4.94 \ 10^{-5}$	$4.14 \ 10^{-3}$

agent is composed of the six optimal thresholds computed in the previous static examples (four thresholds for the output queues). The knowledge of a node is increased at each slot by the output traffic of the node as a function of the arrival rate and the square coefficient of variation of the traffic. The cell loss probabilities for the CLP = 0 cells are given in Table I and Figs. 7–9 for the dynamically controlled system through the multi-agent control scheme.

To compare these values, we also give in this table, results obtained through a simulation of the push-out algorithm. This mechanism is as follows: when the queue is full upon arrival a cell with CLP = 0 pushes out a cell with CLP = 1 if available

in the queue. If no CLP = 1 cell is waiting in the queue, the cell with CLP = 0 is discarded.

When we enter a congested situation, the improvement is very important by just discarding the cells with the CLP = 1 a long time before these cells reach the congested nodes. In any case, these cells will be lost, but in our model, they are often discarded in the entering node of the network. Therefore, these cells do not contribute to the congestion. The advantages of the intelligent multi-agent system to control the traffic and, more generally, to tune the values of the parameters are obvious regarding previous examples.

VII. CONCLUSION

ATM techniques have been developed for high speed and multimedia purposes. So, the ATM switching technique is well-adapted for future networks. Unfortunately, traffic and congestion control schemes are increasingly difficult to perform due to the complexity and distribution of the system. To tune the different parameters (the thresholds in the congestion control scheme of our model) we proposed a semi-autonomous multi-agent system. We have shown that a large benefit on the performance of the network may be expected even using a simple procedure in the agent at the condition that an intelligent management be introduced in the system.

A framework for defining an ATM performance management architecture was described. We used OAM flows to provide the communication between intelligent agents that support the performance monitoring scheme. The main idea in using distributed intelligent agents was to reduce the complexity of the management process. We dealt with the complexity by introducing hierarchical and multiple intelligent managers.

Future issues in distributed artificial intelligence concepts will be to take charge of real-time control and work on a fast time scale. Indeed, in this paper, we simulate agents working in real-time. These agents are prototypes in research laboratories (see, for example, [4]). We assume that these new kinds of intelligent agents (called reactive agents) will permit results described here.

In the area of performance management, we pointed out that OAM capabilities should play a key role in the viability and success of the emerging ATM networks. Mixing OAM capabilities and DAI concepts, as proposed in this paper, results to a better control in ATM networks. We proposed a performance management scheme powerful and flexible enough to handle the technologies expected in the 21st century.

ACKNOWLEDGMENT

The authors gratefully acknowledge Z. J. Ping for his help in building the simulation results in this paper.

REFERENCES

[1] J. J. Bae and T. Suda, "Survey of traffic control protocols in ATM networks," in *Proc. GLOBECOM'91*, 1991, pp. 300.1.1–300.1.6.
[2] H. Breuer, "ATM layer OAM: principles and open issues," *IEEE Commun. Mag.*, vol. 29, no 9, pp. 44–48, Sept. 1991.
[3] M. Butto and E. Cavallero, "Effectiveness of the leaky bucket policing mechanism in ATM networks," *IEEE J. Select. Areas Commun.*, vol. 9, no. 3, pp. 335–342, Apr. 1991.

[4] A. Collinot and B. Hayes-Roth, "Real-time performance of intelligent autonomous agents," in *Decentralized A.I. 3*, E. Werner and Y. Demazeau, Eds. Amsterdam, The Netherlands: Elsevier, 1992.

[5] R. Engelmore *et al.*, *Blackboard systems*, Reading, MA: Addison-Wesley, 1988.

[6] A. E. Eckberg, B. T. Doshi, and R. Zoccolillo, "Controlling congestion in B-ISDN/ATM: Issues and strategies," *IEEE Commun. Mag.* vol. 29, no 9, pp. 75–78, Sept. 1991.

[7] S.C. Farkouh, "Managing-ATM-based broadband networks," *IEEE Commun. Mag.* vol. 31, no. 5, pp. 82–87, May 1993.

[8] D. Gaïti and G. Pujolle, "On the performance management of ATM networks through a multi-agent system," in *Proc. IEEE Int. Conf. Requirements Techniques Network Management*, Cracow, Poland, May 1993.

[9] D. Gaïti, "I²NMA: An intelligent integrated network management architecture," *Int. J. Network Management*, vol. 4, no. 4, pp. 179–189, Dec. 1994.

[10] L. Gasser, "Distributed artificial intelligence," *AI Expert*, July 1989.

[11] D. K. Hsing, "Simulation and performance evaluation of an ATM multiplexer using priority scheduling," in *Proc. GLOBECOM*, San Francisco, CA, 1990, pp. 1946–1952.

[12] ITU-T Recommendation I.150, *B-ISDN Asynchronous Transfer Mode Functional Characteristics*, 1993.

[13] ITU-T Recommendation I.311, *B-ISDN General Aspects*, 1993.

[14] ITU-T Recommendation I.321, *B-ISDN Protocol Reference Model and its Application*, 1993.

[15] ITU-T Recommendation I.356, *B-ISDN ATM Layer Cell Transfer Performance*, 1994.

[16] ITU-T Recommendation I.361, *B-ISDN ATM Layer Specification*, 1993.

[17] ITU-T Recommendation I.371, *Traffic Control and Congestion Control in B-ISDN*, 1993.

[18] ITU-T Recommendation I.610, *OAM Principles of the B-ISDN Access*, 1993.

[19] V. R. Lesser and D. D. Corkill, "Functionally accurate, cooperative distributed systems" in *Readings in Distributed Artificial Intelligence*, A. H. Bond and L. Gasser, Eds. San Mateo, CA: Morgan Kaufmann, 1988.

[20] T. Okada, H. Ohnishi, and N. Morita, "Traffic control in asynchronous transfer mode," *IEEE Commun. Mag.*, vol. 29, no. 9, pp. 58–63, Sept. 1991.

[21] P. Pancha and M. El Zarki, "Transport of VBR MPEG video in ATM networks," in *International Workshop on Modeling and Performance Evaluation of ATM Technology*. Amsterdam, The Netherlands: North Holland, 1993.

[22] G. Pujolle and D. Gaïti, "ATM flow control schemes through a multi-agent system," in *Proc. SICON/ICIE'93*, Singapore, Sept. 1993, pp. 455–459.

[23] J. W. Roberts, "Variable-bit-rate control in B-ISDN," *IEEE Commun. Mag.*, vol. 29, no 9, pp. 50–56, Sept. 1991.

[24] R. G. Smith and R. Davis, "Frameworks for cooperation in distributed problem solving," in *Readings in Distributed Artificial Intelligence*, A. H. Bond and L. Gasser, Eds. San Mateo, CA: Morgan-Kaufmann, 1988.

[25] K. Sriram, S. Mckinney, and M. H. Shrrif, "Voice packetization and compression in broadband ATM networks," *IEEE J. Select. Areas Commun.*, vol. 9, no. 3, Apr. 1991.

[26] W. Verbiest, L. Pinnoo, and B. Voeten, "The impact of the ATM concept on video coding," *IEEE J. Select. Areas Commun.*, vol. 6, no. 9, Dec. 1988.

[27] N. Yin and M. G. Hluchyj, "A dynamic rate control mechanism for source coded traffic in a fast packet network," *IEEE J. Select. Areas Commun.*, vol. 9, no. 7, Sept. 1991.

Dominique Gaïti received the Ph.D. degree in computer science from the University of Paris VI, France, in 1991 and the Habilitation degree in computer science from the University of Paris IX, France, in 1995.

She is currently an Associate Research Scientist at the Center for Telecommunications Research (CTR), Columbia University, New York, after two years spent as a Visiting Scientist in the same lab. She also works at the University of Paris VI, France, as a member of the Scientific Staff. Her research interests are in network management and control, intelligent networks, and distributed artificial intelligence.

Guy Pujolle (M'86–SM'89) received the Ph.D. and Thèse d'Etat degrees in computer science from the University of Paris IX and Paris XI, France, in 1975 and 1978, respectively.

He is currently a Professor at the University of Versailles, France, and a member of the PRiSM Laboratory. He was a Professor at the University of Paris VI, France, and head of the MASI Laboratory depending on the Centre National de la Recherche Scientifique (CNRS) from 1981 to 1993. He is the chairman of the IFIP WG 6.4 on "High Performance Networking" and member of the IFIP WG 7.3 on "Performance Evaluation." He is also a member of the Scientific Committee of France Telecom and GMD, and chairman of the Telecommunication Regulation expert committee at the French Telecom Ministry. His research interests include the analysis and modeling of data communication systems, protocols, high speed networks, and B-ISDN. He is the author of several books and of many papers on diverse aspects of performance analysis and data communication networks.

Performance Management Issues of Currently Operated ATM Enterprise Networks

Rudolf Jaeger, BetaTechnik

The author proposes a solution for the allocation and balancing of resources to maximize available bandwidth shared among corporate users.

Currently established broadband virtual private networks (BVPNs) based on asynchronous transfer mode (ATM) technology comprise ATM cross-connects (ATM-CCs) and a lot of intelligent customer premises equipment (CPE). The CPE, an intelligent ATM service switch or ATM multiplexer, enables the corporate user to connect routers, private branch exchanges (PBXs), or coders-decoders (codecs) onto the ATM network. One fundamental characteristic of CPE is that it is capable of accumulating asynchronous and synchronous traffic which may belong to different corporate users' sites. Figure 1 shows a typical example of a BVPN configuration serving two corporate network users with four user sites each. In general, each user site needs to exchange asynchronous (connectionless) data streams for the inter-local area network (LAN) communication and synchronous (connection-oriented) data streams with constant bit rates for video/voice communication. Each corporate user site has its own local network management center (LNMC), which acts as a manager from the user's end system's (workstations, PBXs, codecs) point of view. The management of the BVPN is accomplished by the broadband network management center (BNMC). There exist logical connections between the LNMC and BNMC for the exchange of the virtual path connection's (VPC) setup/cancel requests and its related quality of service (QoS) parameter.

The following section starts out with a discussion of the configuration and the performance aspects of interLAN communications employing a connectionless server (CLS). Then the bandwidth allocation aspects of the BVPN having to convey synchronous and asynchronous traffic in an ATM environment without a CLS are discussed. Also included in this section is a bandwidth allocation algorithm, allowing maximized utilization of the allocated bandwidth for the communicating corporate user. The last section briefly summarizes the important characteristics of the proposed algorithm.

CONFIGURATION ASPECTS OF A BVPN

During the first phase of operation of ATM pilots, permanent virtual connections (PVCs) are used for the exchange of the asynchronous and synchronous data streams. The PVCs are established either using the signaling protocol or by means of network management services.

CONNECTIONLESS SERVER METHOD WITH AN OVERLAY NETWORK

The direct method of interLAN data exchange relies on an overlay network with non-ATM switching equipment, the CLS. The ATM header label is used to provide access to the CLS, regardless of the address information in the inter-LAN message. The CLSs are attached to the ATM-CC. Every corporate user site needs at least one VPC to the CLS, and there are VPCs between the CLSs. Figure 2 shows a simple example BVPN configuration employing two CLSs serving two corporate users, each having to serve two corporate user sites.

Although the overlay network method is currently considered the most appropriate solution for interLAN data exchange, there are reasons for using connectionless data service without an overlay network, that is, directly using the ATM switching systems without a CLS. The first concerns the number of addressable entities. If the number of corporate user sites is not very large, the approach without an overlay network is more feasible. Second, having to employ a CLS means one has to manage another piece of equipment, and management is a critical issue. Apart from the expense of buying a CLS, the maintenance costs should not be underestimated. Third, due to the fact that the CLS must handle all interLAN traffic, dimensioning such a system might become very difficult. The fact that all of the interLAN traffic is routed through the CLS raises the issue of where the throughput bottleneck will occur. Is it the peak cell rate (PCR) policing being applied at the user network interface, the service time of the CLS, or the transport protocol itself which limits the throughput of interLAN communication? What are the relationships between these components? Therefore, we are interested in the upper bound of the achievable throughput for interLAN communications.

Throughput Estimation for InterLAN Communication — An analytical model of the interLAN communication that considers the standard transport protocols transmission control protocol/Internet protocol 4 (TCP/IP 4) will be derived. Based on this model, a mean value analysis with infinite buffer size is performed for the estimation of the upper bound of the throughput. For the determination of the upper bound estimate of the throughput we assume large data (images, computer-aided design, X-rays, etc.) transfer between two transport layer entities (TCP/TP4). All logical transport con-

Reprinted from IEEE Communications Magazine, January 1996, pp. 70-76.

nections use the connectionless overlay network. Figure 3 depicts the block diagram, with all relevant components, of an example corporate network with three corporate user sites, including five logical transport connections.

Assumptions for the upper bound throughput estimation:

- There are m nodes (workstations) connected to the LANs involved in the interLAN large data transfer. Within each node there exists one transport connection. The window size w is assumed to be the same for all transport connections.
- Error-free transmission is considered; that is, it is unnecessary to retransmit any transport packets.
- The CPE interworking units for the exchange of the asynchronous traffic use separate processors/buffers to process incoming/outgoing traffic for each connected corporate user site.
- The size of the data transfer transport protocol data units (DT TPDUs) is limited to the maximum size of an Ethernet (IEEE 802.3) or token ring (IEEE 802.5) data frame.
- The processing of the acknowledge (ACK) TPDUs is performed by separate processing units.

The Ethernet LAN is represented by a single server queue with constant delay times (T_{LS} and T_{LR}). The transmission of the Ethernet data frame via the ATM network employing CLSs is modeled as a single-server system with the mean service rate μ_{CLS}. The delays caused by the ATM-CC are assumed to be negligible. This is justified because the functions carried out by the ATM-CC are hardware-implemented. T_{CLS} corresponds to the mean service time of an Ethernet data frame at the CLS.

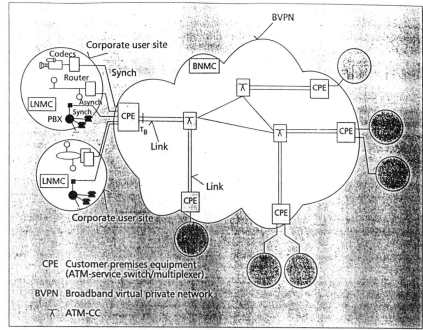

Figure 1. *An example of a BVPN serving two corporate network users.*

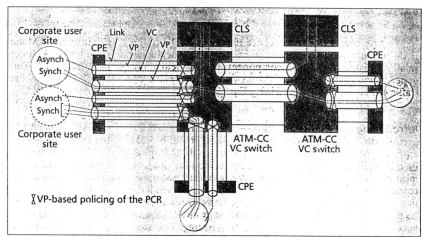

Figure 2. *Connecting two corporate users onto the BVPN employing CLS.*

Thus, we can model the interLAN transport communication part as a number of closed queuing networks, limited by the number of sending transport entities m with a common path (i.e., the CLS—single server). An example of such a queuing network model, again with five interLAN transport connections, is shown in Fig. 4.

Throughput Estimation without PCR Limitation and Infinite Buffer Size

First, we are interested in the upper bound estimate of the throughput which is achievable with m transport connections, each using the window size w without any limitations imposed by the PCR. The maximum number of DT TPDUs, including ACK TPDUs, in the considered communication network is determined by $m * w$. Regardless of the location of the PDUs, we can write

$$(N_{L,S} + N_{R,S} + N_{CPE,S} + N_{CLS} + N_{R,R} + N_{CPE,R} + N_{L,R} + N_{ACK}) \leq m * w \quad (1)$$

Let T_{RND} be the upper bound estimate required for a cor-

rect DT TPDU to be acknowledged (i.e., DT TPDU transmission time + generation and transmission of ACK TPDU); a new DT TPDU will take at least that much time to be admitted into the transmission system. Introducing the throughput of all the queuing networks and applying the Law of Little [1], we have

$$s*T_{RND} = (N_{L,S} + N_{R,S} + N_{CPE,S} + N_{CLS} + N_{R,R} + N_{CPE,R} + N_{L,R} + N_{ACK}) \leq m*w \quad (2)$$

At the common path (CLS single server) of the closed queuing network we also can write, again by applying Little's Law,

$$s * T_{CLS} \leq N_{CLS} \quad (3)$$

For the single server (CLS), the mean number of packets at the server is less or equal to 1; we therefore have

$$s * T_{CLS} \leq 1 \quad (4)$$

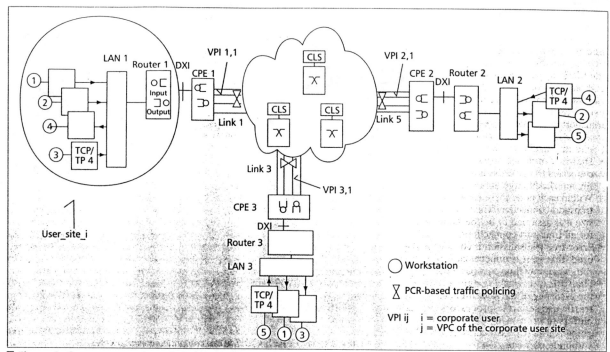

■ Figure 3. *Corporate network employing an overlay network for interLAN traffic exchange.*

We have assumed that the service time for a TPDU of the LAN and the interworking units (CPE, routers) is negligibly small compared to the other components. Consequently, the upper bound of the achievable throughput s of the interLAN traffic can be obtained by combining Eqs. (2) and (4).

$$s = \min[1/T_{CLS}; (m * w)/T_{RND}] \qquad (5)$$

Introducing the PCR Limitation — Now we introduce the access rate limitations imposed by the PCR_j limitations for each corporate user site j. In order to estimate the upper bound of the throughput s_j of each corporate user site j we must consider that the CLS has to serve more than just traffic coming from the user site j. Taking this effect into consideration we introduce the service time T^*_{CLS}. Its value will depend on the interLAN traffic generated by the other interLAN connections and on the employed forwarding strategy (message mode or streaming mode) implemented at the CLS. Under this assumption, the upper bound estimate of the throughput s_j of each user site j is determined by a minimum function:

$$s_j = \min[(m_j * w_j)/T_{RND}; 1/T^*_{CLS}; PCR_j] \qquad (6)$$

Discussion — The throughput achievable by the corporate user site j is determined by three components. Setting $w_j = 1$ (i.e., having only one workstation pair which is sending) causes the upper bound to be determined by w_j/T_{RND}. For $(m_j * w_j)/T_{RND} \gg 1/T^*_{CLS}$, the upper bound is determined by either the service time of the CLS or the PCR_j. Thus, interLAN communications employing CLS is not just a configuration problem of choosing the right value for the PCR and locating the CLS at the right place; it is also a scaling problem, which means selecting the proper processing power of the CLS.

CONNECTIONLESS SERVER METHOD WITHOUT AN OVERLAY NETWORK

The so-called indirect method entirely relies on the CPE and ATM switches for correct interLAN message transfer using the proper ATM application layer (AAL) services. The key issue for the indirect connectionless method concerns virtual path identifier/virtual channel identifier (VPI/VCI) address handling. Several methods exist for routing messages to their destination CPE [2, 3]. The essence of the following approach is to use a direct VPC between the communicating CPE reestablished as a PVC. For each communicating corporate user site pair a VPC, with a certain bandwidth designated as the PCR and its end-to-end QoS, is requested. The ATM service provider tries to satisfy the requested bandwidth with its QoS using the connection admission control functions. The result is either an acceptance or denial of the requested VPC. If the request is admitted, a VPC is established and policed at the user network interface of the ATM-CC. For accumulating the asynchronous traffic there exists one virtual cross-connect (VCC) within the VPC (Fig. 5). The differentiation of the logical interLAN communication is accomplished by the MID field of the ATM adaptation layer (AAL) 3/4 Type PDU. For handling the synchronous connections different VCC connections are used. The VPCs are multiplexed on the physical link.

The advantages of using VPC containing VCC for accumulating asynchronous and synchronous traffic include:

• A clear, logical separation of corporate user site communications is achieved; thus, no traffic interference among the communicating corporate user sites occurs.
• Simple admission and access rate enforcement can be applied; thus, performance evaluation and bandwidth management problems can be treated separately.
• A decrease of setup (pre-established) and transit delays (VPI change only) is the consequence.
• Simple ATM-CC design is allowed because only VP switching is required.

Obtaining High Throughput by Maximizing the Utilization — In exchanging synchronous and asynchronous traffic on a VPC with an upper bound of available bandwidth controlled by the PCR, a bandwidth allocation and congestion problem must be solved. If the traffic mixture sent from the

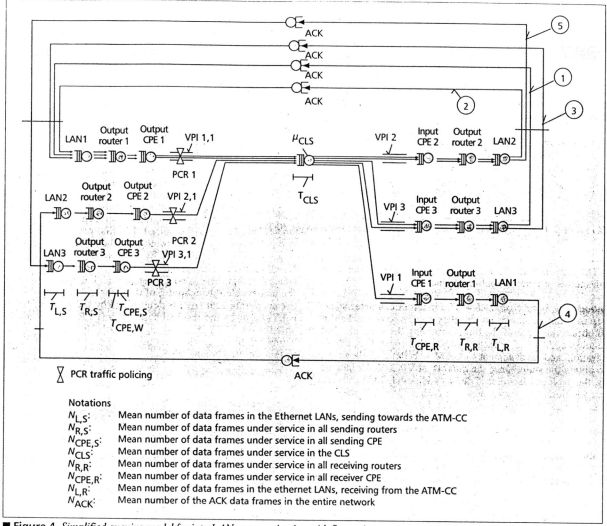

■ Figure 4. *Simplified queuing model for interLAN communication with five active transport connections.*

Notations

$N_{L,S}$:	Mean number of data frames in the Ethernet LANs, sending towards the ATM-CC
$N_{R,S}$:	Mean number of data frames under service in all sending routers
$N_{CPE,S}$:	Mean number of data frames under service in all sending CPE
N_{CLS}:	Mean number of data frames under service in the CLS
$N_{R,R}$:	Mean number of data frames under service in all receiving routers
$N_{CPE,R}$:	Mean number of data frames under service in all receiver CPE
$N_{L,R}$:	Mean number of data frames in the ethernet LANs, receiving from the ATM-CC
N_{ACK}:	Mean number of the ACK data frames in the entire network

CPE and conveyed in a VPC exceeds the PCR for a certain duration of time, an increase of the queuing delay due to bandwidth contention (first stage) and with buffer overflow (final stage), causing ATM cell loss, will occur. A similar problem occurs when exchanging asynchronous and isochronous traffic over a distributed queued dual bus (DQDB) network [4]. Figure 6 depicts an example where at $t = T_1$ an increase of the synchronous traffic due to an additional voice or video connection results in a change of the B_{co} bandwidth used by the synchronous traffic. The currently used bandwidth of the transport connections (sending TP entities) and the new bandwidth occupied by the synchronous users cause an excess of the PCR; bandwidth interference occurs.

Bandwidth Allocation for Asynchronous Traffic — The central problem of requesting bandwidth for interLAN traffic lies in the fact that it is extremely difficult to accurately anticipate or predict the upper bound of the bandwidth required by this bursty traffic. For bursty applications, allocating fixed bandwidth size in advance is not the best way to utilize network resources. It may cause either underutilization or a limitation of the throughput of interLAN communications. In any case a certain amount of bandwidth for the interLAN traffic must be reserved, designated B_{cl} in Fig. 6.

Bandwidth Allocation for Synchronous Traffic — One important QoS parameter requested by synchronous traffic is specified by the blocking probability. Assuming the Poisson process to model the synchronous traffic which may comprise voice connection with n x 64 kb/s bandwidth changes per connection, video connections with n x 1.5 Mb/s (Motion Picture Experts Group 1—MPEG1) or n x 2 Mb/s (H.261) bandwidth changes per connection, with a certain value of the blocking probability, the Erlang formula provides the bandwidth B_{co} requested by the corporate user site as a function of the average offered traffic. The actual number of active voice/video VCC n is a random variable with a maximum value N. For this model the VPC operates most of the time with a number of active synchronous connections with n < N. This means that the bandwidth actually used by the synchronous users is less than the allocated bandwidth B_{co} (Fig. 6).

Due to the VP policing, it is not determined which VCC within the VPC will be affected by cell loss. The problem of cell/packet loss due to congestion (overutilization of resources) in ATM networks is well recognized. Much work [5, 6] has been carried out in attempts to overcome this problem. These solutions rely on the reactive congestion control scheme (closed loop) using either credit or a rate control mechanism, operating on a link-by-link basis, covering the

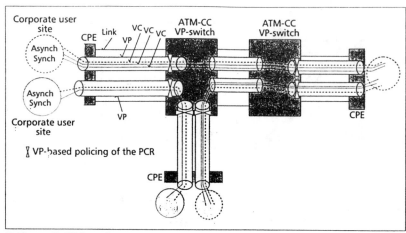

■ **Figure 5.** *VPC configuration connecting two corporate users onto the BVPN.*

ATM network only. The following summarizes the main disadvantages of reactive control schemes.

Introducing Some Overhead — The inherent characteristic of reactive control schemes is that they require some mechanism to obtain the state of the link. Obtaining the state of a link requires adding and extracting information (operation, administration, and management — OAM — cells) that allows you to obtain the state. Once the number of VPCs/VCCs increases, the overhead introduced due to additional OAM cells and the additional processing power at each ATM switch may further degrade the performance of the link.

Reactive Methods Are Too Slow — Congestion control based on the reactive method requires some time to instruct the control points to reduce the rate of offered traffic. This can be a problem in high-speed networks, because the amount of data (cells) still entering the already congested network is much higher than in low-speed networks. Therefore, it is uncertain (no results of real experiments are available) whether reactive methods are suitable for solving congestion in an ATM environment.

Consider the Entire Network — A link-by-link congestion control scheme as proposed by the ATM Forum may transfer a potential congestion problem from one ATM switch to another, allowing the sender to send further packets, thus filling up the queues down to the sender.

Taking these facts into consideration, we propose an approach that uses the proactive control scheme, covering the end-user network as well as the ATM network.

The Approach — The central goal of the proposed scheme is to operate the VPC between a user site pair such that the aggregated traffic (synchronous and asynchronous) by no means exceeds the assigned PCR, that is, the upper bound of the available bandwidth shared by each VPC_j. Thus, we need to establish a mechanism which avoids violation of Eq. (7):

$$B_{coj} + B_{cl_j} < PCR_j \qquad (7)$$

In order to utilize Eq. (7), two tasks are necessary:
• An estimation of the upper bound of the throughput of the interLAN traffic (i.e., the B_{cl} bandwidth) is required.

• An algorithm controlling the upper bound of the bandwidth used by the asynchronous and synchronous users must be defined, making sure that Eq. (7) will not be violated at any instant of time.

The rate-limiting mechanism in the current transport protocols (TCP/TP 4), based on the sliding window mechanism, allows limiting the rate of the sender and thus the upper bound of the bandwidth used by asynchronous (interLAN) traffic. In order to avoid exceeding the PCR of the VPC, a combined bandwidth management and congestion control scheme is required. The first prerequisite is the knowledge of the bandwidth actually used by the asynchronous traffic.

Based on the results obtained previously and taking into consideration that there is no CLS employed, the upper bound of the achievable throughput s_j of the interLAN traffic sent by the corporate user site j is determined by the value of $(m_j * w_j)/T_{RND}$ or by the residual bandwidth $(PCR_j - B_{coj,i})$ available for the VPC_j (Eq. (8)). $B_{coj,i}$ depicts the currently used bandwidth by the synchronous user site j which is less or equal to the allocated bandwidth B_{co}.

$$s_j = \min[(m_j * w_j)/T_{RND}; (PCR_j - B_{coj,i})] \qquad (8)$$

Interpretation of the Result — For $m_j = 1$, the upper bound of the throughput is determined by w_j/T_{RND}. If

$$(m_j * w_j)/T_{RND} \gg (PCR_j - B_{coj,i}),$$

the upper bound of the throughput is determined by the residual bandwidth $(PCR_j - B_{coj,i})$. Knowing the number of connections and the window size used, it is possible to calculate the upper bound of the throughput (i.e., the bandwidth required by the interLAN connections). In order to avoid any bandwidth interference (congestion/cell loss), the main task of the bandwidth management instance is to administer/maintain the bandwidth in such a way that the bandwidth required for the interLAN traffic (upper bound of the throughput) never exceeds the residual bandwidth. Applying this strategy, synchronous traffic is prioritized over asynchronous traffic.

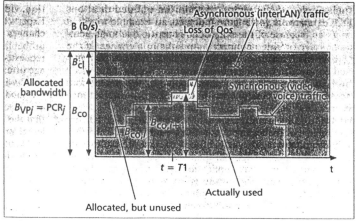

■ **Figure 6.** *Exceeding the PCR due to uncontrolled bandwidth occupancy.*

A Bandwidth Allocation Algorithm — From the analysis above we have learned that it is not sufficient to properly select the bandwidth controlled by the PCR for each VPC. An additional mechanism needs to be employed, preventing the asynchronous traffic from using more bandwidth than the residual value available. Concerning TCP/TP 4 transport protocols, the transport credit window is the most appropriate point to control the residual bandwidth value because the size of the offered credit window directly affects the load on the VPC. Assuming that no dynamic change of the selected PCR is permitted, two possible scenarios have to be considered, which require the performance of the bandwidth allocation algorithm:

• A synchronous user requests/cancels a synchronous connection.
• A change (establishing/closing) of an interLAN transport connection across the ATM network occurs.

In the following the activities of the allocation algorithm with a change of either synchronous and asynchronous connection are discussed in more detail.

A Change of Synchronous Connection — Figure 7 shows the part of the algorithm performed by a bandwidth manager instance after having received a change request (setup/cancellation) for a synchronous VCC. The increase of the synchronous bandwidth B_{co}, causing bandwidth interference (exceeding the PCR), would be recognized by the algorithm upon reception of a ΔB_{co} change request. The actions of path 1 in Fig. 7 will be performed. The remaining bandwidth is calculated serving the interLAN transport connections ($B_{cl,\,i+1}$). Knowing the new bandwidth available, the upper bound of the window sizes of the involved interLAN transport connections will be calculated (TP in Fig. 7). The calculated window sizes are broadcast to the agents involved in the interLAN communication. There, a change of window size at all sending transport entities using the appropriate network management service primitives takes place. Once this is completed, the additional VCC is set up (B in Fig. 7). The closing of a VCC, reducing the use of the synchronous bandwidth B_{co_i}, also induces the bandwidth manager to perform the bandwidth allocation algorithm (path 2 in Fig. 7). If no w limitation has been imposed by the bandwidth allocation algorithm, there will be no update of the window size currently being used.

A Change of InterLAN Transport Connection — A change of interLAN connection may also result in an adjustment of the window size in order to avoid exceeding the PCR. Upon a transport connection change, the upper bound estimate of the bandwidth is calculated. An increase of transport connections results in the performance of path 1 in Fig. 8. The new calculated window size guarantees that the upper bound of the throughput will not exceed the residual bandwidth value ($PCR - B_{co,i}$). A closing of an interLAN transport connection reduces the B_{cl} bandwidth part. The bandwidth allocation algorithm will be performed (path 2 in Fig. 8). If no w limitation has been imposed by the algorithm, there will be no update of the window sizes currently used.

Properties and Their Practical Realization — The scheme operates in a decentralized fashion. Each user site (LNMC) independently handles the assigned bandwidth (PCR) for each VPC employing the allocation algorithm. If a user site encounters the bandwidth (i.e., the PCR subscribed at the BNMC) no longer fulfilling the requirements of the application, a request for an additional bandwidth segment at the BNMC may relieve the bandwidth problem. The proposed allocation scheme can still be used, but a change of the PCR of the particular VPC is necessary. The practical realization of the window size update is accomplished by using appropriate network management services offered by either the common management information protocol (CMIP) or simple network management

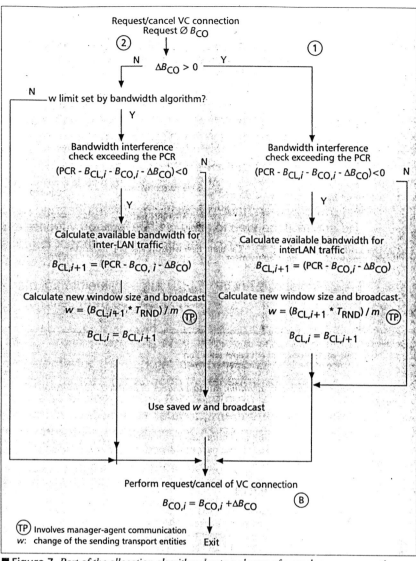

■ Figure 7. *Part of the allocation algorithm due to a change of a synchronous connection.*

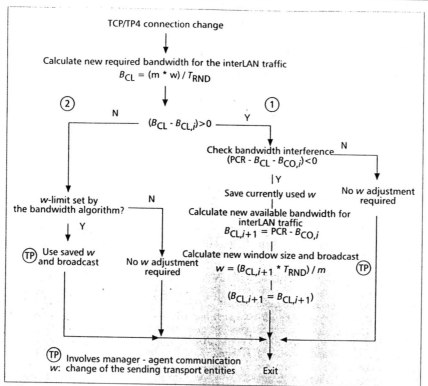

TCP/TP4 connection change

Calculate new required bandwidth for the interLAN traffic
$$B_{CL} = (m * w) / T_{RND}$$

②   N   ①

$(B_{CL} - B_{CL,i}) > 0$ Y

Check bandwidth interference   N
$(PCR - B_{CL} - B_{CO,i}) < 0$

|Y

Save currently used w No w adjustment required

w-limit set by the bandwidth algorithm?   N

Calculate new available bandwidth for interLAN traffic
$$B_{CL,i+1} = PCR - B_{CO,i}$$

Y

(TP) Use saved w and broadcast

No w adjustment required

Calculate new window size and broadcast
$$w = (B_{CL,i+1} * T_{RND}) / m$$

(TP)

$$(B_{CL,i+1} = B_{CL,i+1})$$

(TP) Involves manager - agent communication
w: change of the sending transport entities   Exit

■ **Figure 8.** *Part of the allocation algorithm due to a change of an interLAN transport connection.*

protocol (SNMP). Both parts of the allocation algorithm must be installed at each corporate user site as part of the performance management functional area.

CONCLUSION

The bandwidth allocation aspects of an ATM network serving both asynchronous and synchronous users with a pre-established VPC associated with the PCR have been analyzed. It has been assumed that the LANs/CPE/ATM-CCs have a minimal effect on the performance of the interLAN communication. The proposed algorithm employs the proactive congestion control scheme, which includes the active window control mechanism available at the transport system. It blocks the interLAN burst at the beginning, rather than accepting the bust (bandwidth change) and jeopardize bursts already in progress. This results in substantial improvement of link utilization by ensuring high end-to-end performance for the synchronous user as well as for the asynchronous user (achieving

a controlled high throughput). It takes into account the upper bound of the achievable throughput from the interLAN transport connections, the selected PCR for each VPC, and the bandwidth actually needed to serve the synchronous connections. The activities of the algorithm show that synchronous connections are preferred over interLAN transport connections. The proposed algorithm is adaptive in the sense that a bandwidth allocation scheme, using a dynamic window size control mechanism, adapts to the maximum allowable bandwidth as far as asynchronous users are concerned.

REFERENCES

[1] J. Hammound and P. J. P. O'Reilly, *Performance Analysis of Local Computer Networks*, [Addison-Wesley Publishing Company, 1986].
[2] J. Cherbonnier *et al.*, "ATM direct connectionless service," *Proc. ICC '93*, Geneva, Switzerland, May 23–26, 1993.
[3] N. Kavoc, "Interconnecting 802 LANs through B-ISDN," *Proc. Interworking '93*, Bern, Switzerland, June 1993.
[4] R. Jaeger, "A Bandwidth Management Scheme for Handling Asynchronous and Isochronous Traffic in a LAN/MAN Environment," *Proc. IEEE GLOBECOM '94*, Nov. 1994, pp. 1555–59.
[5] L. Wojnaroski, "Baseline Text for Bandwidth Management," ATM Forum Tech. Committee, Traffic Management Sub-Working Group, Jan. 1994.
[6] J. Scot *et al.*, "Link by Link, Per VC Credit Based Flow Control," ATM Tech. Committee, Mar. 1994.
[7] "ATM User Network Interface Specification (V.3.0)," ATM Forum, 1994.
[8] C. A. Eldridge, "Rate Controls in Standard Transport Layer Protocols," *ACM Sigcomm Comp. Commun. Rev.*, 1992.
[9] V. Jacobsen, "Congestion Avoidance and Control," *Comp. Rev., Proc. SIGCOMM '88*, vol. 18, no 4, Aug. 1988.
[10] G. Ramamurthy and R. R. Dighe, "A Multidimensional Framework for Congestion Control in B-ISDN," *IEEE JSAC*, vol. SAC-9, Dec. 1991.

BIOGRAPHY

RUDOLF JAEGER is a group leader at BetaTechnik working in the Research and Development Department on multimedia systems design. Prior to this assignment, Dr. Jaeger worked for the debis Systemhaus where he was actively involved in the development of bandwidth management strategies for MANs and ATM networks. He earned a Ph.D. in computer science from the Universitaet der Bundeswehr Muenchen (Germany).

The Rate-Based Flow Control Framework for the Available Bit Rate ATM Service

A new ATM service category, the Available Bit Rate service, is currently the subject of intense development. This new service will systematically and dynamically allocate available bandwidth to users by controlling the flow of traffic with feedback. The Rate-Based Flow Control Framework has been identified as the most appropriate for the support of this new service.

Flavio Bonomi and Kerry W. Fendick

Asynchronous transfer mode (ATM) is a networking protocol with the potential to support applications with distinct tolerances for delay, jitter, and cell loss and distinct requirements for bandwidth or throughput. To address this spectrum of needs, the ATM Forum has defined a family of *service categories*. The first two service categories specified, the Constant Bit Rate (CBR) and the Variable Bit Rate (VBR) services, were intended to address applications, like circuit emulation or entertainment-quality video, with precisely defined requirements for throughputs and delays. A third service category, the Unspecified Bit Rate (UBR), was intended for applications, e.g., file transfers submitted in the background of a work station, with minimal service requirements.

The primary goal of a fourth service category currently under development, the Available Bit Rate (ABR) service, is the economical support of applications with *vague* requirements for throughputs and delays. A user might know, for example, that a particular application runs well across a lightly loaded 10-Mb/s Ethernet and miserably through a 9.6 Kb/s modem. That same user, however, could have difficulty selecting a single number to serve as both a guarantee and a bound on the bandwidth for the application, as would be required to set up a CBR connection across an ATM network. Trial and error would help to narrow the range of viable bandwidths for the application, but typically not to a single number. The ABR service is suited for such an application.

While the ABR service is potentially useful for a wide variety of applications, the main motivation for its development has been the economical support of data traffic, where each packet of data is segmented into ATM cells, the loss of any one of which causes the retransmission of the entire packet by a higher protocol layer. After a study by Floyd (Lawrence Berkeley Labs) and Romanow (Sun Microsystems) [1] showed that the indiscriminate

dropping of ATM cells under congestion could lead to the collapse of throughput for packet data applications, the goals of the ABR service were expanded to include the support of *sharply defined* objectives for cell loss. Hence, the class of control mechanisms considered for the ABR service has been restricted to those, based on feedback from the network to the traffic source, that could tightly control cell loss within the network. The ABR service would guarantee a particular cell-loss ratio for all traffic offered in proper response to network feedback. To maximize the odds that the vague requirements of an ABR connection are met by a network's available bandwidth, the class of control mechanism considered for the ABR service has been further restricted to those that can use the available bandwidth efficiently and allocate it evenly among the connections active at a given time.

Vague requirements for throughputs and delays are requirements nonetheless, and are best expressed as ranges of acceptable values. An additional goal of the ABR service is to allow a user to specify, at the time of connection setup, a lower and upper bound on the bandwidth allotted to the connection over its life. The value of allowing users to do so will increase over time as network bandwidths grow and the throughputs required by different types of applications become farther and farther apart. While explicit requests for bounds on delay are not planned as part of the setup procedure for individual ABR connections, network providers are expected to advertise delay bounds for the class of ABR connections as a whole.

A general goal of the ATM protocol is to support connections across local area networks (LANs), metropolitan area networks (MANs), or wide area networks (WANs). The physical link that spans the ATM User Network Interface (UNI), e.g., between a Terminal Adaptor (TA)

FLAVIO BONOMI is a distinguished member of technical staff at AT&T Bell Laboratories.

KERRY W. FENDICK is a distinguished member of technical at AT&T Bell Laboratories and a member of AT&T Interspan™ Data Communications Services.

Reprinted from IEEE Network, March/April 1995, pp. 25-39.

and a switch, may itself extend to arbitrary distances. The ability to work in a variety of environments is particularly important when traffic is controlled using feedback, as with the ABR service, for then the sizes of queue fluctuations depend not so much on the absolute size of network distances as on the amount of data that a connection can transmit during the time it takes feedback to reach the traffic source. Hence, the performance issues experienced by an ABR service for the WAN of today will arise for the MAN of tomorrow that has one-tenth the propagation delay of today's WAN but ten times the link bandwidth.

The approach chosen by the ATM Forum as the best match for the goals of the ABR service is to control the bandwidth of connections *directly*. Since each ATM cell contains the same number of bits, control of a connection's bandwidth, measured as a bit rate, is achieved by directly controlling its cell rate, hence the term *rate-based* flow control. Control of the cell rate for a connection would occur at least at the source TA, which would shape the connection's traffic as directed by feedback from the network. It optionally might occur at points within the network as well. Under a rate-based framework, the share of bandwidth allocated to a connection does not depend on the delays between points where data is shaped on a per-connection basis, so that a rate-based framework is ideal for architectural flexibility. As we will discuss, a rate-based framework can support fair (even) allocations of bandwidth, as well as bandwidth guarantees, even when the simple first-in-first-out (FIFO) discipline is used at network queues. The degree of architectural flexibility allowed by a rate-based framework for the ABR service distinguishes it from other approaches to flow control for high-speed networks.

The following section presents a brief history of the proposal to use a rate-based framework for the support of the ABR service, followed by a section with a rather detailed specification of the rate-based framework, including a preliminary description of its basic operation. The next section examines three important topics, namely, the minimum bandwidth guarantee, the interpretation of fairness, and the issue of policing, in reference to the rate-based support of the ABR service definition. The flexibility offered by the rate-based framework is then illustrated, with a discussion of various complexity-performance trade-offs available to implementors of rate-based schemes. Several simulation results are used in order to provide quantitative assessment of some of these trade-offs. A brief comparative discussion of the rate-based framework and of the two major alternatives proposed for the support of ABR service is presented in the following section. These alternative proposals, known as the credit-based and the integrated proposals, are treated at length elsewhere within this same issue. Finally, our conclusions are discussed.

Evolution of the Rate-Based Framework

The idea of directly controlling the rate of a traffic source was first introduced into the realm of protocols for data networking in the

ANSI Frame Relay standard [2]. The header of a Frame Relay packet contains two bits that the network may optionally use to indicate congestion. Although a source of Frame Relay traffic is under no obligation to respond to these congestion bits, the ANSI standard contained an example of how the source might rationally do so by modulating its transmission rate. The recommended algorithm was a rate-based analog of the Ramakrishnan-Jain algorithm [3] used by the DECnet protocol to adjust window sizes. At fixed intervals, the Ramakrishnan-Jain algorithm makes a binary decision whether to increase the current window size by a *fixed* amount or to decrease it by an amount *proportional* to the current window size. This results in a linear increase or exponential decrease of the window size as a function of time. Congestion is signaled by the network in the forward direction of the connection through a single-bit congestion indicator in each packet, which the destination then copies into acknowledgment packets. In this way, the Ramakrishnan-Jain algorithm employs an *end-to-end* feedback loop.

Closed-loop rate-based control was first proposed in the ATM Forum for the support of the ABR service by Newman (then at Network Equipment Technologies) [4]. In Newman's scheme, a congested point in the network periodically would generate backward congestion messages, in the form of ATM Resource Management (RM) cells. If, over a period of the same length, the traffic source received a backward congestion message, it would decrease its rate by an amount proportional to its current rate. Otherwise, it would increase its rate by an amount also proportional to its current rate. This scheme emphasized simplicity and economy, since the rate changes were implemented by left and right shifts and since RM cells were generated only under congestion. It was designed primarily for use in LANs, however, and its ability to extend to WANs was never demonstrated.

A second closed-loop scheme for rate control was proposed in the ATM Forum by Hluchyj and Yin (then both at Motorola) [5]. Hluchyj would go on to organize the effort to establish a rate-based ABR specification. Their proposed scheme used Explicit Forward Congestion Indication (EFCI), a code-point in the header of ATM data cells, as a single-bit indicator of congestion in the forward direction of the connection. At regular intervals, the destination for the connection would check whether EFCI was set in the most recently received data cell and, if not, would transmit an ATM RM cell back to the traffic source containing permission for the source to increase its rate by a fixed increment. If, over an interval of the same length, the source did not receive permission to increase its rate, it would decrease its allowed rate instead by an amount proportional to its current rate. The allowed rate of a connection would adapt between a minimum and maximum value. This source behavior was similar to a scheme presented to the ATM Forum by Sathe (Stratacom).

The use of a linear increase and exponential decrease of rates   in the Hluchyj-Yin proposal was analogous to the way that the Ramakrishnan-Jain scheme worked, as was the end-to-end span of the feedback loop and the periodic use of binary feedback. As with the Ramakrishnan-Jain scheme, the Hluchyj-Yin scheme was designed for use across WANs as well as LANs. The Hluchyj-Yin scheme departed from the Ramakrishnan-Jain scheme in two critical ways, however. First, it interpreted a set EFCI in a single data cell as sufficient grounds for denying *positive* feedback, unlike the Ramakrishnan-Jain scheme, which based the decision to increase or decrease rates on an average of the single-bit congestion indicators. Second, it interpreted all explicit feedback messages from the network in the backward direction of the connection as positive feedback and interpreted the absence of explicit feedback messages as negative feedback. This made the scheme robust to lost or delayed feedback, although it had the disadvantage of consuming bandwidth for feedback cells when the network was not congested.

The overall approach proposed by Hluchyj and Yin was supported by several of the ATM Forum's companies, which also helped to shape its evolution. The group added the concept of an initial cell rate at which a previously idle connection would begin sending cells. Because of concerns about the amount of bandwidth potentially consumed by the RM cells used for positive feedback, the proposal for a time was modified to use negative feedback instead, as in the Newman scheme. Berger, Bonomi, and Fendick (AT&T), Gun (IBM), Heiss (Siemen's), Makruki (Bell South), and Hooshmand (Stratacom) pointed out the need of service providers to have the option to *police* incoming ABR traffic and to modify the *backward* flow of RM cells to warn the source if the policer was approaching a state where it would take action. Holden (Integrated Telecom/Network Synthesis) proposed the additional option of segmenting the control loop by having intermediate points in the network take on responsibilities of the source and destination.

While the resulting framework succeeded in allowing a high degree of architectural flexibility, it had some weaknesses, as revealed by a set of thought experiments proposed by Bennett and des Jardins (Fore Systems). Some of these weaknesses stemmed from the decision to reverse the polarity of feedback from positive to negative. At least partly in response to the issues raised, Barnhart (Hughes Network Systems) proposed the Proportional Rate Control Algorithm (PRCA). PRCA used positive feedback, like the original Hluchyj-Yin scheme, but constrained the amount of bandwidth consumed by ABR feedback to a fixed proportion of the total bandwidth available to ABR traffic. In PRCA, Barnhart also recognized that if the speed at which a connection's allowed sending rate were to increase in proportion to this rate, then the speed at which the combined sending rates of connections on a link would increase would be proportional to the combined rate, regardless of the number of active sources. This would help make the sizes of queue fluctuations, which depend primarily on fluctuations in the combined sending rate, also invariant to the number of active sources. Such an exponential ramp up was implemented by using fixed-sized increases in rates, as in the Hluchyj-Yin scheme, but at a frequency roughly proportional to the rate of the source. According to PRCA,

the destination would generate one backward RM cell on receipt of every Nrm^{th} forward cell on the connection, *if* this cell did not have a set EFCI. On receipt of an RM cell, PRCA would increase its rate. Otherwise, the rate would automatically decrease. PRCA also had a property, termed *use-it-or-lose-it*, where the allowed rate of a source would decrease to a pre-assigned level if the source was not taking full advantage of it. This helped to guard against coordinated attacks by users, as had been described by Bennett and des Jardins. PRCA retained the concept of an initial cell rate, used for newly active connections, and the options of segmenting the control loop and of signaling congestion in either direction of the connection.

Meanwhile, Adams (British Telecom Laboratories), Charny and Jain (Digital Equipment Corporation and Ohio State, respectively), Lyles (Xerox), and Roberts (ATM Systems) advocated rate-based schemes in which the network would provide the source explicitly with its allowed rate rather than with single-bit feedback. Under some circumstances, this could allow the rate of a source to adapt more rapidly and to oscillate less widely than with single-bit feedback. It also was a natural approach if the network planned to police the ABR traffic, because the network would then need to calculate an explicit rate for the connection anyway. As supporters of explicit-rate feedback pointed out, the communication of an explicit rate was easily implemented if the source would generate a steady stream of RM cells (each containing a field for the explicit rate) and if the destination would loop them back. Each switch in the path could then reduce the explicit rate in the RM cell if it was above the rate that the switch could support for the forward path. Switch vendors would have the options of adjusting the explicit rate field in the forward or backward direction of the connection. As Jain and Charny proposed, the RM cells would also contain the rate that the source was allowed when it generated the forward RM cell. This could help switches to allocate bandwidth fairly.

In a central contribution, Fedorkow (Light-Stream) and A. Jain (Bell Atlantic Network Services) showed how to unify the separate rate-based schemes. They accomplished this by interpreting explicit-rate feedback as a dynamic upper bound on the rate calculated by PRCA. In other words, the algorithm would calculate a rate as PRCA did by using the previous allowed rate and any single-bit feedback received from the network, but then would equate the new allowed rate with the minimum of this calculated rate and the most recent explicit rate received from the network. As required by the explicit-rate scheme, the source would still generate a stream of RM cells, which the destination would loop back. The source would do so at a rate proportional to the allowed cell rate, and each RM cell would contain a single-bit congestion indicator, as required by PRCA, as well as an explicit-rate field. Each switch would then have the option of sending feedback using the explicit-rate field, the congestion indicator, or both.

The synthesis of the two scheme was called the Enhanced Proportional Rate Control Algorithm (EPRCA). In the months since the ATM Forum

The idea of directly controlling the rate of a traffic source was first introduced into the realm of protocols for data networking in the ANSI Frame Relay standard.

Switching
elements
provide the
necessary
resources for
the routing of
ATM cells from
sources to
destinations,
namely port
bandwidth
and buffers.

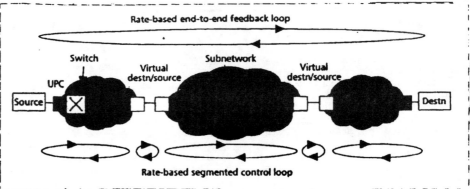

■ Figure 1. *Closed-loop flow-controlled communication network.*

voted to adopt a rate-based framework for ABR, this framework has continued to evolve. Nevertheless, the changes to the rate-based framework since the inception of EPRCA primarily have been enhancements to EPRCA or abstractions of it.

The Rate-Based Congestion Control Framework

*I*n this section we describe the rate-based congestion control framework currently under development for the support of the ABR service. We discuss here only the exchange of data at the level of ATM cells (the ATM layer). It is important to consider this presentation with the awareness that some of the elements of this framework are still being defined at this time.

Figure 1 presents the key elements of a typical communication network implementing a closed-loop (or feedback) control scheme that dynamically regulates the flow of data transported through the network between sources and destinations. These elements are defined as follows.

Source End System and Destination End System — The source end system (SES) and destination end system (DES) are the generation and recipient points, respectively, of the ATM cells transported through the network. The SES and DES typically reside in the Terminal Adaptors, or Network Interface Cards, at the extreme points of an ATM Virtual Connection. The virtual connection is routed through the network and includes a forward (from SES to DES) and a backward (from DES to SES) path. For both bidirectional point-to-point and point-to-multipoint connections the forward and backward components of a virtual connection use the same connection identifiers, and pass through identical transmission facilities.

Within the rate-based framework discussed here, one key functionality of the SES is its ability to submit cells into the network at a variable, controlled, or shaped *rate*. Characterizing the data exchange between an end system (user) and a network in terms of a rate (cells submitted over a given time interval) is the most natural paradigm for ATM, which already defines the CBR and VBR services through rate-based algorithms.

Network Switch (SW) — Switching elements provide the necessary resources for the routing of

ATM cells from sources to destinations, namely, port bandwidth and buffers. These are the limited resources, the contention for which may lead to congestion and, as a consequence, to the possible disruption of normal network operation, involving the potential loss or excessive delay of ATM cells. A switching element implements both *cell scheduling mechanisms* for port bandwidth management and a *cell buffer management mechanism*, which includes a cell discard strategy. Also, a switching element needs to monitor the level of congestion in its resources based on a chosen measure of congestion. With such a measure, a switching element is thus able to support effective *congestion detection* and can then contribute in the process of *congestion indication* to the end systems.

Feedback Mechanisms — Feedback from the network to the end systems gives the users the information necessary to respond, by appropriately modifying their submission rates, to changes in the available bandwidth, so that congestion is controlled or even avoided and the available bandwidth is used. The decision to implement congestion control via a feedback mechanism is motivated directly by the service models adopted for the ABR service, and by the successful experience gained with other data network protocols (e.g., TCP/IP) [3, 6]. It nevertheless has profound performance consequences, given the higher bandwidth available in ATM and the global span envisioned for the evolving ATM networks. The control loop active at the ATM level will need to interact efficiently with other control loops working at higher protocol levels (e.g., TCP/IP).

Virtual Source/Destination (Optional) — While at least one control loop between Source and Destination End Systems is required, as shown in Fig. 1, *segmentation of the control loop* can be optionally implemented by way of Virtual Sources and Destinations, also shown in Fig. 1. An intermediate switching element can close the control loop and initiate a new control loop by functionally behaving as a destination and as a new source. The main motivations for a Virtual Source/Destination are to reduce the length of the control loop, leading to performance improvements, and to create separate control domains for administrative reasons.

Usage Parameter Control (Optional) — Usage Parameter Control (UPC), or Policing (at the UNI) of

Name	Field length	Units	Full name	Comments
PCR	16 bits*	Cells/s	Peak cell rate	Will be policed by network
MCR	16 bits*	Cells/s	Minimum cell rate	Will be guaranteed
ICR	16 bits*	Cells/s	Initial cell rate	Start up rate after source being idle
AIR	16 bits*	Cells/s	Additive increase to rate	Rate increase permitted
Nrm	8 bits	Cells	Number of cells/RM	$Nrm = 2 \char94 N$ (Nrm-1) data cells between RM cells
RDF	8 bits	None	Rate decrease factor	$RDF = 2 \char94 RD$ Used when EFCI bit set or RMs delayed

■ **Table 1.** *Source and destination parameters.*

the traffic submitted by an end system, is an essential requirement for public networks supporting multiple services. Many of these services guarantee to support lower bounds on bandwidth, as well as QoS guarantees applying to delays and cell loss. The need for mechanisms that protect users of the ABR service from misbehaving users of the same service, and limit how various services can affect each other, is satisfied via the joint action of policing and of scheduling and buffer management at the switch ports. This issue has been presented nicely in Lefelhocz [7], where the authors argue that while previous networks based on the "best effort" paradigm succeeded within an educated and cooperative community, future ATM networks offering ABR service will develop in a potentially less cooperative, commercial environment. Policing is not always needed in a private network environment, although efficient mechanisms to ensure fair access to resources are still of importance there.

The main goal of the rate-based proposal for the support of the ABR service, overwhelming endorsed during the September 1994 ATM Forum meeting in Ottawa, is to define a flexible *framework* or family of rate-based closed-loop schemes for congestion control, which includes, as particular instances, a broad range of possible implementations characterized by varying degrees of cost and complexity. In particular, the rate-based framework does the following:
- Supports end-to-end flow control, but also defines the option for intermediate switches or networks to segment the control loop.
- Allows switches to limit their participation in the support of ABR connections to using the simple 1 bit EFCI mechanism, but also to provide more detailed feedback that dynamically changes an explicit upper bound on the source rate.
- Defines mechanisms and control-information formats to allow switches implementing any of the above types of feedback to coexist within the same control loop and interoperate with the end systems.

The flexibility inherent in the specification of the rate-based framework should offer service and network equipment providers a broad latitude in the selection of implementations appropriate to their various markets. It should allow a graceful evolution toward more sophisticated future solutions. The present generation of ATM switches, which will be widely deployed in the next couple of years, will be able, within this framework, to support early instances of the ABR service via the simple EFCI capability. At the same time, the various possible implementations, while obviously supporting the ABR service definition with different levels of performance, should interwork in an adequate fashion within a complex, possibly multivendor, network.

The approach adopted in the rate-based proposal to achieve the ultimate goals listed above consists not in the identification of a single mechanism for implementation, but in a set of requirements that specify the following:
- The content and format of the ATM RM cells used to convey feedback information along the path of each virtual connection.
- A precise definition of the SES behavior (also applying in the case of the Virtual Source) with respect to the generation, handling, and response to the receipt of RM cells.
- A precise definition of the Destination End System behavior (also applying in the case of the Virtual Destination) with respect to the handling of RM cells.
- A broad definition of a range of feasible Switching Element behaviors.

The balance of this section is devoted to a description of the basic operation of congestion control schemes encompassed by the rate-based framework. A further subsection will present and intuitively motivate the specification of the rate-based proposal as outlined above.

Basic Operation

For ABR data calls, the source creates a connection with a call setup request. During this call setup, the values for a set of ABR-specific parameters are identified. Table 1 describes the set of parameters currently considered. Some values are requested by the source and possibly modified by the network (e.g., Peak Cell Rate or Minimum Cell Rate), while others are directly chosen by the network (e.g., the parameters characterizing the process for dynamically updating rates, such as AIR, *Nrm*, or RDF).

Once the source has received permission, it begins cell transmission. The rate at which an ABR source is allowed to schedule cells for transmission is denoted by Allowed Cell Rate (ACR). The ACR is initially set to the Initial Cell Rate (ICR) and is always bounded between the Minimum Cell Rate (MCR) and the Peak Cell Rate (PCR). Transmission is initiated by the sending of an RM cell followed by data cells. The source will continue to send an RM cell after every (*Nrm*-1) user cells transmitted. The source rate is controlled by the return of these RM cells, which contain the information contained in the fields listed in the text box titled "RM Cell Fields." Further fields are being proposed by various authors. The ultimate format and content of the RM cells used within the ABR service is thus not completely determined today. An effort toward the global standardization of such format, also enabling other uses of the same cell type, is currently underway.

The source places the rate at which it may transmit cells (the ACR) in the CCR field of the RM cell, and the rate at which it wishes to transmit cells (usually the PCR) in the ER field. The

RM cell travels *forward* through the network, providing the switches in its path with the information in its content for their use in determining the allocation of bandwidth among ABR connections. Switches may also decide at this time to reduce the value of the explicit rate indication field ER, or set the Congestion Indication bit CI to 1. Switches only supporting the EFCI mechanism will ignore the content of the RM cell.

When the cell arrives at the destination, the destination should change the direction bit in the RM cell and return the RM cell to the source. If the destination is congested and cannot support the rate in the ER field, the destination should then reduce ER to whatever rate it can support. If, when returning a RM cell, the destination had observed a set EFCI in the last data cell received, then it should set the RM cell's CI bit to indicate congestion.

As the RM cell travels *backward* through the network, each switch may examine the cell and determine if it can support the rate ER for this VC. If ER is too high, the switch should reduce it to the rate that it can support. No switch should increase the ER, since prior switch congestion information then would be lost. The switches should try to modify the ER for only those VCs for which it is a bottleneck, since this promotes a fair allocation of bandwidth, as we describe later. Also, switches should modify the ER content of the RM cells traveling on either their forward or backward journeys, but not on both.

When the RM cell arrives back to the source, the source should reset its rate, ACR, based on the information carried back by the RM cell. If the congestion indication bit is not set (CI = 0), then ACR is allowed to increase (as discussed in detail in a following section) toward (or up to) the ER value returned, but never exceeding PCR. If the congestion indication bit is set (CI = 1), then an automatic decrease in the ACR is allowed to occur; and the ACR is further decreased to the returned ER, although never below the MCR.

The Rate-Based Congestion Control Specification

In this section we discuss preliminary specifications for the source, destination, and switching element. (Some changes to these specifications have occured since the typesetting of this article.) These specifications, presented in the accompanying text boxes, define the framework of congestion control mechanisms supporting the ATM ABR service and ensure their interoperability.

The text box titled "Source (and Virtual Source) End System Behavior" provides the specification of the Source End System. As mentioned above, an RM cell is always sent as the first cell after an idle period for the source, where a source is considered *idle* if no data cell is transmitted over an interval of length corresponding to Nrm cell intervals at the current allowed rate ACR. (A source may not become aware of its idleness until it again has a cell to transmit). The use of the Block Start bit has interesting implications (as discussed in a following section) and, in particular, can help to achieve much more aggressive start up or ramp up times.

Specification (4) aims at protecting the network from the impact of sources that, having gone idle at a high ACR, otherwise could claim large amounts of bandwidth as soon as they became active in possibly different load and congestion situations, thus causing large queue fluctuations. This is a simple requirement for a form of *use-it-or-lose-it* mechanism.

Specifications (5) and (6) define the approach for updating rates. The proposed scheme is clearly based on a *positive feedback* control idea: a source can only increase its sending rate when given an explicit positive indication to do so (in our case CI = 0 in returning RM cell); in the absence of such positive indication the source continually decreases it rate. This approach provides for robust control.

From (5) and (6) it follows that the frequency of rate decreases and of possible rate increases is *proportional* to the current sending rate ACR (with proportionality factor $1/Nrm$). Alternative methods discussed in the literature [3, 8] use periodic updating. Finally, note that if large values

---

RM Cell Fields

DIR Direction of the RM cell (forward or return).

CI Congestion indicator (0 = no congestion, 1 = congestion).

BS Block Start bit (1 for start of new block after idle, else 0).

CCR Current cell rate, in effect when forward RM cell is generated.

MCR Minimum cell rate, put in by source.

ER Explicit rate, initially set to PCR, and possibly modified downward by intermediate networks along the path.

Source (and Virtual Source) End System Behavior

1. The source shall send an RM cell for every Nrm cells transmitted. It will always put an RM cell at the start of each transmission after being idle. It will mark the first RM cell after being idle with BS = 1 and all other RM cells with BS = 0.

2. The source shall never send at a rate exceeding PCR.

3. The source may always send at a rate of at least MCR.

4. When a souce starts transmitting after being idle, the ACR should be decreased by at least ACR/RDF for each interval Nrm/ACR cell which has passed, down to ICR (a linear decrease). (*Controversial*).

5. An active source should decrease its ACR by at least ACR/RDF every interval Nrm/ACR, down to MCR (an exponential decrease).

6. Only when a backward RM cell is received with CI = 0, may the source increase the ACR by an amount, AIR, negotiated at call setup and restore any previous decrease since receipt of the previous RM cell.

7. When any backward RM cell is received, the source must set its rate to the minimum of the ER from the RM cell and the ACR resulting from 5 and 6.

---

for AIR (e.g., AIR=PCR) and for RDF are selected at the time the connection is established, then (6) and (7) result in the source responding to the RM cells by always setting ACR=ER, whenever MCR <= ER <= PCR.

Next, the box titled "Destination (and Virtual Destination) End System Behavior" provides the specifications of the Destination End System. The destination has the main role, as specified by (9), of supporting the current generation of switches that communicate congestion only through the EFCI code point.

The box titled "Switch Behavior" specifies the minimal Switch Element behavior. The specification listed obviously leaves an immense range of feasible solutions from which the switch manufacturer may choose. There is flexibility in the definition and detection of congestion in the switch, the type of congestion indication used, the direction of the RM flow (forward/backward) used by the switch for congestion indication, the switch cell scheduling mechanisms adopted, and the algorithms implemented in the switch to determine the appropriate explicit rate.

Specification (13) provides an intermediate switch with a powerful mechanism to communicate with the source without waiting for the first RM cell of the busy period to crisscross the network. By reducing the length of the feedback loop at the beginning of periods of source activity, this option can allow higher ICR values, particularly when the likely point of congestion feedback is near the source, as when the feedback comes from a UPC unit (or policer) at the network edge.

Three Important Topics: Minimum Cell Rate, Rate Fairness, and Policing

This section is devoted to three important issues related to resource allocation, which have profound implications on both how the ABR service will be perceived by the users (QoS), and on how networks will allocate and protect their resources in a multiservice ATM environment that includes ABR. Although much progress has been made in recent months toward the definition of the role played by these aspects within the ABR service definition, they are still object of intense study and debate.

Minimum Cell Rate

The support of a non-negligible MCR as a bandwidth guarantee was not always a goal of the ABR service. ABR was originally envisioned as a best-effort service, as patterned after Ethernet and Token-Ring technologies, and today's Internet. The ATM Forum followed the lead of ANSI in introducing the MCR as a bandwidth guarantee, in order to expand the scope of the ABR service in the follow ways:
- To support the replacement of fixed-bandwidth resources with ABR connections.
- To allow the prioritization of ABR traffic.
- To support quasi-real-time applications.
- To interoperate with other emerging protocols, e.g., RSVP [9].

The capability in the first item typically would apply when a single-ABR connection supports a

Destination (and Virtual Destination) End System Behavior

8. The destination should turn all RM cells received around to return to the source. The direction bit should be changed from "forward" to "backward."

9. If an EFCI bit set = 1 has been received on the prior data cell, then the destination should indicate congestion in the backward RM cell. There are two possible options to be considered:
   a. Set the ER Field to reduce the source rate.
   b. Set the CI bit in the RM cell.
   If the destination is a Virtual Destination, the data cells forwarded to downstream switches should have their EFCI bit reset to 1.

10. If the destination is congested, it may reduce ER to whatever rate it can support.

bundle of applications, whereas the latter three apply when each ABR connection supports a single application.

The prospect of replacing a fixed-bandwidth resource with an ABR connection is best viewed from the perspective of a telecommunications manager who is contemplating the replacement of a network of private lines with a network of ABR connections obtained from an ATM service provider. The current bandwidth of the private lines may have been chosen through trial and error, with degraded performance observed at lower bandwidths. The manager may know, however, that the demands for bandwidth vary widely over the day, so that much of the private-line bandwidth is wasted much of the time. A best-effort service might handle much of the demand much of the time, but would provide no assurance of approaching the support of the peak-hour bandwidth requirements. Introducing a bandwidth guarantee would greatly reduce the risks faced by the telecommunications manager in moving to the ABR network, even if the guarantee did not fully cover peak-hour requirements. The service provider would probably support an ABR connection with a given bandwidth guarantee more economically than a private-line with the same bandwidth, because it could allow other ABR users to take advantage of the unused portion of the connection's guaranteed bandwidth on a best-effort basis.

A non-negligible MCR also provides the easiest path to extending the ABR service to prioritize applications. Prioritized treatment is generally useful, e.g., for SNA traffic, and is especially needed for *quasi-real-time* applications. The VBR and CBR service categories were originally targeted for real-time applications, which have a low delay tolerance to minimize the buffering needed in specialized equipment at ATM endpoints (which convert a cell stream into a continuous bit stream). Meanwhile, the Internet community, often using computers with their large buffers as endpoints of connections, has developed quasi-real-time applications with similar capabilities to real-time ones but with much larger tolerances to delays. Quasi-real-time applications typically require some guarantee on bandwidth, e.g., corresponding to a minimum encoding rate for a video

*Policing an
ABR source,
whose cell
submission
rate will vary
with time
under the
control of
feedback from
the network,
poses a
set of new
challenging
problems.*

stream, but can take advantage of spare bandwidth, as Ramamuthy (NEC) and Kanakia, Mishra, and Reibman [10] (AT&T) have shown. Internet protocols like RSVP allow bandwidth reservation to support quasi-real-time applications.

The use of a non-negligible MCR has met some resistance from members of the ATM Forum who question whether its benefits outweigh the added complexity required. A clear consensus does not exist on whether the ABR service should attempt to address quasi-real-time applications or whether a separate service should be introduced for this purpose. Bandwidth guarantees require bandwidth reservation, so that an ABR service may need to reject call requests if sufficient bandwidth is not available. Note, however, that a user can assure acceptance of an ABR call by requesting the lowest MCR supported (e.g., MCR = 0). For established calls, supporting an MCR may introduce significant additional complexity if sophisticated scheduling mechanisms are used at ports. Supporting an MCR is straightforward, though, with many approaches. Today, the balance of ATM Forum members support the use of an MCR as a bandwidth guarantee, as one way of assuring that the ABR service will meet the needs of evolving applications.

Fairness

At an intuitive level, a bandwidth allocation scheme is fair if it does not offer a different treatment to connections, either based on the time order in which they request a share of the available bandwidth, or on the particular location of their source and destination end points. While many different definitions of fairness may be conceived, the ATM Forum has recently converged toward a particular definition, called *max-min fairness*. [11, 12] This definition applies in an unambiguous way if no ABR connections receive bandwidth guarantees (MCR = 0), but various conflicting interpretations exist if connections use different, non-zero MCR values.

We believe that a reasonable amount of flexibility in the interpretation of fairness should be left to ABR service providers. A common definition of fairness does not appear necessary for different ABR services to interoperate. In addition, some ATM users may wish to depart from a strict definition of fairness, for example, in taking advantage of the low feedback delays of local connections on a LAN to allow them more complete access to LAN bandwidth than connections that leave the LAN and span longer distances. The issue of fairness is intimately related to the way network service providers manage their networks in terms of service billing and other complex network optimization problems.

In the unambiguous case when MCR = 0, the max-min fairness principle, as it applies to bandwidth allocation in a data network, can be interpreted as follows. Connections competing for bandwidth at a node may be divided into 1) *constrained* connections, which cannot achieve their fair (equal) share of the bandwidth at that node because of constraints imposed by their PCR or by limited bandwidth available at other nodes along the route of that connection, and 2) *unconstrained* connections, whose access to higher bandwidth is limited by the bandwidth available at the considered node (which is usually referred

to as a bottleneck node for that connection). The key ideas behind max-min fairness are:
- Each connection must have at least one bottleneck node (or switch port) along its route.
- Rates allocated to unconstrained connections at a node (or switch port) should be equal, and given by the fair share Λ

$$\Lambda = \frac{\mu - \sum_{i \in Constrained\ Set} \lambda_i}{N - M}, \qquad (1)$$

where μ is the link capacity, λ_i is the rate achievable by constrained connection i ($\lambda_i < \Lambda$ for all i), N is the total number of connections, and M is the number of constrained connections at the considered link.

The max-min principle can be shown to lead to the maximization of total throughput. Extensions of the above definition to the case of connections with non-zero and possibly different minimum bandwidths, or to the general case of weighted fairness have been discussed in the literature, and brought to the attention of the ATM Forum by Lyles (Xerox), Hughes (Stratacom), and Yin (Bay Networks), among others.

Rate-based schemes that use explicit-rate feedback to the source have taken direct advantage of Equation 1 above to compute the bottleneck bandwidth that is communicated to the traffic source; see, e.g., Charny [12]. Rate-based schemes based on single-bit feedback also can exploit the definition of max-min fairness. For example, consider first the behavior of the Hluchyj-Yin algorithm in a network with a single node. During periods of positive feedback, fixed increments at regular intervals in the rate used by each source imply that the rates of different sources tend to increase in parallel. During periods of no positive feedback (interpreted as negative feedback), decrements at regular intervals in the rate of each source, in proportion to the source's current rate, imply that all source rates decreases exponentially fast; so, high source rates decrease more rapidly than low ones. Because the algorithm produce oscillatory queue lengths, periods of positive and negative feedback alternate; the rates of different sources ultimately converge, although at a time lag to one another because of differences in feedback delays. Given that the source algorithm results in a fair allocation of bandwidth in the case of one node, max-min fairness results for multinode connections, if nodes refrain from sending negative feedback to "constrained" connections, as defined above.

PRCA achieves max-min fairness in an analogous way: the linear increments and multiplicative decrements in rate that occur at a frequency proportional to the current rate correspond to an exponential decrease and linear increase, as a function of *time*, in the interval at which a source may transmit cells. Hence, intercell intervals for different PRCA sources converge in the same way that rates converge for the Hluchyj-Yin scheme. Since the intercell interval for a source is the inverse of its rate, the rates for different sources themselves converge.

Policing Adaptive Rate Control Algorithms

Policing an ABR source, whose cell submission rate will vary with time under the control of feedback from the network, poses a set of new challenging problems. The hardest challenges come from the differences in time when the policing point (UPC) and the source receive feedback information. Furthermore, other relevant and yet unresolved topics must include policing the correct behavior of the source and the destination in their generation and handling of RM cells. This includes, for example, policing the rate of generation of RM cells, the correct advertised rate inserted in the RM cells, and the correct mapping of information into backward RM cells by the destination.

The natural starting point in deciding how to police an adaptive rate-control algorithm for an ABR service is the framework based on the Generic Cell Rate Algorithm (GCRA), in which conformance to the CBR and VBR services is already defined by the ATM Forum. The GCRA is equivalently viewed as a *virtual scheduling algorithm* and as a *continuous state leaky bucket*. In the former view, the algorithm keeps track of when cells should have arrived if the source were shaping traffic to the allowed rate. It then identifies cells as "non-conforming" if they arrive in advance of their expected arrival times by more than the *delay tolerance* selected for the connection. We primarily limit our discussion of policing algorithms to extensions of the GCRA, although scheduling disciplines also can play a role in limiting how a non-conforming source can affect other traffic.

Two approaches to ABR policing based on the GCRA illustrate the main issues. In the first approach, the rate allowed by the GCRA algorithm would adapt based on feedback that crosses the UNI, in much the same way that the source rate is expected to adapt based on the feedback that it receives. If the UPC algorithm and the source algorithm were properly designed and were to receive identical feedback, but at a lag to one another, then their rates could be expected to converge, but again at a lag to one another. This lag would correspond to the one-way delay between the UPC and the source. Since data also would experience a delay from the source to the UPC, the rate at which the UPC algorithm receives data from the source would lag the rate of the UPC algorithm by one full round-trip delay between the UPC and the source. To accommodate this lag, a UPC algorithm that mirrored the reference behavior for the source would typically require a delay tolerance greater than the round-trip delay to and from the source. This would have the side effect of allowing bursts exceeding the "bandwidth-delay" product, with "bandwidth" corresponding to the allowed cell rate for the connection and "delay" corresponding to the round-trip delay to and from the source. Such a UPC would assure that the source is following the reference algorithm, modulo such bursts.

In the second approach, the UPC would appropriately delay the enforcement of new rates, dictated by the network feedback, to take into account the lag with which the source receives such feedback. A delayed enforcement of new rates would certainly help in reducing the size of the delay tolerance required in the dynamic UPC. For example, if the new rate were enforced at a lag that exactly corresponded to the time for feedback to reach the source and the effects of the new rate to reach the UPC, then the size of the delay tolerance for the GCRA algorithm would need to depend

only on the allowed jitter in the data introduced by scheduling algorithms between the source and the UPC.

We believe that the ideal approach to policing rate-controlled sources should combine these two approaches. The ATM Forum plans to address this difficult but extremely important area in the near future.

Implementation of Rate-Based Schemes for ABR: Performance and Complexity Trade-Offs

We have already mentioned how the rate-based framework provides many degrees of freedom in the definition of network elements suitable for the support of the ABR service. In this section we go one step deeper in the exploration of possible implementation trade-offs at the level of the various elements contributing to the service of ABR traffic. In a few selected cases, we go beyond the identification of feasible alternatives, and also provide performance comparisons based on simulation, in order to assess quantitatively the benefits of more complex solutions.

Our general conclusions, which can only partially be supported by the few quantitative results of this section, confirm that the rate-based framework offers a wide range of effective flow control solutions, and that even simple schemes can work well in a variety of environments. Remarkable further improvements can be achieved without the need to rely on complex cell scheduling schemes at the switches.

Congestion Detection

The selection of the measure of resource congestion used for ABR flow control has broad implications for the implementation complexity and the stability and performance of the corresponding system. It should take into account the switch architecture at hand, the desired behavior of the overall control loop, the resource (buffers or bandwidth) which needs to be more tightly protected, and the time scale over which the control objective can be achieved. This topic has not yet been sufficiently investigated in the research literature, although

---

The selection
of the measure
of resource
congestion
used for ABR
flow control
has broad
implications
for the
implementation
complexity
and the
stability and
performance
of the
corresponding
system.

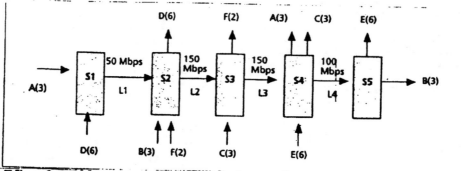

■ **Figure 2.** *Generic fairness configuration (GFCI).*

some contributions are now beginning to appear; see, e.g., Jain *et al.* [13], Altman *et al.* [14], Keshav [15], and and Fendick and Rodrigues [16].

The simplest approach, and the one most commonly implemented, consists in observing the instantaneous length of the queue of cells waiting to be transmitted out of a switch port. The switch port is then considered congested whenever the queue length is found to be larger than a given threshold. This mechanism may seem rather rudimentary because it relies on a 1 bit congestion measure, but it can detect excessive use of both buffer and bandwidth resources, since the presence of a queue reflects a temporary bandwidth demand exceeding the available port bandwidth.

Beyond this basic approach, there exist a multitude of alternatives available. A few illustrative examples proposed in the literature include: 1) the use of multiple thresholds on the queue length; 2) the use of the derivative (differential) of the queue length, where an increasing queue reflects more directly an instantaneous bandwidth demand exceeding the available port bandwidth; 3) the explicit estimation of the aggregate bandwidth demand at a port; and 4) the estimation of the variation of the delay perceived in the service of successive cells from the same connection at a switch port.

An interesting theoretical insight on the stability of rate-based congestion control systems is presented by Altman *et al.* [14], who show that queue-length information must supplement bandwidth information for the stable rate-based control of systems achieving 100 percent utilization of the available bandwidth.

Feedback Congestion Indication: Impact on Fairness and Transient Performance

Once congestion is detected, some form of congestion indication needs to be transmitted to the traffic sources. The basic option offered by the rate-based framework described above consists of single-bit congestion feedback, supported via the EFCI mechanisms in the switches and the CI bit in the RM cells. This basic option imposes very small implementation burdens on the switches and possibly no need to process RM cells. This is an important advantage in the case of very high speed ports, as when processing cells at 622 Mb/s or 2.4 Gb/s rates today. The other extreme of the spectrum is provided by sophisticated switch mechanisms, which compute an explicit rate value that is fed back in the appropriate RM field. This

more advanced approaches require various degrees of processing of the content of the RM cells, and various amounts of memory necessary to store information needed, possibly on a per-connection basis, to determine the explicit rate used for feedback.

Implementers can gracefully move away from the basic EFCI option and toward more and more powerful solutions by progressively adding intelligence in the single bit marking, and then in the computation of explicit rates. In complicated topologies, intelligent 1 bit marking or explicit rate evaluation can surpass the performance of cruder single-bit schemes with respect to

- Efficiency and fairness in the steady-state allocation of the bandwidth.
- Transient behavior experienced in the presence of sudden traffic changes.

Many proposals, characterized by various degrees of implementation complexity, have been introduced in order to provide performance improvements in the two dimensions listed above.

Siu and Tzeng [17] (University of California at Irvine); Barnhart, Lyles (Xerox), and Lin (Cisco); and Roberts (ATM Systems) have proposed examples of more sophisticated switch mechanisms featuring intelligent marking and/or explicit rate evaluation, which demonstrate the enormous potential of the rate-based framework approach. In these schemes the switches may use the CCR information carried in the RM cells or may resort to more complex schemes for measuring rate and queue lengths.

It is interesting to observe that great improvements with respect to the performance of the basic option can be achieved with rather simple schemes, imposing small processing and memory requirements in the switches. This is true of the simple mechanism proposed by Siu and Tzeng [17]. It does not require either per-VC accounting or per-VC queuing, and it computes an estimate of the fair share of bandwidth at a port as a moving average over the rates (CCR) carried by forward or backward RM cells. Although based on a heuristic approach, this scheme fairly allocates bandwidth and also yields a value for the explicit-rate feedback. Recently, Barnhart (Hughes Networks Systems) has proposed an alternative switch mechanism that aims at keeping the aggregate rate of ABR connections at a switch port near a target value, and uses direct measurement of such aggregate rate. This approach is inspired by Jain *et al.* [13].

We now focus on the performance of a few rate-based schemes with respect to the max-min

Parameters for Fig. 4

PCR = 150 Mb/s	MCR = PCR/1000	ICR = PCR/20
AIR = PCR/2900	RDF = 256	Nrm = 32
Network configuration = see Fig. 2	Link distances = 400 m	Host distances = 400 m
Congestion threshold T = 50	High congestion threshold	
VCS = DPF = 7/8	DQT = 500	
	AV = 1/16	

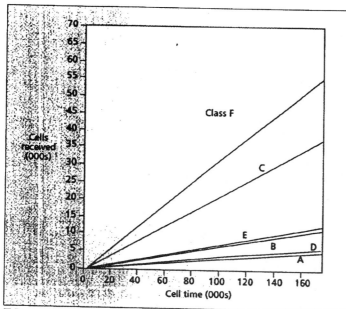

■ Figure 4. *GFC1 fairness test configuration (LAN). Intelligent 1 bit marking mechanism.*

by the rate-based framework. The parameters used in these simulations are as shown in the accompanying box.

Figure 6 shows the performance of the simplest single bit version of the rate-based schemes, with threshold-based congestion detection and FIFO service at the ports. Figure 7 uses the explicit-rate, congestion-avoidance scheme recently introduced by Barnhart. This scheme is based on direct measurement of the current aggregate rate of ABR connections experienced at the switch ports, and aims at maintaining the aggregate rate in the vicinity of a target value, an approach inspired by work of Jain and Lyles. Barnhart's scheme does not require per connection accounting or scheduling. The results in Fig. 7 are obtained using simple FIFO scheduling at the switch ports. Also, to allow immediate access to bandwidth, the parameter AIR for the source systems is equated to PCR, while RDF has a very large value. Thus, immediate response to the explicit-rate feedback is achieved. Note, however, that setting AIR = PCR is not advisable in the WAN environment, where more damped dynamics are required. Without additional damping, actions that reduce the sizes of queue oscillations and improve the efficiency with which bandwidth is used in LANs may increase queue oscillations and reduce bandwidth efficiencies in WANs, where

connections often send bursts of data that do not last as long as the round-trip feedback delay.

By inspecting Fig. 6, we observe that a scheme based on single-bit feedback also can ramp up quickly to the fair rate, though with the oscillatory behavior typically associated with single-bit feedback. Note that such oscillations may not be noticeable at the application level, where average throughputs over intervals exceeding one second are often relevant. Although not presented here, throughputs achieved in this experiment are very high (about 95 percent), and queue lengths are always below 200 cells. The more sophisticated explicit rate scheme in Fig. 7 show better performance in terms of even faster ramp ups and no noticeable oscillations in the rate allocation. Queues, not shown, are even smaller than in the simple EFCI case.

Cell Scheduling and Buffer Management

The rate-based framework does not impose a specific method for scheduling cells and managing buffers at the switches supporting ABR traffic. This enables a wide range of possible architectures.

The simplest and most commonly implemented solution uses a shared port buffer served in a FIFO fashion. While this solution is simple and thus easily implementable, particularly at very high-speed ports, it does not provide any local mechanism to enforce a fair access to buffers and bandwidth; and it leaves such resources open to abuse by malicious users.

The other end of the spectrum is achieved by schedulers that use Weighted Fair Queuing (WFQ) [19] (or approximations thereof) [20], together with per-connection buffer management. Such schemes can protect well-behaved users from less well behaved users, provide fair access to resources even over relatively small time intervals, and preserve the characteristics of traffic as it travels through a network.

Within a rate-based flow control framework, more sophisticated scheduling and buffer management yield improved performance in terms of transient performance, fairness, delay, and delay variability. Higher layer protocols, such as TCP/IP, also may observe better throughput. Finally, policing is simplified when more sophisticated scheduling and buffer management schemes are implemented.

End-to-End versus Segmented Control Loop

Segmentation of the rate control loop is an important option provided by the rate-based framework. It is achieved by closing the control loop at intermediate switches, which then need to act as virtual sources/destinations. A virtual source

36

typically must maintain separate queues for each connection, and a virtual destination must maintain information for each connection.

Abdoul-Magd (Northern Telecom) quantitatively assessed the improvements in performance achieved by segmenting the control loop in a complex configuration with link distances typical of a large WAN (1000 Km/link). For the model of segmented (or link-by-link) control, every switch along the path of an ABR connection implemented the behavior of a virtual source/destination. The explicit-rate version of the simple switch mechanism of Siu and Tzeng [17] was used at each port queue in both the unsegmented and segmented models and at the per-connection queue for each virtual source in the segmented model. For both models, the switches inserted the explicit rate value in the RM cells as they traveled along their backward path. Segmenting the control loop improved fairness and raised link utilizations. The amount of data queued within the network increased when the control loop was segmented, but did not raise delays significantly.

The Roads Not Traveled

The ABR service is not the first to address the vague requirements of data applications for throughputs and delays. LAN protocols like Ethernet and Token Ring at the MAC layer and LAN/WAN protocols like TCP, DECnet, and X.25 at the transport layer have long provided bandwidth on demand to data applications. These protocols will continue to serve users well in many contexts, and packet-based protocols such as TCP and DECnet will continue to run over ATM at the transport layer. Nevertheless, sensitivities to *delays* of the approaches to flow control used by all these protocols make each a less-than-ideal match for the ABR service. The approaches taken by Ethernet and Token Ring are strictly limited in the distances over which they can operate effectively, which excludes them from use for the ABR service.

The sensitivity of TCP, DECnet, and X.25 to delays is more subtly related to their use of mechanisms that directly control the number of outstanding bytes for the connection, that is, the connection's outstanding window size. A window-based protocol is the natural choice for the transport layer, which must guarantee reliable delivery and hence must bound the amount of outstanding data that it might need to retransmit. Nevertheless, because the average throughput for a connection is equal to the ratio of its average window size to it average round-trip delay, achieving an even allocation of bandwidth through the allocation of *window sizes* alone is difficult. As an example, by much the same arguments that showed that the Hluchyj-Yin rate-based scheme tends toward an even allocation of bandwidth among competing connections,

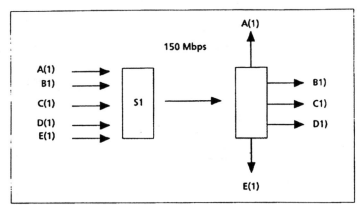

■ Figure 5. *Single bottleneck link, two-node configuration.*

the Ramakrishnan-Jain window-based scheme, which uses the linear increase or exponential decrease of window sizes as a function of time, will tend toward an even allocation of window sizes. (Since window sizes are in units of bytes, one might infer from this that the Ramakrishnan-Jain scheme fairly allocates *buffer space* in the network, rather than bandwidth.) To achieve a fair allocation of bandwidth, the window sizes of different connections would need to tend toward values proportional to the round-trip times for their respective control loops. One way to accomplish this is to alter the Ramakrishnan-Jain scheme to make the linear speed of increase for a

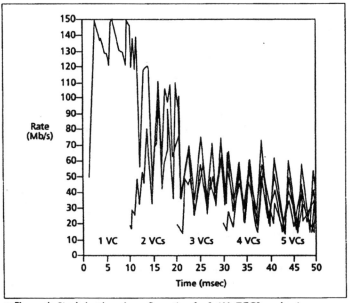

■ Figure 6. *Single bottleneck configuration for LAN. EFCI mechanism.*

Parameters for Fig. 6		
PCR = 150 Mb/s	MCR = PCR/1000	ICR = 20 Mb/s
AIR = PCR/500	RDF = 128	Nrm = 32
Network configuration = see Fig. 5	Link distances = 400 m	Host distances = 400 m
Congestion threshold T = 50		

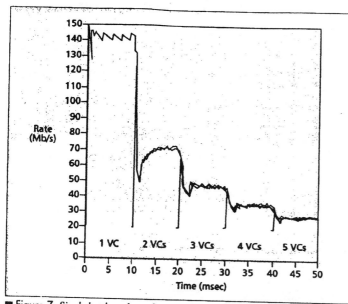

■ Figure 7. *Single bottleneck configuration for LAN. Explicit rate mechanism.*

connection proportional to the round-trip time for the control loop. This later quantity depends on the collective action of the adaptive sources, however, and may vary substantially over time depending on network activity. More robust approaches are to mark the congestion bit selectively based on the monitored throughput for each connection or to use a service discipline at each transmission facility that serves data at the fair rate for each connection and queues incoming data above this rate. (The former approach was proposed by Ramakrishnan *et al.* [21]) Both approaches amount to running a rate-based mechanism underneath the window-based mechanism.

With a fair scheduling discipline at network queues, a window-based scheme still must address two issues to achieve the goals of an ABR service. First, the scheme must allocate a window size to each connection that is large enough to sustain the connection's fair share of the throughput. Second, the scheme must allocate enough buffer space at each scheduler to avoid losing data. Two distinct proposals in the ATM Forum for *Hop-by-Hop Credit-Based Flow Control* addressed these two issues. In both schemes, a separate window for each connection spanned each link and took the form of a credit allocation given by the receiver at one side of a link to the scheduler at the other side of the link. Each credit received for a connection by the scheduler allowed it to transmit one cell. The receiver only allocated credits when it had a corresponding amount of free buffer space per VC, so that the allocated buffer size per VC constrained throughput just as a protocol window does. In particular, the maximum average throughput per connection was constrained by the ratio of its allocated buffer size to its round-trip time across the link. The hop-by-hop control limited the relevant round-trip time to the fixed round-trip propagation delay for a single link, thus minimizing it and avoiding the complications that would have arisen with the variable round-trip times of wider control loops. Still,

both schemes required the precise measurement of round-trip times across each link to minimize buffer sizes without constraining throughput.

The two schemes differed in how they allocated buffer space. The earlier *static credit* scheme reserved enough buffer space per VC to support a throughput equal to the link rate at all times. This was feasible for a LAN at current rates, but not for a WAN with hundreds or thousands of connections. The later *dynamic credit* scheme addressed WANs as well as LANs by varying the buffer allocations depending on the number of active sources and their bandwidth demands. This required a more complex protocol since deallocating buffer space required the receiver to take back credits that it already had allocated across the link.

Ultimately, the Traffic Management Subworking Group of the ATM Forum chose a rate-based framework, rather than the proposed credit-based flow control, primarily because the former required *neither* hop-by-hop control *nor* fair scheduling algorithms at each transmission queue to achieve fairness, although it allowed both as options. Hence, the ATM Forum opted for architectural flexibility. The sensitivity to link delays of the credit schemes also was a concern, particularly for the dynamic credit scheme, as Hughes (Stratacom) demonstrated in an example where a change in the delay for one link in the network could affect the optimal allocation of buffer space per VC throughout the network. Nevertheless, the credit schemes helped to shape the goals of the ABR service by serving as existence proofs that bandwidth could be dynamically allocated without losing cells because of congestion. In addition, the rate-based framework borrowed important traits from the credit scheme, such as the use of positive feedback that was constrained to occupy a fixed proportion of the ABR bandwidth.

The ATM Forum also considered a contribution called the *Integrated Proposal* that advocated the use of a default rate-based congestion-control mechanism within a framework that provided for the transparent use of other mechanisms as options. "Other mechanisms" potentially would have included the credit-based scheme. Supporters of the Integrated Proposal argued that the freedom to introduce new schemes was needed to take full advantage of advances in dynamic flow control and to address any problems that might occur with the default scheme. The drawback was that each new option would require changes in the Network Interface Cards (NICs) that implemented the algorithms, e.g., at each workstation supporting ATM. Because an installed base of NICs is expensive and difficult to change, many members worried that the prospect of additional ABR schemes would slow the deployment of ATM. Furthermore, the architectural flexibility of the rate-based proposal already allowed for many directions of evolution without changing NICs. In particular, the option in the rate-based framework for network equipment to provide explicit-rate feedback did not constrain in any way how the network would derive the explicit rate. The Traffic Management Subworking Group of the ATM Forum therefore chose the path of specifying a single rate-based protocol, thus assuring that innovation would help users with prior investment in ABR NICs as well as users new to the ATM market.

Conclusions

The rate-based protocol under consideration by the ATM Forum for the support of the ABR service is a platform for developing an ever widening family of rate-based schemes in switching equipment. It is grounded, however, in a single set of behaviors implemented by the source and destination of the ABR connection, so it will allow prospective users to deploy ABR terminal adaptors with confidence that their investment will hold its value. The rate-based framework can allow a high degree of architectural flexibility in network equipment, because the allocated bandwidth under a rate-based framework does not depend strongly on delays across the control loop. In other words, the architectural flexibility is a natural outcome of the close match between a rate-based framework and the central requirement for the ABR service to allocate bandwidth fairly.

Some issues, whose creative resolution is crucial for the success of an ABR service supported by the rate-based framework, still need more work. Among these we would mention the further simplification of the required end system behavior, leading to cost savings for the Network Interface Cards, the effective policing of ABR traffic, and the definition of connection admission control for ABR traffic with non-zero minimum rate within networks also supporting VBR and CBR traffic. While unfinished work remains, this presentation offers a broad overview of the impressive progress toward the definition and support of a successful ABR service achieved in the past few months.

Acknowledgments

We are grateful to A. Barnhart for supplying the data that we used in Fig. 7 and to O. Abdoul-Magd for data on his study. The evolving rate-based ABR framework has benefited from the involvement of the many active delegates to the ATM Forum's Traffic Management Subworking Group and the guidance of the chair, N. Giroux.

References

[1] S. Floyd and A. Romanow, "Dynamics of TCP traffic over ATM networks," Proc. ACM SIGCOMM'94, Sept. 1994, pp. 79-88.
[2] DSS1 - Core Aspects of Frame Protocol for the Use with Frame Relay Bearer Service, American National Standards Institute, Telecommunications Committee (ANSI T1S1), Dec. 1990.
[3] K. K. Ramakrishnan and R. Jain, "A Binary Feedback Scheme for Congestion Avoidance in Computer Networks," ACM Trans. Comput. Sys., vol. 8, no. 2, 1990, pp. 158-181.
[4] P. Newman, "Traffic Management for ATM Local Area Networks," IEEE Commun. Mag., vol. 32, no. 8, Aug. 1994, pp. 44-50.
[5] M. Hluchyj and N. Yin, "On closed-loop rate control for ATM networks," Proc. INFOCOM 94, 1994, pp. 99-108.
[6] V. Jacobson, "Congestion Avoidance and Control," Proc. of SIGCOMM' 88, Aug. 1988.
[7] C. Lefelhocz et al., "Congestion Control for Best Effort Service: why we need a new paradigm," Submitted to IEEE JSAC, Spring 1995.
[8] F. Bonomi, D. Mitra, and J. Seery, "Adaptive Algorithms for Closed Loop Flow Control in ATM Networks Based on Binary, Periodic Feedback," submitted to IEEE JSAC, 1995.
[9] L. Zhang et al., "RSVP: A new resource reservation protocol," IEEE Network, vol. 7, no. 5, Sept. 1993.
[10] H. Kanakia, P. Misra, and A. Reibman, "An adaptive congestion control scheme for real-time packet video transport," Proc. ACM SIGCOMM' 93, Sept., 1993.
[11] D. Bertsekas and R. Gallager, "Data Networks," (Prentice Hall, 2nd Edition, 1987).
[12] A. Charny, "An Algorithm for Rate Allocation in a Packet-Switching Network with Feedback" Master's Thesis, MIT Lab for Computer Science, 1994.
[13] R. Jain, S. Kalyanaraman, and R. Viswanathan, "The OSU Scheme for Congestion Avoidance using Explicit Rate Indication," OSU Technical Report, Sept. 1994.
[14] E. Altman, F. Baccelli, and J.-C. Bolot, "Discrete-Time Analysis of Adaptive Rate Control Mechanisms," Proc. 5th Int. Conference on Data Communications, Raleigh, N.C., Oct. 1993, pp. 121-140.
[15] S. Keshav, "Packet-Pair Flow Control," submitted for publication.
[16] K. W. Fendick and M. A. Rodrigues, "Asymptotic Analysis of Adaptive Rate Control for Diverse Sources with Delayed Feedback," IEEE Trans. Info. Theory, vol. 40, no. 6, Nov. 1994, pp. 2008-2025.
[17] K.-Y. Siu and H.-Y. Tzeng, "Adaptive Proportional Rate Control for ABR Service in ATM Networks," UC Irvine Technical Report No. 1102, Electrical and Computer Engineering, July 1994.
[18] Detailed pseudocode is available on request from the authors.
[19] A. Demers, S. Keshav, and S. Shenker, "Analysis and Simulation of a Fair Queuing Algorithm," Proc. of ACM SIGCOMM, 1989, pp. 3-12.
[20] S. J. Golestani, "A Self-Clocked Fair Queuing Scheme for Broadband Applications," Proc. IEEE INFOCOM, 1994, pp. 636-646.
[21] K. K. Ramakrishnan, D.-M. Chiu, and R. Jain, "Congestion Avoidance in Computer Networks with a Connectionless Network Layer. Part IV: A Selective Binary Feedback Scheme for General Topologies," DEC TR-510, Nov. 1987.

Biographies

Flavio Bonomi received a Laurea in electrical engineering from Pavia University, in 1978, and M.S. and Ph.D. degrees in electrical engineering from Cornell University in 1981 and 1989, respectively. From 1985 to 1991 he was with the Department of Performance Analysis at AT&T Bell Laboratories, Holmel, New Jersey, where he worked on performance modeling and analysis in the areas of computer systems and telecommunication systems. Since 1991 he has been with the ATM Platform Organization of AT&T Network Systems, Red Bank, New Jersey, where he is currently a distinguished member of technical staff. His interests and responsibilities within both development and research on ATM broadband systems include switch architecture design, performance analysis, design of traffic management schemes, and network engineering. His e-mail address is: fgb@mtott.com.

Kerry W. Fendick received B.A. in 1982 from Colgate University and an M.S. in mathematics in 1984 from Clemson University. Since 1984 he has worked at AT&T Bell Laboratories in the Data Network Analysis Department, Holmdel, New Jersey, where he is a distinguished member of technical staff. He is also a member of AT&T's InterSpan Data Communications Services and a representative of AT&T in the area of traffic management at the ATM Forum. His interests include the analysis of queueing systems and the control and engineering of high-speed data networks. His e-mail address is: kerry@qsun.att.com.

The rate-based protocol under consideration by the ATM Forum for the support of the ABR service is a platform for developing an ever widening family of rate-based schemes in switching equipment.

Credit-Based Flow Control for ATM Networks

Simulation, analysis, and experiments on switching hardware have shown that for a wide variety of traffic patterns, credit control is fair, uses links efficiently, minimizes delay, and guarantees no cell loss due to congestion. The credit-based mechanism proposed by the authors provides flow control tailored to ATM networks.

H. T. Kung and Robert Morris

H. T. KUNG is a professor of electrical engineering and computer science at Harvard University.

ROBERT MORRIS is a graduate student in computer science at Harvard University.

Congestion control ensures that network resources are divided fairly and efficiently among competing connections. Although congestion control has been studied by researchers for a long time, very high-speed networks using ATM pose a new set of challenges.

The proposed credit-based mechanism provides flow control tailored to ATM networks. Simulation, analysis, experiments on switching hardware have shown that for a wide variety of traffic patterns, credit control is fair, uses links efficiently, minimizes delay, and guarantees no cell loss due to congestion. The credit system is especially well suited to data traffic that is bursty, unpredictable, and has little tolerance for delay.

Other approaches to flow control, including rate-based flow control, may require less expensive hardware and may be effective for steady traffic, but do not handle bursty traffic well. While no one can predict what kind of traffic will dominate future networks, recent evidence suggests that it will be bursty. Thus a major challenge for network research will be to find congestion control mechanisms that blend the hardware simplicity of rate-based flow control with credit-based flow control's ability to handle bursts. This research, in turn, will depend on more experience with real applications and high-level protocols running over ATM.

The high-speed networking market is solidifying quickly, and basic issues in congestion control should be well understood before the market is forced to choose a solution with unknown properties. The lessons learned from the credit-based approach should be incorporated into whatever flow control system that is finally standardized or widely implemented.

Over the last year, the ATM standards community has recognized that data traffic often requires no firm guarantee of bandwidth, but instead can be sent at whatever rate is convenient for the network. This is called "Available Bit Rate" (ABR) traffic by the ATM Forum. ABR traffic gives the network the opportunity to offer guarantees to high priority traffic, and divide the remaining bandwidth among ABR connections.

To support ABR traffic, the network requires a feedback mechanism in order to tell each source how much data to send. A number of such mechanisms have been proposed for ATM, with considerable debate as a result. The two main mechanisms are called credit-based flow control and rate-based flow control. In late 1994, the ATM Forum voted for rate-based flow control, but without committing to the details of any particular algorithm.

This article summarizes the technical basis for credit flow control, including some fundamental advantages of credit which could be adopted by other mechanisms. We hope thereby to speed the evolution of ATM flow control, and minimize the risk of standardizing inadequate solutions. This article avoids political and short-term pragmatic issues, such as migration paths and interoperability, noting that flow control mechanisms adopted now may be in use long after such issues are forgotten.

The first section introduces the problem that flow control solves, along with desirable properties of any solution. The second section presents two general kinds of network traffic that flow control must cope with. The third section provides details of the credit mechanism, and then the fourth gives some intuition as to why it works well. The fifth section outlines the rate-based scheme, and the sixth describes how to add benefits of credit control to rate-based systems. The seventh section summarizes some flow control simulation studies and actual experimental results on ATM switching hardware. The eighth section contains fundamental reasons why credit flow-control has advantages over rate-based, and the concluding section suggests ways in which the advantages of both may be combined.

Reprinted from IEEE Network, March/April 1995, pp. 40-48.

Flow Control Problem

Any data network has bottlenecks: points when more data can arrive than the network can carry. These points are often in switches with multiple ports; congestion arises when data, destined for a single output port, arrives at many inputs. The universal short-term solution involves buffer memory in which a switch can temporarily queue data directed at overloaded outputs. In the longer term, no amount of buffering is sufficient: instead, each source of traffic flowing through a bottleneck must be persuaded to send no more than its fair share of the bottleneck's capacity.

This is fundamentally a feedback control problem, and many control ideas and principles apply. Each network switch collects information about congestion, and informs, directly or indirectly, the sources of data. This feedback is usually based on the amount of buffer space available or in use in the switch. The sources act to control how much data they send. This control loop has a delay of at least twice the propagation delay between the switch and control point. Control systems should seek to minimize this delay, since switches will need to buffer any data that arrives after they signal the congestion status but before the end of the delay.

A variety of technical goals, some of them conflicting, are desirable for any flow control mechanism. Data should rarely, if ever, be discarded due to exhaustion of switch buffer memory. Such data may have to be retransmitted after a possibly lengthly time-out period, further contributing to network congestion and the delay seen by the user. Links between switches should be used at full capacity whenever possible. For instance, if one connection sharing a link reduces the rate at which it sends, the others should increase as soon as possible. All the connections which are constrained by a bottleneck link should get fair shares of that link. The flow control mechanism should be robust; loss or delay of control messages, for instance, should not cause increased congestion. The network administrator should not have to adjust any complex parameters to achieve high performance. Finally, the flow control mechanism should have a cost commensurate with the benefits it provides.

Two Traffic Models

Any prediction of how well a flow control scheme will work requires a model for the behavior of network traffic. A full-blown model might involve characteristics of applications and higher-level protocols. For our purposes it is enough to distinguish between *smooth* and *bursty* traffic.

A smooth traffic source offers a constant and predictable load, or only changes in time scales that are large compared to the amount of time the flow control mechanism takes to respond. Such traffic is easy to handle well; the sources can be assigned rates corresponding to fair shares of the bottleneck bandwidth with little risk that some of them will stop sending and lead to underutilized links. Switches can use a small amount of memory, since bursts in traffic intensity are rare.

Sources of smooth traffic include voice and video with fixed-rate compression. The aggregate effect of a large number of bursty sources may also be smooth, particularly in a wide-area network

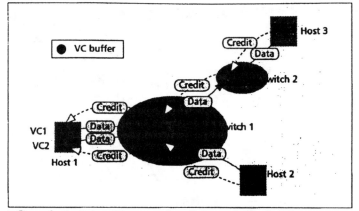

■ Figure 1. *Credit-based flow control applied to each link of a VC.*

where the individual sources are relatively low-bandwidth and uncorrelated. Rate-based flow control works well with smooth traffic.

Bursty traffic lacks any of the predictability of smooth traffic, as observed in some computer communications traffic [5]. Some kinds of bursts stem from users and applications. A Mosaic user clicking on a link, for instance, wants to see a page or image as soon as possible. The network cannot predict when the clicks will occur. Nor should it smooth out the resulting traffic, since doing so would hurt Mosaic's interactive response. Other sources of bursts result from network protocols that break up transfers into individual packets, windows, or RPCs, which are sent at irregular intervals. These bursts are sporadic, and typically do not last long enough on a high-speed link to reach steady state over the link round-trip time.

The most visible sign of network overload due to traffic bursts is usually buffer exhaustion. Credit flow control works well with such traffic because it directly controls buffer allocation.

Credit-based Flow Control

We briefly review credit-based flow control in this section. Implementing link-by-link, per-VC (virtual circuit) flow control, the scheme generally works over a VC link as follows. As depicted by Fig. 1, before forwarding any data cell over the link, the sender needs to receive credits for the VC from the receiver. At various times, the receiver sends credits to the sender indicating availability of buffer space for receiving data cells of the VC. After having received credits, the sender is eligible to forward some number of data cells of the VC to the receiver according to the received credit information. Each time the sender forwards a data cell of a VC, it decrements its current credit balance for the VC by one.

There are two phases in flow controlling a VC. In the first *buffer allocation* phase, the VC is given an allocation of buffer memory, Buf_Alloc, in the receiver. In the second *credit control* phase, the sender maintains a nonnegative credit balance, Crd_Bal, to ensure no overflow of the allocated buffer in the receiver.

Implementing credit-based flow control, an experimental ATM switch [2], with 622 Mb/s ports, has been developed by BNR and Harvard University.

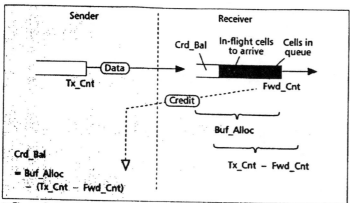

■ Figure 2. *Credit update protocol (CUP).*

An ATM network testbed involving multiple copies of this switch and a variety of ATM host adapter cards is operational. Experiments on this testbed have confirmed the benefit of credit-based flow control as described in this article. Independently, Digital Equipment Corporation has also developed a credit-based ATM network.

For the remainder of this section, we first describe a protocol for the credit control phase; then we introduce the notion of static vs. adaptive credit control, reflecting if the buffer allocation is static or adaptive; next, we overview the sender- and receiver-oriented adaptive approaches; and finally, we describe in some detail a receiver-oriented adaptive buffer allocation scheme.

Credit Update Protocol

The *Credit Update Protocol* (CUP) [8] is an efficient and robust protocol for implementing credit control over a link. As depicted in Fig. 2, for each flow-controlled VC, the sender keeps a running total Tx_Cnt of all the data cells it has transmitted, and the receiver keeps a running total Fwd_Cnt of all the data cells it has forwarded. (If cells are allowed to be dropped within the receiver, Fwd_Cnt will also count these dropped cells). The receiver will enclose the up-to-date value of Fwd_Cnt in each credit record transmitted upstream via a credit cell. When the sender receives the credit record with value Fwd_Cnt, it will update the credit balance, Crd_Bal, for the VC:

$$Crd\_Bal = Buf\_Alloc - (Tx\_Cnt - Fwd\_Cnt) \quad (1)$$

where Buf_Alloc is the total number of cells allocated to the VC in the receiver. Note that the quantity, Tx_Cnt Fwd_Cnt, represents the "outstanding credits" which correspond those cells of the VC which the sender has transmitted, but the receiver has not forwarded. As depicted in Fig. 2, these cells are "in-flight cells to arrive" and "cells in queue" at the time when the receiver sends credit record Fwd_Cnt to the sender. Thus Crd_Bal computed by the sender using Eq.(1) is the proper new credit balance. See [8] for a scheme of using *credit_check cells* periodically sent from the sender to the receiver, to recover from possible loss of data or credit cells.

The frequency at which the receiver sends credit records for a VC depends on the VC's progress. More precisely, each time after the receiver has forwarded "*N2*" cells for some positive integer

N2, the receiver will send a credit record upstream. The value of *N2* can be set statically or adaptively.

The Buf_Alloc value given to a VC determines the maximum bandwidth allowed to the VC by credit flow control. For the rest of this section we make a simplifying assumption that all links have the same peak bandwidth of 1, and represent the rate of a VC as a fraction of 1. Let *RTT* be the round-trip time, in cell transmission times, of the link between the sender and the receiver (Fig. 2) including both link propagation delays and credit processing time. Assume that the receiver uses a fair scheduling policy between VCs with Crd_Bal > 0, when forwarding cells out from its output link. Then if there are *N* active VCs competing for the same output link, the maximum average bandwidth over *RTT* that the VC can achieve is:

$$BW = Buf\_Alloc / (RTT + N2 * N) \quad (2)$$

Note that when there is only one VC using the output port, i.e., *N* = 1, the VC's bandwidth can be as high as Buf_Alloc / (*RTT* + *N2*).

The CUP scheme is a lower level and lighter weight protocol than typical sliding window protocols used in, e.g., X.25 and TCP. In particular, CUP is not linked to retransmission of lost packets. In X.25 or TCP, loss of any packet will stop advancing the window until the dropped packet has been retransmitted successfully. To implement this, each data packet carries a sequence number. In contrast, in CUP the sender does not retransmit lost data cells, the receiver does not reorder received cells, and data cells do not carry sequence numbers.

It can be shown [10] that CUP produces the same buffer management results as the well-known "incremental" credit updating methods (e.g., [3,6]). In these other methods, instead of sending Fwd_Cnt values upstream the receiver sends incremental credit values to be added to Crd_Bal at the sender.

Static vs. Adaptive Credit Control

We call a credit-based flow control *static* or *adaptive*, if the buffer allocation is static or adaptive, respectively. In a static credit control, a fixed value of Buf_Alloc will be used for the lifetime of a VC. Requiring only the implementation of CUP in the previous section or some equivalent protocol, the method is extremely simple.

There are situations, however, where adaptive credit control is desirable. In order to allow a VC to operate at a high rate, Eq.(2) implies that Buf_Alloc must be large relative to *RTT* + *N2* * *N*. Allocating a small buffer to a VC can prevent the VC from using otherwise available link bandwidth. On the other hand, committing a large buffer to a VC can be wasteful, because sometimes the VC may not get sufficient data and scheduling slots to transmit at the desired high rate. The proper rate at which a VC can transmit depends on the behavior of traffic sources, competing traffic, scheduling policy, and other factors, all of which can change dynamically or may not be known *a priori*. In this case, adaptive credit control, which is static credit control plus adaptive adjustment of Buf_Alloc of a VC according to its current bandwidth usage, can be attractive.

Generally speaking, for configurations where a large Buf_Alloc relative to *RTT* + *N2**N is not prohibitively expensive, it may be simplest just to implement static credit control. This would give excellent performance. Otherwise, some adaptive buffer allocation scheme may be used to adjust `Buf_Alloc` adaptively. The adaptation can be carried out by software.

Adaptive Buffer Allocation

Adaptive buffer allocation allows multiple VCs to share the same buffer pool in the receiver node adaptively, according to their needs. That is, `Buf_Alloc` of a VC will automatically decrease, if the VC does not have sufficient data to forward, cannot get sufficient scheduling slots, or is back-pressured due to downstream congestion. The freed-up buffer space will automatically be assigned to other VCs which have data to forward and are not congested downstream.

Adaptive buffer allocation can be implemented at the sender or receiver node. As depicted by Fig. 3, in a sender-oriented adaptive scheme [8, 11] the sender adaptively allocates a shared input-buffer at the receiver among a number of VCs from the sender that share the same buffer pool. The sender can allocate buffer for the VCs based on their measured, relative bandwidth usage on the output port p [8].

Receiver-oriented adaptation [9] is depicted by Fig. 4. The receiver adaptively allocates a shared output-buffer among a number of VCs from one or more senders that share the same buffer pool. The receiver can allocate buffer for the VCs based on their measured, relative bandwidth usage on the output port q [9].

Receiver-oriented adaptation is suited for the case where a common buffer pool in a receiver is shared by VCs from *multiple* upstream nodes. Figure 4 depicts such a scenario: the buffer pool at output port q of the receiver switch *Rcv* is shared by four VCs from two switches *Snd1* and *Snd2*. Note that the receiver (*Rcv*) can observe the bandwidth usage of the VCs from *all* the senders (i.e., *Snd1* and *Snd2* for Fig. 4). In contrast, each sender can only observe the bandwidth usage of those VCs going out from the same sender. Therefore, it is natural to use receiver-oriented adaptation in this case.

Moreover, receiver-oriented adaptation naturally supports the adaptation of *N2* values for individual VCs, in order to minimize credit transmission overhead and increase buffer utilization. Since only the receiver needs to use *N2* values, it can conveniently change them locally, as described in the next section.

Receiver-oriented Adaptive Buffer Allocation

We describe the underlying idea of the receiver-oriented adaptive buffer allocation algorithm in [9]. In referring to Fig. 4, let *RTT* be the maximum of all the *RTT*s and *M* be the size, in cells, of the common buffer pool in the receiver.

For each allocation interval, which is set to be at least *RTT*, the receiver will compute a new allocation and an *N2* value for each VC according its relative bandwidth usage. Over the allocation interval, let *VU* and *TU* be the number of cells forwarded for the VC and that forwarded for all the *N* active VCs, respectively. Then for the VC, the new allocation is:

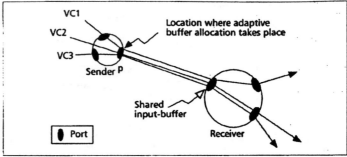

■ **Figure 3.** *Sender-oriented adaptation.*

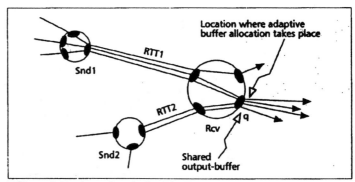

■ **Figure 4.** *Receiver-oriented adaptation.*

$$\texttt{Buf\_Alloc} = (M/2 - TQ - N) * (VU/TU) \quad (3)$$

and the new *N2* value is:

$$N2 = \texttt{Buf\_Alloc}/4 \quad (4)$$

where *TQ* is the total number of cells currently in use in the common buffer pool at the receiver. For the purpose of presenting the basic adaptive idea here, it is without loss of generality that in this section floor and ceiling notations for certain quantities are ignored, such as those in the righthand sides of the above two equations. See [9] for precise definitions and analysis of all quantities.

It is easy to see that the adaptive formula of Eq.(3) will not introduce cell loss. The equation says that for each allocation interval, the VCs divide the "pie" of size $M/2 - TQ - N$ according to their current relative bandwidth usage. Thus, the total allocation for all the VCs is no more than $(M/2 - TQ - N) + N$ or $M/2 - TQ$, assuming the each VC is always given at least one cell in its allocation. Since allocation intervals are at least *RTT* apart, after each new allocation, the total number of in-flight cells is bounded by the total *previous* allocation. Note that the total previous allocation is no more than $M/2 - TQ_{prev}$, where TQ_{prev} is the *TQ* value used therein. Therefore, the total memory usage will never exceed $(M/2 - TQ) + M/2 + TQ$ or *M*. This analysis also explains why *M* is divided by 2 in Eq.(3).

Equation (4) allows the frequency of transmitting credit cells of the VC, i.e., the *N2* value, to adapt to the VC's current `Buf_Alloc`, or equivalently, its relative bandwidth usage. That is, VCs with relatively large bandwidth usage will use large *N2* values, and thus will reduce their bandwidth overhead of transmitting credit records upstream. (In fact, by adapting *N2* value and by packing up to six credit credits in each transmitted credit cell, the transmission overhead for credit cells can be kept very low. Simulation results in [9] show that this overhead is generally below a few percent and sometimes below one percent.) On the other hand, an inactive VC could be given an $N2$ value as small as one. With a smaller $N2$ value, the receiver can inform the sender of the availibity of buffer space sooner, and thus increase memory utilization. The $N2$ value would increase only when the VC's bandwidth ramps up. Thus, the required memory for each VC could be as small as one cell.

From Eqs. (2), (3) and (4), we can show that the adaptive scheme guarantees that a VC will ramp up to its fair share. A sufficient condition is that a fair scheduling policy is employed, the switch buffer size

$$M = 4 * RTT + 2 * N \qquad (5)$$

or larger is used, and a significant portion of the switch buffer is not occupied, i.e., $TQ < 2*RTT/3$.

Assume that there are $N - 1$ active VCs which in aggregate already get the full-link bandwidth of an output port of the receiver. Now a new VC using the same output port starts and wishes to get its fair share, i.e., $1/N$, of the link bandwidth. Suppose that the VC's current buffer allocation X is insufficient for achieving this target bandwidth. That is, by Eqs. (2) and (4),

$$\frac{X}{RTT + \frac{X}{4} \cdot N} < \frac{1}{N}$$

or, equivalently,

$$X < \frac{4 \cdot RTT}{3 \cdot N}$$

Note that with the current allocation X, by Eq.(2) the relative bandwidth that the VC can achieve satisfies:

$$\frac{VU}{TU} \geq \frac{X}{RTT + \frac{X}{4} \cdot N}$$

Since $TQ < 2*RTT/3$, it follows from Eq.(5) and the last two inequalities above that:

$$\left(\frac{M}{2} - TQ - N \right) \cdot \frac{VU}{TU}$$

$$\geq \left(2 \cdot RTT - TQ \right) \frac{X}{RTT + \frac{X}{4} \cdot N} > X$$

Thus the new allocation for the VC computed by Eq.(3) will be strictly larger than X. In this way the buffer allocation for the VC will keep increasing after each round of new allocation, as long as the achievable bandwidth allowed by the current `Buf_Alloc` X is less than $1/N$ and the total queue length TQ is less than 2*RTT/3.

In fact, the ramp up rate for a VC is exponential in number of allocations initially, when the bandwidth allowed by the credit control is small and when TQ is small. We can easily explain this exponential ramp up, using the last inequality expression above, for the simplifying case that TQ = 0. When RTT is large and $XN/4$ is much smaller than RTT, the middle term is about a factor of two larger than the third term. That is, X is ramped up roughly by a factor two every new allocation. In general, from the inequality expres-

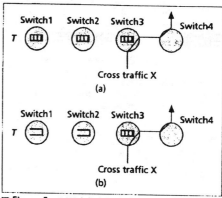

■ **Figure 5.** *a) With link-by-link flow control, all buffers on the path leading to the congestion point (Switch3) where traffic T meets traffic X can be used for preventing cell loss; b) without link-by-link flow control, only the buffer in Switch3 can be used.*

sion we see that if $M = 2 * RTT + 2 + N$, then the ramp up rate for each allocation is about α. Therefore, the larger α or M is, the faster the ramp up will be.

Rationale

We discuss some key reasons behind the credit-based approach. In fact, the same rationale, perhaps formulated in a different form, is applicable to any flow control scheme.

Resource Overallocation to Achieve High Efficiency

For efficiency reasons, the size M of the *total* allocated buffer in the receiver generally needs to be larger than RTT. This is overallocation in the sense that if traffic is 100 percent steady state, M need only be RTT for sustaining the peak bandwidth of the output link. However, for bursty traffic, we need M to be larger than RTT to allow high link utilization and reduce transmission time.

First consider static credit control. If it is affordable, we can let `Buf_Alloc` be $RTT + N2$ for every one of the N active VCs. Then by Eq.(2) the maximum bandwidth the VC can achieve is at least $1/N$ for any value of N. When a scheduling slot for the output link becomes available, an "eligible" VC at the sender that has data and credit can transmit *instantly* at the peak link rate. When there are no other competing VCs, i.e., $N = 1$, any single VC can sustain the peak rate by Eq.(2). Thus, link utilization is maximized and transmission time is minimized.

Now consider adaptive credit control. As in the static case, M needs to be large for increased link utilization and reduced transmission time. For adaptive buffer allocation, M needs to be large also for fast ramp up, as analyzed in the end of the previous section.

Intuitively, receiver-oriented adaptation needs RTT more buffer than sender-oriented adaptation, because receiver-oriented adaptation involves an extra round-trip delay for the receiver to inform the sender of the new allocation. Thus the minimum buffer size for receiver-oriented adaptation is increased from RTT to $2*RTT$. Suppose that the total memory size is larger than the minimum 2*RTT, e.g., as given by Fig. 5. Then the part of the memory that is above the minimum 2*RTT will provide "headroom" for each VC to grow its bandwidth usage under the current buffer allocation. If the VC does increase its bandwidth usage, then as described in the section on the adaptive buffer allocation, the adaptation scheme will notice the increased usage and will subsequently increase the buffer allocation for the VC [8, 9].

The receiver-oriented adaptive buffer allocation scheme in [9] uses M given by Eq.(5). Analysis and simulation results have shown that with this choice of M the adaptive scheme gives excellent performance in utilization, fairness, and ramp-up [9].

Link-by-link Flow Control to Increase Quality of Control

Link-by-link flow control has shorter and more predictable control loop delay than end-to-end flow control. This implies smaller memory requirements for switching nodes and higher performance in utilization, transmission time, fairness, etc. Link-by-link flow control is especially effective for handling transient "cross" traffic. Consider Fig. 5, where T is an end-to-end, flow-controlled traffic, using some transport-level protocol such as TCP, and X is high priority cross traffic. If X uses the whole bandwidth of the Switch3's output link, then the entire window of T for covering the end-to-end round-trip delay would have to be buffered to avoid cell loss. With link-by-link flow control, all the buffers on the path from the source of T to Switch3 can be used to prevent cell loss. In contrast, without link-by-link flow control, only the buffer at the congestion point (i.e., Switch3 in this case) can be used for this purpose.

Moreover, sufficient predictability in the control loop delay is necessary if the receiver is to perform policing. After issuing a flow control command to the sender, the receiver will start policing the traffic according to the new condition only after the control loop delay. Effective policing will not be possible if control loop delay cannot be bounded.

Per-VC Queuing to Achieve High Degree of Fairness

To achieve fairness between bursty VCs sharing the same output, it is necessary to have separate queuing for individual VCs. Using a fair round-robin scheduling policy among these queues, cells from different VCs will be sent out in a fair manner.

Rate-based Flow Control

Rate-based flow control consists of two phases: *rate setting* by sources and network, and *rate control* by sources. These two phases correspond to the buffer allocation and credit control phases in credit-based flow control.

Rate control is a shaping function, for which various implementations are possible. For example, when a cell of a VC with a given rate r arrives, the cell will be scheduled for output at time $1/r$ after the previous output of the same VC. By sorting arriving cells into buckets according to

their departure times, rate control can be implemented without per-VC queuing (although per rate-bucket queuing may be needed).

Suppose that traffic is so steady-state that it is possible to set the rate for each VC perfectly against some performance criteria, and these rates need not change over time to sustain the target performance. Then, if the VCs are shaped at the sources according to the set rates, the rate-based flow control method should work just fine. There would be no need for link-by-link flow control and per-VC queuing in the network. The buffer in a switch can also be kept at the minimum, almost like in a synchronous transfer mode (STM) switch.

However, setting rates perfectly or near optimally is a complicated matter. Consider, for example, the configuration of Fig. 6, known at the ATM Forum as "Generic Fairness Configuration" (GFC) [14]. All traffic sources are assumed to be persistently greedy, and can transmit at the peak link rate when the bandwidth is available.

Note that both traffic B and E share the same link between S4 and S5, and the source of E is closer to the link than that of B. This is analogous to a parking lot scenario in which E starts from a position closer to the exit than B. In a normal, real-world parking lot, E would have an unfair advantage over B by being able to move itself in front of B and get out first. However, in a good ATM network with separate virtual circuits for B and E, they ought to share fairly the bandwidth of the link, as long as they are not bottlenecked elsewhere in the network.

With this fairness objective in mind, we naturally consider the performance criterion described below. First, the VCs on the most congested link will share the link bandwidth equally, and this determines the rates to be set for these VCs. Then, apply the procedure to the other VCs with the remaining bandwidth of the network. Continue repeating the procedure until rates for all the VCs have been assigned. Table 1 shows the resulting rates assigned to individual VC groups.

Translating the above mathematical rate-setting procedure into an efficient and robust implementation is a major challenge. First, under highly bursty ABR traffic, because load changes rapidly, there would be no static rate setting that can be ideal for any significant period of time. When traffic changes, "optimal" rates to be assigned to the affected VCs must change accordingly.

For this reason, adaptive rate setting is necessary for bursty traffic, and has been subject to inten-

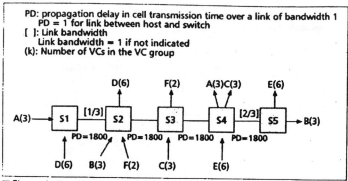

■ Figure 6. *Generic fairness configuration (GFC).*

192

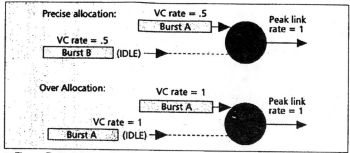

Figure 7. *Both bursts A and B complete transmission earlier and make higher utilization of switch output link in the over-allocating case than in the precise case.*

Group	Bandwidth	Bottleneck link
A	1/27 = 0.037	S1-S2
B	2/27 = 0.074	S4-S5
C	2/9 = 0.222	S3-S4
D	1/27 = 0.037	S1-S2
E	2/27 = 0.074	S4-S5
F	1/3 = 0.333	S2-S3

Table 1. *Expected rates for VC groups in generic fairness configuration (GFC).*

sive research for many years. The "Enhanced Proportional Rate-Control Algorithm (EPRCA)" [12] is one of the latest schemes considered at the ATM Forum, and represents the kind of adaptive rate setting schemes this article assumes.

Rate adaptation cannot be so precise that the newly derived rates will be just right with respect to current load, for at least two reasons. First, information and measurements, based on which adaptation is performed, cannot be totally complete nor up-to-date due to various cost and implementation constraints. Second, feedback control time which the adaptation takes to inform sources, can vary due to disparities in propagation delay and link speed, congestion conditions, scheduling policies, and many other factors.

Rate adaptation should not be precise either. To achieve high utilization under bursty traffic, it is necessary that the total assigned rate for all the VCs over a link is higher than the peak link rate. Consider a simple scenario of Fig. 7 involving only two VCs, A and B. Assume that the two VCs share the same switch output link of bandwidth 1, and each have a data burst that would take a unit time to transmit over a link of bandwidth 1. Suppose that the B burst arrives one unit time later than the A burst. Then as Fig. 7 depicts, in the precise rate setting case where each VC is set with a rate of .5, it would take a total of three time units to complete the transmission of both the A and B bursts. In contrast, in the over-allocating rate setting case where each VC is set with a rate of 1, it would take only two time units to do the same. This need of over-allocating resources is similar to that discussed in the section on resource overallocation for credit control.

As discussed above, since adaptation *can not* and *should not* be precise, rates set by the adaptation

may not be totally correct. Bounding the liability of overrunning switch buffers is then a first order issue. Ideas from the credit control's method for preventing buffer overflow may be exploited. This is the subject of the next section.

Rate-based Control in Credit Style

Rate control can use the credit style of buffer overflow prevention, if the sender reduces its transmission when the receiver's buffer gets to be full. In credit control, the receiver in this case will send upstream reduced credit and allocation amounts, as described in the section on credit-based flow control. In rate control, the receiver can similarly send upstream reduced rates, as described below. Unlike in other rate-based methods we are aware of, it is now the size of the *unoccupied* memory in the receiver that determines the total of rates allocated to the senders. As in adaptive credit schemes, the current relative bandwidth usage of individual VCs determines the rates allocated to them.

We describe this rate-based control scheme in credit style, in referring to the configuration of Fig. 4. Let *RTT* be the maximum of all the *RTT*s. We assume that the senders implement shaping to enforce rates of outgoing VCs as set by the receiving end of each link. A sender could be a switch, a source host, or any "virtual source" on the network edge (see text box on the following page).

The basic idea of this credit-style rate-based scheme is that as soon as the receiver realizes that UM gets to be "too small," i.e., UM ≤ 2 * RTT * TAR, a New_TAR smaller than current Cur_TAR will be computed and resulting ARs for individual VCs will be sent upstream. (One can easily see that New_TAR ≤ Cur_TAR/2.) Before the New_TAR takes effect *RTT* time later, some in-flight cells under Cur_TAR may still arrive. These will be no more than RTT * Cur_TAR cells. Thus, UM will never get below RTT * Cur_TAR when New_TAR takes effect. This proves that like credit control this rate-based scheme will not lose cells due to congestion.

On the other hand, when UM gets to be "too large," i.e., UM > 8 * RTT * TAR, a New_TAR larger than Cur_TAR will be computed and resulting ARs for individual VCs will be sent upstream. (One can easily see that New_TAR > Cur_TAR * 2.) The increased New_TAR will help improve network utilization and reduce transmission time. Note that New_TAR will not be too large that there could be a danger that it will cause buffer overflow. When New_TAR takes effect, UM will still be at least 7 * RTT * Cur_TAR or 3.5 * RTT * New_TAR. If in the future UM decreases and gets as low as 2 * RTT * New_TAR, another smaller New_TAR will be computed and used to set new rates in time to prevent buffer overflow.

This method can achieve zero cell loss and bound the total memory requirement for achieving this. However, the method still needs careful parameter tuning to ensure fairness and efficiency under bursty traffic. For example, exactly how fast the TAR should be increased or decreased under various network and load conditions needs to be determined. (We will report on simulation results in a forthcoming paper.)

Summary of Some Simulation and Experimental Results

Substantial simulations done by ATM Forum members have revealed performance differences between flow control mechanisms in three areas: fairness, link utilization, and switch memory use. Most of these simulations have been performed on the GFC topology shown in Fig. 6, and would ideally yield the per-VC bandwidths given in Table 1. While in many circumstances credit and rate flow control perform similarly, only credit so far has demonstrated its robustness in achieving high performance under stressful conditions. Here we present a brief summary of these simulation results, with a focus on work done at Harvard. For details the reader should contact responsible researchers and look into the references.

A thorough simulation study of credit flow control [9] shows that it is almost perfectly fair not just with steady traffic in the GFC configuration, but also with highly bursty traffic over links of widely varying bandwidths and propagation delays. A study by Su, Golmie, Chang, and Benmohamed of NIST confirms the fairness and high link utilization of credit over GFC. Simulation results in [9] show that the same high performance can actually be achieved with a large number of VCs, e.g., 500 active VCs, sharing the same output link.

To evaluate the effectiveness of the adaptive buffer algorithm during severe congestion, the simulation suite in [9] includes a case where the bandwidth of a bottleneck link is suddenly reduced 100-fold. The simulation results show that during the bandwidth reduction period, not only do new VCs still ramp up quickly (modulo to link RTT), but also they ramp up in a fair manner.

Similar simulations by Bennett, Chang, Kung, and Lin of Fore Systems and Harvard, reported in the ATM Forum, pinpoint situations in which credit control has unique advantages. For instance, if one connection alternates short bursts with long silences, a competing connection can fill in all the gaps with credit control, ensuring full link utilization.

A good deal of traffic over future ATM networks may well use existing transport protocols such as TCP/IP. TCP has its own window-based flow control mechanism [7] which interprets lost or delayed packets as evidence of congestion. Studies by Fang and Chen of Sandia National Laboratories show that TCP connections over credit get close to fair shares of bandwidth and achieve full link utilization.

We have recently conducted flow control experiments on the experimental Harvard/BNR ATM switch, as mentioned previously. The experimental results with TCP and video confirm that credit-based flow control substantially increases efficiency under congestion. For example, for reasons similar to those discussed in the section entitled "Rationale," when multiple TCP sessions compete for bandwidth over a single link through a switch with a 200-cell buffer, the efficiency is only 30 percent without flow control. With flow control, the efficiency rises to over 98 percent. Flow control also helps insulate different connections, which experiments have proved to be particularly important for traffic such as video which does not provide transport-layer flow control and error correction.

Notations

UM   Unoccupied memory in the shared buffer pool at the receiver
AR   Allocated rate for a VC
TAR   Total allocated rate for all VCs sharing the same buffer
MR   Measured rate for a VC at the output. (To simplify presentation, measurement code is omitted here.)
TMR   Total measured rate for all VCs

Rate setting algorithm at receiver

```
begin
if (UM ≤ 2*RTT*Cur_TAR) or (UM > 8*RTT*Cur_TAR)
  Update rates allocated to senders:
    New_TAR = UM/(4*RTT);
      // Note New_TAR ≤ Cur_TAR/2 or New_TAR >
Cur_TAR*2,
      // respectively.
    Compute new allocated rate for each VC:
    AR = (MR/TMR)*New_TAR;
      //AR is proportional to VC's usage.
  Send updated ARs upstream
```

Further study is needed in this area. For example, it would be of interest to understand the performance of various flow control methods for distributed computing and for large networking scenarios involving many users and a wide range of link propagation delays and bandwidths. We encourage additional simulation and field tests.

Fundamental Issues

Credit flow control enjoys some fundamental advantages over rate-based control. We summarize them here in the hope of contributing to general understanding of flow control.

Rate-based control assumes that the rates for the circuits sharing a link can be made to converge on sensible values. However, the network load may change faster than the control system can react. On a very fast network, transfers may also take too little time to achieve a steady state. For instance, TCP sessions often transfer no more than a few dozen KBytes [13] and the required transmission time on a link of OC-3 rate, 155 Mb/s, is only a few milliseconds. (An extensive Unix file size survey [4] has shown that the average file length is only around 22 Kbytes and most files are smaller than 2 Kbytes.) This situation will only get worse with increasing network capacity, and with the increasing differences in bandwidth available in different parts of the network.

For this and other reasons discussed previously, rate adaptation can not and should not be precise. Since rates may not be set correctly, controlling the liability of overrunning switch buffers in an efficient and robust manner is critical to a flow control method.

In particular, when a network is heavily loaded with high priority traffic, switches may want the option of temporarily turning off particular virtual circuits. It might seem natural to simply give a circuit a rate of zero. However, most proposed scheduling mechanisms for hosts and switches use inter-cell gaps to enforce rates. No intercell gap corresponds to a rate of zero. Some other mechanism may be needed to handle cases in which a switch would like to set a rate to zero. More generally, it is difficult to design hardware to provide a wide range of accurate rates.

194

Analysis, simulation, and actual experiments on switching hardware of credit flow control show that it works well over a wide range of network conditions.

Credit flow control is explicit about how much data a sender may transmit without receiving further credit. Lost or delayed feedback messages will not hurt, as the sender would just use the previous allowance. When necessary, the sender's transmission can be stopped completely, i.e., effectively making the rate equal to zero. When receiver-oriented adaptive buffer allocation is used, the receiver can send upstream credit information (e.g., Fwd_Cnt) together with the new allocation in the same management cell. If the management cell is lost or delayed, the sender would just use the previously received credit and allocation; the liability of overrunning the receiver's buffer is bounded.

Rate-based methods can be enhanced in controlling the buffer overflowing problem and thus deciding their memory requirements, by using ideas of credit control as outlined previously. However, the resulting rate-based control still cannot easily handle situations in which management cells for rate updating are lost or delayed. Sources could slowly decrease the rate toward zero if no management cells arrive, but this would be at the expense of lowered network utilization and increased traffic delay. Ideally, sources should actually operate at over-allocated rates for efficiency reasons, as we have discussed previously. In contrast, credit flow control does not have to worry about all these issues about how rates should be increased or decreased. Just imagine how hard it would be to make TCP work reliably and efficiently by using rate instead of window control over the Internet.

Conclusions

Significant differences separate credit and rate flow control. Credit provides precise control over buffer use, and can stop transmission automatically to avoid buffer overrun. Typical rate control methods provide no similar guarantee, partially to avoid some of the expense involved in implementing credit hardware. However, in the long run, rate-based switches will probably need similarly complex hardware anyway, in order to enforce fairness and shape traffic at each switch.

Analysis, simulation, and actual experiments on switching hardware of credit flow control show that it works well over a wide range of network conditions. At one extreme, static allocation of buffers to circuits guarantees no loss due to congestion, high utilization and fairness, regardless of traffic patterns. This kind of guarantee may be a requirement, not just a luxury, in order to provide acceptable service under harsh conditions. The adaptive credit system can reduce memory requirements to just a few round-trip times worth of cells, while maintaining no loss and high performance. Thus a credit system can provide good performance even if future networks are nothing like current predictions. In addition, credit flow control is an existence proof that congestion control can enforce guaranteed no data loss.

As our field experience with ATM networks expands, we will have much to learn, especially on the interaction of ATM flow control with higher lever protocols. Future research in congestion control should explore the patterns of real traffic on high-speed networks. Working prototypes

of the competing flow control systems should be compared. Without such experience it is not possible to make proper trade-offs between performance and cost.

Standards work and implementations should not exclude the possibility of experimenting with different flow control schemes. A system rushed to market is not likely to stand the test of time, and should have built-in possibilities for evolution. As a minimum, negotiated use of different flow control protocols should be allowed. Effective mechanisms to let switches send out rate-management messages in time to prevent buffer overflow, such as those described in the section titled "Rate-based Control in Credit Style," can be studied. Moreover, a sequence number field can be included in rate-management messages. This field would be able to capture Fwd_Cnt values and thus allow CUP implementation. Independently, sequence numbers would be useful for policing anyway. For example, after a switch receives a sequence number originally generated by it and later echoed back by the source, the switch can start policing.

References

[1] ATM Forum, "ATM User-Network Interface Specification," Version 3.0, (Prentice Hall, 1993).
[2] Blackwell *et al.* "An Experimental Flow Controlled Multi-cast ATM Switch," Proceedings of First Annual Conference on Telecommunications R & D in Massachusetts, vol. 6, Oct. 25, 1994. pp. 33-38.
[3] S. Borkar *et al.*, "Integrating Systolic and Memory Communication in iWarp," Conference Proceedings of the 17th Annual International Symposium on Computer Architecture, Seattle, Washington, June 1990, pp. 70-81.
[4] G. Irlam, "Unix File Size Survey 1993," Usenet comp.arch.storage, <URL:http://www.base.com/gordoni/ufs93.html>, last updated Sept. 1994.
[5] W. E. Leland *et al.*, "On the Self-Similar Nature of Ethernet Traffic," Proc. ACM SIGCOMM '93 Symposium on Communications Architectures, Protocols and Applications, Sept. 1993, pp. 183-193.
[6] M. G. H. Katevenis, "Fast Switching and Fair Control of Congested Flow in Broadband Networks," *IEEE J. on Selected Areas in Commun.*, vol. SAC-5, no. 8, Oct. 1987, pp. 13151326.
[7] V. Jacobson, "Congestion Avoidance and Control," Proc. SIGCOMM '88 Symposium on Communications Architectures and Protocols, Aug. 1988.
[8] H. T. Kung, T. Blackwell, and A. Chapman, "Credit-Based Flow Control for ATM Networks: Credit Update Protocol, Adaptive Credit Allocation, and Statistical Multiplexing," Proc. ACM SIGCOMM '94 Symposium on Communications Architectures, Protocols and Applications, Aug. 31-Sept. 2, 1994, pp. 101-114.
[9] H. T. Kung and K. Chang, "Receiver-Oriented Adaptive Buffer Allocation in Credit-Based Flow Control for ATM Networks," Proc. INFOCOM '95, April 1995.
[10] H. T. Kung and A. Chapman, "The FCVC (Flow-Controlled Virtual Channels) Proposal for ATM Networks," Version 2.0, 1993. A summary appears in Proc. 1993 International Conf. on Network Protocols, San Francisco, California, 1993, pp. 116-127, Oct. 1922. (Postscript files of this and other related papers by the authors and their colleagues are available via anonymous FTP from virtual.harvard.edu: /pub/htk/atm.)
[11] C. Ozveren, R. Simcoe, and G. Varghese, "Reliable and Efficient Hop-by-Hop Flow Control," Proc. ACM SIGCOMM '94 Symposium on Communications Architectures, Protocols and Applications, Aug. 31-Sept. 2, 1994, pp. 89-100.
[12] L. Roberts, "Enhanced PRCA (Proportional Rate-Control Algorithm)," ATM-Forum/94-0735R1, Aug. 1994.
[13] A. Schmidt and R. Campbell, "Internet Protocol Traffic Analysis with Applications for ATM Switch Design," ACM SIGCOMM Computer Communication Review, vol. 23, no. 2, pp. 39-52, April, 1993.
[14] R. J. Simcoe, "Configurations for Fairness and Other Test," ATM_Forum/ 94-0557, 1994.

Biographies

H. T. Kung is Gordon McKay Professor of Electrical Engineering and Computer Science at Harvard University, Cambridge, Massachusetts. Prior to joining Harvard in 1992, he was on the computer science faculty at Carnegie Mellon University, where he received his Ph.D. in 1974. His current research is directed toward the design of high-speed computer and communications networks. At Harvard, his research team studies ATM switch arthitectures, congestion control, and implementation of high-level protocols over ATM. His em-mail address is: kung@das.harvard.edu.

Robert Morris is a Ph.D. student in computer science at Harvard University, Cambridge, Massachusetts. He has published in the areas of congestion control and mobile internetworking. His work experience includes implementation of TCP and network file systems at Bell Labs, and of prototype parallel programming languages at DEC and Thinking Machines. He received an A.B. from Harvard College in 1988.

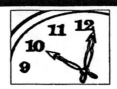

Integration of Rate and Credit Schemes for ATM Flow Control

The authors make the case in favor of an integrated approach to ATM flow control. They contend that both rate and credit schemes have advantages and disadvantages, and that to a large extent they can be viewed as complementary.

K. K. Ramakrishnan and Peter Newman

synchornous transger mode (ATM) is the first switching technology that can support both fixed bandwidth services similar to circuit switching, and highly variable bandwidth services similar to packet switching, in a single integrated environment [1]. Definitions for traffic management for services with a fixed traffic profile were completed by the ATM Forum in their version 3.0 specification [2]. For the last year and a half the Traffic Management Group of the ATM Forum has been working on flow control for the highly variable bandwidth services typically supported by packet switching networks. In such services there is no explicit contract between the network and the user specifying the traffic profile and quality of service expected. Rather, the network is expected to provide each user with a fair share of the amount of bandwidth dynamically available. It is expected that if the user adjusts the transmission rate according to the feedback from the network, then cell loss will remain low. The ATM Forum has termed such services available bit rate (ABR) services.

A congestion control loop is required between the network and the user to support an ABR service. Two separate schools of thought (religions) developed during the ABR debate as to how to implement the control loop: rate and credit. In the rate-based view the network sends information to the user specifying the bit rate at which the user should be transmitting, and the control loop may extend end-to-end across the network. The credit-based approach sends information about the available buffer space independently on each link of the network and is thus a link-by-link mechanism. A third alternative was also proposed, which observed that both rate and credit solutions have their pros and cons and that to a large extent they can be viewed as complementary.

This third alternative was the integrated proposal which attempted to allow these different control mechanisms to coexist. The integrated proposal suggested that rate control was the most appropriate for the wide area, but that static credit control had distinct advantages in the local area (i.e., it had been built and proven to work). It was an attempt to combine the advantages of both approaches into a single proposal for ATM flow control. In this article we present the argument in support of an integrated approach (while remaining cognizant of the fact that rate-based control was selected by the ATM Forum in their September 1994 meeting).

Why Rate in the Wide Area

Wide area networks (WANs) may be classified as such for one very simple reason: they operate across a wide geographical area. Distance means propagation delay and propagation delay may in fact be greater than queuing delay in a wide area, high-speed network [3]. The same dynamic response available in a local area network (LAN) is simply not available from a wide area network due to the limitations imposed by the speed of light. This is physics — it will not change with improved implementation.

Several observations result from the fact that the propagation delay is not negligible. The buffer sizes that would be required to support a static hop-by-hop credit scheme are impractical because of the propagation delay of the long distance links. Thus the only credit scheme that could be applied to the wide area would require dynamic buffer allocation. Also, the speed at which a user can adjust to changing network conditions is a function of the propagation delay and will be much slower in the wide area than in the local area. In addition, the customer understands this and has a different expectation of

K. K. RAMAKRISHNAN is a member of technical staff at AT&T Bell Laboratories.

PETER NEWMAN has recently joined Ipsilon Networks Inc.

Reprinted from IEEE Network, March/April 1995, pp. 49-56.

the performance available from the wide area than that of the local area.

The customer does not expect the same performance from a server physically located on the other side of the country as is expected from a local server, e.g., on campus. It will always be true that bandwidth is plentiful in the local area and will always be a more expensive and more highly shared in the wide area. Thus we have a different expectation from a wide area network than we do for a local area network. So we might expect a different performance from a control loop designed for the wide area than one optimized for the local area.

Conversely, we do not wish to impose the performance limitations of the wide area upon the local area by mandating a single control mechanism that cannot be optimized for both. During the development of the rate-based approach, several proposals were made in which a user began transmission of a burst at a minimum rate and slowly ramped up to a fair share of the bandwidth over a period of about 5 ms. This may be a reasonable method in the wide area, but the local area expects immediate access to the full bandwidth available. Remote procedure call and client server applications with moderate size, but bursty, traffic would perform poorly in such an environment.

The rate-based approach seems the more natural choice for public wide area networks. With the distances involved in the public network, a static credit scheme requires an inordinate amount of buffering to permit a very large number of connections to operate at high speed. While credit schemes with dynamic buffer allocation [4, 5] have been proposed, they are not yet of sufficient maturity. It would be unduly optimistic to expect the public carriers to endorse a dynamic credit scheme at its current stage of development.

In addition, some of the public carriers have a very different view of the timescales involved in an ABR service. They have a very different concept of the rate of variation of bandwidth on a connection than that envisaged in the local area. For example, one of the rate-based solutions proposed by a carrier suggests an ABR service in which the bandwidth of a connection changes in the order of once every 30 seconds. Clearly, one would employ a rate-based mechanism to implement such a service.

A public carrier will need to deploy high-speed switches with a large number of access ports. It is felt that implementing per-VC queuing (as required for a credit scheme) on such a switch will incur unacceptable expense. Further, the larger carrier switches will operate with port speeds of 2.4 Gb/s and above. It is felt that at these speeds it will be difficult to implement anything more complex than EFCI marking. Also, EFCI marking is the only congestion control mechanism specified in the ATM Forum Version 3.0 specification, so compatibility with EFCI marking switches was seen as important to the carriers and wide area network vendors. Finally, public carriers like to charge for their services. Many felt that it was much easier to perform billing when the rate was adjusted explicitly by the network than for a credit-based scheme.

Why Credit-Based Control in Local Area Networks

The initial adoption of ATM in the local area will mostly be driven by the desire to efficiently support existing applications in a high-speed LAN. The ABR class of service will essentially be used as a "best effort" service that emulates the current behavior of existing LAN technologies. This means that bandwidth must be available on a timely basis, allowing applications to "almost instantaneously" utilize all or most of the available bandwidth, while maintaining packet loss low enough for existing applications to work well. It is important to maintain low loss, as a very small cell loss rate results in a significantly higher packet loss rate. The natural question arises as to what cell loss rate is acceptable: packet loss results in inefficient usage of both the network's and the end systems' resources.

To allow for a wide dynamic range of parameters for higher layer protocols, it would be preferable for congestion management schemes to maintain the overall congestion related packet loss rate as low as possible. In essence, the smaller the packet loss rate the better. Among the proposals put forth at the ATM Forum [4-6], the hop-by-hop per-VC credit flow control scheme (FCVC, based on static allocation of buffers) achieves the "ideal" from this perspective: the packet loss rate due to congestion is zero. This makes the overall behavior of LAN applications, which use existing protocol stacks (e.g., TCP/IP, UDP/IP, IPX, etc.) much more predictable. The fact that the loss probability is zero makes the behavior of applications relatively insensitive to parameter settings in many of the algorithms used throughout the protocol stack (e.g., TCP retransmission timers, the extent of the change on the window size when a retransmission occurs, sensitivity to retransmission algorithms, network layer timers, etc.). In a LAN, the link distances are modest. The number of cell buffers needed for a VC to fully utilize the link is of the order of 10 or 12 cells. The number of VCs that a typical LAN switch needs to support are also claimed to be in the 1 K range, with smaller switches having substantially smaller numbers of active VCs to support and larger switches being capable of supporting at most an order of magnitude larger. As a result, even for a switch supporting 1 K VCs, the amount of cell buffering needed is of the order of 10 K cell buffers, which is about 0.5 Mbytes of memory, which may be considered a reasonable amount of memory per port. Thus, the use of the static allocation of buffers for the hop-by-hop per-VC credit flow control scheme appeared to be quite suitable for the LAN.

The competition from both shared LANs (e.g., different Fast Ethernet proposals, FDDI) and switched versions of these LANs promise cost and aggregate bandwidth efficiencies that compete well with those possible on ATM. Therefore, from a purely ABR perspective, the peak available bandwidth of these competing technologies are comparable to the "typical" ATM bandwidths being currently considered. The perception that the QoS guarantees provided by ATM are advantageous will come gradually. We see other service classes, such as CBR and VBR coexisting with ABR service, as being in more widespread use in the future. However, in the immediate future, it will be to the advantage of ATM LANs to achieve high efficiency in its use for data communication using ABR. The opportunistic behavior of ABR in utilizing unused bandwidth will initially (and likely in the long term) be very important. We see efficient use of unused bandwidth, and the responsiveness to the changes in the available bandwidth as significant design considerations for a congestion control scheme in the local area.

It is possible that CBR and VBR flows use bandwidth in such a fashion that the "troughs" in their bandwidth usage may last from a few microseconds to several tens of milliseconds. A scheme for controlling ABR flows that is responsive in using a link's available bandwidth within a few microseconds (few cell times) of its being available is highly desirable. We see the hop-by-hop schemes have a potential for this desired responsiveness. With a static buffer allocation for the hop-by-hop credit based scheme, it has been demonstrated that the efficiency of using this available bandwidth is quite high.

Perhaps one of the most significant performance advantages of hop-by-hop credit over end-end rate is that its performance is independent of the incident traffic pattern. Data traffic contains a large proportion of short, transient, bursts of traffic. An end-end scheme can only control traffic bursts that are longer than round trip time of the connection. Transient bursts can only be accommodated by providing sufficient buffering. The static hop-by-hop credit scheme, however, allows control of all traffic, short transient bursts as well as large file transfers. It offers "zero congestive loss" performance regardless of the arriving traffic pattern.

An obvious, but inadequate, implementation of hop-by-hop credit-based flow control "without per-VC buffering" would not be sufficient. This would not assure that the queuing delays through the network are maintained at sufficiently small levels (operating at the "knee" of the throughput and delay curves [7]). However, by separating the flows on a per-VC basis, we ensure that the queue for one VC does not interfere with that for another VC [8]. Given enough credits for each of the VCs so that it can potentially fully utilize a link, each VC can opportunistically take advantage of the available bandwidth on a hop without interfering with other VCs, while operating at the "knee."

An important area, particularly relevant in a LAN, is the overall fairness and efficiency of operation even when there exist one or more sources (users of the network) that do not cooperate with the other flows in the congestion management scheme. This has been a long-standing question impeding the widespread implementation of schemes for congestion management that require/assume cooperation by all the users of the network. While a policing mechanism at the entry into a WAN is frequently considered, such a policing mechanism may be expensive in a LAN, for an end-to-end rate-based scheme. If it is necessary, it would in fact have to be implemented in every node (particularly switches) in the network, based on our current understanding. Thus, it is desirable to have the non-cooperating flows separated in such a way that they do not interfere with those that are cooperating or "well behaved" from the view of the congestion management scheme. Per-VC credit-based flow control implicitly allows the network to protect itself from a non-cooperating user, and isolates these from the well behaved users. When a non-cooperating user misbehaves, the consequence is additional loss for that VC only, without any concomitant loss experienced by other users. We see this as being desirable for use of a technology, particularly in LANs.

Another complementary issue is that of a switch not participating in the congestion management scheme. Consider a credit scheme in the LAN operating with one or more intervening switches not participating in the credit protocol. This has been addressed using the concept of "tunneling." The two switches on either side of the portion of the subnet that has non-credit switches (let us call it a "non-credit cloud") that participate in the credit update protocol (CUP) communicate the credit cells on a VC that is set up across the "non-credit cloud." This allows for reasonable management of the buffers at the switches that participate in CUP. If the other switches that exist in the path that do not participate in CUP have adequate buffering, then the burst load into these switches are limited by the credits issued by the remote "cooperating switch." This minimizes the amount of loss experienced by the VCs that span the "non-credit cloud," while not providing the strict guarantee of loss-free behavior. The idea of tunneling is explained in more detail in [9].

Interworking Multiple Congestion Control Schemes

Rate-based control is the only solution acceptable to the public carriers for congestion control across the wide area. Static credit control requires excessively large buffers and dynamic credit algorithms are still under development. Rate-based control is very flexible and permits a variety of implementations within the switch. This makes possible product differentiation while maintaining compatibility with the standard. The more complex rate-based implementations will offer a higher performance service, yet the expectations of the customer are lower for a wide area service than for one within the local area.

Static credit-based control permits the lowest cost adapters and the highest performance in the LAN. While there is increased complexity in the switch to support the required per-VC queuing, this may not translate to greatly increased cost for the modest sizes of switch likely to be found in a LAN (5 Gb/s capacity with 2000 VCs per OC-3 port). Indeed, it is not certain that an explicit rate-based approach will offer a much lower cost to attain a similar performance.

Therefore, in order to combine the flexibility of rate with the performance of credit, several integrated approaches were considered:
• Rate in the WAN/credit in the LAN.
• Rate is default, credit is optional.
• One size fits all.

Rate-based control is very flexible and permits a variety of implementations within the switch. This makes possible product differentiation while maintaining compatibility with the standard.

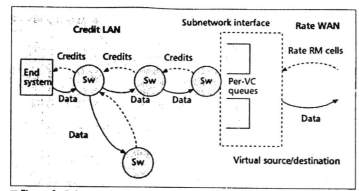

Figure 1. *Subnetwork interface connecting a credit LAN to a rate WAN.*

The first two approaches are combinations of rate and credit while the third is a true integration.

Rate in the WAN, Credit in the LAN

This is perhaps the simplest attempt at an integrated solution, yet it suffers the major drawback of creating two types of ATM interfaces. The proposal is simply that a rate-based scheme be used in the wide area and a static credit-based scheme in the local area.

Figure 1 illustrates the concept. There is an interface located on the trunk port card of the campus backbone switch that connects to the wide area. This interface acts as a virtual source and virtual destination, terminating the credit and rate control loops and interconnecting them. Thus, the LAN looks like a rate-based source to the WAN, and the WAN looks like a credit-based subnet to the LAN. The credit scheme on the LAN side is terminated by returning credit cells for VCs whose data cells are forwarded on to the WAN. The buffer at the interface from the LAN to the WAN direction needs to be sized only to the extent of having an adequate amount of buffering for each VC to go at the full rate of the LAN link. However, the interface from the WAN to the LAN link may in fact need substantially more buffering to accommodate the potentially large end-to-end round-trip feedback delay.

Fundamentally, this virtual source/destination function is a traffic shaper for the ABR service. It is very likely that a traffic shaper will be required in this location to shape the other services, VBR and CBR, on entrance to the wide area. Thus it is not necessarily an excessive burden to require such a function at this interface. In addition, even if the LAN was also rate-based, a virtual source/destination function is likely to be required at the LAN/WAN boundary in order to police the ABR service.

With this solution, we have achieved the performance of credit in the local area and a simple, low-cost end-station adapter card. However, we have divided the ATM world into two types of interface, credit-based LAN and rate-based WAN. Our experience with the Ethernet/Token Ring duality suggests that it would be far better to attempt a single interface even at the expense of somewhat increased cost. Also this solution perpetuates the boundary between the LAN and the WAN. This boundary is artificial. Indeed it is more of a political boundary than a physical boundary and there will be many instances when it is unclear which side of the fence a particular product falls, thus requiring the support of both types of interface. Interoperability problems also surface in this approach. It is unclear how one would propose to support an adapter card only capable of rate-based operation within a credit-based LAN, and also how to support a version 3.0 switch within a credit-based LAN.

Rate is Default, Credit is Optional

In this solution, rate-based control is required in the WAN and it is the default scheme in the LAN. Static credit-based control is permitted as an option within the LAN, selected on a per connection basis, when a connection is established. (Selection on a per link basis is impractical because it will force every switch port to be capable of implementing the virtual source/destination function.)

In this proposal the simple, low-cost, credit-only end-station adapter must be forfeit. All adapters must be capable of the default rate mechanism and multiple control loops may coexist within the same set of nodes. The scheduling hardware for the rate mechanism is the most complex component of the adapter. The additional hardware required to support the credit approach is modest in comparison. If we accept that the adapter must be capable of rate control and should optionally be capable of credit control, then the control scheme may be selected on a per-VC basis. If all entities on the path of the VC are capable of credit then credit control may be selected. If not, the rate-based default is used. This will permit the customer the choice of low-cost rate control switches in the LAN or high performance credit switches.

The virtual source/destination interface between the LAN and the WAN is still required if the credit option is selected on the local area portion of the connection. If credit-based control is only selected for connections that remain within the local area, then wide area connections may use rate-based control throughout the entire connection. Thus the virtual source/destination need no longer be mandatory and no artificial boundary need be defined to separate LAN from WAN. However, a virtual source/destination function is still likely to be necessary at the boundary between a LAN and a public ATM service for traffic shaping and to assist in policing the ABR service.

For the adapter manufacturer, the cost of adopting this compromise is that market pressure will probably force them to implement both schemes. For the switch manufacturer, the credit switch must implement a default rate scheme. Also, congestion control protocol selection is required as part of the signaling process. While this does add additional complexity, it allows multiple traffic management protocols to coexist in the same network. This is not necessarily a bad idea, considering the speed at which the ABR congestion control scheme is being developed by the ATM Forum.

One Size Fits All

The third proposal is to use an encoding in the resource management (RM) cell to provide not only rate information in the cell specifying the rate that a VC can flow, but also to have a validity count field in the RM cell that is associated with the rate. The validity count field may be interpreted as the number of cells transmitted by a VC before the rate that it is currently using becomes invalid. At that point the source has to cease transmission on the VC until a new RM cell is received, updating the rate to use and its validity. Another interpretation of the validity count field is that it is a time value, particularly suited for the end-end rate scheme. This would allow a much longer period for which the rate conveyed in an RM cell would be valid.

With this proposal, a switch that is part of an ATM network may choose to participate in one or the other of the congestion control algorithms. Figure 2 illustrates this concept. "C" is a credit switch, and "R" is a rate switch. If the switch wants to participate in the end-end rate-based congestion management algorithm, it would mark the RM cell with an explicit rate R1. R1 may be based on its calculation of the desired rate for that VC (possibly an allocation based on the max-min fairness criterion [10]). Along with the rate, the switch would mark the RM cell with (potentially) a large value for the validity count field. The count may be set based on the period over which the switch re-computes the rate, or the maximum time it perceives is safe, within which to see a new RM cell in order to communicate a new rate to the VC. This adds a degree of robustness to the algorithm to allow recovery from the loss of RM cells. The validity field may be a constant value that is inserted in each of the RM cells communicated to the VCs. If necessary, depending on the conservativeness of the switch designer, this value may in fact be variable, i.e., set to smaller values as the switch gets more and more congested.

If the switch wants to participate in the hop-by-hop credit scheme, then the explicit rate R2 that is conveyed in the RM cell would be the peak rate assigned to the VC, and the validity count field would be a much smaller variable count that indicates to the upstream node the number of cells that it may send at the explicit rate R2. When the upstream node exhausts the count, it will then have to await a replenishment of credits from a downstream node, just as in the hop-by-hop credit scheme defined in [4].

As far as the end-station adapter network interface card (NIC) is concerned, there is only one interface. The NIC transmits cells at the rate conveyed in an RM cell until the count runs out.

The end-end rate scheme operates as follows: the source of the VC indicates the desired rate in the RM cell. This RM cell is on the same VC, and is therefore allowed to flow all the way to the destination end system. The destination NIC reflects the RM cell, with an indicator to show that the RM cell is now making progress in the reverse direction. The intermediate switches then mark down the rate (the explicit rate allocated to the VC) in the reverse RM cell. The smallest allocation is therefore the value in the RM cell when it reaches the source. The source may then use this rate for subsequent transmissions until a new RM cell is received.

The hop-by-hop credit scheme operates as follows: the source indicates the rate (peak rate, if it wants to set it to a value lower than the link rate) it desires to transmit at in the forward RM cell.

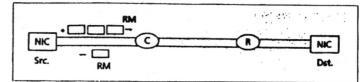

■ Figure 2. *Interworking credit and rate switches.*

The destination end system NIC reflects the RM cell, and the switch then updates the count field in the reverse RM cell. The switch also needs the ability to generate additional RM cells on the local link so as to enable a more timely hop-by-hop indication of credits to the upstream node when necessary (e.g., to initiate data flow on a VC or to support dynamic buffer allocation).

This scheme permits rate and credit switches to be mixed within the local area without any special interface equipment. A rate switch can operate downstream from a credit switch because the RM cell contains the sum of the rate and credit control information. The source will not transmit at a rate greater than that permitted by the rate switch and will send no more cells than is permitted by the credit switch. To support a credit switch downstream from a rate switch, the credit switch must fill in the count field in the backward RM cell with the number of credits that is allowed for the flow, and then the rate switch fills in the explicit rate field in the same backward RM cell. In this way, the source is limited by both the rate at which the "rate-switch" can service the VC, as well as the number of cells that the downstream credit switch is willing to buffer for that VC and ensure no cell loss.

In addition, to support a credit switch downstream from a rate switch, the credit switch must fill in the explicit rate field in the backward RM cell. It will do this by computing the actual throughput of the VC within the credit switch and use this value to mark the RM cells. This is particularly important when the outbound link of the credit switch is the bottleneck. This rate is fed back to the source in the RM cell, to minimize cell loss. It is also likely that the credit switch may require larger per-VC buffers than a pure static credit switch to cope with the additional delay through the rate switch. Thus, the network looks like a rate subnet up to the input to the credit switch, and as a credit subnet downstream from that switch. This requires additional hardware to that of a pure credit switch, but seems a small price to pay for an integrated scheme.

Implementation Issues

The choice among different congestion management mechanisms influences the implementations in a significant way. In the past, with lower speed networks, the issue of implementation of the congestion management algorithms was somewhat less important, since much of it was implemented in software. However, because ATM is meant to be scalable to much higher speeds, the implementation of a significant part of the congestion management algorithms needs to be performed in hardware, both in switches and in the end systems.

The implementation of the two ATM conges-

One of the major issues for switch designs is that of buffering, and where it is located relative to the switching function.

tion control schemes has been viewed to have widely varying complexity. To a large extent, this is due to the differing perspectives of the designers of the switches versus those implementing the end system. It is important to consider the implementation of the scheme from a complete system perspective. Addressing the implementation complexity from an entire system perspective is not often feasible in a standards environment, since representatives tend to focus on one or the other depending on their particular "corporate" emphasis.

Switch Implementation Issues

Switches are relatively expensive to design and build. There is a wide range of switch capacities, from small LAN switches having a small number of ports and a relatively small maximum number of VCs supported per port, to large WAN carrier switches that may have a large number of ports and also potentially a large maximum number of VCs supported per port. There is also the fact that a large number of switch designs are in existence and there is an existing base of deployed switches. This influences what we can accomplish with the introduction of a new congestion management algorithm into an environment that has already deployed older switch designs.

One of the major issues for switch designs is that of buffering, and where it is located relative to the switching function. There are three major ways buffers are placed in switches [11, 12]:
• Input buffered switches.
• Output buffered switches.
• Shared memory switches.

With a hop-by-hop credit scheme, the perception has been that an input buffered switch is most suitable. This is because the occupancy of the buffer is sensed, and when a cell is forwarded from the buffer, is quickly available and can be communicated to the upstream node in a timely fashion. However, even in such a switch, there is the need for feedback across the switch fabric to communicate the credits received from the upstream node. In the output buffered switch, there is the need to communicate credit information across the switch fabric back to the upstream node. In either case, the need to pass credit information across the fabric to the point of control is unavoidable.

The implementation of the hop-by-hop credit scheme in the switch involves a reasonable amount of complexity. This is to maintain state on a per-VC basis, at each port (input or output) and the need to recognize that it is time to communicate credits by transmitting a resource management (RM) cell when a threshold has been reached [4, 5]. In addition, the switching function has to recognize that a credit is available for a VC before the cell is forwarded.

The implementation of the end-end rate scheme has a range of complexity, depending on the particular rate scheme adopted. With almost all of the schemes proposed, there has to be some form of monitoring of the buffer occupancy to determine if the switch or switch links are congested. With the simple EFCI scheme [7, 13], the ability to indicate congestion in the cell header is needed, which requires a small amount of hardware support. However, this function is already

part of the existing standards and is implemented in current switches. With the schemes that require indication of congestion in an RM cell, there is the added complexity of receiving and processing the RM cells.

The significant complexity arrives when an explicit rate computation has to be performed for each VC, and the rate has to be communicated in an RM cell by the switch [14]. In this, a fair allocation of the bottleneck capacity is provided to each VC. The fair allocation is based on a criterion termed "max-min" fairness. The need for allocation of capacity based on a max-min fair allocation has been extensively studied in the recent past [10, 15, 16]. The notion is to provide all VCs that have a "low" demand of the capacity of a resource their entire requirement. The VCs that have a "higher" demand are then provided at least an equal share of the left over bandwidth. This allows VCs that have been bottlenecked elsewhere to not be further limited by this switch, and the VCs for which this switch is the bottleneck are the ones that will be bottlenecked. In informal terms, a switch is supposed to not limit a VC to a rate that is lower than its demand if there are other VCs that are flowing through this switch which have a higher allocation of bandwidth. A straightforward implementation of the explicit rate scheme requires state to be maintained for each VC, of the rate that has been allocated for the VC. A further modified proposal [17] for explicit rate-based congestion attempts to estimate the fair allocation of the capacity for a VC by performing an exponentially weighted averaging of the rates seen from each of the VCs. In this way, there is no need to maintain the explicit rates for each of the VCs, and instead only an estimate of the fair share. A comparison has to be performed between the average rate (which is an approximation of the max-min fair share) and the requested rate by the source of the VC, that is indicated in the RM cell. Furthermore, the implementation needs to be able to capture an RM cell flowing in the reverse direction and write the allocated rate. There is a need to perform a small amount of arithmetic in the switch as well.

The most significant issue related to switch implementation complexity lies in the fact that the hop-by-hop per-VC-based credit scheme requires buffering/queuing on a per-VC basis. This allows each of the VCs to flow independently. If there was a common queue for all the VCs, this potentially results in deadlocks. With a single FIFO queue for all VCs, when a VC is bottlenecked downstream, this results in credits not being issued to the upstream node. This can cause other VCs that may potentially take a different path to also be blocked at the upstream node. Not only does this cause unfairness, but it is relatively easy to arrive at topologies and workloads in which deadlocks may arise. One of the ways this is avoided is to use routing that is "deadlock-free." However, a better approach that not only solves this problem, but also provides considerable benefits in other ways, is to provide queuing on a per-VC basis. This implies that the buffer (e.g., a buffer for an input port) may now be allocated on a per-VC-basis (i.e., the accounting of the occupancy of the buffer is performed on an individual VC basis). This results in additional complexity in the switch, which needs to be considered in the early stages of the switch design. With an end-end rate-based congestion control scheme, there is no strict dependency on the availability of per-VC queuing in the switches. Thus, the complexity of the switch due to queuing and buffering is considerably reduced.

The queuing on a per-VC basis has additional desirable characteristics that have been propounded in the past in the context of Fair Queuing for congestion management [8]. Having a separate queue for each of the VCs allows the scheduling of switching cells from each VC in a fair manner. This also allows the delay and loss behavior of individual VCs to be isolated from each other. When there is a single common queue for all the VCs, this can lead to potentially undesirable interactions between different flows. For example, a VC that has a small amount of data to transfer may have its cells queued behind a large burst of cells from another VC that in fact may be going through a more severe bottleneck downstream. This form of transient "head of the line" blocking results in unpredictable interaction between the VCs. At a high level, the fact that cells rather than larger packets are switched mitigates the effect of this interaction. But, the notion of an ABR service where a VC may flow at the peak rate still allows for a large burst of cells from a VC being queued ahead of cells for a latency sensitive VC. A per-VC queue with a suitably fair (e.g., weighted round-robin) service policy allows for controlling latency better.

In the future, we may envisage being able to specify at least weak bounds on the end-end latency experienced by a cell/packet. Specification of the latency bounds is more easily accomplished when we have a per-VC queue with a fair per-VC service policy [18]. While this notion of specifying delay bounds is strictly not envisaged for ABR service, it may still be desirable in the future for the incorporation of weak real-time traffic (e.g., video teleconferencing). In any case, we clearly see the need for separating the flows from different VCs on a class by class basis in a switch. This requires implementation support for recognizing the class a VC belongs to and queuing and servicing in accordance with the class characteristics. The incremental complexity of per-VC queuing and service may not be particularly significant beyond the existing cost of per service-class queuing.

Many of the first generation switches were implemented with discrete FIFO queues, which made per-VC queuing impossible and, in general, two or at most four per service-class queues were offered. In more recent designs, custom silicon is being employed to reduce cost and increase capacity and functionality. Frequently, the queuing function is now implemented with custom silicon and static RAM permitting queues to be implemented as linked lists of cells. With this implementation, the additional cost of per-VC queuing over per service-class queuing is very low and the flexibility of the scheduler becomes the more significant differentiator. Some advanced designs are already considering incorporating traffic shaping within the main switch queuing function by implementing complex scheduling capabilities within custom silicon.

While most shared memory designs implement queuing with linked lists of cells, all of the queues are implemented in a single, centralized shared memory. This makes it difficult for such designs to offer per-VC queuing or advanced scheduling due to the large number of VCs passing across the center of the switch.

Input or output buffered designs are more likely to offer per-VC queuing than shared memory designs.

Adapter Design Issues

The most cost-sensitive network component for an ATM network appears to be the end-station adapter card. The switch port is cost sensitive, but there is more opportunity for sharing functions across a number of ports. The adapter stands alone. The cost of an adapter is very often determined by the amount of memory used. For ATM, the use of reassembly buffering is an important reason for adding memory on the adapter, in contrast to other technologies. The smaller this is, the more competitive ATM technology would be relative to Fast Ethernet, FDDI, etc.

On the receive side of the ATM adapter, the amount of buffering needed for reassembly in the most simplistic case, without taking advantage of statistical multiplexing is given by: {number of active VCs * max. packet size}. This can be excessive. However, statistical multiplexing arguments typically suggest that the amount of buffering needed is much smaller than this. The downside of this reduced buffering is that when the buffers fill up, because there are too many packets undergoing simultaneous reassembly, we can encounter significant packet loss. In fact, with cheaper adapter designs, we may see that the primary point where loss occurs is in the receiving end system, rather than at the more expensive switches which can be designed to have more buffering.

With a credit-based adapter, we can choose to provide credits to a selected number of VCs to enable reassembly, while allowing the other VCs to more wisely use the buffering at the source end system or in the intermediate switches. This is especially true when static buffer allocation schemes are used. It allows us to bring down the buffering requirement at the receive side of an adapter to "almost arbitrarily" small levels, so that the cost of building an ATM adapter is not substantially more than that of building a Fast Ethernet or FDDI adapter. One must note that the added cost of an ATM switch port for every connection into an ATM network (in contrast to Fast Ethernet, for example) encourages us to make the cost of an ATM adapter as small as possible. Therefore, we see using a credit-based scheme allows us to drive down the cost of building an ATM adapter.

On the transmit side, SAR chips often will queue packets awaiting segmentation on a per-connection basis. The simplest possible scheduler is a list of connections to serve that have packets queued for segmentation. The simplest enhancement of this scheduler that is capable of implementing an ABR service is to queue only those connections that have permission to send. This how the scheduler for the credit scheme is implemented.

The most cost sensitive network component for an ATM network appears to be the end-station adapter card.

This proposal appeared particularly attractive, as the different congestion control schemes being combined offered different optimizations of cost and performance.

For a rate-based scheme, each connection needs to be transmitted at its own particular rate. This is the same problem as traffic shaping. A scheduler capable of supporting a reasonable number of connections for the rate-based scheme is certainly more complex to implement than one for the credit scheme. The rate-based scheme in effect requires both the SAR function and a traffic shaper function.

Summary

We have suggested a means of integrating rate- and credit-based control for ABR traffic management. Why? Because at the time the ATM Forum was due to vote to select a single control mechanism, both the rate- and dynamic credit-based proposals were still under development. At that time it was not clear that one could select between rate and credit as a fundamental approach in the absence of a stable and implementable mechanism.

Static credit control was simple in concept and could be proven to work. It would satisfy the most stringent demands of the local area both now and into the future. It also offered the simplest and lowest cost adapter cards for ABR service. The local area market is a fast moving market, it was ready for ATM product, and it required a stable traffic management scheme rather than one that was still under development.

However, a static credit scheme is not suitable for the wide area. The wide area requires a rate scheme for both technical and political reasons, not the least of these being that this is what the carriers want. Carriers need to provision virtual circuits, apply tariffs, and police on the rate at which the VC is sending information. The wide area market moves more slowly and the same stringent performance may not be required in the wide area as for the local area. There seemed to us less of an immediate need for ABR service in the wide area, so it appeared there was more time to develop a rate scheme for the wide area. By decoupling the schemes for the local and wide areas, there was an opportunity to enhance the wide area scheme over time.

Due to these differing requirements, we felt that one cannot mandate a single congestion control mechanism for all application areas for all time. There is also a desirable goal of being able to support future development. So, it seemed that if we could show how these schemes might interwork, it would be reasonable to permit a choice of control schemes in the local area. This was the basis for the integrated proposal, described here. This proposal appeared particularly attractive, as the different congestion control schemes being combined offered different optimizations of cost and performance.

The ATM Forum has chosen to use a rate scheme for traffic management of the ABR service. Since that decision, considerable development has taken place on the end-end rate scheme, most significantly the inclusion of an explicit rate control capability as an option and the focus on congestion avoidance techniques within the switch. Work continues on the scheme, and the explicit rate enhancements appear to be addressing the requirements of the local area.

References

[1] P. Newman, "Traffic Management for ATM Local Area Networks," *IEEE Commun. Mag.*, vol. 32, no. 8, Aug. 1994, pp. 44-50.
[2] ATM Forum, "ATM User-Network Interface Specification," Version 3.0, (Prentice-Hall, Sep. 1993).
[3] L. Kleinrock, "The Latency/Bandwidth Tradeoff in Gigabit Networks," *IEEE Commun. Mag.* vol. 30, no. 4, Apr. 1992, pp. 36-40.
[4] H. T. Kung, "The FCVC (Flow-Controlled Virtual Channels) Proposal for ATM Networks," *Proc. Int. Conf. Network Protocols*, San Francisco, Oct. 1993.
[5] H. T. Kung et al., "Use of Link-by-Link Flow Control in Maximizing ATM Network Performance: Simulation Results," *Proc. IEEE Hot Interconnects Symp.*, Palo Alto, CA, Aug. 1993.
[6] H. T. Kung, *IEEE Network*, in this issue.
[7] K. K. Ramakrishnan and R. Jain, "A Binary Feedback Scheme for Congestion Avoidance in Computer Networks," *ACM Trans. on Computer Sys.*, May 1990.
[8] A. Demers, S. Keshav, and S. Shenker, "Analysis and Simulation of a Fair Queuing Algorithm," *Proc. ACM Sigcomm Symposium*, 1989.
[9] D. Hunt et al., "Flow Controlled Virtual Connections for ATM Traffic Management," ATM Forum contribution 94-0632R2, Ottawa, Canada, Sept. 1994.
[10] D. Bertsekas and R. Gallagher, *Data Networks*, (Prentice Hall, 1987).
[11] P. Newman, "ATM Technology for Corporate Networks," *IEEE Commun. Mag.*, vol. 30, no. 4, April 1992, pp. 90-101.
[12] R. Rooholamini, V. Cherkassy, and M Garver, "Finding the Right ATM Switch for the Market," *IEEE Computer*, April 1994, pp. 16-28.
[13] M. Hluchyj et al., "Closed-Loop Rate-Based Traffic Management," ATM Forum contribution 94-0438R2, Ottawa, Canada, Sept. 1994.
[14] Anna Charny, "An Algorithm for Rate Allocation in a Packet Switching Network with Feedback," MIT Thesis, MIT/LCS TR-601, April 1994.
[15] K. K. Ramakrishnan, D.-M. Chiu, and R. Jain, "Congestion Avoidance in Computer Networks with a Connectionless Network Layer, Part IV: A Selective Binary Feedback Scheme for General Topologies," (DEC TR-510, Nov. 1987).
[16] S. Shenker, "A Theoretical Analysis of Feedback Flow Control," *Proc. of the ACM Sigcomm Symposium*, 1990.
[17] L. Roberts, "Enhanced Proportional Rate Control Algorithm," ATM Forum contribution 94-0735R1, Ottawa, Canada, Sept. 1994.
[18] A. Parekh, "A Generalized Processor Sharing Approach to Flow Control in Integrated Services Networks," MIT Thesis, MIT/LIDS-TH 2089, Feb. 1992.

Biographies

K. K. RAMAKRISHNAN [M '84] is a member of technical staff at AT&T Bell Laboratories, Murray Hill, New Jersey. Until 1994, he was a consulting engineer at Digital Equipment Corporation, and was most recently a technical director for High Performance Networks. His research interests are in performance analysis and design of algorithms for computer communication networks and distributed systems. He holds a B.S. in electrical engineering from Bangalore University in India and an M.S. in automation from the Indian Institute of Science in 1978. He joined Digital after completing his Ph.D. in computer science from the University of Maryland in 1983. He has worked and published papers in the areas of load balancing, congestion control and avoidance, algorithms for FDDI, distributed systems performance and issues relating to network I/O. He is a member of the End-End Group, as part of the Internet Research Task Force. He is a technical editor for *IEEE Network*. His e-mail address is: kkrama@research.att.com

PETER NEWMAN [M '90] has recently joined Ipsilon Networks Inc., Menlo Park, California, another new networking startup. Previously he was a staff scientist responsible for ATM systems architecture at Adaptive/NET and a survivor of the Traffic Management Group of the ATM Forum. He was a research fellow at the Computer Laboratory of the University of Cambridge, where in 1988 he received a Ph.D. for research in fast packet switching. He began working on fast packet switching in 1981 for the Telecommunications and Computer Systems Research Laboratories of the G.E.C. (U.K.). His e-mail address is: pn@ipsilon.com.

224   IEEE/ACM TRANSACTIONS ON NETWORKING, VOL. 4, NO. 2, APRIL 1996

On Hop-by-Hop Rate-Based Congestion Control

Partho Pratim Mishra, *Member, IEEE*, Hemant Kanakia, *Member, IEEE*,
and Satish K. Tripathi, *Senior Member, IEEE*

Abstract—The current activity in building gigabit speed networks has led many researchers to re-examine the issue of congestion control. In this paper, we describe a rate-based hop-by-hop congestion control mechanism in which the service rates of connections are dynamically adjusted at a switch, using feedback information provided by the neighboring switches. The desired service rate is computed based on a control equation that utilizes a model of the system with feedback information used to correct inaccuracies in the model. We use an analytical model to prove that the expected value of the queue occupancy and throughput of a controlled connection converge to the desired operating point. We also study the variation of the queue occupancy and throughput in steady-state as well as the transient response. The analytical results provide insights into how the parameter values chosen affect performance. We use simulations to compare the performance of the scheme with an equivalent end-to-end control scheme. Our analytical and simulation results show that the hop-by-hop scheme reacts faster to changes in the traffic intensity and, consequently, utilizes resources at the bottleneck better and loses fewer packets than the end-to-end scheme.

I. INTRODUCTION

THE CURRENT activity in building Gigabit speed networks has led many researchers to re-examine the issue of congestion control. The goal of congestion control is to control (input) traffic flows so as to provide a reasonable trade-off between packet losses and overall network throughput. Existing data networks typically use end-to-end control mechanisms to control the flow of traffic. In this class of schemes, explicit or implicit information about network loading is used to adjust the window size or the sending rate of a connection at the source. The DECbit scheme [32], that uses explicit signals from networks, and the Slow-Start scheme [16], that uses packet loss as an implicit signal of congestion, were among the first schemes of this class. Since the introduction of these schemes, many other schemes have been proposed that attempt to further improve performance [11], [20], [30]. Most of the proposed schemes operate on an end-to-end basis with the window or rate adjustments being done in the transport protocol. An alternative approach that has emerged in recent years is based on open-loop rate control where a connection is limited to transmit within certain constraints determined at connection set up time [34], [37].

Manuscript received December 20, 1993; revised December 5, 1994; approved by IEEE/ACM TRANSACTIONS ON NETWORKING Editor M. Sidi.

P. P. Mishra and H. Kanakia are with AT&T Bell Laboratories, Murray Hill NJ 07974 USA (e-mail: partho@research.att.com and kanakia@research.att.com).

S. K. Tripathi is with the Department of Computer Science, University of Maryland, College Park, MD 20742 USA (e-mail: tripathi@cs.umd.edu).

Publisher Item Identifier S 1063-6692(96)02735-5.

We pursue a fundamentally different approach we refer to as hop-by-hop rate-based congestion control. As the name *hop-by-hop* suggests, control is exercised at each switch along the path of a traffic stream. Intuitively, hop-by-hop control mechanisms have certain advantages, particularly in networks with a large propagation delay bandwidth product. First, feedback information is available more quickly because of the smaller distances between hops. Due to the reduced lag time, the control mechanisms can react more quickly resulting in a lower likelihood of packet losses during overloads. Also, with hop-by-hop control packets can be stored not only at the bottleneck node but at earlier nodes along the path of the connection also. As a result, if the bottleneck capacity increases suddenly, a hop-by-hop mechanism can utilize the increased capacity more quickly. Second, as the propagation delay bandwidth product of a network gets larger, one would expect a larger number of applications to transmit data with a transmission duration comparable to or less than the end-to-end delay through a network. A good way to control such short bursts of traffic is to aggregate several bursty traffic streams into a group and subject the group to feedback-based control. Since traffic aggregation occurs at a switch, a hop-by-hop control mechanism is a natural choice for this kind of control. Finally, since hop-by-hop control mechanisms restrict traffic overloads to the periphery of a network, well-behaved users are protected from malicious users. These intuitive arguments are supported by the analytical and simulation results presented in this paper.

The hop-by-hop control mechanisms proposed in the literature may be classified as either, per connection hop-by-hop window mechanisms [3], [24] or per link on–off mechanisms [6], [9]. The hop-by-hop (HBH) control scheme that we describe in this paper differs significantly from these schemes. In our scheme, the service rates of individual connections or aggregates of connections are dynamically adjusted at a switch, using feedback information provided by the neighboring switches. The desired service rate is computed using a control equation that utilizes a model of the system. Old feedback information is used to correct inaccuracies in the model and to predict future service rates. Such a hop-by-hop control mechanisms can be implemented on the next generation of packet switches that are being designed to play an active role in ensuring quality of service for traffic streams such as compressed video, using reservation and scheduling mechanisms [7], [12], [13], [15], [18].

The main focus of this paper is on studying the performance of the HBH scheme using analysis and simulations. We use an analytical model to study the asymptotic stability and covari-

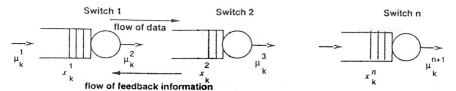

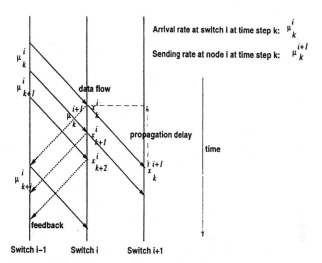

Fig. 1. Model of system.

ance properties of a HBH controlled connection in steady-state. We also use the analytical model to study the transient behavior of a controlled connection when the available bandwidth available at the bottleneck changes abruptly. The analytical results provide insights into how to choose parameter values for good performance. We also compare the performance of the HBH mechanism with an end-to-end control mechanism. Analytical as well as simulation results show that the HBH scheme reacts faster to changes in the traffic intensity and, consequently, utilizes resources at the bottleneck better and loses fewer packets, as compared to the end-to-end scheme.

The rest of the paper is organized as follows. In Section II, we describe the proposed control mechanism. In Section III, we develop the model of the system and study its performance for several different traffic models. In this section, we also examine how the values for the parameters of the scheme may be chosen. In Section IV, we make the comparison with the end-to-end control. Section V discusses related work. We conclude with a summary of the results and observations.

II. CONTROLLER DESIGN

The control mechanism we describe in this paper, henceforth referred to as HBH, is based on nearest-neighbor interaction. Each switch monitors the queue occupancy level of active connections and periodically transmits this state information to its *upstream* neighbors, i.e., toward the source. Although upstream switches can calculate the mean packet sending rate at the downstream switch from the buffer occupancy values,[1] in this paper, we assume that this information is also provided explicitly by the downstream switch. The feedback information is used by upstream switches to compute a target sending rate for a single connection or a group of connections. We have assumed in this paper that each switch has the capability to ensure that the rate at which packets are sent out for a particular connection is *bounded* by the target sending rate.[2] We assume that the source can also adjust its sending rate in response to the feedback provided by the nearest switch. In the rest of this section, we explain how the target sending rate is computed.

Consider a connection routed along a series of switches (see Figs. 1 and 2). The state of the connection is observed in a discrete time space at time instants when feedback is received. As shown in Fig. 2, the kth time instants at switch $i - 1$, and switch i, differ by an interval of time equal to the one-way

Fig. 2. Timing diagram of system.

propagation delay between the two switches, as observed with respect to a global clock. Let x_k^i be the number of queued packets, μ_k^i be the mean rate of packet arrivals, and μ_k^{i+1} be the mean rate of packet departures for the controlled connection at switch i. The time interval between feedback messages being sent is denoted as d, such that j messages are sent in an interval of time equal to the round-trip propagation delay between adjacent switches. In our analysis and simulations, we have assumed that the values of d and j are the same for all neighbors. The timing relationships between the state variables at each switch for this connection is illustrated in Fig. 2.

Making a fluid approximation [21] for the queue occupancy evolution and incorporating the effect of the buffer boundaries we may write

$$x_k^i = \min\left[\max\left(x_{k-1}^i + d.(\mu_{k-1}^i - \mu_{k-1}^{i+1}), 0\right), B_{\max}\right] \quad (1)$$

where B_{max} denotes the maximum buffering available to a connection.[1]

To derive the control law used to compute the value of the sending rate for every connection, we make the following observations. The primary goal of the control mechanism is to ensure that the sending rate of a connection at a switch matches the sending rate for the connection at the downstream switch. It is also desirable to maintain a reservoir of waiting packets at each hop. This allows a connection to quickly increase its sending rate if additional bandwidth becomes available,

---

[1] By subtracting the number of packets transmitted by the upstream switch over a measurement interval from the increase in the queue occupancy value over the same interval.

[2] An implementation of this is described in detail in [28].

---

[1] A fluid model is a good approximation when the discontinuity of jumps in the original process is small relative to the scale of the system, in terms of buffer size or transmission time.

thereby getting higher average throughput. Both goals may be achieved by always attempting to keep the queue occupancy, at each switch, at a target value between zero and B_{max}. The trade-off between higher throughput and lower losses may be adjusted by the choice of this target value, henceforth referred to as the *setpoint*.

In the proposed control mechanism, a switch computes the *target* sending rate to drive the future state of the system, i.e., the number of queued packets for the controlled connection at the downstream switch to the setpoint x^*. We refer to this as a predictive control mechanism because it controls the future evolution of the state of the controlled connection over a finite time horizon. The controller uses the fluid model of (1), ignoring the buffer boundary conditions, to compute how the queue occupancy at the downstream switch will evolve.[2]

Switch $i-1$ computes the target sending rate for the controlled connection at the kth time step as

$$\lambda_k^i = \mu_k^{i+1} + \frac{(x^* - x_k^i)}{d} \cdot g. \qquad (2)$$

In the above equation, g is a gain parameter that controls the rate of convergence to the desired buffer occupancy level; typically its value is less than one for reasons discussed in Section III. Due to the propagation delay between adjacent switches, the values of x_k^i and μ_k^{i+1} are not available at switch $i-1$ at time step k; this switch only knows the value of x_{k-j}^i and μ_{k-j-1}^{i+1} (see Fig. 1). Hence, the switch cannot use (2) directly. Instead, it uses the *predicted* values $\hat{x}_k^i$ and $\hat{\mu}_k^{i+1}$ in (2).

The value of μ_k^{i+1}, depends on the traffic characteristics of each of the input sources, the service discipline used at the downstream switch and the sending rate computed by the downstream switch for this connection. The predictor used for μ_k^{i+1} can be designed to exploit any knowledge available about these characteristics. In this paper, we do not attempt to design such specialized predictors. Instead, we use a first order auto-regressive filter [14] with the parameter α controlling the speed of convergence. At time slot k, switch $i-1$ knows the value of μ_{k-j-1}^{i+1} from which it estimates

$$\hat{\mu}_{k-j}^{i+1} = \alpha \cdot \mu_{k-j-1}^{i+1} + (1-\alpha) \cdot \hat{\mu}_{k-j-1}^{i+1}. \qquad (3)$$

The value of x_k^i is predicted as

$$\hat{x}_k^i = x_{k-j}^i + \sum_{p=k-j}^{k-1} \mu_p^i - \sum_{p=k-j}^{k-1} \hat{\mu}_p^{i+1}. \qquad (4)$$

We assume that in (4) the estimated service rates $\hat{\mu}_{k-j+1}^{i+1}$ to $\hat{\mu}_{k-1}^{i+1}$ are the same as $\hat{\mu}_{k-j}^{i+1}$, which is computed according to (3) when the feedback arrives.

Equation (2) ignores the dependence of the value of μ_k^{i+1} on μ_k^i. When the queue occupancy dips to zero, the sending rate may be less than the maximum possible available to this connection and the current value of μ_k^{i+1} becomes a poor indicator of the available bandwidth. To address this problem,

we modify (2) to allow a connection to react quickly when more capacity opens up. In the modified equation, the sending rate is increased at a fixed rate, δ, as long as the feedback indicates that the number of queued packets at the end of a control period is less than one.[3] The modified design equation is

$$\lambda_k^i = \lambda_{k-1}^i + \delta, \text{ if } x_{k-j}^i \leq 1$$
$$= \hat{\mu}_{k-j}^{i+1} + \frac{(x^* - \hat{x}_k^i)}{d} \cdot g, \text{ otherwise.} \qquad (5)$$

Readers should note that the actual sending rate μ_k^i for a connection at switch $i-1$, can differ from the target sending rate, λ_k^i, depending on the cross-traffic at this switch and the rate at which the upstream switch sends packets. Denoting the maximum bandwidth available to the controlled connection, at switch $i-1$ at time k, as c_k^i, the sending rate for a connection at each switch may be expressed as the minimum of three quantities: the target sending rate, λ_k^i (assuming that it is positive), the available link capacity, c_k^i (which is equal to the total link capacity minus the cross-traffic), and the rate at which packets arrive from the previous switch plus the buffer flushing rate, $\mu_k^{i-1} + \frac{x_k^i}{d}$. Thus, the actual sending rate at switch $i-1$ is given as

$$\mu_k^i = \min \left[\max (0, \lambda_k^i), c_k^i, \mu_k^{i-1} + \frac{x_k^{i-1}}{d} \right]. \qquad (6)$$

III. ANALYSIS

In this section, we define the system model and use it to study the steady-state behavior of a controlled connection in terms of the asymptotic stability and the covariance properties. We also study the transient response characteristics of the system and present simulation results that validate the analysis.

A) Model of System

We study the performance of a single controlled connection routed along several switches with traffic offered by other connections referred to as cross-traffic. Fig. 1 depicts the system that we are modeling. The state of a controlled connection at a switch is fully captured by four state variables: the arrival rate, μ_k^i, the departure rate, μ_k^{i+1}, the queue occupancy, x_k^i, and the estimate of the departure rate, $\hat{\mu}_k^{i+1}$. Since the arrival rate for a connection at a switch is merely the departure rate from the previous node, we need $j * (3 * n + 1)$ state variables to represent the state of a controlled connection that has n nodes on its path (j represents the *age* of the feedback information). The evolution of the queue occupancy, sending rate and estimated sending rate of the downstream switch for the controlled connection at each switch is given by (1), (3), and (6), respectively.

---

[2] Such model-based predictive controls were originally proposed in the field of process control [36] to improve the performance of time-delayed control systems.

[3] The choice of the threshold of one packet is based on our simulation experience that suggests the use of values close to one does not have a significant impact on the achievable throughput. However, the use of values significantly higher than one serves to generate oscillations in which the queue occupancy alternately empties and fills up, thereby, negating the benefits of predictive control.

B) Models of Cross-Traffic

The behavior of the controlled connection depends on the nature of the cross-traffic at each node and the value of the controller parameters. The cross-traffic corresponds to traffic load offered by other connections. For an integrated service network, some of the connections may correspond to voice and video traffic and, thus, may be subject to a different set of controls.

Several different models have been proposed in the literature to capture the effect of cross-traffic, including white noise, Brownian motion and ARMA models [5], [10], [20]. In this paper, only two models of the cross-traffic, namely, white noise and step-change models, have been used for the purpose of analysis. We have used simulations to study the performance when each (HBH-controlled) source generates data in short bursts. We refer the interested reader to [19], [29], and [27] which describe simulations studying the performance of the HBH scheme for many different source traffic models and network configurations.

The first cross-traffic model assumes that the bottleneck service rate can be approximated as a constant value plus white noise. This models a situation where a fixed number of (relatively) long lived bulk data transfers share the capacity at the bottleneck. The randomness models the effect of a large number of short lived connections. This analysis provides insight into the choice of parameters to provide good steady-state performance.

The second cross-traffic model we use is one in which the bottleneck service rate is constant over small intervals of time with step changes from time to time. This analysis provides information about the convergence time and the size of the buffer overshoots/undershoots, which can be used for choosing the controller parameters to ensure a good transient response. This model assumes that the effect of noise is a higher order effect compared to the effect of the change in service capacity.

1) White Noise Model: The system described by (1), (3), and (6) is nonlinear. In general, analytical solutions of such systems are either very complex or intractable. Hence, we linearize the system model by ignoring the queue occupancy boundary conditions. We also assume that the bottleneck is the last node along the path of the connection and that

$$\mu_k^{i+1} = M + \epsilon_k, \quad \text{if node } i \text{ is the bottleneck}$$
$$= \lambda_k^{i+1}, \quad \text{if node } i \text{ is before the bottleneck}$$

where M is a constant value and ϵ_k is a sample of white noise process [35] with zero mean and variance σ^2

$$E[\epsilon_k] = 0$$

$$E[\epsilon_k . \epsilon_j] = 0 \text{, if } k \neq j$$
$$= \sigma^2, \text{ otherwise.}$$

To simplify the analysis, we define a representation of the state of the controlled connection in terms of *deviation* variables, $\underline{x}_k^i = (x_k^i - x^*)$, $\underline{\mu}_k^i = (\mu_k^i - M)$, and $\underline{\hat{\mu}}_k^i = (\hat{\mu}_k^i - M)$ as

$$X_k = [\underline{x}_k^1, \underline{\mu}_k^1, \underline{\hat{\mu}}_k^2, \cdots \underline{x}_k^n, \underline{\mu}_k^n, \underline{\hat{\mu}}_k^{n+1}, \underline{\mu}_k^{n+1}]^T \quad (7)$$

and based on the linearizing assumptions, we combine (1), (3), (5), and (6) to write

$$X_k = A_1.X_{k-1} + A_2.X_{k-2} + \cdots + A_j.X_{k-j} + \underline{W}_{k-1} \quad (8)$$

where

$$\underline{W}_k = \begin{bmatrix} O \\ O \\ . \\ . \\ \epsilon_k \end{bmatrix}.$$

The structure of matrices A_1 to A_j is described in the Appendix. We may rewrite (8) more concisely as

$$Y_k = A.Y_{k-1} + W_{k-1} \quad (9)$$

where

$$A = \begin{bmatrix} O & I & O & O & \dots & O \\ O & O & I & O & \dots & O \\ . & . & . & . & & . \\ . & . & . & . & & . \\ A_j & A_{j-1} & . & . & . & A_1 \end{bmatrix}$$

$$W_k = \begin{bmatrix} O \\ O \\ . \\ . \\ \underline{W}_k \end{bmatrix}$$

and

$$Y_k = \begin{bmatrix} X_{k-j} \\ X_{k-j+1} \\ . \\ . \\ X_{k-1} \end{bmatrix}.$$

O and I denote the zero and identity matrices, respectively. The solution of the above system may be written as

$$Y_n = A^n.Y_0 + \sum_{i=0}^{n-1} A^{n-i-1}.W_i.$$

From this, we obtain

$$E[Y_n] = A^n E[Y_0]$$

A system is asympotically stable if the expected value of the system state converges to a particular steady-state vector, irrespective of the initial conditions. For our system, we are interested in proving convergence of the state vector X_k in the limit to $[x^*, M, M, \cdots, x^*, M, M, M]^T$. This is equivalent to proving that

$$\lim_{n \to \infty} E[Y_n] = 0.$$

A necessary and sufficient set of conditions for stability of the sytem as defined above may be derived by using standard results from linear algebra which show that the limit $\lim_{n \to \infty} A^n$ exists and is equal to zero if all the eigenvalues of A have modulus less than one [31]. In the Appendix, we prove that the only nonzero eigenvalues of A are $(1 - q)$ and α.

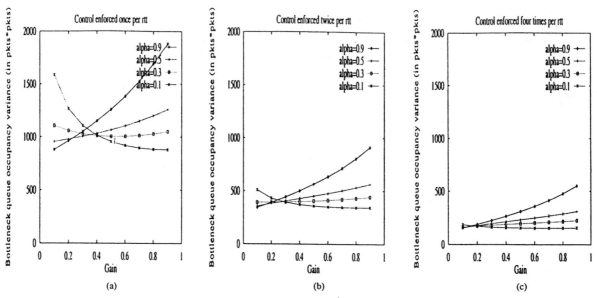

Fig. 3. Variance of bottleneck queue occupancy for various values of g and α.

Therefore, if $-1 < \alpha < 1$ and $0 < g < 2$, $\forall\ i\ \in (0, N)$

$$\lim_{n \to \infty} E[x_n^i] = x^*.$$

$$\lim_{n \to \infty} E[\mu_n^i] = M.$$

$$\lim_{n \to \infty} E[\hat{\mu}_n^i] = M.$$

The above proof shows that the system is stable for values of α in the range $(-1, 1)$. For negative values of α, the system is *underdamped*. In other words, the values of the system state variables (expressed in terms of the deviation from the steady-state values) are alternately positive and negative, as the system coverges to the steady-state. In contrast, for positive values of α, the convergence is *overdamped*, i.e. the values of the system state variables are always either positive or negative depending on the initial state. Most practical adaptive control mechanisms used in networks, such as the adaptive end-to-end rate control mechanisms proposed in the DECbit schemes [32], or the adaptive retransmission timer algorithms used in TCP [16], use an overdamped mode of control. Hence, in the rest of this paper, we choose to study the performance of the systems for values of α in the range $(0, 1)$.

We remark that due to the much larger number of state variables involved, analytical techniques used for nonlinear analysis, such as in [1], do not extend easily to the HBH control scheme we are investigating here.

The proof of stability implies that the expected value of the system state converges to the desired operating point. The sample path, however, will fluctuate around the operating point. From the point of view of effectiveness of congestion control, it is important to study the magnitude of these fluctuations. A measure of this is the queue occupancy variance at each switch. To derive this value, we study the evolution of the covariance matrix, $Cov(Y_k)$, of the state vector Y_k, $Cov(Y_k) = E[Y_k Y_k^T]$. The diagonal elements of this covariance matrix give the variance of each of the components of the

state vector. Let $Cov(W_k)$ be the covariance matrix of W_k. We can use (9) to write[4]

$$Cov(Y_k) = A.Cov(Y_{k-1})A^T + Cov(W_k). \qquad (10)$$

The proof of asymptotic stability also proves that the covariance of the state vector converges to a semidefinite matrix Σ which is the unique solution of the linear equations given by $\Sigma = A.\Sigma.A^T + Cov(W_k)$ [35]. These equations can be solved to obtain the exact expressions for each of the terms. These expressions, however, are very complicated. Instead, we use numerical solutions of (10) to obtain the covariance matrix for various values of the controller parameters. The variance of the queue occupancy and sending rate at each node is obtained from the covariance matrix.

For the numerical results, we study the behavior of a connection routed along four switches. The value of M is 5 pkts/ms (20Mb/s) and the hop round trip delay is 20 ms. The value of σ is 20 pkts/hop round trip time. Fig. 3 shows the variance of the bottleneck queue occupancy for different values of g and α with the control being enforced once, twice, or four times per round trip time.

The results show that for low values of α, an increasing value of g reduces the variance in queue occupancy while the converse is true for higher values of α. This may be explained as follows. For high values of α, the estimated sending rate is *following* the value of the actual sending rate very closely and is, therefore, always out of date. Consequently, the predicted queue occupancy is erroneous and using a high value of g results in unnecessary fluctuation. For low values of α, the tracking is more sluggish. In this case, a deviation of the predicted queue occupancy from the setpoint reflects a deviation of the actual queue occupancy and, therefore, it is desirable to react to this quickly, hence, the better performance

[4]*Covariance* $(A.Y_{k-1}) = A.$ *Covariance* $(Y_{k-1}).A^T$ [35].

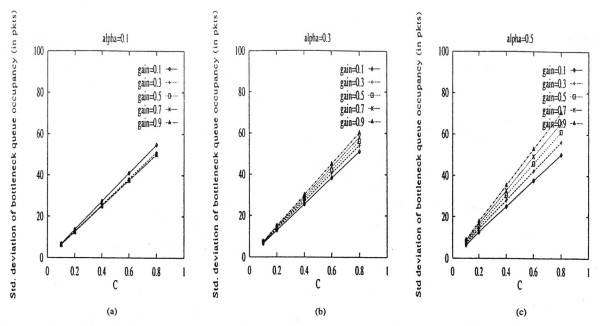

Fig. 4.   Standard deviation of bottleneck queue occupancy variance versus coefficient of variation of bottleneck bandwidth ($C = \sigma/M$).

with a high value of g. Fig. 3 also shows the effect of increasing the frequency of control. Clearly increasing the frequency of control leads to better control, i.e. lower variance of the bottleneck queue occupancy. The minimum value of the standard deviation is about 29.7, 18.5, and 12.5 packets when control is enforced once, twice, and four times per hop round trip time, respectively.

Figure 4 shows that the standard deviation of the bottleneck queue occupancy is a linear function of the coefficient of variation of the bottleneck bandwidth, $C = \sigma/M$. This suggests that the buffering required at the bottleneck needs to be linearly proportional to σ to allow the network to operate in a low-loss regime. We also use numerical solutions of (10) to derive the variance of the packet arrival rate at the bottleneck. The value of this quantity affects the variation in queue occupancy at the previous node. Fig. 5 shows the variance of the queue occupancy at the bottleneck and the previous node and the variance of the arrival rate at the bottleneck. These results indicate that while a high value of g is useful in reducing the variance of the bottleneck queue occupancy, it may cause the variance of the queue occupancy at previous nodes to *increase*.

The information about the queue occupancy variance is important because it provides information about the buffer occupancy requirements in steady-state. The setpoint should be chosen based on the maximum buffering available and the fluctuation of the queue occupancy in steady-state so as to trade packet losses versus higher throughput.

a) Effect of buffer boundaries: In the analysis, we have so far ignored the effect of the buffer boundaries. In an actual system, the buffer boundaries will result in packet losses and a drop in throughput when the buffers fill up and empty out, respectively. How much of an impact does this nonlinearity

have and how does it affect the stability and covariance results we have derived? To examine this, we use Monte-Carlo simulations [38] to compare the performance of the linear system that we have modeled and a nonlinear system in which the buffer boundaries are taken into account. As before, the cross-traffic at the bottleneck is modeled as white noise. We run this for a single node system for 10 000 discrete time steps, assuming the lower and upper buffer boundaries to be zero and 100 packets, respectively. The setpoint is chosen as 50 packets. In Fig. 6, we compare a small trace of the bottleneck queue occupancy for the linear and nonlinear systems. Both systems behave very similarly except at the buffer boundaries. This is reflected in the steady-state measures of the mean and standard deviation of the queue occupancy shown in Table I. These values are computed using the method of batch means [25] with the figures in brackets indicating the 95% confidence intervals.

2) Step Change Model: We next study the behavior of the controlled connection when the available bottleneck service capacity increases or decreases by a fixed amount abruptly. The goal of this analysis is to study the transient behavior in terms of the evolution of the queue occupancy and the sending rate at each node. To simplify the analysis, we assume that the value of α is equal to one and that the change in the bottleneck service rate occurs immediately after the start of a discrete time step. This results in the largest possible queue occupancy over/undershoot. We also make the linearizing assumptions made earlier and assume that the system is initially in equilibrium.

a) Reduction in available capacity: Let the available capacity at the bottleneck reduce from C to $C - \Delta_C$ at (discrete) time step K^0. We assume that the bottleneck is the Bth node on the path of the connection. We can show that the arrival

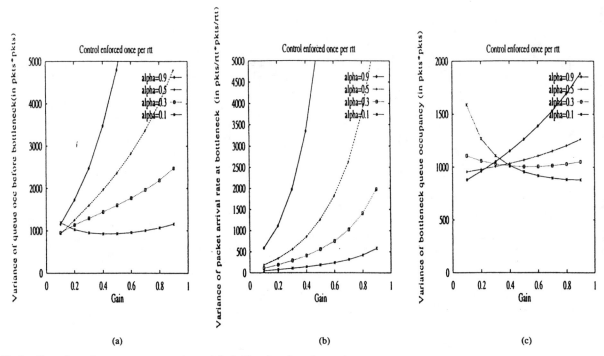

Fig. 5. Comparison of queue occupancy variance at the bottleneck and previous node.

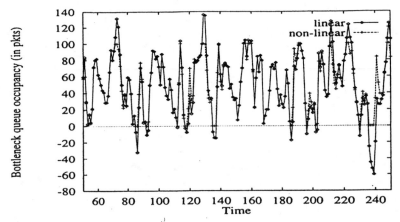

Fig. 6. Effect of buffer boundaries.

TABLE I
IMPACT OF LINEARITY ASSUMPTIONS

	Mean	Standard Deviation
Linear	49.988 (49.187,50.788)	8.653
Non Linear	49.985 (49.277,50.692)	7.648

rate at the bottleneck is given by

$$\mu_k^B = C, \text{ if } k < K^1$$
$$= C - \Delta_C + f_k^1, \text{ otherwise} \qquad (11)$$

where

$$f_k^1 = a^1 \cdot (1-g)^{k-K^1}$$
$$a^1 = -g \cdot (j+1) \cdot \Delta_C$$
$$K^1 = K^0 + (j+1).$$

Thus, the arrival rate at the bottleneck starts to decrease $(j+1)$ time steps after the reduction in capacity. After this the sending rate drops below the new capacity, $C - \Delta_C$, to flush the buildup in packets and then increases at a geometric rate toward $C - \Delta_C$, with the rate of convergence being controlled by the value of g. In general, we can show that the arrival rate at the node m nodes before the bottleneck, μ_k^{B-m}, is given by (see the Appendix)

$$\mu_k^{B-m} = C, \text{ if } k < K^{m+1}$$
$$\approx C - \Delta_C + f_k^{m+1} \text{ otherwise} \qquad (12)$$

where

$$f_k^{m+1} = a^{m+1} \cdot (1-g)^{k-K^{m+1}}$$
$$a^m = a^{m-1} - g \cdot (j+1) \cdot (\Delta_C - a^{m-1})$$

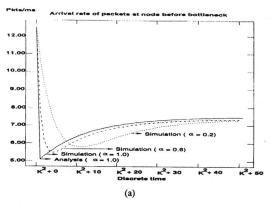

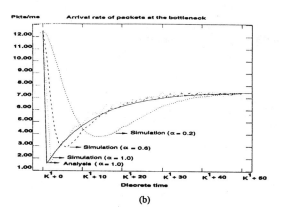

Fig. 7. Arrival rate of packets following a decrease in bottleneck capacity.

$$a^0 = 0$$
$$K^{m+1} = K^0 + (m+1).(j+1).$$

Figure 7 shows the evolution of the arrival rate at the bottleneck and the previous node as predicted by the analysis, compared to the values obtained by simulation. The analytical values closely match those obtained by simulation. The topology used is a chain of five nodes with the bottleneck capacity reduces from 12.5 pkts/ms to 7.5 pkts/ms; the packet size is 500 bytes. The control is enforced every 4 ms and the hop round trip propagation delay equals 20 ms. Fig. 7 also shows results of simulations for values of α less than one, providing insights about how the dynamic behavior changes for different values of α.

From (12) and the linearized version of (1), the evolution of the queue occupancy at the node, m hops before the bottleneck, may be expressed as

$$
\begin{aligned}
x^{B-m}_{k+1} &= x^*, \quad \text{if } k < K^m \\
&\approx x^{B-m}_k + d.\Delta_C - d.a^m.(1-g)^{k-K^m}, \\
&\quad \text{if } K^m \le k < K^{m+1} \\
&= x^{B-m}_k + d.a^{m+1}.(1-g)^{k-K^{m+1}} \\
&\quad - d.a^m.(1-g)^{k-K^m}, \quad \text{otherwise.} \quad (13)
\end{aligned}
$$

It is shown in (13) that the queue occupancy increases from the setpoint to the maximum value and then decreases at a geometrically fast rate. The increase to the maximum value is linear at the bottleneck but is negative geometric at the other nodes. The maximum queue size at the node m steps before the bottleneck is reached at the end of the $K^m + j$th step and is given by

$$x^* + (1+j).d.\Delta_C - d.\sum_{k=K^m}^{k=K^{m+1}-1} a_m.(1-g)^k. \quad (14)$$

In Fig. 8, we show the evolution of the queue occupancy at the bottleneck and the previous node as predicted by the analysis compared to the values obtained by simulation. The difference between the queue occupancy as predicted by the analysis and the simulation is mainly due to two factors. First, the analysis assumes a fluid model. In an actual system, a calculated rate may not always be sustainable because packets

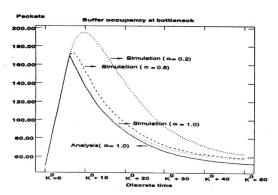

Fig. 8. Queue occupancy following a decrease in capacity.

are finite sized resulting in a certain minimum granularity of allocation. The second reason is that (12) is a first order approximation and ignores higher order terms.

There are several additional insights provided by the above expressions. First, they show that for large values of g, the overshoot at each of the nodes is quickly reduced but only at the cost of large overshoots at the previous nodes. In other words there is a trade-off between the duration and the amplitude of the overshoot. Second, the expressions show the benefits of multiple controls per round trip time. For very high values of k, the overshoot at the bottleneck is about half what it would be with $k = 1$. These observations corroborate the insights obtained by calculating the variation of the queue occupancy in steady-state.

b) Increase in service capacity: Let the service capacity at the bottleneck increase from C to $C + \Delta_C$ at time K^0. In this case, also, the sending rate and queue occupancy evolution are given by (12) and (13), provided that the queue occupancy for the controlled connection at each node does not touch zero. The condition for this is that the value of the queue occupancy as given by (14) should be positive for all values of m.

However, if the queue occupancy at any node touches zero while evolving according to (13), the trajectory changes. This is because the upstream switch changes to the linear probe up mode, clause one of (5), when it gets this information. Also, (14) implies that if an intermediate queue empties then all the queues before it are guaranteed to empty, since $a^{m+1} > a^m$

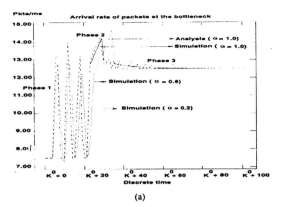

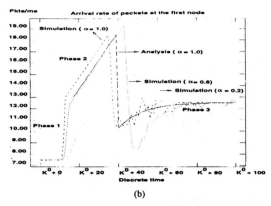

(a)   (b)

Fig. 9. Arrival rate of packets following an increase in bottleneck capacity.

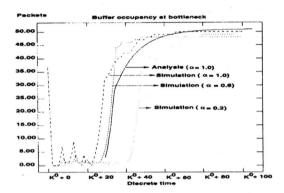

Fig. 10. Queue occupancy following an increase in capacity.

for all values of m. The new trajectory consists of three phases. In phase one, each switch that is upstream of an empty queue attempts to linearly probe up the sending rate. However, the maximum rate at which it can send packets is limited to the rate at which it is receiving packets from the previous node plus the buffer flushing rate, see (6). Hence, in this phase, the sending rate fluctuates and all the intermediate queues empty. The exact behavior is difficult to express analytically. As a result of the intermediate queues emptying out, the sending rate at all nodes becomes dependent on the sending rate of the source. Since the source is B hops from the bottleneck, it learns about the increase in bottleneck capacity at time $K^0 + B.(j+1)$ (see Fig. 1). This is the instant at which phase two begins. Let C' be the rate from which the source starts to probe up its sending rate. This value is dependent on the the time instant at which the queue at the first node empties; call this l. From (12), it follows that

$$C' = C + \Delta_C + a^B.(1-g)^{l-[K^0+B.(j+1)+2]},$$
$$\text{if } l > K^0 + B.(j+1) + 1,$$
$$= C, \text{ otherwise.}$$

As a result of the linear probe up, the arrival rate at the bottleneck exceeds the value $C + \Delta_C$ at time step $P^0 = K^0 + B.(j+1) + l + \lceil \frac{C+\Delta_C - C'}{\delta} \rceil$. This is the start of phase three. Subsequently, the evolution of the queue occupancy at each of the nodes is similar to what happens when there is a decrease in service capacity. In particular, the sending rate at

the node m steps before the bottleneck, may be approximated as

$$\mu_k^{B-m} = C' + [k - (K^0 + B.(j+1) + l)].\delta,$$
$$\text{if } K^0 + B.(j+1) + l < k < K^{m+1}$$
$$= C + \Delta_C + b^{m+1}.(1-g)^{k-K^{m+1}},$$
$$\text{otherwise} \qquad (15)$$

where

$$K^{m+1} = P^0 + (m+1).(j+1)$$
$$b^0 = 0$$
$$b^m = \frac{g.x^*}{d} - b^{m-1}$$
$$\qquad - g.(j+1).[(C' + \lceil \frac{C + \Delta_C - C'}{\delta} \rceil.\delta)$$
$$\qquad - (C + \Delta_C) + b^{m-1} + \delta.(m.j + m - j/2)].$$

The evolution of the sending rate, in phase three, depends on the sign of b^m. If it is positive then the sending rate geometrically decreases to $(C + \Delta_C)$ starting from the value $(C+\Delta_C) + |b^m|$, otherwise it geometrically increases to $(C + \Delta_C)$ starting from the value $(C+\Delta_C) - |b^m|$. This corresponds to two possible queue occupancy evolution trajectories. In the first one the queue occupancy approaches the setpoint at a geometric rate starting from zero, whereas, in the other the queue, occupancy overshoots the setpoint and then decreases at a geometric rate toward the setpoint. Note that different nodes may have different patterns although the monotonicity of the b^m values implies that if a particular node has a setpoint overshoot then all the previous nodes will also have setpoint overshoots. The largest amount by which the setpoint is exceeded (if at all) occurs at the first node at the end of time step $P^0 + j + B.(j+1)$ and is given by

$$d.(j+1).m + \sum_{k=0}^{k=j+1} b^{i+1}.(1-g)^k$$
$$+ [\delta.(j+1).(B.j + B - j/2)] - x^*. \qquad (16)$$

Thus, the time taken to increase to the new sending rate is dependent on the distance of the bottleneck from the source and the value of δ. The above expressions indicate that if δ is large then a connection quickly grabs the available bandwidth but may cause a large overshoot at each node with the largest overshoot occurring at the first node in the chain.

IV. COMPARISON WITH END-TO-END CONTROL

In the previous section, the performance of the HBH control scheme was considered in isolation. How well does this scheme perform *vis-a-vis* end-to-end control schemes? To answer this question we have compared the performance of the HBH scheme with several popular end-to-end control schemes [19], [29]. However, these studies cannot address the question of what advantages are provided by hop-by-hop control over end-to-end control because the difference in performance is partly dependent upon the choice of control policy. Hence, in this paper, we have chosen to compare the performance of the HBH scheme with an *equivalent* end-to-end scheme, referred to as E2E. In the E2E scheme, all switches are assumed to send feedback information back to the source. The source uses the feedback information from the bottleneck node to compute the sending rate for individual connections according to (5). This rate computation is done only at the source unlike in the HBH scheme where it is done at each switch.

One of the advantages of using hop-by-hop control is that the feedback information is available more quickly because of the smaller distances between hops. As a result, the control mechanisms should react more quickly, resulting in a lower likelihood of packet losses during overloads. This intuition is supported by the analytical results obtained in Section III. These results can be used to study the effect of the larger propagation delays on performance by modeling an E2E controlled connection as a single queue at the bottleneck node.[5] Note that the proof of stability applies to the E2E scheme as well, and indicates that the expected values of the sending rate and queue occupancy converge. However, the transient queue occupancy evolution expressions show that the magnitude of the propagation delay has a direct impact on the degree of deviation from the setpoint. Equation (14) shows that the size of the overshoot at the bottleneck is proportional to $(j+1)*d$ which is approximately the delay in the feedback control cycle. Hence, with end-to-end control, the likelihood of buffer overflow is greater for the same value of the buffer setpoint.

Another advantage of using hop-by-hop control is that the capacity of the bottleneck is efficiently utilized, especially when the cross-traffic reduces suddenly. For an HBH controlled connection, packets are stored not only at the bottleneck node but at earlier nodes along the path of the connection also. As a result, if the bottleneck capacity increases suddenly, the HBH mechanism can utilize the increased capacity more quickly.

We use simulations to corroborate these observations. In the simulations there is a primary controlled connection which is assumed to always have data to send for the duration of the experiment. Cross-traffic is provided by a constant rate traffic source that switches on at time 2000 ms and then switches off at 3000 ms. The network configuration used is shown in Fig. 11. Multiple switches along the path of the primary

[5] This is a very commonly used model [5], [10], [20]

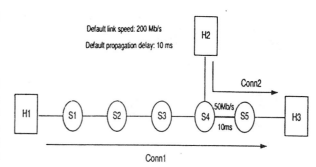

Fig. 11. Simulation configuration one.

connection allow the interactions among the hop-by-hop controllers at each switch to be studied. In this configuration, the end-to-end propagation delays for the controlled connection and the cross-traffic are 60 ms and 30 ms, respectively. The rise rate, δ, is picked to be 1/4 of the bottleneck rate per end-to-end round trip time. The values α and g used for HBH are 0.4 and 0.09, respectively. The value of g used for the E2E scheme is 0.45 and two values of α are used, 0.4 and 1.0. The control period duration is 4 ms leading to five updates in one hop round trip time. The relative performance of the schemes depends on the value chosen for the buffer setpoint. In the HBH scheme, packets are buffered at each hop for any connection, while in the E2E scheme packets are queued only at the bottleneck node. Hence, we choose to compare the performance of the HBH mechanism with a setpoint of either 50 or 200 with that of the E2E scheme with a setpoint of 200. We remark that these buffer setpoint values are much smaller than the *pipe* size, which is 1500 packets for connection one when the entire bottleneck link capacity is used.

In Fig. 12, we show the evolution of buffer occupancy for connection one at the bottleneck, the output link from switch four to switch five. The graphs show that the buffer overshoots for the HBH scheme are much smaller than those for E2E. When the cross-traffic switches off, the buffered packets allow a connection to quickly take advantage of the available bandwidth. As shown in Fig. 12, the HBH scheme with 200 buffers is capable of reacting more rapidly than the E2E scheme with 200 buffers. Also, using a higher value of α does not significantly reduce the magnitude of the overshoot for the E2E scheme. The utilization of the additional capacity depends both on the buffer setpoint as well as the time delay in adjusting the sending rate at the source. In Fig. 12, we show the actual sending rate at the source; with both HBH and E2E the source sending rate takes about the same time to stabilize to the new value.

Another advantage provided by hop-by-hop control over end-to-end control for networks with a large propagation delay bandwidth product is the ability to control aggregates of connections. This is useful because, as the propagation delay bandwidth product of a network gets larger, one would expect a larger number of users to transmit data with a transmission duration comparable to or less than the end-to-end delay through a network. Intuitively, the performance of feedback control mechanisms based on per connection control deteriorates in such a situation. Aggregated control is not

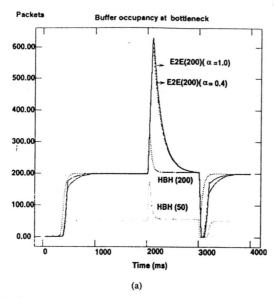

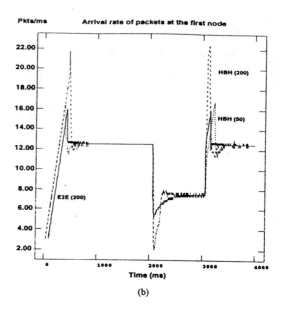

(a)   (b)

Fig. 12.   Comparison of end-to-end and hop-by-hop schemes.

feasible for end-to-end control mechanisms (such as *slow start*) because they are implemented at the transport layer.

To study the impact of relatively small transfer times, we use bursty sources that alternately generate a block of data and then idle. The metric of performance we use is the average burst transfer time. The configuration used in this simulation is shown in Fig. 13. A simpler topology was used in order to speed up the simulations and to obtain very tight confidence intervals (less than 2% of the mean transfer time). For the topology used, both E2E and HBH have the same delay in the feedback control path so that the only reason for the difference in performance results from aggregation. With the aggregated HBH mechanism, control is enforced in the network layer at both hosts and switches. Thus connections 1-20, 21-40, 41-60, 61-80, and 81-100 form the groups. Each of the connections is assumed to generate bulk data according to an exponentially distributed random variable with a mean of 1, 0.25, or 0.05 Mbytes (2000, 500, and 100 packets). The idle time is also assumed to be exponentially distributed so that the average load is approximately 80% or 55%, corresponding to high or medium load.

The results for this set of experiments are summarized in Table II. The experiments show that controlling aggregates of connections using HBH control results in significantly improved performance. Moreover, the overall improvement in performance increases as the burst size decreases: 20% for a burst size of 2000 packets, 40% for a burst size of 500 packets and 75% for a burst size of 100 packets.

The results of this section show that the smaller feedback control delays allow hop-by-hop control to react faster to traffic changes, thus, leading to better utilization of link capacity and smaller queue occupancy increases than with end-to-end control. Moreover, under circumstances where the transmission duration of a unit of application data is small, controlling aggregates of connections using the HBH mechanism leads to superior performance.

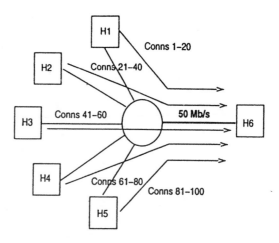

Default link speed: 200 Mb/s

Default propagation delay: 20 ms

Fig. 13.   Simulation configuration two.

V. RELATED WORK

There is a large and growing body of work on the design of end-to-end flow/congestion control schemes for data traffic [11], [16], [20], [26], [30], [32]. There has been relatively little work done in designing hop-by-hop control schemes (although there has been some recent interest in the area [9], [24]). Most of the schemes proposed in the literature may be classified as per connection hop-by-hop *static* window mechanisms [3], [24] or link by link on–off mechanisms [6], [9]. In hop-by-hop window mechanisms, a switch can only send a window's worth of unacknowledged packets to the downstream switch for each connection; window sizes are determined based on the number of buffers available at a switch. In link by link on–off mechanisms, the traffic flow on a link is turned off

TABLE II
EFFECT OF SMALLER TRANSFERS

Scheme	Mean Burst size	Mean Idle time	Mean Transfer time
E2E	2000 pkts	20 secs	827.48 ms
HBH(aggr)	2000 pkts	20 secs	697.99 ms
E2E	2000 pkts	30 secs	523.24 ms
HBH(aggr)	2000 pkts	30 secs	433.81 ms
E2E	500 pkts	5 secs	336.69 ms
HBH(aggr)	500 pkts	5 secs	236.28 ms
E2E	500 pkts	7.5 secs	227.57 ms
HBH(aggr)	500 pkts	7.5 secs	170.83 ms
E2E	100 pkts	1 secs	114.50 ms
HBH(aggr)	100 pkts	1 secs	65.48 ms
E2E	100 pkts	1.5 secs	106.22 ms
HBH(aggr)	100 pkts	1.5 secs	55.17 ms

in response to a switch-off message from a congested node; the flow resumes either through a *timeout* mechanism or when an switch-on message is received. The HBH mechanism we have proposed differs significantly from these schemes. We control rates and not windows. Hence, with the HBH scheme, it is possible to have packet losses, however, the utilization of link bandwidth and switch buffers is far more efficient in a wide area network than with per-connection hop-by-hop window mechanisms. Link-by-link on–off mechanisms result in unfair service to users and spread congestion to other nodes because they are *source-blind* [17]. Also, on–off mechanisms can cause large oscillations in the queue occupancy [8] when there are large time delays in the feedback control loop. The proposed HBH scheme does not demonstrate either of these characteristics.

An alternative approach for congestion control is to subject all connections to an admission control mechanism and police the offered traffic at the access points to the network [34], [37]. This philosophy is acceptable if one believes that sources can be accurately modeled and their demands can be predicted. The proposed hop-by-hop control mechanism does not make such an assumption. It would work well with or without call admission controls and does not require an *a-priori* characterization of source behavior.

Most of the feedback-based flow control schemes proposed for wide area data networks are *reactive* mechanisms. These systems base their control decisions on the old values of buffer occupancy or traffic conditions and exclude any considerations of the predicted future state of the system. Theoretical results reported in [11] prove that oscillations are inevitable for a fairly general form of feedback based controls due to the delay in the feedback. To improve the performance of time-delayed control systems, special control strategies, called model-based predictive controls, have been developed in the field of process control [36].

In a model-based predictive strategy, a controller uses a model of the controlled system to compute the value of the output so as to satisfy some objective function. If the model is reasonably accurate, the performance of a predictive control scheme is better than that of a purely feedback control scheme. This is because decisions are made based on a predicted future system state and not on the old state of the system. In a model-based predictive control system, feedback messages are used to compensate for prediction errors or inaccuracies in the model so as to minimize the drift of the model from the real state of the system.

The first use of predictive control mechanisms for congestion control is reported in [22] and [23]. The control strategy used was a split-range control. The horizon of control was one time step with only one decision being taken per round trip time. The evolution of the queue was predicted with a model-based fluid approximation while the service rate was predicted using a moving average estimator. The predictive control mechanism used in this paper was first presented in [29] and derives from our experience in designing the control mechanisms described in [22] and [23].

In recent years, other researchers have examined the utility of using predictive control mechanisms for congestion control. An end-to-end predictive model-based control strategy is investigated in [20]. Instead of using feedback from switches, the bottleneck rates are estimated in this scheme by a *novel* packet-pair probe mechanism. The goal of the control policy is to drive the buffer occupancy at a future point to a particular value. The queue occupancy at the bottleneck is estimated using a fluid model. Two filters are used for predicting the service rate, a Kalman filter and a fuzzy exponential predictor. An end-to-end predictive control mechanism is reported in [4] that uses an ARMAX model to predict the queue occupancy and attempts to keep the queue occupancy at a setpoint. The parameters of the model are updated using feedback information. A hop-by-hop predictive control mechanism is described in [33] that uses an ARMA model to predict the service rates and a fluid model to predict the queue occupancy. A hop-by-hop predictive control scheme based on packet dropping is described in [2].

VI. CONCLUSIONS

In this paper, we have described a novel hop-by-hop backpressure mechanism for controlling congestion in a packet switched network. We have used an analytical model to prove that the expected value of the queue occupancy and throughput of a controlled connection converge to the desired operating point. We have also studied the variation of the queue occupancy and throughput in steady-state as well as the transient response. The analytical results provide insights into how the parameter values chosen affect performance. We have used simulations to compare the performance of the scheme with an equivalent end-to-end control scheme. Our analytical and simulation results show that the hop-by-hop scheme reacts faster to changes in the traffic intensity and, consequently, utilizes resources at the bottleneck better and loses fewer packets than the end-to-end scheme.

The analytical and simulation results discussed in this paper and in our related work [19], [29], [27] shows that the following popular beliefs about hop-by-hop controls are really myths.

- Myth #1 *Hop-by-hop control is inherently unstable:* It is often stated that hop-by-hop control results in unstable behavior because it causes congestion to spread and results in large oscillations in buffer occupancy. We have found no theoretical or experimental evidence to support these beliefs. We have used simulations to study the behavior for a variety of network configurations and traffic conditions [19], [29], [27]. In none of these experiments have we observed any unstable behavior. When a node became congested, the congestion remained localized and no catastrophic traffic conditions occurred. This fear of instability may stem from past experience with nondiscriminatory on–off type controls and does not seem relevant to the scheme we propose. Theoretical results reported in [11] prove that oscillations in buffer occupancy are inevitable for a fairly general form of feed-back based controls due to the delay in the feedback. Our analytical and simulation results show that the oscillations that do occur with the HBH scheme are small and are quickly damped.

- Myth #2 *Back pressure is slow:* Another common belief about hop-by-hop control is that the source takes a long time to react to changes in network conditions. As is clear from the analytical results discussed in Section III, the time taken by the source to adjust to changes in capacity is less than a few end-to-end round trip times, for typical parameter values. In general, the responsiveness of the control is determined by the exact nature of the controller and the parameter values that are used.

The proposed hop-by-hop scheme requires that each packet switch generate information about buffer occupancy and enforce current service rates per traffic stream. The current generation of commercial ATM offerings features switches that implement per-connection queuing, e.g., the FORE ASX-200E switch, the DEC AN2 switch etc. Once the per-connection queuing and associated bookkeeping operations are implemented, it is but a small step computationally to do rate-based control. The solution being proposed does use a shared buffer pool of free buffers and can, therefore, be implemented in a cost-effective manner. Moreover, with the HBH scheme, fewer acknowledgment packets need to be sent by the transport layer component at the receiver because these packets do not serve any clocking functions in contrast to the role played in end-to-end control schemes such as TCP. Also, in applications where a forward error-correction method is used or where the data has real-time significance, one could suppress acknowledgment traffic without affecting flow control.

With a fixed buffer setpoint, the establishment of a new connection at a switch causes an increase in the total number of occupied buffers at the switch. When the number of buffers available at a switch is shared among all the active connections, an adaptive scheme may be used to decide the buffer setpoint value. We explore this idea in [29]. In a homogeneous environment where all switches employ HBH controls, there is no reason to use additional end-to-end controls at the transport layer. We have shown here that HBH can handle large amounts of data as well as short data bursts better than the corresponding end-to-end scheme. In a heterogeneous environment, some subnetworks may not use HBH controls. In such environments, an end-to-end control is likely to be used at the transport layer. In this environment, the HBH controlled subnetworks may be viewed as single links,

with the virtual service capacity of the link being determined by the HBH control mechanism.

APPENDIX A
PROOF OF STABILITY

In this proof, we will assume with no loss of generality that $d = 1$

$$A_1 = \begin{bmatrix} 1 & -1 & 0 & 0 & 1 & 0 & 0 & \cdots & 0 \\ 0 & -g & 0 & 0 & 0 & 0 & 0 & \cdots & 0 \\ 0 & 0 & \alpha & 0 & 1-\alpha & 0 & 0 & \cdots & 0 \\ 0 & 0 & 0 & 1 & -1 & 0 & 1 & \cdots & 0 \\ \cdot & \cdot & \cdot & \cdot & \cdot & \cdot & \cdot & & \cdot \\ \cdot & \cdot & \cdot & \cdot & \cdot & \cdot & \cdot & & \cdot \end{bmatrix}$$

$$A_2 = \begin{bmatrix} 0 & 0 & 0 & 0 & 0 & 0 & 0 & \cdots & 0 \\ 0 & -g & 0 & 0 & 0 & 0 & 0 & \cdots & 0 \\ 0 & 0 & 0 & 0 & 0 & 0 & 0 & \cdots & 0 \\ 0 & 0 & 0 & 0 & 0 & 0 & 0 & \cdots & 0 \\ 0 & 0 & 0 & -g & 0 & 0 & 0 & \cdots & 0 \\ \cdot & \cdot & \cdot & \cdot & \cdot & \cdot & \cdot & & \cdot \\ \cdot & \cdot & \cdot & \cdot & \cdot & \cdot & \cdot & & \cdot \end{bmatrix}.$$

A_3 through A_{j-1} are identical to A_2

$$A_j = \begin{bmatrix} 0 & 0 & 0 & 0 & 0 & 0 & 0 \\ -g & -g & 1+j*g & 0 & 0 & 0 & 0 \\ 0 & 0 & 0 & 0 & 0 & 0 & 0 \\ 0 & 0 & 0 & 0 & 0 & 0 & 0 \\ 0 & 0 & 0 & -g & -g & 1+j*g & \cdot \\ \cdot & \cdot & \cdot & \cdot & \cdot & \cdot & \cdot \end{bmatrix}.$$

From (9), we may express the characteristic polynomial of A (after some algebra) as

$$P(A) = |M|$$

where

$$M = A_j + \lambda.A_{j-1} + \lambda^2.A_{j-2} + ... + \lambda^{j-1}A_1 - \lambda^j.I.$$

We may express M as

$$\begin{bmatrix} C & D & 0 & \cdots & 0 \\ 0 & C & D & \cdots & 0 \\ 0 & 0 & C & \cdots & 0 \\ \cdot & \cdot & \cdot & \cdot & \cdot \\ \cdot & \cdot & \cdot & \cdot & \cdot \end{bmatrix}$$

from which we obtain

$$P(A) = P(C)^n.$$

$P(C)$ may be written as

$$[\lambda^{j-1} - \lambda^j][-g(1 + \lambda + ... + \lambda^{j-1}) - \lambda^j][\alpha.\lambda^{j-1} - \lambda^j] + \lambda^{j-1}.g.(\alpha.\lambda^{j-1} - \lambda^j).$$

This expression may be simplified after some algebra to

$$\lambda^{3j-2}.(-\lambda + \alpha).[\lambda + (g-1)].$$

Since the eigenvalues of A are the roots of the characteristic polynomial, the only nonzero eigenvalues are α and $1 - g$.

Appendix B
Derivation of Expressions Describing Evolution of State Following a Decrease in Bottleneck Capacity

We first consider the evolution of the arrival rate and the queue occupancy at the bottleneck. Since the decrease in service capacity at the bottleneck occurs at time K^0, we have

$$\mu_k^{B+1} = C - \Delta_C, \quad \forall k > K^0. \tag{17}$$

The previous node $(B-1)$ receives the information about the decrease in $\mu_{K^0}^{B+1}$ at time step $K^0 + j + 1$ (see Fig. 1). Prior to this, the value of μ_k^{B+1} was C and, hence, we may write

$$x_k^B = x_{k-1}^B + (\Delta_C).d, \quad \forall k \in (K^0, K^0 + j + 1). \tag{18}$$

After receiving the new information at time step $(K^0 + j + 1)$, node $(B-1)$ computes its sending rate as

$$\lambda_{K^0+j+1}^B = \frac{x^* - \hat{x}_{K^0+j+1}^B}{d}.g + \hat{\mu}_{K^0+j+1}^{B+1}. \tag{19}$$

Since α is equal to one, we may write from (3)

$$\hat{\mu}_{K^0+j+1}^{B+1} = C - \Delta_C \tag{20}$$

and from (4) and (20)

$$x^* - \hat{x}_{K^0+j+1}^B = -d.(\Delta_C).(j+1)$$
$$\Rightarrow \frac{x^* - \hat{x}_{K^0+j+1}^B}{d}.g = -g*(j+1)*(\Delta_C)$$
$$= a^1 \text{ say}$$
$$\Rightarrow \lambda_{K^0+j+1}^B = C - \Delta_C + a^1$$
$$\Rightarrow \mu_{K^0+j+1}^B = C - \Delta_C + a^1,$$
$$\text{since } \mu_{K^0+j+1}^{B-1} \text{ equals } C.$$

Similarly, we can write

$$\mu_{K^0+j+2}^B = C - \Delta_C + a^1(1-g)$$
$$\mu_{K^0+j+3}^B = C - \Delta_C + a^1(1-g)^2. \tag{21}$$

Using (12), (21), and the linearized version of (1), we may write

$$x_k^B = x_{k-1}^B + d.a^1.(1-g)^{k-(K^0+j+2)}$$
$$\forall k > K^0 + j + 1. \tag{22}$$

Equations (22) and (21) define the evolution of the queue occupancy and the arrival rate at the bottleneck, respectively.

We next consider the evolution of the queue occupancy and the arrival rate at the node before the bottleneck. The information about the decrease in the sending rate of node $B-1$ is received by node $B-2$ at time $K^0 + 2.j + 2$ (see Fig. 1). At this instant, it computes the sending rate as

$$\lambda_{K^0+2.j+2}^{B-1} = \frac{x^* - \hat{x}_{K^0+2.j+2}^{B-1}}{d}.g + \hat{\mu}_{K^0+2.j+2}^B.$$

As before, we may write

$$\hat{\mu}_{K^0+2.j+2}^B = C - \Delta_C + a^1$$

and

$$x^* - \hat{x}_{K^0+2.j+2}^{B-1} = x^* - x_{K^0+j+2}^{B-1}$$
$$- \sum_{k=0}^{j-1} (\mu_{K^0+j+2+k}^{B-1}$$
$$- \hat{\mu}_{K^0+j+2+k}^B).d$$
$$= x^* - (x^* + d.(\Delta_C - a^1)$$
$$+ d.(j.\Delta_C - j.a^1)$$
$$= -d.(\Delta_C - a^1)(j+1)$$
$$\Rightarrow \frac{x^* - \hat{x}_{K^0+2.j+2}^{B-1}}{d}.g = -g*(j+1)*(\Delta_C - a^1)$$
$$= a^{2'} \text{ say}$$
$$\Rightarrow \lambda_{K^0+2j+2}^{B-1} = C - \Delta_C + a^1 + a^{2'}$$
$$= C - \Delta_C + a^2$$
$$\Rightarrow \mu_{K^0+2j+2}^{B-1} = C - \Delta_C + a^2,$$
$$\text{since } \mu_{K^0+2j+2}^{B-2} \text{ equals } C.$$

The remainder of the proof is, however, a little different from the case of the bottleneck node because the sending rate at node $B-1$ is not constant. As before, we may write

$$\lambda_{K^0+2.j+3}^{B-1} = \frac{x^* - \hat{x}_{K^0+2.j+3}^{B-1}}{d}.g + \hat{\mu}_{K^0+2.j+3}^B$$

$$\hat{\mu}_{K^0+2.j+3}^B = C - \Delta_C + a^1(1-g)$$

and

$$x^* - \hat{x}_{K^0+2.j+3}^{B-1} = -d.(j+1)[\Delta_C - a^1.(1-g)]$$
$$+ (a^2 - a^1)$$
$$\Rightarrow \frac{(x^* - \hat{x}_{K^0+2.j+3}^{B-1})}{d}.g = -g.(j+1).(\Delta_C - a^1.(1-g))$$
$$- g.(a^2 - a^1)$$
$$= -g.(j+1).(\Delta_C - a^1) - g.a^2$$
$$+ g.a^1 - (j+1).a^1.g^2$$
$$= a^{2'} - g.a^2 + g.a^1 - (j+1).a^1.g^2$$
$$\Rightarrow \lambda_{K^0+2j+3}^{B-1} = C - \Delta_C + a^1.(1-g) + a^{2'}$$
$$- g.a^2 + g.a^1 - (j+1).a^1.g^2$$
$$= C - \Delta_C + a^2 - g.a^2$$
$$- (j+1).a^1.g^2$$
$$\approx C - \Delta_C + a^2(1-g).$$

In similar fashion, we can derive the expressions for the evolution of the sending rate at earlier nodes. Thus, we may write

$$\mu_k^{B-m} = C, \text{ if } z < K^{m+1}$$
$$\approx C - \Delta_C + a^{m+1}.(1-g)^{k-K^{m+1}} \text{ otherwise.}$$

From (8) and (12) it can be easily shown that the queue occupancy evolution at the node m steps before the bottleneck is given by (13).

APPENDIX C
DERIVATION OF EXPRESSIONS DESCRIBING EVOLUTION OF STATE FOLLOWING AN INCREASE IN BOTTLENECK CAPACITY

As in the previous derivation, we first consider the evolution of the arrival rate at the bottleneck (node B). Since the new service capacity at the bottleneck $C + \Delta_C$ is exceeded (due to the linear probe up) at time P^0, the previous node $(i - 1)$ receives this information at time step $P^0 + j + 1$ (see Fig. 1). Prior to this, the sending rate was being linearly probed up and, hence, we may write

$$\mu_k^{B-1} = M + \delta * [k - K^0 + B(j+1) + l],$$
$$\text{if } K^0 + B(j+1) + l < k < P^0 + j + 1.$$

Thus, we may write

$$x_k^B = x_{k-1}^B + (M + \delta * [(k-1) - K^0 + B(j+1) + l] - (C + \Delta_C).d, \ \forall l \in (P^0, P^0 + j + 1).$$

After receiving the new information at time step $(P^0 + j + 1)$, node $B - 1$ computes its sending rate as

$$\lambda_{P^0+j+1}^B = \frac{(x^* - \hat{x}_{P^0+j+1}^B)}{d}.g + \hat{\mu}_{P^0+j+1}^{B+1}.$$

We have

$$\hat{\mu}_{P^0+j+1}^{B+1} = C + \Delta_C$$

and

$$x^* - \hat{x}_{P^0+j+1}^B = x^* - x_{P^0+1}^B$$
$$- \sum_{l=0}^{j-1} (\mu_{P^0+1+k}^B - \hat{\mu}_{P^0+1+k}^{B+1}.d)$$
$$= x^* - d.[(C' + \lceil \frac{C + \Delta_C - C'}{\delta} \rceil.\delta$$
$$- (C + \Delta_C))(j + 1)$$
$$+ \delta.(1 + 2.. + j)]$$
$$\Rightarrow \frac{(x^* - \hat{x}_{P^0+j+1}^B)}{d}.g = g * \frac{x^*}{d}$$
$$- g.[(C' + \lceil \frac{C + \Delta_C - C'}{\delta} \rceil.\delta$$
$$- (C + \Delta_C))(j + 1)$$
$$+ \delta.(1 + 2.. + j)]$$
$$v = b^1 \text{ say}$$
$$\Rightarrow \lambda_{P^0+j+1}^B = C + \Delta_C + b^1$$
$$\Rightarrow \mu_{P^0+j+1}^B = C + \Delta_C + b^1.$$

Similarly, we can write

$$\mu_{P^0+j+2}^B = C + \Delta_C + b^1(1 - g)$$
$$\mu_{P^0+j+3}^B = C + \Delta_C + b^1(1 - g)^2.$$

We can write for the previous node

$$\lambda_{P^0+2.j+2}^{B-1} = \frac{x^* - \hat{x}_{P^0+2.j+2}^{B-1}}{d}.g + \hat{\mu}_{P^0+2.j+2}^B.$$

As before

$$\hat{\mu}_{P^0+2.j+2}^{B-1} = C + \Delta_C + b^1 \quad (23)$$

and

$$x^* - \hat{x}_{P^0+2.j+2}^{B-1} = x^* - x_{P^0+j+2}^{B-1}$$
$$- \sum_{k=0}^{j-1} (\mu_{P^0+j+2+k}^{B-1} - \hat{\mu}_{P^0+j+2+k}^{B+1}).d$$
$$\Rightarrow \frac{(x^* - \hat{x}_{P^0+j+2}^i)}{d}.g = g * \frac{x^*}{d}$$
$$- g.(j + 1)[C' + \lceil \frac{C + \Delta_C - C'}{\delta} \rceil.\delta$$
$$- (C + \Delta_C) + b^1] + \delta.(1..j)$$
$$= b^{2'} \text{ say.}$$
$$\Rightarrow \lambda_{P^0+j+2}^{B-1} = C + \Delta_C + b^1 + b^{2'}$$
$$= C + \Delta_C + b^2.$$

In a manner similar to the previous proof, we can now show that the sending rate at each node is given by (15).

ACKNOWLEDGMENT

The authors would like to thank J.-C. Bolot and L. Shi for many useful discussions.

REFERENCES

[1] E. Altman, F. Baccelli, and J.-C. Bolot, "Discrete-time analysis of adaptive rate control mechanisms," in *Proc. 5th Int. Conf. Data Commun. Syst. Performance*, Raleigh, NC, 1993.
[2] J. Amenyo, A. A. Lazar, and G. Pacifici, "Proactive cooperative scheduling and buffer management for multimedia networks," *Multimedia Syst.*, vol. 1, no. 1, 1993.
[3] D. Bertsekas and R. Gallagher, *Data Networks*. Englewood Cliffs, NJ: Prentice-Hall, 1992.
[4] J. Bolot, "A self-tuning regulator for adaptive overload control in communication networks," in *Proc. 31st IEEE Conf. Decision Control*, Tucson, Arizona, Dec. 1992.
[5] J. Bolot and A. U. Shankar, "A discrete-time stochastic approach to flow control dynamics," in *Proc. IEEE GLOBECOM*, Orlando, Florida, Dec. 1992.
[6] D. R. Cheriton, "Sirpent: A high-performance internetworking approach," in *Proc. ACM SIGCOMM*, Austin, TX, Sept. 1989, pp. 158–169.
[7] D. D. Clark, S. Shenker, and L. Zhang, "Supporting real-time applications in an integrated services packet network: Architecture and mechanism," in *Proc. ACM SIGCOMM*, Baltimore, MD, 1992, pp. 14–26.
[8] A. Erramilli and L. J. Forys, "Traffic synchronization effects in teletraffic systems," in *Teletraffic and Datatraffic in a Period of Change*, A. Jensen and V. B. Iversen, Eds. Copenhagen, Denmark: North-Holland, 1991, pp. 201–206.
[9] M. Schroeder *et al.*, "Autonet: A high-speed, self-configuring local area network using point-to-point links," *IEEE J. Select. Areas Commun.*, pp. 1318–1335, Oct. 1991.
[10] K. W. Fendick and M. A. Rodrigues, "An adaptive framework for dynamic access to bandwidth at high speed," in *Proc. ACM SIGCOMM*, Baltimore, MD, Sept. 1993.
[11] K. W. Fendick, M. A. Rodrigues, and A. Weiss, "Analysis of a rate-based feedback control strategy for long haul data transport," *Performance Evaluation*, 1992.
[12] D. Ferrari and D. Verma, "A scheme for real-time channel establishment in wide-area networks," *IEEE J. Select. Areas Commun.*, vol. 8, pp. 368–379, Apr. 1990.
[13] S. J. Golestani, "A stop-and-go queueing framework for congestion management," in *Proc. ACM SIGCOMM*, Philadelphia, PA, Sept. 1990, pp. 8–18.
[14] G. C. Goodwin and K. S. Sin, *Adaptive Filtering Prediction And Control*. Englewood Cliffs, NJ: Prentice-Hall, 1984.
[15] J. M. Hyman, A. A. Lazar, and G. Pacifici, "Real time scheduling with quality of service constraints," *IEEE J. Select. Areas Commun.*, vol. 9, pp. 1052–1063, Sept. 1991.

[16] V. Jacobson, "Congestion avoidance and control," in *Proc. ACM SIG-COMM*, Stanford, California, Aug. 1988.

[17] R. Jain, "Congestion control in computer networks: Issues and trends," *IEEE Network Mag.*, vol. 4, no. 3, pp. 24–30, May 1990.

[18] C. R. Kalmanek, H. Kanakia, and S. Keshav, "Rate controlled servers for very high-speed networks," in *Proc. IEEE GLOBECOM*, San Diego, CA, Dec. 1990.

[19] H. Kanakia, S. Keshav, and P. P. Mishra, "A comparison of congestion control schemes," in *Proc. Fourth Ann. Workshop Very High Speed Networks*, Baltimore, MD, Mar. 1993.

[20] S. Keshav, "A control theoretic approach to flow control," in *Proc. ACM SIGCOMM*, Sept. 1991, submitted to *ACM Trans. Comput. Syst.*

[21] L. Kleinrock, *Queueing Systems — Computer Applications*, vol. 2. New York: Wiley, 1976.

[22] K. Ko, P. P. Mishra, and S. K. Tripathi, "Predictive congestion control in high-speed wide area networks," in *Protocols for High-Speed Networks, II*, Johnson, Ed.   Amsterdam, The Netherlands: North Holland, 1991.

[23] _____, "Interaction among virtual-circuits using predictive congestion control," *Comput. Networks ISDN Syst.*, Jan. 1993.

[24] H. T. Kung and A. Chapman, "The FCVC proposal for ATM networks: A summary," in *Proc. Int. Conf. Network Protocols*, Oct. 1993.

[25] S. Lavenberg, *Computer Performance Modeling Handbook - Generation Methods For Discrete Event Simulation*.   New York: Academic, 1983, pp. 223-268.

[26] A. Mankin, "Random drop congestion control," in *Proc. ACM SIG-COMM'90*, Philadelphia, PA, Sept 1990, pp. 1–7.

[27] P. P. Mishra, *Congestion Control in High Speed Integrated Service Networks*, Ph.D. dissertation, University of Maryland, College Park, Sept. 1993.

[28] P. P. Mishra and H. Kanakia, "A hop by hop rate based congestion control scheme," AT&T Bell Labs, Tech. memo., 1992.

[29] _____, "A hop by hop rate based congestion control scheme," in *Proc. ACM SIGCOMM*, Baltimore, MD, Aug. 1992.

[30] D. Mitra, "Dynamic adaptive windows for high speed data networks: Theory and simulations," in *Proc. ACM SIGCOMM*, Philadelphia, PA, Sept. 1990, pp. 20–30.

[31] B. Noble, *Applied Linear Algebra*.   Englewood Cliffs, NJ: Prentice-Hall, 1969.

[32] K. K. Ramakrishnan and R. Jain, "A binary feedback scheme for congestion avoidance in computer networks," *ACM Trans. Comput. Syst.*, vol. 8, no. 2, pp. 158–181, May 1990.

[33] G. Ramamurthy and B. Sengupta, "A predictive congestion control policy for broadband integrated wide area networks," in *Proc. IEEE INFOCOM*, San Franscisco, CA, Mar. 1993.

[34] E. Rathgeb, "Modeling and performance comparison of policing mechanisms for ATM networks," *IEEE J. Select. Areas Commun.*, vol. 9, no 3, pp. 325–334, Apr. 1991.

[35] M. Schwartz and L. Shaw, *Signal Processing: Discrete Spectral Analysis, Detection and Estimation*.   New York: McGraw-Hill, 1975.

[36] D. Seborg, T. Edgar, and D. Mellichamp, *Process Dynamics and Control*.   New York: Wiley, 1989.

[37] M. Sidi, W. Liu, I. Cidon, and I. Gopal, "Congestion control through input rate regulation," in *Proc. IEEE GLOBECOM*, Dallas, Texas, Nov. 1989, pp. 1764–1768.

[38] H. Watson and J. Blackstone, *Computer Simulation*.   New York: Wiley, 1989.

Partho Pratim Mishra (M'95) received the B.Tech. degree from the Indian Institute of Technology, Kharagpur, India, in 1988, and the M.S. and Ph.D. degrees from the University of Maryland, College Park, in 1991 and 1993, respectively, all in computer science.

He is currently a Member of the Technical Staff in the Networked Computing Research Department at AT&T Bell Laboratories, Murray Hill, NJ. His research interests are in the design and analysis of integrated service networks.

Hemant Kanakia (M'89) received the B.Tech. degree from the Indian Institute of Technology, Bombay, India, in 1975, and the Ph.D. degree from Stanford University, CA, in 1990.

He is currently a Member of the Technical Staff in the Computing Science Research Center at AT&T Bell Laboratories, Murray Hill, NJ. His research interests are in the design of integrated service networks, packet video services, and packet switching systems.

Satish K. Tripathi (M'86–SM'86) received the Ph.D. degree in computer science from the University of Toronto. He attended the Banaras Hindu University, the Indian Statistical Institute, the University of Alberta, and the University of Toronto.

He is a Professor in the Department of Computer Science at the University of Maryland, College Park. He has been on the faculty at the University of Maryland since 1978 and served as the Department Chair from 1988 to 1995. For the past 20 years, he has been actively involved in research related to performance evaluation, networks, real-time systems, and fault tolerance. He has more than a hundred papers in international journals and referred conferences. In the networking area, his current projects are on mobile computing, ATM networks, and operating systems support for multimedia information. In the real-time domain he has been working on language design, fault tolerance and predictive communication protocols. He has served as the member of the Program Committee and Program Chairman for various international conferences. He has guest edited special issues of many journals and serves on the editorial boards of *Theoretical Computer Science*, *ACM/Springer Multimedia Systems*, and IEEE TRANSACTIONS ON COMMUNICATIONS. He has edited books in the areas of performance evaluation and parallel computing.

Neural Networks for Adaptive Traffic Control in ATM Networks

Neural networks have several valuable properties for implementing ATM traffic control. The authors present NN-based solutions for two problems arising in connection admission control, affecting the GOS at both the cell and call levels, and propose that neural networks may increase the network throughput and revenue.

Ernst Nordström, Jakob Carlström, Olle Gällmo, and Lars Asplund

uture broadband integrated services digital networks (B-ISDNs) will be based on the Asynchronous Transfer Mode (ATM) technology. ATM is a packet- and connection-oriented switching and multiplexing technique that is designed to support a wide variety of services with different traffic characteristics and grade of service (GoS) requirements at the cell and call levels. Bandwidth flexibility, the capability to handle services in a uniform way, and the possible use of statistical multiplexing are advantageous properties of ATM.

In order to meet the GoS expectations of network users (e.g., in terms of cell loss probability and call blocking probability) the use of network resources at cell and call levels must be carefully controlled. Moreover, resources should be handled so that the network operator revenue is maximized over time. Two types of cell traffic control mechanisms are expected in ATM networks — preventive and reactive traffic control. Preventive traffic control is most important for real-time services, and consists of connection admission control (CAC) and traffic enforcement.

Neural Networks (NNs) have several properties that are valuable when implementing ATM traffic control. First, NNs can implement direct adaptive control, tailored to the actual characteristics of the cell and/or call traffic. No explicit model of the traffic is needed, as in traditional methods, only a good representation of the problem. Second, the parallel structure of NNs can be exploited in hardware implementations, which provides short and predictable response times.

In this article, the authors present NN-based solutions for two problems arising in CAC, which affect the GoS at both the cell and call levels. We argue that NNs may increase the network throughput and revenue, and point out their potential for bursty, non-interactive call traffic.

ERNST NORDSTRÖM is working on his Ph.D. at Uppsala University.

JAKOB CARLSTRÖM is working on his Ph.D. at Uppsala University.

OLLE GÄLLMO is working on his Ph.D. at Uppsala University.

LARS ASPLUND is an associate professor at Uppsala University.

ATM Traffic Control

The nature of ATM makes traffic control a challenging task. In ATM, user cells are asynchronously multiplexed onto high capacity links according to actual communication needs. Calls allocate network resources only virtually, and statistical gain is possible when users are bursty, i.e., they alternate between active and silent states. At the switching nodes, output buffers are required to resolve switching conflicts which arise when several cells are switched simultaneously to the same destination link. However, when too many cells arrive at the same time, or if switching conflicts arise repeatedly, the buffer will saturate and subsequent cells must be discarded. The probability of cell loss is therefore an important GoS measure in an ATM network. The buffer queues also affect the cell delay and cell delay variation, which are important GoS measures for real-time traffic.

Traffic control in ATM networks is likely to be implemented in a multilevel architecture (Fig. 1), which separates the control at the network, call, and cell levels [1]. The network level allocates resources to virtual paths, given the offered call traffic and tolerated call blocking probabilities. The virtual path concept allows several calls to be switched and handled together, which simplifies CAC, but decreases the network utilization, in particular if the path capacities are reserved deterministically. The call level performs CAC within the path network and allocates bandwidth and switch buffer capacity to individual calls. The cell level allocates resources during the cell transfer phase, and is responsible for cell traffic enforcement at access switches and arbitration of cells during switch overload.

Connection Admission Control

The objective of CAC is to restrict the access of new calls so that the cell- and call-level GoS is maintained within the path network. An additional objective is to maximize the network

Reprinted from IEEE Communications Magazine, October, 1995, pp. 43-49.

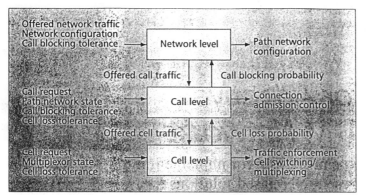

Offered network traffic
Network configuration
Call blocking tolerance → Network level → Path network configuration

Offered call traffic ← → Call blocking probability

Call request
Path network state
Call blocking tolerance
Cell loss tolerance → Call level → Connection admission control

Offered cell traffic ← → Cell loss probability

Cell request
Multiplexor state
Cell loss tolerance → Cell level → Traffic enforcement
Cell switching/
multiplexing

■ **Figure 1.** *Multilevel traffic control in ATM networks.*

revenue over time. The CAC is implemented by routing, link allocation, and link admission control (LAC).

Routing

The purpose of the routing function is to find an economical route among a set of possible route alternatives (called a route network), connecting the origin-destination node pair. The route network may contain all acyclic path sequences between the two nodes. Here, we assume that the route is selected in a two-step procedure. First, each alternative in the route network is investigated to see if it is feasible, i.e., can offer sufficient cell level GoS to the new call as well as to already established calls. Then, all feasible routes are examined to find the route that is most economical in terms of long-term revenue, under the constraint that the call-level GoS is maintained.

A solution to the revenue analysis problem is presented in [2]. The network is modeled as a controlled Markov process, where the Markov state is given be the active network calls. Dynamic programming techniques are used to formulate a state-dependent routing strategy, given an explicit model of the decision task. In order to reduce the computational complexity, the load and revenue generation on successive links/paths are assumed to be independent. More naturally, the load and revenue generation on parallel links/paths are also assumed to be independent. The proposed method is near-optimal when the offered call traffic has Poisson arrivals and exponentially distributed holding times. In order to be optimal the method must detect route states where "intelligent blocking" of narrowband calls improves the long-term revenue. This typically occurs when the route has a free capacity that is equal to the size of a wideband call. By rejecting a narrowband call request, bandwidth is reserved for the wideband call type which increases the long-term revenue.

Link Allocation

When the offered call-level traffic volume is large, some of the paths have to use several parallel physical links for cell transport, in order to avoid excessive call blocking. However, due to the path independence assumption, the routing function can solve these *link allocation* tasks separately. In fact, link allocation involves the same

steps as in routing, i.e., first find the feasible links and then the link which maximizes the long-term revenue. The model-based dynamic programming method [2] is again applicable, with the same assumptions on independence between load and revenue generation on parallel links, if the link group is large. In this case, each link is analyzed in isolation from the others, and the task is to accept/reject call requests optimally.

In this article, we present two NN-based alternatives to the model-based dynamic programming method. The rationale is that assumption on Poisson call arrivals and exponential holding times is only valid for interactive services. But a flexible solution to the ATM traffic control problem must also manage non-Poisson arrivals and other holding-time distributions, which can arise in the B-ISDN.

Link Admission Control

The task of LAC is to maintain the cell- and call-level GoS while using link resources as efficiently as possible. LAC with respect to cell and call-level GoS is performed when determining the set of feasible paths, and maximizing the long-term revenue, respectively.

A route is feasible if the end-to-end cell transport performance is acceptable to the new and already established calls. For computational reasons, the performance is usually evaluated link by link and the change in cell burstiness due to multiplexing at previous switches is neglected.

The total traffic stream offered to an ATM multiplexer is usually analyzed in two time scales, called the cell scale and the burst scale. The cell scale considers queue build-up (congestion) at the switch output buffer due to simultaneous cell arrivals. The burst scale considers queue build-up due to fluctuations in the total arrival rate, which may exceed the link capacity during some periods. The cell scale is typically neglected when evaluating congestion, since the buffer can be dimensioned to resolve the cell scale conflicts.

The burst scale traffic of each call can be modeled as a Markov process with two states, corresponding to an active source state, where cells are generated at a constant peak rate, and a silent source state where no cells are generated. The duration of the active period is chosen so that the Markov process represents the worst case output of the traffic enforcement function. The queue build-up of a multiplexer loaded with two state Markov sources can be analyzed using the fluid flow queueing model [1]. The performance measures (e.g., cell loss probability) derived from this model are very accurate but require large computational efforts, which prevents them from being used in real-time CAC. The main problem is that the number of states of the aggregate traffic process increases exponentially with the number of calls. One conventional solution approach is therefore to find and analyze a simpler traffic process with similar dynamics. Another approach is to analyze the original traffic process using analytical upper bounds on the congestion probability. However, the approximations result in over-restrictive CAC and prevents optimal use of network resources.

Here, we describe a hybrid approach, based on NNs and analytical approximations, which improves the resource utilization.

Neural Network Learning

A Neural Network (NN) is a non-linear function approximator that maps input vectors to output vectors. Structurally, an NN consists of many simple interconnected processing elements that cooperate to produce an output value. A processing element receives input from the environment and/or the other processing elements. The inputs of a processing element are mapped to a scalar output value by a simple function: a weighted sum of the inputs passed through an activation function. The processing elements communicate their outputs to other elements, or to the environment. The input weights of the processing elements are set according to some learning procedure.

Supervised Learning

In *supervised learning* (Fig. 2a), the environment has apprehension of the target function in the form of a set of input-output vector pairs. For each input, the network produces an output which is then compared to the desired output (target). The learning algorithm tries to minimize the error, i.e., the difference between the target and the actual output, by adjusting the network weights. The most well known supervised learning algorithm is Back Propagation (e.g., [7]), which in effect implements gradient descent optimization in weight space.

Supervised learning is supervised in the sense that someone has to supply input-target vector pairs which give explicit instructions as to the desired network response. This is most often done off-line (learning phase), until the network is considered to have learned the task. The network is then put into operation (recall phase), where no learning takes place. The goal of the learning phase is to find a mapping which generalizes well to previously unseen data (encountered in the recall phase).

Reinforcement Learning

In control applications there is often a need for an *agent* which can be adaptive on-line, in a closed loop with the environment (Fig. 2b), and learn from its success and/or mistakes rather than from examples of input-output pairs. This is called *reinforcement learning* (RL), and its main property is that the feedback is an evaluation of the environmental state and, therefore, only an indirect evaluation of the agent's actions in this environment.

The agent can be anything from a simple lookup table to a complex system of several collaborating modules, some of which may be neural networks. In any case, the agent is fed with environmental state vectors and produces actions according to some *policy function*, which in turn causes effects in the environment. The only feedback to the agent is a scalar *reward*, and the goal of learning is to find a policy which maximizes the long-term reward it receives.

The policy function is often designed to map states to actions in two stages. First, a *merit func-*

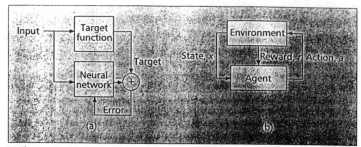

■ **Figure 2.** *(a) Supervised learning and (b) reinforcement learning.*

tion maps states to *merit values*, one for each possible action (assumed to be finitely many). A merit value is an estimate of the relative merit of selecting the corresponding action. An *action selector* then uses these merits to choose an action. In the simplest (deterministic) case the selected action is the one with the highest merit. However, the agent should be allowed to explore its environment, to learn how its actions affect the environment and, consequently, the reward it receives. Therefore, a stochastic action selector is often used, where actions are selected randomly with higher probability of selecting actions with high merits.

To improve its policy, the agent must evaluate the goodness of each action performed. But the total reward obtained gives only the cumulative effect of all actions performed. The agent thus needs a method for assigning credit to individual actions. This is referred to as the *temporal credit assignment problem* and can be solved either implicitly, or by an explicit *evaluation function* in the agent.

Reinforcement Learning by Construction of Hypothetical Targets

A monolithic approach to reinforcement learning, where the agent consists of a sole neural network, is proposed in [5]. The network is used as a merit function and maps state vectors to real valued, *M*-dimensional output vectors of action merits, where *M* is the number of possible actions. The action selector then transforms this merit vector to a binary *action vector* of the same dimensionality, where all values are 0 except the one corresponding to the chosen action, which has a value of 1.

How to train this network is perhaps not obvious. Actions not only affect the current state of the environment, but also future states, which may also depend on other events (e.g., other agents) beyond control. In other words, no target vectors are known at the time of a decision. The only feedback is the reward, which may or may not be available for every action.

The lack of target vectors does not disqualify the use of a supervised training algorithm, however. If it is assumed that the current action will eventually turn out to be a good one, the action vector in itself should be a good *hypothetical target vector* since training on it would enforce the action just taken (pushing the corresponding merit estimate toward 1) and inhibit all others (pushing the merit estimates toward zero). This is called an *optimistic* target vector. Similarly, a *pessimistic* target vector can be constructed

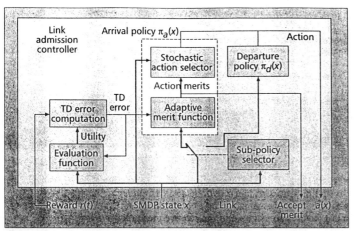

■ **Figure 3.** *The architecture of the modified actor-critic method.*

under the hypothesis that the current action will turn out to be bad. One way to do this is to invert the optimistic one, but better strategies can be found. For example, the pessimistic target vectors can be used to inject rules into the network about actions which, given the current state, are illegal or known to be bad.

The network can not use these target vectors to update its weights directly, since it does not know which one to apply until the reward is received. But, it can use the hypothetical target vectors to accumulate two weight change values for each of its weights, one optimistic and one pessimistic. This can be done using any supervised algorithm. Here, the Back Propagation algorithm (e.g., [7]) is used and the method is therefore called BP_{HT} (Back Propagation on Hypothetical Targets).

The weight changes are accumulated (and discounted) over time until the reward $r \in [-1,1]$ arrives. The sign of r decides whether to use the optimistic or the pessimistic weight change values when updating the weights. Thus, BP_{HT} makes the implicit assumption that if the reward is positive, all actions leading to it were good, and vice versa. This is, of course, not a very good assumption in each single case, but in the long run the bad effects cancel out.

Temporal-Difference Learning

A well-known approach to temporal credit assignment is temporal-difference (TD) methods [3]. These methods have a solid mathematical foundation, closely related to dynamic programming. In TD methods, the total reward expected to be received starting from an environment state is explicitly modeled.

In this work, the actor-critic method is used — Fig. 3 shows the architecture of the variant of this method employed in this work. This method solves the problem of finding an optimal policy by using two function approximators: an evaluation function $eval(x)$ which learns to predict the total future reward $V(x)$ from each state x, given the current policy, and a policy function $\pi(x)$, which indicates what action a to select in each state. For learning, we use the simplest form of TD learning: the TD(0) algorithm. In this algorithm, the agent estimates the total expected

reward from a state, and performs an action according to its present policy. During learning, actions are chosen by a stochastic action selector. The non-zero probability of choosing an action with low merit enables the agent to search for better policies. After learning, actions are chosen deterministically. The algorithm is summarized in Fig. 4.

Performing an action results in a transition to a new state, and an associated immediate reward is received. The difference between the expected total reward in the previous state and the expected total reward in the new state, plus the immediate reward, should then equal zero. If not, the difference is used to update the estimated total reward in the previous state as well as the action merits.

In most applications, representing the total reward function and the policy function exactly is infeasible, because of the amount of time and data storage required for exploring the entire state space completely. A better alternative is to employ parametric function approximators, e.g., neural networks. The neural networks' capability of generalizing between similar input patterns makes the RL agent able to find reasonable estimates in states not visited before, based on experience of similar states.

Neural Networks for Connection Admission Control

Link Admission Control

LAC with respect to cell transport performance is a complex task for which accurate analytical models exist, but they are too complex to be used in a real ATM network. To obtain a practical solution feasible in real-time, a trade-off between computational complexity and evaluation accuracy is needed. NNs offer an alternative to conventional approximation methods and can increase the link utilization if properly applied. The function approximation ability of NNs can be employed to implement accurate performance functions, computed off-line. Moreover, additional performance data can be collected and applied during on-line operation, to compensate for possible errors in the traffic and/or performance model. In [6], a hybrid LAC approach is proposed, based on analytical approximations and supervised NNs, with performance data derived from the accurate fluid flow model [1]. An analytical upper bound on the cell loss probability controls the admission at low links loads, while the NN performs admission at higher loads, where the use of a complex performance model is motivated. The restriction to high load situations speeds up the (off-line) NN learning procedure, and increases the approximation accuracy where actually needed. The input vector to the NN characterizes the aggregate cell arrival rate, and is obtained after preprocessing of the peak cell rate, mean cell rate, and maximum cell burst size parameters of each call. Experiments presented in [6] show that the complementary knowledge supplied by the NN indeed increases the resource utilization.

Link Allocation with BP_{HT}

The BP_{HT} algorithm offers a simple adaptive approach to link allocation. The state vector contains load measures for each of the links and information on the requesting call type. The action vector points out a suitable link for the call. The environment (the switch) generates a reward for every action, equal to +1 if the call fitted where it was placed by the allocator, and -1 otherwise. In the latter case, the call is rejected.

Using this reward scheme, maximizing the long-term reward is to maximize the number of accepted calls. An agent with a poor policy will be forced to reject calls more often than necessary. These rejects will lead to negative reward, pushing the agent away from such decisions (using the pessimistic weight change values). This in itself is not necessarily a good thing, since the reject may have been the only decision possible in the given state. But, due to the accumulation of weight change values, the agent will also be forced away from the previous decisions which lead to the reject situation. Thus, the agent is forced to change its policy by temporal credit assignment.

Experiments on a simple model of the link allocation problem show that BP_{HT} is able to learn this task, reaching a level of performance comparable to conventional (non-adaptive) methods on stationary call inter-arrival and holding time distributions [5]. But, BP_{HT} makes no assumptions on these distributions, and can adapt to changes in them. Furthermore, other (larger) state descriptions than the ones used by the static methods are feasible. For example, the state vector could be extended to include for how long the calls already on the links have been active.

It should also be noted that the allocator is trained by a slight modification of a supervised algorithm, which implies that explicit target information, if available at some time during training, can be used directly. For example, the allocator could be given an initial guess of a good solution by first training it supervised to approximate some conventional method, such as First Fit, and then setting it free to explore by reinforcement learning.

A Temporal-Difference Learning Scheme for Adaptive Link Allocation

In the temporal-difference learning scheme for ATM link allocation presented in [4], the link allocation task is decomposed into a set of link admission control sub-tasks. These sub-tasks are formulated as semi-Markov Decision Problems (SMDPs). A semi-Markov process is a continuous time dynamic system consisting of a countable state set, X, and a finite action set, A. At each state $x \in X$, an action $a \in A$ is applied, resulting in a new state $y \in X$, according to the system-specific transition probabilities. Provided that the next state is y, the time until the transition from x to y occurs follows a state-specific probability distribution. A reward rate $r(t)$ describes the rate of revenue received between the transitions.

Similarly to [2], the reinforcement learning

1. Compute the evaluation function output $eval(x)$ for the current state x.
2. Select and perform an action randomly, according to the action merits. This results in a transition to a new state y, and a reward r associated with the transition.
3. Compute the new evaluation function output $eval(y)$.
4. Update $eval(x)$ by adding a fraction of the TD error $\varepsilon = r + \gamma\, eval(y) - eval(x)$, where $0 < \gamma < 1$ is a learning parameter. If a neural network is used as a function approximator, update the network using the TD error as the output error.
5. Update the policy by adding a fraction of ε to the merit value of the action chosen in x. This increases the probability of selecting actions who turn out to give a higher $eval$ value than expected, and decreases the probability of actions whose $eval$ value is lower than expected.
6. Go to 1.

■ **Figure 4.** *The TD(0) algorithm.*

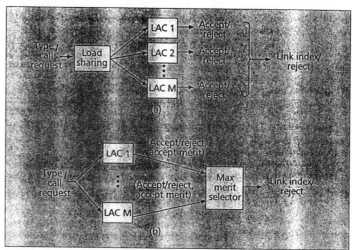

■ **Figure 5.** *Link allocation using the modified actor-critic method; a) during adaptation; b) after adaptation.*

approach in [4] views the link allocation problem as a controlled semi-Markov process, but whereas [2] proposes an indirect approach where the underlying process is modeled explicitly, reinforcement learning solves the problem directly. In the semi-Markov process describing an ATM link, a state x comprises the current number of active calls of each traffic type, and an event descriptor indicates if a call is arriving or departing and identifies the call type of this call. The action set A has two elements: *ACCEPT* and *REJECT*, indicating whether the call arrival or departure is accepted or not. For obvious reasons, a call departure must always be accepted, but by controlling whether arriving calls are accepted or not, a policy which increases the long-term reward can be found. For this reason, the link admission control policy is divided into two sub-policies, an adaptive arrival policy π_a, and a departure policy π_d, which accepts all departures. The motivation for this arrangement is that it allows the evaluation function to be updated also when calls depart, resulting in better estimates and faster and safer convergence. The reward rate is the aggregate cell transmission rate, and the immediate reward received upon a state transition is the integral of this rate, giving the number of cells transmitted on the link since the previous state transition.

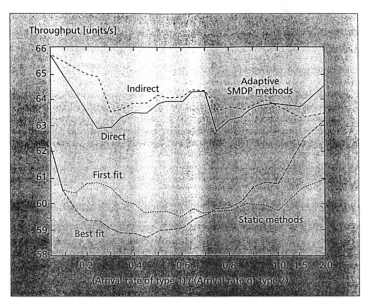

Throughput [units/s]

Figure 6. *Call level throughput vs. arrival rate for different methods. In the simulation, a group of three links, each having a capacity 24 units/s, was offered traffic from two call types. Call type 1 had a bandwidth requirement of 1 unit/s and type 2 bandwidth requirements are 6 units/s. The SMDP methods adapted to the traffic for four adaptation periods, with duration 1000 and 15,000 simulated call arrivals or departures, for the indirect and direct methods, respectively. The throughput values are based on 300,000 arrivals or departures after policy covergence.*

The link admission controllers used (Fig. 3) are based on the actor-critic method [3] and temporal-difference learning, using the TD(0) algorithm. During adaptation, each link admission controller adapts to a constant-rate call flow, in a number of periods (see Fig. 5a). The constant rate is achieved by setting probabilities, called load-sharing coefficients, for selecting the different links within the link group for each traffic type. A selected link admission controller can then accept or reject the call, and learns an optimal policy given the offered traffic. After all LAC policies have converged, new load-sharing coefficients are determined so that more traffic will be offered to links with a relatively high rate of accepting calls during the next adaptation period. After a few (typically three to five) adaptation periods, the load sharing coefficients converge, and the adaptation ends.

After adaptation, the load-sharing policy is abandoned. Instead, on an arrival of a call of some call type, each link is checked to see if it has sufficient free capacity to accept the call. Provided this is the case, the controller selects the action (*ACCEPT* or *REJECT*), which has the highest merit value. The controller outputs the resulting action along with the accept merit value. The link allocator then selects the link with the highest accept merit value (among the links that accept the call) (Fig. 5b). If all the link admission controllers reject the call, so does the link allocator.

As discussed above, neural networks are useful for function approximation when the state space is large. They also allow incorporation of other system parameters, providing the agent with information which may improve its perfor-

mance. However, in the simulations described below, lookup tables were used for function representation.

In [4], the throughput of a link group controlled by the direct SMDP scheme is compared to an indirect, dynamic-programming-based scheme [2], as well as to the First Fit and Best Fit algorithms. The diagram in Fig. 6 shows simulation results from these methods, where they allocate calls of two types with exponentially distributed inter-arrival time and holding time to three links with equal capacity. The aggregate traffic mean load is constant, but the arrival rate ratio is varied. The diagram shows that the adaptive SMDP methods yield up to 7 percent higher long-term revenue than the static methods. The diagram also shows that the direct SMDP scheme yields a performance similar to the indirect scheme's.

Compared to dynamic programming, the reinforcement learning scheme has two main advantages — lower computational complexity and computer memory requirements, and one main disadvantage — a requirement for longer interaction with the system for convergence. In realistic systems, the state space grows large, which makes it very hard to use traditional dynamic programming. By, instead, using reinforcement learning with neural networks for function approximation, this problem can be overcome, due to the neural network's ability to generalize between states. Methods also exist for speeding up the convergence of reinforcement learning.

Summary

*T*raffic control in ATM networks is a challenging task, and a flexible solution is needed to meet the performance requirements of future B-ISDNs. The multi-level control architecture that separates the control in the network, call, and cell levels is assumed in this article. These levels implement control on different time scales, but have strict performance relationships. Here, we focus on the call level, and the realization of two Connection Admission Control sub-functions, which are concerned with cell and call-level GoS control.

Neural networks have features that motivate their use in ATM traffic control. The parallelism, exploited in hardware implementations, enables fast and time-predictable control actions, the adaptability offers independency from traffic and performance models, typically restricting the efficiency of conventional methods.

Conventional methods for LAC with respect to cell level GoS face an accuracy-simplicity dilemma. To obtain implementations that meet the short response time requirements of CAC, approximations must be introduced, that result in over-restrictive CAC, and thereby under-utilization of the network resources. We argue that the function approximation ability of NNs can be employed to implement accurate but complex performance functions, computed off-line. Moreover, performance data can be collected and applied during on-line operation, in order to compensate for modeling errors.

The link allocation problem arises during routing when a virtual path consists of several physical links. The objective of the link allocation function is to maximize the long-term revenue, while maintaining the call-level GoS. A near-optimal solution can be formulated using dynamic programming with an explicit model of the decision task [2]. However, this requires that the offered call traffic has Poisson call arrivals and exponentially distributed holding times.

A flexible solution to the ATM link allocation problem must also manage non-Poisson arrivals and other holding-time distributions, which can arise in the B-ISDN. We have described two adaptive methods based on NNs and reinforcement learning.

In the first method, called BP_{HT}, a single NN is trained on bipolar reward, indicating if the performed link allocation action was a success or failure. For each action, weight changes are computed by supervised training on two hypothetical target vectors, one under the assumption that the action will turn out to be good and one under the opposite assumption. The weight changes are accumulated and discounted over time, and the sign of the reward indicates which one to apply when updating the weights. Future work on the BP_{HT} approach includes a more realistic reward strategy, to exploit BP_{HT}'s ability to switch between reinforcement and supervised learning, and to test the approach in a non-stationary environment.

The second method is a direct (model-free) variant of the model-based dynamic programming method [2]. The proposed method adapts the link allocation policy to the offered call traffic such that long-term revenue is maximized. It decomposes the link allocation task into a set of LAC tasks, formulated as SMDPs. The LAC policies are directly adapted by reinforcement learning, using the temporal-difference learning scheme. Simulations with Poisson call traffic shows that the reinforcement method yields a long-term revenue comparable to the model-based dynamic programming method. The advantage of reinforcement learning is that the computational complexity and computer memory requirements can be reduced by using neural networks for function approximation. In our future work, we will consider link allocation of non-Poisson traffic, thus exploiting this advantage.

References

[1] COST 224, "Performance Evaluation and Design of Multiservice Networks," Final Report, Luxembourg, 1992.
[2] Z. Dziong and L. Mason, "An Analysis of Near Optimal Call Admission Control and Routing Model for Multiservice Loss Networks," *Proc. INFOCOM '92*, Session 2A.1.1, Florence, Italy, May 1992.
[3] A. Barto, R. Sutton, and C. Watkins, "Learning and Sequential Decision Making," Report COINS 89-95, Dept. of Computer and information Science, University of Massachusetts, Amherst, Sept. 1989.
[4] E. Nordström and J. Carlström, "A Reinforcement Learning Scheme for Adaptive Link Allocation in ATM Networks," in J. Alspector, R. Goodman & T. X. Brown (Eds.), *Proc. of the Int'l Workshop on Applications of Neural Networks to Telecommunications 2 (IWANNT-95)*, Stockholm, Sweden, 1995, pp. 88-95.
[5] O. Gällmo and L. Asplund, "Reinforcement Learning by Construction of Hypothetical Targets", in J. Alspector, R. Goodman & T. X. Brown (Eds.), *Proc. of the Int'l Workshop on Applications of Neural Networks to Telecommunications 2 (IWANNT-95)*, Stockholm, Sweden, 1995, pp. 300-307.
[6] H. Brandt *et al.*, A Hybrid Neural Network Approach to ATM Admission Control, *Proc. of the International Switching Symposium (ISS '95)*, p. P.b6, Berlin, April 1995.
[7] J. Hertz, A Krogh, and R. G. Palmer, "Introduction to the Theory of Neural Computation," (Redwood City, CA: Addison-Wesley, 1991).

Biographies

ERNST NORDSTRÖM received an M.Sc. in engineering physics from Uppsala University in 1991. He is currently working on his Ph.D. at the department of computer systems, Uppsala University, Sweden. His research focuses on traffic control and resource allocation in broadband telecommunications, with the application of neural networks a major interest.

JAKOB CARLSTRÖM received an M.Sc. in engineering physics from Uppsala University in 1994. He is currently working on his Ph.D. at the department of computer systems, Uppsala University, under the supervision of Lars Asplund. For his thesis he is looking at applications of neural networks and reinforcement learning to resource allocation problems in broadband telecommunication networks.

OLLE GÄLLMO received an M.Sc. in computer science from Uppsala University in 1991 and is currently working on his Ph.D.. His main interests are neural network learning algorithms in general and reinforcement learning in particular. He has also been involved in a project on pulse coded hardware implementation of neural networks.

LARS ASPLUND [M '93] is an associate professor at the department of computer system and head of the department at Uppsala University. He leads two research groups. One in artificial neural networks; hardware implementations and applications in telecom. The other research is in distributed real-time system; hardware implementations of run time systems and high speed communications. He received a B.Sc. from Uppsala University in 1972 and a Ph.D. in 1977.

Traffic control in ATM networks is a challenging task, and a flexible solution is needed to meet the performance requirements of future B-ISDNs.

ELSEVIER

Computer Networks and ISDN Systems 28 (1996) 453–469

COMPUTER
NETWORKS
and
ISDN SYSTEMS

A flexible traffic shaper for high speed networks: design and comparative study with leaky bucket

S. Radhakrishnan [a], S.V. Raghavan [a,*], Ashok K. Agrawala [b]

[a] *Department of Computer Science and Engineering, Indian Institute of Technology, Madras, India*
[b] *Institute for Advanced Computer Studies and Department of Computer Science, University of Maryland, College Park, MD, USA*

Abstract

Maximizing bandwidth utilization and providing performance guarantees, in the context of multimedia networking, are two incompatible goals. Heterogeneity of the multimedia sources calls for effective traffic control schemes to satisfy their diverse Quality of Service (QoS) requirements. These include admission control at connection set up, *traffic control* at the source ends and efficient scheduling schemes at the switches. The emphasis in this paper is on traffic control at the source end.

Most multimedia sources are bursty in nature. Traffic shapers have been mainly studied hitherto from the point of view of their effectiveness in smoothing the burstiness. The Leaky Bucket (LB) scheme, to cite an example, is a mean rate policer smoothing at the token generation rate. Studies on bursty sources show that burstiness promotes statistical multiplexing at the cost of possible congestion. Smoothing, on the other hand, helps in providing guarantees at the cost of utilization. Thus need for a flexible scheme which can provide a reasonable compromise between utilization and performance is imminent. Recent studies have also questioned the suitability of LB for policing real-time traffic due to the excessive delays. We argue for a policy which is less stringent on short term burstiness than the LB.

We propose a new traffic shaper which can adjust the burstiness of the input traffic to obtain reasonable bandwidth utilization while maintaining statistical service guarantees. The performance study is conducted in two parts. In the first part, we study the effect of varying the shaper parameters on the input characteristics. In the second part, we dimension our scheme and a LB equivalently and compare the mean and peak rate policing behavior with delay and loss as the performance parameters. Adopting a less stringent attitude towards short term burstiness is shown to result in considerable advantage while policing real-time traffic. Future research possibilities in this topic are explored.

Keywords: High-speed networks; Congestion control; Traffic shaping

1. Introduction

Advances in optical transmission media and high speed switching have paved the way for many exciting multimedia applications, such as teleconferencing and real-time distributed computing, to be supported on computer networks. Most of these new applications, constituted of heterogeneous mix of video, voice and data, are characterized by stringent QoS requirements in

* Corresponding author. E-mail: svr@iitm.ernet.in.

0169-7552/96/$15.00 © 1996 Elsevier Science B.V. All rights reserved
SSDI 0169-7552(95)00076-3

terms of throughput, delay, jitter and loss guarantees. The heterogeneity of the sources calls for effective congestion control schemes to meet the diverse Quality of Service (QoS) requirements of each application. These include admission control at connection set up, traffic enforcement and shaping at the edges of the network and multiclass scheduling schemes at the intermediate switches. Latency effects apparent at the gigabit speeds make the conventional feedback techniques ineffective. Thus the responsibility of preventing congestion lies with the admission control and traffic enforcement schemes.

Some of the admission control, resource reservation and scheduling schemes proposed for integrated broad band networks in the recent past and the related issues are surveyed in a previous paper [13]. Admission control restricts the number of connections that can be supported by the network. Admission control is decided by an algorithm which expects that the user provides an estimate of the traffic parameters and abides by their negotiated values. Resource reservation schemes manage the allocation of the resources at each of the nodes so that per-node QoS requirements can be met for each connection. Scheduling policies provide sharing of bandwidth among the various classes and the various streams within each class so that the individual requirements can be met for each connection.

In a resource sharing packet network, admission control and scheduling schemes by themselves are not sufficient to provide guarantees. This is due to the fact that the users may, inadvertently or otherwise, attempt to exceed the rates specified at the time of connection establishment. Traffic policing schemes proposed in the literature include mainly Leaky Bucket (LB), Jumping Window (JW), Moving Window (MW), Exponential Weighted Moving Average (EWMA) and associated variations. A performance comparison among these schemes from the point of view of violation probability, sensitivity to overloads, dynamic reaction time and worst case traffic admitted into the network can be found in [11]. It has been shown that the LB and the EWMA are the most promising mechanisms to cope with short-term fluctuations and hence suited for policing bursty traffic. Several improvements of the LB has been proposed for increasing utilization in an ATM environment [3,5,15]. Traffic enforcement schemes police the source streams to check that their characteristics conform to the declared values throughout the life of the connection. The various schemes have been studied from the point of view of their capability to smooth the burstiness in the source. Traffic Shaping, on the other hand, conditions the input stream so that the characteristics are amenable to the scheduling mechanisms to provide the required QoS guarantees. Although, one may imply the other, there are subtle differences. The former checks the conformance to the declared values whereas the latter shapes it to be more agreeable to the scheduling policies.

Traffic shapers have been mainly studied hitherto from the point of view of their effectiveness in smoothing the burstiness. The leaky bucket scheme, to cite an example, is a mean rate policer smoothing at the token generation rate. Studies on bursty sources show that burstiness promotes statistical multiplexing at the cost of possible congestion. Smoothing, on the other hand, helps in providing guarantees at the cost of utilization. Thus need for a flexible scheme which can provide a reasonable compromise between utilization and performance is imminent. Recent studies [10,12] have also questioned the suitability of LB for policing real-time traffic. LB, in its attempt to enforce smoothness often introduces excessive access delays thereby making it incapable of regulating real-time traffic. A policy which is less stringent on short term burstiness while bounding long term behavior with a LB-bound would be better suited for time critical traffic. This was the second motivation which led us to the new proposal.

We propose a new traffic shaper which can adjust the burstiness) of the input traffic to obtain reasonable bandwidth utilization while maintaining statistical service guarantees. It uses a window based shaping policy which captures the essence of the LB scheme, permits short term burstiness in a more flexible manner and is inherently peak rate enforced. The decision to admit an arriving packet is based on the temporal image of the past data maintained in a shift register. We will refer to the new scheme as the SRTS (Shift Register Traffic

Shaper). A single sliding window mechanism for traffic shaping was incorporated for traffic regulation by Rigolo and Fratta in [14]. In that paper, the shaper consisted of a sliding window followed by a server operating at a constant rate. Our scheme employs more than one window, which jointly provide a more general control over the burstiness of the input stream. The motivation for our scheme is derived by studying the characteristics of the traffic generated by the leaky bucket scheme.

The performance characteristics of SRTS is studied in this paper in two parts. In the first part, we investigate the controlling effect of shaper parameter variations on the input traffic characteristics. Delay, loss and burstiness behavior at the output is studied for different window parameters and input burstiness. The adjustable burstiness feature is demonstrated in this study. In the second part, we dimension the proposed SRTS shaper and a LB shaper equivalently and compare the mean and peak rate policing behavior with delay and loss as the performance parameters. Adopting a less stringent attitude towards short term burstiness is shown to result in considerable advantage for policing real-time traffic.

The rest of the paper is organized as follows: Section 2 discusses qualitatively how burstiness of the source decides the bandwidth that needs to be allocated for specified QoS guarantees. A quantitative means of representing burstiness bounds is defined. Section 3 presents the general requirements of a traffic shaper and briefly describes LB and EWMA schemes. Effect of shaping on delays and bandwidth requirement is discussed in Section 4. Sections 5 and 6 describe the proposed SRTS scheme and its variable burstiness feature. Section 7 presents the simulation results, observations and inferences. Finally Section 8 summarizes and concludes this paper.

2. Burstiness and bandwidth allocation

2.1. Introduction

Traffic sources in multimedia applications can be basically classified into five categories, viz.,

data, voice, video, image and graphics. But we confine our discussion to mainly data, voice and video. Data sources are generally bursty in nature whereas voice and video sources can be continuous or bursty, depending on the compression and coding techniques used. Continuous sources are said to generate constant bit rate (CBR) traffic and bursty sources are said to generate variable bit rate (VBR) traffic. Most of the multimedia sources are bursty in nature.

A CBR source needs peak rate allocation of bandwidth for congestion-free transmission. For a VBR source, the average rate of transmission λ_a can be a small fraction of the peak rate λ_p. Thus a peak rate allocation would result in gross under utilization of the system resources. With peak rate allotment, providing performance guarantees is easy. On the other extreme, average allotment may lead to buffer overflows and consequent losses/delays. No meaningful guarantees can be offered in such cases. An effective bandwidth λ_{eff}, whose value lies between the average and the peak rates is determined for various sources [6,7]. An allocation corresponding to the effective bandwidth optimizes the network utilization and performance guarantees. An allocation nearer to the peak rate allows providing tighter probabilistic guarantees. In the extreme, with peak rate allotment, the guarantees can be deterministic.

2.2. Bursty model and bandwidth requirement

The source model that is used for measuring performance is the ON-OFF bursty model [2,17,19]. ON-OFF model is characterized by interspersed ON and OFF periods each exponentially distributed with mean T_{ON} and T_{OFF} respectively. During an ON period, cells are periodically transmitted at peak rate λ_p (intercell time during an ON period is $\tau_p = 1/\lambda_p$). The average rate λ_a for this model is $\lambda_p \cdot T_{ON}/(T_{ON} + T_{OFF})$ and the burstiness $\hat{r} = (T_{ON} + T_{OFF})/T_{ON}$. The effective bandwidth requirement for this source λ_{eff} is such that $\lambda_a \leq \lambda_{eff} \leq \lambda_p$.

The ON-OFF bursty model can be justifiably used in modeling many of the sources, currently of interest in multimedia networks. For example, voice sources using talkspurt and video sources after compression and coding, generate bursty streams. Since voice and video sources are *basically* of the CBR type, cell generation during ON period is periodic in nature. To model a generalized data source, as in the case of a large data file transfer application, the ON-OFF model can be modified to make the ON period intercell times exponentially distributed. This assumption will result in an Interrupted Poisson Process (IPP). Further generalizations will lead to 2-state and n-state Markov Modulated Poisson Process (MMPP) models [8].

In this paper, we use an ON-OFF bursty model for the source. The burstiness can be varied by altering the T_{ON} or T_{OFF} keeping the other constant.

2.3. Defining smoothness for a general stream

In order to compare the proposed scheme with other enforcement schemes, we define the smoothness of a traffic stream as follows:

Definition. A generalized packet stream is defined to be $(n_1, T_1; n_2, T_2; \ldots; n_k, T_k)$ smooth if, over any time window of duration T_1, number of packets $\leq n_1$ *and* ... over any time window of duration T_2, number of packets $\leq n_2$ *and* ... over any time window of duration T_k, number of packets $\leq n_k$, where k denotes the number of windows for characterizing the smoothness of the

stream. A larger k can provide a more flexible description of the stream.

3. General model for traffic shaping

A general framework for studying the performance of a traffic shaper is presented in this section. Source is characterized by a peak rate λ_p, an average rate λ_a and mean ON duration T_{ON}. We assume that the network access link at the output of the traffic shaper has a capacity equal to the peak rate of the source stream. Thus any burst arrival is serviced fastest at the peak rate. A traffic shaper which closely fits the model above is the Leaky Bucket with a Peak rate Policer (LBP). In the following sections, we first describe the characteristics of a LBP output traffic. These characteristics motivated the development of the scheme proposed in this paper. A brief description of EWMA, a window based policer is also given for comparison with the proposed scheme.

3.1. Leaky Bucket scheme

Leaky Bucket [18] and its variant schemes are described in [3,5,11,15]. In a generalized model of the leaky bucket shown in Fig. 1, tokens are generated at a fixed rate as long as the token buffer of size b is not full.

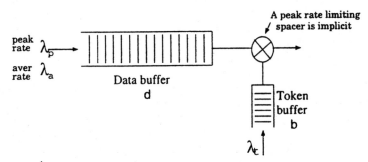

Fig. 1. A generalized Leaky Bucket scheme.

When a packet arrives from the source, it is released into the network only if there is at least one token in the token buffer. This scheme enforces the token arrival rate λ_t on the input stream. Clearly, λ_t should be greater than the average arrival rate λ_a for stability and less than the peak arrival rate λ_p for achieving bandwidth utilization. An input data buffer of size d permits statistical variations. An arriving packet finding the input buffer full is said to be a violating packet and can be dropped or tagged for a preferential treatment at the switching nodes.

In this paper, we assume that a peak-rate limiting spacer is an integral part of the leaky bucket mechanism. When a burst of data arrives at the input, even if enough tokens are present, the packets are not instantaneously released into the network. Successive packets are delayed by τ, the transmission time at negotiated peak rate λ_p, where $\tau = 1/\lambda_p$. We will use LBP to designate the leaky bucket with peak rate policer.

For the leaky bucket parameters defined above, maximum burst size at the output is $b' = b/(1 - \lambda_t/\lambda_p)$. This includes the new tokens that arrive during the transmission of the first b packets. The output of the leaky bucket is characterized as follows:

1. *maximum burst size*: For the LBP, maximum burst size at the output is $b' = b/(1 - \lambda_t/\lambda_p)$, obtained as follows. If we assume the largest burst starts at t_1, the token buffer should be full at t_1. This would be possible only if the source generated an input burst after a prolonged OFF period of b/λ_t, where b is the token buffer size. Since the burst service is not instantaneous due to peak rate policer, more tokens may arrive during the consumption of the existing tokens. Since tokens are removed at λ_p and arrive at λ_t, the instantaneous token count in TB will be $b(t) = b + (\lambda_t - \lambda_p) \cdot t$ and hence TB empties at time $b/(\lambda_p - \lambda_t)$. The maximum burst size b' then becomes $b/(1 - \lambda_t/\lambda_p)$.

2. *long term output smoothness*: over a large time duration T, number of packets sent out by the leaky bucket, $n(T)$ is $\leq \lambda_t \cdot T = n_t$. This relationship is also true for any time duration T' starting from zero or any epoch when token

buffer becomes empty. It is assumed here that the token buffer is empty at $t = 0$.

3. *short term burstiness*: Over durations smaller than T mentioned in the previous item and exceeding the maximum burst size, leaky bucket output can be modeled as a Linear Bounded Arrival Process (LBAP) with parameters (σ, ρ) [4]. Here, σ represents the maximum burst size b' and ρ represents the token rate λ_t.

In terms of the smoothness definition given in Section 2.3, we can state that for any T starting from 0 (or from any epoch when token buffer is empty), LBP output is (n_t, T) smooth.

3.2. Exponentially weighted moving average scheme

EWMA is a window based scheme [11] where the maximum number of cells permitted within a fixed time window is limited. If we consider the connection time to consist of consecutive windows of same size, the maximum number of cells accepted in the ith window N_i is a function of the mean number of cells per window N and an exponentially weighted sum of the cells accepted in the preceding windows as given below

$$N_i = \frac{\left(N - (1 - \gamma)\left(\gamma X_{i-1} + \ldots + \gamma^{i-1} X_1\right)\right) - \gamma^i S_0}{(1 - \gamma)}$$

where S_0 is the initial value for the EWMA. The weight factor γ decides the number of relevant preceding windows which influence the number of packets permitted in the current window. A nonzero value of γ permits more burstiness. For a value of $\gamma = 0.8$, up to 5 times N number of packets can occur in the first window. Thus a large value of γ increases the reaction time and it is shown in [11] that the dynamic behavior of EWMA is the worst. Moreover, the implementation complexity of this scheme is higher than LB and other window based schemes.

4. Shaping and BW allocation

The bandwidth that needs to be allocated to the shaped stream depends on the shaper parameters. For instance, a LB produces a stream which requires, at a minimum, bandwidth equal to the token arrival rate, to be allocated at the access multiplexer. A larger token arrival rate reduces the access delay at the policer but needs a larger bandwidth allocation. For a source characterized by a peak rate λ_p and burstiness $\hat{r}$, bandwidth allocation λ_{bw} is such that $\lambda_p/\hat{r} \leq \lambda_t \leq \lambda_{bw} \leq \lambda_p$. At the access multiplexer, the capacity of the output link $\lambda_o = \sum_{i=1}^{m} \lambda_{bw}(i)$ for m streams multiplexed to the same output. Since most multimedia traffic is bursty in nature, a large statistical multiplexing gain is possible only if λ_t is near the average arrival rate $\lambda_a = \lambda_p/\hat{r}$. On the other hand, the smaller λ_t, the larger the access delay and/or violation probability incurred by the source. A lenient enforcement policy can increase the delay at the multiplexing/switching nodes due to buffer overflows. Thus there is a trade off between the access delay introduced by the policer and the network delay at the switches. From the end user's point of view, the delay incurred by the application includes the access delay and the network delay. For a constant bandwidth allocation, the effect of input rate control can be summarized by the following observations [10,12]:

1. The total delay experienced by a cell is the sum of the access delay due to queuing at the shaper and the network delay at the switch. The policer simply transfers the network delay on to the input side thereby avoiding overflow losses/delays within the network. Thus unless the source has a large buffer and can tolerate excess delay, the input rate control as performed by the LB can hardly improve the network performance [12]. For many real time applications, this access delay could be prohibitive.

2. A stringent input rate control may unnecessarily increase the user end-to-end delay by a significant amount [12].

3. The minimum total average delay is achieved when no traffic enforcement is invoked [10,12]. This observation is applicable when the network bandwidth is considerably greater than the source transmission rate, in which case the effect of individual streams is smoothed by statistical multiplexing. Nevertheless, to check

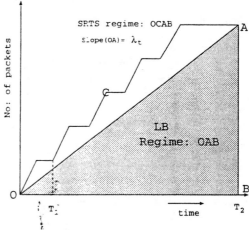

Fig. 2. Permitted number of packets vs. time.

excessive burstiness and prolonged rate violations, input policer is practically needed.

It is evident from the aforementioned points that the access delay introduced by the traffic policer can be significant. One way of reducing the access delay would be to permit more short term burstiness subject to

· the maximum burst size should be bounded and burst arrivals must be peak rate enforced;
· the number of arrivals over a larger time durations to be bounded at the average policing rate.

LB and the EWMA mechanisms perform the above two in different ways. The short term burstiness permitted by the LB is decided by the size of the token buffer b. As explained earlier, over any time duration T starting from 0 (or any epoch when the token buffer becomes empty), the number of packets admitted into the network are bounded by $\lambda_t * T$. With reference to Fig. 2 which shows the number of admitted packets versus time, the operating region for LB operation is below the line OA corresponding to the average policing rate. A source is permitted to send a burst only if it remains inactive for a sufficient amount of time to gather enough number of tokens in the token buffer. Thus the operating point is always below the line OA. A well behaved source transmitting uniformly at the token arrival rate will operate along OA.

The short term burstiness in the EWMA mechanism is influenced by the factor γ as described earlier in Section 3.2. The dynamic response for the EWMA is however poor for reasonable values of γ. EWMA output is not peak rate enforced and the implementation complexity is also considerable compared to the other schemes.

We describe in the next section a traffic shaper which has the following features:

1. permits short term burstiness but bounds long term behavior so that the number of packets admitted over a long time is same as that admitted by an equivalent leaky bucket;
2. variable burstiness easily incorporated;
3. it is inherently peak rate enforced;
4. it is a window based shaper consisting of two or more windows and the shaper behavior can be more flexibly set unlike the EWMA which has only one control parameter γ;
5. it is designed using a shift register and two counters and hence can easily be implemented in hardware.

5. Shift Register Traffic Shaper (SRTS)

5.1. Motivation for the new scheme

Two basic concepts motivated the development of the SRTS:

1. provide burstiness variation for possible multiplexing gain;
2. reduce the access delays by adopting a less stringent attitude towards short term burstiness following the observations made in Section 4.

These are elaborated below. We have seen that in a Leaky Bucket (LBP) policer, the number of packets over any time duration T starting from 0 is bounded by $\lambda_t \cdot T$. One possible modification to this boundedness is as follows:

· Over any predecided time duration of value T_1 (constant), we can bound the number of packets as in the LBP case.
· Over sub-durations within T_1, we can allow more burstiness, *of course*, with bounds.

The advantage that is foreseen in *permitting*

controlled burstiness is improvement of the statistical multiplexing gain at the switches. *This is of at most relevance in the current scenario since most of the multimedia traffic sources are bursty in nature.* These include naturally stream based sources which are also rendered bursty by the efficient compression and coding mechanisms employed.

In Fig. 2, the operating region of the LB was depicted. Previous section described how LB introduces access delays which can become prohibitive for real-time applications. With an aim to *reduce the access delays*, what we need is a traffic shaper which performs like the LB over longer durations, but allows short-term burstiness in a more liberal sense than is permitted by the LB. With reference to Fig. 2, we attempt to operate above line OA over short durations while confining to the LB bound over a large interval (say OB). As mentioned in the previous section, OA is the upper boundary for LB operation. A typical upper boundary for the proposed shaper can be the piecewise linear line OCA. Thus by virtue of its short term operation above line OA, short term burstiness is more flexibly permitted by the proposed shaper. In the case of LB, a stream has to gather enough number of tokens by remaining inactive before it can afford to drive in a burst of data. On the contrary, a larger operating region of SRTS permits the source to have short term overdrafts as long as it confines within the operating region. A simple implementation of the scheme using 2 windows is outlined in the following section.

5.2. Description of the new scheme

The Shift Register Traffic Shaper (SRTS) makes use of the temporal profile [1] of the packet stream admitted by the shaper over the immediate past N time slots, where a time slot τ refers to the reciprocal of the peak rate. This temporal history can be maintained by a shift register with 1 bit corresponding to every packet sent. The shift register is shifted right every time slot τ. The entry of the bits into the shift register is as per the following:

Let $f_d = 1$ if data buffer is not empty and 0

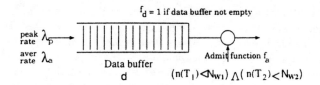

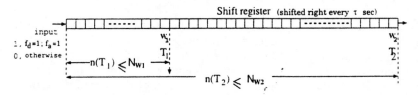

Fig. 3. Shift Register Traffic Shaper (SRTS).

otherwise; Similarly, let f_a denote the admit control function defined as $f_a = (n(T_1) < n_1)$ and $(n(T_2) < n_2)$ and $(n(T_3) < n_3)\ldots$ depending on the number of windows. Here T_i refers to a time window. The size of the corresponding window is denoted by W_i and maximum number of packets permitted in W_i by N_{Wi} (note that $N_{Wi} = n_i$).

The data bit shifted in is

1   if $f_d = 1, f_a = 1$,

0   otherwise.

Thus the bit contents of the shift register at any instant, provides an image of the history of the packets sent. All the time durations mentioned with reference to the shift register start from the time point corresponding to the entry point of the shift register. To determine the num-

ber of packets in any time duration, a counter is used. It increments whenever a "1" enters the shift register and decrements when a "1" shifts out of the right edge of the corresponding window monitored by the counter.

Fig. 3 describes an enforcement scheme using two windows. This scheme generates an $(n_1, T_1; n_2, T_2)$ smooth traffic, which means that over any period of duration T_1, the number of packets $n(T_1) \le n_1$ and over any period of duration T_2, the number of packets $n(T_2) \le n_2$. Even though we have described the scheme with two windows, further flexibility in moulding the burstiness is possible using the appropriate number of windows. Since the restriction on the number of packets permitted in a time window is enforced at the entry point of the shift register and the win-

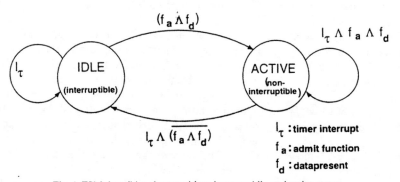

Fig. 4. FSM describing the transitions between idle and active states.

dow shifts to the right every τ seconds, the smoothness is guaranteed over *any time window over the entire duration of the connection.*

One limitation that arises in the above arrangement is due to the discretization of time into slots of τ. A slot is termed active if a cell is transmitted during that slot and idle, otherwise. Since the cell arrival instant need not synchronize with the output slots, a cell arriving during an idle slot will have to wait till the end of that slot for transmission. *This limitation is removed* in our current scheme by using "soft" discretization. If a cell arrives during an idle slot, say after τ' elapses (out of τ), idle slot is frozen and an active slot is initiated immediately. At the termination of this active slot, if either data is absent or the admit function is false, the residual idle slot of duration $(\tau - \tau')$ commences. The end of a slot is indicated by the timer interrupt shown in Fig. 4. The shift register is shifted right at the end of every slot, active or passive. The essence of the above arrangement is that an idle slot is interruptible whereas an active slot is not. Every time an idle slot is interrupted, the residual idle time is saved for future use up.

The modification described above is illustrated as an FSM in Fig. 4.

The key features are:
- Idle to Active state transition is fired by the event $(f_a \wedge f_d)$ where f_a = admit function and f_d = data present flag. The following actions ensue:
  1. save residual time by freezing the counter,
  2. initiate transmission and go to active state,
  3. every slot timer interrupt in idle state will cause transition to itself after resetting the counter.
- Active to Idle state transition is fired by the timer interrupt:
  1. if $(f_a \wedge f_d) = 1$, initiate another active slot,
  2. else initiate an idle slot and go to idle state.

6. Providing adjustable burstiness

Using 3 counters and associated SRTS parameters N_{W1}, W_1, N_{W2}, W_2 and N_{W3}, W_3, it is possible to tune the burstiness at the output of the SRTS while complying with the LB bounds over a predecided time duration. Window parameters can be derived from the key observations about the characteristics of the LBP output.

LBP has essentially 2 parameters. The bucket size b which decides the maximum burst size and the token arrival rate λ_t which provides a measure of the effective bandwidth allotted to the source. The model proposed in this paper has 3 parameters. One window, W_1 which limits the maximum burst size and a second window (W_3) for long term average policing correspond conceptually to the 2 LBP parameters. The third window, namely W_2, is the one for providing the variable burstiness feature. An adjustable burstiness feature can be provided in SRTS by the following choice of parameters:
1. The parameters of the smallest window T_1 are

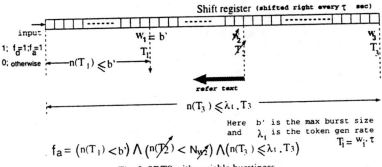

$$f_a = \left(n(T_1) < b' \right) \wedge \left(n(T_2) < N_{W2} \right) \wedge \left(n(T_3) \leqslant \lambda_t . T_3 \right)$$

Fig. 5. SRTS with variable burstiness.

chosen as $W_1 = b'$ and $N_{W1} = b'$. This bounds the maximum burst size.

2. Window-3 parameters can enforce the average policing characteristics exhibited by the LBP over large time durations. If λ_{eff} is the effective bandwidth allotted for the bursty source (λ_p, λ_a), then the token arrival rate λ_t of the equivalent leaky bucket should be equal to the effective bandwidth. Thus the window parameters are chosen as follows: for $W_3 = $ large value T, $N_{W3} = \lambda_{eff} \cdot \tau \cdot W_3$.

3. Window-2, the main control parameter of the shaper can be suitably tuned to incorporate the burstiness control feature. If we assume a LBAP (σ, ρ) for the output of the LBP over durations larger than and of the order of maximum burst size, σ will be b' and ρ equals λ_t. Then for a chosen value of W_2, $N_{W2} = b' + \lambda_t \cdot (W_2 - W_1) \cdot \tau$. The region of operation to permit higher burstiness is shown by the shaded arrow in Fig. 5. The burstiness can be varied by adjusting N_{W2} or W_2. For instance, increasing N_{W2} or reducing W_2 increases the output burstiness.

Example. For a bursty model with mean ON period of 200 ms, minimum intercell time τ of 10 ms and burstiness 5, $\lambda_p = 100$ and $\lambda_a = 20$. If we choose λ_{eff} to be 40, for a bucket size (of an equivalent LBP) of 18, max burst size $b' = b/(1 - \lambda_t/\lambda_p) = 30$. Thus $W_1 = N_{W1} = 30$. For $W_2 = 75$, $N_{W2} = 30 + 45 \cdot 40/100 = 48$. W_3 corresponds to the large duration over which the average policing is enforced.

For a choice of $W_3 = 450$, $N_{W3} = \lambda_{eff} \cdot \tau \cdot W_3 = 450 \cdot 40/100 = 180$.

The exact choice of W_2 and W_3 is currently arbitrary and can be tailored to suit the specific application-stream. The only criteria is that over W_2, we assume the equivalent LBP to generate a LBAP stream whereas over the larger window W_3, an averaging property is expected. The influence of the source leading to a judicious choice of W_2 and W_3 is yet to be investigated.

7. Performance study and results

The performance characteristics of SRTS is studied in this paper in two parts. In the first part, we investigate the controlling effect of shaper parameters on the input traffic characteristics. Delay, loss and burstiness behavior at the output is studied for different window parameters and input burstiness. The adjustable burstiness

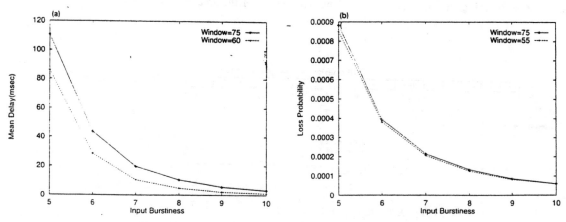

Fig. 6. (a) Mean delay and (b) loss characteristics vs. input burstiness.

feature is demonstrated in this study. In the second part, we dimension the proposed SRTS shaper and a LB shaper equivalently and compare the mean and peak rate policing behavior with delay and loss as the performance parameters.

7.1. SRTS characteristics and features

7.1.1. Simulation experiments

The experiments performed to study the controlling effect of shaper parameters on input characteristics is described in this section. As mentioned in Section 2.2., the source is assumed to be of ON-OFF bursty type. Three simulation experiments are performed as detailed below. In all the cases, $W_1 = N_{W1} = 30$; $W_3 = 450$, $N_{W3} = 180$; $N_{W'2} = 48$; Size of control window W_2 is a variable parameter. Each simulation run is performed with 10^7 packets. These values are chosen based on the discussion in the previous section.

Experiment 1. In this experiment, we study the delay characteristics of the traffic shaper as a function of the input burstiness for different window parameters. Size of data buffer is very large to keep losses close to zero. The input burstiness is varied by adjusting the ON period, keeping the

OFF period constant. Intercell time is 10 ms and hence $\lambda_p = 100$. Since the long term average policed rate is λ_t, the range of ON period variation is such that λ_a remains $\leq \lambda_t$ for stability. Thus $(T_{ON}/(T_{ON} + T_{OFF}) \cdot 100) < \lambda_t$, which is fixed at 40. Input burstiness is varied from 5 to 10 by keeping the OFF period constant at 800 ms and adjusting the ON period. Fig. 6(a) gives the delay distribution for window sizes of 75 and 60. The number of simulation runs are such that the results are accurate to within 5% with 95% confidence level.

Experiment 2. In this experiment, we study the loss characteristics incurred by SRTS shaping as a function of the input burstiness for different window parameters. Data buffer size is finite. In this case, the input burstiness is varied by keeping the ON period constant at 200 ms and varying the OFF period.

Simulation is conducted for sufficient number of packets to yield loss probability values of up to 10^{-6} (see Fig. 6(b)).

Experiment 3. In this experiment, we study the output burstiness as a function of window parameters, for the same source burstiness. Since the output stream is of an arbitrary nature unlike the

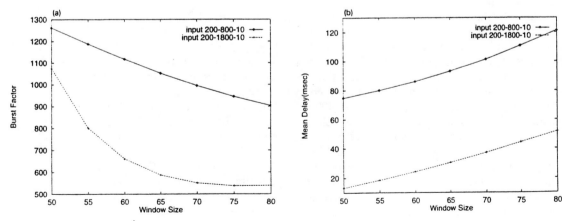

Fig. 7. (a) Output burst factor and (b) mean delay vs. window size.

input stream which is described by a bursty ON-OFF model parameters, we use ratio of Variance to Mean of cell interarrival times [9,16] for characterizing the burstiness. We will use the term "burst factor" for this ratio to differentiate this definition of burstiness from the definition given in Section 2.2. Fig. 7a presents the result for 2 source ON-OFF characteristics. Keeping the ON time at 200 ms, measurements are taken for two OFF period values, namely 800 ms and 1800 ms respectively.

Fig. 7(b) illustrates the effect of window size on mean delay. The number of simulation runs are such that the results are accurate to within 5% with 95% confidence level.

7.1.2. Observations and inference

Main observations in the simulation results and inferences drawn, thereof, are as follows:

1. Increase in input burstiness (as defined in Section 2.2.) causes a reduction in the mean delay. This is expected since a larger burstiness implies a shorter source active period for a constant OFF period. As can be seen in Fig. 6(a), a smaller window size W_2 for the same N_{W2} admits burstier streams than would be admitted by a correspondingly larger window size for the same N_{W2}.

2. For the finite buffer case, the loss characteristics are presented in Fig. 6(b). For reasons similar to the results in the previous experiment, a smaller window reduces the losses. The difference is however not as much pronounced as in the previous case.

3. The output burst factor variation demonstrated in Fig. 7(a) is a significant result in concurrence with our concept of a "controllable" burstiness. A shaper with a larger control window size generates a smoother output stream. The burstiness of the output can be tuned to provide higher bandwidth utilization at the switches.

4. The results of Fig. 7(b) provide a means of selecting the window parameters suitable for the delay requirements of the application. By judiciously selecting the window-2 parameters, namely W_2 and N_{W2}, it is possible to tune the shaper behavior based on the application char-

acteristics and the performance requirements. Although the general influence of the parameters is apparent, the precise correspondence between the source behavior and the window parameters needs to be established for different practical sources.

7.2. Comparison of SRTS and LB policing

7.2.1. Establishing equivalence

For comparing the performance of SRTS with the LBP scheme, the parameters of the two schemes have to be chosen to establish a functional equivalence. In this paper, we use a SRTS with two windows. Our aim in this experiment is to obtain the transfer characteristics OCA depicted in Fig. 2 and study its effects. The shaping parameters are the window sizes W_1, W_2 and the maximum number of packets permitted in each window N_{W1}, N_{W2}. The window parameters can be derived from the key observations made earlier regarding the LBP scheme.

The maximum burst size b' for the LBP is $b' = b/(1 - \lambda_t/\lambda_p)$. If we observe the number of packets within a window of size W (say), the maximum number of packets allowed N_W within W is

for $W \leq b'$, $N_W = W$; $\qquad$ (a)

for $W > b'$, $N_W = b' + \lambda_t \cdot (W - b') \cdot \tau$; $\qquad$ (b)

for $W \gg b'$, $N_W \cong W \cdot \tau \cdot \lambda_t$. $\qquad$ (c)

The values assumed for the LBP in the current simulation are $b = 18$; $\lambda_p = 100$ and $\lambda_t = 40$. Then max burst size $b' = b/(1 - \lambda_t/\lambda_p) = 30$. The first window W_1 is chosen as 50 to satisfy (b). Thus to admit more short term burstiness than what is permitted by the LBP, N_{W1} should be $\geq 30 + 20 \cdot 40/100 = 38$. For the current simulation, we have chosen this value of 38 for N_{W1}. For the LBP, the distribution of these packets within W_1 should be subject to operation within the shaded region in Fig. 2. Whereas, for the SRTS, they can be more flexibly distributed since the SRTS operating regime is bigger than that of LBP. Window-2 parameters can enforce the average policing characteristics exhibited by the LBP over large time durations. Hence the window size, in this case, follows (c). Consequently, the number of packets policed over a time duration $T_2(= W_2 \cdot \tau)$ for the LBP and the SRTS are identical. For the current study, we have chosen $W_2 = 10 \cdot W_1 = 500$ and $N_{W2} = 500 \cdot \tau \cdot \lambda_t = 200$.

The exact choice of W_1 and W_2 is currently arbitrary and can be tailored to suit the application stream. The only criteria is that over W_1, we assume the "equivalent" LBP to generate a LBAP stream whereas over the larger window W_2, an averaging property is expected.

7.2.2. Simulation experiments

In this section, we compare and study the effectiveness of SRTS and LBP as mean and peak rate policers. Two simulation experiments are performed. The source model is the bursty ON-OFF model explained in Section 2.2. Since we intend to vary the burstiness of the source, the mean ON time is kept at 200 ms. The OFF times and τ_p are appropriately adjusted to obtain the required mean rate.

SRTS is a mean as well as a peak rate policer. In the two experiments, we assume an overdi-

mensioning factor $C = 1.5$ relating the policed rate and the mean rate of the source (as in [11]). The peak enforced rate is 100 and hence the minimum delay between consecutive packets at the output of the shaper τ is 10 ms. Each simulation run is performed with 10^7 packets.

Experiment 1. In this experiment, we study the loss and delay characteristics for different source mean rates. The mean rate variation is achieved by varying the OFF time keeping mean ON time = 200 ms and mean policed rate, $\lambda_t = 40$. With the overdimensioning factor of 1.5, the negotiated mean rate = 26.67. The OFF time is varied such that $\lambda_p/(1 + T_{OFF}/200) \le 26.67$. Thus $T_{OFF} > 550$ for a well behaved source. X-axis shows the normalized mean rate. For the first part which estimates the violation probability, a finite data buffer of size 20 is assumed. In a practical case, the size can be based on the maximum access delay that can be tolerated by a particular application. For the second part of the experiment which studies the access delay, size of the data buffer is kept very large so as to keep losses close

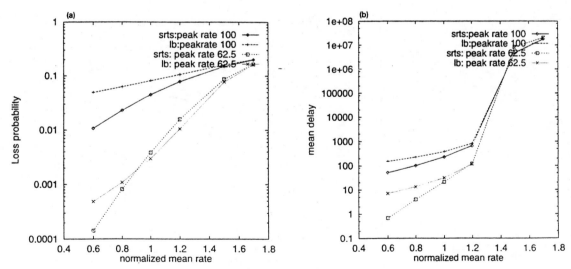

Fig. 8. (a) Loss and (b) delay characteristics vs. normalized mean rate.

to zero. The experiment is performed for two values of the peak rate, 100 ($\tau_p = 10$) and 62.5 ($\tau_p = 16$). The results are shown in Fig. 8.

The number of simulation runs are such that the results are accurate to within 5% with 95% confidence level.

Experiment 2. In this experiment, we study the loss and delay characteristics for different source peak rates. Thus we compare the peak rate enforcement provided by the SRTS and the LBP. For each run, the peak rate and the OFF duration are adjusted to keep the mean rate constant. X-axis plots the normalized peak rates. The experiment is repeated for two values of the mean rate, 25 and 20. Both these values are within the negotiated rate of 26.67. Other parameters are as in the previous experiment. The results are shown in Fig. 9.

7.2.3. Observations and inference

The main observations in the simulation results and inferences drawn, thereof, are as follows.

With reference to Fig. 8(a), for an input stream with peak rate 100 (corresponding to the peak rate limit built in the shaper), SRTS has much lesser loss probability for mean rates up to the policed rate (1.5 · source mean). Beyond this, both the curves converge quickly. At the lower peak rate of 62.5, however, there is a crossover between the SRTS and LBP loss curves. This we attribute to the fact that the source traffic is smooth in this region and the advantage of SRTS in favoring short term burstiness is not made use of. In both the cases, the steeper gradient of the SRTS curve is an indicator of its effectiveness as a mean rate policer. The flexible admission of short term burstiness results in a lower access delay for the SRTS. This fact is evident from Fig. 8(b). For well behaved sources with mean rate below the negotiated value, lower the mean rate, better the performance of the SRTS. This is true from the point of view of loss probability as well as access delay. At 0.6 times the mean rate, the access delay introduced by the SRTS is one order less than that introduced by the equivalent LBP.

Fig. 9 depicts the response of the shapers to peak rate violation. For the loss curves, violation

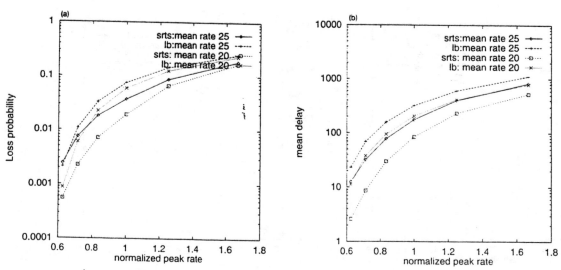

Fig. 9. (a) Loss and (b) delay characteristics vs. normalized peak rate.

is more gradual than in the mean rate case. For our simulation which assumed a data buffer of size 20, SRTS yields lower values of violation probability than the LBP for traffic conforming to the negotiated rate. This is due to the more liberal admission policy for burstiness existing over short durations. The access delay curves for the two shapers are almost parallel to each other. As in the previous case, SRTS shaped streams have a consistently smaller access delay compared to the LBP case. However, compared to the delay characteristics for mean rate violation behavior, peak rate violation curves for SRTS as well as LBP do not exhibit steep gradients.

The advantages of the SRTS policy in terms of lower violation probability and access delay for traffic *within the negotiated rates* is due to the larger operating regime shown in Fig. 2. The above advantage of the SRTS however comes at a cost. The SRTS output is burstier than its LB counterpart. This would necessitate a more careful buffering and scheduling design at the switches to prevent congestion at the intermediate nodes. Since the network link transmission rate is generally much higher than the maximum source transmission rate, we expect that the fluctuations at the SRTS output will be effectively smoothed by the statistical multiplexing effect at the switches. Also, since the maximum burst size is limited and the long term behavior is bounded, the buffers and the schedulers can be dimensioned appropriately at the switches to provide the required degree of loss and delay guarantees.

From the point of view of minimizing congestion within the network, the policy adopted by the LB is quite effective. LB reduces the delays within the network by transferring them on to the input side. However, the stringent enforcement increases the access delay and hence raises questions regarding the suitability of LB for real time traffic. We show through this study that the access delays can be reduced by adopting a more liberal attitude over shorter durations while maintaining the LB bounds over larger durations. For the same bandwidth allocation at the switches, such a policy is shown to perform better for real time source traffic.

8. Summary and conclusion

In this paper, we proposed a flexible traffic shaper and compared its performance with a LBP. The motivation for the new scheme is derived from the output characteristics exhibited by the LBP. Two main goals were set. One is to provide an adjustable burstiness feature so that higher bandwidth utilization along with reasonable guarantees can be obtained. The second was to reduce the access delays for real-time traffic by being more liberal in permitting short term burstiness. The window based shaping policy adopted in the SRTS scheme can be used to achieve both the goals.

The performance of the proposed shaper is studied in two parts. In the first we study the effect of window parameters on input characteristics and demonstrate the adjustable burstiness feature. In the second part, we compare the loss and delay performance of a 2-window SRTS and a LBP. By adopting a more liberal, yet bounded attitude over short durations, SRTS reduces the access delays for time critical traffic.

For providing the desired utilization and guarantees, a traffic shaper must work in unison with the buffer management and scheduling schemes at the switches. A composite study involving the shaper and the scheduler is necessary to see the effect of SRTS shaping on end-to-end performance. Such a study will constitute our future research.

References

[1] A.K. Agrawala, Temporal profile capture, Personal Communication, 1994.
[2] J.J. Bae and T. Suda, Survey of traffic control schemes and protocols in ATM networks, *Proc. IEEE* **79** (2) (1991) 170–189.
[3] K. Bala, I. Cidon and K. Sohraby, Congestion control for high speed packet switched networks, *Proc. IEEE INFOCOM*, 1990, pp. 520–526.
[4] R.L. Cruz, A calculus for network delay, part I: network elements in isolation, *IEEE Trans. Information Theory* **37** (1) (1991) 114–131.

[5] A.E. Eckberg, D.T. Luan and D.M. Lucantoni, Bandwidth management: a congestion control strategy for broadband packet networks—characterizing the throughput-burstiness filter. *Comput. Networks ISDN Systems* **20** (1990) 415–423.

[6] A.L. Elwalid and D. Mitra, Effective bandwidth of general Markovian traffic sources and admission control of high speed networks, *Proc. IEEE INFOCOM'93*, San Francisco, Calif., March 1993, pp. 256–265.

[7] R. Guerin, H. Ahmadi and M. Naghshineh, Equivalent capacity and its application to bandwidth allocation in high speed networks, *IEEE J. Select. Areas Comm* **9** (7) (1991) 968–981.

[8] H. Heffes and D.M. Lucantoni, A Markov modulated characterization of packetized voice and data traffic and related statistical multiplexer performance, *IEEE J. Select. Areas Comm.* **4** (6) (1986) 856–868.

[9] J.Y. Hui and E. Arthurs, A broadband packet switch for integrated transport, *IEEE J. Select. Areas Comm.* **5** (1987) 1264–1273.

[10] M. Murata, Y. Ohba and H. Miyahara, Analysis of flow enforcement algorithm for bursty traffic in ATM networks, *Proc. IEEE INFOCOM'92*, Firenze, Italy, May 1992, pp. 2453–2462.

[11] E.P. Rathgeb, Modelling and performance comparison of policing mechanisms for ATM networks, *IEEE J. Select. Areas Comm.* **9** (3) (1991) 325–334.

[12] S.Q. Li and S. Chong, Fundamental limits of input rate control in high speed networks, *Proc. IEEE INFOCOM'93*, San Francisco, Calif., March 1993, pp. 662–671.

[13] S. Radhakrishnan and S.V. Raghavan, Network support for distributed multimedia – issues and trends, *Proc. SEACOMM'94, Int. Conf. on Communications and Computer Networks*, Kuala Lumpur, Malaysia, 1994.

[14] G. Rigolio and L. Fratta, Input rate regulation and bandwidth assignment in ATM networks: an integrated approach, *Proc. ITC-13: Queueing, Performance and Control in ATM*, Copenhagen, Denmark, June 1991, pp. 123–128.

[15] M. Sidi, W. Liu, I. Cidon and I. Gopal, Congestion control through input rate regulation, *Proc. GLOBECOM'89*, Dallas, Texas, November 1989, pp. 1764–1768.

[16] K. Sriram and W. Whitt, Characterizing superposition arrival processes in packet multiplexers for voice and data, *IEEE J. Select. Areas Comm.* **4** (1986) 833–846.

[17] G.D. Stamoulis, M.E. Anagnoustou and A.D. Georgantas, Traffic source models for ATM networks: a survey, *Comput. Comm.* **17** (6) (1994) 428–438.

[18] J.S. Turner, New directions in communications (or which way to the information age?), *IEEE Comm.* **24** (10) (October 1986) 8–15.

[19] D. Yates, J. Kurose, D. Towsley and M.G. Hluchyj, On per-session end-to-end delay distributions and the call admission problem for real-time applications with QoS requirements, *Proc. ACM SIGCOMM'93*, Ithaca, N.Y., September 1993, pp. 2–12.

S. Radhakrishnan received B.Sc. (Engg) degree in Electronics and Communication with first rank and distinction from University of Kerala in 1982. During 1983, he worked as an Engineer in Vikram Sarabhai Space Center, Trivandrum after which he joined College of Engineering, Trivandrum as a lecturer. In 1988, he received an M.Tech in Computer Science and Engineering from Indian Institute of Technology, Madras. Since 1988, he has been a member of the faculty of Government Engineering College, Trichur. He is currently pursuing his doctoral studies in the Department of Computer Science and Engineering, I.I.T Madras. His areas of interest are high speed networks, congestion control and performance evaluation.

S.V. Raghavan is a Professor in the Department of Computer Science and Engineering, Indian Institute of Technology, Madras. He is also the Chief Investigator of the project on Education and Research in Computer Networking jointly sponsored by the Department of Electronics, Government of India, and the United Nations Development Programme. Dr. Raghavan is a life member of the Computer Society of India, a member of the Institution of Engineers and a fellow of the Institute of Electronics and Telecommunication Engineers. He is presently serving on the Board of Editors of the Journal of Institute of Electronics and Telecommunication Engineers (IETE) for computers and control. He is also a member of the Editorial Advisory Board for Computer Communications. His research interests are networks, protocols, multimedia systems and performance.

Ashok K. Agrawala is a Professor of Computer Science at the University of Maryland, College Park. He earned the A.M. and Ph.D. degrees in Applied Mathematics from Harvard University, Cambridge, Mass. in 1970. From 1968 to 1970, Dr. Agrawala was a Senior Engineer in the Applied Research Department, Honeywell, Inc. Waltham, Mass. In 1970, he joined the Honeywell Information Systems as Principal Engineer in the Optical Character Recognition Department. Since 1971, he has been on the Faculty of the Department of Computer Science, University of Maryland, College Park. He has been actively involved in research on several aspects of computer systems. He introduceed the idea of clustering for characterizing the workload of computer systems. He developed techniques for transient analysis of queues. Recently, he has been working on the design problems for hard real-time systems and has developed the system, MARUTI, which addresses the needs of next generation real-time systems operating in distributed environments and supporting fault tolerant operations. He has also developed deterministic analysis techniques for computer networks and applied them to flow and congestion control problems. In the past, he has published on microprogramming, computer architectures, local area networks and pattern recognition. He is the author of many papers and books.

Dr. Agrawala is a fellow of the IEEE and a member of the Association for Computing Machinery, American Association for Advancement of Science and Sigma Xi.

CHAPTER IV

ROUTING

This chapter provides an in-depth treatment of routing in ATM networks.

Routing Subject to Quality of Service Constraints in Integrated Communication Networks

With increasingly diverse QOS requirements, it is impractical to continue to rely on conventional routing paradigms that emphasize the search for an optimal path based on a predetermined metric, or a particular function of multiple metrics. Modern routing strategies must not only be adaptive to network changes but also offer considerable economy of scope.

Whay C. Lee, Michael G. Hluchyj, and Pierre A. Humblet

WHAY C. LEE is with the Networking Research Department at Motorola.

MICHAEL G. HLUCHYJ is Vice President and Chief Technology Officer at Summa Four. This work was performed while he was with Motorola.

PIERRE A. HUMBLET is with Eurecom Institute.

This paper was presented in part at INFOCOM '93, San Francisco, CA [1]

Traditional communication network architectures were designed to support users with homogeneous and simple quality of service (QOS) requirements. With increasing demand for a wide spectrum of network services, networking technologies that thrived on economy of scale are gradually giving way to new technologies that offer economy of scope. Modern communication networks must cater to users with diverse, fine-grain, and subjective QOS requirements. This task is accomplished by means of a wide spectrum of network control mechanisms operating over various time-scales. In a connection-oriented communication network, the transfer of information between two end users is accomplished by network functions that select and allocate network resources along an acceptable path. The logical association between the communicating end users is referred to as a call. The "chain" of network resources that support a call is a connection. Routing is a call-level network control mechanism through which a path is derived for establishing communication between a source and a destination in a network. This article proposes a call-level QOS framework in which QOS is specified in terms of QOS constraints, examines issues of routing subject to QOS constraints, and presents a call-by-call source routing scheme with rule-based fallbacks that depend on connection states.

Path selection within routing is typically formulated as a shortest path optimization problem, i.e., determine a series of network links connecting the source and destination such that a particular objective function is minimized. The objective function may be the number of hops, cost, delay, or some other metric that corresponds to a numeric sum of the individual link parameters along the selected path. Efficient algorithms for computing shortest paths have been used in communication networks (e.g., Dijkstra, Bellman-Ford) [2]. However, within the context of satisfying diverse QOS requirements, the computation becomes more difficult as constraints are introduced in the optimization problem. These constraints typically fall into two categories: link constraints and path constraints. A link constraint is a restriction on the use of links for path selection, e.g., available capacity on a link must be greater than or equal to that required by the call. Link constraints are relatively straightforward, as one simply removes links from the topology for shortest path computation that do not meet the link selection criteria. A path constraint is a bound on the combined value of a performance metric along a selected path (e.g., end-to-end delay through the network must not exceed what the call can tolerate). Path constraints make a routing problem intractable. In fact, a shortest path problem with even one path constraint is known to be NP-complete (see Shortest Weight-Constrained Path Problem in [3]).

The subjectivity of today's QOS requirements and the complex trade-off among them make it difficult to define an appropriate routing metric. Moreover, with distinct characteristics of different traffic types, the same metric is not universally applicable. The introduction of QOS negotiation further renders the meaning of an optimal path indeterminable. There is little or no additional utility for having a path whose associated QOS is more desirable than the user-specified QOS. On the other hand, there is considerable disutility for failing to find a path that meets the user-specified QOS. Hence, a new routing paradigm that emphasizes searching for an acceptable path satisfying various QOS requirements is needed for integrated communication networks.

Apart from issues of user-specified QOS requirements, there is also the problem of routing in a dynamic environment due to transient fluctuations in offered load, time-of-day changes in service demand, and incidental disruptions in the network (e.g., link failure and call preemption). In addition, the routing topology may also

0890-8044/95/$04.00 1995 © IEEE

change because of the possibility of dynamically adding and removing transmission facilities. Thus, modern routing strategies must be designed to adapt to changes in the network.

In this article, we consider the problem of routing in networks subject to QOS constraints. After providing an overview of prior routing work in the second section, we define various QOS constraints in the third section. In the fourth section, we present a call architecture that may be used for QOS matching. In the following section, we present a connection management mechanism for network resource allocation. Next, we discuss routing subject to QOS constraints. Following that we present fallback routing, and review some existing routing frameworks. In the following section, we present a new rule-based, call-by-call source routing strategy for integrated communication networks. A brief conclusion is provided in the final section.

Overview of Existing Routing Technologies

Many routing algorithms or strategies for connection-oriented and connectionless networks are found in the literature. We provide an overview below for a few that address issues of QOS and dynamic networks.

Alternate routing is widely used in telephone networks to provide dependable services. In [4], two fundamentally different classes of alternate routing algorithms, deterministic and randomized alternate routing algorithms, were investigated. Dynamic Non-Hierarchical Routing (DNHR) is a deterministic alternate routing scheme where the assignment of alternate paths is static, subject to time-of-day changes [5]. It was later extended to allow periodic update of the alternate assignment via a trunk status map [6]. DNHR eventually evolved into a more robust adaptive routing method in which a predetermined one-hop path is attempted first on a per-call basis, and if there is not enough capacity, all two-hop alternate paths are scanned to determine, if available, the one with the least load [7]. A similar approach known as Dynamic Traffic Management (DTM) makes routing decisions for groups of calls instead of on a call-by-call basis, and allows them to attempt a direct path and a recommended alternate path with the largest number of free circuits [8]. In addition to the previous techniques on which existing systems are based, a variety of other approaches have been suggested. In randomized alternate routing, each alternate path is selected with a given probability for a call. The probability assignment for each alternate path is continuously updated to reflect the likelihood of a successful attempt with the path. The more likely an alternate path permits a successful attempt, the higher is its probability of being selected. Early versions of stochastic routing are found in [9, 10]. In a recent version, known as Dynamic Alternate Routing (DAR), routing choices are reset whenever a call fails [11]. When a one-hop path is busy, the alternate two-hop path last successfully used is used once again for the next call overflow. If the alternate path is busy, calls are blocked and a new alternate path is selected at random. In fuzzy alternate routing, each alternate path is assigned a value between 0 and 1, determined by a "fuzzy membership" function, to indicate the relative order of selection of the path [12].

Conventional routing paradigms for data networks emphasize the search for an optimal path based on a predetermined metric, or a particular function of multiple metrics. In [13], an algorithm was proposed to solve a routing and flow control problem for an operating point with the optimal trade-off among delay, throughput, and fairness. In [14], a routing problem is formulated as a nonlinear combinatorial optimization problem, with the objective of maximizing a total traffic-dependent reward for the admitted calls subject to constraints on end-to-end cell loss probability and delay. In [15], a dynamic routing method that minimizes a long-run average cost of lost calls, using an optimization technique based on Markov decision theory, was proposed. Intra-domain routing protocols, such as the Open Shortest Path First (OSPF) protocol, support assignment of different type-of-service routing metrics based on different combinations of delay, throughput, and reliability [16].

Policy routing incorporates policy related constraints into path computation and packet forwarding functions for inter-domain communication [17]. It uses explicit policy advertisement along with topology information and a link-state style source routing protocol. Each administrative domain is governed by an autonomous administration, with distinct goals as to the class of customers it intends to serve, the QOS it intends to deliver, and the means for recovering its cost. The abstract policy route, a series of administrative domains, is specified by the end administrative domain as a form of source route, and each policy gateway selects the next actual policy gateway that is to be used to forward the packets.

Routing subject to multiple path constraints (e.g., cost and delay constraints) is a desirable feature in today's integrated networks in spite of its intractability. In [18], two heuristic approaches for solving a shortest path problem subject to multiple path constraints were proposed. In [19], an intractable multicast routing problem subject to a path constraint is heuristically reduced to constrained shortest path subproblems. It is common to formulate a routing problem subject to multiple path constraints as a multicriteria shortest path problem where each constrained path metric is taken to be a routing objective. A simple approach for multicriteria routing is to assume that the "optimal" path is a non-dominated path, one such that every other path has at least one path value greater than the corresponding path value of that path. With this assumption, one can generate the set of non-dominated paths so that the utility function can be applied to each non-dominated path to determine the desired path. A number of methods to generate these paths for a shortest path problem with two objective functions were reported in [20].

Call preemption has become increasingly useful for prioritized resource allocation in applications where there is a wide variety of traffic types. In [21], several versions of an optimal call preemption problem were shown to be computationally intractable, and some heuristic algorithms were proposed. Less efficient, but robust, preemption algorithms are found in [22]. In these algorithms, calls are normally routed using a table-driven routing algorithm, without considering their priority levels. When a high-priority call is blocked,

Routing subject to multiple path constraints (e.g., cost and delay constraints) is a desirable feature in today's integrated networks in spite of its intractability.

the call is routed, with preemption, along a path determined by means of flooding search messages all over the network. Some non-preemptive routing strategies for networks with priority classes are surveyed in [23]. These strategies resort to some means of either reserving resources for high-priority calls (e.g., separate networks, trunk reservation, trunk subgrouping), or extending the search for feasible paths (e.g., more choices for alternate paths, limited waiting for resources).

Work on rule-based routing is relatively scarce. In [24], Stach proposed an Expert Router that can monitor and predict a network's configuration to decide which path to use for each new call. By establishing a profile of the application and associating it with the speeds of the terminals, the Expert Router can quickly determine whether a call is delay-tolerant or not. Calls with high delay tolerance are assigned the "poorest acceptable paths," whereas calls with low delay tolerance are assigned the "best" available paths.

Optimization techniques using artificial neural networks have found their way into adaptive routing in communication networks [25]. A neural network architecture implemented in each node in a communication network is continuously trained to recognize the current status or topology of the communication network as long as there are messages passing through or received by the node. Despite its potential, many open issues remain to be resolved before the suitability of this approach could be adequately established for routing in today's integrated networks.

Quality of Service Constraints

QOS may be considered as a degree of conformance to user-specified service criteria. Many existing QOS frameworks either focus heavily on traffic management performance criteria (e.g., [26]), or accommodate fine-grain user-oriented quality requirements (e.g., [27]). The QOS framework in emerging ATM networks distinguishes QOS at different time scales [28]. It supports a set of individually specified QOS parameters (e.g., available cell rate, cell transfer delay, etc.), and permits them to be configured as standard profile sets [29]. Additional work on QOS framework can be found in [30-34]. An important element and challenge in the architecture of integrated networks is the ability to offer the diversity of QOS required by the different applications that use the network, and yet still make efficient use of network resources. In [35], one finds a survey of a large volume of research on QOS issues focusing on performance-oriented call admission control in high speed networks.

We propose a call-level QOS framework in which QOS is specified in terms of three classes of QOS constraints which may depend on the type of service of the call: performance constraints (e.g., throughput, delay), resource constraints (e.g., transmission medium, channel security), and priority constraints (e.g., establishment priority, retention priority) [36]. A performance constraint is a constraint on a directly perceivable measure of the quality of information transfer over a connection. A resource constraint is a restriction on the use of a given type of network resource with a particular set of characteristics. A priority constraint is a condition imposed on network resource allocation to provide different blocking probabilities to traffic of different priority classes.

Performance constraints may be negotiable or non-negotiable among the network and the end users. A negotiable constraint is specified in terms of a range of values bounded by a requested value and an acceptable value. A requested value is the most desirable performance level the user would like to have if resources are readily available. An acceptable value is the least desirable performance level the user would tolerate. A non-negotiable constraint is specified in terms of only an acceptable value. Although each performance constraint is basically a path-dependent QOS constraint, it can be implemented as a constraint on either a link attribute (e.g., throughput) or a path attribute (e.g., delay). A link attribute is a link parameter that is considered individually to determine whether a given link is acceptable for carrying a given connection, whereas a path attribute is an accumulation of an additive link parameter along a given path to determine whether the path is acceptable for carrying a given connection.

Resource constraints, which are subject to user definition, may be directly related to QOS (e.g., security), or indirectly related to QOS (e.g., carrier selection). Resources may refer to basic network elements (e.g., links), or aggregations of network elements (e.g., administrative domains). The effective topology used for path selection is determined by availability and acceptability of network resources with various resource attributes. Each resource attribute (e.g., transmission medium) is associated with a set of possible discrete attribute values (e.g., satellite, microwave). A resource constraint can be specified in terms of a subset of this set. A network resource is not acceptable for a call unless each of its resource attribute values belongs to the corresponding resource constraint set. The simplest resource constraints determine whether or not a given resource is acceptable for routing a call. They are predetermined and do not depend on the status of the network.

Priority constraints may be implemented in one of two approaches in a routing architecture: preemptive routing and non-preemptive routing. In a preemptive approach, network resources that have already been allocated to existing calls may be retrieved and used to accommodate new calls of greater importance. Thus, the blocking performance of high-priority calls is improved at the expense of disruption to low-priority calls. In a non-preemptive approach, calls of high priority are granted preferential access to network resources without bumping existing calls off the network. Thus, the blocking performance of high-priority calls is improved at the expense of the blocking performance of low-priority calls.

Call Architecture

We now describe a call architecture that may be used to support QOS matching [37]. Call Processing and Routing are two key network control components residing in each node representing a switching system in a network. Together, they are used to provide each call a connection that satisfies all QOS constraints, and to maintain an acceptable level of QOS throughout the duration of the call. The flow of control signals between a pair of end users during a typical call setup is shown in Fig. 1.

When a source user initiates a connect request, Call Processing at the source node queries its peer entity at the destination node for destination-specific QOS information. Call Processing at the destination node in turn queries the destination user, and then returns the information obtained to Call Processing at the source node. The QOS constraints derived from the end users' QOS requirements are then consolidated into a consistent set of constraints that are assigned to the connection to be established between the end users. A set of QOS constraints is acceptable for call setup only if it is acceptable to both end users. QOS translation is carried out whenever it is needed in the QOS consolidation phase to account for various protocol processing overheads and to provide a bridge between the different interpretations of QOS on opposite sides of each protocol interface. Subsequently, Call Processing at the source node obtains from Routing an acceptable path that satisfies the consolidated QOS constraints. The QOS associated with this selected path is referred to as the available QOS. QOS negotiation is a procedure involving the network and the end users during call setup to determine the level of QOS that is agreeable by the end users and can be supported by the network. For each negotiable performance constraint, an agreed value is determined. During QOS negotiation, if it is determined that a path is available such that the network can provide a performance value that is better than the requested value, the path is accepted, but only the requested value would be guaranteed. If the network can only provide a performance value that is worse than the acceptable value, the call would be blocked, or it may have to preempt other calls.

When QOS negotiation is completed, a remote connect request is sent across the network and indicated to the destination user. The response is relayed back to Call Processing at the source node, which finally notifies the source user of the completion of QOS negotiation. Finally, Call Processing builds the network path by allocating resources from the source to the destination. In this phase, Call Processing derives from the agreed QOS meaningful network status information, and submits it to Routing for topology update. Call Processing also derives from the agreed QOS useful information for allocating network resources such that the agreed QOS can be guaranteed. Note that a call setup that involves QOS negotiation takes an amount of time that is of the order of two times the end-to-end round-trip delay. Compared to this delay, the time to compute a path for routing in a typical network is relatively small.

Connection Management

Connection management is a connection-level network control mechanism that is responsible for setting up, maintaining, and taking down connections. We show in Fig. 2 the transitions among four distinct connection states for connection management: Connection Establishment, Connection Reestablishment, Information Transfer, and Connection Release. Establishment refers to the setting up of a connection. Reestablishment is needed after

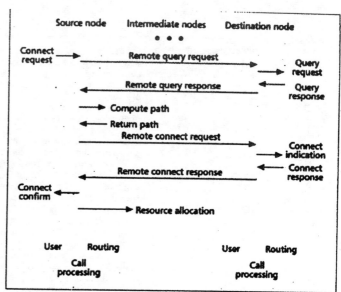

■ Figure 1. *Call architecture.*

an existing connection has been disrupted either by a network failure or by preemption. Reoptimization is performed by the network to conserve network resources utilized by established connecti

When a call arrives at a network node, it enters the Establishment state. If there are not enough resources to support the call, the call is rejected. Otherwise, upon successful connection establishment (i.e., a path is available such that all QOS constraints are satisfied), the call enters the Information Transfer state. When a call in the Information Transfer state is completed, it enters the Release state, and the connection is subsequently taken down. When a call is in the Information Transfer state, its connection may fail or be preempted. Should this happen, the call enters the Reestablishment state, so that the network may automatically attempt to reestablish the connection by finding a new acceptable path. During reestablishment, the QOS constraints associated with an affected call are adjusted according to update rules that take into consideration the previously agreed value. Any missing or out-of-sequence protocol data units (e.g., cells in an ATM network) due to reestablishment could be taken care of by error recovery protocols at the link or transport layers. Provided an acceptable path is found, network resources are allocated along the new path from source to destination. Upon successful reestablishment, the call reenters the Information Transfer state. The length of time in which a connection reestablishment attempt may be repeated is limited by the connection reestablishment delay. Beyond this delay, the reestablishment procedure is aborted, and the call enters the Release state.

Reoptimization is carried out by the network, without direct user involvement, to find a more economical path or one that satisfies more stringent QOS constraints. It is useful for preventing connections from permanently using unnecessarily costly paths in the event that they happen to be established when the network is congested. Reoptimization can be triggered by the network admin-

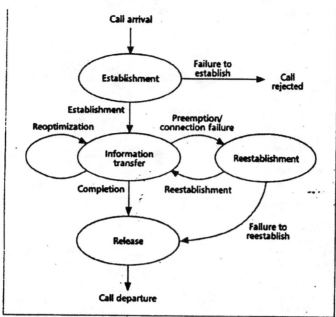

■ Figure 2. *Connection states.*

istrator (periodically), or by time-of-day. The procedure for reoptimization is similar to that for reestablishment. During reoptimization for a call, the QOS constraints associated with the call are adjusted according to update rules such that they become more stringent, and the call remains in the Information Transfer state.

During call preemption, the preempting call must be in either the Connection Establishment state or the Connection Reestablishment state. During path computation, a call may only preempt lower priority calls that are in the Information Transfer state. However, for preemption due to resource contention while resources are being allocated to a new connection, the preempted call may be in any connection state.

Routing Subject to QOS Constraints

*I*n this section, we examine issues of routing subject to performance constraints, resource constraints, and priority constraints.

Routing Subject to Performance Constraints

For each performance parameter, a path constraint is derived from its acceptable value. Unfortunately, a shortest path problem with path constraints is intractable [3]. The value of each constrained path metric may itself be a criterion for minimization to improve the chance of finding a path that satisfies the particular path constraint. However, a multicriteria shortest path problem is not a well defined optimization problem unless all the criteria are embedded in one utility function used as a single objective function for the shortest path problem.

There exists no efficient algorithm to solve the multicriteria shortest path problem with a general utility function. However, if a linear utility function (e.g., a weighted sum of delay and cost) is assumed, the problem reduces to a single-criterion shortest path problem with linearly combined link attribute values. One considerable drawback for using a linear combination of routing objectives is that the resulting routing performance is quite sensitive to the selected relative weights. For example, consider the routing problem shown in Fig. 3: Determine an acceptable path from source *s* to destination *t*. Let $P(m, n)$ denote the *n*th link on the *m*th path. For each link, the parameters C and D represent the respective cost and delay of the link. The first path is clearly the minimum cost path, and the second the minimum delay path. If the overall routing objective weighs cost and delay equally, then one can verify that the third path is indeed the optimal path. Should the relative weights be biased sufficiently one way or the other, either the first or the second path may be the optimal path. Note that it is not known beforehand that with equal weighting of cost and delay, the optimal path traverses many more hops than either the minimum cost path or the minimum delay path.

Routing Subject to Resource Constraints

To accommodate preferential selection of network resources, it is common practice to assign weights to links, and let link weights be incorporated in the routing objective function. The less desirable a resource attribute value of a link is, the heavier is the weight assigned to the link. This approach cannot consistently satisfy the user resource preference, since the minimization of the sum of link weights along a path does not guarantee that the weights of individual links are also minimized. Moreover, routing performance is also very sensitive to the weights assigned to the links. Consider the example shown in Fig. 4. In this example, the weight *W* for each link is indicated, with one exception. We let *X* be the unknown weight of the link. We examine how the minimum weight path depends on the value of *X*. For $0 \le X < 4$, the first path is optimal, and it includes the link with weight *X*. For $X > 4$, the second path is optimal. Note that the second path traverses many more hops than the first path.

Resource attributes used to be specified with binary (include/exclude) choices when preferential resource selection is desirable. Today, many users demand multi-level preferential specification of resource attributes to support policy-oriented routing. For example, a user may specify each attribute value of a resource attribute in terms of one of four levels of resource preference: "required," "preferred," "don't_care," and "don't_use." A resource attribute is said to be preferentially dependent on another if its preference structure depends on that associated with the other resource attribute. For example, consider the following attribute sets: CONFIDENTIALITY with values "encrypted" and "unencrypted," and INTEGRITY with values "protected" and "unprotected." Suppose that a user permits either the combination of "unencrypted" and "protected," or the combination of "encrypted" and "unprotected." Then, no combination of confidentiality and integrity constraint sets can adequately represent this user's resource constraints. If all resource attributes are preferentially independent of one another, the user can specify preferences for one resource attribute at a time. For

251

simplicity, it is desirable that all resource attributes are preferentially independent of one another.

Routing Subject to Priority Constraints

Preemptive routing algorithms that rely on flooding to determine desirable paths (e.g., [22]) are not very efficient in utilizing network resources. However, they may be acceptable for a military network where the QOS requirements for the high-priority calls are stringent and cannot be compromised. Non-preemptive routing algorithms that reserve network resources for high-priority calls are not very efficient either, since unclaimed reserved resources cannot be used by low-priority calls. Preemptive routing is a better approach, provided that there is an efficient means of path selection and a minimally disruptive connection establishment.

For the preemptive approach, flooding can be avoided if all the relevant information for routing is made available at each node via an efficient topology distribution protocol. Priority constraints can be specified with respect to connection states, and implemented as link constraints. Specifically, each call is assigned a priority number for the Connection Establishment state (establishment priority), the Connection Reestablishment state (reestablishment priority), and the Information Transfer state (retention priority). A preemption is permitted only when the priority of the preempting call is higher than the priority of the call to be preempted. The appropriate priority number used for comparison is the one that is associated with the connection state of the given call. The admissibility of the call on a given link thus depends on the appropriate priority level of the call. The priority numbers are also used to resolve resource contention when multiple calls are simultaneously trying to utilize the same network resources. In this case, the call with the highest appropriate priority is processed first.

There is an undesirable cyclic effect, which occurs when a call with a high reestablishment priority preempts an existing call with a low retention priority, and is subsequently preempted by the latter because the retention priority of the former is lower than the reestablishment priority of the latter. As a result, the two calls may alternately switch between the Connection Reestablishment state and the Information Transfer state. The cyclic effect can be avoided if the retention priority of each call is required to be at least as high as its reestablishment priority.

Routing Framework

We now introduce fallback routing, review some existing routing frameworks, and compare their suitability for routing in integrated communication networks. Specifically, we consider five desirable aspects: economy of scale, economy of scope, fine granularity, path optimality, and adaptive capability. The comparisons are summarized in Table 1.

Call-by-Call Routing versus Table-Driven Routing

Call-by-call routing offers the flexibility of tailoring a path to the characteristics and QOS requirements of each call. Since path computation is done upon the arrival of each call, it permits fine-grain network control. There are increasing

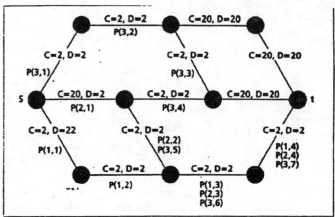

■ Figure 3. *Routing with cost and delay metrics.*

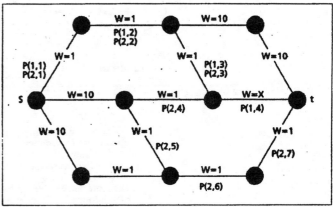

■ Figure 4. *Link weight approach.*

returns to scope because the computational overhead is independent of the number of call types. The approach also permits optimization of the path selected for each call. In today's integrated networks requiring call-level QOS matching, the time to compute a path is typically small compared to the round-trip delay of signaling to obtain the end users' QOS information for call setup. Provided that networks are well designed to support given call request rates, call-by-call routing offers great potential for QOS-sensitive routing.

In table-driven routing, all paths are precomputed and stored in routing tables. There are increasing returns to scale due to many calls being routed over the same path. However, this approach lacks fine-grain network control, and the selected paths cannot be optimal for all traffic types, unless a different table is used for each traffic type. The routing tables must adapt to topological changes.

Source Routing versus Hop-by-Hop Routing

In source routing, decisions for routing a call are made entirely at the source, based on global network configuration and status that are updated via a topology distribution protocol. Routing functions at intermediate nodes are thus relatively simple. With sufficient topology information available to the

Routing framework	Economy of scope	Economy of scale	Fine granularity	Path optimality	Adaptive capability
Call-by-call routing	x		x	x	x
Table-driven routing		x			
Source routing	x		x	x	
Hop-by-hop routing		x			x
Fallback routitng	x		x	x	x
Alternate Routing		x			x

■ Table 1. *Routing framework comparison.*

source, it is possible to have fine-grain network control and optimization of desired paths. There are increasing returns to scope since the same topology information may be used for many traffic types. Source routing is hence very promising for path selection in modern integrated networks where there are increasingly many traffic types due to multimedia applications.

In hop-by-hop routing, routing decisions are distributed. Routing computation at intermediate nodes is non-trivial. With the use of routing tables, there are opportunities for economy of scale. However, routing tables require storage. In this approach, steps are needed to prevent loops. Although the approach can respond to failures quickly, the recovery is suboptimal because it retains the segment of the path from the source to the point of failure. It is difficult to use hop-by-hop routing to support call-level QOS matching (e.g., call preemption) because there is insufficient call specific information where routing decisions are made.

Fallback Routing versus Alternate Routing

In fallback routing, one sequentially computes paths based on a sequence of routing instances, until an acceptable one is available or the call will be blocked upon completion of a predetermined fallback sequence (Fig. 5). An instance of a constrained shortest path problem consists of link constraints, path constraints, and a routing objective function. Fallback routing adapts to changes in the network status, and permits alternate path computations to accommodate preferential resource constraints, call preemption, and other routing features that require multiple path computations per call setup. Fallback routing offers considerable economy of scope, for it accommodates heterogeneous users by computing alternate paths as they are needed. The sequence of fallback routing instances is either predetermined or selected in real time according to established rules. The routing instances can be specified to support fine granularity, provided pertinent QOS information is available.

In alternate routing, a set of predetermined paths stored in routing tables are attempted sequentially during each call setup for resource allocation until there is a successful attempt or the call will be blocked upon completion of the attempt sequence. The alternate paths may depend on traffic classes and the time-of-day. The use of routing tables offers economy of scale, but significant storage is needed. The routing tables may be periodically updated to adapt to existing network conditions. The manner in which alternate paths are attempted distinguishes among existing variations of alternate routing. Under

light loads, alternate routing minimizes blocking probability. But, under heavy loads, blocking probability may be increased drastically as alternate paths used tend to consume more network resources.

Rule-Based Call-by-Call Source Routing

Using the terminology defined in the previous section, we propose a call-by-call source routing strategy with rule-based fallbacks for communication networks with integrated traffic subject to diverse QOS requirements. The strategy is to efficiently determine an acceptable path for each call given the current state of the network. As opposed to the traditional routing paradigm where the primary goal is to minimize the value of a routing objective function, the routing paradigm described below emphasizes meeting various routing constraints. Nonetheless, the shortest path algorithm is still used as a means to identify acceptable paths.

Routing with Rule-Based Fallbacks

The proposed rule-based routing strategy makes use of all available information to dynamically modify the fallback sequence of path computations according to network status and connection states. The strategy begins path computation with an initial routing instance that is determined by the connection state and the user QOS requirements. If no feasible path is found, stopping rules are used to decide whether a fallback computation is in order. In the fallback, a new routing instance with relaxed constraints is selected according to fallback rules. If a feasible path is found, the network will attempt to allocate network resources along the path for the call. This attempt may sometimes fail because of resource contention due to latency in topology updates. If this attempt fails, the call is blocked. A more sophisticated alternative to this approach is to allow crankback so that the source will select a new routing instance to fall back on, using the latest information derived from the unsuccessful attempt. Crankback routing is similar to alternate routing, except that alternate paths are not predetermined, but computed one at a time after each unsuccessful attempt to establishment a connection.

The proposed rule-based routing strategy follows a generic rule-based model for expert systems. The model consists of three modules: data base, knowledge base, and inference engine. The data base contains topology information that is updated via a topology distribution protocol. The knowledge base contains rules that are used to generate routing instances based on a predetermined routing policy and the QOS demanded by the users. Examples of these rules are described in the next three subsections. The inference engine is basically a sequential shortest path computer that also verifies path feasibility.

Fallback on Performance Constraints — Instead of computing an optimal path for the intractable constrained shortest path problem, the proposed rule-based routing strategy uses the following heuristic for fallbacks. The original routing problem without path constraints is first solved, and then the selected path is checked against the path constraints to determine feasibility. If the path constraints are not satisfied for the selected path, fallback allows the call to have one or more additional opportunities to search for a feasible path.

Instead of dealing with an unknown multi-dimensional utility function, the proposed rule-based routing strategy assumes that the routing criteria are ranked by the network user according to relative importance. The ordered criteria are then used to determine the shortest path objective functions for the initial and fallback path computations. For example, the initial objective function may be minimizing cost. Should the computed path fail to meet the specified delay constraint, a fallback objective function of minimizing delay could be used to find an acceptable path. This ordinal ranking approach is different from a cardinal ranking approach which relies on relative weightings.

Fallback on Resource Constraints — The proposed rule-based routing strategy can accommodate preferential resource constraints. User preference for resources can be translated into preferential sets of resource constraints. Each of these sets can be selected to define a routing instance according to some predetermined rules. Suppose that each attribute value of a resource attribute is specified in terms of one of the following levels of resource preference.

- REQUIRED: At most, one attribute value from a given attribute set may be configured "required." When an attribute value is configured so, only resources characterized by this attribute value may be used.
- PREFERRED: Resources characterized by attribute values configured "preferred" must be considered with priority over those characterized by attribute values configured otherwise, except for "required."
- DON'T_CARE: Resources characterized by attribute values configured "don't_care" may be considered, in addition to any configured "preferred," only when no acceptable path can be found otherwise.
- DON'T_USE: Resources characterized by attribute values configured "don't_use" must be avoided. At least one attribute value from a given attribute value set should be configured differently from "don't_use."

We translate the four levels of resource preference into two sets of resource constraints, namely "requested resource constraints," denoted Requested_RC, and "acceptable resource constraints," denoted Acceptable_RC. An attribute value may be included in one or both sets of constraints, and if it is not included in a set, it is considered excluded from it. For each resource attribute, the resource translation algorithm sequentially checks the numbers of attribute values specified "required," "preferred," and "don't_care." It detects an invalid configuration when there is more than one attribute value specified "required," or none specified other than "don't_use." If there is only one attribute value specified "required," it is included in both Requested_RC and Acceptable_RC. If no attribute value is specified "required," and at least one is specified "preferred," then those that are specified "preferred" are included in both Requested_RC and Acceptable_RC, whereas those specified "don't_care" are included only in

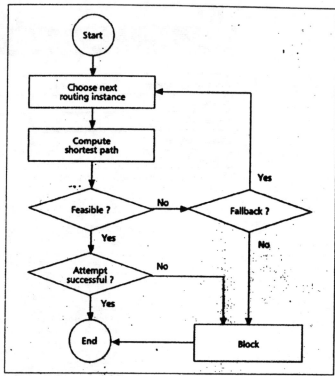

■ Figure 5. *Routing with fallbacks.*

Acceptable_RC. Else, if no attribute value is specified "required" or "preferred," and there is at least one attribute value specified "don't_care," those specified "don't_care" are included in both Requested_RC and Acceptable_RC.

With fallback routing, paths are first computed using only resources satisfying the requested resource constraints, with a fallback to the less restrictive acceptable resource constraints.

Fallback on Priority Constraints — Preemptive routing for networks with priority classes can be disruptive, and the overall throughput is not increased because of call preemption. Nonetheless, since no resources are reserved for high-priority calls, low-priority calls are not likely to be blocked when the network is lightly loaded. Using source routing where topology information is made available to the source for efficient path selection, there is no need to flood search messages throughout the network to determine desirable paths. It is often possible to relax the resource constraints of a call so that its performance constraints can be met without unnecessary disruption to calls of lower priority. Since preemption is inherently disruptive, routing without preemption should be attempted first before preemption is considered. We refer to this approach as look-around-first preemption. The fallback approach to routing permits look-around-first preemption to avoid unnecessary preemption, by first attempting to find a feasible path without preempting any existing calls. If this should fail, then in searching for a feasible path, the fallback routing instance only accounts for the resources consumed by the same or higher priority calls.

254

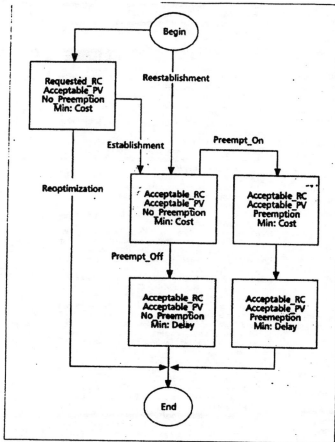

Begin

Requested_RC
Acceptable_PV
No_Preemption
Min: Cost

Reestablishment

Establishment

Reoptimization

Preempt_On

Acceptable_RC
Acceptable_PV
No_Preemption
Min: Cost

Acceptable_RC
Acceptable_PV
Preemption
Min: Cost

Preempt_Off

Acceptable_RC
Acceptable_PV
No_Preemption
Min: Delay

Acceptable_RC
Acceptable_PV
Preemption
Min: Delay

End

■ Figure 6. Rule-based routing.

State-Dependent Fallback Rules

To facilitate call-level QOS matching, existing alternate routing strategies make use of simple rules for selecting predetermined alternate paths. Some intra-domain routing protocols, such as OSPF, rely on predetermined routing instances that depend on type of service. The proposed rule-based routing strategy makes use of a knowledge base that contains a variety of rules for selecting routing instances in real-time as they are needed for initial and fallback path computations. Its main features include rules for selecting constrained routing instances, rules for falling back from one routing instance to another, and rules for determining when to fallback and when to stop.

A specific implementation of the proposed rule-based routing strategy is described below, and illustrated in Fig. 6. In this implementation, resource constraints are specified with preferences, as described earlier. In Fig. 6, PV stands for "performance value." The fallback scenario for each call depends on its connection state. In a normal situation for connection establishment without preemption, the initial routing instance is defined by the requested resource constraints, the path constraints, and the minimization of cost. If the initial routing attempt is unsuccessful, there will be a fallback on the resource constraints (i.e., the

acceptable resource constraints will be used instead of the requested resource constraints). If the second attempt fails because the delay path constraint could not be satisfied, there will be a fallback on the routing objective function (i.e., delay instead of cost). If the third attempt is unsuccessful, the call will be blocked. If preemption is allowed, there will be a fallback on preemption before the fallback on the routing objective function. It is important to note that if the network is designed and dimensioned properly, routing fallbacks are rare except when the network is overloaded.

Reestablishment follows a similar fallback scenario, except that the first routing instance is skipped. For reestablishment, both the requested and acceptable values associated with each negotiable performance constraint are set to the previously agreed value, so that this value continues to be guaranteed. No fallback is allowed for reoptimization. A connection will not be reoptimized unless the fractional improvement in the path cost exceeds a predetermined threshold.

A connection may be interrupted when resources along its path degrade excessively in performance or are disabled. If preemption is allowed, a connection may also be bumped by another connection of greater importance. When a connection is interrupted, an attempt is made to reestablish the connection so that it resumes service quickly. Connection reestablishment must be completed within a predetermined interval, known as the connection reestablishment delay, or the connection must be released.

Conclusion

With increasingly diverse QOS requirements, it is impractical to continue to rely on conventional routing paradigms that emphasize the search for an optimal path based on a predetermined metric, or a particular function of multiple metrics. Modern routing strategies must not only be adaptive to network changes but also offer considerable economy of scope. To satisfy the need for future integrated networks (e.g., ATM) to accommodate traffic with diverse QOS requirements, we have proposed a call-by-call source routing strategy that makes use of rule-based fallbacks. This strategy provides a flexible platform on which routing can be efficiently carried out subject to performance constraints, resource constraints, and priority constraints.

Fallback routing, an integral part of the proposed strategy, is an iterative path calculation approach wherein routing constraints may be modified in each iteration based on the QOS requirements of the call, the connection state of the call, and dynamic network information. The outcome of a fallback path calculation is either a selected path or that there is no path that satisfies all the QOS constraints. Without fallbacks, a single-pass rule-based routing can neither accommodate preferential resource constraints nor look-around-first call preemption. Although alternate routing offers economy of scale (in the sense that the same computation performed can be used for many calls), it cannot efficiently support integrated traffic with diverse QOS requirements. The predetermined alternate paths impose unnecessary restriction on the search for a suitable path. Policy routing can accommodate to some extent various QOS constraints. However, the constraints must be translated into domain-based resource constraints, and there is no mechanism to deal with preferential resource constraints.

QOS-sensitive routing is an important feature in the emerging implementation of routing in ATM networks [38]. Here, the proposed routing architecture is hierarchical source routing with optional crankbacks. A variety of traffic-dependent QOS-related topology state parameters are advertised to support call-level QOS matching. Topology information at each hierarchical level is aggregated to trade-off fine-grain QOS matching for scaling in very large networks. Rule-based, call-by-call source routing is ideal for QOS-sensitive path selection within a routing domain where it is easy to distribute relatively accurate topology information. For inter-domain routing, where only partial topology information is available and different domains may use different intra-domain routing algorithms for path selection, it is difficult to guarantee efficient use of network resources. Nonetheless, fallback routing is still useful for preferential resource selection, prioritized multicriteria routing, look-around-first call preemption, and improving the chance of success for crankback and/or reroute after failure or call preemption.

Acknowledgment

The authors thank P. Kamat, D. Faulkner, and R. Constantin for many valuable comments and suggestions.

References

[1] W. Lee, M. Hluchyj, and P. Humblet, "Rule-Based Call-by-Call Source Routing for Integrated Communication Networks," *Proc. IEEE INFOCOM '93*, 1993, pp. 987-993.
[2] D. Bertsekas and R. Gallager, *Data Networks*, (Prentice-Hall, 1987).
[3] M. R. Garey and D. S. Johnson, *Computers and Intractability: A Guide to the Theory of NP-Completeness*, (W. H. Freeman, 1979).
[4] D. Mitra and J. B. Seery, "Comparative Evaluations of Randomized and Dynamic Routing Strategies for Circuit-Switched Networks," *IEEE Trans. on Commun.*, vol. 39, no. 1, Jan. 1991, pp. 102-116.
[5] G. R. Ash, R. H. Cardwell, and R. P. Murray, "Design and Optimization of Networks with Dynamic Routing," *Bell Labs. Tech. Journal*, vol. 60, no. 8, Oct. 1981.
[6] G. R. Ash, "Use of a Trunk Status Map for Real-Time DNHR," *Proc. of the 11th Int'l Teletraffic Congress*, Kyoto, Japan, Sept. 1985.
[7] G. R. Ash and B. D. Huang, "An Analytical Model for Adaptive Routing Networks," *IEEE Trans. on Communications*, vol. 41, no. 11, Nov. 1993, pp. 1748-1759.
[8] J. Regnier and W. H. Cameron, "State-Dependent Dynamic Traffic Management for Telephone Networks," *IEEE Commun. Mag.*, vol. 28, no. 10, Oct. 1990, pp. 42-53.
[9] K. S. Narendra, E. A. Wright, and L. G. Mason, "Application of Learning Automata to Telephone Traffic Routing and Control," *IEEE Trans. on Systems, Man, and Cybernetics*, vol. SMC-7, no. 11, Nov. 1977, pp. 785-792.
[10] V. V. Marbukh, "Investigation of a Fully Connected Channel Switching Network with Many Nodes and Alternative Routes," *Simulation of Behavior and Intelligence*, (Plenum Publishing Corporation, 1984), pp. 1601-1608.
[11] P. B. Key and G. A. Cope, "Distributed Dynamic Routing Schemes," *IEEE Commun. Mag.*, Oct. 1990, pp. 54-64.
[12] A. Krasniewski, "Fuzzy Automata as Adaptive Algorithms for Telephone Traffic Routing," *Proc. IEEE ICC '84*, pp. 61-66, May 1984.
[13] S. Chong, "Fair Integration of Routing and Flow Control in Communication Networks," *IEEE Trans. on Commun.*, vol. 40, no. 4, April 1992, pp. 821-834.
[14] F. Lin and J. R. Yee, "A Real-Time Distributed Routing and Admission Control Algorithm for ATM Networks," *Proc. IEEE INFOCOM '93*, 1993, pp. 792-801.
[15] A. Kolarov and J. Hui, "Least Cost Routing in Multiple-Service Networks," *Proc. IEEE INFOCOM '94*, 1994, pp. 1482-1489.
[16] J. Moy, "OSPF Version 2," RFC 1247, July 1991.
[17] D. D. Clark, "Policy Routing in Internetworks," *Internetworking: Research and Experience*, vol. 1, 1990, pp. 35-52.
[18] J. M. Jaffe, "Algorithms for Finding Paths with Multiple Constraints," *Networks*, vol. 14, 1984, pp. 95-116.
[19] V. P. Kompella, J. C. Pasquale, and G. C. Polyzos, "Multi-cast Routing for Multimedia Communication," *IEEE/ACM Trans. on Networking*, vol. 1, no. 3, June 1993.
[20] M. I. Henig, "The Shortest Path Problem with Two Objective Functions," *European Journal of Operational Research*, 25, 1985, pp. 281-291.
[21] J. A. Garay and I. S. Gopal, "Call Preemption in Communication Networks," *Proc. IEEE INFOCOM '92*, 1992, pp. 1043-1050.
[22] R. P. Lippmann, "New Routing and Preemption Algorithms for Circuit-Switched Mixed-Media Networks," *Proc. IEEE MILCOM '85*, 1985, pp. 660-666.
[23] G. Gopal, A. Kumar, and A. Weinrib, "Routing in a Circuit-Switched Network with Priority Classes," *Proc. IEEE INFOCOM '89*, April 1989, pp. 792-799.
[24] J. F. Slach, "Expert Systems Find a New Place in Data Networks," in *Networking Software*, Ungaro, ed., Data Communication Book Series, (McGraw Hill, 1987), pp. 75-83.
[25] C. Wang and P. N. Weissler, "The Use of Artificial Neural Networks for Optimal Message Routing," *IEEE Network Mag.*, March/April 1995, pp. 16-24.
[26] ANSI X3.102-1983, "American National Standard for Information Systems—Data Communications Systems and Services — User-Oriented Performance Parameters."
[27] J. S. Richters and C. A. Dvorak, "A Framework for Defining the Quality of Communications Services," *IEEE Commun. Mag.*, vol. 26, no. 10, Oct. 1988.
[28] H. Gilbert, O. Aboul-Magd, and V. Phung, "Developing a Cohesive Traffic Management Strategy for ATM Networks," *IEEE Commun. Mag.*, vol. 29, no. 10, Oct. 1991, pp. 36-45.
[29] ATM Forum Traffic Management Draft Specification, Version 4.0, April 1995.
[30] A. Campbell, G. Coulson, and D. Hutchison, "A Quality of Service Architecture," *ACM SIGCOMM Computer Communication Review*, vol. 24, no. 2, April 1994, pp. 6-27.
[31] A. A. Lazar, A. Temple, and R. Gidron, "An Architecture for Integrated Networks that Guarantees Quality of Service," *Int'l J. Digital and Analog Comm. Systems*, vol. 3, no. 2, 1990.
[32] A. A. Lazar and G. Pacifici, "Control of Resources in Broadband Networks with Quality of Service Guarantees," *IEEE Commun. Mag.*, vol. 29, no. 10, Oct. 1991, pp. 66-73.
[33] J. Jung and A. Gravey, "QoS Management and Performance Monitoring in ATM Networks," *Proc. IEEE GLOBECOM '93*, 1993, pp. 708-712.
[34] J. Jung and D. Seret, "Translation of QoS Parameters into ATM Performance Parameters in B-ISDN," *Proc. IEEE INFOCOM '93*, 1993, pp. 748-755.
[35] J. Kurose, "Open Issues and Challenges in Providing Quality of Service Guarantees in High-Speed Networks," *ACM SIGCOMM Computer Commun. Review*, vol. 23, no. 1, Jan. 1993, pp. 6-15.
[36] W. Lee and P. Kamat, "Integrated Packet Networks with Quality of Service Constraints," *Proc. IEEE GLOBECOM '91*, Dec. 2-5, 1991, pp. 8A.3.1- 8A.3.5.
[37] W. Lee and P. Kamat, "Quality of Service Matching for Integrated Fast Packet Networks," *Proc. IEEE GLOBECOM '92*, Dec. 6-9, 1992, pp. 931-937.
[38] ATM Forum PNNI Draft Specification, April 1995.

Biographies

WHAY C. LEE [M '89] received a B.S. in economics, B.S., M.S., E.E., and Ph.D. degrees in electrical engineering from MIT. In 1982, he was an intern at COMSAT Laboratories. In November 1988, he joined the Networking Research Department of Motorola Codex, Mansfield, Massachusetts, where he conducted applied research in routing, connection management, and quality of service issues in high speed integrated cell relay networks. Since 1994, he has been representing Motorola in the PNNI Subworking Group of the ATM Forum.

MICHAEL G. HLUCHYJ [F '94] received a B.S.E.E. from the University of Massachusetts-Amherst, and S.M., E.E., and Ph.D. degrees in electrical engineering from the Massachusetts Institute of Technology. In 1981, he joined the technical staff at AT&T Bell Laboratories, and in 1987, he became director of Networking Research at Motorola Codex, where he led efforts in the architecture, design, and analysis of all levels of traffic management for high-speed, integrated cell relay networks. In 1994, he became vice president and chief technology officer at Summa Four, Manchester, New Hampshire, where he is currently responsible for identifying and assessing strategic market requirements, technology trends and architectural directions for Summa Four's future products.

PIERRE A. HUMBLET [F '93] received his electrical engineering degree from the University of Louvain, Belgium, in 1973, and M.S.E.E. and Ph.D. degrees from MIT, where he became a professor of electrical engineering in 1978. In 1993, he joined the Eurecom Institute, France. His teaching and research interests are in the area of communication systems, particularly digital mobile networks and optical networks. He is a consultant with a number of companies, most recently with Motorola and IBM.

Although alternate routing offers economy of scale, it cannot efficiently support integrated traffic with diverse QOS requirements.

Competitive Routing of Virtual Circuits in ATM Networks

Serge Plotkin

(*Invited Paper*)

Abstract— Classical routing and admission control strategies achieve provably good performance by relying on an assumption that the virtual circuits arrival pattern can be described by some *a priori* known probabilistic model. Recently a new on-line routing framework, based on the notion of *competitive analysis*, was proposed. This framework is geared toward design of strategies that have provably good performance even in the case where there are *no statistical assumptions* on the arrival pattern and parameters of the virtual circuits. The on-line strategies motivated by this framework are quite different from the min-hop and reservation-based strategies. This paper surveys the on-line routing framework, the proposed routing and admission control strategies, and discusses some of the implementation issues.

I. INTRODUCTION

FUTURE broadband integrated services digital networks (B-ISDN) will carry a wide spectrum of new consumer services, such as video-on-demand, video teleconferencing, etc. A key characteristic of these services is that they require quality-of-service (QoS) guarantees. Assuring QoS requires reservation of resources. As a result, B-ISDN will likely allocate resources in terms of virtual circuits (or virtual paths). In particular, creating a virtual circuit will require reservation of bandwidth on some path between the endpoints of the connection. Since network resources are limited, some requests for establishment of virtual circuits will be denied.

Thus, there is a need for an *admission control* and *routing* strategy that addresses the following two questions:

- What path should be used to route a given circuit?
- Which circuits should be routed and which ones should be rejected?

The admission control and routing strategy has to take into account the limitations of the underlying network. In particular, due to the high bandwidth-dely product, each circuit has to be routed on a single path. Moreover, rerouting circuits is either heavily discouraged or outright forbidden. For some applications it is more efficient to use *multicast* circuits, where instead of a single destination there are multiple destinations. Examples include teleconferencing, video on demand, database updates, etc. In this case the routing strategy has to choose a *tree* that spans the nodes participating in the multicast.

The problem of bandwidth reservation and management in the context of circuit-switched networks has been studied extensively. Until recently, most of the analysis and design

Manuscript received September 30, 1994; revised April 1, 1995. This work was supported by NSF CCR-9304971, ARO DAAH04-95-1-0121, and Terman Fellowship.

The author is with Stanford University, Stanford, CA 94305 USA.

IEEE Log Number 9412661.

effort concentrated on achieving provably good performance under the assumption that the arrival pattern of virtual circuit requests can be described by a simple probabilistic model with known parameters. This approach, starting from the work of Kelly [26], lead to the development of many practical routing strategies. Examples include the dynamic non-hierarchical routing (DNHR) [2], [4], [1] and real time network routing (RTNR) [3] strategies developed in AT&T, as well as dynamically controlled routing (DCR) developed at Bell Northern Research [16], [17], [24]. Dynamic state-dependent routing strategies based on reservation were thoroughly analyzed by Mitra *et al.* in [34], [35].

Recently, a new framework was proposed that leads to routing strategies that can achieve provably good performance without relying on any assumptions about the probabilistic behavior of the traffic [20], [5], [19], [8], [9]. The first step in developing such strategies was to develop an appropriate way to compare these strategies one to another. The difficulty lies in the fact that traditionally, the performance of routing strategies is measured as a function of the parameters characterizing the input traffic; this approach is not appropriate when there is no *a priori* knowledge of these parameters. Thus, it was necessary to develop a measure that will allow us to compare different strategies and that is meaningful independent of whether or not there are assumptions about the input traffic.

The idea, proposed in [20], [5], is to use the concept of the *competitive ratio*. This concept was introduced in [39] and further developed in [25], [15], [33]. (Some of the earlier papers on approximation algorithms, e.g., [40], can be viewed as optimizing the competitive ratio as well.) A competitive ratio is defined with respect to two algorithms; both algorithms have to deal with the incoming requests, which in our case are requests for establishing virtual circuits. One is the *on-line* algorithm whose performance we want to measure. The on-line algorithm has to deal with the requests one-by-one and can not use any knowledge of the future requests. The other is the best possible (in terms of performance) *off-line* algorithm; this algorithm is omniscient in the sense that it is assumed to have a *complete a priori knowledge* of the entire request sequence, including future requests. Informally, the competitive ratio measures how much the on-line algorithm loses in performance as a result of not making optimum decisions. In particular, it measures how much is lost due to lack of knowledge of future requests.

Formally, the competitive ratio of a given on-line algorithm is defined as the supremum over all input sequences of the performance achieved by the optimum off-line algorithm and

Reprinted from IEEE Journal on Selected Areas in Communications, Vol. 13, No. 6, Aug. 1996, pp. 1128-1135.

the performance achieved by this on-line algorithm. Roughly speaking, the statement that a particular strategy has competitive ratio α means that its performance is at most a factor of $1/\alpha$ of the performance of the best possible off-line algorithm.

Clearly, the "best" strategy with respect to the competitive ratio depends on the parameter chosen to measure the performance. Recently, two measures were proposed for computing the competitive ratio of the on-line routing and admission control algorithms—the *throughput* and the *congestion* measure. In the first, we measure the proportion of the routed (accepted) circuits. A variation on this measure is the total routed bandwidth-duration product, i.e., total throughput. In the second, we measure the maximum link congestion, i.e., maximum ratio of the allocated bandwidth on a link to its total bandwidth. Clearly, to use this measure we have to disallow rejections. Consequently, disallowing rejections implies that the on-line algorithm should be allowed to use more than 100% of the edge capacity.

A competitive strategy for the *congestion-minimization* model was developed by Aspnes, Azar, Fiat, Plotkin, and Waarts in [5]. This strategy achieves a competitive ratio of $O(\log n)$ for permanent (i.e., infinite holding time) virtual circuits (PVC's), where n is the number of nodes in the network. It was extended to the case of finite holding time circuits (SVC's) where the holding time of a circuit becomes known upon its arrival in [13]. For this case, the strategy achieves $O(\log nT)$ competitive ratio, where T is the maximum holding time.

Competitive strategies for the *throughput-maximization* model were given by Garay and Gopal for the case of a single link [20], by Garay, Gopal, Kutten, Mansour, and Yung [19] for a line network, and by Awerbuch, Azar, and Plotkin [8] for general network topologies. In particular, if the bandwidth requested by a single circuit never exceeds $O(1/\log L)$ fraction of link capacity, the strategy in [8] achieves a competitive ratio of $O(\log L)$ for PVC routing, where L is the maximum number of hops taken by a virtual circuit. In the SVC case where the duration of a circuit becomes known upon its arrival and the requested bandwidth never exceeds $O(1/\log LT)$ fraction, this strategy achieves $O(\log LT)$ ratio. It was shown that polylogarithmic competitive ratio is not achievable if the bandwidth of a single circuit exceeds $O(1/\log L)$ fraction of single link bandwidth for the PVC case and $O(1/\log LT)$ fraction for the SVC case [8].

Roughly speaking, the main idea behind the new competitive strategies is to assign each link a "length" that is a highly non-linear (e.g., exponential) function of its current congestion. The new circuit is routed along the *shortest path* with respect to this length. In the throughput-maximization model, the circuit is rejected if the length of the shortest path exceeds some predefined threshold that depends on the profit (e.g., bandwidth-duration product) associated with this circuit.

The intuition of routing along shortest paths with respect to a length function that is exponential in the congestion is based on viewing the routing problem as an instance of *multicommodity flow problem*. (See [14] for a thorough treatment of this relationship.) The multicommodity flow problem involves simultaneously shipping of several different commodities from their respective sources to their sinks in a single network so that the total amount of flow going through each edge is no more than its capacity. Associated with each commodity is a demand, which is the amount of that commodity that we wish to ship. In the routing context, commodities correspond to virtual circuits, demands correspond to the requested bandwidth, and capacity corresponds to the link bandwidth.

Roughly speaking, the multicommodity flow solution is optimal if all flows are routed along shortest paths, where the length is defined to be an appropriate function of the link congestion. Recently, several multicommodity flow algorithms that are based on repeated rerouting of flow onto shortest paths were developed [37], [28], [31]. By defining the length function to be exponential in the current congestion, these algorithms produce an approximate multicommodity flow in polynomial time.

It is important to note that although these (off-line) multicommodity flow algorithms provide the intuition behind the idea of routing along shortest paths with respect to an exponential function of congestion, they can not be used directly to construct dynamic on-line routing strategies. The main reason is that these algorithms rely on repetitive rerouting. Moreover, they work only if we have a complete knowledge of the entire request sequence.

While the $O(\log LT)$ competitive ratio does not seem sufficiently small from a practical point of view, it is important to observe that this ratio is achieved without any *a priori* knowledge about the input. The guarantee on competitive ratio can be greatly improved if we can introduce some probabilistic assumptions. The resulting strategies work well if the assumptions are satisfied, and do not "break down" if the assumptions turn out to be wrong.

We discuss several possible classes of assumptions in Section IV. For example, to achieve an $O(\log LT)$ competitive ratio in the throughput-maximization case, it is sufficient to know the distribution on the holding time of each arriving circuit rather than having the specific holding time. In particular, if the holding times are exponentially distributed, then it is possible to further improve the competitive ratio to $O(\log L \log \log L)$ [22]. This bound does not rely on the frequently made assumption that the arrival patterns to different links are independent. It is interesting to note that there can be no strategy (deterministic or randomized) that achieves a polylogarithmic competitive ratio in case there is no *a priori* information (and hence no probabilistic assumptions) about the holding times [12], [32].

Several practical routing and admission control strategies derived from the competitive strategies were studied in [21] for the PVC case and in [22] for the SVC case. Simulations show that these strategies outperform the minimum-hop and reservation-based strategies for sparse networks. Reservation based strategies are usually based on the notion of "primary paths" that are preferred paths for routing; other, "alternate" paths, are used only if the primary paths are totally congested. Selection of primary paths is a nontrivial problem and usually has to involve knowledge of the traffic matrix for general topologies. Since the strategies based on the competitive analysis do not rely on the notion of primary versus alternate traffic, they seem more suitable for sparse networks with nonsymmetric traffic matrices.

Section II introduces the general framework. Section III presents competitive strategies for PVC routing in the throughput-maximization and congestion-minimization models and Section IV addresses the issues involved in extending these strategies to the SVC case. Section V considers the problem of routing multicast circuits. Section VI discusses some results of applying these theoretical algorithms to realistic networks.

II. MODEL AND DEFINITIONS

The network is represented as a capacitated (directed or undirected) graph $G(V, E, u)$ with n nodes and m edges, where $u(e)$ represents the capacity of the edge $e \in E$. The input sequence is a collection of k requests: $\beta_1, \beta_2, \cdots, \beta_k$, where each request β_i is described by the tuple

$$\beta_i = (s_i, t_i, r(i, \tau), T^s(i), T^f(i), \rho(i)).$$

Nodes s_i and t_i are the source and destination of the request, $r(i, \tau)$ is the bandwidth required by β_i as a function of time; $T^s(i)$ and $T^f(i)$ are the start and finish times for the request. Let $T(i) = T^f(i) - T^s(i)$ denote the *holding time* (i.e., duration) of the requested circuit, and let T denote the maximum possible value of $T(i)$. We use $r(i)$ instead of $r(i, \tau)$ if the requested bandwidth does not depend on τ. $\rho(i)$ denotes the "profit" that we get if the request is routed (accepted). For example, $\rho(i)$ might be defined to be proportional to the bandwidth-duration product $r(i)T(i)$.

For convenience $r(i, \tau)$ is defined to be 0 for $\tau \notin [T^s(i), T^f(i)]$ and also if i is rejected. In most cases, the requested bandwidth $r(i, \tau)$ remains fixed over the duration of the circuit. The *relative load* at time τ on an edge e just before considering the jth request is defined by

$$\lambda_e(j, \tau) = \sum_{e \in P_i, i < j} \frac{r(i, \tau)}{u(e)}$$

where P_i is the path along which the ith connection is routed. Let $\lambda(j) = \max_{e \in E, \tau} \lambda_e(j, \tau)$. Similarly, define $\lambda_e^*(j, \tau)$ and $\lambda^*(j)$ to be the corresponding quantities for the routes produced by the off-line algorithm. For simplicity we will abbreviate $\lambda(k)$ as λ and $\lambda^*(k)$ as λ^*, where k is the index of the last request.

In this paper we concentrate on two related models. In the *congestion-minimization* model, the routing strategy is required to accept all of the requests. The goal is to minimize the maximum congestion λ. The competitive ratio used to measure the performance of strategies in this model is defined as the supremum over all request sequences of λ/λ^*, where λ^* is the congestion produced the the optimum off-line algorithm.

In the *throughput-maximization* model, the routing strategy is allowed to reject some of the requests. The goal in this case is to maximize the total profit $\sum_i \rho(i)$ associated with the accepted requests. The competitive ratio in this model is the supremum over all possible request sequences σ of the ratio between the profit of the optimum off-line algorithm on σ and the profit of the on-line algorithm on the same σ. Note that the optimization goal depends on the exact definition of the profit. For example, if the profit is constant per request, then the goal is to maximize the total number of satisfied requests. If the profit is proportional to the bandwidth-duration product, then the goal is to maximize the total routed bandwidth.

III. ROUTING PERMANENT VIRTUAL CIRCUITS

A. Competitive PVC Routing in Throughput-Maximization Model

In this section, we describe a competitive routing and admission control strategy for the throughput-maximization model [8]. We start by identifying some additional restrictions that have to be imposed on the traffic, and then present a simplified strategy for routing PVC circuits. The discussion of the more general routing and admission control strategy for the SVC case is deferred to Section IV.

1) Assumption and Restrictions: Let L be the maximum number of hops allowed for a single circuit. First, we assume that the profit is scaled such that the following condition is satisfied

$$1 \leq \frac{1}{L} \cdot \frac{\rho(i)}{r(i)} \leq F. \tag{1}$$

Note that it is always possible to satisfy the above condition if we choose large enough F. For example, if the profit is defined to be proportional to the bandwidth, than we can take $\rho(j) = Lr(j)$ and $F = 1$.

We assume that the rates $r(i)$ of the requests are small compared to the link capacities. More precisely, we assume that for every request

$$r(i) \leq \frac{\min_e\{u(e)\}}{\log(2LF + 1)}. \tag{2}$$

It was shown in [8] that such restriction is necessary. More precisely, they showed that if we allow requests with rates $r(j)$ larger than $\min\{u(e)\}/k$, then there can be no on-line strategy that achieves a competitive ratio smaller than $\Omega(L^{1/k} + F^{1/k})$. In other words, without assumption (2) it is impossible to design a strategy that achieves a polylogarithmic competitive ratio in the general case. If we restrict the underlying network topology to a tree or a hypercube, it is possible to achieve logarithmic competitive ratio without the above assumption [11], [10].

2) PVC Routing Algorithm: In the PVC case, each arriving circuit has infinite holding time. The idea is to assign each link a *length* that is *exponential* in the current congestion of this link. More precisely, define the base $\mu = 2LF + 1$. (This choice will become clear after the proof of Lemma 3.) The *length* of an edge e just before job j is considered, is defined by

$$c_e(j) = u(e)\left(\mu^{\lambda_e(j)} - 1\right).$$

The on-line routing strategy, proposed in [8], is as follows:

- When request j arrives, check if there exists a path P in the graph from s_j to t_j satisfying the following condition

$$\sum_{e \in P} \frac{r(j)}{u(e)} c_e(j) \le \rho(j).$$

- If such a path P exists, accept the connection and use P to route the connection; otherwise, reject the request.

The proof of competitiveness of the above strategy is based on three lemmas. Lemma 1 shows that the sum of the lengths of all the edges at any point in time is within $O(\log \mu)$ factor of the already accrued profit. Lemma 2 shows that the total profit of circuits that were rejected by the on-line algorithm but accepted by the off-line algorithm is bounded by the total length. Finally, Lemma 3 shows that appropriate choice of μ implies that the routing strategy never violates capacity constraints. In other words, if the algorithm decides to route a circuit, then there is always sufficient available capacity.

Lemma 3.1: Let $\mathcal{A}$ be the set of accepted requests and k be the index of the last connection. Then

$$2 \log \mu \sum_{j \in \mathcal{A}} \rho(j) \ge \sum_e c_e(k+1).$$

Proof: By induction on k, the number of arrived requests. For $k = 0$, both sides are 0. Rejected connections do not matter since they neither affect the length nor the profit. Therefore we are done if we show the following for an *accepted* connection β_j

$$\sum_e (c_e(j+1) - c_e(j)) \le 2\rho(j) \log \mu.$$

Consider an edge $e \in P_j$. From the definition of the length we have

$$c_e(j+1) - c_e(j) = u(e) \left(\mu^{\lambda_e(j) + \frac{r(j)}{u(e)}} - \mu^{\lambda_e(j)} \right)$$
$$= u(e) \mu^{\lambda_e(j)} \left(\mu^{\frac{r(j)}{u(e)}} - 1 \right)$$
$$= u(e) \mu^{\lambda_e(j)} \left(2^{\frac{r(j)}{u(e)} \log \mu} - 1 \right).$$

Assumption (2) implies that $r(j) \le \frac{u(e)}{\log \mu}$. Since $2^x - 1 \le x$ for $x \in [0, 1]$, we get

$$c_e(j+1) - c_e(j) \le \mu^{\lambda_e(j)} r(j) \log \mu$$
$$= \log \mu \left(\frac{r(j)}{u(e)} c_e(j) + r(j) \right).$$

Summing up over all the links and using the fact that the request β_j was accepted, we get

$$\sum_e (c_e(j+1) - c_e(j)) \le \log \mu (\rho(j) + |P_j| \cdot r(j)).$$

Using the fact that the number of hops in the path is less than L, and the assumption (1) that the profit was scaled appropriately, implies

$$\sum_e (c_e(j+1) - c_e(j)) \le 2\rho(j) \log \mu.$$

$\square$

The next step is to show that the profit due to requests that were routed by the off-line algorithm but were rejected by the on-line algorithm is bounded by the sum of the lengths of all the edges.

Lemma 3.2: Let Q be the set of indices of the requests that were admitted (routed) by the off-line algorithm but not by the on-line algorithm, and denote $\ell = \max\{Q\}$. Then $\sum_{j \in Q} \rho(j) \le \sum_e c_e(\ell)$.

Proof: Let P'_j be the path used by the off-line algorithm to route β_j, for $j \in Q$. The fact that β_j was not admitted and monotonicity in j of the lengths $c_e(j)$ imply

$$\rho(j) \le \sum_{e \in P'_j} r(j) \frac{c_e(j)}{u(e)} \le \sum_{e \in P'_j} r(j) \frac{c_e(\ell)}{u(e)}.$$

Summing over all $j \in Q$, we get:

$$\sum_{j \in Q} \rho(j) \le \sum_{j \in Q} \sum_{e \in P'_j} \frac{r(j)}{u(e)} c_e(\ell)$$
$$\le \sum_e c_e(\ell) \sum_{j \in Q : e \in P'_j} \frac{r(j)}{u(e)} \le \sum_e c_e(\ell).$$

The last inequality follows from the fact that the off-line algorithm cannot exceed unit relative load at any instance in time. $\square$

Lemmas 1 and 2 imply a polylogarithmic bound on the maximum possible ratio between the profits of the off-line algorithm and the profit due to requests that were accepted by the on-line algorithm. It remains to show that if the on-line strategy decides to accept a request and route it along some path P, then there is indeed sufficient available capacity along P. The intuition is that the length of an edge when it is close to saturation is so large that it will never be chosen by the on-line algorithm. In the following lemma $\mathcal{A}$ denotes the set of requests that were *routed* by the on-line algorithm.

Lemma 3.3: For all edges $e \in E$, $\sum_{j \in \mathcal{A}, e \in \mathcal{P}_j} r(j) \le u(e)$.

Proof: Let β_j be the first request that caused the capacity violation on an edge e. This implies that $\lambda_e(j) > 1 - \frac{r(j)}{u(e)}$. Using assumption (2) and the definition of length, we have

$$c_e(j)/u(e) = \mu^{\lambda_e(j)} - 1 > \mu^{1 - \frac{1}{\log \mu}} - 1 = \mu/2 - 1 = LF.$$

Assumption (1) gives

$$\frac{r(j)}{u(e)} c_e(j) > LF \cdot r(j) \ge \rho(j)$$

which means that request β_j could not have been routed through edge e. $\square$

Note that the total profit of the off-line algorithm can be bounded by the profit of the on-line algorithm plus the profit due to circuits that were accepted by the off-line but rejected by the on-line. This fact, together with Lemmas 1, 2, and 3, implies that the competitive ratio of the algorithm is bounded by $O(\log \mu)$. Note that if profit is proportional to the bandwidth, we have $O(\log \mu) = O(\log L)$, matching the lower bound in [8].

$\text{SVC\_ROUTE}(\beta_j = (s, t, r(\tau), T^a, T^f, \rho))$:

$\forall \tau, e \in E : \ c_e(j, \tau) \leftarrow u(e)(\mu^{\lambda_e(j,\tau)} - 1);$

if $\exists$ path P in $G(V, E)$ from s to t s.t.

$$\sum_{e \in P} \sum_{T^a \leq \tau < T^f} \frac{r(\tau)}{u(e)} c_e(j, \tau) \leq \rho$$

then route the connection on P, and set:

$\forall e \in P, T^a \leq \tau \leq T^f,$
$\lambda_e(j+1, \tau) \leftarrow \lambda_e(j, \tau) + \frac{r(\tau)}{u(e)}$

else reject the connection

Fig. 1. The SVC routing and admission control strategy for the through-put-maximization model.

Theorem 3.4 ([8]): The PVC routing and admission control strategy shown in Fig. 1 never violates the capacity constraints and accrues at least $O(1/\log \mu)$-fraction of the profit accrued by the optimal off-line algorithm.

B. PVC Routing in Congestion-Minimization Model

In this section, we will describe an on-line strategy for the PVC case that is competitive in the congestion-minimization model. This strategy was developed in [5]; we will present the analysis from [9]. As before, we defer the discussion of the SVC case to Section IV.

As in the throughput-maximization model, we define the length of a link to be exponential in the current congestion on this link. More precisely, we set

$$c_e(j) = \mu^{\lambda_e(j)}(\mu^{r(j)/u(e)} - 1)$$

where $\mu = 1 + \gamma/2$ for some $0 < \gamma < 1$. The on-line strategy routes on the shortest path with respect to this length. (Recall that, in contrast to the throughput-maximization model, no rejections are allowed.)

For simplicity, we will assume that the congestion of the off-line algorithm is 1. If it is not, one can use a binary doubling procedure to guess an approximation to this congestion, and scale the input appropriately [5]. The key to the proof of competitiveness of the above strategy is the following "stability condition."

Definition 3.5 ([9]): Let P be some existing $s - t$ route satisfying request β_j, and let P' be any $s - t$ path in G. We say that the algorithm is in a stable state if, for any P, P' and $k \geq j$, we have

$$\sum_{e \in P} \mu^{\lambda_e(j)}(\mu^{r(j)/u(e)} - 1) \leq 2 \sum_{e \in P'} \mu^{\lambda_e(k)}(\mu^{r(j)/u(e)} - 1).$$

We will show that as long as the stability condition is satisfied, the congestion is small. First, observe that this condition is inductively satisfied since the relative loads do not decrease. Moreover, applying the condition with P' being the path P_j^* used by the optimum off-line algorithm to route connection β_j, and using the fact that $\forall x \in [0, 1]$:

$2(\mu^x - 1) \leq \gamma x$, we get

$$\sum_{e \in P_j} \mu^{\lambda_e(j)}(\mu^{r(j)/u(e)} - 1) \leq 2 \sum_{e \in P^*} \mu^{\lambda_e(k)}(\mu^{r(j)/u(e)} - 1)$$

$$\leq \gamma \sum_{e \in P_j^*} \mu^{\lambda_e(k)} r(j)/u(e).$$

Let $\mathcal{P}, \mathcal{P}^*$ be the sets of paths used by the on-line and the off-line algorithms to route the currently active connections, respectively. Summing over all currently active connections, and exchanging the order of summation yields

$$\sum_{e \in E} \sum_{P_j \in \mathcal{P} | e \in P_j} \mu^{\lambda_e(j)}(\mu^{r(j)/u(e)} - 1)$$

$$\leq \gamma \sum_{e \in E} \mu^{\lambda_e(k)} \sum_{P_i^* \in \mathcal{P}^* | e \in P_i^*} r(i)/u(e).$$

Notice that the left-hand-side is a telescopic sum for each edge e. Since the normalized load of the off-line algorithm never exceeds 1, we have $\sum_{e \in E} \mu^{\lambda_e} \leq m/(1 - \gamma)$. Thus, the ratio between the congestion of the on-line algorithm and the congestion of the off-line algorithm (which we assumed to be 1) never exceeds $O(\log m)$, which implies the following claim.

Theorem 3.6 ([5]): The congestion-minimization routing algorithm is $O(\log n)$-competitive.

IV. SWITCHED VIRTUAL CIRCUITS ROUTING

The strategies presented in Sections III-A and III-B work only for routing PVC circuits. In this section, we describe how to adapt these strategies to routing switched virtual circuits (SVC's).

A. Known Holding Times

The PVC routing and admission control strategies described above can be easily extended to the SVC case when the holding time of a circuit becomes known upon the arrival of this circuit. We will refer to this case as the known holding times case. The idea, proposed in [13], is to "flatten" the time, i.e., duplicate the network for each time unit.

More precisely, let $\lambda_e(j, \tau)$ denote the congestion on edge e at time τ as measured upon arrival of request β_j. In other words, this is the congestion on e at time τ due to the load created by requests $\beta_1, \cdots, \beta_{j-1}$. Observe that $\lambda_e(j, \tau)$ is nondecreasing with j. For the throughput-maximization case, the length associated with edge e and time instance τ is defined by

$$c_e(j, \tau) = u(e)(\mu^{\lambda_e(j,\tau)} - 1) \tag{3}$$

where $\mu = 2LTF + 1$, and F is defined by (1). If $e \in P_j$, then e's contribution to the length of the path P_j is computed as

$$\sum_\tau \frac{r(j, \tau)}{u(e)} c_e(j, \tau) = \sum_\tau r(j, \tau)(\mu^{\lambda_e(j,\tau)} - 1). \tag{4}$$

If there exists a path whose length is bounded by the profit $\rho(j)$, then this path is used to route the connection β_j. Otherwise, the connection is rejected. The modified algorithm is presented in Fig. 1.

It is straightforward to adapt the proofs of Lemmas 1, 2, and 3 to the SVC case. The additional requirement needed to satisfy Lemma 1 is that $\rho(j) \geq Lr(j)T(j)$, and the condition that is sufficient for Lemma 3 is that $\mu/2 - 1 \geq \rho(j)$. Thus, instead of the assumptions (1) and (2) we have to assume that

$$1 \leq \frac{1}{L} \cdot \frac{\rho(j)}{r(j,\tau)T(j)} \leq F \qquad (5)$$

$$r(j,\tau) \leq \frac{\min_e\{u(e)\}}{\log(2LTF + 1)}. \qquad (6)$$

As in the PVC case, (5) can be always satisfied by taking a large enough value of F. Also, without assumption (5), it is impossible to achieve a polylogarithmic competitive ratio [8]. For example, setting $\rho(j) = LT(j)r(j)$ and $\mu = 2LT + 1$ satisfies the above assumption and leads to $O(\log \mu) = O(\log LT)$ competitive ratio. Maximizing $\sum_j \rho(j)$ in this case corresponds to maximizing the total bandwidth-duration product, i.e., throughput. If the goal is to maximize the total acceptance rate, then the profit should be constant per request. For example, defining $\rho(j) = LT_{max}r_{max}$ leads to competitive ratio of $O(\log(L(T_{\max}/T_{\min})(r_{\max}/r_{\min})))$.

The same idea of "flattening" the time scale can be applied to design competitive algorithms for congestion-minimization case. More precisely, define the length of an edge as follows

$$c_e(j,\tau) = \mu^{\lambda_e(j,\tau)}(\mu^{r(j,\tau)/u(e)} - 1)$$

where μ is defined as in Section III-B. The strategy is to route request β_j on path P_j that minimizes

$$\sum_{e \in P_j, \tau \in [T^s, T^j]} c_e(j,\tau).$$

The stability condition (Definition 3.5) can be adapted to the SVC case in a natural way by adding a summation over time. See [13] for a complete proof that the above strategy achieves $O(\log nT)$ competitive ratio.

B. Unknown Holding Times

The SVC routing strategies described above rely on a priori knowledge of holding times. In many real applications holding times become known only after termination of the call, and hence it is important to develop strategies for this case, which we refer to as the unknown holding times case.

If we have no information whatsoever about the holding times, it is easy to show that there can be no competitive throughput-maximization algorithm. Roughly speaking, the reason is as follows. First, observe that the on-line algorithm has to reject a request at some point. Say, it rejects the kth request in some sequence. Now assign arbitrary long holding time to this rejected request and make it the last request in the sequence. The off-line algorithm will reject all the requests except this last one, and thus will get arbitrary larger throughput than the on-line algorithm. Similar argument shows that there can be no competitive algorithm that maximizes the number of routed requests [9].

The situation is not much better for the congestion-minimization case. It is easy to adapt the lower bound of Azar, Broder, and Karlin [12] to show $\Omega(n^{1/4})$ lower bound

for the competitive ratio in this case,[1] assuming the underlying graph is directed. This adaptation results in a sequence where holding times of some of the requests are exponential in n, and hence does not preclude an $O(\log T)$-competitive algorithm. Ma and Plotkin [32] showed how to construct a different sequence where all holding times are polynomial, and improved this lower bound to $\Omega(\min\{n^{1/4}, T^{1/3}\})$. The lower bounds in [12], [32] apply even if the on-line algorithm is allowed to use randomization. It is interesting to note that no nontrivial lower bounds are known for the case where the underlying graph is undirected.

These lower bounds indicate that we should consider alternate models. One natural model, considered in [23], is to assume that the distribution on the holding time becomes known with the arrival of the request. Observe that in this case we have to compare to an off-line algorithm that does not have a complete knowledge of the request sequence. More precisely, it should have a complete knowledge of the request parameters except the holding time. In this case it is possible to modify the throughput-maximization algorithm so that the expected throughput achieved by this strategy will be within $O(\log LT)$ factor of the expected throughput achieved by the optimum off-line algorithm. Roughly speaking, the idea is to route a circuit with constant rate $r(j)$ as if its rate depends on time and is equal to $r(j,\tau) = r(j) \cdot \Pr\{j \text{ alive at } \tau\}$.

In case the holding times are distributed exponentially, the algorithm in [23] becomes significantly simpler and achieves $O(\log L \log \log L)$ competitive ratio with respect to expected throughput. This improvement is based on two ideas. First, the fact that the holding times are distributed according to an exponential distribution implies that the result of summing the cost of an edge over time is a function of the current load only, and hence can be written in a closed form. Second, μ can be taken to be independent of T. Intuitively, the reason that μ was taken to be proportional to T in the throughput-competitive SVC routing algorithm described in the previous section was to make sure that even if a link is currently saturated but will be free from the next time step on, the cost of this link (summed up over time) will exceed the maximum profit, preventing the algorithm from using this link. The fact that the holding times are distributed exponentially implies that the probability of such even is very low.

An alternative model is to allow rerouting. Observe that if the number of reroutings per connection is not limited, it is trivial to maintain optimum relative load, i.e., competitive ratio of 1. Thus, we should allow only limited rerouting. In [9], it was shown that by allowing each circuit to be rerouted at most $O(\log n)$ times during its lifetime, we can maintain $O(\log n)$ competitiveness with respect to maximum congestion. Roughly speaking, the idea is to make sure that the stability condition (Definition 3.5) is always satisfied. If one of the routed circuits does not satisfy the condition, it is rerouted onto the shortest possible path. Since this causes its length to go down by at least a factor of 2, one can show that it will not be rerouted more than $O(\log n)$ times.

---

[1] The result in [12] is an $\Omega(\sqrt{n})$ lower bound in the context of load-balancing. Adaptation of this lower bound to the routing model results in an $\Omega(\sqrt[4]{n})$ lower bound.

V. ROUTING MULTICAST CIRCUITS

Similar to a virtual circuit request, a *multicast* request is specified by the required bandwidth, holding time, and the set of participating nodes. In order to satisfy a multicast request, we need to allocate the required bandwidth along a *tree* connecting the *set* of participating nodes. This is in contrast to the virtual circuit routing problem, where we needed to allocate bandwidth along an appropriate path.

The multicast case can be treated in exactly the same way as we have treated the virtual circuit routing problem in the previous sections, leading to strategies with exactly the same bounds. The only difference is that instead of finding a shortest path connecting the source and the sink nodes, we need to find a *minimum-cost Steiner tree* spanning the set of participating nodes. For example, to see that this is true for the throughput-maximization case, consider the proof of Theorem 1. Observe that the fact that we route along a path rather than some other subgraph of the network is used only in one place: in (1) we used the fact that the path can include at most L links. Thus, the same approach will work for multicast routing, with L replaced by L', the maximum number of links in the tree.

Although finding minimum-cost Steiner trees is NP-hard, it is sufficient to use a simple polynomial-time 2-approximation algorithm. One interesting variant of multicast routing is when we are allowed to choose a subset of the nodes participating in the multicast group, and allocate a tree spanning only these nodes. Naturally, the profit in this case should be proportional to the number of spanned (satisfied) nodes. A profit-competitive strategy for this case is to find the largest subset of the multicast group that can be spanned by a Steiner tree whose cost is below the profit scaled by the size of this subset [8]. This is an NP-hard problem. Heuristics for solving this problem were given in [18]; an $O(\log^2 n)$-approximation algorithm is described in [7].

VI. IMPLEMENTATION ISSUES

The previous sections presented the competitive routing and admission control strategies from a purely theoretical point of view. In this section, we will discuss some of the issues involved in applying these ideas to realistic scenarios.

Should we implement the throughput-maximization strategy analyzed in Section IV "as is"? This question was studied in [22], where it was observed that using this strategy "as-is" does not lead to sufficiently good results. In fact, the resulting performance was observed to be always worse than the performance of a simple greedy min-hop strategy.

The main problem is that the analysis suggests a huge value of $\mu = 2LTF + 1$, proportional to the largest holding time T, which leads to a very conservative admission control strategy. Indeed, consider a single link network ($L = 1$) where at time t_0 we are trying to route request β_j with unit holding time. Consider the case where the current congestion of the link is $\lambda(j, t_0) = 1/\log T$. Observe that if we follow the throughput-maximization strategy exactly, then we will not be able to route this request, even though the link is essentially unused.

Recall that μ was determined in order to satisfy Lemma 3. Roughly speaking, the analysis suggested that μ should

be large enough so that the cost of any path that has a saturated link will exceed the maximum profit. In [23] it was observed that in many realistic situations the cases where the link is saturated at t and is totally unused at $t + 1$ are rare. Using this observation they showed that if one assumes exponential distribution of the holding times, then a much smaller $\mu = O(L \log L)$ is sufficient if the strategy is modified to reject a request that has a saturated link on each one of the shortest paths connecting its endpoints.

Simulation studies of this modified strategy (referred to as the "EXP" strategy in [41]) show that it outperforms many natural algorithms, including several variants of min-hop and reservation-based algorithms on several commercial topologies. Somewhat surprisingly, the EXP strategy leads to shorter average hop-count than the min-hop-based algorithms.

An important question is how to implement shortest-path-based strategies in a distributed environment. Namely, in the environment where there is no central node that makes all the routing decisions and that has a complete knowledge of the state of the system. There are two main issues that have to be addressed. First, the routing should be *concurrent*, i.e., several nodes might be trying to create routes at the same time. Second, the strategy has to work even with *outdated data* about the global state of the system.

Concurrent routing was considered from a theoretical point of view by Awerbuch and Azar in [6]. They showed that by *iterative flooding* over all of the possible routes, one can route all of the requests in a logarithmic number of "flooding rounds" if several nodes are trying to route concurrently. Their strategy leads to a polylogarithmic competitive ratio if the number of different possible routes between any two points is very small. Moreover, their strategy is resilient against nonmalicious failures of the nodes. It is not known how to treat the case where there are node pairs that are connected by a large number of different possible routes.

In order to make sure that each node in the network has a recent view of the global state of the network, one can periodically flood the network with state updates. An alternative approach, suggested in [22], is to allow each node to update its view of the network only when it decides on a route. More precisely, during the creation of the route, the node should update its information about all the edges on the route. If during the creation of the route a saturated edge is encountered, the strategy is to try again, up to some parameter k tries, and then reject the request.

The advantage of this approach is that has relatively low overhead and does not require an external "update procedure." Simulation results described in [22] indicate that although for $k = 1$ (i.e., reject if the path chosen by looking only at the locally available information has a saturated link) the performance is worse than the performance of the centralized strategy, it is significantly better than the performance of min-hop based strategies. Simulations also indicate that already for small values of k, the performance essentially reaches that of the centralized algorithms.

Intuitively, the distributed strategy based on the exponential length function outperforms the min-hop strategy because it tries to choose paths that are the least saturated according

263

to its (outdated) information. This is in contrast to min-hop based strategy, that tries to route over arbitrary paths that had sufficient available capacity according to the (same) outdated data. Thus, the paths chosen by the exponential-length based strategy are more likely to have sufficient available capacity at present.

VII. CONCLUSIONS

In this paper we have surveyed a class of routing and admission control strategies based on assigning each link a length that is an exponential function of the current congestion on this link, and routing along the shortest path with respect to this length; if no sufficiently short path exists, the request is rejected. From the theoretical point of view, this approach is attractive because it unifies the routing and admission control decisions. Moreover, it was shown that the appropriate choice of the length function results in algorithms that outperform min-hop based and reservation-based algorithms on sparse network topologies.

The algorithms were motivated by using *competitive ratio* to compare performance of various strategies. The main advantage of this measure is that it allows us to compare strategies without any assumptions on the statistical behavior of the offered traffic. By incorporating statistical assumptions into algorithms motivated by competitive analysis we get algorithms that have good performance under these assumptions, and at the same time do not "break down" when these assumptions are not satisfied.

Although all of the strategies presented in this paper are dealing with managing the available bandwidth, similar competitive approaches can be applied to design strategies for managing other resources in the network, such as the available buffer space, processing load, etc.

Much work remains to be done. One potential problem with the strategies described in this paper is that they do not address the fairness issues. For example, it is easy to see that the admission control strategy described in Section IV will be much more inclined to reject high-bandwidth requests than low-bandwidth ones. Another problem stems from the fact that the competitive ratio is too pessimistic a measure, since it compares to a very powerful omniscient off-line algorithm that can not be implemented. Several new measures that are more refined than competitive ratio were recently proposed in [29]. An interesting research direction is to try to design strategies based on these new measures. Another promising research direction is to combine the ideas of the competitive on-line routing with the more traditional reservation-based approaches [3], [27], [34], [35], [36], [30], [38] in order to derive strategies that have good performance both for dense and for sparse topologies.

ACKNOWLEDGMENT

The author would like to thank B. Awerbuch, Y. Azar, R. Gawlick, A. Kamath, D. Mitra, O. Palmon, R. Ramakrishnan, and O. Waarts for helpful discussions; A. Borodin's comments helped in improving the clarity of the presentation. He would

also like to thank J. Oldham for his numerous comments on the early draft of this paper.

REFERENCES

[1] G. R. Ash, "Use of trunk status map for real-time DNHR," in *Proc. ITC-12*, Torino, Italy, 1988.
[2] G. R. Ash, R. H. Cardwell, and R. P. Murray, "Design and optimization of networks with dynamic routing," *Bell Syst. Tech. J.*, vol. 60, pp. 1787–1820, 1981.
[3] G. R. Ash, J. S. Chen, A. E. Frey, and B. D. Huang, "Real-time network routing in an integrated network," in *Proc. ITC-13*, Copenhagen, Denmark, 1991.
[4] G. R. Ash, A. H. Kafker, and K. R. Krishnana, "Servicing and real-time control of networks with dynamic routing," *Bell Syst. Tech. J.*, vol. 60, pp. 1821–1845, 1981.
[5] J. Aspnes, Y. Azar, A. Fiat, S. Plotkin, and O. Waarts, "On-line machine scheduling with applications to load balancing and virtual circuit routing," in *Proc. 25th Ann. ACM Symp. Theory Comput.*, pp. 623–631, May 1993.
[6] B. Awerbuch and Y. Azar, "Local optimization of global objectives: Competitive distributed deadlock resolution and resource allocation," in *Proc. 35th IEEE Ann. Symp., Foundations Comput. Sci.*, Nov. 1994, pp. 240–249.
[7] B. Awerbuch, Y. Azar, A. Blum, and S. Vempala, "Improved approximation guarantees for minimum-weight k-trees, prize-collecting salesmen, and bank robbers," unpublished, 1994.
[8] B. Awerbuch, Y. Azar, and S. Plotkin, "Throughput competitive on-line routing," in *Proc. 34th IEEE Ann. Symp. Foundations Comput. Sci.*, Nov. 1993, pp. 32–40.
[9] B. Awerbuch, Y. Azar, S. Plotkin, and O. Waarts, "Competitive routing of virtual circuits with unknown duration," in *Proc. 5th ACM-SIAM Symp. Discrete Algorithms*, Jan. 1994, pp. 321–327.
[10] B. Awerbuch, R. Gawlick, T. Leighton, and Y. Rabani, "On-line admission control and circuit routing for high-performance computing and communication," in *Proc. 35th IEEE Ann. Symp. Foundations Comput. Sci.*, Nov. 1994, pp. 412–423.
[11] B. Awerbuch. Y. Bartal, A. Fiat, and A. Rosen, "Competitve non-preemptive call control," in *Proc. 5th ACM-SIAM Symp. Discrete Algorithms*, 1994.
[12] Y. Azar, A. Broder, and A. Karlin, "On-line load balancing," in *Proc. 35th IEEE Ann. Symp. Foundations Comput. Sci.*, 1992, pp. 218–225.
[13] Y. Azar, B. Kalyanasundaram, S. Plotkin, K. Pruhs, and O. Waarts, "On-line load balancing of temporary tasks, " in *Proc. Workshop Algorithms, Data Structures*, Aug. 1993, pp. 119–130.
[14] D. Bertsekas and R. Gallager, *Data Networks*, 2nd ed. Englewood Cliffs, NJ: 1992.
[15] A. Borodin, N. Linial, and M. Saks, "An optimal on-line algorithm for metrical task systems," *J. ACM*, vol. 39, pp. 745–763, 1992.
[16] W. H. Cameron, J. Regnier, P. Galloy, and A. M. Savoie, "Dynamic routing for intercity telephone networks," in *Proc. ITC-10*, Montreal, Québec, Canada, 1983.
[17] F. Caron, "Results of the Telecom Canada high performance routing trial," in *Proc. ITC-12*, Torino, Italy, 1988.
[18] S. Y. Cheung and A. Khumar, "Efficient quorumcast routing algorithms," in *Proc. INFOCOM '94*, vol. 2, 1994.
[19] J. Garay, I. Gopal, S. Kutten, Y. Mansour, and M. Yung, "Efficient on-line call control algorithms," in *Proc. 2nd Ann. Israel Conf. Theory Computing, Syst.*, 1993.
[20] J. A. Garay and I. S. Gopal, "Call preemption in communication networks," in *Proc. INFOCOM '92*, Florence, Italy, vol. 44, 1992, pp. 1043–1050.
[21] R. Gawlick, C. Kalmanek, and K. Ramakrishnan, "On-line permanent virtual circuit routing," in *Proc. IEEE Infocom*, Apr. 1995.
[22] R. Gawlick, A. Kamath, S. Plotkin, and K. Ramakrishnan, "Routing and admission control of virtual circuits in general topology networks," AT&T Bell Laboratories, Tech. Rep. BL011212-940819-19TM, 1994.
[23] ——, "Routing of virtual circuits with unknown holding times," unpublished, 1994.
[24] A. Girard and M. A. Bell, "Blocking evaluation for networks with residual capacity adaptive routing," *IEEE Trans. Commun.*, vol. 37, pp. 1372–1380, 1989.
[25] A. R. Karlin, M. S. Manasse, L. Rudolph, and D. D. Sleator, "Competitive snoopy caching," *Algorithmica*, vol. 1, no. 3, pp. 70–119, 1988.
[26] F. P. Kelly, "Blocking probabilities in large circuit-switched networks," *Advanced Appl. Probab.*, vol. 18, pp. 473–505, 1986.
[27] ——, "Network routing," *Phil. Trans. R. Soc. London*, pp. 343–367, 1991.

[28] P. Klein, S. Plotkin, C. Stein, and É. Tardos, "Faster approximation algorithms for the unit capacity concurrent flow problem with applications to routing and finding sparse cuts," *SIAM J. Computing*, vol. 23, no. 3, pp. 466–487, June 1994.

[29] E. Koutsoupias and C. H. Papadimitriou, "Beyond competitive analysis," in *Proc. 35th IEEE Ann. Symp. Foundations Comput. Sci.*, Nov. 1994, pp. 394–400.

[30] K. R. Krishnan and T. J. Ott, "Forward-looking routing: A new state-dependent routing scheme," in *Proc. ITC-12*, Torino, Italy, 1988.

[31] T. Leighton, F. Makedon, S. Plotkin, C. Stein, É. Tardos, and S. Tragoudas, "Fast approximation algorithms for multicommodity flow problem," in *Proc. 23rd ACM Symp. Theory Computing*, May 1991, pp. 101–111.

[32] Y. Ma and S. Plotkin, "Improved lowered bounds for load balancing of tasks with unknown duration," unpublished, 1995.

[33] M. S. Manasse, L. A. McGeoch, and D. D. Sleator, "Competitive algorithms for on-line problems," in *Proc. 20th Ann. ACM Symp. Theory Computing*, 1988, pp. 322–332.

[34] D. Mitra, R. J. Gibbens, and B. D. Huang, "State-dependent routing on symmetric loss networks with trunk reservations—I," *Annals Oper. Res.*, vol. 35, pp. 3–30, 1992.

[35] _____, "State-dependent routing on symmetric loss networks with trunk reservations—II," *IEEE Trans. Commun.*, vol. 41, no. 2, Feb. 1993.

[36] T. J. Ott and K. R. Krishnan, "State-dependent routing of telephone traffic and the use of separable routing schemes," in *Proc. ITC-11*, Kyoto, Japan, 1985.

[37] F. Shahrokhi and D. Matula, "The maximum concurrent flow problem," *J. Assoc. Comput. Mach.*, vol. 37, pp. 318–334, 1990.

[38] S. Sibal and A. DeSimone, "Controlling alternate routing in general-mesh packet flow networks," AT&T, Tech. Rep. BL045370F-940603-01TM, June 1994.

[39] D. D. Sleator and R. E. Tarjan, "Amortized efficiency of list update and paging rules," *Commun. ACM*, vol. 28, no. 2, pp. 202–208, 1985.

[40] A. C. Yao, "New algorithms for bin packing," *J. ACM*, vol. 27, pp. 207–227, 1980.

[41] R. Gawlick, A. Kamath, S. Plotkin, K. Ramakrishnan, "Routing and admission control in general topology networks," Stanford Univ., Stanford, CA, Tech. Rep. STAN-CS-TR-95-1548.

Serge Plotkin received the Ph.D. degree in computer science from the Massachusetts Institute of Technology, Cambridge, in 1988.

In 1989, he joined the Department of Computer Science at Stanford University, Stanford, CA. His main research interests include design and analysis of algorithms, on-line algorithms, and combinatorial optimization with applications to high-speed networks design and management.

The PIM Architecture for Wide-Area Multicast Routing

Stephen Deering, *Member, IEEE*, Deborah L. Estrin, *Senior Member, IEEE*,
Dino Farinacci, Van Jacobson, Ching-Gung Liu, and Liming Wei

Abstract— The purpose of multicast routing is to reduce the communication costs for applications that send the same data to multiple recipients. Existing multicast routing mechanisms were intended for use within regions where a group is widely represented or bandwidth is universally plentiful. When group members, and senders to those group members, are distributed sparsely across a wide area, these schemes are not efficient; data packets or membership report information are occasionally sent over many links that do *not* lead to receivers or senders, respectively. We have developed a multicast routing architecture that efficiently establishes distribution trees across wide area internets, where many groups will be sparsely represented. Efficiency is measured in terms of the router state, control message processing, and data packet processing, required across the entire network in order to deliver data packets to the members of the group. Our protocol independent multicast (PIM) architecture: a) maintains the traditional IP multicast service model of receiver-initiated membership, b) supports both shared and source-specific (shortest-path) distribution trees, c) is not dependent on a specific unicast routing protocol, and d) uses soft-state mechanisms to adapt to underlying network conditions and group dynamics. The robustness, flexibility, and scaling properties of this architecture make it well-suited to large heterogeneous internetworks.

I. INTRODUCTION

THIS paper describes an architecture for efficiently routing to multicast groups that span wide-area (and inter-domain) internets. We refer to the approach as protocol independent multicast (PIM) because it is not dependent on any particular unicast routing protocol.

The architecture proposed here complements existing multicast routing mechanisms such as those proposed by Deering in [9] and [10] and implemented in MOSPF [26] and distance vector multicast routing protocol (DVMRP) [29]. These traditional multicast schemes were intended for use within regions where a group is widely represented or bandwidth is universally plentiful. However, when group members, and

senders to those group members, are distributed *sparsely* across a wide area, these schemes are not efficient. Data packets (in the case of DVMRP) or membership report information (in the case of MOSPF) are occasionally sent on links, and associated state is stored in routers, that do *not* lead to receivers or senders, respectively. The purpose of this work is to develop a multicast routing architecture that efficiently establishes distribution trees even when some or all members are sparsely distributed. Efficiency is measured in terms of the router state, control message processing, and data packet processing required across the entire network in order to deliver data packets to the members of the group.

A. Background

In the traditional IP multicast model, established by Deering [9], a *multicast address* is assigned to the collection of receivers for a multicast group. Senders simply use that address as the destination address of a packet to reach all members of the group. The separation of senders and receivers allows any host, member or nonmember, to send to a group. A group membership protocol [8] is used for routers to learn the existence of members on their directly attached subnetworks. This receiver-initiated joint procedure has very good scaling properties. As the group grows, it becomes more likely that a new receiver will be able to splice onto a nearby branch of the distribution tree. A multicast routing protocol, in the form of an extension to existing unicast protocols (e.g., DVMRP, an extension to a RIP-like distance-vector unicast protocol, or MOSPF, an extension to the link-state unicast protocol OSPF), is executed in routers to construct multicast packet delivery paths and to accomplish multicast data packet forwarding.

In the case of link-state protocols, changes of group membership on a subnetwork are detected by one of the routers directly attached to that subnetwork and that router broadcasts the information to all other routers in the same routing domain [24]. Each router maintains an up-to-date image of the domain's topology through the unicast link-state routing protocol. Upon receiving a multicast data packet, the router uses the topology information and the group membership information to determine the source-specific, "shortest-path" tree (SPT) from the packet's source subnetwork to its destination group members.

Throughout this paper, when we use the term SPT, we mean shortest from the perspective of unicast routing. If the unicast routing metric is hop counts, then the branches of the multicast

Manuscript received February 8, 1995; approved by IEEE/ACM TRANSACTIONS ON NETWORKING Editor C. Partridge.

S. Deering is with Xerox PARC, Palo Alto, CA 94304 USA (e-mail: deering@parc.xerox.com).

D. L. Estrin is with the Computer Science Department/ISI, University of Southern California, Los Angeles, CA 90089 USA (e-mail: estrin@usc.edu).

D. Farinacci is with Cisco Systems Inc., San Jose, CA 95134 USA (e-mail: dino@cisco.com).

V. Jacobson is with the Lawrence Berkeley Laboratory, Berkeley, CA 94720 USA (e-mail: van@ee.lbl.gov).

C.-G. Liu is with the Computer Science Department, University of Southern California, Los Angeles, CA 90089 USA (e-mail: charley@catarina.usc.edu).

L. Wei is with Cisco Systems Inc., San Jose, CA 95134 USA (e-mail: lwei@cisco.com).

Publisher Item Identifier S 1063-6692(96)02719-7.

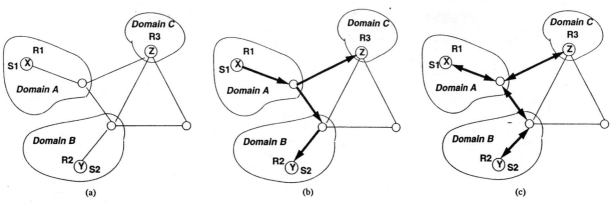

Fig. 1. Example of multicast trees.

SPT are minimum hop; if the metric is delay, then the branches are minimum delay. Moreover, in situations where paths are asymmetric, the multicast SPT's are actually reverse SPT's because we use unicast routings shortest path from the receiver to the source to build the branch of the distribution tree from the source to the receiver. Where route asymmetry results in poor quality distribution trees, it would be useful to obtain a shortest-path from route from unicast routing in order to build true SPT's.

Broadcasting of membership information is one major factor preventing link-state multicast from scaling to larger, wide-area, networks. Every router must receive and store membership information for every group in the domain. The other major factor is the processing cost of the Dijkstra SPT calculations performed to compute the delivery trees for all active multicast sources [25], thus limiting its applicability on an internet wide basis.

Distance-vector multicast routing protocols construct multicast distribution trees using variants of reverse path forwarding (RPF) [7]. When the first data packet is sent to a group from a particular source subnetwork, and a router receiving this packet has no knowledge about the group, the router forwards the incoming packet out of all interfaces except the incoming interface. Some schemes reduce the number of outgoing interfaces further by using the unicast routing protocol information to keep track of child-parent information [9], [29]. A special mechanism is used to avoid forwarding of data packets to leaf subnetworks with no members in that group (aka, truncated broadcasting). Also, if the arriving data packet does not come through the interface that the router uses to send packets to the source of the data packet, the data packet is silently dropped; thus the term RPF [7]. When a router attached to a leaf subnetwork receives a data packet addressed to a new group, if it finds no members present on its attached subnetworks, it will send a prune message upstream toward the source of the data packet. The prune messages prune the tree branches not leading to group members, thus resulting in a source-specific reverse-SPT with all leaves having members. Pruned branches will "grow back" after a time-out period. These branches will again be pruned if there are still no multicast members and data packets are still being sent to the group.

Compared to the total number of destinations within the greater Internet, the number of destinations having group members of any particular *wide-area* group is likely to be small. In the case of distance-vector multicast schemes, routers that are not on the multicast delivery tree still have to carry the periodic truncated-broadcast of packets, and process the subsequent pruning of branches for all active groups. One protocol, DVMRP, has been deployed in hundreds of regions connected by the multicast backbone (MBONE) [18]. However, its occasional broadcasting behavior severely limits its capability to scale to larger networks supporting much larger numbers of groups, many of which are sparse.

B. Extending Multicast to the Wide Area: Scaling Issues

The scalability of a multicast protocol can be evaluated in terms of its overhead growth with the size of the internet, size of groups, number of groups, size of sender sets, and distribution of group members. Overhead is measured in terms of resources consumed in routers and links, i.e., router state, processing, and bandwidth.

Existing link–state and distance–vector multicast routing schemes have good scaling properties only when multicast groups densely populate the network of interest. When most of the subnets or links in the internetwork have group members, then the bandwidth, storage and processing overhead of broadcasting membership reports (link–state), or data packets (distance–vector) is warranted, since the information or data packets are needed in most parts of the network, regardless. The emphasis of our proposed work is to develop multicast protocols that will also efficiently support the sparsely distributed groups that are likely to be most prevalent in wide-area internetworks.

C. Overhead and Tree Types

The examples in Fig. 1 illustrate the inadequacies of the existing mechanisms. There are three domains that communicate via an internet. There is a member of a particular group, G, located in each of the domains. There are no other members of this group currently active in the internet. If a traditional IP multicast routing mechanism such as DVMRP is used, then, when a source in domain A starts to send to the group, its data packets will be broadcast throughout the entire internet. Subsequently, all those sites that do not have local members will send prune messages and the distribution tree will stabilize to that illustrated with bold lines in Fig. 1(b). Periodically, however, the source's packets will be broadcast throughout the entire internet when the pruned-off branches time out.

Thus far, we have motivated our design by contrasting it to the traditional dense-mode IP multicast routing protocols. More recently, the core based tree (CBT) protocol [1] was proposed to address similar scaling problems. CBT uses a single delivery tree for each group, rooted at a "core" router and shared by all senders to the group. As desired for sparse groups, CBT does not exhibit the occasional broadcasting behavior of earlier protocols. However, CBT does so at the cost of imposing a single shared tree for each multicast group.

If CBT were used to support the example group, then a core might be defined in domain A and the distribution tree illustrated in Fig. 1(c) would be established. This distribution tree would also be used by sources sending from domains B and C. This would result in concentration of all the sources' traffic on the path indicated with bold lines. We refer to this as *traffic concentration*. This is a potentially significant issue with CBT, or any protocol that imposes a single shared tree per group for distribution of all data packets. In addition, the packets traveling from Y to Z will not travel via the shortest path used by unicast packets between Y and Z.

We need to know the kind of degradations a core-based tree can incur in average networks. David Wall [30] proved that the bound on maximum delay of an optimal core-based tree (which he called a *center-based* tree) is two times the shortest-path delay. To get a better understanding of how well optimal core-based trees perform in average cases, we simulated an optimal core-based tree algorithm over a large number of different random graphs. We measured the maximum delay within each group, and experimented with graphs of different node degrees. We show the ratio of the CBT maximum delay versus SPT maximum delay in Fig. 2(a). For each node degree, we tried 500 different 50-node graphs with 10-member groups chosen randomly. It can be seen that the maximum delays of core-based trees with optimal core placement, are up to 1.4 times those of the SPT's. Note that although some error bars in the delay graph extend below one, there are no real data points below one (the distribution is not symmetric, for more details see [33]).

For interactive applications where low latency is critical, it is desirable to use the trees based on shortest-path routing to avoid the longer delays of an optimal core-based tree.

With respect to the potential traffic concentration problem, we also conducted simulations in randomly generated 50-node networks. In each network, there were 300 active groups all having 40 members, of which 32 members were also senders. We measured the number of traffic flows on each link of the network, then recorded the maximum number within the network. For each node degree between three and eight, 500 random networks were generated, and the measured maximum number of traffic flows were averaged. Figure 2(b) plots the measurements in networks with different node degrees. It is

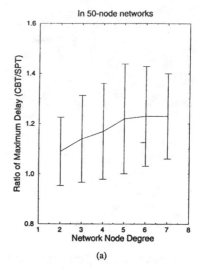

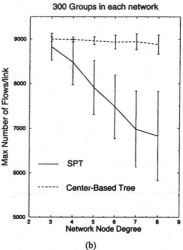

Fig. 2.   Comparison of SPT's and center-based tree.

clear from this experiment that CBT exhibits greater traffic concentrations.

Despite the disadvantages of longer path length and traffic concentration, shared-tree schemes such as CBT (and PIM's shared tree) have the significant advantage of reduced multicast routing state. This is particularly true for applications that are not highly delay sensitive or data intensive.

It is evident to us that both tree types have their advantages and disadvantages. One type of tree may perform very well under one class of conditions, while the other type may be better in other situations. For example, shared tress may perform very well for large numbers of low data rate sources (e.g., resource discovery applications), while SPT's may be better suited for high data rate sources (e.g., real-time teleconferencing), a more complete analysis of these trade-offs can be found in [33]. It would be ideal to flexibly support both types of trees within one multicast architecture, so that the selection of tree types becomes a configuration decision within a multicast protocol.

PIM is designed to address the two issues addressed above: to avoid the overhead of broadcasting packets when group members sparsely populate the internet, and to do so in a way that supports good-quality distribution trees for heterogeneous applications.

In PIM, a multicast group can choose to use SPT's or a group-shared tree. The first-hop routers of the receivers can make this decision independently. A receiver could even choose different types of trees for different sources.

The capability to support different tree types is the fundamental difference between PIM and CBT. There are other significant protocol engineering differences as well. Two obvious engineering trade-offs are:

a) *Soft-State versus Explicit Reliability Mechanism:* CBT uses explicit hop-by-hop mechanisms to achieve reliable delivery of control messages. As described in the next section, PIM uses periodic refreshers as its primary means of reliability. This approach reduces the complexity of the protocol and covers a wide range of protocol and network failures in a single simple mechanism. On the other hand, it can introduce additional message protocol overhead.

b) *Incoming Interface Check on All Multicast Data Packets:* If multicast data packets loop, the result can be severe. Unlike unicast packets, multicast packets can fan. out each time they loop. Therefore, we assert that all multicast data packets should be subject to an incoming interface check comparable to the one performed by DVMRP and MOSPF.

D. Paper Organization

In the remainder of this paper, we enumerate the specific design requirements for wide-area multicast routing (Section II), describe a specific protocol for realizing these requirements (Section III), and discuss open issues (Section IV).

II. REQUIREMENTS

We had several design objectives in mind when designing this architecture:

- *Efficient Sparse Group Support:* We define a sparse group as one in which a) the number of networks or domains with group members present is significantly smaller than number of networks/domains in the Internet, b) group members span an area that is too large/wide to rely on a hop-count limit or some other form of limiting the "scope" of multicast packet propagation, and c) the internetwork is not sufficiently resource rich to ignore the overhead of current schemes. Sparse groups are not necessarily "small," therefore, we must support dynamic groups with large numbers of receivers.

- *High-Quality Data Distribution:* We wish to support low-delay data distribution when needed by the application. In particular, we avoid *imposing* a single shared tree in which data packets are forwarded to receivers along a common tree, independent of their source. Source-specific trees are superior when a) multiple sources send data simultaneously and would experience poor service when the traffic is all concentrated on a single shared tree, or b)

the path lengths between sources and destinations in the SPT's are significantly shorter than in the shared tree.

- *Routing Protocol Independence:* The protocol should rely on existing unicast routing functionality to adapt to topology changes, but at the same time be independent of the particular protocol employed. We accomplish this by letting the multicast protocol make use of the unicast routing tables, independent of how those tables are computed.

- *Robustness:* The protocol should be capable of gracefully adapting to routing changes. We achieve this by a) using *soft-state* refreshment mechanisms, b) avoiding a single point of failure, and c) adapting along with (and based on) unicast routing changes to deliver multicast service so long as unicast packets are being serviced.

- *Interoperability:* We require interoperability with traditional RPF and link-state multicast routing, both intra- and inter-domain. For example, the intra-domain portion of a distribution tree may be established by some other IP multicast protocol, and the inter-domain portion by PIM. In some cases, it will be necessary to impose some additional protocol or configuration overhead in order to inter-operate with some intra-domain routing protocols.

In support of this inter-operation with existing IP multicast, *and* in support of groups with very large numbers of receivers, we should maintain the logical separation of roles between receivers and senders.

III. PIM PROTOCOL

In this section, we start with an overview of the PIM protocol and then give a more detailed description of each phase.

As described, traditional multicast routing protocols designed for densely populated groups rely on data driven actions in all the network routers to establish efficient distribution trees; we refer to such schemes as *dense mode* multicast. In contrast, *sparse mode* multicast tries to constrain the data distribution so that a minimal number of routers in the network receive it. PIM differs from existing IP multicast schemes in two fundamental ways:

a) Routers with local (or downstream) members join a PIM sparse mode distribution tree by sending explicit join messages; in dense mode IP multicast, such as DVMRP, membership is assumed and multicast data packets are sent until routers without local (or downstream) members send explicit prune messages to remove themselves from the distribution tree.

b) Dense mode IP multicast tree construction is all data driven, PIM must use per-group *Rendezvous points* (RP) for receivers to "meet" new sources. Rendezvous points are used by senders to announce their existence and by receivers to learn about new senders of a group. Source-specific trees in PIM are data driven, however, and the RP-tree is receiver-join driven in anticipation of data.

The SPT state maintained in routers is of the same order as the forwarding information that is currently maintained by routers running existing IP multicast protocols such as MOSPF, i.e., source (S), multicast address (G), outgoing

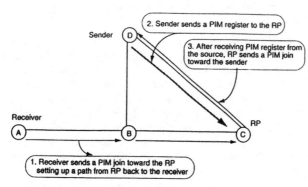

Fig. 3. How senders rendezvous with receivers.

interface set (oif), incoming interface (iif). We refer to this forwarding information as the *multicast forwarding entry* for (S, G). The oif's and iif's of (S, G) entries in all routers together form an SPT rooted at S.

An entry for a shared tree can match packets from any source for its associated group if the packets come through the right incoming interface, we denote such an entry $(*, G)$. A $(*, G)$ entry keeps the same information an (S, G) entry keeps, except that it saves the RP address in place of the source address. There is an RP-flag indicating that this is a shared-tree entry.

Figure 3 shows a simple scenario of a receiver and a sender joining a multicast group via an RP. When the receiver signals that it wants to join a PIM multicast group (i.e., by sending an IGMP message [8]), its first hop PIM router (A in Fig. 3) sends a PIM-join message toward the RP advertised for the group. Processing of this message by intermediate routers sets up the multicast tree branch from the RP to the receiver. When sources start sending to the multicast group, the first hop PIM-router (D in Fig. 3) sends a PIM-register message, piggybacked on the data packet, to the RP's for that group. The RP responds by sending a join toward the source. Processing of these messages by intermediate routers (there are no intermediate routers between the RP and the source in Fig. 3) sets up a packet delivery path from the source to the RP.

If source-specific distribution trees are desired, the first hop PIM router for each member eventually joins the source-rooted distribution tree for each source by sending a PIM-join message toward the source. After data packets are received on the new path, router B in Fig. 3 sends a PIM-prune message toward the RP. B knows, by checking the incoming interface in its routing table, that it is at a point where the SPT and the RP tree branches diverge. A flag, called SPT bit, is included in (S, G) entries to indicate whether the transition from shared tree to SPT has completed. This provides a smooth transition, e.g., there is no loss of data packets.

An RP is used *initially* to propagate data packets from sources to receivers. An RP may be any PIM-speaking router that is close to one of the members of the group, or it may be some other PIM-speaking router in the network. A sparse mode group, i.e., one that the receiver's directly connected PIM router will join using PIM, is identified by the presence of RP addresses associated with the group in question. The mapping information may be configured, derived algorithmically, or may be learned through another protocol mechanism.

PIM avoids explicit enumeration of receivers, but does require enumeration of sources. If there are very large numbers of sources sending to a group but the sources' average data rates are low, then one possibility is to support the group with a shared tree, which has less per-source overhead. If SPT's are desired, then when the number of sources grows very large, some form of aggregation or proxy mechanism will be needed; see Section IV. We selected this trade-off because in many existing and anticipated applications, the number of receivers is much larger than the number of sources. And when the number of sources is very large, the average data rate tends to be lower (e.g., resource discovery).

The remainder of this section describes the protocol design in more detail.

A. Local Hosts Joining a Group

A host sends an IGMP-report message identifying a particular group, G, in response to a directly-connected router's IGMP-query message, as shown in Fig. 4. From this point on, we refer to such a host as a receiver, R, (or member) of the group G.

When a *designated router* (DR) receives a report for a new group G, it checks to see if it has RP addresses associated with G. The mechanism for learning this mapping of G to RP's is somewhat orthogonal to the specification of this protocol, however, we require some mechanism in order for the protocol to work. For the purposes of this description, we assume that each DR listens to a "well-known" multicast group to obtain the group-address (or group-address-range) to RP mappings for all multicast groups.

The DR (e.g., router A in Fig. 4) creates a multicast forwarding cache for $(*, G)$. The RP address is included in a special record in the forwarding entry, so that it will be included in upstream join messages. The outgoing interface is set to that over which the IGMP report was received from the new member. The incoming interface is set to the interface used to send unicast packets to the RP. A wildcard (WC) bit associated with this entry is set, indicating that this is a $(*, G)$ entry.

B. Establishing the RP-Rooted Shared Tree

The DR router creates a PIM-join message with the RP address in its join list with the RP and wildcard bits set; nothing is listed in its prune list. The RP bit flags an address as being the RP associated with that shared tree. The WC bit indicates that the receiver expects to receive packets from new sources via this (shared tree) path and, therefore, upstream routers should create or add to $(*, G)$ forwarding entries. The PIM-join message payload contains the IGMP information multicast-address = G, PIM-join = RP, RPbit, WCbit, PIM-prune = NULL.

Each upstream router creates or updates its multicast forwarding entry for $(*, G)$ when it receives a PIM-join with the WC and RP bits set. The interface on which the PIM-join

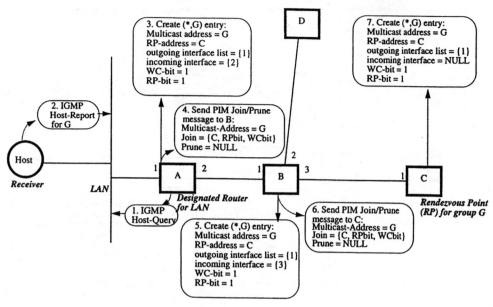

Fig. 4. Example: How a receiver joins, and sets up shared tree. Actions are numbered in the order they occur.

message arrived is added to the list of outgoing interfaces for $(*, G)$. Based on this entry, each upstream router between the receiver and the RP sends a PIM-join message in which the join list includes the RP. The packet payload contains multicast-address $= G$, PIM-join $=$ RP, RPbit, WCbit, PIM-prune $=$ NULL.

The RP recognizes its own address and does not attempt to send join messages for this entry upstream. The incoming interface in the RP's $(*, G)$ entry is set to null.

C. Switching from Shared Tree (RP Tree) to SPT

When a PIM-router with directly-connected members receives packets from a source via the shared RP-tree, the router can switch to a source-specific tree. We refer to the source-specific tree as an SPT, however, if unicast routing is asymmetric, the resulting tree is actually a reverse-SPT. As shown in Fig. 5, router A initiates a new multicast forwarding entry for the new source, Sn which, in turn, triggers a join message to be sent toward Sn with Sn in the join list. The newly-created Sn, G forwarding entry is initialized with the SPT bit cleared, indicating that the SPT branch from Sn has not been completely setup. This allows the router to continue to accept packets from Sn via the shared tree until packets start arriving via the source specific tree. A timer is set for the (Sn, G) entry.

A PIM-join message will be sent upstream to the best next hop toward the new source, Sn, with Sn in the join list: multicast-address $= G$, PIM-join $= Sn$, PIM-prune $=$ NULL. The best next hop is determined by the unicast routing protocol.

When a router that has an (Sn, G) entry with the SPT bit cleared starts to receive packets from the new source Sn on the interface used to reach Sn, it sets the SPT-bit. The router will send a PIM-prune toward the RP if its shared tree incoming interface differs from its SPT incoming interface, indicating

that it no longer wants to receive packets from Sn via the RP tree. In the PIM message toward the RP, it includes Sn in the prune list, with the WC-bit set indicating that a negative cache should be set up on the way to the RP. A negative cache entry is an (S, G) entry with null outgoing interface list. Data packets matching the negative cache are discarded silently.

When the Sn, G entry is created, the outgoing interface list is copied from $(*, G)$, i.e., all local shared tree branches are replicated in the new SPT. In this way, when a data packet from Sn arrives and matches on this entry, all receivers will continue to receive source packets along this path unless and until the receivers choose to prune themselves.

Note that a DR may adopt a policy of not setting up a (S, G) entry (and therefore, not sending a PIM-join message toward the source) until it has received m data packets from the source within some interval of n seconds. This would eliminate the overhead of (S, G) state upstream when small numbers of packets are sent sporadically (at the expense of data packet delivery over the suboptimal paths of the shared RP tree). The DR may also choose to remain on the RP-distribution tree indefinitely instead of moving to the SPT. Note that if the DR does join the SPT, the path changes for all directly connected and downstream receivers. As a result, we do not guarantee that a receiver will remain on the RP tree; if receiver A's RP tree overlaps with another receiver B's SPT, receiver A may receive its packets over the SPT. A multicast distribution tree is a resource shared by all members of the group. To satisfy individual receiver-specific requirements or policies the multicast tree might degenerate into a set of receiver-specific unicast paths.

D. Steady-State Maintenance of Router State

In the steady state, each router sends periodic refreshers of PIM messages upstream to each of the next hop routers that is en route to each source, $(S, *)$ for which it has a multicast

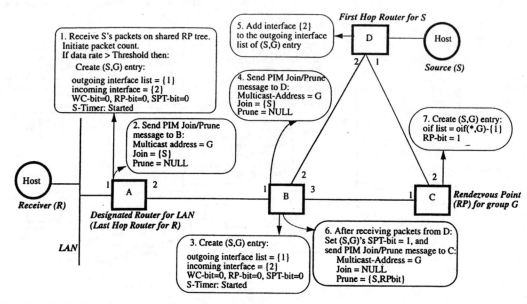

Fig. 5. Example: Switching from shared tree to SPT. Actions are numbered in the order they occur.

forwarding entry (S, G), as well as for the RP listed in the $(*, G)$ entry. These messages are sent periodically to capture state, topology, and membership changes. A PIM message is also sent on an event-triggered basis each time a new forwarding entry is established for some new (Sn, G) (note that some damping function may be applied, e.g., a merge time). Optionally, the PIM message could contain only the incremental information about the new source. The delivery of PIM messages does not depend on positive acknowledgment; lost packets will be recovered from at the next periodic refresh time.

E. Multicast Data Packet Processing

Data packets are processed in a manner similar to existing multicast schemes. An incoming interface check is performed and if it fails, the packet is dropped, otherwise the packet is forwarded to all the interfaces listed in the outgoing interface list (whose timers have not expired). There are two exception actions that are introduced if packets are to be delivered continuously, even during the transition from a shared to SPT.

1) When a data packet matches on an (S, G) entry with a cleared SPT bit, if the packet does not match the incoming interface for that entry, then the packet is forwarded according to the $*, G$ entry, i.e., it is sent to the outgoing interfaces listed in $*, G$ *if* the incoming interface matches that of the $*, G$. The $*, G$ RPF check is needed because the packet should be dropped if it does not pass the RPF check of either the $*, G$ or Sn, G entry. The iif of the $*, G$ entry points toward the RP.
2) When a data packet matches on an (S, G) entry with a cleared SPT bit, *and* the incoming interface of the packet matches that of the (S, G) entry, then the packet is forwarded and the SPT bit is set for that entry.

Data packets never trigger prunes. Data packets may trigger actions which, in turn, trigger prunes. In particular, data

packets from a new source can trigger creation of a new (S, G) forwarding entry. This causes S to be included in the prune list in a triggered PIM message toward the RP, just as it causes $(S, *)$ to be included in the join list in a triggered PIM message toward the source.

F. Timers

A timer is maintained for each outgoing interface listed in each (S, G) or $*, G$ entry. The timer is set when the interface is added. The timer is reset each time a PIM-join message is received on that interface for that forwarding entry [i.e., (S, G) or $(*, G)$]. Recall that all PIM, control messages are periodically refreshed.

When a timer expires, the corresponding outgoing interface is deleted from the outgoing interface list. When the outgoing interface list is null a prune message is sent upstream and the entry is deleted after three times the refresh period.

G. PIM Routers on Multiaccess Subnetworks

Certain multiaccess subnetwork configurations require special consideration. When a local area network (LAN)-connected router receives a prune from the LAN, it must detect whether there remain other downstream routers with active downstream members. The following protocol is used when a router whose incoming interface is the LAN has all of its outgoing interfaces go to null, the router multicasts a prune message for (S, G) onto the LAN. All other routers hear this prune and if there is any router that has the LAN as its incoming interface for the same (S, G) and has a non-null outgoing interface list, then the router sends a join message onto the LAN to override the prune. The join and prune should go to a single upstream router that is the right previous hop to the source or RP; however, at the same time we want others to hear the join and prune so that they suppress their own joins/prunes or override the prune. For this reason, the join is sent to a special multicast group of which all routers on the same LAN (and only those on the same LAN) are members. The IP address of the intended recipient of the message is included in the IGMP header.

H. Unicast Routing Changes

When unicast routing changes an RPF check is done and all affected multicast forwarding entries are updated. In particular, if the new incoming interface appears in the outgoing interface list, it is deleted from the outgoing list.

The PIM-router sends a PIM-join message out its new interface to inform upstream routers that it expects multicast datagrams over the interface. It sends a PIM-prune message out the old interface, if the link is operational, to inform upstream routers that this part of the distribution tree is going away.

I. Protocol Summary

In summary, once the PIM-join messages have propagated upstream from the RP, data packets from the source will follow the (S, G) distribution path state established. The packets will travel to the receivers via the distribution paths established by the PIM-join messages sent upstream from receivers toward the RP. Multicast packets will arrive at some receivers before reaching the RP if the receivers and the source are both "upstream" from the RP.

When the receivers initiate shortest-path distribution, additional outgoing interfaces will be added to the (S, G) entry and the data packets will be delivered via the shortest paths to receivers.

Data packets will continue to travel from the source to the RP in order to reach new receivers. Similarly, receivers continue to receive some data packets via the RP tree in order to pick up new senders. However, when source-specific tree distribution is used, most data packets will arrive at receivers over a shortest path distribution tree.

IV. OPEN ISSUES

Before concluding, we discuss several open issues that require further research, engineering, or experimental attention.

- *Aggregation of Information in PIM:* One of the most significant scaling issues faced by PIM and other known multicast routing schemes is the amount of memory consumed by multicast forwarding entries as the number of active sources and groups grows.

  The most straightforward approach for reducing source-specific state is to aggregate across source addresses, for example by using the highest level aggregate available for an address when setting up the multicast forwarding entry. This is optimal with respect to forwarding entry space. It is also optimal with respect to PIM message size. However, PIM messages will carry very coarse information and when the messages arrive at routers closer to the sources where more specific routes

exist, there will be a large fanout, and PIM messages will travel toward all members of the aggregate, which would be inefficient in most cases.

On closer consideration, it seems that source-specific state might not be the dominant concern. In PIM, as well as other multicast schemes such as DVMRP, source-specific state is created in a data-driven manner. Moreover, in PIM, source-specific state is only created when the source's data rate exceeds some threshold. Therefore, we know that the amount of source-specific state can not grow without bound, because the amount of available bandwidth, and therefore the number of active sources, is bounded. In fact, the number of simultaneously-active sources is not just bounded by the capacity of the links (which may be quite large in the future), but by the limited input capacity of the members of the group (which is growing but not at the same rate as backbone link bandwidth, for example).

Of greater concern is the potential explosion of simultaneously-active multicast groups, and the associated group-specific state. Unlike source-specific trees, group-specific shared trees are not built or maintained in a data-driven manner and therefore are not subject to the same bounds described above. Two approaches to group-specific state reduction are under consideration. Both are targeted for central backbone regions of the network where group-specific state proliferation is of most concern. In the first, a region does not maintain group-specific shared tree state in the absence of data traffic. Instead, only the border routers of the region retain group specific state, and only when data packets arrive for a particular group is routing state built inside of the region. In effect, the region emulates dense mode behavior. To carry this out, border routers must still maintain group-specific state in order to stay on the shared group tree, and PIM-join messages must still be propagated across the region to reach the border routers on the other side. In other words, state reduction can be reduced for low duty-cycle groups, however, control messaging is not affected. In the second approach for group-specific state reduction, a region can aggregate (S, G) entries into $(S, *)$ or $(S, \text{group-range})$ entries. This approach appears quite promising, particularly when (S, G) entries are only aggregated when their outgoing interface lists are the same.

- *Interaction with Policy-Based and TOS Routing:* PIM messages and data packets may travel over policy-constrained routes to the same extent that unicast routing does, so long as the policy does not prohibit this traffic explicitly.

  To obtain policy-sensitive distribution of multicast packets, we need to consider the paths chosen for forwarding PIM-join and register messages.

  If the path to reach the RP, or some source, is indicated as having the appropriate quality of service (QoS), and as being symmetric, then a PIM router can forward its joins upstream and expect that the data packets will be allowed to travel downstream. This implies that BGP/IDRP [20],

[28] should carry two QoS flags: symmetry flag and multicast willing flag.

If the generic route computed by hop-by-hop routing does not have the symmetry and multicast bits set, but there is an SDRP [16] route that does, then the PIM message should be sent with an embedded SDRP route. This option needs to be added to PIM-join messages. Its absence will indicate forwarding according to the router's unicast routing tables. Its presence will indicate forwarding according to the SDRP route. This implies that SDRP should also carry symmetry and multicast QoS bits *and* that PIM should carry an optional SDRP route inside of it to cause the PIM message and the multicast forwarding state to occur on an alternative distribution tree branch.

- *Interaction with Receiver Initiated Reservation Setup such as RSVP [36]:* Many interesting opportunities and issues arise when PIM-style explicit join multicast routing is used to support reservations, particularly, receiver-oriented reservations.

For example, RSVP reservation messages travel from receivers toward sources according to the state that multicast routing installs. When a reservation is shared among multiple sources (e.g., a shared audio channel where there is generally only one or two speakers at a time), it is appropriate to set up the reservation on the shared, RP-tree. However, for source-specific reservations (e.g., video channels), one wants to avoid establishing them over the shared tree if, shortly thereafter, receivers are going to switch to a source-specific tree. In this situation, routing could be configured to not send source-specific reservations over a shared-tree, for example.

Another interesting issue involves the need for alternate path routing when and if reservation requests are denied due to insufficient resources along the route that unicast routing considers to be best. To support this situation, PIM should be updated to allow explicit routing (i.e., often referred to as source routing) of PIM-join messages so that the reservation may be attempted along an alternate branch.

V. CONCLUSION

We have presented a solution to the problem of routing multicast packets in large, wide area internets. Our approach uses 1) constrained, receiver-initiated, membership advertisement for sparsely distributed multicast groups, 2) supports both shared and shortest path tree types in one protocol, 3) does not depend on the underlying unicast protocols, and 4) uses soft-state mechanisms to reliably and responsively maintain multicast trees. The architecture accommodates graceful and efficient adaptation to different network conditions and group dynamics.

A prototype of PIM has been implemented using extensions to existing IGMP message types. Simulation and implementation efforts conducted characterize configuration criteria and deployment issues. A complete specification document is available as an IETF internet-draft.

Due to the complexity of the environments within which PIM expects to operate, there are still several issues not completely resolved. Solutions to some of the issues require coordination with efforts in other areas such as interdomain routing and resource reservation protocols.

REFERENCES

[1] A. J. Ballardie, P. F. Francis, and J. Crowcroft, "Core based trees," in *Proc. ACM SIGCOMM*, San Francisco, 1993.
[2] M. W. Bern and R. L. Graham, "The shortest-network problem," *Scientific American*, pp. 84–89, Jan. 1989.
[3] C. Topolcic (Ed.), *Experimental Internet Stream Protocol:* Version 2 (st-ii), RFC1190, Oct. 1990.
[4] B. Cain, A. Thyagarajan, and S. Deering, *Internet Group Management Protocol*, Version 3, Working draft, July 1995.
[5] S. Casner, "Second ietf internet audiocast," in *Internet Society News*, vol. 1, no. 3, p. 23, 1992.
[6] D. D. Clark, "The design philosophy of the darpa internet protocols," in *Proc. ACM SIGCOMM*, 1988.
[7] Y. K. Dalal and R. M. Metcalfe, "Reverse path forwarding of broadcast packets," *Commun. ACM*, vol. 21, no. 12, pp. 1040–1048, 1978.
[8] S. Deering, *Host Extensions for IP Multicasting*, RFC1112, Aug. 1989.
[9] ——, "Multicast Routing in a Datagram Internetwork," *Ph.D. Thesis*, Stanford University, 1991.
[10] S. Deering and D. Cheriton, "Multicast routing in a datagram internetworks and extended lans," in *ACM Trans. Comput. Syst.*, pp. 85–111, May 1990.
[11] S. Deering, D. Estrin, D. Farinacci, and V. Jacobson, *Protocol Independent Multicast (PIM), Dense Mode Protocol: Specification*, Internet Draft, Mar. 1994.
[12] S. Deering, D. Estrin, D. Farinacci, V. Jacobson, C. Liu, and L. Wei, *Protocol Independent Multicast (PIM): Motivation and Architecture*, Working Draft, Nov. 1994.
[13] ——, *Protocol Independent Multicast (PIM): Specification*, Working Draft, Nov. 1994.
[14] ——, *Protocol Independent Multicast (PIM), Sparse Mode Protocol: Specification*, Working Draft, Sept. 1995.
[15] M. Doar and I. Leslie, "How bad is naive multicast routing," in *Proc. IEEE INFOCOM'93*, 1993.
[16] D. Estrin, T. Li, Y. Rekhter, and D. Zappala, *Source Demand Routing Protocol: Packet Format and Forwarding Specification*," IETF Working Draft, Mar. 1995.
[17] S. Floyd, V. Jacobson, C. Liu. S. McCanne, and L. Zhang, "A reliable multicast framework for light-weight sessions and application level framing," in *Proc. ACM SIGCOMM*, 1995.
[18] R. Frederick, "Left audio & videocast," *Internet Society News*, vol. 1, no. 4, p. 19, 1993.
[19] E. N. Gilbert and H. O. Pollak, "Steiner minimal trees," *SIAM J. Applied Mathematics*, vol. 16, no. 1, pp. 1–29, Jan. 1968.
[20] S. Hares and J. Scudder, *Idrp for IP*, Working Draft, Sept. 1993.
[21] R. M. Karp, *Reducibility Among Combinatorial Problem.* New York: Plennum, 1972.
[22] L. Kou, G. Markowsky, and L. Berman, "A fast algorithm for steiner trees," *Acta Informatica*, vol. 15, pp. 141–145, 1981.
[23] G. Malkin, *RIP Version 2 Carrying Additional Information*, RFC1388, June 1993.
[24] J. Moy, *OSPF Version 2*, RFC1247, Oct. 1991.
[25] ——, *MOSPF: Analysis and Experience*, Mar. 1994, RFC1585.
[26] ——, *Multicast Extension to OSPF*, RFC1584, Mar. 1994.
[27] V. J. Rayward–Smith and A. Clare, *On Finding Steiner Vertices*, Networks, vol. 16, pp. 284–294, 1986.
[28] Y. Rekhter and T. Li (Eds.), *A Border Gateway Protocol 4 (BGP-4)*, RFC1771, Mar. 1995.
[29] D. Waitzman, S. Deering, and C. Partridge, *Distance Vector Multicast Routing Protocol*, RFC1075, Nov. 1988.
[30] D. Wall, "Mechanisms for broadcast and selective broadcast," Ph.D. thesis, Stanford University, Stanford, CA, Tech. Rep., no. 190, June 1980.
[31] B. M. Waxman, "Routing of multipont connections," *IEEE J. Select. Areas Commun.*, vol. 6, no. 9, Dec. 1988.
[32] L. Wei and D. Estrin, "A comparison of multicast trees and algorithms," Computer Science Department, University of Southern California, Tech. Rep. USC-CS-93-560, Sept. 1993.
[33] ——, "The trade-offs of multicast trees and algorithms," in *Proc. 1994 Int. Conf. Comput. Commun. Networks*, San Francisco, CA, Sept. 1994.

IEEE/ACM TRANSACTIONS ON NETWORKING, VOL. 4, NO. 2, APRIL 1996

[34] L. Wei, F. Liaw, D. Estrin, A. Rowmano, and T. Lyon, "Analysis of a resequencer model for multicast over ATM networks," in *3rd Int. Workshop Network Operating Syst. Support Digital Audio Video,* San Diego, CA, Nov. 1992.

[35] P. Winter, "Steiner problem in networks: a survey," in *Networks,* vol. 17, no. 2, pp. 129–167, 1987.

[36] L. Zhang, R. Braden, D. Estrin, S. Herzog, and S. Jamin, *Resource Reservation Protocol (RSVP),* Version 1, Functional Specification, IETF Working Draft, July 1995.

Dino Farinacci has worked on transport and network layer protocols for 15 years. Currently, he works for Cisco Systems, Inc., San Jose, CA, where he has been designing and implementing IP and OSI routing protocols. He is a member of the IPng Directorate of the IETF where he has been involved in prototyping IP next generation proposals. In the last couple of years, he has been involved in the design, implementation, and deployment of IP multicast routing technology, notably PIM and DVMRP. Dino has been an active member of the Internet Engineering Task Force (IETF) for six years.

Stephen Deering (S'84–M'87) received the B.Sc. and M.Sc. degrees from the University of British Columbia, Canada, in 1973 and 1982, and the Ph.D. degree from Stanford University, Stanford, CA, in 1991, respectively.

He is currently a member of the research staff at Xerox PARC, engaged in research on advanced internetwork technologies, including multicast routing, mobile internetworking, scalable addressing, and support for multimedia applications over the Internet. He is present or past chair of numerous Working Groups of the Internet Engineering Task Force (IETF), a co-founder of the Internet Multicast Backbone (MBone), and the lead designer of the next generation Internet Protocol, IPv6.

Van Jacobson photo and biography not available time of publication.

Deborah L. Estrin (S'78–M'80–SM'95) received the Ph.D. degree in 1985 and the M.S. degree in 1982 from the Massachusetts Institute of Technology and the B.S. degree in 1980 from the University of California, Berkeley.

She is currently an Associate Professor of Computer Science at the University of Southern California, Los Angeles, where she joined the faculty in 1986. Estrin is a co-PI on the National Science Foundation (NSF) Routing Arbiter project at USC's Information Sciences Institute. She co-chairs the Source Demand Routing Working Group of the IETF and is an active participant in the Inter-Domain Multicast Routing and RSVP working groups. Estrin is a member of the ACM and AAAS. She has served on several panels for the NSF and National Research Council/CSTB, and is currently a member of ARPA's ISAT. Estrin was one of the founding Editors of Wiley's *Journal of Internetworking Research and Experience* and is currently an editor of the ACM/IEEE TRANSACTIONS ON NETWORKS.

Dr. Estrin received the NSF Presidential Young Investigator Award for her research in network interconnection and security in 1987.

Ching-Gung Liu (ACM S'95) received the M.S. degree from the University of Southern California, Los Angeles, in 1991 and the B.S. degree from National Taiwan University, China, in 1988. He joined the Ph.D. program at the University of Southern California and started working on the design and implementation of PIM in 1993.

Liu is currently working on scalable reliable multicast protocol toward the Ph.D. degree.

Liming Wei received the Ph.D. and M.S. degrees from the University of Southern California in 1995 and 1990 and the B.S. degree from Xian JiaoTong University, China, in 1985.

He currently works in the internetwork operating systems (IOS) division of Cisco Systems, Inc., San Jose, CA. His research interests include the design and evaluations of multicast routing mechanisms, and transport protocol performance. He developed the first version of PIMSIM, a packet level protocol simulator for PIM, and is now working on the realization of ubiquitous multicast routing services.

Distributed Algorithms for Multicast Path Setup in Data Networks

Fred Bauer, *Student Member, IEEE*, and Anujan Varma, *Member, IEEE*

Abstract— Establishing a multicast tree in a point-to-point network of switch nodes, such as a wide-area asynchronous transfer mode (ATM) network, can be modeled as the NP-complete Steiner problem in networks. In this paper, we introduce and evaluate two distributed algorithms for finding multicast trees in point-to-point data networks. These algorithms are based on the centralized Steiner heuristics, the *shortest path heuristic* (SPH) and the *Kruskal-based shortest path heuristic* (K-SPH), and have the advantage that only the multicast members and nodes in the neighborhood of the multicast tree need to participate in the execution of the algorithm. We compare our algorithms by simulation against a baseline algorithm, the pruned minimum spanning-tree heuristic that is the basis of many previously published algorithms for finding multicast trees. Our results show that the competitiveness (the ratio of the sum of the heuristic tree's edge weights to that of the best solution found) of both of our algorithms was, on the average, 25% better in comparison to that of the pruned spanning-tree approach. In addition, the competitiveness of our algorithms was, in almost all cases, within 10% of the best solution found by any of the Steiner heuristics considered, including both centralized and distributed algorithms. Limiting the execution of the algorithm to a subset of the nodes in the network results in an increase in convergence time over the pruned spanning-tree approach, but this overhead can be reduced by careful implementation.

Index Terms—Multicasting, Steiner problem in networks, distributed algorithms.

I. INTRODUCTION

MANY FUTURE applications of computer networks such as distance education, remote collaboration, and teleconferencing will rely on the ability of the network to provide multicast services. Indeed, many recent standards for packet-switched networks, notably asynchronous transfer mode (ATM), frame relay, and SMDS, include support for multicasting. Thus, multicasting will likely be an essential part of future networks.

Multicasting is sometimes supported in a point-to-point packet network by setting up a multicast tree connecting the members of the multicast group. We concern ourselves in this paper with networks that use virtual circuit routing, such as ATM and frame relay. In such a network, a multicast virtual circuit is set up from the source of the multicast to the destinations before data transmission occurs. Determining this optimal multicast tree for the virtual circuit is a difficult problem. Previous authors have established that the multicast tree problem can be modeled as the *Steiner problem in networks* (SPN) [2], [3], [8], [20], and that finding explicit solutions in large networks is prohibitively expensive. For example, two popular explicit algorithms, the *spanning tree enumeration algorithm* and the *dynamic programming algorithm* [20], have algorithmic complexities of $O(p^2 2^{(n-p)} + n^3)$ and $O(n3^p + n^2 2^p + n^3)$, respectively, where n is the number of nodes in the graph and p is the number of multicast members. A number of good, inexpensive, centralized heuristics exist for the SPN and have been reviewed extensively elsewhere [3], [8], [10], [15], [16]–[20]. Some have been shown, through analysis, to produce solutions no worse than twice the optimal solution [20]. Empirical evidence from our previous papers indicate that these heuristics find solutions much better than twice the optimal with reasonable speed in most cases [1].

Most of the algorithms proposed in the literature for SPN are serial in nature, however, a few distributed heuristics exist [4], [12]. Many of these algorithms are based on reducing the SPN to the minimum spanning tree (MST) problem, and using a distributed MST algorithm such as the one described by Gallager *et al.* [6]. A Steiner tree is created by pruning the MST by removing subtrees containing no multicast members. For example, Chen *et al.* [4] finds a Steiner tree by applying a distributed minimum spanning tree algorithm twice. First, the algorithm is applied to the original graph. This first minimum spanning tree is used to create a *shortest path forest* composed of disjoint trees and edges that together, form a connected subgraph of the original graph. The distributed minimum spanning tree algorithm is then applied a second time to this subgraph. The solution is obtained by pruning unnecessary leaves and branches from this second minimum spanning tree. Likewise, Kompella *et al.* [12] describe two distributed versions of earlier centralized heuristics proposed by the same authors [11]. Both of these distributed heuristics first build a *constrained Steiner tree* that reflects the combined criteria of cost and delay. A distributed MST algorithm is applied to this constrained Steiner tree and the solution tree is pruned. The two heuristics differ in their criteria for choosing edges while constructing the MST.

Distributed Steiner heuristics based on a minimum spanning tree algorithm suffer from two drawbacks: First, all the nodes in the network must participate in the execution of the algorithm. This may be impractical in a large network with

Manuscript revised January 1996; approved by IEEE/ACM TRANSACTIONS ON NETWORKING Editor J. Crowcroft. This research was supported by the Advanced Research Projects Agency (ARPA) under Contract F19628-93-C-0175 and by the National Science Foundation (NSF) Young Investigator Award MIP-9257103. This paper was presented in part at GLOBECOM'95, Singapore, November 1995.

The authors are with the Computer Engineering Department, University of California, Santa Cruz, CA 95064 USA.

Publisher Item Identifier S 1063-6692(96)02722-7.

sparse multicast groups. Second, the theoretical upper bound on *competitiveness* of a pruned MST to that of an optimal Steiner tree has been shown to be $s + 1$ where s is the number of nonmulticast nodes [17]. Here, competitiveness is defined to be the ratio of the sum of the heuristic tree's edge weights to that of an optimal tree [9], [18], [19]. Other equivalent terms for this measure include *inefficiency* and *quality of solution*. Thus, the competitiveness of a multicast tree decreases with the size of the multicast group. In comparison, the equivalent theoretical upper bound for the shortest path heuristic (SPH) for the Steiner tree problem is $2(1 - (1/p))$ [20], where p is the size of the multicast group. Our empirical evidence suggests that pruned MST heuristics often produce solutions of inferior quality as compared to those produced by shortest path Steiner heuristics.

In this paper, we present two distributed algorithms for the Steiner problem in networks. The algorithms are based on the SPH and the Kruskal-based shortest path heuristic (K-SPH) described in [1]. We analyze their message and convergence-time complexities and compare their simulation results against those from a pruned MST algorithm. We choose the distributed MST algorithm due to Gallager *et al.* [6] as our baseline algorithm for comparison. This algorithm is perhaps the simplest of all pruned MST algorithms, yet produces Steiner trees that are representative of other, more elaborately pruned MST heuristics such as those described in [4] and [12]. The distributed heuristics are compared on the basis of three criteria: competitiveness, number of messages exchanged, and convergence time.

Our simulations of the algorithms are performed on a large set of sparse, randomly-generated network topologies. We use the distance propagation delay model, using the distance between nodes as the weight of the edge between them. We restrict our analysis to sparse networks for two reasons: i) they are more representative of real point-to-point networks, and ii) they are inherently more difficult to solve because, in general, fewer solutions exist in a sparse network than in a dense one. Similarly, the simulated multicast groups are small relative to the size of the network, reflecting likely multicast applications such as video conferencing, distance learning, resource discovery and replicated database updating. Note that our results are not specific to any particular type of network such as ATM, but may be applied to any virtual circuit-based point-to-point network.

The remainder of this paper is organized as follows. Section II introduces and analyzes our two distributed heuristics, based on the centralized Steiner heuristics, K-SPH and SPH, respectively. Section III compares the algorithms in terms of their competitiveness, convergence time, and number of messages exchanged. We show that the distributed shortest-path heuristics produced multicast trees with competitiveness within 5% of that of the best solution found by any heuristic, both centralized and distributed, in more than 90% of our test networks. In contrast, only 0.3% of the solutions produced by the pruned MST algorithm fell within 5% of the best solutions in terms of their cost (sum of edge weights). Finally, Section IV concludes the paper with a discussion of the results.

II. STEINER TREE HEURISTICS

In this section, we summarize previous Steiner heuristics and introduce the two distributed Steiner heuristics.

Before continuing, we make the following basic definitions and notations. Z is the set of multicast destinations, S is the set of nonmulticast nodes $V - Z$, $P_{i,j}$ is the shortest path between nodes i and j, $d_{i,j}$ is the distance of the shortest path between nodes i and j as well as the weight of the edge between nodes i and j, and $C(T)$ is the cost of tree T (the sum of T's edge weights). Graph distances will be defined as follows: The distance between two nodes is the distance of the shortest path between them. Likewise, the distance between a node and a tree is the distance of the shortest path between the node and any node in the tree. Finally, the distance between two trees is the distance of the shortest among all paths between any node in one tree and any node in the other tree. As in [6], we append the weight of an edge or path with the index of its destination node in determining shortest paths so that, in case of a tie, the actions of the individual nodes would be consistent. Since we do not allow multiple edges between the same pair of nodes, this ensures that all the nodes select the same edge or path, given the same set of edge weights.

To be suitable for distributed implementation, a heuristic must satisfy four criteria. It must i) use the existing routing information available at each node in the network, ii) use minimal computational and network resources, iii) require a minimum of coordination between neighbors, and iv) limit itself to nodes directly involved in the multicast. Of the centralized heuristics evaluated in [1], we chose the following four heuristics as candidates for distributed implementation: the SPH, a variant of SPH known as SPH-Z, the K-SPH, and the *average distance heuristic* (ADH). Each of these heuristics is described in [15]. A brief summary of heuristics SPH and K-SPH follows.

SPH: Heuristic SPH, introduced in [16], initializes the multicast tree to an arbitrary multicast member. It then grows the tree by successively adding the next closest multicast member to the multicast tree by the shortest path between the multicast member and the tree. The algorithm terminates when all the multicast members have joined the tree.

K-SPH: Heuristic K-SPH, introduced in [13], differs from SPH in the manner in which the multicast tree is expanded. Instead of growing the tree one node at a time, the algorithm joins subtrees pairwise repeatedly until all the multicast nodes are part of a single tree. The algorithm initially starts with Z subtrees, each a multicast member itself. In the expansion step, it finds two subtrees that are closest to each other and joins them along the shortest path between them to form a single subtree. This heuristic is a refinement of the average distance heuristic first proposed by Rayward–Smith and Clave [14].

A. Distributed Steiner Heuristics

After further consideration, only two of the four heuristics, SPH and K-SPH, remain as suitable candidates for distributed implementation. Both heuristics SPH-Z and ADH fail our criteria for conversion. Although heuristic SPH-Z initially appears attractive as a distributed heuristic, its component distance information for each of the Z instances could be distinct. This forces as many as Z copies of component information at each node and a virtual storm of network messages before convergence. Likewise, ADH fails our criteria because its calculation of the most central node requires excessive overhead for coordination between nodes in the network. In addition, our earlier results indicate that, on the average, the solutions produced by K-SPH and ADH are of nearly identical quality [1]. Of these two heuristics, K-SPH is the more attractive candidate because of its relative simplicity and lower running time.

Distributed heuristics SPH and K-SPH are designed to run as asynchronous, independent processes running one per node in a network.

We assume that each such node knows its shortest path to all other nodes in the network. The distributed heuristics that each node in the network is a router; the routing tables in each such node are up-to-date; all shortest paths are *symmetric* in the sense that nodes i and j share shortest paths between them; no topology changes occur during the execution of the algorithm; the network is connected; every node has a unique index; each multicast member has knowledge of the indices of all other multicast members; and each multicast member is able to determine the distance to every other node from its routing table.

Heuristic SPH is inherently a serial algorithm since there is only one subtree expanding itself at any time during the execution of the algorithm and nodes must join the tree serially. Heuristic K-SPH, on the other hand, allows many of the join operations to proceed in parallel. The latter, however, is substantially more difficult to parallelize because of the significant amount of coordination that may be needed while combining subtrees. In the following, we present distributed K-SPH first, followed by a similar distributed implementation of SPH.

1) Distributed Heuristic K-SPH: Like its centralized version, distributed K-SPH starts with a forest of Z multicast members (Z-nodes) and connects them pairwise into successively larger subtrees until a single multicast tree remains or no further connections are possible. We refer to the subtrees during the execution of the algorithm as *fragments*. Thus, at the beginning of the algorithm, there are Z fragments, each a trivial subtree consisting of one Z-node. As the algorithm proceeds, these fragments grow into increasingly larger collections of multicast members.

At any instant during the execution of the algorithm, each node in the network is either part of a fragment or has not been yet been included in the multicast tree. Note that every Z-node is always a fragment node and every nonmember node (S-node) is initially a nonfragment node. When two fragments merge, the nodes in both fragments and the nodes that lie on the path connecting them become the fragment nodes of the new, merged fragment.

Each fragment has a *fragment leader* coordinating the activities of the fragment. This fragment leader is the fragment Z-node with the lowest index. Each fragment leader executes the finite state machine shown in Fig. 1. Initially, each multicast member is the leader of its own one-node fragment; when

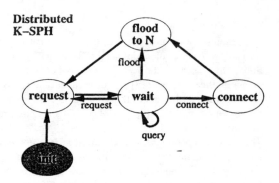

Fig. 1. The finite state machine for fragment leaders in distributed K-SPH.

```
while fragments remain do

    # algorithm discovery step
    update fragment information for nearby fragments
    f ← closest fragment

    # algorithm connection step
    request merger with fragment f
    if merger requests exchanged with fragment f then
        attempt connection to fragment f
        if connection established then
            merge fragments
        else
            restore original fragments
        end if
    end if
end while
```

Fig. 2. Pseudo-code for fragment leaders in distributed K-SPH.

two fragments merge, leadership is assigned to the fragment leader with the lower index. To identify fragments uniquely, each has the same index as its leader and each fragment node is aware of its fragment index.

At the highest level, each fragment, guided by its leader, executes the pseudo-code shown in Fig. 2. During the execution of the algorithm, each fragment attempts to merge with its closest neighboring fragment. This is accomplished in two steps; a *discovery* step and a *connection* step. During the discovery step, the leader gathers and updates its information on other fragments and graph nodes. Based on the information gathered, it determines the closest fragment with which to merge. During the connection step, it communicates with the closest neighbor fragment's leader, requesting a merge. This closest fragment leader is simply the Z-node with the same index as the closest fragment. If accepted, the leader with the lowest index attempts to connect the two fragments. Regardless of the outcome (the request is rejected, the fragments are connected, or the connection attempt fails), the cycle repeats until the algorithm terminates.

Distributed K-SPH processes running on each node rely on the shortest path information assumed available at its node, as well as information maintained by the fragment leaders. Each node also stores the index of its fragment. Initially, only multicast nodes have a fragment index. Each leader maintains additional shortest path information for its fragment. This

```
# request merger with fragment f
do
      send request to fragment f's leader
      wait for response
until accept or reject

leader ← this fragment index < fragment f's index
if accept and leader then
      # attempt connection to fragment f
      send connect message to head of shortest path


      wait for connection success or failure
      if failure then
            send reject to fragment f's leader
end if
```

Fig. 3.   Fragment leader pseudo-code for the connection step in distributed K-SPH.

information augments the shortest path information at each node. For example, the leader stores only the distance, and the head and tail of the shortest path between its fragment and every other fragment. The additional details necessary to build the path between fragments is stored at the head of the path, a node in the leader's subtree. Note that the shortest path between fragments needs not start or end at a leader node.

2) The Finite State Machine of Heuristic K-SPH:

State init: When distributed K-SPH starts, each Z-node, the leader of its own trivial one-node fragment, already knows its distance to every other fragment as provided by the initial distance tables and no discovery step is necessary. Instead, each distributed K-SPH leader starts with the connection step, described below.

States request, wait, and connect: States *request, wait* and *connect*, in Fig. 1, comprise the connection step. During this step, each leader attempts to connect its fragment with the closest fragment, known as its *preferred fragment* (Fig. 3 shows the pseudo-code for this step). It does so by sending a *merge request* message to the leader of the preferred fragment (that is, the Z-node with the same index as the preferred fragment). A leader receives one of three responses to its request:

Buy   A fragment leader returns the busy response when a request arrives during its discovery step. Upon receiving a busy response, a fragment will retransmit its merge request.

Reject   A fragment node returns a reject message when i) it receives a connection request from a fragment other than its preferred fragment, ii) when a connection attempt fails, or iii) when it is no longer a fragment leader.

Accept   A fragment leader returns an accept response when it exchanges merge requests with its preferred fragment. Once an accept message is sent, the fragment may not leave the connect step or accept a request from another fragment until the connection attempt completes.

Connecting Fragments: Upon receiving the accept response, the fragment leader with the lowest index attempts to

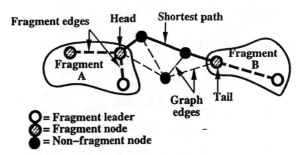

Fig. 4.   Example of fragments A and B merging in distributed K-SPH.

```
# send update request to all children
for all fragment children do
      send fragment index, distance to closest fragment,
            and shortest path information to each child
end for

# query all nodes closer than closest fragment
for nodes nearer than closest fragment do
      send nodes query for component information
end for

wait for responses
update shortest path information information

# forward results
if not leader then
      send summary of shortest path information
            to parent
end if

if leader then
      f ← closest fragment
```

Fig. 5.   Fragment leader pseudo-code for the discovery step in distributed K-SPH.

connect the two fragments together using a shortest path. To do so, a connect message is sent down this shortest path. The message may either reach the target fragment or be *blocked*. Blocking occurs when the message reaches a node in a third fragment before reaching the target fragment.

Figure 4 illustrates a successful connection where fragments A and B are connected by their shortest path. This path has its head in one fragment, its tail in the other, and passes through only nonfragment nodes. The connect message stops at the first node in the target fragment it reaches and sends a status message back along the same path.

If the connect message is blocked, the blocked node returns a status message back along the shortest path. Each intermediate node, upon receiving this status message, reverts to its previous nonfragment status. Upon receiving the status message, the initiating fragment leader sends a reject message to the other fragment leader.

After the connection step, fragment leaders enter the discovery step.

The discovery step: The discovery step accomplishes three tasks: i) it informs every node in the fragment of its new fragment index, ii) it gathers fragment information about

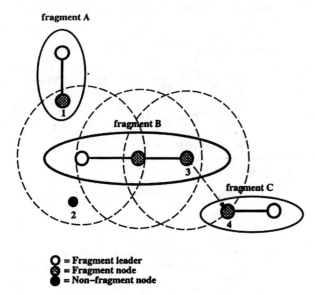

Fig. 6. Example of the discovery phase in distributed K-SPH. Fragment B's leader believes that fragment C is the closest fragment. During fragment B's discovery step, it instructs fragment nodes to query those nodes closer than fragment C. This distance is the distance between node 3, the head of the path to fragment C, and node 4, its tail, and is marked by the dotted circles around each of fragment B's nodes. Since nodes 1 and 2 fall within one such circle, they receive queries and fragment B's leader discovers the closer fragment A.

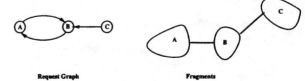

Fig. 7. An example for request graph.

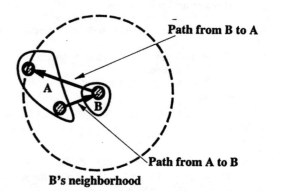

Fig. 8. Two subtrees with different shortest paths.

nodes close to the fragment, and iii) it refreshes information on shortest paths to other fragments. The pseudo-code for the discovery step is shown in Fig. 5. Each fragment leader achieves these tasks by performing a multicast on its fragment rooted at itself. In the multicast message, the leader includes the fragment index, the distance to the preferred fragment and shortest paths to other fragments. As each node in the fragment receives the multicast, it updates its fragment index, queries *nearby* nodes and passes the multicast message to its children. Nearby nodes are defined as those nodes that lie within the shortest distance from this fragment to the preferred fragment. Nearby nodes are queried for fragment index information. The objective of queries to nearby nodes is to find fragment nodes closer than those already known by the leader. Fig. 7 illustrates a case where this is useful. Queries could be sent to all nodes in the graph, but are limited to nearby nodes for two reasons: i) a set distance avoids broadcast storms and ii) new shortest paths discovered should be shorter than those already available. The discovery step is implemented by state *flood-to-N* in Fig. 1.

Analysis of Distributed K-SPH Algorithm: Having described the distributed K-SPH in the previous section, we now turn to its properties. We use a directed *request graph* to show the relationship of fragments to one another during the execution of the algorithm. Each fragment in the network is represented by a node in the request graph and its current choice of preferred fragment by a directed edge. Fig. 6 illustrates an example graph with three vertices representing fragments A, B, and C. In this example, the fragment pair A and B request each other, while a third, more distant fragment C requests fragment B. Fragments A and B will

merge, creating a new fragment that will form a pair with fragment C and merge. A fragment is considered *stable* when it is in the states wait or request since its choice of preferred partner is unknown when the fragment is in states connect, flood-to-N, or init.

The request graph can be used to show that the distributed K-SPH algorithm does not deadlock. To prove that the algorithm will terminate, we need to only show that at any time during the execution of the algorithm, the shortest-path distances maintained by two of the fragments to each other will converge to the same value in a finite time (that is, a cycle of length two in the request graph). These two fragments will then merge to form a new fragment. Thus, by induction, the algorithm will terminate in finite time.

Lemma 1: At any time during the execution of the algorithm, the shortest-path distances maintained by two stable fragments to each other will converge to the same value within a finite time.

Proof: Initially, the shortest path between any two single-node multicast members is the shortest path between their fragments. This path is symmetric in the sense that both paths consist of the same nodes and edges. This is because of the strict ordering of all shortest paths. Suppose that at some later time, the shortest paths between two fragments differ in distance as shown in Fig. 8. Suppose further, that one fragment, in this case fragment B, has the longer path. The next time fragment B enters state flood-to-N, it will query every node in its neighborhood for fragment information. Any node in fragment A closer to B must fall within B's neighborhood and will become the tail of a new shorter path to fragment A. The shortest of all such paths will become fragment B's new shortest path to fragment A. By a symmetrical argument, the paths between fragments A and B must converge on the same distance.

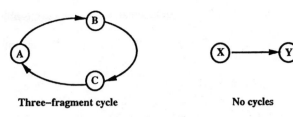

Three–fragment cycle   **No cycles**

Fig. 9. A request graph demonstrating deadlock.

TABLE I
MESSAGE BOUNDS FOR DISTRIBUTED HEURISTICS K-SPH AND SPH

Bound	Distributed K-SPH	Distributed SPH
Lower Bound	$Z \log Z$	Z^2
Upper Bound	ZN	ZN

TABLE II
CONVERGENCE-TIME BOUNDS FOR DISTRIBUTED HEURISTICS K-SPH AND SPH

Bound	Distributed K-SPH	Distributed SPH
Lower Bound	$\log Z$	DZ
Upper Bound	DZ	DZ

Inconsistencies may also occur when a path is blocked. Assume that only one of a pair of fragments finds the shortest path between them blocked. Assume fragment A has a shortest path to B, but B's shortest path to A is blocked. The shortest path between fragments can only be blocked by a node belonging to a third fragment C. In this case, fragment A will query the blocking node in fragment C the next time A enters the discovery phase (state flood-to-N). In addition, C will also update its distance to A during its recovery phase, resulting in consistent values for the distance between A and C.

A deadlock occurs when no two-fragment cycle exists in the request graph even when all fragments are stable. Fig. 9 shows two such examples. In the first case, three fragments are locked in a cycle and in the other, one fragment has no outgoing edges and cannot merge with any other fragment. Either of these cases could mean that distributed K-SPH would never terminate. In the following, we show that such deadlocks cannot occur.

Lemma 2: Distributed K-SPH does not deadlock.

Proof: Let $d(I, J)$ represent the distance between fragments I and J. In Fig. 9, stable fragments A, B, and C are locked in a three-node cycle. Since each fragment prefers the closest fragment, the following inequalities must hold: $d(A, B) < d(A, C), d(B, C) < d(B, A)$, and $d(C, A) < d(C, B)$. We know from Lemma 1, however, that at least two of the fragments, say A and B, must have equidistant shortest paths. This leads to a contradiction. A similar argument holds for any cycle of more than two fragments. Consider the case where no cycle exists as shown by fragments X and Y in Fig. 9. Fragment Y has no outgoing edge, which indicates that it has no shortest path to any fragment. This means that Y's path to X must be blocked and, by Lemma 1, will eventually be discovered. Distributed K-SPH terminates with an error when both X and Y have no outgoing edges.

Convergence Time and Number of Messages: We now derive some simple asymptotic bounds on the number of messages and convergence time of the distributed K-SPH algorithm.

Distributed K-SPH uses the least number of messages when the network has $Z = 2^i$ multicast nodes, any number of nonmulticast nodes, and fragments always find a partner. Under these conditions, a total of $Z/2^1 + Z/2^2 + \cdots + Z/2^i = Z(2^i - 1/2^i = 2^i(2^i - 1/2^i)) = 2^i - 1$ merges occur during i rounds. Each fragment merges using a relatively small number of messages and the new fragment enters the discovery phase. In the discovery phase, each fragment node queries every child and neighbor for fragment and distance information. Assume that, on average, each fragment node queries a finite

number of neighbors and children approximated by c. The total number of messages sent by multicast members during each round is $cZi = cZ \log Z = \Omega(Z \log Z)$. During each of the $\log Z$ rounds, the longest round-trip message time between leader and fragment root dominates. This round-trip time can be, at worst, twice the diameter of the graph and, at best, a constant. Thus, the time to converge is lower-bounded by $c \log Z = \Omega(\log Z)$.

In the worst case, only one fragment finds a partner during any round. Thus, $Z - 1$ rounds occur before a solution is found. If fragments are always relatively large, the number of messages would be the number of rounds times the number of nodes on all fragments, $c(Z - 1)N = O(ZN)$. If the round-trip times during each of the $Z - 1$ rounds is large and close to twice the graph diameter, $2D$, then the convergence time for this case is $2D(Z - 1) = O(DZ)$.

These bounds are summarized in Tables I and II, along with the bounds for the other algorithm considered in this paper. Our results from simulations of the algorithm show that the rates of increase of both the convergence time and the number of messages with the number of nodes fell within these bounds as shown in Section III.

3) Distributed SPH: The distributed SPH is a special case of distributed K-SPH described in Section II-A1. In distributed SPH, any one of the multicast members may act as the source of the multicast, referred to here, simply, as the *source node*. In contrast to distributed K-SPH, only one fragment grows, the *source fragment*, connecting multicast members to itself until all the multicast members are part of the same fragment. The heuristic terminates when a single tree remains.

In SPH, the preferred fragment of every fragment is always the source fragment. The sole exception, of course, is the source fragment itself which prefers its closest fragment. Note that all other fragments are trivial one-node subtrees containing one multicast member each. However, to maintain uniformity with our previous heuristic description, we will continue to use the term fragment instead of multicast member. Using the same connection step outlined for heuristic K-SPH, the source fragment merges with its closest fragment. As the source fragment grows, it uses the same discovery step to determine the new, closest fragment. The source fragment never changes its index. This preserves the source fragment's

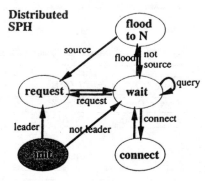

Fig. 10.   The finite state machine for each node performing distributed SPH.

original index so that nonsource fragments never need to change their preferred fragment index. As a consequence, nonsource fragments do not enter the discovery phase. In all other respects, distributed SPH is very similar to distributed K-SPH. Fig. 10 shows the finite state machine used by each node.

Algorithm Analysis: Since distributed SPH is a special case of distributed K-SPH, its analysis proceeds similarly to that of distributed K-SPH. For example, it too will not deadlock as shown by Lemma 3.

Lemma 3: Heuristic SPH does not deadlock.

Proof: Consider Fig. 9 again. A three-node cycle, such as the one in Fig. 9, cannot occur in distributed SPH because every fragment except the source prefers the source fragment. Thus, the longest request graph cycle in distributed SPH has a length of two: an edge from the source to a fragment and the return edge. A longer request cycle is an error. Likewise, a zero-node cycle indicates an error since every fragment except the source fragment always prefers the source fragment and the source fragment prefers its closest fragment.

Messages and Convergence Time: Like distributed K-SPH, distributed SPH uses the least number of messages when $Z = 2^i$ multicast members exist. Distributed SPH differs from distributed K-SPH in that only two fragments merge during a round. Assume that, on average, each fragment node queries a finite number of neighbors and children approximated by c. The number of messages in this case would be $c + 2c + 3c + \cdots + (Z-1)c = c((Z-1)^2 - (Z-1)^2/2 = O(Z^2)$. The round-trip time during each of the $Z-1$ rounds cannot be greater than twice the graph diameter and the convergence time is $c(2D)(Z-1) = \Omega(DZ)$.

In the worst case, assume that the source fragment grows quickly and the round-time distance for messages approaches twice the graph diameter, $2D$. The number of messages in this case, is $c(Z-1)N = O(ZN)$. Likewise, the convergence time becomes $2D(Z-1) = O(DZ)$.

The message and convergence time bounds for the distributed heuristics are summarized in Tables I and II, respectively.

III. SIMULATION RESULTS

To evaluate the two distributed heuristics presented in the last section, we implemented the algorithms in a simulator and performed extensive simulations on randomly generated test networks. We chose the distributed MST algorithm due to Gallager *et al.* [6] as our baseline algorithm to compare the results. This algorithm was used to produce a minimum spanning tree of the network graph that was then pruned to obtain a Steiner tree. We chose this MST algorithm as our baseline algorithm because the majority of previously reviewed distributed algorithms find multicast trees are based on finding minimal spanning trees [4], [12]. This algorithm differs from our algorithms, distributed K-SPH and SPH, in the fact that all the network nodes must participate in the execution of the algorithm in the former, while only the multicast members and nodes in the vicinity of the multicast tree being set up execute the algorithm in the latter.

This section summarizes the simulation results and compares the algorithms in terms of their convergence time, competitiveness, and the number of messages exchanged.

A. Evaluation Methodology

1) Network Model: Because our choice of existing network topologies and multicast applications was small, we chose to compare Steiner heuristics using randomly generated networks. Each algorithm was run on a total of 1000 test networks. Each of the 1000 networks is a sparse 200-node network. We consider an n-node graph to be sparse when less than 5% of the possible $\binom{n}{2}$ edges are present in the graph. Note that the number of edges in an n-node connected graph can vary from $n-1$ for a tree to $\binom{n}{2}$ for the complete graph on n nodes. For our test networks on 200 nodes, the number of edges must fall in the narrow range from 199 to 5% of maximum edges possible equals 995. Fig. 11 shows the distribution of the number of edges for our test networks. We believe such a graph describes a plausible wide area network (WAN) because a large network is likely to be loosely interconnected. Likewise, the simulated networks have 10% or 30% of their nodes in the multicast group because multicast applications running on such a WAN are likely to involve only a minority of nodes in the network. For example, consider a video conference in a large corporate network. The conference is most likely to directly involve a minority of nodes in the network. The choice of 10% and 30% of the nodes was made since these figures represent more difficult cases of the Steiner problem. Later, in Section III-C, we discuss how these heuristics scale with increasing multicast membership size (10% to 90%) and network size (20 to 200 nodes).

The 1000 networks were generated to resemble real networks in a manner similar to that of Doar [5]. Each of the 200 nodes is distributed across a Cartesian coordinate plane with minimum and maximum coordinates (0, 0) and (400, 400), creating a forest of 200 nodes spread across this plane. The nodes are then connected by a random spanning tree. This tree is generated by iteratively considering a random edge between nodes and accepting those edges that connect distinct components. The remaining edges of the graph are chosen by examining each possible edge (x, y) and generating a random number $0 \le r < 1$. If r is less than a probability function $P(x, y)$ based on the distance between x and y, then the edge is accepted. Each edge's distance is its rectilinear distance plus

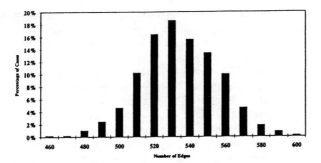

Fig. 11.   The histogram of the number of edges in the test graphs.

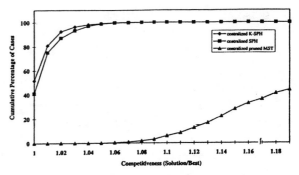

Fig. 12.   Competitiveness distribution for centralized Steiner heuristics.

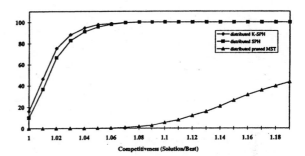

Fig. 13.   Competitiveness distribution for distributed Steiner heuristics.

a small constant. This distance is also the time it takes for a message to traverse this edge. We used the probability function

$$P(x,y) = \beta e(-d_{x,y}/2\alpha n)$$

where $d_{x,y}$ is the rectilinear distance between nodes x and y [5]. The parameters α and β govern the density of the graph. Increasing α increases the number of connections to nodes far away and increasing β increases the number of edges from each node. After some experimentation, we chose $\alpha = 0.10$ and $\beta = 0.20$ for generating the graphs used in this simulation. These values produced graphs of realistic density.

We performed two different simulations on each generated graph by varying the multicast group size in two ways; the number of multicast nodes was chosen as either 20 or 60 of the 200 nodes. Results are presented for both combinations for each graph. The nodes in a multicast group were chosen randomly in each case. The random numbers were chosen from a uniform distribution. To ensure fairness, each heuristic was run on the same 1000 networks.

B. Evaluation Metrics

The metrics we use for comparison are the competitiveness, convergence time, and messages passed. Competitiveness is the ratio of heuristic tree cost $C(T)$ to that of the best solution C_{best} found by any heuristic. To determine the best solution, we considered solutions produced by the two distributed heuristics described in this paper and the distributed MST algorithm, as well as the serial heuristics described in [1]. We use the best heuristic solution found for each test network rather than an optimal solution because explicit algorithms to find optimal solutions are prohibitively expensive on large networks. The convergence time was found by measuring the elapsed time in the simulated network from the start of simulation to the time at which the last message reaches its destination. Since message-passing delays are likely to dominate processing delays on the convergence time of the algorithm in a wide-area network, we considered only the former in computing the simulation time. We used the distance between two nodes as the delay to pass a message between them. Messages passed is the total number of messages passed between nodes before convergence.

C. Simulation Results

Having described the algorithms and the simulation environment, we now turn to the results of our simulations.

Figure 12 shows the competitiveness distribution for the centralized versions of SPH, K-SPH, and pruned MST algorithms. Each of the three plots shows the cumulative percentage of cases whose competitiveness is less than or equal to a given value. Fig. 13 shows the same distributions for the distributed versions of the three algorithms. Note that the distributed versions of SPH and K-SPH may provide inferior solutions compared to their centralized versions because of the lack of global topology information in each node in the former. The degradation in the competitiveness, however, was small in our test networks. In fact, the competitiveness produced by distributed K-SPH was often superior to that of centralized SPH.

When comparing the competitiveness, heuristics SPH and K-SPH consistently outperformed the pruned MST heuristic in both centralized and distributed cases. This result is consistent with the known theoretical upper bounds on the heuristics. It has been shown that the cost of a solution produced by either SPH or K-SPH is within twice the cost of an optimal solution [20]. In contrast, the ratio between the cost of a solution produced by pruning a minimum spanning tree and that of an optimal solution can be as large as the number of nonmulticast nodes [17]. In our case, the cost of pruned MST solutions was rarely worse than twice that of the best solution found, but was often significantly worse than that produced by shortest path heuristics. Fig. 14 displays the complete cumulative distribution for the pruned minimum spanning tree algorithm. In Fig. 13, 90% of the solutions

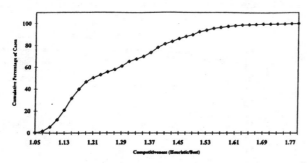

Fig. 14. Competitiveness distribution for the distributed pruned minimum spanning tree heuristic.

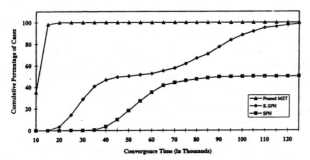

Fig. 15. Cumulative distribution for the number of messages transmitted by the three distributed Steiner heuristics.

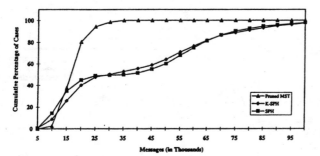

Fig. 16. Convergence time distribution for distributed Steiner heuristics.

produced by both distributed K-SPH and SPH were within 4% of the best in terms of their cost. In comparison, when the best 90% of the solutions produced by the pruned MST algorithm were considered, some of the solutions had costs as high as 50% more than that of the optimal algorithm. Thus, if competitiveness is the most important criterion in the choice of the algorithm, distributed K-SPH is the heuristic of choice.

Heuristics SPH and K-SPH also enjoy the advantage that neither requires the participation of all the nodes in the network. Only the nodes in the multicast tree and within its neighborhood need to participate in the execution of the algorithm. The pruned minimum spanning tree algorithm, on the other hand, requires participation from every node of the network, a condition difficult to satisfy in practice in a large wide-area network.

Viewed from the perspective of messages exchanged and convergence-time, however, the pruned MST heuristic enjoys

an advantage over shortest path heuristics SPH and K-SPH. Fig. 15 displays the cumulative percentage of networks solved within a given number of messages for the three algorithms. Likewise, Fig. 16 displays the cumulative percentage of networks solved within a given convergence time. Both the number of messages and the convergence time for the solutions produced by pruned MST algorithm fell well within a much narrower range as compared to the results for distributed K-SPH and SPH. This is again consistent with the known theoretical bounds on the number of messages generated by the heuristics. In the case of the pruned MST heuristic, the additional effort to prune the minimum spanning tree is inconsequential as compared to the effort required to find the minimum spanning tree. Thus, the theoretical upper bound on the number of messages in the pruned MST heuristic is $O(N \log_2 N + E)$ [6]. In comparison, the upper bound on the number of messages for both SPH and K-SPH is $O(ZN)$. Thus, when the number of multicast nodes is large in comparison to $\log N$, the pruned MST heuristic has a smaller upper bound on the number of messages.

On comparing the SPH and K-SPH algorithms, it is interesting to observe that the algorithms had the same level of communication complexity in terms of the number of messages generated, yet the range of convergence times produced by K-SPH was significantly tighter. This is primarily due to the disparate approaches used by the algorithms in growing the multicast tree. Distributed SPH grows the tree by adding one multicast member at a time to the source fragment, concentrating much of the work at the source, while distributed K-SPH allows multiple fragments of the tree to combine in parallel. This allows distributed K-SPH to provide lower convergence times without increasing the number of messages substantially.

To answer the question of how the distributed heuristics scale with multicast group and network size, we performed 3600 additional simulations summarized by Figs. 17–19. Figs. 17 and 18 show the average convergence time passed for both SPH and K-SPH when either the multicast group size is varied from 10% to 90% in a 200-node graph or when network size is varied from 20 nodes to 200 nodes. Each graph point summarizes the average value for 200 test networks. Minimum and maximum values for each are displayed using error bars. Similarly, Fig. 19 summarizes the average messages passed when membership size and graph size are varied. The equivalent graphs for distributed heuristic SPH are omitted since they mirror the results shown in the convergence time graphs. These graphs demonstrate that distributed heuristics SPH and K-SPH scale reasonably well for both multicast-group and network size.

Even though the convergence times for distributed K-SPH in Fig. 16 are higher than those of the pruned MST algorithm by as much as 10 times, we believe that the former can be brought down by modifying distributed K-SPH in the following ways:

1) If a fragment receives a reject message because the preferred fragment has already merged with another, the fragment enters the discovery step and looks for the next closest fragment. If the rejecting fragment indicates its new fragment index, a fragment could skip

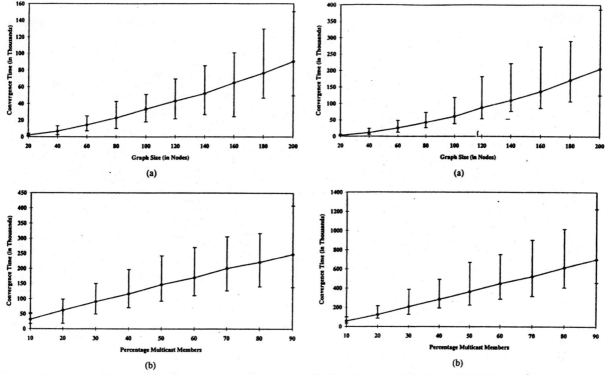

Fig. 17. Convergence time of the distributed K-SPH algorithm (a) as a function of network size with 30% multicast membership, and (b) as a percentage of multicast membership in a 200-node network.

Fig. 18. Convergence time of the distributed SPH algorithm (a) as a function of network size with 30% multicast membership, and (b) as a percentage of multicast membership in a 200-node network.

the discovery step and send a merge request to the new merged component. Preliminary tests indicate that this can reduce convergence time by 5%.

2) Inefficiencies result when a large fragment merges with a small fragment. This inefficiency is evident in distributed SPH because the largest fragment, the source fragment, always merges with a fragment containing a single multicast member. Although such merges cannot be avoided in distributed K-SPH, the duration of such a merge can be reduced by taking into account the fragment size when merging fragments as follows: if a small fragment is added to a large fragment, the discovery step can be shortened by performing a *partial* discovery step. A partial discovery step updates the fragment leader's knowledge of fragment distances using existing fragment distance information and new information gathered by propagating a multicast through the smaller fragment's nodes. Such a partial discovery step is significantly faster; as much as 35% in our tests. The new fragment, however, may be unaware of fragment distance information it might otherwise have found through a full discovery step and, hence, the competitiveness may suffer. Thus, this approach trades off competitiveness for speed.

3) In our simulations, we observed that few connection attempts between fragments are blocked in practice. This allows the connection and discovery steps to be overlapped, reducing the time it takes for two fragments to

complete a merge. The price paid is an occasional failed connection attempt requiring longer discovery steps in both the original fragments to restore the fragments to their original states.

IV. CONCLUDING REMARKS

In this paper, we introduced two distributed heuristics based on shortest path Steiner hueristics, and evaluated their performance relative to a baseline pruned minimum spanning-tree heuristic. The primary advantage of our distributed algorithms over previous algorithms is that they require participation from only the nodes in the multicast tree and within their neighborhood. Among the two algorithms studied, distributed K-SPH emerged as the clear winner. In comparison to distributed SPH, it has substantially lower convergence time and slightly better competitiveness.

The heuristics developed are an improvement over existing distributed Steiner heuristics based on the minimum spanning tree [4], [12] for two reasons: they produce solutions of superior quality in most cases and require the participation of only a subset of network nodes. Our results show that the competitiveness of the solutions produced by both of our algorithms were, on the average, at least 25% better in comparison to those produced by the pruned spanning-tree approach. In addition, the competitiveness found by our algorithms was, in almost all cases, within 10% of the best solution found by any of the Steiner heuristics considered, including both centralized and distributed algorithms.

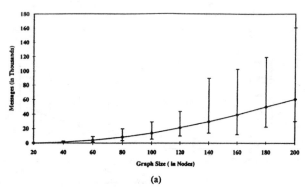

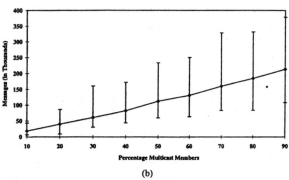

Fig. 19. Number of messages generated by the distributed K-SPH algorithm (a) as a function of network size with 30% membership, and (b) as a percentage of multicast membership in a 200-node network.

Limiting the execution of the algorithm to a subset of the nodes in the network can result in an increase in convergence time over the pruned spanning-tree approach. Indeed, the convergence time of distributed K-SPH was as large as 10 times that of the pruned MST algorithm in many of our test networks. However, we believe that the distributed K-SPH algorithm can be streamlined in several ways to narrow this gap, as discussed in the last section.

Areas for future research include provisions for robustness of the algorithms in an environment where node and link failures occur. As stated here, the heuristics assume reliable delivery of messages and a stable topology during their execution. If an environment is assumed where nodes and links do fail during execution, a combination of schemes to ensure convergence and correctness needs to be applied. These would certainly include an adaptive all-paths distributed algorithm such as the one described by Humblet [7] and a timeout mechanism to detect rejected merger requests. Additional work is required to study the effectiveness and performance of these schemes.

REFERENCES

[1] F. Bauer and A. Varma, "Degree-constrained multicasting in point-to-point networks," in *Proc. IEEE INFOCOM*, Boston, Apr. 1995, pp. 369–376.
[2] J. Beasley, "An SST-based algorithm for the Steiner problem in graphs," *Networks*, vol. 19, pp. 1–16, 1989.
[3] K. Bharath-Kumar and Jaffe, "Routing to multiple destinations in computer networks," *IEEE Trans. Commun.*, vol. COM-31, no. 3, pp. 343–351, Mar. 1983.
[4] G. Chen, M. Houle, and M. Kuo, "The Steiner problem in distributed computing systems," *Information Sciences*, vol. 74, no. 1–2, pp. 73–96, Oct. 1993.
[5] M. Doar and I. Leslie, "How bad is naive multicast routing?" in *Proc. IEEE INFOCOM*, San Francisco, CA, Apr. 1993, pp. 82–89.
[6] R. Gallager, P. Humblet, and P. Spira, "A distributed algorithm for minimum-weight spanning trees," *ACM Trans. Programming Languages Syst.*, vol. 5, no. 1, pp. 66–77, Jan. 1983.
[7] P. Humblet, "Another adaptive distributed shortest path algorithm," *IEEE Trans. Commun.*, vol. 39, no. 6, pp. 995–1003, Jun. 1991.
[8] F. Hwang and D. Richards, "Steiner tree problems," *Networks*, vol. 22, pp. 55–89, 1992.
[9] M. Imase and B. Waxman, "Dynamic Steiner tree problem," *SIAM J. Disc. Math.*, vol. 4, no. 3, pp. 369–384, Aug. 1991.
[10] V. Kompella, J. Pasquale, and G. Polyzos, "Multicasting for multimedia applications," in *Proc. IEEE INFOCOM*, New York, NY, May 1992, pp. 2078–2085.
[11] ——, "Multicast routing for multimedia communications," *IEEE/ACM Trans. Networking*, vol. 1, no. 3, pp. 286–292, Jun. 1993.
[12] ——, "Two distributed algorithms for the constrained Steiner tree problem," in *Proc. Comput. Commun. Networking*, San Diego, CA, Jun. 1993.
[13] J. Kruskal, "On the shortest spanning subtree of a graph and the traveling salesman problem," *Proc. Amer. Math. Soc.*, vol. 7, pp. 48–50, 1956.
[14] V. Rayward-Smith and A. Clare, "On finding Steiner vertices," *Networks*, vol. 16, pp. 283–294, 1986.
[15] M. Smith and P. Winter, "Path-distance heuristics for the Steiner problem in undirected networks," *Algorithmica*, vol. 7, no. 2–3, pp. 309–327, 1992.
[16] H. Takahashi and A. Matsuyama, "An approximate solution for the Steiner problem in graphs," *Math. Japonica*, vol. 24, no. 6, pp. 573–577, 1980.
[17] S. Voss, "Steiner's problem in graphs: Heuristic methods," *Discrete Applied Mathematics*, vol. 40, pp. 45–72, 1992.
[18] B. Waxman, "Routing of multipoint connections," *IEEE J. Select. Areas Commun.*, vol. 6, no. 9, pp. 1617–1622, Dec. 1988.
[19] J. Westbrook and D. Yan, "Greedy algorithms for the on-line Steiner tree and generalized Steiner problems," in *Proc. Algorithms Data Structures. Third Workshop, WADS '93*, Montreal, Quebec, Canada, Aug. 1993, pp. 621–633.
[20] P. Winter, "Steiner problem in networks: A survey," *Networks*, vol. 17, no. 2, pp. 129–167, 1987.

Fred Bauer (S'90) received the B.S. degree from the University of California, Berkeley, the M.S. degree from Santa Clara University, CA, and is working toward the Ph.D. degree at the University of California, Santa Cruz.

He is a research assistant at the University of California, Santa Cruz, where he is engaged in the research of serial and distributed multicast routing algorithms in point-to-point networks under constraints. His research interests include computer networks, multicasting, and routing in point-to-point networks.

Anujan Varma (S'83–M'85) received the Ph.D. degree from the University of Southern California, Los Angeles, in 1986.

He is an Associate Professor of computer engineering at University of California, Santa Cruz. He was with the IBM Thomas J. Watson Research Center, Yorktown Heights, NY, until 1991. His research interests lie in the areas of high speed switching, ATM networks, and optical networks. He has published more than 60 papers in these areas and holds five patents.

Dr. Varma received the National Science Foundation Young Investigator Award in 1992, the IEEE Darlington Award for the best paper published in the IEEE TRANSACTIONS ON CIRCUITS AND SYSTEMS in 1991, and a teaching innovation award from the University of California in 1993. He also received two Invention Achievement Awards from IBM for his work on switching networks.

A Thermodynamic Theory of Broadband Networks with Application to Dynamic Routing

Joseph Y. Hui, *Senior Member, IEEE*, and Ezhan Karasan, *Student Member, IEEE*

Abstract—We propose a thermodynamic theory for broadband networks relating quantities such as grade of service (GoS), bandwidth assignment, buffer assignment, and bandwidth demand. We propose a scalability postulate for these four quantities. Useful thermodynamic type relationships are then derived. The scalability postulate and thermodynamic type relations are then reexamined via statistical methods using the moment generating function. Large deviations theory is applied, and in the process, notions such as effective bandwidth are defined. We apply this theory to networks which allow dynamic routing of different call types. The probability of rare events expressed in conjunctive forms is characterized using large deviations theory. Based on this theory, a new dynamic routing method called effective bandwidth network routing (EBNR) is proposed.

I. INTRODUCTION

NETWORKS are large dynamical systems. The interactions of various components are complex, and the analytical computation of detailed phenomena very often is intractable, inaccurate, and sometimes irrelevant. Analytical approaches for network performance so far focus primarily on detailed and microscopic modeling and derivations of node and network dynamics. There is a need for a macroscopic theory which is more concerned with large quantities and qualitative behavior on a larger scale. There is also a need for a fundamental understanding concerning how these quantities scale with respect to each other. Given the scale of the network and the large capacity of network components such as memory and capacity, we could be more interested in the asymptotes and exponents of aggregated quantities. Qualitative behavior such as conditions for system equilibrium may generate more insight concerning resource allocation and system control than a detailed calculation based on often unverifiable data and models. After all chaotic phenomena, so prevalent in complex systems, soon render such detailed calculations irrelevant. Instead, appropriately defined aggregated quantities, which could be measured via empirical methods and related using a macroscopic theory, could render a better understanding and engineering of complex broadband networks.

While we are still far from attaining such an understanding, this paper is an attempt to define interesting quantities and relationships among these quantities. Section II examines a number of system parameters such as the grade of service (GoS) G, the bandwidth in the network C, the buffer capacity in the network B, and the bandwidth demands N. These quantities can be vector quantities denoting multiple commodities throughout the whole network. Basic relations are given among these extensive quantities and their corresponding intensive marginals. A fundamental postulate, called the scalability postulate, is used to derive a myriad of fundamental relationships. The approach taken is similar to that of the classical theory of Thermodynamics. Section III reexamines these quantities using large deviations theory and moment generating functions, focusing on the asymptotics and exponential behavior of such systems. The approach taken is similar to that of Statistical Mechanics, allowing description and computation of system parameters by modeling the microscopic dynamics. Section IV applies large deviations theory to analyzing events of a conjunctive form, with an application to network routing using alternative paths of multiple links. Section V concludes the paper and proposes an application of the above theory called effective bandwidth network routing (EBNR).

A model of traffic in interconnection networks using thermodynamics is presented by Benes in [4]. In this model the entropy of the system is defined as the Shannon entropy of the random variable denoting the state of the network. This entropy functional is not a measurable quantity on a real network contrary to the entropy defined in this paper. The statistical description of the traffic in Benes' model is characterized only through average values and blocked calls are omitted which is an important performance measure of the network. Furthermore, this model can not be extended to multirate traffic.

Large deviations techniques have been used to obtain the asymptotics for small probabilities in network applications. The relationship between capacity, loss probability and offered traffic for multirate traffic on a blocking link is obtained by using transform domain methods [17]. The effect of changes in the parameters such as capacity and offered traffic on the performance of the network for routing and capacity allocation problems is discussed in [20]. Hui [15], [16] used the Chernoff bound to compute the tail of the probability distribution for Poisson offered traffic and showed that, for unbuffered networks, there is a notion of engineered bandwidth for each source, which depends on the statistics of the source

Manuscript received September 30, 1994; revised April 1, 1995. This work was supported in part by the National Science Foundation under contract NSF NCR 90-58079-02 and with matching funds from Bellcore and NEC. This paper was presented in part at the Third INFORMS Telecommunications Conference, Boca Raton, FL, March 1995.

The authors are with the Department of Electrical and Computer Engineering, Rutgers University, Piscataway, NJ 08855 USA.

IEEE Log Number 9412649.

Reprinted from IEEE Journal on Selected Areas of Communications, Vol 13, No. 6, Aug. 1995, pp. 991-1003.

TABLE I
COMPARISONS OF QUANTITIES IN THERMODYNAMICS, NETWORK THEORY, AND BENES' MODEL

Thermodynamics		Network Theory		Benes' model
S	Entropy $-\sum p_s \log p_s$	G	Grade of Service (GoS)	Shannon entropy of the random variable corresponding to the state of the network
E	Energy	C	Capacity	Number of calls in progress
	Particle		Traffic source	Call
N_i	Number of particles of type i	N_i	Number of sources with traffic demand of type i	Number of calls (no type)
V	Volume	B	Buffer size	Number of ways of connecting calls
T	Temperature	θ^{-1}	Capacity price for GoS	[log(calling rate per path)]$^{-1}$
P	Pressure	ζ/θ	Capacity price for buffer	Not interpreted
μ	Chemical potential	μ_i/θ	Effective bandwidth cost per traffic demand i	Not interpreted
$-\log Q$	Partition function	ψ	Logarithmic moment generating function of the resource requirement (bandwidth and buffer) $\sum N_i \mu_i$	Logarithm of the generating function for the number of ways of connecting calls

as well as the characteristics of the channel. Kelly [18] extended the notion of effective bandwidth to GI/G/1 queues using Kingman's bound. The similarity between the effective bandwidths for unbuffered and buffered sources is also noted.

For queues driven by point arrival processes, the fluid-flow approximation is valid when the mean buffer length and the buffer size are large. The motivation for this approximation lies in the fact that the magnitudes of the discontinuous jumps are small as compared to the average queue length. Thus, the original discrete queue can be represented by a continuous fluid flow. The tail probabilities for multiple on-off sources sharing a large buffer is obtained with a fluid-flow model [1]. Using large deviations techniques it is shown that the fluid-flow approximation corresponds to the most probable path for continuous time Markov processes [22]. The effective bandwidth for multiple Markov modulated fluid-flow sources sharing a statistical multiplexer with a large buffer is obtained [11], [14].

Large deviations techniques have also been used to bound traffic parameters to obtain exponential upper bounds on the queue length and delay in queueing networks [6], [8]. The application of Chernoff bound for the waiting time of a single queue using martingales is given in [13].

A limiting regime similar to the one used in Section IV is discussed in [7], [19] for Poisson arrival process and fixed routing in a circuit-switched network. When the capacity of links and offered traffic are increased together the blocking probability of a path is given by a product form, as if links are blocked independently. The analysis is also generalized to networks with alternative routing using Erlang fixed point approximation. An independence assumption has been used in networks to evaluate the probability of joint events (Kleinrock's assumption for queueing networks and Lee's assumption for alternative routing). The dynamic routing method EBNR proposed in Section V is closely related to the real-time network routing (RTNR) policy [2], in which routing

decisions are based on the current number of idle circuits in each of the links throughout the network.

II. A THERMODYNAMICAL THEORY OF NETWORKS

The physical theory of thermodynamics is a fundamental study of the relationship among macroscopic quantities such as volume V, energy E, entropy S, and the number of particles N. A typical relation is expressed in the functional form $E(S, N, V)$ among many other possible forms. These four quantities are termed extensive quantities in the sense that a functional quantity scales in the same manner as its arguments, i.e., $E(\alpha S, \alpha N, \alpha V) = \alpha E(S, N, V)$. Certain physical laws, such as the conservation of energy (the first law) and the nondecreasing entropy of closed systems (the second law) further constrain the evolution of these quantities in time.

A modest parallel in networking similarly deals with the functional form $C(G, N, B)$, in which C represents capacity, G represents GoS, N represents the number of connections, and B represents buffer resources. These could be vector quantities for entities throughout the network. We call this functional form the bandwidth demand (BD) equation, which gives the required bandwidth for carrying a traffic intensity N with a buffer size B, while meeting the GoS requirement G. The bandwidth demand is the minimum bandwidth required for satisfactory GoS, while an actual network may have more or less bandwidth than required. An alternative functional form, which is often more useful, is the GoS equation $G(C, N, B)$ which gives the GoS for given network resources and traffic.

The quantities C, G, N, B bear a certain remarkable parallel, respectively, with the thermodynamic quantities E, S, N, V as shall be pointed out later. This resemblance is due largely to the mathematical structures of scalable systems rather than physical resemblance, and hence one should not overextend the interpretation of the parallels. Nevertheless, Table I lists the analogous quantities between Thermodynamics and our

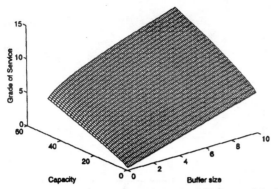

Fig. 1. GoS versus buffer size and capacity for fluid flow model with $\rho = 0.6$.

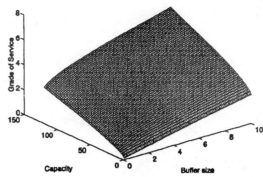

Fig. 2. GoS versus buffer size and capacity for fluid flow model with $\rho = 0.8$.

network theory. The analogies made by Benes are stated in the third column. It is noteworthy that though there is a certain mathematical resemblance between our theory and that of Benes, the parameters and their interpretations are quite different between the two theories. Their applications are also different: Benes' work is largely concerned with enumerating equally likely states in a switching network, while we are concerned with computing GoS and BD using large deviations theory.

So far, the definition of G is deliberately abstract, similar to the notion of entropy for Thermodynamics before the days of Statistical Mechanics. A fundamental question is whether these four network parameters are extensive, that is how they scale with respect to the other parameters. In this section, we propose the following scalability postulate

$$G(\alpha C, \alpha N, \alpha B) = \alpha G(C, N, B). \quad (1)$$

This postulate, which seems implausible at first sight is justifiable a priori for the resulting elegant structures; and aposteriori for simple systems such as the M/M/1/B queue and the M/M/C/C+B queue (see Appendix A), and for systems with no buffers ($B = 0$). The scalability property for the fluid flow model is asymptotically shown in [12], [22] for large C, B and N. In each of these cases, the GoS is defined as the negative logarithm of the loss probability. The following theorem proves the linear scalability property for slotted time queueing systems as C, B and N go to infinity, such that bandwidth per source $c = C/N$ and buffer per source $b = B/N$ are kept constant.

Theorem 2.1: For a slotted time queueing system, G, defined as the negative logarithm of the loss probability, satisfies

$$\lim_{N \to \infty} \frac{G(\alpha N c, \alpha N, \alpha N b)}{N}$$

$$= \alpha \lim_{N \to \infty} \frac{G(Nc, N, Nb)}{N} \triangleq \alpha g_N(c, b) \quad (2)$$

for any $\alpha > 0$.

Theorem 2.1 is proved by using Gärtner-Ellis Theorem and the proof is given in Appendix B. To demonstrate how fast linear scaling is achieved in practical systems, we consider a numerical example of multiplexing fluid flow on-off sources [1]. We plot various aspects of the function $G(C, N, B)$ and

show that there is a strong linearity even for small values. The fluid flow model has N identical on-off sources, with on and off periods of mean durations of 1 and 2 unit times, respectively, and each source require 1 unit of bandwidth when on. We define $\rho = N\delta/C$, where δ is the average bandwidth demand per source. We also define $\gamma = B/C$. Figs. 1 and 2 plot GoS versus C and B for different values of ρ (buffer size B has units of 1 unit bandwidth times 1 unit time). In Figs. 3 and 4, G versus C is plotted for different values of ρ and γ. We observe that the linear scalability holds for even small values of B and C. In Figs. 5 and 6, G versus B is plotted while keeping C fixed for different values of ρ and C. We observe that G becomes a linear function of B as B increases.

We now explore further the implications of linear scaling. The following equation expresses the marginal change of the effective bandwidth in terms of the differentials of the parameters G, N and B

$$dC = \left(\frac{\partial C}{\partial G}\right)_{N,B} dG + \left(\frac{\partial C}{\partial N}\right)_{G,B} dN + \left(\frac{\partial C}{\partial B}\right)_{G,N} dB. \quad (3)$$

These partial derivatives can be viewed as the shadow prices of capacity relative to GoS, traffic, and buffering, respectively.[1] The computation of these quantities depends on the underlying dynamics. In parallel for Thermodynamics, the corresponding equation is

$$dE = \frac{\partial E}{\partial S} dS + \frac{\partial E}{\partial N} dN + \frac{\partial E}{\partial V} dV = TdS + \mu dN - PdV$$

in which T represents the absolute temperature, μ represents the chemical potential of the particles, and P represents the pressure exerted by the volume. These quantities are intensive in the sense that scaling the system does not change these quantities.

We summarize the implications of the scalability property (1) in the following theorem.

[1] In a network C, G, N, B represent vectors, whereas their derivatives become Jacobian matrices. For example, the matrix $\partial C/\partial G = [\partial C_i/\partial G_j]$ corresponds to the matrix of shadow prices for capacities with respect to GoS's of all nodes, whereas $\partial C_i/\partial G = [\partial C_i/\partial G_j]$ is the gradient vector representing the shadow prices.

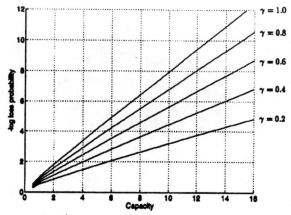

Fig. 3. GoS versus capacity for fluid flow model with $\rho = 0.6$ and $\gamma = 0.2, 0.4, 0.6, 0.8, 1.0$.

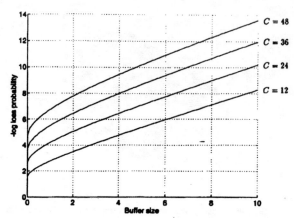

Fig. 5. GoS versus buffer size for fluid flow model with $\rho = 0.6$ and $C = 12, 24, 36, 48$.

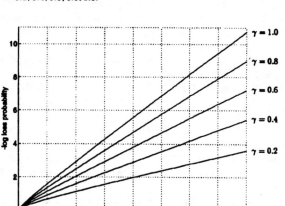

Fig. 4. GoS versus capacity for fluid flow model with $\rho = 0.8$ and $\gamma = 0.2, 0.4, 0.6, 0.8, 1.0$.

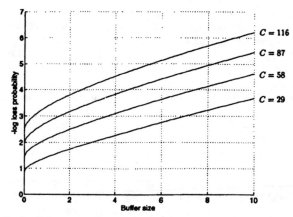

Fig. 6. GoS versus buffer size for fluid flow model with $\rho = 0.8$ and $C = 29, 58, 87, 116$.

Theorem 2.2: (i) The quantities G, C, N, B are simultaneously extensive, e.g., $C(\alpha G, \alpha N, \alpha B) = \alpha C(G, N, B)$ given the scaling equation for G in (1). (ii) The partial derivatives of G with respect to C, N, B are intensive, e.g., $(\partial G(\alpha C, \alpha N, \alpha B)/\partial(\alpha C))_{N,B} = (\partial G(C, N, B)/\partial C)_{N,B}$. (iii) The Euler form holds for the GoS equation, which is given by

$$G = \left(\frac{\partial G}{\partial C}\right)_{N,B} C + \left(\frac{\partial G}{\partial N}\right)_{C,B} N$$
$$+ \left(\frac{\partial G}{\partial B}\right)_{N,B} B \triangleq \theta C - \mu N + \zeta B. \quad (4)$$

For multiple call types with N_i denoting the number of connections of type i, Euler form for the GoS is given by

$$G = \theta C - \sum_i \mu_i N_i + \zeta B \text{ where } \mu_i = \left(\frac{\partial G}{\partial N_i}\right)_{C,B,\{N_j\}_{j \neq i}}$$

(iv) G is linear in C (or B, N) for given $\rho = N/C$ (assume $\delta = 1$), and $\gamma = B/C$, i.e., $G = g_C(\rho, \gamma)C$ (for given $c = C/N$ and $b = B/N$, $G = g_N(c, b)N$).

Proof: (i) $C_1 = C(G, N, B)$ is the solution to the GoS equation $G = G(C_1, N, B)$. Using the scalability property (1), we obtain $\alpha G = \alpha G(C_1, N, B) = G(\alpha C_1, \alpha N, \alpha B)$, which implies that αC_1 is the solution to the bandwidth equation $\alpha C_1 = C(\alpha G, \alpha N, \alpha B)$. (ii) The proof follows by differentiating both sides of (1) with respect to C while keeping N and B fixed. (iii) Differentiating both sides of (1) with respect to α, we have

$$\frac{\partial G(\alpha C, \alpha N, \alpha B)}{\partial(\alpha C)} C + \frac{\partial G(\alpha C, \alpha N, \alpha B)}{\partial(\alpha N)} N$$
$$+ \frac{\partial G(\alpha C, \alpha N, \alpha B)}{\partial(\alpha B)} B = G(C, N, B). \quad (5)$$

Setting $\alpha = 1$ in (5), we obtain the Euler form (4).

(iv) For given ρ and γ, we have (C, N, B) being the scaling of $(1, \rho, \gamma)$ by C, and hence by the scalability property, there exists a $g_C(\rho, \gamma)$ such that $G = g_C(\rho, \gamma)C$. □

In Fig. 7, the function $g_C(\rho, \gamma)$ is plotted versus ρ for different values of γ for the fluid flow model described previously. The simplicity of these curves allows for further parametric reduction.

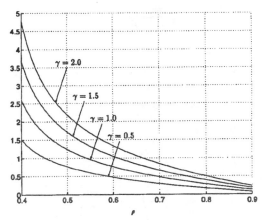

Fig. 7. $g_C(\rho, \gamma)$ versus ρ for $\gamma = 0.5, 1.0, 1.5, 2.0$.

TABLE II
FIRST-ORDER RELATIONS BETWEEN EXTENSIVE QUANTITIES

$\left(\frac{\partial G}{\partial C}\right)_{N,B} = \theta$	$\left(\frac{\partial G}{\partial B}\right)_{C,N} = \zeta$	$\left(\frac{\partial G}{\partial N_i}\right)_{C,B} = -\mu_i$
$\left(\frac{\partial C}{\partial B}\right)_{G,N} = -\frac{\zeta}{\theta}$	$\left(\frac{\partial C}{\partial N_i}\right)_{G,B} = \frac{\mu_i}{\theta}$	$\left(\frac{\partial B}{\partial N_i}\right)_{G,C} = \frac{\mu_i}{\zeta}$

An immediate application of linear scaling is that the performance of a queueing system can be obtained by scaling down the parameters of the system, computing the GoS for the scaled system through simulation and then rescaling the resulting GoS to obtain the GoS for the original system. This approach provides computational savings over the direct study of the given system since the loss probability is much larger in the scaled down system. Since effective bandwidth function is also linearly scalable, the effective bandwidth for a system can be computed by scaling down the system. The Euler form of (4) for the GoS equation allows us to express G in terms of its marginals corresponding to intensive variables (in thermodynamics we have correspondingly the well-known energy equation $E = TS + \mu N - PV$). Equation (4) allows us to eliminate one variable and express the functional dependence more succinctly as stated in part (iv) of Theorem 2.2, which states that G is linear in C for g (given ρ and γ).

The intensive variables θ, ζ and μ_i can be used to explore the differential relations between extensive variables as listed in Table II. The relations in the second row of Table II can be obtained from the definitions of θ, ζ and μ_i by using the identity

$$\left(\frac{\partial X}{\partial Y}\right)_Z = -\left(\frac{\partial Z}{\partial Y}\right)_X \Big/ \left(\frac{\partial Z}{\partial X}\right)_Y.$$

For example, $\partial G/\partial C$ and $\partial G/\partial B$ represent the shadow prices of GoS with respect to capacity and buffer, whereas $\partial C/\partial B$ is the shadow price for capacity with respect to buffer and hence explains the trade-off between transmission and buffering. $\partial G/\partial N_i$ is the shadow price for GoS when an additional call of type i joins the system. $\partial C/\partial N_i$ and $\partial B/\partial N_i$ are the effective bandwidth and effective buffer for a connection of type i, which correspond to shadow prices for capacity and buffer relative to traffic demand. Also, $\partial N_i/\partial N_j = \mu_j/\mu_i$ represents the relative price of a connection of type i with respect to a connection of type j. These partial derivatives, which are given as ratios among the intensive parameters μ_i, θ, and ζ are useful for resource allocation and admission control. They will be used later for dynamic routing.

Many interesting partial differential relationships can also be obtained by using Legendre transformation: Given that we may measure the intensive parameters instead of the extensive parameters, different independent parameters could be chosen as the basis for further calculations. There are a total of 8 such bases, since we have a choice of either the extensive parameter or the associated intensive parameter for each independent variable of the GoS equation $G(C, N, B)$. Let $G_{P_1 P_2 P_3}$ be the function obtained by choosing (P_1, P_2, P_3) as the set of independent variables and let (Q_1, Q_2, Q_3) be the set of dependent variables with $\partial G_{P_1 P_2 P_3}/\partial P_i = Q_i$ (this follows from the properties of Legendre transformation). By using the property that mixed partial derivatives are equal independent of the order of differentiation, we write

$$\frac{\partial^2 G_{P_1 P_2 P_3}}{\partial P_1 \partial P_2} = \frac{\partial^2 G_{P_1 P_2 P_3}}{\partial P_2 \partial P_1} \quad \text{or} \quad \frac{\partial Q_1}{\partial P_2} = \frac{\partial Q_2}{\partial P_1}. \quad (6)$$

As mentioned, we have eight different choices of independent variables (P_1, P_2, P_3) among the intensive and extensive quantities. Also, we have three choices among (P_1, P_2, P_3) for taking second order partial differentiation. Therefore, there are a total of 24 equations of the type (6), which are called Maxwell relations. These relations are useful for calculating partial derivatives from other measured partial derivatives. All Maxwell relations are listed in Table III. We note that the derivation of Maxwell relations does not require the scalability property. The use of these relationships is subject to further research.

So far the discussion has been general. Though the equations present useful relationships between the quantities, no practical means is provided to compute their values. A particular method of computation is given by using large deviations theory. The suggested analogy between the parameters of a network versus the parameters of thermodynamics will then be clarified.

III. LARGE DEVIATIONS THEORY APPLIED TO NETWORK

The scalability of GoS is largely a consequence of considering the asymptotic behavior of the exponent for GoS figures of interest, such as the loss probability p. Typically, such GoS is plotted on a logarithmic scale on the y-axis versus a linear scale for other parameters of interests, such as buffer size, traffic load, or capacity on the x-axis. It is often observed [11], [14] that $\log p/B$ becomes a constant for large B, and hence

TABLE III
MAXWELL RELATIONS (SECOND ORDER) OBTAINED FROM GOS EQUATION

Function	Ind. vars.	Base	Maxwell equations	
$dG_{CNB} = \theta dC - \mu dN + \zeta dB$	C	C, N	$-\left(\frac{\partial\mu}{\partial C}\right)_{B,N} = \left(\frac{\partial\theta}{\partial N}\right)_{B,C}$	(T3.1)
	N	C, B	$\left(\frac{\partial\zeta}{\partial C}\right)_{B,N} = \left(\frac{\partial\theta}{\partial B}\right)_{C,N}$	(T3.2)
	B	N, B	$\left(\frac{\partial\zeta}{\partial N}\right)_{B,C} = -\left(\frac{\partial\mu}{\partial B}\right)_{C,N}$	(T3.3)
$dG_{\theta NB} = -Cd\theta - \mu dN + \zeta dB$	θ	θ, N	$\left(\frac{\partial C}{\partial N}\right)_{\theta,B} = \left(\frac{\partial\mu}{\partial\theta}\right)_{B,N}$	(T3.4)
	N	θ, B	$\left(\frac{\partial\zeta}{\partial\theta}\right)_{B,N} = -\left(\frac{\partial C}{\partial B}\right)_{\theta,N}$	(T3.5)
	B	N, B	$-\left(\frac{\partial\mu}{\partial B}\right)_{\theta,N} = \left(\frac{\partial\zeta}{\partial N}\right)_{\theta,B}$	(T3.6)
$dG_{C\mu B} = \theta dC + Nd\mu + \zeta dB$	C	C, μ	$\left(\frac{\partial N}{\partial C}\right)_{\mu,B} = \left(\frac{\partial\theta}{\partial\mu}\right)_{C,B}$	(T3.7)
	μ	C, B	$\left(\frac{\partial\zeta}{\partial C}\right)_{\mu,B} = \left(\frac{\partial\theta}{\partial B}\right)_{C,\mu}$	(T3.8)
	B	μ, B	$\left(\frac{\partial\zeta}{\partial\mu}\right)_{C,B} = \left(\frac{\partial N}{\partial B}\right)_{C,\mu}$	(T3.9)
$dG_{CN\zeta} = \theta dC - \mu dN - Bd\zeta$	C	C, N	$-\left(\frac{\partial\mu}{\partial C}\right)_{N,\zeta} = \left(\frac{\partial\theta}{\partial N}\right)_{C,\zeta}$	(T3.10)
	N	C, ζ	$-\left(\frac{\partial B}{\partial C}\right)_{N,\zeta} = \left(\frac{\partial\theta}{\partial\zeta}\right)_{C,N}$	(T3.11)
	ζ	N, ζ	$\left(\frac{\partial B}{\partial N}\right)_{C,\zeta} = \left(\frac{\partial\mu}{\partial\zeta}\right)_{C,N}$	(T3.12)
$dG_{\theta\mu B} = -Cd\theta + Nd\mu + \zeta dB$	θ	θ, μ	$-\left(\frac{\partial C}{\partial\mu}\right)_{\theta,B} = \left(\frac{\partial N}{\partial\theta}\right)_{\mu,B}$	(T3.13)
	μ	θ, B	$\left(\frac{\partial\zeta}{\partial\theta}\right)_{\mu,B} = -\left(\frac{\partial C}{\partial B}\right)_{\theta,\mu}$	(T3.14)
	B	μ, B	$\left(\frac{\partial\zeta}{\partial\mu}\right)_{\theta,B} = \left(\frac{\partial N}{\partial B}\right)_{\theta,\mu}$	(T3.15)
$dG_{\theta N\zeta} = -Cd\theta - \mu dN - Bd\zeta$	θ	θ, N	$\left(\frac{\partial\mu}{\partial\theta}\right)_{N,\zeta} = \left(\frac{\partial C}{\partial N}\right)_{\theta,\zeta}$	(T3.16)
	N	θ, ζ	$\left(\frac{\partial B}{\partial\theta}\right)_{N,\zeta} = \left(\frac{\partial C}{\partial\zeta}\right)_{\theta,N}$	(T3.17)
	ζ	N, ζ	$\left(\frac{\partial B}{\partial N}\right)_{\theta,\zeta} = \left(\frac{\partial\mu}{\partial\zeta}\right)_{\theta,N}$	(T3.18)
$dG_{C\mu\zeta} = \theta dC + Nd\mu - Bd\zeta$	C	C, μ	$\left(\frac{\partial N}{\partial C}\right)_{\mu,\zeta} = \left(\frac{\partial\theta}{\partial\mu}\right)_{C,\zeta}$	(T3.19)
	μ	C, ζ	$-\left(\frac{\partial B}{\partial C}\right)_{\mu,\zeta} = \left(\frac{\partial\theta}{\partial\zeta}\right)_{C,\mu}$	(T3.20)
	ζ	μ, ζ	$-\left(\frac{\partial B}{\partial\mu}\right)_{C,\zeta} = \left(\frac{\partial N}{\partial\zeta}\right)_{C,\mu}$	(T3.21)
$dG_{\theta\mu\zeta} = -Cd\theta + Nd\mu - Bd\zeta$	θ	θ, μ	$\left(\frac{\partial N}{\partial\theta}\right)_{\mu,\zeta} = -\left(\frac{\partial C}{\partial\mu}\right)_{\theta,\zeta}$	(T3.22)
	μ	θ, ζ	$\left(\frac{\partial B}{\partial\theta}\right)_{\mu,\zeta} = \left(\frac{\partial C}{\partial\zeta}\right)_{\theta,\mu}$	(T3.23)
	ζ	μ, ζ	$-\left(\frac{\partial B}{\partial\mu}\right)_{\theta,\zeta} = \left(\frac{\partial N}{\partial\zeta}\right)_{\theta,\mu}$	(T3.24)

indicating an asymptotically linear scaling of GoS with respect to buffer size. On the other hand, $\log p$ often resembles a "water fall" for increasing C, if load is kept constant. However, the linear scaling of $\log p$ versus C is often restored if we allow load to scale linearly as C. In this case, the utilization level of the capacity is kept constant. Combining the scaling of GoS with respect to buffer size with the scaling of GoS with respect to load and capacity, we formulated the scalability postulate of GoS with respect to buffer size, traffic load, and capacity in the previous section.

Large deviations theory has been used to obtain asymptotic results that apply to communication networks. The application of large deviations theory to statistical mechanics can be found in [10]. A better known technique of this theory is the Chernoff bound, used to bound the tail of random variables with known moment generating functions [13]. Chernoff bounds will be used to provide the link between thermodynamic theory of networks and large deviations theory.

Consider a node where X and Y denote random variables corresponding to traffic rate and buffer occupancy, respectively. The Chernoff bound is derived as follows

$$
\begin{aligned}
&-\log P\{X > C, Y > B\} \\
&= -\log \int_B^\infty \int_C^\infty f_{XY}(x,y)\,dx\,dy \\
&\geq -\log \int_B^\infty \int_C^\infty e^{\theta(x-C)} e^{\zeta(y-B)} f_{XY}(x,y)\,dx\,dy \\
&\geq -\log \left(e^{-\theta C} e^{-\zeta B} \int_0^\infty \int_0^\infty e^{\theta x} e^{\zeta y} f_{XY}(x,y)\,dx\,dy \right) \\
&= \theta C + \zeta B - \psi(\theta, \zeta) \qquad (7)
\end{aligned}
$$

where $f_{XY}(x, y)$ and $\psi(\theta, \zeta)$ denote, respectively, the joint probability density and logarithmic moment generating functions of X and Y. We define the GoS function G as given by the right-hand side of (7), namely

$$G \triangleq \theta C + \zeta B - \psi(\theta, \zeta). \qquad (8)$$

The Laplace parameters θ and ζ are chosen to maximize the value of G. Since $\psi(\theta, \zeta)$ is convex, θ and ζ, which maximize the right-hand side of (7), are the solutions to the equations

$$\frac{\partial \psi(\theta, \zeta)}{\partial \theta} = C, \qquad \frac{\partial \psi(\theta, \zeta)}{\partial \zeta} = B \qquad (9)$$

where both partial derivatives are taken with C, N and B are kept fixed.

There is a remarkable similarity between equation (8), i.e., $G = \theta C + \zeta B - \psi(\theta, \zeta)$, and the Euler equation (4) resulting from the scalability postulate, i.e., $G = \theta C - \mu N + \zeta B$. In (4), $\theta = \partial G / \partial C$ and $\zeta = \partial G / \partial B$ by definition, which we now derive from (8) and (9) for the GoS function resulting from large deviations theory.

Using (8), the partial derivative of G with respect to C, keeping B and N fixed can be written as

$$\left(\frac{\partial G}{\partial C}\right)_{B,N} = \theta + C\frac{\partial \theta}{\partial C} + B\frac{\partial \zeta}{\partial C}$$
$$- \frac{\partial \psi(\theta, \zeta)}{\partial \theta}\frac{\partial \theta}{\partial C} - \frac{\partial \psi(\theta, \zeta)}{\partial \zeta}\frac{\partial \zeta}{\partial C} = \theta \qquad (10)$$

where the last equality follows from (9). Similarly, we obtain

$$\left(\frac{\partial G}{\partial B}\right)_{C,N} = \zeta. \qquad (11)$$

Furthermore from (8), the partial derivative of G with respect to N_i, where N_i denotes the number of traffic sources of type i, is given by

$$\left(\frac{\partial G}{\partial N_i}\right)_{C,B} = C\frac{\partial \theta}{\partial N_i} + B\frac{\partial \zeta}{\partial N_i} - \left(\frac{\partial \psi(\theta, \zeta)}{\partial N_i}\right)_{C,B,\theta,\zeta}$$
$$- \frac{\partial \psi(\theta, \zeta)}{\partial \theta}\frac{\partial \theta}{\partial N_i} - \frac{\partial \psi(\theta, \zeta)}{\partial \zeta}\frac{\partial \zeta}{\partial N_i} = -\left(\frac{\partial \psi(\theta, \zeta)}{\partial N_i}\right)_{C,B,\theta,\zeta} \qquad (12)$$

where the last equality follows from (9). The intensive parameter $\mu_i = -(\partial G/\partial N_i)_{C,B}$ defined in Section II corresponds to the large deviation parameter $\mu_i = \partial \psi(\theta, \zeta)/\partial N_i$. If the GoS function G defined by (8) is linearly scalable in C, B and N_i, then by using (10), (11) and (12) we can write $\psi(\theta, \zeta)$ as

$$\psi(\theta, \zeta) = \sum_i N_i \frac{\partial \psi(\theta, \zeta)}{\partial N_i}. \qquad (13)$$

Table IV lists the first-order relations between extensive and intensive quantities obtained by using Chernoff bound that are not listed in Table II. The last equation can be obtained from (9) by using the identity

$$\left(\frac{\partial X}{\partial Y}\right)_Z = \left(\frac{\partial W}{\partial Y}\right)_Z \Big/ \left(\frac{\partial W}{\partial X}\right)_Z.$$

TABLE IV
FIRST-ORDER RELATIONS BETWEEN EXTENSIVE AND INTENSIVE QUANTITIES

$\left(\frac{\partial C}{\partial B}\right)_{G,N} = -\frac{\zeta}{\theta}$	$\left(\frac{\partial C}{\partial N_i}\right)_{G,B} = \frac{\mu_i}{\theta}$	$\left(\frac{\partial B}{\partial N_i}\right)_{G,C} = \frac{\mu_i}{\zeta}$

A. Notions of Effective Bandwidth with Small and Large Buffers

In our scalability postulate, we scale up C, N and B simultaneously. Previous works in the literature for effective bandwidth focus primarily on either the small buffer case [15], [16] or the large buffer case [11], [14]. In this subsection, we seek to harmonize these two views. Assuming linear scalability we summarize the results of the earlier part of this section by

$$G = \theta C + \zeta B - \sum_i N_i \mu_i$$

$$\text{where } \mu_i = -\left(\frac{\partial G}{\partial N_i}\right)_{C,B} = \left(\frac{\partial \psi(\theta, \zeta)}{\partial N_i}\right)_{C,B,\theta,\zeta}. \qquad (14)$$

For the small buffer case, the aggregate effective bandwidth $\hat{C}$ is given by

$$\hat{C} = \frac{G}{\theta} + \sum_i N_i \frac{\mu_i}{\theta} \qquad (15)$$

where μ_i/θ is defined as the per source effective bandwidth $\hat{c}$, and G/θ is an added provision for GoS. For the large buffer case, the per source effective bandwidth $\hat{c}$ is defined by the following equation

$$\hat{c} = \lim_{B \to \infty, G/B \to \zeta} C(G, 1, B) \qquad (16)$$

and it has been proved that the aggregate effective bandwidth, $\hat{C}$, is additive, i.e.,

$$\hat{C} = \lim_{B \to \infty, G/B \to \zeta} C(G, N, B) = N\hat{c}. \qquad (17)$$

For the large buffer case [11], [14], the aggregate effective bandwidth is defined as minimum bandwidth required such that $G = \zeta B$ for large B. We observe from (14) that the effective bandwidth $\hat{C}$ satisfies

$$\hat{C} = \sum_i N_i \frac{\mu_i}{\theta}. \qquad (18)$$

The value of θ in (18) can be determined by using (9), and θ is given by the solution of the equation

$$\frac{\psi(\theta, \zeta)}{\theta} = \frac{\partial \psi(\theta, \zeta)}{\partial \theta}. \qquad (19)$$

Since $\psi(\theta, \zeta)$ is convex and $\psi(0, \zeta) > 0$ for $\zeta > 0$, the solution to (19) uniquely exists. The solution has also a geometric interpretation as the value of θ for which the tangent line to $\psi(\theta, \zeta)$ passes through the origin.

To unify the two notions of effective bandwidth for the small and large buffer cases, it should be noted that the effective bandwidth for a connection of type i is given by

$$\hat{c}_i = \frac{\mu_i}{\theta} = \left(\frac{\partial C}{\partial N_i}\right)_{G,B} \qquad (20)$$

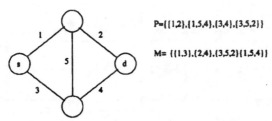

P={{1,2},{1,5,4},{3,4},{3,5,2}}

M= {{1,3},{2,4},{3,5,2}{1,5,4}}

Fig. 8. The set of alternatives and the set of cutsets between s and d.

which is the additional bandwidth required for the connection if G and B are to be kept constant. The interpretation in (20) can be used for resource trade-off.

B. Measurement of Intensive Variables

To apply the above thermodynamical and statistical theories, it is necessary to develop either analytical or experimental methods to measure parameters such as ψ, θ, ζ, or μ_i. Among these parameters ψ is probably the most important and can be measured on line using the following procedure.

Denote the moment generating function as $\phi(\theta)$, i.e., $\psi(\theta) = \ln \phi(\theta)$. Consider in discrete time step k, we obtain a measurement X_k, which is the average value of parameters such as bit rate or buffer occupancy over the duration of the time step. Here, X_k could be a vector with θ_k being the associated vector of marginal prices. For simplicity of notations, we treat X_k as a scalar instead. We update the moment generating function $\phi(\theta)$ at each step as

$$\phi_{k+1}(\theta) = (1 - \alpha)\phi_k(\theta) + \alpha e^{\theta X_k}. \qquad (21)$$

We use the Taylor series expansions of ϕ and ψ with finite number of coefficients M. Experimental results indicate that the choice of $M = 5$ is sufficient to obtain the estimates with a reasonable amount of error. Let $a[m]$ and $d[m], 0 \le m \le M - 1$ denote the mth coefficients of Taylor series expansions of ϕ and ψ, respectively. In each iteration, we upgrade the following values.

1) Update the coefficients $a[.]$ by using the Taylor series expansion of (21)

$$a_{k+1}[m] = (1 - \alpha)a_k[m] + \alpha \frac{(X_k)^m}{m!}$$

for $m = 0, \cdots, M - 1$, and update the coefficients $d[.]$ recursively as (see [16])

$$d_{k+1}[0] = 0, d_{k+1}[1] = a_{k+1}[1]$$

and

$$d_{k+1}[m] = a_{k+1}[m] - \frac{1}{m} \sum_{j=1}^{m-1} j a_{k+1}[m-j] d_{k+1}[j]$$

for $m = 2, \cdots, M - 1$.

2) Use Newton's method to find θ_{k+1} given as the solution of the implicit equation given by (9)

$$\sum_{m=1}^{M-1} m d_{k+1}[m](\theta_{k+1})^{m-1} = C.$$

Currently, we are testing the stability and convergence properties of this algorithm for empirical measurements of the shadow prices.

IV. PROBABILITY OF EVENTS IN HIGH-SPEED NETWORKS EXPRESSED IN CONJUNCTIVE FORM

Earlier discussion was primarily focused on the single component systems even though the extensive and intensive parameters can be defined as vector quantities for multicomponent systems. In the rest of the paper, we shall be dealing with multicomponent systems using the Gärtner-Ellis Theorem. An event in a multicomponent system can be written as a logical expression and the set of points corresponding to an event can be expressed in a conjunctive form, namely the intersection of union of subsets, where each subset represents the set of points corresponding to a subevent.

In this section, by using the theory of large deviations, we show that the asymptotic probability of a rare event expressed as a union of a set of subevents is governed by the subevent with the largest probability. As an illustration of the results, consider the graph in Fig. 8 corresponding to a network with alternative routing. P and M denote, respectively, the set of paths and the set of cutsets between nodes s and d. Our results show that the probability of the event for a single path is given exclusively by the most critical link on the path. The probability of the event for all paths in P is given by the most critical cutset in M, which can be obtained by using the logarithmic moment generating function. The results apply to networks with unbuffered or buffered resources. In the following analysis, the occurrence probability of a rare event is evaluated by using the logarithmic moment generating function which can be expressed analytically if possible or measured by monitoring the statistical quantities relevant for the computation of the rare event.

Let $G = (N, E)$ be the graph corresponding to the network. $P_{sd} = \{P_1, \cdots, P_m\}$ denotes the set of all possible paths between nodes s and d, where $P_i = (l_{i1}, \cdots, l_{iq_i})$, $l_{ij} \in E$ is the jth link in P_i and q_i is the number of links in P_i. We assume that a rare event A corresponding to nodes s and d can be written in a conjunctive form, which is intersection of union of events

$$A = \bigcap_{i=1}^{m} \bigcup_{j=1}^{q_i} A_{ij} \qquad (22)$$

where A_{ij} is an event corresponding to link l_{ij}. $\bigcap$ and $\bigcup$ denote the intersection and union of events, respectively. A typical event that can be expressed in the form (22) is the blocking between nodes s and d under alternative routing where all possible paths are allowed, with the event A_{ij} corresponding to blocking on link l_{ij}.

Definition 4.1: A subset $E' \subset E$ is called a (s, d)-cutset if s and d are in different components in $G' = (N, E - E')$.

Let $M_{sd} = \{M_1, \cdots, M_r\}$ be the set of minimal (s, d)-cutsets, where $M_k = (l_{k1}, \cdots, l_{kt_k})$, with t_k being the number of links in M_k. The following lemma gives the disjunctive form (union of intersection of events) corresponding to (22) which will be used in Theorem 4.4 to obtain the probability of a rare event between s and d. When A_{ij} corresponds to congestion on l_{ij}, Lemma 4.1 demonstrates the fact that all paths between s and d are congested if and only if there exists a congested cutset between s and d.

Lemma 4.1:

$$\bigcap_{i=1}^{m} \bigcup_{j=1}^{q_i} A_{ij} = \bigcup_{k=1}^{r} \bigcap_{l=1}^{t_k} A_{kl}.$$

Proof: Let A be an event such that $A \in \bigcap_{l=1}^{t_k} A_{kl}$ for some k, $1 \le k \le r$. A is contained in A_{kl} for all links of cutset M_k and each path between s and d uses at least one link from M_k. Therefore, for any path i, A is contained in A_{ij} for some link l_{ij}, $1 \le j \le q_i$. Hence

$$A \in \bigcap_{i=1}^{m} \bigcup_{j=1}^{q_i} A_{ij}.$$

Conversely, let $A \in \bigcap_{i=1}^{m} \bigcup_{j=1}^{q_i} A_{ij}$. For each path P_i, A is contained in A_{ij} for some link l_{ij_i}, $1 \le j_i \le q_i$. $\{l_{ij_i}\}_{i=1}^{M}$ is a (s,d)-cutset since P_{sd} contains all possible (s,d) paths in G and by deleting an edge from each path, s and d become disconnected in $(N, E - \{l_{ij_i}\})$. There exists a cutset M_k in M_{sd} which is a subset of $\{l_{ij}\}$ since M_{sd} contains all minimal (s,d)-cutsets. Hence

$$A \in \bigcup_{k=1}^{r} \bigcap_{l=1}^{t_k} A_{kl}.$$

$\square$

This lemma is useful in two ways as we shall see later. First, it simplifies the calculation by expressing the events in terms of critical cutsets. Second, the disjunctive expression of the event is critical in the following proofs.

Consider a sequence of networks indexed by n (each having the same topology), where $\underline{Z}_n$ denotes a random vector representing a set of random variables each corresponding to a resource occupancy measure in the nth network. We assume that $E[\underline{Z}_n] = nE[\underline{Z}_1]$, i.e., the average values of the random variables constituting $\underline{Z}_n$ increase linearly as n gets larger. Let A_n be an event corresponding to congestion in the nth network, that can be written as a union of subevents such that

$$A_n = \bigcup_i A_{ni}$$

with $\Pr\{A_{ni}\} = \Pr\{\underline{Z}_n \in nS_i\}$ where $S_i \subset \Re^d$ is a convex set. Since $A_n = \bigcup_i A_{ni}$, we have $\Pr\{A_n\} = \Pr\{\underline{Z}_n \in nS\}$, where $S = \bigcup_i S_i$.

We show that the probability of A_n as $n \to \infty$ is governed by the probability of the subevent with the largest probability. The motivation under this result lies in the fact that the probability of A_n can be upperbounded (by union bound) as a sum of exponentials with large negative exponents, which is dominated by the term with the exponent of smallest magnitude (Laplace's principle).

This result can be applied to a queueing network, where A_n denotes the event that a packet will be lost at some buffer on its route. $\underline{Z}_n$ is the random vector corresponding to buffer occupancies and S is the set of points for which the occupancy

of one of the buffers on the path exceeds the buffer size. The computation of this probability requires the analysis of the queue with largest loss probability along the path. Thus, using this analysis all methods applicable to a single buffer can be extended to a network of buffers. In the remaining part of this section, we analyze the congestion between two nodes in a network.

We evaluate the probability of events expressed in the disjunctive form derived earlier in this section in Lemma 4.1. We consider a network with $\underline{C} = (C_1, \cdots, C_M)^T$ denoting a threshold vector above which congestion occurs. This threshold vector may contain both transmission and buffering constraints. The network operates under alternative routing, where a connection request blocked on a path can try other paths. A connection request is rejected when all paths between origin and destination are blocking. The notion of a path here is more general than a physical path of links in a circuit-switched network. Paths could be considered as a constituent comprising an alternative and links could be considered as components of a path which may be a transmission or a buffering facility. $\psi(\underline{\theta})$ is the logarithmic moment generating function corresponding to a measure of congestion.

We show that when the threshold vector and amount of the traffic are increased together, asymptotically the loss probability on a path is given by the most congested link along the path. We then characterize the congestion between a node pair which corresponds to the congestion of all possible paths.

Consider a sequence of networks indexed by n. Let the random vector $\underline{Z}_n$ denote a measure of utilization in the nth network. Let $\underline{C}_n$ denote the vector corresponding to congestion thresholds in the nth network. We set $E[\underline{Z}_n] = nE[\underline{Z}_1]$ and $\underline{C}_n = n\underline{C}$ so that the ratios of average utilizations to congestion thresholds are kept fixed. Assume that the logarithmic moment generating function $\psi_n(\underline{\theta})$ of $\underline{Z}_n$ satisfies the assumptions of Gärtner-Ellis Theorem given in Appendix C.

Theorem 4.1 Gärtner-Ellis [5]: If Assumptions C.1 and C.2 are true, then

$$\limsup_{n \to \infty} \frac{1}{n} \log \Pr\{\frac{\underline{Z}_n}{n} \in F\} \le - \inf_{\underline{x} \in F} I(\underline{x})$$

for any closed F.

If Assumptions C.1, C.2 and C.3 are true, then

$$\liminf_{n \to \infty} \frac{1}{n} \log \Pr\{\frac{\underline{Z}_n}{n} \in G\} \ge - \inf_{\underline{x} \in G} I(\underline{x})$$

for any open G, where $I(\underline{x})$ is the Legendre transform of $\psi(\underline{\theta})$ defined by

$$I(\underline{x}) = \sup_{\underline{\theta} \in \Re^d} [<\underline{\theta}, \underline{x}> - \psi(\underline{\theta})]$$

where

$$\psi(\underline{\theta}) = \lim_{n \to \infty} \psi_n(\underline{\theta})/n \text{ and } \psi_n(\underline{\theta}) = \log E[e^{<\underline{\theta}, \underline{Z}_n>}].$$

In the nth network, for a path $P_i \in P_{sd}$

$$\Pr\{P_i \text{ is congested}\} = \Pr\{\bigcup_{l_j \in P_i} \{Z_{nj} > nC_j\}\}$$

where Z_{ij} denotes the utilization on link l_{ij}.

Before discussing the applications of Gärtner-Ellis Theorem for alternative routing in high-speed networks, we present the following min-max theorem which will be used later in the proofs of Theorems 4.3 and 4.4. The proof of Theorem 4.2 follows from the fact that $< \underline{\theta}, \underline{x} > -\psi(\underline{\theta})$ is a saddle-function [21].

Theorem 4.2: For a closed convex set F,

$$\inf_{\underline{x} \in F} \sup_{\underline{\theta}} [< \underline{\theta}, \underline{x} > -\psi(\underline{\theta})] = \sup_{\underline{\theta}} \inf_{\underline{x} \in F} [< \underline{\theta}, \underline{x} > -\psi(\underline{\theta})].$$

The following theorem states that the probability that P_i is congested is given by the most congested link along P_i.

Theorem 4.3:

$$\limsup_{n \to \infty} \frac{1}{n} \log \Pr\{ \bigcup_{l_j \in P_i} \{Z_{nj} > nC_j\} \} \leq - \inf_{j: l_j \in P_i} [C_j \theta_j^* - \psi^j(\theta_j^*)]$$

where $\psi^j(\theta_j) = \psi(\underline{\theta}) |_{\theta_i = 0, i \neq j}$ and θ_j^* is given by $\frac{\partial \psi^j(\theta_j^*)}{\partial \theta_j^*} = C_j$.

Proof:

$$\limsup_{n \to \infty} \frac{1}{n} \log \Pr\{ \bigcup_{l_j \in P_i} \{Z_{nj} > nC_j\} \}$$

$$= \limsup_{n \to \infty} \frac{1}{n} \log \Pr\{ \frac{Z_n}{n} \in G_i \}$$

$$\leq - \inf_{x \in \overline{G}_i} I(\underline{x})$$

where $G_i = \{ \underline{x} : \underline{x} \geq \underline{0} \text{ and } x_j > C_j \text{ for some } j \text{ such that } l_j \in P_i \}$ and $\overline{G}_i$ denotes the closure of G_i. Define $F_j = \{ \underline{x} : \underline{x} \geq \underline{0} \text{ and } x_j > C_j \}$. We have $\overline{G}_i = \bigcup_{l_j \in P_i} \overline{F}_j$.

$\{\overline{F}_j\}$ are closed and convex, hence we can apply min-max theorem

$$\inf_{\underline{x} \in \overline{G}_i} I(\underline{x}) = \inf_{\underline{x} \in \bigcup_{j: l_j \in P_i} \overline{F}_j} I(\underline{x}) = \inf_{j: l_j \in P_i} \inf_{\underline{x} \in \overline{F}_j} I(\underline{x})$$

$$= \inf_{j: l_j \in P_i} \sup_{\underline{\theta}} \inf_{\underline{x} \in \overline{F}_j} [< \underline{\theta}, \underline{x} > -\psi(\underline{\theta})]$$

$$\inf_{\underline{x} \in \overline{F}_j} < \underline{\theta}, \underline{x} > = \begin{cases} C_j \theta_j, & \text{if } \underline{\theta} \geq \underline{0} \\ -\infty, & \text{otherwise.} \end{cases}$$

We obtain

$$\inf_{\underline{x} \in \overline{G}_i} I(\underline{x}) = - \inf_{j: l_j \in P_i} \sup_{\underline{\theta} \geq \underline{0}} [C_j \theta_j - \psi(\underline{\theta})]$$

$$= - \inf_{j: l_j \in P_i} \sup_{\theta_j \geq 0} [C_j \theta_j - \psi^j(\theta_j)]$$

$$= - \inf_{j: l_j \in P_i} [C_j \theta_j^* - \psi^j(\theta_j^*)]$$

where $\psi^j(\theta_j)$ is the marginal logarithmic moment generating function for link j, and the second equality follows from

$$\frac{\partial \psi_n(\underline{\theta})}{\partial \theta_k} = \frac{E[Z_{nk} e^{<\underline{\theta}, \underline{Z}_n>}]}{E[e^{<\underline{\theta}, \underline{Z}_n>}]} \geq 0 \quad \text{since} \quad \underline{Z}_n \geq \underline{0} \text{ all } n$$

and from the uniform convergence of $\frac{\psi_n(\underline{\theta})}{n}$, i.e., $\psi(\underline{\theta})$ is increasing in θ_k. The last equality is obtained by using the concavity of $C_j \theta_j - \psi^j(\theta_j)$, with θ_j^* defined in the statement of the theorem. □

Next, we look at the probability that all paths between s and d are congested. In proving the following result, we use the disjunctive form proved in Lemma 4.1, in order to be able to express the set corresponding to congestion as a union of convex sets. The theorem states that the probability of a rare event is dominated by the most critical cutset. It is also mentioned as a consequence that when the links in a cutset are independent, the upper bound can be written as a sum over links constituting the critical cutset, where each term corresponds to the exponent of the upper bound for individual links.

Theorem 4.4:

$$\limsup_{n \to \infty} \frac{1}{n} \log \Pr\{ \bigcup_{i=1}^{m} \bigcap_{j: l_j \in M_i} \{Z_{nj} > nC_j\} \}$$

$$\leq \inf_i \left[\sum_{j: l_j \in M_i} C_j \theta_{ij}^* - \psi(\underline{\theta}_i^*) \right]$$

where $\underline{\theta}_i^*$ satisfies

$$\frac{\partial \psi(\underline{\theta}_i^*)}{\partial \theta_{ij}^*} = C_j$$

for $j \in M_i$ and $\theta_{ij}^* = 0$ otherwise.

Proof:

$$\limsup_{n \to \infty} \frac{1}{n} \log \Pr\{ \bigcup_{i=1}^{m} \bigcap_{j: l_j \in M_i} \{Z_{nj} > nC_j\} \}$$

$$= \limsup_{n \to \infty} \frac{1}{n} \log \Pr\{ \frac{Z_n}{n} \in S \}$$

$$\leq - \inf_{\underline{x} \in \overline{S}} I(\underline{x})$$

where $S = \bigcup_{i=1}^{m} \bigcap_{j: l_j \in M_i} F_j$, and F_j is as previously defined

$$\inf_{\underline{x} \in \overline{S}} I(\underline{x}) = \inf_i \inf_{\underline{x} \in \bigcap_{j: l_j \in M_i} \overline{F}_j} I(\underline{x})$$

since $\bigcap_j \overline{F}_j$ is closed and convex. We have from the min-max theorem

$$\inf_{\underline{x} \in \bigcap_{j: l_j \in M_i} \overline{F}_j} I(\underline{x}) = \sup_{\underline{\theta}} \inf_{\underline{x} \in \bigcap_{j: l_j \in M_i} \overline{F}_j} [< \underline{\theta}, \underline{x} > -\psi(\underline{\theta})].$$

We can write

$$\inf_{\underline{x} \in \bigcap_{j: l_j \in M_i} \overline{F}_j} < \underline{\theta}, \underline{x} > = \begin{cases} \sum_{j: l_j \in M_i} C_j \theta_j, & \text{if } \underline{\theta} \geq \underline{0} \\ -\infty, & \text{otherwise.} \end{cases}$$

Hence, we obtain

$$\inf_{\underline{x} \in \bigcap_{j: l_j \in M_i} \overline{F}_j} I(\underline{x}) = \sup_{\underline{\theta} \geq \underline{0}} \left[\sum_{j: l_j \in M_i} C_j \theta_j - \psi(\underline{\theta}) \right]$$

$$= \sum_{j: l_j \in M_i} C_j \theta_{ij}^* - \psi(\underline{\theta}_i^*)$$

where $\underline{\theta}_i^*$ satisfies

$$\frac{\partial \psi(\underline{\theta}_i^*)}{\partial \theta_{ij}^*} = C_j$$

for $j \in M_i$ and $\theta_{ij}^* = 0$ otherwise. The last equality is obtained by using the fact that $\psi(\underline{\theta})$ is increasing in θ_k for all k and using the concavity of $< \underline{x}, \underline{\theta} > -\psi(\underline{\theta})$ with respect to $\underline{\theta}$. □

Remark: If the links belonging to the same cutset are blocked independently, $\psi(\underline{\theta}_i^*)$ can be written as a sum of the individual logarithmic moment generating functions each corresponding to a link constituting cutset M_i. We have

$$\limsup_{n \to \infty} \frac{1}{n} \log \Pr\{\bigcup_{i=1}^{m} \bigcap_{j:l_j \in M_i} \{Z_{nj} > nC_j\}\}$$

$$\leq \inf_i \left[\sum_{j:l_j \in M_i} C_j \theta_j^* - \psi^j(\theta_j^*) \right] \quad (23)$$

where θ_j^* satisfies

$$\frac{\partial \psi^j(\theta_j^*)}{\partial \theta_j^*} = C_j$$

and $\psi^j(\theta_j)$ is the marginal logarithmic moment generating function for link j.

The loss probability between s and d with multiple paths is given asymptotically by the loss probability of the most congested (s,d)-cutset. The probability of congestion for a cutset can be computed by numerical differentiation for the solution of the corresponding Laplace parameter for each link in the cutset. It is noteworthy that for events consisting of subevents, the right-hand side of (23) is an upperbound, not just an asymptotic result.

If the function $I(\underline{x})$ is continuous on the boundaries of the sets $\{F_j\}_{j=1}^M$, then the infimum taken over the closure set $\overline{F}_j$ will be same as the infimum taken over F_j. In this case, by using the lower bound in the Gärtner-Ellis Theorem, we conclude that the upper bound is actually reached as the limit.

V. EFFECTIVE BANDWIDTH NETWORK ROUTING AND CONCLUSION

In this section we propose a dynamic network routing strategy for which decisions are based on the residual effective bandwidth on network components. This policy is similar to RTNR method [2] used for circuit-switched networks. The EBNR mechanism is applicable to any network containing both unbuffered and buffered resources. The routing decisions are done according to the following criteria: For a connection to be established we choose the path that maximizes the residual effective bandwidth. The residual effective bandwidth on a path is determined by the component of the path with the smallest residual effective bandwidth. The motivation for this rule is twofold. First, the effective bandwidth is a good measure of the required bandwidth to achieve a given GoS criteria on a component as a function of the traffic demand and buffer size. Second, as proven in Section IV, the probability of a congestion on a path is dominated by the most congested component.

The routing rule for EBNR is expressed as: For a connection request between s and d of traffic demand type i, first try the direct connection, say component j, if any. Use the direct connection if

$$C_j \geq C_j(G_j^r, N_j + e_i, B_j)$$

where C_j is the capacity for component j and $C_j(G_j^r, N_j, B_j)$ is the required bandwidth for component j as a function of the required GoS G_j^r, current traffic demand N_j and buffer size B_j which is given by the BD equation. e_i is the unit vector in the ith component with appropriate dimension. Otherwise, choose the alternative path $P_k \in P_{sd}$ that maximizes

$$R_k = \min_{l \in P_k} C_l - C_l(G_l^r, N_l, B_l) \quad (24)$$

and use P_k if

$$R_k \geq C_l(G_l^r, N_l + e_i, B_l) - C_l(G_l^r, N_l, B_l) \quad (25)$$

where component l on path P_k is the one that achieves the minimum in (24). Otherwise, the connection request is rejected. The actual GoS G_l may be larger or smaller than the required GoS G_l^r. When the number of traffic sources using component l is large, the right-hand side of (25) can be approximated by the derivative of the aggregate effective bandwidth with respect to N_i given in Table II. (25) is then equivalent to

$$R_k \geq \frac{\mu_i(\theta_l, \zeta_l)}{\theta_l} \quad (26)$$

where θ_l and ζ_l are the intrinsic variables corresponding to component l. The right-hand side of (26) corresponds the additional effective bandwidth required for routing a traffic demand of type i through component l. The change in actual GoS for component l after routing demand i is given by $(\partial G_l / \partial N_{li})_{C_l, B_l} = -\mu_i(\theta_l, \zeta_l)$, where N_{li} is the number of traffic demands of type i on component l.

The implementation of the routing algorithm requires the monitoring of extensive parameters. The effective bandwidth of a network component l can be obtained from the measurements of the intensive parameters θ_l, ζ_l and μ_l for component l as described in Section III,

$$C_l(G_l^r, N_l, B_l) = \frac{G_l^r}{\theta_l} + \frac{1}{\theta_l} \sum_i N_{li}\mu_i - \frac{\zeta_l}{\theta_l}B_l.$$

The algorithm also requires the exchange of the necessary information between components. The stability of the routing method need to be addressed. A bandwidth reservation technique similar to the trunk reservation method used in circuit-switched networks may be incorporated into the algorithm.

In this paper, we have addressed the problem of identifying the fundamental relations between quantities such as GoS, transmission capacity, buffer resources and traffic demand in a network. The way these parameters scale with respect to each other defines the set of very useful intensive variables. In this context the problem of effective bandwidth for buffered resources is revisited. These parameters can be obtained either analytically or by measurements. Empirical methods to measure these quantities are discussed. The theory is applied to networks with dynamic routing and the probabilities of rare events expressed in conjunctive forms are characterized by using large deviations theory. Further research in this area should be directed at the scalability problem in general systems, measurement methods and stability issues.

APPENDIX A

In this part we justify the scalability property for M/M/1/B and M/M/C/C+B queues when C and B are large.

I. M/M/1/B:

The logarithm of the loss probability is given by

$$\log p_B = \log(1 - \rho) - \log(1 - \rho^B) + B \log \rho$$

where $\rho = \lambda/\mu < 1$ is the utilization factor with λ and μ denoting the arrival and transmission rates, respectively. The logarithm of the loss probability is asymptotically given by

$$\log p_B = B \log \rho \qquad (27)$$

since $\log(1 - \rho)$ and $\log(1 - \rho^B)$ become very small compared to $B \log \rho$. When λ, μ and B are all scaled by a large α (ρ is kept constant), the GoS equation (27) shows that the logarithm of the loss probability is scaled by α.

II. M/M/C/C+B:

The logarithm of the loss probability is given by

$$\log p_{C+B} = \log p_0 + C \log C - \log C! + (C + B) \log \rho$$

where $\rho = \lambda/C\mu < 1$ is the utilization factor with λ and μ denoting the arrival rate and transmission rate per channel, respectively, and p_0 is given by

$$p_0 = \left[\sum_{n=0}^{C} \frac{(C\rho)^n}{n!} + \frac{C^C}{C!} \sum_{n=C+1}^{B+C} \rho^n \right]^{-1}.$$

When C is large, using Stirling's formula we obtain

$$\log p_{C+B} = \log p_0 + (C + B) \log \rho + C.$$

Using Stirling's formula we have

$$e^{C\rho} = \max_{0 \le n \le C} \frac{(C\rho)^n}{n!} < \sum_{n=0}^{C} \frac{(C\rho)^n}{n!} < \sum_{n=0}^{\infty} \frac{(C\rho)^n}{n!} = e^{C\rho}$$

and

$$\frac{C^C}{C!} \sum_{n=C+1}^{B+C} \rho^n = \frac{(C\rho)^C}{C!} \sum_{n=1}^{B} \rho^n = (e\rho)^C \sum_{n=1}^{B} \rho^n.$$

$-\log p_0$ is asymptotically given by

$$-\log p_0 = C\rho + \log\left(1 + \left(\frac{e\rho}{e^\rho}\right)^C \sum_{n=1}^{B} \rho^n\right) \approx C\rho$$

since $e\rho < e^\rho$ for $\rho < 1$ and the summation is upper bounded by $\rho/(1 - \rho)$. The logarithm of the loss probability is asymptotically given by

$$\log p_{C+B} = (C + B) \log \rho + C(1 - \rho). \qquad (28)$$

When λ, C and B are scaled together by a large α (keeping μ and thus ρ fixed), we observe from (28) that the logarithm of the loss probability is also scaled by α. Hence, the GoS equation for M/M/C/C+B queue is scalable.

In Fig. 9, we plot GoS versus capacity for $\rho = 0.8$ and different values of γ. We observe that linear scalability holds even for small values of C and B.

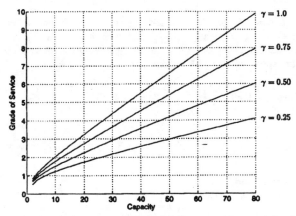

Fig. 9. GoS versus capacity for M/M/C/C+B queue with $\rho = 0.8$ and $\gamma = 0.1, 0.25, 0.5, 1.0$.

APPENDIX B

Proof of Theorem 2.1: Consider a slotted time queueing system with N statistically independent sources multiplexed into the system. The multiplexer is served with a fixed rate channel of capacity $C = Nc$ bits per time slot. Bits arriving when the bandwidth is fully utilized are placed in a buffer of size $B = Nb$ bits. Let X_j^n denote the number of bits arriving during time slot j generated by source n. Assume the system is in steady state and let $p(Nc, N, Nb)$ denote the loss probability. The random variable $Y_i = \sum_{n=1}^{N} \sum_{j=1}^{i} X_{-j}^n$ denotes total number of bits arriving at the system in the interval $[-i, 0]$. Let A_i denote the event that the system overflows at time 0 and the buffer was last empty at time $-i$. We have $p(Nc, N, Nb) = \Pr(\bigcup_{i=1}^{\infty} A_i)$. By using arguments similar to Laplace principle, it can be shown that for large N, $p(Nc, N, Nb) \approx \sup_{i \ge 1} \Pr\{A_i\}$. A necessary condition for A_i is that $Y_i > Nci + Nb$. Hence

$$\Pr(A_i) \le \Pr\{Y_i > Nci + Nb\}. \qquad (29)$$

Since the right-hand side of (29) is a lower bound on $p(Nc, N, Nb)$ for any i, we have for large N

$$p(Nc, N, Nb) \approx \sup_{i \ge 1} \Pr\{Y_i > Nci + Nb\}. \qquad (30)$$

We use Gärtner-Ellis Theorem to obtain

$$\lim_{N \to \infty} \frac{1}{Ni} \log \Pr\left\{ \frac{1}{Ni} Y_i > c + \frac{b}{i} \right\} = -I_i\left(c + \frac{b}{i}\right) \qquad (31)$$

where

$$I_i(x) = \sup_{\theta \ge 0} [\theta x - \psi_i(\theta)]$$

$$\psi_i(\theta) = \lim_{N \to \infty} \frac{1}{Ni} \log E(e^{\theta Y_i}) = \frac{1}{i} \log E(e^{\theta W})$$

where W is a random variable having the same distribution as i.i.d. random variables $\{\sum_{j=1}^{i} X_{-j}^n\}_{n=1}^{N}$. Hence, we have

$$\lim_{N \to \infty} \frac{G(Nc, N, Nb)}{N} = \inf_{i \ge 1} \sup_{\theta \ge 0} [b\theta + i(c\theta - \psi_i(\theta))]. \qquad (32)$$

Equation (32) establishes the claim of Theorem 2.1. $\qquad \square$

APPENDIX C

In this appendix, we present the assumptions under which Gärtner-Ellis Theorem holds. Consider a sequence of random vectors $\underline{Z}_n \in \Re^d$ which has a logarithmic moment generating function

$$\psi_n(\underline{\theta}) = \log E[e^{<\underline{\theta}, \underline{Z}_n>}]$$

where $\underline{\theta} \in \Re^d$ and $<., .>$ denotes the inner product operation. It can proved that $\psi_n(\underline{\theta})$ is convex and lower semicontinuous [9].

Assumption C.1: For each $\underline{\theta} \in \Re^d$, the limit defined as

$$\psi(\underline{\theta}) = \lim_{n \to \infty} \frac{1}{n} \psi_n(\underline{\theta})$$

exists as an extended real number. Furthermore, $\psi(\underline{\theta})$ is convex and lower semi-continuous.

Assumption C.2: The origin belongs to the interior of the domain D_ψ of ψ defined by $D_\psi = \{\underline{\theta} : \psi(\underline{\theta}) < \infty\}$.

Definition C.1: A convex function $\psi : \Re^d \to \Re$, differentiable on the domain D_ψ, is steep if a sequence $\{\underline{\theta}^n\} \subset \Re^d$ with $\underline{\theta}^n \to \underline{\theta}$ where $\underline{\theta}$ is on the boundary of D_ψ implies that $\lim_{n \to \infty} \| \nabla \psi(\underline{\theta}^n)\| = \infty$.

Assumption C.3: $\psi(\underline{\theta})$ is steep.

Remarks: Since $\{\psi_n(\underline{\theta})\}$ are convex functions, $\psi(\underline{\theta})$ is convex if D_ψ is a convex set. $\psi(\underline{\theta})$ is lower semi-continuous if $\psi_n/n \to \psi$ uniformly. Assumption C.2 is rather a mild condition and holds for almost all random vectors sequences.

ACKNOWLEDGMENT

The authors would like to thank B. Hajek for his valuable comments and suggestions concerning the presentation of the paper.

REFERENCES

[1] D. Anick, D. Mitra, and M. M. Sondhi, "Stochastic theory of a data-handling system with multiple sources," *Bell Syst. Tech. J.*, vol. 61, 1982.
[2] G. R. Ash, J.-S. Chen, A. E. Frey, and B. D. Huang, "Real-time network routing in a dynamic class-of-service network," in *Proc. 13th ITC*, Copenhagen, Denmark, 1991.
[3] J. P. Aubin, *Explicit Methods of Optimization*. Paris: Bordas, 1984.
[4] V. E. Benes, *Mathematical Theory of Connecting Networks and Telephone Traffic*. New York: Academic, 1965.
[5] J. A. Bucklew, *Large Deviation Techniques in Decision, Simulation, and Estimation*. New York: Wiley, 1990.
[6] C. S. Chang, "Stability, queue length and delay, Part II: Stochastic queueing networks," IBM Res. Rep. RC17709, 1992.
[7] S.-P. Chung and K. W. Ross, "Reduced load approximations for multirate loss networks," *IEEE Trans. Commun.*, vol. 41, no. 8, 1993.
[8] R. L. Cruz and H.-N. Liu, "Non-recursive identities for tandem queueing networks," preprint, 1993.
[9] A. Dembo and O. Zeitouni, *Large Deviation Techniques and Applications*. Boston: Jones and Bartlett, 1993.
[10] R. S. Ellis, *Entropy, Large Deviations and Statistical Mechanics*. New York: Springer-Verlag, 1985.
[11] A. I. Elwalid and D. Mitra, "Effective bandwidths of general Markovian traffic sources and admission control of high-speed networks," *IEEE/ACM Trans. Networking*, vol. 1, no. 3, 1993.
[12] A. Elwalid, D. Heyman, T. V. Lakshman, D. Mitra, and A. Weiss, "Fundamental bounds and approximations for ATM multiplexers with applications to video teleconferencing," *IEEE J. Select. Areas Commun.*, vol. 13, no. 6, pp. 1004–1016, Aug. 1995.
[13] R. G. Gallager, *Discrete Stochastic Processes*, ch. 7, 1994.
[14] R. J. Gibbens and P. J. Hunt, "Effective bandwidths for the multi-type UAS channel," *Queueing Syst.*, vol. 9, 1991.
[15] J. Y. Hui, "Resource allocation for broadband networks," *IEEE J. Select. Areas Commun.*, vol. 6, 1988.
[16] ———, *Switching and Traffic Theory for Integrated Broadband Networks*. Boston, MA: Kluwer, 1990, sec. 8.5.
[17] ———, "A congestion measure for call admission and traffic engineering for multi-layer multi-rate traffic," *Int. J. Dig., Anal. Commun. Syst.*, vol. 3, 1990.
[18] F. P. Kelly, "Effective bandwidths at multi-class queues," *Queueing Syst.*, vol. 9, 1991.
[19] ———, "Blocking probabilities in large circuit-switched networks," *Advances Appl. Probab.*, vol. 18, 1986.
[20] ———, "Routing in circuit-switched networks: optimization, shadow prices and decentralization," *Advances Appl. Probab.*, vol. 20, 1988.
[21] R. T. Rockafellar, *Convex Analysis*. Princeton, NJ: Princeton University Press, 1970.
[22] A. Weiss, "A new technique for analyzing large traffic systems," *Advances Appl. Probab.*, vol. 18, 1986.

Joseph Y. Hui (S'82–M'83–SM'90) received the S.B., S.M., E.E., and Ph.D. degrees in electrical engineering from the Massachusetts Institute of Technology, Cambridge, in 1981, 1981, 1982, and 1983, respectively.

After graduation in 1983, he joined Bell Communications Research, Morristown, NJ. He joined Rutgers University, New Brunswick, NJ, in 1989, as an Associate Professor in the Department of Electrical and Computer Engineering. For periods between 1979–1981, he was with Comsat Laboratories under the M.I.T. Cooperative Program. He was also an Adjunct Professor at the Center for Telecommunications Research, Columbia University, New York, NY, during 1987–1988. His current research interests include coding and information theory, wireless information networks, as well as switching, protocol, traffic, and security issues for integrated broadband networks. He is the author of a book entitled *Switching and Traffic Theory for Integrated Broadband Networks* (Kluwer, 1990). His work on multiple access communications and switching networks has resulted in several patents.

Dr. Hui is the recipient of the 1985 William Bennett Prize Paper Award given by the IEEE Communications Society. He also received Presidential Young Investigator Award from the National Science Foundation.

Ezhan Karasan (S'89) received the B.S. degree from Middle East Technical University, Ankara, Turkey, and the M.S. degree from Bilkent University, Ankara, Turkey, in 1987 and 1990, respectively, both in electrical engineering. He is currently working toward the Ph.D. degree in electrical engineering at Rutgers University, New Brunswick, NJ.

His research interests include performance analysis of broadband networks and multimedia systems.

Mr. Karasan was awarded a fellowship from NATO Science Scholarship Program between 1991–1994.

CHAPTER V

PERFORMANCE/DELAY ANALYSIS

This chapter covers performance and delay analysis of ATM switching and networks.

Network Delay Analysis of a Class of Fair Queueing Algorithms

S. Jamaloddin Golestani, *Member, IEEE*

Abstract— A self-clocked fair queueing (SCFQ) scheme has been recently proposed [6], [5] as an easily implementable version of fair queueing. In this paper, the worst case network delay performance of a class of fair queueing algorithms, including the SCFQ scheme, is studied. We build upon and generalize the methodology developed by Parekh and Gallager [10], [11] to study this class of algorithms based on the leaky-bucket characterization of traffic. Under modest resource allocation conditions, the end-to-end session delays and backlogs corresponding to this class of algorithms are shown to be bounded. For the SCFQ scheme, these bounds are larger, but practically as good as the corresponding bounds for the PGPS scheme [11]. It is shown that the SCFQ scheme can provide adequate performance guarantees for the delay-sensitive traffic in ATM.

I. INTRODUCTION

THIS paper studies the worst case delay performance of a class of fair queueing algorithms, including the recently proposed self-clocked fair queueing (SCFQ) [6], [5].

In recent years, there has been an increasing interest in employing some form of fair queueing in packet networks [4], [8], [9], [13], [1], [10], [7]. This interest stems from the isolation that fair queueing provides among different users, allowing them to share resources without overriding each other. Unlike FIFO queueing where a session can increase its share of service by presenting more demand and keeping a larger number of packets in the queue, the underlying idea in fair queueing is to serve sessions in proportion to some prespecified service shares, independent of the queueing load presented by each session.

While it is simple to define fair queueing for an idealized fluid-flow traffic model, the extension of this definition to the actual packet-based service scenario is not straightforward. Demers, *et al.*, [4] define fair queueing for the packet-based model by using the idealized fluid-flow traffic model as reference. In what they call *packet-by-packet fair queueing*, packets are served in essentially the same order in which they would finish service in the hypothetical fluid-flow fair queueing system. Parekh and Gallager [10], [11] adopt the same definition for fairness, in order to derive bounds on the end-to-end session delays based on the leaky-bucket characterization of traffic. Following their terminology, in this paper we refer to the fluid-flow fair queueing and the packet-by-packet fair queueing, as the GPS and PGPS schemes, respectively.

Manuscript received September 30, 1994; revised April 1, 1995.
The author is with Bellcore, Morristown, NJ 07962 USA.
IEEE Log Number 9412655.

The PGPS scheme does not lend itself to easy implementation since it is based on real-time simulation of an external reference system. Even the more efficient virtual-time implementation proposed by Greenberg and Madras [7], involves a relatively high degree of computational complexity. An alternative approach to fair queueing is the SCFQ scheme [6], [5]. This scheme, which is based on an internally generated virtual time, is simpler and more feasible for high-speed implementation. Zhang's *virtual clock* algorithm [13], which was proposed earlier, constitutes an important, albeit incomplete step [6] toward the formulation of fair queueing based on the notion of virtual time.

An objective of this paper is to analyze the worst case network performance of the SCFQ scheme, based on the leaky-bucket characterization of traffic. However, we carry out this analysis for a more general class of packet-based queueing algorithms. In the algorithms of this class, the amount of service provided to each active session loosely follows a common index of work progress in the system, referred to as the virtual time. In order to analyze the network performance of this class of algorithms, we build upon and generalize the methodology developed in [11] for the GPS scheme. Our study shows that the network delay properties of the PGPS scheme are shared by a larger class of packet-based queueing algorithms.

In Section II, the impact of multiplexing on the leaky-bucket characterization of a traffic stream is discussed. Section III introduces the class of fair queueing algorithms that we study in this paper. In Sections IV and V, we analyze the worst case performance of this class of algorithms over a single server and a network of servers, respectively. Finally, in Section VI, we interpret the results of this paper for the special cases of interest. We conclude that the delay and the backlog bounds of the SCFQ scheme are larger but, from a practical standpoint, almost as good as the corresponding bounds for the PGPS scheme.

II. IMPACT OF MULTIPLEXING ON THE LEAKY-BUCKET CHARACTERIZATION

In this section, the impact of multiplexing on the leaky-bucket characterization of traffic is discussed. The main concepts in this section have been originally studied by Cruz [2], [3]. Here, we develop a concise presentation for the background material needed later, and present some new results.

Reprinted from IEEE Journal on Selected Areas of Communications, Vol 13, No. 6, Aug. 1995, pp. 1057-1070.

Leaky-bucket characterization of a traffic stream is based on specifying a two-parameter envelop on the volume of arriving traffic [12]. Let $A(t)$ denote the total amount of traffic arrived on a stream up to, but not including, the time t. In this paper, all functions are assumed to be left continuous, i.e., $f(t) = f(t^-)$, for any function $f(.)$. Also, we define $f(t_1, t_2) \triangleq f(t_2) - f(t_1)$. Following these conventions, the total traffic arrived on the stream $A(t)$, during $[t_1, t_2)$, is denoted by $A(t_1, t_2)$.

Definition 1: Given $\sigma > 0$, and $\rho > 0$, the traffic stream $A(t)$ is called (σ, ρ)-*regular*, if for any interval $[t_1, t_2)$

$$A(t_1, t_2) \leq \sigma + \rho(t_2 - t_1).$$

We refer to σ and ρ as the *burstiness* and the *average rate* of $A(t)$.

Lemma 1: A necessary and sufficient condition for $A(t)$ to be (σ, ρ)-regular is that there be some function $\alpha(t)$ satisfying the following bounds for any instant t and any interval $[t_1, t_2)$

$$0 \leq \alpha(t) \leq \sigma \qquad (1)$$

$$A(t_1, t_2) \leq \rho(t_2 - t_1) - \alpha(t_1, t_2). \qquad (2)$$

Proof: Proof of sufficiency is straight forward. To prove the necessity of (1) and (2), assume that $A(t)$ is (σ, ρ)-regular and define $a(t)$ as

$$a(t) \triangleq \inf_{\forall \tau \leq t} [\sigma + \rho(t - \tau) - A(\tau, t)]. \qquad (3)$$

It can be shown that (1) and (2) are satisfied with $\alpha(t) = a(t)$.
$\square$

$a(t)$ specifies the maximum size of a traffic burst that can arrive at t, without violating the (σ, ρ)-regularity of $A(t)$. In the physical interpretation commonly used for the leaky-bucket characterization [12], $a(t)$ corresponds to the amount of permits available at t. Therefore, we refer to $a(t)$ as the *permit function* associated with the (σ, ρ)-regular stream $A(t)$.

Next, consider a multiplexer serving traffic from different sessions and let us focus on the traffic stream of a given session k as it enters and leaves the multiplexer. Let $A_k(t)$ represent the arriving traffic of k to the multiplexer. In this paper, we mainly deal with packet-based noncut-through multiplexors where the transmission of a packet cannot begin until it has been completely received. In accordance with this point of view, we interpret $A_k(t)$ as representing a *packet* stream and define it as the aggregated length of packets *fully* received up to the time t. It follows that $A_k(t)$ has a staircase shape, with each step corresponding to the arrival of a packet. Let (σ_k, ρ_k) be a leaky-bucket characterization for $A_k(t)$, and $a_k(t)$ be the corresponding permit function. Therefore

$$0 \leq a_k(t) \leq \sigma_k, \text{ for all } t \qquad (4)$$

$$A_k(t_1, t_2) \leq \rho_k(t_2 - t_1) - a_k(t_1, t_2),$$
$$\text{for all } t_1 \text{ and } t_2, t_1 < t_2. \qquad (5)$$

For the departing traffic stream of session k from the multiplexer, we use both a continuous bit-oriented and a packet-oriented representation, respectively, denoted by $W_k(t)$ and $W'_k(t)$. $W_k(t)$ is the total number of bits from k transmitted up to the time t, whereas $W'_k(t)$ is the total length of packets of k which are fully transmitted by t. We treat $W_k(t)$ as a continuous function, while $W'_k(t)$ has a staircase shape.

Denote by $Q_k(t)$ the *backlog* of session k at time t, including the residue of partially transmitted packets

$$Q_k(t) \triangleq A_k(t) - W_k(t). \qquad (6)$$

Definition 2: The *potential backlog* of session k at time t is defined as

$$\omega_k(t) \triangleq a_k(t) + Q_k(t). \qquad (7)$$

Although the backlog $Q_k(t)$ is discontinuous, $\omega_k(t)$ is continuous because packet arrivals cause a corresponding drop in $a_k(t)$. The notion of potential backlog plays a helpful role in this paper. In particular, it helps determine a leaky-bucket characterization for $W_k(t)$. Notice that for any interval $[t_1, t_2)$

$$W_k(t_1, t_2) = A_k(t_1, t_2) - Q_k(t_1, t_2)$$
$$\leq \rho_k(t_2 - t_1) - a_k(t_1, t_2) - Q_k(t_1, t_2) \quad (8)$$
$$= \rho_k(t_2 - t_1) - \omega_k(t_1, t_2).$$

According to Lemma 1, (8) constitutes a leaky-bucket characterization for $W_k(t)$, if $\omega_k(t)$ is both nonnegative and bounded. Since $Q_k(t)$ and $a_k(t)$ are both nonnegative

$$\omega_k(t) \geq 0. \qquad (9)$$

Furthermore, assuming that $Q_k(t)$ has the upper bound $Q_k^{\max}$

$$\omega_k(t) \leq \sigma_k + Q_k^{\max}$$

which indicates that $W_k(t)$ is $(\sigma_k + Q_k^{\max}, \rho_k)$-regular. The following lemma establishes a tighter characterization for $W_k(t)$ by showing that, in spite of the apparent implication of (7), $\omega_k(t)$ never exceeds $Q_k^{\max}$.

Lemma 2: Let $Q_k(t) \leq Q_k^{\max}$, for any (σ_k, ρ_k)-regular stream $A_k(t)$. It follows that

$$\omega_k(t) \leq Q_k^{\max} \qquad (10)$$

and $W_k(t)$ is $(Q_k^{\max}, \rho_k)$-regular.

Proof: At any time τ, it is possible for $A_k(t)$ to undergo a jump of size $a_k(\tau)$ without violating its (σ_k, ρ_k)-regularity. In case of such a jump, we have $A_k(\tau^+) = A_k(\tau) + a_k(\tau)$. Since $W_k(t)$ is continuous, $W_k(\tau) = W_k(\tau^+)$. We conclude from (6) and (7) that

$$Q_k(\tau^+) = Q_k(\tau) + a_k(\tau) = \omega_k(\tau).$$

Therefore, since $Q_k(t) \leq Q_k^{\max}$ for all t, we have $\omega_k(\tau) \leq Q_k^{\max}$. Finally, it follows from Lemma 1 and (8)–(10) that $W_k(t)$ is $(Q_k^{\max}, \rho_k)$-regular. $\square$

Notice that $a_k(\tau)$ is the size of the largest burst that can arrive on session k at time τ. Therefore, $\omega_k(\tau) = Q_k(\tau) + a_k(\tau)$ equals the maximum backlog that session k can acquire at τ^+, hence the name *potential backlog*.

Next, define the *packet backlog* of session k at time t as

$$Q'_k(t) \triangleq A_k(t) - W'_k(t). \qquad (11)$$

A partially transmitted packet of k remains fully included in $Q'_k(t)$ until the transmission is completed. Again, combining (5) and (11) we get

$$W'_k(t_1, t_2) \leq \rho_k(t_2 - t_1) - \omega'_k(t_1, t_2) \qquad (12)$$

for any interval $[t_1, t_2]$, where

$$\omega'_k(t) \triangleq a_k(t) + Q'_k(t) \geq 0. \qquad (13)$$

Moreover, we have the following lemma:

Lemma 3: Let $Q_k(t) \leq Q_k^{\max}$, for any (σ_k, ρ_k)-regular stream $A_k(t)$. Denote the transmission speed by C, and the maximum packet length of session k by $L_k^{\max}$. Assume that the multiplexer is nonpreemptive, i.e., the transmission of a packet is always completed before the service is shifted to another packet. Then

$$Q'_k(t) \leq \omega'_k(t) \leq Q_k^{\max} + \frac{\rho_k}{C} L_k^{\max}. \qquad (14)$$

Furthermore, $W'_k(t)$ is $(Q_k^{\max} + L_k^{\max} \rho_k / C, \rho_k)$-regular.

Proof: The first inequality in (14) follows from (13). To show the second inequality, consider any time t. If $Q'_k(t) = Q_k(t)$, then $\omega'_k(t) = \omega_k(t)$, and (14) follows from Lemma 2. So, let $Q'_k(t) \neq Q_k(t)$, which means that some packet p from k is under transmission at t. Let the transmission of p start at $\tau < t$. By definition

$$Q'_k(t) = Q'_k(\tau) + A_k(\tau, t) = Q_k(\tau) + A_k(\tau, t).$$

Also from (5)

$$a_k(t) = a_k(\tau) + a_k(\tau, t) \leq a_k(\tau) + \rho_k(t - \tau) - A_k(\tau, t).$$

Therefore

$$\omega'_k(t) = a_k(t) + Q'_k(t) \leq \omega_k(\tau) + \rho_k(t - \tau) \leq \omega_k(\tau) + \frac{\rho_k}{C} L_k^{\max}$$

where the last inequality follows since, by assumption, the multiplexing is nonpreemptive and transmission of p takes no longer than $L_k^{\max}/C$. We can now conclude (14) from Lemma 2. Finally, according to (12) and Lemma 1, $W'_k(t)$ is $(Q_k^{\max} + L_k^{\max} \cdot \rho_k / C, \rho_k)$-regular. □

Notice that the results in Lemmas 2 and 3 regarding the service provided to session k have been derived without making any specific assumption about the arriving traffic of other sessions, or considering a particular nonpreemptive queueing scheme for the multiplexer. The impact of the queueing scheme and the traffic characteristics of other sessions on the worst case performance of session k, will be manifested in the parameter $Q_k^{\max}$. In the subsequent sections, we study this impact for the case of fair queueing and leaky-bucket characterization for all of the sessions.

III. A CLASS OF FAIR QUEUEING ALGORITHMS

In this section, we introduce the class of fair queueing algorithms studied by this paper.

Consider the queueing system at a link with the transmission speed C. Denote by $\mathcal{K}$ the set of sessions k set up on this link, and by $\phi_k, k \in \mathcal{K}$, the service share allocated to session k. Ideally, a fair queueing algorithm is expected to provide service to the active sessions in proportion to the allocated service shares. Assume, without loss of generality, that the session service shares add up to one, i.e.,

$$\sum_{k \in \mathcal{K}} \phi_k = 1. \qquad (15)$$

Define a session k as *backlogged* at time t, if $Q_k(t)$ is nonzero. Denote by $\mathcal{B}(t)$ the set of sessions that are backlogged at t, and by $\mathcal{B}(t_1, t_2)$ the set of sessions that are backlogged during the entire interval (t_1, t_2), i.e.,

$$\mathcal{B}(t) \triangleq \{k, \text{s.t.} \quad Q_k(t) > 0\}$$

$$\mathcal{B}(t_1, t_2) \triangleq \{k, \text{s.t.} \quad Q_k(\tau) > 0 \text{ for, } t_1 < \tau < t_2\}.$$

Finally, assume that the queueing scheme is work-conserving and define a *busy period* as a maximal interval of time during which the server is busy, without interruption.

Definition 3: Given a set of session service shares ϕ_k, $k \in \mathcal{K}$, a work-conserving queueing algorithm is called fair if for any busy period, there exists a function $v(t)$ and a set of bounded functions $\delta_k(t)$, $k \in \mathcal{K}$, for which the following are satisfied during any subinterval (t_1, t_2) of the busy period

$$\frac{1}{\phi_k} W_k(t_1, t_2) \leq v(t_1, t_2) - \delta_k(t_1, t_2), \qquad k \in \mathcal{K} \qquad (16)$$

with equality if $k \in \mathcal{B}(t_1, t_2)$, and

$$\delta_k^{\min} \leq \delta_k(t) \leq \delta_k^{\max}, \qquad k \in \mathcal{K} \qquad (17)$$

where $\delta_k^{\min}$ and $\delta_k^{\max}$ are fixed and supposedly small parameters. We refer to $v(t)$ as the system's *virtual time*.

The above definition implies that the services received by different backlogged sessions, normalized to the corresponding service shares, always remain within a bounded difference from each other. This property conforms to our notion of fairness.

The simplest queueing algorithm that satisfies Definition 3 is the GPS scheme discussed in [4], [10]. For the GPS scheme, $\delta_k(t) = 0$, for all times and all sessions. This scheme, however, is based on an idealized fluid-flow model of traffic and is not directly applicable to packet-based multiplexing. An example of a packet-based queueing algorithm that satisfies Definition 3 is the SCFQ scheme [6], [5], for which $\delta_k^{\max} = L_k^{\max}/\phi_k$, and $\delta_k^{\min} = 0$. The SCFQ scheme has the additional property that while a session k is not backlogged, or each time a packet from k finishes service, $\delta_k(t) = 0$. As said earlier, an important feature of the SCFQ algorithm is its computational simplicity and the relative ease with which it can be implemented. Other examples of the class of queueing algorithms defined in Definition 3 will not be discussed in this paper.

Equation (16) suggests viewing $v(t)$ as the index of work progress in the system, and $\delta_k(t)$ as the normalized service lag of session k, measured against this index. With this interpretation in mind, the quantity

$$\delta(t) \triangleq \sum_{j \in \mathcal{K}} \phi_j \cdot \delta_j(t) \qquad (18)$$

305

is the combined service lag of all sessions, as measured against $v(t)$. Now let us define

$$\bar{v}(t) \triangleq v(t) - \delta(t)$$

and use it as the new index of system's work progress. From (16), we can write

$$W_k(t_1, t_2) \leq \phi_k \Big(\bar{v}(t_1, t_2) - \tilde{\delta}_k(t_1, t_2) \Big), \qquad k \in \mathcal{K} \quad (19)$$

with equality if $k \in \mathcal{B}(t_1, t_2)$, where

$$\tilde{\delta}_k(t) \triangleq \delta_k(t) - \delta(t), \qquad k \in \mathcal{K}. \quad (20)$$

According to (19), $\tilde{\delta}_k(t)$ may be viewed as the normalized service lag of session k, measured against the new index $\bar{v}(t)$. Notice that

$$\sum_{j \in \mathcal{K}} \phi_j \cdot \tilde{\delta}_j(t) = \sum_{j \in \mathcal{K}} \phi_j \cdot \delta_j(t) - \delta(t) \sum_{j \in \mathcal{K}} \phi_j = \delta(t) - \delta(t) = 0. \quad (21)$$

Therefore, the service lag of all sessions add up to zero, suggesting that $\bar{v}(t)$ is an unbiased index of work progress in the system.[1] As one would expect, during a busy period, $\bar{v}(t)$ is an increasing function of time. This property may be verified by summing up (19) over $k \in \mathcal{K}$, and noting that $\sum_{k \in \mathcal{K}} W_k(t_1, t_2) = C(t_2 - t_1)$, for any subinterval (t_1, t_2) of a busy period.

Since the functions $\delta_k(t)$ are bounded by the constants $\delta_k^{\max}$ and $\delta_k^{\min}$, it follows from (18) and (20) that $\tilde{\delta}_k(t)$, $k \in \mathcal{K}$, are also bounded, allowing the following definitions

$$\tilde{\delta}_k^{\max} \triangleq \sup \tilde{\delta}_k(t), \qquad k \in \mathcal{K} \quad (22)$$

$$\tilde{\delta}_k^{(\text{init}) \min} \triangleq \inf \Big\{ \tilde{\delta}_k(t),$$

given that k becomes backlogged at $t \}$, $\quad k \in \mathcal{K}$, $\quad (23)$

$$\Delta_k \triangleq \phi_k \Big(\tilde{\delta}_k^{\max} - \tilde{\delta}_k^{(\text{init}) \min} \Big), \qquad k \in \mathcal{K}. \quad (24)$$

The maximization and minimization in (22) and (23) are taken over all times and all possible event sequences. Δ_k represents the maximum possible increase that the service lag of a session k can undergo, beginning with a time at which k becomes backlogged. In the case of GPS scheme, we get $\tilde{\delta}_k(t) = 0$, for all k. Therefore, $\Delta_k = \tilde{\delta}_k^{\max} = \tilde{\delta}_k^{(\text{init}) \min} = 0$. For the SCFQ scheme, we can show that [5]

$$\Delta_k = (1 - \phi_k) L_k^{\max} + \phi_k \sum_{j \in \mathcal{K}, \ j \neq k} L_j^{\max}. \quad (25)$$

In the subsequent sections, we will find that the worst case delay performance of a fair queueing scheme can be characterized in terms of the associated parameters Δ_k, $k \in \mathcal{K}$.

---

[1] This interpretation is not accurate since the service lag of the *backlogged* sessions, as measured against $\bar{v}(t)$, do not always add up to zero.

IV. FAIR QUEUEING AND LEAKY-BUCKET TRAFFIC

In this section, we consider a fair queueing system and study the maximum session backlogs based on the leaky-bucket characterization of the arriving traffic.

To summarize the model, consider a queueing system S at a link with the transmission speed C, which multiplexes the traffic of sessions k, $k \in \mathcal{K}$. Assume that the arriving packet stream of each session k, $A_k(t)$, is (σ_k, ρ_k)-regular, and denote by $a_k(t)$ the corresponding permit function. The departing traffic of session k is represented both by the continuous function $W_k(t)$, which shows the exact service received by session k, and by the staircase function $W_k'(t)$, which reflects the completion time of packet transmissions for k. Unlike Section II, where we needed to model the arriving traffic of only one session, here a leaky-bucket characterization is assumed for the arriving traffic of all sessions. The queueing scheme satisfies the fairness conditions given in Definition 3, and the session service shares ϕ_k, $k \in \mathcal{K}$, are subject to (15). In order to have a stable queue, we assume that

$$\sum_{j \in \mathcal{K}} \rho_j < C. \quad (26)$$

Our goal in this section is to determine the maximum backlog $Q_k(t)$ that can accumulate for each session k, in the queueing system S. We begin, however, by analyzing the worst case evolution of the potential session backlogs $\omega_k(t)$. As discussed earlier, $\omega_k(t)$ and $Q_k(t)$ share the same maximum. By focusing our attention on the potential session backlogs, we are able to capture the essence of session interactions in the queueing system.

A. Analysis of Potential Session Backlogs

Let the queueing system S be at *initial rest* at t_0, i.e., let $Q_k(t_0) = 0$, and $a_k(t_0) = \sigma_k$, for $k \in \mathcal{K}$. It follows that

$$\omega_k(t_0) = Q_k(t_0) + a_k(t_0) = \sigma_k, \qquad k \in \mathcal{K}. \quad (27)$$

Let a busy period start at t_0, and extend to t. We first study the combined potential backlog of all sessions, $\sum_{j \in \mathcal{K}} \omega_j(t)$. According to (27), initially we have

$$\sum_{j \in \mathcal{K}} \omega_j(t_0) = \sum_{j \in \mathcal{K}} \sigma_j. \quad (28)$$

The total service provided to the sessions during (t_0, t), equals $C(t - t_0)$. Therefore, in view of (8)

$$\sum_{j \in \mathcal{K}} \omega_j(t_0, t) \leq \sum_{j \in \mathcal{K}} \rho_j(t - t_0) - \sum_{j \in \mathcal{K}} W_j(t_0, t)$$

$$= \sum_{j \in \mathcal{K}} \rho_j(t - t_0) - C(t - t_0)$$

$$= - \Big(C - \sum_{j \in \mathcal{K}} \rho_j \Big)(t - t_0) < 0 \quad (29)$$

where the last inequality follows from the stability condition (26). We conclude that, during the busy period, the combined potential backlog of sessions is cleared at a minimum rate of $C - \sum_{j \in \mathcal{K}} \rho_j$.

Does the potential backlog $\omega_k(t)$ of an individual session k also reduce, during a busy period? Intuitively, we expect from a fair queueing scheme to serve a backlogged session k at the minimum average rate

$$r_k \stackrel{\triangle}{=} \phi_k \cdot C \qquad (30)$$

or at a higher average rate, if some sessions are not backlogged. Assuming that the session service shares are chosen such that

$$r_k > \rho_k \qquad (31)$$

we expect that the potential backlog of session k decreases at a minimum clearing rate $r_k - \rho_k$, except for momentary fluctuations caused by the lack of perfect fairness in the packet-based queueing scheme. Following [11], we shall refer to (31) as the *local stability condition* for session k. In general, the service share allocations may not satisfy the local stability condition for all of the sessions. For a locally unstable session, the potential backlog can initially increase, during a busy period. However, (26) guarantees that some of the sessions are locally stable. Once the backlog of these sessions drop to zero, the service provided to other sessions will increase, ultimately bringing their backlogs down to zero.

We see from the above discussion that the evolution of a session's potential backlog is related, in general, to the backlogs of other sessions. The order at which the backlogs of different sessions are cleared, depends on the set of session service shares ϕ_k, and the average rates ρ_k. The essence of this dependency is best captured by the following definition, taken from [10].

Definition 4: Consider an ordering of sessions in $\mathcal{K}$, denoted by integers $1, 2, \cdots, K$. We call this ordering feasible if for any k, $k = 1, 2, \cdots, K$

$$\frac{\phi_k}{\sum_{j=k}^{K} \phi_j} \left(C - \sum_{j=1}^{k-1} \rho_j \right) > \rho_k \qquad (32)$$

where, by convention, $\sum_{j=1}^{0} \rho_j = 0$.

Definition 4 plays a key role in our study of fair queueing, as it does in the analysis of the GPS scheme in [10]. It is shown in [10] that, given the stability condition (26), at least one feasible ordering exists. One can easily verify from (30) and (31) that any locally stable session is the first session in some feasible ordering.

The following theorem provides a bound on the combined potential backlog of the first k sessions, $k = 1, \cdots, K$, in any feasible session ordering.

Theorem 1: Let $1, 2, \cdots, K$, be a feasible ordering of sessions. At any time t of a busy period

$$\sum_{j=1}^{k} \tilde{\omega}_j(t) \leq \sum_{j=1}^{k} \left(\sigma_j - \phi_j \cdot \tilde{\delta}_j^{(\text{init}) \min} \right), \qquad k = 1, \cdots, K$$

$$(33)$$

where

$$\tilde{\omega}_j(t) \stackrel{\triangle}{=} \omega_j(t) - \phi_j \cdot \tilde{\delta}_j(t), \qquad j = 1, \cdots, K. \qquad (34)$$

For the proof see Appendix A.

We noticed in Section III that $\phi_j \cdot \tilde{\delta}_j(t)$ is the overdue service to session j at time t, as measured against the index $\tilde{v}(t)$. Therefore, $\tilde{\omega}_j(t)$ may be interpreted as the potential backlog of session j, adjusted for the overdue service $\phi_j \cdot \tilde{\delta}_j(t)$. Theorem 1 shows that the combined adjusted potential backlog of the first k sessions, in any feasible ordering of sessions, is bounded by the combined burstiness of those sessions, minus the term $\sum_{j=1}^{k} \phi_j \cdot \tilde{\delta}_j^{(\text{init}) \min}$. This correcting term is due to the lack of perfect fairness, reflected in the nonzero values of $\tilde{\delta}_j(t)$. For the GPS scheme, which is the idealized form of fair queueing, $\tilde{\delta}_j^{(\text{init}) \min} = \tilde{\delta}_j(t) = 0$, and the correcting term disappears.

The bound in Theorem 1 is tight for $k = 1$, but is not tight for larger values of k. The tightness of the bound for $k = 1$, can be verified by inspecting Step 1 of the proof in Appendix A. To show that the bound is not tight in general, notice from (34) and (21), that

$$\sum_{j=1}^{K} \tilde{\omega}_j(t) = \sum_{j=1}^{K} \omega_j(t) - \sum_{j=1}^{K} \phi_j \cdot \tilde{\delta}_j(t) = \sum_{j=1}^{K} \omega_j(t) \leq \sum_{j=1}^{K} \sigma_j$$

where the last inequality follows from (28) and (29). This result is a tighter bound for $k = K$, compared to (33). However, as we next show, (33) cannot be significantly tightened. Let the system be at initial rest at t_0, and assume that a busy period starts at this time. Since $\omega_j(t)$ is a continuous function, we see from (27) that

$$\omega_j(t_0^+) = \omega_j(t_0) = \sigma_j, j = 1, \cdots, K.$$

Therefore, in view of (22)

$$\sum_{j=1}^{k} \tilde{\omega}_j(t_0^+) = \sum_{j=1}^{k} \omega_j(t_0^+) - \sum_{j=1}^{k} \phi_j \cdot \tilde{\delta}_j(t_0^+)$$

$$\geq \sum_{j=1}^{k} \sigma_j - \sum_{j=1}^{k} \phi_j \cdot \tilde{\delta}_j^{\max}, \qquad 1 \leq k \leq K.$$

We conclude that the bound in Theorem 1 cannot be tightened by more than $\sum_{j=1}^{k} \Delta_j$, where Δ_j is given in (24).

Next, consider the following lemma, which is established in Appendix A as an intermediate step in the proof of Theorem 1:

Lemma 4: For any subinterval (t_1, t_2) of a busy period and any nonempty subset $\mathcal{M}$ of $\mathcal{K}$

$$\tilde{v}(t_1, t_2) \geq \frac{1}{\sum_{j \in \mathcal{M}} \phi_j} \left[\left(C - \sum_{j \in \mathcal{M}^c} \rho_j \right) (t_2 - t_1) \right.$$

$$\left. + \sum_{j \in \mathcal{M}^c} \tilde{\omega}_j(t_1, t_2) \right] \qquad (35)$$

where $\mathcal{M}^c \stackrel{\triangle}{=} \mathcal{K} - \mathcal{M}$.

Lemma 4 provides a set of lower bounds on the progress of work in the queueing system, as expressed by the index $\tilde{v}(t)$. These bounds depend on the combined potential backlog of sessions in the sets $\mathcal{M}^c$. On the other hand, Theorem 1 provides an upper bound on the combined potential backlog of certain sets of sessions. In the following theorem, the above results are joined together to establish a set of lower bounds on the amount of service received by a backlogged session.

Theorem 2: Let $k \in B(t_1, t_2)$. Then

$$W_k(t_1, t_2) \geq \frac{\phi_k}{\sum_{j \in \mathcal{M}} \phi_j} \left[\left(C - \sum_{j \in \mathcal{M}^c} \rho_j \right)(t_2 - t_1) \right.$$
$$\left. - \sum_{j \in \mathcal{M}^c} (\sigma_j + \Delta_j) \right] - \phi_k \cdot \bar{\delta}_k(t_1, t_2)$$

for any set $\mathcal{M}$ that consists of the last m sessions, $1 \leq m \leq K$, in some feasible session ordering.

For the proof see Appendix A.

In the following section, Theorem 2 will be used to characterize the worst case session backlogs.

B. Worst Case Reference Model of a Fair Queueing System

In this section we will use a reference GPS model as the basis for characterizing the worst case performance of the fair queueing system S. This approach facilitates a concise treatment of the network problem in Section V, since the network performance of the GPS scheme has been previously studied [10], [11]. As the first step in this direction, let us apply Theorem 2 to a GPS server. Under the GPS scheme, $\Delta_k = \bar{\delta}_k(t) = 0, k \in \mathcal{K}$. Therefore

$$W_k^{GPS}(t_1, t_2) \geq \frac{\phi_k}{\sum_{j \in \mathcal{M}} \phi_j} \left[\left(C - \sum_{j \in \mathcal{M}^c} \rho_j \right)(t_2 - t_1) \right.$$
$$\left. - \sum_{j \in \mathcal{M}^c} \sigma_j \right] \quad (36)$$

where k is backlogged during (t_1, t_2), and $\mathcal{M}$ satisfies the condition given in Theorem 2.

Comparison of (36) and Theorem 2 suggests that we may be able to establish a link between the worst case performances of a GPS system and the more general fair queueing system S, by increasing the burstiness of sessions in the GPS system from σ_j to $\sigma_j + \Delta_j$. The following definition, borrowed from [10], helps us investigate this possibility by identifying a worst case scenario under which the lower bound in (36) is met.

Definition 5: A traffic stream $A(t)$ with the leaky-bucket characterization (σ, ρ), is called *greedy* starting at time t_1, if the bucket of permits associated with the stream is full at t_1, and the traffic arrives after t_1, as fast as possible, i.e.

$$A(t_1, t_2) = \sigma + \rho(t_2 - t_1), \quad \text{for all } t_2 > t_1. \quad (37)$$

Notice that, according to (37), $A(t_1, t_1^+) = \sigma$. Therefore, (37) implicitly requires that a full bucket of permits be available at t_1, i.e., $a(t_1) = \sigma$. Moreover, Definition 5 requires that $A(t)$ be continuous after the initial jump at t_1. Therefore, this definition is only relevant to continuous bit streams and is not applicable to a packet-oriented stream for which $A(t)$ has a staircase shape. We solely discuss the greedy traffic streams in the context of a GPS server where the continuous view of traffic is consistent with the server model.

Definition 6: Consider a fair queueing system S, based on the model articulated at the beginning of Section IV. The reference queueing system $\mathcal{R}$ is constructed from system S by

1) changing the queueing scheme to GPS,
2) increasing the burstiness of the arriving traffic of sessions to

$$\hat{\sigma}_k \stackrel{\triangle}{=} \sigma_k + \Delta_k, \quad k \in \mathcal{K} \quad (38)$$

and

3) assuming that the sessions are greedy, starting at $t = 0$.

The parameters ρ_k, ϕ_k, and C are the same for both systems. Where necessary, we use a hat sign over the variables associated with $\mathcal{R}$, to distinguish them from the variables of S. For example, $B(t_1, t_2)$ and $\hat{B}(t_1, t_2)$ respectively refer to the set of sessions that are backlogged in S and $\mathcal{R}$, during (t_1, t_2). Denote by $\hat{e}_k > 0$, $k = 1, 2, \cdots, K$, the time at which the backlog of session k in $\mathcal{R}$ reaches zero. Notice that the stability condition (26) also applies to $\mathcal{R}$ and guarantees that all session backlogs will eventually clear. Without loss of generality, assume that $\hat{e}_1 \leq \hat{e}_2 \cdots \leq \hat{e}_K$. The behavior of system $\mathcal{R}$ is summarized in the following lemma:

Lemma 5: In the reference system $\mathcal{R}$,

1) Once the backlog of a session reaches zero, it remains zero afterward.
2) The service $\hat{W}_k(0, \tau)$ received by each session k in $\mathcal{R}$ satisfies the following

$$\hat{W}_k(0, \tau) = \min [\phi_k \cdot \hat{v}(0, \tau), \hat{\sigma}_k + \rho_k \cdot \tau]$$
$$= \begin{cases} \phi_k \cdot \hat{v}(0, \tau), & 0 \leq \tau \leq \hat{e}_k \\ \hat{\sigma}_k + \rho_k \cdot \tau, & \tau \geq \hat{e}_k \end{cases} \quad (39)$$

where

$$\hat{v}(0, \tau) \stackrel{\triangle}{=} \frac{1}{\sum_{j \in \hat{B}'(0, \tau)} \phi_j} \left[\left(C - \sum_{j \notin \hat{B}'(0, \tau)} \rho_j \right) \tau \right.$$
$$\left. - \sum_{j \notin \hat{B}'(0, \tau)} \hat{\sigma}_j \right], \quad \tau \geq 0 \quad (40)$$

and $\hat{B}'(0, \tau) \stackrel{\triangle}{=} \hat{B}(0, \min(\tau, \hat{e}_K))$.

3) The order $k = 1, 2, \cdots, K$, in which session backlogs reach zero, is a feasible ordering.

The proof easily follows from the results established in [10]. A direct proof can also be constructed in the context of the present analysis, as outlined in Appendix B.

It can be shown that $\hat{v}(\tau)$ is a continuous, increasing, convex $\cup$, and piecewise linear function, with break points at $\tau = \hat{e}_k, k = 1, 2, \cdots, K-1$, [10]. During the busy period $(0, \hat{e}_K)$, $\hat{v}(\tau)$ is equal to the virtual time of $\mathcal{R}$, as defined in Definition 3. For notational convenience, in (40), we have extended the definition of $\hat{v}(\tau)$ beyond the busy period $(0, \hat{e}_K)$. This extension is such that, for $t \geq \hat{e}_K$, $\hat{v}(\tau)$ maintains the slope that it has during the interval $(\hat{e}_{K-1}, \hat{e}_K)$. Fig. 1 illustrates the relationship between the functions $\hat{W}_k(0, \tau)$, $\phi_k \cdot \hat{v}_k(0, \tau)$, and $\hat{\sigma}_k + \rho_k \cdot \tau$, for a simple case with $k = 2$, and $K = 3$.

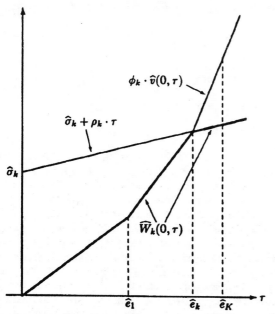

Fig. 1. Illustration of the functions $\widehat{W}_k(0,\tau)$, $\phi_k \cdot \hat{v}(0,\tau)$, and $\sigma_k + \rho_k \cdot \tau$, for the case of $K = 3$, and $k = 2$.

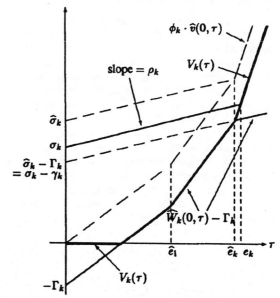

Fig. 2. Comparison of the reference service curve $V_k(\tau)$ with $\widehat{W}_k(0,\tau) - \Gamma_k$, in an example with $k = 2$, and $K = 3$.

The following theorem combines the results of Theorem 2 and Lemma 5 to compare the services received by a session in systems S and $\mathcal{R}$.

Theorem 3: Consider a session $k \in \mathcal{B}(t)$. Denote by τ_k, $\tau_k < t$, the most recent time that k has become backlogged in S. The service received by k in system S, during (τ_k, t), satisfies the following lower bounds

$$W_k(\tau_k, t) \geq \phi_k \cdot \hat{v}(0, t - \tau_k) - \Delta_k \geq \widehat{W}_k(0, t - \tau_k) - \Delta_k \quad (41)$$

and

$$W'_k(\tau_k, t) \geq V_k(t - \tau_k) \geq \widehat{W}_k(0, t - \tau_k) - \Gamma_k \quad (42)$$

where the *reference service curve* $V_k(\tau)$ is defined as

$$V_k(\tau) \triangleq \max[0, \phi_k \cdot \hat{v}(0, \tau) - \Gamma_k], \qquad \tau \geq 0 \quad (43)$$

$$\Gamma_k \triangleq \Delta_k + \gamma_k, \quad (44)$$

$$\gamma_k \triangleq \begin{cases} L_k^{\max}, & \text{in general,} \\ \phi_k \cdot L_k^{\max}, & \text{if } S \text{ is based on} \\ & \text{the SCFQ scheme.} \end{cases} \quad (45)$$

For the proof see Appendix B.

Theorem 3 provides two lower bounds on $W'_k(\tau_k, t)$, i.e., the departing packet stream of session k after τ_k. These bounds are expressed either in terms of the service $\widehat{W}_k(0,\tau)$ that k receives in the reference system $\mathcal{R}$, or in terms of the reference curve $V_k(\tau)$. As Fig. 2 illustrates, the latter bound is tighter during the intervals immediately after $\tau = 0$, and $\tau = \hat{e}_k$. Between these two intervals, the two bounds are identical. Notice in particular, that the line $\sigma_k + \rho_k \cdot \tau$, crosses $V_k(\tau)$ at $e_k > \hat{e}_k$, and that the duration of activity period of session k in S never exceeds e_k. Since k cannot remain backlogged in

S for longer than e_k seconds, the form of the above bounds after $\tau = e_k$ does not concern us.

Both of the above bounds are used in the rest of this paper. In the following lemma, we will use the bound expressed in terms of $\widehat{W}_k(0,\tau)$, to compare the maximum backlogs of a session in S and $\mathcal{R}$. As may be observed from Fig. 2, the backlog of k in either system is maximized at the intermediate values of τ, where the two bounds are identical. The tighter bound given in (42) will be used in section V-B, where we analyze a session's total backlog in a network of fair queueing servers.

Lemma 6: Let $\widehat{Q}_k^{\max}$ denote the maximum backlog of session k in $\mathcal{R}$. The bit-oriented and packet-oriented backlogs of k in system S always satisfy

$$Q_k(t) \leq \widehat{Q}_k^{\max}$$

and

$$Q'_k(t) \leq \widehat{Q}_k^{\max} + \mu_k \quad (46)$$

where

$$\mu_k \triangleq \min[\gamma_k, \frac{\rho_k}{C} L_k^{\max}]. \quad (47)$$

For the proof see Appendix B.

Using an argument similar to Lemma 2, we can conclude from (46) that

$$\omega'_k(t) \leq \widehat{Q}_k^{\max} + \mu_k.$$

Considering Lemma 1 and (12), we finally reach at the following important corollary:

Corollary 1: The departing *packet* stream $W'_k(t)$ of each session k in S is $(\widehat{Q}_k^{\max} + \mu_k, \rho_k)$-regular, where $\widehat{Q}_k^{\max}$ is the maximum backlog of session k in the reference system $\mathcal{R}$, and μ_k is given in (47).

V. NETWORK OF FAIR QUEUEING SERVERS WITH LEAKY-BUCKET TRAFFIC

In this section, we extend the analysis to a network of fair queueing servers. To summarize the model, consider a network $\mathcal{N}$ composed of a set of interconnected links and shared by a number of sessions. Each session is assigned a fixed route in the network. Denote by $\mathcal{L}, \mathcal{K}_\ell$, and $\mathcal{K}$ the set of links, the set of sessions sharing link ℓ, and the set of all sessions in the network, respectively. Denote by S_ℓ the queueing system at link ℓ. We use a superscript ℓ over the parameters associated with S_ℓ. Each queueing system S_ℓ is based on a fair queueing scheme of the class defined by Definition 3. In general, the service shares ϕ_k^ℓ, assigned to a session k at different links ℓ of its route, can be different. Assume that the packet stream of each session k, upon arrival to the first server in the network, is (σ_k, ρ_k)-regular. The following stability condition is assumed to apply to each queueing system S_ℓ

$$\sum_{j \in \mathcal{K}_\ell} \rho_j < C_\ell$$

where C_ℓ is the speed of link ℓ.

In Section V-A, we study the internal characterization of the traffic, based on the session leaky-bucket parameters at the edge of the network. The end-to-end session delays and backlogs will then be analyzed in Section V-B. In both sections, we use the worst case reference model developed earlier to exploit the similarities between a GPS network and the more general fair queueing network $\mathcal{N}$.

A. Internal Characterization of Network Traffic

Consider the traffic of a session k as it passes through the network. Denote by $A_k^\ell(t)$ the packet stream of k upon arrival to the queueing system of each link ℓ, along its route. Our goal is to find a leaky-bucket characterization (σ_k^ℓ, ρ_k) for $A_k^\ell(t)$, using the same average rate ρ_k at each hop. Let ℓ and ℓ' represent two successive links in the route of session k. Clearly

$$A_k^{\ell'}(t) = W_k^{\prime \ell}(t). \tag{48}$$

Consider the queueing system S_ℓ and assume that a leaky-bucket characterization (σ_j^ℓ, ρ_j) exists for the arriving traffic $A_j^\ell(t)$ of each session $j \in \mathcal{K}_\ell$. Denote by $\mathcal{R}_\ell$ the reference GPS queueing system associated with S_ℓ, as defined in Definition 6. Corollary 1 provides a leaky-bucket characterization for $W_k^{\prime \ell}(t)$ based on the maximum backlog of session k in the reference system $\mathcal{R}_\ell$. We conclude from (48) that $A_k^{\ell'}(t)$ is $(\sigma_k^{\ell'}, \rho_k)$-regular, with

$$\sigma_k^{\ell'} = \widehat{Q}_k^{\ell, \max} + \mu_k^\ell \tag{49}$$

where $\widehat{Q}_k^{\ell, \max}$ is the maximum backlog of session k in the reference system $\mathcal{R}_\ell$, and μ_k^ℓ is the parameter defined in (47), as applied to system S_ℓ. The maximum backlog $\widehat{Q}_k^{\ell, \max}$ can be determined in terms of the burstiness $\widehat{\sigma}_j^\ell$ of the arriving traffic of each session j to the reference system $\mathcal{R}_\ell$, as described

in [10]. Using the multi-variable function f to represent the dependency of $\widehat{Q}_k^{\ell, \max}$ on $\widehat{\sigma}_j^\ell, j \in \mathcal{K}_\ell$, we may write

$$\widehat{Q}_k^{\ell, \max} = f\{\widehat{\sigma}_j^\ell, j \in \mathcal{K}_\ell\}. \tag{50}$$

Since

$$\widehat{\sigma}_j^\ell = \sigma_j^\ell + \Delta_j^\ell, \qquad j \in \mathcal{K}_\ell$$

it follows from (49) and (50) that

$$\sigma_k^{\ell'} = \mu_k^\ell + f\{\sigma_j^\ell + \Delta_j^\ell, j \in \mathcal{K}_\ell\}. \tag{51}$$

In (51), ℓ' refers to the link following ℓ along the route of session k. The set of equations given in (51) for different k and ℓ, should be solved to determine $\sigma_k^\ell, k \in \mathcal{K}_\ell, \ell \in \mathcal{L}$, in terms of the initial burstiness parameters $\sigma_k, k \in \mathcal{K}$.

As (51) illustrates, the burstiness of a session k at the input of link ℓ' depends on the burstiness σ_j^ℓ of sessions passing through the preceding link ℓ. Each σ_j^ℓ in turn depends on the burstiness of other sessions at some other links, and so on. The simplest scenario for solving the equation set (51) is when there are no loops in the chain of dependencies among the parameters $\sigma_j^\ell, j \in \mathcal{K}_\ell, \ell \in \mathcal{L}$. In this case, the equations in (51), once properly arranged, can be successively solved by substituting the result of one equation into the next ones. In addition to simplicity, the existence of bounded results is guaranteed in this scenario.

For a GPS network, a condition called consistent relative session treatment (CRST) has been developed in [11], which ensures that no loop exists in the chain of dependencies among the burstiness of sessions at different links. This condition is based on the established property that, in the GPS system $\mathcal{R}_\ell$, $\widehat{Q}_k^{\ell, \max}$ does not depend on $\widehat{\sigma}_j^\ell$, for any session $j, j \neq k$, for which

$$\frac{\phi_j^\ell}{\rho_j} \leq \frac{\phi_k^\ell}{\rho_k}. \tag{52}$$

The CRST condition basically requires that there be some network-wide session ordering, such that if k is less than j, (52) is satisfied at any link ℓ traversed by both k and j. This condition guarantees that, in the equation set (51), the same session ordering can be followed to successively compute the internal burstiness of sessions.

While the above property has been shown in [11] for a GPS network, the same result would clearly apply to the more general fair queueing network $\mathcal{N}$. In solving the equation set (51), the only difference between $\mathcal{N}$ and a more specific GPS network is that the terms μ_k^ℓ and Δ_j^ℓ are zero for the GPS network. Neither the logical dependencies among the parameters σ_j^ℓ in (51), nor the CRST condition are affected by the values of μ_k^ℓ or Δ_j^ℓ, thereby the following theorem.

Theorem 4: Let the CRST condition apply to network $\mathcal{N}$, i.e., let there be a network-wide session ordering for which (52) holds for any link ℓ and any session pair k and j, $k < j$, that traverse ℓ. It follows that a leaky-bucket characterization (σ_k^ℓ, ρ_k) exists for any session k along its route. The parameters σ_k^ℓ can be sequentially computed from (51), following the same session ordering.

B. End-to-End Session Delays and Backlogs

Once the network internal burstiness parameters σ_k^ℓ are computed, the maximum backlog or delay of a session at each hop of its route may be determined, based on Lemma 6. The simplest bound on the total backlog or delay of a session emerges by adding up the session's maximum backlog or delay at individual links along its route. Such a bound, however, can be very loose since, in general, the session's backlog (delay) at different links cannot be maximized, simultaneously. For a network of GPS servers, tight bounds on the total backlog or delay of a session have been determined in [11], through an elaborate analysis. In this section, we extend that analysis to the more general fair queueing network $\mathcal{N}$. The basis of our analysis are the following equations, which respectively express the exchange of traffic between different queueing systems in $\mathcal{N}$, and the worst case behavior of each individual queueing system

$$A_k^{\ell'}(t) = W_k^{\prime\ell}(t), \qquad k \in \mathcal{K}_\ell, \quad \ell \in \mathcal{L},$$
$$W_k^{\prime\ell}(\tau_k^\ell, t) \geq V_k^\ell(t - \tau_k^\ell), \qquad k \in \mathcal{B}^\ell(t)$$

where ℓ' refers to the link following ℓ along the route of session k, τ_k^ℓ is the most recent time, prior to t, that k has become backlogged in S_ℓ, and $V_k^\ell(\tau)$ is the reference service curve associated with session k in S_ℓ, as defined in (43). In comparison, the following equations form the basis of the parallel analysis carried out in [11], for the GPS network

$$A_k^{\ell'}(t) = W_k^\ell(t), \qquad k \in \mathcal{K}_\ell, \quad \ell \in \mathcal{L},$$
$$W_k^\ell(\tau_k^\ell, t) \geq \hat{S}_k^\ell(0, t - \tau_k^\ell), \qquad k \in \mathcal{B}^\ell(t)$$

where $\hat{S}_k^\ell(0, t - \tau_k^\ell)$ is defined in [11] as the service that k receives in the GPS system of link ℓ, under greedy traffic arrivals. A careful inspection shows that, once the network internal burstiness parameters σ_k^ℓ are determined, the problems of finding bounds on the total session delays and backlogs, based on these two equation sets, are structurally identical. In particular, the function $V_k^\ell(\tau)$ shares all the properties of $\hat{S}_k^\ell(0, \tau)$ that have been used in [11] in order to characterize the worst case session delays and backlogs. Both functions pass through the origin and are continuous, nondecreasing, piecewise linear, and convex $\cup$, over the range of interest. The range of interest for each function extends from $\tau = 0$, to where the line $\sigma_k^\ell + \rho_k \cdot \tau$ is crossed. One difference between these two functions is that the slope of the first linear segment in $V_k^\ell(\tau)$ is zero (Fig. 2), whereas $\hat{S}_k^\ell(0, \tau)$ is always increasing. This difference, however, does not impact any of the results reached in [11]. We conclude that the analysis of GPS networks in [11] can be carried over to network $\mathcal{N}$, basically by replacing $W_k^\ell(t)$ with $W_k^{\prime\ell}(t)$, and $\hat{S}_k^\ell(0, \tau)$ with $V_k^\ell(\tau)$. The complexity of the analysis notwithstanding, this conversion is straightforward. Therefore, in the rest of this section, we only present the end results.

Let the internal burstiness parameters σ_j^ℓ, be determined for the network $\mathcal{N}$. Consider the reference queueing systems $\mathcal{R}_\ell$, and the reference service curve $V_k^\ell(\tau)$, associated with each queueing system S_ℓ in $\mathcal{N}$. Recall that the arriving traffic of each session j in $\mathcal{R}_\ell$ has the burstiness $\hat{\sigma}_j^\ell = \sigma_j^\ell + \Delta_j^\ell$.

Consider any session k and, without loss of generality, let it traverse links $\ell = 1, \cdots, H$. Denote by $Q_k^{\prime\max}$ the maximum end-to-end backlog of packets from session k, and by $D_k^{\prime\max}$ the maximum end-to-end delay of any packet from session k. In order to express bounds on $Q_k^{\prime\max}$ and $D_k^{\prime\max}$, we use a set of auxiliary piece-wise linear functions $J_k^\ell(t), \ell = 1, \cdots, H$, which parallel the functions $G_k^\ell(t)$ in [11]. We define these functions, along the route of session k, iteratively and based on the reference service curves $V_k^\ell(t)$

$$J_k^\ell(t) \triangleq \begin{cases} \widehat{W}_k^1(0, t), & \ell = 1 \\ \min_{\tau \in [0,t]}\{J_k^{\ell-1}(t) \\ \quad + V_k^\ell(0, t - \tau)\}, & t - \tau \leq e_k^\ell, \quad \ell = 2, \cdots, H. \end{cases}$$

See [11] for a better description of these functions and a simple algorithm to construct them. The following result parallels Theorem 3 in [11].

Theorem 5: For any session k in $\mathcal{N}$

$$Q_k^{\prime\max} \leq \max_{\tau \geq 0}\{\sigma_k + \rho_k \cdot \tau - J_k^H(\tau)\} \tag{53}$$

and

$$D_k^{\prime\max} \leq \max_{\tau \geq 0}\left\{\min\{t : J_k^H(t) = \sigma_k + \rho_k \cdot \tau\} - \tau\right\}. \tag{54}$$

VI. SPECIAL CASES

In this section, we evaluate the results of this paper for two cases of special interest: locally stable sessions and the SCFQ scheme. After discussing these cases, we will compare the performance of the PGPS and the SCFQ schemes, for a locally stable session.

A. Locally Stable Sessions

A session k is called *locally stable* in the network $\mathcal{N}$, if it is locally stable at each link along its route, i.e., if

$$r_k^\ell = \phi_k^\ell \cdot C_\ell > \rho_k \tag{55}$$

for each link ℓ traversed by k. Define the *minimum expected service rate* of session k as

$$r_k \triangleq \min r_k^\ell \tag{56}$$

with the minimization taken over the links ℓ traversed by k. Clearly, r_k is the *fair* share of service to k at the bottleneck of its route, when all of the competing sessions are backlogged, hence the name minimum expected service rate. It follows from (56) that for a locally stable session k, $r_k > \rho_k$.

In studying the performance of a locally stable session k, we let the burstiness parameters of all other sessions be arbitrarily large. Obviously, this assumption can only lead to an increase in the worst case delay and backlog of k. Consider the reference system $\mathcal{R}_\ell$ of any link ℓ, along the route of k. Since the burstiness of all other sessions in $\mathcal{R}_\ell$ are assumed to be arbitrarily large, k will be the first session to clear its backlog, once the greedy regime of operation starts. Therefore, the first breakpoint in the function $\phi_k^\ell \cdot \hat{v}^\ell(0, \tau)$, corresponds to the time that k seizes to be backlogged in $\mathcal{R}_\ell$. It should be clear that the slope of the first segment of $\phi_k^\ell \cdot \hat{v}^\ell(0, \tau)$ is equal to r_k^ℓ. Therefore, the reference service curve $V_k^\ell(\tau)$

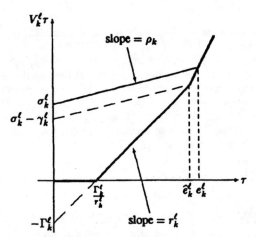

Fig. 3.   The reference service curve $V_k^\ell(\tau)$ for a locally stable session k at link ℓ, assuming arbitrarily large burstiness for other sessions. Notice that, in general, $\sigma_k \leq \sigma_k^\ell$.

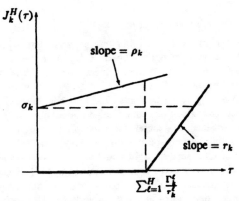

Fig. 4.   Illustration of $J_k^H(\tau)$, and $\sigma_k + \rho_k \cdot \tau$, for a locally stable session. The bounds on the backlog and delay of session k respectively correspond to the maximum vertical and horizontal distances between these two curves.

has the form illustrated in Fig. 3. Finally, using the reference curves $V_k^\ell(\tau), \ell = 1, \cdots, H$, and the algorithm described in [11], $J_k^H(\tau)$ can be constructed. Fig. 4 illustrates the first two linear segments of $J_k^H(\tau)$ that are needed to carry out the optimizations in (53) and (54). Notice that the slope of $J_k^H(\tau)$, after these two segments, may only increase [11]. Therefore, as a careful inspection of Fig. 4 reveals, the maximizations in (53) and (54) are respectively achieved at $\tau = \sum_{\ell=1}^H \Gamma_k^\ell / r_k^\ell$, and $\tau = 0^+$, thereby the following theorem:

Theorem 6:   Consider a network of fair queueing servers of the class defined in Definition 3. Let session k conform to (σ_k, ρ_k), and assume that it is locally stable, i.e., $r_k > \rho_k$, where r_k is given by (56) and (55). Then, regardless of traffic characteristics of other sessions, the total backlog and delay of session k satisfy the following bounds

$$Q_k'^{\max} \leq \sigma_k + \rho_k \cdot \sum_{\ell=1}^H d_k^\ell \qquad (57)$$

and

$$D_k'^{\max} \leq \frac{\sigma_k}{r_k} + \sum_{\ell=1}^H d_k^\ell \qquad (58)$$

where

$$d_k^\ell \triangleq \frac{\Gamma_k^\ell}{r_k^\ell}. \qquad (59)$$

Notice that the bound on the end-to-end delay of session k consists of the term σ_k/r_k, which depends on the session's burstiness, and the terms d_k^ℓ, each corresponding to one link of the route. To evaluate the above bounds for a GPS network, first we recall from Section III that for a GPS server, $\Delta_k^\ell = 0$. Next, we argue that since a GPS network is based on the fluid flow model of traffic, for the purpose of computing delays and backlogs, we may assume that $L^{\max} = 0$. It follows that $\Gamma_k = \Delta_k + L_k^{\max} = 0$. Therefore, for a locally stable session in a network of GPS servers, (57) and (58) hold with $d_k^\ell = 0$, as previously established in [11].

In Theorem 6, no requirement has been placed on the arriving traffic of sessions other than k. In fact the assumption of arbitrarily large burstiness that we made for sessions $j \neq k$, is practically equivalent to relaxing all restrictions on these sessions. The reason is that, during a bounded interval of time, any bounded stream $A(t)$ is (σ, ρ)-regular for an arbitrary ρ and sufficiently large σ.

B. Locally Stable Sessions in a Network of SCFQ Servers

The impact of any particular fair queueing scheme on the internal characterization of traffic and the performance bounds derived in this paper, appears through the parameters Γ_k^ℓ. For the SCFQ scheme, from (25), (44), and (45) we get

$$\Gamma_k^\ell = L_k^{\max} + \phi_k^\ell \sum_{j \in \mathcal{K}_\ell, \ j \neq k} L_j^{\max}, \qquad \ell \in \mathcal{L}, \quad k \in \mathcal{K}_\ell.$$

Therefore, the backlog and delay of a locally stable session in a network of SCFQ servers obey the bounds of Theorem 6 with

$$d_k^\ell = \frac{L_k^{\max}}{r_k^\ell} + \frac{1}{C_\ell} \sum_{j \in \mathcal{K}_\ell, \ j \neq k} L_j^{\max}, \qquad \ell \in \mathcal{L}, \quad k \in \mathcal{K}_\ell. \qquad (60)$$

We see that d_k^ℓ, or the contribution of link ℓ of the session's route to the delay bound is composed of two terms. The first term equals the transmission time of a maximum-sized packet from k, by a server with the rate r_k^ℓ. The second term in d_k^ℓ equals the time needed to transmit one maximum-sized packet from each other session, at the link speed C_ℓ. The relative significance of these two components of d_k^ℓ depend on the number of sessions sharing link ℓ, as well as the session share $\phi_k^\ell = r_k^\ell / C_\ell$. As the session share gets larger, or the number of competing sessions increases, the second component tends to dominate d_k^ℓ.

We believe that for a locally stable session in a network of SCFQ servers, the backlog bound given by (57) and (60) is tight, but it should be possible to tighten the delay bound expressed by (58) and (60), by the amount $L_k^{\max}/r_k$ [5].

C. Comparison of the PGPS and the SCFQ Schemes

We compare the worst case delay performance of the SCFQ and the PGPS schemes for a locally stable session. Based on the analysis in [11], the following delay bound applies to a locally stable session k in a network of PGPS servers[2]

$$\mathbf{D}_k'^{\max} \leq \frac{1}{r_k}(\sigma_k - L_k^{\max}) + \sum_{\ell=1}^{H} d_k^\ell \qquad (61)$$

where

$$d_k^\ell = \frac{L_k^{\max}}{r_k} + \frac{1}{C_\ell}L^{\max}$$

and $L^{\max}$ is the maximum packet size in the network. The first term in this bound is almost equal to the corresponding term σ_k/r_k in (58). However, the terms d_k^ℓ in the delay bound of the PGPS scheme are smaller compared to the corresponding terms for the SCFQ scheme.

We now consider a numerical example. Consider an ATM link ℓ with the transmission speed $C_\ell \approx 150$ Mb/s. The atomic unit of data in ATM is a cell with the fixed length $L = 424$ b. The transmission time of a cell at the above speed is about 2.83μs. Let the number of sessions sharing the link be $K = 37$. Assume that link ℓ is the bottleneck on the route of a session k with $\rho_k < r_k = r_k^\ell = 1.5$ Mb/s. The contribution of link ℓ to the worst case delay of session k is $d_k^\ell \approx 385\mu$s under the SCFQ scheme, and $d_k^\ell \approx 285\mu$s under the PGPS scheme. In comparison, for a session k with $\rho_k < r_k = r_k^\ell = 30$ Mb/s, we would have $d_k^\ell \approx 120\mu$s under the SCFQ scheme, and $d_k^\ell \approx 20\mu$s under the PGPS scheme. For both sessions, the per-link difference between the maximum delays of the SCFQ and the PGPS schemes is about 100μs. This difference would have been 1 ms, if either the number of sessions using the link was $K = 360$, or the packet size was $L = 4200$ b, or if the link speed was $C_\ell = 15$ Mb/s.

VII. CONCLUSION

In this paper, a class of fair queueing schemes was defined using a virtual-time representation of work progress in the queueing system. Based on this definition, the worst case performance of a network of fair queueing servers with leaky-bucket traffic was studied and the end-to-end session delays and backlogs were shown to be bounded, under moderate resource allocation conditions. As a special case, a network of self-clocked fair queueing (SCFQ) servers was considered, and the end-to-end delay bound for a locally stable session was determined. Compared to a network of PGPS servers [11], the session delay bounds associated with the SCFQ scheme are larger, abut the difference is typically insignificant.

While in this paper, we have discussed fair queueing in the context of achieving fairness among individual sessions, the more pragmatic approach is to apply fair queueing among several classes of sessions, as proposed by Clark, et al. [1]. In this approach, sessions are grouped into different

classes based on the compatibility of their traffic characteristics and performance requirements. With such an architecture in mind, the term "session" in this paper should be replaced by "session class." Accordingly, in the example considered in Section VI-C, K should be interpreted as the number of session classes sharing a given link. While the number of sessions sharing a broadband transmission link can be very large, the number of session classes needed for effective application of fair queueing is much smaller. As noticed earlier, with a small K, the difference between the worst case performance of the PGPS and the SCFQ schemes diminishes.

In the numerical example of Section VI-C, only locally stable sessions were considered. Obviously, the maximum end-to-end delays will be larger if a session (or session class) is not locally stable. However, in case of a delay-sensitive session (or session class), it is only natural to make the session (session class) locally stable by allocating to it sufficient service shares at different links of the route.

Given the simplicity and the fairness property of the SCFQ scheme [6], [5] and its network delay properties, we think that this scheme is well-suited for implementation in broadband multi-media networks. A more complex version of fair queueing, such as the PGPS scheme, might be justifiable where delay-sensitive traffic is transmitted in a network with slow transmission speeds or large packet sizes, or where service shares are assigned to a very large number of competing entities.

APPENDIX A

We prove Theorem 1 after establishing Lemma 4 and two more intermediate results.

Proof of Lemma 4: Let $\mathcal{M}$ be any nonempty subset of $\mathcal{K}$. Since the queueing system is work conserving and (t_1, t_2) is contained in a busy period

$$\begin{aligned}
C(t_2 - t_1) &= \sum_{j\in\mathcal{K}} W_j(t_1, t_2) \\
&= \sum_{j\in\mathcal{M}} W_j(t_1, t_2) + \sum_{j\in\mathcal{M}^c} W_j(t_1, t_2) \\
&\leq \sum_{j\in\mathcal{M}} \phi_j[\tilde{v}(t_1, t_2) - \tilde{\delta}_j(t_1, t_2)] \\
&\quad + \sum_{j\in\mathcal{M}^c} [\rho_j(t_2 - t_1) - \omega_j(t_1, t_2)]
\end{aligned}$$

where the inequality follows from (19) and (8). It follows that

$$\tilde{v}(t_1, t_2) \geq \frac{1}{\sum_{j\in\mathcal{M}}\phi_j}\left[\left(C - \sum_{j\in\mathcal{M}^c}\rho_j\right)(t_2 - t_1) + \sum_{j\in\mathcal{M}^c}\omega_j(t_1, t_2) + \sum_{j\in\mathcal{M}}\phi_j\cdot\tilde{\delta}_j(t_1, t_2)\right].$$

According to (34)

$$\omega_k(t_1, t_2) = \tilde{\omega}_k(t_1, t_2) + \phi_k\cdot\tilde{\delta}_k(t_1, t_2), \qquad k\in\mathcal{K}.$$

[2] The delay bound in (61) is tighter compared to (39) in [11]. We think that the factor 2 in (37)–(39) of [11] is not necessary.

Therefore

$$\tilde{v}(t_1, t_2)$$

$$\geq \frac{1}{\sum_{j \in \mathcal{M}} \phi_j} \left[\left(C - \sum_{j \in \mathcal{M}^c} \rho_j \right)(t_2 - t_1) + \sum_{j \in \mathcal{M}^c} \tilde{\omega}_j(t_1, t_2) \right.$$
$$\left. + \sum_{j \in \mathcal{M}^c} \phi_j \cdot \tilde{\delta}_j(t_1, t_2) + \sum_{j \in \mathcal{M}} \phi_j \cdot \tilde{\delta}_j(t_1, t_2) \right]. \quad (62)$$

In view of (21), the last two sums in (62) add up to zero, verifying the lemma. □

Now, let $1, 2, \cdots, K$, be any feasible ordering of sessions in $\mathcal{K}$. Choose an arbitrary session k and consider Lemma 4 for $\mathcal{M} = \{k, \cdots, K\}$. Since $\mathcal{M}^c = \{1, \cdots, k-1\}$, we get the following corollary by combining (35) and (32):

Corollary 2: Let $1, 2, \cdots, K$ be a feasible ordering of sessions. Then for any session k

$$\tilde{v}(t_1, t_2) > \frac{\rho_k}{\phi_k}(t_2 - t_1) + \frac{1}{\sum_{j=k}^{K} \phi_j} \sum_{j=1}^{k-1} \tilde{\omega}_j(t_1, t_2).$$

Lemma 7: Let $1, 2, \cdots, K$, be a feasible ordering of sessions. For any $k \in \mathcal{B}(t_1, t_2)$, we have

$$\tilde{\omega}_k(t_1, t_2) < \frac{-\phi_k}{\sum_{j=k}^{K} \phi_j} \sum_{j=1}^{k-1} \tilde{\omega}_j(t_1, t_2).$$

Proof: From (34) and (8), we have

$$\tilde{\omega}_k(t_1, t_2) = \omega_k(t_1, t_2) - \phi_k \cdot \tilde{\delta}_k(t_1, t_2)$$
$$\leq \rho_k(t_2 - t_1) - \left[W_k(t_1, t_2) + \phi_k \cdot \tilde{\delta}_k(t_1, t_2) \right].$$

Since $k \in \mathcal{B}(t_1, t_2)$, (19) holds with equality. Therefore

$$\tilde{\omega}_k(t_1, t_2) \leq \rho_k(t_2 - t_1) - \phi_k \cdot \tilde{v}(t_1, t_2). \quad (63)$$

The lemma follows from (63) and Corollary 2. □

Proof of Theorem 1: Consider any fixed time t in a busy period. For each session k, define τ_k, $\tau_k \leq t$, as the most recent time for which $Q_k(\tau_k) = 0$. It follows from this definition that either k is not backlogged at t and $\tau_k = t$, or k is backlogged during (τ_k, t). Furthermore, since $\omega_k(\tau_k) = a_k(\tau_k)$, we conclude from (4) and (23), that

$$\tilde{\omega}_k(t) = \tilde{\omega}_k(\tau_k, t) + \tilde{\omega}_k(\tau_k)$$
$$= \tilde{\omega}_k(\tau_k, t) + a_k(\tau_k) - \phi_k \cdot \tilde{\delta}_k(\tau_k)$$
$$\leq \tilde{\omega}_k(\tau_k, t) + \sigma_k - \phi_k \cdot \tilde{\delta}_k^{(\text{init}) \min},$$
$$k = 1, \cdots, K. \quad (64)$$

We now apply induction on k to prove the theorem.

Step 1: First, we show that

$$\tilde{\omega}_1(\tau_1, t) \leq 0. \quad (65)$$

If $\tau_1 = t$, (65) follows with equality. Otherwise, session 1 is backlogged during (τ_1, t), in which case (65) follows from Lemma 7. Next, we apply (64) to $k = 1$, and use (65) to get

$$\tilde{\omega}_1(t) \leq \sigma_1 - \phi_1 \cdot \tilde{\delta}_1^{(\text{init}) \min}$$

verifying the theorem for $k = 1$.

Step 2: Assume that the theorem is valid for $k = \ell - 1$, i.e.

$$\sum_{j=1}^{\ell-1} \tilde{\omega}_j(t) \leq \sum_{j=1}^{\ell-1} (\sigma_j - \phi_j \cdot \tilde{\delta}_j^{(\text{init}) \min}). \quad (66)$$

To show the validity of the theorem for $k = \ell$, we consider two cases:

Case a: Assume that session ℓ is not backlogged at t. In this case, by definition, $\tau_\ell = t$. Therefore, $\tilde{\omega}_\ell(\tau_\ell, t) = 0$, and according to (64)

$$\tilde{\omega}_\ell(t) \leq \sigma_\ell - \phi_\ell \cdot \tilde{\delta}_\ell^{(\text{init}) \min}. \quad (67)$$

Adding (67) to (66), we get (33) for $k = \ell$.

Case b: Assume that session ℓ is backlogged at t. It follows that $\tau_\ell < t$, and ℓ is backlogged during (τ_ℓ, t). Apply Lemma 7 to session $k = \ell$ and the interval (τ_ℓ, t), to get

$$\tilde{\omega}_\ell(\tau_\ell, t) < \frac{-\phi_\ell}{\sum_{j=\ell}^{K} \phi_j} \sum_{j=1}^{\ell-1} \tilde{\omega}_j(\tau_\ell, t). \quad (68)$$

By adding the sum $\sum_{j=1}^{\ell-1} \tilde{\omega}_j(\tau_\ell, t)$ to both sides of (68), we get

$$\sum_{j=1}^{\ell} \tilde{\omega}_j(\tau_\ell, t) < \left(1 - \frac{\phi_\ell}{\sum_{j=\ell}^{K} \phi_j} \right) \sum_{j=1}^{\ell-1} \tilde{\omega}_j(\tau_\ell, t). \quad (69)$$

Now, there are two possibilities regarding the sign of the sum $\sum_{j=1}^{\ell-1} \tilde{\omega}_j(\tau_\ell, t)$, which appears on the right hand side of both (68) and (69). First, we assume $\sum_{j=1}^{\ell-1} \tilde{\omega}_j(\tau_\ell, t) \leq 0$. It then follows from (69) that

$$\sum_{j=1}^{\ell} \tilde{\omega}_j(\tau_\ell, t) < 0. \quad (70)$$

Since ℓ is not backlogged at τ_ℓ, according to Case a, (33) is valid for $k = \ell$ and time τ_ℓ. Therefore, it follows from (70) that

$$\sum_{j=1}^{\ell} \tilde{\omega}_j(t) = \sum_{j=1}^{\ell} \tilde{\omega}_j(\tau_\ell) + \sum_{j=1}^{\ell} \tilde{\omega}_j(\tau_\ell, t)$$
$$< \sum_{j=1}^{\ell} \tilde{\omega}_j(\tau_\ell) \leq \sum_{j=1}^{\ell} (\sigma_j - \phi_j \cdot \tilde{\delta}_j^{(\text{init}) \min})$$

establishing (33) for $k = \ell$ and time t.

Next, assume that $\sum_{j=1}^{\ell-1} \tilde{\omega}_j(\tau_\ell, t) \geq 0$. It follows from (68) that

$$\tilde{\omega}_\ell(\tau_\ell, t) < 0. \quad (71)$$

We now conclude (67) from (71) and (64). Finally, by adding (67) to (66), we get (33) for $k = \ell$. This completes the proof of Step 2. The theorem follows by induction from Steps 1 and 2. □

Proof of Theorem 2: Let the set $\mathcal{M}$ in Lemma 4 consist of the last m sessions, $1 \leq m \leq K$, in some feasible ordering of sessions. It follows that $\mathcal{M}^c$ consists of the first $K - m$ sessions in that ordering. Applying Theorem 1 to the sessions in $\mathcal{M}^c$, we conclude that for any time t

$$\sum_{j \in \mathcal{M}^c} \tilde{\omega}_j(t) \leq \sum_{j \in \mathcal{M}^c} (\sigma_j - \phi_j \cdot \tilde{\delta}_j^{(\text{init}) \min}). \quad (72)$$

On the other hand, since $\omega_j(t)$ is nonnegative, for any time t we have

$$\tilde{\omega}_j(t) = \omega_j(t) - \phi_j \cdot \tilde{\delta}_j(t) \geq -\phi_j \cdot \tilde{\delta}_j^{\max}, \qquad j = 1, \cdots, K. \quad (73)$$

We conclude from (72) and (73) that

$$\sum_{j \in \mathcal{M}^c} \tilde{\omega}_j(t_1, t_2)$$
$$= \sum_{j \in \mathcal{M}^c} \tilde{\omega}_j(t_2) - \sum_{j \in \mathcal{M}^c} \tilde{\omega}_j(t_1)$$
$$\geq - \sum_{j \in \mathcal{M}^c} \phi_j \cdot \tilde{\delta}_j^{\max} - \sum_{j \in \mathcal{M}^c} (\sigma_j - \phi_j \cdot \tilde{\delta}_j^{(\text{init}) \min})$$
$$= - \sum_{j \in \mathcal{M}^c} (\sigma_j + \Delta_j). \quad (74)$$

Combining (74) and Lemma 4, we get the following important lower bound on $\tilde{v}(t_1, t_2)$

$$\tilde{v}(t_1, t_2) \geq \frac{1}{\sum_{j \in \mathcal{M}} \phi_j} \left[\left(C - \sum_{j \in \mathcal{M}^c} \rho_j \right) (t_2 - t_1) \right.$$
$$\left. - \sum_{j \in \mathcal{M}^c} (\sigma_j + \Delta_j) \right].$$

The theorem follows, since $k \in \mathcal{B}(t_1, t_2)$, and (19) holds with equality. $\square$

APPENDIX B

Proof of Lemma 5: The first property follows from the stability condition (26) and the fact that, with greedy sessions, no traffic burst can arrive after $\tau = 0$. For the GPS system $\mathcal{R}$, we have $\hat{\delta}_k(\tau) = 0$. Since $k \in \hat{\mathcal{B}}(\tau)$, for $0 \leq \tau < \hat{e}_k$, it follows from (16) that $\widehat{W}_k(0, \tau) = \phi_k \cdot \hat{v}(0, \tau)$. The second part of (39) follows from (6) and (37), since $\widehat{Q}_k(\tau) = 0$, for $\tau \geq \hat{e}_k$. The third property can be shown by first arguing that in a GPS system, for a greedy session k, (8) holds with equality; then showing that for $\mathcal{M} \triangleq \mathcal{B}(t_1, t_2)$, Lemma 4 and, subsequently, Theorem 2 hold with equality. $\square$

Proof of Theorem 3: We begin by proving (41). According to Lemma 5

$$\widehat{W}_k(0, t - \tau_k) \leq \phi_k \cdot \hat{v}(0, t - \tau_k). \quad (75)$$

Using (40), $\hat{v}(0, t - \tau_k)$ can be expressed in terms of the set $\hat{\mathcal{B}}'(0, t - \tau_k)$. Note that, according to part 3 of Lemma 5, $\hat{\mathcal{B}}'(0, t - \tau_k)$ consists of the last m sessions, $1 \leq m \leq K$, in a feasible session ordering. Therefore, $\hat{\mathcal{B}}'(0, t - \tau_k)$ satisfies the requirements for the set $\mathcal{M}$ in Theorem 2. Since by assumption, $k \in \mathcal{B}(\tau_k, t)$, we can apply Theorem 2 to the interval (τ_k, t) and the set $\mathcal{M} = \hat{\mathcal{B}}'(0, t - \tau_k)$. The result, after considering (38) and (40), simplifies to

$$W_k(\tau_k, t) \geq \phi_k \cdot \hat{v}(0, t - \tau_k) - \phi_k \cdot \tilde{\delta}_k(\tau_k, t). \quad (76)$$

On the other hand, from (22)–(24) we have

$$\phi_k \cdot \tilde{\delta}_k(\tau_k, t) = \phi_k \cdot \tilde{\delta}_k(t) - \phi_k \cdot \tilde{\delta}_k(\tau_k)$$
$$\leq \phi_k \left(\tilde{\delta}_k^{\max} - \tilde{\delta}_k^{(\text{init}) \min} \right) = \Delta_k \quad (77)$$

where the inequality follows since k becomes backlogged at τ_k. Finally, we obtain (41) by combining (75)–(77).

To show (42), denote by $\epsilon_k(t)$ the length of the transmitted portion of the packet from session k that receives service at t. If no packet from k is served at t, let $\epsilon_k(t) = 0$. It follows that

$$W_k'(t) = W_k(t) - \epsilon_k(t).$$

Noting that $\epsilon_k(\tau_k) = 0$, it follows from (76) that

$$W_k'(\tau_k, t) \geq \phi_k \cdot \hat{v}(0, t - \tau_k) - \phi_k \cdot \tilde{\delta}_k(\tau_k, t) - \epsilon_k(t). \quad (78)$$

Since $W_k'(\tau_k, t) \geq 0$, we can also write

$$W_k'(\tau_k, t) \geq \max[0, \phi_k \cdot \hat{v}(0, t - \tau_k) - \phi_k \cdot \tilde{\delta}_k(\tau_k, t) - \epsilon_k(t)].$$

In general, $\epsilon_k(t) \leq L_k^{\max}$. Therefore, in view of (77) and (75), (42)–(44) follow with $\gamma_k = L_k^{\max}$.

Next we show that, for the special case of the SCFQ scheme, γ_k can be set to $\phi_k \cdot L_k^{\max}$. First, notice that if no packet from k is receiving service at t, then by definition $\epsilon_k(t) = 0$, and (42)–(44) follow for any $\gamma_k \geq 0$. So, assume that some packet p of session k receives service at t, and let t' denote the beginning of transmission of p. Since no new packet starts service during (t', t), it follows from the SCFQ definition [6], [5] that $v(t'^+, t) = 0$. On the other hand, by definition, $\epsilon_k(t') = 0$, and $\epsilon_k(t)$ equals the service given to k during (t', t). Therefore, using the results in [6], [5]

$$\delta_k(t'^+, t) = -v_k(t'^+, t) = -\frac{1}{\phi_k} \epsilon_k(t)$$

and

$$\delta_j(t'^+, t) = -v_j(t'^+, t) = 0, \qquad j \in \mathcal{K}, j \neq k$$

where $v_j(t)$ is the *virtual time of session j*, as defined in [6], [5]. We conclude that

$$\tilde{\delta}_k(t'^+, t) = \delta_k(t'^+, t) - \delta(t'^+, t)$$
$$= \delta_k(t'^+, t) - \sum_{j \in \mathcal{K}} \phi_j \cdot \delta_j(t'^+, t) = (1 - \frac{1}{\phi_k}) \epsilon_k(t).$$

Therefore, since $\epsilon_k(t) \leq L_k^{\max}$

$$\phi_k \cdot \tilde{\delta}_k(\tau_k, t) + \epsilon_k(t)$$
$$= \phi_k \cdot \tilde{\delta}_k(\tau_k, t'^+) + \phi_k \cdot \tilde{\delta}_k(t'^+, t) + \epsilon_k(t) \quad (79)$$
$$= \phi_k \cdot \tilde{\delta}_k(\tau_k, t'^+) + \phi_k \cdot \epsilon_k(t)$$
$$\leq \Delta_k + \phi_k \cdot L_k^{\max}$$

where the inequality follows from (77), as applied to time t'^+ instead of t. Combining (75), (78), and (79), we obtain (42)–(44) with $\gamma_k = \phi_k \cdot L_k^{\max}$. $\square$

Proof of Lemma 6: Let session k be backlogged in S at time t. Denote by τ_k, $\tau_k \leq t$, the most recent time for which $Q_k(\tau_k) = 0$. It follows that

$$Q_k(t) = Q_k(\tau_k, t)$$
$$= A_k(\tau_k, t) - W_k(\tau_k, t)$$
$$\leq \sigma_k + \rho_k(t - \tau_k) - W_k(\tau_k, t).$$

Since sessions in $\mathcal{R}$ are greedy from time zero

$$\widehat{Q}_k(t - \tau_k) \geq \widehat{Q}_k(0, t - \tau_k) = \widehat{A}_k(0, t - \tau_k) - \widehat{W}_k(0, t - \tau_k)$$
$$= \widehat{\sigma}_k + \rho_k(t - \tau_k) - \widehat{W}_k(0, t - \tau_k).$$

It follows that

$$Q_k(t) - \widehat{Q}_k(t - \tau_k) \leq \sigma_k - \widehat{\sigma}_k + \widehat{W}_k(0, t - \tau_k) - W_k(\tau_k, t) \leq 0$$

where the last inequality follows from (38) and (41), knowing that $k \in \mathcal{B}(\tau_k, t)$. We conclude that

$$Q_k(t) \leq \widehat{Q}_k(t - \tau_k) \leq \widehat{Q}_k^{\max} \tag{80}$$

establishing the first part of the lemma.

Similarly, using (11) and (42), we can conclude that

$$Q_k'(t) \leq \widehat{Q}_k(t - \tau_k) + \gamma_k \leq \widehat{Q}_k^{\max} + \gamma_k.$$

On the other hand, from Lemma 3 and (80) we get

$$Q_k'(t) \leq \widehat{Q}_k^{\max} + \frac{\rho_k}{C} L_k^{\max}. \tag{81}$$

Finally, (46) follows from the last two inequalities. □

REFERENCES

[1] D. D. Clark, S. Shenker, and L. Zhang. "Supporting real-time applications in an integrated services packet network: Architecture and mechanism," in *Proc. ACM SIGCOMM Symp.*, 1992, pp. 14–26.
[2] R. L. Cruz, "A calculus for network delay, pt. I: Network elements in isolation," *IEEE Trans. Inform. Theory*, vol. 37, no. 1, pp. 114–131, Jan. 1991.
[3] ———, "A calculus for network delay, pt. II: Network analysis," *IEEE Trans. Inform. Theory*, vol. 37, no. 1, pp. 132–141, Jan. 1991.
[4] A. Demers, S. Keshav, and S. Shenkar, "Analysis and simulation of a fair queueing algorithm," in *Proc. SIGCOMM'89*, Austin, TX, Sept. 1989, pp. 1–12.
[5] S. J. Golestani, "A self-clocked fair queueing scheme for high speed applications," submitted for publication to the *ACM/IEEE Trans. Networking.*
[6] ———, "A self-clocked fair queueing scheme for broadband applications, in *Proc. IEEE INFOCOM*, 1994, pp. 636–646.
[7] A. G. Greenberg and N. Madras, "How fair is fair queueing?," *J. Assoc. Computing Machinary*, vol. 39, no. 3, pp. 568–598, July 1992.
[8] A. T. Heybey and J. R. Davin, "A simulation study of fair queueing and policy enforcement," *ACM Comput. Commun. Rev.*, vol. 20, no. 5, Oct. 1990.
[9] E. L. Hahne, "Round-robin scheduling for max-min fairness in data networks," *IEEE J. Select. Areas Commun.*, vol. 9, no. 7, pp. 1024–1039, Sept. 1991.
[10] A. K. Parekh and R. G. Gallager, "A generalized processor sharing approach to flow control in integrated services networks: The single node case," *ACM/IEEE Trans. Networking*, vol. 1, no. 3, pp. 344–357, June 1993.
[11] ———, "A generalized processor sharing approach to flow control in integrated services networks: The multiple node case," *ACM/IEEE Trans. Networking*, vol. 2, no. 2, pp. 137–150, Apr. 1994.
[12] J. S. Turner, "New directions in communications or which way to the information age," *IEEE Commun. Mag.*, vol. 24, no. 10, pp. 8–15, Oct. 1986.
[13] L. Zhang, "Virtual clock: A new traffic control algorithm for packet switching," *ACM Trans. Comput. Syst.*, vol. 9, no. 2, pp. 101–124, May 1991.

S. Jamaloddin Golestani (M'85) was born in Najafabad, Iran, in May 1955. He received the B.S. degree from Sharif University of Technology, Tehran, Iran, in 1973, and the M.S. and Ph.D. degrees from the Massachusetts Institute of Technology, Cambridge, in 1976 and 1979, respectively, all in electrical engineering.

From 1980 to 1988, he was with the faculty of Isfahan University of Technology, Isfahan, Iran, where he taught and did research in communications theory, communication networks, and radar systems. During this period, he also served as a consultant to the Telecommunications Company and Telecommunications Research Center of Iran. In 1988, he joined Bell Communications Research, Morristown, NJ, where he is currently a Member of the Information Networking Research Laboratory. His research interests include high-speed networks, distributed network algorithms, congestion control, error control, and wireless networks.

Multi-Hour, Multi-Traffic Class Network Design for Virtual Path-Based Dynamically Reconfigurable Wide-Area ATM Networks

D. Medhi, *Member, IEEE*

Abstract—Virtual path (VP) concept has been gaining attention in terms of effective deployment of asynchronous transfer mode (ATM) networks in recent years. In a recent paper, we outlined a framework and models for network design and management of dynamically reconfigurable ATM networks based on the virtual path concept from a network planning and management perspective. Our approach has been based on statistical multiplexing of traffic within a traffic class by using a virtual path for the class and deterministic multiplexing of different virtual paths, and on providing dynamic bandwidth and reconfigurability through virtual path concept depending on traffic load during the course of the day. In this paper, we discuss in detail, a multi-hour, multi-traffic class network (capacity) design model for providing specified quality-of-service in such dynamically reconfigurable networks. This is done based on the observation that statistical multiplexing of virtual circuits for a traffic class in a virtual path, and the deterministic multiplexing of different virtual paths leads to decoupling of the network dimensioning problem into the bandwidth estimation problem and the combined virtual path routing and capacity design problem. We discuss how bandwidth estimation can be done, then how the design problem can be solved by a decomposition algorithm by looking at the dual problem and using subgradient optimization. We provide computational results for realistic network traffic data to show the effectiveness of our approach. We show for the test problems considered, our approach does between 6% to 20% better than a local shortest-path heuristic. We also show that considering network dynamism through variation of traffic during the course of a day by doing dynamic bandwidth and virtual path reconfiguration can save between 10% and 14% in network design costs compared to a static network based on maximum busy hour traffic.

Index Terms—Wide–Area ATM networks, dynamic virtual path routing, multi–hour network capacity design, optimization model, duality and subgradient optimization, on–off fluid flow model.

I. INTRODUCTION

BROADBAND networks will support a variety of services such as: voice, video, data, and image with different traffic characteristics, different qualities of service, different bandwidth requirements, and holding times in an integrated environment. ATM is considered the preferred transfer mode to support various services on broadband networks. In an ATM

network, traffic can be considered at the VP level, the call level, the burst level, and the cell level [14]. Discussion on control issues at different levels can be found in [22], [28]. A connection-oriented transport mechanism is to be used for ATM networks. This means a virtual connection is required to be set up between the origin and the destination for a connection request. The call then uses this connection. There are two operational steps. During call setup, network resources are checked before the connection is allowed. Once the call is accepted, network traffic management monitors the traffic status and performs a policing function to ensure that resources are properly used and accordingly, controls can be applied at different levels to satisfy quality of service (QOS). There are two operational steps. During call setup, network resources are checked before the connection is allowed. Once the call is accepted, network traffic management monitors the traffic status and performs a policing function to ensure resources are properly used and controls can be applied at different levels to satisfy QOS.

Statistical multiplexing is possible at all levels of ATM-based networks. There are different implications due to introduction (or nonintroduction) of statistical multiplexing at different levels. For example, consider a network that does not use any virtual path connection (VPC); then all the traffic can be statistically multiplexed on virtual channel connections (VCC) sharing common network links. Though this may result in minimum capacity networks, the VCC call establishment cost could be significant. Furthermore, this scenario may require complex admission control schemes. This is because each VCC would need to negotiate a connection request at each intermediate node between source and destination [10]. On the other hand, if peak rates are allocated at each level, then resources would be poorly utilized. Thus, techniques are needed to make better use of available resources while providing probabilistic guarantees of QOS. Use of virtual path as an effective transport technique, and for routing and resource management for ATM networks, it has recently gained considerable attention [1], [2], [9]–[10],[11], [13], [21], [25], [27], [32], [38], [40]. By grouping virtual circuits into a virtual path, an ATM-based network can be better managed. This can result in reduction of call set up time if there exists a virtual path (with enough capacity) between an origin and a destination since there is no need for extra processing at the intermediate nodes. This will also allow calls of similar traffic characteristics to be statistically multiplexed between an

Manuscript received August 1994; revised April 1995; approved by IEEE/ACM TRANSACTIONS ON NETWORKING Editor V. Sahin. This paper was presented in part at the IEEE INFOCOM'95, Boston, MA, April 1995.

D. Medhi is with the Department of Computer Networking, a unit of Computer Science Telecommunications at the University of Missouri–Kansas City, Kansas City, MO 64110 USA (e-mail: dmedhi@cstp.umkc.edu).

IEEE Log Number 9415895.

origin–destination pair. Simple call admission control schemes may be needed. For ease of network management and control, virtual paths may be defined for dissimilar traffic types and can be deterministically multiplexed. This deterministic multiplexing of different virtual paths is likely to result in requirements of more network capacity than if *everything* is statistically multiplexed. However, at the same time, dynamic bandwidth control and virtual path rearrangement can be provided using VP concept with less complex admission control schemes. Thus, we consider statistical multiplexing of similar traffic within a virtual path and deterministic multiplexing of various virtual paths along with dynamic bandwidth control and virtual path reconfiguration.

In a companion paper [34], we have outlined a framework and models for network design and management for a wide-area, dynamically reconfigurable ATM network based on the virtual path concept from a network planning and management perspective. In this paper, we present an approach for network dimensioning of such ATM networks. Our approach is based on the observation that statistical multiplexing of virtual circuits for a traffic class in a virtual path, and the deterministic multiplexing of different virtual paths leads to decoupling of the network dimensioning problem into the bandwidth estimation problem *and* the combined virtual path routing and capacity design problem. Based on this observation, we present here a multi-hour, multi-traffic class network design model for providing specified quality of service in dynamically reconfigurable networks and present a decomposition algorithm by looking at the dual problem and using subgradient optimization. We provide computational results on network saving for realistic network traffic data. Multi-hour design has been used for (single service) dynamic call routing circuit-switched networks with considerable network saving [5]. The concept of dynamic reconfigurability has been addressed for circuit-switched networks [6], [7], [18], [19]. There has been some work on ATM network dimensioning [17], [30], [31], [36], [37] and for VP layout design [2]. All this work takes varying approaches to ours. To our knowledge, a multi-hour, multi-traffic class network design model has not been addressed to date. Our approach can be used by network designers/planners for network capacity planning of wide-area public or private ATM-based networks.

The rest of this paper is organized as follows: in Section II, we start with a discussion of the role of virtual paths in ATM networks and present the multi-hour network design model. In Section III, we present a decomposition algorithm. In Section IV, we present computational results for realistic network traffic data. Finally, in Section V, we summarize our approach and discuss how our approach may be useful to network designers.

II. NETWORK DESIGN MODEL

Use of virtual path as an effective transport technique for ATM-based networks has been gaining considerable attention [1], [38]. (For discussion on the role of VP in resource management, refer to [9]–[11], [22], [27], [32].) A virtual path provides a logical direct link between virtual path terminators. Using virtual paths, an ATM network can be better managed by

grouping virtual circuits into bundles [38]. Flexibility in traffic management is possible with the use of VP's, due to separation of the logical transport network from the physical transmission network. For our work here, we assume VC's of *similar* traffic characteristics and QOS requirements are statistically multiplexed on a virtual path. For brevity, we will refer to it as *STQOS types* or *classes*. Note that more than one STQOS type may be preferable between an origin-destination pair for traffic of significantly different traffic characteristics and requirements. For example, it may be minimally preferable to have an STQOS type defined for real-time services and another for nonreal-time services. Use of VP simplifies B-ISDN call processing and reduces call establishment time since there is no processing required at the intermediate nodes. As presented in [38], for example, the explicit scheme can be used in the cell header organization of virtual paths. This way, processing on a call-by-call basis at each intermediate node can be eliminated during call establishment and release. Consequently, call set up time can be significantly reduced. Alternately, the network can be a collection of ATM switches and ATM cross-connect systems where the traffic demand between two-end ATM switching nodes can be cross-connected at intermediate nodes using ATM cross-connect systems [11], [32], [34]. There are also other advantages in using virtual path concept as noted in [22]: Class of service control is easier to implement than when different types of traffic are supported over the same virtual path. Dynamic bandwidth control is easier to implement per path due to similar traffic characteristics. Multiplexing several classes of traffic with different characteristics decreases the multiplexing gain compared to the multiplexing of traffic with the same characteristics. Based on these advantages, we assume the following for effective network design and management: We allow statistical multiplexing between calls of the same STQOS class over virtual circuits *within* the virtual path allocated for this STQOS type, however, we assume *no* statistical multiplexing between different virtual paths for different STQOS classes (i.e., only deterministic multiplexing). As mentioned before, a key advantage is that call processing time can be significantly reduced due to the introduction of VP's. In addition to the benefits already discussed, each virtual path for each STQOS type is assigned a certain bandwidth which determines the number of virtual channels it can support to provide satisfactory QOS. We still use dynamic path bandwidth control to adjust the required bandwidth based on anticipated demand at different times during the day. Following [9], we consider when bandwidth is reserved on a VP, a limit is placed on the number of calls and bursts in progress on that VP at any time. This also simplifies the control decision to verify the number of calls and bursts in progress compared to allocated maximum. Furthermore, the use of the concept of statistical multiplexing among VC's of same STQOS type in a VP and deterministic multiplexing of different VP's simplifies the nonlinear optimization problem of network dimensioning to meet certain QOS guarantees for a given traffic demand and class. Specifically, it has the following major advantage: it *decouples* the network dimensioning problem into the problem of determining the bandwidth needed on each virtual path for each STQOS type

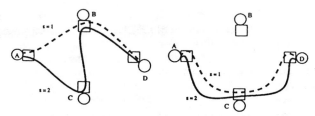

Fig. 1. Virtual paths shown for two different STQOS classes for a demand pair at two different load periods during the day, morning at left, and afternoon at right. □—cross-connect node; ○—switching node.

and the associated problem of determination of virtual path routing for each STQOS type and sizing of the network. The work here is based on this key observation/advantage of *decoupling* the bandwidth estimation problem *and* the VP routing and network sizing problem.

We first discuss the second problem, i.e., our model for the *dynamic* VP routing and network sizing problem. In the framework of a network, there are a number of possible virtual paths that an STQOS type can take between two switching end points (or a demand pair). There are possible demands between any two ATM switching nodes in the network (demand pairs). Thus, we consider the determination of virtual path for each STQOS type and each demand pair in the network. Specifically, given the estimated required bandwidth for a particular STQOS type and between two ATM switching end points, we need to determine one virtual path (nonbifurcated routing) from the list of the possible (candidate) virtual paths between the end points that use ATM cross-connect nodes at intermediate points (for setting up a VP). Note that a virtual path is constructed by connecting one or more network links. Additionally, for a particular demand pair, different virtual paths may be taken by different STQOS types at different times during a day due to network dynamism (with different upper bound bandwidth requirements to satisfy the request for connections at that time of the day). For example, consider Fig. 1. For the demand pair A-D in the morning, calls for STQOS type $s = 1$ may take the route A-B-D, while STQOS type $s = 2$ may take the route A-C-B-D. In the afternoon, however, the calls for both STQOS types $s = 1$ and $s = 2$ may take the VP route A-C-D. It should be understood that a VP route A-B-D means that the connection requests at ATM switch A for destination ATM switch D goes from ATM switch A to ATM cross-connect A to ATM cross-connect B to ATM cross-connect D to ATM switch D (note that it does *not* enter ATM switch B). Due to the flow of traffic on different virtual paths at different times of the day, we can determine the total traffic on each link of the network at different times during the day by adding, for different pairs and different STQOS types that use this link (this is due to deterministic multiplexing of different STQOS types). For the formulation we are about to present for the VP routing and network sizing problem, we assume we are given a set of ATM switching and ATM cross-connect locations and a set of possible links for which capacity has to be determined (network sizing). Change of VP routes for different times during the day provides us with *dynamic* virtual path

bandwidth control and dynamic VP based reconfigurability for better use of resources. Thus, to summarize, our work here considers dynamic bandwidth control with dynamic network reconfigurability based on virtual path for broadband networks such that optimal capacity on links can be provided to satisfy QOS requirements for each STQOS class and for traffic variation during the day. We assume the day has been clustered into several load periods ($\mathcal{H}$) and we introduce a superscript $h \in \mathcal{H}$ to represent different load periods. Note that $\mathcal{H}$ need not be all the hours of a day; it can be clustered into important traffic load change periods during a day. To mathematically represent the problem, we introduce the following notation:

$\mathcal{K}$	The set of node (demand) pairs in the network.
$\mathcal{S}$	The set of STQoS types.
$\mathcal{L}$	The set of links in the network.
$\mathcal{P}_k^{sh}$	The set of possible candidate virtual paths for STQoS type $s \in \mathcal{S}$, demand pair $k \in \mathcal{K}$ used for all $h \in \mathcal{H}$.
x_{kj}^{sh}	Virtual path routing variables – 1 if STQoS type $s \in \mathcal{S}_k$, $k \in \mathcal{K}$ uses path $j \in \mathcal{P}_k^{sh}$ in $h \in \mathcal{H}$; 0 otherwise,
$b_k^{sh} = bw(A_k^{sh}, T_s, QoS_s)$	Estimated bandwidth requirement for traffic amount A_k^{sh} (with traffic descriptor T_s and quality of service requirement QoS_s) for STQoS $s \in \mathcal{S}$ for $k \in \mathcal{K}$ in $h \in \mathcal{H}$ (discussed later).
$\delta_{kj}^{s\ell h}$	Link-path incidence matrix; 1 if path $j \in \mathcal{P}_k^{sh}$ for STQoS $s \in \mathcal{S}$ and for pair $k \in \mathcal{K}$ in $h \in \mathcal{H}$ uses link $\ell \in \mathcal{L}$; 0 otherwise,
y_ℓ	Sizing (topology) variables; the number of units of high capacity on traffic link $\ell \in \mathcal{L}$.
α	Capacity of a high capacity link unit.
c_ℓ	Cost of a high capacity unit on link $\ell \in \mathcal{L}$.

The following model, to be referred to as problem (P), can be used for multi-hour, multi-STQOS class network dimensioning of a dynamically reconfigurable VP routing network

$$v_P = \min_{\{x,y\}} \sum_{\ell \in \mathcal{L}} c_\ell y_\ell \qquad (1a)$$

subject to

$$\sum_{j \in \mathcal{P}_k^{sh}} x_{kj}^{sh} = 1, \quad s \in \mathcal{S}, \quad k \in \mathcal{K}, \quad h \in \mathcal{H} \qquad (1b)$$

$$\sum_{k \in \mathcal{K}} \sum_{s \in \mathcal{S}} b_k^{sh} \sum_{j \in \mathcal{P}_k^{sh}} \delta_{kj}^{s\ell h} x_{kj}^{sh} \le \alpha y_\ell, \quad \ell \in \mathcal{L}, \quad h \in \mathcal{H} \qquad (1c)$$

$$x_{kj}^{sh} = 1/0, \quad j \in \mathcal{P}_k^{sh}, s \in \mathcal{S}, k \in \mathcal{K}, h \in \mathcal{H} \qquad (1d)$$

$$y_\ell \ge 0 \text{ and integer}, \quad \ell \in \mathcal{L}. \qquad (1e)$$

In this model (1a), the objective function (1a) represents the total capacity cost for network links. (1b) and (1d) are the decisions of choosing a virtual path for a STQOS type for a node pair at different times during the day. One out of several possible VP paths is chosen. The left hand quantity in (1e) is the total link capacity required at a particular load period for virtual paths set up using that link by different source–destination node pairs. Thus, constraint (1c) says the link flow in each load period is going to force the determination of capacity on the link to cover for any time during the day. Different sets of candidate paths for each load period and service for each traffic pair may be explicitly provided through the notation $\mathcal{P}_k^{sh}$. This model takes possible candidate paths as an input; these candidate paths, for example, can be generated using a k-shortest path algorithm [29]. The idea of candidate paths is advantageous in restricting (or allowing) choice of certain paths due to information available from various network elements based on network growth, and restricting the maximum number of links allowed for a path (often the case in existing telecommunications networks) to limit the number of intermediate cross-connect ports used or to limit the delay for certain service types, thereby, preprocessing the set of candidate virtual paths (hence the link–path formulation). Note that this approach is an integrated approach since the solution of the model provides network capacity as well as VP routing at different times of the day.

We now discuss the bandwidth (often referred to as the *equivalent bandwidth*) estimation problem (i.e., how the quantity b_k^{sh} can be estimated for each STQOS class for different traffic pairs at different load periods during the day). Although in theory, each conceivable traffic type can be an STQOS class by itself, in practice this would generate too many classes and could become an administrative nightmare for network operations and management. Classifying various traffic types under a single STQOS class or putting them into different STQOS classes is itself a complex problem. For example, Suruagy Monteiro [42] addressed this problem in terms of whether to integrate or not [43]. This issue certainly deserves further investigation, and is, however, beyond the scope of this paper. For the purpose of the rest of the work here, we consider an STQOS class to have homogeneous traffic with same QOS requirements.

Suppose for an STQOS class s, a parameter (grade-of-service) for QOS is given in terms of acceptable connection denial probability, q_s, and the offered traffic for pair k in load period h is given by A_k^{sh} erlangs. Recall with decoupling we arrive at essentially providing a virtual link from origin to destination switching node for a STQOS class. Thus given offered load in erlangs, A_k^{sh}, and connection denial probability, q_s, we can use inverse the Erlang-blocking formula [26], $E^{-1}(A_k^{sh}, q_s)$, to estimate the maximum number of virtual circuits needed to be connected for this class, i.e., $N_k^{sh} = N(A_k^{sh}, q_s) = \lceil E^{-1}(A_k^{sh}, q_s) \rceil$ ($\lceil x \rceil$ denote the smallest integer greater than or equal to x). A similar discussion as above is also given by [37]. This puts a limit on the maximum number of connections allowed. Now, if each connection for a particular STQOS type requires peak rate allocation, e.g., class 1 traffic in BISDN [8], the traffic descriptor T_s will be the peak rate, $(R_{\text{peak}})_s$, per connection for this service class, and the

bandwidth estimate is $b_k^{sh} = N_k^{sh}(R_{\text{peak}})_s$. Thus, in the case of class 1 traffic in BISDN, there is no statistical multiplexing of connections within an STQOS class. On the other hand, if an STQOS class can be characterized by an on–off model, the traffic descriptor in this case can be given by

$$T_s = \{\rho_s, m_s, (R_{\text{peak}})_s\}$$

where ρ_s is the utilization, m_s is the mean burst period, and $(R_{\text{peak}})_s$ is the peak rate ([20]). To allow N_k^{sh} connections (sources) to be admitted to the network based on A_k^{sh} and q_s, we adapt here an approach, to be referred as InvAMS, based on the the fluid–flow approach given by [3], to estimate b_k^{sh} for each STQOS type $s \in \mathcal{S}$, pair $k \in \mathcal{K}$ in $h \in \mathcal{H}$ for a second parameter (besides grade-of-service mentioned above) for the quality-of-service, QOS, given in terms of buffer overflow probability, p_s, see appendix for detail. It is worth noting other approaches for bandwidth estimation: e.g., Guérin *et al.* [20] have presented an approximate equivalent bandwidth estimation method based on the approach by Anick *et al.* [3] for computation in real-time; Suruagy Montiero *et al.* [43] provide an approach based on the finite buffer fluid–flow model by Tucker [44]. The capacity design for a *single* entity (link or path) based on a quality of service requirement specified by pth percentile delay of m cells has been presented by Sato and Sato [39].

It should also be noted that if a more detailed traffic descriptor than the on–off model suits some emerging service, then an appropriate bandwidth estimation procedure has to be used instead of InvAMS procedure. This requires only a new module for bandwidth estimation for this emerging service *without* needing any change in problem (P). Further, in case different types of heterogeneous sources are decided to be multiplexed in an STQOS class, an approach based on the work by Elwalid and Mitra [12] may be pursued toward estimating bandwidth requirement for that class. However, for the rest of the discussion and clarity, we will refer only to InvAMS procedure with the 3-tuple traffic descriptor and consider statistical multiplexing of a homogeneous traffic type within an STQOS class.

III. A DECOMPOSITION ALGORITHM

In this section, we describe a decomposition algorithm for the problem (P) using Lagrangean relaxation with duality and subgradient optimization [23]. This type of approach has been used successfully for solving data network routing and design problems (see, [15], [16]), but have not been addressed in the context of multi-hour, multi-STQOS class design. Convergence results for subgradient optimization can be found, for example, in [35]. The essence of this decomposition algorithm is to consider the dual problem of (P) by relaxing constraints (1c) to arrive at simpler subproblems that can be solved easily, and then use updating of dual variables to iteratively solve simpler subproblems to drive toward the optimal solution of the original problem (P). First, we add an artificial upper bound on the variables y [its use will be seen in the dual problem, (5)]. Specifically, let the bound be $\hat{y}_\ell, \ell \in \mathcal{L}$, i.e.,

$$y_\ell \le \hat{y}_\ell, \quad \ell \in \mathcal{L}$$

and in compact form, $y \leq \hat{y}$. Let $u = (u_\ell^h)$ be the dual multiplier associated with the constraint (1c). Then the Lagrangean is

$$L(x, y, u) = \sum_{\ell \in \mathcal{L}} c_\ell y_\ell + \sum_{\ell \in \mathcal{L}} \sum_{h \in \mathcal{H}} u_\ell^h \qquad (2)$$
$$\times \left(\sum_{k \in \mathcal{K}} \sum_{s \in \mathcal{S}} b_k^{sh} \sum_{j \in \mathcal{P}_k^{sh}} \delta_{kj}^{s\ell h} x_{kj}^{sh} - \alpha y_\ell \right).$$

Rearranging

$$L(x, y, u) = \sum_{\ell \in \mathcal{L}} \left(c_\ell - \alpha \sum_{h \in \mathcal{H}} u_\ell^h \right) y_\ell$$
$$+ \sum_{h \in \mathcal{H}} \sum_{k \in \mathcal{K}} \sum_{s \in \mathcal{S}} b_k^{sh} \sum_{j \in \mathcal{P}_k^{sh}} \sum_{\ell \in \mathcal{L}} u_\ell^h \delta_{kj}^{s\ell h} x_{kj}^{sh}. \qquad (2')$$

The dual problem (D) is

$$v_D = \max_{u \geq 0} g(u) \qquad (3a)$$

where

$$g(u) = \min_{x,y} L(x, y, u). \qquad (3b)$$

Note that for given u, the Lagrangean is separable in x and y and reduces (2) to solving two independent subproblems, i.e.,

$$\min_{x,y} L(x, y, u) = \min_y L_1(y, u) + \min_x L_2(x, u)$$
$$= g_1(u) + g_2(u) \qquad (4a)$$

where

$$g_1(u) = \min_y L_1(y, u)$$
$$= \min_y \left\{ \sum_{\ell \in \mathcal{L}} \left(c_\ell - \alpha \sum_{h \in \mathcal{H}} u_\ell^h \right) y_\ell \mid 0 \leq y \leq \hat{y} \right\} \qquad (4b)$$

and

$$g_2(u) = \min_x L_2(x, u)$$
$$= \min_x \left\{ \sum_{h \in \mathcal{H}} \sum_{k \in \mathcal{K}} \sum_{s \in \mathcal{S}} b_k^{sh} \sum_{j \in \mathcal{J}_k^{sh}} \left(\sum_{\ell \in \mathcal{L}} u_\ell^h \delta_{kj}^{s\ell h} \right) x_{kj}^{sh} \mid \right.$$
$$\sum_{j \in \mathcal{J}_k^{sh}} x_{kj}^{sh} = 1, \ s \in \mathcal{S}, \ h \in \mathcal{H}, \ k \in \mathcal{K}; \qquad (4c)$$
$$\left. x_{kj}^{sh} = 0/1, \ j \in \mathcal{J}_k^{sh}, s \in \mathcal{S}, k \in \mathcal{K}, h \in \mathcal{H} \right\}.$$

For subproblem (4b), observe that $L_1(y, u)$ is further separable to each link variable since it has only bounding constraints on the link variables, and thus the solution to (4b) for each ℓ can be easily obtained by setting

$$y_\ell^*(u) = \begin{cases} 0, & \text{if } c_\ell \geq \alpha \sum_{h \in \mathcal{H}} u_\ell^h \\ \hat{y}_\ell, & \text{if } c_\ell < \alpha \sum_{h \in \mathcal{H}} u_\ell^h. \end{cases} \qquad (5)$$

Further note the other subproblem (4c) is also separable for each k, h, and s since there is no dependency constraint among k, h, s. Also, the solution is easily obtainable by setting the variable for the appropriate path j to 1 for which the "path cost," $\sum_{\ell \in \mathcal{L}} u_\ell^h \delta_{kj}^{s\ell h}$, is the least among all the paths for that

specific k, h, s. We denote this path index by j^* so that $x_{kj^*}^{sh}(u) = 1$.

Note that the problem (D) is nonsmooth and as such, we use a subgradient approach to solve the dual problem [23]. This method iterates on the dual variable u. Thus, given u, once the solutions to the subproblems (4b) and (4c) are obtained, a dual subgradient, $\pi = (\pi_\ell^h)$, for $g(\cdot)$ is computed using

$$\pi_\ell^h = \sum_{k \in \mathcal{K}} \sum_{s \in \mathcal{S}} b_k^{sh} \delta_{kj^*}^{s\ell h} x_{kj^*}^{sh}(u) - \alpha y_\ell^*(u), \ \ell \in \mathcal{L}, h \in \mathcal{H}. \quad (6)$$

Then the dual multiplier, u, is updated using

$$u_\ell^h \leftarrow \max \left\{ 0, u_\ell^h + \lambda \pi_\ell^h \right\}, \quad \ell \in \mathcal{L}, h \in \mathcal{H} \qquad (7)$$

where the step size, λ, is given by [23]

$$\lambda = \rho \frac{\tilde{g} - g(u)}{\|\pi\|^2} \qquad (8)$$

and where $\tilde{g}$ is an upper bound on the dual objective and the relaxation parameter, ρ, is chosen such that $0 < \rho \leq 2$.

A primal feasible point for problem (P) can be easily obtained at each iteration by considering the solution $x_{kj^*}^{sh}(u) = 1$ to compute the left hand side of (1c) to generate a feasible y, and in turn, we also can compute a primal objective function value. As the dual iteration progresses, we check for decrease in the primal objective value and store the best primal solution, and the best primal cost so far.

Note if the integrality of link variable y is relaxed in the original problem (P), then we have a mixed integer programming (MIP) problem and it is clear the optimal objective function value for this mixed integer problem is, $v_{MIP} \leq v_P$. Coupling this fact with the result of the weak duality theorem ([35], p. 203), we have the relation:

$$v_P \geq v_{MIP} \geq v_D.$$

Given this observation, the upper bound on the dual objective, $\tilde{g}$, is set to be the lowest value of the objective function of the MIP problem as the iteration progresses. For notational convenience, we will denote the lowest network cost obtained using the decomposition algorithm for problem (P) by C_P, for the MIP problem by C_{MIP}, and the best dual cost by C_D.

In our implementation, coded in C language, we set the maximum dual iterations to 1000. ρ was initially set to 2 and was halved whenever the dual objective value did not improve in 40 iterations.

To summarize, we have the following algorithmic steps to solve the entire multi-hour, multi-STQOS class network design problem:

Step 1 Generate candidate set of virtual paths $\mathcal{P}_k^{sh}$ for $s \in \mathcal{S}$, $k \in \mathcal{K}$, $h \in \mathcal{H}$.

Step 2 For given QOS and the traffic descriptor for different STQOS classes, and traffic amount for different node pairs and for different load periods, compute b_k^{sh} using the InvAMS procedure for $s \in \mathcal{S}$, $k \in \mathcal{K}$, $h \in \mathcal{H}$.

Step 3 Size network by solving multi-hour, multi-STQOS class model (P) using the decomposition algorithm.

TABLE I
NETWORK TOPOLOGY INFORMATION FOR SAMPLE NETWORKS

Network	No. of ATM Switches	No. of Traffic Pairs, $\#(\mathcal{K})$	No. of ATM Cross-Connect Nodes	No. of Links, $\#(\mathcal{L})$
EN-1	7	21	10	14
EN-2	10	45	18	27
EN-3	15	105	23	33

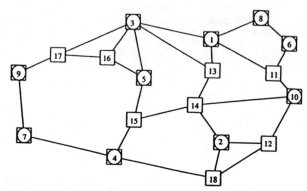

Fig. 3. Topology of EN-2 (10 ATM switching nodes, 18 ATM cross-connect nodes).

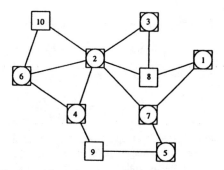

Fig. 2. Topology of EN-1 (7 ATM switching nodes, 10 ATM cross-connect nodes). □ – cross-connect node; ○ – switching node.

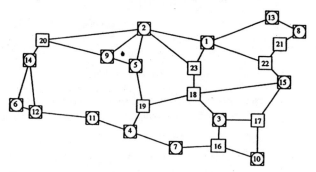

Fig. 4. Topology of EN-3 (15 ATM switching nodes, 23 ATM cross-connect nodes).

IV. COMPUTATIONAL RESULTS

For computational work, we use STQOS classes, each with one homogenous traffic type as already discussed in Section II. To illustrate our approach, we limit two STQOS classes where each class has different on–off traffic descriptor values and quality of service requirements. We use three realistic example networks we have used in other work [33]. These sample networks are extracted from an actual voice network spanning the continental US. Topological information for these networks are given in Table I (also see Figs. 2–4). Note that in these networks a circle and a square together means an ATM switching node is co-located (same city) with an ATM cross-connect node. Although Fig. 1 more accurately depicts the relation of cross-connect and switching nodes, we have put the same city cross-connect and switching node together here to avoid cluttering the picture. The link between two cross-connect nodes is the possible link placements for which capacity is to be determined by our approach. Buffering is provided with the ATM switches. (For this architectural view, see also [11].) The maximum number of sources (connections) to be admitted for the voice traffic of these networks for three different times during a day (morning, early afternoon and late afternoon) i.e. $\#(\mathcal{H}) = 3$, are considered based on the offered load and connection denial probability (see Section II). For brevity, we refer to these three load periods as ld-1, ld-2, and ld-3, respectively, and this service as $s = 1$. (Certainly, VP routing can be updated more often than three times in a day; our choice of three is to present computational results with VP dynamism.) Since, at this point, we do not have realistic traffic data available to us for any other traffic, we used fictitious traffic for the second STQOS class ($s = 2$). The number of connections (sources) to be admitted for this STQOS class for different traffic pairs in the network for

TABLE II
SUMMARY OF NETWORK TRAFFIC (IN TERMS OF TOTAL NUMBER OF SOURCES/CONNECTIONS TO BE CONNECTED) FOR SAMPLE NETWORKS

Network	ld-1 $s=1/s=2$	ld-2 $s=1/s=2$	ld-3 $s=1/s=2$	Max. Busy Hour $s=1/s=2$
EN-1	1652/168	1091/139	1530/189	1661/247
EN-2	2687/263	2830/321	3226/349	3531/473
EN-3	4687/488	4082/395	4956/491	5442/691

various times of the day are generated using a uniform random number generator by picking a number between 0 and 20% of the number of sources for the voice traffic (i.e, $N_k^{2h} = \lceil \text{Uniform } (0, 1) \times 0.2 N_k^{1h} \rceil$, where N_k^{sh} is the number of traffic sources to be admitted for service s, traffic pair k in load period h, and where $\lceil x \rceil$ returns the smallest integer higher than x). The total traffic in terms of number of sources to be admitted for different times of the day are listed in Table II.

For the voice traffic ($s = 1$), following [41], we have used the following parameters for the traffic descriptor for packetized voice procedure: utilization (ρ) = 0.6487, mean burst period (m) = 352 ms, peak rate (R_{peak}) = 32 Kbps (for ADPCM coding); these values are used in computing bandwidth requirement using the InvAMS procedure for buffer overflow probability, p, of 10^{-4}. The parameters used for the second STQOS class are: $\rho = 0.2$, $m = 300$ ms, $R_{\text{peak}} = 300$ Kbps; the buffer overflow probability used is 10^{-7}. The

TABLE III
TRAFFIC DESCRIPTOR PARAMETERS AND QOSS FOR TWO STQOS CLASSES

Services	ρ	m	R_{peak}	Buffer overflow probability, p
s=1	0.6487	352 ms	32 Kbps	10^{-4}
s=2	0.2	300 ms	300 Kbps	10^{-7}

traffic descriptor parameters and the QOS requirements are summarized in Table III. Note the difference between these two traffic types: The second type has a peak rate, is an order of magnitude greater than the voice traffic, has lower utilization and mean burst period, while the overflow probability is much more stringent for the second type. We assume the buffer size (r) to be 1 Mbit for each class (see InvAMS procedure in the Appendix).

Given the maximum number of connections to be admitted (and the parameters listed in Table III), InvAMS procedure is used to compute the bandwidth requirements, i.e.,

$$b_k^{sh} = InvAMS(N_k^{sh}, \rho_s, m_s, (R_{\text{peak}})_s, r, p_s),$$
$$s \in \mathcal{S}, h \in \mathcal{H}, k \in \mathcal{K}.$$

We have used the modular grouping value, α, for capacity unit of a link to be 1.5 Mbps $\approx$ T1 rate. (It should be noted that this link speed is used only for illustration purpose and that our model is not limited to using this value.) Given the trend that the fiber cost is comparatively low compared to port cost at the nodes, we have computed the unit cost of links of 1.5 Mbps using 100 as the cost of each termination port and 0.1 to be the distance cost per mile. Thus, $c_\ell = 2 \times 100 + 0.1 \times D_\ell$, where D_ℓ is the distance in miles for 1.5 Mbps pipe for link ℓ. The candidate paths are generated based on distance using a k-shortest path algorithm [29]. For each k, s, h, we generated a maximum of six candidate paths for EN-1, ten for EN-2 and fifteen for EN-3.

Our computational work is aimed at addressing the following items: 1) duality gap obtained using the decomposition algorithm, 2) a measure of effectiveness of our approach compared to a local shortest path based heuristic, 3) cost saving compared to (static) virtual path based maximum busy hour network design with "worst" case and observed case. We discuss these items in some detail below.

The dual-based approach for the multi-hour (MuH) design provides us with a (best) dual objective value, C_D, which provides us with a lower bound on the objective value for the problem (P), C_P. We can, in turn, obtain a bound on the duality gap (in percentage) by using $100(C_P - C_D)/C_D$. Further, the mixed integer problem provides us with an objective function value, C_{MIP}, that is lower than the one for problem (P) and a tighter bound on duality gap if the nonintegral link capacities were acceptable.

The local shortest path heuristic (LSPH) is a fairly naïve rule where the bandwidth required for a traffic pair is always routed on the shortest distance route, then the network cost is computed based on the link flow produced as a result of

this rule. We will denote the network cost obtained using LSPH by C_{LSPH}. This cost is primarily used to obtain some quantitative measure on gain or effectiveness due to the decomposition algorithm compared to LSPH.

Maximum busy hour refers to the maximum load for all hours (for each k and s), i.e., $N_k^{s,\max} = \max_{h \in \mathcal{H}} \{N_k^{sh}\}$. This is usually used for *static* virtual path design providing for the grade-of-service at any time during the day. We will refer to this as the maximum busy hour (MaxBH) scenario. Total network traffic for each service with maximum busy hour scenario is listed in Table II. When the subscript h is omitted from model (1a), it reduces to the maximum busy hour model (with $\#(\mathcal{H}) = 1$ and bandwidth computed for $N_k^{s,\max}$). We can use the algorithm described in the previous section for computing the best primal and dual objective values. The cost for the MaxBH scenario when compared to the cost for MuH design obtained using the decomposition algorithm provides us with a yardstick on saving with dynamic VP routing. We refer to this saving as the observed case scenario. Note that this would be the maximum saving possible if the cost obtained were the *actual* optimal values. Finally, if we compare the primal cost for the multi-hour design with the dual cost for the single-hour design we, in essence, get a feel for the "worst" case saving achieved by MuH approach since the (actual) optimal dual objective for MaxBH case provides us with the maximum possible value for the primal cost if static VP routing was used.

The cost results for the sample networks with multi-hour traffic and maximum busy hour traffic are tabulated in Table IV using the decomposition algorithm of the previous section. In this table, we show the best cost for problem (P), the best cost for mixed integer program (MIP), the best dual cost, the LSPH cost as well as the duality gap and saving of dual-based decomposition algorithm compared to LSPH. The decomposition algorithm appears to provide reasonable results as the duality gap is bounded by not more than 13% for the objective function value for problem (P), and by not more than 5% for the objective function value for the MIP. Furthermore, observe that our decomposition algorithm method provides between 6% and 20% cost saving compared to the local shortest path heuristic. In Table V, we show the iteration number when the lowest primal value, C_P, reported in Table IV is obtained along with the computing time in seconds (step 2 and step 3) for running to 1000 dual iterations. This is on a DEC Alpha AXP running OSF/1 operating system (DEC Model 3000/400, 64 MB main memory, *SPECfp 92* benchmark = 112.5). The computing time for generating candidate paths for all traffic pairs using the k-shortest path method (step 1) was 0.12, 0.89 and 2.70 s for EN-1, EN-2 and EN-3, respectively. Thus, we observe a good solution to problem (P) can be obtained in a reasonable computing time.

Finally, in Table VI, we report gain due to multi-hour design. Specifically, we found that, for the test problems, although the multi-hour design approach with dynamic bandwidth and virtual path reconfigurability may save a minimum of 3% in the "worst" case compared to maximum busy-hour design static VP routing design, the observed case saving is a significant gain of between 10% and 14%.

TABLE IV
COST OF NETWORK DESIGN, DUALITY GAP, AND COMPARISON

	C_P	C_{MIP}	C_D	C_{LSPH}	1 (%)	2 (%)	3 (%)
EN-1 (MaxBH)	15278.90	13821.93	13821.60	17568.00	10.54	0.00	14.98
EN-1 (MuH)	13402.00	12571.76	12257.29	16016.30	9.34	2.57	19.51
EN-2 (MaxBH)	57129.90	54100.36	54045.99	61875.70	5.71	0.10	8.31
EN-2 (MuH)	51485.10	47980.03	45760.05	54710.70	12.51	4.85	6.27
EN-3 (MaxBH)	91098.90	87818.22	87799.59	97790.00	3.76	0.02	7.34
EN-3 (MuH)	81599.10	77892.32	74766.10	89328.60	9.14	4.18	9.47

(1 - duality gap $= \frac{(C_P - C_D)100}{C_D}\%$; 2 - duality gap with MIP $= \frac{(C_{MIP} - C_D)100}{C_D}\%$; 3 - saving compared to LSPH $= \frac{(C_{LSPH} - C_P)100}{C_P}\%$; MaxBH = Maximum busy hour; MuH = Multi-Hour)

TABLE V
ITERATION NUMBER AT LOWEST COST AND
COMPUTATIONAL TIME FOR SAMPLE NETWORKS

	Iteration # at lowest cost	Time (sec)
EN-1 (MaxBH)	1	1.43
EN-1 (MuH)	136	4.18
EN-2 (MaxBH)	136	9.13
EN-2 (MuH)	508	26.98
EN-3 (MaxBH)	114	42.33
EN-3 (MuH)	680	127.25

TABLE VI
COST SAVING DUE TO MULTI-HOUR DYNAMIC VP ROUTING DESIGN
COMPARED TO MAXIMUM BUSY HOUR STATIC VP ROUTING DESIGN

	"worst" case saving (%)	observed saving (%)
EN-1	3.13	14.00
EN-2	4.97	10.96
EN-3	7.60	11.64

V. SUMMARY AND DISCUSSION

In this paper, we present an approach for dimensioning wide-area, ATM-based networks. We consider the scenario where traffic types of similar traffic characteristics and QOS requirements are grouped under an STQOS class for statistical multiplexing of connections using the virtual path concept while different virtual paths are deterministically multiplexed on a network link. We present a discussion to show how this concept leads to the key observation that the network dimensioning problem can be decoupled into two manageable subproblems: the bandwidth estimation problem *and* the combined virtual path routing and capacity design problem. We further consider the traffic pattern behavior due to the traffic load variation depending on the time of day for different traffic pairs and traffic classes in the network to address a dynamically reconfigurable virtual path-based ATM network environment; this is captured in the dimensioning process as well. We then present computational procedure to efficiently determine network sizing while providing computational bound on the solution quality using duality theory. We show for the test prob-

lems considered, our approach does between 6% to 20% better than a local shortest path heuristic. Furthermore, for the same test problems, we have shown that considering network dynamism through variation of traffic during the course of a day can save between 10% and 14% in network design costs compared to a static network based on maximum busy hour traffic.

Two important observations come from this work: 1) although we have used an on–off model for demonstration of the bandwidth estimation procedure, other, more accurate models may be used for the bandwidth estimation part depending on the type of service. Importantly, this does not change the network design paradigm present since the estimation problem is decoupled from the routing/capacity design problem. 2) Our approach allows for the scenario where different node pairs may have a different number of STQOS classes. This means a newly emerging service may be deployed for selected traffic pairs based on the community of interest and demand forecast since the virtual path concept is used. It is hoped that our approach will be useful to network designers involved in planning, design and deployment of wide-area ATM-based networks. The interested reader is referred to [34] for models for network servicing and monitoring of ATM networks.

APPENDIX

We present the InvAMS procedure here. For simplicity, consider one STQOS type and one demand pair. InvAMS procedure requires a subroutine to compute overflow probability based on the two-state, fluid flow model due to Anick *et al.* [3]. Here, each traffic source is either in an idle state (no transmission) or a burst state (transmission at peak rate). We present an approach that can be used for off-line computation as is the case with the network design phase of network planning and management. We assume the burst and idle period are i.i.d. and exponentially distributed, then a traffic source can be characterized by the following three parameters:

$\rho :=$ utilization, fraction of time the source is active

$m :=$ mean burst period

$R_{\text{peak}} :=$ peak rate.

If $1/\lambda$ and $1/\mu$ are mean idle and burst period, then

$$\mu = 1/m, \qquad \lambda = \rho/\{m(1-\rho)\}.$$

Consider N sources. If $F_i(r)$ is the equilibrium probability that i sources are active and the buffer length does not exceed r and $F_i = 0$ for $i \notin [0, N]$, then the set of differential equations governing the equilibrium buffer distribution can be given by [3]

$$(iR_{\text{peak}} - b)\frac{dF_i(r)}{dr} = (N - i + 1)\lambda F_{i-1}$$
$$- \{(N-i)\lambda + i\mu\}F_i + (i+1)\mu F_{i+1}, \ i \in [0, N]$$

where $b :=$ capacity (bandwidth). In matrix notation

$$\mathbf{D}\frac{d}{dx}\mathbf{F}(r) = \mathbf{M}\mathbf{F}(r), \qquad r \geq 0.$$

The following eigen problem can be solved analytically [3]

$$z\mathbf{D}\phi = \mathbf{M}\phi$$

(z is some eigen value of $\mathbf{D}^{-1}\mathbf{M}$, and ϕ is the associated right eigenvector). The probability of overflow beyond r is given by

$$p = 1 - \mathbf{1}^T\mathbf{F}(r) = - \sum_{i=0}^{N-\lfloor b/R_{\text{peak}}\rfloor -1} e^{z_i r}a_i(\mathbf{1}^T\phi_i).$$

(Here $\mathbf{1}^T$ is a vector of 1's.) Thus, given N, ρ, m, R_{peak}, b, and buffer size, r, the overflow probability can be computed based on the above approach by [3]. For brevity, we denote this procedure as $AMS(N, \rho, m, R_{\text{peak}}, b, r)$.

To compute the bandwidth required for given N, ρ, m, R_{peak}, r and acceptable overflow probability $\hat{p}$ (QOS), a simple bisection scheme as given below can be used (this is what we refer to as InvAMS procedure):

```
procedure InvAMS(N, ρ, m, R_peak, r, p̂):
    Estimate b_l and b_h such that
        p = AMS(N, ρ, m, R_peak, b_h, r) < p̂ < AMS(N, ρ, m,
        R_peak, b_l, r)
    while (|log(p) - log(p̂)| > δ) do /* for some
            tolerance δ > 0 */
        b = (b_l + b_h)/2
        p = AMS(N, ρ, m, R_peak, b, r)
        if (p > p̂) then
            b_l = b
        else
            b_h = b
        endif
    endwhile
    return(b)
```

ACKNOWLEDGMENT

The traffic data used in this work is based on data provided for another work [33] by Sprint Corporation and is greatly appreciated.

REFERENCES

[1] R. G. Addie, J. L. Burgin, and S. L. Sutherland, "B-ISDN protocol architecture," in *Proc. IEEE GLOBECOM*, 1988, pp. 22.6.1–5.
[2] S. Ahn, R. P. Tsang, S. R. Tong and D. H. C. Du, "Virtual path layout design in ATM networks," in *Proc. of IEEE INFOCOM*, 1994, pp. 192–200.
[3] D. Anick, D. Mitra, and M. M. Sondhi, "Stochastic theory of a data-handling system with multiple sources," *Bell Syst. Tech. J.*, vol. 61, no. 8, pp. 1871–1894, 1982.
[4] A. Arvidsson, "Management of reconfigurable virtual path networks," in *Proc. 14th Int. Teletraffic Congress*, 1994, pp. 931–940.
[5] G. R. Ash, R. H. Cardwell, and R. P. Murray, "Design and optimization of networks with dynamic routing," *Bell Syst. Tech. J.*, vol. 60, no. 8, pp. 1787–1820, 1981.
[6] G. R. Ash, K. K. Chan, and J. F. Labourdette, "Analysis and design of fully shared networks," in *Proc. 14th Int. Teletraffic Congress*, 1994, pp. 1311–1320.
[7] G. R. Ash and S. D. Schwartz, "Network routing evolution," in *Network Management and Control*, A. Kershenbaum *et al.*, Eds. New York: Plenum, 1990 pp. 357–367.
[8] D. Bertsekas and R. Gallager, *Data Networks*, 2nd ed. Englewood Cliffs, NJ: Prentice–Hall, 1992.
[9] J. Burgin, "Broadband ISDN resource management," *Computer Networks & ISDN Systems*, vol. 20, pp. 323–331, 1990.
[10] J. Burgin and D. Dorman, "Broadband ISDN resource management: the role of virtual paths," *IEEE Commun. Mag.*, vol. 29, no. 9, pp. 44–48, Sept 1991.
[11] M. De Prycker. "ATM switching on demand," *IEEE Network*, vol. 6, no. 2, pp. 25–28, Mar. 1992.
[12] A. I. Elwalid and D. Mitra, "Effective bandwidth of general markovian traffic sources and admission control of high speed networks," *IEEE/ACM Trans. Networking*, vol. 1, pp. 329–343, 1993.
[13] S. P. Evans, "Optimal bandwidth management and capacity provision in a broadband network using virtual paths," *Performance Evaluation*, vol. 13, pp. 27–43, 1991.
[14] J. Filipiak, "M-architecture: a structural model of traffic management and control in broadband ISDN," *IEEE Commun. Mag.*, vol. 27, no. 5, pp. 25–31, 1989.
[15] B. Gavish and I. Newman, "Capacity and flow assignment in large computer networks," in *Proc. IEEE INFOCOM*, 1986, pp. 275–284.
[16] ——, "Routing in a Network with Unreliable Components," *IEEE Trans. Commun.*, vol. 40, pp. 1249–1258, 1992.
[17] M. Gerla, J. A. Suruagy Monteiro, and R. Pazos, "Topology design and bandwidth allocation in ATM nets," *IEEE J. Select. Areas Commun.*, vol. 7, pp. 1253–1262, 1989.
[18] G. Gopal, C. Kim, and A. Weinrib, "Dynamic network configuration management," in *Proc. IEEE Int. Conf. Commun.*, 1990, pp. 295–301.
[19] ——, "Algorithms for reconfigurable networks," in *Proc. 13th Int. Teletraffic Congress*, 1992, pp. 341–347.
[20] R. Guérin, H. Ahmadi, and M. Naghshineh, "Equivalent capacity and its application to bandwidth allocation in high-speed networks," *IEEE J. Select. Areas Commun.*, vol. 9, pp. 968–981, 1991.
[21] S. Gupta, K. Ross, and M. El Zarki, "Routing in virtual path based ATM networks," in *Proc. IEEE GLOBECOM*, Dec. 1992, pp. 571–575.
[22] I. W. Habib and T. N. Saadawi, "Controlling flow and avoiding congestion in broadband networks," *IEEE Commun. Mag.*, vol. 29, no. 10, pp. 46–53, Oct. 1991.
[23] M. Held, P. Wolfe, and H. Crowder, "Validation of subgradient optimization," *Mathematical Programming*, vol. 6, pp. 62–88, 1974.
[24] J. Hui, M. Gursoy, N. Moayeri and R. Yates, "A layered broadband switching architecture with physical or virtual path configurations," *IEEE J. Select. Areas Commun.*, vol. 9, pp. 1416–1425, 1991.
[25] R. H. Hwang, J. F. Kurose and D. Towsley, "MDP routing in ATM networks using virtual path concept," in *Proc. IEEE INFOCOM*, 1994, pp. 1509–1517.
[26] D. L. Jagerman, "Methods in traffic calculation," *AT&T Bell Labs. Tech. J.*, vol. 63, no. 7, pp. 1283–1310, 1984.
[27] R. Kawamura, K. I. Sato, and I. Tokizawa, "Self-healing ATM networks based on virtual path concept," *IEEE J. Select. Areas Commun.*, vol. 12, no. 1, pp. 120–127, 1994.

[28] K. Kawashima and H. Saito, "Teletraffic issues in ATM networks," *Computer Networks & ISDN Systems*, vol. 20, pp. 369–375, 1990.

[29] E. L. Lawler, *Combinatorial Optimization: Networks and Matroids*. New York: Holt, Rinehart, and Winston, 1976.

[30] M. J. Lee and J. R. Yee, "A design algorithm for reconfigurable ATM networks," in *Proc. IEEE INFOCOM*, 1993, pp. 144–151.

[31] K. Lindberger, "Dimensioning and design methods for integrated ATM networks," in *Proc. 14th Int. Teletraffic Congress*, 1994, pp. 897–906.

[32] M. Logothetis and S. Shioda, "Centralized virtual path bandwidth allocation scheme for ATM network," *IEICE Trans. Comm.*, vol. E75-B, no. 10, pp. 1071–1080, 1992.

[33] D. Medhi, "A unified approach to network survivability for teletraffic networks: models, algorithms and analysis," *IEEE Trans. Commun.*, vol. 42, pp. 534–548, 1994.

[34] ——, "Models for network design, servicing and monitoring of ATM networks based on the virtual path concept," *Computer Networks and ISDN Systems*, to appear (available by anonymous ftp: `ftp://ftp.cstp.umkc.edu/papers/dmedhi/m_cnisdn_9x.ps`).

[35] M. Minoux, *Mathematical Programming—Theory and Algorithms*. New York: Wiley, 1986.

[36] C. M. D. Pazos, J. A. Suruagy Monteiro, and M. Gerla, "Topological design of multiservice ATM networks," in *Proc. SBT/IEEE ITS*, 1994, pp. 385–389.

[37] H. Saito, *Teletraffic Technologies in ATM Networks*. Boston, MA: Artech House, 1994.

[38] K. I. Sato, S. Ohta, and I. Tokizawa, "Broad-band ATM network architecture based on virtual paths," *IEEE Trans. Commun.*, vol. 38, pp. 1212–1222, 1990.

[39] Y. Sato and K. I. Sato, "Virtual path and link capacity design for ATM networks," *IEEE J. Select. Areas Commun.*, vol. 9, pp. 104–111, 1991.

[40] R. Siebenhaar, "Optimized ATM virtual path bandwidth management under fairness constraints," in *Proc. IEEE GLOBECOM*, 1994, pp. 924–928.

[41] K. Sriram and W. Whitt, "Characterizing superposition arrival processes in packet multiplexers for voice and data," *IEEE J. Select. Areas Commun.*, vol. SAC-4, no. 6, pp. 833–846, 1986.

[42] J. A. Suruagy Monteiro, "Bandwidth allocation in broadband integrated services digital networks," Ph.D. dissertation, Report no. CSD-900018, Computer Science Department, University of California–Los Angeles, CA, July 1990.

[43] J. A. Suruagy Monteiro, M. Gerla, and L. Fratta, "Statistical multiplexing in ATM networks," *Performance Evaluation*, vol. 12, pp. 157–167, 1991.

[44] R. C. F. Tucker, "Accurate method for analysis of a packet–speech multiplexer with limited delay," *IEEE Trans. Commun.*, vol. 36, pp. 479–483, 1988.

D. Medhi (M'89/ACM'90) received the B.Sc. (with honors) in mathematics from Cotton College, Gauhati University, Assam, India, M.Sc. in Mathematics from the University of Delhi, India, the M.S. and Ph.D. degrees in Computer Sciences from the University of Wisconsin–Madison, in 1981, 1983, 1985 and 1987, respectively.

He is currently an Assistant Professor in the Department of Computer Networking, a unit of Computer Science Telecommunications at the University of Missouri–Kansas City (UMKC). Prior to joining UMKC, he was a Member of Technical Staff at AT&T Bell Laboratories, Holmdel, NJ, from 1987 to 1989. His current research interests are in survivable network design, dynamic routing, broadband network design, large-scale optimization algorithms, network architecture and network management. He is on the editorial board of the *Journal of Network and Systems Management* and is a member of council of INFORMS Section on Telecommunications.

Dr. Medhi is a member of ACM, INFORMS (formerly, ORSA/TIMS), and SIAM.

Performance Analysis of Reactive Congestion Control for ATM Networks

Kenji Kawahara, Yuji Oie, *Member, IEEE*, Masayuki Murata, *Member, IEEE*, and Hideo Miyahara, *Member, IEEE*

Abstract—In ATM networks, preventive congestion control is widely recognized for efficiently avoiding congestion, and it is implemented by a conjunction of connection admission control and usage parameter control. However, congestion may still occur because of unpredictable statistical fluctuation of traffic sources even when preventive control is performed in the network. In this paper, we study another kind of congestion control, i.e., reactive congestion control, in which each source changes its cell emitting rate adaptively to the traffic load at the switching node (or at the multiplexer). Our intention is that, by incorporating such a congestion control method in ATM networks, more efficient congestion control is established. We develop an analytical model, and carry out an approximate analysis of reactive congestion control algorithm. Numerical results show that the reactive congestion control algorithms are very effective in avoiding congestion and in achieving the statistical gain. Furthermore, the binary congestion control algorithm with push-out mechanism is shown to provide the best performance among the reactive congestion control algorithms treated here.

I. INTRODUCTION

IN packet-switching networks, congestion control methods are mainly divided into two categories: preventive control and reactive control [1]. In conventional packet-switching networks, reactive controls are generally adopted in which the source node recognizes network congestion by means of the feedback information sent from the destination node or intermediate ones. Then, the source node limits the packet injection into the network by some appropriate method. However, in high-speed networks of today, propagation delay of such congestion information are no longer negligible compared to the packet transmission times. This sort of congestion control policy results in severe performance degradation for real-time applications during the congestion period, which is greater than round-trip propagation delay. Therefore, preventive controls are now being recognized as an attractive way of treating congestion problems in high-speed networks. For example, in ATM networks, congestion is prevented by limiting the number of connections on each link in connection admission control (CAC) and usage parameter control (UPC), which ensure required quality of service (QOS) for the established connections (see, e.g., [2]).

Manuscript received March 2, 1994; revised September 12, 1994.

K. Kawahara and Y. Oie are with the Department of Computer Science and Electronics, Faculty of Computer Science and Systems Engineering, Kyushu Institute of Technology, Iizuka 820, Japan.

M. Murata and H. Miyahara are with the Department of Information and Computer Sciences, Faculty of Engineering Science, Osaka University, Toyonaka 560, Japan.

IEEE Log Number 9407073.

However, it often happens that users do not have enough information related to the characteristics of their traffic before transmitting it, as mentioned in [3]. It is therefore desirable that the CAC is performed based upon simple parameters associated with incoming traffic. Gersht and Lee [3] have proposed congestion control at two levels, VC level and cell level. In their mechanism, the simple CAC at VC level successfully prevents congestion in combination with reactive congestion control at cell level, which is applied only to nonreal-time traffic. Abould-Magd and Gilbert [4] and Newman [5] have shown by means of simulations that reactive congestion control, referred to as explicit congestion notification (ECN) mechanism, is effective in ATM networks in allowing an efficient use of network resources while maintaining adequate QOS. In particular, Newman [5] has focused on ATM LAN's and shown that a backward ECN mechanism is very effective in achieving high link utilization in ATM LAN's of up to at least 50 km. The analytical approach for reactive congestion control was developed by Wang and Sengupta [6], in which propagation delay between sources and a congested node is taken into account, and packets are assumed to be always transmitted in available slots from each source according to a Poisson distribution.

The main objective of the current paper is to provide insights into the benefits gained by using the reactive control algorithm and its limitations. For this purpose, we treat the two-stage queueing network where the output from the multiple *sources* in the first stage is multiplexed at the switching node, called *server*, in the second stage with some propagation delay between two stages. In this model, the cell transmission rate at each source can be adjusted according to the queue length in the server because each source is equipped with buffers. For the cell arrival processes at each source, we employ the two-state Markov-modulated Bernoulli process (MMBP) which is intended to model the superposition of bursty traffic [7]. By using this model, we provide an approximate analysis to examine the impact of propagation delay, buffer size, and traffic characteristics such as average arrival rate and burstiness on the performance of some reactive congestion control algorithms. In particular, we are interested in ATM LAN's in which propagation delay is very low, and reactive congestion controls are thus expected to be very effective.

Our modeling intends to treat the following case of practical interest; the ECN is sent along the forward path to the destination, referred to as the *forward* ECN, and each source

0733–8716/95$04.00 © 1995 IEEE

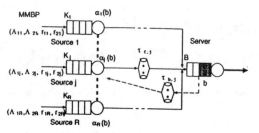

Fig. 1.   Analytical model for reactive congestion control.

stops/begins to transmit its cells according to the ECN. The *backward* ECN mechanism can be also treated in which the latency experienced by the ECN is smaller than in the forward ECN mechanism.[1] Another type of congestion control which we will treat is that each source controls its cell transmission depending on its own queue length as well as the ECN. More specifically, the latter mechanism forces each source to *push out* its head-of-line cell to the server when there is no space in its own buffer for a newly arriving cell. If at most one cell arrives at a source per slot, cell loss does not occur at the source in this case. Furthermore, the pushed-out cells from some sources can enter the server buffer if there is any space in the buffer, whereas these cells, in turn, increase the server queue, causing the sources to stop their cell transmission for a longer duration. Accordingly, this should lead to performance improvement with respect to cell loss at the cost of some additional waiting time incurred in the buffer, along with an appropriate ECN-based congestion control. Within an acceptable waiting time, performance improvement can actually be obtained, which will be shown in our numerical examples.

The remainder of the paper is organized as follows. In Section II, we describe our analytical model. Section III provides an approximate analysis for deriving the cell-loss probability and the average waiting time under reactive congestion controls considered in this paper. Numerical results and discussions are given in Section IV. Section V presents concluding remarks.

II. ANALYTICAL MODEL

In this section, we describe our model for analyzing the reactive congestion control algorithms. Our queueing system consists of two-stage queues with finite capacity in series, as illustrated in Fig. 1. In the first stage, there are R sources in parallel. S_{1j} denotes the jth source in the first stage, which has a cell buffer of K_j in length. Cells transmitted from these sources are multiplexed at the server S_2 in the second stage, which is equipped with a buffer of B in length.

We consider a discrete time queueing system with time slot being equal to a cell transmission time on the output link. It is assumed that cells arrive at each source S_{1j} according to a two-state MMBP, which is characterized by a set of parameters,

$(\Lambda_{1j}, \Lambda_{2j}, r_{1j}, r_{2j})$. It has two states, state 1 and state 2. At each slot, the process changes its state from state 1 to state 2 with probability r_{1j}, and from state 2 to state 1 with probability r_{2j}. The mean number of cells arriving at the jth source per slot is Λ_{1j} during state 1 and Λ_{2j} during state 2, respectively. Thus, the average arrival rate at the jth source queue is given by

$$\Lambda_j = \frac{r_{2j}}{r_{1j} + r_{2j}}\Lambda_{1j} + \frac{r_{1j}}{r_{1j} + r_{2j}}\Lambda_{2j}, \qquad (1 \le j \le R). \quad (1)$$

Suppose that $\Lambda_{1j} \ge \Lambda_{2j}$. In addition to the average arrival rate, we define the burstiness, β_j, which is commonly used to represent how the arrival traffic is bursty, and the burst-length, L_{b_j}, as follows

$$\beta_j \triangleq \frac{\Lambda_{1j}}{\Lambda_j}, \qquad L_{b_j} \triangleq \frac{1}{r_{1j}}, \qquad (1 \le j \le R). \quad (2)$$

We introduce the probability matrix of state transition and that of cell arrival for each MMBP at source queues, T_j and $a_{i,j}$, respectively, as follows

$$T_j = \begin{pmatrix} 1 - r_{1j} & r_{1j} \\ r_{2j} & 1 - r_{2j} \end{pmatrix}$$
$$a_{i,j} = \begin{pmatrix} a_{1j}(i) & 0 \\ 0 & a_{2j}(i) \end{pmatrix}, \qquad (1 \le j \le R). \quad (3)$$

Each element, $a_{lj}(i)\,(l = 1, 2)$, in the above matrix $a_{i,j}$ corresponds to the probability that the number of i cells arrive at the jth source queue at each slot when MMBP is in state l, and is given by

$$a_{lj}(i) = \binom{N_{lj}}{i}\left(\frac{\Lambda_{lj}}{N_{lj}}\right)^i\left(1 - \frac{\Lambda_{lj}}{N_{lj}}\right)^{N_{lj}-i}, \qquad (1 \le j \le R) \quad (4)$$

where N_{lj} is the maximum number of cells arriving at each slot at the jth source when it is in state l.

We introduce a control function $\alpha_j(b)$ for each source S_{1j}, which is a function of the queue length, b, of the server, and takes values ranging from 0 to 1. At each slot, by using $\alpha_j(b)$ as a probability of transmitting a cell, the jth source determines whether it transfers the cell in its buffer to the server or not. Apparently, as the number of cells at the server becomes large, i.e., when the server is congested, the cells should be held momentarily in the sources to relieve congestion at the server quickly. In this case, the transmission rate at each one of the sources should be decreased. However, if the transmission rate is kept low at sources even after congestion is relieved at the server, cell loss at sources would unnecessarily happen.

Furthermore, we take into account propagation delay between the source and the server; let $\tau_{f,j}$ be cell propagation delay from the jth source to the server, and $\tau_{b,j}$ be delay experienced by the congestion notification from the server to the jth source, as illustrated in the top of Fig. 2. Namely, the jth source transmits its cell to the server according to the state of the server queue at the $\tau_{b,j}$th slot preceding the current slot.

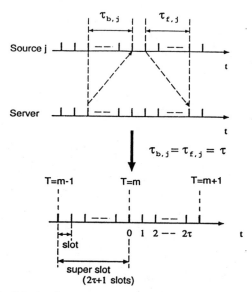

Fig. 2. Behavior of cell transmission and outline of *super-slot*.

The state of the server at the current slot thus depends on the state of the jth source at the $\tau_{f,j}$th slot behind the current slot. As a result, it is very hard to carry out an exact analysis of this system on a slot basis.[2]

We set $\tau_{f,j}$ and $\tau_{b,j}$ to the same value, τ, for all the sources. A block of consecutive $2\tau + 1$ slots will be called a *super-slot* (see the bottom of Fig. 2). Furthermore, we use the following model which makes the analysis tractable, and then obtain the cell loss and the average waiting time characteristics at an arbitrary slot by using the steady-state probability at the beginning of the super-slot. It is worth noting that the following model is the exact one when τ is equal to 0.

1) The server receives cells transmitted during a super-slot from each source only at the end of the super-slot. Since cells transmitted at the ith slot ($i = 0, 1 \cdots, 2\tau$) of a super-slot arrive at the server in $2\tau - i$ slots, the average delay time of cells transmitted from sources to the server is equal to $[\Sigma_{i=0}^{2\tau}(2\tau - i)]/(2\tau + 1)$, resulting in τ.

2) Each source is assumed to receive the information of congestion notification from the server only at the beginning of a super-slot with no delay. The value of the control function $\alpha_j(b)$ is changed only at the beginning of a super-slot, and is kept fixed all over the super-slot. Since the feedback delay at the ith slot of a super-slot is actually equal to i slots, the average feedback delay time per super-slot from the server to sources becomes $(\Sigma_{i=0}^{2\tau} i)/(2\tau + 1)$. This is also equal to τ.

---

[2] Wang and Sengupta [6] proposed a sophisticated approach for analyzing a similar system by taking into account propagation delay between sources and the server as mentioned in Section I. It is also of interest to investigate a manner to apply their approach to the system considered here. Since we are in particular interested in ATM LAN's with very low propagation delay, we derive here an exact analysis of the system under no propagation delay, and then approximately analyze the system based upon the analysis under some propagation delay.

III. DERIVATION OF STEADY-STATE PROBABILITY OF BUFFER CONTENTS

The state of our system can be completely described by a set of 1) the queue length, D_2, of the server, 2) the queue length, D_{1j}, of each source, and 3) the MMBP state, S_j, of each source. Since it forms a Markov chain on a super-slot basis, we can derive the steady-state probability at the beginning of a super-slot $P(b, k_1, s_1, \cdots, k_R, s_R) \triangleq \Pr(D_2 = b, D_{11} = k_1, S_1 = s_1, \cdots, D_{1R} = k_R, S_R = s_R)$ by using the transition probability matrix Q obtained below for this process, and then also derive the overall system cell-loss probability.

A. Transition Probability Matrix for System State, Q

In order to derive Q, we below obtain the following matrices: 1) the transition probability matrix per slot, $G_{b,j}(x)$, of the jth source, 2) the transition probability matrix per slot, $G_b(y)$, of all the sources, and 3) the transition probability matrix per super-slot, $L_{b,b'}$, concerning the server.

1) Transition Probability Matrix for Each Source: To represent the transition probability matrix per slot for each source, we assume that the events on each source at a slot occur in the following sequence:

1) At the beginning of a slot, each source decides whether it transmits its head-of-line (HOL) cell according to $\alpha_j(b)$. The value of $\alpha_j(b)$ at the beginning of a super-slot is assumed to be used throughout that super-slot as mentioned earlier. If the jth source can transmit a cell at the slot, it starts to send the HOL cell to the server.

2) New cells arrive at the sources and are stored in their buffers. If the jth source contains k_j cells at the beginning of a slot, it can store at most $K_j - k_j + 1$ new cells. When more than $K_j - k_j + 1$ cells arrive, some of them will be lost. If there is no cell in the buffer at the beginning of a slot, the source immediately starts to send one of the newly arriving cells.[3]

3) The source finishes sending the HOL cell at the end of a slot.

Let $G_{b,j}(x)$ denote the transition matrix associated with the jth source on the condition that the server contains b cells in the buffer. Its (k, l)-block element corresponds to the probability that the number of x cells are transmitted from the jth source to the server, and that the number of cells, D_{1j}, at the jth source is changed from k to l. As mentioned in Section II, each source transmits its HOL cell to the server with probability $\alpha_j(b)$, which will be specified for each control algorithm in Section IV.

As mentioned in Section I, we deal with two congestion control mechanisms, *discipline A* and *discipline B*, which are different in the buffer management at the sources. $G_{b,j}(x)$ is obtained below for these two disciplines:

1) *discipline A (basic one)*

Whether the HOL cell is transmitted or not depends only on $\alpha_j(b)$. $G_{b,j}(x)$ takes the form of (5), shown at the bottom of the next page, under this discipline, where $0[m]$ represents a zero matrix of dimension $m \times m$.

---

[3] Some assumptions other than this one (cut-through assumption) can be used. This one is chosen only as one of available assumptions.

2) *discipline B* (pushout *discipline*)

When cell arrivals cause buffer overflow at the jth source, the HOL cell is pushed out to the server regardless of the value of $\alpha_j(b)$, thereby enabling one of the new cells to enter the source buffer. Thus, the transition matrix $G_{b,j}(x)$ under discipline B is different from that under discipline A only in the rightmost column, which is related to the case where the buffer of the jth source becomes fully occupied. Under this discipline, we obtain $G_{b,j}(x)$ as (6), at the bottom of this page.

2) Transition Probability Matrix of Cells Transmission of All Sources: We introduce $G_b(y)$ which represents the probability

that the number of y cells are transmitted at a slot from the sources to the server in total, and it can be expressed by the Kronecker product of cell arrival matrices from the sources, i.e.

$$G_b(y) = \sum_{\Sigma_{j=1}^{R} x_j = y} G_{b,1}(x_1) \otimes \cdots \otimes G_{b,R}(x_R),$$

$$(0 \leq y \leq R). \quad (7)$$

3) Transition Probability Matrix Concerning the Queue Length of Server per Super-Slot: To obtain the probability matrix which denotes the transition per super-slot with respect

$$G_{b,j}(0) = (1 - \alpha_j(b)) \times \begin{pmatrix} \dfrac{a_{0,j}T_j}{(1-\alpha_j(b))} & a_{1,j}T_j & \cdot & a_{K_j-1,j}T_j & \displaystyle\sum_{i=K_j}^{\infty} a_{i,j}T_j \\ 0[2] & a_{0,j}T_j & \cdots & a_{K_j-2,j}T_j & \displaystyle\sum_{i=K_j-1}^{\infty} a_{i,j}T_j \\ \vdots & \ddots & \ddots & \vdots & \vdots \\ \vdots & \cdots & \ddots & a_{0,j}T_j & \displaystyle\sum_{i=1}^{\infty} a_{i,j}T_j \\ 0[2] & \cdots & \cdots & 0[2] & a_{0,j}T_j \end{pmatrix}$$

$$G_{b,j}(1) = \alpha_j(b) \times \begin{pmatrix} a_{1,j}T_j & a_{2,j}T_j & \cdots & a_{K_j,j}T_j & \displaystyle\sum_{i=K_j+1}^{\infty} a_{i,j}T_j \\ a_{0,j}T_j & a_{1,j}T_j & \cdots & a_{K_j-1,j}T_j & \displaystyle\sum_{i=K_j}^{\infty} a_{i,j}T_j \\ 0[2] & \ddots & \ddots & \vdots & \vdots \\ \vdots & \ddots & a_{0,j}T_j & a_{1,j}T_j & \displaystyle\sum_{i=2}^{\infty} a_{i,j}T_j \\ 0[2] & \cdots & 0[2] & a_{0,j}T_j & \displaystyle\sum_{i=1}^{\infty} a_{i,j}T_j \end{pmatrix}, \quad (0 \leq b \leq B, \quad 1 \leq j \leq R) \quad (5)$$

$$G_{b,j}(0) = (1 - \alpha_j(b)) \times \begin{pmatrix} \dfrac{a_{0,j}T_j}{(1-\alpha_j(b))} & a_{1,j}T_j & \cdots & a_{K_j-1,j}T_j & a_{K_j,j}T_j \\ 0[2] & a_{0,j}T_j & \cdots & a_{K_j-2,j}T_j & a_{K_j-1,j}T_j \\ \vdots & \ddots & \ddots & \vdots & \vdots \\ \vdots & \cdots & \ddots & a_{0,j}T_j & a_{1,j}T_j \\ 0[2] & \cdots & \cdots & 0[2] & a_{0,j}T_j \end{pmatrix}$$

$$G_{b,j}(1) = \alpha_j(b) \times \begin{pmatrix} a_{1,j}T_j & a_{2,j}T_j & \cdots & a_{K_j,j}T_j & \displaystyle\sum_{i=K_j+1}^{\infty} \dfrac{a_{i,j}T_j}{\alpha_j(b)} \\ a_{0,j}T_j & a_{1,j}T_j & \cdots & a_{K_j-1,j}T_j & \displaystyle\sum_{i=K_j}^{\infty} \dfrac{a_{i,j}T_j}{\alpha_j(b)} \\ 0[2] & \ddots & \ddots & \vdots & \vdots \\ \vdots & \ddots & a_{0,j}T_j & a_{1,j}T_j & \displaystyle\sum_{i=2}^{\infty} \dfrac{a_{i,j}T_j}{\alpha_j(b)} \\ 0[2] & \cdots & 0[2] & a_{0,j}T_j & \displaystyle\sum_{i=1}^{\infty} \dfrac{a_{i,j}T_j}{\alpha_j(b)} \end{pmatrix}, \quad (0 \leq b \leq B, \quad 1 \leq j \leq R). \quad (6)$$

330

to the queue length of the server, we assume the events on the server at a slot occur in the following sequence,

1) The server begins to forward its HOL cell.
2) Cells arrive from each source. If the server contains b cells at the beginning of the slot, it can store at most $B - b + 1$ cells of arriving cells. If the server contains no cells at the beginning of a slot, it immediately begins to forward one of the arriving cells.
3) The server finishes forwarding the cell at the end of a slot.

In what follows, we obtain the transition matrix $L_{b,b'}$, which represents the transition of the number of cells stored at the server from b to b' at the beginning of two consecutive super-slots.

For this purpose, we temporarily define the matrix $M_{b,t}(x)$, whose elements represent the probabilities that the server queue length is equal to x at the end of the tth slot in a super-slot, given that it is equal to b at the beginning of the super-slot. $L_{b,b'}$ is related to this matrix as follows

$$L_{b,b'} \triangleq M_{b,2\tau}(b'). \qquad (8)$$

Suppose that $x + 1 - b$ cells arrive at the server at the zeroth slot, which includes b cells at the beginning of the zeroth slot. One of the b cells will be transmitted, and x cells will be kept at the server at the end of the zeroth slot. One of the b cells will be transmitted by the end of zeroth slot, and the server thus has x cells at the end of zeroth slot. Therefore, we have $M_{b,0}(x)$ at the end of the zeroth slot in a super-slot as follows

$$
M_{b,0}(x) = \begin{cases}
\sum_{j=0}^{1} G_b(j - b), \\
\qquad \text{if } x = 0 \quad \text{and} \quad b \leq 1 \\
G_b(x + 1 - b), \\
\qquad \text{if } 1 \leq x \leq B - 1 \\
\sum_{j=1}^{R - B + b} G_b(B + j - b), \\
\qquad \text{if } x = B.
\end{cases} \qquad (9)
$$

In a similar manner, we obtain the following relation between $M_{b,t}(x)$ and $M_{b,t-1}(y)$

$$
M_{b,t}(x) = \begin{cases}
\sum_{j=0}^{1} \sum_{i=0}^{\min(j,R)} M_{b,t-1}(j - i) G_b(i), \\
\qquad \text{if } x = 0 \\
\sum_{i=0}^{\min(x+1,R)} M_{b,t-1}(x + 1 - i) G_b(i), \\
\qquad \text{if } 1 \leq x \leq B - 1 \\
\sum_{j=1}^{R} \sum_{i=j}^{\min(B+j,R)} M_{b,t-1}(B + j - i) G_b(i), \\
\qquad \text{if } x = B
\end{cases}
$$
$$(1 \leq t \leq 2\tau). \qquad (10)$$

We can obtain $M_{b,2\tau}(b')$ by using (9) and (10) iteratively.

B. Derivation of Steady-State Probability

Using the matrix $L_{b,b'}$, the whole transition probability matrix Q can be built as follows

$$
Q = \begin{pmatrix}
L_{0,0} & L_{0,1} & \cdots & L_{0,B} \\
L_{1,0} & L_{1,1} & \cdots & L_{1,B} \\
\vdots & \vdots & \ddots & \vdots \\
L_{B,0} & L_{B,1} & \cdots & L_{B,B}
\end{pmatrix}. \qquad (11)
$$

Note that the dimension of Q is given by

$$(B+1)q \times (B+1)q, \quad (q \triangleq 2^R (K_1+1) \cdots (K_R+1)). \qquad (12)$$

Consequently, we can obtain the steady-state probability vector by solving the following equation

$$PQ = P, \quad Pe((B+1)q) = 1 \qquad (13)$$

where $e(m)$ represents a column vector of dimension m, whose elements are all equal to 1, and

$$P = [P_0, \cdots, P_b, \cdots, P_B],$$
$$P_b = [\cdots, P(b, k_1, s_1, \cdots, k_R, s_R), \cdots],$$
$$0 \leq k_j \leq K_j, \quad s_j = 1, 2, \quad (0 \leq j \leq R) \qquad (14)$$

whose elements are ordered appropriately in accordance with the configuration of the transition matrices.

It may be difficult to directly solve (13) since the number of states grows explosively as the size of buffer capacity at sources and/or the server becomes large (See (12)). We thus employ the computational algorithm proposed in [8], by which the computational cost is determined by the buffer size of the source queue and independent of that of the server queue.[4]

C. Derivation of Cell-Loss Probabilities

In this subsection, we will derive the cell-loss probability at an arbitrary slot by using the steady-state probability at the beginning of a super-slot, which has been obtained in the previous section. It is noted that no cell loss occurs at sources under discipline B, if at most one cell arrives at each source at a slot.

1) Average Number of Lost Cells at the Source Queue: Using the steady-state probability vector P derived in the previous subsection, we first obtain the average number of lost cells, $R_{\text{loss}1,j,t}$, at the tth slot of a super-slot at the jth source, and then get the average number of lost cells, $R_{\text{loss}1,j}$, at an arbitrary slot.

In order to obtain $R_{\text{loss}1,j,t}$, we define the state probability at the beginning of a super-slot on the condition that the queue length D_2 of the server is equal to b, as follows

$$\pi_{b,0}(k_1, s_1, \cdots, k_R, s_R)$$
$$\triangleq \Pr(D_{11} = k_1, S_1 = s_1, \cdots, D_{1R} = k_R,$$

---

[4] The dimension of the submatrices $L_{i,j}$ is a function of the source buffer size, but is not a function of the server buffer size. In addition, if propagation delay and the number of sources are relatively small, many of the submatrices $L_{i,j}$ become 0 ones when $|i - j|$ is relatively large. Furthermore, the computational scheme in [8] enables us to obtain the solution to (13) only by means of nonzero sub-matrices. Therefore, the computational cost becomes less expensive as propagation delay becomes lower; that is, this computational scheme is very effective in ATM LAN's we have focused on here.

$$S_R = s_R | D_2 = b)$$
$$= P(b, k_1, s_1, \cdots, k_R, s_R) / \Pr(D_2 = b) \quad (15)$$

and introduce its vector representation

$$\boldsymbol{\Pi}_{b,0} \triangleq [\cdots, \pi_{b,0}(k_1, s_1, \cdots, k_R, s_R), \cdots]. \quad (16)$$

Note that $\Pr(D_2 = b) = \boldsymbol{P}_b e(q)$ in which q indicates the dimension of vector $\boldsymbol{P}_b$. The conditional state probability vector, at the beginning of the tth slot of a super-slot, $\boldsymbol{\Pi}_{b,t}$, can be given in terms of $\boldsymbol{\Pi}_{b,0}$ as

$$\boldsymbol{\Pi}_{b,t} = \boldsymbol{\Pi}_{b,0} \boldsymbol{G}_b^t, \qquad (1 \le t \le 2\tau) \quad (17)$$

where $\boldsymbol{G}_b \triangleq \Sigma_{i=0}^R \boldsymbol{G}_b(i)$, in which $\boldsymbol{G}_b(i)$ is given in (7).

Noting that $\alpha_j(b)$ at the beginning of a super-slot is used over it, we can derive $R_{\text{loss}1,j,t}$ for the jth source controlling its traffic under discipline A as follows

$$R_{\text{loss}1,j,t} = \sum_{\sigma} \Pr(D_2 = b) \pi_{b,t}(k_1, s_1, \cdots, k_R, s_R)$$
$$\times \left\{ \alpha_j(b) \sum_{i=K_j+2-k_j}^{N_{s_j,j}} a_{s_j,j}(i) \right.$$
$$\cdot [i + k_j - (K_j + 1)]$$
$$+ [1 - \alpha_j(b)] \sum_{i=K_j+1-k_j}^{N_{s_j,j}} a_{s_j,j}(i)$$
$$\left. \cdot (i + k_j - K_j) \right\} \quad (18)$$

where σ represents all combinations of $(b, k_1, s_1, \cdots, k_R, s_R)$ for b, k_i and s_i that satisfy $0 \le b \le B, 0 \le k_i \le K_i$ and $s_i = 1, 2 (1 \le i \le R)$. In the above equation, the first (the second) term in the braces corresponds to the case where the jth source is (not) permitted to transmit its cell.

On the other hand, under discipline B (namely, HOL cell pushout scheme), the jth source transmits its HOL cell regardless of the value of $\alpha_j(b)$ when newly arriving cells cause buffer overflow. Thus $R_{\text{loss}1,j,t}$ is simply given under discipline B by

$$R_{\text{loss}1,j,t} = \sum_{\sigma} \Pr(D_2 = b) \pi_{b,t}(k_1, s_1, \cdots, k_R, s_R)$$
$$\times \sum_{i=K_j+2-k_j}^{N_{s_j,j}} a_{s_j,j}(i)[i + k_j - (K_j + 1)]. \quad (19)$$

Finally, we can obtain $R_{\text{loss}1,j}$ as follows

$$R_{\text{loss}1,j} = \frac{\sum\limits_{t=0}^{2\tau} R_{\text{loss}1,j,t}}{2\tau + 1}. \quad (20)$$

2) Average Number of Lost Cells at the Server Queue: We obtain below the average number of lost cells, $R_{\text{loss}2,t}$, at the tth slot of a super-slot at the server queue. Suppose that the queue length of the server is equal to x at the end of the $t-1$-st slot; its associated probability matrix is $\boldsymbol{M}_{b,t-1}(x)$. At the tth slot, y cells arrive at the server from all the sources with probability $\boldsymbol{G}_b(y)$. In this case, one of the x cells is transmitted, and $B+1-x$ of the y cells are then stored in the server buffer. However, other $x + y - (B+1)$ cells are lost. Accordingly, we have $R_{\text{loss}2,t}$ given by

$$R_{\text{loss}2,t}$$
$$= \begin{cases} \sum\limits_{b=B+2-R}^{B} \sum\limits_{y=B+2-b}^{R} \\ \boldsymbol{P}_b \boldsymbol{G}_b(y) e(q) \{b + y - (B+1)\} \\ \quad \text{if } t = 0, \\ \sum\limits_{b=0}^{B} \sum\limits_{x=B+2-R}^{B} \sum\limits_{y=B+2-x}^{R} \\ \boldsymbol{P}_b \boldsymbol{M}_{b,t-1}(x) \boldsymbol{G}_b(y) e(q) \{x + y - (B+1)\} \\ \quad \text{if } 1 \le t \le 2\tau. \end{cases} \quad (21)$$

The average number of lost cells at each slot at the server, $R_{\text{loss}2}$, is given by

$$R_{\text{loss}2} = \frac{\sum\limits_{t=0}^{2\tau} R_{\text{loss}2,t}}{2\tau + 1}. \quad (22)$$

3) Overall System Cell-Loss Probability: By using (20) and (22), we finally obtain the overall system cell-loss probability as

$$P_{\text{loss}} = \frac{\sum\limits_{j=1}^{R} R_{\text{loss}1,j} + R_{\text{loss}2}}{\sum\limits_{j=1}^{R} \Lambda_j} \quad (23)$$

where Λ_j is the arrival rate of the arriving traffic at the jth source, which has been defined in (1).

D. Average Waiting Time

Let $P_{s_{1j},t}(k_j)$ and $P_{s_2,t}(b')$ denote the probability that the queue length at the jth source and the server are equal to k_j and b', respectively, at the tth slot of a super-slot. By using $\boldsymbol{M}_{b,t}(b')$ given by (10) and $\pi_{b,t+1}(k_1, s_1, \cdots, k_R, s_R)$ given by (17), we obtain these probabilities as follows

$$P_{s_{1j},t}(k_j) = \sum_{\sigma_{k_j}} \Pr(D_2 = b)$$
$$\times \pi_{b,t+1}(k_1, s_1, \cdots, k_j, s_j, \cdots, k_R, s_R),$$
$$(1 \le j \le R)$$
$$P_{s_2,t}(b') = \sum_{b=0}^{B} \boldsymbol{P}_b \boldsymbol{M}_{b,t}(b') e(q) \quad (24)$$

where σ_{k_j} represents all combinations of $(b, k_1, s_1, \cdots, k_{j-1}, s_{j-1}, s_j, k_{j+1}, s_{j+1}, \cdots, k_R, s_R)$

for b, k_i and s_i that satisfy $0 \leq b \leq B$, $0 \leq k_i \leq K_i$ $(i = 1, \cdots, j-1, j+1, \cdots, R)$ and $s_i = 1, 2$ $(1 \leq i \leq R)$. Note that $\pi_{b,t+1}(k_1, s_1, \cdots, k_R, s_R)$ is the state probability at the beginning of the $t+1$st slot, and that it can be regarded as the state probability at the end of the tth slot as well. Hence, we have the average queue length at the jth source and the server, denoted by $L_{q,1j}$ and $L_{q,2}$, as follows

$$L_{q,1j} = \frac{\sum_{t=0}^{2\tau}\sum_{k_j=0}^{K_j} k_j P_{s_{1j},t}(k_j)}{2\tau + 1}, \qquad (1 \leq j \leq R)$$

$$L_{q,2} = \frac{\sum_{t=0}^{2\tau}\sum_{b'=0}^{B} b' P_{s_2,t}(b')}{2\tau + 1}. \qquad (25)$$

By using Little's formula, we obtain the total average waiting time at the jth source and the server

$$W_j = \frac{L_{q,1j}}{\Lambda_j - R_{\text{loss}1,j}} + \frac{L_{q,2}}{\sum_{i=1}^{R}(\Lambda_i - R_{\text{loss}1,i}) - R_{\text{loss}2}}. \qquad (26)$$

IV. NUMERICAL RESULTS AND DISCUSSIONS

In this section, we investigate the effectiveness of reactive congestion control schemes by means of numerical results, which can be obtained by using our analytical method presented in the previous section. We can study various types of reactive congestion control schemes in a way to determine $\alpha_j(b)$ appropriately according to their schemes.

A. Numerical Parameters

The numerical results presented here are obtained under the following conditions:

- source nodes

  Sources are homogeneous in terms of the input traffic characteristics, buffer size and the function $\alpha_j(b)$. Namely, for any j such that $1 \leq j \leq R$

  $$(\Lambda_{1j}, \Lambda_{2j}, r_{1j}, r_{2j}) = (\lambda_1, \lambda_2, r_1, r_2),$$
  $$\Lambda_j = \lambda,$$
  $$\beta_j = \beta, \quad L_{b_j} = L_b,$$
  $$N_{lj} = \mathcal{N}_l, \quad (l = 1, 2),$$
  $$K_j = K, \quad \alpha_j(b) = \alpha(b).$$

Now, we define the total arrival rate at the server, λ_{all}, and that becomes equal to $R\lambda$.

- cell arrival model

  The interrupted Bernoulli process (IBP) is used as a cell arrival process to sources for simplicity of discussion although the analytical model can treat more general processes, MMBP. Namely, $\mathcal{N}_1 = 1, \mathcal{N}_2 = 0$ and $\lambda_2 = 0$, i.e., a cell arrives with probability λ_1 during state 1, and no cell arrives during state 2.

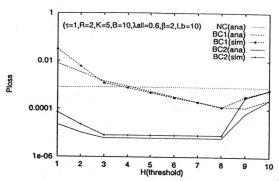

Fig. 3. Cell-loss probability as a function of H: comparison between analysis and simulation.

We will show the sensitivity of the cell-loss probability to the reactive congestion control algorithms. For this purpose, we consider a rather simple algorithm, in which cases $\alpha(b)$ takes only two values, i.e., 0 and 1. Namely, each source can emit its HOL cell until the queue length of the server, b, exceeds some threshold denoted by H. This type of control is below referred to as the *binary control*, BC for short. The binary control is of practical interest from an implementation point of view because the ECN sent by the server is a simple binary information, i.e., choking or relieving signal (or cell).

1) *BC1*:

$$\alpha(b) = \begin{cases} 1, & b \leq H - 1 \\ 0, & H \leq b \leq B. \end{cases}$$

2) *BC2*: a combination of BC1 and pushout discipline (discipline B, see Section II)

Numerical results in the case without any congestion control are also provided just for comparison; this case is denoted by No control (NC).

B. Numerical Results

First, we verify the accuracy of our analysis by comparing numerical results with simulation ones, and next discuss the optimum threshold H_{opt} at which the overall cell-loss probability, P_{loss}, is minimized under BC1 and BC2. Finally, we investigate the effectiveness of the reactive congestion control schemes.

1) Optimum Threshold H_{opt}: Fig. 3 illustrates the cell-loss probability as a function of the threshold H. We fix the buffer size of the server $B = 10$, that of each source $K = 5$, the number of sources $R = 2$, and propagation delay $\tau_l = 1$. With regard to input traffic characteristics of each source, we fix the input rate $\lambda = 0.3$, the burstiness $\beta = 2$, and the burst-length $L_b = 10$; the total arrival rate at the server λ_{all} is thus set to 0.6. In this figure, a comparison between analytical results and simulation ones is also shown.

We first see from this figure that analytical results agree with simulation ones very well over a wide range of H. Furthermore, the optimum threshold that minimizes P_{loss} is equal to 8 in BC1 from the analytical result. If H is set to a value smaller than 8, it may happen that sources are not allowed to transmit their HOL cells to the server in spite of the fact that the server queue has some space to store arriving cells. This results in increasing cell loss at sources. On the other hand, if H is larger than 8, more cells from each source will be dropped at the server queue. First, focusing on cell loss in the server, we will consider the condition on the optimum threshold. Since one-way propagation delay is τ slots, sources keep sending cells to the server during $(2\tau+1)$ slots even after the server sends a choking signal (or cell (see Fig. 2)). As a result, at most $(2\tau+1)\times R$ cells arrive at the server in this period, while the server can forward $2\tau+1$ cells in the same period. The server should thus send the ECN signal to each source when its queue length exceeds $B-(2\tau+1)(R-1)$ in order to prevent cell loss at the server. Finally, the optimum threshold for the server is $B+1-(2\tau+1)(R-1)$ or less. On the contrary, larger H is better for the sources because they are less frequently prevented from sending cells. The optimum threshold thus depends on the cell-loss performance at both the server and the sources. When cell loss at the server is dominant in the total cell loss, the optimum threshold can be given as follows

$$H_{\text{opt}}^{*} = B + 1 - (2\tau+1)(R-1), \quad \text{in case of BC1.} \quad (27)$$

By using this H_{opt}^{*}, P_{loss} is improved about one order of magnitude compared with that under NC.

Suppose that, under BC2, the binary control with pushout scheme, the server sends the choking signal when its queue length exceeds H_{opt}^{*} given in the above equation. For example, cell loss will occur if all R sources send their cells during $2\tau+1$ slots until they receive the choking signal and two cells or more are further pushed out in the following slot. In addition, it is noted that the sources push out their HOL cells to the server only when i) their buffers are filled up, and ii) newly cells arrive at them. Thus, a sequence of these events will happen with very small probability. In fact, BC2 drastically reduces the cell-loss probability about two orders of magnitude compared with NC. Moreover, BC2 successfully minimizes P_{loss} over a wide range of H. If H is set to a value smaller than H_{opt}^{*} for BC1, the pushout occurs more often on each source, and it will be more likely that pushed-out cells enter the server buffer because of the larger space remained at the server. Therefore, we can expect that P_{loss} is almost the same value as that in the case of $H = H_{\text{opt}}^{*}$. However, when a value smaller than $2\tau+1$ is chosen as H, the server queue can become empty after relieving cells are transferred to sources. As a result, the server utilization decreases, thereby increasing the cell-loss probability as shown in Fig. 3 (see the cases of $H = 1, 2$). Therefore, the range of optimum threshold of BC2 can be given as follows

$$2\tau+1 \leq H_{\text{opt}} \leq B+1-(2\tau+1)(R-1), \quad \text{in case of BC2.} \quad (28)$$

It is worth noting that a wider range of the optimum threshold H_{opt} is available under BC2 than under BC1. Therefore, the threshold can be determined based upon a rather rough estimation on propagation delay between the server and the sources. This is a very desirable feature because it is often

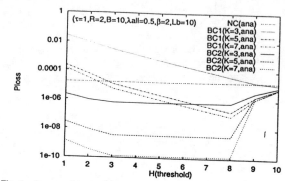

Fig. 4.   Impact of the buffer size of sources, K.

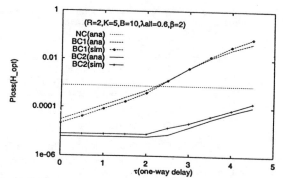

Fig. 5.   Cell-loss probability as a function of τ: Comparison between analysis and simulation.

very difficult for the server to know exactly the propagation delay.

We investigate the impact of the source buffer size K in Fig. 4, where we set the parameters as in Fig. 3 except for λ_{all}, which is set to 0.5. It is shown that both BC1 and BC2 reduce the cell-loss probability with larger K, and that BC2 is further superior to BC1 in terms of cell-loss performance. We observe that the range of the optimum threshold in BC2 does not vary with K, while the optimum threshold H_{opt} in BC1 is larger than H_{opt}^{*} given in (27) when K is small. This implies that H_{opt} in BC1 can be affected by the buffer size K.

2) The Impact of the Propagation Delay: Fig. 5 shows the cell-loss probability as a function of one-way propagation delay τ. In this figure, H is chosen in a manner to minimize P_{loss} in BC1 and BC2; the resulting P_{loss} is denoted by $P_{\text{loss}}(H_{\text{opt}})$, in what follows. Other parameters are set as in Fig. 3 except for τ. The comparison between analytical and simulation results are also shown. The analytical results there agree with the simulation ones very well, as in Fig. 3 τ is larger than 2, there exists no H satisfying (27) and inequality (28). In such cases, BC1 is not effective in reducing the cell-loss probability, while BC2 is still effective there.

Fig. 6 illustrates the impact of the server buffer size B in NC and BC2. We see from this figure that we can gain almost the same improvement in terms of cell-loss reduction for various values of B, when H_{opt} given in inequality (28) is available.

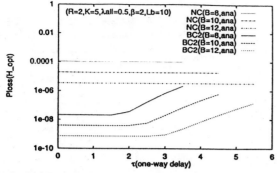

Fig. 6. Impact of the buffer size of server, B.

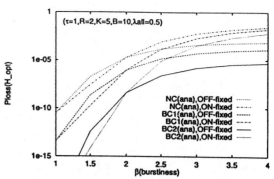

Fig. 8. Cell-loss probability versus traffic burstiness.

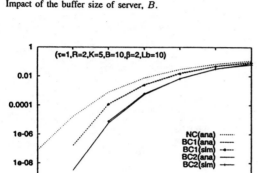

Fig. 7. Cell-loss probability versus total offered traffic rate at server.

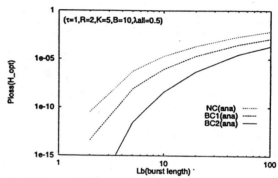

Fig. 9. Cell-loss probability versus traffic burst-length.

3) The Impact of the Traffic Characteristics: Fig. 7 shows the sensitivity of $P_{\text{loss}}(H_{\text{opt}})$ to the total arrival rate at the server λ_{all}. Under BC1, the optimum threshold H_{opt} is larger than H_{opt}^* given in (27) when λ_{all} is large. The improvement due to the congestion control such as BC1 and BC2 becomes larger as λ_{all} decreases. Supposing that the quality of service (QOS) in terms of the cell-loss probability is less than 10^{-6}, we see that, under BC2, the maximum amount of traffic that the server can accommodate increases up to about 0.57 from 0.44, while that under BC1 increases up to 0.52.

We show the sensitivity of $P_{\text{loss}}(H_{\text{opt}})$ to the input traffic burstiness β in Fig. 8. From (1) and (2), β is obtained as follows

$$\beta = \frac{\lambda_1}{\lambda} = \frac{r_1 + r_2}{r_1}. \qquad (29)$$

Keeping λ_{all} constant, we vary β by changing λ_1 and either r_1 or r_2, both of which denote the phase transition probabilities of the input traffic. In this figure *ON-fixed (OFF-fixed)* denotes the case where r_2 (r_1) is varied. In the case of ON-fixed, the cell-loss probability increases monotonously as β becomes larger. On the other hand, in the case of OFF-fixed, there is a plateau in terms of P_{loss}; it is noted that the average ON period decreases here as β increases.

We also present the sensitivity of $P_{\text{loss}}(H_{\text{opt}})$ to the burst-length L_b in Fig. 9. Again, from this figure, it is shown that BC2 improves the performance over a wide range of L_b. Suppose here that the QOS with regard to P_{loss} is less

than 10^{-6}. BC2 can accept the input traffic of the burst-length which is four times as long as that allowed by NC.

So far, we have focused on the situation where there are only two sources in the system. Fig. 10 depicts the cell-loss probability in cases with three and four sources. This figure demonstrates that the reactive control will work well even in a system consisting of a larger number of sources; i.e., the effectiveness of the control algorithms is less sensitive to the number of sources given a total traffic rate. However, it is worth noting that, from inequality (28), the range of the optimum threshold H_{opt} depends on the number of sources R.

4) Average Waiting Time: Fig. 11 shows the total average waiting time spent at the source and the server. Cells are kept waiting in the buffer for a longer duration under congestion control than under no congestion control. The average waiting time is larger in BC2 than in BC1 because pushed-out cells entering the server increases the server queue length; this additional waiting time in BC2 is traded for cell-loss improvement, as shown in several figures. We see that the average waiting time is kept within an acceptable level for nonreal-time applications over a wide range of λ_{all}.

V. CONCLUDING REMARKS

An analytical model has been developed to provide insights into the benefits obtained through reactive congestion control and its limitations in ATM LAN's with relatively low propa-

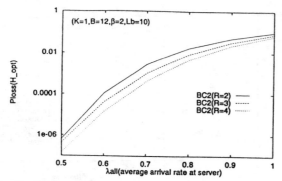

Fig. 10. Cell-loss probability versus total offered traffic rate: cases of 2, 3 and 4 sources in case of BC2.

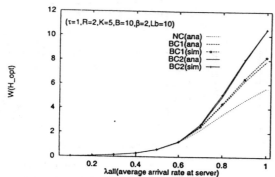

Fig. 11. Average waiting time versus total offered traffic rate

amount of offered traffic, the burstiness and the burst-length. For example, in the case treated in Fig. 7, BC2 successfully increases the maximum amount of traffic that can be accommodated by the server up to about 0.57 from 0.44 under no congestion control, keeping the cell-loss probability less than 10^{-6}.

REFERENCES

[1] I. W. Habib and T. N. Saadawi, "Controlling flow and avoiding congestion in broadband networks," *IEEE Commun. Mag.*, vol. 29, no. 10, pp. 46–53, Oct. 1991.
[2] H. Gilbert, O. Aboul-Magd, and V. Phung, "Developing a cohesive traffic management strategy for ATM networks," *IEEE Network*, vol. 29, no. 10, pp. 36–45, Oct. 1991.
[3] A. Gersht and K. J. Lee, "A congestion control framework for ATM networks," *IEEE J. Select. Areas Commun.*, vol. 9, no. 2, pp. 1119–1130, 1991.
[4] O. Aboul-Magd and H. Gilbert, "Incorporating congestion feedback in B-ISDN traffic management strategy," in *Proc. ISS'92*, Oct. 1992.
[5] P. Newman, "Backward explicit congestion notification for ATM local area networks," in *Proc. IEEE Globecom'93*, Nov./Dec. 1993, pp. 719–723.
[6] Y. T. Wang and B. Sengupta, "Performance analysis of a feedback congestion control policy under non-negligible propagation delay," in *Proc. Sigcomm'91*, 1991, pp. 149–157.
[7] H. Heffes and D. M. Lucantoni, "A Markov modulated characterization of packetized voice and data traffic and related multiplexer performance," *IEEE J. Select. Areas Commun.*, vol. SAC-4, no. 6, pp. 856–868, Sept. 1986.
[8] W. J. Stewart, "Recursive procedures for the numerical solution of Markov chains," *Queueing Networks with Blocking*, H. G. Perros and T. Altiok, Eds. New York: Elsevier, 1989, pp. 229–247.

gation delay. Our model is exact in cases without propagation delay, and is approximate in cases of nonzero propagation delay. As illustrated in Fig. 1, our analytical model consists of several sources and the server, which represents a congested node. The MMBP is employed as a cell arrival process at the source, which enables us to handle bursty traffic.

By the use of our model, we carried out an approximate analysis of two types of reactive congestion control algorithms. Numerical results agree with simulation ones, and indicate that a significant reduction in cell-loss probability can be achieved with the reactive congestion control, in particular, when propagation delay and utilization are rather low, like in ATM LAN's. The results obtained here are summarized below.

1) The binary congestion control algorithm combined with pushout discipline (BC2) provides better performance than the binary control (BC1).

2) We can determine the optimum threshold, H_{opt}, of the queue length in a congested node that minimizes the overall cell-loss probability, P_{loss}, quantitatively, under both BC1 and BC2. Under BC2, it is a function of the number of sources R and propagation delay τ, and can be determined based upon a rather rough estimation of R and τ. As a result, we see that BC2 is better than BC1 in that it is easier to determine H_{opt} under BC2 than under BC1.

3) The statistical gain can be increased by the reactive congestion control algorithms over a wide range of the

Kenji Kawahara was born in Nagasaki, Japan, in 1968. He received the B.E. and M.E. degrees in computer sciences and electronics from Kyushu Institute of Technology, Fukuoka, Japan, in 1991 and 1993, respectively.

He is currently with the graduate school of Kyushu Institute of Technology. His research interests include computer networks and error and congestion control in high-speed networks.

Mr. Kawahara is a member of the Institute of Electronics, Information, and Communication Engineers (IEICE) of Japan.

Yuji Oie (M'83) received the B.E., M.E., and D.E. degrees from Kyoto University, Kyoto, Japan, in 1978, 1980, and 1987, respectively.

From 1980 to 1983, he was with Nippon Denso Company Ltd., Kariya, Japan. From 1983 to 1990, he was with the Department of Electrical Engineering, Sasebo College of Technology, Sasebo, Japan. Since 1990, he has been an Associate Professor in the Department of Computer Science and Electronics, Faculty of Computer Science and Systems Engineering, Kyushu Institute of Technology, Iizuka, Japan. His research interests include performance evaluation of computer communication networks, high-speed networks, and queueing systems.

Dr. Oie is a member of IPSJ and IEICE.

Masayuki Murata (M'89) received the B.E., M.E., and Dr.E. degrees from Osaka University, Osaka, Japan, in 1982, 1984, and 1988, respectively, all in information and computer sciences.

In April 1984, he joined Tokyo Research Laboratory, IBM Japan, as a Researcher. From September 1987 to January 1989, he was an Assistant Professor with the Computation Center, Osaka University. In February 1989, he moved to the Department of Information and Computer Sciences, Faculty of Engineering Science, Osaka University, and has been an Associate Professor since December 1992. His research interests include computer communication networks, performance modeling and evaluation, and queueing systems.

Dr. Murata is a member of ACM and IEICE.

Hideo Miyahara (S'68–M'72) received the M.E. and D.E. degrees from Osaka University, Osaka, Japan, in 1969 and 1973, respectively.

From 1973 to 1980, he was an Assistant Professor in the Department of Applied Mathematics and Physics, Faculty of Engineering, Kyoto University, Kyoto, Japan. From 1980 to 1986, he was an Associate Professor in the Department of Information and Computer Sciences, Faculty of Engineering Science, Osaka University, and from 1986 to 1989, he was a Professor at the Computation Center. Since 1989, he has been a Professor in the Department of Information and Computer Sciences, Faculty of Engineering Science. From 1983 to 1984, he was a Visiting Scientist at IBM Thomas J. Watson Research Center, Yorktown Heights, NY. His research interests include performance evaluation of computer communication networks, broadband ISDN, and multimedia systems.

Dr. Miyahara is a member of IPSJ and IEICE.

337

Performance Evaluation of Adaptation Functions in the ATM Environment

George I. Stassinopoulos, *Member, IEEE*, Iakovos S. Venieris, *Member, IEEE*,
K. P. Petropoulos, and Emmanuel N. Protonotarios

Abstract—The paper models and evaluates key design issues for the Adaptation Layer in ATM networks. The role and efficient design of the adaptation layer is crucial for future B–ISDN based on ATM. We concentrate on packet-mode adaptation services analyzing and simulating relevant protocols employed for narrowband ISDN signaling and packet data. Processing and transmission resources are modeled. In particular we investigate the performance of software based solution resident in microprocessors and interfaces to the ATM world via a generic interface component. This set-up which is currently under development is found adequate to handle narrowband ISDN signaling and data traffic. It offers a cost effective and readily available solution for the transition phase towards fully customized broadband components.

I. Introduction

THE ATM adaptation layer (AAL) functionality is by definition service dependent, i.e., the AAL protocols have to provide to its service users the required quality of service (QOS) by enhancing the transmission and switching service offered by ATM. The adoption, however, of a huge number of AAL protocols, one for each service with different QOS requirements, would result in a complex B-ISDN protocol stack. To preserve a cost effective, easily extensive and modular broadband network, CCITT has accepted two main methods for classifying services and protocols according to the AAL requirements. That is service grouping and AAL sublayering. Services with common adaptation requirements and common traffic characteristics are grouped together in distinct service classes in the way appearing in Table I of CCITT draft recommendation I.362. Four service classes have currently been identified. Class A and B refer to constant bit rate (CBR) and variable bit rate (VBR) connection oriented services which require timing relation between source and destination. Class C and D refer to VBR connection oriented and connectionless services which do not require timing relation between source and destination.

Commonalties between the adaptation functions required for services belonging to the same or even different service classes

Paper approved by E. G. Sable, the Editor for Communications Switching of the IEEE Communications Society. Manuscript received August 10, 1990; revised May 14, 1991 and March 18, 1992. This work was supported in part by the European Community R&D in Advanced Communications—Technologies in Europe (RACE), programs R1022, R1044. This paper was presented in part at the 7th International Teletraffic Congress Seminar on Broadband Technologies: Architectures, Applications, Control, and Performance, Morristown, NJ, October 1990.

The authors are with the Department of Electrical and Computer Engineering, Division of Computer Science, National Technical University of Athens, 157 73 Zographou, Athens, Greece.

IEEE Log Number 9401431.

TABLE I
Bandwidth Utilization

	Signaling		Data	
	Alt A	Alt B	Alt A	Alt B
mean	0.661	0.697	0.861	0.877
max	0.858	0.887	0.872	0.887

enable sublayering of the AAL into distinct functional groups. On top of the ATM layer the AAL is further decomposed in the following two sublayers [1], [2], the segmentation and reassembly (SAR) sublayer and the convergence Sublayer (CS). This decomposition allows a conceptually clearer definition of functional groups. The protocols operating in the SAR sublayer generate ATM service data units (SDU's) which are fixed size 48-octet packets. Depending on the particular traffic profile of a service the SAR protocol either packetizes/depacketizes bits or performs segmentation/reassembly of packet-like SAR SDU's. The packetization/depacketization function of SAR refers to class A and B services which will be referred as continuous bit-stream oriented (CBO) services. The segmentation/reassembly functionality of SAR refers to the class C and D services or else to Packet Mode (PM) services; i.e., services offering a packet-like AAL SDU. Signaling in the control plane and data transfer in the user plane are typical examples of PM services. A number of services may use the same lower functions of the AAL protocol, i.e., the same SAR protocol, and simultaneously each service may require a different set of AAL higher functions. The higher AAL functions constitute the convergence sublayer (CS) protocol. The functionality of CS is clearly the convergence of different AAL service users of the same or different service class to a common SAR. In extreme cases no CS services are required (e.g., signaling as studied in [3]). Four SAR protocols have currently been identified in CCITT [2], each one corresponding to a different class of services. However, since these have not yet been finalized in the standardization bodies, enhancement of the number of SAR protocols and service classes is still an open issue. We thus feel free to present and concentrate on a further class, known as class 0, which has also been proposed in ETSI/NA5 [1]. This class is served by SAR protocols devoted to support narrowband ISDN service users for which the QOS offered by ATM is more easily provided. This implies that no CS protocols operating over SAR for class 0 services are required.

The adaptation functions undertaken by the SAR protocol for class 0 services are those centred around segmentation and reassembly of Layer 2 (L2) PDU's to and from ATM cells.

Reprinted from IEEE Transactions on Communications, Vol. 42, No. 6, June 1994, pp. 2335-2344.

The applications of SAR protocols for class 0 services is of crucial importance, especially in the transition phase towards full ATM oriented B–ISDN, in order to ensure compatibility of existing narrowband ISDN equipment and ATM. We will demonstrate that software algorithms in modern processors can cover the processing needs for narrowband services, arising from the segmentation/reassembly of frames to and from ATM cells.

In this paper the performance of SAR class 0 protocols for services when adapting existing OSI L2 protocols to the ATM bearer service is considered. Adaptation functions are assumed to be realized on the subscriber side, i.e., in Terminal Adaptors (TAs) connected to narrowband ISDN terminal equipments (TE's). This implies that the proposed SAR protocols should provide for a cost effective solution. To this end, two segmentation/reassembly methods, comprising two simple SAR protocol alternatives are presented in Section II. A processor executing the SAR protocol software algorithms, as well as other accompanying interfacing components are assumed for two scenarios differing on the transmitting but being equal on the receiving side. L2 frame streams belonging to different virtual connections are converted to the resulting cell streams and vice versa. Concrete characteristics of these interface components under development are given in Section III.1. Both SAR protocol alternatives are applied in the two scenarios: In the first a TA performing SAR protocol functions is attached to each narrowband TE, while in the second more than one TE's share a common TA. In both cases we assume a many-to-one communication reflecting the need to evaluate a worst case frame delay distribution in the receiving side. The scenarios considered are described in detail in Section III-B. With the above we can observe in detail the effect of cell interleaving. It is shown that the end-to-end delay performance depends heavily on whether cells belonging to a frame are consequent or intertwined with cells of other frames. Results are highlighted in Section IV.

II. SAR PROTOCOLS SUPPORTING NARROWBAND ISDN SERVICE USERS

As stated in the introduction the AAL protocols supporting existing narrowband ISDN service users protocols mainly involve segmentation and reassembly of L2 frames to and from ATM cells. Other functions like error detection and correction, retransmission and flow control are provided on a L2 frame basis in the well known manner appearing in data link protocol standards (see [4] for LAP-D as an example of signaling data link protocol). Here we assume that these functions are kept on a frame level, since the high reliability of the newly developed physical media can guarantee a performance at least as reliable as present day narrowband transmission set-ups [5], [14].

Reassembly of L2 frames is possible only when the receiver is aware of the particular connection an incoming frame belongs 1) as well as the beginning and the end of a frame so that consecutive frames of the same connection are distinguished 2).

We first turn our attention in 1). Currently ISDN provides a single physical channel for signaling and data transfer

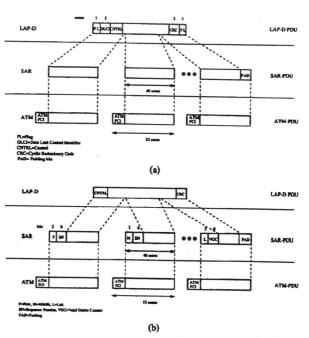

Fig. 1. Segmentation/reassembly alternatives. (a) Segmentation/reassembly Alternative (A). (b) Segmentation/reassembly Alternative (B).

(D-channel) so that the L2 containing the LAP-D protocol distinguishes signaling and data connections through the TEI and SAPI fields [4] of the LAP-D PCI. In the B–ISDN environment the multiplexing feature of LAP-D is moved to the ATM layer and is provided on a cell basis. Following this concept signaling and data exchange in an ATM-based network is assumed to be realized by assigning separate Virtual Channel/Path Identifiers (VCI's, VPI's) for each connection. Each signaling or data connection endpoint will be associated with its own ATM VCI/VPI that corresponds to a DLCI (data link connection identifier) value of LAP-D. At both ends corresponding tables must be kept and updated each time VCI's/VPI's for signaling or data are created or removed. This means that the reassembler of L2 frames accepts cells based on their VCI's/VPI's and forwards them to the upper layer through a SAP corresponding to the VCI/VPI value.

To address 2) we first remark that in ISDN frame delimitation is provided on a L2 frame basis using the well-known flagging and bitstuffing techniques appearing in HDLC oriented protocols [see Fig. 1(a)]. Frame delimitation may be alternatively provided on a cell level by the SAR protocol, without affecting the performance of the system. The SAR PCI subfields responsible for this task are denoted as F/M/L/S and VOC in Fig. 1(b). The main advantage in moving frame delimitation functions down to the lower SAR is the applicability of the same class 0 protocol to service users also with non-delimited L2 frames. An example appears in [14] where the SAR class 0 protocol serves LLC (logical link control). To overcome duplication of functions between adjacent layers the L2 frame assumed for this alternative should not be delimited. In Fig. 1(b) the LAP-D PDU is illustrated without flags and bitstuffing. Since multiplexing is provided on ATM layer the

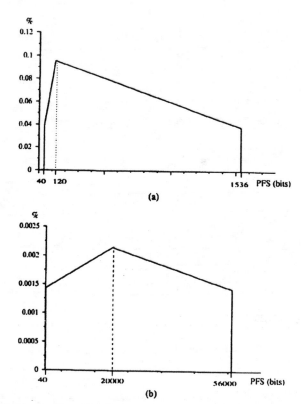

Fig. 2. Pure Frame Size distribution in bits. (a) Signaling frames. (b) Data frames.

TABLE II
INPUT PARAMETERS

Arrival rate of L2 signalling and data frames	1/(10,000 δ)	
Pure Frame Size distribution of signalling frames (PFS)	Fig. 2(a)	
Pure Frame Size distribution of data frames (PFS)	Fig. 2(b)	
Segmentation Alternative	A	B
Segmentation into cells according to	Fig. 1(a)	Fig. 1(b)
SAR processing time of a cell (segm./reass.) $J: F, M, L, S$	$T_{s,r}^J = 6\,\delta$	$T_{s,r}^F = 7\,\delta$ $T_{s,r}^L = 12\,\delta$ $T_{s,r}^M = 8\,\delta$ $T_{s,r}^S = 10\,\delta$
ATM servicing rate	2 out of 10 cells are free to carry the traffic of the connections considered	
Virtual Connections	8 signaling 3 data	

Note: δ is the 53-octet cell transmission time.

the envisaged hardware/software set-up in Section III-A and present its modeling in Section III-B.

A. Resources at the Transmit and Receive Side

At the transmit side we examine the handling of a L2 frame waiting for transmission in a microprocessor memory. In the case of alternative (A) it is bitstuffed and properly flagged. All SAR functions are performed by software so that the frame is then mapped into a sequence of ATM cells residing in the same memory. Upon completion the microprocessor resorts to a microprocessor-ATM interface (μP–IF) component for transmission. This component, currently under development [13] is accessible from the microprocessor side via an 8 bit data, 8 bit address, 6 bit control bus. The microprocessor passes the ATM cell octet by octet on a μP–IF FIFO. On the ATM transmit side this FIFO is emptied, while ATM empty cells are generated whenever the FIFO is empty. All cell multiplexing functions are undertaken by the microprocessor software. In particular priority schemes can be implemented, since a FIFO-empty signal from the μP–IF initiates the download of a new cell, which is selectable by the microprocessor software.

On the receive side the μP–IF chip is aware of the requested VPI/VCI values through an internal register bank updatable from the microprocessor. A cell arriving on the ATM side is accepted if its VPI/VCI is matched by any of the predefined values (max 64 values) and after hardware implemented header error checking it is passed to the 8 bit parallel data bus again through the intervention of a receive FIFO in the μP–IF. This FIFO also undertakes rate adaption between ATM 150 Mb/s rate and the slower rate towards the microprocessor side.

On the microprocessor side we work with a DMA access. Cells are written directly into memory, arranged on different banks according to their VPI/VCI. Adaptation layer reassembly is again performed by software. Typical processing time values in ATM cell transmission time for 150 Mbit/s rate for each alternative appear in Table II.

SAR SDU may be a L2 frame without the DLCI field [see Fig. 1(b)]. This allows a simplified LAP-*D* version to operate over SAR [3].

The segmentation/reassembly alternatives appearing in Fig. 1 can be compared to the bandwidth utilization of the ATM cell η, that is the fraction of the pure frame size (PFS) in bits divided by the total number of bits carried by the ATM cells used to transfer a frame. PFS is the number of significant bits of the frame. For example in the case of LAP-*D* the PFS is the ISDN LAP-*D* without flags, bitstuffing and DLCI field. This comprises the L3 PDU, CRC and control fields. Assuming signaling and data PFS distributions in bits according to Fig. 2 the mean bandwidth utilization values for each segmentation/reassembly alternative are given in Table I. For alternative A, we have assumed that bitstuffing adds about 3.2% overhead [9].

III. PACKET MODE PROCESSING AND TRANSMISSION

Sections III and IV examine in detail the performance of the processing and transmission functions, when following the SAR protocols for packet-mode traffic. The main resources which come into play are as follows:

1) the processors employed at the transmit and receive side;
2) the multiplexing and transmission resources in the ATM network.

Regarding 2) we take a macroscopic view modeled in detail in Section III-B below. For 1) we briefly describe

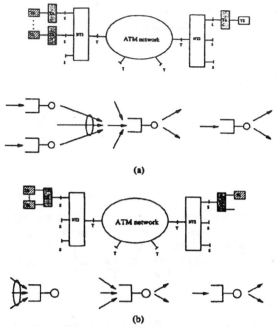

Fig. 3. Multiplexing scenarios. (a) Scenario 1, multiplexing on cell level. (b) Scenario 2, multiplexing on frame level. Note: Reference points S, T are ATM reference points [11].

B. Scenarios and Modeling

We study the situation where a group of narrowband ISDN users communicate with an individual remote narrowband ISDN user through the ATM network. This users group is connected to the same network termination 2 (NT2) and accesses the ATM network through the same T interface of the reference configuration model adopted for the user network interface (UNI) [11]. As stated in Section II we assume that separate virtual channel/path point-to-point connections have been established between each user in the group and the remote ISDN user. In the case of signaling connections the metasignaling procedure described in [12] has been followed. For data connections the normal signaling procedures have been used [12].

We examine the two scenarios illustrated in Fig. 3. In the first [Fig. 3(a)] a TA performing SAR class 0 protocol functions is attached to each narrowband TE. All L2 frames originating from different TE's are segmented separately and the resulting ATM cell streams are multiplexed in the NT2. In the second [Fig. 3(b)] all the TE's of the group share a common TA. This common TA is of the same processing power as each one of the TA's of the first scenario. The TA multiplexes arriving L2 frames originated from different TE's and then segments the composite frame stream into cells. For both cases at the receiving side a single TA performs reassembly of cells into the original frames and passes them to the destination TE.

We now model the processing activities provided by the SAR class 0 protocol on each L2 frame as well as the transmission of this frame using ATM cells (Fig. 3). The passage of a L2 frame across the SAR segmentor service boundary is modeled as a burst arrival of cells. The number

of cells in the burst is given by the particular segmentation procedure implemented in the SAR. The L2 frame length in cells follows a distribution derived from the distribution of the PFS in bits (Fig. 2) after taking into account the segmentation alternatives used by the SAR protocol.

The processing time T_s devoted to each segment for each segmentation/reassembly alternative derives from Table II. The model for the SAR segmentor is complete by specifying the L2 frame arrival statistics. We assume that frames originated from each TE follow an exponential distribution. The waiting time of a frame in the SAR segmentor queue is denoted by Fw_s.

The receiver TA is modeled as a queue that accepts only cells marked with particular recognizable VCI's/VPI's and performs reassembly of the original L2 frames according to the segmentation/reassembly alternative employed. The waiting time of a cell in the SAR reassembler buffer is denoted by Cw_r and the processing time consumed for reassembly by T_r.

The pattern of the ATM cell stream entering the reassembler buffer clearly depends on the ATM network topology, the ATM switch architecture as well as the ATM traffic load in the following manner:

a) In an ATM network cells destined to a common TE through distinct virtual connections may possibly follow different routes. A route is characterized by the involving number of intermediate ATM switches. Each ATM switch contributes to the ATM cell delay (C_{ATM}) due to buffering in a manner depending on the specific switch architecture.

b) Multiplexing of cells belonging to other virtual connections than these considered here is performed in each ATM switch of a route.

Since the key issue of our study is the AAL functions performed at the TA(s) rather than the ATM performance we resort to simplifications regarding ATM modeling. As far as a) is concerned we assume that all cells belonging to one of the virtual connections considered here use the same route for the common destination. The intervening ATM switches are modeled as a single queue where the multiplexed stream of all cells originated from the TE's considered above arrives. By this component decoupling we provide a model less sensitive to ATM network topology changes [16].

Regarding b) complex analytical models have recently been introduced to derive the input and output statistics of an ATM switch [10], as well to determine the resource reservation strategy required for each connection. Most of them encapsulate the performance characteristics of ATM switches with specific architectures [6]–[8]. In our study we assume that a resource reservation scheme for our connections has been applied to all ATM switches of the route independently of the switching architecture. The mean bandwidth allocated for our connections derives from their number, the mean PFS in cells, and the mean arrival rate of frames, as proposed by [16]. This mean bandwidth appears in Table II as μ giving the percentage of cells allocated to our connections. The resource allocation scheme guarantees a total prespecified bandwidth (say μ) for all connections as studied here. This resource reservation scheme does not correspond to peak bandwidth allocation usually employed for the synchronous transfer mode (STM). Thus, in order to show the implications

341

TABLE III
END-TO-END FRAME DELAY DECOMPOSITION

Fd:	end-to-end delay of a signaling or data frame
Fw_s:	waiting time of a frame in the segmentor queue
T_s:	processing time consumed on the segmentation of the frame by the segmentor server
C_{ATM}:	waiting time for transmission in ATM caused by the statistical multiplexing feature of ATM
Cw_r:	waiting time for each cell of the frame in the reassembler buffer
T_r:	processing time consumed for the reassembly of the frame by the reassembler server

$$Fd = \begin{cases} T_s^S + T_r^S + Fw_s + C_{ATM}^S + Cw_r^S & \text{for frame size} = 1 \text{ cell} \\ T_s^F + (n-2)T_s^M + T_s^L + T_r^L + Fw_s + C_{ATM}^L + CS_r^L & \text{for frame size} = n \text{ cells} \end{cases} \tag{1}$$

where superscript J denotes the sequence of a segment inside a frame;
$J = (F)$irst, (M)iddle, (L)ast or (S)ingle subscript i denotes the SAR
operation; $i = (s)$egmentation or (r)eassembly

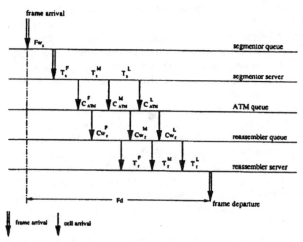

Fig. 4. Timing diagram.

of statistical multiplexing, i.e., the presence of other cells than the ones considered in the ATM switching fabric, we assume as a worst case a geometric service distribution. No concrete further assumptions can be made regarding the interarrival distribution of these cells offered to our connections as this is heavily depended on the implementation of the resource allocation policy. The elementary time interval corresponds to the transmission time for an ATM cell for a bit rate of 150 Mb/s. The output of the ATM queue is a multiplexed cell stream which includes cells belonging to different virtual connections, i.e., cells destined to other TE's than the one considered here as the target destination.

The end-to-end delay decomposition of a signaling or data frame (Fd) is summarized in Table III. These components are highly correlated. Their significance varies according to the segmentation/reassembly alternative employed as well as the multiplexing scenario assumed. The timing diagram in Fig. 4 displays the way the above components constitute the end-to-end delay of an L2 frame, i.e., the time interval between the frame arrival at the segmentor and the delivery of the reassembled frame from the reassembler to the layer above. This leads to relation 1) of Table III. As can be verified in the multiple cell frame case the frame delay is composed of Fw_s and the delay encountered by the last cell. This again is composed of its time-in-queue and its processing delays. The

time-in-queue of the last cell equals the processing time of the cells preceding it (first and middles). For single cell frames Fig. 4 should be simplified in an obvious way. The timing diagram of Fig. 4 and the corresponding delay decomposition 1) apply to both multiplexing scenarios.

IV. RESULTS

We present here results obtained by simulation and following the decomposition for the end-to-end frame delay as given in 1). In individual delay components of the transmitter for which an analytical method is given in [3], we compare analytic and simulation results. Characteristics of the end-to-end delay are better displayed for the signaling frames which are short sized. As such we have assumed the signaling PFS distribution as in Fig. 2(a) and we shall primarily concentrate on them. The same results can easily be generalized for data frames. Fig. 5 illustrated the distribution of Fd for signaling frames and for both multiplexing scenarios. A background of data traffic through the same segmentation, reassembly and ATM transmission functions is also assumed but not included in the statistics. Input parameters for our simulation study are recapitulated in Table II.

In all figures we can clearly discern different regions extending from one peak to the next. Each region corresponds to the end-to-end delay of frames with a certain size in cells. Therefore, one could see the distribution of the frame size in cells by comparing the areas of each region but allowing at the same time for the error caused by the overlapping decaying tails. In Fig. 5(b) and (d) this observation is more vividly illustrated. For the discussion below we regard all Fig. 5 as a composition of overlapping decaying distribution impulses. Each impulse corresponds to frames of a certain size in cells. Its front corresponds to frames segmented in cells which do not encounter any queueing delay ($Fw_s = C_{ATM} = Cw_r = 0$). For small queueing delay values (values on the right of the front) the segmentation/reassembly alternative heavily affects the processing effort and hence the impulse shape. The impulse tail is extended to larger values due to queueing caused by increased signaling and/or background data traffic. This can be further justified by comparing Figs. 5 and 6. In Fig. 6 the Fd of signaling frames is depicted in an environment with no background of data traffic. Due to the short size of signaling frames and to the relatively low mean frame arrival rate, queueing has insignificant consequences on Fd.

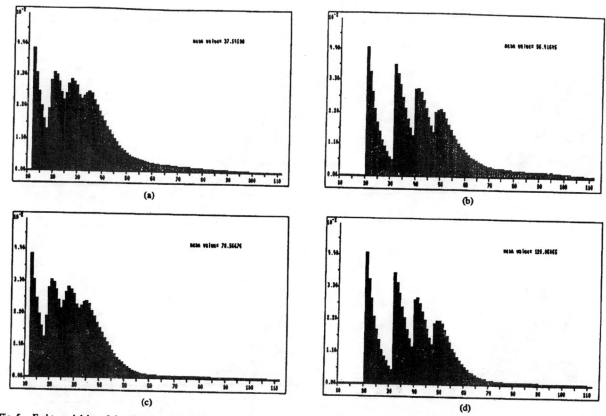

Fig. 5. End-to-end delay of signaling frames (Fd) in an environment with signaling and data frames. (a) Scenario 1, segmentation/reassembly Alternative (A). (b) Scenario 1, segmentation/reassembly Alternative (B). (c) Scenario 2, segmentation/reassembly Alternative (A). (d) Scenario 2, segmentation/reassembly Alternative (B). Note: Abscissa in ATM cell transmission time units at 150 Mb/s.

As expected Fig. 6 appears to be completely analogous with Fig. 5 apart from the tails presenting the effect of queueing. The multiplexing scenario affects both the queueing delay in the segmentor (scenario 2 is in disadvantage) and the delay caused by waiting for the last cell at the reassembler (scenario 1 is in disadvantage due to cell interleaving). By comparing Fig. 5(a) with (c) and Fig. 5(b) with (d) we see that the multiplexing scenario affects the tails.

In the sequel we examine in detail the end-to-end frame delay components and at the same time demonstrate the grade of their dependency on the segmentation/reassembly alternative assumed and the multiplexing scenario employed.

A. Impact of Segmentation/Reassembly Alternative

Starting from the segmentation/reassembly alternatives the differences in functionality are translated to considerable higher processing times for alternative B), which yields to longer mean end-to-end frame delay (Table IV). Thus, as expected, the mean frame waiting time in the segmentor buffer is much higher for alternative B) since the difference in service times between alternatives is more critical than the difference in the number of cells a frame is translated. The same result derives also from the analytical model where the mean values of Fw_s are smaller reflecting our assumptions regarding the L2 frame discrete time arrival statistics (see

[3, Appendix A]). For both alternatives C_{ATM} follows a geometrical distribution depicted in Fig. 7. However the mean waiting time experienced by a cell in the ATM queue is less for alternative B). This can be explained if one considers the cell arrival statistics in the ATM queue. The cell stream issued when segmentation of frames according to alternative B) is performed appears less bursty, due to longer processing in the SAR server. Therefore the ATM server is allowed to transmit outstanding cells, before the arrival of a cell that leaves the SAR processor immediately following the servicing of its forerunner. The mean ATM waiting time appearing in Table IV almost equals to the analytical result increased by $\delta/2$ which corresponds to the probability that a cell completes its service in the middle of a time unit δ (see [3, Appendix D]).

We now turn our attention to the mean waiting time of a cell in the reassembler buffer. For better understanding of that delay component we consider Fig. 8 illustrating the distribution of Cw_r for different alternatives and multiplexing scenarios. As previously we discern different regions corresponding to different states of the reassembler buffer. The probability that Cw_r is zero equals the probability that the reassembler server is empty. This zero probability is greater for alternative B) and at the same time its distribution function decreases faster within the region of the lower values of the random variable Cw_r. This situation contradicts with what one expects, since

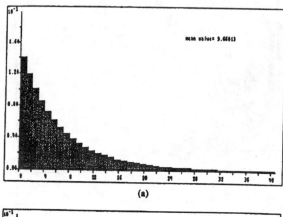

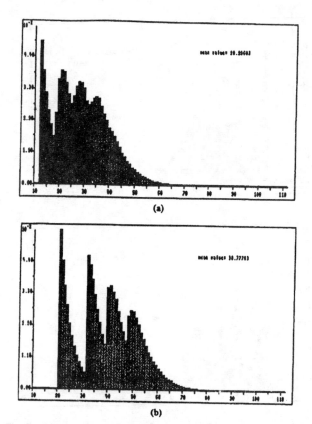

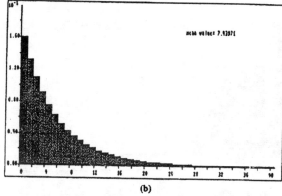

Fig. 6. End-to-end delay of signaling frames (Fd) in an environment with signaling frames only. (a) Scenario 1, segmentation/reassembly Alternative (A). (b) Scenario 1, segmentation/reassembly Alternative (B). Note: Abscissa in ATM cell transmission time units at 150 Mb/s.

Fig. 7. Cell waiting time in the ATM queue (C_{ATM}). (a) Scenario 1, segmentation/reassembly Alternative (A). (b) Scenario 1, segmentation/reassembly Alternative (B). Note: Abscissa in ATM cell transmission time units at 150 Mb/s.

alternative B) consumes more processing time for reassembly. It also contradicts the intuitive law that less waiting time in the ATM queue would result to greater waiting times in the reassembler buffer. The explanation is that in case of alternative B) the time devoted for segmentation of the last cell of a frame is considerable greater than the one for other cells processing. This allows the reassembler to process the preceding cells of the last cell before its arrival at the reassembler buffer. Note here that due to the short size of signaling frames the probability that a cell is the last cell of a frame is considerably high, i.e., about 40%. Since for data frames this probability is much lower the above phenomenon is no longer valid.

To avoid confusion we repeat once more that the above remarks are valid only for the lower values of Cw_r within each impulse. As stated before, these values correspond to the case where no collision between signaling and data frames has been occurred when even data frames are also present. In case of collision much greater waiting times for an incoming cell in the reassembler are expected, since preceding data cells will probably keep the reassembler busy for relatively longer periods. Due to longer processing these periods will be longer with alternative B). Therefore the mean cell waiting time in the reassembler buffer is finally longer with alternative B) (Table IV). In an environment with only signaling sources

the opposite would happen (Table V). The distribution of the higher values of the random variable Cw_r within each impulse depends on the multiplexing scenario employed and will be assessed later.

Taking into consideration the above remarks we can now easily interpret Fig. 5. In alternative B) all curves corresponding to different regions drop faster than in alternative A). This is a result of the distributions of C_{ATM} and Cw_r delay components. However, although these delay components equal to zero with higher probability, their superposition appearing within each region of Fig. 5, does not always present a peak at the begin of the region, i.e., to the value corresponding to the fixed T_i^J delay. This is explained by the correlation of the delay components C_{ATM} and Cw_r. For example a cell experienced no delay in the ATM queue waits in the reassembler buffer with greater probability, due to its preceding cells. As expected this situation does not appear for single cell frames, while it becomes more apparent for longer frames and for bursty cell arrivals in the reassembler buffer, i.e., the case in alternative A).

B. Impact of the Multiplexing Scenarios

Apart from the segmentation/reassembly alternatives considered so far, we now turn to the implications of the multiplexing scenarios on the delay components. To do so we

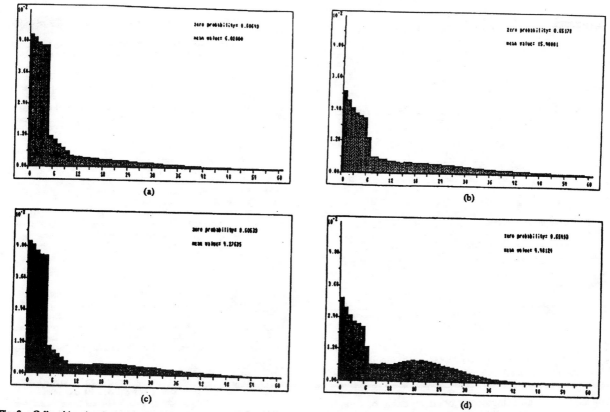

Fig. 8. Cell waiting time in the reassembler buffer (Cw_r). (a) Scenario 1, segmentation/reassembly Alternative (A). (b) Scenario 1, segmentation/reassembly Alternative (B). (c) Scenario 2, segmentation/reassembly Alternative (A). (d) Scenario 2, segmentation/reassembly Alternative (B).

observe the higher values of Fd corresponding to collision situations as they appear in Fig. 5. Collisions are more probable in an environment with signaling and data frames. This is the reason why the multiplexing scenario has no significant effect when an environment with signaling frames only is considered (see Fig. 6).

When multiplexing on a frame level is provided, i.e., the case in the second scenario, the most significant delay component of Fd is Fw_s. On the other hand since the multiplexing on a cell level, results in interleaving of cells belonging to frames originated from different sources, longer values of C_{ATM} and Cw_r are expected. It is of particular interest to examine in detail the influence of the multiplexing scenario on the Cw_r distribution. Let us consider the case where a signaling frame appears just after a data frame. In the first scenario a stream of multiplexed signaling and data cells will be send to the reassembler. As expected the cell waiting time in the reassembler buffer will take higher values, since a signaling cell has to wait not only for its preceding cells in the same signaling frame, but also for its preceding data cells. In the second scenario the signaling cells queue in the segmentor and are serviced only after the last data cell has been transmitted. That gives time for the reassembly of consequent outstanding data cells of the same frame. Therefore signaling cells arriving in the reassembler buffer will probably have to wait for just a few remaining data cells to be serviced.

This explains the distribution of the higher values of Cw_r. As shown in Fig. 8 the probability distribution function of Cw_r for the first scenario is much more expanded to larger values, while in the second scenario an appreciable peak appears.

From what has been stated so far it can be easily derived that the exponential tails appearing in Fig. 5 are mainly due to the longer values of Cw_r [Fig. 5(a), (b)] and Fw_s [Fig. 5(c), (d)]. By consulting also Table IV we observe that signaling frames, due to their relatively short size are favored by the first scenario. The expected increase in Cw_r values is relatively small when compared to Fw_s values of the second scenario. This is expressed by the longer tails appearing in Fig. 5(c), (d). The reverse situation appears with data frames. The increase of Cw_r values in case of scenario 1 is more critical than the additional Fw_s delay introduced by scenario 2 (see Table IV). This fact becomes more pronounced for higher arrival rates of data frames.

V. CONCLUSIONS

Segmentation/reassembly alternatives and multiplexing scenarios have been compared. In general, alternative B) employing frame delimitation on a cell level exhibits higher end-to-end frame delay due to more complicated processing requirement. However, it better regulates cell traffic, which is of advantage at the receiver. In particular the last cell of a signaling frame, which requires the maximal processing at the

TABLE IV
MEAN DELAY IN AN ENVIRONMENT WITH SIGNALING AND DATA FRAMES

		Scenario 1		Scenario 2	
		Alt *A*	Alt *B*	Alt *A*	Alt *B*
Signaling	Fd	37.545	56.416	78.567	128.059
	Fw_s	0.013	0.027	46.231	86.009
	C_{ATM}	9.660	7.439	6.652	5.138
	Cw_r	6.028	15.481	4.276	4.481
Data	Fd	547.725	742.050	531.844	711.554
	Fw_s	13.960	24.773	46.677	86.641
	C_{ATM}	31.668	18.527	11.821	6.537
	Cw_r	30.474	69.451	16.445	15.963

Note: The delay is expressed in time units δ where δ is the 53-octet cell transmission time.

TABLE V
MEAN DELAY IN AN ENVIRONMENT WITH SIGNALING FRAMES ONLY

		Scenario 1		Scenario 2	
		Alt *A*	Alt *B*	Alt *A*	Alt *B*
Signaling	Fd	28.286	38.778	28.278	38.787
	Fw_s	0.013	0.027	0.107	0.222
	C_{ATM}	5.670	4.985	5.624	4.938
	Cw_r	1.052	0.858	1.026	0.788

Note: The delay is expressed in time units δ, where δ is the 53-octet cell transmission time.

segmentor allows the receiver to process waiting cells. Hence, the reassembly can occur immediately upon arrival of this last cell.

Concerning multiplexing scenarios, intervening of cells by multiplexing on a cell level causes an increased total delay for long size frame (e.g., data) and a reduced total delay for short size frame (e.g., signaling). Explanation have been given by examining individual delay components.

In general it has been demonstrated that software based implementation assisted by specially designed hardware components with limited functionalities is sufficient for coping with narrowband packet traffic in the future ATM-based broadband networks.

REFERENCES

[1] G. I. Stassinopoulos and I. S. Venieris, "An ATM adaptation layer protocol model for packet mode services," *ETSI/NA5*, Newcastle, Nov. 1989.

[2] CCITT, "ATM adaptation layer (AAL) specification—Rec. I.363," *SGXVIII*, TD 23, Geneva, Jan. 1990.

[3] G. I. Stassinopoulos and I. S. Venieris, "ATM adaptation layer (AAL) protocols for signalling," *Comput. Networks ISDN Syst. J.*, vol. 23, pp. 287–304, 1992.

[4] CCITT, "ISDN user-network interface—Data link layer specification—Rec. I.441," *CCITT Red Books Fascicle*, vol. III.5, pp. 201–237, 1984.

[5] H. Mulder, "ISDN layer 2 message error protection in an ATM environment," Race Proj. 1022, SWP3, DNL_321_013, Nov. 1989.

[6] A. Pattavina, "Multichannel bandwidth allocation in a broadband packet switch," *IEEE J. Select. Areas Commun.*, vol. 6, pp. 1489–1499, Dec. 1988.

[7] M. G. Hluchyj and M. J. Karol, "Queueing in high performance packet switching," *IEEE J. Select. Areas Commun.*, vol. 35, pp. 1347–1356, Dec. 1987.

[8] J. Y. Hui and E. Arthur, "A broadband packet switch for integrated transport," *IEEE J. Select. Areas Commun.*, pp. 1264–1273, Oct. 1987.

[9] H. Jablecki, R. Misra, and I. Saniee, "A call processing traffic study for integrated digital loop carrier applications," *IEEE Trans. Commun.*, vol. 36, pp. 1053–1061, Sept. 1988.

[10] M. Murata, Y. Oie, T. Suda, and H. Miyahara, "Analysis of a discrete-time single-server queue with bursty inputs for traffic control in ATM networks," *IEEE J. Select. Areas Commun.*, vol. 8, pp. 447–458, Apr. 1990.

[11] CCITT, "ISDN user-network interface with broadband capabilities—Draft Rec. I.413," *SGXVIII*, TD 25, Geneva, Jan. 1990.

[12] R. Carli and I. S. Venieris, "ATM adaptation layer protocol at B-ISDN user-network interface," in *Integrated Broadband Communications: Views from RACE*. New York: Elsevier, Science (North Holland), 1991, vol. 16.

[13] H. E. Koukoutos, A. I. Papadopoulos, and G. I. Stassinopoulos, "Generic microprocessor adapter for ATM—A framed data packet assembler-disassembler," Version 5.2, RACE Proj. R1022, NTUA_SWP4_1006, Apr. 1990.

[14] G. I. Stassinopoulos, I. S. Venieris, and R. Carli, "ATM adaptation layer protocols and IEEE LAN interconnection," in *Proc. 15th IEEE LCN Conf.*, Minneapolis, MN, Oct. 1990.

[15] B. Pauwells, "A survey of alternatives for some functions of the OSI Layer 2 for signalling and packet switched data," *TC 2nd Workshop*, Race Project 1022, Aveiro, Nov. 1988.

[16] G. M. Woodruff and R. Kositpaiboon, "Multimedia traffic management principles for guaranteed ATM network performance," *IEEE J. Select. Areas Commun.*, vol. 8, pp. 437–446, Apr. 1990.

George I. Stasinopoulos (M'82) was born in Athens in 1951. He received the electrical engineering degree from the Swiss Federal Institute of Technology (ETH Zurich) in 1974, and the Ph.D. degree in automatic control from the Imperial College, London, Department of Computing and Control in 1977.

From 1977 to 1981 he gained Industrial experience in the design and manufacture of microprocessor based industrial controllers in the cement industry (AGET General Cement Company) as well as in computer networking and industrial process control. From 1981 he is a member of the staff of the National Technical University of Athens, Department of Computer Science where he is currently a professor. Current research interests are in the fields of data communication networks LAN's, MAN's, packet, circuit, and hybrid switching systems, analysis and synthesis of communication networks, routing, flow control and queueing theory. He has over 40 publications in the above areas. He has participated in several national research programs dealing with data communications networks. These included development of modeling, simulation, analysis and design packages for packet and circuit switched data networks. He has also participated in many Race projects.

Dr. Stassinopoulos is a reviewer for the IEEE TRANSACTIONS ON COMMUNICATIONS, the IEEE JOURNAL ON SELECTED AREAS IN COMMUNICATIONS and the *Computer Networks and ISDN Systems*. He is a member of the Technical Chamber of Greece.

Iakovos S. Venieris (S'88–M'92) was born in Naxos, Greece, on March 3, 1965. He received the Dipl.-Ing. degree from the University of Patras, Patras, Greece in 1988, and the Ph.D. degree from the National Technical University of Athens (NTUA), Athens, Greece, in 1990, all in electrical engineering.

In January 1988 he joined the Telecommunications Laboratory of NTUA, where he is now a research associate. His research interests are in the fields of B-ISDN, high speed LAN's and MAN's, all optical networks, internetworking, signaling, resource scheduling and allocation for network management, modeling, performance evaluation and queueing theory. He has over 20 publications in the above areas.

Dr. Venieris has received several national and international awards for academic achievement. He has been exposed to standardization body work and has contributed to NA5 of ETSI and SG XVIII of CCITT. He is participating in several RACE and ESPRIT projects dealing with B-ISDN protocols. ATM switching and MAC techniques. He is a reviewer for the IEEE TRANSACTIONS ON COMMUNICATIONS and the IEEE JOURNAL ON SELECTED AREAS IN COMMUNICATIONS.

Dr. Venieris is a member of the Technical Chamber of Greece.

K. P. Petropoulos was born in Kalamata, Greece in 1968. He received the Diploma in Electrical Engineering from the National Technical University of Athens, Athens, Greece in 1990 and the M.Sc. degree in Communications from Columbia University, New York in 1991.

He is currently a doctoral student at Columbia University, Department of Electrical Engineering, working in the area of lightwave communications.

Emmanuel N. Protonotarios was born in Naxos, Greece, on February 23, 1940. He received the degree in mechanical and electrical engineering (summa cum laude) from the National Technical University of Athens (NTUA), Athens, Greece, in July 1963, and the Ph.D. degree in electrical engineering from Columbia University, New York, NY, in 1966.

From 1963 to 1966 he performed graduate studies under a Fullbright Travel Grant and a Fellowship from Columbia. From May 1966 to August 1968 he worked at Bell Laboratories, Holmdel, NJ, as a Member of the Technical Staff in the Digital Transmission Laboratory, doing fundamental work in PCM and DPCM transmission systems. From 1968 to 1973 he was an Assistant Professor and then an Associate Professor of Electrical Engineering at Columbia, where he taught and performed research in digital communication systems. He has been Director of the Computer Science Division, Chairman of the Department of Electrical Engineering and Vice Rector for Academic Affairs at NTUA, where he has been a professor since 1973, teaching and performing research in communication systems, computer networks, local area networks, etc.

Dr. Protonotarios received nine prizes for academic achievement while studying at NTUA, earning first place in the entire University for five consecutive years. He serves on many committees for evaluation of research in Greece. From 1981 to 1983 he was Managing Director of the National Research Foundation of Greece. He has organized international conferences on electrical engineering in general and on communication systems in particular, having served as General Chairman, Technical Program Committee Chairman, and member of steering or organizing committees.

Dynamics of TCP Traffic over ATM Networks

Allyn Romanow, *Member, IEEE,* and Sally Floyd, *Member, IEEE*

Abstract— We investigate the performance of TCP connections over ATM networks without ATM-level congestion control and compare it to the performance of TCP over packet-based networks. For simulations of congested networks, the effective throughput of TCP over ATM can be quite low when cells are dropped at the congested ATM switch. The low throughput is due to wasted bandwidth as the congested link transmits cells from "corrupted" packets, i.e., packets in which at least one cell is dropped by the switch. We investigate two packet-discard strategies that alleviate the effects of fragmentation. *Partial packet discard*, in which remaining cells are discarded after one cell has been dropped from a packet, somewhat improves throughput. We introduce *early packet discard*, a strategy in which the switch drops whole packets prior to buffer overflow. This mechanism prevents fragmentation and restores throughput to maximal levels.

I. INTRODUCTION

WE investigate basic questions of congestion control for best-effort traffic in asynchronous transfer mode (ATM) networks. ATM is the 53-byte cell-based transport method chosen by ITU-TSS (formerly CCITT) for broadband ISDN [12]. ATM is also under development for use in high-speed LAN's. In the ATM context, best-effort traffic is data traffic that does not have stringent real-time requirements. It is called available bit rate (ABR) traffic in the ATM Forum.[1] Despite its importance, few studies prior to this one have investigated the performance of ATM for best-effort data traffic (exceptions are [7], [17], [28]) [34].

Since ATM does not provide media access control, it has been a concern that the throughput will be low if an ATM network experiences congestion; in fact there is already practical evidence to this effect [11]. This paper uses simulation studies to investigate the throughput behavior of TCP over ATM for best-effort traffic when there is network congestion. First, we consider the throughput performance of TCP over ATM without any additional ATM/AAL-level[2] congestion control mechanisms, such as hop-by-hop flow control or ATM-level rate-based traffic management. We compare this TCP over *plain* ATM with the performance of *packet TCP*, TCP that

is not over ATM and therefore is not fragmented into cells by the link layer.

The simulation results comparing TCP over plain ATM with packet TCP show that the former can have arbitrarily low throughput performance, whereas packet TCP has quite good performance. We examine these results and explain the dynamics causing the poor behavior. Based on this analysis, we explore two simple control mechanisms: partial packet discard (PPD) and early packet discard (EPD). In PPD [3], if a cell is dropped from a switch buffer, the subsequent cells in the higher layer protocol data unit are discarded. We find that PPD improves performance to a certain degree, but that throughput performance is still not optimal. To improve performance further, we propose a mechanism called EPD that brings throughput performance to its optimal level. In EPD, when the switch buffer queues reach a threshold level, entire higher level data units (e.g., TCP/IP packets) are dropped.

This study is focused on the dynamics of Transport Control Protocol (TCP) over ATM networks.[3] The performance of TCP is important as the protocol is widely used in today's Internet and private networks [32]. Although this study is specific to TCP, the results are relevant to any packet-based protocol running over ATM. Thus the general results apply to User Datagram Protocol (UDP), or to other transport protocols such as DECnet [19], IPX, VMTP [9], and AppleTalk [31].

Analysis of throughput behavior shows that the poor performance of TCP over plain ATM is caused by the well-known problem of fragmentation. In this case, TCP/IP packets are fragmented at the ATM layer. When the ATM switch drops a cell, the rest of the higher-level packet is still transmitted, clogging the congested link with useless data. Thus some additional control mechanism is required to achieve acceptable performance for TCP in ATM networks. Our simulations also show that for plain ATM, smaller switch buffers, larger TCP windows, and larger TCP packet sizes can each reduce the overall effective throughput.

This paper focuses on the specific traffic goal of achieving high throughput for TCP over ATM. Several additional goals of traffic management for best-effort traffic not under consideration here include fairness, low average delay and the control of misbehaving users. We assume the network context of fully supported Quality of Service, in which best-effort traffic is one of several traffic classes, each of which is handled according to its respective service requirements.

Section II describes the experimental design. Sections III, IV, and V discuss the simulation results for TCP over plain ATM, for PPD, and for EPD. Section VI considers the use

Manuscript received March 2, 1994; revised September 6, 1994. This work was supported in part by the Director, Office of Energy Research, Scientific Computing Staff, of the U.S. Department of Energy under Contract DE-AC03-76SF000098.

A. Romanow is with Sun Microsystems Inc., Mountain View, CA 94043 USA.

S. Floyd is with Lawrence Berkeley Laboratory, Berkeley, CA 94720 USA.

IEEE Log Number 9407076.

[1] The ATM Forum is an international consortium whose goal is to accelerate the use of ATM products and services through the development of interoperability specifications and the promotion of industry cooperation.

[2] The ATM Adaptation Layer (AAL) is the layer above the ATM layer that adapts the fixed-size ATM cell to the next higher-level data unit, which may be either signaling or user data [5], [12].

[3] For the purposes of this paper, IP is relevant only in that it determines the size of the higher level packet.

Reprinted from IEEE Journal on Selected Areas in Communications, Vol. 13, NO. 4, May 1995, pp. 633–641.

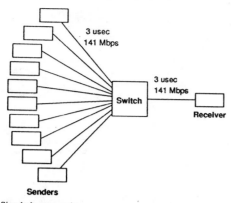

Fig. 1. Simulation scenario.

of additional congestion control mechanisms along with EPD, and Section VII discusses future work.

II. SIMULATION SETUP

This section describes the simulation environment. We compare simulations of TCP traffic over ATM networks with simulations of packet TCP. The simulations use the network topology shown in Fig. 1.

A simple topology was chosen to make it easier to understand performance dynamics. Because a LAN environment has fewer switches, and connections have a shorter roundtrip time, the congestion control issues are more straightforward than in a wide-area environment. To model a LAN environment, we used a propagation delay of 3 μs for each link. Note that in this setting, the delay-bandwidth product is only four cells.

Simulations were run with ten "bulk-data" TCP connections. The number 10 was chosen to represent a relatively large number of simultaneous TCP's contending for the same resources. Each TCP connection is assumed to have an infinite supply of data. The simulation time was 15 s, which is reasonably long, relative to the average roundtrip time, and allows an aggregate transfer of more than 250 MB of data. In both the packet switch and ATM switch, the output ports use FIFO queuing.

All simulations were run for a range of values for the TCP packet size, switch buffer size, and TCP window size. Packet sizes were chosen according to common link level maximum transfer units (MTU's). The TCP packet size often used in IP networks is 512 bytes; 1500 bytes is the packet size for ethernet networks; 4352 bytes is for FDDI networks; and 9180 is the default for IP over ATM [2]. Buffer size per output port ranges from 256 cells to 8000 cells. A buffer size of 1000 or 2000 cells per port for a small switch (e.g., 16–32 ports) would not be considered unusual. TCP window size uses common values of 8 kbyte, 16 kbyte, 32 kbyte, and 64 kbyte.

In the simulations of TCP over ATM, each TCP connection has its own virtual channel (VC), identified by a virtual channel identifier (VCI) [4]. The link bandwidth was set to 141.333 Mb/s, so that the cell transmission time for a 53-byte cell is an integral number of microseconds (3 μs). The ATM simulator is a modified version of one developed by Zhang [37]. The simulations for packet TCP use a modified version of the REAL simulator [21], with extensive enhancements by McCanne and Jamin [15].

Both simulators implement the same version of TCP based on the 4.3-Tahoe BSD release [18]. Briefly, there are two phases to TCP's window-adjustment algorithm. A threshold is set initially to half the receiver's advertised window. The connection begins in slow-start phase, and the current window is essentially doubled each roundtrip time until the window reaches the threshold. Then the congestion-avoidance phase is entered, and the current window is increased by roughly one packet each roundtrip time. The window is never allowed to increase to more than the receiver's advertised window.

In 4.3-Tahoe BSD TCP, packet loss (a dropped packet) is treated as a "congestion experienced" signal. The source uses the *fast retransmit* procedure to discover a packet loss: if four ACK packets are received acknowledging the same data packet, the source decides that a packet has been dropped [32]. The source reacts to a packet loss by setting the threshold to half the current window, decreasing the current window to one, and entering the slow-start phase. The source also uses retransmission timers to detect lost packets.

To improve the performance of TCP in the high-speed low-propagation-delay environment modeled in these simulations, we adjusted some parameters in TCP's algorithm for setting the retransmit timeout values. The current TCP algorithms for measuring the roundtrip time and for computing the retransmit timeout are coupled [18] and assume a coarse-grained clock. We changed the clock granularity for measuring the roundtrip time to 0.1 ms, and we changed the initial values used to set the retransmit timeout. These changes were necessary in order for the simulation results not be dominated by the specifics of current implementations of TCP. Our goal is to explore the possible limitations that ATM networks place on the performance of TCP-style protocols, and this must be distinguished from artifacts of specific implementation choices. TCP's retransmit timer algorithms are discussed in more detail in Appendix B.

The simulated ATM switch is based on a design by Lyles [35]. The switch modeled is a 16-port output-buffered Batcher-banyan design. The switch architecture is of a sufficiently general design that the performance results are not architecturally dependent. In particular, the simulation results are not dependent on whether the switch is input-buffered or output-buffered. In the simulated ATM switch, the input cell queues are served in round robin fashion. In one cell time, a cell from each of two input port queues can be queued onto the same output port. If the output buffer is full, then only one of the two cells can be queued and the other cell must be dropped. In this case, each of the two contending cells has equal probability of being dropped.

For the simulations with packet TCP, the router has an output-buffered switch with a Drop-Tail packet-dropping discipline. That is, when the output buffer overflows, packets arriving at the output buffer are dropped.

III. TCP OVER PLAIN ATM

It has been known for some time that packet fragmentation can result in wasted bandwidth and packet retransmission [20]. Because the network might drop only one fragment from a

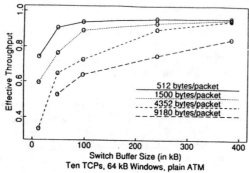

Fig. 2. TCP over plan ATM.

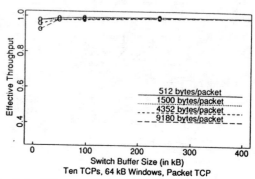

Fig. 3. Packet TCP over non-ATM networks.

packet, "the loss of any one fragment means that the resources expended in sending the other fragments of that datagram are entirely wasted" ([20], p. 392). In this section we quantify the effect of fragmentation with simulations of TCP traffic over plain ATM. Following sections discuss ways to avoid wasted bandwidth.

Fig. 2 shows effective throughput as a function of switch buffer size and TCP packet size for TCP over plain ATM. We define the *effective throughput* or goodput as the throughput that is "good" in terms of the higher-layer protocol. That is, the effective throughput does not include cells that are part of a retransmission or an incomplete packet.[4]

The simulations are shown for ten TCP connections, with a maximum TCP window of 64 kbyte. The y-axis shows the effective throughput as a fraction of the maximum possible effective throughput. On the x-axis is the switch output buffer size in kilobytes (ranging from 256 to 8000 cells). Circles are shown in the plots at 256, 1000, 2000, 5000, and 8000 cells. Different line types represent simulations with different packet sizes.[5]

Fig. 3 shows the simulation results for ten TCP connections with packet TCP, for the same range of buffer sizes and packet sizes used in Fig. 2. Comparing the two figures, it is clear that TCP over plain ATM can have lower throughput than packet TCP. For the simulations with packet TCP, the effective throughput is always at least 90% of the maximum possible, while for simulations of TCP over plain ATM the effective throughput can be as low as 34%.[6]

Fig. 2 shows that smaller switch buffers and larger TCP packet sizes both reduce the effective throughput for TCP over plain ATM. The TCP window size also affects the effective throughput of TCP over plain ATM. Simulations with the TCP window ranging from 8 kbyte to 64 kbyte show a lower effective throughput with larger windows. Simulations of TCP

over plain ATM with both five and ten TCP connections show that the effective throughput is lower with increased congestion caused by a larger number of TCP connections [36].

As Fig. 3 shows, the effective throughput for packet TCP is not greatly affected by either buffer size or packet size. Similarly, aggregate effective throughput is high even with many TCP connections or large TCP windows.

The following section explains these effects in detail.

Analysis

In this section we consider three possible causes for low effective throughput for TCP over ATM. These are the delivery of inactive cells, link idle time, and the retransmission of packets that have already been received.

The primary reason for the low effective throughput of TCP over ATM in our simulations is that when cells are dropped at the switch, the congested link transmits other cells from "corrupted" packets (that is, packets with at least one cell dropped by the switch). In the absence of fragmentation, this phenomenon does not occur in packet TCP, where packets dropped at the switch are not transmitted over the congested link. This problem of lost throughput due to "dead" cells transmitted on the congested link is made worse by any factor that increases the number of cells dropped at the switch, such as small buffers, large TCP packets, increased TCP window size, or an increase in the number of active connections.

Larger packet sizes increase the number of wasted cells that the congested link transmits when the switch drops a single cell from one packet. In addition, the use of larger TCP packets substantially increases the aggressiveness of TCP's window increase algorithm, which in the congestion avoidance phase increases the congestion window by roughly one packet per roundtrip time. While larger packet sizes may be considered advantageous because they do not fragment network file system (NFS) packets (that default to 8 kbyte), and because some end-nodes can process larger packets more cheaply than smaller packets [2], large packets are a performance disadvantage in a congested local-area ATM network.

A secondary reason for the low effective throughput in some of the simulations is that the congested link is occasionally idle. However, except for a few simulations with very small buffers, where link idle time reached 20% of the link bandwidth, the amount of link idle time was typically close to

---

[4]For a packet that does not break down into an integer number of cells, the effective throughput does not include bytes from the "padding" in the last cell. See [8] for proposals to reduce bandwidth inefficiencies due to such size mismatch.

[5]For the case of a 256-cell buffer and packet size of 9180 bytes, the data point is not shown because results were segregated. Segregation is discussed in more detail in Appendix A.

[6]Although the simulations in Figs. 2 and 3 were run on different simulators, we have made substantial efforts to reduce secondary effects in the simulations that could obscure the main dynamics. This is described in more detail in the appendices.

zero. For the scenarios explored in this paper, this global synchronization is not a significant problem; connections recover fairly quickly from a dropped packet, and a single connection with a small window is sufficient to keep the congested link highly utilized.

Despite the fact that link idle time is not an important factor in these simulations, it could be a significant problem with TCP over plain ATM. The phenomenon of link idle time due to synchronization of the TCP window adjustment algorithms has been studied for packet TCP [30]. This synchronization could be exacerbated in ATM networks, where cells from different packets are usually interleaved at the switch, causing several TCP connections to synchronize and go through slow-start at roughly the same time. Link idle time can be affected by details of the retransmit timer algorithms (discussed in Appendix B).

A third possible reason for low effective throughput, but one that is not a significant factor in our simulations, is that the congested link could retransmit packets that have already been correctly received. With current TCP window adjustment algorithms, this can only occur when multiple packets are dropped from one window of packets. In these ATM LAN simulations, due to the congestion, windows generally do not become sufficiently large for this to be a significant problem.

The importance of network configuration parameters—switch buffer size, TCP packet size, and TCP window size—should not suggest that the fragmentation problem can be completely solved by appropriate configuration settings, which offer only partial solutions. Large buffers can result in unacceptably long delay, and it is not always possible to use small packets in an Internet environment. In addition, the beneficial effect of small windows, small packets, or large buffers can be offset if the number of contending connections increases.

IV. ATM WITH PARTIAL PACKET DISCARD

Since the main problem with TCP over plain ATM is that useless cells congest the link, an alternative strategy is for the ATM switch to drop all subsequent cells from a packet as soon as one cell has been dropped. We refer to this strategy as PPD. It was called "selective cell discarding" in [3]. A similar cell-dropping mechanism was developed in the Fairisle ATM switch ([24], p. 330). In a different context, [27] proposed dropping subsequent packets of video frames after the loss of a subset of packets invalidates the entire frame.

Implementing PPD would be quite straightforward with AAL5 [3], an adaptation layer designed for data and standardized by ITU-TSS [6], [1]. PPD could be signaled on a per-VC basis. With PPD, once the switch drops a cell from a VC, the switch continues dropping cells from the same VC until the switch sees the ATM-layer user-to-user (AUU) parameter set in the ATM cell header, indicating the end of the AAL packet. The end-of-packet cell (EOP) itself is not dropped. Because AAL5 does not support the simultaneous multiplexing of packets on a single VC, the AUU parameter can be used to delimit packet boundaries.

The implementation of PPD requires the switch to keep additional per-VC state in order to recognize that VC's are

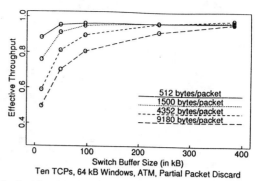

Fig. 4.   Partial packet discard.

using AAL5 and want to use PPD; this can be established through ATM-level signaling. Also, the switch must keep state on which VC's are currently having cells dropped. A related approach that would not require using the AUU parameter would be for the switch to discard a significant number of cells from a single VC when the switch is forced to drop cells. The performance of this approach should be somewhat worse that the performance of PPD, because the switch could transmit dead cells from the first part of one corrupted packet, along with dead cells from the last part of another corrupted packet.

Fig. 4 shows the throughput results for simulations with PPD, using the same configuration as in previous simulations. As Fig. 4 shows, the effective throughput is improved with PPD. However, improvement is limited because the switch begins to drop cells only when the buffer overflows. The first cell dropped by the switch might belong to a packet that contains queued cells or cells already transmitted on the congested link.[7] Thus, the congested link can still transmit a significant fraction of cells belonging to corrupted packets.

V. EARLY PACKET DISCARD

Effective throughput for TCP over ATM can be much improved if the switch drops entire packets prior to buffer overflow. This strategy, called EPD, prevents the congested link from transmitting useless cells and reduces the total number of corrupted packets. As with PPD, EPD can be signaled on a per-VC basis.

With EPD, when a switch buffer becomes in danger of overflowing, the switch drops all of the cells in an AAL5 frame (i.e., it drops a packet). This is a violation of layering consistent with the growing trend towards application level framing and integrated layer processing, which hold that "layering may not be the most effective modularity for implementation" ([10], p. 200).

In the implementation of EPD for our simulation study, the switch drops packets whenever the proportion of the buffer in use exceeds a fixed threshold; in our simulations this threshold is set to half the buffer size. When the threshold is reached,

---

[7] In our implementation of PPD, when the switch first drops a cell, the switch does not look in the buffer for earlier cells that belong to the same packet, as such a search through the queue would be expensive to implement in hardware.

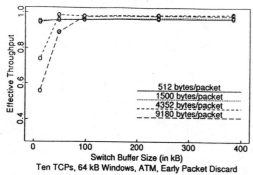

Fig. 5. Early packet discard.

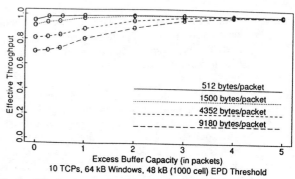

Fig. 6. Effective throughput versus excess buffer capacity.

the switch drops the first arriving cell and all subsequent cells of any incoming packet belonging to a VC designated as using EPD. As long as the buffer queue exceeds the fixed threshold, the switch continues to drop packets from multiple connections. In terms of the cell-dropping strategy, the ATM switch emulates a packet-based switch, dropping complete packets of cells.

Fig. 5 shows the results using EPD in the same congestion scenario previously investigated. Note that except for very small buffer sizes, high effective throughput is achieved.

The EPD mechanism does not require cooperation among ATM switches. It also does not rely on end-to-end congestion control to prevent uncontrolled buffer overflows. Thus higher level protocols such as user datagram protocol (UDP) that do not use end-to-end congestion control can benefit from EPD.

EPD affects congestion within a shorter time frame than do end-to-end congestion control mechanisms. EPD prevents useless data from being immediately transmitted. In contrast, TCP's end-to-end congestion control removes congestion in the longer term by reducing its congestion window in response to dropped packets.

In addition to keeping per-VC state, which is also required with PPD, the implementation of EPD requires the switch to monitor the active buffer queue size. The difficulty in supporting EPD depends on the details of a particular switch architecture; specifically, whether the functions of queue monitoring and packet dropping are located near each other in the hardware. In many switch designs these functions are colocated and it is relatively inexpensive to implement EPD.

TCP over ATM with EPD shares many of the dynamics of TCP in packet-switched networks. This includes a lack of protection from misbehaving users, global synchronization [33], a bias against connections with longer roundtrip ;imes [15], and a bias against connections with multiple contested gateways [14]. EPD could have an additional bias against connections with shorter packets. If the congestion epoch is short and there are two active connections, one with small packets and one with large packets, the switch is likely to find the beginning of one of the smaller packets first, and might never need to drop cells from the connection with larger packets. These biases could be avoided by using additional congestion control mechanisms, as discussed in Section VI.

Preliminary Investigations on Setting the EPD Threshold

The goal of EPD is to prevent frequent buffer overflows by dropping complete packets before the buffer fills, rather than preventing *all* buffer overflows. Occasional buffer overflows do not have serious negative effects on performance.

The placement of the EPD threshold determines how efficiently the buffer is used, and how often cell dropping will occur. Setting the threshold depends on a great many factors and we have not made a complete study of the issue. This section offers some preliminary work.

We find it useful to distinguish two conceptually different aspects of buffer use. The EPD threshold essentially functions as the *effective buffer size*. The *excess buffer capacity*, referring to the buffer in excess of the EPD threshold, is used to accommodate cells from outstanding packets, those that have cells in transmission on the link. Consider an ATM network where the largest packet (i.e., AAL5 unit) contains m cells. If cells from different packets were never interleaved, then it would be sufficient to have an excess buffer capacity of m cells.

We show the relationship between excess buffer capacity and throughput for the restricted case that we have been using as an example—i.e., 64-kbyte windows, 10 TCP's, infinite traffic source model, fixed size packets. Fig. 6 plots the effective throughput as a function of the excess buffer capacity, measured in numbers of packets. Here the EPD threshold, and thus the effective buffer size, is set to 1000 cells. The actual buffer size is set to 1000 cells plus a small multiple (from 1 to 5) of the packet size m. Different line types show the simulation results for different packet sizes. As Fig. 6 shows, the effective throughput drops below 90% in those cases where the excess buffer capacity is less than $3m$ cells. Simulations with an effective buffer size of 2000 cells show similar results.

Further investigation is needed to determine the desired excess buffer capacity for more diverse and typical scenarios. A number of factors are relevant in determining the placement of the threshold that will lead to efficient operation. Among the most important considerations are the distribution of packet sizes and the traffic distribution. In addition, important factors include the duration of the congestion epoch; the proportion of the incoming cells during the congestion epoch that belong to outstanding packets, and thus need to be buffered; and the interaction with ATM-level or transport-level congestion control mechanisms. Also the amount of excess buffer capacity needed depends on how the buffer is shared with non-EPD traffic.

Determining the optimal value for the EPD threshold, that is, the effective buffer size, is a distinct issue from determining the optimal value for the excess buffer capacity. The question of the optimal effective buffer size depends primarily on the network context, e.g., LAN or WAN, trade-offs between throughput and delay, the mix of non-EPD traffic, etc.

VI. SPECULATIONS ON EARLY PACKET DISCARD WITH OTHER ATM CONGESTION CONTROL MECHANISMS

Although the EPD mechanism achieves high effective throughput for TCP or other best-effort traffic over ATM networks, it does not address other traffic management concerns. Issues that may warrant further control mechanisms at the ATM level include controlling average delay for delay-sensitive best-effort traffic (e.g., telnet traffic), providing more stringent fairness requirements, protecting against misbehaving users, and reducing packet drops. This section considers how EPD might be used in conjunction with other ATM control mechanisms.

One possible way to achieve greater traffic control is to incorporate EPD with a random early detection (RED) gateway strategy. RED gateway mechanisms [16] are designed to maintain a low *average* queue size in cooperation with end-to-end congestion control mechanisms. If EPD and RED mechanisms were used together, the ATM switch would have two separate queue thresholds for two separate purposes. The EPD threshold, which would be fairly high, would be used so that the switch could drop complete packets of cells before being forced by a buffer overflow to drop partial packets of cells. The RED threshold, which would be lower, is a threshold for the *average* queue size. When the average queue size indicates persistent congestion, the switch would begin to inform sources to use their end-to-end flow control mechanisms to reduce the load on the network.

Two traffic management schemes for best-effort traffic are currently under development by the ATM Forum traffic management working group. One scheme is a feedback control scheme to operate at the ATM level, similar in nature to DECbit and TCP. In this scheme, the ATM-level source adjusts its sending rate in response to congestion indications from the ATM switches. Early versions appear in [25], [26]. EPD could be used to make rate-based feedback control schemes more robust. By using EPD, feedback control schemes would be more tolerant of occasional cell loss, and could be designed to focus more heavily on other traffic management goals. This tolerance of occasional cell loss might be particularly useful in a switch designed to carry wide-area as well as local traffic.

The second proposal under investigation in the ATM Forum is a hop-by-hop credit-based strategy [22], [29]. This proposal is based on the goal of avoiding cell drops by allowing a VC to transmit cells on a link only when it is known that sufficient buffer capacity is available at the receiving switch. Given such a goal, EPD mechanisms would have little relevance. However, with the memory-sharing modifications that have

been developed to adapt the hop-by-hop proposal to a wide-area environment [23], problems could result if best-effort VC's receiving high bandwidth suddenly have their throughput reduced as a result of downstream congestion. In this case, the addition of EPD mechanisms to drop a packet of cells from stalled connections could free-up valuable memory, and at the same time provide early notification of congestion to the TCP source. Mechanisms similar to those in [13] could be explored to implement EPD for ATM switches with per-VC buffers.

VII. CONCLUSIONS AND FUTURE WORK

As we have shown in this paper, TCP can perform poorly over plain ATM, primarily due to fragmentation. This situation is ameliorated by larger switch buffers and smaller sized TCP packets. PPD improves performance to some extent. However, the fragmentation problem can be obviated by EPD, easily implemented with many switch designs.

For ATM networks with occasional transient congestion, PPD may be an adequate method to provide high effective throughput. Further investigations would be of interest of PPD and EPD strategies in different traffic environments, including a mix of packet sizes, diverse types of data, and different traffic flow models. It would also be interesting to study EPD and PPD with different ATM-level congestion-control mechanisms, such as those mentioned above. Also it would be useful to explore further the behavior of both discard mechanisms in an environment of multiple switches and a large number of VCs.

Of course, if ATM best-effort service is defined to require a cell-loss rate below 10^{-6}, then EPD is of little relevance. An important issue to consider is whether elimination of cell loss is desirable for best-effort traffic, which typically uses modern transport protocols such as TCP that have congestion control mechanisms at the transport layer. Currently such transport protocols rely on packet drops as the indication of congestion in the network. If packets are not dropped, the transport protocol will not be able exercise congestion control and may behave problematically. Further investigation of these issues is needed.

This work has pointed toward several relatively minor ways that TCP could be changed to accomodate native ATM. First, in order to allow high bandwidth utilization in a congested ATM LAN with high bandwidth and low propagation delay, we decreased the TCP clock granularity in our simulators by several orders of magnitude. Further investigation is needed on the effect of TCP clock granularity on overall network performance.

Another change in TCP that would accomodate ATM would be to dynamically vary the packet size. Smaller packet sizes could be used in LANs, where the advantages of larger packets are not as great, and where a less-aggressive window increase algorithm is appropriate.

A third change to TCP that would facilitate interactions with ATM-level congestion control mechanisms would be for TCP congestion control mechanisms to respond to explicit congestion notification, in addition to using packet drops as indications of congestion. We are currently exploring such modifications to TCP [38].

APPENDIX A
SIMULATION DETAILS

We used two different simulators for these experiments, one for the simulations of packet TCP, and another for the simulations of TCP over ATM. Neither simulator is capable of running both kinds of simulations.

Occasionally in simulations one or more connections can be starved out (prevented from attaining any bandwidth by the other connections). This phenomenon, called segregation, has been explained in relation to phase effects in [15]. In order to avoid these phase effects the simulations in this paper add a small random component to the roundtrip time for each packet [15]. In addition, both the packet TCP and the ATM simulations include an added telnet connection that uses less than 1% of the link bandwidth. The telnet connection further offsets phase effects by sending short packets at random times.

In the packet TCP simulations, the link speed ranges from 141.176 Mb/s to 141.528 Mb/s, depending on the packet size. This gives a packet transmission time that is an integer number of microseconds, ranging from 29 μs for a 512-byte packet to 520 μs for a 9180-byte packet.

APPENDIX B
TCP RETRANSMIT TIMERS

The clock granularity for TCP can contribute to poor TCP performance in a high-speed low-propagation-delay environment with ATM. In TCP, the retransmission timer is set as a function of the roundtrip time. The minimum value for the retransmit timer is twice the TCP clock tick, where the TCP clock tick refers to the granularity of the clock used for measuring the TCP roundtrip time. If a retransmitted packet is itself dropped, an exponential backoff is triggered.

In the TCP Tahoe release, the clock granularity is typically 300–500 ms; this clock granularity can be too coarse for the high-speed low-propagation-delay ATM environment. With a clock granularity of 300 ms, when a TCP packet is dropped due to congestion, the retransmit timer gets set to a relatively large value, compared to the actual roundtrip time.

For the simulations reported here, we set the TCP clock granularity to 0.1 ms, which worked reasonably well for this environment.[8] Setting the clock to a finer granularity did not work well. Because the algorithms for setting the retransmit timer assume a somewhat coarse granularity for the TCP clock, relative to the measured roundtrip times, simulations with the clock granularity set to 1 μs result in spurious retransmissions.

To further explore the effects of clock granularity, we ran simulations of EPD with the TCP clock granularity set to 300 ms instead of 0.1 ms. For simulations with mild congestion, the effective throughout is still high, but there

[8] In addition, we adjusted time constants for initial values of the retransmit timer, so that if the first packet of a connection is dropped, the retransmit timer is 0.2 s. We staggered the start times of the various connections to reduce the probability of having the network drop the first packets of a connection, thereby reducing the impact of initial values of the retransmit timer.

can be extreme unfairness, with several connections caught in exponential backoff while other connections receive most of the bandwidth. For simulations with severe congestion, a TCP clock granularity of 300 ms results in lower effective throughput.

However, the clock granularity may not be of critical importance in state-of-the-art and future TCP implementations, which rely less on the retransmit timer. One result of TCP Reno's reduced use of the slow-start procedure [32] is a decreased reliance on the retransmit timer. Newer TCP implementations with Reno-style congestion control algorithms are becoming widely available. Also, the use of intelligent congestion detection mechanisms in switches would reduce TCP's reliance on retransmit timers. Further, with congestion detection mechanisms such as those in RED algorithms, connections that use only a small fraction of the link bandwidth are unlikely to have packets dropped at the switch or gateway. In this case, packets are less likely to be dropped from connections with small windows, where the retransmit timer rather than the fast retransmit procedure might be required for recovery.

For TCP connections whose entire path is over ATM networks, reducing the duplicate ACK threshold from three to one can also improve performance by decreasing reliance on the retransmit timer. Because ATM networks should not reorder or duplicate cells, TCP connections transmitted over all-ATM networks do not necessarily have to wait for three duplicate ACK's to reliably infer a dropped packet, and could retransmit after one duplicate ACK.

APPENDIX C
PACKET RETRANSMISSION RATES

In the simulations of TCP over ATM with EPD, the effective throughput is generally high; the exceptions are simulations where the buffer contains only a few packets worth of cells. Nevertheless, the packet retransmission rate for the active TCP connections can be high even when the effective throughput on the congested link is close to optimal. The throughput can be high even while packet loss and retransmission rates are high because the throughput measures the efficiency of the link, how much "good" data is received across the link. Under high congestion, some connections experience dropped packets, while other packets from those connections are transmitted on the congested link. In this way the loss/retransmission rate can be high, while the overall link throughput is optimal.

Fig. 7 shows the cell loss rates for simulations with TCP over plain ATM. Figs. 8–10 show the packet retransmission rates for simulations with TCP over plain ATM, TCP over ATM with EPD, and packet TCP. The switch buffer size is shown on the x-axis; the y-axis shows the number of retransmitted packets, as a percentage of the total number of packets, disregarding duplicates. If packets are retransmitted more than once, the percentage retransmission can be over 100. For simulations with EPD, the cell loss rate is comparable to the packet retransmission rate.

As Figs. 8 and 9 show, EPD reduces the number of retransmitted packets. However, even with packet TCP the

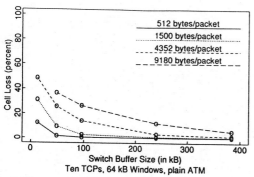

Fig. 7.   Cell loss rates for TCP over plan ATM.

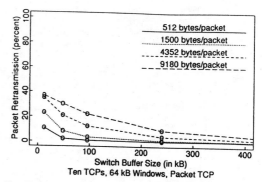

Fig. 10.   Packet retransmission rates for packet TCP.

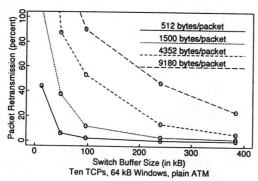

Fig. 8.   Packet retransmission rates for TCP over plain ATM.

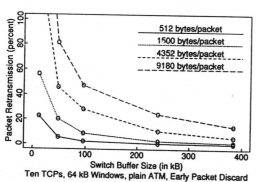

Fig. 9.   Packet retransmission rates for EPD.

retransmission rate can be high. For TCP connections with small roundtrip times and large packets, the TCP window increase algorithm is fairly aggressive, and this can result in a significant fraction of dropped packets.

The important performance parameters for TCP traffic are not the cell loss rates but the average end-to-end packet delay (for interactive TCP traffic such as telnet traffic) and the total time for a connection to complete a transfer (for bulk-data TCP traffic such as FTP file transfers). These performance parameters are not unaffected by cell loss rates, but they depend at least as much on the effective throughput, average queue sizes, retransmission procedures of the transport protocol, and the underlying fairness of the network than on cell-loss rates.

ACKNOWLEDGMENT

The authors thank L. Zhang for generous help with the ATM simulator and issues related to TCP dynamics. This work has also benefited from discussions with V. Jacobson, T. Lyon, B. Lyles, P. Newman, C. O'Neill, V. Paxson, the Traffic Management Working Group of the ATM Forum, and others, and from feedback from anonymous reviewers. They also thank S. Jamin for his useful comments on the paper and J. Haslam for her help.

REFERENCES

[1] "AAL5- A new high speed data transfer AAL," ANSI T1S1.5 91-449, Nov. 1991.
[2] R. Atkinson, "Default IP MTU for use over ATM AAL5," IETF RFC-1626, May 1994.
[3] G. Armitage and K. Adams, "Packet reassembly during cell loss," IEEE Network Mag., vol. 7, no. 5, pp. 26–34, Sept. 1993.
[4] CCITT, "B-ISDN asynchronous transfer mode functional characteristics," draft recommend. I.150, COM XVIII-R109, July 1992.
[5] CCITT, "B-ISDN ATM adaptation layer (AAL) functional description," draft recommend. I.362, COM XVIII, June 1992.
[6] CCITT, "B-ISDN ATM adaptation layer (AAL) specification," draft recommend. I.363, Section VI, COM XVIII, Jan. 1993.
[7] R. Cáceres, "Efficiency of ATM networks in transporting wide-area data traffic," TR-91-043, Int. Comput. Sci. Inst., Berkeley, CA, July 1991.
[8] R. Cáceres, "Multiplexing traffic at the entrance to wide-area networks," Ph.D. dissertation, rep. UCB/CSD 92/717, Univ. Calif., Berkeley, Dec. 1992.
[9] D. Cheriton, "VMTP: Versatile message transaction protocol-protocol specification," IETF RFC-1045, Feb. 1988.
[10] D. Clark and D. Tennenhouse, "Architectural considerations for a new generation of protocols," in Proc. SIGCOMM '90, Sept. 1990, pp. 201-208.
[11] M. Csenger, "Early ATM users lose data," Commun. Week, May 16, 1994.
[12] M. DePrycker, Asynchronous Transfer Mode, 2nd ed. London: Ellis Horwood, 1993.
[13] C. Fang, H. Chen, and J. Hutchins, "A simulation study of TCP performance in ATM networks," in Proc. IEEE GLOBECOM '94 (San Francisco, CA), Nov. 94.
[14] S. Floyd, "Connections with multiple congested gateways in packet-switched networks Part 1: One-way traffic," Comput. Commun. Rev., vol. 21, no. 5, pp. 30–47, Oct. 1991.
[15] S. Floyd and V. Jacobson, "On traffic phase effects in packet-switched gateways," Internetworking: Res., Experience, vol. 3, no. 3, pp. 115–156, Sept. 1992.
[16] S. Floyd and V. Jacobson, "Random early detection gateways for congestion avoidance," IEEE/ACM Trans. Networking, vol. 1, no. 4, pp. 397–413, Aug. 1993.
[17] E. Hahne, C. Kalmanek, and S. Morgan, "Dynamic window flow control on a high-speed wide-area data network," Comput. Networks, ISDN Syst., vol. 26, no. 1, pp. 29–41, Sept. 1993.
[18] V. Jacobson, "Congestion avoidance and control," in Proc. SIGCOMM '88, Aug. 1988, pp. 314–329.

[19] R. Jain and K. K. Ramakrishnan, "Congestion avoidance in computer networks with a connectionless network layer: Concepts, goals, and methodology," in *Proc. IEEE Comp. Networking Symp.* (Washington, DC), Apr. 1988, pp. 134–143.

[20] C. Kent and J. Mogul, "Fragmentation considered harmful," in *Proc. SIGCOMM '87*, Aug. 1987, pp. 390–401.

[21] S. Keshav, "REAL: A network simulator," rep. 88/472, Comput. Sci. Dept., Univ. Calif., Berkeley, 1988.

[22] H. Kung and A. Chapman, "The FCVC (flow-controlled virtual channels) proposal for ATM networks," version 2.0, 1993.

[23] H. Kung, T. Blackwell, and A. Chapman, "Credit-based flow control for ATM networks: Credit update protocol, adaptive credit allocation, and statistical multiplexing," in *Proc. SIGCOMM '94*, Sept. 1994.

[24] I. Leslie and D. McAuley, "Fairisle: An ATM network for the local area," in *Proc. SIGCOMM '91*, Sept. 1991, pp. 327–336.

[25] B. Makrucki, "On the performance of submitting excess traffic to ATM networks," in *Proc. IEEE GLOBECOM '91*, Dec. 1991.

[26] P. Newman, "Backward explicit congestion notification for ATM local area networks," in *Proc. IEEE GLOBECOM '93*, Dec. 1993, pp. 719–723.

[27] S. Ramanathan, P. Rangan, and H. Vin, "Frame-induced packet discarding: An efficient strategy for video networking," in *Proc. Fourth Int. Workshop Network. Operating Sys. Support Digital Audio, Video* (Lancaster, U.K.), Nov. 93, pp. 175–186.

[28] A. Schmidt and R. Campbell, "Internet protocol traffic analysis with applications for ATM switch design," *ACM Comput. Commun. Rev.*, vol. 23, no. 2, pp. 39–52, Apr. 1993.

[29] M. Schroeder *et al.*, "Autonet: A high-speed, self-configuring local area network using point-to-point links," *IEEE J. Select. Areas Commun.*, vol. 9 no. 2, pp. 1318–1335.

[30] S. Shenker, L. Zhang, and D. Clark, "Some observations on the dynamics of a congestion control algorithm," *Comput. Commun. Rev.*, vol. 20, no. 4, pp. 30–39, Oct. 1990.

[31] G. Sidhu, R. Andrews, and A. Oppenheimer, *Inside AppleTalk*. Reading, MA: Addison-Wesley, 1990.

[32] W. Stevens, *TCP/IP Illustrated*, vol. 1. Reading, MA: Addison-Wesley, 1994.

[33] L. Zhang and D. Clark, "Oscillating behavior of network traffic: A case study simulation," *Internetworking: Res., Experience*, vol. 1, no. 2, pp. 101–112, Dec. 1990.

[34] R. Cáceres, "Multiplexing data traffic over wide-area cell networks," unpub. tech. rep., Matsushita Information Technology Laboratory, Princeton, NJ, Mar. 1993.

[35] B. Lyles, D. Swinehart, and A. Bell, "Anatomy of an ATM Switch: The BADLAN local area ATM design," (working title), in preparation, 1994.

[36] A. Romanow and S. Floyd, "Dynamics of TCP traffic over ATM networks: Extended version," unpub. tech. rep., Lawrence Berkeley Laboratory, Berkeley, CA, July 1994.

[37] L. Zhang, private communication.

[38] S. Floyd, "TCP and explicit congestion notification," to be published.

Allyn Romanow (S'88–M'88) received the M.S. and Ph.D. degrees from Stanford University, Stanford, CA, in 1980 and 1983, respectively.

She was with Yale University, New Haven, CT, from 1983–1985, where she was an Assistant Professor with the Yale School of Organization and Management, and also did research in applied data analysis and statistics. From 1987–1990 she was with Olivetti Research, where she developed software to support networked multimedia applications and became interested in ATM. In 1990, she joined Sun Microsystems, Mountain View, CA, where she was Project Lead for an ATM research group and worked on STREAMS performance. In addition to congestion control, her areas of interest are congestion control, network resource management, IP multicast, and network performance.

Sally Floyd (S'88–M'89) received the B.A., M.S., and Ph.D. degrees from the University of California at Berkeley. She received the graduate degrees in theoretical computer science in 1987 and 1989.

The undergraduate degree in sociology and mathematics in 1971 was followed by nearly a decade of work on computer systems for Bay Area Rapid Transit (BART). She is now with Lawrence Berkeley Laboratory, Berkeley, CA, as a Research Scientist.

IEEE JOURNAL ON SELECTED AREAS IN COMMUNICATIONS, VOL. 13, NO. 6, AUGUST 1995

Entropy of ATM Traffic Streams: A Tool for Estimating QoS Parameters

N. G. Duffield, J. T. Lewis, Neil O'Connell, Raymond Russell, and Fergal Toomey

(Invited Paper)

Abstract—For the purposes of estimating quality-of-service parameters, it is enough to know the large deviation rate-function of an ATM traffic stream; modeling procedures can be bypassed if we can estimate the rate-function directly, exploiting the analogy between the rate-function and thermodynamic entropy. We show that this proposal is soundly based on statistical sampling theory. Experiments on the Fairisle ATM network at the University of Cambridge have established that it is feasible to collect the required data in real time.

I. INTRODUCTION

HOW will ATM carriers allocate the band-width required to guarantee the quality-of-service promised in their customer contracts? How can customers exploit to their advantage the tariff structures offered by the carriers? Both carrier and customer will need to measure quality-of-service (QoS) parameters. Existing proposals involve modeling: fitting a statistical model to the input traffic and calculating QoS parameters from the model. Doubts have been expressed about this procedure because data traffic is bursty and cannot be described by a model with a small number of parameters. Our approach is more radical: we estimate directly the thermodynamic entropy of the data-stream at an input-port; from this, the QoS parameters can be calculated rapidly. The algorithms are simple enough to be programmed onto the port-controllers of an ATM switch.

II. THE PROBLEM

ATM switches are buffered. Cells may be lost if a buffer overflows; cells may be delayed by being stacked in a buffer. In this paper, we are concerned with the components of cell-loss and cell-delay which are attributable to a single buffer of finite size. The QoS parameters we are concerned with are:

- cell-loss ratio;
- cell-delay variation;
- mean cell-delay;
- "jitter" (the variance of the cell-delay).

The problem we address is the estimation of these parameters for ATM traffic which is stacked in a buffer emptied at a fixed service-rate. This is a queueing problem: the QoS parameters can be estimated easily provided we know the tail of the

queue-length distribution. Estimating the tail is a problem in large deviation theory; as we shall see, the large deviation rate-function of the arrivals process (the number of cells entering the buffer in each clock-cycle) yields an estimate of the tail of the queue-length distribution. The current practice is to model the arrivals process:

- choose a statistical model;
- fit the parameters of the model to the traffic (using moments, for example);
- compute QoS parameters, using the model.

There are objections to the implementation of this program:

- it is difficult to automate the selection of a model;
- bursty traffic cannot be modeled using a small number of parameters;
- the computational requirements make it difficult to perform the estimation in real time;
- it wastes resources—A good model contains more information about the arrivals process than is required for the estimation of QoS parameters.

This has triggered the search for alternatives to modeling (see Courcoubetis *et al.* [5] for another proposal). Since all that is required for the estimation of QoS parameters is a knowledge of the large deviation rate-function of the arrivals process, why not estimate the rate-function itself? There are good reasons for believing this to be possible: since the work of Ruelle [13] and Lanford [11], it has been well known (but not widely) that the rate-function of large deviation theory is the same kind of mathematical object as the entropy-function of equilibrium thermodynamics. (The connection between large deviation theory and equilibrium thermodynamics is explained briefly in Appendix B.) The rate-function and the entropy-function have this in common: they encapsulate concisely the relevant information about the system. For an ideal gas, the entropy-function can be calculated from first principles; for a real gas, one could choose a statistical model, fit the parameters of the model to measured properties of the gas (virial coefficients, for example), compute the entropy-function from the model and use the entropy-function to compute the bulk properties of the gas. This is not the practice of chemical engineers: they measure the entropy-function or use the tables of measured values available in the literature.

Our claim is this:

For the purposes of estimating QoS parameters, it is enough to know the rate-function of the ATM traffic stream; the modeling procedure can be by-passed if we can estimate the rate-function directly.

Manuscript received September 30, 1994; revised April 1, 1995.

N. G. Duffield is with the School of Mathematical Sciences, Dublin City University, Dublin 9, Ireland. He is also with the Dublin Institute for Advanced Studies, Dublin 4, Ireland.

J. T. Lewis, N. O'Connell, R. Russell, and F. Toomey are with the Dublin Institute for Advanced Studies, Dublin 4, Ireland.

IEEE Log Number 9412648.

Reprinted from IEEE Journal on Selected Areas in Communications, Vol. 13, No. 4, Aug. 1995, pp. 981-990.

III. BASIC THEORY

In the previous section we stated somewhat vaguely that QoS parameters for a traffic stream passing through a buffer can be estimated using the rate-function of the arrivals process. We will now make that statement more precise with an overview of the underlying theory.

A. Estimating QoS Parameters

Suppose we have a single server queue with stationary arrivals (X_k) and constant service rate s. For stability we require that $s > EX_1$; in other words, the service rate exceeds the mean input rate. The rate function of the arrivals process is defined, for $x > EX_1$, by

$$I(x) := \lim_{n \to \infty} \frac{1}{n} \log P\left(\sum_{k=1}^{n} X_k > nx\right) \qquad (1)$$

whenever this limit exists. The theory of large deviations tells us that, provided I satisfies some mild technical conditions [8]–[10], the tails of the queue-length distribution are asymptotically log-linear

$$\lim_{q \to \infty} \frac{1}{q} \log P(Q > q) = -\delta \qquad (2)$$

moreover

$$\delta = \inf_{w>0} I(w+s)/w. \qquad (3)$$

A related result [14] is that, for a large finite buffer, the log-frequency of cell-loss is approximately linear in the buffer-size, with slope $-\delta$. To obtain an upper bound on the log-frequency of cell-loss, we suggest using the straight line $-\mu - \delta q$, where q denotes the buffer-size and $-\mu$ is the log-frequency with which the queue is nonempty.[1] Using this bound, one can estimate the cell-loss ratio, cell-delay variation, mean cell-delay, variance of the cell-delay ("jitter"). The cell-loss ratio is given approximately by the frequency of cell-loss divided by the mean input rate; the cell-delay variation is just the distribution of the queue-length divided by the service rate (up to "round-off" error), and the mean and variance of the cell-delay are just the mean and variance of this distribution.

Now that we have established the role of the rate-function in the problem of estimating QoS parameters, we turn to the question of how to estimate it using traffic observations. It turns out that it is easier to estimate a transform of the rate-function, namely the scaled cumulant generating function (cgf), rather than the rate-function itself. The scaled cgf λ is defined by

$$\lambda(\theta) = \lim_{n \to \infty} \frac{1}{n} \log E \exp\left(\theta \sum_{k=1}^{n} X_k\right) \qquad (4)$$

whenever this limit exists; it is related to the rate-function $I(x)$ by

$$\lambda(\theta) = \sup_{x} \{x\theta - I(x)\} \qquad (5)$$

moreover, δ can be calculated directly from the scaled cgf using the formula

$$\delta = \sup\{\theta : \lambda(\theta) \leq s\theta\}. \qquad (6)$$

A sufficient condition for the validity of the theory we have described is that the arrivals process, in addition to being stationary, should be *mixing*: there is no long-range dependence.

B. Estimating the Scaled cgf

The mixing condition has a second consequence which we exploit in constructing an estimator for λ: there exists a block size b for which the block sums

$$\tilde{X}_1 := \sum_{k=1}^{b} X_k, \tilde{X}_2 := \sum_{k=b+1}^{2b} X_k, \cdots \qquad (7)$$

are approximately independent and identically distributed. Furthermore

$$\lambda(\theta) \approx \lambda_b(\theta) := \frac{1}{b} \log E e^{\theta \tilde{X}_1} \qquad (8)$$

and so the problem of estimating λ is roughly equivalent to the problem of estimating the distribution of $\tilde{X}_1$. This suggests using the (normalized) cgf of the empirical distribution of the block sums as an estimator for λ and the corresponding solution to (6) as an estimator for δ

$$\hat{\lambda}_b^n(\theta) := \frac{1}{b} \log \frac{b}{n} \sum_{i=1}^{[n/b]} e^{\theta \tilde{X}_i} \qquad (9)$$

$$\hat{\delta}_b^n := \sup\{\theta : \hat{\lambda}_b^n(\theta) \leq s\theta\}. \qquad (10)$$

To apply this method in practice, one is faced with the following questions:

- How much data do we need to get a good estimate?
- What is a suitable block size?
- Can we assume stationarity?

The analytic and simulation results that follow are intended to provide some insight and rough heuristics for the first two. The question of stationarity is not specific to this problem: it is a fundamental requirement for prediction. (That is not to say that data with trends, cycles and "external forces" cannot be dealt with; it is often the case that nonstationarity can be "removed" from the data once it is "explained.") We anticipate that the method of estimating δ proposed in this paper will be most useful for short-term prediction, where stationarity is required only over relatively short time periods. For example, it provides a basis for characterizing traffic "on the fly" so that resources can be allocated dynamically.[2]

C. Sampling properties of $\hat{\delta}_b^n$

1) Sampling Theory: For a given model, the sampling distribution of $\hat{\delta}_b^n$ can be calculated using the formula

$$P(\hat{\delta}_b^n < d) = P(\hat{\lambda}_b^n(d) > sd) \qquad (11)$$

or by using the fact (proved in Appendix A) that, for large n, the distribution of $\sqrt{n}(\hat{\delta}_b^n - \delta_b)$ is approximately normal with

---

[1] This is not a rigorous upper bound in general, but we suspect that a sufficient condition for it to be so is that the arrivals are nonnegatively correlated, which is typically the case in practice.

[2] We are grateful to A. Dembo for a private communication in which he suggested using (9) as an estimator for λ. We thank also D. Daley for his comments on an earlier version of this paper.

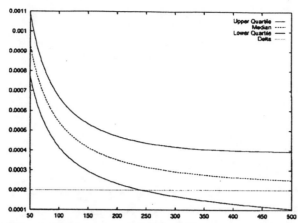

Fig. 1. Gaussian first-order autoregressive process: IQR versus block size.

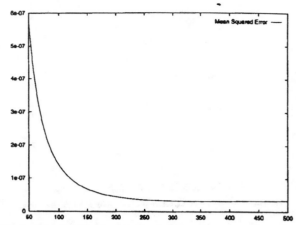

Fig. 2. Gaussian first-order autoregressive process: mean squared error versus block size.

zero mean and variance given by

$$\sigma_b^2 := \lim_{n \to \infty} \frac{b}{\phi_b'(\delta_b)^2} \Bigg[\phi_b(2\delta_b)$$
$$+ \sum_{k=1}^{[n/b]-1} 2 \left(1 - \frac{k}{[n/b]} \right) E e^{\delta_b(\tilde{X}_1 + \tilde{X}_{1+k})} - [n/b] \Bigg] \quad (12)$$

where

$$\delta_b = \sup\{\theta : \lambda_b(\theta) \le s\theta\} \quad (13)$$

and

$$\phi_b(\theta) = e^{b\lambda_b(\theta) - sb\theta}. \quad (14)$$

As $n \to \infty$, $\hat{\delta}_b^n$ converges in probability to δ_b, and $\delta_b = \delta$ if the block sums are independent; in general we have $\delta_b \approx \delta$ for large b. The sampling distribution tells us how good the estimator is; it can also be used to obtain confidence intervals for δ_b and hence approximate confidence intervals for δ. From the approximation (12) we can immediately see the effect of increasing the sample size: as $n \to \infty$ the variance of our estimator decays like σ_b^2/n. However, this is not strictly true, because the variance of $\hat{\delta}_b^n$ is generally infinite! This is a technical hitch due to the fact that in general there is a small but positive probability that most or all of the block sums do not exceed bs, leading to huge or even infinite values of $\hat{\delta}_b^n$; this probability goes to zero as $n \to \infty$ provided $P(X_1 > bs) > 0$, and the effect disappears in the normal approximation. Incidentally, it can be shown (see Appendix A) that if the block sums are independent and we condition on at least three block sums exceeding bs, the variance of $\hat{\delta}_b^n$ becomes finite; in general we have finite kth moments when we condition on there being $k+1$ block sums exceeding bs.

We will now apply the normal approximation to an example to see the effect of varying the block size and service rate on the precision of our estimator. A good model for this purpose is the (stationary) first-order auto-regressive process: let ϵ_k be a sequence of independent normal random variables with zero mean and unit variance, $0 \le \alpha < 1$, and define the X's recursively by

$$X_k = \alpha X_{k-1} + \epsilon_k \quad (15)$$

with $X_1 = \epsilon_1/\sqrt{1 - \alpha^2}$. Note that the arrivals may be positive or negative, and the mean input rate is zero: this is only a mathematical convenience; what we call the "service rate" should really be thought of as the difference between the actual service rate and the actual mean input rate. The parameter α reflects the "burstiness" of the traffic: the larger the value of α the more strongly correlated the arrivals are and this has the effect of encouraging trends, or "bursts"; if $\alpha = 0$ we have independent, Gaussian arrivals. For this model

$$\phi_b(\theta) = \exp \left[\frac{1}{2} \left(b - 2\alpha \left(\frac{1 - \alpha^b}{1 - \alpha^2} \right) \right) \left(\frac{\theta}{1 - \alpha} \right)^2 - bs\theta \right] \quad (16)$$

$$\delta_b = 2(1 - \alpha)^2 s \left[1 - \frac{2\alpha(1 - \alpha^b)}{b(1 - \alpha^2)} \right]^{-1} \quad (17)$$

and

$$\delta = 2(1 - \alpha)^2 s. \quad (18)$$

The asymptotic variance is given by

$$\sigma_b^2 = \frac{b}{\phi_b'(\delta_b)^2} \left[\phi_b(2\delta_b) - 1 + 2 \sum_{k=0}^{\infty} \left(e^{C\alpha^{bk}} - 1 \right) \right] \quad (19)$$

where

$$C = \frac{1}{2} \frac{\alpha}{1 - \alpha^2} (1 - \alpha^b)^2 \left(\frac{\delta_b}{1 - \alpha} \right)^2 (1 + \alpha^{b+1}). \quad (20)$$

(For details of these calculations, see Appendix A.)

In Fig. 1 we have plotted the (approximate) interquartile range (IQR) of $\hat{\delta}_b^n$ against block size b, for fixed service rate $s = 1$, $\alpha = 0.99$ and sample size $n = 10^7$. This illustrates the trade-off between

- increasing the block size to reduce bias, and
- decreasing the block size to reduce variance.

One way of optimising this trade-off is to minimize the *mean squared error* of the estimator. Again, strictly speaking this does not exist, but for the normal approximation it is given by

$$\sigma_b^2/n + (\delta_b - \delta)^2. \quad (21)$$

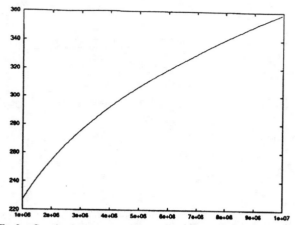

Fig. 3. Gaussian first-order autoregressive process: optimal block size versus sample size.

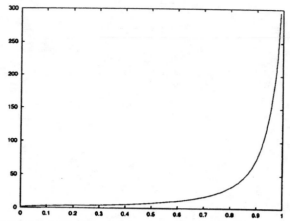

Fig. 5. Gaussian first-order autoregressive process: optimal block size versus α.

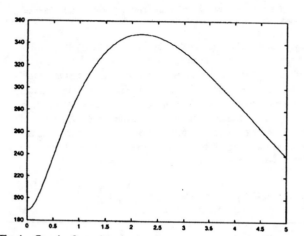

Fig. 4. Gaussian first-order autoregressive process: optimal block size versus service rate.

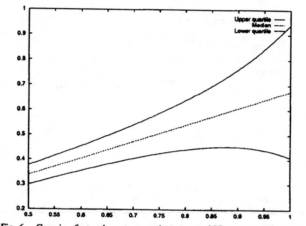

Fig. 6. Gaussian first-order autoregressive process: IQR versus service rate.

This is plotted in Fig. 2 (against block size). From this we can read off the optimal block size, which in this case is in the region 350–400. Note that the optimal block size depends on the sample size (n), service rate (s) and burstiness (α); in Figs. 3–5 we have plotted the optimal block size against each of these parameters.

Finally, we consider the effect of increasing the service rate on the precision of the estimator. Fig. 6 is a plot of the approximate IQR of $\hat{\delta}_b^n$ against s, for fixed block size $b = 5$, sample size $n = 800$ and $\alpha = 0.5$. Clearly the estimator loses precision as the service rate increases. Intuitively, this is because a higher service rate gives rise to shorter queues and hence less information about the tails of the queue-length distribution.

We have made similar calculations for the two-state Markov model described in the next subsection. The formula for the asymptotic variance is considerably more cumbersome in this case; we do not reproduce it here. Moreover, the results show the same qualitative features as those for the stationary AR(1) process, at least for block-sizes less than 50; beyond 50, it is more convenient to investigate the two-state Markov model by simulation, described in the next subsection.

2) Simulation Results: The results of this section are intended to complement the analytic approximations of the previous section; here we investigate the sampling properties of $\hat{\delta}_b^n$ with "exact" calculations based on simulations of two traffic models; note that, in both models, the traffic streams have the same mean activity.

- *Bernoulli:* The arrivals X_k are independent and identically distributed with

$$P(X_1 = 1) = 1 - P(X_1 = 0) = 1/4.$$

- *Two-State Markov:* Here the arrivals are modeled by a two-state Markov chain with transition probabilities

$$P(X_2 = 1|X_1 = 0) = 1/16; \quad P(X_2 = 0|X_1 = 1) = 3/16.$$

First we consider the sample size: Figs. 7 and 8 show how the empirical interquartile range varies with sample size for each model. In both cases the service rate is fixed ($s = 0.3$) and for the two-state Markov traffic we have used the block size $b = 500$ (by independence there is no need to aggregate the Bernoulli traffic). In the Bernoulli case we have superimposed the analytic approximation of Section III-C1: clearly it is a

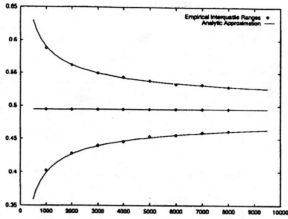

Fig. 7. Interquartile range versus sample size for Bernoulli traffic.

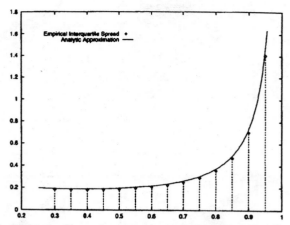

Fig. 9. Interquartile spread versus service rate for Bernoulli traffic.

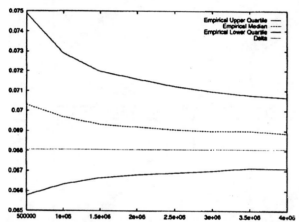

Fig. 8. Interquartile range versus sample size for two-state Markov traffic.

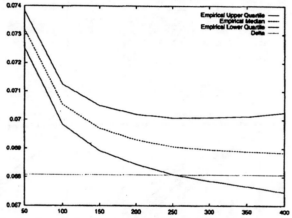

Fig. 10. Interquartile versus block size for two-state Markov traffic.

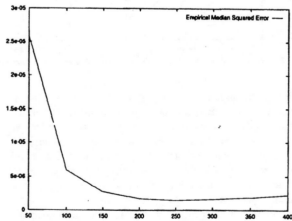

Fig. 11. Median squared error versus block size for two-state Markov traffic.

good approximation; the analytic approximation is difficult to compute for the two-state Markov model.

Next we consider the service rate: Fig. 9 is a plot, for fixed sample size $n = 1024$, of the empirical interquartile spread against service rate for the Bernoulli traffic, with the analytic approximation. Again we see that for large service rates, the precision of our estimator is reduced quite dramatically.

Finally we consider the effect of varying the block size for correlated traffic, with a view to finding an optimal block size. In Fig. 10 we have plotted, for fixed sample size $n = 4.2(10)^6$ and service rate $s = 0.3$, the empirical interquartile range of the estimator against block size for the two-state Markov traffic: just as we expect, increasing the block size reduces bias on one hand, but increases spread on the other. Since we are now dealing with a finite sample where the variance does not exist, we consider minimizing the *median* squared error of the estimator as a criterion for choosing the optimal block size. This is asymptotically equivalent to the mean squared error of Section III-C1, and is a more robust quantity than the sample mean squared error. The empirical median squared error, for fixed sample size $n = 4.2(10)^6$ and service rate $s = 0.3$, is plotted in Fig. 11: this is minimized at about $b = 250$.

D. Watermarking

Recall that the parameter δ we are trying to estimate is given by

$$\delta = -\lim_{q \to \infty} \frac{1}{q} \log P(Q > q) \qquad (22)$$

where $P(Q > q)$ is the frequency with which the queue-length exceeds the level q. In other words, if we plot $\log P(Q > q)$

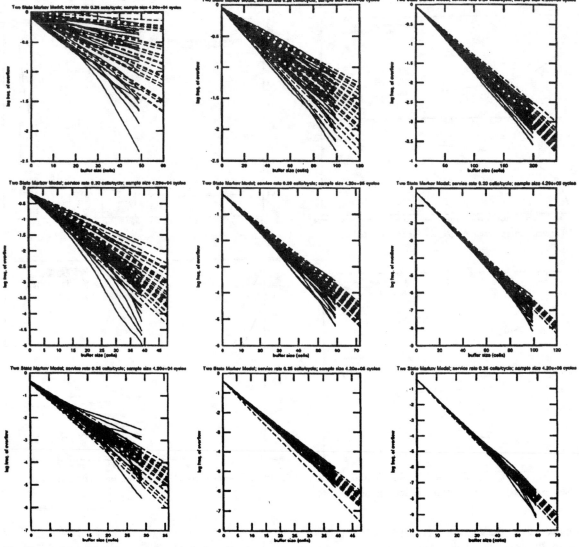

Fig. 12. Watermarks and δ -estimates for a variety of sample sizes and service rates

against q, the asymptotic slope is $-\delta$. To observe this empirically, we feed simulated data through a virtual buffer and plot the log-frequencies with which each level is exceeded; we call this a *watermark plot*. Given sufficient data, a watermark plot will typically have a "straight part" with slope close to $-\delta$ before becoming "wobbly" at levels which are rarely exceeded. It is important to keep in mind that a watermark plot is a random object.

In this section we compare the variation in our δ-estimates with the variation in the corresponding watermark plots using simulated two-state Markov arrival streams with transition probabilities 1/16 (0 to 1) and 3/16 (1 to 0). The estimates are based on optimal block sizes which, in each case, were found using the procedure described in Section III-C2. Fig. 12 shows the results of 30 simulations for different sample sizes and service rates; for each simulation, the watermark is plotted along with our estimated value of δ. The variation in the

δ-estimates is comparable with the variation in the slopes of the (straight part of the) watermarks in all cases.

E. The Relation of Cell-Loss Ratio to Watermarking

In Section III-A we proposed the linear upper bound $-\mu - \delta q$ on the log-frequency of cell-loss from a finite buffer of size q; this, in turn, provides an upper bound on the log of the cell-loss ratio. In this section, we compare the watermark plot (the log-tail-frequencies of the queue-length distribution in an *infinite buffer*), the cell-loss ratios at each finite buffer-size, and the queue-length distribution in a finite buffer, using simulated Bernoulli and two-state Markov traffic.

In Fig. 13, we demonstrate the relation between watermark and cell-loss ratio in a simulation of 10^7 cycles of Bernoulli traffic with activity 0.38 and service rate 0.4 up to buffer-size 40, and the queue-length distribution in a buffer of size 40.

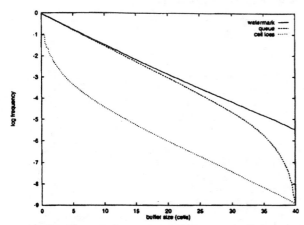

Fig. 13. Watermark, finite buffer queue-length and cell-loss ratio for Bernoulli arrivals.

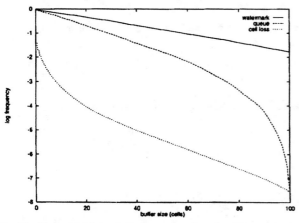

Fig. 14. Watermark, finite buffer queue-length and cell-loss ratio for two-state Markov arrivals.

In Fig. 14, we do the same for 10^6 cycles of two-state Markov traffic up to buffer-size 100 (in this case the log-tail-frequencies of the queue-length distribution in a buffer of size 100 are plotted). As before, the parameters of the source are 1/16, 3/16, and the service rate is 0.26.

IV. CONCLUSIONS

This investigation has shown that the proposal to use an empirical entropy function to estimate QoS parameters is theoretically sound. Experiments, made on the Fairisle network at the University of Cambridge by S. Crosby, have established that it is feasible to collect the required data in real time.

Our experience so far with real traffic has been promising. For our method to be applicable, the traffic must be stationary and mixing over periods long enough to ensure adequate precision. The requirement of stationarity is not specific to this method: inconsistent behavior cannot be predicted. We anticipate that our method will be most useful for short-term prediction where stationarity is only required only for relatively short time-periods. For example, it provides a basis for characterising traffic on the fly, so that resources can

be allocated dynamically. The question of the applicability of our analysis to real switches has been investigated by running simulated two-state Markov data through the Fairisle switch and comparing the observed end-to-end delay with that predicted by the rate-function. The observed delay distribution was in close agreement with the predicted, demonstrating that a single buffer with constant service rate is a fairly good representation of the actual situation in the Fairisle switch when configured as an output-buffered switch with FIFO queueing. Preliminary experiments to test the usefulness of the estimator with "real" ATM traffic have also been carried out; a report on these and the other experiments referred to here can be found in [15].

APPENDIX A

A. The Central Limit Theorem

An alternative expression for $\hat{\delta}_b^n$ is

$$\hat{\delta}_b^n = \sup\{\theta : \hat{\phi}_b^n(\theta) \leq 1\} \tag{23}$$

where

$$\hat{\phi}_b^n(\theta) = \frac{b}{n} \sum_{i=1}^{[n/b]} e^{\theta(\tilde{X}_i - b s)}. \tag{24}$$

Thus

$$P(\hat{\delta}_b^n < d) = P(\hat{\phi}_b^n(d) > 1). \tag{25}$$

Set $\phi_b(\theta) := E\hat{\phi}_b^n(\theta)$. By the central limit theorem for weakly dependent stationary processes we have that, for each θ, $\sqrt{n}[\hat{\phi}_b^n(\delta_b) - 1]$ converges weakly as $n \to \infty$ to a normal distribution with zero mean and variance given by

$$\tau_b^2 := \lim_{n \to \infty} n\mathrm{var}\, \hat{\phi}_b^n(\delta_b)$$
$$= \lim_{n \to \infty} b[\phi_b(2\delta_b)$$
$$+ \sum_{k=1}^{n/b-1} 2\left(1 - \frac{kb}{n}\right) E e^{\delta_b(\tilde{X}_1 + \tilde{X}_{1+k})} - \frac{n}{b}]$$

provided this limit exists. Assuming ϕ_b is smooth on the interior of its effective domain (the set where it is finite) and finite in a neighborhood of δ_b, the weak law of large numbers tells us that $\hat{\phi}_b^{n\prime}(\delta_b)$ converges in probability to $\phi_b'(\delta_b)$ and $\hat{\phi}_b^{n\prime\prime}(\theta)$ converges in probability to $\phi_b''(\theta)$ for $\theta \leq \delta_b$. Combining these facts with (25) we have that as $n \to \infty$

$$P(\sqrt{n}(\hat{\delta}_b^n - \delta_b) < d)$$
$$= P(\hat{\delta}_b^n < d/\sqrt{n} + \delta_b)$$
$$= P(\hat{\phi}_b^n(\delta_b + d/\sqrt{n}) > 1)$$
$$= P\left(\hat{\phi}_b^n(\delta_b) + \frac{d}{\sqrt{n}}\hat{\phi}_b^{n\prime}(\delta_b) + \frac{1}{n}O_p(1) > 1\right)$$
$$= P\left(\sqrt{n}[\hat{\phi}_b^n(\delta_b) - 1] > -d\hat{\phi}_b^{n\prime}(\delta_b) - \frac{1}{n}O_p(1)\right)$$
$$\to P(Z > -\phi_b'(\delta_b)/\tau_b)$$

where $O_p(1)$ means "convergent in probability" and Z is a standard normal random variable. The last step follows from

Slutzky's theorem (see, for example, [3]). It follows that $\sqrt{n}(\hat{\delta}_b^n - \delta_b)$ converges weakly to a normal random variable with zero mean and variance $\tau_b^2/\phi_b'(\delta_b)^2$.

B. The Conditional Moments of $\hat{\delta}_b^n$

For notational convenience set $m = n/b$, $Z_i = \check{X}_i - bs$, and drop the subscripts and superscripts on $\hat{\delta}_b^n$ and $\hat{\phi}_b^n$. Let N denote the number of block sums exceeding bs, that is

$$N = \#\{i : Z_i > 0\}. \tag{26}$$

Note that $\hat{\delta} = \infty$ on $\{N = 0\}$. Now, assuming the block sums are independent and identically distributed

$$
\begin{aligned}
&P(\hat{\delta} \geq \theta | N \geq k) \\
&= P(\hat{\phi}(\theta) \leq 1 | N \geq k) \\
&= P(\hat{\phi}(\theta) \leq 1 | Z_1, \cdots, Z_k > 0) \\
&= P(\sum_{i=2}^m e^{\theta Z_i} \leq m - e^{\theta Z_1}, e^{\theta Z_1} \leq m | Z_1, \cdots, Z_k > 0) \\
&\leq P(\sum_{i=2}^m e^{\theta Z_i} \leq m, e^{\theta Z_1} \leq m | Z_1, \cdots, Z_k > 0) \\
&= P(\sum_{i=2}^m e^{\theta Z_i} \leq m | Z_2, \cdots, Z_k > 0) P(e^{\theta Z_1} \leq m | Z_1 > 0) \\
&\vdots \\
&\leq P(\sum_{i=k+1}^m e^{\theta Z_i} \leq m) P(e^{\theta Z_1} \leq m | Z_1 > 0)^k.
\end{aligned}
$$

Thus, to ensure that

$$E(\hat{\delta}^r | N \geq k) < \infty \tag{27}$$

it suffices to have, for some $\epsilon > 0$

$$\lim_{\theta \to \infty} \theta^{r+\epsilon} P(0 < Z_1 \leq \log m/\theta) = 0 \tag{28}$$

if we assume that there exists $\gamma > 0$ for which Z_1 has a density on $(0, \gamma)$ then (28) is guaranteed once $k > r$.

C. Calculations for the Autoregressive Process

The stationary AR(1) (first-order autoregressive) process $\{X_i\}_{i \geq 1}$ can be defined recursively by

$$
\begin{aligned}
X_1 &= \alpha \frac{\xi_0}{\sqrt{1-\alpha^2}} + \xi_1 \\
X_{i+1} &= \alpha X_i + \xi_{i+1} \ \forall \ i \geq 1
\end{aligned}
$$

where $\{\xi_j\}_{j \geq 1}$ is a sequence of independent Gaussian random variables with zero mean and unit variance: $\xi_j \sim N(0,1), \forall j \geq 1$. Thus

$$X_i = \sum_{j=1}^i \alpha^{i-j} \xi_j + \frac{\alpha^i}{\sqrt{1-\alpha^2}} \xi_0.$$

The stationary distribution of this process is Gaussian with mean 0 and variance $(1-\alpha^2)^{-1}$, so we can start it off in the stationary regime by choosing ξ_0 to be also Gaussian with

zero mean and unit variance. We choose a block size b, and define the aggregated process $\{\check{X}_k\}_{k \geq 1}$ by

$$
\begin{aligned}
\check{X}_{k+1} &:= \sum_{i=kb+1}^{kb+b} X_i \\
&= \sum_{j=kb+1}^{kb+b} \frac{1-\alpha^{kb+b+1-j}}{1-\alpha} \xi_j + \frac{1-\alpha^b}{1-\alpha} \sum_{j=1}^{kb} \alpha^{kb+1-j} \xi_j \\
&\quad + \frac{1-\alpha^b}{1-\alpha} \frac{\alpha^{kb+1}}{\sqrt{1-\alpha^2}} \xi_0.
\end{aligned}
$$

We wish to calculate $E[e^{\theta \check{X}_k}]$ and $E[e^{\theta(\check{X}_k + \check{X}_l)}]$. The $\check{X}_i$'s are stationary, since the X_i's are, and so

$$
\begin{aligned}
E[e^{\theta \check{X}_k}] &= E[e^{\theta \check{X}_1}] \\
E[e^{\theta(\check{X}_k + \check{X}_l)}] &= E[e^{\theta(\check{X}_{|k-l|+1} + \check{X}_1)}].
\end{aligned}
$$

If X and Y are two independent Gaussian random variables with zero mean and unit variance, then

$$\log E[e^{\theta(aX+bY)}] = \frac{1}{2}(a^2 + b^2)\theta^2.$$

We use this fact repeatedly on the ξ_j's which make up the $\check{X}_k$'s to get

$$
\begin{aligned}
\log E[e^{\theta \check{X}_1}] &= \frac{1}{2}\left(b - \frac{2\alpha}{1-\alpha^2}(1-\alpha^b)\right)\left(\frac{\theta}{1-\alpha}\right)^2 \\
\log E[e^{\theta(\check{X}_{k+1}+\check{X}_1)}] &= \frac{1}{2}\frac{\alpha}{1-\alpha}(1-\alpha)^2(1+\alpha^{b+1}) \\
&\quad \cdot \alpha^{(k-1)b}\left(\frac{\theta}{1-\alpha}\right)^2 + 2\log E[e^{\theta \check{X}_1}]
\end{aligned}
$$

for $k \neq 1$. Thus

$$
\begin{aligned}
\phi_b(\theta) &:= E[\frac{b}{n}\sum_{k=1}^{n/b} e^{\theta(\check{X}_k - s)}] \\
&= \exp\left\{\frac{1}{2}\left(b - \frac{2\alpha}{1-\alpha^2}(1-\alpha^b)\right)\left(\frac{\theta}{1-\alpha}\right)^2 - \theta s\right\}
\end{aligned}
$$

and

$$
\begin{aligned}
\delta_b &:= \sup\{\theta : \phi_b(\theta) \leq 1\} \\
&= \frac{2(1-\alpha)^2 s}{b - \frac{2\alpha}{1-\alpha^2}(1-\alpha^b)}.
\end{aligned}
$$

Now $E[e^{\theta(\check{X}_{k+1}+\check{X}_1)}] = e^{C\beta^{k-1}}$, where $\beta = \alpha^b$ and

$$C = \frac{1}{2}\frac{\alpha}{1-\alpha^2}(1-\beta)^2\left(\frac{\delta_b}{1-\alpha}\right)^2(1+\alpha\beta).$$

Finally

$$
\begin{aligned}
\sigma_b^2 &= \lim_{n \to \infty} \frac{b}{\phi_b'(\delta_b)}\left[\phi_b(2\delta_b) - 1 \right. \\
&\quad \left. + 2\sum_{k=1}^{n/b-1}\left(1 - \frac{kb}{n}\right)\left(E[e^{\delta_b(\check{X}_{k+1}+\check{X}_1)}] - 1\right)\right] \\
&= \frac{b}{\phi_b'(\delta_b)}\left[\phi_b(2\delta_b) - 1 + 2\sum_{k=0}^{\infty}\left(e^{C\beta^k} - 1\right)\right]
\end{aligned}
$$

since

$$\lim_{n \to \infty} \sum_{k=1}^{n/b-1} \frac{kb}{n} \left(e^{C\beta^k} - 1 \right) = 0$$

for $\beta < 1$.

Appendix B

Here we recall the rudiments of thermodynamics and explain briefly the connection with the theory of large deviations. For a readable account of this approach to thermodynamics (which goes back to Gibbs in 1873), see Callen [4].

For simplicity, we consider the thermodynamics of a gas consisting of molecules of a single chemical species. The entropy per unit volume of the gas is a function $s(u, \rho)$ of u, the internal energy per unit volume, and ρ, the mass per unit volume. The function $s(u, \rho)$ is continuously differentiable (expressing the continuity of the intensive variables, such as pressure) and concave (expressing thermodynamic stability). All bulk properties of the gas can be derived from the entropy function, using standard formulae (see [4]). For example, the entropy function of an ideal gas is given (up to an additive constant) by

$$s(u, \rho) = k\rho \left\{ \frac{f}{2} \ln u - \left(1 + \frac{f}{2} \right) \ln \rho \right\} \qquad (29)$$

where k is Boltzmann's constant and f is a constant depending on the chemical species. From this function we may derive, for example, the two equations of state

$$p = kT\rho, \qquad u = \frac{f}{2} kT. \qquad (30)$$

Boltzmann's remarkable formula

$$S = k \ln W \qquad (31)$$

relating the thermodynamic entropy S of a macroscopic equilibrium state to the number W of microscopic states which correspond to the macroscopic state, gives rise to problems of interpretation. To have any hope of giving the formula a precise meaning, we should pass to the limit in which the volume V of the system become infinite. In this limit we might expect a formula

$$s(u, \rho) = \lim_{V \to \infty} \frac{k}{V} \ln W[H_V = uV, N_V = \rho V] \qquad (32)$$

where $W[H_V = uV, N_V = \rho V]$ is the phase-space volume of those macroscopic states for which the Hamiltonian H_V takes the value uV and the number of particles N_V takes the value ρV. However, the existence of the limit on the right-hand side of (32) poses obvious difficulties. These were resolved by Ruelle [13] in 1965.

Ruelle's idea can be illustrated simply: let B_a be a disc of radius a centered on the point (u, ρ); one can prove that the limit

$$s[B_a] = \lim_{V \to \infty} \frac{k}{V} \ln W[(H_V/V, N_V/V) \in B_a] \qquad (33)$$

exists. Now let B_a shrink to a point, defining

$$s(u, \rho) := \inf_{a>0} s[B_a]. \qquad (34)$$

The argument used to establish the existence of the limit (33) proves also that $s(u, \rho)$ is a concave function. In the case of an ideal gas, it is easy to verify (using Stirling's Formula) that Ruelle's procedure yields (29).

This simple idea was developed by Ruelle and Lanford to provide a rigorous treatment of statistical thermodynamics, described in detail in Lanfords's 1971 Battelle Lectures [11]. Ruelle's idea turned out to have a surprising ramification in probability theory: Lanford used it to give a completely new proof of Cramèr's Theorem; this was the first step in an important development in the theory of large deviations.

The modern theory of large deviations began with Cramèr's refinement [6] of the weak law of large numbers.

Theorem 1: Let $X_1, X_2, \cdots$ be a sequence of bounded, identically distributed independent random variables. There exists a concave function s such that, for every open interval J

$$\lim_{n \to \infty} \frac{1}{n} \ln P[n^{-1}(X_1 + X_2 + \cdots + X_n) \in J] = \sup_{x \in J} s(x). \qquad (35)$$

Lanford first proved that, for each open interval $B_a := (x - a, x + a)$, the limit

$$\lim_{n \to \infty} \frac{1}{n} \ln P[n^{-1}(X_1 + X_2 + \cdots + X_n) \in B_a] \qquad (36)$$

exists (the value $-\infty$ is allowed). Lanford then defined $s(x)$ by

$$s(x) := \inf_{a>0} s[B_a] \qquad (37)$$

and proved that (34) holds for each open interval J.

This approach to the theory of large deviations was taken up by Bahadur and Zabell [2]; they developed it to prove a powerful generalization of Cramèr's Theorem. Azencott [1] and, later, Deuschel and Stroock [7], systematised these developments. A detailed review of thermodynamic aspects of large deviation theory, including an account of the part played by the grand canonical pressure (the scaled cumulant generating function used in Section III), is given in [12].

We have illustrated how, from the mathematical point of view, the rate-function of large deviation theory is the same kind of object as the entropy function of thermodynamics. They have this in common: they encapsulate concisely the relevant information about the system; for this reason it makes sense to measure them.

References

[1] R. Azencott, "Grandes déviations et applications", in *Lecture Notes in Mathematics*. Berlin: Springer, 1980, oo, 2–176.
[2] R. R. Bahadur and S. L. Zabell, "Large deviations of the sample mean in general vector spaces," *Ann. Prob.*, vol. 7, pp. 587–621, 1979.
[3] P. Billingsley, *Convergence of Probability Measures*. New York: Wiley, 1968.
[4] H. B. Callen, *Thermodynamics and an Introduction to Thermostatistics*. New York: Wiley, 1985.
[5] C. Courcoubetis, G. Kesidis, A. Ridder, J. Walrand, and R. Weber (1993). "Admission control and routing in ATM networks using inferences from measured buffer occupancy," to be published.
[6] H. Cramèr, "Sur un théorème-limite de la théorie des probabilités", *Actualités Scientifiques et Industrielles*, vol. 736, no. 5, p. 23, 1938.
[7] J.-D. Deuschel and D. W. Stroock, *Large Deviations*. New York: Academic, 1989.
[8] G. de Veciana, C. Courcoubetis, and J. Walrand, "Decoupling bandwidths for networks: A decomposition approach to resource management," Mem. UCB/ERL M93/50, Univ. Calif., 1993.

[9] N. G. Duffield and N. O'Connell, "Large deviations and overflow probabilities for the general single server queue, with applications," to be published.

[10] P. W. Glynn and W. Whitt, "Logarithmic asymptotics for steady-state tail probabilities in a single-server queue," *J. Appl. Prob.*, vol. 31A, pp. 131–159, 1994.

[11] O. E. Lanford, "Entropy and equilibrium states in classical statistical mechanics," in *Lecture Notes in Physics.* Berlin: Springer, 1973.

[12] J. T. Lewis and C.-E. Pfister, "Thermodynamic probability theory: some aspects of large deviations, to be published.

[13] D. Ruelle, "Correlation functionals," *J. Math. Phys.*, vol. 6, pp. 201–220, 1965.

[14] F. Toomey, "Queues of bursty traffic in finite buffers," in *Proc. 3rd Int. Workshop Queueing Networks Finite Capacity*, Bradford, U.K., July 1995.

[15] S. Crosby *et al.*, "Bypassing modeling: An investigation of entropy as a traffic descriptor in the fairisle ATM network," in *Proc. 12th U.K. Teletraffic Symp.*, Windsor, London, U.K., Mar. 1995.

Neil O'Connell received the B.S. degree with first class honors and a Gold Medal, in 1989, the M.S. degree in 1990, and the the Ph.D. degree from the University of California, Berkeley, in 1993.

He was with the Department of Statistics, University of California, after 1990. Currently, he is a Lecturer in the Department of Statistics, Trinity College, Dublin, Ireland, where he is a Scholar.

Dr. O'Connell was an invited speaker at the IMA Workshop on Mathematical Population Genetics in Minnesota, January 1994.

Raymond Russell received the B.S. degree with first class honors and the Synge Medal, in 1993.

In 1992, he was with the Mathematics Department, University of California, Berkeley, writing computer code implementing algorithms for the numerical solution of systems of polynomial equation.

Mr. Russell is a Scholar of Trinity College, Dublin, Ireland.

N. G. Duffield received the Ph.D. degree from the University of London, London, U.K., in 1987.

He was with IBM in London and Oslo, Norway, before studying at Christ's College, Cambridge, U.K. As a postdoctoral fellow at DIAS, he worked on the application of probability theory to statistical mechanics. Currently, he is a Lecturer in the School of Mathematics, Dublin City University, Dublin, Ireland, where he teaches a graduate course on queueing systems. He has held visiting fellowships at the Australian National University and at the Tinbergen Institute, Amsterdam, The Netherlands.

J. T. Lewis received the Ph.D. degree from The Queen's University of Belfast, Northern Ireland.

From 1955 to 1972, he was with the Mathematical Institute, Oxford, U.K. He was a Member of the Institute for Advanced Studies, Princeton, NJ, 1969 to 1970. He has been at DIAS since 1972 and Director of the School of Theoretical Physics since 1975. His current research interest is applications of Large Deviation Theory.

Dr. Lewis served on the Executive of the International Association of Mathematical Physics from 1982–1988 and the Council of the Royal Irish Academy from 1982–1988.

Fergal Toomey received the B.S. degree with first class honors from Trinity College, Dublin, Ireland, in 1992, and the M.S. degree in theroetical physics in 1993.

In 1992, he was with the Hitachi Dublin Laboratory, writing programs for mesh generation, as part of their automatic differential-equations-solving package.

Performance Limitation of the Leaky Bucket Algorithm for ATM Networks

Naoaki Yamanaka, Youichi Sato, and Ken-Ichi Sato

Abstract— The performance limitation of the "Leaky Bucket algorithm" is analyzed for usage parameter control and traffic management in Asynchronous Transfer Mode (ATM) networks. Simulation results show that the conventional statistical bandwidth allocation method, which uses "the worst pattern derived from the cell interarrival time moments" permitted by the Leaky Bucket algorithm, can not guarantee the QOS. As a result, this paper proves that the VC/VP bandwidth allocation method based on the Leaky Bucket algorithm is unsatisfactory.

I. INTRODUCTION

A SYNCHRONOUS TRANSFER MODE (ATM) has been adopted by ITU-T as the transport and switching technique for broadband integrated services digital network (B-ISDN) due to its flexibility in providing bandwidth on-demand and the potential bandwidth efficiency offered by the statistical multiplexing of bursty traffic.

Two basic traffic control functions, connection admission control and usage parameter control (UPC) [1] are necessary for guaranteeing QOS, the quality of service. UPC ensures that during the information transfer phase, connections exceeding their specified traffic rates do not deteriorate the QOS of other connections.

The bandwidth allocation algorithm is related to the UPC mechanism [2]–[4]. In particular, the "Leaky Bucket algorithm" [1], and its performance have been analyzed world wide. This is because of the simplicity of the algorithm and its low hardware demands [5]–[8].

The bandwidth allocation method proposed in [2] uses "the worst pattern" (heaviest or burstiest traffic pattern derived from the cell interarrival time moments) for bandwidth allocation. This letter illustrates the performance limitation of the Leaky Bucket algorithm and the danger of conventional statistical bandwidth allocation methods based on the "worst pattern" Leaky Bucket. The performance of the Leaky Bucket algorithm and its bandwidth allocation method for B-ISDN/ATM network are not reliable.

II. TRAFFIC CONTROL AND USAGE PARAMETER CONTROL (UPC)

The network allocates bandwidth to all VC's and VP's accepted by CAC (call admission control) [9]. The bandwidth requirement of a VC/VP connection is indicated in the form of traffic descriptors. It is important to develop a simple but

Paper approved by J. F. Kurose, the Editor for Networking Systems of the IEEE Communications Society. Manuscript received December 15, 1991; revised September 15, 1992 and March 15, 1994.

N. Yamanaka is with NTT Network Service Systems Laboratories, Musashino-shi, Tokyo 180, Japan.

Y. Sato and K.-I. Sato are with NTT Optical Network Systems Laboratories, Kanagawa 238-03, Japan.

IEEE Log Number 9411091.

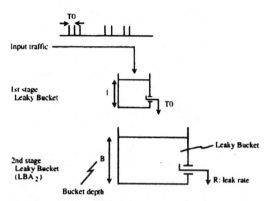

Fig. 1. Leaky bucket algorithm for variable bit-rate services (VBR).

accurate bandwidth allocation algorithm applicable to all traffic types.

During the information transfer period, UPC ensures that the cell traffic of every connection does not exceed the negotiated traffic rate, as one or more excessive rates may deteriorate the QOS of other connections. The "Leaky Bucket" algorithm is considered to be one of the simplest UPC algorithms and is discussed in the following section.

III. LEAKY BUCKET ALGORITHM FOR UPC

A traffic descriptor is a set of parameters that characterize the traffic offered by an ATM connection. In general, the Leaky Bucket algorithm is characterized by its bucket depth or threshold (B) and its leak rate (R) as shown in Fig. 1.

To monitor peak and average traffic rates of variable bit-rate (VBR) services, the dual Leaky Bucket algorithm has been proposed as one UPC technique [11], [12]. The minimum time (T_0) between consecutive cells determines the peak traffic rate. A first stage Leaky Bucket with the following parameters monitors the peak rate T_0.

First stage leaky Bucket leak rate $R0 = T0$.
First stage leaky Bucket depth $B0 = 1$.

To set the average traffic rates according to the leaky bucket algorithm and thereafter control traffic, the following two leaky bucket parameters will be used as the average rate traffic descriptors [10] of $T0$, T and X.

Second stage leaky bucket leak rate $R = X/T$.
Second stage leaky bucket depth.

$$B = X - R(X - 1)T0. \qquad (1)$$

The second stage Leaky Bucket (LBA$_2$) of the dual Leaky Bucket algorithm monitors these parameters. This paper discusses the performance of the two stage Leaky Bucket.

Reprinted from IEEE Transactions on Communications, Vol. 43, No. 8, Aug. 1995, pp. 2298-2300.

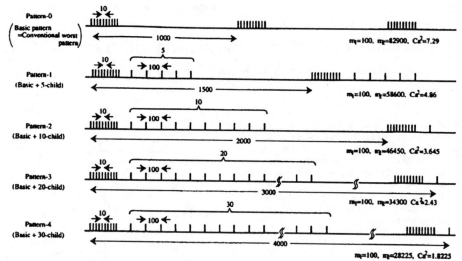

Fig. 2. Some examples of LBA$_2$ permitted patterns used in the simulation. (m_1: first moment of cell interarrival time, m_2: second moment of cell interarrival time, C_a^2: Squared coefficient of variation of cell interarrival time).

There are a number of traffic patterns that correspond to peak rate $1/T_0$ and mean rate R. The maximum number (X) of ATM cells sent in a burst with a peak rate of $1/T_0$ is determined by the following equation derived from formula (1)

$$X = \text{int} \frac{\lceil B - T0 \bullet R \rceil}{1 - T0 \bullet R} \qquad (2)$$

where int $\lceil r \rceil$ is the smallest integer larger than the real number r. The pattern characterized by a maximum burst length of $T0 \bullet X$ cells spaced by the minimum cell interarrival time of $T0$, and a burst interarrival time of T, is called the basic pattern. The patterns derived from the basic pattern and also permitted by LBA$_2$ are called child patterns.

Fig. 2 is an example of a combination of child patterns interleaved into the basic pattern. If the burst length and interarrival time relationships between basic and child patterns follow (3) and (4) below, the combination patterns are also permitted by LBA$_2$

$$K(\text{child}) = m \bullet K(\text{basic}) \qquad (3)$$

$$T(\text{child}) = m \bullet T(\text{basic}) \qquad (4)$$

where $0 < m \leq 1$.

For those combination patterns, the interarrival time T' is larger than the basic pattern's interarrival time T, and the bucket depth does not exceed the threshold B.

IV. BANDWIDTH ALLOCATION METHOD USING LEAKY BUCKET

According to 2, bandwidth allocation should be determined according to "the worst" LBA$_2$ permitted pattern. A shown hereafter, this method does not give an upper-bound of the bandwidth required for the traffic permitted by LBA$_2$. The basic pattern in Fig. 2 is taken as "the worst" LBA$_2$ permitted pattern. This pattern is the burstiest pattern, i.e. it has the highest cell interval time coefficient of variation. In addition,

all the higher moments of the cell interval time are larger for the basic pattern than for any other LBA$_2$ permitted pattern.

According to our simulation results, however, there are LBA$_2$ permitted patterns that have more impact on the queue length than the above mentioned "worst pattern." One such pattern is described below. When the Leaky parameters are

$$T0 = 10, \quad R = 0.01, \quad B = 9.1$$

the corresponding LBA$_2$ "worst pattern" is determined as;

$$T0 = 10, \quad X = 10, \quad \text{and} \quad T = 1000.$$

This pattern is denoted pattern-0 and is shown in Fig. 2. As was described before, combinations of the basic pattern and some children patterns such as pattern-1 to pattern-4, shown in Fig. 2, are also permitted by LBA$_2$.

As shown in Fig. 2, studying the interarrival time moments for all patterns shows that pattern-0 (basic pattern) has the largest second moment and the largest squared coefficient of variation of cell interarrival time. The first and second moments m_1 and m_2, and the squared coefficient of variation Ca^2 may be calculated as follows.

$$m_1 = \frac{1}{n}(t_1 + t_2 + t_3 + \cdots + t_n) \qquad (5)$$

$$m_2 = \frac{1}{n}(t_1^2 + t_2^2 + t_3^2 + \cdots + t_n^2) \qquad (6)$$

$$C_a^2 = \frac{m_2 - m_1^2}{m_1^2} \qquad (7)$$

where t_i is the cell interarrival time between ith cell and $(i + 1)$th cell, and n is the total number of cells in T' period. The basic pattern also has the largest higher moments of cell interarrival time.

Since interarrival times T and T' are constant for each VP/VC and, hence, cell arrivals from each VP/VC are periodic, probability $P[N = q]$ is determined by the phase difference of the arrival processes. Therefore, this letter derives

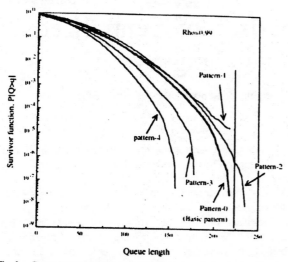

Fig. 3.   Queue length simulation results of "the worst pattern" and the newly discovered LBA$_2$ permitted pattern with more impact.

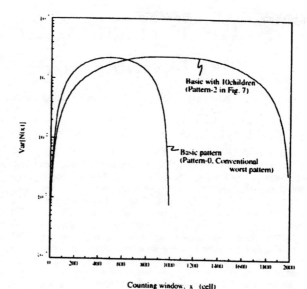

Fig. 4.   Variation in cell arrival number versus counting window size.

the probability distribution by simulations where the phases of the arrival processes with periods T and T' were randomly varied for each VP. In other words, the phases were uniformly distributed. Total output link efficiency ρ was fixed at 0.99.

Simulation results of survivor function, $P[Q > q]$, which can be used for approximating cell loss rate, are shown in Fig. 3. According to what is suggested in existing works [2], all LBA$_2$ accepted patterns should lie under the curve of pattern-0 in Fig. 3. That is, a 225-cell buffer should guarantee a cell-loss rate of 10^{-8}. Our simulations show, however, that some combined patterns yield much higher cell-loss rates, worse than 10^{-6}. Such patterns are pattern-1 and pattern-2 in Fig. 2. In other words, the worst pattern has not yet been identified.

To explain why some basic-child combination patterns shown in Fig. 2 (pattern-1 and -2) have a stronger impact than the basic pattern, we introduce the counting process [13] to characterize cell traffic patterns. The variations in the number of arriving cells versus the counting window size x are analyzed for pattern-0 and -1 and shown in Fig. 4. If the counting window size x is 1000 cells, the first moment of the number of arriving cells $N(x = 1000)$ is 99 for both basic and combined patterns. However, the second moment, or the deviation, $\mathrm{Var}[N(x = 1000)]$, of pattern-2 is larger than that of pattern-0 as shown in Fig. 4. The second moment strongly impacts the queue length. The second moment $\mathrm{Var}[N(x)]$ of the number of arriving cells depends on the counting window size x.

V.   CONCLUSION

The performance limitation of the existing bandwidth allocation algorithm which uses the worst pattern based on the Leaky Bucket algorithm has been demonstrated. Computer simulations revealed that the existing statistical bandwidth allocation method does not always guarantee the QOS of

VP/VC connections. The VC/VP bandwidth allocation method based on the Leaky Bucket algorithm is shown to have a significant shortcoming.

REFERENCES

[1] J. S. Turner, "New directions in communications (or which way to the information age?)," *IEEE Commun. Mag.*, vol. 24, pp. 8–15, 1986.
[2] R. Kositpaiboon and V. Phung, "Usage parameter control and bandwidth allocation for B-ISDN/ATM variable bit rate services," in *Multimedia '90. Sess. 4*, Bordeaux, France, Nov. 1990.
[3] E. P. Rathgeb and T. H. Theimer, "Policing function in ATM network," in *ISS '90, Session A8, Paper #4*, vol. V, Stockholm, Sweden, 1990, pp. 127–130.
[4] W. Kowalk and R. Lehnert, "The 'Policing function' to control user access in ATM network—Definition and implementation," in *ISSLS '88, Session 12.2.1*, 1988, pp. 240–245.
[5] H. Ahmadi, R. Guerin, and K. Sohraby, "Analysis of leaky bucket access control mechanism with batch arrival process," in *GLOBECOM '90, Session 400 B.1*, 1990, pp. 344–349.
[6] A. W. Berger, A. E. Eckberg, T.-C. Hou, and D. M. Lucantoni, "Performance characterizations of traffic monitoring, and associated control, mechanisms for broadband 'Packet' networks," in *GLOBECOM '90, Session 400 B.1*, pp. 350–354.
[7] J.-B. Suk and C. G. Cassandras, "Performance comparison of two window flow control schemes with admission delay," in *GLOBECOM '90, Session 506.3*, 1990, pp. 892–896.
[8] G. Niestegge, "The 'Leaky bucket' policing method in the ATM (asynchronous transfer mode) network," *Int. J. Digital Analog Commun. Syst.*, vol. 3, pp. 187–197, 1990.
[9] K.-I. Sato, S. Ohta, and I. Tokizawa, "Broad-band ATM network architecture based on virtual paths," *IEEE Trans. Commun.*, vol. 38, pp. 1212–1222, 1990.
[10] CCITT Recommendation, "Broadband aspects of ISDN," I. 121, 1990.
[11] CCITT SGXVIII USA Contribution, "Cell transfer capacity parameters and their measurement," *CCITT, D.1021/XVIII*, Nov. 1990.
[12] K. Bala, I. Cidon, and K. Sohraby, "Congestion control for high speed packet switched networks," in *Proc. IEEE INFOCOM '90*, 1990, pp. 520–526.
[13] H. Heffes and D. M. Lucantoni, "A Markov modulated characterization of packetized voice and data traffic and related statistical multiplexer performance," *IEEE J. Select. Areas Commun.*, vol. SAC-4, pp. 856–868, 1986.

A Traffic-Handling Comparison of Centralized and Distributed ATM Switching Systems

Anthony S. Acampora, *Fellow, IEEE*, and Jean-François P. Labourdette, *Member, IEEE*

Abstract— This paper describes a geographically distributed ATM switching architecture that exploits new possibilities offered by lightwave technology. Small modules that provide both an access and an ATM switching function are distributed over some extended geographical area and connected to a passive optical medium. Each module is equipped with some small number of electrooptic transmitters and receivers that provide access to the medium. Assignment of wavelengths to transmitter/receiver pairs create logical channels that are wavelength-multiplexed onto the medium, thus creating a logical connection diagram among the modules.

Advantages of the lightwave-based distributed architecture are the huge bandwidth of the medium, a high degree of modularity to facilitate growth, high reliability, and the ability to provide "clear channels" among modules. On the other hand, if the externally offered flow of ATM cells among modules is too uniform, then each module may be capable of supporting only a fraction of the load that could be carried by any port of a fully connected centralized ATM switch with output queueing. Fortunately, under the much more realistic assumption of nonuniform traffic, the independence between the logical connection diagram and the physical topology of the medium can be exploited by reconfiguring the connection diagram to "match" the nonuniformity of the cell traffic. Simulation results show that, as the nonuniformity becomes larger, the reconfiguration technique allows the traffic-handling capability of a distributed switch to match that of a centralized switch.

I. INTRODUCTION

ASYNCHRONOUS transfer mode (ATM) is rapidly emerging as a universal format for transporting multimedia information: voice, data, image, full-motion video. By exploiting the relative ease with which both constant bit rate and variable bit rate bursty packet traffic can be segmented into fixed-length cells, which are then statistically multiplexed, transported, and reassembled at their destinations, ATM holds forth the potential for an integrated telecommunications infrastructure offering bandwidth-upon-demand via universal access ports, each supporting a multiplicity of simultaneous virtual connections. Key to ATM is the self-routing switch,

Paper approved by I. Chlamtac, the Editor for Computer Networks of the IEEE Communications Society. Manuscript received September 25, 1991; revised May 18, 1992, July 27, 1992, and March 16, 1993. This work was supported by NSF Contract ECD-88-11111. This paper was presented in part at IEEE GLOBECOM '91, Phoenix, AZ, 1991. The Center for Telecommunications Research at Columbia University is an NSF Engineering Research Center.

A. S. Acampora is with the Department of Electrical Engineering and the Center for Telecommunication Research, Columbia University, New York, NY 10027 USA.

J.-F. P. Labourdette was at the Department of Electrical Engineering, Columbia University, New York, NY 10027 USA. He is now with AT&T Bell Laboratories, Holmdel, NJ 07733 USA.

IEEE Log Number 9406293.

and a variety of switch architectures using custom hardware to read each ATM cell header and effect real-time routing decisions have been proposed [1]–[4].

While heavily dependent on VLSI, these centalized ATM switch fabrics do not exploit a second breakthrough technology: photonics. In this paper, we consider a geographically distributed ATM fabric in which the switching function is embodied in small, self-routing electronic access modules which are connected to, and intercommunicate over, a passive optical medium, and we compare its traffic-handling capability against that of a centralized switch with the same number of user access ports. Many independent high-speed channels, each interconnecting an optical transmitter in one switching module to an optical receiver in another, are wavelength-multiplexed onto the medium. Each module is equipped with a small number p (say, 2–4) of transmitters and receivers, along with a small $(p + 1) \times (p + 1)$ fully connected output buffered self-routing ATM switch. Assignment of wavelengths to transmitter/receiver pairs defines the logical connectivity among modules. The multihop approach is used to route ATM cells from source to destination along the various links of the connection graph (each link corresponding to one of the WDM channels), with each switching module providing cell relay in addition to user access [5]–[7]. Since all channels are wavelength-multiplexed onto a common optical medium, the logical connectivity diagram and the physical topology of the medium (the fiber routes, position of optical couplers, power splitters, power combiners, etc.) are independent. Optical amplifiers would be deployed as needed to maintain adequate signal levels and signal-to-noise ratios [8].

Interest in the optically based distributed approach arises from several observations. First, the optical medium possesses enormous bandwidth (several tens of terahertz over the low-loss optical window). Several totally independent networks might thereby be supported over the same physical medium. In fact, many of the WDM channels might be used in the so-called "clear channel" mode, carrying information between select user pairs in arbitrary transmission formats, including analog if appropriate. Second, the medium might be viewed as "permanent plant." As new technologies are developed, these can be embodied in new access modules which provide an overlay network on the same optical medium. Third, the distributed ATM approach is highly modular: access modules (and wavelengths) can be simply added by physical attachment to the medium. Fourth, implementation and development of small, distributed ATM switch fabrics might be considerably simpler and less expensive than a large centralized switch,

Reprinted from IEEE Transactions on Communications, Vol. 43, No. 6, June 1995, pp. 2070-2076.

especially at high access rates (1 Gb/s). Finally, since optical filter technology permits slow (milliseconds) tuning of optical receivers over a large fraction of the optical band [9], [10], the logical connectivity among access modules, being independent of the physical topology of the medium, can be changed in response to varying traffic patterns (the main subject of this paper) and to route around module failures (improved reliability). A heuristic previously developed to maximize the amount of traffic carried in a single hop is used for this adaptation [11]–[13].

Our intention is to offset the multihop disadvantage: if the instantaneous traffic matrix is uniform (each arriving ATM cell is equally likely to be destined for any output), then the maximum traffic intensity that can be offered by each user is limited to $Cp/E[hops]$, where $E[hops]$ is the average number of hops taken by a representative cell from its source to its destination, and C is the data rate of both the user access link and each optical channel. For small p and large N, this intensity is less than C (for example, an 896-module multihop network, each equipped with two 1 Gb/s transmitters and receivers, offers a sustainable throughput per user of only 200 Mb/s under instantaneously uniform loading). By contrast, for a fully connected centralized switch, with output buffering, each user can always offer and accept a sustainable traffic intensity equal to C, independent of N and independent of the degree of traffic nonuniformity.

The multihop inefficiency can be offset by suitable combinations of three techniques. The first technique involves increasing the speed of the optical links by a factor sufficiently high to offset the inefficiency. By itself, and assuming uniform instantaneous cell traffic, the required factor is equal to $E[hops]/p$; much lower factors are adequate when used in combination with the other techniques. The second technique involves a modest increase in p; this has the effect of richly increasing the connectivity of the logical connection diagram, causing rapid decrease in $E[hops]$, but suffers the disadvantage of requiring additional optical transmitters/receivers per access module. The third and perhaps most powerful technique is to exploit any nonuniformity in the traffic pattern: the assumption of instantaneously uniform traffic intensity, while permitting simple throughput calculations, is highly artificial, would rarely be encountered in practice, and leads to distorted conclusions which are overly pessimistic. A more realistic (although still pessimistic) assumption is that the expected number of one-way virtual connections between all $N(N-1)$ user pairs is a constant, but that the instantaneous number of virtual connections actually established between user pairs are independent random variables drawn from some common discrete probability distribution. The connection diagram can then be adapted, if necessary, to the instantaneous matrix of virtual connections, with a preference for assigning optical channels between those pairs having the greatest number of virtual connections.

The traffic-handling capability of an ideal, centralized switch is compared against that of the distributed rearrangeable switch through a combination of analysis and simulation. Virtual circuit traffic matrices are generated at random, with each element drawn independently from a common discrete

probability distribution, under the assumption that all virtual circuits produce the same ATM cell generation statistics (another pessimistic assumption, considering that many virtual circuits may correspond to low bandwidth connections in a multimedia environment). A traffic matrix is "accepted" for the multihop approach if and only if a connection diagram and flow of information among the links can be found such that the average data rate on each inbound and outbound access link is less than the capacity of an access link, and the average data rate on each optical link is less than the capacity of an optical link. For the centralized switch, a much simpler acceptance criterion applies: a traffic matrix is accepted if and only if the average datum on each inbound and outbound access link is less than the capacity of an access link.

Note that, for the multihop system, it is not necessary to compute a new connection diagram in response to each new call attempt. First, the call processor would try to accommodate the new request over the existing connection diagram without affecting existing connections. If this fails, the call processor might then try to reroute traffic away from heavily used links, again maintaining the existing connection diagram. Only if this fails would a new connection diagram be computed. These steps provide a practical approach to implement rearrangeability since, for most new call attempts, out of sequence cell delivery, possible transient congestion during the reconfiguration phase, and possibly long setup delay associated with computation of a new connection diagram are avoided.

Results for a network with $N = 24$ access modules show that if the average traffic intensity per virtual connection is equal to 1/10 of the input port capacity, and a design rejection ratio is, say, 10^{-2}, then the distributed switch can carry the same offered load per input port as the centralized switch, with neither speeding up of the optical channels nor increasing the fan-in/fan-out of the access modules being necessary. When the intensity of each connection is 1/100 of the input port capacity (implying more uniform cell traffic), a speed-up of 1.5 and a load reduction of 10% with respect to the centralized switch are needed to achieve the same design rejection ratio. Thus, as the intensity of each virtual connection becomes larger, the performance of the distributed approach becomes indistinguishable from the centralized approach, with neither speed-up of the optical channels nor enriched connectivity being required. These results, along with other passive optical network opportunities mentioned earlier, are suggestive of the strong potential of the distributed approach. Techniques such as these can readily be applied to much larger distributed ATM switches.

In Section II, we briefly describe the distributed and centralized switch architectures to be studied, and in Section III, we describe the traffic model. Performance results appear in Section IV.

II. DISTRIBUTED AND CENTRALIZED SWITCH ARCHITECTURES

The geographically distributed ATM switch, functionally appearing as shown in Fig. 1, consists of a set of modules that provide both an access and a switching function. Those are connected to, and intercommunicate over, an all-optical

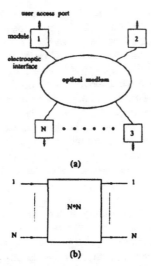

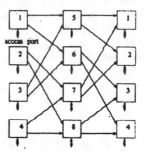

Fig. 2. Recirculating perfect shuffle connection diagram for an eight-module switch with two transmitters and receivers per module.

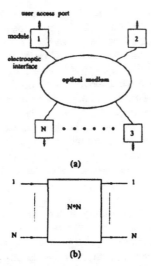

Fig. 1. Switch architectures. (a) Distributed switch. (b) Centralized switch.

medium which is totally devoid of any optical logic elements. The optical medium may have a variety of physical topologies (bus, tree, star, etc.), spanning a very wide geographical area, and may include couplers, power dividers and combiners, wavelength multiplexers and demultiplexers, and optical amplifiers.

Each module is equipped with an access and exit port that receive and transmit information, respectively, from and to network end users. We will refer to these simply as users. The ability of the modules to tap into the optical medium is achieved by mean of electrooptic transmitters and receivers allocated in some small number p to each module. If a transmitter at a particular module and a receiver at some other module emit and receive, respectively, on some common wavelength, a directed optical connection is created over the fiber from the transmitting module to the receiving module. By assigning wavelengths to transmitter/receiver pairs, a logical, directed connectivity pattern is created among the modules. Such logical connections will be referred to as internal links. Since the number of transmitters and receivers allocated to each module is relatively small (compared to the number of modules), the connection diagram among the modules falls far short from providing full connectivity. Thus, a directed connection between every pair of modules will not always exist, and traffic originating at the sending module may need to be relayed through intermediate modules before reaching its destination (multihop). The recirculating Perfect Shuffle graph shown in Fig. 2 for $N = 8$ modules and $p = 2$ transmitters and receivers per module has a regular structure that tends to minimize the number of hops [5], [6].

The distributed switch can be defined by the following system parameters:

N = number of modules (size of the switch);
p = number of transmitters and receivers per module;
C = access and exit port speed;
S = speed of each internal wavelength-multiplexed optical link;
$r = S/C$ = speed-up factor.

Uniform traffic patterns would rarely be experienced in practice, and the number of virtual connections instantaneously in progress between distinct input-output port pairs would, in general, be different for different pairs. This in turn implies that, at the cell level, the flow of traffic at the switch input and output ports would be unbalanced [14], [15]. Such traffic imbalances can be exploited by the distributed switch. Since the logical connection diagram among modules is independent of the physical topology of the medium, it can be adapted to particular nonuniform virtual connection traffic patterns by using transmitters and/or receivers that can be slowly tuned over all or part of all wavelengths in use on the medium.

The flow and wavelength assignment (FWA) problem for finding the logical connectivity and routing pattern that minimize the maximum flow on any internal link for some given matrix of traffic $t = (t_{ij})$ was previously studied [11], [12]. For the distributed ATM switch, element t_{ij} represents the number of virtual connections requested between input port i and output port j, multiplied by the bandwidth or duty cycle of each virtual connection. A heuristic algorithm was proposed in [11], which seeks a connectivity diagram that literally "matches" as best as possible the traffic matrix by maximizing the amount of traffic carried in one hop. Then, using a flow deviation method, the routing of each virtual connection is found for that particular connection graph to minimize the largest flow of traffic on any link.

III. DISTRIBUTED VERSUS CENTRALIZED SWITCH UNDER NONUNIFORM TRAFFIC

A. Traffic Model

We assume that the point-to-point call (virtual circuit) arrival processes (calls arriving on input link i and destined to output link j) are independent Poisson processes with rate $\lambda_{ij} = \lambda/N$, and the call holding times are independent and identically governed by some general distribution with mean $1/\mu$. Thus, the average call loading per user pair is $\rho_N \equiv \lambda/N\mu$, in Erlangs. We also assume that all calls have the same bandwidth (cell duty cycle) b, measured in the same units as the access or external link capacity C and the internal link capacity S. We define the call granularity g^{-1} as

$$g^{-1} = \frac{\text{call bandwidth}}{\text{external link bandwidth}} = \frac{b}{C}. \qquad (1)$$

Note that g represents the maximum number of calls that can be accommodated on any input or output link.

The traffic is uniform at the call level, in the sense that the statistics of calls (arrival process, holding time distribution, bandwidth) offered to all input–output link pairs are identical. However, the actual number of calls in progress at any given moment will generally be different for different source/destination pairs. Let n be the matrix describing the instantaneous number of calls in progress:

$$n = (n_{ij}) \qquad (2)$$

where n_{ij} represents the number of calls in progress between input link i and output link $j, 1 \leq i, j \leq N$. The resulting cell traffic $t = bn$ will, therefore, not be uniform. Indeed, each time a call arrives or terminates, the call matrix n and the cell flow pattern t change.

B. Performance Analysis

Performances of the distributed rearrangeable switch with nonuniform traffic will now be compared against that of the centralized switch. A possible performance measure of interest is the probability that a call offered to the switch cannot be accommodated and is thus blocked or rejected. For the centralized switch, a call arriving on input link i and destined to output link j could be blocked for either of two reasons: either the number of calls already in progress on input link i is such that there is not enough remaining capacity to accept the new call, or the number of calls already in progress on output link j is such that there is not enough remaining capacity to accept the new call. For the distributed rearrangeable switch, an offered call would also be blocked if one or both of these conditions apply. Furthermore, a new call would also be rejected if it could not be routed through the switch without causing the flow on some internal link to exceed the link capacity S. However, by reconfiguring the logical connectivity and computing a new routing pattern, it might be possible to accommodate the new call. It follows that while the distributed switch will always experience a larger blocking probability than the centralized switch, the difference might be quite small if traffic nonuniformities are exploited; internal link speed-up and increased fan-in/fan-out may or may not be needed.

For the centralized switch, let $\{\pi(n)\}$ be the probability distribution for the matrix state description $n = (n_{ij}), 1 \leq i, j \leq N$. In the steady state, a deceptively simple product form solution exists [16] from which the blocking probability can be found. Unfortunately, because of constraints on the traffic matrix n (namely, no station can establish more than g simultaneous virtual connections, and no station can accept more than g simultaneous virtual connections), this solution is computationally useless. Thus, rather than using the blocking probability as the evaluation criterion, we shall use, instead, a closely related measure, the rejection ratio, a good approximation which can be more readily computed. This criterion also simplifies the simulations needed to study the behavior of the distributed switch.

Let us consider input and output links without any capacity constraints, that is, suppose that each input and output link

could support an infinite number of calls. The number n_{ij} of calls in progress between any input–output link pair could then take any integer value. Among all such matrices, only a portion could actually be supported by a centralized switch of finite link capacity C: those matrices for which the sum of the number of calls in progress on each input and output link, multiplied by the call bandwidth b, is less than the link capacity C (or, equivalently, the number of calls on any link must be less than g). We thus define the rejection ratio R_{rej} for the centralized switch as the probability mass associated with those matrices that would be rejected by a switch with finite link capacity C, that is, those matrices for which any row or any column sum exceeds g.

We introduce the random variables $s_i = \sum_{s=1}^{N} n_{is}$ and $d_j = \sum_{s=1}^{N} n_{sj}, 1 \leq i, j \leq N$, describing the number of calls in progress on any input or output link, respectively. Since the call arrival process on any input–output pair is Poisson with rate λ/N, and the processes between any pair are independent, it follows that the call arrival process on any input link is Poisson with rate λ. Similarly, without capacity constraints on the links, the call arrival process on any output link is Poisson with rate λ. The call holding time for each connection is assumed to be exponential with mean $1/\mu$. The number of calls in progress on each input and output link, without capacity constraints, is therefore a random variable, identically distributed for each link, with probability distribution P_k (where, for all $i, j, P_k = \text{Prob}[s_i = k] = \text{Prob}[d_j = k]$) given by

$$P_k = \frac{\rho^k}{k!} e^{-\rho}, \qquad k = 0, 1, \cdots \qquad (3)$$

with $\rho \equiv \lambda/\mu$. The mean number of calls in progress on any input or output link is simply ρ. The probability L that the number of calls in progress on any link is less than g is given by

$$L = \sum_{k=0}^{g} P_k = e^{-\rho} \sum_{k=0}^{g} \frac{\rho^k}{k!}. \qquad (4)$$

Let P be the probability that all input and output links have fewer than g calls in progress: $P = \text{Prob}[s_i \leq g, d_j \leq g \; \forall i, j]$. Because of the dependency among the s_i and the d_j (the number of calls in progress among all input links $\sum_{i=1}^{N} s_i$ is equal to the number of calls in progress among all outputs $\sum_{j=1}^{N} d_j$), the probability P cannot be written in simple product form. However, we would expect that as the switch dimensionality N grows large, the number of calls in progress on any pair of input and output links should approach statistical independence, with the result that $P \simeq L^{2N}$, yielding for the rejection ratio $R_{rej} = 1 - P$

$$R_{rej} \simeq 1 - L^{2N}. \qquad (5)$$

Expression (5) is an approximation for the rejection ratio of a centralized switch with input and output links of finite capacity. The validity of the approximation was established by simulation over a wide range of parameters; numerical results obtained both by the approximation (5) and by simulations are presented and discussed in the next section.

We shall now evaluate the rejection ratio for the distributed rearrangeable switch. An element n_{ij} of the matrix n represents the number of calls in progress from input link i to output link j. From such a matrix, we can construct a cell traffic matrix $t = (t_{ij}), 1 \leq i, j \leq N$, where $t = bn$. When there are no link capacity constraints, the cell flow matrices t span an infinite space. For such a flow matrix t to be accepted by the distributed switch with finite input and output link capacity $C(= bg)$ and finite internal link capacity S, it is necessary that the flow on each input and output link does not exceed the link capacity C (as was the case with the centralized switch):

$$\sum_{s=1}^{N} t_{is} \leq C, \qquad 1 \leq i \leq N \tag{6}$$

$$\sum_{s=1}^{N} t_{sj} \leq C, \qquad 1 \leq j \leq N. \tag{7}$$

Furthermore, the maximum flow F on any internal optical link, given by the heuristic solution of the flow and wavelength assignment problem [11] must not exceed the internal link capacity S:

$$F \leq S. \tag{8}$$

For the distributed rearrangeable switch, call traffic matrices were randomly generated under the assumption that, for all i, j, the request process from input i to output j is Poisson with rate λ/N and the call holding time is exponential with mean $1/\mu$ (these are the same conditions as applied when studying the rejection ratio of the centralized switch). For each matrix which was generated, conditions (6)–(8) were applied to determine whether or not that matrix could be accommodated. The fraction of matrices which could not be accommodated defines the rejection ratio for the distributed switch.

IV. RESULTS

We compare the distributed rearrangeable switch and the centralized switch using the rejection ratio as the performance measure. The rejection ratio for the centralized switch provides a lower bound for the distributed rearrangeable switch, and is evaluated via the approximation (5) and also via simulation. The rejection ratio for the distributed switch is evaluated via simulation. For a particular load per input link ρ, we determine if the centralized and distributed switches can accept each matrix generated, and the rejection ratio is found by dividing the number of rejected matrices by the total number of matrices generated. Note that for $g \leq p$, all call matrices that can be accommodated by the centralized switch can also be accommodated by the distributed switch, with a direct logical link assigned to each call, given that internal links operate at the same speed as external links (speed-up = 1). The distributed switch would then achieve the same rejection ratio as the centralized switch.

We consider a switch with $N = 24$ modules and $p = 2$ transmitters and receivers per module. Two granularities are studied, corresponding to call bandwidths of 1% and 10% of the access link capacity ($g = 100$ and $g = 10$, respectively). The curves in Fig. 3 show the rejection ratio as a function of

the offered load per input link ρ normalized by g. The solid curves represent the rejection ratio for the centralized switch as computed from (5). The stars represent simulation points for the centralized switch. Each point was estimated from 2000 call traffic matrices. These points follow closely the solid curve in both cases, $g = 10$ [Fig. 3(a)] and $g = 100$ [Fig. 3(b)], thus demonstrating both that the approximation (5) is quite accurate for a switch size $N = 24$, and also that enough matrices were generated for each point to be statistically valid.

Fig. 3(a) shows the simulation points obtained for the distributed switch with $g = 10$ and internal link speed-up of 0.5 (crosses) and 0.75 (circles) (both cases corresponding to an actual slowdown of the optical links, relative to the external links). With a speed-up of 1 (stars, no speed-up), the simulation points for the distributed switch correspond exactly with the simulation points for the centralized switch. In the case $g = 100$ [Fig. 3(b)], simulation points are shown for a speed-up $r = 1.5$ (crosses), a speed-up $r = 1.75$ (circles), and a speed-up $r = 2$ (stars). The simulation points for $r = 1.75$ fall slightly above those for the centralized switch, and a speed-up of 2 is enough to achieve the rejection ratio of the centralized switch, as appearing in Fig. 3(b).

From these curves, we can determine the difference in permissible offered loading for the centralized and distributed approaches to guarantee a given design rejection ratio. For example, in the case $g = 10$ and with a slow-down $r = 0.75$, the distributed switch can carry the same offered load as a centralized switch to achieve a design rejection ratio of 10^{-2}. To achieve the same design rejection ratio in the case $g = 100$, with a speed-up of 1.5, the permissible normalized loading for the distributed switch must decrease approximately from 0.69 to 0.62 (a 10% decrease relative to the centralized switch). With a speed-up of 2, the same loading could be supported by the distributed switch.

Comparing the two cases $g = 10$ and $g = 100$, it appears that the distributed rearrangeable switch performs better for small values of g, corresponding to highly nonuniform traffic patterns at the cell level. This result is consistent with intuition and with the previous observation that, for g sufficiently small, the distributed switch achieves the same rejection ratio as the centralized switch. For larger values of g, the law of large numbers would imply that the cell traffic tends to become uniform, requiring a speed-up factor greater than unity to match the throughput performance of the centralized switch (as discussed in Section III).

V. CONCLUSION

An architecture for broad-band ATM switches was considered for which modules that provide both access and switching functions are distributed over an extended geographical area. The modules are equipped with electrooptic transmitters and receivers and have access to a passive optical medium. By assigning wavelengths to the transmitters and receivers, a logical connectivity diagram is created among the modules that is independent of the physical topology of the optical medium. Furthermore, the logical connectivity can be optimally reconfigured for different traffic conditions, providing switch

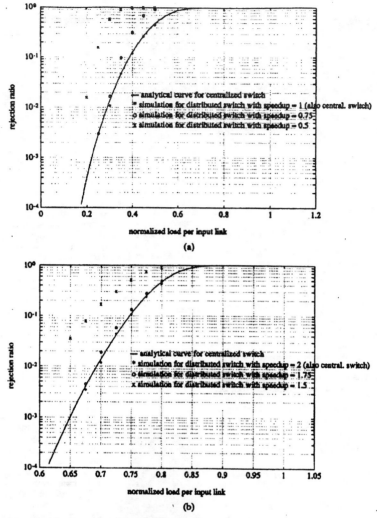

Fig. 3. Rejection ratio versus normalized load per input link for $N = 24$. (a) $g = 10$. (b) $g = 100$.

performance that may match those of a centralized switch. Depending on the degree of traffic nonuniformity, some combination of optical link speed-up, increased fan-in/fan-out per access module to enrich connectivity, and dynamic reconfiguration of the connection diagram can always be found to reduce the load on each internal link to a value below that which exists on the output links. The multihop disadvantage can thereby be completely offset, and performance identical with that of the ideal nonblocking centralized ATM switch with output buffering can be achieved. When the call statistics produce highly nonuniform cell traffic patterns, performance comparable to the centralized switch can be achieved through logical reconfiguration alone, without requiring link speed-up or increased fan-in/fan-out.

Reconfiguring the switch implies temporary disruption of some existing connections, which may cause cell desequencing. These cells would need to be reordered prior to exiting the switch or at their network destination. Fortunately, when the distributed rearrangeable switch is presented with a request for a new connection, that connection will usually be accommodated without the need to invoke the reconfiguration algorithm. Only when the call cannot be accepted by an existing connection diagram will an attempt be made to reconfigure the switch and accommodate the new call. If a configuration is found that could accept the incoming call, a decision to reconfigure and accept that call would then be made, considering the number of logical links that would need to be changed (by returning of transmitters or receivers) and the number of existing virtual circuits that would be disrupted.

The distributed rearrangeable switch offers great capabilities to deal with heterogeneous traffic, such as voice, data, and video, that extend beyond ATM transport. For example, a "clear channel" can be set up between two modules to establish a circuit-switched video connection (the transmitter and receiver involved in the logical connection would be temporarily removed from the pool of equipment available for logically interconnecting the ATM switching modules). Going one step further, one could allocate the transmitters and receivers to create distinct logical subnetworks for distinct classes of traffic. Such an allocation would depend on the mix of traffic offered to the network and would require some form of bandwidth management. Once the allocation is made, the subnetworks could be configured independently of each other, taking into account the specific quality of service required by the type of traffic carried by each subnetwork respectively. Other potential benefits include enhanced reliability, since reconfigurability can avoid failed transmitters and/or receivers, and enhanced modularity, since it is relatively easy to attach a new access module to the optical medium.

REFERENCES

[1] F. A. Tobagi, "Fast packet switch architectures for broadband integrated services digital networks," *Proc. IEEE*, vol. 78, Jan. 1990.
[2] A. Huang and S. Knauer, "Starlite: A wideband digital switch," in *Proc. GLOBECOM '84*, Atlanta, GA, Dec. 1984.
[3] J. Y. Hui and E. Arthurs, "A broadband packet switch for integrated transport," *IEEE J. Select. Areas Commun.*, vol. SAC-5, Oct. 1987.
[4] Y. S. Yeh, M. G. Hluchyj, and A. S. Acampora, "The knockout switch: A simple, modular architecture for high-performance packet switching," *IEEE J. Select. Areas Commun.*, vol. SAC-15, Oct. 1987.
[5] A. S. Acampora, "A multichannel multihop local lightwave network," in *Proc. GLOBECOM '87*, Tokyo, Japan, Nov. 1987.
[6] M. G. Hluchyj and M. J. Karol, "ShuffleNet: An application of generalized Perfect Shuffle to multihop lightwave networks," in *Proc. INFOCOM '88*, New Orleans, LA, Mar. 1988.
[7] A. S. Acampora and M. J. Karol, "An overview of lightwave packet networks," *IEEE Network Mag.*, vol. 3, Jan. 1989.
[8] C. R. Giles and E. Desurvire, "Propagation of signal and noise in concatenated erbium-doped fiber optical amplifiers," *J. Lightwave Technol.*, vol. 9, Feb. 1991.
[9] H. Kobrinski and K. W. Cheung, "Wavelength-tunable optical filters: Applications and technologies," *IEEE Commun. Mag.*, vol. 27, Oct. 1989.
[10] C. A. Brackett, "Dense wavelength division multiplexing networks: Principles and applications," *IEEE J. Select. Areas Commun.*, vol. 8, Aug. 1990.
[11] J.-F. P. Labourdette and A. S. Acampora, "Logically rearrangeable multihop lightwave networks," *IEEE Trans. Commun.*, vol. 39, Aug. 1991.
[12] ——, "Partially reconfigurable multihop lightwave networks," in *Proc. GLOBECOM '90*, San Diego, CA, Dec. 1990.
[13] J.-F. P. Labourdette, "Rearrangeability techniques for multihop lightwave networks and application to distributed ATM switching systems," Ph.D. dissertation, Dep. Elec. Eng., Columbia Univ., New York, NY, Oct. 1991.
[14] M. Eisenberg and N. Mehravari, "Performance of the multichannel multihop lightwave network under nonuniform traffic," *IEEE J. Select. Areas Commun.*, vol. 6, Aug. 1988.
[15] S.-Q. Li and M. J. Lee, "A study of traffic imbalances in a fast packet switch," in *Proc. INFOCOM '89*, Ottawa, Ont., Canada, Apr. 1989.
[16] D. Y. Burman, J. P. Lehoczky, and Y. Lim, "Insensitivity of blocking probabilities in a circuit-switching network," *J. Appl. Prob.*, vol. 21, 1984.

Anthony S. Acampora (S'68–M'75–SM'86–F'88) received the Ph.D. degree in electrical engineering from the Polytechnic Institute of Brooklyn, Brooklyn, NY.

He is a Professor of Electrical Engineering at Columbia University and Director of the Center for Telecommunications Research, a national engineering research center. He joined the faculty at Columbia in 1988 following a 20 year career at AT&T Bell Laboratories, most of which was spent in basic research where his interests included radio and satellite communications, local and metropolitan area networks, packet switching, wireless access systems, and lightwave networks. His most recent position at Bell Laboratories was Director of the Transmission Technology Laboratory, where he was responsible for a wide range of projects, including broadband networks, image communications, and digital signal processing. At Columbia University, he is involved in research and education programs concerning broadband networks, wireless access networks, network management, optical networks, and multimedia applications. Many of these projects enjoy active industrial participation and involve cross-disciplinary research teams to develop new system approaches, analytical methodologies, VLSI circuitry, lightwave devices, and telecommunications software.

Dr. Acampora has published over 140 papers, holds 24 patents, and has authored a recently completed textbook entitled, *An Introduction to Broadband Networks: MANs, ATM, B-ISDN, Self-Routing Switches, Optical Networks, and Network Control for Voice, Data, Image, and HDTV Telecommunications*. He sits on numerous telecommunications advisory committees and frequently serves as a consultant to government and industry. He is a former member of the IEEE Communications Society Board of Governors.

Jean-François P. Labourdette (M'91) was born in Blois, France, in 1963. He received the "Diplome d'Ingenieur" from Ecole Nationale Superieure des Telecommunications, Brest, France, in 1986, and the M.S. and Ph.D. degrees in electrical engineering from Columbia University, New York, in 1988 and 1991, respectively.

From 1987 to 1991, he was a Graduate Research Assistant at the NSF Center for Telecommunications Research, Columbia University, working on reconfigurable lightwave networks. He spent the summer of 1990 at Motorola Codex, Mansfield, MA, investigating the design of fast packet networks for integrated traffic. Since 1991, he has been with AT&T Bell Laboratories, Holmdel, NJ, in the Network Planning Department, working on circuit-switched network routing, dynamically reconfigurable T1/T3 network architectures, and ATM networking. His research interests include lightwave network architectures, network performances, and optimization techniques for network design and network reconfiguration.

Dr. Labourdette was a recipient of a Lavoisier Scholarship from the French government in 1986–1987, and has been a Motorola Scholar in 1989–1990 and 1990–1991. He received the Eliahu I. Jury award for best doctoral dissertation in Electrical Engineering at Columbia University in 1992.

ATM Performance Evaluation Under Transparencies of a Distributed System Environment (DSE)

E. D. Kollias, *Student Member, IEEE*, and G. I. Stassinopoulos, *Member, IEEE*

Abstract—Management architectures as well as protocols for accessing managed entities and exchanging management information are well developed in standards. On the other hand recent developments in Open Distributed Processing (ODP) are of recognized importance for network and service management. Their generic features fit well into the geographically extended, multiple vendor and heterogeneous environment of communication networks. As a third ongoing development Asynchronous Transfer Mode (ATM) Broadband Integrated Services Digital Networks (B-ISDN) offer challenging problems for resource allocation, network performance and Quality of Service (QoS) evaluation in real time. The paper shows how performance monitoring and evaluation for ATM networks can greatly profit from the features of a Distributed System Environment (DSE). The extreme flexibility offered by the ATM principle requires a rich and reusable set of servers accomplishing coordinated performance evaluation tests. DSE transparencies are an excellent match to corresponding Management Applications (MA) requirements, so that tests can be performed in a distributed, flexible and adaptable way under a conceptually simple architecture. The paper draws extensively from a non-distributed counterpart, i.e., an existing sophisticated ATM test and analysis tool developed under the "Research for Advanced Communications in Europe" (RACE) program, R1083 PARASOL project.

I. INTRODUCTION

NETWORK MANAGEMENT emerges today as a prominent concept encompassing short or long term activities related to Broadband Integrated Services Digital Networks (B-ISDN). Architectures have been suggested [22] which encompass the managed network, managed objects as proxies to real managed entities, general purpose servers and management applications. In parallel, conceptual models (like the Netman Cube Model in [2]) classify and categorize network management requirements, activities and information. We exclude service management, address only network management and furthermore focus exclusively on performance evaluation of ATM networks.

The Asynchronous Transfer Mode (ATM) principle utilizes short, equally sized packets, called cells for the transport of information and signalling messages associated with any narrow or broadband service. A prominent goal of current developments is to provide a unified access to a single network being able to cope with all present and future communication needs. B-ISDN is envisaged as a single network providing all services, thus accomplishing both network and service integration. In the ATM based B-ISDN, network and service integration is effected at the lowest of possible levels, namely at the ATM layer residing directly on top of the physical layer. An accompanying important feature within the ATM layer is label multiplexing, i.e., the ability to multiplex different connections through the use of connection identifiers. By avoiding fixed positioning of bits of multiplexed channels in a recurring time frame, one obtains the widest possible bandwidth allocation possibilities, but also new causes of impairments due to the inherently statistical multiplexing principle. The same labels are also used for switching. Testing at this level becomes crucial because all important networking functions are realized within the ATM layer.

Testing is also extremely versatile. Network performance monitoring and evaluation requires for ATM a much wider range of measurements, conducted under a variety of possible background loads and active connections under test. Close couplings exist between network performance parameters and the interpretation of results requires heavy processing where again different options, degrees of compression and modes of presentation are conceivable. Presentation of ATM layer performance measurements is interesting in its own right, but the value of well specified and controlled measurements extends far beyond.

Broadband services impose stringent network performance parameters for the underlying network, specially for ATM based B-ISDN, where statistical multiplexing can lead to cell loss, misrouting, sequence integrity violation and other ATM layer specific impairments on top of better understood physical bit level phenomena. The mapping between network performance and Quality of Service (QoS) becomes complicated and cannot be easily calculated by closed form formulas or easily expressible tabulated relationships [3]. On another line, network performance information is needed virtually on-line in order to enable complex resource allocation (mainly bandwidth) and call admission control policies. Both areas are crucial for the large scale introduction of ATM. Charging

Manuscript received October 21, 1993. This work was supported in part by the "Research for Advanced Communications in Europe" (RACE) program, R1083 PARASOL project.

The authors are with the National Technical University of Athens, Electrical and Computer Engineering Department, Computer Science Division, 157 73 Zographou, Athens, Greece.

IEEE Log Number 9401460.

Reprinted from IEEE Journal on Selected Areas in Communications, Vol. 12, No. 6, Aug. 1994, pp. 1059-1071.

ATM network. The fact that the platform itself will draw communication resources, required for its own purposes, from the monitored ATM network, does not alter the validity of the previous statement.

Furthermore the significance of a DSE can be estimated via the number and level of transparencies it provides to its users. Transparencies essentially aim at hiding the basic features of distribution, in particular aspects like geographical distance, heterogeneity, partial system failure, resource redundancy, etc. We can mention access, location, concurrency, replication, failure, migration, resource, federation and name transparencies. Some of these will provide welcome features for our environment and will be examined in Section IV.

The increased size and number of interconnected networks and the desire to arrive at vendor independent solutions for network management leads to the development of concepts, methods and appropriate equipment as part of a Telecommunications Management Network (TMN). TMN requires that architecturally and procedurally both networks, TMN and the managed network, are closely related. This places implementation restrictions on management applications. To counter these, the recent trend is to see network management as any distributed application and profit from advances in ODP.

International Standards Organization's (ISO) Network Management gives the ability to monitor and control network resources, which are represented as "managed objects." In ISO Network Management we can encounter application processes called "managers" residing on managing systems (or management stations), and application processes called "agents" residing on managed systems (or network elements being managed). The concept of Network Management appears when managers and agents exchange monitoring and control information (via protocols and a shared conceptual schema) useful to the management of a network and its components. Agents are accessed using the CMIP/CMISE protocol [23]. Managed objects represent system and networking resources (e.g., a modem, a protocol entity, a TCP connection) that are subject to management. Using the provided services and protocols, the manager orders the agent to perform an operation on a managed object for which it is responsible. Relevant operations might be the return of certain values associated with a managed object (read a variable), the modification of values associated with a managed object (set a variable), the accomplishment of an action on the managed object (switch the module on/off). Furthermore the managed object may also asynchronously generate notifications that are forwarded by agents to the manager (events or traps). Application processes however, on managing or managed systems may well be able to play both roles at the same time. The protocol mechanisms usually supplied are fully symmetric between the manager and agent.

In modern Network Management, management information is modelled using object-oriented techniques. Thus we have multiple "managed objects," as abstractions of "manageable" physical or logical resources of the network. Each managed object belongs to a particular object class. A particular managed object existing in a particular network is defined as an "object instance" of the object class to which it belongs. Managed objects are fully defined by specifying the "attributes" or properties the object has, the operations and specific actions (e.g., self-test) that can be performed on the object, any constraints on these operations, events that the object can generate and information about various relationships the object may be involved in. Managed objects also participate in relationships with each other. These relationships can be used to construct hierarchies of managed objects.

Management applications concern five well identified areas (see [14]): Configuration, Fault, Performance, Accounting and Security Management. In the sequel we will confine ourselves to Performance and Fault Management. Moreover within these areas a target network infrastructure based on the Asynchronous Transfer Mode (ATM) will be assumed. To operate in the forementioned areas, OSI committees have identified a number of generic functions that apply to performance management, fault management, etc. Thus we have functions like object management, event management, software management, alarm reporting, configuration management, relationship management, workload monitoring, state management, etc. The control of management information is being performed using some central information site, where agents register and where managers acquire information for potentially managed entities. Information is accessed using CMIP, through the intervention of agents, each being attached to a separate Management Information Tree (MIT).

In Table I we can observe basic requirements of a modern Network Management framework mapped onto operations or services provided by a DSE. To better illustrate the issues for DSE services we mention those already existing in a typical, available product, e.g., the ANSA platform [9].

The client-server model is the approach followed in a modern management framework. The management application, acting as a client, issues calls to the agent (server) in order to collect useful information. Asynchronous notifications may be generated by a server to inform the manager about an abnormal situation. In ANSA a module is able to act both as client and as server and the platform design itself is based on that model.

Multi-point connections required by network management applications are supported by ANSA. Furthermore with the provision of a threads mechanism the potential servers interact in parallel with their clients in the same address space thus improving overall performance.

Binding operations are being performed using a common location scheme, while in the case of agents resident in fixed locations the address is well known in advance. The ANSA trading service allows dynamic naming and addressing, whereas it can re-establish an association broken by e.g., server failure, through the use of the locator service.

ing as a QoS degradation. This fact must be reflected to any testing and performance analysis setup. High resolution measurements are necessary and post processing of measured data must allow terminal behavior emulation. It is moreover clear that a definite selection of guidelines cannot be made today. On the other hand one should instead strive towards a flexible measurement architecture, where components and modules handling the measurement and analysis task are easily upgradable, removable and exchangeable. This will be presented in Section IV.

A. The PARASOL Architecture for ATM Layer Measurements.

For the ATM specific reasons outlined before, considerable effort has been invested in test tools. In particular we give here a very brief outline of the PARASOL test tool, developed in the RACE 1083 project. This is arguably the most complete ATM test tool, having as scope the generation and analysis of ATM traffic. It is realized as a standalone, self contained collection of ATM Traffic Generator (ATG), ATM Traffic Analyzer (ATA) and Equipment (i.e., ATG and ATA) Controller (EC). Its realization is highly modular and large commonalities (in hardware) exist between ATA and ATG. This will be fully exploited below. Larger configurations with more than one ATG and possibly ATA are possible. It is a discrete, centralized tool not incorporated within the network under test. However its structure and modular design is amenable to distribution and, aided by developments in distributed processing, the realization of a distributed platform for performance analysis and evaluation for ATM network management becomes feasible.

1. The Centralized Setup: The centralized setup, as depicted in Fig. 1 is on one hand what has been achieved today and on the other serves as instantiation of a particular configuration possible to set-up within the targeted distributed environment. In the existing centralized setup we speak of testing, having in mind testing of ATM systems during development or commissioning. In the envisaged distributed setup (Section IV below) testing will be replaced by monitoring or performance evaluation.

The ATM Traffic Generator (ATG) in Fig. 1 generates statistical traffic patterns for isolated Virtual Circuits (VC's), Virtual Paths (VP's) or ATM links. For VP or link traffic a pseudo-statistical mix of a multitude of individual sources is possible. The effect of impairments can be also emulated in the generated cell streams, so that the reaction of the ATM Network Under Test (NUT) on already corrupted cells can be analyzed. For example errored cell headers can trigger transition to various states of the physical layer cell delineation procedure and/or provoke intentional cell misrouting. ATG traffic models are also used for background load. The setting of the external background load generators is controlled by the test operator. All test operator interactions with the test setup are effected through the equipment controller. A broadband interface at the T_B reference point is assumed between the ATM NUT, ATG, and ATA ([19]).

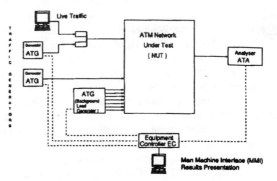

Fig. 1. The PARASOL set-up for ATM layer measurements.

Normally, the ATG produces the complete test pattern required to perform measurements. The ATA receives the generated test cell streams after its transfer through the ATM NUT. It extracts cell subsequences of interest according to various criteria (VP, VC identifier, time stamps, bit patterns) and performs basic on-line analysis calculations. Subsequent extensive processing on the extracted data is possible within the EC, so that blocks of sequentially gathered data have to be passed from ATA to EC. In addition, it is possible to insert a controlled amount of test cells in an existing connection serving live traffic (cut-through mode). Measurements are then carried out, whereby mechanisms are provided to extract test cells from the compound cell stream.

The EC communicates with the ATA, ATG and the ATM NUT to set up the connections between inputs and outputs of the NUT, to read states and download parameters from and to ATG/ATA, to coordinate the measurement procedure, etc. Finally it undertakes presentation of results, though a sophisticated Man Machine Interface (MMI).

2. Modularity and Functional Decomposition: A prerequisite for distribution is the modular design and implementation of functions related to the generation and analysis of traffic, filtering and presentation of results. The PARASOL test tool has been designed on the basis of an essential and an architectural model. The essential model has described the required functions through structured design methods, away from any implementation detail. As such it is largely still applicable for a distributed version. The architectural model, on which the essential model has been mapped, takes heavily into account the centralized nature of the existing tool as depicted in Fig. 1. It has to be totally replaced by another one, suitable for the distributed environment.

Any measurement to be performed by an ATM Test Tool can be generally subdivided into a cell scale real time part and into a longer term real time or off-line part. In the real time part appropriate cell sequences are injected somewhere in the ATM NUT, received cells are identified and collected elsewhere, where also some limited real time processing and extraction of subsequences according to certain criteria takes place. This processing includes measured data reduction like averaging, derivation of histograms and other functions possible in hardware and real time. All generation and analysis functions can be accomplished at the full cell rate of the interface, e.g., with a speed corresponding to 155 or even 622 Mbit/s. Considerable pre- and post processing is required, through longer term real time, or even off-line software processes. One can draw parallels here with the Connection Timeline of the Timeline Model in [18]. The setting up of measurement parameters and their downloading to the generation and analysis hardware elements can be seen as preparatory steps resembling the connection set-up procedure. Immediately after the collection of measured data, off-line analysis by software will yield the desired result of the test experiment. This is a concluding procedure like connection clearing. Still longer term analysis beyond the cell scale or Connection Timeline can give more general performance indices, show trends, etc. Tight coupling with the ATM NUT is here no longer required and this operation is outside the scope of this paper.

Some emerging architectural implications can be given. Simple, real time hardware based generating and analyzing functions have to be embedded within the ATM NUT at various critical points. Although in principle different measurements require different hardware one can exploit commonalities and build configurable modules able for a multitude of operations. This is particularly true for generators, where a basic memory based hardware can realize an impressive array of even qualitatively distinct generated patterns. Thus, although these elementary hardware based functions have fixed locations, their role and contribution can greatly vary from measurement to measurement. The situation is even more flexible with pre- and post-processing functions and indeed this is the main target where distribution advantages and transparencies can aim at. As we will outline below an open ended array of such functions can be available to the management application, so that the place and kind of performance measurement can be freely decided.

B. Servers and Interfaces in a DSE for Distributed Performance Measurements

1. Traffic Analysis Aspects: We first present options available today for analyzing, filtering, and presenting outcomes of measurements. A hardware module, resident at the receiving end of an ATM VC or VP or a whole ATM link connection (sink), is able to identify and extract relevant cells from the incoming stream and perform all necessary filtering functions, so that sequences of values related to any one of several measurements are collected. The most used criterion for cell extraction is based on the VCI/VPI, i.e., all cells belonging to the same channel connection are extracted. Another interesting alternative is the extraction of test cells interleaved with cells carrying live traffic on the same VC (cut-through mode). Only one measurement can be performed by each module at each particular time, the same module is however capable of collecting the required data for anyone of

the identified measurements. We focus on the analyzer part to gain more easily insight into the overall problem as well as the required aspects of distribution.

An Elementary Measurement is an interface offered by an appropriate hardware module installed at some appropriate ATM network elements. This module must have access on the ATM cell stream at standardized, B-ISDN specific reference points or interfaces. Elementary Measurements (EM) as suggested below, are drawn from measurements conducted with the PARASOL Test Tool and presented in [19], [20].

EM1: **Cell Delay.** The interface offers a stream of values representing delay information based on time stamps. Cell delay over a VC connection is the sum of a fixed cell assembly delay, a fixed transmission delay and a variable queuing delay term.

EM2: **Cell Interarrival Time.** The interface offers a stream of values representing the difference of time stamps between consecutive cells. Transmit or receive time stamps are of interest.

EM3: **Payload Bit Errors.** The interface offers a stream of values representing the number of errored bits at successive cell payloads. Each cell has to be evaluated independently of the others as the occurrence of cell loss would render multi-cell tests invalid.

EM4: **Errored Cell Interarrival Time.** The interface offers a stream of values representing the period (in cell times) between successive errored cells.

EM5: **Consecutive Correct Cells.** The interface offers a stream of values representing the numbers of sequential correct cells.

EM6: **Cell Sequence Numbers.** The interface offers a stream of values representing the cell sequence number of each cell. This information can be the basis of very elaborate cell sequence integrity observations, helping in depth debugging activities on top of performance evaluation. A typical secondary outcome is the Cell Loss Ratio.

EM7: **Cell Insertion Probability.** The interface offers the number of inserted cells against the total number of cells received. This measurement can be performed both on VP/VC basis and on link basis.

Most of the above Elementary Measurements can be performed only on test cell streams since they require time stamping, sequence numbers, etc., which can only be accommodated in the cell payload. An alternative is to interleave specially demarcated test cells with the live traffic of an existing VC or VP at controllable intervals (cut-through mode). Some measurements, like Cell Insertion on a link basis do not require test cells; the analyzing hardware module is informed in advance on all valid VCI/VPI on the link under test and can detect unknown identifier values. The Cell Insertion Probability measurement does not have anything in common with the cut-through mode, since it concerns parasitically and not intentionally inserted cells. Thus measurements can be conducted on live traffic of user connections, on test traffic inserted into user connections or on test traffic on specially established test connections. Only the last two cases involve generator functionalities as will be explained below. In any case measurement methods should prevent that results are adversely effected, due to the presence of excessive test traffic, either on a connection basis, or as a general background load. It makes sense that some of the Elementary Measurements present their output also in histogram form.

Since elementary measurements are in effect interfaces, which have fixed location we denote by $EMk(j)$ the elementary measurement k as above, presenting measurements at the physical interface j of the ATM network. How j is practically specifying the real interface is not further elaborated. We envisage a situation, where new, further elementary measurements are added in evolutionary steps (new k values) as well as existing elementary measurements are performed at additional physical interfaces (new j values). In contraposition to interfaces of other modules as given below, the $EMk(j)$ interfaces are assumed fixed, without migration possibilities, since at least initially, the corresponding functionality is intimately tied to hardware.

Analysis Servers are software modules offering their services above a distributed platform. They perform filtering, analysis and to some extent presentation functions on the data provided by the Elementary Measurements $EMk(j)$. Typical services are given below distinguished by the form of their output.

AS1: Calculation of single parameter statistical measures. These include (moving) averages, higher moments, probability of exceeding thresholds. The list and available options is open ended.

AS2: Calculation of histograms. Typical options are compression and reduction of resolution of histograms generated by appropriate $EMk(j)$.

AS3: Calculation of autocorrelation values.

AS4: Transformation of raw data. Typical examples are normalization, extraction of subsequences according to different criteria (like thresholds), etc.

The above items, as well as the particular option for each one, are of course open ended. One of the main methods of working in a DSE is the possibility to add/ remove/modify the Analysis Servers through provided platform functionalities. Analysis Servers are denoted by ASq. The index q refers exclusively to different services. Each ASq, fully software implemented and integrated as a platform server, shares all merits of the platform features like migration, fault tolerance, subject to trading, replication, etc.

2. Traffic Generation Aspects: The advantages of a DSE can be equally observed in the traffic generation aspects of the overall performance measurement setup. Measurements can only be performed if appropriately generated test cell streams are generated and injected into the ATM NUT, again at standardized B-ISDN specific reference points or interfaces. Special VC's/VP's might have to be set up to accommodate the test cell traffic, in which case the generating hardware module must also perform, or assist in performing signalling. In the cut-through mode test cells are injected at existing live connections. In all cases two main tasks are involved: the construction of the sequence of test cells with each of their bits valued appropriately and the generation of the desired statistical patterns for interdeparture times, distribution of intended errors and ATM protocol violations, etc. Hence there is a considerable statistical, traffic engineering part to be performed off-line before the start of the measurement. Parameters are then deduced and downloaded to Elementary Sources (ES) realized in hardware and embedded within the ATM NUT. One expects a smaller number of ESn's in comparison to EMk's. There are indeed few basic hardware set-up propositions for real time ATM traffic generation and we will present only two. For an excellent exposition along with queue theoretic foundations see [21].

An Elementary Source is thus an interface offered by an appropriate hardware module installed within the ATM NUT like:

ES1: Memory based generator. A FIFO memory is filled off-line with pointers to predefined cell patterns. Timing information for play-out time is also reported.

ES2: State model based generator. The source assumes a limited number of distinct states (usually only two, representing active end silent periods) and at each state a regenerated version of an older cell-pattern is outputted.

With ES1 there is a complete control on the generated cells as entailed in the downloaded memory content. In contraposition ES2 concerns a coarser generating process, highly appropriate also for background traffic.

As with Analysis Servers, Generation Servers (GS) are software processes dealing with all preprocessing for obtaining the actual generator setup. This then is downloaded through the $ESn(i)$ interfaces to hardware. Here the array of possible options can be impressive, exhausting a theoretically based service specific catalogue. Based on traffic engineering for ATM one can distinguish connection, dialogue, burst or source level modelling of sources, single or multiplexed source models, models based on several levels of activity, etc. Reference [16] exposes relevant work conducted within the RACE program. A distinction relying more directly to real sources is also possible. Voice, data, constant and variable bit rate video service based source models are candidates, with [17] being a typical example.

Here again $ESn(i)$ is an interface at the fixed location i and the nature of the Elementary Source denoted by n can interact with some GSp's, where p ranges within a numerous, open ended set of Generation Servers implemented in software. Index p refers exclusively to the kind of generating process, since the location of GS is immaterial as will be seen below.

Analysis and Generation Servers are examples of Mediator Servers. According to [14] mediation functions are used to transfer, adapt and filter information between functions capturing information from the managed network and network management applications. The introduction of Mediator Servers in a DSE allows software modules from independent providers to be encapsulated in the network management platform easily, as well as to remove/modify existing services without notification of the management application. This implies that service entities, accessed through a remote interaction model, still respect old external interfaces so as to be upgraded transparently (version upgrade [9], [22]).

C. Management Applications (MA)

As made clear before we are only concerned with Management Applications (MA's) in the area of performance and to a lesser degree with fault management. We strive at network wide measurements to be performed at arbitrary times and to be typically extended over connection duration periods. To this end GSp and ASq represent in Fig. 2 the available functional resources and $ESn(i)$ and $EMk(j)$ the installed hardware base for performing measurements. The distribution of Elementary Sources and Measurements represent functional as well as quantitative resources. Indeed the installed hardware base for testing within the ATM NUT is directly related to the breadth and topological spread of possible performance evaluation experiments.

The MA itself can benefit from the underlying distributed environment, since it will most likely enjoy its own high modularity. A typical decomposition would include a separate module for Man Machine Interface (MMI), database servers to the Management Information Trees (MIT's) and other external databases. Attached to the MMI, a User Interface Management System (UIMS) server is an additional module used for the creation and tailoring of the MMI, but also for managing a dynamic windowing system during run time. Concerning the scope of MA's one could mention call acceptance policies, resource allocation, load balancing, verification of billing and charging through well predefined test scenaria at various ATM traffic levels. Also in a longer time scale provisioning can be assisted through extended and robust in time performance measurements. Fault management can also be aided by specially designed MA's. Many ATM layer faults will manifest themselves through a degradation of some performance parameters related to the mentioned Elementary Measurements and not with a complete breakdown of a network element. Such cases are extremely difficult to identify and locate without quantitative analysis of test results. Our scope is not to present or describe even a preliminary list of conceivable MA's. On the other hand, with typical realistic scenaria serving as examples, we intend to illustrate how key features of a

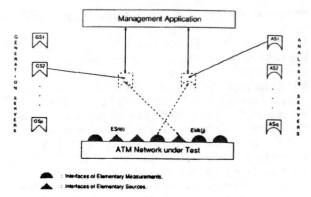

Fig. 2. Invocation scheme for servers.

DSE can be exploited giving impressively flexible and future safe support to MA's.

IV. DSE TRANSPARENCIES FOR ATM PERFORMANCE EVALUATION

As suggested in Fig. 2 and in Section III, the task of the distributed platform is to enable the functional and possibly also topological match between Management Application, Generation and Analysis Servers and Elementary Sources and Measurements. The final outcome of such a match can be seen in Fig. 3, where all these entities are in separate locations. In principle only $EMk(j)$ and $ESn(i)$ are fixed and it is likely that before staring an experiment, the platform will enable ASq/GSp to become corresident with $EMk(j)/ESn(i)$ respectively. This would avoid long distance transfer of setup and measurement data for generation and/or analysis. Notice also that Fig. 3 stipulates that the ATM NUT also provides communication resources as required for the distributed platform. We have this particular feature for network management, where the tested system also constitutes a functional part of the testing system. Fig. 3 further shows the possibility of direct access to the platform's communication resources (in our case drivers for ATM connections) by sidestepping the platform kernel during the actual transfer of data. In general the platform kernel contributes to the preparatory phase of an information exchange by providing required utilities and means of varying sophistication. Trading is such an example, which will be exploited below.

A. Location Transparency Through Trading Service

We have seen that in addition to functions resident in network hardware elements, there exist a large variety of functions necessary for the initial setup, definition of the measurement mode, calculation of raw data and presentation of results. This set of functions under the composition and allocation principles of Section III-B constitute a set of generic servers (termed AS and GS). It is desirable, for the sake of flexibility, extendibility, software maintenance, etc., to establish and offer these services free

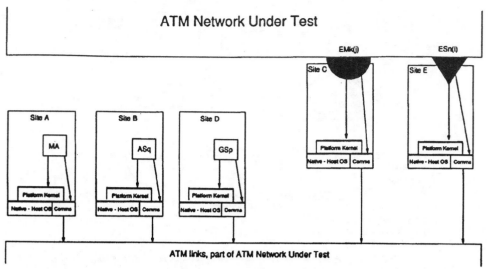

Fig. 3. Realization of server invocation and interfacing with ATM Network and test in a DSE.

from any location constraints. Location transparency should go to the point where not even a centralized registration and look-up procedure for locating and addressing these servers is required.

The trading service of a typical DSE provides exactly the desired possibility. Thus, each generic server offers its interface by exporting to a so called **trader** its.type, naming context and attributes/constraints. No rigid naming schemes are imposed and several servers of the same type might coexist, offering the desired variety in attributes/constraints. A client, in our case the Management Application, needs only to refer to a type with associated optional attributes/constraints and obtains through the matching functionality of the trading service an interface reference to the appropriate server. Furthermore with the use of the relocation service (usually coupled with the trader, see ANSA locator in [9]), connections broken due to system/service failure can be reestablished transparently from the initiator of the invocation. This feature is also useful in cooperation with migration aspects as described in Section IV-B.

In ANSA [9], the trader organizes the offers' information database using hierarchical trees in two levels: **context** and **types**. The type of an offer is used to determine the kind of service provided. Types are stored in a hierarchical order similarly to the object oriented class declaration. Furthermore types reside in a special context space allowing a second level coding according to the specific application requirements. Context are stored in a tree structure like the UNIX directory structure. A third utility for the looking-up procedure is provided. This is the **constraint** mechanism that allows special information for each offer to be included in the trader's space. Thus, a server indicates its willingness to engage in service provision by *exporting* (registering) an interface reference, together with the additional information of its type, context space it wishes to register to, as well as special in-

formation required for the constraint mechanism. A client finds an appropriate server by performing an *import* (lookup) operation on the trader. During its import operation the client supplies its requirements about type, context and/or special constraints to be included in the lookup operation. Especially the naming context in an import request designates the root of a tree of context in which the trading service will search for matching offers (see Fig. 4). The result of a successful import is an interface reference to the server.

In ATM performance specific terms the above advantage can be seen in the following scenario. The services associated with analyzing as outlined in Section II-B.1 can now be organized according to the above. Let AS1 be an Analysis Server for single statistical parameter calculation. The export operation (offer) to the trader as expressed in the DPL language looks like:

! { } ←*traderRef$Export*("*Single Value*",

"*/ansa/analysis_servers*", "*minimum value*", ir)

where

"Single Value" (AS1)	→ type of server (single value calculation)
"/ansa/analysis_servers"	→ naming context to store that offer
"minimum value"	→ special attribute of that server
ir	→ interface reference to the trader

We can probably have a second ASI server differing from the first one at e.g., the parameter to be calculated. The export operation will look like:

! { } ←*traderRef$Export*("*Single Value*",

"*/ansa/analysis_servers*", "*average*", ir)

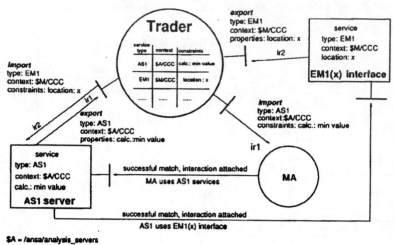

Fig. 4. Trading provides the required matching between MA, AS, EM, etc.

We can classify the different services of Section III-B.1 according to the following scheme, where

AS1 type stands for single parameter statistical measurement calculation,

AS2 type stands for histogram,

AS3 type stands for calculation of autocorrelation values,

AS4 type stands for raw data transformation, etc.,

and context denotes Cell Delay, Payload Bit Errors, Consecutive Correct Cells (CCC), Errored Cell Interarrival time (ECC), Cell Interarrival Time (CIT), etc. This then gives offers as in Table II. We have distinguished different context according to a broad classification of measurements. The criterion is chosen, so as to ensure, that for each context the same format for the data passed from EMk to the ASq server prevails.

Similarly we can classify Generation Servers according to context (memory based or state model) and to type. For type we chose the long possible array of options of modelling traffic theoretically or obtaining it through idealization of real sources. Generation Server offers are shown in Table III.

We can now describe the contribution of the trader. Take for example the simple situation, where an MA wants to set-up a performance evaluation measurement (e.g., cell delay mean value) using one distinct traffic generation Elementary Source ES$n(i)$ and one Elementary Measurement EM$k(j)$. The MA decides on the locations i, j, i.e., the endpoints between which the measurement has to take place.

Actions taken are as follows:

(i) The MA asks the trader for a GSp server, whose type corresponds to the appropriate traffic profile (GS1, GS2). If the trader finds such a software module, it returns the interface reference to MA and the con-

TABLE II
ANALYSIS SERVER OFFERS

Type	Naming Context	Properties
Single Value (AS1)	/ansa/analysis_servers/cell_delay	average
Single Value (AS1)	/ansa/analysis_servers/cell_delay	prob. of exceeding threshold
Single Value (AS1)	/ansa/analysis_servers/CCC	minimum value
Histogram (AS2)	/ansa/analysis_servers/ECC	histogram logarithm
Histogram (AS2)	/ansa/analysis_servers/ECC	histogram high resolution
Raw data (AS4)	/ansa/analysis_servers/CIT	raw_data
Raw data (AS4)	/ansa/analysis_servers/CIT	values exceeding threshold

TABLE III
GENERATION SERVER OFFERS

Type	Naming Context	Properties
burst (GS1)	/ansa/generation_services/memory_based	null
voice (GS2)	/ansa/generation_services/state_model	null
multiplexed traffic (GS3)	/ansa/generation_services/state_model	null

nection MA $\leftrightarrow$ GSp is now established. Further information about the source type is forwarded from MA to GSp. The corresponding DPL statement is:

$$! \ \{ir\} \leftarrow traderRef\$Export(``GS1'',$$

$$``ansa/generation\_services'',0)$$

(ii) The MA asks the trader for a single value (AS1) calculation server, whose context corresponds to cell delay and 'average' as constraint. If the trader finds such a software module, it returns the interface reference to MA and the connection MA $\leftrightarrow$ AS1 is also established. Further information about the measurement type (cell delay) and location j is forwarded by subsequent invocations from MA to AS1. The location j must be part of this information. The corresponding DPL statement is:

! {ir} ←*traderRef$Export*("*AS1*",

"*ansa/analysis_services*", "*average*")

(iii) The GS*p* server using the information forwarded by MA, will have to connect (through the trader) to multiple sources of type ES*n*(*i*) having as properties their geographic location.

(iv) Now the AS1 server connects to the EM1 interface. Again we should note that MA may wish to measure cell delay in multiple points in the network. The EM1 interface present at multiple network elements distinguishes itself by including in its properties the geographic location; the client (AS1) includes in the constraint field during successive calls to the trader the location where MA will obtain results from.

The setup as in Fig. 3 has now been established. MA starts the measurement, which runs for some time on its own, i.e., without MA control. Results are gathered at the analyzing site *j* and the measurement is completed when certain conditions are fulfilled. The setup as realized through the trader, is either retained until the end of the measurement or it is released and resetup at the end to collect and process the results. This can be achieved without invocation of the trader, since interface references are already known and can be stored in the MA. We assumed above the previously given use of type and context regarding AS, GS. For the classification of EM*k*(*j*), ES*n*(*i*), it is mandatory that the location parameter *i*, *j* appears either as context or as property.

The GS*p* functionality essentially providing the traffic profile is only used at the beginning of the measurement. Similarly the AS*q* functionality is only used at the end of the measurement, in order to process the results. To avoid the above as well as the complication of setting up the EM*k*(*j*) through the AS*q*, one could have a direct line from MA to EM*k*(*j*) based on accessing information originally given by AS (or design the MA to explicitly ask the trader for an EM*k*(*j*) interface). It is worth noting that not all combinations of EM/AS are possible. For example calculation of histograms cannot be performed on Cell Sequence Integrity measurements. This however, is taken care by the AS or the MA.

An ATM network as a large-scale distributed system, consist of a multitude of domains, authorities (e.g., separate enterprises, autonomous departments etc.). In such cases, interworking can only be achieved via cooperation in federal style. ANSA federation mechanism allows multiple traders to co-exist in a large distributed environment, each one being responsible for its own domain. Clients and servers address their calls only to their local trader, whereas communication between separate domains is achieved through a higher layer communication scheme between traders. The federation of separate domains directly affects the architectural view of naming (and trading). ANSA trader federation provides features like separation of naming domains, naming conventions, naming context, naming networks, distinct path names and name

transparency. ANSA federated traders are able to internetwork and exchange information about their local configuration entities [9].

B. Migration Transparency and Placement Management

Another feature found in modern DSE's is the option of moving resources (those not coupled with hardware) from one network element to another, in order to satisfy specific needs. When this happens as part of the initialization procedure during system start-up, we speak of placement management. Migration then refers to dynamic change of location of modules during operation, due to functional and system specific reasons. Migration of components can achieve better distribution of load, minimal use of communication resources and protection from expected forthcoming system degradation.

Through migration, modules may move to network elements if and when their functions are actually required. This prevents the need for replication of the same module at different sites or the remote interaction between modules during the performance of their actual tasks. This would load communication resources and/or introduce inappropriate delays for on-line tasks. Moreover, in our case, migration is necessary to bring together servers and hardware coupled generation or analysis modules.

A further step can be considered by removing the assumption that EM*k*(*j*), ES*n*(*i*) are resident in fixed locations. These interfaces could belong to software modules (agents) that can migrate from one network element to another to be loaded on generic hardware. In this case the same hardware must be software configurable to support more than one EM*k*/ES*n* interfaces. This has been accomplished to a large degree in the PARASOL Test Tool ([19], [21]). Another example in the same spirit is quoted in [24], where a simple PC board can be configured as memory based analyzer/generator or a mix of both.

An interesting ATM specific migration example is shown in Fig. 5. The Management Application deals with remote debugging at VC or VP level. Elementary Measurements and Elementary Sources do not have the *i*, *j* indices, which indicate fixed location. Instead each ES*n* or EM*k* can move to specific locations *A*, *A'*, *A"* respectively *B*, *B'*, *B"* where appropriate hardware is installed. Between two distinct network nodes *A*, *B* we want to measure the Cell Loss Ratio. The MA resides in the network operator host and GS*p* and AS*q* are anywhere in the network. In order to set-up this measurement we need hardware support for traffic generator in *A* and traffic analyzer in *B*. Furthermore we will need an ES interface at *A* and an EM6 interface at *B*. Initially the MA collects Cell Loss Ratio results between points *A* and *B*. If significant Cell Loss is determined, the MA proceeds to locate the responsible link. Thus, it decides to perform again the same experiment between *A'* and *B'*. Assuming that there is hardware support for generation and analysis functions, ES and EM6 migrate to new positions, *A'* and *B'* respec-

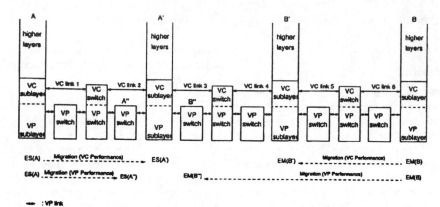

Fig. 5. Remote debugging.

tively, to conduct again the same measurement. The description so far deals with performance evaluation at VC level, so that candidate positions to migrate must be VC switching nodes. Fig. 5 shows also, with positions A'', B'', the same scenario on VP basis. Migration makes this example feasible and allows efficient use of testing resources.

C. Replication Transparency

Replication transparency is already implemented in some of the existing ODP platforms (e.g., file services) to provide increased dependability and availability. Replication allows the user or MA to keep several copies of the original resource, so as to enable fast and concurrent access to remotely located resources. Use of replication speeds up measurement processing and security of results. Both improvements occur, because communication through the network supporting the platform is avoided. Mechanisms enabling replication are similar to those supporting migration but include additionally procedures to ensure consistency of replicas [22].

ATM will be a widely extended public backbone network. Taking also into account administrative aspects it is likely that the establishment, use, modifications of each server would be centrally administered. The replication mechanism allows multiple copies of a "prototype" module to be replicated locally as part of the underlying platform functionality and it is thus useful in our context.

A typical case calling for extensive use of replication is the generation of background load, through a large number of replicated ESn's at various network elements. We have seen in Section III-B.2 that a Generation Server interacts with the ES$n(i)$ interface to set-up and activate the generation hardware. The replication mechanism ensures here that all background load generators, whose interface is a replica to an ESn prototype, can be set-up and controlled in one go.

V. CONCLUSION

Drawing experience from designing and implementing ATM layer test and performance evaluation tools, we have examined in some detail the possibility for a correspond-

ing distributed version. This is highly desirable and appropriate due to the size of backbone networks and the complexity and flexibility of ATM. The paper has shown that Open Distributed Processing concepts and properties harmoniously meet the requisites of the examined case. Open System Platforms have previously been considered for network management in B-ISDN, however only in general terms and from the point of view of a general architecture encompassing all areas of network management. Here by focusing exclusively on performance and fault management in ATM we have been able to arrive at much more concrete propositions, giving also examples explaining key platform functionalities such as trading, migration and replication.

REFERENCES

[1] J-Y. Le Boudec, "The Asynchronous Transfer Mode, a tutorial," *Comp. Networks ISDN Systems*, vol. 24, no. 4, pp. 279–309, 1992.
[2] "The Netman Cube Model," *RACE Common Functional Specifications*, document 7, issue B, Dec. 1991.
[3] J. G. Markopoulos, C. I. Costopoulou, M. E. Theologou, and E. N. Protonotarios, "An object-oriented approach for quality of service and network performance modelling," *IFIP Trans.*, C-5 Performance of Distributed Systems and Integrated Communications Networks, 1992.
[4] A. E. Eckberg, "B-ISDN/ATM traffic and congestion control," *IEEE Network.*, vol. 6, pp. 28–37, Sept. 1992.
[5] Chin-Tan Lea, "What should be the goal for ATM," *IEEE Network.*, vol. 6, pp. 60–66, Sept. 1992.
[6] E. D. Sykas, K. M. Vlakos, I. S. Venieris, and E. M. Protonotarios, "Simulative analysis of optimal resource allocation and routing in IBCN's," *IEEE J. Select. Areas Commun.*, vol. 9, pp. 486–492, Apr. 1991.
[7] Technical Committee 32 Technical Group 2 (TC32-TG2), "Support environment for Open Distributed Processing (SE-ODP)," July 1989.
[8] G. Coulouris and J. Dollimore, "Distributed Systems," Queen Mary College, 1988.
[9] "The ANSA Reference Manual," *Advanced Networked Systems Architecture Project*, Cambridge, UK.
[10] "DCE Reference Manual," Open Software Foundation, 1991.
[11] "The Comandos Guide," version 1.3, *Comandos Consortium*, Mar. 1991.
[12] A. Balis, A. Dede, K. Flokos, B. Martin, and R. v. Riet, "HARNESS, An evolving standard for distributed processing," SIGDIS-OMG Workshop, Berlin, Germany, Sept. 1993.
[13] S. Mullender, "Distributed systems," in *The Advanced Networked Systems Architecture*. New York: Addison Wesley, 1989.
[14] CCITT Draft Recommendation M.3010.
[15] I. Miloutcheva, "XTP and ST-II Facilities for Provision of the QoS

Requirements of Connection-mode Transport Services" TU Berlin, Res. Note, Sept. 1992.

[16] R. Kleinewillinghofer-Kopp and R. Lehnert, "ATM reference traffic sources and traffic mixes," RACE workshop "Traffic and performance aspects in IBCN," Munich, Germany, July 3-4, 1990.

[17] B. Maglaris et al., "Performance analysis of statistical multiplexing for packet video sources," in Proc. GLOBECOM'87, Nov. 1987, paper 47.8.

[18] "The Timeline Model," RACE Common Functional Specifications, document 3, CFS D510.

[19] G. Crawford and W. Grupp, "Network performance measurements in ATM systems," Telecommun., pp. 22-32, Aug. 1991.

[20] G. Crawford and W. Grupp, "Testing in the ATM environment," Commun. Int.,Oct. 1991.

[21] H. G. Diavolitsis, B. E. Helvik, R. Lehnert, and J. G. Michelsen, "Traffic generation for ATM systems testing environment, modelling and feasibility studies," in Proc. ITC 13th Queueing, Performance, and Control in ATM, Copenhagen, Denmark, June 1991, vol. 15, pp. 83-90.

[22] V. Wade, "A framework for TMN computing platforms," in Proc. 5th RACE TMN Conf., London, U.K., Nov. 20-22, 1991, I.3/5, pp. 2-17.

[23] "Common Management Information Service Definition," ISO/IEC 9595, JTC1/SC21 CMIP, N-3874R2, Dec. 1989.

[24] K. Kassapakis, J. S. Giamnadakis, M. G. Bakouris, and T. G. Sardis, "Analyzing and testing ATM network equipment using the traffic analyzer/generator (Atmospheric test tool)," in 4th Int. Conf. Advances in Commun. & Control, Rhodes, Greece, June 14-18, 1993.

[25] "High Speed Transport Service Definition (HSTS)," Preliminary Draft Proposal, American National Standard, contribution by Paramax System Corporation, in ISO/IEC SC6 Meeting, San Diego, CA, July 13-24, 1992.

E. D. Kollias (S'90) received the Diploma in electrical engineering from the National Technical University of Athens, Greece, in 1990.

He is currently Senior Researcher at the Division of Computer Science, National Technical University of Athens, working in the areas of computer network protocols, distributed processing, ATM testing, and evaluation and network management architectures.

G. I. Stassinopoulos (M'81) received the Diploma in electrical engineering from the Swiss Federal Institute of Technology (ETH), Zurich, Switzerland, in 1974, and the D.I.C. and Ph.D. degrees in computing and control from Imperial College, London, U.K., in 1977.

He spent three years in industry designing and implementing microprocessor-based industrial control systems. Since 1981 he has been a member of the staff of the Department of Computer Science at the National Technical University of Athens, Greece, where he is now a Professor. He is involved in various European Community research programs in the area of broad-band integrated networks. His research interests include optimal control theory, computer network protocols, routing and flow control, distributed systems, and design of components for asynchronous transfer mode (ATM) networks.

Performance Analysis of a Random Packet Selection Policy for Multicast Switching

Mustafa K. Mehmet Ali and Shaying Yang

Abstract—This paper studies a random packet selection policy for the multicast switching. An input packet generates a fixed number of primary copies plus a random number of secondary copies. Assuming a constant number of contending packets during a slot, the system is modeled as a discrete time birth process. A difference equation describing the dynamics of this process is derived, the solution of which gives a closed form expression for the distribution of the number of packets chosen. Then this result is extended to the steady state distribution through a Markov chain analysis. It is shown that the old packets have larger fanout than the fresh packets and the copy distribution of the mixed packets is determined. The packet and copy throughput taking into account the old packets have been obtained. We determined the mean packet delay as well as an upperbound for packet loss probabilities for finite buffer sizes. The asymptotic distribution of the number of packets is also given for large switch sizes under saturation by applying results from the renewal theory. Finally, simulations are done to determine the performance of the switch under mixed (unicast plus multicast) traffic.

I. INTRODUCTION

IMPLEMENTATION of broadband-ISDN over optical fiber will enable offering of a wide range of services. Among these services, there will be a demand for delivery of the same information to several destinations. Teleconferencing, entertainment video, LAN internetworking, and distributed data processing provide examples of such applications. An essential component of such a system will be a multicasting switch which will transmit copies of an input packet to several outputs. The number of copies generated by a packet is known as fan out. The objective of this paper is to give a performance analysis of such a multicast switch under random packet selection policy.

In recent years, various switch architectures have appeared in the literature [1]–[3]. These architectures assume that the underlying transmission format is the asynchronous transfer mode (ATM) with fixed length packets. The time is slotted of which size equals to the packet duration. A typical switch implementation consists of a copy network which generates packet copies, followed by a nonblocking point-to-point routing network. The buffers are provided at the inputs of both the copy and routing networks to store the packets and copies respectively. This work assumes such an input queuing architecture operating in the ATM environment.

When a packet reaches to the head-of-line (HOL) position at an input queue, it generates a number of copies to be transmitted to different outputs. Each output may receive only a single copy from the inputs during a slot. If more than one HOL packet has a copy destined for the same output, this results in contention. The performance of the switch depends on the way this contention is resolved at the outputs. The contention resolution algorithms may be broadly classified into two depending on whether or not the fan out is splitted. In fan out splitting discipline the packet transmission is spread over several slots; while in no fan out splitting all the copies of a packet are transmitted in a single slot. In [4], a fan out splitting discipline has been studied where in each slot, among the copies contending for an output one of them would have been chosen randomly. Several variations of this policy have also been analyzed in [5] under more accurate assumptions. This work also studies a random packet selection policy under no fan out splitting discipline through simulation. In [6], performance of this discipline has been determined under the assumption that input ports have rotating priority in each slot. Finally, in [7], both fan out splitting and not splitting disciplines have been analysed under rotating priority assumption using matrix-geometric techniques.

In this paper, we shall study the random packet selection policy under no fan out splitting. In the following, a small and large packet will refer to the relative size of a packet in terms of its fan out, the number of copies that it has generated. The simulation studies in [5] have shown that the performance of random policy is comparable to the fan out splitting discipline at relatively small fan out. However, in practice, the unicast and multicast traffic will exist together and thus the former will provide enough small packets including to the destinations that cannot be selected by large packets. This will prevent lowering of the throughput at large fanouts, which is confirmed by simulation studies to be presented. At this writing, the random packet selection policy is considered to be a viable service discipline for the multicast switching.

The organization of the paper is as follows. The next section describes the random packet selection policy under consideration, the packet arrival process to the system and the copy generation process. Section III, assuming a constant number of contending HOL packets during a slot, models the random selection policy as discrete time birth process. A difference equation describing the dynamics of this process

Paper approved by A. Jajszczyk, the Editor for Switch Theory & Fabrics of the IEEE Communications Society. Manuscript received January 4, 1994; revised April 13, 1994, and May 25, 1995.

M. K. M. Ali is with Concordia University, Department of Electrical and Computer Engineering, 1455 de Maisonneuve Boulevard West, Montreal, Quebec, H3G 1M8, Canada.

S. Yang was with Concordia University, Department of Electrical and Computer Engineering, 1455 de Maisonneuve Boulevard West, Montreal, Quebec, H3G 1M8, Canada. She is now with Bell Northern Research, Ontario, Canada.

Publisher Item Identifier S 0090-6778(96)01784-9.

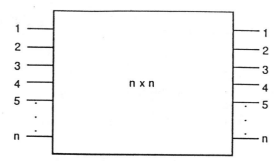

Fig. 1. A multicast packet switch.

is derived, the solution of which gives the distribution of the number of packets chosen for transmission during that slot. Section IV removes the assumption that the number of contending HOL packets is constant through a Markov chain analysis however no input queuing is allowed. An input generates a new packet after the present one has been transmitted. We determine the packet and copy throughput and demonstrate that the old HOL packets have larger fan out than the new HOL packets. In Section V, we drop the assumption that no input queuing is allowed and derive the mean packet delay and give an upper bound for packet loss probabilities for finite buffer sizes. In Section VI, the asymptotic distribution of the number of packets chosen for transmission during a slot is derived by applying results from the renewal theory. Section VII presents some numerical and simulation results and finally Section VIII presents conclusions of the paper.

II. MODELING

In the following, we assume an $n * n$ multicast switch with infinite input queuing (Fig. 1). The arrival of the packets to each input is according to an independent Bernoulli process, a single packet is generated with probability λ during a slot. In certain applications user information is sent in large units which are segmented into ATM cells, therefore successive arrivals to a given input are strongly correlated. The independence assumption can be justified by the distance between consecutive cells of the same VC, which implies rather low peak rates as compared with channels and switch capacities.

The random packet selection policy serves to the HOL packets at the inputs. If two packets have copies simultaneously destined to the same outputs they are said to be interfering with each other and only one of them may be transmitted during a slot. Those HOL packets not served in the present slot contend in the next slot together with the new HOL packets. At the beginning of a slot, the random selection process determines from among the contending packets those to be transmitted in that slot. This process consists of a number of rounds during which the packets to be transmitted are selected. In each round a packet is chosen randomly from among the remaining contending packets, and then the packets interfering with the chosen packet is eliminated from further contention in the subsequent rounds. This process keeps going on until no more noninterfering packets is left and then the chosen packets are transmitted to the outputs in the same slot. Clearly, this

is an extension of the corresponding random packet selection policy for the unicast switching. Those packets that have been eliminated from the contention, as well as new HOL packets contend for selection in the following slot.

In the above description of the random policy, a chosen packet will not interfere with any of the packets chosen in the earlier rounds. This observation led us to the following equivalent implementation of this policy. In this case, the selection process consists of as many trials as the number of the contending packets during a slot. In the first trial a packet is picked up randomly from among the contending packets and it is kept as a chosen packet. In the second trial, another packet is picked up randomly, however this is kept only if it does not interfere with the first chosen packet otherwise discarded. These trials are continued each time picking a contending packet and keeping it if it does not interfere with any of the packets chosen in the earlier trials. Again this process goes on until the contending packets are exhausted and then the chosen packets are transmitted during that slot.

Clearly both implementations describe the same policy and therefore give the same performance. The two of them differ in the way the interfering packets are discarded, the first one discarding them concurrently while the second one sequentially and we shall refer to them with these names (see Table I for an example). In practice, the concurrent policy will be the choice for implementation efficiency, however, its analysis does not result in a closed form solution and will not be presented here. The sequential random selection policy lends itself to analysis more easily and in the following the results will be derived using this version.

Next, we describe the copy generation process. Each packet is assumed to generate two types of copies to be referred as primary and secondary copies. The distinction between two types is only for the modeling purposes. First, a packet generates fixed number of primary copies, ζ, which are distributed to the outputs according to the random sampling without replacement. Thus, the first primary copy is randomly selected to go to any of the n outputs, the second primary copy to any of the remaining $(n-1)$ outputs, and so and so forth. After that secondary copies are generated to each of the outputs not selected by the primary copies according to independent Bernoulli trials with probability p. This will be referred to as the modified Binomial copy generation process and results in the generalization of the corresponding policy for the unicast switching. The probability generating function (PGF) of the distribution of the number of copies generated by a packet is given by

$$B(z) = z^{\zeta}(pz + 1 - p)^{n-\zeta}. \tag{1}$$

Letting $\zeta = 1$ and $p \to 0$ in the above, each packet generates a single copy reducing to the unicast switching. On the other hand, $\zeta = 0$ and $p \neq 0$ results in the pure binomial copy distribution.

In the following, the words "generation of a copy for an output" and "selecting an output" will be used interchangeably. The phrase "choosing a packet" will be reserved for packets successfully chosen for transmission during a slot.

IEEE TRANSACTIONS ON COMMUNICATIONS, VOL. 44, NO. 3, MARCH 1996

TABLE I

AN EXAMPLE FOR THE CONCURRENT AND SEQUENTIAL IMPLEMENTATION OF THE RANDOM PACKET SELECTION POLICY IN AN $(8 * 8)$ SWITCH

Outputs / Packets	1	2	3	4	5	6	7	8
1	0	0	1	1	0	0	0	0
2	1	0	1	0	0	0	0	0
3	0	1	0	0	1	0	0	1
4	0	0	0	0	0	0	1	1
5	1	0	0	1	0	0	0	0
6	0	0	0	1	0	0	1	0

Copy matrix: one indicates a primary or secondary copy to an output; zero indicates no copy.

Rounds	Chosen Packets	Discarded Packets	Remaining Packets
1	2	1, 5	3, 4, 6
2	4	3, 6	-

Concurrent policy

Trial No.	Packet No.	Interference	Outcome
1	1	-	Success
2	5	1	Failure
3	2	1	Failure
4	3	-	Success
5	4	3	Failure
6	6	1	Failure

Sequential policy

III. DISTRIBUTION OF THE NUMBER OF CHOSEN PACKETS FOR A GIVEN NUMBER OF CONTENDING PACKETS

The objective of the present section is determining the distribution of the number of chosen packets given a fixed number of HOL packets contending at the inputs during a slot. There will be α contending packets and this assumption will be dropped in the next section. Due to its simplicity, the analysis will keep track of the remaining number of unselected outputs instead of the selected ones. First, the PGF of the number of unselected outputs after the choice of the jth packet will be determined, and this will lead to the probability that a contending packet will not interfere with the first j chosen packets. Then a difference equation describing the dynamics of the packet selection process will be derived, the solution of which will give the desired probability distribution. Assuming that a packet has not generated a primary copy to output i, let the random variable $\tilde{x}_i$ denote the outcome of the Bernoulli trial for generation of a secondary copy to this output

$$\tilde{x}_i = \begin{pmatrix} 1, & \text{with probability } p; \\ 0, & \text{otherwise.} \end{pmatrix} \quad (2a)$$

Clearly, $\tilde{x}_i$'s are i.i.d, with a PGF given by

$$\tilde{X}(z) = \tilde{X}_i(z) = pz + 1 - p. \quad (2b)$$

For convenience, also the r.v. x_i will be defined as the compliment of $\tilde{x}_i$

$$x_i = 1 - \tilde{x}_i, \text{with a PGF given by} \quad (3a)$$

$$X(z) = X_i(z) = (1-p)z + p. \quad (3b)$$

In the following between $X(z)$ and $\tilde{X}(z)$, whichever one is more appropriate will be used.

A. PGF of the Number of Unselected Outputs After the Choice of jth Packet

Let r_j denote the number of unselected outputs after the choice of the jth packet. At the beginning of the selection policy, the number of available ouputs and its PGF are given by

$$r_0 = n, \quad R_0(z) = E[z^{r_0}] = z^n. \quad (4)$$

The remaining number of unselected outputs following the jth choice are related to that of after the $(j-1)$st choice by

$$r_j = \sum_{i=0}^{r_{j-1}-\zeta} x_i, \quad \text{with } r_0 = n. \quad (5)$$

The minus ζ in the upper limit accounts for the compulsory primary copies of the jth packet. From the independence of r_{j-1} and x_i,

$$R_j(z) = E[z^{r_j}] = (z^{-\zeta} E[z^{r_{j-1}}])|_{z=X(z)} \quad (6)$$

with

$$R_j(z) = [z^{-\zeta} R_{j-1}(z)]|_{z=X(z)}. \quad (7)$$

The repeated application of the above equation with (4) as an initial condition results in

$$R_j(z) = \frac{[1 - (1-p)^j(1-z)]^n}{\prod_{i=1}^{j}[1 - (1-p)^i(1-z)]^\zeta}. \quad (8)$$

Next we shall determine the number of outputs selected by the jth packet, n_j. Number of outputs available for selection is r_{j-1}, and ζ of them are selected by the primary copies and a Bernoulli trial is performed for each of the remaining $(r_{j-1} - \zeta)$ outputs for secondary copies. Thus

$$n_j = \zeta + \sum_{i=0}^{r_{j-1}-\zeta} \tilde{x}_i \quad \text{and}$$

$$N_j(z) = E[z^{n_j}] = z^\zeta [z^{-\zeta} R_{j-1}(z)]|_{z=\tilde{X}(z)}. \quad (9)$$

Substituting from (8) and (2b)

$$N_j(z) = \frac{z^\zeta [1 - p(1-p)^{j-1}(1-z)]^n}{[1 - p(1-z)]^\zeta \prod_{i=1}^{j-1}[1 - p(1-p)^i(1-z)]^\zeta}. \quad (10)$$

From the above average number of outputs selected by the jth packet is given by

$$\bar{n}_j = \frac{dN_j(z)}{dz}\bigg|_{z=1} = \mu(1-p)^{j-1} \quad (11)$$

where $\mu = \zeta + (n - \zeta)p$ is the average number of copies generated by a contending packet. As may be seen, only the first chosen packet has the same average number of copies as a contending packet and sizes of the subsequently chosen packets drop down.

Next, we shall determine the total number of outputs selected by the first chosen j packets, m_j. Then m_j and its PGF are given by

$$m_j = \sum_{i=0}^{j} n_i = n - r_j,$$

$$M_j(z) = E[z^{m_j}] = z^n R_j(z^{-1})$$

$$= \frac{z^{j\zeta}[z - (1-p)^j(z-1)]^n}{\prod_{i=1}^{j}[z - (1-p)^i(z-1)]^\zeta} \qquad (12)$$

where we substituted for $R_j(z^{-1})$ from (8). Then, the average number of outputs selected by the j chosen packets is given by

$$\overline{m}_j = \frac{dM_j(z)}{dz}\bigg|_{z=1}$$

$$= n[1 - (1-p)^j] + \frac{\zeta[(1-p) - (1-p)^{j+1}]}{p}. \qquad (13)$$

B. Derivation of the Probability that a Packet Will not Interfere with the j-Chosen Packets

Next, we shall determine the probability that a packet picked up for trial following the jth chosen packet will not interfere with any of the earlier chosen packets, P_j. A packet will interfere with the first j chosen packets, if it generates copies to the outputs also selected by these packets. Let U_j be the total number of copies that a contending packet has interfering with the first chosen j packets, and u the number of primary copies that a contending packet has interfering with the first j chosen packets.

Then U_j is given by

$$U_j = u + \sum_{i=0}^{m_j - u} \tilde{x}_i.$$

Conditioning on u and m_j

$$U_j(z|u, m_j) = z^u[\tilde{X}(z)]^{m_j - u}. \qquad (14)$$

Next, we determine the probability distribution of u. The n outputs may be considered as consisting of two types of objects, ζ of them that have a primary copy of the contending packet destined for them and the $(n - \zeta)$ of them that do not have. Let us define success if a primary copy is destined to one of the m_j outputs selected by the j chosen packets. Then u is equal to the number of successes in a random sample of size m_j chosen without replacement from among the n outputs. The random variable u has the hypergeometric distribution given by [8]

$$\Pr(u|m_j) = \frac{\binom{\zeta}{u}\binom{n-\zeta}{m_j - u}}{\binom{n}{m_j}}. \qquad (15)$$

Finally, unconditioning wrt both u and m_j

$$U_j(z) = \sum_{m_j} \sum_{u=0}^{\zeta} z^u[\tilde{X}(z)]^{m_j - u}$$

$$\cdot \frac{\binom{\zeta}{u}\binom{n-\zeta}{m_j - u}}{\binom{n}{m_j}} \Pr(m_j). \qquad (16)$$

Substitution of $z = 0$ gives the probability that a contending packet will not interfere with the first j chosen packets, P_j. Clearly in the inner summation, only the value of $u = 0$ will contribute to this probability, thus

$$P_j = U_j(z)|_{u=z=0}$$

$$= \left\{ \frac{(n-\zeta)!}{n!} \sum_{m_j} \frac{(n-m_j)!}{(n-m_j-\zeta)!}[\tilde{X}(z)]^{m_j} \Pr(m_j) \right\}\bigg|_{z=0}. \qquad (17)$$

It has not been possible to find a closed form expression for the above probability, therefore a number of specific cases will be given with the help of the following Z-transform property [9]

$$m_j(m_j - 1)(m_j - 2) \cdots (m_j - k + 1)\Pr(m_j)$$

$$\Leftrightarrow z^k \frac{d^k M_j(z)}{dz^k} \qquad (18)$$

which results in

$$m_j \Pr(m_j) \Leftrightarrow z\frac{dM_j(z)}{dz}, \qquad (19a)$$

$$m_j^2 \Pr(m_j) \Leftrightarrow z^2\frac{d^2 M_j(z)}{dz^2} + z\frac{dM_j(z)}{dz} \qquad (19b)$$

$\zeta = 0$:

$$P_j = \left\{ \sum_{m_j}[\tilde{X}(z)]^{m_j} \Pr(m_j) \right\}\bigg|_{z=0}.$$

$$= \{[M_j(z)|_{z=\tilde{X}(z)}]\}|_{z=0}$$

Substituting from (2b) and (12)

$$P_j = [1 - p + p(1-p)^j]^n \qquad (20)$$

which corresponds to the pure Binomial copy generation process.

$\zeta = 1$:

$$P_j = \left\{ \frac{1}{n}\sum_{m_j}(n - m_j)[\tilde{X}(z)]^{m_j} \Pr(m_j) \right\}\bigg|_{z=0}$$

$$= \left\{ \frac{1}{n}\left[nM_j(z) - z\frac{dM_j(z)}{dz} \right]\bigg|_{z=\tilde{X}(z)} \right\} \qquad (21)$$

where above we used (19a) and results in

$$P_j = \frac{[1 - p + p(1-p)^j]^n}{\prod_{i=1}^{j}[1 - p + p(1-p)^i]}\left\{ (1-p)^j\left(1 - \frac{j}{n}\right) \right.$$

$$+ (1-p)^{j+1} \left[\frac{1}{n} \sum_{i=1}^{j} \frac{1-(1-p)^i}{[1-p+p(1-p)^i]} \right.$$
$$\left. - \frac{1-(1-p)^j}{[1-p+p(1-p)^j]} \right] \Bigg\}. \qquad (22)$$

The P_j corresponding for $\zeta = 2,3$ have also been determined but due to their length will not be given here. Next the limiting case of $p \to 0$ will be considered with each packet generating only ζ number of primary copies. Then m_j is simply a constant, $m_j = j\zeta$, and substituting it into (17) gives P_j as

$$P_j = \prod_{i=0}^{\zeta-1} \left(1 - \frac{j\zeta}{n-i} \right). \qquad (23)$$

Finally setting $\zeta = 1$ gives

$$P_j = 1 - \frac{j}{n} \qquad (24)$$

in which case each packet generates a single copy that is equally likely to go to any output. Clearly, this corresponds exactly to the unicast switching.

C. Distribution of the Number of Chosen Packets

Now we are ready to determine the distribution of the number of chosen packets given that α packets are contending during a slot. As has been described in the introduction, the sequential random selection policy performs as many Bernoulli trials as the number of contending packets. This process may be modeled as a discrete time birth process, where the trial number corresponds to the discrete time. The birth corresponds choosing a packet successfully and the population size at any time is the number of packets chosen by the end of that trial. The birth coefficients are independent of time and dependent on the population size and are given by P_j for the population size j. Let us define $P_j(i)$ as

$$P_j(i) = \Pr \{ j \text{ packets will be chosen by the end}$$
$$\text{of the } i\text{th trial} \}.$$

The dynamics of the system may be described by the following difference equation

$$P_j(i+1) = (1-P_j)P_j(i) + P_{j-1}P_{j-1}(i),$$
$$1 \le j \le i \text{ and } P_j(i) = 0, \text{ for } j > i \qquad (25)$$

with the initial conditions

$$P_j(0) = \begin{cases} 1, & j=0; \\ 0, & j>0 \end{cases} \qquad (26)$$

and P_j given by (17) for $j \ge 1$ and $P_j = 1$ for $j = 0$ which guarantees that the first trial will always succeed. Equation (25) relates the state of the system at the end of the $(i+1)$st trial to that of the ith trial. Let us define

$$P_j(z) = \sum_{i=0}^{\infty} P_j(i) z^i. \qquad (27)$$

Now taking the transform of of both sides of the (25) wrt i gives

$$\frac{1}{z}[P_j(z) - P_j(0)] = (1-P_j)P_j(z) + P_{j-1}P_{j-1}(z), \quad j \ge 1$$

with $P_j(0) = 0$ for $j \ge 1$ results in

$$P_j(z) = \frac{zP_{j-1}P_{j-1}(z)}{1-z(1-P_j)}, \qquad j \ge 1. \qquad (28)$$

The repeated application of the above equation with the initial distribution, $P_0(z) = 1$, results in the following transform:

$$P_j(z) = \frac{z^j}{P_j} \prod_{k=1}^{j} \frac{P_k}{[1-(1-P_k)z]}$$
$$= \frac{z^j}{P_j} \sum_{k=1}^{j} \frac{A_k}{[1-(1-P_k)z]} \qquad (29)$$

where, in the second equation above, the product expression has been replaced by a summation using partial fraction expansion with A_k given by

$$A_k = P_k \prod_{\substack{x=1 \\ x \ne k}}^{j} \frac{P_k}{[1-(1-P_k)z]} \Bigg|_{z=(1/1-P_k)}$$
$$= P_k \prod_{\substack{x=1 \\ x \ne k}}^{j} \frac{1-P_k}{1-\frac{P_k}{P_x}}. \qquad (30)$$

The above equation may be inverted to give

$$P_j(i) = \frac{1}{P_j} \sum_{k=1}^{j} P_k (1-P_k)^{i-j} \prod_{\substack{x=1 \\ x \ne k}}^{j} \frac{1-P_k}{1-\frac{P_k}{P_x}}$$
$$1 \le j \le i. \qquad (31)$$

For α contending packets, the result is determined by setting $i = \alpha$ in the above equation

$$P_j(\alpha) = \frac{1}{P_j} \sum_{k=1}^{j} P_k (1-P_k)^{\alpha-j} \prod_{\substack{x=1 \\ x \ne k}}^{j} \frac{1-P_k}{1-\frac{P_k}{P_x}},$$
$$1 \le j \le \alpha. \qquad (32)$$

The above gives the distribution of the number of chosen packets given α contending packets in a slot and as may be seen, it has a nice closed form. Setting $\alpha = n$ gives the distribution for a switch in saturation.

IV. THE STEADY-STATE DISTRIBUTION OF THE NUMBER OF PACKETS CHOSEN

In this section, we drop the assumption that the number of contending packets during a slot is a constant. We determine the steady-state probability distribution of the number of packets chosen during a slot through a Markov chain analysis by embedding at the end of the slots. The packets at an embedded point are those not chosen in the previous slot and left for the next slot and they will be called old packets. We assume that the arrival of the packets to each input is according to an independent Bernoulli process with parameter λ, however no input queuing is allowed. Thus an input does not generate a new packet until the present one has been transmitted. The sum of the (old and fresh) HOL packets will be contending for random selection in that slot, and the chosen packets will be transmitted in the same slot. The ones not chosen become old packets for the following slot. We will also show that the distribution of the number of copies generated by an old packet is different than that of a new HOL packet, and its effect on the throughput will be determined. Let us introduce the following additional notation:

p_{mt} Transition probability of having t old packets at an embedded point given m old packets at the previous embedded point.

$\nu(f)$ Probability of f new HOL packets at the beginning of a slot.

$\tau(i)$ Probability that a sum of i (old and new) packets will be contending during a slot.

π_k Probability of having k packets at an embedded point at the steady state.

W_j Probability that j packets will be chosen in a slot at the steady state.

ρ Probability that an input is busy.

First let us determine

$$\nu(f|m) = \Pr\{f \text{ new HOL packets } |m \text{ old packets at an embedded point}\}$$
$$= \binom{n-m}{f}\lambda^f(1-\lambda)^{n-m-f}. \tag{33}$$

and then (34) (see equation at the bottom of the page). Then the transition probabilities are given by

$$p_{mt} = \begin{cases} \displaystyle\sum_{i=t+1}^{n} P_{i-t}(i)\tau(i|m), & t > 0; \\ \displaystyle\sum_{i=0}^{n} P_i(i)\tau(i|m), & t = 0 \end{cases} \tag{35}$$

where $P_{i-t}(i)$ is the probability that $(i-t)$ packets will be chosen from a total of i contending packets in a slot and is given by (31). Following the determination of the transition probability matrix, the steady-state distribution of the number of packets at an embedded point (π_k) may be solved for, after which the distribution of the number of packets chosen during a slot is given by

$$W_j = \begin{cases} \displaystyle\sum_{k=0}^{n-1}\sum_{i=j}^{n} P_j(i)\tau(i|k)\pi_k, & j > 0; \\ \tau(0|0)\pi_0, & j = 0. \end{cases} \tag{36}$$

Next, we determine packet and copy throughput per port T_p and T_c, respectively. They are defined as the average number of packets and copies transmitted per port per slot respectively, given by

$$T_p = \frac{1}{n}\sum_{j=1}^{n} jW_j \tag{37}$$

$$T_c = \frac{1}{n}\sum_{j=1}^{n} \overline{m}_j W_j$$
$$= \sum_{j=1}^{n}\left\{1 - (1-p)^j + \frac{\zeta[(1-p)-(1-p)^{j+1}]}{np}\right\}W_j \tag{38}$$

where we have substituted for $\overline{m}_j$ from (13).

Further, let μ_d denote the average number of copies in a chosen packet, then

$$\mu_d = \sum_{j=1}^{n} \frac{\overline{m}_j}{j}\frac{W_j}{1-W_0}. \tag{39}$$

Next, we determine the probability that an input is busy, ρ. Each input alternates between idle and service periods, together which will be referred to as a cycle. Let the mean idle, service and cycle periods be denoted by $\overline{i}, \overline{s}$ and $\overline{c}$, respectively. Since the number of slots to generate a new packet is geometrically distributed with parameter λ, then

$$\overline{i} = \frac{1-\lambda}{\lambda}. \tag{40}$$

Clearly, the mean cycle duration is given by $\overline{c} = 1/T_p$. Thus the mean service time is given by

$$\overline{s} = \overline{c} - \overline{i} = \frac{1}{T_p} - \frac{1-\lambda}{\lambda}. \tag{41}$$

Finally, the probability than an input is busy is given by the product of packet throughput and the mean service time

$$\rho = T_p\overline{s} = 1 - \frac{(1-\lambda)T_p}{\lambda}. \tag{42}$$

The above gives us a relation between input busy probability and packet throughput.

D. The Mixed Packet Copy Distribution and Its Effect on the Throughput

As explained above, the contending packets at the input will be a mix of new and old HOL packets left over from the previous slots. The average number of copies generated by the jth chosen packet was determined in (11) and it was shown that the overall average size of chosen packets is smaller than average of the contending packets in terms of number of copies generated. As a result of this, the packets left behind (old packets) will be larger packets and their secondary copy

$$\tau(i|m) = \Pr\left\{i \text{ packets contending in a slot}\,\middle|\,\begin{matrix}m \text{ old packets at the previous} \\ \text{embedded point}\end{matrix}\right\}$$
$$\tau(i|m) = \begin{cases} \nu(i-m|m) & i \geq m \\ 0 & i < m \end{cases} \tag{34}$$

generation probability to each output will be higher than the fresh HOL packets and assumed to be given by p_0 and p_f, respectively, where $p_f < p_0$. The corresponding PGF of the number of copies generated by these packets will be

$$b_f(z) = z^\zeta (p_f z + 1 - p_f)^{n-\zeta} \tag{43a}$$

$$b_0(z) = z^\zeta (p_0 z + 1 - p_0)^{n-\zeta}. \tag{43b}$$

It will be assumed that the PGF of the distribution of the number of copies generated by a mixed packet at the input will be given by

$$B(z) = z^\zeta (pz + 1 - p)^{n-\zeta} \tag{44}$$

where p is a function of both p_f and p_0. Clearly the meaning of p is same as before and the approximate copy distribution (44) is identical to that given in (1); therefore, all the previous results remain valid. However, now, p is an internal parameter and it is very desirable to plot the results against the external parameter, p_f. Thus we have to express p_f in terms of p, and this is possible from the following observation. At the steady state the average number of copies that a fresh packet generates must be equal to the average number of copies of a departing packet at the output since every arriving packet to the system will eventually depart. The former average is given by $\mu_f = \zeta + (n - \zeta)p_f$, and the latter by (39). Substituting for $\overline{m}_j$ from (13) and solving $\mu_f = \mu_d$ for p_f gives

$$p_f = \frac{1}{n-\zeta} \left\{ \sum_{j=1}^{n} \left\{ n[1 - (1-p)^j] \right. \right.$$
$$\left. \left. + \frac{\zeta[(1-p) - (1-p)^{j+1}]}{p} \right\} \frac{W_j}{j} - \zeta \right\}. \tag{45}$$

Finally, the results are obtained in terms of p_f as follows. First, we determine the steady-state distribution and the throughput as a function of the mixed packet copy generation probability p, from (37)–(38) and then express it as a function of p_f from the above equation.

V. MEAN PACKET DELAY AND BUFFER LOSS PROBABILITIES

As in the previous section we assume Bernoulli process for packet arrivals, however we drop the assumption that no input queuing is allowed. We first present the mean packet delay result assuming infinite input queues and then give an upperbound for packet loss probabilities for finite buffer sizes. A direct analysis of this system is not mathematically tractable, therefore we will make use of the results derived in the previous section.

Assuming that no queuing and infinite input queuing systems are operating under the same packet throughput, since the dynamics of the service discipline remains the same, then they will have the same mean service time. This observation has also been confirmed by simulation results. Thus the probability that an input is busy will be same for both systems when they have the same packet throughput (T_p). As a result, busy input probability of the infinite queuing system for any particular value of T_p is also given by (42). We note that while for the no queuing system packet arrival rate is greater than throughput

($\lambda > T_p$), for the infinite queuing system ($\lambda = T_p$). Thus we have related the packet arrival rate (λ), the probability that an input is busy (ρ) and the parameters of the copy generation (ζ, p_f) for the infinite queuing system. This is the multicast equivalent of the following relation derived in [10]

$$(2 - \rho)\lambda^2 - 2(1 + \rho)\lambda + 2\rho = 0 \tag{46}$$

for the unicast switching with $n = \infty$. However, the complexity of the multicast switching does not allow us to obtain such a simple expression.

Now we are ready to determine the mean packet delay. In the following, an input queue is modeled as independent of the other input queues and HOL contention is taken into account through the service time distribution. Further, we assume that a HOL packet being served is independent from slot to slot and has the probability q. Thus each input queue may be modeled as a single server discrete time queue with Bernoulli arrival process and geometrically distributed service times with parameters λ and q respectively. The corresponding queue length distribution has been derived in [10] for the unicast switching which also applies to the multicast switching model. The two differ only through the values assumed by q, probability that a HOL packet will be served during a slot. Thus from [10]

$$p_k = \Pr(k \text{ packets in the buffer})$$
$$= \frac{\lambda(2 - \lambda)}{2(1 - \lambda)}(1 - w_\lambda)w_\lambda^{k-1}, \qquad k > 0$$
$$p_0 = 1 - \rho, \quad \rho = \lambda/q, \quad w_\lambda = \frac{\lambda(1 - q)}{(1 - \lambda)q}. \tag{47}$$

From the above the average number of packets in the buffer ($\overline{k}$) may be determined, then the mean packet delay through the Little's result

$$\overline{d} = \frac{\overline{k}}{\lambda} = \frac{1 - \lambda}{q - \lambda}. \tag{48}$$

The unknown parameter q may be determined from $q = \lambda/\rho$. In the case of unicast switching ρ is related to λ through (46). In the case of multicast switching, for a given value of ρ, the corresponding input load $\lambda = T_p$ is determined from (37) and (45). Thus we may plot the mean delay as a function of λ from the above equation.

The packet loss probability for a finite buffer size of B is upperbounded by the corresponding probability of $(k > B)$ for the infinite buffer case [10]. Thus

$$\Pr(\text{packet loss}) < \Pr(k > B) = 1 - \Pr(k \le B)$$
$$\Pr(\text{packet loss}) < \frac{\lambda(2 - \lambda)}{2(1 - \lambda)}w_\lambda^B. \tag{49}$$

VI. THE ASYMPTOTIC DISTRIBUTION OF THE NUMBER OF PACKETS CHOSEN UNDER HEAVY TRAFFIC

The numerical difficulties of evaluating the distribution given in (32) for large values of n has led to a search for asymptotic results. The objective has been the derivation of the distribution of the number of packets chosen during a slot for large switches under saturation. In the following, we shall limit ourselves to pure Binomial copy generation process and derive the results in terms of the mixed packet copy generation probability, p. In each slot, the random packet selection policy performs a sequence of independent Bernoulli trials where the choice of a packet is considered to be a success. The main characterstic of these trials is that after each success, the success probability changes. The success probability after the jth success is given by P_j in (20). The limiting form of this probability for large switches is obtained by substituting for $p = \mu/n$ in (20) and letting $n \to \infty$

$$\hat{P}_j = \lim_{n \to \infty} \left\{ 1 - \frac{\mu}{n} \left[1 - \left(\left(1 - \frac{\mu}{n} \right)^n \right)^{j/n} \right] \right\}^n$$
$$= e^{-\mu(1 - e^{-\mu j/n_\infty})} \tag{50}$$

where n_∞ stands for a large n. Clearly the interarrival time of the successes in the number of trials will be independent with the geometric distribution each with a different parameter. The mean and variance of the jth interarrival time will be given by

$$\beta_j = \frac{1}{\hat{P}_j}, \quad \sigma_j^2 = \frac{1 - \hat{P}_j}{\hat{P}_j^2}. \tag{51}$$

The sequential random packet selection policy may be modeled as a discrete time renewal process with the renewal points taken as those trials that packets have been chosen successfully. The distribution of the number of packets chosen may also be derived using this approach, but this is not followed here [11]. The renewal process generated by the random policy falls into the category of independent, but not identically distributed renewal times. There has been a considerable amount of research to determine asymptotic results for this problem and next, such a result is given from [12, ch. 9] and [13].

Theorem 1: As the number of trials goes to infinity, the distribution of the number of packets chosen, W_j, approaches to a normal distribution with the mean $\beta_N = n/\beta$ and variance $\sigma_N^2 = \sigma^2 n/\beta^3$ where $\beta = \lim_{j \to \infty} 1/j \sum_{k=1}^{j} \beta_k, \sigma^2 = \lim_{j \to \infty} 1/j \sum_{k=1}^{j} \sigma_k^2$ and β_k, σ_k^2 are finite. Let

$$f_N(x) = \frac{1}{\sqrt{2\pi}\sigma_N} e^{-(1/2)((x - \beta_N)/\sigma_N)^2}. \tag{52}$$

Then W_j is given by

$$W_j = \int_{j-1/2}^{j+1/2} f_N(x) \, dx. \tag{53}$$

Then the packet throughput per port is given by $T_p = \beta_{N/n}$ and the copy throughput per port by (40) with $\zeta = 0$

$$T_c = \lim_{n \to \infty} \left[1 - \sum_{j=1}^{n} (1-p)^j W_j \right]$$
$$= \lim_{n \to \infty} \left\{ 1 - \sum_{j=1}^{n} \left[\left(1 - \frac{\mu}{n} \right)^n \right]^{j/n} W_j \right\} \tag{54}$$

which may be shown to be given by

$$T_c = 1 - e^{-\mu/\beta} e^{\mu^2 \sigma^2/2n\beta^2}. \tag{55}$$

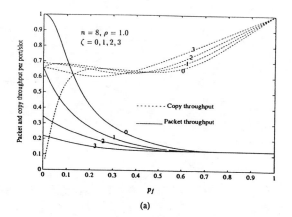

(a)

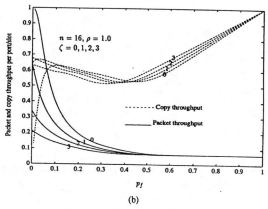

(b)

Fig. 2. The steady-state packet and copy throughputs per port/slot as a function of the fresh packet copy generation probability for the load $\rho = 1.0$, different no. of primary copies ζ, and the switch sizes of $n = 8, 16$.

The corresponding results, as a function of the average number of copies in a fresh packet, $\mu_f = np_f$, are determined by using (45) and (53).

VII. NUMERICAL RESULTS

This section presents numerical examples as well as simulation results which justify the approximations in the paper. Figure 2 presents the steady-state packet and copy throughput per port against fresh packet copy generation probability, p_f. We assume that the system is under saturation ($\rho = 1$) for which no queuing and infinite input queuing systems are equivalent since they achieve the same throughput. The results are given for a different number of primary copies, $\zeta = 0, 1, 2$, and 3, and for switch sizes of $n = 8, 16$. $\zeta = 0$ corresponds to the pure Binomial copy distribution. As may be seen packet throughput (T_p) drops monotonically as secondary copy generation probability (p_f) increases due to increasing interference among the packets. In the limit, T_p approaches to $1/n$ which corresponds to the choice of a single packet. On the other hand, following its initial value, T_c rises to a maximum due to larger packet sizes as p_f increases. After the maximum, T_c drops slightly and then increases linearly and in the limit single packet is chosen which generates copies to most of the outputs. The maximum value of T_c, will be a good operating

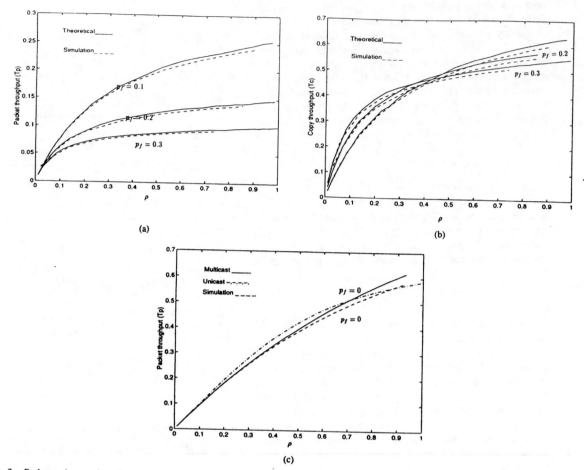

Fig. 3. Packet and copy throughput versus probability of busy input with single primary copy ($\zeta = 1$) and secondary copy generation probability (p_f) as a parameter.

point of the system since both the packet and copy throughput are relatively high.

Next we assume a system with single primary copy ($\zeta = 1$), secondary copy generation probability (p_f) as a parameter and a switch size of $n = 16$. We present both theoretical and simulation results. Figure 3 shows the packet and copy throughput against probability of busy input for this system. Fig. 3(a) and (b) plot the results for $p_f = 0.1$, 0.2, and 0.3, while Fig. 3(c) for $p_f = 0$. The latter figure also includes the unicast result corresponding to $n = \infty$ from (46). Under light and moderate traffic result of this paper is closer to simulation than the unicast results. Figure 4 shows the average packet delay as a function of packet arrival rate (λ). The corresponding simulation results show good agreement with the theoretical results. Table II gives the 99% confidence interval of the mean delay for simulation results. As may be seen the maximum error is quite low—less than 10%. Finally Fig. 5 presents the upperbound for packet loss probabilities for the same system with buffer size as a parameter. We note that the loss probability is negligible for buffer sizes larger than $B = 20$.

Figure 6 gives asymptotic packet and copy throughput as a function of the average number of copies generated by a fresh

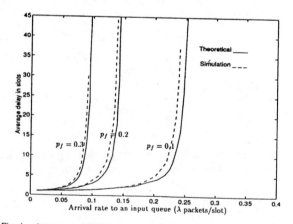

Fig. 4. Average packet delay versus arrival rate of the packets to an input queue (λ) with single primary copy and secondary copy generation probability (p_f) as a parameter.

packet for a switch size of $n = 1024$ and under saturation. As may be seen, simulation results show very good agreement with the theoretical results. Further, it was found that the copy throughput remains same for switch sizes in hundreds and more.

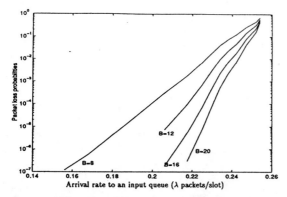

Fig. 5. Buffer overflow probability versus arrival rate of the packets to an input queue (λ) with buffer size (B) as a parameter (single primary copy, $\zeta = 1$, and secondary copy generation probability $p_f = 0.1$).

TABLE II
THE 99% CONFIDENCE INTERVAL OF MEAN DELAY FOR SIMULATION RESULTS WITH SINGLE PRIMARY COPY ($\zeta = 1$) SECONDARY COPY GENERATION PROBABILITY (p_f) AND PACKET ARRIVAL RATE (λ PACKETS/SLOT) AS PARAMETERS AND A SWITCH SIZE OF $n = 16$

λ	$p_f = 0.1$	$p_f = 0.2$	$p_f = 0.3$
0.025	1.07 ± 0.006	1.15 ± 0.007	1.25 ± 0.017
0.050	1.17 ± 0.008	1.44 ± 0.020	1.90 ± 0.069
0.075	1.29 ± 0.015	2.01 ± 0.046	4.94 ± 0.367
0.100	1.50 ± 0.018	3.56 ± 0.141	
0.125	1.76 ± 0.025	9.51 ± 0.845	
0.150	2.22 ± 0.068		
0.175	3.07 ± 0.081		
0.200	4.78 ± 0.252		
0.225	11.28 ± 1.234		

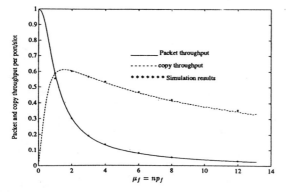

Fig. 6. Asymptotic packet and copy throughput per port/slot against the average number of copies generated by a fresh packet and simulation results for the switch size of $n = 1024$.

Finally, Fig. 7 gives simulation results for the packet and copy throughput both for multicast traffic only, as well as for mixed (40% multicast plus 60% unicast) traffic as a function of the packet fanout and under saturation load ($\rho = 1.0$). Simulations are done by giving priority to the multicast over unicast packets in the selection process. Thus, intitially, only the multicast packets contend for selection during a slot. When no non-interfering multicast packets are left, then the unicast

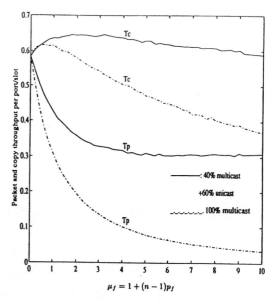

Fig. 7. Asymptotic packet and copy throughputs per port/slot against the average no. of copies generated by a fresh packet for the load $\rho = 1$, single primary copy, $\zeta = 1$, switch size of $n = 256$ and a mix of (multicast + unicast) traffic.

packets contend for the remaining unselected outputs. As may be seen the mixed traffic shows higher throughput than the multicast traffic only, and the copy throughput of mixed traffic approaches asymptotically that of the unicast traffic (0.586).

VIII. CONCLUSIONS

We have determined the performance of random packet selection policy under the assumption that all copies of a packet has to be transmitted during the same slot, no fan out splitting. We have derived a relation between the input load, traffic intensity and the copy generation parameters which is the multicast equivalent of a similar result for the unicast switching. It has been shown that the old packets have a larger number of copies than the new HOL packets. We determined the delay-throughput characteristic of the switch that takes this effect into account. While the packet throughput decreases monotonically as the number of copies generated by a packet increases, the copy throughput exhibits a maximum which will be a convenient operating point for the system. The simulation results show that the switch will have higher throughput in the presence of mix traffic, multicast plus unicast traffic, as will be the case in a practical system.

The throughput of this policy is somewhat lower than the policy that allows the transmission of the copies of a packet to spread over several slots. Since the load presented to the switch will be multiple of the input load as a result of the copy generation, the higher throughput of this policy will be inadequate to overcome this problem. We will need solutions such as switches with more outputs than the inputs, and higher internal speed than the input lines. The simplicity of the implementation makes the random packet selection policy with no fan out splitting an attractive solution for the multicast switching despite of its lower throughput.

ACKNOWLEDGMENT

The authors would like to thank J. Fang for performing the initial simulations.

REFERENCES

[1] J. S. Turner, "Design of a broadcast packet switching network," in *Proc. IEEE INFOCOM '86*, 1986, pp. 667–675.

[2] T. T. Lee, R. Boorstyn, and E. Arthurs, "The architecture of a multicast broadband packet switch," in *Proc. IEEE INFOCOM '88*, New Orleans, LA, 1988, pp. 1–8.

[3] T. T. Lee, "Non-blocking copy networks for multicast packet switching," *IEEE J. Select. Areas Commun.*, vol. 6, pp. 1455–1467, Dec. 1988.

[4] J. F. Hayes, R. Breault, and M. K. Mehmet-Ali, "Performance analysis of a multicast switch," *IEEE Trans. Commun.*, vol. 39, no. 4, pp. 581–587.

[5] J. Y. Hui and T. Renner, "Queueing analysis for multicast packet switching," *IEEE Trans. Commun.*, vol. 42, no. 2/3/4, pp. 723–731.

[6] X. Chen, J. F. Hayes, and M. Mehmet-Ali, "Performance comparison of two input access methods for multicast switching," *IEEE Trans. Commun.*, vol. 42, no. 5, pp. 2174–2178, May 1994.

[7] X. Chen, I. Lambadaris, and J. F. Hayes, "A general unified model for performance analyses of multicast switching," in *Proc. GLOBECOM '92*, Orlando, FL, Dec. 1992, pp. 1498–1502.

[8] W. Feller, *An Introduction to Probability Theory and Its Applications*. New York: Wiley, 1971.

[9] L. Kleinrock, *Queueing Systems Volume 1: Theory*. New York: Wiley, 1975.

[10] J. Y. Hui and E. Arthurs, "A broadband packet switch for integrated transport," *IEEE J. Select. Areas Commun.*, vol. SAC-5, pp. 1264–1273, Oct. 1987.

[11] M. Mehmet-Ali and S. Yang, "The performance analysis of a multicast switch with random selection policy," in *Proc. 17th Biennial Symposium on Communications*, Kingston, Ont., 1994, pp. 331–334.

[12] D. R. Cox, *Renewal Theory*. London, U.K.: Methuen, 1962.

[13] Y. S. Chow and H. E. Robbins, "A renewal theorem for random variables which are dependent or non-identically distributed," *Ann. Math. Statist.*, vol. 34, pp. 390–401, 1963.

Mustafa K. Mehmet Ali received the B.Sc. and M.Sc. degrees from Bogazichi University, Istanbul, Turkey, in 1977 and 1979, respectively, and the Ph.D. degree from Carleton University, Ottawa, Ontario, Canada, in 1983, all in electrical engineering.

He worked as a Research Engineer at TELESAT Canada until the end of 1984. Since then he has been at the Department of Electrical and Computer Engineering at Concordia University, Montreal, Canada, where at present he is an Associate Professor. His current research interest is performance analysis of the broadband networks.

Shaying Yang received the Master of Engineering degree from NorthWest Telecommunication Engineering Institute, P.R.O.C., in 1986, and the Master of Applied Science degree in electrical and computer engineering from Concordia University, Canada, in 1994.

After teaching in Beijing Information Technology Institute, China for several years, she moved to Canada and studied at Concordia University. She is a software engineer presently with Bell Northern Research, Ontario. Her field of interest includes communication protocols and object-oriented system design.

ELSEVIER

Performance Evaluation 21 (1994) 111–129

PERFORMANCE
EVALUATION
An International
Journal

Approximate analysis of a shared-medium ATM switch under bursty arrivals and nonuniform destinations

Atef O. Zaghloul [a], Harry G. Perros [b]

[a] IBM Corporation, Department C15, Research Triangle Park, NC, 27709, USA
[b] Department of Computer Science, and Center for Communications and Signal Processing,
North Carolina State University, Raleigh, NC 27695-8206, USA

Abstract

In this paper, we present an approximate analysis of a generic shared-medium ATM switch with input and output queueing. Input traffic is assumed to be bursty and is modelled by an Interrupted Bernoulli Process (IBP). Three different bus service policies are analyzed: Time Division Multiplexing (TDM), Cyclic, and Random. The output links may have constant or geometric service time. The analysis is based on the notion of decomposition whereby the switch is decomposed into smaller sub-systems. First, each input queue is analyzed in isolation after we modify its service process. Subsequently, the shared medium is analyzed as a separate sub-system utilizing the output process of each input queue. Finally, each output queue is analyzed in isolation. The results from the individual sub-systems are combined together through an iterative scheme. This method permits realistic system characteristics such as limited buffer size, asymmetric load conditions, and nonuniform destinations to be taken into consideration in the analysis. The model's accuracy is verified through simulation.

1. Introduction

The Asynchronous Transfer Mode (ATM) is the adopted transfer mode solution for broadband ISDN. ATM must be capable of efficiently multiplexing a large number of highly bursty sources, such as voice, video, and large file transfer. As a result, there is an increasing interest in the performance analysis of ATM based networks and in particular in ATM switches. There are several ATM switch architectures that have been proposed recently in the literature (see for instance [1], and [15]). ATM switch architectures can be classified into three classes: *shared-memory*, *shared-medium*, and *space-division*. Tobagi [13] gives a detailed review of the different switch architectures and their implementation issues. In this study, we are interested in the analysis of the shared-medium architecture. In a shared-medium switch, all packets arriving on the input links are routed to the output links over a common high-speed medium such as a parallel bus. Each of the output links is capable of receiving all packets transmitted on the bus. The PARIS system described by Cidon et al. [1] and the ATOM switch

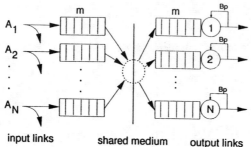

Fig. 1. Queueing model of a shared-medium switch.

proposed by Suzuki et al. [11] are two examples of such a switch architecture. One of the main advantages of the shared-medium architecture is the simplicity with which the multicast function is achieved since a transmitted packet over the shared-medium can be received by all output links simultaneously. Thus, the need to send multiple copies is eliminated. Also, priority among input links can be easily implemented within the bus arbitration policy. A shared-medium packet switch can provide packet queueing at the input links, the output links, or both the input and the output links (see [6] and [9]).

A queueing model of a generic shared-medium packet switch with input and output queueing is shown in Fig. 1. The input queues are attached to the shared bus and contend for access when they have one or more packets to transmit. The order in which input queues are served is determined by the bus service policy. In order to model such a system accurately, it is essential to take into consideration system characteristics such as finite buffer capacities, bursty input traffic, nonsymmetric load conditions, and nonuniform destinations. Cells arriving to a full input queue will be lost. Furthermore, if one of the output queues is full, the flow of customers destined to it may be momentarily stopped. This situation is commonly referred to as blocking. Because of the finite buffer capacities and blocking, closed-form solutions are difficult to obtain. As a result, such queueing networks are typically analyzed approximately using the notion of decomposition.

In this paper, we analyze the shared-medium switch shown in Fig. 1 under three bus service policies: Time division multiplexing (TDM), Cyclic, and Random selection. The switch is analyzed approximately using the notion of decomposition. First, each input queue is analyzed in isolation after we modify its service process. Next, we analyze the shared bus as a separate sub-system utilizing the departure process from each input queue. Finally, we analyze each output queue in isolation. Each sub-system is analyzed numerically as a Markov chain. The results from individual sub-systems are combined together through the means of an iterative algorithm. The accuracy of the approximation algorithm is verified via simulation.

The shared-medium switch, under cyclic and random selection bus service policies, can be viewed as a finite capacity discrete-time polling system with blocking. The literature contains hundreds of papers on the subject of polling systems (see [12]). However, most of the studies reported were for one-message buffer systems or infinite buffer systems. Very few papers have dealt with finite buffer polling systems in discrete-time or in continuous-time. Jou, Nillson, and Lai [5] analyzed a discrete-time polling system with finite buffer capacity under bursty arrival process. Their approach gives an upper bound for the cell loss probability. Tran-Gia [14] gives an approximate algorithm for polling systems with finite capacity and non-exhaustive service. The analysis is based on the technique of the imbedded Markov chain and the evaluation of discrete convolution operations taking advantage of fast convolution algorithms, e.g., the Fast Fourier Transform. Ibe and Trivedi [4] considered finite-population and finite-capacity polling systems. Generalized stochastic Petri nets are used to describe the system. The major drawback of this method is the large state space of the system. Ganz and Chlamtac [2] presented an approximate solution to slotted communication systems in continuous time with finite population and finite buffer capacity. Similarly, very little has been reported in the literature on discrete-time queueing networks with blocking. Gershwin [3] analyzed a discrete-time queueing network with blocking that represents a synchronized production assembly system. It is often referred to as the transfer line model. The transfer line model has been analyzed by decomposing the network to sub-systems each consisting of two successive servers and the buffer in-between. Recently, Morris and Perros [7] developed an approximation algorithm for the analysis of a buffered Banyan ATM switch. The switch is analyzed by decomposing it into the individual switching elements. Further references for the analysis of multi-stage interconnection networks can be found in [7]. A sub-system of this switch was analyzed approximately in [16]. See [10] for a comprehensive review of queueing networks with blocking.

The paper is organized as follows. In Section 2, a description of the system under study is presented. Section 3 covers the analysis of the three sub-systems. Numerical results are presented and compared against simulation results in Section 4. Finally, conclusions are given in Section 5.

2. The queueing model under study

In this paper, we consider a single-stage $N \times N$ shared-medium switch with queue size (input and output) equal to m as shown in Fig. 1. Cells may be queued before switching at the inputs, if the output queue is full, as well as after switching at the outputs. A cell at the top of input queue i is destined for output queue j with probability d_{ij}, where $\sum_{j=1}^{N} d_{ij} = 1$, $i = 1, 2, \ldots, N$. Each input queue containing one or more packets arbitrates for the bus by activating the *bus-request* signal. A bus arbiter is used to select the input queue to be served next according to the bus service policy. Once an input queue has been granted the bus, only one cell is forwarded to its destination output buffer. If the output buffer is full, then the cell will be blocked. The blocked cell remain at the top of its input queue until the queue is granted the bus again. At that time, the cell will be forwarded to output queue j with probability d_{ij}.

The bus bandwidth is N times the speed of a single input link, where N is the number of input links. The arrival process to each input queue is slotted, with a slot size equal to the transmission time of an ATM cell. The bus is also slotted, with a slot size equal to $1/N$ of the transmission time of an ATM cell. For instance, if $N = 6$, then there are 6 bus slots within the boundary of each arrival slot as shown in Fig. 2. Three different bus service policies are considered in this paper: Time Division Multiplexing (TDM), cyclic order, and random selection. These service policies are described in detail in Section 3.1. We assume zero

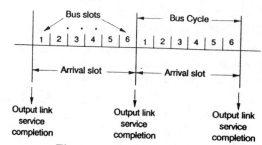

Fig. 2. Bus slots and arrival slots.

switch-over time which means that when the bus completes serving the current queue, it switches instantaneously and starts serving the next queue. This is normally accomplished by separating the control signals, which are used for bus arbitration, and data signals, which are used for data transmission. This scheme permits arbitration for the bus to be performed in parallel to data transmission; thus, justifying the zero switch-over assumption. Finally, the service time of each output link consists of n arrival slots, where n is geometrically distributed with parameter B_p. The servers of the N output links are synchronized. That is, they all begin and end a slot at the same time.

The arrival process to each of the input queues is assumed to be bursty and it is modelled by an Interrupted Bernoulli Process (IBP). That is, the incoming link into an input queue is slotted. Each slot is long enough to contain one cell. An arriving slot may or may not contain a cell. In an IBP, we have a geometrically distributed period during which no arrivals occur (idle state), followed by a geometrically distributed period during which arrivals occur in a Bernoulli fashion (active state). Given that the process is in the active state at slot t, it will remain in the active state during the next slot $t + 1$ with probability p, or it will change to the idle state with probability $1 - p$. If the process is in the idle state at slot t, it will remain in the idle state during the next slot $t + 1$ with probability q, or it will change to the active state with probability $1 - q$. During the active state, a slot contains a cell with probability α. The quantity α is also known as the peak bandwidth, i.e., the rate of arrivals during the active period. In [8], the average arrival rate, i.e., the probability that any slot contains a cell, is calculated as

$$\rho = \frac{\alpha(1-q)}{2-p-q},$$

and the squared coefficient of variation, C^2, of the time between successive arrivals is

$$C^2 = 1 + \alpha \left[\frac{(1-p)(p+q)}{(2-p-q)^2} - 1 \right].$$

Because of the finite buffer space at the input links, a cell arriving to a full input queue is lost. However, once a cell has been received, it will not be lost within the switch. In this paper, we assume that α is equal to 1 for each arrival process.

3. The analysis

The shared-medium switch described in the previous section is analyzed approximately by decomposing it into smaller sub-systems. First, each input queue is analyzed separately after we revise its service process. This revised service process which we will call the *effective service time* consists of three components. The possible delay due to bus contention, the actual bus transmission time (one bus slot), and the blocking delay due to a full destination queue. Having analyzed each input queue, we proceed to analyze a sub-system that represents the bus. The arrival process to this bus sub-system from each input queue i is obtained from the departure process of input queue i. Finally, each output queue is analyzed in isolation. The attempted departure process out of the bus sub-system serves as the input process for the output queues.

Each sub-system is analyzed numerically as a Markov chain. However, in order to analyze each sub-system, information is needed from the other sub-systems. This information is updated through an iterative scheme. The algorithm iterates until convergence. Sections 3.1 and 3.2 describe the analysis of the input queues and the bus respectively. The analysis of the output queues is presented in Section 3.3. Finally, a summary of the algorithm is given in Section 3.4.

3.1. Analysis of the input queues

As stated earlier, each input queue is analyzed in isolation after we revise its service process. This revised service process is described in Sections 3.1.1, 3.1.2, and 3.1.3 for TDM, Cyclic, and Random selection policies respectively. In Section 3.1.4 we derive the cell loss probabilities for the input links.

3.1.1. TDM

Time Division Multiplexing (TDM) is the simplest bus allocation scheme. In TDM each bus slot i is preassigned to input queue i. Each input queue is only allowed to transmit during the bus slot assigned to it. If input queue i is empty, but slot i is wasted since other busy input queues are not allowed to use it. The slot assignments follow a predetermined pattern that repeats itself periodically as shown in Fig. 2. Each such period is called a bus cycle. Once, a cell reaches the head of an input queue, it waits for its slot number and then it is forwarded to the output buffer, if the output buffer is not full. If the output buffer is full, then the cell will be blocked and will wait for its slot number in the next bus cycle. We note that this blocking mechanism is different from the first-blocked-first-unblocked mechanism that has been typically used in continuous-time queueing networks with blocking. The blocking probability Pb_i for input queue i is calculated from the steady-state probabilities of the output queues in Section 3.3.

The state of an input queue is fully described by the state vector $X = \{x_0, x_1, x_2\}$ where x_0 takes the following values: 0 if the input process is in the idle state, 1 if the input process is in the active state. Variable x_1 represents the number of cells in the queue, and it takes the values $0, 1, 2, 3, \ldots, m$, where m is the maximum queue capacity. Variable x_2 represents the present bus slot number and it takes the values: $1, 2, 3, \ldots, N$. The stationary probability vector π of the input queues is obtained by solving the system of linear equations $\pi A = \pi$, where A is the

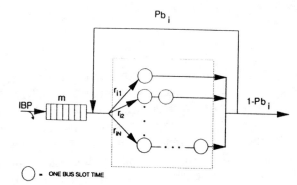

Fig. 3. Effective service time of an input queue (Cyclic case).

transition probability matrix. In this paper, π was obtained for all three bus service policies using the Gauss–Seidel method.

3.1.2. Cyclic service

In this policy, the busy input queues are served in a cyclic fashion. The service policy in limited, i.e. only one cell is transmitted from the input queue being served before the server (the bus) switches to the next input queue. Once the present input queue has been served, the server proceeds in cyclic order until it finds an input queue which is non-empty. We assume zero switch-over time. Due to this cyclic policy, once a cell has reached the front of an input queue, it may be blocked for $0, 1, 2, \ldots, N-1$ bus slots before it is granted the bus. This leads to representing the effective service time of each of the input queues by the phase-type structure shown in Fig. 3. The upper path in Fig. 3 represents the event that a cell at the top of input queue i will be transmitted immediately across the bus without delay. In this event, the effective bus service time is equal to one bus cycle. The probability of this event is denoted by r_{i1} for input queue i. The other paths in the figure represent the events that the cell at the top of input queue i finds one or more busy input queues already waiting for the bus. In this case, the cell from input queue i will have to wait for its turn in the polling cycle. This waiting time varies from 1 bus slot to $N-1$ bus slots. For example, the second path in the figure represents the event where the effective bus service time is equal to 2 bus slots. During the first slot the cell is blocked at its respective input queue. During the second slot the cell is transmitted across the bus. The probabilities, $r_{i1}, r_{i2}, \ldots, r_{iN}$ are derived from the bus sub-system discussed in the Section 3.2. If the destination output buffer is full, then the cell will be blocked and consequently, one bus slot will be wasted. The blocked cell remains at the top of input queue i until the queue is granted the bus again. At that time, the cell will attempt to enter a destination queue j with probability d_{ij}.

The state of an input queue is fully described by the state vector $X = \{x_0, x_1, x_2, x_3\}$ where x_0 takes the following values: 0 if the input process is in the idle state, 1 if the input process is in the active state. Variable x_1 represents the number of cells in the node, and it takes the values $0, 1, 2, 3, \ldots, m$, where m is the maximum queue capacity. Variable x_2 represents the current bus slot number $(1, 2, \ldots, N)$ which is used as a counter to keep track of the arrival slot boundaries. Variable x_3 represents the number of remaining service bus slots $(1, 2, \ldots, N)$.

3.1.3. Random selection

In this service policy the bus arbiter will select one input queue among the busy ones randomly. All busy input queues have equal probability of being selected. For instance, if there are N busy input queues at selection time, each busy input queue is selected with probability $1/N$. On the other hand, if there is only busy input queue, it will be selected with probability 1. This policy could easily be modified to give one or more input queues a higher probability of being selected. Because we have random selection, when a cell reaches the front of input queue i, it may be selected (i.e. granted the bus) with probability c_i. This selection probability c_i, obviously, is a function of the number of busy input queues at selection time. The probabilities, $c_1, c_2, \ldots, c_N$ are derived from the bus sub-system discussed in the Section 3.2. If the output buffer is full, then the cell will be blocked. The blocked cell remains at the top of its input queue until the queue is granted the bus again. As a result, one bus slot is wasted.

The state of an input queue is fully described by the state vector $X = \{x_0, x_1, x_2, x_3\}$ where x_0 takes the following values: 0 if the input process is in the idle state, 1 if the input process is in the active state. Variable x_1 represents the number of cells in the node, and it takes the values 0, 1, 2, 3,..., m, where m is the maximum queue capacity. Variable x_2 represents the current bus slot number (1, 2,..., N). Variable x_3 indicates whether the input queue is in service (granted the bus) or not and takes the values: 0 if the queue is not in service, 1 if the queue is in service.

3.1.4. The cell loss probability

Because of the finite buffer space at the input links, arriving cells to a full input queue will be lost. This loss probability P_L is calculated from the input queue stationary probability vector as follows. Let G be the set of states of the input queue in which the arrival process is in the idle state, H be the set of states of the input queue in which the arrival process is in the active state, F_I be the set of the states of the input queue in which the queue is full and the arrival process is in the idle state, and F_A be the set of the states of the input queue in which the queue is full and the arrival process is in the active state. Then, we have

$$P_L = \frac{\sum_{X \in F_I} P(X)(1-q) + \sum_{X \in F_A} P(X)p}{\sum_{X \in G} P(X)(1-q) + \sum_{X \in H} P(X)p}$$

where $P(X)$ is the steady-state probability that the input queue is in state X.

3.2. Analysis of the bus

The bus is analyzed as a separate sub-system. This sub-system is modeled as a single server, representing the bus, with a hypothetical queue that contains one customer from each busy input queue. Customers present in this hypothetical queue are served according to the bus service policy, i.e. TDM, Cyclic, or Random. After a cell from input queue i receives service equal to one bus slot, another cell from input queue i may join the hypothetical queue with probability p_i. On the other hand, a cell from input queue i which is not in the system during the present bus slot may arrive to the hypothetical queue with probability $1 - q_i$. The values for

p_i and q_i for each of the input queues are obtained from the steady-state probability vector of the input queues as follows.

The states of input queue i are divided into three groups. Those states from which it is possible to have a departure will be called *departure states*. Those states from which it is not possible to have a departure because of an empty queue will be called *idle states*. The third group consists of all the states in which the input queue has at least one customer; however, a departure is not possible. These states are called *wait states*. The probability p_i can then be obtained as the probability that input queue i will be in a departure state or a wait state in the next slot, given that it is currently in a departure state. The probability q_i can be obtained as the probability that input queue i will be in one of the idle states in the next slot, given that it is currently in one of the idle states. Let $P(X)$ be the steady-state probability that the input queue is in state X, and let $t(X \to X')$ be the transition probability from state X to state X'. Then, we have

$$p_i = \frac{\sum\limits_{X \in D} \left(P(X) \left[\sum\limits_{X' \in D,W} t(X \to X') \right] \right)}{\sum\limits_{X \in D} P(X)} \quad \text{and} \quad q_i = \frac{\sum\limits_{X \in I} \left(P(X) \left[\sum\limits_{X' \in I} t(X \to X') \right] \right)}{\sum\limits_{X \in I} P(X)}$$

where D denotes the set of departure states, I denotes the set of idle states, and W denotes the set of wait states. Since the departure process is approximated by an IBP with $\alpha_i = 1$, this simplifies the task of selecting the appropriate departure, idle, and wait states as shown below.
(1) TDM: Departure states: $x_1 > 0$ and x_2 (bus slot number) equal to the input queue number. Wait states: $x_1 > 0$ and $x_2 \neq$ input queue number. Idle states: $x_0 = x_1 = 0$.
(2) Cyclic: Departure states: $x_1 > 0$ and $x_3 = 1$. Wait states: $x_1 > 0$ and $x_3 > 1$. Idle states: $x_0 = x_1 = 0$.
(3) Random: Departure states: $x_1 > 0$ and $x_3 = 1$. Wait states: $x_1 > 0$ and $x_3 = 0$. Idle states: $x_0 = x_1 = 0$.
For Cyclic and Random policies, the state of the bus sub-system is described by the state vector $(W; S)$, where W denotes the input queues which have requested to use the bus. These are the queues that contain one or more cells waiting to be transmitted. The variable S represents the input queue number that is presently being served. For a system with 3 input queues numbered 1, 2, 3, W takes on the values (0), (1), (2), (3), $(1, 2)$, $(1, 3)$, $(2, 3)$, and S takes on the values 1, 2, and 3. For the TDM case, the state of the bus is described by the state vector $(W; B, S)$ where W denotes the input queues that have requested the bus, B denotes the current bus slot number ($B = 1, 2, \ldots, N$), and S denotes the state of the server (i.e. the bus), idle or busy. The bus sub-system is analyzed as a Markov chain using the Gauss–Seidel method.

Next, we derive the *effective bus service time* distribution for each input queue. The effective bus service time consists of the possible delay due to bus contention plus the actual bus transmission time (one bus slot). Note that the effective service time, mentioned earlier in the paper, consists of the effective bus service time plus the blocking delay due to a full destination queue. In the TDM case, the time it takes for an input queue to be granted the bus is deterministic since it is independent of the state of the other input queues. This is because, every input queue is served for exactly one bus slot in every bus cycle. In Cyclic and Random bus service policies, however, the time it takes for an input queue to be granted the bus is dependent upon the state of the other input queues. The input queue effective bus service time for the cyclic and random bus allocation policies are derived in the next two sections.

3.2.1. Effective bus service time — cyclic case

For the cyclic bus service policy, the effective bus service time is calculated by marking an arriving cell and following it until it departs. The distribution of the time that a cell spends in the system is viewed as the first passage time distribution between pairs of states (j, k) where j belongs to those states from which an arrival is permitted, and k belongs to those states where the cell is in service. The distribution of the first passage time between arbitrary pairs of states j and k is defined by

$$f_{jk}^{(n)} = P(Y_n = k, Y_{n-1} \neq k, \ldots, Y_1 \neq k \mid Y_0 = j), \quad n = 1, 2, \ldots \tag{1}$$

where Y_n is the state of the system at transition n. The effective bus service time distribution for each input queue is calculated from the steady-state probabilities as follows. First, we aggregate the bus states into three groups as they pertain to each of the input queues.
- S_i = set of states in which a cell from input queue i is in service,
- Q_i = set of states in which a cell from input queue i is requesting service, i.e. the cell is waiting in the bus queue,
- R_i = set of states in which a cell from input queue i is not in the system.

The probability that the effective bus service time for a cell from input queue i is n bus slots is equal to the first passage time $f_{jk}^{(n)}$ where j is the *arrival state* and k is the *service state*. In our model, the arrival states for input queue i are those states from which an arrival is possible, i.e. the union of the set of states S_i and R_i. The service states for input queue i are those states in which a cell from input queue i is in service, i.e. the set of states S_i. Note that all intermediate states between the arrival states and the service states, belong to the set Q_i.

The probability $f_i^{(n)}$ that the effective bus service time for input queue i is n bus slots is calculated from Eq. (1) by considering all arrival states and all service states for input queue i. Let $P(Y)$ be the steady-state probability that the bus is in state Y, and $\lambda_i(Y)$ be the probability that in the next slot there will be an arrival from input queue i given that the bus is in state Y. Furthermore, let $t(Y \to Y')$ be the transition probability from state Y to state Y' and $t^n(Y \to Y')$ be the nth power of the transition probability from state Y to state Y'. Then, the probability $f_i^{(n)}$ that the effective bus service time for input queue i is n bus slots is

$$f_i^{(1)} = \frac{\sum\limits_{Y \in S_i, R_i} \left(P(Y) \left[\sum\limits_{Y' \in S_i} t(Y \to Y') \right] \right)}{\sum\limits_{Y \in S_i, R_i} P(Y)\lambda_i(Y)},$$

$$f_i^{(2)} = \frac{\sum\limits_{Y \in S_i, R_i} \left(P(Y) \left[\sum\limits_{Y' \in Q_i} t(Y \to Y') \sum\limits_{Y'' \in S_i} t(Y' \to Y'') \right] \right)}{\sum\limits_{Y \in S_i, R_i} P(Y)\lambda_i(Y)},$$

and for $n > 2$,

$$f_i^{(n)} = \frac{\sum_{Y \in S_i, N_i} \left(P(Y) \left[\sum_{Y' \in Q_i} t(Y \to Y') \sum_{Y' \in Q_i} t^{n-2}(Y' \to Y') \sum_{Y'' \in S_i} t(Y' \to Y'') \right] \right)}{\sum_{Y \in S_i, R_i} P(Y) \lambda_i(Y)}$$

Note that $\lambda_i(Y) = p_i$ when $Y \in S_i$, and $\lambda_i(Y) = 1 - q_i$ when $Y \in R_i$. The transition probabilities $t(Y \to Y')$ are obtained readily from the bus transition matrix since the bus states are aggregated into three groups for each input queue as it was explained earlier. Finally, the above first passage probabilities $f_i^{(1)}, f_i^{(2)}, \ldots, f_i^{(n)}$ are substituted for the branching probabilities $r_{i1}, r_{i2}, \ldots, r_{in}$ shown in Fig. 3.

3.2.2. Effective bus service time — random selection case

In random selection bus service policy, the service time of input queue i is geometrically distributed with probability c_i. This is the probability that input queue i will be selected (granted the bus) during the next bus slot given that input queue i is busy. Note that the probability of being selected is dependent upon how many other input queues are arbitrating for the bus. Furthermore, the probability of selection is equally distributed among the busy queues.

The probability that input queue i will be selected to be served during the next bus slot can be directly obtained from the steady-state probabilities of the bus sub-system. Let $P(Y)$ be the steady-state probability that the bus is in state Y, and $\lambda_i(Y)$ be the probability that in the next slot there will be an arrival from input queue i given that the bus is in state Y. Let $t(Y \to Y')$ be the transition probability from state Y to state Y'. Then, the probability of selecting input queue i is

$$c_i = \frac{\sum_Y \left(P(Y) \left[\sum_{Y' \in S_i} t(Y \to Y') \right] \right)}{\sum_Y P(Y) \lambda_i(Y)}$$

where $\lambda_i(Y) = p_i$ when $Y \in S_i$, $\lambda_i(Y) = 1$ when $Y \in Q_i$, and $\lambda_i(Y) = 1 - q_i$ when $Y \in N_i$.

3.2.3. The bus attempted departure process

Next, we characterize the attempted departure process from the system bus. We use the attempted departure process rather than the actual departure process. The actual departure process is associated with departure instances where a cell leaves the input queue. The attempted departure process is associated with all instances of service completion independent of whether the cell leaves or gets blocked and is forced to receive another service. The aggregate attempted departure process from the bus is split into N different IBP processes which serve as the offered arrival processes to the output queues. The aggregate attempted departure process is approximated by an IBP with parameters p_d, q_d, and α_d. We set $\alpha_d = 1$. The values for p_d and q_d are obtained using the same method as the case of p_i and q_i obtained in Section 3.2. The states of the bus are divided into two groups; those states from which it is possible to have an attempted departure (active states), and those states from which it is not possible to have an attempted departure (idle states). The probability p_d can then be obtained as the probability that the bus will be in one of the active states in the next slot, given that it is currently in an active state. Similarly, the probability q_d can be obtained as the probability that the bus will be in one of the idle states in the next slot, given that it is currently in one of the idle states. Let $P(Y)$ be the steady-state probability that the bus is in state Y, and $t(Y \to Y')$ be the transition probability of state Y to state Y'. Then, we have

$$p_d = \frac{\sum\limits_{Y \in A} \left(P(Y) \left[\sum\limits_{Y' \in A} t(Y \to Y') \right] \right)}{\sum\limits_{Y \in A} P(Y)} \quad \text{and} \quad q_d = \frac{\sum\limits_{Y \in I} \left(P(Y) \left[\sum\limits_{Y' \in I} t(Y \to Y') \right] \right)}{\sum\limits_{Y \in I} P(Y)}$$

where the set of active states A consists of any state where the bus sub-system has one or more customers in the hypothetical queue.

The next step is to split the aggregate attempted departure process out of the bus sub-system into N separate processes which in turn become the arrival processes to the output queues. Let p_j, q_j, and α_j be the IBP parameters associated with the arrival process to output queue j. In this analysis, we assume that $p_j = p_d$ and $q_j = q_d$, for $j = 1, 2, \ldots, N$. The parameter α_j is calculated by equating throughputs at the output of the input queues and the input of the output queues. Let T_i be the throughput of of input queue i and d_{ij} be the routing probability that a cell from input queue i is destined for output queue j. Let T_j be the throughput of the traffic destined for output queue j. Then, we have

$$\alpha_j = \frac{T_j(2 - p_d - q_d)}{(1 - q_d)} \quad \text{for} \quad j = 1, 2, \ldots, N$$

where $T_j = \sum_{i=1}^{N} T_i(1 - Pb_i)d_{ij}$. The blocking probability Pb_i for input queue i is derived in the following section.

3.3. Analysis of an output queue

The arrival process to each output queue is modeled by an IBP as discussed above. The service process is assumed geometric. The state of the output queue is described by a state vector that keeps track of the state of the input process (idle or active), the number of customers in the queue, and the bus slot number. The output queue state vector is denoted $Z = \{z_0, z_1, z_2\}$ where z_0 takes the following values: 0 if the input process is in the idle state, 1 if the input process is in the active state. The variable z_1 represents the number of cells in the node, and takes the values $0, 1, \ldots, m$ where m is the queue size. The variable z_2 represents the current bus slot number, and takes the values $1, 2, \ldots, N$ where N is the number of input queues. The output queue is analyzed as a Markov chain using the Gauss–Seidel method.

Next, the blocking probability for each input queue is calculated. The blocking probability Pb_i for input queue i is the probability that given that the bus has been granted to input queue i, the cell at the top of input queue i is blocked from entering its chosen destination output queue. Let Pb_{ij} be the probability that output queue j is full, given that the bus has been granted to input queue i and the cell at the top of input queue i is destined for output queue j. Then, $Pb_i = \sum_{j=i}^{N} d_{ij} Pb_{ij}$, for $i = 1, 2, \ldots, N$. Pb_{ij} is obtained as follows. Let F_j be the set of all states in which output queue j is full. Recall that S_i is the set of states of the bus in which a customer from input queue i is in service. Then, we have

$$Pb_{ij} = \frac{\sum_{Z \in F_j} \left(P(Z) \sum_{Y} P(Y) \sum_{Y' \in S_i} t(Y \to Y') d_{ij} \right)}{\sum_{Y} P(Y) \sum_{Y' \in S_i} t(Y \to Y') d_{ij}}.$$

3.4. Summary of the algorithm

The switch is analyzed by decomposing it into smaller sub-systems. First, each input queue is analyzed in isolation after its service process has been modified. Subsequently, the bus is analyzed as a separate sub-system utilizing the output process of each input queue. Finally, each output queue is analyzed as a separate sub-system. The approximation algorithm can be summarized as follows:

Step 1. For each input queue, initialize the service time distribution $r_{i1}, r_{i2}, \ldots, r_{iN}$ (Cyclic case), the selection probability c_i, $i = 1, 2, \ldots, N$, (random selection case), and the blocking probability Pb_i.

Step 2. Analyze numerically each input queue. Calculate new values for p_i and q_i for each input queue i.

Step 3. Analyze numerically the common bus. Calculate the effective service time distribution for each input queue ($r_{i1}, r_{i2}, \ldots, r_{iN}$ for TDM, and c_i for random selection). These new values are used in the next iteration. Calculate new values for p_j, q_j, and α_j that characterize the arrival process to each output queue.

Step 4. Analyze numerically each output queue. Calculate the queue length distribution and new values for the blocking probability Pb_i of each input queue.

Step 5. Repeat Steps 2, 3, and 4 until a convergence test criterion has been met. The convergence test compares the queue length distribution of each input queue from one iteration to the next.

Step 6. Calculate performance measures such as queue length distribution, system throughput, and cell loss probabilities.

4. Numerical results

The approximation algorithm described in the previous section was implemented on an IBM 3090. The following performance measures were obtained for validation purposes: mean queue length (input and output queues), switch throughput, blocking probability, and cell loss probability. The approximate results were compared to results obtained by simulation. A representative sample of these comparisons is given for a 6×6 switch with queue size (input and output) equal to 32. The blocking probability at the output links B_p was set to 0.1.

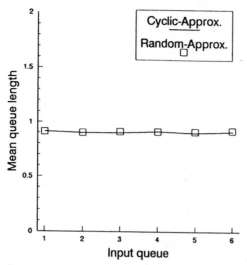

Fig. 4. Mean input queue length: uniform destinations, $\rho = 0.7$, $C^2 = 100$.

Confidence intervals for the simulation results were small and, therefore, they were not plotted.

Figs. 4 to 9 have been obtained assuming a uniform destination distribution. That is, the routing probability d_{ij} was equal to 1/6 for all cells traversing the switch. Figs. 4 and 5 compare the performance of the Cyclic and the Random bus allocation policies under symmetric arrivals and uniform destinations. The mean input queue length and the cell loss probability under the two policies are contrasted in Figs. 4 and 5 respectively. In general, the results for the cyclic and the random selection policies were similar. Therefore, in Figs. 6–9, the comparisons are made between either Random selection and TDM, or Cyclic and TDM. Fig. 6

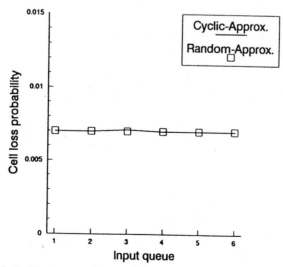

Fig. 5. Cell loss probability: uniform destinations, $\rho = 0.7$, $C^2 = 100$.

A.O. Zaghloul, H.G. Perros / Performance Evaluation 21 (1994) 111–129

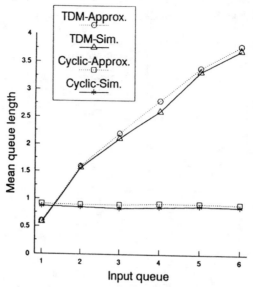

Fig. 6. Mean input queue length: uniform destinations, $\rho = 0.7$, $C^2 = 100$.

gives the mean input queue length for TDM and cyclic bus service policies under symmetric arrivals and uniform destinations. The arrival process is an IBP with $\alpha = 1$, such that $\rho = 0.7$ and $C^2 = 100$. We observe that under the cyclic bus service policy, the mean input queue lengths are equal. On the other hand, under TDM, the mean input queue length increases as the input queue number is increased from 1 to 6. This is due to the fact that if two or more input queues are waiting to transmit a cell to the same output queue which has only one empty space, then the input queue with the lowest queue number will transmit successfully, whereas

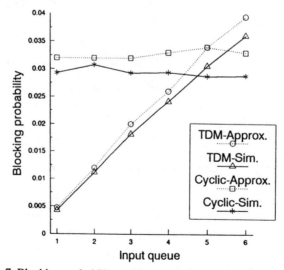

Fig. 7. Blocking probability: uniform destinations, $\rho = 0.7$, $C^2 = 100$.

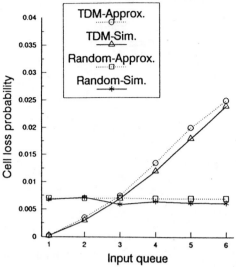

Fig. 8. Cell loss probability: uniform destinations, $\rho = 0.7$, $C^2 = 100$.

the other queues will be blocked. Since, the state of the output queue does not change within a bus cycle, the input queue blocking probability will increase as the input queue number is increased, e.g. input queue 6 will have the largest blocking probability. The results show that, due to blocking, TDM policy has a fairness problem. There is a big difference, nearly 7-fold, in the mean queue length between input queue 1 and queue 6. The maximum, minimum, and average relative errors for the results in Fig. 6 are 8.1%, 1.9%, and 4.8% respectively. Figs. 7 and 8 show the blocking probability (the probability that the cell at the top of queue i will be

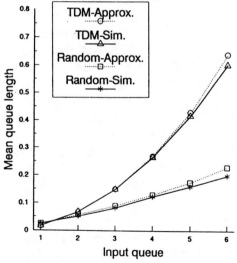

Fig. 9. Mean queue length: asymmetric arrivals, uniform destinations.

A.O. Zaghloul, H.G. Perros / Performance Evaluation 21 (1994) 111–129

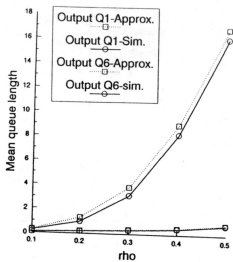

Fig. 10. Mean queue length: TDM, nonuniform destinations.

blocked due to a full destination queue) and the cell loss probability for each input queue for the same example considered in Fig. 6. Again, under TDM, we note that input queue 6 suffers the most in terms of cell loss probability. We note that the fairness problem can be solved by rotating the bus slot assignments within bus cycles (i.e. (1, 2, 3, 4, 5, 6), (2, 3, 4, 5, 6, 1), (3, 4, 5, 6, 1, 2),... etc.). The maximum, minimum, and average relative errors for results in Fig. 7 are 14.0%, 3.9%, and 9.8% respectively and for results in Fig. 8 are 14.1%, 2.3%, and 9.4% respectively. Fig. 9 gives the mean queue length of each input queue for TDM and Random bus service policies under asymmetric IBP arrivals with parameters: $\rho_1 = 0.1$, $\rho_2 = 0.2$, $\rho_3 = 0.3$, $\rho_4 = 0.4$, $\rho_5 = 0.5$, $\rho_6 = 0.6$, and $C_i^2 = 100$ for $i = 1, 2, ..., 6$. We note that random selection is considerably superior to TDM since the selection is made among only the busy input queues. Thus, bus slots are not wasted on empty input queues as in TDM. The maximum, minimum, and average relative errors for the results in Fig. 9 are 14.5%, 0.9%, and 5.2% respectively.

Results in Figs. 10–13 were obtained under a nonuniform destination distribution. In particular, for each input queue 30% of the traffic was destined to output queue 1 and the remainder of the traffic was uniformly distributed among the rest of the output queues, i.e. output queues 2 to 6 get 14% each. This type of traffic pattern is referred to in the literature as the *hot-spot* pattern. Figs. 10 to 12 give the mean queue length of output queue 1 (hot output) and output queue 6 (a non-hot output) for the three bus service policies, TDM, Random, and Cyclic respectively. The arrival process to each input queue was an IBP with $C^2 = 50$ and ρ increasing from 0.1 to 0.5. Note that when ρ is equal to 0.5, the average rate of arrivals destined for output 1 (hot output) is equal to 0.9 which is the output link capacity. For all three bus service policies, although not shown, the input queues were virtually empty. This is due to the fact that the bus speed is equal to the sum of the input link capacities and as a result, most of the queueing within the switch occurs in the output queues. We note that there is a good agreement between the approximation results and the simulation data. The maximum, minimum, and average relative errors for the results in Fig. 10 are 8.1%, 2.6%, and 4.9%, and for

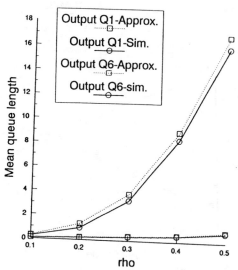

Fig. 11. Mean queue length: Random selection, nonuniform destinations.

the results in Fig. 11 are 14.5%, 6.1%, and 10.6% respectively. Maximum, minimum, and average relative errors for results in Fig. 12 are 14.8%, 4.9%, and 10.7% respectively. Fig. 13 gives the blocking probability for each input queue under asymmetric arrival process ($\rho_1 = 0.1$, $\rho_2 = 0.2$, $\rho_3 = 0.3$, $\rho_4 = 0.4$, $\rho_5 = 0.5$, $\rho_6 = 0.6$, and $C_i^2 = 100$ for $i = 1, 2, \ldots, 6$) and nonuniform traffic destination distribution (the same destination distribution mentioned above). This pattern gives wide variation of traffic crossing the switch. Under TDM bus service policy, the blocking probability increases as the input queue number is increased from 1 to 6 which is expected. On the other hand, under cyclic service, the blocking probability is highest for the

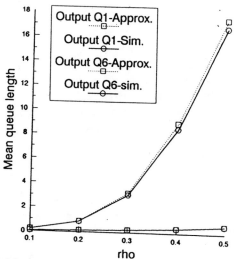

Fig. 12. Mean queue length: Cyclic, nonuniform destinations.

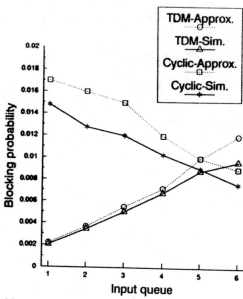

Fig. 13. Blocking probability: asymmetric arrivals, nonuniform destinations.

input queue with the lowest arrival rate and vice versa. This can be explained, intuitively, by the fact that the heavily utilized input queues keep the hot spot output full most of the time. Thus, blocking probabilities of the input queues with low arrival rates is increased. The maximum, minimum, and average relative errors for the results in Fig. 13 are 16.7%, 3.3%, and 11.6% respectively.

In general, the accuracy of the algorithm is good. It was observed that if the input or output queue size is small (i.e. less than 16) the results are not very good when C^2 is high (i.e. greater than 100). When the queue size is large (i.e. equal to or greater than 32) the accuracy is good for values of C^2 up to 150. Also, as the load on the system increases beyond 75% of the system capacity, the accuracy of the algorithm worsens (relative error is greater than 20%).

5. Conclusions

In this paper, we presented an approximate analysis of a generic shared-medium ATM switch under realistic system characteristics such as limited buffer size, asymmetric load conditions, and nonuniform destinations. Three different bus service policies were analyzed: Time Division Multiplexing (TDM), Cyclic, and Random.

The analysis is based on the notion of decomposition whereby the switch is decomposed into smaller subsystems. First, each input queue is analyzed in isolation after we modify its service process. Subsequently, the shared medium is analyzed as a separate sub-system utilizing the output process of each input queue. Finally, each output queue is analyzed in isolation. The results from the individual sub-systems are combined together through an iterative scheme. The model's accuracy is verified through simulation. It was shown that it has an acceptable accuracy.

References

[1] I. Cidon, I. Gopal, G. Grover and M. Sidi, Real-time packet switching: a performance analysis, *IEEE J. S.A.C.* **6** (9) (1988).

[2] A. Ganz and I. Chlamtac, A linear solution to queueing analysis of synchronous finite buffer networks, *IEEE Trans. Comm.* **38** (4) (1990).

[3] S. Gershwin, An efficient decomposition algorithm for unreliable tandem queueing systems with finite buffers, *Proc. 1st Int. Workshop on Queueing Networks with Blocking* (North-Holland, Amsterdam, 1989).

[4] O. Ibe and K. Trivedi, Stochastic Petri net models of polling systems, *IEEE J. S.A.C.* **8** (9) (1990).

[5] F. Jou, A. Nilsson and F. Lai, The upper bounds for delay and cell loss probability of bursty ATM traffic in a finite capacity polling system, *2nd Int. Workshop on Queueing Networks with Blocking*, RTP, North Carolina (1992).

[6] M. Karol, M. Hluchyj and S. Morgan, Input versus output queueing on a space-division packet switch, *IEEE Trans. Comm.* **35** (12) (1987).

[7] T. Morris and H. Perros, Performance analysis of a multi-buffered Banyan ATM switch under bursty traffic, *INFOCOM 92*, Florence, Italy.

[8] A. Nilsson, F. Lai and H. Perros, An approximate analysis of a bufferless $N \times N$ synchronous Clos ATM switch, in: Cohen and Pack (Eds.), *Queueing, Performance, and Control in ATM* (North-Holland, Amsterdam, 1991) 39–46.

[9] A. Pattavina, Performance evaluation of ATM switches with input and output queueing, *Int. J. Digital Analog Comm. Systems* **3** (1990).

[10] H.G. Perros, Approximation algorithms for open queueing networks with blocking, in: Takagi (Ed.), *Stochastic Analysis of Computer and Communication Systems* (North-Holland, Amsterdam, 1990) 451–498.

[11] H. Suzuki, H. Nagano, T. Takeuchi and S. Iwasaki, Output-buffer switch architecture for asynchronous transfer mode, *Int. Conf. on Communications*, Boston, MA (1989).

[12] H. Takagi, Queueing analysis of polling models: an update, in: Takagi (Ed.), *Stochastic Analysis of Computer and Communication Systems* (North-Holland, Amsterdam, 1990) 267–318.

[13] F. Tobagi, Fast packet switch architectures for broadband integrated services digital networks, *Proc. IEEE* **78** (1) (1990).

[14] P. Tran-Gia, Analysis of polling systems with general input process and finite capacity, *IEEE Trans. Comm.* **40** (2) (1992).

[15] J. Turner, Design of a broadcast packet switching network, *IEEE Trans. Comm.* **36** (6) (1988).

[16] A. Zaghloul and H. Perros, Approximate analysis of a discrete-time polling system with bursty arrivals, *IFIP Workshop on Modelling and Performance Evaluation of ATM Technology*, Martinique (1993).

Telecommunication Systems 3(1995)379-395

Discrete-time analysis of cell spacing in ATM systems

F. Hübner[1]

Telecom Australia Research Laboratories, Network Analysis Section,
770 Blackburn Road, Clayton, Victoria 3168, Australia
E-mail: f.huebner@trl.oz.au

P. Tran-Gia

Institute of Computer Science, University of Würzburg,
Am Hubland, 97074 Würzburg, Germany
E-mail: trangia@informatik.uni-wuerzburg.d400.de

Received May 1994; revised October 1994

In this paper, an analysis of a general spacer mechanism as used in ATM systems and being part of the usage parameter control functions is developed. The cell process which is subject to spacing can be an arbitrarily chosen renewal process. The algorithm aims at the calculation of the spacer output process in terms of the cell inter-departure time distribution which gives insights to understand the traffic stream forming properties of the spacing mechanism. Two spacer variants are taken into account, where cell rejection and non-rejection versions of the spacing scheme are considered. It is shown that the state process of the $GI/D/1$ queue and $GI/D/1$ queue with bounded delay can be used to analyze the spacer process. Numerical results are presented to show the system performance for different traffic conditions and system parameters. Beyond the consideration of the pure spacing mechanism, we also take into account that the cell streams are changed between the ATM connection endpoints and the spacer. We model this by considering the output process of a discrete-time $GI/G/1$ queue as the spacer input process. We also take the spacer output process as input for a discrete-time $GI/G/1$ queue to investigate how the spaced cell stream is again changed until reaching the private/public UNI.

1. Cell spacing mechanism

The design of the user network interface (UNI) in accordance with the incorporated usage parameter control (UPC) function plays an important role in the current ATM development and standardization process. Figure 1 shows a configuration which defines the sequence of reference points and functional groups that the ATM cells

---

[1] The work for this paper was performed while the author was with the Institute of Computer Science, University of Würzburg, Germany.

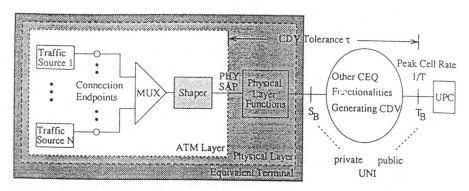

Fig. 1. Reference configuration from ITU-TSS Draft Rec. I.371.

pass on their way from the endpoints of a connection to the UPC. The configuration serves as a reference configuration in the International Telecommunication Union-Telecommunication Standardization Sector (ITU-TSS) [6].

After multiplexing, a traffic shaping function must be performed to avoid that misbehaving traffic sources[2] can deteriorate network performance by generating cells excessively. Leaky-bucket based regulation schemes just as cell spacing have been proposed to perform the traffic shaping function. It should be noted that the leaky-bucket based regulation schemes (contrary to the cell spacing schemes) do not reshape conforming cell streams. At the physical layer service access point (PHY SAP), the peak cell rate of an ATM connection is defined as the inverse of the minimum cell inter-arrival time. Cell delay variation (CDV) is introduced by some physical layer and customer equipment (CEQ) functions between the physical layer service access point (PHY SAP) and the T_B reference point (public UNI). A peak cell rate monitor algorithm that tolerates the CDV (for which the users are not responsible) is proposed by the ITU-TSS [6] and is also adopted by the ATM Forum [1]. Discussions of the dimensioning of the monitor algorithm can be found in [4, 9, 12, 13].

The leaky bucket mechanism has been proposed and investigated as a traffic shaper in several performance studies. In [11], an analytical study has revealed that the usage of a leaky bucket can be very inefficient. Only when the transmission rate that is assigned to a connection is above the leaky bucket permit rate and cells are rejected/marked with a probability greater than 10^{-2}, can the leaky bucket protect the network from misbehaving connections.

The fluid flow approach was used to investigate ON/OFF source traffic and the so-called buffered leaky bucket in [7] and [14]. In [14], two different shaping schemes have been taken into account to incorporate a possibility to give priority

---

[2] The misbehavior of a source (according to its traffic contract) can be intentionally initiated by the user or can stem from a malfunction of the technical equipment.

to real time over non-real time traffic. In the first scheme, the leaky bucket tokens are accessible for both traffic types and in the second, one dedicated token pool for each of the traffic types is provided. It turned out that the latter scheme provides better flexibility and bandwidth utilization. In [7], the performance of a buffered leaky bucket mechanism and its output process was investigated. An approximation of the output process as coupled Markov Modulated Fluid Sources was proposed and shown to be quite accurate in terms of identical moments of the Markovian approximation and the rate processes.

In the following, we consider cell spacing as a traffic shaping function as it is discussed in recent literature [3–5, 8, 10, 18]. A description of the basic cell spacing functionality is given in section 2.1. The advantage of cell spacing over regulating ATM traffic using a leaky bucket scheme is that cell spacing not only limits the traffic volume, but also reduces its burstiness. This is done at the expense of introducing delay and, therefore, the cell spacing mechanisms must be dimensioned carefully to guarantee the negotiated quality of service (QoS) for each ATM connection.

In [4, 8, 10, 18], architectures and the corresponding traffic models for cell spacers have been proposed. The effects of cell spacing on ATM traffic streams have been discussed in [4, 5, 18] and for a so-called N-level shaper, which constitutes a generalization of the basic cell spacing mechanism in [2]. All performance studies mentioned used either simulation or analytical approaches which are quite limited in terms of not being able to consider realistic ATM traffic scenarios.

In this paper, we derive a very potential analytical approach which allows us to model the ATM traffic which arrives at the shaper (cf. fig. 1) in a very realistic manner. We focus on the change in ATM traffic streams by passing through a cell spacer and derive the cell inter-departure time distribution. Our results are exact if we consider the cell spacer solely and offer a stream of ATM cells which forms a renewal process with general inter-arrival time distribution (see section 2). Then, we take into account that the cell streams are changed between the ATM connection endpoints and the spacer. We propose an approximate solution for the case where cells which are subject to spacing are given by the output process of a discrete-time $GI/G/1$ queueing system which models these changes in the cell streams (see section 3). We also propose an approximate solution for the case where the spacer output process serves as an input process for a discrete-time $GI/G/1$ queue. By this constellation, we are able to investigate how the spaced traffic streams are changed between the spacer and the private/public UNI. The numerical results are compared with simulation results and it turns out that the approximate results are extremely accurate.

2. Performance analysis

2.1. BASIC MODEL

The relation between the shaper and the spacer is illustrated in fig. 2. Traffic entering the spacer is logically demultiplexed, since each spacer is responsible for

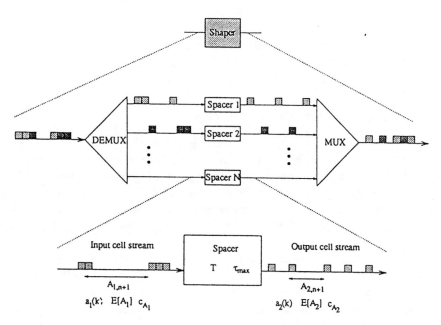

Fig. 2. Basic spacer model.

the cells from exactly one ATM connection. After spacing the different cell streams, they are again multiplexed together. The basic function of a spacer device is to enforce a minimum cell inter-departure time. The bottom part of fig. 2 shows the basic spacer model and the related parameters.

The spacer has to influence the input cell stream in such a way that the time between consecutive cells in the output stream is at least T.[3] This cell stream forming is done by delaying cells which arrive too close together. The time a cell should be delayed is bounded by τ_{max}. Cells which would experience a larger delay are rejected. The purpose is to prevent cells from being delayed too long due to real-time constraints (e.g. according to the negotiated QoS) and to save buffer capacity in the cell spacer.

The time between cells n and $n + 1$ is denoted by the random variable (r.v.) $A_{i,n+1}$ ($i = 1$ denoting the input and $i = 2$ the output stream). The corresponding stationary discrete-time distributions and their means and coefficients of variation (CoV) are denoted by $a_i(k)$, $E[A_i]$, and c_{A_i}.

In the next two subsections, we present an exact analysis for the cell inter-departure time distribution $a_2(k)$. In general, the output process is a non-renewal process. The inter-departure time distribution is thus given in conjunction with a

---

[3] As appropriate for ATM systems, time is discretized into slots of cell duration length. Therefore, we refer to the time interval $x \cdot$ *cell duration* simply as time x.

renewal assumption. The discrete-time inter-arrival time distribution $a_1(k)$ can be chosen as an arbitrary renewal process. In section 2.2, we omit the mechanism of cell rejection, whereas we take it into account in section 2.3.

2.2. ALGORITHM FOR PURE CELL SPACING

If we omit the cell rejection mechanism, the spacer simply delays cells as long as necessary to leave the spacer with inter-cell times of at least T. We present an iterative algorithm to derive the cell inter-departure time distribution of the spacer. The inter-departure time between cell n and $n + 1$ is T if cell $n + 1$ arrives not later than T after cell n departed from the spacer. Only when a cell arrives more than time T after the preceding cell departed is the cell inter-departure time exactly the inter-arrival time.

The basic idea for the analysis is to introduce a *spacer state* denoted by the r.v. Z_n. Depending on the spacer state Z_n a cell sees upon arrival, the cell has to be delayed a specific amount of time or departs immediately from the spacer. The following notation is used:

Z_n^- r.v. for the spacer state just before the arrival instant of cell n. If Z_n^- is positive, the cell will be delayed by Z_n^- slots, otherwise it will immediately depart from the spacer.

Z_n^+ r.v. for the spacer state immediately after the arrival instant of cell n.

The distributions of the discrete-time r.v.'s Z_n^- and Z_n^+ are denoted by $z_n^-(k)$ and $z_n^+(k)$, respectively. A sample evolution of the r.v.'s Z_n^- and Z_n^+ is shown in fig. 3.[4]

Starting the process in fig. 3 with cell n which needs not be spaced, Z_n^+ is set to T and is then decreased by one in each slot. If cell $n + 1$ would arrive within T time slots after the arrival instant of cell n (i.e. Z_n would not be negative), cell $n + 1$ would depart T slots after cell n. Since cell $n + 1$ arrives later then T time slots after cell n, the inter-departure time $A_{2,n+1}$ is the same as the inter-arrival time $A_{1,n+1}$. Just before the arrival of cell $n + 1$, Z_{n+1}^- is negative and therefore Z_{n+1}^+ is set to T. Cell $n + 2$ arrives so early that Z_{n+2}^- is positive. Therefore, Z_{n+2}^+ is given by increasing Z_{n+2}^- by T and the departures of cells $n + 1$ and $n + 2$ are spaced by T. Cell $n + 3$ arrives later than T at the spacer but cell $n + 2$ is delayed for some slots. According to fig. 3, it happens that cell $n + 3$ departs also after T slots. As can be seen, it is possible that under certain circumstances the cell inter-departure intervals are smaller than the cell inter-arrival intervals, although each of the cells has to pass the spacer. This can occur when two consecutive cells are delayed, but the latter cell is delayed less than the former one.

---

[4] The decrease of the state process values occurs stepwise, since we consider a slotted time axis, but to simplify the illustration we depict it as linear decrease (45° lines).

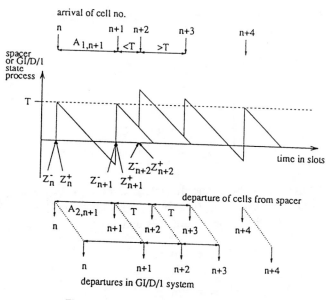

Fig. 3. Snapshot of the spacer state process.

It should be noted here that the state process of the spacer is equivalent to the process of the unfinished work of the $GI/D/1$ queue [17]. Thus, the analysis can be used here in an analogous way. The main difference is that the spacer does not have a service period per cell but can deliver cells without sojourn time. The output process of the $GI/D/1$ queueing system is shifted by time T compared to the spacer output process (cf. fig. 3).

In the following, we outline an iterative algorithm for the computation of the distributions $z_n^-(k)$ and $z_n^+(k)$, assuming that the cell arrival process constitutes a discrete-time renewal process with general distribution $a_1(k)$. Using the limiting distributions $z^-(k)$ and $z^+(k)$, the cell inter-departure time distribution $a_2(k)$ can be easily derived. We start with the dependencies between the r.v.'s Z_n^- and Z_n^+:

$$Z_{n+1}^- = Z_n^+ - A_{1,n+1}. \tag{1}$$

This equation is driven by the decrease of Z_n by one in each slot. Z_n^+ itself is determined by Z_n^- in the following way:

$$Z_n^+ = \max\{Z_n^-, 0\} + T. \tag{2}$$

According to eq. (2), Z_n^+ is set to T if Z_n^- is negative, otherwise Z_n^+ is given by increasing Z_n^- by T (cf. fig. 3). The related distributions $z_n^-(k)$ and $z_n^+(k)$ can be derived according to eqs. (1) and (2) by

$$z_{n+1}^-(k) = z_n^+(k) * a_1(-k) \tag{3}$$

and

$$z_n^+(k) = \begin{cases} 0, & k < T, \\ \sum_{k'=-\infty}^{0} z_n^-(k'), & k = T, \\ z_n^-(k-T), & k > T. \end{cases} \tag{4}$$

The "*" operation in eq. (3) denotes the discrete convolution operation. $z_{n+1}^-(k)$ is computed using $z_n^+(k)$ and $z_n^+(k)$ using $z_n^-(k)$. Thus, the stationary limiting distributions $z^-(k)$ and $z^+(k)$ are derived (by iterating eqs. (3) and (4) in an alternating manner) as

$$z^-(k) = \lim_{n \to \infty} z_n^-(k) \tag{5}$$

and

$$z^+(k) = \lim_{n \to \infty} z_n^+(k). \tag{6}$$

According to the stability condition for the *GI/D/*1 queue, stability is guaranteed for $T/E[A_1] < 1$ (determinsitic service time of T in the *GI/D/*1 queue). The probability that a cell is delayed upon its arrival p_d is simply given by

$$p_d = \sum_{k=1}^{\infty} z^-(k). \tag{7}$$

By defining the operation $\pi_0(x(k))$ on a distribution $x(k)$ by

$$\pi_0(x(k)) = \begin{cases} 0, & k < 0, \\ \sum_{k'=-\infty}^{0} x(k'), & k = 0, \\ x(k), & k > 0, \end{cases} \tag{8}$$

the distribution for cell delay caused by the spacer can be simply given as

$$P\{\text{spacer delay} = k \text{ slots}\} = \pi_0(z^-(k)) \tag{9}$$

As already described above, the time between the departure of the cells n and $n + 1$ is T if the value of Z_{n+1}^- is not negative. Otherwise, the cell inter-departure time is T plus the number of slots in which the state process was negative until cell $n + 1$ arrived. Thus, the cell inter-departure time $A_{2,n+1}$ is given by

$$A_{2,n+1} = \begin{cases} T, & Z_{n+1}^- \geq 0, \\ T - Z_{n+1}^-, & Z_{n+1}^- < 0. \end{cases} \tag{10}$$

The stationary cell inter-departure time distribution $a_2(k)$ can be derived according to eq. (10) as

$$a_2(k) = \begin{cases} 0, & k < T, \\ \sum_{k'=0}^{\infty} z^-(k'), & k = T, \\ z^-(-k + T), & k > T. \end{cases} \tag{11}$$

2.3. ALGORITHM FOR CELL SPACING WITH REJECTION

The spacing mechanism as discussed in the previous subsection can lead to large spacing delay, i.e. the time between the arrival of a cell at the spacer and the departure from it. Thus, a control scheme to guarantee a maximal cell spacing delay can be useful to cope with specific real-time services and their delay constraints. In this subsection, we consider the spacing scheme with rejection. Therefore, we additionally have to incorporate the impact of the delay bound τ_{max} in the analysis. A cell which would be delayed by the spacer more than τ_{max} slots in rejected and has no longer influence on the spacing mechanism. For analysis purposes, we distinguish between the two cases, $\tau_{max} < T$ and $\tau_{max} \geq T$.

The spacer state process is similar to the unfinished work process of a $GI/D/1$ queueing system with bounded delay, which was analyzed in [16]. Figure 4 shows a sample path of the spacer state evolution for the case $\tau_{max} < T$. The meaning of Z_n^- and Z_n^+ is the same as in the last subsection (cf. fig. 3).

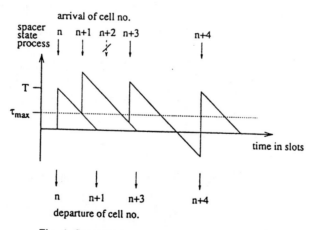

Fig. 4. Spacer state process sample path ($\tau_{max} < T$).

At the arrival instant of cell $n + 1$, the r.v. Z_{n+1}^- equals τ_{max} and therefore this cell is not rejected but experiences the maximum delay τ_{max} until departure from the spacer. Since Z_{n+2}^- is larger than τ_{max}, cell $n + 2$ is rejected and Z_{n+2}^+ is not increased compared to Z_{n+2}^-. Z_{n+1}^- depends in the same way on Z_n^+ as described in eq. (1) and the related distribution $z_{n+1}^-(k)$ is given by eq. (3). Z_n^+ is determined by Z_n^- similarly to eq. (2), but the maximum delay τ_{max} must be taken into account:

$$Z_n^+ = \begin{cases} T, & Z_n^- \leq 0, \\ Z_n^- + T, & 0 \leq Z_n^- \leq \tau_{max}, \\ Z_n^-, & Z_n^- > \tau_{max}. \end{cases} \tag{12}$$

This equation is valid for $\tau_{max} < T$ and $\tau_{max} \geq T$, but the related distributions $z_n^+(k)$ are different. For $\tau_{max} < T$, $z_n^+(k)$ is given as

$$z_n^+(k) = \begin{cases} 0, & k \leq \tau_{max}, \\ z_n^-(k), & \tau_{max} + 1 \leq k \leq T - 1, \\ z_n^-(T) + \sum_{k'=-\infty}^0 z_n^-(k'), & k = T, \\ z_n^-(k) + z_n^-(k - T), & T + 1 \leq k \leq T + \tau_{max}. \end{cases} \tag{13}$$

Again, $z_{n+1}^-(k)$ can be computed using $z_n^+(k)$ and $z_n^+(k)$ using $z_n^-(k)$. Thus, the stationary limiting distributions $z^-(k)$ and $z^+(k)$ are derived by iterating eqs. (3) and (13). The cell rejection probability p_r is determined by

$$p_r = \sum_{k=\tau_{max}+1}^{\tau_{max}+T} z^-(k). \tag{14}$$

The cell delay distribution introduced by the spacer is given as

$$P\{\text{delay} = k \text{ slots}\} = (1 - p_r)^{-1} \cdot \begin{cases} \sum_{k'=-\infty}^0 z^-(k'), & k = 0, \\ z^-(k), & 1 \leq k \leq \tau_{max}. \end{cases} \tag{15}$$

Taking into account the cell rejection probability, the cell inter-departure time $A_{2,n+1}$ is given similarly to eq. (10) by

$$A_{2,n+1} = \begin{cases} T, & 0 \leq Z_{n+1}^- \leq \tau_{max}, \\ T - Z_{n+1}^-, & Z_{n+1}^- \leq 0. \end{cases} \tag{16}$$

Accordingly, the stationary cell inter-departure time distribution $a_2(k)$ is

$$a_2(k) = (1 - p_r)^{-1} \cdot \begin{cases} 0, & k < T, \\ \sum_{k'=0}^{\tau_{max}} z^-(k'), & k = T, \\ z^-(-k + T), & k > T. \end{cases} \tag{17}$$

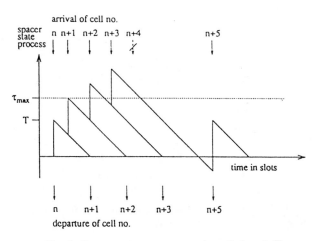

Fig. 5. Spacer state process sample path ($\tau_{max} \geq T$).

A snapshot of the evolution of the spacer state process for $\tau_{max} \geq T$ is depicted in fig. 5.

In contrast to the case $\tau_{max} < T$, several cells can arrive at the spacer close together without being rejected. However, after some time there are too many of them and therefore, for example, cell $n + 4$ is rejected. With the choice of $\tau_{max} \geq T$, it is possible to space bursty input cell streams (e.g. cell arrivals in consecutive slots) without cell rejection. Each of the equations for the iterative algorithm are the same as for $\tau_{max} < T$, except that eq. (13) for $z_n^+(k)$ is altered slightly. For some $\tau_{max} \geq T$, $z_n^+(k)$ is given as

$$
z_n^+(k) = \begin{cases}
0, & k < T, \\
\sum_{k'=-\infty}^{0} z_n^-(k'), & k = T, \\
z_n^-(k - T), & T < k \leq \tau_{max}, \\
z_n^-(k) + z_n^-(k - T), & \tau_{max} < k \leq T + \tau_{max}.
\end{cases}
\tag{18}
$$

2.4. NUMERICAL RESULTS

The algorithms derived above allow considerations of arbitrary discrete-time renewal processes as spacer input. To provide systematic parameter studies, in the following we use a negative binomial distribution for $a_1(k)$ to describe the cell arrival process at the spacer:

$$
a_1(k) = \binom{k + n - 1}{k} p^n (1 - p)^k.
\tag{19}
$$

The mean $E[A_1]$ and CoV c_{A_1} of a negative binomially distributed r.v. A_1 are given according to the parameters p and n by

$$p = (E[A_1]c_{A_1}^2)^{-1} \quad \text{and} \quad n = E[A_1](E[A_1]c_{A_1}^2 - 1)^{-1}. \tag{20}$$

$E[A_1]$ and c_{A_1} can be chosen independently of each other but must fulfill $E[A_1]c_{A_1}^2 > 1$.

In figs. 6–9, we depict some numerical results to show the influences and capabilities of the cell spacing mechanism. Figure 6 shows a specific cell inter-arrival distribution and the corresponding inter-departure time distribution functions for different values of the spacer delay bounds.

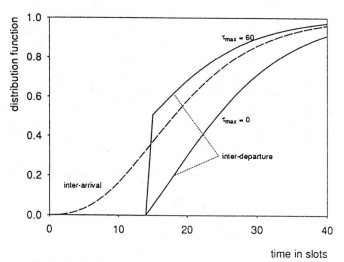

Fig. 6. Comparison of inter-arrival and inter-departure process.

The cell inter-arrival time is negative binomially distributed with mean $E[A_1] = 20$ and CoV $c_{A_1} = 0.5$. The minimum cell inter-departure time from the spacer is chosen at $T = 15$. Accordingly, the inter-departure time distribution function is zero for times smaller than T. Moreover, we can observe a step in the curve for $\tau_{max} = 60$. As shown, due to the spacer function, the inter-departure process can differ considerably from the inter-arrival process.

Table 1 shows some cell delay probabilities p_d (cf. eq. (7)) for the parameter set used in fig. 6 for varying CoV c_{A_1}. It can be observed that more cells are delayed if the CoV increases and this effect demonstrates the capability of cell spacing to form the ATM traffic streams properly.

Table 1

Cell delay probabilities p_d.

c_{A_1}	2.0	1.5	1.0	0.75	0.5	0.25	0.0
p_d	90%	85%	74%	64%	46%	17%	0%

F. Hübner, P. Tran-Gia, Cell spacing in ATM systems

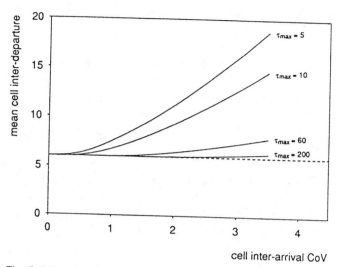

Fig. 7. Influence of spacer delay bound on mean inter-departure time.

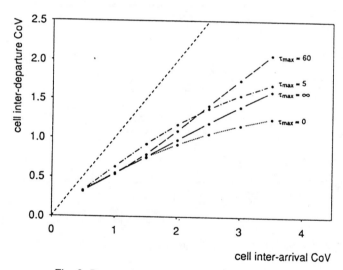

Fig. 8. Process forming capability of cell spacing.

By the employment of the spacer delay bound, cells can be rejected and the inter-departure time distribution (and also its mean) depends strongly on the type of the inter-arrival process and the dimensioning of the maximum spacing delay. This effect is illustrated in fig. 7, where the input process is again described by a negative binomial distribution with mean $E[A_1] = 6$ and minimum inter-departure time $T = 5$. The dotted line indicates the mean cell inter-departure time if no cell spacing would be employed.

The traffic smoothing or variance reduction property of the spacer can be seen in fig. 8, where the CoV of the departure process is plotted as a function of the CoV of the arrival process. The parameters used are the same as for fig. 7. It can be observed that the CoV of the departure process lies below the CoV of the arrival process (we would arrive at the dotted line if no cell spacing would be employed). This effect is intended by the employment of spacing to smooth the cell streams.

By inspecting the curves in fig. 8 more carefully, it can be observed that choosing τ_{max} higher does not necessarily lead to higher CoV in the cell inter-departure process (see e.g. $\tau_{max} = \infty$). The influence of the spacer delay bound on the cell inter-departure process is shown in fig. 9, where the variation reduction property in dependence on the cell delay bound of the spacer is visible.

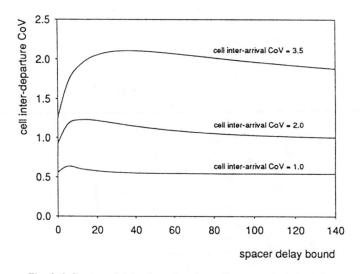

Fig. 9. Influence of delay bound on inter-departure characteristics.

3. Tandem model as overall traffic scenario

In the model presented in the previous section, the input of the spacer was assumed to be a discrete-time renewal process. In this section, we consider the more realistic case that the traffic which is generated by the connection is changed before reaching the spacer and that the spacer output traffic is again changed until reaching the private/public UNI. To model the change in the characteristics of traffic between the ATM connection endpoints, the spacer and the private/public UNI, we adopt a tandem model as depicted in fig. 10.

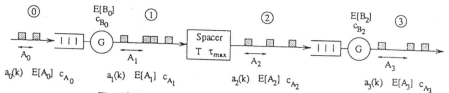

Fig. 10. Tandem model for spacing ATM cell streams.

3.1. CELL PROCESS CHANGES BEFORE SPACER

The change in the characteristics of traffic between the ATM connection endpoints and the spacer output (cf. fig. 1) is investigated by taking the output process of a discrete-time $GI/G/1$ queue as the spacer input process ($\textcircled{0} \rightarrow \textcircled{2}$ in fig. 10). The traffic which is generated by a specific ATM connection is described by a discrete-time GI distribution and the time between the generation instants of two cells is denoted by the r.v. A_0. The corresponding cell generation distribution is denoted by $a_0(k)$ with mean $E[A_0]$ and coefficient of variation c_{A_0}. The delay introduced between the connection endpoints and the spacer is modeled by the service time of the $GI/G/1$ model, which can be arbitrarily chosen. The service time has mean $E[B_0]$ and coefficient of variation c_{B_0}.

In general, the output process of a $GI/G/1$ queue is a non-renewal process. To analyze this part of the tandem model, we approximate the $GI/G/1$ output process by a renewal process and use this as the input process for the spacer. The output process of the $GI/G/1$ queue is evaluated using the algorithm presented in [15].

Since the analytic results for the tandem traffic model as shown in fig. 10 are obtained using a renewal approximation, validations are made by simulations. In fig. 11, the inter-departure time distribution function of the spacer is depicted, where the system configuration is as follows. A $GI/D/1$ queue with negative binomially distributed cell inter-generation time ($E[A_0] = 20$, $c_{A_0} = 0.5$ and $c_{A_0} = 2.0$) and deterministic service time $E[B_0] = 4$ delivers a non-renewal output process. This output process is used as the input process for a spacer with parameters $T = 15$ and $\tau_{max} = 5$. The simulation results show that the approximation is extremely accurate, also if quite different cell generation processes ($c_{A_0} = 0.5/c_{A_0} = 2.0$) are used.

The traffic smoothing characteristics of the spacer are depicted in fig. 12, which shows the CoV of the inter-departure process c_{A_2} as a function of the CoV of the inter-arrival process c_{A_0}. Here, the CoV c_{B_0} of the service time in the $GI/G/1$ queue is additionally taken into account. The dotted line depicts the case where the input cell stream is neither altered by the $GI/G/1$ queue nor by the spacer.

3.2. CELL PROCESS CHANGES AFTER SPACER

The change of the spacer output traffic until reaching the private/public UNI is investigated by taking the output traffic of the spacer as input traffic for the

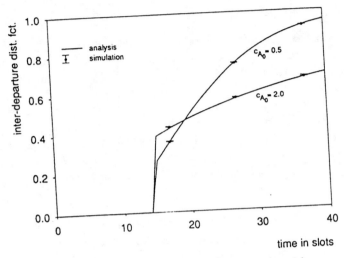

Fig. 11. Approximation accuracy for the tandem model.

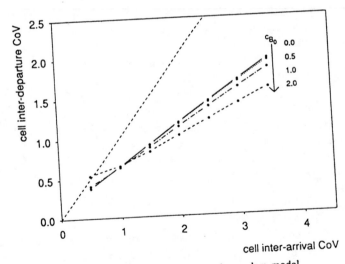

Fig. 12. Smoothing properties in the tandem model.

*GI/GI*1 queue (① → ③ in fig. 10). The input traffic of the spacer follows a discrete-time *GI* distribution $a_1(k)$. The time between the departures of cells from the spacer is described by the r.v. A_2. The CDV introduced after spacing (between the PHY SAP and the S_B/T_B reference point; cf. fig. 1) is modeled by the service time of the *GI/GI*1 queue. The output of the spacer is in general not a renewal process. For analysis

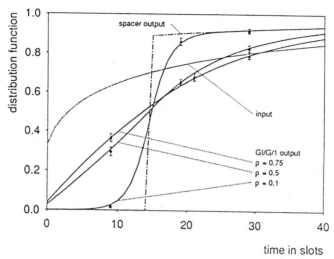

Fig. 13. Change of spacer output process.

purposes, we approximate this output process by a renewal process and take it as the input process for the $GI/G/1$ queue.

Figure 13 shows how the spacer input process is changed after spacing (spacer output) by passing through the $GI/G/1$ queue ($GI/G/1$ output). The input traffic has mean $E[A_1] = 20$ and CoV $c_{A_1} = 2.0$, and the spacer parameters are $T = 15$ and $\tau_{max} = \infty$ (this choice leads to $E[A_2] = E[A_1]$, cf. fig. 7). The service time of the $GI/G/1$ queue follows a negative binomial distribution and has mean $E[B_2]$ and coefficient of variation $c_{B_2} = 1.0$. The distribution function of the $GI/G/1$ queue output process is depicted for different values of $\rho = E[B_2]/E[A_2]$. It can be observed that the smoothed traffic (spacer output) becomes more bursty after passing through the $GI/G/1$ queue. This effect increases with increasing utilization of the resources between the PHY SAP and the private/public UNI (cf. fig. 1), i.e. with larger values for ρ. The renewal approximation again delivers very accurate results, as the simulation results indicate.

4.   Concluding remarks

We presented a discrete-time model for cell spacing which performs the shaping function in ATM systems. Algorithms have been developed to calculate the spacer output process distributions. The analysis was carried out in discrete-time domain, based on queueing systems of the types $GI/D/1$ and $GI/D/1$ with bounded delay. Besides the investigation of the spacing mechanism solely (case (i), where the arrival process at the spacer is an arbitrary renewal process), two submodels have been taken into account: (ii) the arrival process is the output process of a $GI/G/1$ queue, and (iii) the spacer process is the input process of a $GI/G/1$ queue. The results are given in terms of the output process distributions, which give insights into the traffic stream forming properties of the spacing mechanism. Two spacer variants have been taken into account, where cell blocking and non-blocking versions of the spacing scheme have been considered. Numerical examples have been presented to show the spacer performance for different traffic conditions and system parameters. The results are exact for the model considered in case (i). For the tandem model (cases (ii) and (iii), an approximation which delivers very accurate numerical results has been presented.

Acknowledgement

The authors would like to thank N. Vicari for valuable programming support.

References

[1]   ATM Forum, ATM user-network interface specification, Version 3.0 (1993).
[2]   F. Bernabei, L. Gratta, M. Listanti and A. Sarghini, Analysis of ON–OFF source shaping for ATM multiplexing, *INFOCOM 1993*, Paper 11a.3.
[3]   P. Boyer, Y. Rouaud and M. Servel, Méthode et système de lissage et de contrôle de débit de communications temporelles asynchrones, French Patent, INPI No. 90/00770 (1990) and European Patent Office Bulletin 91/30 (1991).
[4]   P. Boyer, F.M. Guillemin, M.J. Servel and J.-P. Coudreuse, Spacing cells protects and enhances utilization of ATM network links, IEEE Network 6(5) (1992).
[5]   F.M. Brochin, A cell spacing device for congestion control in ATM networks, Performance Evaluation 16(1992)107–127.
[6]   ITU-TSS Draft Recommendation I.371, Traffic control and congestion control in B-ISDN (1994).
[7]   A.I. Elwalid and D. Mitra, Analysis and design of rate-based congestion control of high speed networks, I: Stochastic fluid models, access regulation, Queueing Systems 9(1991)29–64.
[8]   F.M. Guillemin, P.E. Boyer and L. Romoeuf, The spacer-controller: Architcture and first assessments, *Workshop on Broadband Communications*, Estoril, Portugal (1992) pp. 313–323.
[9]   F.M. Guillemin and W. Monin, Limitation of cell delay variation in ATM networks, *ICCT*, Beijing, China (1992).
[10] F.M. Guillemin and W. Monin, Management of cell delay variation in ATM networks, *GLOBECOM 1992*, pp. 128–132.
[11] M.G. Hluchyj and N. Yin, On the queueing behavior of multiplexed leaky bucket regulated sources, *INFOCOM 1993*, Paper 6a.3.
[12] F. Hübner, Dimensioning of a peak cell rate monitor algorithm using discrete-time analysis, *ITC-14*, Antibes, France, 1994, pp. 1415–1424.
[13] F. Hübner, Output process analysis of the peak cell rate monitor algorithm, University of Würzburg, Institute of Computer Science Research Report Series, Report No. 75 (1994).
[14] L.K. Reiss and L.F. Merakos, Shaping of virtual path traffic for ATM B-ISDN, *INFOCOM 1993*, Paper 2a.4.
[15] P. Tran-Gia, Discrete-time analysis for the interdeparture distribution of $GI/G/1$ queues, in: *Teletraffic Analysis and Computer Performance Evaluation*, eds. O.J. Boxma, J.W. Cohen and H.C. Tijms (North-Holland, Amsterdam, 1986) pp. 341–357.
[16] P. Tran-Gia, Analysis of a load-driven overlaod control mechanism in discrete-time domain, *ITC-12*, Turino, Italy, 1988, Paper 4.3a.2.
[17] P. Tran-Gia, Discrete-time analysis technique and application to usage parameter control modelling in ATM systems, *8th Australian Teletraffic Research Seminar*, Melbourne, 1993.
[18] E. Wallmeier and T. Worster, The spacing policer, an algorithm for efficient peak bit rate control in ATM networks, *ISS 14* (1992) Paper A5.5.

Fundamental Bounds and Approximations for ATM Multiplexers with Applications to Video Teleconferencing

Anwar Elwalid, *Member, IEEE,* Daniel Heyman, T. V. Lakshman, *Member, IEEE,*
Debasis Mitra, *Fellow, IEEE,* and Alan Weiss

Abstract—The main contributions of this paper are two-fold. First, we prove fundamental, similarly behaving lower and upper bounds, and give an approximation based on the bounds, which is effective for analyzing ATM multiplexers, even when the traffic has many, possibly heterogeneous, sources and models are of high dimension. Second, we apply our analytic approximation to statistical models of video teleconference traffic, obtain the multiplexing system's capacity as determined by the number of admissible sources for given cell-loss probability, buffer size and trunk bandwidth, and, finally, compare with results from simulations, which are driven by actual data from coders. The results are surprisingly close. Our bounds are based on large deviations theory. The main assumption is that the sources are Markovian and time-reversible. Our approximation to the steady-state buffer distribution is called *Chernoff-dominant eigenvalue* since one parameter is obtained from Chernoff's theorem and the other is the system's dominant eigenvalue. Fast, effective techniques are given for their computation. In our application we process the output of variable bit rate coders to obtain DAR(1) source models which, while of high dimension, require only knowledge of the mean, variance, and correlation. We require cell-loss probability not to exceed 10^{-6}, trunk bandwidth ranges from 45 to 150 Mb/s, buffer sizes are such that maximum delays range from 1 to 60 ms, and the number of coder-sources ranges from 15 to 150. Even for the largest systems, the time for analysis is a fraction of a second, while each simulation takes many hours. Thus, the real-time administration of admission control based on our analytic techniques is feasible.

I. INTRODUCTION

RESEARCH on the architecture and design of ATM systems has in recent times been stymied by the inability to effectively analyze multiplexers when the traffic has many, possibly heterogeneous, sources and the dimensions of their models are high. Secondly, there is a growing gap between measurements and models, more generally between real systems and their purported analyses; as a corollary, there are few checks on the efficacy of designs of real systems. The widespread acceptance of ATM and the accompanying richness of services and applications are accentuating these problems.

Manuscript received September 30, 1994; revised April 1, 1995.
A. Elwalid, D. Mitra, and A. Weiss are with AT&T Bell Laboratories, Murray Hill, NJ 07974 USA.
D. Heyman and T. V. Lakshman are with Bell Communications Research, Red Bank, NJ 07701 USA.
IEEE Log Number 9412650.

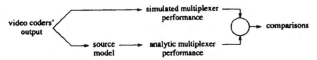

Fig. 1. Methodology.

This paper provides some relief for both these troubling conditions. We prove fundamental upper and lower bounds on loss probabilities in buffered multiplexing systems with time-reversible Markovian sources, which provably mirror true behavior for the full spectrum of buffer sizes. We propose an approximation for all Markovian traffic sources which is based on the upper bound. We call this the Chernoff-dominant eigenvalue (CDE) method since it has only two parameters, one of which is obtained from Chernoff's theorem and the other is the multiplexing system's dominant eigenvalue. Both these quantities have separately been studied extensively in the past. Fast, effective techniques are available for their computation, even for heterogeneous, high-dimensioned source models. In the case of discrete-time systems, which are of particular importance here since video teleconference traffic is framed, we fill a gap in the literature by obtaining an explicit, scalar, monotonic function whose root, which is easily calculated, is the dominant eigenvalue.

The complementary part of the paper starts with the measured output of video teleconference coders. The study then proceeds along two paths, as sketched in Fig. 1.

In the top "simulation" path, the output from several coders is supplied to a simulated finite multiplexing buffer, and the losses monitored. In the bottom "analytic" path the coders' output is used to define a Markovian (DAR(1)) source model, which is both high order (≈ 60 states for each source) and parametrically parsimonious. Only the mean, variance, correlation of the data and the range of the number of cells per frame are required to define the source model, which can therefore be done quickly and easily. The CDE method is then used to analyze the multiplexer performance. The comparisons of the end results are in terms of system capacity. For an upper bound on the cell loss probability of about 10^{-6}, buffer size B and trunk capacity or bandwidth C, we obtain for each of the two paths the capacity of the system as measured by the maximum number of admissible video teleconference

Reprinted from IEEE Journal on Selected Areas in Communications, Vol. 13, No. 6, Aug. 1995, pp. 1004–1016.

sources. The results are surprisingly close. It may therefore be reasonably inferred that our approximation technique is tight, and that our modeling of the available video teleconferencing traffic data by DAR(1) is effective.

The systems investigated have a broad range. The trunk bandwidth C ranges from 45 to 300 Mb/s, the buffer sizes are such that the corresponding maximum delays range from 1 to 60 ms, and, importantly, the number of coder-sources ranges from 15 to 150. Even for the largest systems the time required on a standard workstation for analysis is a fraction of a second, while each simulation takes many hours. Thus, importantly, our analytic techniques can be implemented fast enough for real-time administration of admission control based on the techniques to be feasible.

Our new mathematical results include upper and lower bounds on the probability of buffer overflow, which have similar behavior over the full range of buffer sizes B. The techniques used to arrive at these results are from Large Deviations theory. Specifically, the upper and lower bounds correspond to lower and upper bounds on the large deviations rate function related to buffer overflows. In the homogeneous model there are K identical Markovian traffic sources of arbitrary, but finite, dimensions. The results show that if b denotes the buffer capacity per source, i.e., $b = B/K$, and $W(t)$ represents the buffer occupancy at time t, there exist easily calculated positive constants, C_1 and C_2, such that for every $b > 0$

$$\lim_{K \to \infty} \frac{1}{K} \log \mathbb{P}(W(t) \geq Kb) \leq -C_2 b - C_1. \quad (1)$$

It is also shown that the constants are the best possible since the inequality is tight at the two limits, $b \to 0$ and $b \to \infty$. Furthermore, the companion lower bound to (1) behaves as $-C_2 b - C_3$, for all $b \geq b_0$, where b_0 and C_3 are positive constants. The main assumption that is made in proving the above results is that the sources are Markovian and time-reversible. The sources in the video teleconference application are Markovian and time-reversible.

Consider the following conventional estimate of the stationary overflow probability of a buffer of size B derived from an infinite buffer analysis

$$G(B) = \lim_{t \to \infty} \mathbb{P}(W(t) \geq B). \quad (2)$$

Based on our bounds and experience with numerical experiments, we propose the following approximation for systems with general Markovian sources

$$G(B) \approx e^{-KC_1} e^{-C_2 B}. \quad (3)$$

Note the connection to (1). We have used this approximation for systems with high dimensional Markovian sources that are time-reversible and irreversible, and found it to be effective in both cases. In (3) we let $L = e^{-KC_1}$ and $z = -C_2$, so that

$$G(B) \approx L e^{zB}. \quad (4)$$

This form has considerable appeal since we can show that L is the loss in bufferless multiplexing as estimated from Chernoff's theorem, and z is the dominant eigenvalue in buffered multiplexers, which is known to determine the large buffer behavior in the logarithmic scale. We call the approximation in (4) the CDE method of estimating overflow probability.

In Section II-B we give explicit procedures, which are simple and fast, for calculating z and L for stochastic fluid models. For discrete-time systems the procedure for calculating L is unchanged, while the theory and numerical procedures for calculating the dominant eigenvalue are developed in Section III. These procedures are used in Section V to calculate the CDE approximation for the video teleconference applications.

Coffman *et al.* [3] considered on-off, 2-state sources and gave numerical evidence to support the claim $G(0) \approx L$. (It is easy to show that $G(0) \geq L$.) Simonian and Guibert [32] quote the observation in [3] as partial basis for a related approximation. In [9] the approximation is used for the analysis and admission control of a multi-service multiplexing system in which the services are prioritized. The approximation refines the pure exponential form e^{zB} used in effective bandwidth analyses [12], [13], [8], [23], [37]. Prior studies [18], [20], [30] have noted that the loss in bufferless multiplexing is very well approximated by the Chernoff large deviations approximation. Note that in typical ATM applications where cell loss probabilities are in the range $10^{-6} - 10^{-9}$, a substantial contribution is derived from the mechanism underlying bufferless multiplexing; it is not atypical for L to be in the range $10^{-3} - 10^{-5}$. Hence, the prefactor L typically adds significantly to the accuracy of the effective bandwidth approximation, which otherwise can sometimes be overly conservative [4]. It should also be noted that other approaches for improving the exponential bound are in [31], [4] and [6].

The paper is organized as follows. Section II gives the fundamental bounds from Large Deviations theory. Section III considers discrete-time, discrete-state space systems. Section IV gives the statistical model of teleconference traffic. Section V reports on numerical results from simulations and analyses.

II. BOUNDS AND APPROXIMATIONS FOR MULTIPLEXERS

A. Bounds for Time-Reversible Buffered Systems

In this section we obtain an upper bound on the probability of buffer overflow in a class of models of buffered multiplexers. This upper bound is equivalent to a lower bound on the large deviations rate function related to buffer overflows. We concentrate here on the case of homogeneous sources; the extension of the main results to heterogeneous sources is straightforward and stated in a subsequent section. The models have K traffic sources, trunk capacity or bandwidth C, a constant, and a buffer of size B. Also, b and c are respectively the buffer and trunk capacity per source; i.e., $B = bK$ and $C = cK$. Standard arguments for Markovian traffic sources show that there is a positive constant C_2 such that, if $W(t)$

represents the total buffer occupancy at time t, for each fixed K

$$\lim_{b \to \infty} \frac{1}{Kb} \log \mathbb{P}(W(t) \geq Kb) = -C_2. \tag{5}$$

We show that there exists an easily calculated constant $C_1 > 0$ such that for every $b > 0$

$$\lim_{K \to \infty} \frac{1}{K} \log \mathbb{P}(W(t) \geq Kb) \leq -C_2 b - C_1. \tag{6}$$

The constants are the best possible, since we have

$$\lim_{b \downarrow 0} \lim_{K \to \infty} \frac{1}{K} \log \mathbb{P}(W(t) \geq Kb) = -C_1 \tag{7}$$

and also

$$\lim_{b \to \infty} \lim_{K \to \infty} \frac{1}{Kb} \log \mathbb{P}(W(t) \geq Kb) = -C_2. \tag{8}$$

Furthermore, we derive a similar but less explicit lower bound

$$\lim_{K \to \infty} \frac{1}{K} \log \mathbb{P}(W(t) \geq Kb) \geq -f(b) \tag{9}$$

where $f(b)$ is given by a somewhat complicated formula, but for some fixed b_0 we have

$$f(b) = C_2 b + C_3 \tag{10}$$

for all $b \geq b_0$, where C_3 is a constant that is again given by a somewhat complicated formula. We can easily show the obvious bound $C_3 > C_1$.

An individual source is characterized by (Q, R) and has state space $(1, 2, \cdots, d)$. The $d \times d$ matrix generator $Q = \{Q_{i,j}\}$, where $Q_{i,j}$ (for $i \neq j$) is the rate at which a source in state i jumps to state j, and $Q_{i,i} = -\sum_{j \neq i} Q_{i,j}$. The vector $R = (R_1, R_2, \cdots, R_d)$, where R_i is the rate at which a source in state i generates traffic. The K traffic sources are statistically identical and independent Markov jump processes. To describe the aggregate behavior of the sources we encode each state of an individual source in a different dimension as follows: the vector $q(t) \in \mathcal{Z}^d$, wherein the component $q_i(t)$ denotes the number of sources in state i at time t. A source jumping from state i to state j causes a transition of $q(t)$ in direction $e_j - e_i$, where e_i is the unit vector in direction i ($i = 1, 2, \cdots, d$). The rate of these jumps is $q_i Q_{i,j}$, because there are q_i sources in state i, each jumping at rate $Q_{i,j}$. Therefore, $q(t)$ is a Markov process with infinitesimal generator

$$L\phi(q) = \sum_{i,j} q_i Q_{i,j} (\phi(q + e_j - e_i) - \phi(q)). \tag{11}$$

L is an operator on functions $\phi : \mathbb{R}^d \to \mathbb{R}^1$. We make two assumptions on the process $q(t)$:
1) $q(t)$ is time-reversible.
2) $q(t)$ is irreducible.

In fact, we can eliminate Assumption 2, which we have included only to make a few arguments simpler. We do use Assumption 1 in crucial ways for our proof, though. We do not know whether or not this assumption is necessary for our results.

The final part of the buffer model is the rate at which the buffer (whose content is denoted $W(t)$) drains. We assume that the buffer drains with rate at most C

$$\frac{d}{dt}W(t)$$
$$= \begin{cases} \langle R, q(t) \rangle - C, & \text{if } \langle R, q(t) \rangle - C > 0 \text{ or } W(t) > 0 \\ 0, & \text{otherwise} \end{cases} \tag{12}$$

where $\langle x, y \rangle \triangleq \sum_i x_i y_i$.

We make the standard large deviations scaling of the process $q(t)$ as follows

$$z_K(t) \triangleq \frac{q(t)}{K}. \tag{13}$$

Then $z_K(t)$ is a Markov process whose components represent the fraction of sources in each state. The generator of $z_K(t)$ is L_K, given by

$$L_K \phi(x) = \sum_{i,j} K x_i Q_{i,j} (\phi(x + (e_j - e_i)/K) - \phi(x)). \tag{14}$$

The generator is defined for points $x \in S_d$, where S_d is the set of probability vectors in $\mathbb{R}^d$

$$S_d \triangleq \left\{ x \in \mathbb{R}^d : x_i \geq 0, \sum_i x_i = 1 \right\}. \tag{15}$$

We now define the large deviations local rate function $\ell(x, y)$ associated with the process $z_K(t)$

$$\ell(x, y) \triangleq \sup_{s \in \mathbb{R}^d} \left(\langle s, y \rangle - \sum_{i,j} Q_{i,j} x_i \left(e^{\langle e_j - e_i, s \rangle} - 1 \right) \right). \tag{16}$$

$\ell(x, y)$ is defined for $x \in S_d$ and for y with $\sum_i y_i = 0$, which is a condition satisfied by the difference of probability vectors. Intuitively, $\ell(x, y)$ represents the negative logarithm of the local probability of the process $z_K(t)$ traveling in direction y. For example, we can show that as $K \to \infty$

$$\mathbb{P}_x \left(\sup_{0 \leq t \leq \Delta} |z_K(t) - (x + ty)| < \epsilon \right) = e^{-K\ell(x,y) + O(K\Delta) + o(n)}. \tag{17}$$

Here, $\mathbb{P}_x$ refers to sample paths $z_K(t)$ that start at the point x. A more precise and general statement than (17), is the following statement of the large deviations principle. For any open set of paths $\mathcal{G}$ and for any closed set of paths $\mathcal{F}$, we have the following limits

$$\liminf_{K \to \infty} \frac{1}{K} \log \mathbb{P}(z_K \in \mathcal{G}) \geq -\inf_{r \in \mathcal{G}} I_0^T(r) \tag{18}$$

$$\limsup_{K \to \infty} \frac{1}{K} \log \mathbb{P}(z_K \in \mathcal{F}) \leq -\inf_{r \in \mathcal{F}} I_0^T(r) \tag{19}$$

where

$$I_0^T(r) \triangleq \int_0^T \ell(r(t), r'(t)) dt. \tag{20}$$

The function $I_0^T(r)$ is called the rate function; ℓ is the local rate function. For more information about the rate functions or the large deviations principle, see Varadhan [36], Dembo and Zeitouni [7], Freidlin and Wentzell [11], or Shwartz and Weiss [35].

We can also write the buffer content $W(t)$ as an integral. Let

$$s(t) \triangleq \arg\sup_{u \leq t} \int_u^t (\langle R, q(t)\rangle - C)\, dt. \tag{21}$$

That is, $s(t)$ is the last time before t that the buffer is empty

$$s(t) \triangleq \sup\{u : u \leq t,\ W(u) = 0\}. \tag{22}$$

Then, we have the following representation of $W(t)$

$$W(t) = \int_{s(t)}^t (\langle R, q(t)\rangle - C)\, dt. \tag{23}$$

We define the operator $B(q)(t)$ as the map giving the function $W(t)$ from a path $q(t)$, using either of the equivalent definitions (12) or (23). That is

$$W(t) = B(q)(t). \tag{24}$$

We also have a scaled buffer occupancy

$$w(t) \triangleq \frac{W(t)}{K}. \tag{25}$$

This can be obtained by a transformation on $z_K(t)$ as follows

$$w(t) = \int_{s(t)}^t (\langle R, z_K(t)\rangle - c)\, dt. \tag{26}$$

We define the scaled operator $B_s(z_K)$ by (26), namely, $w(t) = B_s(z_K)(t)$.

The "center" of the process p is defined to be the unique limit of the solution of the fluid equation for the scaled process $z_\infty(t)$

$$\frac{d}{dt} z_\infty(t) = \sum_{i,j} z_{\infty,i}(t) Q_{i,j}(e_j - e_i) = z_\infty(t)Q \tag{27}$$

where $z_{\infty,i}(t)$ means the ith component of $z_\infty(t)$. That is, we define

$$p \triangleq z_\infty(\infty). \tag{28}$$

Assumption 2 assures the uniqueness of p. In fact, for the class of models considered here, p is identical to π, where the component π_i represents the unique stationary probability that a single source is in state i. That is, $\pi \in S_d$ and

$$\pi Q = 0. \tag{29}$$

We now prove 6 and give explicit expressions for the constants C_1 and C_2

$$C_1 = \inf_{r,v,T \in F} \int_0^T \ell(r, r')\, dt,$$
$$C_2 = \inf_{r \in S_d : \langle r, R\rangle > c} \frac{\ell(r, 0)}{\langle r, R\rangle - c} \tag{30}$$

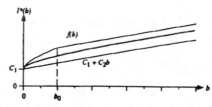

Fig. 2. The cost function $I^*(b)$ and our bounds. $I^*(b)$ was calculated numerically for a two state model. $f(b)$ is linear and parallel to $C_1 + C_2 b$ for $b > b_0$.

where

$$F \triangleq \{r, v, T : r(0) = \pi,\ \langle v, R\rangle = c,\ r(T) = v\} \tag{31}$$

and the function ℓ is defined by (16). Furthermore, we have a much more explicit expression for C_1

$$C_1 = \inf_{x \in H(c)} \ell_1(x) \tag{32}$$

where $\ell_1(x)$ is the rate function for a multinomial random variable

$$\ell_1(x) \triangleq \sum_{i=1}^d x_i \log \frac{x_i}{\pi_i} \tag{33}$$

where π_i is the steady-state probability that a source is in state i, and

$$H(c) \triangleq \{x \in S_d : \langle x, R\rangle = c\}. \tag{34}$$

Here is a precise statement of our main result (See Fig. 2).

Theorem 2.1: Suppose that the underlying process $q(t)$ is reversible and irreducible. Let C_1 be defined by (32), let C_2 be defined by (30), and let $p = \pi$, which is defined by (29). Define

$$I^*(b) \triangleq \inf_{(r,T) \in \mathcal{G}(b)} I_0^T(r) \tag{35}$$

where

$$\mathcal{G}(b) = \{r, T : r(-\infty) = p,\ B_s(r)(T) = b\}. \tag{36}$$

Then, for each $b > 0$

$$I^*(b) \geq C_1 + C_2 b. \tag{37}$$

$\square$

The equivalence of C_1 as defined by (30) and by (32) comes from the same calculations that show that Chernoff's theorem is equivalent to Sanov's theorem; see, e.g., [35, ch. 2].

$I_0^T(r)$ should be thought of as a cost. It is the cost for the process $z_K(t)$ to follow the path $r(t)$. The cost is related to probability by the large deviations principle

$$\mathbb{P}(\sup_{0 \leq t \leq T} |z_K(t) - r(t)| < \varepsilon) = e^{-KI_0^T(r) + o(K)}. \tag{38}$$

The probability of an event is related to the cheapest cost of the paths r that cause the event to occur. That is, to calculate the frequency of an unlikely event's occurrence, think of all the different ways that it might occur, calculate the cost of

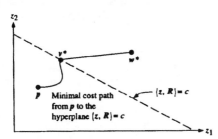

Fig. 3.   A path $r_b(t)$ for Theorem 2.3.

each way, and take the cheapest cost I^*. Then the probability of the event is approximated by $\exp(-KI^*)$.

The idea behind the bound in Theorem 2.1 is the following. The quantity C_1 represents the lowest cost for going from the point p to the point, say v^*, where the buffer begins to fill. See Fig. 3. The quantity C_2 represents the lowest possible cost per unit buffer for a path that doesn't move. The lowest cost of achieving a buffer occupancy b should be larger than $C_1 + C_2 b$, since any path that makes the buffer occupancy reach b will have to cross to the place where the buffer begins to fill, and then will have to make the buffer fill to b, but will also have to be a nearly continuous path, so it can't be near all the minima all the time.

We give a related result. Suppose that

$$C_2 = \frac{\ell(w^*, 0)}{\langle w^*, R \rangle - c} \tag{39}$$

for a unique point $w^* \in \mathcal{S}_d : \langle w^*, R \rangle > c$. Define

$$A \triangleq \frac{1}{\langle w^*, R \rangle - c}. \tag{40}$$

Given $\varepsilon > 0$ and T, define

$$g_\varepsilon(b, T) = \frac{1}{bA} \int_{T-bA}^{T} 1[|z_K(t) - w^*| < \varepsilon] \, dt. \tag{41}$$

Theorem 2.2: For each $\varepsilon > 0$ there is a $\delta > 0$ such that for any T

$$\lim_{K, b \to \infty} \mathbf{P}_{ss}(g_\varepsilon(b, T) > 1 - \varepsilon \mid w_K(T) \geq b) = 1. \tag{42}$$

($\mathbf{P}_{ss}$ refers to steady-state probability.)   □

This theorem states that, if there is a unique w^* such that (39) holds, then we know exactly how the system behaves in order that the buffer occupancy reaches a high level —the system spends almost all the time just before overflow in a small neighborhood of w^*. The proof of this theorem does not use either of the two assumptions; that is, the theorem holds for both reducible and irreversible systems.

We have a lower bound on buffer overflow probability which is a bit harder to write explicitly, but has the same form and asymptotics as the upper bound of (6).

Theorem 2.3: There is a function $f(b)$ such that for every $b > 0$

$$I^*(b) \leq f(b). \tag{43}$$

Furthermore, there is a constant b_0 such that

$$\begin{aligned} f(0) &= C_1 \\ f(b) &= C_3 + C_2 b \quad \text{for} \quad b \geq b_0. \end{aligned} \tag{44}$$

Compare the bounds on $I^*(b)$ given by (44) and Theorem 1; the discrepancy is bounded for all b.   □

The proofs of these results are immediate consequences of the large deviations principle for the process $z_K(t)$ and of the Freidlin-Wentzell theory, plus some new lemmas. The Freidlin-Wentzell theory equates steady-state probabilities with upcrossing probabilities. The large deviations principle equates upcrossing probabilities with solutions to variational problems. The variational problems are integrals of the function $\ell(x, y)$ as in (30). The bound in (37) and the result in (42) follow from some new lemmas, which bound the solutions to the variational problems. The bound (43) follows from a specific construction: consider a path that goes from p to the region $\langle z_K, R \rangle = c$, and from there to a minimizing point w^*, which is defined in (39). Then the minimum of the variational problem has to have lower cost than this particular path. The bound is then established, with the function f being the cost of the particular path. The path is depicted in Fig. 3.

We use the following result in our analysis. It is essentially due to [10]. (See also [34].)

Theorem 2.4: If the process $z_K(t)$ is reversible, and if Kurtz's theorem holds, then given any $x \neq p$ the time reversed path $r(t) = z_\infty^x(-t)$ from p to x is a minimal cost path from p to x. Therefore

$$\lim_{\varepsilon \downarrow 0} \lim_{K \to \infty} \frac{1}{K} \log \mathbf{P}_{ss}(|z_K(t) - x| < \varepsilon) = -I_0^T(r). \tag{45}$$

□

The proofs of Theorems 2.1–2.3 are in the Appendix.

B. Approximation, Numerical Procedures

As mentioned in Section I, see (2), $G(B)$ denotes the estimate of the stationary overflow probability of a buffer of size B. There the following approximation was also proposed

$$G(B) \approx e^{-KC_1} e^{-C_2 B}. \tag{46}$$

This approximation was shown in Section II-A to have attractive asymptotic properties; in our experience it is also both conservative and close to the true overflow probability in typical applications with both reversible and irreversible sources. In (46) we let $L = e^{-KC_1}$ and $z = -C_2$, to obtain the CDE approximation to the overflow probability

$$G(B) \approx L e^{zB}. \tag{47}$$

From the discussion below Theorem 1, L is the loss in bufferless multiplexing as estimated from either Chernoff's theorem or Sanov's theorem; z is the dominant eigenvalue of the buffered multiplexer, which is known to determine the large buffer behavior of the overflow probability. (The dominant eigenvalue in stable irreducible Markovian models is always real and negative.)

The dominant eigenvalue and its calculation have been topics of central importance in most studies of statistical multiplexing based on stochastic fluid models [1], [21], [22], [27], [28], [31], [30]. Here are two results quoted from [8]. Define the diagonal matrix $R_d = \text{diag}(R_1, R_2, \cdots, R_d)$. Observe that for z real and negative, $[R_d - \frac{1}{z}Q]$ is an irreducible matrix with nonnegative off-diagonal elements. Such a matrix has a real eigenvalue, called the maximal real eigenvalue (MRE) that is greater than the real part of all its other eigenvalues. Let

$$g(z) \triangleq \text{MRE}\left(R_d - \frac{1}{z}Q\right). \tag{48}$$

Fact 1: The dominant eigenvalue z of the homogeneous system with K sources, each source described by (Q, R), and channel capacity C is obtained by solving the equation

$$Kg(z) = C. \tag{49}$$

$\square$

Equation (49) is easily solved because $g(z)$ is monotonic decreasing for $z < 0$, and c lies between $\hat{R} \triangleq \max_i R_i = g(-\infty)$, and $\bar{R} = \sum_i \pi_i R_i = \lim_{z \to 0} g(z)$. Now suppose that there are J classes of sources, where each class $j \in [1, \cdots, J]$ is comprised of K_j sources characterized by $(Q^{(j)}, R^{(j)})$. Then we have

Fact 2: The dominant eigenvalue z of the heterogeneous system is obtained by solving

$$\sum_{j=1}^{J} K_j g^{(j)}(z) = C \tag{50}$$

where

$$g^{(j)}(z) \triangleq \text{MRE}\left(R_d^{(j)} - \frac{1}{z}Q^{(j)}\right). \tag{51}$$

$\square$

We may now turn to the procedure for calculating L, the estimate from Chernoff's theorem of the loss in bufferless multiplexing. Let $V_{j,i}(t)$ denote the rate of traffic generation by source i of class j at time t, and let $\{V_{j,i}\}$ be a collection of independent random variables where $V_{j,i}$ has the stationary distribution of $V_{j,i}(t)$. The total traffic generation has a stationary distribution given by a random variable $V = \sum_j \sum_i V_{j,i}$. Loss occurs when the total traffic generation exceeds the level C. Therefore we estimate $\mathbb{P}(V \geq C)$.

Let $\pi^{(j)}$ denote the stationary probability vector of a class j source. Then $V_{j,i}$ has moment generating function

$$M_j(s) \triangleq \mathbb{E}(e^{sV_{j,i}}) = \sum_k \pi_k^{(j)} e^{sR_k^{(j)}}. \tag{52}$$

Chernoff's theorem states that

$$\log \mathbb{P}(V \geq C) \leq -F(s^*),$$

and $\log \mathbb{P}(V \geq C) = -F(s^*)\left[1 + O\left(\frac{\log C}{C}\right)\right]$ (53)

where

$$F(s) \triangleq sC - \sum_j K_j \log M_j(s) \tag{54}$$

and $F(s^*) = \sup_{s \geq 0} F(s)$. Hence, the estimate of the loss $L = \exp(-F(s^*))$. For $C < \max_i R_i$ it is easy to check that $F(s)$ is a strictly concave function with a unique maximum at $s^* > 0$ that can be obtained by solving $F'(s) = 0$.

For our numerical procedures we use a refinement to the estimate of $\mathbb{P}(V \geq C)$ given by (53) [29], [5].

Fact 3: As $C \to \infty$ with $K_j/C = O(1)$, $j = 1, \cdots, J$

$$\mathbb{P}(V \geq C) = \frac{\exp(-F(s^*))}{s^* \sigma(s^*) \sqrt{2\pi}} \left[1 + o(1)\right] \tag{55}$$

where

$$\sigma^2(s) = \frac{\partial^2 \log \mathbb{E}(s^V)}{\partial s^2}. \tag{56}$$

$\square$

More specifically

$$\sigma^2(s) = \sum_{j=1}^{J} K_j \left[\frac{M_j''(s)}{M_j(s)} - \left(\frac{M_j'(s)}{M_j(s)}\right)^2\right]. \tag{57}$$

To summarize, we obtain L by calculating the leading term on the right hand side of the expression for $\mathbb{P}(V \geq C)$ in (55).

III. DISCRETE-TIME MULTIPLEXING SYSTEMS

In this section we obtain the CDE approximation to discrete-time Markov models. Specifically, we let the approximation for the buffer overflow be of the form (47), and we develop the theory and numerical procedures for computing the dominant eigenvalue, which here is given by e^z. The bufferless multiplexing loss L is obtained from Chernoff's theorem exactly as described in Section II-B, and hence is not considered further. Prior work on the analysis of related discrete-time Markov models are in [24], [38], [33], [23]. However, we did not find the specific result of interest here in the literature.

Consider the homogeneous model in which an infinite buffer is supplied by K independent, identical sources and is serviced by a channel which transmits at most C cells in unit time. Here time is divided into units; the natural time unit in the system model in the sequel is the frame. Each source is described by an irreducible Markov chain with transition matrix P. When the source is in state i $(i = 1, 2, \cdots, d)$ at a particular time unit, R_i cells are produced in that time unit. Thus each source is characterized by (P, R). The superposition of the K sources is characterized by M and Λ, where $R_d = \text{diag}(R)$

$$M = P \otimes P \otimes \cdots \otimes P \quad \text{and} \quad \Lambda = R_d \oplus R_d \oplus \cdots \oplus R_d. \tag{58}$$

Here K copies occur in the Kronecker product and sum, so that M and Λ are $d^K \times d^K$. Note that the above representation, while not corresponding to the minimal state representation of the superposition process, is nonetheless essential for the derivation of the decomposition obtained below. We only consider stable systems for which $\bar{R} = \sum_i \pi_i R_i < C/K$, where $\pi \in S_d$ and $\pi P = \pi$.

Let $W(t)$ denote the number of cells in the buffer at the beginning of the tth time unit. Also, let $L(s)$ be the number of cells generated when the source state is s; hence, $L(s) \in \{\lambda_1, \lambda_2, \cdots, \lambda_{d^K}\}$, where λ_i is the ith diagonal element of Λ. The evolution of the buffer content is described by

$$W(t+1) = [W(t) + L(s(t)) - C]^+ \qquad (59)$$

where $[\cdot]^+ = \max(\cdot, 0)$. Let $p(n, k) \triangleq \lim_{t \to \infty} \mathbb{P}(W(t) = n, L(s(t)) = \lambda_k)$ $(k = 1, 2, \cdots, d^K)$, and $p(n) = [p(n,1)p(n,2) \cdots p(n, d^K)]$ $(n = 0, 1, 2, \cdots)$. The system's steady-state balance equations are

$$
\begin{aligned}
p(0) &= \sum_{\ell, m: \lambda_m + \ell \leq C} p(\ell) M_m \\
p(n) &= \sum_{m: \lambda_m \leq n - C} p(n - \lambda_m + C) M_m \qquad (60)
\end{aligned}
$$

where M_m is the matrix obtained from M by replacing every row except the mth by a row of zeros.

Assume independent solutions of (60) of the form

$$p(n) = e^{zn}\phi \quad (n = 0, 1, 2, \cdots). \qquad (61)$$

On substitution of (61) into (60), we obtain the following eigenvalue equation

$$e^{-zC}\phi = \phi e^{-z\Lambda} M \qquad (62)$$

where e^z is an eigenvalue and ϕ is the corresponding eigenvector. Now, for real z, the matrix $A(z) = e^{-z\Lambda} M$ is nonnegative and irreducible, hence its (Perron-Frobenius) eigenvalue of maximum modulus, which we denote by $g(z)$, is real, positive and simple. Utilizing the structure of M and Λ in (58), we obtain

$$A(z) = (e^{-zR_d}P) \otimes (e^{-zR_d}P) \otimes \cdots \otimes (e^{-zR_d}P). \qquad (63)$$

From this structure we may infer [14] that

$$g(z) = \{\mu(z)\}^K \qquad (64)$$

where $\mu(z)$ is the Perron-Frobenius eigenvalue of $e^{-zR_d}P$.

The dominant eigenvalue of the multiplexing system, which dominates the behavior of $p(n)$ for large n, is the largest value of e^z which satisfies (62). This quantity is real, positive and, for stable systems, less than unity, i.e., $z < 0$. From (62) and (64) we have,

Fact 1: The dominant eigenvalue of the discrete-time, homogeneous multiplexing system is e^z, where z is obtained by solving

$$-K \frac{\log \mu(z)}{z} = C. \qquad (65)$$

$\square$

Since $-\{\log \mu(z)\}/z$ is monotonic decreasing for $z < 0$, and C is bounded by $\hat{R} = \max_i R_i$ and $\overline{R}$, and C/K lies between $\hat{R}$ and $\overline{R}$, (65) can be solved without difficulty.

The above analysis easily extends to the case of heterogeneous sources. In particular, if there are J classes of sources, where each class $j \in [1, 2, \cdots, J]$ is comprised of K_j sources characterized by $(P^{(j)}, R^{(j)})$, then we have

Fact 2: The dominant eigenvalue of the heterogeneous multiplexing system is given by e^z, where z is obtained by solving

$$\sum_{j=1}^{J} K_j \left\{ \frac{-\log \mu^{(j)}(z)}{z} \right\} = C \qquad (66)$$

where $\mu^{(j)}(z)$ is the Perron-Frobenius eigenvalue of $e^{-zR_d^{(j)}}P^{(j)}$. $\square$

IV. A STATISTICAL MODEL OF VBR-CODED TELECONFERENCE TRAFFIC

To formulate statistical models of VBR-coded teleconference traffic, we analyzed traffic from three 30 min long video conference sequences coded using three different methods. All of the sequences show head-and-shoulders scenes with moderate motion and scene changes, and with very little camera zoom or pan. Let us call the three coding algorithms A, B, and C. Algorithm A uses intrafield/interframe DPCM coding without DCT nor motion compensation. Algorithm B is a modified version of the H.261 video coding standard. H.261 is a hybrid DPCM/DCT coding scheme with motion compensation. The modified version uses an open loop (no rate control) coding scheme with a fixed quantizer step size $(Q = 2)$. Algorithm C uses a hybrid DPCM/DCT coding algorithm and is similar to algorithm B. However, it does not use motion compensation. The three algorithms also differ in some other aspects of coding, such as picture formats and entropy coding. The key differences to note are that A uses neither motion compensation nor DCT, B uses both motion compensation and DCT, and C uses DCT without motion compensation. The traffic data that we used gives the number of cells per frame. It does not specify how the cells arrive to the network within an interframe interval. Hence, we only model the number of cells per frame.

Let X_n be the number of cells in the nth frame of a VBR-coded video teleconference. In [16] and [17] we showed that X_n has the following properties for all three coding schemes.

1) The number of cells per frame is a stationary Markov chain.
2) The marginal distribution of X_n is negative-binomial.
3) The correlation between X_n and X_{n+k} has the form ρ^k.

The probability function for the negative-binomial distribution is

$$
\begin{aligned}
f_k &= \binom{k + r - 1}{k} p^r q^k \\
&= \binom{-r}{k} p^r (-q)^k, \qquad k = 0, 1, \cdots. \quad (67)
\end{aligned}
$$

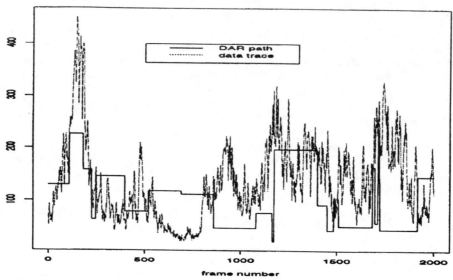

Fig. 4. Comparison of number of cells/frame (y-axis) for 2000 frame trace for one source using actual data and DAR(1) model.

The mean and variance of this distribution are

$$m = \frac{r(1-p)}{p} \quad \text{and} \quad v = \frac{r(1-p)}{p^2} \quad (68)$$

respectively. Here, $0 < p < 1$, $q = 1 - p$ and $r > 0$. The method of moments gives the estimates

$$\hat{p} = \frac{m_0}{v_0} \quad \text{and} \quad \hat{r} = \frac{m_0{}^2}{v_0 - m_0} \quad (69)$$

for p and r in terms of the observed values of m_0 and v_0; $v_0 > m_0$ is required for the estimates to make sense.

From properties (2) and (3), the only parameters that are needed to specify the X_n are the mean and variance of the marginal distribution, and the autocorrelation coefficient. From property (1), the temporal evolution of the process is completely specified once a suitable transition matrix for the Markov chain is given. Estimating the transition matrix $P = (p_{ij})$ for the Markov chain modeling X_n (or some aggregation of the X_n) using

$$\hat{p}_{ij} = \frac{\text{number of transitions } i \text{ to } j}{\text{number of transitions out of } i} \quad (70)$$

is not practical since this has too many parameters.

To be of practical use, we would like the model to be based only on parameters which are either known at call set-up time or can be measured without introducing too much complexity in the network. Hence, we use the discrete autoregressive process of order 1, or DAR(1) process [19], because it provides an easy and practical method to compute the transition matrix and gives us a model based only on three physically meaningful parameters, the mean, variance, and correlation of the offered traffic. Let Q be a square stochastic matrix where each row is $\mathbf{f} = (f_0, f_1, \cdots, f_M)$, where f_i

$(i = 0, 1, \cdots, M - 1)$ are the negative binomial probabilities in (67), $f_M = \sum_{m > M-1} f_m$, and M is the peak rate in cells per frame. If the peak rate is not known, any suitably large number M can be used. The matrix P given by

$$P = \rho I + (1 - \rho)Q \quad (71)$$

where I is the identity matrix, has the desired properties. The rate vector $R = (R_0, R_1, \cdots, R_M)$, where $R_i = i$ $(i = 0, 1, \cdots, M)$. Later we consider aggregating these states. The transition matrix in (71) has the property that if the current frame has i cells say, then the next frame will have i cells with probability $\rho + (1 - \rho)f_i$, and will have k cells, $k \neq i$, with probability $(1 - \rho)f_k$. This makes each sample path more regular than the data traces because the number of cells per frame stays constant for a mean of $((1 - \rho)(1 - f_i))^{-1}$ frames; this is about 100 frames with our data. This can be seen in Fig. 4 which plots a segment of the actual data trace and a trace of the same length produced by the DAR(1) model. However, this difference between the DAR and the actual trace attenuates for an ensemble of sources as more and more sources are superposed. This is evident from Fig. 5 which shows multiplexed traces produced using the actual traffic and using the DAR(1) model.

The stationary probability vector of the DAR(1) process is $\mathbf{f}$, i.e., $\mathbf{f} = \mathbf{f}P$. Also, detailed balance holds, i.e., $f_i P_{ij} = f_j P_{ji}$ for all i and j. Hence,

Fact: The DAR(1) process with transition matrix P is reversible. ☐

Consequently, all eigenvalues of P are real.

This DAR model was introduced in [16] and was shown to accurately predict the blocking probability for a superposition of several identical sources fed to a statistical multiplexer. Algorithm C was used in that study. This result was shown to hold for algorithms A and B in [17]. Further evidence that the

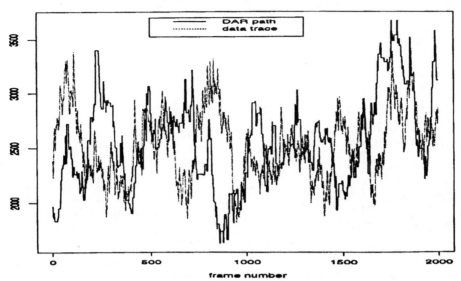

Fig. 5. Comparison of number of cells/frame (y-axis) for 2000 frame trace for 20 multiplexed sources using actual data and DAR(1) model.

DAR model is a good fit to video conference data is given in [26] where the analyzed sequence was generated by a codec different from those used in our studies.

This three parameter model is restricted to video conferences because we have not so far been able to adequately model entertainment video sources using similar models [15].

V. ANALYTIC AND SIMULATION RESULTS

We considered the following traffic engineering problem: How many simultaneous (statistically identical) video conferences can an ATM switch carry with a cell-loss rate (CLR) of about 10^{-6}? We computed this number using the CDE method and compared it to the number obtained by simulation. This was done for the different video sources (using the different coding schemes) described in Section IV. We found the agreement between the two numbers to be sufficiently accurate, for traffic engineering purposes, over a wide range of system characteristics.

For the analytic approximation to the buffer overflow probability with DAR(1) source models we use the expression in (47), where the loss in bufferless multiplexing, L, is obtained from the refinement to Chernoff's theorem, see (55), and the dominant eigenvalue e^z is obtained by the following result. It is assumed here that $R_0 < R_1 < \cdots < R_M$.

Theorem 5.1: The dominant eigenvalue of the multiplexing system with K homogeneous DAR(1) sources, each described by (P, R) is e^z, where z is the unique solution to the scalar equation

$$(1 - \rho) \sum_{i=1}^{M} f_i [e^{z(R_i - C/K)} - \rho]^{-1} = 1 \qquad (72)$$

TABLE I
PARAMETERS OF TRAFFIC SEQUENCES STUDIED

Sequence	Mean Cells/frame	Peak Cells/frame	Variance	Correlation 1-frame lag	Cell Size Bytes
A	1506.4	4818.0	262827.1	0.9731	14
B	104.8	220.0	882.5	0.9795	48
C	130.3	630.0	5536.9	0.9846	64

in the interval $((\log \rho)/(R_{M-1} - C/K), (\log \rho)/(R_M - C/K))$. The function in (72) in this interval is monotonic decreasing. $\qquad \Box$

The proof, which is omitted, exploits the structure of P in (71). For a related result see [8, sect. VI].

To obtain the number of admitted sources by simulation, we used the actual traffic traces giving the number of cells per frame for video teleconferences of approximately 30 min duration. Here, we present results for sequences A and C which are the traffic traces generated by the coding schemes A and C described in Section IV. The relevant parameters for the different sequences are shown in Table I.

For sequence A, the frame rate is 30 frames/s, and the trace is 38 100 frames long. Sequence C is 45 000 frames long and the frame rate is 25 frames/s.

The switch is modeled as a multiplexer with a buffer whose size is determined by the maximum buffering delay. Cell arrivals from each individual source are equally spaced during the interframe interval (33.3 ms for sequence A, 40 ms for sequence B). The recorded data trace is used to generate traffic for each of the sources. Since we do not have hundreds of different 30 min long recorded traces to simulate the different admitted sources, we use the same sequence to generate traffic for all sources. This is done by using different starting points (indices) in the trace. We found by experimentation, that with a random choice of indices the variation of the number of

TABLE II
COMPARISON OF NUMBER OF CODING SCHEME C SOURCES
ADMITTED USING SIMULATION AND THE CDE METHOD

C	45	67	81	103	125	145	195	245	270	310
B	57	9	50	44	5	0.5	9	23	7	1
K_{sim}	20	30	40	50	60	70	98	128	139	156
K_{CDE}	16	25	33	44	53	63	90	120	130	150
$\frac{K_{CDE}}{K_{sim}}$	.80	.83	.83	.88	.88	.90	.92	.94	.94	.96

TABLE III
COMPARISON OF NUMBER OF CODING SCHEME A SOURCES
ADMITTED USING SIMULATION AND USING THE CDE METHOD

C	110	185	280	375
B	8.5	9.5	10	11
K_{sim}	16	30	49	66
K_{CDE}	15	30	50	70
$\frac{K_{CDE}}{K_{sim}}$	.94	1.0	1.02	1.06

admitted sources with choice of indices is generally about 10% (excluding clearly pathological choices such as several sources having the same indices).[1]

Another factor which can affect cell losses is the relative phase between frames arriving from different sources. We use the same relative phases in all experiments. Also, to minimize the effect of phases found in [16] we choose the phases such that the arrival instants of frames from different sources are equally spaced in the 40 ms or 33.3 ms interframe interval. (For a 40 ms interframe interval, if there are 20 sources, the first cells belonging to a new frame from each source arrive at times 2 ms, 4 ms, $\cdots$, 40 ms, and every 40 ms thereafter.)

We use the following notation:

C output rate [Mb/s]
B buffer size [ms] (maximum delay at buffer served at rate C)
K maximum number of sources that approximately achieve CLR = 10^{-6}.

The subscripts sim and CDE denote results from simulation and results from computations using the CDE method.

Table II compares the number of sources using coding scheme C admitted in simulation experiment to the number admitted using the CDE method. The number admitted by simulation was determined by adding sources until the loss rate exceeded the specified bound of approximately 10^{-6}. The CDE computation was done using the DAR(1) source model with the required three parameters of the model (mean, variance, and correlation) being estimated from the traffic trace. From the table, we see that $K_{CDE} < K_{sim}$ and their ratio gets monotonically closer to one as the correctly engineered maximum number of sources gets larger. The peak-to-mean ratio for this traffic is 5, and the mean bit rate is 1.668 Mb/s.

[1] The cell loss probability is sensitive to choice of indices. However, this does not translate to large variations in the number of admitted sources because of the relatively large increments in the offered traffic when new sources are admitted.

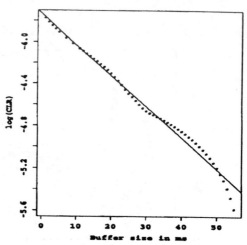

Fig. 6.   Log(CLR) versus buffer size for sequence C, 20 sources, $C = 45$ MByte/s.

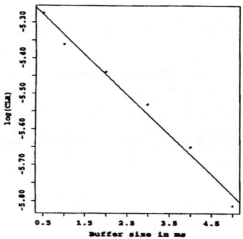

Fig. 7.   Log(CLR) versus buffer size for sequence C, 60 sources, $C = 125$ MByte/s.

Hence, from the table it can be seen that the statistical multiplexing gain is in the 3 to 4 range.

Table III presents results using traffic coded by scheme A. We see that the number admitted using the CDE method is a very close approximation to the "true" number obtained by simulation.

We also tested by simulation one of the basic hypothesis underlying the use of the CDE method. The hypothesis is that $\log(\text{CLR}) \approx \ell + zB$, where ℓ and z are constants. Figs. 6 and 7 plot on a log-linear scale the buffer overflow probabilities for various buffer sizes. The overflow probabilities were obtained by simulation using sequence C for the parameters indicated in the figure. The plots shows that the hypothesis is well founded for this set of parameters. Similar results were obtained for many other parameter settings. For 60 sources, the traffic information in sequence C allows us to simulate 3.5×10^8 cell arrivals to the switch. This does not permit us to reliably

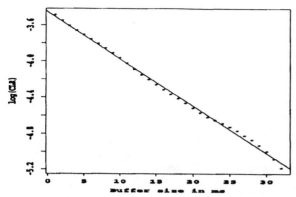

Fig. 8. Log(CLR) versus buffer size for sequence A, 50 sources and $C = 280$ MByte/s.

estimate CLR's much lower than the ranges shown in the figure.

Fig. 8 shows the results from experiments with sequence A. For the 50 source example shown in the figure, the information in sequence A allows us to simulate 2.8×10^9 cell arrivals at the switch allowing us to obtain reliable estimates of CLR for the ranges shown in the figure. Again, we find that the buffer overflow probability decreases exponentially with buffer size. Beran et al. [2] state that our traffic data exhibit long-range dependence. The DAR(1) model has a geometrically declining autocorrelation function. So it takes into accounts only short range dependence. Leland et al. [25] argue (in the context of Ethernet traffic) that when traffic is long range dependent "overall packet loss decreases very slowly with increasing buffer capacity." If these assertions were both valid for the system we model, then the CDE method would not be applicable to video teleconference traffic. Results from our simulation studies using actual data traces (summarized in Figs. 6–8) do not conform to these assertions. Furthermore, the underlying hypothesis necessary for using the CDE method seems to hold for video teleconferences and the results in Tables II and III indicate that this method is accurate enough to be used for admission control and bandwidth allocation of video teleconferences.

APPENDIX
PROOFS OF THEOREMS 2.1 AND 2.3

We need two lemmas. The proof of Lemma 1 is in [35, ch. 13].

Lemma 1: For any path $r(t)$ and time $T > 0$ define

$$\bar{r}(T) \triangleq \frac{1}{T} \int_0^T r(t)\,dt \qquad (73)$$

$$\bar{r}'(T) \triangleq \frac{1}{T} \int_0^T r'(t)\,dt = \frac{r(T) - r(0)}{T}. \qquad (74)$$

Then

$$I_0^T(r) \geq T\ell(\bar{r}(T), \bar{r}'(T)). \qquad (75)$$

$\square$

Lemma 2:

$$I_{-\infty}^T(r) = I_{-\infty}^T(s) = I_{-\infty}^\infty(r) = I_{-\infty}^\infty(s). \qquad (76)$$

Proof: The definition of reversibility is

$$\pi_x Q_{x,y} = \pi_y Q_{y,x} \text{ for every pair } x, y. \qquad (77)$$

Extending this by iteration we find that for any sequence of states $x(1), \cdots, x(n)$ we have

$$\pi_{x(1)} Q_{x(1),x(2)} Q_{x(2),x(3)} \cdots Q_{x(n-1),x(n)}$$
$$= \pi_{x(n)} Q_{x(n),x(n-1)} Q_{x(n-1),x(n-2)} \cdots Q_{x(2),x(1)}. \qquad (78)$$

This means that for cost functions we obtain

$$\mathbb{P}(r(0)) \exp\left(-K I_0^T(r)\right) = \mathbb{P}(r(T)) \exp\left(-K I_0^T(r(T-t))\right). \qquad (79)$$

But for reversible systems it is easy to show (essentially from Theorem 2.4) that

$$\mathbb{P}(r(0)) = \exp\left(-K I_{-\infty}^0(r) + o(K)\right)$$
$$\mathbb{P}(r(T)) = \exp\left(-K I_{-\infty}^0(s) + o(K)\right).$$

This finishes the proof. $\square$

Proof of Theorem 2.1: Recall the definition of $\mathcal{G}(b)$ in (36). Choose a $b > 0$. Suppose that $(r, T) \in \mathcal{G}(b)$, and that r is a minimal cost trajectory. We can shift time by any amount τ and keep $(r(t + \tau), T + \tau) \in \mathcal{G}(b)$. Therefore, we are free to state that 0 is the last time before T that $B_s r(t) = 0$. We can extend r to times larger than T by setting it equal to z_∞. It is easy to see that $B_s r(t) < b$ for every $t > T$, since the path $z_\infty \to p$ and since otherwise we could achieve the buffer content b with lower cost. Therefore the path

$$s(t) \triangleq r(T - t) \qquad (80)$$

has the property that $B_s s(0) = 0$. Now the reversibility of $z_K(t)$ implies that the cheapest path from p to any point y is the time reversal of $z_\infty(t)$ starting at y; that is, the cheapest way to go from the center p to any point y is the time reversal of the most likely way to go from y to p.

Thus, the path $s(t)$ has the same properties as r: (s, T) is a member of $\mathcal{G}$, and s has 0 as the last time before T when $B_s s(t) = 0$. Note that since the cost of $z_\infty(t)$ is zero, $I_T^\infty(r) = I_T^\infty(s) = 0$.

Now, define

$$\begin{matrix} \beta_1 = I_{-\infty}^0(r) & & \beta_2 = I_0^T(r) \\ \beta_3 = I_{-\infty}^0(s) & & \beta_4 = I_0^T(s) \end{matrix}. \qquad (81)$$

Lemma 2 states that $\beta_1 + \beta_2 = \beta_3 + \beta_4$. Now use Lemma 1 to obtain

$$\beta_2 \geq T\ell(\bar{r}(T), \bar{r}'(T)). \qquad (82)$$

Similarly

$$\beta_4 \geq T\ell(\bar{r}(T), -\bar{r}'(T)) \qquad (83)$$

since the average of s' over $(0, T)$ is $-\bar{r}'(T)$, and the average of s over the same interval is $\bar{r}(T)$. Now $\ell(x, y)$ is convex in y, so

$$\frac{1}{2}(\beta_2 + \beta_4) \geq T\ell(\bar{r}(T), 0). \qquad (84)$$

$$r_b(t) = \begin{cases} (1-t)\boldsymbol{v}^* + t\boldsymbol{w}^*, & \text{if } 0 < t < u(b) \\ \boldsymbol{w}^*, & \text{if } 1 \le u(b) \le t \le U(b) \\ (1-(t-U(b)))\boldsymbol{w}^* + (t-U(b))\boldsymbol{v}^*, & \text{if } U(b) < t < U(b)+1 \\ \boldsymbol{z}_\infty(t-U(b)-1), & \text{if } t > U(b)+1. \end{cases} \tag{94}$$

Furthermore, since β_1 and β_3 are each costs of going from the point $\boldsymbol{p}$ to the hyperplane $\langle R, \boldsymbol{z}_K \rangle = c$, each of them is larger than C_1, which is defined to be the minimal cost of all paths to go from $\boldsymbol{p}$ to that hyperplane. Now we use Lemma 2

$$\begin{aligned} I^T_{-\infty}(\boldsymbol{r}) &= \beta_1 + \beta_2 \\ &= \frac{\beta_1 + \beta_2 + \beta_3 + \beta_4}{2} = \frac{\beta_1 + \beta_3}{2} + \frac{\beta_2 + \beta_4}{2} \\ &\ge C_1 + T\ell(\bar{\boldsymbol{r}}(T), \mathbf{0}) \\ &\ge C_1 + bC_2 \end{aligned} \tag{85}$$

since C_2 was defined to be the minimum cost per unit buffer for a path that does not move. □

Proof of Theorem 2.2: By the lower semicontinuity of $\ell(\boldsymbol{x}, \boldsymbol{y})$ and the assumed uniqueness of $\boldsymbol{w}^*$, for any $\varepsilon > 0$ there is a $\delta > 0$ such that if $|\boldsymbol{x} - \boldsymbol{w}^*| > \delta$ then

$$\frac{\ell(\boldsymbol{x}, \mathbf{0})}{\langle \boldsymbol{x}, R \rangle - c} > C_2 + \varepsilon \triangleq \frac{\ell(\boldsymbol{w}^*, \mathbf{0})}{\langle \boldsymbol{x}, R \rangle - c} + \varepsilon. \tag{86}$$

Lemma 1 shows that any path has a cost that is lower bounded by a constant plus the cost of its center. As $b \to \infty$, the point $\bar{\boldsymbol{r}}' \to \mathbf{0}$, since the time tends to infinity and $\boldsymbol{r}(t)$ is bounded. Therefore

$$I^T_0(\boldsymbol{r})/T \ge \ell(\bar{\boldsymbol{r}}, \bar{\boldsymbol{r}}') > \ell(\boldsymbol{w}^*, \mathbf{0}) + \varepsilon \tag{87}$$

unless $|\bar{\boldsymbol{r}} - \boldsymbol{w}^*| < \delta$. Now the inequality of Lemma 1 is strict unless $\boldsymbol{r}(t)$ is a constant. This proves that the fraction of time over which $\boldsymbol{r}(t)$ is close to $\boldsymbol{w}^*$ tends to one as $T \to \infty$ (that is, as $b \to \infty$). □

Proof of Theorem 2.3: There are many ways of arriving at a function $f(b)$ such that (43) and (44) hold. We simply have to find a set of functions $\{r_b(t)\}$ with associated $T(b)$ satisfying the following conditions (see Fig. 3)

$$r_b(0) = \boldsymbol{v}^* = r_b(T(b)) \tag{88}$$

$$\int_0^{T(b)} (\langle r_b(t), R \rangle - c) \, dt = b. \tag{89}$$

Then, we take

$$f(b) = I^{T(b)}_0(r_b). \tag{90}$$

It is not hard to show that there is a choice of the family $\{r_b(t)\}$ such that $f(b) = I^*(b)$. However, for many models it is difficult to find $I^*(b)$ analytically. We therefore propose a set of paths that give only an approximation, but one that has bounded error as $b \to \infty$, and that is tight as $b \to 0$.

For every $b > 0$ we define $r_b(t)$ for $t < 0$ to be the minimal cost path from $\boldsymbol{p}$ to $\boldsymbol{v}^*$ that reaches $\boldsymbol{v}^*$ at time 0. This is, by the reversibility assumption, the time reversal of $\boldsymbol{z}_\infty(t)$ starting at $\boldsymbol{v}^*$ at time 0; see Theorem 4. Let $\boldsymbol{w}^*$ represent any

minimizing point of the fraction that defines C_2, see (39). Then let ω represent the denominator of that fraction

$$\omega \triangleq \langle \boldsymbol{w}^*, R \rangle - c. \tag{91}$$

Now define $b_0 = \omega$, and define

$$u(b) \triangleq \min\left(1, \sqrt{\frac{2b}{\omega}}\right). \tag{92}$$

($u(b)$ is the first time when either $r_b(t) = \boldsymbol{w}^*$ or when the buffer reaches $b/2$; see (95) below.) Furthermore define

$$U(b) \triangleq \begin{cases} u(b), & \text{if } u(b) < 1 \\ \dfrac{b-2\omega}{\omega}, & \text{if } u(b) = 1 \end{cases} \tag{93}$$

($U(b)$ is the time when the path $r_b(t)$ starts going back to $\boldsymbol{v}^*$.) We now define $r_b(t)$ for $t > 0$ as shown in (94), at the top of this page. In words, this makes $r_b(t)$ linear between $\boldsymbol{v}^*$ and $\boldsymbol{w}^*$ for time up to 1, then $r_b(t)$ is equal to $\boldsymbol{w}^*$ for a while, then it goes linearly back to $\boldsymbol{v}^*$ and from there follows $\boldsymbol{z}_\infty(t)$ back to $\boldsymbol{p}$. With these definitions it is easy to see that $T(b) = u(b) + U(b)$.

First we check that $\int_0^{T(b)} (\langle r_b(t), R \rangle - c) \, dt = b$. For $0 \le s \le 1$

$$\int_0^s (\langle r_b(t), R \rangle - c) \, dt = \int_0^s t\omega \, dt = \omega \frac{s^2}{2}. \tag{95}$$

This shows why we chose $u(b)$ as we did. From here it is clear that $\int_0^{T(b)} (\langle r_b(t), R \rangle - c) \, dt = b$.

If $b > b_0$ then we have $f(b) = f(b_0) + C_2(b - b_0)$ (recall that we define $f(b)$ via (90), since the integral of $\ell(r_b, r_b')$ can be broken up into the pieces where $r_b = \boldsymbol{w}^*$ and $r_b \ne \boldsymbol{w}^*$. Those portions where $r_b \ne \boldsymbol{w}^*$ are just the times when $r_b = r_{b_0}$, and those where $r_b = \boldsymbol{w}^*$ give C_2 increase in $I^T_0(r_b)$ per unit increase in b. □

REFERENCES

[1] D. Anick, D. Mitra, and M. M. Sondhi, "Stochastic theory of a data handling system with multiple sources," *Bell Syst. Tech. J.*, vol. 61, pp. 1871–1894, 1982.
[2] J. Beran, R. Sherman, M. S. Taqqu, and W. Willinger, "Variable-bit rate video traffic and long-range dependence," to be published.
[3] E. G. Coffman, B. M. Igelnik, and Y. A. Kogan, "Controlled stochastic model of a communication system with multiple sources," *IEEE Trans. Inform. Theory*, vol. 37, no. 5, pp. 1379–1387, 1991.
[4] G. L. Choudhury, D. M. Lucantoni, and W. Whitt, "On the effectiveness for admission control in ATM networks," in *Proc. ITC14*, pp. 411–420.
[5] N. R. Chaganty and J. Sethuraman, "Strong large deviation and local limit theorems," *Ann. Probab.*, vol. 21, no. 3, pp. 1671–1690, 1993.
[6] N. G. Duffield, "Exponential bounds for queues with Markovian arrivals," *Queueing Syst.*, vol. 17, pp. 413–430, 1994.
[7] A. Dembo and O. Zeitouni, *Large Deviations Techniques and Applications.* Boston, MA: Jones and Bartlett, 1993.

[8] A. I. Elwalid and D. Mitra, "Effective bandwidth of general Markovian traffic sources and admission control of high speed networks," *IEEE/ACM Trans. Networking*, vol. 1, no. 3, pp. 329–343, 1993.

[9] ——, "Analysis, approximations and admission control of a multiservice multiplexing system with priorities," in *Proc. IEEE INFOCOM '95*, pp. 463–472.

[10] M. R. Frater, A. Kennedy, and B. D. O. Anderson, "Reverse-time modeling, optimal control, and large deviations," *Syst. Contr. Lett.*, vol. 12, pp. 351–356, 1989.

[11] M. I. Freidlin and A. D. Wentzell, *Random Perturbations of Dynamical Systems*. New York: Springer-Verlag, 1984.

[12] R. Guerin, H. Ahmadi, and M. Naghshineh, "Equivalent capacity and its application to bandwidth allocation in high-speed networks," *IEEE J. Select. Areas Contr.*, vol. 9, pp. 968–981, 1991.

[13] R. J. Gibbens and P. J. Hunt, "Effective bandwidths for the multi-type UAS channel," *Queueing Syst.* vol. 9, pp. 17–28, 1991.

[14] A. Graham, *Kronecker Products and Matrix Calculus with Applications*. Chichester, U.K.: Ellis Harwood, 1981.

[15] D. P. Heyman and T. V. Lakshman, "Source models for VBR broadcast-video traffic," in *Proc. IEEE INFOCOM 1994*, pp. 664–671.

[16] D. P. Heyman, Ali Tabatabai, and T. V. Lakshman, "Statistical analysis and simulation study of video teleconference traffic in ATM networks," *IEEE Trans. Circuits, Syst. Video Technol.*, vol. 2, no. 1, pp. 49–59, Mar. 1992.

[17] D. P. Heyman, T. V. Lakshman, A. Tabatabai, and H. Heeke, "Modeling teleconference traffic from VBR video coders," in *Proc. ICC 1994*, pp. 1744–1748.

[18] J. Y. Hui, *Switching and Traffic Theory for Integrated Broadband Networks*. Boston: Kluwer, 1990.

[19] P. Jacobs and P. Lewis, "Time series generated by mixtures," *J. Time Series Anal.*, vol. 4, no. 1, pp. 19–36, 1983.

[20] F. P. Kelly, "Effective bandwidths at multi-type queues," *Queueing Syst.*, vol. 9, pp. 5–15, 1991.

[21] L. Kosten, "Stochastic theory of data-handling systems with groups of multiple sources," in *Performance of Computer Communication Systems*, H. Rudin and W. Bux, Eds. New York: Elsevier, 1984, pp. 321–331.

[22] L. Kosten, "Liquid models for a type of information buffer problem," *Delft Prog. Rep. 11*, 1986, pp. 71–86.

[23] G. Kesidis, J. Walrand, and C. S. Chang, "Effective bandwidth for multiclass fluids and other ATM sources," *IEEE/ACM Trans. Networking*, vol. 1, no. 4, pp. 424–428, 1993.

[24] S.-Q. Li, "A general solution technique for discrete queuing analysis of multimedia traffic on ATM," *IEEE Trans. Commun.*, vol. 39, no. 7, July 1991.

[25] W. E. Leland, M. S. Taqqu, W. Willinger, and D. V. Wilson, "On the self-similar nature of Ethernet traffic," in *Proc. ACM SIGCOMM Conf. Comput. Commun.*, pp. 183–193, 1993.

[26] D. Lucantoni, M. Neuts, and A. Reibman, "Methods for performance evaluation of VBR video traffic models," *IEEE/ACM Trans. Networking*, vol. 3, no. 2, pp. 176–180, Apr. 1994.

[27] D. Mitra, "Stochastic theory of a fluid model of producers and consumers coupled by a buffer," *Adv. Appl. Prob.*, vol. 20, pp. 646–676, 1988.

[28] I. Norros, J. W. Roberts, A. Simonian, and J. T. Virtamo, "The superposition of variable bit rate sources in an ATM multiplexer," *IEEE J. Select. Areas Commun.*, vol. 9, pp. 378–387, 1991.

[29] V. V. Petrov, "On the probabilities of large deviations for sums of independent random variables," *Theory of Prob. Applicat.*, vol. X, no. 2, pp. 287–298, 1965.

[30] J. W. Roberts, "Performance evaluation and design of multiservice networks," COST 224 Project, Commission European Communities, Final Rep., 1992.

[31] T. E. Stern and A. I. Elwalid, "Analysis of a separable Markov-modulated rate model for information-handling systems," *Adv. Appl. Prob.*, vol. 23, pp. 105–139, 1991.

[32] A. Simonian and J. Guibert, "Large deviations approximation for fluid queues fed by a large number of on/off sources," in *Proc. ITC14*, 1994, pp. 1013–1022.

[33] K. Sohraby, "On the asymptotic behavior of heterogeneous statistical multiplexer with applications," in *Proc. IEEE INFOCOM '92*, pp. 839–847.

[34] A. Shwartz and A. Weiss, "Induced rare events: Analysis via large deviations and time reversal," *Adv. App. Prob.*, vol. 25, pp. 667–689, 1993.

[35] ——, *Large Deviations for Performance Analysis*. London, U.K.: Chapman & Hall, 1995.

[36] S. R. S. Varadhan, *Large Deviations and Applications*. Philadelphia, PA: SIAM, 1984.

[37] W. Whitt, "Tail probabilities with statistical multiplexing and effective bandwidths for multi-class queues," *Telecommun. Syst.*, vol. 2, pp. 71–107, 1993.

[38] Z. Zhang, "Finite buffer discrete-time queues with multiple Markovian arrivals and services in ATM networks," in *Proc. IEEE INFOCOM '92*, pp. 2026–2034.

Anwar Elwalid (M'91) received the B.S. degree from Polytechnic Institute of New York, Brooklyn, and the M.S. and Ph.D. degrees from Columbia University, New York, NY, all in electrical engineering.

Since 1991, he has been with the Mathematics of Networks and Systems Research Department, Bell Laboratories, Murray Hill, NJ. His research areas include ATM networks, multimedia traffic and queueing, and stochastic systems.

Dr. Elwalid is a member of Tau Beta Pi and Sigma Xi.

Daniel Heyman received the B.S. degree in industrial and electrical engineering from Rensselaer Polytechnic Institute, Troy, NY, in 1960, the M.I.E. degree from Syracuse University, Syracuse, NY, in 1962, and the Ph.D. degree in operations research from the University of California-Berkeley in 1966.

He joined Bell Laboratories and then transfered to Bellcore. His research areas include numerical analysis of stochastic processes, queueing theory, and performance models of data communications systems.

T. V. Lakshman (M'86) received the M.S. degree from the Indian Institute of Science, Bangalore, India, and the M.S. and Ph.D. degrees in computer science from the University of Maryland, College Park, in 1984 and 1986, respectively.

He joined Bellcore in 1986 and is currently a Senior Research Scientist in the Information Networking Research Laboratory. He has been involved in research on several aspects of networks and distributed computing, such as issues related to provision of video services using ATM networks, end-to-end flow control problems in high-speed networks, ATM traffic shaping and policing, ATM switching, and parallel architectures for fast signaling and connection-management in high-speed networks. His current research interests are in the areas of high-speed networking, distributed computing, and multimedia systems.

Dr. Lakshman is a member of the Association for Computing Machinery.

Debasis Mitra (M'75–SM'82–F'89), for a photograph and biography, please see page 936 of this issue.

Alan Weiss, for a photograph and biography, please see page 952 of this issue.

CHAPTER VI

EFFECTIVE BANDWIDTH MANAGEMENT

This chapter describes buffer and bandwidth management in an ATM switching system and network.

Resource Management in Wide-Area ATM Networks Using Effective Bandwidths

G. de Veciana, *Member, IEEE*, G. Kesidis, *Member, IEEE*, and J. Walrand, *Fellow, IEEE*

Abstract—This paper is principally concerned with resource allocation for connections tolerating statistical quality of service (QoS) guarantees in a public wide-area ATM network. Our aim is to sketch a framework, based on effective bandwidths, for call admission schemes that are sensitive to individual QoS requirements and account for statistical multiplexing. Recent results approximating the effective bandwidth required by heterogeneous streams sharing buffered links, including results for the packetized generalized processor sharing service discipline, are described. Extensions to networks follow via the concept of decoupling bandwidths—motivated by a study of the input-output properties of queues. Based on these results we claim that networks with sufficient routing diversity will inherently satisfy nodal decoupling. We then discuss on-line methods for estimating the effective bandwidth of a connection. Using this type of traffic monitoring we propose an approach to usage parameter control (i.e., policing) for effective bandwidth descriptors. Finally, we suggest how on-line monitoring might be combined with admission control to exploit unknown statistical multiplexing gains and thus increase utilization.

I. Introduction

THE asynchronous transfer mode (ATM) is an emerging standard for transport in broadband integrated service digital networks (B-ISDN). B-ISDN traffic is statistically heterogeneous (e.g., voice, video, data, network signaling) requiring varied qualities of service (QoS), ranging from deterministic to statistical bounds on cell loss probability and/or cell delay. From an ATM network's point of view, each connection (or "call") consists of a stream of 53-byte packets called cells; cells associated with a given connection follow the same route, called a virtual circuit, and arrive to the destination(s) in order. ATM can provide users with "bandwidth on demand," which, for example, is advantageous to efficiently accommodate variable rate traffic streams such as real-time video. Streams are statistically multiplexed on network links; thus, in principle, the resources required to satisfy the QoS desired for each stream can be reduced by sharing both bandwidth and buffer memory.

Our simplified model for a public wide-area ATM network consists of output buffered switches with nonblocking switch fabrics. From a connection's point of view, each switch

Manuscript received September 30, 1994; revised April 1, 1995. This work was supported by NSF Grant NCR-9409722 and NSERC of Canada.

G. de Veciana is with the Department of Electrical and Computer Engineering, The University of Texas, Austin, TX 78712 USA.

G. Kesidis is with the Electrical and Computer Engineering Department, University of Waterloo, N2L 3G1 Canada.

J. Walrand is with the Electrical Engineering and Computer Science Department, University of California, Berkeley, CA 94720 USA.

IEEE Log Number 9412657.

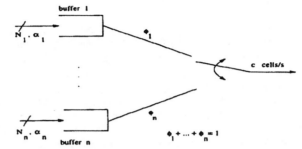

Fig. 1. Priority buffers node.

looks like a constant delay (propagation delay plus overhead) followed by a buffer and a server. As shown in Fig. 1, switch output nodes are organized as parallel FIFO's which share the output link's bandwidth via a "packetized" general processor sharing (PGPS) service policy; see Section II-B2 and [1], [2]. The salient feature of the PGPS service policy is its ability to "fairly" guarantee a particular minimum bandwidth to a given FIFO while being work conserving. This in turn permits differentiation in the QoS received by traffic streams. ATM connections can be grouped into three categories based on their QoS requirements [3]: deterministic, statistical, and best-effort.

There are several proposed approaches to handling traffic in an ATM network. One such approach is to regulate each non-best-effort connection with a leaky bucket at the user-network interface (UNI). A leaky bucket having a constant token arrival rate, ρ, and finite token buffer size, σ, will limit its output stream to bursts of size σ and an average rate not to exceed ρ. Such a stream is said to satisfy a deterministic (σ, ρ) constraint. Based on this type of traffic characterization the network can *reserve* an appropriate size buffer and minimum guaranteed bandwidth such that deterministic end-to-end delay bounds are satisfied with no cell loss due to buffer overflow from the output of the leaky bucket to the destination of the connection [4]–[6]. A traffic stream satisfying a (σ, ρ) constraint upon arriving at the UNI would incur no further delays or loss at the UNI. However, a traffic stream with an unknown or statistical characterization may incur random delays as well as cell loss at the UNI, due to the leaky bucket mechanism, ultimately degrading the overall end-to-end performance.[1] Moreover this approach does not take advantage of potential statistical multiplexing gains since resources are reserved per connection, at each network node, to match each traffic flow's

[1] Marking, instead of dropping, cells at the UNI substitutes a known degradation with potentially improved but unknown performance characteristics within the network.

0733–8716/95$04.00 © 1995 IEEE

deterministic descriptor. Nevertheless, the simplicity as well as the ability of such schemes to guarantee deterministic bounds for real-time traffic satisfying deterministic constraints make this type of framework appealing.[2]

A second approach to ATM network management is based on approximate statistical traffic descriptors as a means to allocate shared network resources for connections with statistical QoS requirements. The main advantage of this approach is the exploitation of statistical multiplexing resulting in increased resource utilization. However, in order to effectively guarantee QoS to individual connections, traffic may need to be segregated, i.e., buffered separately. Ideally, independent connections with identical statistics and the same QoS requirement might share FIFO's at PGPS nodes. More realistically, connections of the same traffic "class" might be grouped on virtual paths and share buffers at each PGPS node, see Section II-C2. The sharing of resources has the disadvantage of making resource allocation within the network difficult. Moreover, traffic monitor and/or policing devices –suitable for connections with statistical traffic descriptors– are required at the UNI for usage parameter control, see Section IV.

Best-effort traffic, such as electronic mail and file transfers, can be buffered both at the network edge and at PGPS nodes within the network without excessively degrading service; other buffering options are discussed in [7]. The best-effort FIFO's receive service when buffers handling deterministic and statistical traffic types are idle. Congestion in FIFO's handling best-effort traffic might be avoided by using higher layer end-to-end protocols; e.g., feedback protocols or window flow control.

In summary: users requiring deterministic QoS constraints specify deterministic traffic descriptors at the outset (possibly established by a leaky bucket UNI) and are handled thereafter via bandwidth and buffer reservation. Connections that can tolerate statistical constraints are partially segregated and managed based on their statistical characteristics and required QoS. Best-effort traffic is allocated storage space and offered the left over (or "idle") bandwidth.

In this context, PGPS is sufficiently flexible to distribute bandwidth "fairly" among the three categories and classes of traffic while being theoretically tractable for both the deterministic [2] and statistical [8] categories. At ATM transmission rates, the PGPS algorithm is somewhat complex to implement on a per-connection basis for thousands of calls [9], [10]. In our view, the added complexity of "fair" redistribution of idle bandwidth versus fixed bandwidth allocation makes sense for a small number of *statistically* shared buffers. Even in this case, the advantage of PGPS over a simple priority service discipline depends on the characteristics of the traffic and the range of QoS requested [11].

Hereafter we focus on ATM resource management for traffic tolerating statistical QoS guarantees using large network buffers; e.g., real-time traffic along paths with small propagation delay (i.e., tolerating large queueing delays) and, possibly, available bit-rate (ABR) traffic that requires a nonzero minimum service bandwidth and can tolerate some cell loss [12]. For such traffic we contend that the "effective bandwidth" is an appropriate traffic descriptor.[3] A connection's traffic descriptor and QoS requirement are basic components of the *traffic contract* to be negotiated at call set-up [16]. The effective bandwidth is a natural measure of a connection's bandwidth requirement relative to the desired QoS constraint, e.g., delay and/or loss experienced by a connection's cells. The bandwidth available for connections with statistical QoS requirements at a PGPS node is equal to the link capacity minus the total bandwidth reserved for connections with deterministic QoS requirements.

In this paper we will not discuss "reactive" congestion control because high bandwidth-delay products render such approaches impractical for most real-time, high-bandwidth users. Instead we focus on preventive congestion control using admission control (cf. Sections II and V) and rate-based throttling (cf. Section IV). As ATM provides bandwidth on demand, traffic will need to be monitored (cf. Section III) to verify that users comply with their connection's traffic descriptors and policed in order to ensure fairness [16]. Monitoring is also important if usage-based pricing is eventually implemented [17].

Our aim in this paper is to draw together recent work to give an overall picture of ATM resource management based on effective bandwidth traffic descriptors in the spirit of [3], [18], [19], [7], [20]. The picture is not complete, so we have endeavored to highlight future research directions. This paper is organized as follows:

I. Introduction
II. Effective Bandwidth as a Traffic Descriptor for Admission Control
   A. Traffic Descriptor and QoS Requirements
   B. Bandwidth Allocation for Buffered Links
   C. Nodal Decomposition and End-to-End QoS Requirements
   D. On Accuracy and Relaxation of Stationarity Assumptions
III. Monitoring Traffic
   A. Direct Approach
   B. Model Fitting Methods
   C. Virtual Buffer Methods
IV. Usage Parameter Control
V. Measuring Statistical Multiplexing Gain for Admission Control
VI. Summary

II. EFFECTIVE BANDWIDTH AS A TRAFFIC DESCRIPTOR FOR ADMISSION CONTROL

Real-time admission control for switched virtual circuits will be based on a user supplied traffic descriptor and the requested QoS. The network uses this information to establish whether sufficient spare resources are available to admit the

---

[2] A possible simplification in the case of (σ, ρ) constrained flows is to use *fixed* rate bandwidth allocation. Indeed we can assign a fixed service rate ρ to a connection in addition to a buffer of size σ at the first node and a one cell buffer thereafter; see the "bottleneck" analysis in [5]. While this approach is not work conserving it permits end-to-end deterministic guarantees with notable advantages over PGPS: a reduction in buffering, complexity, and jitter per connection.

[3] For traffic with very low delay constraints, effective bandwidths based on zero-buffering are more appropriate [13]–[15].

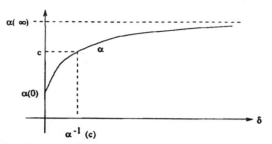

Fig. 2. Effective bandwidth curve.

call through a given route. In turn, routing algorithms rely on suitable "link metrics" [21] to establish possible routing options. Our focus herein, is on suitable "metrics," rather than the routing algorithms; for work on routing see [3], [22], [23] and references therein.

A. Traffic Descriptor and QoS Requirements

The proposed traffic descriptor for a traffic stream is its *effective bandwidth*. It depends on both the statistical nature of the stream of cells and the nature of the required QoS constraint.

Consider a buffered link with capacity c cell/s, supporting a stationary and ergodic arrival packet stream $A(t)$. Let X be distributed as the buffer's stationary workload. Our preliminary QoS aim is to limit the likelihood of large delays or ensure that cell loss probabilities at this link are in fact quite small. In order to do so, we require that

$$P\{X > B\} \leq \epsilon := e^{-B\delta} \ll 1 \qquad (1)$$

for a reasonably large ATM buffer size B if loss is of concern, or for $B = Tc$ when delays exceeding T seconds are to be made unlikely. The parameter δ clearly determines the stringency of the QoS constraint. Extensions to end-to-end QoS requirements are discussed in Section II-C2.

Under mild conditions, for both continuous and discrete-time arrival processes, it has been shown (see, e.g., [14], [24]–[27]), that for all $\delta \geq 0$

$$\alpha(\delta) < c \iff \lim_{B \to \infty} B^{-1} \log P\{X > B\} \leq -\delta \qquad (2)$$

or equivalently

$$P\{X > B\} = \exp[-B\alpha^{-1}(c) + o(B)] \qquad (3)$$

where $o(B)$ is a function satisfying $\lim_{B \to \infty} o(B)/B = 0$. The function $\alpha(\cdot)$, shown in Fig. 2, is given by

$$\alpha(\delta) := \delta^{-1} \lim_{t \to \infty} t^{-1} \log E \exp[\delta A(0, t]] \qquad (4)$$

where $A(0, t]$ denotes the number of cell arrivals to the buffer in the interval of time $(0, t]$. In light of (2), $\alpha(\cdot)$ is called the source's *effective* bandwidth. The effective bandwidth is an nondecreasing function, in δ, with the mean rate of the source being $\alpha(0)$ and the "peak" rate being $\alpha(\infty)$.[4]

---

[4] The peak rate of a traffic stream is well-defined for fluid models, however it requires careful definition for slotted arrivals [28].

The δ-constraint on X given by (1) matches that in (2) to the *first order*; i.e., in the exponent, for large buffers. More will be said on this approximation in Section II-D. Thus, to first order, the effective bandwidth is the minimum bandwidth required by the connection to accommodate its desired δ-constraint.

If the effective bandwidth characteristic is not known apriori, the user can select an "envelope" effective bandwidth from a collection provided by the network [29]. For example, the envelope effective bandwidth for voice would be the "worst-case" measured effective bandwidth characteristic for actual voice sources. Resulting resource allocation based on envelope effective bandwidths would be conservative but would simplify resource management by limiting the number of traffic types.

As this paper unfolds, we will consider the viability of this traffic descriptor. Some issues to keep in mind are: First, the extent to which the descriptor allows for an efficient admission policy; e.g., no over allocation or reservation during and after the admission process. Over allocation of resources, as in the case of peak-rate bandwidth allocation policies, will typically increase the blocking probability of future calls. Second, the traffic descriptor should be reasonably accurate and robust in the sense that the journey from user location to the network and along its virtual circuit should not significantly modify the source's descriptor; otherwise, the traffic descriptor may become useless (cf. Section II-C1). Third, the issue of policing, or the ease with which the network can check (in real-time) that a connection complies with its stated traffic descriptor, see Section IV. Finally, a key goal is to keep things simple. Indeed, the resulting management schemes should be easily implemented and adaptable while maintaining a reasonable level of performance, else the burden of management may outweigh the benefits.

B. Bandwidth Allocation for a Buffered Link

The key relationship needed for resource management is that between the traffic descriptor(s) and the resources necessary to support the desired qualities of service. Below we present a natural relationship between the effective bandwidth traffic descriptor and the bandwidth that should be allocated to a FIFO buffer *shared* by multiple streams. We then discuss a similar relationship for a group of FIFO's sharing an output link via a PGPS service policy.

1) FIFO Buffer: Consider a FIFO buffer with deterministic service rate of c cells/s and arrivals consisting of the superposition of N *independent* sources with effective bandwidths $\alpha_1, \cdots, \alpha_N$, defined as in (4) for the individual packet streams $A_i(t)$. The following result follows directly from (2)–(4) and the independence of the arrival streams

$$\sum_{i=1}^{N} \alpha_i(\delta) < c \iff \lim_{B \to \infty} B^{-1} \log P\{X > B\} \leq -\delta$$

or alternatively

$$P\{X > B\}$$

$$= \exp[-BI(c) + o(B)] \text{ where } I^{-1}(\delta) := \sum_{i=1}^{N} \alpha_i(\delta).$$

Two key characteristics of this result are: first, the additivity of the individual effective bandwidths which makes checking whether the QoS constraint is satisfied quite simple; second, that the result holds for a large class of traffic streams, such as Markov modulated fluids [30], [18], [31], or Markov-modulated Poisson sources, as well as *most* reasonable stationary and ergodic traffic models [24], [25], [32], [33], [27].

In the case of a shared buffer, the δ-constraint should be interpreted as a *performance* constraint on the buffer, say cell loss. Furthermore, when traffic streams are statistically identical, each stream *individually* experiences this QoS constraint.

2) PGPS Buffer Node: As mentioned in the introduction, due to the heterogeneity of services, B-ISDN networks will need to support and guarantee multiple QoS. The proposed approach is to segregate statistically identical streams with similar QoS requirements in "logically" separate buffers, which nevertheless can share the total output link capacity via an appropriate service policy. Below we describe the bandwidth requirements, in terms of effective bandwidths and heterogeneous QoS requirements, for segregated buffers subject to a PGPS service policy described below.

Let N_i be the number of sources, each with effective bandwidth α_i, sharing FIFO i. Let X_i be distributed as the steady state workload of FIFO i, see Fig. 1. The total link capacity is c cells/s.

Under PGPS, the jth cell arriving to FIFO i (at time a_j^i) is assigned a virtual finishing time (VFT) F_j^i. These VFT's satisfy the following recursion [2]

$$F_{j+1}^i = \max\{F_j^i, v(a_j^i)\} + \frac{1}{\phi_i c} \text{ for all } j \geq 0 \text{ with}$$

$$F_0^i := 0$$

where v is the "virtual time" function for PGPS. At each departure epoch, the cell with the smallest VFT in the node is chosen for service. The virtual time function of PGPS is derived from the evolution of a corresponding "GPS" policy so that the departure times under PGPS track those under GPS (Theorem 1 of [2]). The GPS policy is work conserving and has "fluid" dynamics so that each FIFO i receives service bandwidth proportional to ϕ_i where $\phi_1 + \phi_2 + \cdots + \phi_n = 1$.

The following result, taken from [8], relates bandwidth requirements with QoS constraints in this system. A δ_i-constraint is satisfied at Buffer i if the following effective bandwidth inequality is satisfied

$$N_i \alpha_i(\delta_i) + \min\left\{(1 - \phi_i c), \sum_{j \neq i} N_j \alpha_j(\delta_i)\right\} < c$$

$$\Rightarrow \lim_{B \to \infty} B^{-1} \log P\{X_i > B\} \leq -\delta_i. \quad (5)$$

We now discuss the implications of this relationship.

3) Spare Capacity for Call Admission of a PGPS Node: Suppose without loss of generality that a new connection is to be routed through Buffer 1, which is subject to a δ_1 QoS requirement. By (5), the *spare capacity* at Buffer 1 can be taken to be

$$c - N_1 \alpha_1(\delta_1) - \min\left\{(1 - \phi_1 c), \sum_{i=2}^n N_i \alpha_i(\delta_1)\right\}. \quad (6)$$

That is, an additional connection with effective bandwidth $\alpha_1(\delta_1)$ can be routed through this buffer without degrading the desired QoS if

$$\alpha_1(\delta_1) < c - N_1 \alpha_1(\delta_1) - \min\left\{(1 - \phi_1 c), \sum_{i=2}^n N_i \alpha_i(\delta_1)\right\}.$$

A key point to bear in mind, is that in order to determine the spare capacity available to each of the buffers in this system, the effective bandwidth of each stream needs to be known for the various QoS being supported by the node; i.e., $\alpha_i(\delta_j)$ for all $i, j = 1 \ldots n$. Thus to effectively manage a system with heterogeneous QoS requirements, we must have a rough idea of the *entire* effective bandwidth characteristic.

C. Nodal Decomposition and End-to-End QoS Requirements

We have discussed approximate effective bandwidth results for *single* buffered links; as such these are appropriate for use in an ATM LAN. Below we discuss extensions to wide-area networks and consider end-to-end QoS requirements.

1) Nodal Decoupling: In order to apply single buffer results in the network context, we need to ensure that the effective bandwidths of streams traversing a network are preserved. In [28] constraints ensuring that this is indeed the case are considered. The *decoupling bandwidth* of a stream, denoted by $\alpha^*(\cdot)$, is the service rate required to ensure that the characteristics, $\alpha(\cdot)$, of that stream remain unchanged. Thus, if a single stream enters a buffer with capacity c and $\alpha^*(\delta) < c$, we can conclude that the effective bandwidth of the input and output streams are equal for the given QoS at the given δ. If the given stream shares the buffer with other streams, having an aggregate mean rate μ, and they only coincide with the latter at this buffer, then the constraint $\alpha^*(\delta) + \mu < c$ guarantees that the effective bandwidth of the stream of interest remains unchanged. These results hold for arbitrary work-conserving policies. Other studies of the characteristics of network asymptotics [34], [35] show that exact results for bandwidth allocation subject to tail constraints in networks require solving a rather complex collection of nonlinear equations drawing on precise knowledge of traffic statistics within the network.

We propose a simplified outlook based on the notion of decoupling bandwidths. Consider a single buffered node shared by multiple traffic streams operating at a utilization of 90%. One can show that if the peak rate of a particular traffic stream does not exceed 10% of the link capacity, then the effective bandwidth characteristic of that stream at the output is equal to that of the input. We call this the *decoupled regime*.

In order to be viable, guaranteeing decoupling at the network level should be a simple task. We believe that high-speed networks with sufficient "routing diversity" will naturally satisfy this requirement. A network with routing diversity is one in which the proportion of bandwidth allocated to traffic sharing similar routes (i.e., virtual paths) is small relative to the typical link capacity. A conservative rule of thumb for guaranteeing decoupling in a network is derived in [28] suggesting that decoupling is in effect when no more than 5% of the streams at a given buffer also share another downstream buffer. These results are proposed and supported by simulations in [36].

In practice, since the link bandwidths in ATM networks are quite large, we expect that the 10% rule is easily maintained. Similarly, a diversity of 5% should typically be in effect if traffic is fairly well distributed over the network by the routing algorithm.

2) End-to-End QoS Requirements: We now address nodal decomposition of QoS requirements [3], [20]; i.e., the relationship between the constraint of (2) and the end-to-end QoS requirement of a connection. In order to answer these questions, we unfortunately must resort to over-simplifications. The goal is to find appropriate values for the δ-constraints at intermediary nodes, given end-to-end cell loss or delay constraints.

In the sequel, we assume that the end-to-end QoS requirements are based on *steady state* cell loss probability and delay rather than those experienced by "typical" cells. Notice that for some applications it may be necessary to consider the manner in which excessive delays or cell loss occur, i.e., in *clumps* or spread out. Further research on more detailed QoS requirements that are easily and accurately "decomposed" is required [37].

a) Constraints on cell loss probability: Assume that a connection requires that the cell loss probability, F, it experiences in the ATM network must satisfy $F < \epsilon \ll 1$. Let n be the number of buffers along a connection's virtual circuit and F_i denote the cell loss probability of the connection at Buffer i, $i = 1, \cdots, n$. Assuming the cell losses at each Buffer are independent events, we have that

$$1 - F = \prod_{i=1}^{n} (1 - F_i) \Rightarrow F \approx \sum_{i=1}^{n} F_i.$$

Thus if we distribute losses equally over all nodes, that is requiring that $F_i < \epsilon/n$ for all $i = 1, \cdots, n$ we have $F < \epsilon$ as desired. In [37] an argument is made that for *stringent* end-to-end loss constraints, a nonuniform distribution of loss among nodes does not significantly improve "performance."

Let B_i be the size of the buffer at node i in cells. The constraint $F_i < \epsilon/n$ is asymptotically (as $B_i \to \infty$) equivalent to the constraint $P\{X_i > B_i\} < \epsilon/n$ where X_i is the steady state workload in an infinite buffer with the same inputs. Thus, we take $\delta_i = -B_i^{-1} \log(\epsilon/n)$ for the buffer at node i.

This decomposition results in a nodal QoS requirement which depends on the number of nodes visited by a stream. Thus, two video streams visiting a given node may have different QoS requirements if their virtual circuits have different "lengths." Unfortunately, we only allow statistically identical traffic with the *same* QoS requirement to share buffers. One solution is to compute all QoS partitioning based on the "diameter" of the network; i.e., the longest virtual circuit in terms of nodes visited. While this may on occasion be conservative, we believe the advantages of reduced numbers of shared buffers and increased potential for multiplexing gain will outweigh other alternatives.

b) Constraints on cell delay and delay jitter: Let D end-to-end virtual delay distribution for a given connection, ignoring propagation and processing times. Assume that a connection requires a statistical bound on the end-to-end delay jitter

its cells experience; i.e.

$$P\{|D - ED| > T\} < \epsilon \ll 1 \qquad (7)$$

for some threshold $T > 0$. Cells that experience a delay of more than $ED + T$ are essentially lost as far as the receiver is concerned while cells that are delayed less than $ED - T$ can be buffered at the receiver.

It was argued in [38] that "the end-to-end delay jitter is in the range of the maximum transfer time of one node." Intuitively this corresponds to the idea that there is a bottleneck node which determines the end-to-end performance. Consequently, (7) will hold if we constrain $P(X_i > Tc_i) < \epsilon$ for all $i = 1, \cdots, n$ where c_i cell/s is the service capacity of Buffer i. Thus, we take $\delta_i = -(Tc_i)^{-1} \log \epsilon$ at Buffer i in this case.

Note that expressions for maximum and minimum end-to-end delay can be obtained in terms of the virtual circuit's propagation and processing delays and the total amount of buffer memory (i.e., maximum queueing delay) while the dimensioning of "playback" (receive) buffers is related back to delay jitter characteristics of the stream [39].

D. On Accuracy and Relaxing Stationarity Assumptions

The expressions for the spare capacity based on effective bandwidth are typically conservative (recall that only the first order exponential characteristics of the tail distribution are considered). Indeed, for buffers shared by large numbers of streams, it has been shown that additional statistical multiplexing gains are obtained which are not captured by the effective bandwidth approximation [40]. To account for this, one must resort to refined asymptotics such as [41], [15] or combine effective bandwidth results with zero-buffer approximations as in [18]. In general, calculating the additional terms appears to be difficult; thus, in Section V, we propose monitoring of buffer workloads to account for additional gains from statistical multiplexing of large numbers of sources. In addition, the expression in (6) for the spare capacity of a PGPS node is conservative in and of itself though, experimentally, it appears to be quite reasonable [11].

The second underlying approximation in the previous sections has been that the network reaches steady state: the quasistatic approximation. If connection durations are not sufficiently long then the quasistatic approximation may not be accurate. The question remains as to whether the distribution of the transient process associated with a buffer servicing a number of connections, whose effective bandwidth[5] never exceeds the buffer capacity, will in fact satisfy the expected δ-constraint *at each point in time*. Proofs of effective bandwidth results are usually based on transient arguments (i.e., starting the system empty); thus one might expect that, subject to constraints on connection characteristics, the predicted QoS will in fact be met. For simple connections offering i.i.d. arrivals, this type of result is easily developed by coupling and stochastic comparison. Further work will be required to ensure that more realistic connection characteristics will not lead to gross inaccuracies in a nonstationary environment.

---

[5] One might define the effective bandwidth of a finite connection as that of the process consisting of consecutive independent connections of the that type.

III. MONITORING TRAFFIC

In this section we describe approaches to estimating the effective bandwidth, or spare capacity, by monitoring traffic. Recall that in order to determine the spare capacity for buffers at a PGPS node, the effective bandwidth may need to be estimated for several QoS: $\delta_i, i = 1, \cdots, n$. Thus, in practice, we may want to roughly estimate the entire effective bandwidth characteristic. In the sequel, monitoring is proposed for usage parameter control and as a means to account for statistical multiplexing gains.

A. Direct Approach

Recall that the effective bandwidth α of a cell arrival process is given by

$$\alpha(\delta) := \delta^{-1} \lim_{t \to \infty} t^{-1} \log E \exp[\delta A(0, t]] \qquad (8)$$

for $\delta > 0$ where $A(0, t]$ is the number of cell arrivals to the buffer in the interval of time $(0, t]$. By monitoring the cell arrival process, we can obtain an asymptotically consistent (as $k, m \to \infty$) estimator for the effective bandwidth at time $k \times m$

$$\hat{\alpha}_{k \times m}(\delta) := \delta^{-1} k^{-1} \log \left(m^{-1} \sum_{i=1}^{m} \exp[\delta A(k(i-1), ki]] \right).$$

This approach may however take some time to converge. Referring to (8), an accurate estimate of $\alpha(\delta)$ will require that both k and m be large. So, the monitoring time $k \times m$ may in fact be quite lengthy. However, direct estimation of the effective bandwidth is unique in that it circumvents modeling the traffic stream and monitoring network buffers, making it an attractive option.

B. Model Fitting Methods

This is a two-step approach. First, an appropriate parametric model for the arrivals process is selected (e.g., a two-state Markov-modulated Poisson Process) and its parameters are estimated [42], [43], [18], [34]. Second, the effective bandwidth of the traffic model is numerically computed or obtained by off-line simulation (see, e.g., [24], [31], [25]) and used to estimate the bandwidth requirements of the source. The problem with this approach is that some traffic may be too complex to model [44] or may also require that the *order* of the underlying Markov process is estimated. Nevertheless, this type of approach has been carried out successfully. In particular, a modeling method that achieves a good match in terms of predicting the performance indices of interest is reported in [45].

C. Virtual Buffer Methods

We now describe an approach to estimating an effective bandwidth characteristic that is based on real-time buffer measurements. Suppose the mean rate $\alpha(0)$ and the peak rate $\alpha(\infty)$ are estimated "directly" while intermediate points on the effective bandwidth characteristic are estimated via *virtual buffers* at the user-network interface, see Fig. 3. A virtual buffer is not part of the virtual circuit but rather a monitoring

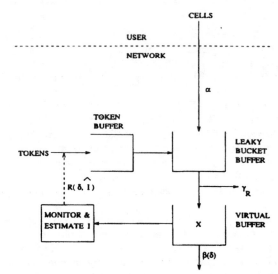

Fig. 3. Leaky bucket and virtual buffer.

device. A virtual buffer "assigned" a deterministic service rate c, $c \in (\alpha(0), \alpha(\infty))$, is used to estimate the associated QoS: $\alpha^{-1}(c)$. The approximate effective bandwidth characteristic is then obtained by interpolating between these estimated points, see Fig. 2.

To estimate $\alpha^{-1}(c)$, recall that $P\{X > B\} = \exp[-B\alpha^{-1}(c) + o(B)]$ where X is distributed as the steady state workload of the virtual buffer. As in [46], take B_1 such that $P\{X > B_1\}$ is not too large and assume $P\{X > B\} \approx Ae^{-bI}$, for $b \geq B_1$, where A and I are quantities to be estimated. The buffer workload is monitored over time and the empirical distribution $\pi(\cdot)$ of the workload beyond B_1 is obtained. A and I are chosen so as to minimize the Kullback-Leibler distance between π and $p(b) = A\exp(-bI)$ for $b \geq B_1$

$$\hat{I} = \log \left(1 + \frac{1 - \Pi(B_1 - 1)}{\sum_{b=B_1}^{\infty} b\pi(b) - B_1(1 - \Pi(B_1 - 1))} \right)$$

$$\hat{A} = (1 - \Pi(B_1 - 1)) \exp[B_1 \hat{I}]$$

where $\Pi(B_1 - 1) := \sum_{b=1}^{B_1 - 1} \pi(b)$. So we take $\hat{I}$ as our estimate of $\alpha^{-1}(c)$ (and $\hat{A}$ is our estimate of $e^{o(B)}$). An indication of the performance of this approach is given by the simulation results of the next section.

Alternatively, we could use the approach of [44] to estimate $\alpha^{-1}(c)$ or an approach based on *generalized extreme value theory* [47], [48].

IV. USAGE PARAMETER CONTROL

In order to prevent gross misuse of network resources, it is reasonable to include mechanism for peak rate policing at all access points for a public ATM network. However, as ATM provides bandwidth on demand, peak rate policing will not suffice to ensure QoS and fairness to other users sharing buffers at a PGPS node. Consequently, connections violating agreed upon traffic descriptors must also be throttled

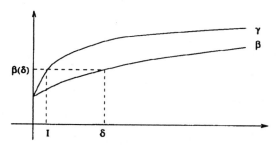

Fig. 4. Policing the effective bandwidth curve at δ.

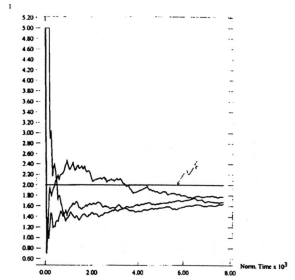

Fig. 5. First source in violation.

into compliance or penalized (with, e.g., excess charges) accordingly. We now describe an approach to accomplish this task for a fixed value of δ [49].

Let β be the user-specified (envelope) effective bandwidth and α be the true effective bandwidth. Referring to the traffic throttle of Fig. 3, let γ_R be the effective bandwidth of the departure process from the leaky bucket (i.e., the process that enters the network) when R is the token arrival rate. Initially, $R = \beta(\infty)$, the pre-specified peak rate of the call. Consequently, the connection is, at first, largely unaffected by the leaky bucket; in particular, if $\alpha(\infty) \leq \beta(\infty)$ (peak rate compliance), then $\gamma_{\beta(\infty)}(\delta) = \alpha(\delta)$.

The relationship between the characteristics of the leaky bucket's output traffic and the user-specified effective bandwidth $\beta(\delta)$ is given by $P\{X > B\} = \exp[-BI + o(B)]$ where $I := \gamma_R^{-1}(\beta(\delta))$. A virtual buffer can be used to obtain an estimate, $\hat{I}_t$, of this quantity over time, see Section III-C. A user is said to have *violated* his/her effective bandwidth descriptor β at δ if

$$\gamma_R(\delta) > \beta(\delta) \Leftrightarrow \hat{I}_t < \delta \qquad \text{(Fig. 4)}.$$

In order to enforce the traffic descriptor, a simple policy can be used to adjust the token rate R. If $\hat{I}_t$ drops below δ (i.e., a violation), then R is set to $\beta(\delta)$ so that the process entering the network will become compliant [50]. R will be reset to $\beta(\infty)$ at the earliest time t such that $\hat{I}_t > \delta$, i.e., compliance. Thus, a connection in violation is allowed limited access to the network based on its traffic descriptor, i.e., $R = \beta(\delta)$. Furthermore when a violating call is once again deemed in compliance, the throttle will return to the role of peak rate policing only ($R = \beta(\infty)$) and thereby become virtually transparent to the user.

Alternatively, when a violation is detected, we could begin to adaptively determine the token rate R such that $\gamma_R(\delta) = \beta(\delta)$, equivalently, $\hat{I} = \delta$. Also, we could replace the leaky bucket throttle with a buffer having variable service rate R; the same policy for modifying R described above would work here too. For the case of several virtual buffers operating in parallel to police several intermediate points on the effective bandwidth characteristic simultaneously, the token rate R would be a function of the estimates made at each virtual buffer. Indeed, if δ_i is the *smallest* "policed" δ for which a violation has been detected, then R could be set to $\beta(\delta_i)$. Although this approach to usage parameter control is complex, we propose its use for policing *aggregations* of streams as suggested in [12].

Because this effective bandwidth policier is difficult to analyze, we now give some simulation results to indicate its performance. Consider a discrete-time Markov chain Y_k with state-space $\{0, 1\}$ and transition probability matrix P with $P_{0,1}$ being the probability that a transition occurs from state 0 to 1. The number of arrivals of the source in the real-time interval $[0, K\Lambda^{-1}]$ seconds is given by

$$\sum_{k=0}^{K} \mathbf{1}\{Y_k = 1\}$$

where $\mathbf{1}$ is the indicator function and Λ is the peak rate of the source in cells/s. Thus, the source has three parameters: $P_{0,1}$, $P_{1,0}$ and Λ. In the simulations described below, the token buffer's capacity was fixed at 10 tokens and we assumed peak rate compliance, i.e., $\alpha(\infty) = \beta(\infty)$.

Our first simulated source had parameters $\Lambda = 60$ cells/s, $P_{0,1} = 0.5$ and $P_{1,0} = 0.9$. We chose $\delta = 2$. Using the formula for the effective bandwidth given in [24] and [25] (Section III-B), we get that $\alpha(\delta) = 26.8$. The parameter of our traffic monitor was taken to be $B_1 = 2$. We simulated the regulator with $\beta(\delta) = 25$, i.e., the source is in violation. The results of this simulation are given in Fig. 5 wherein the value of $\hat{I}$ as a function of normalized time[6] for three typical trials is plotted. Note that $\hat{I}$ begins above $\delta = 2$ but eventually becomes smaller than δ permanently where our regulator is enforcing $\gamma_R(\delta) < \beta(\delta)$. We also simulated the regulator with $\beta(\delta) = 28$, i.e., a compliant source. In Fig. 6 we plotted $\hat{I}$ for three typical trials. The estimates settle to a value of $\hat{I} > \delta$ where no enforcement is occurring.

Our second simulated source had parameters $\Lambda = 1000$ cells/s, $P_{0,1} = 0.7$ and $P_{1,0} = 0.1$. We took $\delta = 0.5$ and, consequently, $\alpha(\delta) = 908$. The parameter of our traffic

---

[6]The normalized time is time in seconds divided by the mean interarrival time of the source.

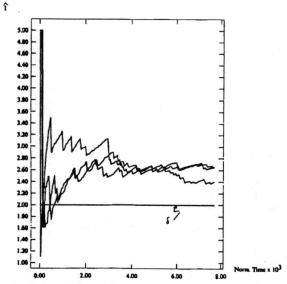

Fig. 6.   First source in compliance.

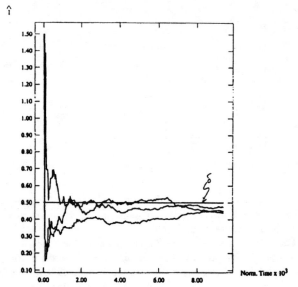

Fig. 7.   Second source in violation.

monitor was taken to be $B_1 = 5$. We simulated the regulator with $\beta(\delta) = 900$ so that the source was in violation. The results were similar to those of the previous example and are given in Fig. 7. We also simulated the regulator with $\beta(\delta) = 915$ so that the source was in compliance. Again, the results were similar to those of the previous example and are given in Fig. 8.

V. MEASURING STATISTICAL MULTIPLEXING GAIN FOR ADMISSION CONTROL

We now describe how online performance monitoring can be used to adjust call admission criteria in order to exploit observed statistical multiplexing gains. A common criticism of the effective bandwidth approach is that it can be conservative (or optimistic) due to its neglect of statistical multiplexing gains. This transpires from the following series of approximations

$$P(X > B) \approx A \exp[-IB] \approx \exp[-IB].$$

That is, not only do we approximate the tail with a single exponential term, but we take the leading constant $A = 1$. A convincing argument is made in [40] that the leading constant A may in fact be quite small or large, reflecting important characteristics of multiplexing. In general for heterogeneous systems, a precise analysis of the leading constant appears to be prohibitive, and can render management based on effective bandwidths inefficient. Thus, we propose to measure the extent of statistical multiplexing gain and change the admission criterion accordingly. This idea was motivated by a reformulation of the effective bandwidth constraint to include the effects of the leading constant in [51].

Suppose we use the Kullback-Leibler approach to obtain a fast estimate $\hat{A} \exp[-B\hat{I}]$ of $P\{X > B\}$ where X denotes

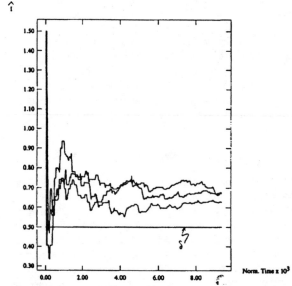

Fig. 8.   Second source in compliance.

the steady state workload of a buffer handling a superposition of independent sources with effective bandwidths $\alpha_i(\cdot)$. Recall that the parameter δ in the constraint $P\{X > B\} < \exp[-B\delta]$ is derived from QoS requirements (Section II-C2) and fixed B. Thus, the "QoS constraint" becomes $\hat{A} \exp[-B\hat{I}] \leq \exp[-B\delta]$; equivalently, $\hat{I} \geq \delta + \log(\hat{A})/B$.

We assume that the effect of adding a single call with effective bandwidth α on the parameter A is negligible. Therefore, we propose to accept the call if

$$\alpha(\delta + \log(\hat{A})/B) < c - \sum_i \alpha_i(\delta + \log(\hat{A})/B)$$

Note that $\hat{A} \ll 1$ ($\log(\hat{A}) < 0$) corresponds to large statistical multiplexing gain and, therefore, larger spare capacity than given by the effective bandwidth results of Section II-B. This can be seen by the previous "admission" equation (the arguments of the effective bandwidth functions are smaller). This reasonably simple call admission scheme allows for more efficient usage of the system's multiplexing capacity.

The approach we propose can be summarized as follows: Measure the multiplexing gain as reflected by the magnitude of the constant term A and use this measurement to adjust the desired quality of service parameter, δ, used for admission control. An underlying assumption is that the impact of a single source is not too strong, or more optimistically, its impact is much stronger on the exponent than on the leading constant. We are currently investigating the effectiveness of on-line estimation schemes such as this. Note that this approach requires that entire effective bandwidth characteristics are specified.

VI. SUMMARY

In summary, we have described an ATM network resource allocation scheme that uses the PGPS service policy to handle connections with differing QoS requirements. Resource allocation for certain statistical QoS connections was based on an effective bandwidth traffic descriptor. The appropriateness of this traffic descriptor was argued in terms of its simplicity, its ability to accurately translate the QoS requirement of the connection to network resources (buffers and bandwidth), its ability to reflect how connections interfere with one another, and finally the ability of the network to police it. Indeed, a preliminary approach for effective bandwidth usage parameter control was proposed and some simulation results were given.

For connections specified by effective bandwidths, we described a simple admission control policy for individual PGPS buffered links and for networks via decoupling bandwidths results. However, this admission control policy does not account for resource utilization gains due to statistical multiplexing. As current theoretical results are unmanageable, we propose measuring statistical multiplexing in real-time. Such measurements are encorporated into the admission control policy initially described.

REFERENCES

[1] A. Demers, S. Keshav, and S. Shenker, "Analysis and simulation of a fair queueing algorithm," *Internet Res., Exper.*, vol. 1, 1990.
[2] A. K. Parekh and R. G. Gallager, "A generalized processor sharing approach to flow control in integrated services networks: The single node case," *IEEE/ACM Trans. Networking*, vol. 1, no. 3, pp. 344–357, June 1993.
[3] D. Ferrari and D. C. Verma, "A scheme for real-time channel establishment in wide-area networks," *IEEE J. Select. Areas Commun.*, vol. 8, no. 3, pp. 368–379, 1990.
[4] R. L. Cruz, "A calculus for network delay, Pt. 1: Network elements in isolation," *IEEE Trans. Inform. Theory*, vol. 37, pp. 114–131, 1991.
[5] S. Low, "Traffic management of ATM networks: Service provisioning, routing, and traffic shaping," Ph.D. dissertation, Elec. Eng., Comput. Sci. Dept. Univ. Calif., Berkeley, 1992.
[6] A. K. Parekh and R. G. Gallager, "A generalized processor sharing approach to flow control: The multiple node case," *IEEE/ACM Trans. Networking*, vol. 2, no. 2, pp. 137–150, Apr. 1994.

[7] K. Sriram, "Methodologies for bandwidth allocation, transmission scheduling, and congestion avoidance in broadband ATM networks," *Comput. Networks, ISDN Syst.*, vol. 26, pp. 43–59, 1993.
[8] G. de Veciana and G. Kesidis, "Bandwidth allocation for multiple qualities of service using generalized processor sharing," Univ. Texas, Austin, Elec., Comput. Eng. Dept., Tech. Rep. SCC-94-01, 1994.
[9] S. J. Golestani, "A self-clocked fair queueing scheme for broadband applications," in *Proc. IEEE INFOCOM*, vol. 2, pp. 636–646, 1994.
[10] A. Hung and G. Kesidis, "Buffer design for wide-area ATM networks," to be published.
[11] C.-F. Su and G. de Veciana, "On the capacity of multi-service networks," to be published.
[12] ATM Forum's Traffic Management Working Group, "DRAFT ATM Forum traffic management specification version 4.0," ATM Forum, Tech. Rep. 95-0013, Dec. 19, 1994.
[13] J. Y. Hui, "Network, transport, and switching integration for broadband communications," *IEEE Network*, pp. 40–51, Mar. 1988.
[14] F. P. Kelly, "Effective bandwidths of multi-class queues," *Queueing Syst.*, vol. 9, no. 1, pp. 5–16, 1991.
[15] I. Hsu and J. Walrand, "Admission control for ATM networks," in *Proc. IMA Workshop Stochastic Networks*, 1994.
[16] The ATM Forum, *ATM User-Network Interface Specification Version 3.0*. Englewood Cliffs, NJ: Prentice-Hall, 1993.
[17] G. de Veciana and R. Baldick, "Pricing multi-service networks," Elec., Comput. Eng. Dept., Univ. Texas, Austin, Tech. Rep. SCC-94-06, 1994.
[18] R. Guérin, H. Ahmadi, and M. Naghshineh, "Equivalent capacity and its application to bandwidth allocation in high-speed networks," *IEEE J. Select. Areas Commun.*, vol. 9, no. 7, pp. 968–981, 1991.
[19] R. Guérin and L. Gun, "A unified approach to bandwidth allocation and access control in fast packet-switched networks," in *Proc. IEEE INFOCOM*, vol. 1, pp. 1–12, 1992.
[20] D. Towsley, "Providing quality of service in packet switched networks," *Performance Evaluation of Computer and Communications Systems*, L. Donatiello and R. Nelson, Eds. New York: Springer-Verlag, 1993, pp. 560–586.
[21] D. Bertsekas and R. Gallager, *Data Networks*, 2nd ed. Englewood Cliffs, NJ: Prentice-Hall, 1992.
[22] R. O. Onvural and I. Nikolaidi, "Routing in ATM networks," *High-Speed Commun. Networks*, pp. 139–150, 1992.
[23] R.-H. Hwang, J. F. Kurose, and D. Towsley, "MDP routing in ATM networks using the virtual path concept," in *Proc. IEEE INFOCOM*, 1994, pp. 1509–1517.
[24] C.-S. Chang, "Stability, queue length and delay of deterministic and stochastic queueing networks," *IEEE Trans. Automat. Contr.*, vol. 39, pp. 913–931, 1994.
[25] G. Kesidis, J. Walrand, and C.-S. Chang, "Effective bandwidths for multiclass Markov fluids and other ATM sources," *IEEE/ACM Trans. Networking*, vol. 1, no. 4, pp. 424–428, Aug. 1993.
[26] W. Whitt, "Tail probabilities with statistical multiplexing and effective bandwidths in multi-class queues," *Telecommun. Syst.*, pp. 71–107, 1993.
[27] N. G. Duffield and N. O'Connell, "Large deviations and overflow probabilities for the general single-server queue, with applications," Dublin Institute for Advanced Studies, Dublin, Ireland, Tech. Rep. DIAS-APG-93-30, 1993.
[28] G. de Veciana, C. Courcoubetis, and J. Walrand, "Decoupling bandwidths for networks: A decomposition approach to resource management for networks," in *Proc. IEEE INFOCOM*, vol. 2, 1994, pages 466–474.
[29] G. Kesidis, "A closed-loop leaky bucket regulator," E&CE Dept., Univ. of Waterloo, Waterloo, Ontario, Canada, Tech. Rep. #93-03, 1992.
[30] R. J. Gibbens and P. J. Hunt, "Effective bandwidths for multi-type UAS channel," *Queueing Syst.*, vol. 9, no. 1, pp. 17–28, 1991.
[31] A. I. Elwalid and D. Mitra, "Effective bandwidth of general Markovian traffic sources and admission control of high speed networks," *IEEE/ACM Trans. Networking*, vol. 1, no. 3, pp. 329–343, June 1993.
[32] G. de Veciana and J. Walrand, "Effective bandwidths: Call admission, traffic policing and filtering for ATM networks," to be published.
[33] P. W. Glynn and W. Whitt, "Logarithmic asymptotics for steady-state tail probabilities in a single-server queue," *J. Appl. Probab.*, vol. 31, 1994.
[34] C. S. Chang, "Approximations of ATM networks: Effective bandwidths and traffic descriptors," IBM, Tech. Rep. 18954, 1993.
[35] N. O'Connell, "Large deviations in queueing networks," Dublin Institute for Advanced Studies, Dublin, Ireland, Tech. Rep. DIAS-APG-94-13, 1994.
[36] W.-C. Lau and S.-Q. Li, "Traffic analysis in large-scale high-speed integrated networks: Validation of nodal decomposition approach," in *Proc. IEEE INFOCOM*, 1993.

[37] R. Nagarajan, "Quality-of-Service issues in high-speed networks," Ph.D. dissertation, Comp. Sci. Dept, Univ. of Mass. at Amherst, 1993.

[38] H. Kröner, M. Eberspächer, T. H. Theimer, P. J. Kühn, and U. Breim, "Approximate analysis of the end-to-end delay in ATM networks," in *Proc. IEEE INFOCOM*, vol. 2, pp. 978–986, 1992.

[39] F. P. Kelly and P. B. Key, "Dimensioning playout buffer from an ATM network," in *11th U.K. Teletraffic Symp.*, Mar. 1994.

[40] G. L. Choudhury, D. M. Lucantoni, and W. Whitt, "Squeezing the most out of ATM," preprint, 1993.

[41] D. D. Botvich and N. G. Duffield, "Large deviations, the shape of the loss curve, and economies of scale in large multiplexers," Dublin Institute for Advanced Studies, Dublin, Ireland, Tech. Rep. DIAS-APG-94-12, 1994.

[42] H. Heffes and D. M. Lucatoni, "A Markov modulated characterization of packetized voice and data traffic and related statistical multiplexer performance," *IEEE J. Select. Areas Commun.*, vol. 4, no. 6, pp. 856–868, 1986.

[43] L. Deng and J. W. Mark, "Parameter estimation for Markov modulated Poisson processes via the EM algorithm with time discretization," *Telecommun. Syst.*, vol. 1, no. 4, pp. 321–338, 1993.

[44] N. G. Duffield, J. T. Lewis, N. O'Connell, R. Russell, and F. Toomey, "The entropy of an arrivals process: A tool for estimating QoS parameters of ATM traffic.," in *Proc. 11th IEE Teletraffic Symp.*, Mar. 1994.

[45] C.-L. Hwang and S-Q. Li, "On the convergence of traffic measurement and queueing analysis: A statistical-match queueing (SMAQ) tool," in *Proc. IEEE INFOCOM*, 1995, pp. 602–612.

[46] C. Courcoubetis, G. Kesidis, A. Ridder, J. Walrand, and R. Weber, "Admission control and routing in ATM networks using inferences from measured buffer occupancy," to be published.

[47] F. Berbnabei, R. Ferretti, M. Listanti, and G. Zingrillo, "ATM system buffer design under very low cell loss probability constraints," in *Proc. IEEE INFOCOM*, 1991, pp. 8c.3.1–8c.3.10.

[48] V. Dijk, E. Aanen, and H. van den Berg, "Extrapolating ATM-simulation results using extreme value theory," *Queueing, Performance and Control in ATM (ITC-13)*. North-Holland: Elsevier, 1991, pp. 97–104.

[49] G. Kesidis, "A traffic regulator for effective bandwidth usage parameter control in ATM networks," E&CE Dept., Univ. of Waterloo, Waterloo, Ontario, Canada, Tech. Rep. 93-03, 1993.

[50] G. de Veciana, "Leaky buckets and optimal self-tuning rate control," in *Proc. IEEE Globecom'94*, San Francisco, CA, 1994.

[51] Z. Liu, P. Nain, and D. Towsley, "Exponential bounds for a class of stochastic processes with applications to call admission control in networks," in *Proc. IEEE CDC*, 1994.

G. de Veciana (S'88–M'94) received the B.S., M.S., and Ph.D. degrees from the University of California at Berkeley, in 1987, 1990, and 1993, respectively, all in electrical engineering.

He is currently an Assistant Professor in Electrical and Computer Engineering at the University of Texas at Austin. His research interests are in the design and control of telecommunication networks. He is particularly interested in monitoring and management of ATM networks.

G. Kesidis (S'91–M'92) was born in Toronto, Canada, in 1964. He received the B.A.Sc. degrees from the University of Waterloo, Waterlo, Ontario, in 1988, and the M.S. and Ph.D. degrees from the University of California at Berkeley in 1990 and 1992, respectively, all in electrical engineering.

He is currently an Assistant Professor in the Electrical and Computer Engineering Department, University of Waterloo. His research interests include resource allocation, congestion control, and performance evaluation of high-speed networks.

J. Walrand (S'71–M'80–SM'90–F'93) is Professor of Electrical Engineering and Computer Science, University of California at Berkeley. He is the author of *An Introduction to Queueing Networks* (Prentice-Hall, 1988) and *Communication Networks: A First Course* (Irwin/Aksen, 1991).

Dr. Walrand was a recipient of the Lanchester Prize from the Operations Research Society of America.

460

A New Approach for Allocating Buffers and Bandwidth to Heterogeneous, Regulated Traffic in an ATM Node

Anwar Elwalid, *Member, IEEE*, Debasis Mitra, *Fellow, IEEE*, and Robert H. Wentworth, *Member, IEEE*

(*Invited Paper*)

Abstract—A new approach to determining the admissibility of variable bit rate (VBR) traffic in buffered digital networks is developed. In this approach all traffic presented to the network is assumed to have been subjected to *leaky-bucket* regulation, and extremal, periodic, on-off regulated traffic is considered; the analysis is based on fluid models. Each regulated traffic stream is allocated bandwidth and buffer resources which are independent of other traffic. Bandwidth and buffer allocations are traded off in a manner optimal for an adversarial situation involving minimal knowledge of other traffic. This leads to a single-resource statistical-multiplexing problem which is solved using techniques previously used for unbuffered traffic. VBR traffic is found to be divisible into two classes, one for which statistical multiplexing is effective and one for which statistical multiplexing is ineffective in the sense that accepting small losses provides no advantage over requiring lossless performance. The boundary of the set of admissible traffic sources is examined, and is found to be sufficiently linear that an *effective bandwidth* can be meaningfully assigned to each VBR source, so long as only statistically-multiplexable sources are considered, or only nonstatistically-multiplexable sources are considered. If these two types of sources are intermixed, then nonlinear interactions occur and fewer sources can be admitted than a linear theory would predict. A qualitative characterization of the nonlinearities is presented. The complete analysis involves conservative approximations; however, admission decisions based on this work are expected to be less overly conservative than decisions based on alternative approaches.

I. INTRODUCTION

RESEARCH in high-speed communications has been dominated in recent years by issues related to services based on the asynchronous transfer mode (ATM). An important issue is congestion control. This issue is intertwined with the notion of the *capacity* of the network measured in users for given quality of service, and the administration of admission control in real-time, where the goal is to admit users upto capacity. The statistical nature of a significant part of the traffic, its burstiness and variability, and the stringency of the quality of service requirements combine to pose challenges of unprecedented difficulty. An essential prerequisite is the regulation of traffic at network edges, as shown in Fig. 1.

Manuscript received September 30, 1994; revised April 1, 1995.

A. Elwalid and D. Mitra are with AT&T Bell Laboratories, Murray Hill, NJ 07974 USA.

R. H. Wentworth is with AT&T Bell Laboratories, Red Bank, NJ 07701 USA.

IEEE Log Number 9412660.

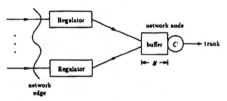

Fig. 1.　Regulated traffic offered to an ATM node.

The leaky bucket regulator [20] has become ubiquitous in current service offerings. In our work we assume that all traffic is subject to regulation by such devices, which have three parameters: the token rate r, which bounds the long-term average rate of the regulated traffic; B_T, the token buffer size, which bounds the burst size; P, which bounds the peak rate. Also shown in Fig. 1 is the network node, which for our purposes is composed of two resources, a buffer of size B and a trunk of transmission bandwidth C.

One approach to network capacity calculations and admission control has been based on statistical source models. See for instance [1], [18], and also [5] for analysis of the combined effects of such models and regulators. The reliability of source models in this approach is a matter of concern, however. A contrasting approach is based on worst case congestion effects at the network nodes, given that regulators exist at the entry points. That is, traffic sources are adversarial to the extent permitted by regulators. Even with this worst case approach there are interesting choices to be made. One option is to proceed with deterministic bounds to ensure that there are no losses in the network nodes. See [16] for an example along these lines. Another option is to allow very small loss probabilities, say 10^{-9}, and to extract multiplexing gains from the statistical independence of traffic processes. This approach, which combines independent, worst case source behavior with a quality of service guarantee in the form of a small loss probability, is taken in this paper. It should counter the overly conservative usage implied by the deterministic bounds [24], and lead to more efficient use of network resources. There is little prior statistical analysis of burst-scale congestion in the multiplexing of periodic, on-off source traffic. Examples are [12] and [19]. In these papers the analysis is approximate and the calculations of the overflow probability, as pointed out in [12], are quite laborious. Also, no attempt is made to carry the

Reprinted from IEEE Journal on Selected Areas in Communications, Vol. 13, No. 6, Aug. 1995, pp. 1115-1127.

analysis through to the stage where it can be used in real-time administration of admission control.

Before proceeding to details we give an overview of the paper in three parts.

1) We examine the capacity of a single network node and its admission control based on a probabilistic quality of service guarantee, specifically that the cell loss probability does not exceed L, a small number. All traffic submitted to the network node is leaky-bucket-regulated and, moreover, is on-off, periodic and extremal in the sense that when the traffic source is on its rate is the maximum permitted, i.e., P, the amount of data generated in an on period, Q, is also maximum, where

$$Q = B_T \frac{P}{P - r} \qquad (1)$$

and the mean rate in each period is r, the maximum permitted. The randomness in the source model stems from the assumption of statistical independence of the traffic processes, specifically in their phases. A key aspect of our work is the heterogeneity of the regulators; in fact, we expect a proliferation quite early in the evolution of the networks. The analysis is based throughout on fluid models.

2) The approach taken in this paper, where one of the two key network resources is the buffer, is novel in its use of established techniques for analyzing *unbuffered* resources, such as the Chernoff large deviations approximation [9]–[11], [14]. The important bridge to the case where bandwidth is the other network resource is based on a technique that allows the two resources to be exchangeable. The first phase of the analysis concludes with a reduction from a two-resource to a one-resource problem, and in the second phase the aforementioned established techniques take over. Even in the second phase we have discovered nonlinear phenomenon which is of utmost importance to multiplexing. When only a single class of statistically homogeneous traffic sources is present, we find that the statistical multiplexing gain exceeds unity only if the capacity of the single resource, say, the bandwidth, exceeds a critical value, C_c, which depends on the source characteristics. Therefore, for given bandwidth at the ATM node, C, in a heterogeneous environment there may exist source classes for which $C_c < C$ and other classes with $C_c \geq C$. We call the two classes "statistically-multiplexable" and "nonstatistically-multiplexable" VBR sources, respectively, and abbreviate the terms to S-VBR and NS-VBR. While this dichotomy has long been appreciated at an intuitive level by researchers, this appears to be the first time that it has been analytically and quantifiably stated. We give a simple and explicit expression for C_c for a source class. The simultaneous presence of both types of sources makes the design and admission control problems harder.

3) This paper pays considerable attention to molding the analytic and qualitative results for the purposes of real-time administration of admission control. A key concept here is effective bandwidth, which has recently received considerable attention for both buffered [7], [8], [6], [21] and unbuffered [9]–[11], [14] network resources. Underlying the concept is the linearity of $\partial \mathcal{A}_L$, the boundary of the admissible set $\mathcal{A}_L$,

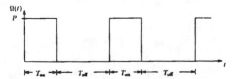

Fig. 2. Periodic, on-off rate process departing from regulator.

which is the set of combinations of sources of various classes for which the quality of service requirement specified by L is satisfied. The linearity of $\partial \mathcal{A}_L$ is sometimes exact in an appropriate asymptotic limit, and sometimes approximate and empirical. We find in our numerical investigations that the boundary of the admissible set often deviates negligibly from linearity if all source classes are either S-VBR or NS-VBR. When both source types are present, the boundary is nonlinear, albeit approximately piece-wise linear, and with very different effective bandwidths in the different regions. Our analytic results identify the boundaries of the regions in $\partial \mathcal{A}_L$.

We proceed to a more detailed description of the traffic sources. As mentioned earlier, and also shown in Fig. 1, all traffic offered to an ATM node is regulated at the network edge. The regulation is performed by leaky bucket devices with parameters (r, B_T, P); the ancillary burst-size parameter Q is obtained as indicated in (1). We assume that the departure process from such a regulator is extremal, on-off and periodic with indeterminate phases. We do not have conclusive proof that such processes are worst-case in the sense of maximizing the steady-state loss probability in the ATM node. However, this is suggested by the results of Doshi [4], Mitra and Morrison [15] and Worster [22] (see also [23]). Doshi has various related results in general frameworks. In [15] it is specifically shown that, for a single-resource problem, which is what we have in this paper after the initial phase of the analysis, the Chernoff estimate of the loss is maximized by extremal, on-off, periodic processes with independent, uniformly distributed random phases. This result holds for heterogeneous regulators.

We denote by $\Omega(t)$ the rate process which is the output of the regulator, see Fig. 2. In the figure

$$T_{\text{on}} = \frac{B_T}{P - r} \qquad \text{and} \qquad T_{\text{off}} = \frac{B_T}{r}. \qquad (2)$$

We let the period be denoted by $T = T_{\text{on}} + T_{\text{off}} = Q/r$. Also, the source activity factor

$$w_\Omega = \Pr(\Omega > 0) = \frac{r}{P}. \qquad (3)$$

The paper is organized as follows. Section II, which follows, is on lossless multiplexing. Here the basic idea of exchangeability of buffer and bandwidth is introduced and an optimum trade-off is struck, which gives rise to the effective bandwidth for lossless multiplexing. This quantity, denoted by e_0, is the benchmark to which comparisons are made later in calculating the statistical multiplexing gain. Section III on statistical multiplexing exploits the noncoincidence of bursts due to the random phases of the regulated traffic. The loss probability is estimated by a well-known refinement of the Chernoff bound. The admissible set and the calculations leading to the

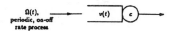

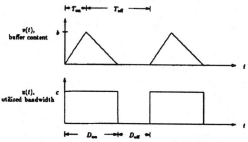

Fig. 3. Virtual buffer/trunk system for a single source.

Fig. 4. Processes of the virtual system for a single source.

effective bandwidth, e, which is based primarily on the work of Hui [10], are reviewed. Section IV on qualitative theory gives, first, the analysis for a homogeneous class of traffic sources, which leads to C_c, the critical bandwidth required for the statistical multiplexing gain e_0/e to exceed unity. The ideas are generalized to the heterogeneous environment, giving rise to results on the nonlinear composition of the boundary of the admissible set. Finally the sensitivity of the statistical multiplexing gain on the token rate r is studied and a corollary establishes a critical value of r_c. Section V reports on extensive numerical investigations on all the topics highlighted by the analysis. Finally, Section VI concludes with discussions on miscellaneous topics.

II. LOSSLESS MULTIPLEXING

In this section we consider the base case where the quality of service requirement is lossless performance. Each virtual circuit is allocated buffer b_0 and bandwidth e_0, and admission is denied if uncommitted resources at the node are inadequate to satisfy the allocations. A key feature is the heterogeneity of the virtual circuits and hence the goal is to characterize the set of admissible combinations of virtual circuits with various associated regulator parameters. We first consider a single source in a framework which we call its virtual buffer/trunk system. Next, in Section II-B, the multiplexing of sources is considered and the admissible set obtained.

A. Virtual Buffer/Trunk System

Consider a single source with periodic, on-off rate process $\Omega(t)$, see Fig. 2, which supplies an infinite buffer with a trunk of bandwidth c, as shown in Fig. 3.

We assume that $c \geq r$, the stability condition. Let $v(t)$ and $u(t)$ respectively denote the *buffer content* and the *utilized bandwidth* at time t, where the latter is an on-off process which takes values c and 0 depending on whether the buffer is not empty or empty, respectively. See Fig. 4.

The stability condition ensures that the buffer is emptied in every cycle of length T. Let D_{on} and D_{off}, respectively, denote the time in each cycle that the buffer and the trunk is utilized. Clearly, $D_{on} + D_{off} = T$, and D_{on} exceeds T_{on} by

the time taken by the buffer to go from its state of maximum occupancy to empty. Let b denote the maximum buffer content, $\sup_{t>0} v(t)$. Then

$$D_{on} = T_{on} + \frac{b}{c}, \qquad D_{off} = T_{off} - \frac{b}{c}. \tag{4}$$

Hence, the fraction of time that the virtual buffer/trunk system is busy

$$w = \frac{D_{on}}{D_{on} + D_{off}} = \frac{T_{on}}{T_{on} + T_{off}} + \frac{b}{c} \cdot \frac{1}{T_{on} + T_{off}}$$
$$= w_\Omega + \frac{b}{c} \cdot \frac{1}{T}. \tag{5}$$

Importantly, $w \geq w_\Omega$. Also

$$b = B_T - \frac{B_T(c - r)}{P - r}. \tag{6}$$

Hence $b \leq B_T$. Note that b decreases linearly with increasing c for $r \leq c \leq P$, and that the extreme points of (b, c) are (B_T, r) and $(0, P)$.

B. Multiplexing

We now use the behavior of the processes of the virtual buffer/trunk system for single sources to design admission control for heterogeneous sources sharing the nodal resources.

First, suppose there is a set of I virtual circuits such that the traffic source for circuit i ($1 \leq i \leq I$), is an on-off process $\Omega_i(t)$. The aggregate traffic $\sum_{i=1}^{I} \Omega_i(t)$ will be associated with buffer content $V(t)$ and a utilized bandwidth $U(t)$, where the latter is an on-off process which takes values C and 0.

Consider assigning each virtual circuit a virtual buffer/trunk. Circuit i would be allocated bandwidth c_i ($r \leq c_i \leq P$), and also buffer b_i, the peak buffer occupancy given in (6). Then, if

$$\sum_{i=1}^{I} c_i \leq C \tag{7}$$

it follows that

$$\sum_{i=1}^{I} u_i(t) \leq C \tag{8}$$

and

$$\sum_{i=1}^{I} v_i(t) \geq V(t). \tag{9}$$

Thus, the sum of the virtual buffer usages bounds the aggregate buffer usage. We shall conservatively use the sum of the virtual buffer usages, $\sum_{i=1}^{I} v_i(t)$, as an estimate of the aggregate buffer usage $V(t)$. Equation (9) implies that if our estimate does not exceed the available buffer B, then neither will the actual buffer usage.

In the case where all sources are identical except for phase, one finds

$$\sum_{i=1}^{I} b_i = \sup_{phases, t} \left\{ \sum_{i=1}^{I} v_i(t) \right\} = \sup_{phases, t} \{V(t)\}. \tag{10}$$

Thus, in this case our estimate accurately predicts the maximum buffer usage, and hence the boundary between lossless

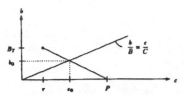

Fig. 5. Determination of buffer and bandwidth allocation (b_0, e_0).

and lossy transmission. The estimate will be less precise when dissimilar sources are involved.

Our main concern now is the selection of the parameters c_i, which are free at this point. If all the sources are known and are heterogeneous, then determining the values c_i which produce the lowest estimated peak buffer usage without exceeding the total bandwidth constraint (7) involves a complicated optimization. A simplification results if the c_i for a particular source must be chosen independent of any knowledge of the character of other sources. Then a little thought makes it clear that optimal resource management requires that the per-circuit allocations (b_i, c_i) be such that both network resources will always be exhausted at the same time for any aggregation of circuits using the same allocation rule. This occurs when

$$\frac{b_i}{B} = \frac{c_i}{C} \qquad (11)$$

i.e., when the allocations are in proportion to their respective nodal capacities. Although we shall sometimes consider cases where all sources are taken to be known, we shall continue to abide by (11) because of the simplification it provides. Using (11) in lieu of doing a calculation invoking simultaneous knowledge of all circuits leads to admission decisions which are exact if all sources are identical, but conservative if sources are heterogeneous.

Observe that for given B and C, (6) and (11) determine a unique allocation which we denote by (b_0, e_0). The solution is depicted in Fig. 5.

The quantity e_0, which is of obvious importance throughout this paper, is referred to as the "effective bandwidth for lossless performance". The justification for the term stems from the fact that if $e_{0,i}$ is the effective bandwidth of the ith virtual circuit, then the set of circuits $\{1, 2, \cdots, I\}$ is admissible if

$$\sum_{i=1}^{I} e_{0,i} \le C. \qquad (12)$$

The admissible set may equivalently be given by $\sum_{i=1}^{I} b_{0,i} \le B$, where $b_{0,i}$ is the "effective buffer requirement" for virtual circuit i; however, we will use the former description.

Exceptions to the above procedure arise if there is no intersection of the straight lines in Fig. 5. An intersection at (b_0, e_0) exists if and only if

$$\frac{C}{B} > \frac{r}{B_T}. \qquad (13)$$

Sources which violate (13) are "bandwidth-limited" and in such cases a natural choice for the allocated bandwidth is

$$e_0 = r. \qquad (14)$$

There are the following options available in the corresponding buffer allocations: 1) $b_0 = rB/C$, or 2) $b_0 = B_T$. The former allocation, which in effect inflates B_T to rB/C and is therefore more liberal, has the advantage that the administration of admission control and resource allocation is routine, i.e., as if (13) holds. This option is recommended if the margin of violation of (13) is small, which is more typical. On the other hand, if the margin is large and the second option is followed then it is necessary to go to the extreme length of recalculating the residual B and C available to the nonbandwidth-limited sources whenever such a bandwidth-limited virtual circuit is admitted to the network.

We end this section by giving formulas for e_0 and w, which will be useful later

$$e_0 = \begin{cases} \dfrac{P}{1 + \dfrac{B/C}{B_T}(P - r)}, & \text{if } r \le \dfrac{B_T}{B/C} \\[4mm] r, & \text{if } \dfrac{B_T}{B/C} \le r < P \end{cases} \qquad (15)$$

$$w = \frac{w_\Omega P}{e_0} = \frac{r}{e_0}. \qquad (16)$$

Note that in the above expressions e_0 and w depend on the nodal buffer B and bandwidth C only through B/C. This important fact should not be surprising since the ratio of buffer and bandwidth allocated to individual sources is equal to the ratio of the buffer and bandwidth at the node.

The formula for e_0 perhaps is most easily remembered when expressed in terms of different variables

$$e_0 = \begin{cases} \dfrac{P}{1 + \dfrac{T_{\text{buf}}}{T_{\text{on}}}}, & \text{if } T_{\text{buf}} \le T_{\text{off}} \\[4mm] r, & \text{if } T_{\text{off}} \le T_{\text{buf}} \end{cases} \qquad (17)$$

where

$$T_{\text{buf}} = \frac{B}{C} \qquad (18)$$

is the maximum delay time of the buffer.

III. STATISTICAL MULTIPLEXING

In contrast to the framework of the preceding section, here we espouse the statistical viewpoint and allow small loss probabilities. We establish a framework for extracting statistical multiplexing gains from 1) the assumption of statistical independence of traffic sources, and 2) the exploitation of the unutilized time-varying portions of the allocated resources to virtual circuits. This typically leads to better utilization of network resources.

It will be helpful to assume that the virtual circuits are grouped by classes. Let J denote the number of classes, where each class is associated with a particular set of parameters for the regulator, (r, B_T, P), and K_j denotes the number of virtual circuits of class j.

A. Reduction to a Single Resource Loss Model

We begin with the characterization of the ith virtual circuit of class j by two stationary random processes $u_{ji}(t)$ and $v_{ji}(t)$, which respectively denote the utilized bandwidth and buffer content for the circuit's virtual buffer/trunk system. As shown in Fig. 4, these two processes are synchronized in their on-off behavior. To make their correspondence closer for ease of analysis, we shall conservatively bound the process $v_{ji}(t)$ by an on-off process, which takes the peak value for the on period. Thus we shall view $u_{ji}(t)$ and $v_{ji}(t)$ as two synchronized on-off processes, which respectively take values $e_{0,j}$ and $b_{0,j}$ while on and 0 while off. The parameters $e_{0,j}$ and $b_{0,j}$ are calculated by the procedure in the preceding section. With this formalism in place we need only to deal with either $u_{ji}(t)$ or $v_{ji}(t)$, and we choose the former.

On account of the assumed statistical independence of traffic sources, the processes $u_{ji}(t)$ ($i = 1, 2, \cdots, K_j$) of the same source class have identical templates and differ only in their phase, i.e.

$$u_{ji}(t) = u_j(t + \theta_{ji}) \qquad (19)$$

where $u_j(t)$ is a deterministic, periodic on-off function with period T_j, which takes values $e_{0,j}$ and 0 for fractions w_j and $(1 - w_j)$, respectively; the phases θ_{ji} are independent random variables uniformly distributed in the interval T_j.

Our performance measure is the loss probability P_{loss}

$$P_{\text{loss}} = \Pr(U > C) \qquad (20)$$

where the total instantaneous load $U = \sum_{j=1}^{J} \sum_{i=1}^{K_j} u_{ji}$. Hence P_{loss} is the fraction of time that the aggregated demand for bandwidth from all sources exceeds the nodal bandwidth. From the earlier discussions, time periods during which losses occur at the network node due to a full buffer are contained in periods during which $U(t) > C$. We shall take for our quality of service requirement

$$P_{\text{loss}} \leq L \qquad (21)$$

where L is a small number, such as 10^{-9}.

B. Chernoff Bound, Admissible Set, Effective Bandwidth

Our primary means for estimating P_{loss} is the Chernoff bound, which is reviewed here, and a refined large deviations approximation based on it, which is described in Section III-C. The instantaneous loads u_{ji} are independent, nonnegative random variables with moment generating functions

$$M_j(s) = E[\exp(s u_{ji})] = \int_0^\infty e^{sx} dW_j(x) \qquad (22)$$

where

$$W_j(x) = \Pr(u_{ji} \leq x). \qquad (23)$$

Chernoff's bound gives [2]

$$\log P_{\text{loss}} \leq -F_K(s^*) \qquad (24)$$

where

$$F_K(s) = sC - \sum_{j=1}^{J} K_j \log M_j(s) \qquad (25)$$

and

$$F_K(s^*) = \sup_{s \geq 0} F_K(s)$$

If $C \to \infty$ and $K_j/C = O(1)$, then [3], [17]

$$\log P_{\text{loss}} = -F_K(s^*)\left[1 + O\left(\frac{\log C}{C}\right)\right]. \qquad (26)$$

Hence the asymptotic large deviations approximation is $P_{\text{loss}} \sim \exp(-F_K(s^*))$.

To avoid trivialities assume the stability condition

$$\sum_{j=1}^{J} K_j E(u_{ji}) < C \qquad \text{and} \qquad \lim_{s \to \infty} \sum_{j=1}^{J} K_j \frac{M_j'(s)}{M_j(s)} > C \qquad (27)$$

(the prime denotes derivative) since without the latter condition there is no loss. Also note that

$$F_K'(s) = C - \sum_{j=1}^{J} K_j \frac{M_j'(s)}{M_j(s)}. \qquad (28)$$

It is easy to verify that $F_K(s)$ is a strictly concave function with a unique maximum at $s = s^*$, which is the positive root of the equation $F_K'(s) = 0$.

Of particular interest here is the case of binomially distributed u_{ji}, where $w_j = \Pr(u_{ji} = e_{0,j})$ and $1 - w_j = \Pr(u_{ji} = 0)$. Then

$$F_K(s) = sC - \sum_{j=1}^{J} K_j \log\{1 - w_j + w_j \exp(s e_{0,j})\} \qquad (29)$$

and s^* is obtained by solving the equation

$$\sum_{j=1}^{J} \frac{K_j w_j e_{0,j} \exp(s e_{0,j})}{1 - w_j + w_j \exp(s e_{0,j})} = C. \qquad (30)$$

In the single-class case, i.e., $J = 1$, the resulting expressions are illuminating: with $a = (C/e_0)/K$

$$s^* = \frac{1}{e_0} \log\left[\frac{a}{1-a} \cdot \frac{1-w}{w}\right] \qquad (31)$$

$$F_K(s^*) = K\left[a \log\left(\frac{a}{w}\right) + (1-a) \log\left(\frac{1-a}{1-w}\right)\right]. \qquad (32)$$

The above expression may be used to obtain $K_{\max}$, which is the value of K for which

$$F_K(s^*) = \log(1/L). \qquad (33)$$

In light of (21) and (24), the quality of service requirement on P_{loss} is satisfied for all $K \leq K_{\max}$. Similarly, in the case of multiple classes, we are interested in the *admissible set*

$$\mathcal{A}_L(B, C) = \{\mathbf{K} : F_K(s^*) \geq \log(1/L)\} \qquad (34)$$

Hui [10] has shown that the complement of the admissible set is convex; hence the points on the boundary, which we denote by $\partial \mathcal{A}_L$, also satisfy (33) with K replaced by J-tuples $(K_1, \cdots, K_J)$.

For a wide variety of conditions the boundary $\partial \mathcal{A}_L$ is closely approximated by an appropriately chosen linear hyperplane. (There are notable exceptions, which the theory in the next section will systematically treat; however, even in these cases the boundary is approximately piece-wise linear and hence the following comments apply with obvious modification.) For instance, following Hui [10] and Kelly [11], we may pick a point $\tilde{K}$ on $\partial \mathcal{A}_L$ and obtain the tangent hyperplane to $\partial \mathcal{A}_L$ which touches $\partial \mathcal{A}_L$ at $\tilde{K}$. Let the region constrained by this hyperplane by denoted by $\tilde{\mathcal{A}}_{L,\tilde{K}}$. Clearly, from the aforementioned concavity of $\mathcal{A}_L$, $\tilde{\mathcal{A}}_{L,\tilde{K}}$ is a conservative bound to $\mathcal{A}_L$. Moreover, denoting

$$\tilde{\mathcal{A}}_{L,\tilde{K}} = \left\{ K : \sum_{j=1}^{J} K_j e_j \le C \right\} \qquad (35)$$

the parameters e_j which define $\tilde{\mathcal{A}}_{L,\tilde{K}}$ are readily obtained [10], [11]

$$e_j = \frac{\log M_j(\tilde{s}^*)}{\tilde{s}^* + (\log L)/C} \qquad (j = 1, 2, \cdots, J) \qquad (36)$$

where $\tilde{s}^*$ is where $F_{\tilde{K}}(s)$ is maximized.

The quantity e_j may justifiably be called the effective bandwidth of class j traffic sources. The statistical multiplexing gain g compares this quantity to $e_{0,j}$, which is the effective bandwidth for lossless performance

$$g_j = e_{0,j}/e_j \qquad (j = 1, 2, \cdots, J). \qquad (37)$$

In our numerical investigations we have found the end results to be fairly insensitive to reasonable choices of $\tilde{K}$. One selection which works well is $\tilde{K}_j = K_{\text{max},j}/2$, where $K_{\text{max},j}$ is the maximum number of admissible sources when only class j sources are admitted.

An optimistic (upper) bound of $\mathcal{A}_L$, which follows from the aforementioned concavity of the admissible region is

$$\left\{ K : \sum_{j=1}^{J} K_j e_j^u = C \right\} \qquad (38)$$

where $e_j^u = C/K_{\text{max},j}$. These optimistic estimates of the effective bandwidths are considerably easier to calculate, since they are obtained by considering each source class in isolation, and in many cases are quite close to the conservative estimates in (36). Such is the case when $\partial \mathcal{A}_L$ is close to being linear. Examples in Section V will demonstrate that this is quite common.

C. Refined Large Deviations Approximations

In our numerical investigations we use a refinement to the large deviations approximation (26) and bound (24) [3], [17]. For the asymptotic scaling in which $K_j/C = O(1)$ and

$C \to \infty$, the refined approximation is

$$P_{\text{loss}} = \frac{\exp\{-F_K(s^*)\}}{s^* \sigma(s^*) \sqrt{2\pi}} [1 + o(1)] \qquad (39)$$

where s^* is obtained by solving $F_K'(s) = 0$, i.e., exactly as before, and

$$\sigma^2(s) = \frac{\partial^2}{\partial s^2} \log E[e^{sU}]$$

where U is the total instantaneous load, see (20). More specifically

$$\sigma^2(s) = \sum_{j=1}^{J} K_j \left[\frac{M_j''(s)}{M_j(s)} - \left\{ \frac{M_j'(s)}{M_j(s)} \right\}^2 \right]. \qquad (40)$$

In the particular case of binomially distributed random variables u_{ji}, the quantities in the above expression have appeared before, except for $M_j''(s)$ which is given by $w_j e_{0,j}^2 \exp(se_{0,j})$.

The dominant exponential (in C) term is common to both the base and refined large deviations approximations. Hence, the fundamental qualitative properties are not affected. We will find it more convenient to conduct our qualitative investigation in terms of the simpler base approximation. In quantitative terms a rough rule of thumb is that the refinement adds about 10% to the calculated nodal capacity.

IV. QUALITATIVE THEORY

In this section we develop a qualitative theory based on the contents of the preceding section. We examine more carefully the existence of solutions K to the equation given earlier for determining the boundary $\partial \mathcal{A}_L$ of the admissible set, namely

$$F_K(s^*) = \log(1/L). \qquad (41)$$

The topic addressed here is whether the admissible set $\mathcal{A}_0$ for lossless performance is a proper subset of $\mathcal{A}_L$, i.e., whether statistical multiplexing gains exist. We also determine conditions under which the sets $\mathcal{A}_0$ and $\mathcal{A}_L$ coincide either completely or partially. When only a single source class exists these results illuminate conditions under which the statistical multiplexing gain, $g = e_0/e$ either exceeds or equals unity. We show that there exist critical values C_c, such that if $C \le C_c$ then $g = 1$ and if $C > C_c$ then $g > 1$. Similar critical values r_c exist for the token rate. Simple expressions for C_c and r_c are obtained. For given nodal bandwidth C we thus obtain statistically-multiplexable and nonstatistically-multiplexable VBR source classes. In the context of multiple source classes we obtain results here on the constitution of the boundary of the admissible set. The results here help to explain the observations from numerical investigations, which are reported in the next section, on the almost-linearity of the boundary of the admissible in the presence of only S-VBR sources, and the qualitatively different boundary, with piece-wise linear segments, which is obtained when both S-VBR and NS-VBR sources are present.

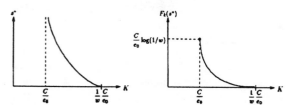

Fig. 6.   Sketches of s^* and $F_K(s^*)$ for model with single source class.

A. Single Source Class

From (32)

$$\frac{\partial}{\partial K} F_K(s^*) = \log\left(\frac{1-a}{1-w}\right) \tag{42}$$

where $a = C/(K e_0)$. From the stability condition (3.9), $w < a$. Hence, $\partial F_K(s^*)/\partial K < 0$. Also, for $K = C/e_0 + 0$, $\partial F_k(s^*)/\partial K = -\infty$, and, importantly

$$F_K(s^*) = \frac{C}{e_0} \log(1/w). \tag{43}$$

From the expression for s^* in (31)

$$s^* = \frac{1}{e_0} \log\left[\frac{1}{K - C/e_0} \cdot \frac{C}{e_0} \cdot \frac{1-w}{w}\right] \tag{44}$$

it follows that $s^* \to \infty$ as $K \to C/e_0 + 0$, and $s^* = 0$ for $K = \frac{1}{w}\frac{C}{e_0}$. The following summarizes the salient features of $F_K(s^*)$. See also Fig. 6.

Proposition 4.1: With C, w, e_0 held fixed, and K in the interval $[\frac{C}{e_0}, \frac{1}{w}\frac{C}{e_0}]$

1) $F_K(s^*)$ is monotonic, strictly decreasing with increasing K.
2) For $K = C/e_0 + 0$, $s^* = \infty$, $\frac{\partial}{\partial K} F_K(s^*) = -\infty$ and $F_K(s^*) = \frac{C}{e_0}\log(1/w)$.

In particular, $\frac{C}{e_0}\log(1/w)$ is the maximum value of $F_K(s^*)$ and it is achieved at $K = C/e_0$. □

Now consider the calculation of $K_{\max}$, the largest value of K for which $P_{\text{loss}} \le L$, which is given by the solution K of $F_K(s^*) = \log(1/L)$. Observe the following dichotomy: if $\log(1/L) < \frac{C}{e_0}\log(1/w)$, the maximum value of $F_K(s^*)$, then $K_{\max} > C/e_0$. Hence the statistical multiplexing gain $g = e_0/e > 1$, since $e = C/K_{\max}$. If, on the other hand, $\log(1/L) \ge \frac{C}{e_0}\log(1/w)$ then no solution to (41) exists; however, we know independently that for $K = C/e_0$, $P_{\text{loss}} = 0$ and hence $K_{\max} = C/e_0$. In this case we obtain $g = 1$. The above facts are now summarized.

Definition: The critical bandwidth C_c is the smallest quantity such that the statistical multiplexing gain exceeds unity for all $C > C_c$.

Tacit to the above definition is the assumption that B varies with C in such a manner that B/C is held fixed.

Proposition 4.2:

$$C_c = \frac{e_0 \log(1/L)}{\log(1/w)} \tag{45}$$

□

Recall from (15) and (16) that an implication of our resource allocation procedure is that e_0 and w depend on the nodal

resource capacities B and C only through B/C. Hence this is also true for C_c.

B. Multiple Source Classes

Conditions in (27) give

$$\sum_{j=1}^{J} K_j w_j e_{0,j} < C < \sum_{j=1}^{J} K_j e_{0,j}. \tag{46}$$

Also, for $C \ge \sum K_j e_{0,j}$ obviously $P_{\text{loss}} = 0$. Our main result is

Proposition 4.3:
1) $F_K(s^*)$ has a maximum value m_F, where

$$m_F = \max_{1 \le j \le J} \frac{C}{e_{0,j}} \log(1/w_j) \tag{47}$$

2) Say that the above maximum is reached at an unique j^*. Then $F_K(s^*)$ reaches its maximum value at the following unique corner point $\mathbf{K}$

$$K_j = C/e_{0,j}, \quad \text{if } j = j^*, \\ = 0, \quad \text{otherwise.} \tag{48}$$

3)

If $\log(1/L) > m_F$ then $\mathcal{A}_L = \mathcal{A}_0$. $\tag{49}$

If $\log(1/L) < \min_j \frac{C}{e_{0,j}} \log(1/w)$ then $\mathcal{A}_0 \subset \mathcal{A}_L$. $\tag{50}$

Otherwise, $\mathcal{A}_0 \subseteq \mathcal{A}_L$, i.e., the boundaries of $\mathcal{A}_0$ and $\mathcal{A}_L$ coincide in part and elsewhere $\mathcal{A}_L$ subsumes $\mathcal{A}_0$. Specifically, $\mathbf{K}$ on the boundary of $\mathcal{A}_0$ such that $\sum K_j \log(1/w_j) \le \log(1/L)$ is also on the boundary of $\mathcal{A}_L$, and when the inequality is false $\mathbf{K}$ is contained in the proper interior of $\mathcal{A}_L$.

Proof: Observe from (30) that as $s^* \to \infty$, $\sum_j K_j e_{0,j} \to C$. Hence, for $\sum_j K_j e_{0,j} = C$, from (29)

$$F_K(s^*) = \sum_{j=1}^{J} K_j \log(1/w_j) + s^*\left(C - \sum_{j=1}^{J} K_j e_{0,j}\right) \\ = \sum_{j=1}^{J} K_j \log(1/w_j). \tag{51}$$

Next,

$$\frac{\partial}{\partial K_i} F_K(s^*) = -\log(1 - w_i + w_i e^{s^* e_{0,i}}) < 0. \tag{52}$$

Similarly, by taking the derivative of both sides of (30) with K_i, we find that

$$\frac{\partial s^*}{\partial K_i} < 0. \tag{53}$$

At this point we observe that various features of the analysis for the single class carry over naturally to the case of multiple classes, namely, on $\partial \mathcal{A}_0 = \{\mathbf{K} : \sum K_j e_{0,j} = C\}$, $s^* = \infty$

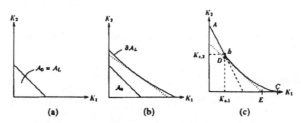

Fig. 7. Illustration of various possibilities for admissible sets and statistical multiplexing gains for two traffic source classes.

and $F_{\mathbf{K}}(s^*) = \sum K_j \log(1/w_j)$, and as $\mathbf{K}$ increases in any direction away from $\partial \mathcal{A}_0$, s^* and $F_{\mathbf{K}}(s^*)$ decrease.

Now consider the behavior of $F_{\mathbf{K}}(s^*) = \sum K_j \log(1/w_j)$ on $\partial \mathcal{A}_0$. Since this function is linear in $\mathbf{K}$, its maximum on $\partial \mathcal{A}_0$ is reached at its boundary, typically a corner point. At the jth corner point, where $K_i = C/e_{0,j}$ if $i = j$ and $K_i = 0$ otherwise, $F_{\mathbf{K}}(s^*) = (C/e_{0,j}) \log(1/w_j)$. Hence we arrive at the results in 1) and 2).

Next consider the multiple class version of the problem considered previously for the single class, namely, the existence of solutions $\mathbf{K}$ in (41). If $\log(1/L) > m_F$ then clearly no solution exists. In this case, as with a single class, the requirement $P_{\text{loss}} \le L$ can only be met by having $P_{\text{loss}} = 0$, i.e., by restricting $\mathbf{K}$ to $\mathcal{A}_0$. Hence, in this case $\mathcal{A}_L = \mathcal{A}_0$. On the other and, if $F_{\mathbf{K}}(s^*) > \log(1/L)$ for all $\mathbf{K}$ on $\partial \mathcal{A}_0$ then, from the aforementioned range and monotonicity of $F_{\mathbf{K}}(s^*)$, solutions $\mathbf{K}$ to (41) exist in the complement of $\mathcal{A}_0$. Hence, $\mathcal{A}_0 \subset \mathcal{A}_L$. Finally, consider the mixed case where $F_{\mathbf{K}}(s^*) \le \log(1/L)$ for some $\mathbf{K}$ on $\partial \mathcal{A}_0$ and the inequality is reversed for other $\mathbf{K}$ on $\partial \mathcal{A}_0$. In this case any $\mathbf{K}$ on $\partial \mathcal{A}_0$ for which the inequality holds is such that (41) does not have a solution and hence such a $\mathbf{K}$ is also an element of $\partial \mathcal{A}_L$. Hence, any $\mathbf{K}$ on $\partial \mathcal{A}_0$ for which $\sum K_j \log(1/w_j) \le \log(1/L)$ is also an element of $\partial \mathcal{A}_L$. Moreover, all other $\mathbf{K}$ on $\partial \mathcal{A}_0$ are contained in the proper interior of $\mathcal{A}_L$.

This concludes the proof of Proposition 4.3.   □

To illustrate the result for a two-class model we need to consider three cases:

1)
$$\log(1/L) > m_F, \text{ i.e., } C < \min(C_{c,1}, C_{c,2}) \qquad (54)$$

2)
$$\log(1/L) < \min_j \left\{ \frac{C}{e_{0,j}} \log(1/w_j) \right\},$$
$$\text{i.e., } C > \max(C_{c,1}, C_{c,2}) \qquad (55)$$

3)
$$C_{c,1} < C < C_{c,2} \qquad (56)$$

where $C_{c,j}$ is the critical bandwidth for class j

$$C_{c,j} = e_{0,j} \log(1/L) / \log(1/w_j), \qquad j = 1, 2. \qquad (57)$$

According to Proposition 4.3, for case 1) we have that $\mathcal{A}_L = \mathcal{A}_0$. This situation is sketched in Fig. 7(a); note that the admissible set is a simplex. The performance implication is that there is no statistical multiplexing gain in this case.

For this reason both source types are NS-VBR, i.e., "bad" in the sense that the sources are too "large" with respect to the node bandwidth. For case (b), the result states that $\mathcal{A}_0$ is a proper subset of $\mathcal{A}_L$, as sketched in Fig. 7(b). In this case the statistical multiplexing gain exists and both source types are S-VBR. The final case 3) is sketched in Fig. 7(c). The boundary of the admissible set is ABC, in which the segment AB is linear and coincides with the boundary of $\mathcal{A}_0$, namely, $\{\mathbf{K} : \sum K_j e_{0,j} = C\}$, while the segment BC is convex. The breakpoint B has coordinates $\mathbf{K}_s$ which the result gives

$$K_{s,1} e_{0,1} + K_{s,2} e_{0,2} = C \qquad (58)$$
$$K_{s,1} \log(1/w_1) + K_{s,2} \log(1/w_2) = \log(1/L). \qquad (59)$$

Note that for $K_1 > K_{s,1}$ the boundary segment BC lies entirely above the linear extension of AB, with the difference attributable to the statistical multiplexing gain. Of course no such gain exists for $K_1 < K_{s,1}$. In this case class 1 is S-VBR and class 2 is NS-VBR for the given node bandwidth (and, implicitly, node buffer). The breakpoint $\mathbf{K}_s$ is clearly important for operations and design because, first, it demarcates between two different sets of effective bandwidths, and secondly, there are obvious performance benefits in operating to the right of the breakpoint since the effective bandwidth of class 1 sources is smaller.

In the sketch of Fig. 7(a) we have also shown the linear segment DE which is tangent to BC at an intermediate point. As our numerical results indicate, in many cases the departure from linearity of boundary segments represented by BC is slight, in which case DE is close to BC throughout.

C. Critical Value of the Token Rate r

An important observation reported in the next section is the sensitivity of the statistical multiplexing gain, $g = e_0/e$, on the token rate r. Here we present a complementary qualitative result which establishes that with all parameters except r held fixed, there exists a critical value of r, denoted by r_c, which separates token rates for which the statistical multiplexing gain exists, i.e., $g > 1$, from those for which $g = 1$. For simplicity we only consider the case of a single class.

Recall from Section IV-A that if $(C/e_0) \log(1/w) \le \log(1/L)$ then the maximum number of sources that is admissible, $K_{\max} = C/e_0$ and hence $e = e_0$. On the other hand, if $(C/e_0) \log(1/w) > \log(1/L)$ then $K_{\max} > C/e_0$, and $e_0 > e$. Denote

$$f(r) \triangleq \frac{C}{e_0} \log(1/w) \qquad (60)$$

so that $g > 1$ if and only if $f(r) > \log(1/L)$. In (60) let r be varied, while the other parameters, B, C, P, and B_T, are held fixed; note that e_0 and w depend on r as given in (15) and (16). As sketched in Fig. 8, $f(r)$ is a monotonic, strictly decreasing function of r for r in $(0, B_T C/B)$. This is because both e_0 and w increase with r.

Moreover, $f(r) \to \infty$ as $r \to 0+$ and $f(B_T C/B) = 0$. For $r > B_T C/B$, as discussed earlier in Section II, $e_0 = r$ and $w = 1$, and hence $f(r) = 0$. Consequently, there exists

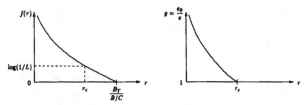

Fig. 8. The token rate r is varied while all other parameters are held fixed in a single source class.

an unique solution r_c to

$$f(r) = \log(1/L) \qquad (61)$$

with the property that $f(r)$ is greater or less than $\log(1/L)$ depending on whether r is less or greater than r_c. Hence, we have:

Proposition 4.4: Let B, C and the source parameters P and B_T be fixed. The statistical multiplexing gain g exceeds 1 if and only if $r < r_c$. The critical token rate r_c is the unique solution r to the equation

$$\frac{C}{e_0} \log(1/w) = \log(1/L) \qquad (62)$$

where e_0 and w depend on r as given in (15) and (16). $\qquad \square$

It is not hard to show the monotonicity of g with respect to r for $r < r_c$, which is also depicted in Fig. 8.

D. Critical Values of the Source Activity Factor w_Ω

It is also of interest to examine the case where the mean rate r and period T are held fixed, and the source activity factor w_Ω is varied. Varying w_Ω is equivalent to varying the peak rate P, since $P = r/w_\Omega$. Some algebraic manipulation of (62) reveals that the critical token rate r_c may be written as

$$r_c = \frac{C}{\log\left(\frac{1}{L}\right)} \left(w_\Omega + \frac{T_{\text{buf}}}{T} \right) \log \left[\left(w_\Omega + \frac{T_{\text{buf}}}{T} \right)^{-1} \right] \qquad (63)$$

for

$$w_\Omega + \frac{T_{\text{buf}}}{T} < 1. \qquad (64)$$

When (64) is violated, $e_0 = r$ and $r_c = 0$.

The character of (63) is as follows. At $w_\Omega = 0$, r_c has the value $r_{c,0} = C/[e \log(1/L)]$. As w_Ω is varied, r_c achieves a peak value $r_{c,\text{max}}$

$$r_{c,\text{max}} = \begin{cases} \dfrac{C T_{\text{buf}}}{T \log(1/L)} \log \left(\dfrac{T}{T_{\text{buf}}} \right), & \text{if } \dfrac{T_{\text{buf}}}{T} < e^{-1} \\[2mm] r_{c,0}, & \text{if } \dfrac{T_{\text{buf}}}{T} \geq e^{-1}. \end{cases} \qquad (65)$$

where here $e = 2.718$. If $r_{c,\text{max}} < r$ then the multiplexing gain g will be 1 for all values of w_Ω. If $r < r_{c,0}$ then there will be a critical value $w_{\Omega,c2}$ such that $g > 1$ for $w_\Omega < w_{\Omega,c2}$ and $g = 1$ for $w_\Omega < w_{\Omega,c2}$. If $T_{\text{buf}}/T < e^{-1}$, then there is a third possibility, namely, that $r_{c,0} < r < r_{c,\text{max}}$. In this case, there is an additional critical value, $w_{\Omega,c1}$, such that if $w_\Omega < w_{\Omega,c1}$, then $g = 1$.

This analysis provides a possible perspective on the ways in which NS-VBR traffic can arise: Statistical multiplexing can be impossible because 1) the mean rate r is too large; 2) the traffic is too smooth (w_Ω is large); or 3) there is little buffering and the peak rate P is large (w_Ω is small).

V. NUMERICAL STUDY

The purpose of this section is to numerically illustrate the mathematical results derived in prior sections and, also, to obtain qualitative results and design guidelines. One of the highlights of the results, which has considerable practical implications, is the linearity of the boundary of the admissible region and the specification of the conditions for it to hold. This result allows us to justifiably define the effective bandwidth for each traffic class independently of the others. The numerical examples in this section address the following issues: 1) the tightness of the Chernoff bound, 2) the behavior of the effective bandwidth, e, with respect to nodal resources (bandwidth and buffer), 3) the sensitivity of e and the multiplexing gain with respect to the mean rate, peak rate and token buffer size, 4) the admission region when the source classes are all S-VBR, 5) the admission region when both S-VBR and NS-VBR sources are present, and 6) the accuracy of our analytical approach to resource allocation and comparison with simulation.

We begin by considering results for a single class of sources. In Fig. 9 we examine the effective bandwidth, $e = C/K_{\text{max}}$ (K_{max} is integer) versus C with B/C held fixed. Our objectives in this figure are to test the accuracy of the Chernoff bound, demonstrate the existence of C_c, and compare the values obtained numerically (for integer K) and from (45). Observe that for $C < 11.1$, e is equal to e_0, the effective bandwidth in lossless multiplexing; for $C > 11.1$ statistical multiplexing gain is in effect and e begins to drop. C_c obtained from (45) is 10.65. (The small discrepancy is due to the integrality of K_{max} in the figures.) Observe that the Chernoff bound on the loss probability results in a bound on e which is quite tight for all values of C and gets tighter as C increases; also, e approaches r for large values of C, as expected. In Fig. 10 we consider a different class and obtain similar qualitative results; in particular, the values of C_c in the figure and that obtained from (45) are 13.1 and 12.6, respectively.

In contrast to Figs. 9 and 10, in Fig. 11 we consider two classes with very different values of C_c. In the figure C_c is 22.1 and 108.5 for classes 1 and 2, respectively, while (45) gives 20.9 and 100.7. This suggests that if the two classes are multiplexed over a link having bandwidth 45, for instance, then class 1 will exhibit statistical multiplexing gain while class 2 will not. The exact value of C_c for the multiplexed classes is examined further below.

Fig. 12 considers the sensitivity of e with respect to r, the mean rate. The figure shows e and the multiplexing gain (e_0/e) as functions of r, for various values of B_T, with all other parameters held fixed, and strikingly exhibits the sensitivity of the multiplexing gain e_0/e with respect to r. For instance, when r increases from 0.1 to 0.2, the gain decreases from 2.7 to 1.54.

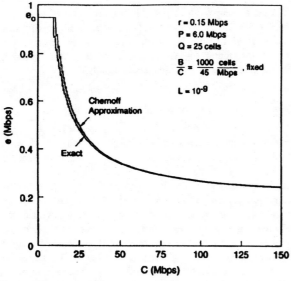

Fig. 9. Effective bandwidth e versus trunk bandwidth C, with B/C held fixed, where B is buffer size.

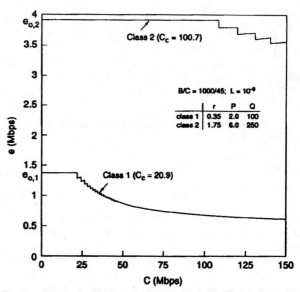

Fig. 11. Effective bandwidth e versus trunk bandwidth C, for two classes with very different values of critical bandwidths, C_c.

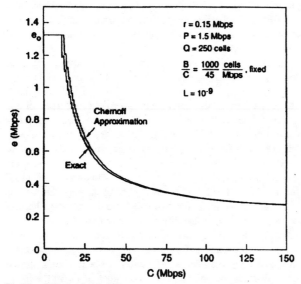

Fig. 10. Effective bandwidth e versus trunk bandwidth C, with B/C held fixed, where B is buffer size.

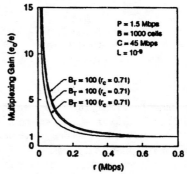

Fig. 12. Sensitivity of the effective bandwidth to the mean source rate, r.

We next examine the multiplexing of multiple classes of sources. Fig. 13 considers two classes, which were individually considered in Figs. 9 and 10. The boundary of the admissible region is plotted for different value of loss probability L. For each L we plot the boundary obtained using Chernoff bound and its linear conservative approximation obtained as the tangent at $K_j = K_{\max,j}/2$, $j = 1, 2$. There are two important observations to make: (1) Statistical multiplexing, even with very small loss probability, provides considerable gain in network capacity (number of connections). For instance, more than 3-fold increase in the maximum number of sources of each class is obtained as L is increased

from 0 to 10^{-7}, (2) The boundary of the admissible region is very close to its linear conservative approximation for all values of L; it is also very close to the optimistic linear approximation defined in (38). The linearity of the admissible region is due to the high degree of sharing allowed among all sources and can be best explained by examining Fig. 13 in conjunction with Figs. 9 and 10. We first note that the value of C_c for each class ($C_{c,1} = 11.1$ and $C_{c,2} = 13.1$) is less than the link capacity $C = 45$, hence the two classes are S-VBR. Second, and more interestingly, e_1, and e_2, obtained from the linearized boundary, correspond to the values read off from Figs. 9 and 10, respectively. The linearity of the admissible region is further tested in Fig. 14 for different values of C with B/C and L held fixed.

In Fig. 15 the effect of varying the peak rate is examined. The boundary of the admissible region is plotted for differentvalues of P_1 and P_2 (the peak rates of class 1 and class 2 respectively)while all other parameters are held fixed. Note that increasing the peak rate reduces the admissible region, but does not alter the linearity of its boundary.

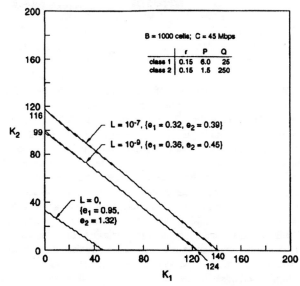

Fig. 13. Admissible region for the multiplexing of two source classes considered in Figs. 9 and 10, for various values of the loss probability L.

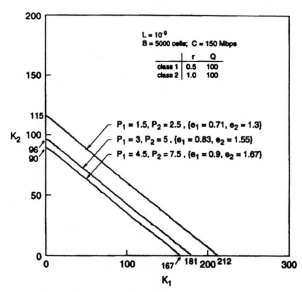

Fig. 15. Effect of peak rates, P_1 and P_2.

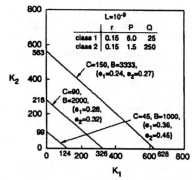

Fig. 14. Similar to Fig. 13, with L fixed, different values of C and B/C fixed.

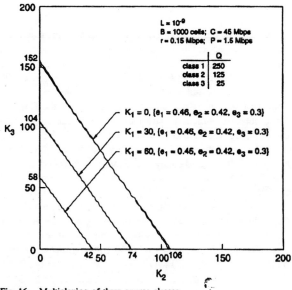

Fig. 16. Multiplexing of three source classes.

In Fig. 16, we consider three classes of S-VBR sources and plot the admissible region in the space of K_1 and K_2 for different fixed values of K_3. Again, the linearity of the boundary persists.

Next, we consider the multiplexing of two source classes, where class 1 is S-VBR and class 2 is NS-VBR, i.e., $C_{c,1} < C < C_{c,2}$. As discussed in Section IV-B such mixture of VBR classes results in a breakpoint in the boundary of the admissible region. Fig. 17 demonstrates this result. Class 1 and class 2 are the same classes considered individually is Fig. 11. The breakpoint in the figure is at $K_1 = 10$ and $K_2 = 8$ which closely matches that given by (58) and (59), where $K_1 = 10.517$ and $K_2 = 7.78$.

The analysis leading to the preceding numerical results involved a number of (generally conservative) approximations which are reviewed in Section VI. The accuracy of these approximations may be assessed by comparing the number of sources predicted by the analysis with that predicted by simulation. We have done some preliminary work in this

regard. We consider a node with a single class of sources, where the source parameters, the link buffer size and the link bandwidth are as given in Fig. 10. Table I gives the number of admissible sources found from analysis and from a fluid-model simulation for different loss probabilities. In the simulation, each periodic on-off source generates fluid at a constant rate during the on period, and the fluid is drained from the buffer at a constant rate. The table is obtained by determining the loss probability from the simulation for each value of K, the number of admissible sources, and then determining the corresponding number of sources for that loss probability from analysis. Note that the number of admissible sources obtained from the analysis is a lower bound on the number found from the simulation.

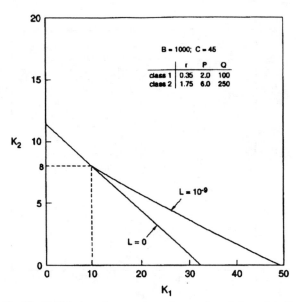

Fig. 17. Multiplexing of two source classes, class 1 is statistically-multiplexable and class 2 is nonstatistically-multiplexable.

VI. DISCUSSION

Our analysis has been based on a number of approximations. Most of the approximations used have been conservative. Each of these approximations essentially replaces the number of sources that can be admitted for a given loss probability with an upper bound on the admissible number of sources. Conservative approximations include (A) use of the Chernoff approximation, which we know to be quite accurate; (B) the use of segregated bandwidth allocations for each circuit so that inequality (9) is taken to be an equality; (C) the optimization of each circuit buffer and bandwidth allocation independent of the nature of the traffic sources for other circuits, leading to (11); (D) the replacement of the virtual buffer usage $v_{ji}(t)$ by an on-off process, which in conjunction with approximations (B) and (C) reduces the problem to one involving a single resource; (E) the use of worst-case leaky-bucket output rather than more typical traffic patterns, albeit it is difficult to know what usage patterns will be typical in ATM networks; and optionally (F) the approximation of the concave admissible set boundary by a tangent plane, leading to (36). Optimistic approximations include (G) the use of the fluid-model as a proxy for a system with discrete traffic; and optionally (H) the approximation of the concave admissible set boundary by a plane determined by single-class effective bandwidths, leading to (38).

The fluid-model simulation results in Section V are suggestive with regard to the magnitude the error introduced by approximations (A), (B), and (D). In the examples considered, the analytic results admit 22%–27% fewer sources than the fluid simulation would allow. Of course, much more work would need to be done before any broad generalizations could be made regarding the accuracy of these approximations. Similarly, work would be needed to evaluate the accuracy of (C); this could be studied via simulations of multiple source classes.

TABLE I
FLUID-MODEL SIMULATION VERSUS ANALYSIS FOR
$r = 0.15$ Mb/s $P = 1.5$ Mb/s AND $Q = 250$ CELLS

Loss Probability	2.2×10^{-8}	1.7×10^{-7}	1.3×10^{-6}	6.0×10^{-6}	2.8×10^{-5}
K (Simulation)	150	160	170	180	190
K (Analysis)	110	119	129	137	147

Regarding (G), the use of the fluid model in lieu of a discrete model is optimistic because it ignores the possible need to buffer cells during some portion of the cell interarrival time of each source. If the number of cells involved in a burst is large and the buffering required in the fluid model is substantial, then the fluid-model predictions are expected to be very close to those produced by a discrete model. In cases where the cell interarrival times for individual sources are large and the number of sources in a burst is small, the predictions of the fluid model may be significantly optimistic. While optimism is dangerous in an admission control criterion, 1) this optimism may be counterbalanced by the conservatism of other approximations, and 2) we anticipate that relatively simple methods of accounting for errors due to the fluid approximation will be forthcoming.

The numerical results of Section V suggest that approximations (F) and (H), linear approximations to the boundary of the admissible set, should be fairly accurate as long as S-VBR and NS-VBR traffic is not intermixed. The potential for using the optimistic linear approximation, (H), is tremendously important for practical on-line admission control, insofar as it allows one to incrementally tally the total effective bandwidth used in a buffer/trunk system as sources are added and dropped, without any need to take into account future traffic or recalculate the effective bandwidths of previously added traffic. How to attain this sort of efficiency in cases where S-VBR and NS-VBR traffic are intermixed will be the subject of future work.

Throughout this work we have focused on a single buffer/trunk system. It is important to examine the effect of buffering and multiplexing on the characteristics of the source traffic as it traverses the network. While the total traffic multiplexed into a node gets smoothed out due to buffering, and hence its effective bandwidth decreases, some sources experience increase and others experience decrease in their effective bandwidth. The traffic burstiness of an individual source increases if the traffic passes through the multiplexing node when its buffer is nonempty and few other sources are on. In this case, the peak rate of the output traffic increases, and can reach the link bandwidth if the traffic arrives to nonempty buffer while all other sources are off. This increase in burstiness will be of concern in subsequent downstream nodes if the source follows a downstream path which is shared by only few other sources. However, when the source peak rate is small compared to the link rate, i.e., the number of sources multiplexed is large, the probability that only few sources are on is small. In [13] simulation studies using source models with exponentially-distributed on and off periods confirm that the the change in the characteristics of the source traffic due to buffering and multiplexing in a network node is negligible provided that the source peak rate is a small fraction of the link bandwidth, and, thus, network analysis based on nodal decomposition is justified.

ACKNOWLEDGMENT

The authors gratefully acknowledge the benefit of discussions and support of our colleague F. Bonomi who saw early the need for a new approach to resource allocation and admission control to ATM networks.

REFERENCES

[1] D. Anick, D. Mitra, and M. M. Sondhi, "Stochastic theory of a data handling system with multiple sources," *Bell Syst. Tech. J.*, vol. 61, pp. 1871–1894, 1982.

[2] P. Billingsley, *Probability and Measure*, 2nd ed. New York: Wiley, 1986.

[3] N. R. Chaganty and J. Sethuraman, "Strong large deviation and local limit theorems," *Ann. Probab.*, vol. 21, no. 3, pp. 1671–1690, 1993.

[4] B. T. Doshi, "Deterministic rule based traffic descriptors for broadband ISDN: Worst case behavior and connection acceptance control," in *Proc. ITC-14*, J. Labetoulle and J. W. Roberts, Eds. New York: Elsevier, 1994, pp. 591–600.

[5] A. I. Elwalid and D. Mitra, "Analysis and design of rate-based congestion control of high speed networks, I: Stochastic fluid models, access regulation," *Queueing Syst.*, vol. 9, pp. 29–63, 1991.

[6] ———, "Effective bandwidth of general Markovian traffic sources and admission control of high speed networks," *IEEE/ACM Trans. Networking*, vol. 1, pp. 329–343, 1993.

[7] R. Guerin, H. Ahmadi, and M. Nagshineh, "Equivalent capacity and its application to bandwidth allocation in high-speed networks," *IEEE J. Select. Areas Commun.*, vol. 9, pp. 968–981, 1991.

[8] R. J. Gibbens and P. J. Hunt, "Effective bandwidths for the multi-type UAS channel," *Queueing Syst.*, vol. 9, pp. 17–28, 1991.

[9] J. Y. Hui, "Resource allocation for broadband networks," *IEEE J. Select. Areas Commun.*, vol. 6, pp. 1598–1608, 1988.

[10] ———, *Switching and Traffic Theory for Integrated Broadband Networks*. Boston, MA: Kluwer, 1990.

[11] F. P. Kelly, "Effective bandwidths at multi-type queues," *Queueing Syst.*, vol. 9, pp. 5–15, 1991.

[12] K. Kvols and S. Blaabjerg, "Bounds and approximations for the periodic on/off queue with applications to ATM traffic control," in *Proc. IEEE INFOCOM*, 1992, pp. 487–494.

[13] W. C. Lau and S. Q. Li, "Traffic analysis in large-scale high-speed integrated networks: validation of nodal decomposition approach," in *Proc. IEEE INFOCOM*, 1993, pp. 1320–1329.

[14] D. Mitra and J. A. Morrison, "Erlang capacity and uniform approximations for shared unbuffered resources," *IEEE/ACM Trans. Networking*, vol. 2, pp. 558–570, 1994.

[15] ———, "Independent regulated processes to a shared unbuffered resource which maximize the loss probability," preprint, 1994.

[16] A. K. Parekh and R. G. Gallager, "A generalized processor sharing approach to flow control in integrated services network—the single-node case," *IEEE/ACM Trans. Networking*, vol. 1, pp. 344–357, 1993.

[17] V. V. Petrov, "On the probabilities of large deviations for sums of independent random variables," *Theory Probab., Applicat.*, vol. 10, pp. 287–298, 1965.

[18] "Performance Evaluation and Design of Multiservice Networks," J. W. Roberts, Ed., Commission of the European Communities, Final Rep., COST 224 project, 1992.

[19] J. W. Roberts, B. Bensaou, and Y. Canetti, "A traffic control framework for high speed data transmission," in *Proc. IFIP Workshop Modeling, Performance Eval. ATM Technol.*, 1993, pp. 243–262.

[20] J. S. Turner, "New directions in communications (Or which way to the information age?)," *IEEE Commun. Mag.*, Oct. 1986.

[21] W. Whitt, "Tail probabilities with statistical multiplexing and effective bandwidths for multi-class queues," *Telecommun. Syst.*, vol. 2, pp. 71–107, 1993.

[22] T. Worster, "Modeling deterministic queues: the Leaky Bucket as an arrival process," *Proc. ITC-14*, J. Labetoulle and J. W. Roberts, Eds. New York: Elsevier, 1994, pp. 581–590.

[23] N. Yamanaka, Y. Sato and K. I. Sato, "Performance limitations of leaky bucket algorithm for usage parameter control of bandwidth allocation methods," *IEICE Trans. Commun.*, vol. E75-B, no. 2, 1992, pp. 82–86.

[24] D. Yates, J. Kurose, D. Towsley, and M. Hluchyj, "On per-session end-to-end delay and call admission problem for real-time applications with QOS requirements," in *Proc. SIGCOMM '93*, 1993.

Anwar Elwalid (S'89–M'90), for a photograph and biography please see page 1016 of this issue.

Debasis Mitra (M'75–SM'82–F'89), for a photograph and biography please see page 936 of this issue.

Robert H. Wentworth (M'93) received the B.S. and B.A. degrees in physics and applied mathematics, respectively, from the University of Rochester, Rochester, NY, and the M.S. and Ph.D. degrees in applied physics from Stanford University, Stanford, CA.

While at Stanford, he investigated novel optical communication and sensing schemes, and developed new models for the noise associated with multimode semiconductor lasers, and for the ultrafast nonlinear optical response of liquids. In 1989, he joined AT&T Bell Laboratories, where his initial research emphasized understanding the noise and distortion properties of semiconductor lasers for use in lightwave cable television systems. Since 1993, his work has involved the admission and routing of virtual circuits in ATM networks.

Effective Bandwidth Vectors for Multiclass Traffic Multiplexed in a Partitioned Buffer

V. G. Kulkarni, L. Gün, *Senior Member, IEEE*, and P. F. Chimento

Abstract—We consider a traffic model where a single source generates traffic having J ($J \geq 2$) quality of service (QoS) classes. QoS in this case is described by a cell loss probability objective ϵ_j for QoS class j. We assume that $\epsilon_1 \geq \epsilon_2 \geq \cdots \geq \epsilon_J$, in other words, class J has the most stringent QoS requirements and class 1 the least. The traffic from K such independent heterogeneous Markov-modulated fluid sources is multiplexed into a single buffer of size B. There are $J - 1$ thresholds $\{B_j, 1 \leq j \leq J-1\}$ such that $0 < B_1 < B_2 < \cdots < B_{J-1} < B$. Let $B_0 = 0$ and $B_J = B$. If the buffer content is in $(B_{j-1}, B_j), 1 \leq j \leq J$ only traffic of class index j or above is accepted and all other traffic is rejected. For this system of K sources we define an effective bandwidth vector of size J such that QoS requirements for all classes are satisfied if each component of the vector is less than the channel capacity. We propose several bandwidth vectors that can be computed for each source separately. Numerical studies are reported on the efficacy of these bandwidth vectors.

I. INTRODUCTION

THE emerging high speed networks achieve efficiency and higher resource utilization by using statistical multiplexing. Under statistical multiplexing the traffic from several sources gets superimposed onto a single buffer and is transmitted to the network in a first-come-first-served fashion. In the high-speed networks using asynchronous transfer mode (ATM), each source is assured a given quality of service (QoS), and the admission control scheme is designed to assure that a source is admitted into the network only if there is sufficient capacity in the network to guarantee the QoS.

Stochastic fluid models and the theory of large deviations have been used in the literature to define what is called *effective bandwidth* or *equivalent capacity* for each source. The effective bandwidth is a number that depends on the source characteristic, the QoS requirement of the source and the buffer size. The most useful property of the effective bandwidth is the following: If the sum of the effective bandwidths of all the sources multiplexed onto a buffer is less than the speed of

the channel removing data from the buffer then (in certain asymptotic sense) the QoS requirements of all the sources are satisfied. This is what makes the concept of effective bandwidths very useful in admission control. Several authors have studied this concept from different angles [3], [6]–[8], [9], [11].

The above method of admission control indeed works very satisfactorily as long as the QoS requirements of all the sources are the same or at least close. In practice all the sources get the QoS of the most stringent source, since they all get the same QoS. This manifests itself in less than optimal resource allocation. This is a major drawback of this method.

When the source QoS requirements are varied, or when every source generates traffic belonging to multiple classes with varying QoS requirements (such as MPEG-2 multilayered video, or sources policed by leaky bucket regulators), the above call admission procedure needs to be changed. In particular, when a source, such as a multilayered video codec, transmits, the information from different layers that emanate from that single source may have very different QoS requirements. So, for example, some signals may have only enhancement effects on the final image, or enhancements of sound quality, and so can be transmitted at a much lower QoS than signals having to do with the more fundamental quality of the way the information is presented [13].

One method is to classify the traffic into multiple classes according to their QoS requirements and to employ a separate buffer for each class of traffic. Then the effective bandwidth methodology can be applied to each buffer separately. This, however, has several drawbacks: First, we need a scheduler to schedule the transmission from the various buffers to ensure first in first out discipline for each connection (source). Second, the buffer utilization is inferior. Third, if the cells of different priorities emanate from a single source (that is, they are part of a single stream), then having seperate buffers for differing QoS requirements forces resequencing at the destination, which is highly undesirable. Fourth, having seperate logical buffers for each QoS requirement complicates the implementation.

To overcome the above disadvantages one can consider a shared buffer scheme. Under this scheme the traffic is classified as before. Suppose there are J classes, indexed 1, 2, $\cdots$, J. We assume that class J has the most stringent QoS and class 1 has the least stringent one. The buffer is of size B. There are $J - 1$ thresholds $\{B_j, 1 \leq j \leq J-1\}$ such that $0 < B_1 < B_2 < \cdots < B_{J-1} < B$. For convenience, define $B_0 = 0$ and $B_J = B$. If the buffer content is in the interval $(B_{j-1}, B_j), (1 \leq j \leq J)$ only traffic of class index

Manuscript received September 30, 1994; revised April 1, 1995. This work was supported in part by NSF Grant NCR-9406823. This paper was presented in part at the INFORMS Telecom Conference, Boca Raton, FL, March 1995.

V. G. Kulkarni was a visitor at IBM High Bandwidth Networking, Network Analysis Center, Research Triangle Park, NC 27709 USA. He is now with the Department of Operations Research, University of North Carolina, Chapel Hill, NC 27599 USA.

L. Gün was with IBM High Bandwidth Networking, Network Analysis Center, Research Triangle Park, NC 27709 USA. He is now with Motorola Codex, Mansfield, MA 02048 USA.

P. F. Chimento is on leave with IBM High Bandwidth Networking, Network Analysis Center, Research Triangle Park, NC 27709 USA. He is now with Tele-Informatics and Open Systems, University of Twente, Enschede, The Netherlands.

IEEE Log Number 9412653.

Reprinted from IEEE Journal on Selected Areas in Communications, Vol. 13, No. 6, Aug. 1995, pp. 1039-1047.

j or above is accepted and all other traffic is rejected. The admission policy is more complicated when the buffer content is exactly at a threshold and will be stated precisely in the next section.

The above scheme of differentiating traffic from different traffic classes is called a buffer sharing scheme. It is intuitively clear that the above mechanism would provide highest QoS to class J and lowest QoS to class 1 traffic. Furthermore, the scheme maintains the first-in-first-out ordering among all accepted traffic and eliminates the need for schedulers. It is also easy to analyse [3], [13] and is shown to be optimal within a large class of service policies [2], [12], [14]. For these reasons this scheme is very attractive.

In this paper we analyse this scheme and show how the concept of effective bandwidths can be extended to this configuration. The aim is construct a vector of size J (called the effective bandwidth vector) for each source such that the QoS requirements are satisfied for all classes if the each component of the sum of the effective bandwidth vectors is less than the channel speed.

The purpose of constructing such a vector is to try to reduce the bandwidth requirements of the source stream as a whole. So, for example, if no priority differentiation is made, then all the cells from that particular source must be treated as though they required the most stringent QoS. Intuitively, one would expect the bandwidth requirements to be less when there is priority differentiation. For a given number of sources and for a given trunk capacity, bandwidth savings can be defined as the difference between the total effective bandwidth required by the sources with no differentiation and that required by the sources with two or more levels of priority.

The paper is organized as follows: The model is described in detail, and the bulk of the notation is introduced in Section II. Section III contains the relevant results from the descriptive analysis of this model. This section essentially restates the results of [3] using our notation. In Section IV we present the asymptotic analysis of the loss probability (QoS). The asymptotic region is precisely defined in this section. It also states a sufficient condition for the priority differentation to produce savings. Using the results of this section, we construct an effective bandwidth vector for the system of K sources in Section V. Unfortunately, this bandwidth vector is not additive, i.e., it cannot be written as a sum of K effective bandwidth vectors, one for each source. Hence we study several possible candidates for effective bandwidth vectors for a single source. The most logical candidate, unfortunately, provides only an approximation, and not a bound. Hence, we propose several candidates that can be proved to provide bounds, although loose. In Section VI we discuss numerical algorithms to compute the effective bandwidth vectors. We

illustrate the concepts in Section VII by numerical examples using a voice-multiplexing example.

II. THE MODEL

In this section we describe the precise model of multiplexing K Markov modulated fluid sources, each producing fluid belonging to J different classes onto a single buffer of size B that is serviced by a channel of capacity c. Let $Z_k(t)$ be the state of the kth source (i.e., the state of the external environment that controls the traffic stream generated by the kth source) at time t. $\{Z_k(t), t \geq 0\}$ is assumed to be an irreducible continuous time Markov chain (CTMC) with state space $\mathcal{N}_k = \{1, 2, \cdots, \mathcal{N}_k\}$ and generator matrix $G_k, (1 \leq k \leq K)$. When the kth source is in state i, it generates class j fluid at rate $\lambda_{k,i}^j$. As explained in the introduction, the admission policy is based upon a space reservation scheme, using thresholds $\{B_j, 1 \leq j \leq J-1\}$.

Let $X(t)$ be the amount of fluid (of all classes) in the buffer at time t. When $B_{j-1} < X(t) < B_j$, only fluid belonging to classes $\{j, j+1, \cdots, J\}$ is admitted into the buffer. Thus, when $0 \leq X(t) < B_1$, fluid of all classes is admitted, while when $B_{J-1} < X(t) < B_J$, only fluid of class J is admitted. At threshold B_j fluid of class j is admitted at such rate that the buffer content does not rise above B_j. To make this precise, we give an expression for $I_j(t)$, the rate at which the fluid of class j is admitted into the buffer at time t. First, we need the following notation

$$\Lambda_{k,i}^j = \sum_{r=j}^{J} \lambda_{k,i}^r. \tag{1}$$

With this we can write (2), seen at the bottom of this page, for $1 \leq j \leq J$. We use $(x)^+ = \max(0, x)$ and $(x)^- = \min(0, x)$. Now, let $\Phi(B_j)$ be the long-run probability that the buffer content is above the threshold B_j. We take this probability to be the surrogate for the loss fraction for fluid of class j. The QoS guarantee is that this loss fraction is kept below a prespecified quantity ϵ_j. Obviously, $\epsilon_1 > \epsilon_2 > \cdots > \epsilon_J > 0$. Thus, using the surrogate, the QoS is satisfied for all the classes of traffic if

$$\Phi(B_j) < \epsilon_j, \qquad \text{for all } 1 \leq j \leq J. \tag{3}$$

III. THE ANALYSIS

Let $Z(t) = (Z_1(t), Z_2(t), \cdots, Z_K(t))$ be the state vector of the K sources. It is clear that $\{(X(t), Z(t)), t \geq 0\}$ is a Markov process with piecewise deterministic paths. The

$$I_j(t) = \begin{cases} \sum_{k=1}^{K} \lambda_{k,Z_k(t)}^j, & \text{if } X(t) < B_j \\ \min\{\sum_{k=1}^{K} \lambda_{k,Z_k(t)}^j, (c - \sum_{k=1}^{K} \Lambda_{k,Z_k(t)}^{j+1})^+\}, & \text{if } X(t) = B_j \\ 0, & \text{if } X(t) > B_j \end{cases} \tag{2}$$

dynamics of the process is given by

$$\frac{dX(t)}{dt} = \begin{cases} (\sum_{j=1}^{J} I_j(t) - c)^+, & \text{if } X(t) = 0 \\ \sum_{j=1}^{J} I_j(t) - c, & \text{if } 0 < X(t) < B \quad (4) \\ (\sum_{j=1}^{J} I_j(t) - c)^-, & \text{if } X(t) = B. \end{cases}$$

Now, $\{Z(t), t \geq 0\}$ is a CTMC with state-space $\mathcal{N} = \mathcal{N}_1 \times \mathcal{N}_2 \times \cdots \times \mathcal{N}_K$ where $\mathcal{N}_k = \{1, 2, \cdots N_k\}$ is the state-space of $\{Z_k(t), t \geq 0\}$. The generator of $\{Z(t), t \geq 0\}$ is given by

$$G = G_1 \oplus G_2 \oplus \cdots \oplus G_K \quad (5)$$

where $\oplus$ represents the Kronecker sum. Let

$$p_k(i) = \lim_{t \to \infty} P\{Z_k(t) = i\}, \qquad (i \in \mathcal{N}_k, k = 1, 2, \cdots, K) \quad (6)$$

$$p(n) = \lim_{t \to \infty} P\{Z(t) = n\}, \qquad (n \in \mathcal{N}) \quad (7)$$

be the limiting distribution of Z. Now let

$$\pi(x, n) = \lim_{t \to \infty} P\{X(t) \geq x, Z(t) = n\}, \qquad (x \geq 0, n \in \mathcal{N}) \quad (8)$$

and

$$\pi(x) = [\pi(x, n)]_{n \in \mathcal{N}}. \quad (9)$$

For $1 \leq j \leq J$, we use the notation

$$\pi^j(x) = \pi(x), \qquad B_{j-1} < x < B_j. \quad (10)$$

Next, we state the differential equations satisfied by $\pi^j(x)$. First, we need the following notation

$$\Lambda_k^j = \text{diag}(\Lambda_{k,1}^j, \Lambda_{k,2}^j, \cdots, \Lambda_{k,N_k}^j), \qquad 1 \leq j \leq J \quad (11)$$

$$\Lambda^j = \Lambda_1^j \oplus \Lambda_2^j \oplus \cdots \oplus \Lambda_K^j, \qquad 1 \leq j \leq J \quad (12)$$

$$D_j = \Lambda^j - cI, \qquad 1 \leq j \leq J. \quad (13)$$

The $\{\pi^j(x), 1 \leq j \leq J\}$ satisfy the following differential equations

$$\frac{d}{dx}\pi^j(x)D^j = \pi^j(x)G, \qquad B_{j-1} < x < B_j. \quad (14)$$

Next, we state the boundary conditions. For $1 \leq j \leq J$, let

$$\mathcal{N}_+^j = \{n \in \mathcal{N} : D^j(n, n) > 0\} \quad (15)$$

$$\mathcal{N}_-^j = \{n \in \mathcal{N} : D^j(n, n) < 0\}. \quad (16)$$

For simplicity we assume that $\{n \in \mathcal{N} : D^j(n, n) = 0\} = \emptyset$. (The final results hold true even when this assumption is not satisfied.) Note that

$$\mathcal{N}_+^j \cup \mathcal{N}_-^j = \mathcal{N}, \qquad 1 \leq j \leq J \quad (17)$$

$$\mathcal{N}_-^1 \subseteq \mathcal{N}_-^2 \subseteq \cdots \subseteq \mathcal{N}_-^J \quad (18)$$

$$\mathcal{N}_+^1 \supseteq \mathcal{N}_+^2 \supseteq \cdots \supseteq \mathcal{N}_+^J. \quad (19)$$

With this notation we can write the boundary conditions as follows (See Elwalid and Mitra [3] for their derivation.)

$$\pi^1(0, n) = p(n), \qquad n \in \mathcal{N}_+^1 \quad (20)$$

$$\pi^j(B_j-, n) = \pi^{j+1}(B_j+, n), \qquad n \in \mathcal{N}_-^j \cup \mathcal{N}_+^{j+1} \quad (21)$$

$$\pi^J(B_J-, n) = 0, \qquad n \in \mathcal{N}_-^J. \quad (22)$$

The above boundary conditions are intuitive. Equation (21), for example, says that there is no mass at (B_j, n) in steady state if the drift on either side of B_j is away from B_j. The spectral solution to (14) is given by

$$\pi^j(x) = \sum_r a_r^j \phi_r^j e^{\eta_r^j x}, \qquad 1 \leq j \leq J \quad (23)$$

where each (η_r^j, ϕ_r^j) pair is an (eigenvalue, eigenvector) pair satisfying

$$\eta \phi D^j = \phi G. \quad (24)$$

Elwalid and Mitra in [4] show how the (eigenvalue, eigenvector) problem of the above equation involving the large G matrix can be reduced to a coupled (eigenvalue, eigenvector) problem invoving the smaller matrices G_k. We briefly state the main result. For $j, 1 \leq j \leq J$, and $k, 1 \leq k \leq K$, define

$$A_k^j(\eta) = \Lambda_k^j - \frac{1}{\eta}G_k. \quad (25)$$

Theorem 3.1–Elwalid-Mitra: Let $1 \leq j \leq J$ be fixed. i) A pair (η, ϕ) satisfies (24) if and only if the following equations hold

$$g_k^j(\eta)\phi_k^j = \phi_k^j A_k^j(\eta), \qquad 1 \leq k \leq K \quad (26)$$

$$\sum_{k=1}^{K} g_k^j(\eta) = c \quad (27)$$

$$\phi = \phi_1^j \otimes \phi_2^j \otimes \cdots \otimes \phi_K^j. \quad (28)$$

ii) For $\eta < 0$ the solution $g_k^j(\eta)$ to (26) with the maximum real part is a simple real solution, called the maximal real eigenvalue, denoted by $g_k^{j*}(\eta)$ and it decreases monotonically from $\Lambda_k^{j,max}(= \max_{i=1,\cdots,N_k} \Lambda_{k,i}^j)$ to $\Lambda_k^{j,mean}(= \sum_{i=1}^{N_k} p_k(i)\Lambda_{k,i}^j)$ as η increases from $-\infty$ to 0. iii) For $\Lambda^{j,mean}(= \sum_{k=1}^{K} \Lambda_k^{j,mean}) < c < \Lambda^{j,max}(= \sum_{k=1}^{K} \Lambda_k^{j,max})$, the dominant eigenvalue η^{j*}, is given by the unique solution in $(-\infty, 0)$ to

$$\sum_{k=1}^{K} g_k^{j*}(\eta^{j*}) = c. \quad (29)$$

Furthermore, η^{j*} is a monotonic, strictly decreasing function of $c \in (\Lambda^{j,mean}, \Lambda^{j,max})$.

We consider the case of distinct eigenvalues, in which case we have $|\mathcal{N}|$ eigenvalues. The unknowns $\{a_r^j, 1 \leq j \leq J, r = 1, 2, \cdots, |\mathcal{N}|\}$ are obtained by using (20)–(22) which provide the correct number of equations for them. Now, for $1 \leq j \leq J$

$$\Phi(B_j) = P\{\text{BufferContent} \geq B_j\} \quad (30)$$

$$= \sum_{n \in \mathcal{N}} \pi^j(B_j, n). \quad (31)$$

Thus, the QoS requirements can be roughly written as

$$\Phi(B_j) \leq \epsilon_j, \qquad 1 \leq j \leq J. \quad (32)$$

Now that we have a way of computing the QoS requirements, we next study the asymptotic behavior of $\Phi(B_j)$ as buffer size gets large and the QoS requirements get more stringent.

IV. ASYMPTOTICS

In this section we study the following asymptotic case

$$B_j \to \infty, \qquad 1 \le j \le J \qquad (33)$$

$$\text{and } \epsilon_j \to 0, \qquad 1 \le j \le J \qquad (34)$$

$$\text{so that } \frac{B_j - B_{j-1}}{B_J} \to b_j, \qquad 1 \le j \le J \qquad (35)$$

$$\text{and } \frac{\log \epsilon_j}{B_j} \to \gamma_j, \qquad 1 \le j \le J \qquad (36)$$

where $b_j > 0, \sum_{j=1}^{J} b_j = 1$ and $-\infty < \gamma_j < 0$. Note that the condition $b_j > 0$ implies that all threshold separations $B_j - B_{j-1}$ tend to infinity in the asymptotic region. The next theorem gives the asymptotic behavior of $\Phi(B_j)$.

Theorem 4.1: In the asymptotic case described by (33) and (35) we have

$$\Phi(B_j) = \exp\{\sum_{r=1}^{j} \eta^{r*}(B_r - B_{r-1})\}\{\text{constant} + o(1)\},$$

$$1 \le j \le J. \quad (37)$$

Proof: The proof is a tedious exercise in matrix algebra. We start by introducing the required notation

$$\mathcal{R}_+^j = \{r : \text{Re}(\eta_r^j) \ge 0\} \qquad (38)$$

$$\mathcal{R}_-^j = \{r : \text{Re}(\eta_r^j) < 0\} \qquad (39)$$

$$a^j = [a_r^j]_{r=1,\cdots,\mathcal{N}} \qquad (40)$$

$$a_+^j = [a_r^j : r \in \mathcal{R}_+^j] \qquad (41)$$

$$a_-^j = [a_r^j : r \in \mathcal{R}_-^j] \qquad (42)$$

$$\phi^j(A) = [\phi_r^j(n)]_{n \in A}, \text{ for } A \subseteq \mathcal{N} \qquad (43)$$

$$\phi_+^j(A) = [\phi_r^j(n)]_{n \in A, r \in \mathcal{R}_+^j} \qquad (44)$$

$$\phi_-^j(A) = [\phi_r^j(n)]_{n \in A, r \in \mathcal{R}_-^j} \qquad (45)$$

$$p(A) = [p(n)]_{n \in A} \qquad (46)$$

$$E^j(x) = \text{Diag}[e^{\eta_r^j x}]_{r=1,\cdots,\mathcal{N}} \qquad (47)$$

$$E_+^j(x) = \text{Diag}[e^{\eta_r^j x}]_{r \in \mathcal{R}_+^j} \qquad (48)$$

$$E_-^j(x) = \text{Diag}[e^{\eta_r^j x}]_{r \in \mathcal{R}_-^j}. \qquad (49)$$

With the above notation the QoS requirements of (32) can be written as

$$\Phi(B_j) = a^j E^j(B_j)\phi^j(\mathcal{N})1 \le \epsilon_j, \qquad \text{for } 1 \le j \le J \quad (50)$$

where 1 is a column vector of dimension $|\mathcal{N}|$. Using the above notation we shall prove the theorem for the case $J = 2$. The general case follows in a similar fashion. The boundary conditions in (20)–(22) can be written as

$$a^1\phi^1(\mathcal{N}_+^1) = p(\mathcal{N}_+^1) \qquad (51)$$

$$a^1 E^1(B_1)\phi^1(\mathcal{N}_-^1) = a^2 E^2(B_1)\phi^2(\mathcal{N}_-^1) \qquad (52)$$

$$a^1 E^1(B_1)\phi^1(\mathcal{N}_+^2) = a^2 E^2(B_1)\phi^2(\mathcal{N}_+^2) \qquad (53)$$

$$a^2 E^2(B_2)\phi^2(\mathcal{N}_-^2) = 0. \qquad (54)$$

Equation (54) yields

$$a_+^2 E_+^2 \phi_+^2(\mathcal{N}_-^2) + a_-^2 E_-^2 \phi_-^2(\mathcal{N}_-^2) = 0 \qquad (55)$$

which yields

$$a_+^2 E_+^2(B_2) = -a_-^2 E_-^2(B_2)\phi_-^2(\mathcal{N}_-^2)\phi(\mathcal{N}_-^2)^{-1}. \qquad (56)$$

Next, (53) yields

$$a^1 E^1(B_1)\phi(\mathcal{N}_+^1)$$

$$= a_+^2 E_+^2(B_1)\phi_+^2(\mathcal{N}_+^2) + a_-^2 E_-^2(B_1)\phi_-^2(\mathcal{N}_+^2) \qquad (57)$$

$$= a_+^2 E_+^2(B_2)E_+^2(B_1 - B_2)\phi_+^2(\mathcal{N}_+^2) + a_-^2 E_-^2(B_1)\phi_-^2(\mathcal{N}_+^2) \qquad (58)$$

$$= a_-^2 E_-^2(B_2)[-\phi_-^2(\mathcal{N}_-^2)\phi_+^2(\mathcal{N}_-^2)^{-1}E_+^2(B_1 - B_2)\phi_+^2(\mathcal{N}_+^2)$$

$$+ E_-^2(B_1 - B_2)\phi_-^2(\mathcal{N}_+^2)]. \qquad (59)$$

The last equation follows by substituting (56) in (58). Now, in the asymptotic region under consideration, $E_+^2(B_1 - B_2)$ remains bounded above by 1, while $E_-^2(B_1 - B_2)$ goes to ∞. Hence the first term in the square brackets in (59) can be ignored in the asymptotic region. Hence, we get

$$a_-^2 E_-^2(B_2) = a^1 E^1(B_1)[\cdot]E_-^2(B_2 - B_1) \qquad (60)$$

where $[\cdot]$ represents a matrix that does not dependent on B_1 or B_2. Using this convention we get

$$a^2 E^2(B_2) = a_+^2 E_+^2(B_2) + a_-^2 E_-^2(B_2) \qquad (61)$$

$$= a_-^2 E_-^2(B_2)[\cdot] \qquad (62)$$

$$= a^1 E^1(B_1)[\cdot]E_-^2(B_2 - B_1)[\cdot]. \qquad (63)$$

A similar analysis shows that

$$a^1 E^1(B_1) = p(\mathcal{N}_+^1)[\cdot]E_-^1(B_1). \qquad (64)$$

Combining (63)–(64) we get

$$a^2 E^2(B_2) = [\cdot]E_-^1(B_1)[\cdot]E_-^2(B_2 - B_1)[\cdot]. \qquad (65)$$

Now, (64) shows that, in the asymptotic region, $\Phi(B_1)$ is a linear combination of terms of the type $e^{\eta_r^1 B_1}, r \in \mathcal{R}_-^1$, and (65) shows that $\Phi(B_2)$ is a linear combination of terms of the type $e^{\eta_r^1 B_1 + \eta_s^2(B_2 - B_1)}, r \in \mathcal{R}_-^1, s \in \mathcal{R}_-^2$. Using the dominant terms corresponding to η^{1*} and η^{2*} we get the theorem. □

Since there can be a nonzero probability mass at B_j, it is important to realize that $\Phi(B_j)$ in the above theorem is in fact $\Phi(B_j+)$, that is, it includes that mass. The next theorem gives a sufficient condition to check if the QoS criterion is satisfied for the traffic of all classes.

Theorem 4.2: The QoS criterion of (32) is satisfied in the asymptotic region of (33)–(36) if there exist negative numbers $\{\gamma_{jr}, 1 \le j \le J, 1 \le r \le j\}$ such that

$$\sum_{r=1}^{j} b_r \gamma_{jr} = \gamma_j \sum_{r=1}^{j} b_r \qquad (66)$$

and

$$\sum_{k=1}^{K} g_k^{r*}(\gamma_{jr}) < c, \qquad 1 \le r \le j. \qquad (67)$$

Proof: From Theorem 2, in the asymptotic region of (33)–(36) we can write

$$\frac{\Phi(B_j)}{\epsilon_j} = \exp\{\delta_j B_J\}\{\text{constant} + o(1)\}, \qquad 1 \le j \le J. \tag{68}$$

where

$$\delta_j = \sum_{r=1}^{j} \eta^{r*} b_r - \gamma_j \sum_{r=1}^{j} b_r. \tag{69}$$

Now, $\Phi(B_j)/\epsilon_j \to 0$ if $\delta_j < 0$ and $\Phi(B_j)/\epsilon_j \to \infty$ if $\delta_j > 0$ in the asymptotic region under consideration. It can be easily seen that $\delta_j < 0$ if and only if there exists a set of negative numbers $\{\gamma_{jr}, 1 \le r \le j\}$ satisfying (66) and

$$\eta^{r*} < \gamma_{jr}, \qquad 1 \le r \le j. \tag{70}$$

Now, from EM it follows that $\eta^{r*} < \gamma_{jr}$ if $\sum_{k=1}^{K} g_k^{r*}(\gamma_{jr}) < c$. Hence the theorem follows. □

One basic question in priority traffic is: Will the creation of several priority classes always result in savings? The next theorem shows that the answer is a conditional "yes."

Theorem 4.3: The priority differentiation results in savings if

$$\gamma_1 \ge \gamma_2 \ge \cdots \ge \gamma_J. \tag{71}$$

Proof: We shall give a very restricted proof, but it will provide an idea behind the general result. Consider two systems, each with K sources, that are identical in all respects except that priority one traffic of system one is treated as priority two traffic in system two. Using an additional superscript l to denote the system index $l = 1, 2$, we have

$$\lambda_{k,i}^{j,2} = \begin{cases} 0, & \text{for } j = 1 \\ \lambda_{k,i}^{1,1} + \lambda_{k,i}^{2,1}, & \text{for } j = 2 \\ \lambda_{k,i}^{j,1}, & \text{for } j = 3, \cdots, J. \end{cases} \tag{72}$$

This implies that

$$g_k^{j*,2}(\eta) = \begin{cases} g_k^{1*,1}(\eta), & \text{for } j = 1, 2 \\ g_k^{j*,1}(\eta), & \text{for } j = 3, \cdots, J. \end{cases} \tag{73}$$

Now for system two, the sufficient conditions of Theorem 3 need to be satisfied only for $j = 2, \cdots, J$. Suppose this is the case. The condition in (67) for $j = 2$, when applied to system two, becomes

$$\sum_{k=1}^{K} g_k^{2*,1}(\gamma_{21}) < c \tag{74}$$

$$\sum_{k=1}^{K} g_k^{2*,2}(\gamma_{22}) < c. \tag{75}$$

Using (73) and the fact that $g_k^{1*,1}(\eta)$ is a decreasing function of η the above equations can be written as

$$\sum_{k=1}^{K} g_k^{1*,1}(\min\{\gamma_{21}, \gamma_{22}\}) < c. \tag{76}$$

Since the maximum value of $\min\{\gamma_{21}, \gamma_{22}\}$ is γ_2 we see that the above equation implies

$$\sum_{k=1}^{K} g_k^{1*,1}(\gamma_2) < c. \tag{77}$$

Now, if $\gamma_2 \le \gamma_1$, then (77) implies

$$\sum_{k=1}^{K} g_k^{1*,1}(\gamma_1) < c. \tag{78}$$

Furthermore, $g_k^{2*,1}(\eta) \le g_k^{1*,1}(\eta)$ implies

$$\sum_{k=1}^{K} g_k^{2*,1}(\gamma_2) < c. \tag{79}$$

Thus, condition (67) is satisfied for system one for $j = 1$ with $\gamma_{11} = \gamma_1$ and for $j = 2$ with $\gamma_{21} = \gamma_{22} = \gamma_2$. For $j = 3, \cdots, J$ the conditions in (67) are the same for both the system. Thus, if the sufficient conditions of Theorem 3 are satisfied for system two, then they are satisfied for system one, provided $\gamma_2 \le \gamma_1$. This proves the result in this case. The general result follows in a similar fashion. □

Note that the condition in (71) implies that the ratio B_j/B_{j-1} must be larger than $\log(\epsilon_j)/\log(\epsilon_{j-1})$ in order to achieve savings through priority differentiation. In fact, when $\log(\epsilon_j)/B_j$ is a constant, (independent of j) one can see that the bandwidth requirements of a source with priority differentiation is the same as the one which treats all traffic as the highest priority traffic. This analytic insight is itself a benefit of this analysis.

We note here that in [1], Choudhury, Lucantoni, and Whitt discuss the notion of effective bandwidth and point out some of its drawbacks. In general, an effective bandwidth approximation based only on large buffer asymptotics can significantly overestimate or underestimate the number of sources that can be multiplexed on a trunk. If the sources are more "bursty" than Poisson, then effective bandwidth tends to underestimate the number of sources that can be multiplexed, and if the sources are less "bursty" then the number of sources are overestimated. This argues that effective bandwidth results should be used carefully, perhaps combined with other procedures as in [5].

V. EFFECTIVE BANDWIDTH VECTORS

The sufficient condition of Theorem 3 can be written in the following form

$$c^{j*}(K) < c, \qquad 1 \le j \le J, \tag{80}$$

where $c^{j*}(K) = \min_{(\gamma_{j1}, \cdots, \gamma_{jj}) \in \Delta_j} \max_{r=1, \cdots, j} \{\sum_{k=1}^{K} g_k^{r*}(\gamma_{jr})\}$,

$$1 \le j \le J, \tag{81}$$

where $\Delta_j = \{(x_1, \cdots, x_j) : x_r < 0, 1 \le r \le j, \sum_{r=1}^{j} x_r b_r$

$$= \gamma_j \sum_{r=1}^{j} b_r\}. \tag{82}$$

This leads to the following natural definition:

Definition: The vector

$$c^*(K) = (c^{1*}(K), c^{2*}(K), \cdots, c^{J*}(K)) \qquad (83)$$

is called the *effective bandwidth vector* for the system of K sources multiplexed onto a single buffer. However, it is clear from the definition that the effective bandwidth vector of the K-source system cannot be represented as a sum of K effective bandwidth vectors, each associated with a single source. In the next section we study one candidate for effective bandwidth vectors of a single source, which will serve as an approximation.

An Approximate Bandwidth Vector

Here we consider the case of independent and identical sources. Thus the generator matrix of the external environment driving each source is G, and the rate at which a source produces traffic of class j in state i is λ_i^j. Thus the maximal real eigenvalues are the same for all the sources, i.e. $g_k^{j*}(\eta) = g^{j*}(\eta)$. Then we get

$$c^{j*}(K) = \min_{(\gamma_{j1}, \cdots, \gamma_{jj}) \in \Delta_j} \max_{r=1,\cdots,j} \left\{ \sum_{k=1}^{K} g_k^{r*}(\gamma_{jr}) \right\} \quad (84)$$

$$= K c^{j*} \qquad (85)$$

$$\text{where } c^{j*} = \min_{(\gamma_{j1}, \cdots, \gamma_{jj}) \in \Delta_j} \max_{r=1,\cdots,j} \{ g^{r*}(\gamma_{jr}) \}. \quad (86)$$

Thus, we can define

$$c^* = (c^{1*}, c^{2*}, \cdots, c^{J*}) \qquad (87)$$

as the effective bandwidth vector of a single source. (This is a direct generalization of the effective bandwidth vector defined in [10]). Thus as long as the sources are identical and independent, the effective bandwidth vector of the K-source system is the sum of the effective bandwidth vectors of the individual sources, i.e.

$$c^*(K) = K c^*. \qquad (88)$$

This motivates us to study the effective bandwidth vector defined by (87) as a candidate even if the sources are distinct.

Now, consider the K distinct sources as described in Section II. For the kth source, define the effective bandwidth vector as $c_k^* = (c_k^{1*}, c_k^{2*}, \cdots, c_k^{J*})$ where

$$c_k^{j*} = \min_{(\gamma_{j1}, \cdots, \gamma_{jj}) \in \Delta_j} \max_{r=1,\cdots,j} \{ g_k^{r*}(\gamma_{jr}) \}. \quad (89)$$

The question is, how does $\sum_{k=1}^{K} c_k^*$ compare with the system bandwidth vector $c^*(K)$ defined by (81)? Unfortunately, the sum provides neither an upper bound nor a lower bound. It only provides an approximation. This is because moving the sum in (81) outside the max operator increases the right-hand side, while further moving it outside the min operator decreases the right-hand side.

The next theorem gives an important result. Let $\gamma_k^{jr*}, 1 \leq r \leq j$ be the point where the minimum on the right-hand side of (89) is achieved. Also let $\gamma^{jr*}, 1 \leq r \leq j$ be the point

where the minimum on the right-hand side of (81) is achieved. We introduce the following notation

$$q^{jr*} = \max_{k=1,2,\cdots,K} \gamma_k^{jr*}, \quad 1 \leq r \leq j \leq J \quad (90)$$

$$q^{j*} = (q^{j1*}, q^{j2*}, \cdots, q^{jj*}) \qquad (91)$$

$$w_i = \frac{1}{b_i} \sum_{r=1}^{j} (\gamma_j - q^{jr*}) b_r, \quad 1 \leq i \leq j \leq J \quad (92)$$

$$\Gamma_i^{j*} = (\Gamma_i^{j1*}, \Gamma_i^{j2*}, \cdots, \Gamma_i^{jj*}) \qquad (93)$$

$$= q^{j*} + w_i e_i^j, \quad 1 \leq i \leq j \leq J \qquad (94)$$

where e_i^j is a vector with j components, all of which are zero, except the ith one, which is equal to one. Note that the definition of (94) implies that $\Gamma_i^{j*} \in \Delta_j$.

Theorem 5.1: The vector $(\gamma^{j1*}, \gamma^{j2*}, \cdots, \gamma^{jj*})$ is a convex combination of the j vectors $\{\Gamma_i^{j*}, i = 1, 2, \cdots, j\}, 1 \leq j \leq J$.

Proof: The theorem is obvious for $j = 1$ since in that case $\Delta_1 = \{(\gamma_1)\}$ is a singleton. Now consider the case where $2 \leq j \leq J$. We further assume that the vectors $\{\gamma_k^{j*} = (\gamma_k^{j1*}, \cdots, \gamma_k^{jj*}), k = 1, \cdots, K\}$ lie in the interior of Δ_j. (The theorem holds even when they are on the boundary, but the proof is more tedious.) Then, from (89), we have

$$g_k^{r*}(\gamma_k^{jr*}) = c_k^{j*}, \quad \text{for all } 1 \leq r \leq j. \quad (95)$$

Now consider a fixed r, $1 \leq r \leq j$. Since $g_k^{r*}(\eta)$ is a decreasing function of η, it follows that for all $x \in \Delta_j$ with $x_r \geq \gamma_k^{jr*}$ we have $g_k^{r*}(x_r) \leq c_k^{j*}$ and there exists at least one $i \neq r$ such that $g_k^{i*}(x_i) \geq c_k^{j*}$. Hence

$$\max_{i=1,\cdots,j} g_k^{i*}(x_i) = \max_{i=1,\cdots,j; i \neq r} g_k^{i*}(x_i). \quad (96)$$

Now, let $x \in \Delta_j$ be such that $x_r < \gamma_k^{jr*}$. Then, there exists a $y \in \Delta_j$ such that $x_r < y_r \leq \gamma_k^{jr*}$ and $y_i < x_i$, for $i \neq r$. Hence we have

$$\max_{i=1,\cdots,j} g_k^{i*}(x_i) = \max_{i=1,\cdots,j; i \neq r} g_k^{i*}(x_i) \quad (97)$$

$$\geq \max_{i=1,\cdots,j; i \neq r} g_k^{i*}(y_i) \quad (98)$$

$$= \max_{i=1,\cdots,j} g_k^{i*}(y_i). \quad (99)$$

Hence, for each $r, 1 \leq r \leq j$, and $x \in \Delta_j$ such that $x_r > q^{jr*}$ there is a $y \in \Delta_j$ such that $x_r > y_r \geq q^{jr*}$ and $y_i > x_i$, for $i \neq r$, and

$$\max_{i=1,\cdots,j} g_k^{i*}(x_i) \geq \max_{i=1,\cdots,j} g_k^{i*}(y_i) \quad (100)$$

for all $k = 1, \cdots, K$. This implies that $\gamma^{jr*} \leq q^{jr*}$. The set $\{x \in \Delta_j : x_r \leq q^{jr*}\}$ is the convex hull of the vectors $\{\Gamma_i^{j*}, i = 1, \cdots, j\}$. Hence the theorem follows. $\square$

The above theorem can be used in two ways: First, it reduces the space over which one has to search for the system-optimal vector $(\gamma^{j1*}, \cdots, \gamma^{jj*})$. Secondly, it provides another candidate for an effective bandwidth vector with desirable properties, as described in the next section.

Additive Bandwidth Vectors

We begin by defining a class of effective bandwidth vectors. For $k = 1, 2, \cdots, K$ define

$$e_k^{j*} = \max_{r=1,\cdots,j} \{g_k^{r*}(\xi_{jr}^*)\}, \qquad \text{for } 1 \le j \le J \qquad (101)$$

where $\{\xi_{jr}, 1 \le r \le j \le J\}$ is a given set of numbers so that $\xi_j = (\xi_{j1}, \cdots, \xi_{jj}) \in \Delta_j$. Define

$$e_k^* = (e_k^{1*}, e_k^{2*}, \cdots, e_k^{J*}). \qquad (102)$$

We study e_k^* as a possible candidate for an effective bandwidth vector for the kth source.

Theorem 5.2:

$$(i) \quad e_k^* \ge c_k^*, \quad \text{where } c_k^* \text{ is as defined in (89).} \qquad (103)$$

$$(ii) \quad \sum_{k=1}^{K} e_k^* \ge c^*(K) \text{ where } c^*(K) \text{ is defined by (81).} \qquad (104)$$

Proof: (i) Using (101) and (89) we get

$$e_k^{j*} = \max_{r=1,\cdots,j} \{g_k^{r*}(\xi_{jr}^*)\}, \qquad (105)$$

$$\ge \min \max_{r=1,\cdots,j} \{g_k^{r*}(\gamma_{jr})\} \qquad (106)$$

$$= c_k^{j*}. \qquad (107)$$

The inequality follows because ξ_{jr}^* belongs to the set of γ_{jr} over which the minimum is taken. (ii) Using (101) and (89) we get

$$\sum_{k=1}^{K} e_k^{j*} = \sum_{k=1}^{K} \max_{r=1,\cdots,j} \{g_k^{r*}(\xi_{jr}^*)\} \qquad (108)$$

$$\ge \max_{r=1,\cdots,j} \sum_{k=1}^{K} \{g_k^{r*}(\xi_{jr}^*)\} \qquad (109)$$

$$\ge \min \max_{r=1,\cdots,j} \sum_{k=1}^{K} \{g_k^{r*}(\gamma_{jr})\}. \qquad (110)$$

□

The property in (104) provides the justification for calling e_k^* an additive bandwidth vector.

Note that e_k^* is not an effective bandwidth vector of the usual type, i.e., it is not defined in terms of the characteristics of the kth source alone. In fact, it depends upon the source characteristics of all the sources in the system. However, it still provides an implementable method of call admission.

Next we consider two special sets of vectors $\{\xi_j, 1 \le j \le J\}$.

1) *Average of extreme points:* As a first choice, consider

$$\xi_j = \frac{1}{j} \sum_{i=1}^{j} \Gamma_i^{j*}, 1 \le j \le J \qquad (111)$$

where Γ_i^{j*} is an extreme point of Δ_j as defined in (93). Clearly, $\xi_j \in \Delta_j$ for all $1 \le j \le J$.

2) *Average over sources:* As a second choice, consider

$$\xi_{jr} = \frac{1}{K} \sum_{k=1}^{K} \gamma_k^{jr*}, 1 \le r \le j \le J \qquad (112)$$

where $\gamma_k^{j*} = (\gamma_k^{j1*}, \cdots, \gamma_k^{jj*})$ is the point where the minimum over the right-hand side of (89) is achieved. Thus the vector ξ_j is an average of the vectors γ_k^{j*} and hence is in Δ_j.

A Special Case

Here we consider a special case where each source produces a single-priority fluid. However, the total number of priorities is still J. The motivation is to study the multiplexing of sources of differing QoS requirements into a single buffer.

We say that a source is of type j if it produces traffic with QoS requirement ϵ_j (i.e., priority j traffic). Let K_j be the set of sources of type j. Now, consider a source $k \in K_t$. We have

$$\lambda_{k,i}^j = \begin{cases} 0, & \text{if } j \ne t \\ \lambda_{k,i}^j, & \text{if } j = t \end{cases} \qquad (113)$$

and

$$\Lambda_{k,i}^j = \begin{cases} 0, & \text{for } t < j \le J \\ \lambda_{k,i}^t, & \text{for } 1 \le j \le t. \end{cases} \qquad (114)$$

This, along with (25) implies that

$$A_k^j(\eta) = \begin{cases} A_k^t(\eta), & \text{for } 1 \le j \le t \\ -\frac{1}{\eta} G_k, & \text{for } t < j \le J \end{cases} \qquad (115)$$

which further implies that

$$g_k^{j*}(\eta) = \begin{cases} g_k^{t*}(\eta), & \text{for } 1 \le j \le t \\ 0, & \text{for } t < j \le J. \end{cases} \qquad (116)$$

Now consider the computation of the approximate bandwidth vector c_k^* as defined in (89). We have

$$c_k^{j*} = \min_{(\gamma_{j1}, \cdots, \gamma_{jj}) \in \Delta_j} \max_{r=1,\cdots,j} \{g_k^{r*}(\gamma_{jr})\}, \quad 1 \le j \le J \qquad (117)$$

$$= \min_{(\gamma_{j1}, \cdots, \gamma_{jj}) \in \Delta_j} \max_{r=1,\cdots,j} \{g_k^{t*}(\gamma_{jr})\}, \qquad 1 \le j \le t \qquad (118)$$

$$= \min_{(\gamma_{j1}, \cdots, \gamma_{jj}) \in \Delta_j} \max \{ \max_{r=1,\cdots,t} \{g_k^{t*}(\gamma_{jr})\}, 0 \}, \\ t < j \le J. \qquad (119)$$

The above minimum is achieved at $\gamma_{jr} = \gamma_k^{jr*}$ where

$$\gamma_k^{jr*} = \begin{cases} \gamma_j, & \text{for } 1 \le r \le j \le t \\ 0, & \text{for } 1 \le r \le j, t < j \le J. \end{cases} \qquad (120)$$

Thus, computing the ξ_j vectors (using the average over sources method) for the additive bandwidth vectors using (25) is easy.

We get

$$\xi_{jr} = \frac{\sum_{t=1}^{r} |K_t|}{K} \gamma_j, \qquad 1 \le r \le j \le J. \qquad (121)$$

Note that this method is particularly easy to use, since it involves using the fixed parameters γ_j and keeping track of $|K_t|$ for each $t = 1, 2, \cdots, J$.

VI. COMPUTATIONAL ALGORITHM

We begin by describing a numerical algorithm to compute the minimum in (81) and (89). The algorithm uses ideas of steepest descent as well as of binary search, and is based upon the following simple theorem, which we state without proof.

Theorem 6.1: Let $h_i : (-\infty, 0] \to [0, \infty), 1 \le i \le j$ be bounded monotone decreasing functions. Let $(\eta_1, \eta_2, \cdots, \eta_j)$ be the value of $x = (x_1, x_2, \cdots, x_j)$ where the function $h(x) = \max_{i=1,2,\cdots,j} h_i(x_i)$ achieves its minimum over $x \in \Delta_j$. If, for a given $x \in \Delta_j$, $h_r(x_i) = \max_{i=1,\cdots,j} \{h_i(x_i)\}$ then, $\eta_r \ge x_r$.

This is a direct result of the structure of the minimization problem and the monotone nature of the h_i functions. It yields the following algorithm to find $(\eta_1, \eta_2, \cdots, \eta_j)$.

Algorithm A: **Given:** Monotone decreasing bounded functions $h_i : (-\infty, 0] \to [0, \infty)$. Two small positive numbers tolerance1 and tolerance2 to dictate the stopping criterion.

Aim: To find $(\eta_1, \eta_2, \cdots, \eta_j)$ as defined in Theorem 6.1.

Step 0: Set $L = \gamma_j \sum_{i=1}^{j} b_i(\frac{1}{b_1}, \frac{1}{b_2}, \cdots, \frac{1}{b_j})$.

Step 1: Compute

$$\delta = \frac{\gamma_j \sum_{i=1}^{j} b_i}{\sum_{i=1}^{j} L_i b_i}.$$

Set $x = \delta L$.

Step 2: Let

$$h_{\max} = \max_{i=1,2,\cdots,j} h_i(x_i)$$

and

$$h_{\min} = \min_{i=1,2,\cdots,j} h_i(x_i).$$

If $h_{\max} - h_{\min} \le$ tolerance1, stop. x is the desired η. If $-\max_{i=1,2,\cdots,j}\{x_i\} \le$ tolerance2, stop. x is the desired η.

Step 3: Set $L_r = x_r$ and go to step 1.

Remark: If the desired η vector is in the interior of Δ_j, the algorithm stops due to the first stopping condition in Step 2. If η is on the boundary of Δ_j , the algorithm stops due to the second stopping condition in Step 2.

Note that this algorithm can be used to compute c_k^{j*} in (89) as well as $c^{j*}(K)$ in (84) because both $g_k^{i*}(x_i)$ and $\sum_{k=1}^{K} g_k^{i*}(x_i)$ satisfy the properties of Theorem 6.1. Once the algorithm produces the (γ_k^{jr*}) vectors, they can be used to compute the additive bandwidth vector defined by (102). This algorithm is used in all the numerical work reported below.

VII. NUMERICAL RESULTS

Though most of this paper has concentrated on theoretical results, and the construction of approximate bandwidth vectors, we will show some numerical results. One can reasonably ask whether the procedures outlined above actually produce enough benefit to be worthwhile. In this short section, we give an example to show that priority differentiation may indeed be worthwhile. We use the same example as in [10]. Here we extend the voice source example of that paper to explore the effects of multiple priorities and multiple homogeneous sources.

Once again, we assume that the peak bit rate, including ATM overhead, is 72 170 b/s. The parameters of the two-state Markov chain controlling the source are: average talkspurt = 350 ms. and average silence duration = 650 ms. We used four different configurations:

1) *No priority differentiation:* In this case, there is only one buffer threshold, 100 cells, which is the size of the buffer. The target loss probability used was the most stringent requirement of the traffic stream, 10^{-10}.

2) *Two priorities:* In this case, we used two buffer thresholds: 55 cells, for low-priority traffic and 100 cells, for high-priority traffic. The target loss probability for low-priority traffic is 10^{-1} and for high-priority traffic it is 10^{-10}. The peak bit rate is split evenly between the priorities.

3) *Three priorities:* For three priorities, we set the buffer thresholds at 55 cells (low priority), 91 cells (medium priority), and 100 cells (high priority). The target loss probabilities we set to 10^{-1} for low priority, 10^{-7} for medium priority, and 10^{-10} for high priority. We split the peak bit rate among the priorities as follows: 25% each for high and low priority traffic and 50% for medium priority.

4) *Four priorities:* Finally, for four priorities we set the buffer thresholds to 55 cells, 60 cells, 91 cells, and 100 cells (lowest priority to highest). We set the target loss probabilities to 10^{-1}, 10^{-4}, 10^{-7}, and 10^{-10} (again, lowest priority to highest). The peak bit rate was again split evenly among all the priorities.

In this experiment, we computed the additive effective bandwidth vector e_k^* defined in (102). Recall that the e_k^* vectors provide an upper bound for $c^*(K)$ (104) but that since all the sources in this case are identical, the system effective bandwidth vector and the additive effective bandwidth vectors are the same.

Table I shows the result of the computation of the effective bandwidth for the four different configurations described above.

The entries in Table I show the total effective bandwidth (in bits per second) required to support a given number of sources with a given number of priorities differentiated. We can look at the savings achieved from two different points of view: First is to look at the total effective bandwidth required by each of the priority configurations. Having two priorities saves about 8% of the bandwidth over no differentiation. Three priorities saves about 11% of the bandwidth and having four priorities

TABLE I
HOMOGENEOUS SOURCES: TOTAL BANDWIDTH USED

Sources	Number of Priorities			
	1	2	3	4
21	1,515,568	1,399,466	1,353,172	1,294,818
22	1,587,738	1,466,107	1,417,608	1,356,476
23	1,659,908	1,532,749	1,482,045	1,418,134
24	1,732,078	1,599,390	1,546,481	1,479,792
25	1,804,248	1,666,031	1,610,918	1,541,450

saves about 15% of the bandwidth in this case. Second, we can look at the savings from the point of view of the number of connections that would fit on a 1.544 Mb/s link. Note that we have ignored the usual framing and that also, ATM overhead prevents the usual 24 64kb/s connections from fitting in the DS1.

In this example, using four priorities, we can fit about 19% more connections into the given bandwidth than with no priority differentiation. With two and three priorities, we can fit 9.5% more connections.

In this case, we did not find optimal buffer thresholds, as we did in [10] and so the bandwidth savings are less than shown in that paper.

REFERENCES

[1] G. L. Choudhury, D. M. Lucantoni, and W. Whitt, "On the effectiveness of effective bandwidths for admission control in ATM networks," in *Proc. ITC-14*, 1994, pp. 411–420.

[2] I. Cidon, R. Guerin, and A. Khamisy, "On protective buffer policies," IBM Research Division, tech. rep. RC 18113, 1992.

[3] A. I. Elwalid and D. Mitra, "Fluid models for the analysis and design of statistical multiplexing with loss priorities on multiple classes of bursty traffic," *IEEE Trans. Commun.*, vol. 42, no. 11, pp. 2989–3002, 1994.

[4] ——, "Effective bandwidth of general Markovian traffic sources and admission control of high speed networks," *IEEE/ACM Tran. Networking*, vol. 1, no. 3, pp. 329–343, June 1993.

[5] I. Cidon, R. Guèrin, and A. Khamisy, "A unified approach to bandwidth allocation and access control in fast packet-switched networks," in *Proc. INFOCOM-92*, 1992, pp. 1–12.

[6] R. J. Gibbens and P. J. Hunt, "Effective bandwidths for the multi-type UAS channel," *Queueing Syst.*, vol. 9, pp. 17–28, 1991.

[7] L. Gun, A. Narayan, and V. G. Kulkarni, "Bandwidth allocation and access control in high speed networks," *Annals Op. Res.*, 1994.

[8] J. Y. Hui, "Resource allocation for broadband networks," *IEEE J. Select. Areas Commun.*, vol. 6, pp. 1598–1608, 1988.

[9] G. Kesidis, J. Walrand, and C. S. Chang, "Effective bandwidths for multiclass Markov fluids and other ATM sources," *IEEE/ACM Trans. Networking*, vol. 1, no. 4, pp. 424–428, 1993.

[10] V. G. Kulkarni, L. Gun, and P. F. Chimento, "Effective bandwidth vectors for two-priority ATM traffic," in *Proc. INFOCOM '94*, 1994.

[11] V. G. Kulkarni and T. E. Tedijanto, "Optimal cell discarding policy for color-coded voice traffic in ATM networks," IBM Corp., tech. rep. TR 29.1584, 1993.

[12] A. Y. M. Lin and J. A. Silvester, "Priority queueing strategies and buffer allocation protocols for traffic control at an ATM integrated broadband switching system," *IEEE J. Select. Areas Commun.*, vol. 9, no. 9, pp. 1524–1536, 1991.

[13] K. Lindberger, "Analytical methods for traffic problems with statistical multiplexing in ATM networks," in *Proc. 13th Int. Teletraffic Cong.*, 1991.

[14] L. Tassiulas, Y. C. Hung, and S. S. Pannar, "Optimal buffer control during congestion in an ATM network node," in *Proc. 1992 Conf. Inform. Syst., Sci.*, 1992.

V. G. Kulkarni was born in Solapur, India, in 1955. He received the B.Tech. degree in mechnaical engineering from the Indian Institute of Technology, Bombay, in 1976, and the M.S. and Ph.D. degrees from Cornell University, Ithaca, NY, in 1978 and 1980, respectively.

After a year at Georgia Institute of Technology as a Visiting Faculty, he moved to the University of North Carolina, Chapel Hill, in 1981, where he is currently a Professor in the Department of Operations Research. His main research interest is stochastic models. He has published numerous papers containing applications of stochastic processes to retrial queues, computer performance, fault tolerant systems, stochastic Petri nets, database systems, communications systems, effective bandwidths, stochastic fluid models, among others. He authored the graduate textbook *Modeling and Analysis of Stochastic Systems* (Chapman-Hall, 1995).

Dr. Kulkarni is an Associate Editor of *Operations Research Letters* and is a member of the editorial boasrd of *Stochastic Models*.

L. Gün (S'85–M'90–SM'93) was born in Brussels, Belgium, in July 1961. He received the B.A. degree in mathematics and the B.S. degree in electrical engineering from Bogazici University, Turkey, in 1983. He received the M.S. and Ph.D. degrees in electrical engineering from the University of Maryland, College Park, in 1986 and 1989, respectively.

He has held visiting positions at IBM, AT&T Bell Laboratories, INRIA, and George Mason University, Fairfax, VA. From August 1989 to January 1995, he was with the IBM High Bandwidth Architecture group, Research Triangle Park, NC, where he was the Lead Architect for bandwidth management and congestion control issues of IBM's Networking BroadBand Services (NBBS) architecture. From 1993 to January 1995, he was Manager of the NBBS Architecture and Emerging Technologies Departments. During 1993, he was an Adjunct Professor in the Operations Research Department, University of North Carolina, Chapel Hill. He is now with Motorola Information Systems Group, Mansfield, MA, where he heads the Networking Research Department. His current research interests are in ATM traffic management and quality of service issues, wireless ATM, and multimedia distribution over the cable plant. He has published numerous research papers in the areas of bandwidth management, congestion control, and dynamic routing issues for fast packet-switched networks, as well as computational probability, queueing theory, and stochastic control.

Dr. Gün served as the technical cochair and member of technical program committees of several international conferences. He is an active contributor to the traffic management and QoS groups in the ATM Forum.

P. F. Chimento was born in Monesson, PA, in 1950. He received the A.B. degree in philosophy from Kenyon College, Gambier, OH, in 1972, the M.S. degree in computer science from Michigan State University, East Lansing, in 1978, and the Ph.D. degree in computer science from Duke University, Durham, NC, in 1988.

He was with IBM Corporation from 1978 to 1994, holding various positions in design, development, testing, and architecture. Most recently, he was a member of the core team that developed IBM's Broadband Networking Services Architecture for high-speed packet and cell switching. In 1994, he took a leave of absence from IBM to accept a Visiting Faculty position at the University of Twente, The Netherlands, where he is a Member of the Centre for Telematics and Information Technology (CTIT) and the Tele-Informatics and Open Systems (TIOS) group, working on B-ISDN signaling and resource allocation issues and participating in Dutch and European telecommunications projects. He has published in the IEEE TRANSACTIONS ON COMPUTERS, *Operations Research*, and several conferences.

Dr. Chimento is a member of the ACM and ORSA (INFORMS).

CHAPTER VII

ATM NETWORK MANAGEMENT

This chapter describes network management of ATM networks and switching systems.

Network Management of ATM Networks: A Practical View

Mehmet Toy
LT Bell Laboratories
Room: 3A-409G, 200 Schulz Drive, Red Bank, NJ 07701
mtoy@mtatm.att.com

1. INTRODUCTION

The complexity and richness of ATM technology provide a great challenge to manage ATM networks. Users expect the cost of ATM networks operations to be lower than that for the conventional networks, and manage the network from a single point. The network management system must be highly reliable and secure, and scalable [1].

ATM networks as the conventional data and voice networks consist of CPEs, access facilities, traffic concentrators/protocol converters, backbone switches and backbone facilities. CPEs such as set-top boxes and traffic concentrators/protocol converters mostly use SNMP protocol to talk to a network management system, while backbone switches use CMIP protocol for the same purpose. Facilities are mostly SONET facilities in the US, SDH in Europe and Japanese SDH in Japan. Equipment in the network is usually provided by multivendors. Interworking between different vendor equipment is essential to the operation.

In order to reduce complexity of the network management, it is divided into layers: Service Management Layer (SML), Business Management Layer (BML), Network Management Layer (NML), Network Element Management Layer (NEML), and Network Element Layer (NEL) as described in M.3010 [2]. In this paper, we will describe a high level end-to-end operational architecture for ATM networks and explain how each TMN functions defined in M.3010 (provisioning, fault management, performance management, security management and accounting management) can be performed.

ATM Forum has been defining the protocols and functionalities for various network management interfaces. Service providers are divided into two camps about the functionalities of the operational interface to network elements:

while some service providers want just the element level view, others want the subnetwork level view. ATM equipment vendors are struggling with optimization of the effort in satisfying both types of service providers. Those who want the element level view will implement the subnetwork level view and higher layer network management functions in their Operations Support System (OSS), while those require subnetwork level view will only add higher layer network management functions to their OSS to manage a large ATM network. Each solution has its own advantages and disadvantages. However, the first solution is more costly to service providers. This paper examines ATM operations at NEML level from a practical perspective.

2. OPERATIONAL ARCHITECTURE

An ATM network is likely to compromise variety of equipment depending on applications as shown in Figure 1. ATM products at customer premises such as hubs, routers, DSUs, multiplexers, and switches provide LAN functions and access to an ATM wide area network. In the central office, larger switches will provide the backbone for public and private networks, complemented by multiplexers and servers such as video servers. Common approaches to manage the ATM network are:

1. A management system (or multiple management systems of the same kind) is (are) assigned for each type of devices such as routers and facilities such as SONET facilities. Coordination between these management systems is provided either via human operators or an OSS. All network management systems can be located in a single or multiple network operation centers.

2. A management system is assigned to per device type. Coordination between management systems is performed via an OSS.

3. Approaches in 1 and 2 are mixed.

Reprinted from ICT'96, April 1996, pp. 19-24.

The centralized and integrated management of these networks allows more timely and less error prone information to be passed to network managers. In turn, this allows network managers to efficiently eliminate immediate network problems, and reduce the possibility of more serious problems arising. Furthermore, the centralized-integrated network management system presents meaningful, coordinated and summary information about alarms and messages

Network management functions to be supported by these systems are defined in M.3010 as TMN functions that are partitioned as BML, SML, NML, NEML and NEL. BML is where agreements between operators are made. SML provides point of contact with customers for all service transactions such as opening a new account, service provisioning, service creation, service contracts. NML provides an end-to-end view of the network. It receives aggregated data from NEML to create a global view within its domain. NEML that is also called subnetwork management layer (SNML) manages a collection of Network Elements (NEs). NEL is responsible for management of NEs (i.e. Element Management) and is provided by either intelligent NEs or element managemnet systems (EMSs)). These functions include basic TMN functions. Two types of TMN physical realizations are given in Figures 2 and 3. In this paper we will use the term OSS to describe a network management system that supports at least the Network Management Layer of Figures 2 and 3 and can manage multivendor equipment. The OSS may support SML and BML in addition to NML. For large networks, the capacity of OSS may become unreasonable large and execution of certain operations such as provisioning become unreasonably slow. It is practical to add another level, SML, that resides between the OSS and the network element.

Given this integrated and centralized approach, the standard interface between network management systems and networks are described in Figure 4 below. The M1 interface is for the management of ATM CPE devices. The M2 interface is for managing a private ATM network. The M3 interface is for end customers to control their portion of a public ATM network. The M4 interface is for managing resources

within a public network. It can use only the element level, or subnetwork level view, or both. The M5 interface allows to exchange

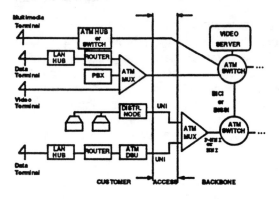

Figure 1: A typical ATM Broadband

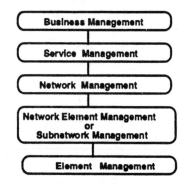

Figure 2: A TMN Implementation

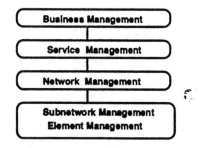

Figure 3: A TMN Implementation

information between two public network managers. An example to M5 is the X-Coop interface described in [3].

Another interface that is not depicted in Figure 4 is the local interface. The local interface could be a simple async interface or a user friendly graphical interface (GUI).

3. INTERFACE PROTOCOLS

The common application protocol for M4 and M5 is CMIP while the common application protocol

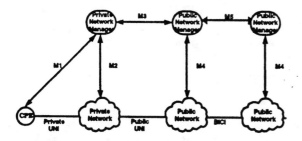

Figure 4: The ATM Forum Management Interface Architecture [4].

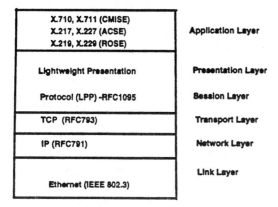

Figure 5: CMOT Protocol Stack for M4 Interface

for M1, M2 and M3 is SNMP. Although CMIP is an OSI protocol and expected to use lower OSI protocols such as X.25, in ATM networks, CMIP is implemented over TCP/IP rather than X.25 due to throughput limitation of X.25. Some of protocol stack alternatives for M1, M2, M3 and M4 are illustrated in Figures 5, 6, 7 and 8.

4. CONFIGURATION MANAGEMENT

Configuration management of an ATM network is the configuration management of end-to-end physical resources such as hardware, software and facility, and logical resources such as circuits. Configuration of hardware and software for equipment is usually performed from a local interface of an element management system or automatically discovered by the equipment, and the OSS is notified about the completion of configuration of each component. Logical resources are usually configured from an OSS with the help of management systems below.

The network configuration begins with configuration of equipment components such as racks, shelves, slots, circuit boards and ports for

X.710, X.711 (CMISE) X.217, X.227 (ACSE) X.219, X.229 (ROSE)	Application Layer
X.215 , X.226	Presentation Layer
X.225	Session Layer
TP 0 TCP (RFC793)	Transport Layer
IP (RFC791)	Network Layer
Ethernet (IEEE 802.3)	Link Layer Physical Layer

Figure 6: RFC1006 Protocol Stack for M4 Interface

each equipment in the network. The equipment components can be provisioned from a local interface and reported to an OSS via M3 and M4 interfaces. They can be provisioned from an OSS as well, or be automatically discovered when they are plugged in [5]. Automatic discovery of components makes the provisioning simpler for network administrators.
It is convenient to provision them via the local interface since there has to be an administrator at the site to attach these components to the system. The local administrator may or may not have an access to the OSS, but will have access to the local interface.

After provisioning of physical hardware and software, logical ports (UNI, BISSI, and BICI) need to be provisioned. It is convenient to provision them from the OSS since there is no need for the administrator to be present at the equipment site to perform the function and most of the parameters of logical resources are independent of underlying physical resources. The next step in the configuration is provisioning of facilities (trunks) between each equipment. This can be achieved by either OSS talking to NEML systems, where each NEML is responsible from management of a subnetwork consisting of equipment possibly delivered by the same vendor and facilities, or OSS talking to EMSs where each EMS system is responsible from management of a single equipment, and has no knowledge of facilities between two equipment. Configuration management of the facilities (such as SONET/SDH point-to-point or ring

X.710, X.711 (CMISE) X.217, X.227 (ACSE) X.219, X.229 (ROSE)	Application Layer
X.215 , X.226	Presentation Layer
X.225	Session Layer
TP 0	Transport Layer
X.25	Network Layer
HDLC LAPB	Link Layer
V.35/RS232 C	Physical Layer

Figure 7 : Complete OSI Protocol Stack for M4 Interface

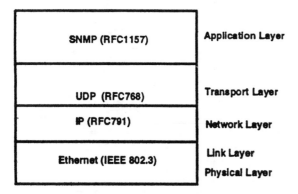

Figure 8: Protocol Stack for M1,M2 and M3 Interfaces

topologies) can be performed from the element management system for facilities.

After the completion of physical and logical ports, and facilities, VP/VC cross connections or circuit connections can be configured. NEML systems are capable of determining the best route for the connection within the subnetwork. This reduces the functionalities to be implemented in service providers' OSSs and makes the circuit provisioning faster. On the other hand, EMSs are not capable of routing. The OSS must perform routing and equipment that slows down the circuit provisioning process. In any configuration alternative, the centralized network management system (or the network administrator) must ensure the completion of

each component provisioning before the completion of end-to-end provisioning.

Configuration events, as results of the configuration management activities from the local interface of an EMS, or an NEML system, or an OSS, will be reported to the OSS using event reports. These events will help the OSS database to synchronize itself with databases of individual equipment.

5. FAULT MANAGEMENT

End-to-end fault management requires setting appropriate thresholds for objects, collecting measurements, reporting of alarms, generating event reports conducting tests and problem sectionalization, and identifying causes.

Threshold are mostly set for measurement counts as described in the following section. Alarms are generated at the physical layer and ATM layer. Some of physical layer alarms are: alarm indication signal (AIS), remote defect indication (RDI), loss of pointer (LOP), loss of signal (LOS), loss of frame (LOF), degraded signal, payload type mismatch, and path trace mismatch. At the ATM layer, AIS and RDI are the two common types of alarms.

Alarms with their severity level will be displayed on a map and correlated by the OSS.They are also logged in EMS and NEML systems for retrieval by the OSS. The OSS has the control over what events are logged and reported, via log and event forwarding discriminator objects [6].

In addition to threshold events and alarms, event reports are generated for changes of operational and administrative states of equipment, physical and logical ports, termination points and connections; and changes of attributes of objects representing these components.

After receiving event reports and alarms, if they are not adequate for identifying the problem and cause, testing will be performed via facility loopback and VP/VC loopback, and hardware/software tests. The VP/VC loopback is performed by inserting OAM cells into the traffic and examining the captured OAM cells. The VP/VC loopback helps to identify ATM layer problems while the facility loopback helps to identify physical layer problems. The testing can be performed either manually or automatically upon the detection of alarm or being prescheduled. One approach for performing automatically is to have EMS or NEML systems to execute the test based on the OSS request. A given VP/VC is first tested for an end-to-end connectivity. If the test is failed, then a loopback testing is conducted at segment level to sectionalize the problem.

Diagnostics tests for hardware and software are mainly conducted from the local interface of EMS systems to identify the location and cause of the problem.

6. PERFORMANCE MANAGEMENT

The performance management is gathering statistical data and correcting the behavior and effectiveness of the network by correcting the behavior of network components such as equipment, physical and logical ports, and connection termination points. The data is collected for 15-minute and 24-hour intervals. Thresholds are set for erred blocks, severely erred blocks, lost information cells, misinserted cells and excessive cell transfer delay occurrences. A Threshold Crossing Alert (TCA) is generated when the threshold is crossed. The network management layer application correlates ATM layer TCAs, physical layer TCAs, and TCAs from different VPs and VCs established over the same set of links.

At the physical layer, measurements are collected for SONET ports: Coding Violations-STS3c Path, Erred Seconds-STS3c Path, Coding Violations-STS3c Path-Far-End, Erred Seconds-STS3c Path-Far-End, Severely Erred Seconds-STS3c Path, Severely Erred Seconds-STS3c Path-Far-End, Unavailable Seconds-STS3c Path, and Unavailable Seconds-STS3c Path-Far-End. For DS3 facilities, Coding Violations-P-bits, Coding Violations-CP-bits, Coding Violations-CP-bits -Path Far-End, Erred Seconds-P-bits, Erred Seconds-CP-bits, Erred Seconds-CP-bits-Path-Far-End, Severely Erred Seconds-P-bits, Severely Erred Seconds-CP-bits, Severely Erred Seconds-CP-bits-Path-Far-End, Severely Erred Frame/AIS Seconds-P-or-CP-bits, Severely Erred Frame/AIS Seconds-CP-bits-Path-Far-End, Unavailable Seconds, and

Unavailable Seconds-CP-bits-Path-Far-End are collected.

At the ATM layer, cell level protocol performance data, UPC/NPC disagreement performance data, congestion data and traffic load data are collected for logical ports such as UNI and BISSI, equipment and termination points [7]. The data consists of incoming cells, outgoing cells, HEC erred cells, incoming cells discarded, outgoing cells discarded, incoming CLP0 cells discarded, outgoing CLP0 cells discarded, discarded cells with invalid header, and number of OAM cells.

At the ATM adaptation layer (AAL), incorrect and invalid segmentation and reassembly (SAR) field errors, and invalid convergence sublayer (CS) field errors are counted.

The management system sets multiple sets of threshold values for the these parameters and selectively assigns to one or more interfaces terminating on an ATM equipment. TCAs are autonomously reported as part of fault management.

Cell level protocol monitoring that involves in collecting and thresholding data counts, measures an ATM network element ability to successfully process and deliver incoming ATM cells. Monitoring of UPC/NPC disagreement, which is the non-compliance with prenegotiated traffic descriptors described in ATM Forum UNI and BICI specifications [8, 9], involves in cells discarded due to UPC/NPC functions (a fault of the user).The M4 interface shall support management system requests to initiate UPC/NPC disagreement monitoring on a limited number of VP/VC links at any one point in time (e.g., 30 ATM links per DS3 and 90 ATM links per STS-3c) [10].

Failures, testing routines, and reconfigurations of UNIs, BICIs, and PVCs may affect the collection of data. When such events occur, the ATM NE is expected to flag the collected data as "suspect".

7. CUSTOMER NETWORK MANAGEMENT

Most of the service providers partition their backbone switches to multiple customers in such a way that certain access ports are dedicated to certain customers. However the backbone ports and trunks are usually shared among customers' traffic.

Each customer desires to monitor its ports (UNIs) by retrieving configuration information, performance data and alarm information. Configuration and performance data are provided on demand. Alarm information is provided autonomously. With this information the user can draw a map of its network, display alarms, and retrieve measurement data. It is also possible to allow customers to provision their connections given that issues related to security and unconfirmed messaging are resolved.

The communication protocol for this M3 interface, which is also called Customer Network Management Interface (CNM), is SNMP. The SNMP manager resides in the customer's workstation while the SNMP Proxy agent resides in the service provider's network management system.

8. BILLING
Service providers generate, format and transmit billing records, and then produce customer invoices. The billing process can be summarized as usage data collection, usage data formatting into Bellcore AMA formatted record, and usage record transporting to Network Management Layer application for rating and bill rendering. Total cells delivered to the egress location is an accepted metric for the usage. The EMS accumulates unidirectional cell count numbers, QoS, time and duration of recording interval, call loss ratio, erred cell ratio, misinserted cell rate, and cell transfer delay. The EMS will release the usage data either on demand or periodically to NEML application for formatting and rating/billing application.

9.RELIABILITY,SCALABILITY, SECURITY and COST
One of the fundamental advantages of ATM technology is to be able to use the same technology for local and wide area networks, and voice and data applications. From operational perspective, it means that the same network management tools and systems can be used across the network. This will simplify network operations and reduce its cost by reducing number of network management systems and time for training staff.

Network management systems should be scalable. It means that their capacity can be expanded. It also means that network management architecture is suitable for small networks (i.e. 10 nodes or less) as well as large networks (i.e. a couple hundred nodes). Appropriate use of TMN realizations given in Figure 2 and 3 will help to achieve that.

Reliability and security are also important factors. Network management systems hardware and software should be fault tolerant. Communications infrastructure for network management systems should use duplicate communication paths.

Good login/password checking is necessary for accessing network management systems and the network. Network management systems should be informed of unauthorized user attempts.

10. CONCLUSION
Despite of the complexity of managing ATM networks, the industry has made substantial progress in this area. This paper presented some of the progress from a practical perspective. Many issues remain to be worked such as management of SVCs, performance of each operational interfaces, and functions of NML, BML and SML for ATM networks.

11. REFERENCES
1. M. Toy, "GlobeView-2000 Broadband System Management via Open Interfaces", AT&T 1995 Network Management Workshop, Holmdel, NJ, June 1995.
2. CCITT Rec. M. 3010, 10/92.
3. T.Baker, et. all., "The management of Pan-European ATM Networks, The X-Interface", Broadband Communications -II, IFIP 1994.
4. ATM Forum, "Customer Network Management (CNM) for ATM Public Network Service", Revision 1.04, Oct. 5, 1994.
5. ATM Forum, "M4 Interface Requirements and Logical MIB: ATM Network Element View, Version 1.0", Oct. 14, 1994.
6. ITU Rec. M.3100, 8/02/95.
7. Bellcore GR-1114-CORE, Issue 1, Jan., 1995.
8. ATM Forum, "User Network Interface (UNI) Specification Version 3.1", Sept., 1994.
9. The ATM Forum, "B-ICI Specification 2.0", Sept., 1995.
10. Bellcore GR-1248-CORE, Issue 1, Aug., 1994.

Managing ATM-based Broadband Networks

Industry is reaching agreements on standard ATM-layer operations early in the BISDN development process.

Stephen C. Farkouh

T he various players in the telecommunications arena have been engaged in a focused effort to specify and standardize operations functions that would allow broadband network providers to effectively and efficiently manage their high-speed, high-performance ATM networks. This is evident by activities currently underway in CCITT and T1 to develop international and national standards on ATM layer operations [1, 2], as well as by activities that have begun in the recently developed ATM Forum [3]. One reason industry has turned its attention to the management of ATM-based broadband networks is to ensure that operations impacts and needs are identified and addressed early in the BISDN development process. Another motivating factor is the general understanding that even high-performance ATM-based networks will, at times, experience failures, congestion, and periods of degraded performance; and without the appropriate management tools to anticipate, detect, and overcome these problems, the viability of the broadband network would be in jeopardy.

This paper discusses some of the management tools that are being addressed throughout industry to aid network providers in dealing with these unfortunate, yet inevitable, occurrences. Specifically, this paper highlights some of the ATM virtual path connection (VPC) and virtual channel connection (VCC) performance, fault, and traffic management functions that are currently being addressed in CCITT and T1 standards committees, as well as in the ATM forum.

ATM VP/VC Connection Management

M anaging VPCs and VCCs includes monitoring transmission performance, detecting and reporting failures, and running various on-demand tests. Considering the large number of VPCs and VCCs that may be configured in a broadband ATM network, it would be neither practical nor cost-effective to individually manage (to the degree

suggested herein) every one of them. Fortunately, not every ATM connection configured in the network will require extensive management. For example, VPCs and VCCs that have relatively short holding times (ultimately accounting for the bulk of network-supported virtual connections) probably would not require such management. This is because these connections would, in most cases, be set up and torn down (released) before any meaningful performance data could be collected or maintenance action taken. Conversely, VPCs and VCCs with long holding times, i.e., permanent virtual connections (PVCs), are perfect candidates for detailed management. The types of PVCs that a network/service provider would be most inclined to maintain include those used to communicate control information (e.g., signaling or operations information), as well as those used to interconnect ATM switch-supported service modules (e.g., switched multimegabit data service (SMDS) modules). In addition, as part of a service agreement, a network/service provider may choose to maintain a select set of end-to-end (customer-to-customer) cell relay service PVCs.

ATM Layer Operations Flows

B roadband operations procedures sometimes require the exchange of operations information between various nodes in a network. For example, at the physical layer, termination devices located at each end of a physical facility exchange operations information through well-defined overhead fields included in the signal format. In a similar manner, peer ATM-layer management entities in each node will also need to communicate to support VPC/VCC management. Specifically, in-band connection-specific operations information such as failure indications, performance monitoring data, and test requests will need to be communicated between the various nodes supporting each VPC or VCC. Mechanisms to transmit such information at the VP and VC levels are referred to in relevant CCITT/T1 standards [1, 2] as F4 and F5 flows, respectively.

VPC (F4) and VCC (F5) operations flows are made possible through the exchange of specially

STEPHEN C. FARKOUH is a member of technical staff at Bellcore.

 0163-6804/93/$03.00 1993© IEEE

Reprinted from IEEE Communications Magazine, May 1993, pp. 82-86.

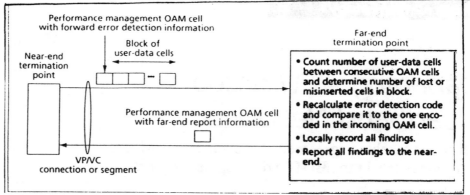

Figure 2. *VPC/VCC level performance monitoring scheme.*

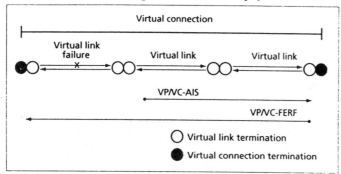

Figure 3. *VPC/VCC failure indications.*

Various performance parameters may be measured using the results of the aforementioned performance-monitoring scheme. For example, Table 1 illustrates the extent to which this scheme can be used to monitor the ATM layer quality of service (QOS) parameters defined in the CCITT Draft Recommendation I.35B [5].

This performance-monitoring scheme is flexible enough so that other ratio-based and even time-based performance parameters (e.g., errored seconds, severely errored seconds, and coding violations) for constant bit-rate connections can be monitored.

The ATM-switch function of collecting performance data for a particular VPC or VCC need not always be active in the public network. At times when it is not, it may be desirable to relieve the connection endpoints from performing the OAM cell generation and processing functions described

previously. An activation/deactivation procedure, which also makes use of OAM cells, has been defined in the CCITT and T1 standards committees [1, 2] to meet this need.

VPC/VCC Failure Reporting

Similar to physical connections, virtual connections may also experience failures. VPC or VCC failures may result from physical link failures as well as from ATM-related troubles such as corrupted VPI/VCI translation tables or the inability to delineate ATM cells from the payload of the underlying physical link. When a VPC or VCC failure is detected, an alarm indication must be forwarded to the local network management system (to initiate repair and restoration procedures) and to the various nodes along the failed connection. The latter function is satisfied by the following two alarm indications, both of which are communicated through OAM cells.

VP-AIS and VC-AIS

The alarm indication signal (AIS) is generated by the intermediate node detecting a failure to alert the downstream nodes that a failure has been detected upstream.

VP-FERF and VC-FERF

The far-end received failure (FERF) signal is generated by the node terminating the failed connection to alert the upstream nodes that a failure has been detected downstream.

An illustration of these failure indications is

I.35B Parameters	VPC/VCC PM Parameters	Notes
Cell loss ratio	Cell loss ratio	Offsetting lost and misinserted cells will not be captured
Cell misinsertion rate	Cell misinsertion rate Cell misinsertion ratio	
Cell error ratio	Cell error ratio Cell block error ratio	Overhead objectives (1% of total user traffic) restrict ability to measure cell error ratio
Severely errored cell block ratio	Severely errored cell block ratio	
Cell transfer delay (CTD)	OAM CTD	OAM cell delay measurements should accurately reflect the delay experienced by the user-data cells carried by the virtual connection
Mean Cell Transfer Delay	Mean OAM CTD	
Cell Delay Variation (CDV)	OAM CDV OAM CDV threshold crossing events	

Table 1. *Performance Parameters and Relationship to CCITT Rec. I.35B*

provided in Fig. 3. Note that physical link alarm indications may result in the generation of VPC alarm indications that, in turn, may result in the generation of VCC alarm indications. The interaction or propagation of physical layer and ATM layer alarms is demonstrated in Fig. 4.

VPC/VCC Continuity Checking

VPC and VCC failures resulting from ATM layer malfunctions are not as readily detectable as those resulting from physical layer troubles. This is partly because, without special operations mechanisms, most VPC or VCC nodes will not be able to distinguish between an idle, yet working, connection, and one that has failed. The way to resolve this is to transmit an OAM cell carrying a continuity indication from one end of the connection to the other in a manner that ensures a working connection does not remain idle (i.e., without traffic) for more than a prenegotiated amount of time. Therefore, if a connection endpoint does not receive any cells (not even an OAM cell) for a longer duration than that which was prenegotiated, it can assume that VP/VC level connectivity has been lost.

VPC/VCC OAM Cell Loopback Testing

The OAM cell loopback capability allows for operations information to be inserted at one location along a virtual (path/channel) connection and returned (or looped back) at a different location, without disrupting service. This capability is performed by inserting an OAM cell at any accessible point along the virtual connection (i.e., at a local endpoint or intermediate point) with instructions in the OAM cell payload for the cell to be looped back at one or two other identifiable points along the connection. For illustrative purposes, four example scenarios have been identified in Fig. 5.

In the first scenario, an OAM cell is inserted and looped back within a single network. The second scenario shows an end-to-end OAM cell loopback that extends across a multiple networks. In the third scenario, an OAM cell is inserted at the edge of one network and looped back at an endpoint of the virtual connection. In the fourth and final scenario, Network No. 2 performs an end-to-end loopback by inserting an OAM cell at an intermediate point with instructions for it to be looped back at both endpoint locations (in series). Note that other scenarios exist which have not been explicitly shown here.

The OAM cell loopback capability is expected to be a key tool in enabling network managers to conveniently perform such essential functions as pre-service connectivity verification, fault sectionalization, and on-demand cell delay measurements.

Traffic Management Functions

Control actions will be needed to improve VPC and VCC traffic performance during overloads and ATM network failures. For example, during periods of excessive congestion, a switch could begin selectively discarding ATM cells, with the intent of maximizing delivery of high-

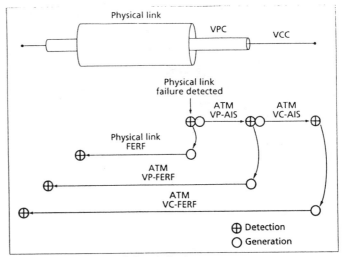

■ Figure 4. *Propagation of alarm indications.*

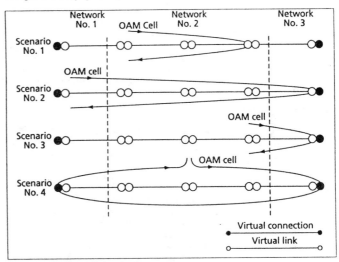

■ Figure 5. *Example loopback scenarios.*

priority traffic (i.e., ATM cells with the priority bit set to zero) for as long as possible. During congested periods, ATM switches also could transmit ATM layer congestion notifications in both the forward and backward directions of VPC/VCC transmission. Upon reception of a congestion notification, VPC/VCC terminating equipment could take measures to help alleviate network congestion (e.g., reduce load on the network). Recognizing the need for a forward congestion notification capability, CCITT has defined an explicit forward congestion indication (EFCI) tag in the format of the ATM cell header [4]. Although there are no standards agreements on a backward congestion notification capability, proposals to support this function using OAM cells have been presented in standards. One advantage of backward congestion notifications over forward congestion notifications is that the congestion reports are sent directly to the source of the user traffic, rather than the recipient. It should be noted that, in general, the use of OAM cells for reporting congestion (as opposed to simple cell tagging) allows for additional information (such as level and cause of congestion) to be supplied along with the congestion indication

Figure 6. OAM cells.

(a) Performance management OAM cell

Cell header fields	OAM cell type	OAM function type	Forward error detection information					Far-end report			
			Monitoring cell sequence number	Total user cell count	BIP-16	Time-stamp	Unused (6AH)	Block error results	Lost/misinserted cell count	Unused (0s)	CRC-10
40 bits	4 bits	4 bits	8 bits	16 bits	16 bits	32 bits		8 bits	16 bits	6 bits	10 bits

(b) Fault management OAM cell

Cell header fields	OAM cell type	OAM function type	Failure type	Failure location	Unused (0s)	Loopback indication	Loopback location	Correlation tag	Source ID	Unused (0s)	CRC-10
40 bits	4 bits	4 bits	8 bits	72 bits	6 bits	2 bits	72 bits	32 bits	72 bits	6 bits	10 bits

(c) Activation/deactivation OAM cell

Cell header fields	OAM cell type	OAM function type	Message ID	Direction of action	Correlation tag	PM block sizes A-B	PM block sizes B-A	Unused (6AH)	Unused (0s)	CRC-10
40 bits	4 bits	4 bits	6 bits	2 bits	8 bits	4 bits	4 bits	336 bits	6 bits	10 bits

itself. One problem, however, is that it involves inserting additional OAM cells into a network that may be already overburdened with ATM traffic.

OAM Cell Format

A number of OAM cell types have been defined to handle the variety of ATM layer operations functions defined for VPCs and VCCs. The following three cell types have been recognized in standards and forums:
- Performance management OAM cell.
- Fault management OAM cell.
- Activation/deactivation OAM cell.

The purpose of the performance management OAM cell is to support VPC/VCC performance monitoring and network traffic management functions such as backward congestion notifications.

The purpose of the fault management OAM cell is to provide in-band alarm reporting and end-to-end continuity check capabilities, as well as provide fault localization capabilities such as the OAM cell loopback function.

In support of both performance and fault management, the activation/deactivation OAM cell provides the ability to enable and disable the previously described VPC/VCC performance monitoring and continuity check functions.

The differences between all of these OAM cells lie in the format of the OAM cell payload (Figs. 6a, b, and c). Although the payloads of these cells are quite different, some payload fields are common across all OAM cells. As shown in Fig. 6, the common part of the OAM cell consists of fields that identify the type of OAM cell (e.g., performance management or fault management) and its function (e.g., performance monitoring, alarm reporting, or loop-back testing), and a field that contains an error detection code generated over the entire 48-byte payload.

Conclusion

Operations and management capabilities play a key role in the viability and success of the emerging broadband (ATM) networks. Substantial progress has been made in standards and throughout the industry to define and establish the operations functions required to manage an ATM transport network. As the details of the functions discussed in this paper are resolved, one can expect more focus on other aspects of ATM transport network management (e.g., VPC/VCC survivability aspects) and the extension of the previously mentioned functions to support multipoint VPC and VCC arrangements.

References

[1] CCITT Study Group XVIII, Recommendation I.610—OAM Principles and Functions for BISDN, June 1992.
[2] Standards Committee T1S1.5, Broadband ISDN Operations and Maintenance Principles: Technical Report, T1S1.5/91-006R3, Aug. 1992.
[3] ATM User-Network Interface Specification, Version 2.0, ATM Forum, June 1992.
[4] CCITT Study Group XVIII, CCITT Recommendation I.361—BISDN ATM Layer Specification, June 1992.
[5] CCITT Study Group XVIII, Draft Recommendation I.358, June 1990.

Biography

Stephen C. Farkouh has been a member of technical staff at Bellcore, Red Bank, New Jersey, since 1987. He has been involved in the specification of operations requirements and standards for ISDN network elements and, more recently, broadband ATM switching systems.

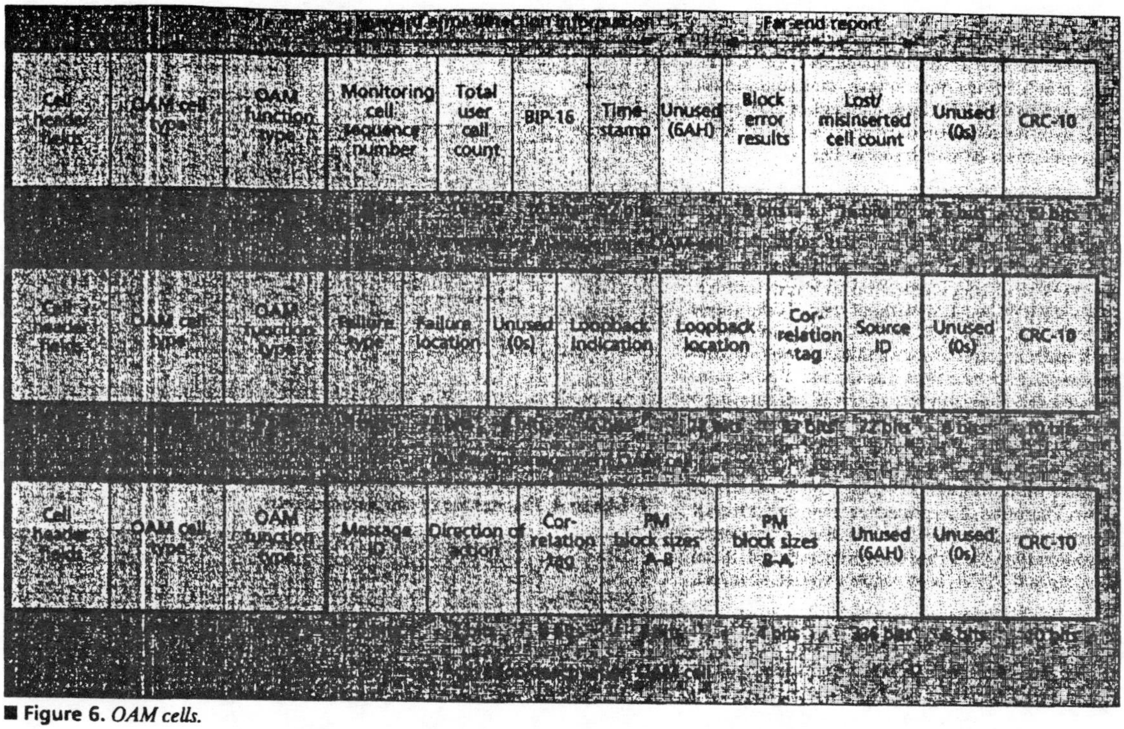

Figure 6. *OAM cells.*

itself. One problem, however, is that it involves inserting additional OAM cells into a network that may be already overburdened with ATM traffic.

OAM Cell Format

A number of OAM cell types have been defined to handle the variety of ATM layer operations functions defined for VPCs and VCCs. The following three cell types have been recognized in standards and forums:
- Performance management OAM cell.
- Fault management OAM cell.
- Activation/deactivation OAM cell.

The purpose of the performance management OAM cell is to support VPC/VCC performance monitoring and network traffic management functions such as backward congestion notifications.

The purpose of the fault management OAM cell is to provide in-band alarm reporting and end-to-end continuity check capabilities, as well as provide fault localization capabilities such as the OAM cell loopback function.

In support of both performance and fault management, the activation/deactivation OAM cell provides the ability to enable and disable the previously described VPC/VCC performance monitoring and continuity check functions.

The differences between all of these OAM cells lie in the format of the OAM cell payload (Figs. 6a, b, and c). Although the payloads of these cells are quite different, some payload fields are common across all OAM cells. As shown in Fig. 6, the common part of the OAM cell consists of fields that identify the type of OAM cell (e.g., perfor-

mance management or fault management) and its function (e.g., performance monitoring, alarm reporting, or loop-back testing), and a field that contains an error detection code generated over the entire 48-byte payload.

Conclusion

Operations and management capabilities play a key role in the viability and success of the emerging broadband (ATM) networks. Substantial progress has been made in standards and throughout the industry to define and establish the operations functions required to manage an ATM transport network. As the details of the functions discussed in this paper are resolved, one can expect more focus on other aspects of ATM transport network management (e.g., VPC/VCC survivability aspects) and the extension of the previously mentioned functions to support multipoint VPC and VCC arrangements.

References

[1] CCITT Study Group XVIII, Recommendation I.610—OAM Principles and Functions for BISDN, June 1992.
[2] Standards Committee T1S1.5, Broadband ISDN Operations and Maintenance Principles: Technical Report, T1S1.5/91-006R3, Aug. 1992.
[3] ATM User-Network Interface Specification, Version 2.0, ATM Forum, June 1992.
[4] CCITT Study Group XVIII, CCITT Recommendation I.361—BISDN ATM Layer Specification, June 1992.
[5] CCITT Study Group XVIII, Draft Recommendation I.358, June 1990.

Biography

Stephen C. Farkouh has been a member of technical staff at Bellcore, Red Bank, New Jersey, since 1987. He has been involved in the specification of operations requirements and standards for ISDN network elements and, more recently, broadband ATM switching systems.

CHAPTER VIII

APPLICATIONS

This chapter covers various applications of ATM, including voice, video, data, satellite and wireless.

Broadband Applications and Services Prospectus

Michael DeMaio

Henry J. Kafka

Not too long ago, network traffic was almost entirely comprised of voice or voice-grade traffic. Today, networks must support a rapidly growing percentage of several different kinds of high-bandwidth or broadband traffic—data, image, and video—in addition to conventional voice traffic. There are several factors that create the demand for these new capabilities. Telecommunication customers want faster performance, better quality, customization, lower costs, and an ever increasing variety of advanced information services. For network-service providers, increasing competition requires an accentuated focus on providing timely, reliable, flexible, and evolvable information-network services. But, while network-service providers require new networking technologies to enable the deployment of advanced services, they must also increase network efficiencies to maintain control of their operating expenses. How might asynchronous transfer mode (ATM) technology be used to address these needs? This paper discusses some of the expected broadband applications and services enabled with ATM technology, as well as applications and services involving more than a 1-Mbit/s peak transport capability. In addition, the prospects for broadband services and applications deployment are also presented.

Introduction

Dramatic changes in the global marketplace suggest extraordinary telecommunications changes in the not-too-distant future. While basic telephony may remain a centerpiece of telecommunications for many years to come, several new information-networking services promise to have a profound effect on the next-generation telecommunications network. These new services are driven by several converging factors. Among them are: changes in the business climate; technology-driven change; legal and regulatory changes; and new consumer demands.

Changes in the Business Climate. Due to intense competition in today's business environment, cost management and time-to-market factors have become critical for the ongoing success of businesses. Consequently, fundamental changes take place in the organizational structure and scope of most large businesses, and even some moderate-size companies. Many are moving toward cross-functional work groups with geographically disparate (even mobile) staffs, responding dynamically to rapidly changing market conditions. Moreover, the acceptance of company-endorsed work-at-home arrangements (telecommuting) appears to be rising.

Many corporations are also becoming more multinational and global; they are pursuing competitively driven, strategic partnerships on a worldwide scale. Finally, the universal "push" for increased quality in every phase of the product life cycle has expanded communications requirements between the business' suppliers and its customers.

In addition to these commercial business changes, there is also a strong stimulus for change coming from governments all around the world. For example, in the United States, the end of the cold-war era has provided the incentive to invest in the conversion of the military-industrial complex into an information-networking and computing complex. Many envision this transformation as a key element in revitalizing the world economy. The interplay between government and commercial sectors in implementing this vision will increase the already intense interest in high-speed, multimedia information networking for non-military applications.

These changes validate several new information-networking needs: increased data networking; growth in public-carrier (non-private) information networking; the use of a variety of diverse network services-on-demand through a common network interface; new applications requiring high-resolution graphics and images; visual telecommunications; and multimedia. In addition, the deployment of new network-based "mission-critical" applications requires that networks provide increased service flexibility, a greater variety of services, higher service reliability, and high-speed performance.

Technology-Driven Change. At the same time, rapid advances in technology can be seen: the decreasing cost of processing power; decreasing memory costs; the decreasing cost of bandwidth; the increasing use of desktop client-networked and server-networked computing and "user-friendly" graphical interfaces; and the convergence of telecommunications and computing. These changes have not only intensified computing capabilities, but they also have spawned the development of many new applications involving graphical and visual communications. These new applications will greatly intensify interface-bandwidth requirements, a trend that is expected to continue for the foreseeable future.

Legal and Regulatory Changes. In the United States, recent Federal Communications Commission (FCC) rule modifications and proposed rule changes will have a significant effect on both the kinds of services offered, as well as the companies that are legally permitted to offer telecommunication services. Specifically, the local exchange carriers (LECs) are permitted to offer "video dial tone," and the FCC has recommended elimination of telephone company and cable television (CATV) company cross-ownership restrictions. The impact that these changes may have is already evident from the aggressive plans of the LECs and CATV companies to expand into each other's former businesses.

Significant legal and regulatory changes aren't restricted to wire-line carriers. The recent FCC decision to allocate unoccupied radio spectrum in the 900-MHz band for narrowband personal communications services (PCS), and the anticipated allocation of frequencies in the 1,800 MHz band, are expected to spur the development of next-generation, wireless, high-speed voice and data PCS. These capabilities may well blur the distinction between services offered via traditional networks versus wireless-access networks.

In Europe, the development of the European economic community (EEC) is having an equally dramatic effect on telecommunications policy throughout western Europe—even in the non-EEC countries—and will also affect most of eastern Europe over time. Similar, though less pronounced, telecommunication policy changes are also occurring in several Pacific-rim countries—most notably Japan. These changes are encouraging more and more competition.

New Consumer Demands. There are a number of economic, social, and lifestyle changes that are dramatically altering consumer demands for information services. On the economic front, transportation costs continue to rise, and the cost of living close to one's workplace is often prohibitively expensive. Consequently, research confirms that a growing number of employees are opting for work-at-home arrangements and "flex-time" work schedules. Similarly, concerns about the environment and crime have many people seeking ways to minimize personal travel through telecommuting. Finally, for a variety of reasons, studies show a marked shift toward spending more leisure time at home, as well as the growing acceptance and use of PC-like equipment in the home. Coupled with these changes is the desire for entertainment and information that fits the consumer's schedule, rather than the producer's.

Summing It Up. In the business world, the changing organizational structure and scope—coupled with the increased use of high-capacity, high-speed networked computing—suggests an increasing demand for high-bandwidth, broadband communications. On the technical front, improvements in transmission and switching technology promise decreasing costs for high-bandwidth communications and more cost-effective visual telecommunication applications. These phenomena may be synergistic, leading to an overall increase in the demand for high-bandwidth communications by a broader segment of the market than would otherwise be the case.

On the residential front, non-business consumers will want fundamentally more advanced telecommunication services than traditional, basic telephony services. But, will the price be right and will consumers buy? How quickly will the synergism help bring down the cost of broadband services, so that even typical residential customers can afford them? Several market trials are underway to help answer these questions. One thing is clear: the telecommunications network will be dramatically changed in the coming years.

Broadband Application and Service Evolution

The deployment of broadband ATM communications will evolve through multiple phases. Initial "niche" services, such as frame relay, Switched Multimegabit Data Service (SMDS), and 1.544 Mbits/s (DS-1) switched services will evolve to include early, provisioned ATM network services. Finally, as new applications develop and network capabilities mature, fully integrated, broadband-ATM switched services will emerge. The starting point for this evolution is the combination of today's communication networks, available telecommunication standards, and the most pressing near-term demands for broadband applications (the mechanisms used to achieve what people want to do at work or at play) and services (the

telecommunications capabilities by which applications are implemented). Differences between the business and residential markets suggest that ATM applications and services will follow different introduction schedules.

Business-Market Evolution. In the business market (assumed to include work-at-home situations), ATM services will initially augment the currently available set of voice-networking and data-networking services. Today's business networks carry a wide range of applications, which can be sorted into various classes. These classes include voice service, low-speed terminal data communication, higher-speed local-area network (LAN) interconnect and LAN backbone transmissions, imaging data services, bulk data transfers, and video teleconferencing sessions. These applications are carried over a correspondingly wide range of communication networks. Typically, each application structures its own subnetwork around a communication-network service that is best matched to its needs.

Current market-driven applications—LAN interconnect, collaboration using high-resolution imaging data, and video teleconferencing—have hastened the introduction of several new high-speed services, based on relatively mature circuit-oriented and packet-oriented technologies. As new ATM-based customer premises equipment and networking capabilities become available, demand for semi-permanent (provisioned) ATM public-network services will emerge.

These network service offerings will enable end-users to design private and virtual private networks at broadband rates. New service offerings will coexist with today's non-switched and switched network services. The initial use of ATM services in this environment will be to extend further the available set of networking options so that high-speed, packet-like applications—including LAN interconnect, LAN backbones, and high-resolution image transfers—can take advantage of ATM's efficiency, high transmission speeds, and its ability to handle "bursty" data traffic. In some cases, existing application networks will move to ATM, possibly using protocol adaptations between existing application protocols and ATM. In other cases, new applications that were not practical earlier (because of cost or performance limitations) will become possible due to the availability of ATM services.

As applications move to ATM, ATM-based networks could be used to consolidate multiple, separate data networks. These applications will take advantage of the fact that many carriers and equipment manufacturers will transport communications protocols, such as frame-relay and SMDS services, over ATM backbone networks. By taking advantage of protocol adaptations, current applications (using frame-relay and SMDS services) as well as new applications (running over ATM services) can be combined onto a single data-networking environment based on ATM. Eventually, as multimedia applications become more prevalent in data networks, many will evolve to employ the ATM protocol directly. Over time, this will reduce the need for protocol adaptations.

As broadband ATM becomes more cost effective and ubiquitous, end-users will take advantage of ATM's ability to carry many different types of traffic, and will extend the trend toward network consolidation to areas beyond data networking. For example, the ATM backbone, which will initially be deployed to support data networking traffic, can readily be used to transport high-speed circuit payloads, such as video traffic and voice trunks, at 1.544 Mbits/s (DS-1 rate) or higher. This consolidation trend will lead to the use of ATM-based, integrated, wide-area-network access. Integrated access involves converting all of a customer's communication

services to ATM at the customer's premises, and then carrying them into the wide-area network by means of a single, high-speed ATM access line. Each service may still be treated as a part of its own subnetwork, but the common ATM access line allows transport efficiency and bandwidth sharing among the services and subnetworks.

As this continues, the desire for on-demand (real-time switched) networking capabilities will emerge. The addition of intelligent switching capabilities to the network will enable the introduction of many new and useful features. First, the required bandwidth can be allocated and de-allocated on demand and in real time. Second, connections beyond a company's private or virtual private network can be established when and where they are needed around the globe. More significantly, features now available for voice services through the intelligent network can be applied to broadband ATM services—for example, "700," "800," and "900" switched services, call screening, and call forwarding, to name a few. All the while, the more "bursty" traffic—data and image—will be statistically multiplexed to maximize bandwidth, thereby increasing transport-network facility utilization.

Over time, as multimedia applications become more prevalent and as other applications increasingly demand flexible service capabilities, the multiple services provided over integrated access lines will evolve toward fully integrated network solutions. In an integrated network environment, a wide range of services—with various levels of performance and intelligence—will still be available. However, these services may be offered in selectable grades within a single, integrated networking environment. The resulting integrated communications environment will provide the full service and bandwidth flexibility needed to meet, most efficiently, the diverse and rapidly evolving applications that will likely characterize the progressive business environment.

Panel 2 identifies business applications that have good prospects for three classes of broadband ATM services: high-speed image networking, interactive multimedia, and wide-area-network distributed computing.

Residential Market Evolution. Advanced residential information services have achieved only limited market penetration to date. On the other hand, with the trend toward more leisure time spent at home, residential video-entertainment services have been very successful. For reasons that follow, ATM technology will play a key role in the evolution of advanced video-entertainment services. This may provide the stimulus for widespread demand for residential, broadband data and multimedia services, in addition to video-entertainment services.

While today's video-entertainment delivery systems are based on analog technology, there is considerable consumer demand for higher quality and more reliable CATV services. Consequently, the industry is quickly moving toward systems now in development that will use digital channels and rapidly advancing, digital video-compression technology. These systems will provide brand-new capabilities, such as video-on-demand, high-definition television (HDTV), and 500-channel CATV.

In several of these capabilities, multiple, compressed, digital video channels are carried over a single digital bit stream. Digital video-compression technology permits encoding video signals at variable bit rates. In many applications, a single bit stream may carry multiple digital channels running at different bit rates. (Various aspects of the program material can affect the desired video bit rate, such as the amount of motion, and whether the original source material was from film or videotape.)

Within a telecommunications network, ATM technology is ideally suited to serve as the multiplexing technique for carrying multiple, compressed, digital video signals over a single digital bit stream to the home. ATM technology is highly effective in carrying multiple channels of arbitrary bandwidth over a single digital bit stream. In addition, ATM is well suited to the additional flexibility demanded by some digital video-entertainment applications. In many cases, a single video program can be associated with multiple audio signals (multiple languages) or data overlays (closed captioning or ordering information). All of these signals and overlays can be carried efficiently as ATM virtual circuits in a single, multiplexed bit stream.

The value of ATM in carrying compressed digital video is reinforced by recent video-compression standards work from the Motion Picture Experts Group (MPEG). The MPEG-2 standard has been designed to enable MPEG-2 compressed video information to be transported via ATM calls over an ATM network.

Initial residential use of digital compressed video will be for CATV systems with an extended number of channels. Early services will probably include an expanded channel selection, a wider range of pay-per-view events, and an enhanced pay-per-view system, which might provide the most recent movie releases at

---

Panel 3. Residential Applications Envisioned Through Broadband ATM-Based Services

Distribution Video
— Broadcast TV/HDTV
— Broadcast distance learning
— Enhanced pay-per-view (near video-on-demand)
— Video-on-demand
— Video catalog/advertising
— Tele-shopping

Interactive Multimedia
— Multimedia electronic mail
— Multimedia "700," "800," and "900" services
— Sports event simulcasting/tele-wagering
— Interactive distance learning
— Multimedia videotext/"Yellow Pages"
— Interactive TV/games
— Multimedia telephony and virtual reality

15-minute intervals. These services will be followed by video-on-demand service, which will use the extended number of channels to provide interactive and fully controllable viewing of movies supplied by video servers.

The network and customer-premises equipment used to provide these video entertainment services includes key underlying capabilities, which facilitate the deployment of more advanced residential services. The underlying capabilities of a CATV channel-expansion system with video on demand include:
- Broadband channels to the residence,
- The ability to select and process broadband digital channels, and
- The ability to transmit information in the "upstream" direction from the residence into the network.

With the flexibility of ATM, these basic capabilities will help to provide a full range of audio, video, data, and multimedia applications to the home. Applications will include entertainment, education, and telecommuting services. Thus, the initial deployment of ATM video-entertainment services will lead to the widespread deployment of high-bandwidth equipment for the home. This equipment will have the flexibility to offer the sophisticated capabilities expected by today's media-conscious residential consumers.

Fiber-based and coaxial-cable-based distribution systems, which are being installed today, can deliver 50 to 80 analog channels to communities ranging in size from a few hundred homes to a few thousand homes. With the technology described earlier, these types of installations could provide a dynamically "sharable" bandwidth of 1.5 Gbits/s to 2.4 Gbits/s (or more) to each community. These broadband distribution systems, when combined with the bandwidth flexibility provided by ATM networks, create an astounding array of opportunities for service and application evolution.

Panel 3 lists some of the residential applications that are envisioned through the use of broadband distribution video and interactive multimedia services.

Conclusions

The development of broadband ATM services will be driven by end-user application demands. In the business environment, explosive growth in data networking will drive the deployment of ATM campus-backbone networks. Deployment will be accelerated by client and server distributed-network computing, and applications utilizing progressively more graphic and video-oriented content. Moreover, the requirement to extend local campus-network capabilities to the entire wide-area corporate enterprise will spur demand for initial, carrier-based, ATM-provisioned services. Emergence of cost-effective client workstations will encourage the development of many new multimedia applications. And finally, the need to extend the information "superhighway" to corporations' external clients (both its customers and its suppliers) and to its telecommuting employees will usher in the evolution to intelligently switched, broadband ATM services—on premises and across public networks.

In the residential market, consumer preferences, new regulatory rules, and technology advances will encourage the development of an exciting array of advanced video-entertainment services to the home. Some of the most advanced video-distribution services have already been field tested and are in the early market-deployment stage. Consumer demand for interactive video applications will encourage the introduction of early multimedia service offerings. Some of these include interactive TV, interactive tele-education, and perhaps even event simulcasting with tele-wagering.

Initial success in broadband market development in the business and residential sectors—coupled with the technology trends discussed earlier—may reinforce each other in much the same way that the cellular telephone

market has developed. This market "churn" will further encourage competition between traditional LECs, access providers, and CATV companies—thereby stimulating the rapid introduction of broadband services and capabilities based on ATM technology. Then, as market penetration rises and prices fall, the dream of advanced multimedia telephony services for the mass market can become reality.

At the core of this change is ATM, a technology that can dynamically support a broad range of applications. ATM will provide the communications infrastructure to support the convergence of telecommunications, computing, and video (television). It is difficult to predict whether ATM technology will deliver on all its promises, but there is compelling evidence that suggests it will do so in the near future.

Acknowledgments

The authors wish to acknowledge the excellent comments and helpful suggestions provided by Len Gilchrist (AT&T Network Systems U. S.-customer switching systems business unit), Roger Levy (AT&T Network Systems division ATM platform organization) and Dave Rajala (AT&T Network Systems transmission systems business unit) in the development of this paper.

(Manuscript approved October 1993)

Michael DeMaio *is a technical manager in the AT&T Network Systems division ATM systems department in Red Bank, New Jersey. He is responsible for researching and developing ATM platform system requirements. Mr. DeMaio has B.S. and M.S. degrees in electrical engineering, both from Drexel University in Philadelphia, Pennsylvania. He joined AT&T Bell Laboratories in 1976.*

Henry J. Kafka *is a technical manager in the new business opportunities and visual communications department at AT&T Bell Laboratories in Lisle, Illinois. He is responsible for researching and developing emerging applications that rely on broadband ATM technology, as well as for system engineering and architecture for interactive video products. Mr. Kafka joined AT&T in 1979. He has a B.S. in electrical engineering from Northwestern University in Evanston, Illinois, and an M.S., also in electrical engineering, from the University of Illinois, Urbana-Champaign.*

ATM VP-Based Broadband Networks for Multimedia Services

Technical advances and a sound introduction strategy could permit the debut of multimedia leased-line services by the mid-1990s.

Tomonori Aoyama, Ikuo Tokizawa, and Ken-ichi Sato

TOMONORI AOYAMA is executive manager of NTT's intellectual property department.

IKUO TOKIZAWA is a group leader of broadband transport research group in NTT Transmission Systems Laboratories.

KEN-ICHI SATO is a supervisor in the Transport Processing Laboratory at NTT.

The advancement of ATM techniques saw the first set of B-ISDN Recommendations in 1990 [1]. Succeeding efforts toward the completion of B-ISDN techniques have reached a level sufficient for network providers to introduce ATM techniques into their telecommunication networks. This introduction is essential because demand for high-speed multimedia communication has increased significantly. In this context, we are considering application of ATM techniques in the provision of cost-effective and flexible multimedia ATM leased-line services to interconnect private networks, LANs, and MANs. For the first time, this paper describes details of the intended ATM system.

For the successful introduction of B-ISDN, one of the most critical issues for network providers is the introduction strategy. Any strategy must comply with two major requirements: the realization of an effective infrastructure and creation of new network services.

The strategy must assure graceful network evolution and also enable network cost reduction so that B-ISDN can replace existing network facilities. By offering effective network services, network providers can increase their revenue and, therefore, spur introduction of B-ISDN.

We have proposed the virtual path (VP) concept for ATM networks. Its effectiveness has been widely discussed, thus the benefits have been elucidated [3-6]. It also has been demonstrated that the application of the VP concept satisfies the aforementioned requirements and that it will play a key role in the introduction of B-ISDN [7-9]. On the basis of the above context, we are considering first applying VP-based B-ISDN techniques in providing ATM multimedia leased-line services.

This paper first describes the VP-based ATM transport network architecture that supports leased-line services. Next, services that will be provided by the multimedia leased-line are summarized. This will demonstrate how VP benefits can be exploited. There are various VP-related technical issues that must be resolved before these services can fully exploit the VP benefits. This paper will high-light our latest technical advances that will enable realization of the services. The introduction strategy and our technical developments described herein will pave the way to realization of the services.

VP-based Transport Network Architecture

A layered transport network architecture is an important concept on which the network should be built [10, 11]. This is because it simplifies the design, development, and operation of the network, and allows smooth network evolution to keep pace with user demands. This is made possible by the assignment of necessary functions to the related layers. The introduction of the layered concept also makes it easy for each network layer to evolve independently of the other layers, thus capitalizing on introduction of new technology specific to each layer.

The transport layer can be divided into three layers: the circuit, path, and transmission media layers [10], as illustrated in Fig. 1. This layering concept is being extensively discussed by CCITT for the SDH transport network [11]. The circuit is an end-to-end connection established/released dynamically or on the basis of short-term provisioning. The transmission media (facility) network which interconnects nodes and/or subscribers is constructed based on long-term provisioning; geographical conditions are taken into consideration. The path layer bridges these two layers and plays a significant role in constructing reliable and flexible networks [6]. Effective network restoration (service protection) can be realized through the path layer. Flexibility of the network also can be enhanced with path layer control, which can be utilized by end-customer control of the leased-line networks. Thus, the importance of a path-layer management scheme that utilizes intelligent digital cross-connect systems is increased significantly. To date, the circuit and path layer have been realized in existing digital networks with STM techniques. We are planning to introduce ATM techniques in the path layer by introducing VPs.

The VP strategy enables fully logical realiza-

Reprinted from IEEE Communications Magazine, April 1993, pp. 30-39.

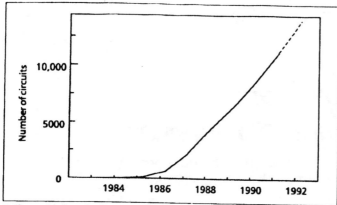

■ Figure 3. *Growth of high-speed digital leased-line services.*

ATM Multimedia Leased-line Services

Existing Leased-line Services in Japan

Before discussing the ATM leased-line services, let us briefly examine the current growth of high-speed digital leased-line services in Japan (STM) (Fig. 3). The services were started in 1984, and now provide 12 speeds ranging from 64 kb/s to 6.1 Mb/s with point-to-point, point-to-multipoint, and multiple access capabilities. Almost all large business customers in Japan have built private networks by utilizing these leased-line services. At the beginning of 1991 the number of end-to-end circuits exceeded 10,000, and continues to increase rapidly. The demand for speeds higher than 1.5 Mb/s is increasing. The ATM multimedia leased-line service will cover the anticipated demand with enhanced service capability.

Services

Table 1 summarizes the major characteristics of envisaged ATM multimedia leased-line services. These services provide maximum flexibility to the customers. Service attributes follow.

User Access to VPs — Services are provided across user-to-user VPs. ATM leased-line customers can access VPs through standardized UNIs and all the virtual channels accommodated within each VP are transported transparently. The choice of how to use the virtual channels is left to the customers. According to the clients' demands they can freely determine the number of virtual channels defined between path end points, individual virtual channel capacity, and VCI values. Moreover, the clients can alter these factors. This provides flexible customer networking capability.

Tailored VP Capacity — Customers can capitalize on the tailored path capacity capability of VPs. The alteration of VP capacity can be attained without any modification of the interface structure. This reduced kind of interface structure will result in the cost-effective deployment of leased-line services.

Guaranteed QOS — This service provides guaranteed quality of service (QOS) for VPs. For example, the most stringent requirement for cell loss rate (10^{-8} or less) will be met and the quality will be guaranteed for end-to-end connection. This cell loss rate is guaranteed not only for constant bit rate (CBR) VPs, but also for variable bit rate (VBR) VPs, even while ensuring statistical multiplexing gain for VBR VPs. Thus, when VP connections are accepted, guaranteed QOS is provided and the network reactive congestion control (as

User-to-user connection		Virtual path (maximum 256 VPI)
User network interface		B-ISDN UNI (156 Mb/s)
VP bandwidth		Peak rate: 64 Kb/s ~ 122 Mb/s
		Peak rate + average rate
Connection	Symmetry	Unidirectional
	Mode	Permanent
		Reserved (including fast reservation)
Quality	Blocking probability for bandwidth increase	Non-zero (reserved mode)
	Cell loss rate	10^{-8} or less (end-to-end, guaranteed)
Traffic management	Connection admission control	Deterministic
	Traffic control	VP-UPC (discarding of violating cells)
Service protection		Hitless protection switching of VPs (when rerouting/replacing transmission lines/equipment
End customer control		VP: via network operation
		VC: via end customer operation
Charging		On the basis of reserved VP bandwidth and duration

■ Table 1. *Principle characteristics of multimedia ATM leased-line services.*

32

506

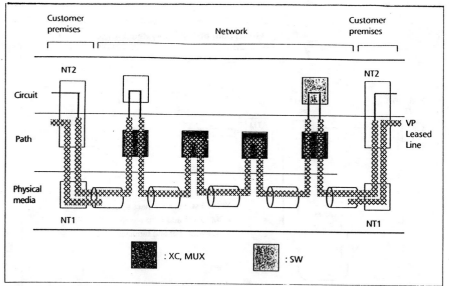

■ Figure 1. *Layered architecture of transport network for public telecommunication network.*

tion of path functions and will greatly enhance network capability and reliability. The benefits of the VPs over digital paths in STM networks already have been described in detail [2-6]. The VP networks will allow both the development of the B-ISDN infrastructure and provision of multimedia leased-line services from the outset by providing users access to VPs. In other words, the leased-line services can spur introduction of the VP layer. This is possible because leased-line services can be completed by the path and transmission media layers (Fig. 1). Thus, the network infrastructure and provision of new services can be realized simultaneously with the introduction of VPs.

The functional configuration of the envisaged target ATM network is shown in Fig 2. The specific architecture for ATM multimedia leased-line services with VPs will be described later. The network consists of a VP network and two types of virtual channel networks: private and public. The VP network is shared by the private and public-switched virtual circuit networks. The private virtual channel network is constructed on the VP leased-line network by customers and will be used for private business communication. The public virtual channel network is constructed by utilizing the ATM switching systems installed in central offices. It provides B-ISDN public-switched services.

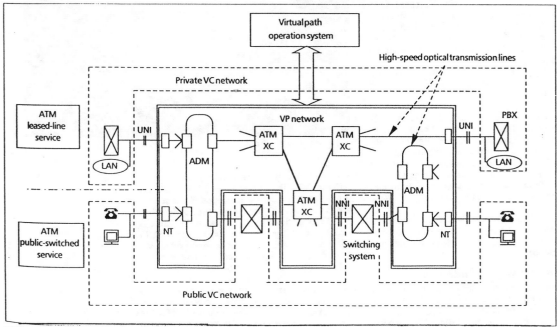

■ Figure 2. *VP-based ATM network configuration.*

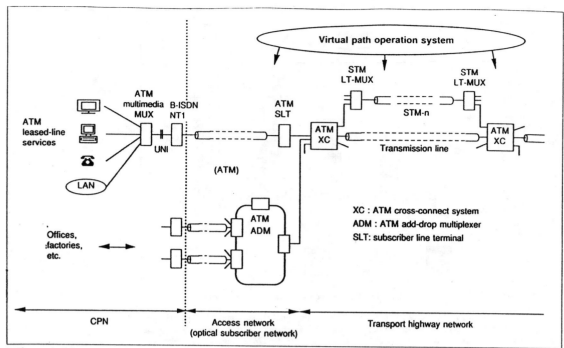

■ Figure 4. *Organic network architecture for ATM leased-line services.*

in the frame relay service or flow control mechanism of the SMDS services) is not required. Technical details are presented later.

Reduced Transmission Cost — If this broadband service with high transmission quality can be provided at low cost, rapid penetration will be assured. To enable this, two types of network resource sharing mechanisms will be implemented. One type of network resource sharing is the reserved connection mode, wherein VP bandwidth can be increased/decreased according to the user's demands, and thus network resources are shared all the time (variable capacity VP services). The second type of network resource sharing employs cell statistical multiplexing capability among VBR VPs.

Enhanced OA&M Capabilities — OAM cells will be utilized to implement VP maintenance signal transfer functions, in-service VP performance monitoring, and VP testing and path tracing functions. Moreover, hitless protection switching capability will be provided which does not disturb active VPs during transmission line rerouting and transmission equipment replacement.

Not all the attributes previously described will be available from the very beginning of service provisioning. The techniques needed to enable them are described later.

Organic Network Architecture

The organic network architecture for multimedia ATM leased-line services is depicted in Fig. 4. The customer premises network (CPN) will utilize ATM Multimedia MUX which has a service-dependent terminal interface. It terminates VPs and

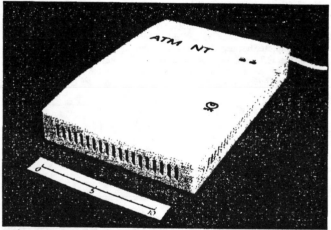

■ Figure 5. *Network terminal.*

also will terminate VCs and multiplex them into different VPs. The CPN includes the network terminal (NT). A recently developed NT that provides 156 Mb/s T_B interface standardized in CCITT is depicted in Fig. 5. Its total volume is about 1000 cc. The subscriber line terminal (SLT) will be implemented in the service nodes. VP UPC function is implemented here and after the UPC, VPs from different customers are multiplexed and fed to the ATM cross-connect systems. The ATM cross-connect systems route the cells according to their VPIs. Alteration of VP capacity can be completed without any communication with the ATM cross-connect systems [2, 6]. This is because no processing at cross-connect nodes along paths is

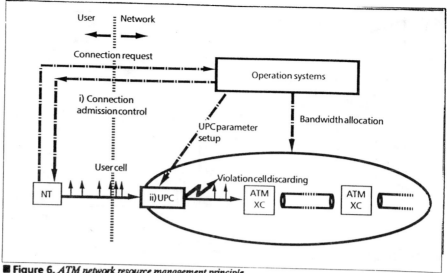

■ Figure 6. *ATM network resource management principle.*

required when the VP bandwidth is altered. This is one of the remarkable features of the ATM cross-connect system, and it enables rapid VP bandwidth control and increases the flexibility of end-customer control.

ATM cross-connect systems will be interlinked directly by the SDH transmission systems of STM-N (cells are mapped into VC-4-Nc, where N = 4, 16) or by STM-1 in STM systems according to the traffic requirement. In the subscriber access network, ATM add/drop multiplexer (ADM) systems forming a physical ring structure may be applied according to customer distribution and density.

Technologies

ATM Network Resource Management

In ATM networks, traffic must be managed to guarantee the QOS of VCs/VPs and to effectively utilize network resources. The principles of ATM network resource management are illustrated in

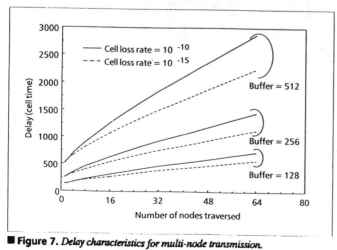

■ Figure 7. *Delay characteristics for multi-node transmission.*

Fig. 6. The traffic management procedure consists of connection (VC/VP) admission control (CAC) and usage parameter control (UPC) for each VC/VP. These two processes are tightly related and the procedure should be optimized as a whole [12]. This section discusses VP-related techniques, however, most of the discussion also is applicable to VCs. Connection admission control should be done based on the VP accommodation design algorithm within transmission links.

VP Accommodation Design and Multiplexing Buffer Size — As mentioned earlier, two types of VPs exist in terms of the bandwidth: CBR and VBR paths. Requirements for the VP accommodation design are an acceptable calculation time, conservativeness (provides conservative cell loss rate), and reasonable statistical gain for VBR VP accommodation. We already have developed an algorithm suitable for CBR/VBR VPs that satisfies the aforementioned requirements [13, 14].

At the outset of VP introduction, however, it appears that network-network VPs [1] (such as VPs connecting ATM switching systems) and most of the user-user VPs [1] will use CBR VPs. In this context, we have developed an effective algorithm applicable for CBR VPs. The algorithm takes into consideration the cell jitter caused by ATM cross-connect/multiplexing systems and the mixture of VPs given the wide variety of path bandwidths. This algorithm uses the M/D/1 model to evaluate link utilization. It guarantees a conservative QOS for VP accommodation within the links [14]. The maximum queuing delay versus number of XC/ADM/SLT nodes traversed is shown in Fig. 7. This was evaluated by applying the above algorithm assuming the cell loss rates at each node are 10^{-10} and 10^{-15}, and the buffer size of each node is altered. The upper bound of the tandem queuing delay for CBR VPs, shown in Fig. 7, is given by the convolution of the cell delay distribution obtained with M/D/1 model [14]. The delay time is normalized by the time required to transmit one cell into the transmission link. When the

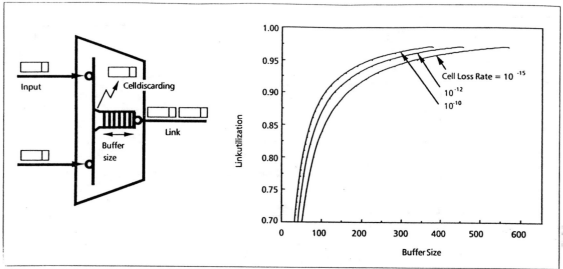

■ Figure 8. *Link utilization vs. buffer size.*

buffer size of each node is 256, specified cell loss rate is 10^{-10}, transmission link speed is 2.4 Gb/s, and the maximum number of nodes traversed is 30; the maximum delay jitter is calculated to be 160 μs (0.18 μs x 900). When the transmission link speed is 156 Mb/s, it is 2.5 ms. Using these evaluations, the maximum buffer size and the maximum number of nodes that can be traversed were determined. It was found that a buffer size of 256 causes insignificant delay (cell delay jitter).

Next, the algorithm was used to determine necessary buffer size for SLT/XC/ADM systems. Buffer size versus available maximum traffic load (link utilization) for CBR VP accommodation is shown in Fig. 8. The major observations are:

- Link utilization significantly increases with increased buffer size, if buffer size is less than 200.
- Link utilization is almost independent of buffer size, if buffer size is larger than 300.

From this, and the cell delay considerations described before, we adopted the minimum buffer size (Q) of 256 for the systems being developed. When Q equals 256, and the specific cell loss rate is 10^{-10} (10^{-12}), the maximum link utilization efficiency is 0.956 (0.94).

Usage Parameter Control — After VP connection admission control is performed, the UPC function is utilized during communication phase in order to monitor and control user traffic to ensure it conforms to the value negotiated at the CAC phase [15]. The UPC function should satisfy the following requirements:

- Simple hardware.
- Deterministic cell traffic monitoring capability.
- Least probability to accept violating cells (mispolicing).
- Least probability to treat conforming cells as violating cells (faulty-policing).

We have developed a new UPC algorithm which satisfies these requirements and is applicable to a wide range of traffic parameter values [12, 16]. The algorithm effectively combines the so-called dangerous bridge (sliding window type) method, the DB-method, and the 2-phase T-X (cred-it window type) method. The algorithm uses the DB method for cell traffic specified with relatively small traffic parameter values, while the two-phase T-X method is applied for cell traffic with relatively large values. The proposed algorithm realizes precise UPC without elaborate hardware [12, 16]. The algorithm reduces the effect of mispolicing cells to the point that it can be neglected from the viewpoint of VC/VP bandwidth allocation [12, 16]. The reduction in this effect also allows better network resource (link) utilization. Thus, the proposed algorithm will be a credible solution for the requirements given herein. The UPC circuit is implemented in the SLT.

ATM Network Utilization Enhancement

As described previously, the key to reduce the cost of the leased-line services is to maximize the utilization of network resources. This is attained by capitalizing on the statistical multiplexing effect. Two levels of statistical multiplexing are possible: connection level and cell level. The former is used by reserved mode connections, where the VP bandwidth can be altered according to user demand. When the bandwidth increase is accepted by the network, the QOS of the VP is guaranteed. Decreases in the bandwidth are allowed at any time. The improvement of the link utilization or resultant cost reduction is offset by the introduction of a nonzero blocking probability for bandwidth increase requests and by the increased processing load stemming from the on-demand resource reservation.

The other level of statistical multiplexing is the cell level. This is provided by defining the VBR VPs. The bandwidth of the VBR VPs are defined by a set of parameters such as peak and average cell rates. The VP accommodation design and UPC can guarantee the QOS of VBR VPs in a statistical multiplexing environment. In this context, care should be taken that there is no difference between CBR and VBR VPs in terms of QOS. In other words, VBR VPs can exploit statistical cell multiplexing gain while the QOS remains completely guaranteed [13]. Some calculation results of these two levels of statistical multiplexing will follow.

To realize multimedia ATM leased-line services, the key component is the ATM cross-connect system.

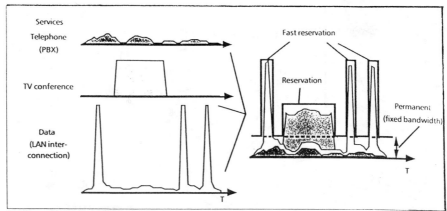

■ **Figure 9.** *Various VP bandwidth reservation schemes.*

Reserved Mode Connection — A comparison of several VP bandwidth reservation schemes is shown in Fig. 9. Fixed or permanent VP bandwidth reservation is required for the constant bit-rate services as PBX use. TV conferences will require the reserved mode, and the beginning and possibly the ending time will be declared by the user. Last, but not least, is the fast bandwidth reservation for LAN-to-LAN interconnection. This can yield large statistical gains.

Our basic concept for variable capacity VP services is explained in Fig. 10. The user can increase the VP bandwidth on demand when there is sufficient unused link capacity along the VP end-to-end. Here CBR VPs are considered for simplicity. Charging will be done based on the bandwidth and duration of each bandwidth, T_1 and T_2, as shown in Fig. 9.

Figure 10 shows analytical results on the statistical gains for a VP traversing n links. The statistical gain is defined here as the ratio of the allowable maximum number of VPs with the reserved mode scheme and that with the permanent mode scheme (peak rate is 50 Mb/s). It was found that the worst blocking probability for a VP which traverses n links occurs when all other VPs traverse only one link [17]. The details of the analytical procedures are

out of the scope of this paper, but will be presented elsewhere [18]. The probabilities of failure to increase the bandwidth were set at 0.1 and 0.01. Each link speed was set at 2.4 Gb/s. The durations of T_1 and T_2 are assumed to have negative exponential distribution with those average values, and the ratio of T_1/T_2 was set at 1/50 and 1/100. The point to be emphasized is that statistical gain is only slightly dependent on n, and a gain of more than 50 can be attained when T_1/T_2 is 1/100.

Cell Level Resource Sharing — As mentioned before, we have developed an algorithm [13] that can effectively capitalize on the statistical cell multiplexing effect. Figure 11 shows an example of the statistical multiplexing gain obtained with the developed algorithm for a wide range of VP bandwidth parameters, where $T0$ is the minimum cell interarrival time to a VP and T is the period defining the average cell rate. The gain is defined as the reciprocal of the required bandwidth normalized to that required with peak cell rate bandwidth allocation. Figure 11 shows that gains of more than 10 are obtained depending on VP bandwidth parameter values. Analytical details are provided in [13].

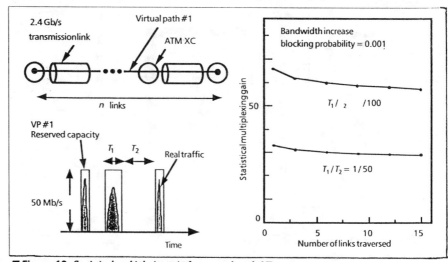

■ **Figure 10.** *Statistical multiplexing gain for reserved mode VP services.*

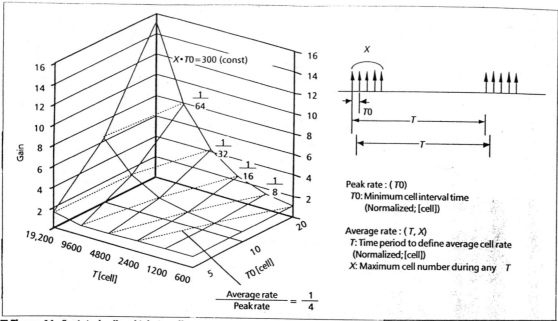

■ Figure 11. *Statistical call multiplexing effect.*

These two types of network resource sharing techniques will allow significant transmission cost reductions.

ATM Cross-connect System Architecture

To realize multimedia ATM leased-line services, the key component is the ATM cross-connect system. The ATM cross-connect system can uniformly handle various VP speeds with the same hardware. On the other hand, in STM networks, different hardware (such as 64 kb/s, 1.5 Mb/s and 50 Mb/s cross-connect systems) has to be implemented to operate networks efficiently, as mentioned previously.

We have been developing ATM cross-connect systems that will allow the construction of VP infrastructure and simultaneously are applicable to VP leased-line services. In other words, the systems are efficient and economical when applied to large or small offices. Also, they should increase the fill factor of transmission facilities and minimize the delay time. The basic cross-connect system architecture we are developing is shown in Fig. 12. Its operating speed is 2.5 Gb/s. The cross-connect system should have a configuration suitable for accommodating high-speed interfaces. If the system supports 2.5 Gb/s interfaces, the configuration that does not use multiplexer/demultiplexer block is most desirable, as shown in Fig. 12. This can be achieved by reducing the inner-hardware operation speed through the use of parallel processing techniques in which the number of parallel lines can be up to the cell length.

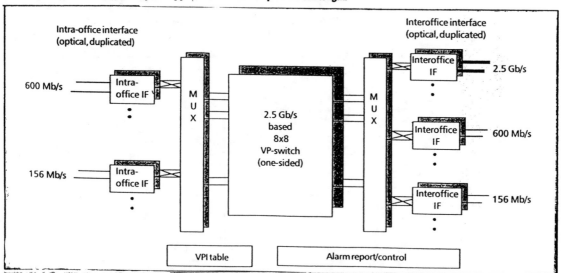

■ Figure 12. *2.5 Gb/s-based ATM cross-connect system architecture.*

512

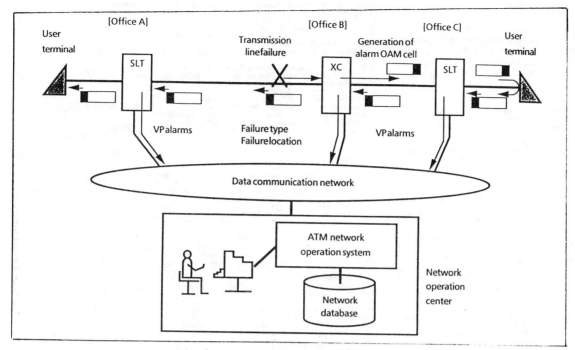

Figure 13. *VP maintenance signal transfer.*

To realize efficient ATM network provisioning, specifications of the ATM cross-connect switch fabric include:
- Nonblocking characteristics.
- No restrictions on the usage condition of the middle link in multistage switching networks.
- Cell sequence integrity.

This means that the switch fabrics should be determined only by the input and output port connection relationship, and should not be restricted by middle link conditions. Even when VP capacity is dynamically altered in the network, blocking caused by the utilization conditions of the inner link also should be avoided. For example, blocking may occur in non-self-routing, three-stage switching networks if VPs are set up through the middle link and the VP bandwidths are dynamically changed. Examples of switch fabrics satisfying the above requirements are one-stage-switching networks or self-routing multistage networks, both of which we are now developing.

OA&M Capability

In order to provide high-quality and highly reliable VPs, we have been developing VP management functions [19]. These functions can be effectively realized with OAM cells. This is explained in the following example using the VP maintenance signal transfer function (Fig. 13). This function notifies transmission link failures to VP endpoints in that case. This function corresponds to the VP availability monitoring function specified in CCITT Recommendation I.610. In order to achieve this function, it is proposed that VP alarm indication signal OAM cells (VP-AIS cells) be inserted into each affected VP by the transport node (XC or ADM) when it detects an upstream transmission failure. In order to notify the opposite side endpoint of the VP failure, it also is proposed that VP far end receive failure OAM cells (VP-FERF cells) be generated at the VP endpoint (ATM switch or user terminal) when VP-AIS cells are detected. In addition to the notification of the VP failure, the failure type and location also can be notified by using the payload of the VP-AIS cell.

The VP-AIS cell must be transferred to the VP endpoint quickly. In order to realize this, the VP-AIS cell has the same VPI value as the affected VP. The VP-AIS cell is identified by a specific VCI value that indicates the VP level OAM cell and a specific value within the payload that indicates its OAM type. Other important VP management functions include VP performance monitoring, VP testing, and VP tracing. An effective ATM network will be created after these management functions have been implemented.

Conclusion

Our strategy of introducing ATM techniques is aimed at the realization of the infrastructure needed for the future advanced information society. From the beginning the strategy includes the provisioning of cost-effective, high-speed multimedia leased-line services. This is made possible by the VP concept. We have been developing the techniques necessary for the new services, and prototype systems were scheduled to be completed in 1992. Some issues remain to be resolved before fully realizing the services. The issues include the definition of source traffic descriptors, protocols for VP bandwidth alteration, end-customer control mechanisms, and VP restoration techniques. The services, however, will be provided step by step considering the progress of international standardization. The customer will first harvest the VP benefits by the mid-1990s.

Acknowledgment

We were able to perform the work addressed in this article through the support of Dr. Tetsuya Miki, executive manager, NTT Transmission Systems Laboratories; and many colleagues who participated in the development of the link system.

References

[1] CCITT Recommendations, I series (B-ISDN), Nov. 1990.
[2] K. Sato, S. Ohta, and I. Tokizawa, "Broadband ATM Network Architecture Based on Virtual Path," *IEEE Trans. Commun.*, vol. 38, no. 8, pp. 1212-1222, Aug. 1990.
[3] I. Tokizawa, T. Kanada, and K. Sato, "A New Transport Network Architecture Based on Asynchronous Transfer Mode Techniques," *Proc. ISSLS '88*, Boston, 11.2.1-11.2.5, 1988.
[4] R. G. Addie and R. E. Warfield, "Bandwidth Switching and New Network Architecture," *Proc. 12th Int. Teletraffic Congress*, Turin, 2.3ii A.1.1-1.7, June 1988.
[5] J. P. Coudreuse and L. Etessa, "ATM: Status of Definition and Discussion of Some Open Issues," presented at the 2nd IEEE COMSOC Int. Multimedia Commun. Workshop, Ottawa, Canada, April 20-23, 1989.
[6] K. Sato and I. Tokizawa, "Flexible Asynchronous Transfer Mode Networks Utilizing Virtual Paths," *Proc. ICC '90*, Atlanta, Ga., 318.4.1-318.4.8, April 16-19, 1990.
[7] K. Sato, R. Kawamura, and I. Tokizawa, "Introduction Strategy of B-ISDN Based on Virtual Paths," *Proc. FORUM '91* (Tech. Symp. of TELECOM 91), Geneva, Switzerland, Session 2.5, pp. 225-229, Oct. 10-15, 1991.
[8] J-P Coudreuse and P. Adam, "ATM Applications," *Proc. FORUM '91*, Geneva, Switzerland, Session 2.5, pp. 231-234, Oct. 10-15, 1991.
[9] O. Funtneider, "Architectural Aspects for ATM Network," *Proc. FORUM '91*, Geneva, Switzerland, Session 2.5, pp. 225-229, Oct. 10-15, 1991.
[10] H. Ishikawa, "New Concept in Telecommunications Network Architecture," *NTT Rev.*, vol. 1, no. 1, pp. 79-86, May 1989.
[11] CCITT Recommendation G. 803, "Architectures of Transport Networks Based on the Synchronous Digital Hierarchy (SDH)," CCITT Meeting Report R-106 (WP XVIII), COM XVIII-R106-E, July 1992.
[12] N. Yamanaka, Y. Sato, and K. Sato, "Usage Parameter Control and Bandwidth Allocation Methods for ATM-based B-ISDN," *Proc. 4th IEEE Int. Workshop MULTIMEDIA '92*, Monterey, Calif., April 1-4, 1992.
[13] Y. Sato and K. Sato, "Evaluation of Statistical Cell Multiplexing Effects and Path Capacity Design in ATM Networks," *IEICE Trans. Commun.*, vol. E75-B, No. 7, pp. 642-648, July 1992.
[14] Y. Sato, N. Yamanaka, and K. Sato, "ATM Network Resource Management Techniques for CBR Virtual Paths/Channels," submitted to the *IEEE/ACM Trans. Networking*.
[15] CCITT Recommendation I.371, 1992.
[16] N. Yamanaka, Y. Sato, and K. Sato, "Usage Parameter Control and Bandwidth Allocation Methods Considering Cell Delay Variation," to appear in *IEICE Trans. Commun.*, vol. E76-B, no. 3, March 1993.
[17] H. Hadama, K. Sato, and I. Tokizawa, "Dynamic Bandwidth Control of Virtual Paths in ATM Networks," presented at 3rd IEEE Int. Workshop on Multimedia Communs, MULTIMEDIA '90, Bordeaux, France, November 14-17, 1990.
[18] H. Hadama, K. Sato, and I. Tokizawa, "Analysis of Virtual Path Bandwidth Control Effects in ATM Networks," to be presented.
[19] Y. Kanayama, Y. Maeda, and H. Ueda, "Virtual Path Management Functions for Broad-band ATM Networks," *Proc. GLOBECOM '91*, Phoenix, Ariz., Session 39, 39.2, Dec. 2-5, 1991.

Biographies

IKUO TOKIZAWA joined NTT Laboratories in 1969, where he did applied research and development in the field of high-capacity FDM multiplexers, digital signal processing, and speech codecs. From 1984 to 1987, he supervised a group doing development of STM digital synchronous multiplexers, including digital cross-connect systems. Currently, he is a group leader of broadband transport research group in NTT Transmission Systems Laboratories.

TOMONORI AOYAMA received B.E., M.E. and Ph.D. degrees from University of Tokyo, Japan, in 1967, 1969, and 1991, respectively. He joined the Electrical Communications Laboratories, Nippon Telegraph and Telephone Public Corporation in 1969. From 1973 to 1974 he was a visiting scientist at the Massachusetts Institute of Technology. In 1991 he was appointed executive manager of Transport Processing Laboratory, NTT Transmission Systems Laboratories. He currently is executive manager of NTT's intellectual property department.

KEN-ICHI SATO received the B.S., M.S., and Ph.D. degrees in electronics engineering from the University of Tokyo. In 1978 he joined Yokosuka Electrical Communication Laboratories, NTT. From 1978 to 1984 he was engaged in the research and development of optical fiber transmission. His research and development experiences cover fiber optic video transmission systems for CATV distribution systems and subscriber loop systems. Since 1985, he has been active in the development of B-ISDN based on ATM techniques. His present responsibilities include information transport network architecture, variable network architecture, broadband transport technology, and network performance analysis. He is currently a supervisor in the Transport Processing Laboratory at NTT.

The customer will first harvest the VP benefits by the mid-1990s.

514

A Vision for Residential Broadband Services: ATM-to-the-Home

To achieve the grand vision of the residential broadband market, thousands of applications must be enabled on these networks. Instead of constantly searching for the single killer application through market studies and speculative guesses, the best insurance policy is to build a platform of thousands of applications such that, collectively, these applications all become killer applications.

Tim Kwok

TIM KWOK is the chief ATM architect for Microsoft.

The convergence of the computer, communication, cable, and television industries has transformed from only a vision of the future to a reality in the past two years. Major network operators, both telcos and cable companies (MSOs, or multiple system operators), around the world are racing to deploy residential broadband services. Cable vendors are selling equipment to telcos, as well as MSOs, to build broadcast and interactive TV networks, while telco vendors are selling equipment to cable operators, in addition to the telcos, to build telephone and interactive TV networks. Meanwhile, all major computer companies (hardware and software) are developing servers, set-top boxes and software for both telcos and MSOs.

This trend is spurred by three powerful forces: deregulation, consumer demand, and technology. For decades, most network operators have had monopolies in their geographical areas or markets. However, deregulation has forced these network operators to rethink their strategies and redefine their markets in order to survive and grow. Otherwise, competition from other network providers and entrepreneurs could significantly affect their market share. Most of them have invested very heavily (in billions of US$) in a new market: residential broadband services. Such services include video on demand, home shopping, video games, (high quality) video telephony, and eventually thousands of residential applications being envisioned or to be invented.

At the same time, consumers have become more accustomed to using new technologies for entertainment, education, and work. One-third of all American homes already has a PC [1], and six out of ten Pentium™-based PCs were sold to consumers and not businesses [2]. About 4.3 percent of all American households use on-line services today, and research has projected that this will grow to 17.6 percent by 1998 [3]. With the arrival of residential broadband networks at much higher data rates than current narrowband access, new residential broadband applications will explode in number.

More importantly, technological advances in software, computing, video compression, and networking have made deploying residential broadband services economically possible within the next few years. The arrival of asynchronous transfer mode (ATM) networks has enabled a wide range of new interactive multimedia applications for the residential market. The objective of this article is to present a vision for supporting universal residential broadband services based on an ATM-to-the-home (ATTH) network architecture [4]. This network architecture applies to the various residential access network (RAN) architectures being deployed today, such as hybrid fiber/coax (HFC), fiber-to-the-curb (FTTC), fiber-to-the-home (FTTH), and asymmetric digital subscriber loop (ADSL) technologies.

First, this article addresses today's residential networks and applications, to understand why a switched broadband residential network is required to support residential broadband services. After exploring residential broadband application requirements, a new class of service is proposed to support a very important class of residential broadband applications that has been not addressed. Then, the technical and strategic motivations for using the ATTH architecture are discussed in detail. A universal model for residential broadband network architecture based on ATTH is described, which is shown to apply to various RAN architectures. Finally, this article discusses the signaling requirements of residential broadband services and explain why the ATM multiconnection per-call model is much more efficient than the DSM-CC session control approach for the ATTH architecture.

Reprinted from IEEE Network, Oct. 1995, pp. 14-28.

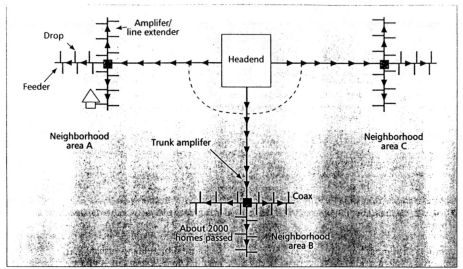

■ Figure 1. *Traditional cable TV network architecture.*

Target Residential Broadband Network

Today's residential networks can be broadly classified as into broadcast and switched networks. A broadcast network, such as the cable TV network, provides a one-way, one-to-many distribution of information. As shown in Fig. 1, analog video received at the headend is broadcast, via the tree and branch architecture of the coaxial cable distribution plant, to each subscriber. A switched network, such as the telephone network, provides two-way, point-to-point communications between any two users on the network (Fig. 2).

Unfortunately, neither the existing cable TV nor the current telco networks can support the envisioned residential broadband services (Table 1). Although the traditional cable network has the advantage of a broadband transmission medium to the home that can potentially deliver information at Gb/s, this is a broadcast network and has no switching capability. Hence, it cannot support point-to-point connectivity or switched interactive services. Another problem is that the "cable network" actually consists of disjointed islands of local cable systems. Communications between these islands of cable networks has not been necessary for their core application: broadcast TV application (except their shared common source of programming from national headends). Today's telephone network provides the key value of ubiquitous communication between any two phones on the network anywhere in the world, by providing a sophisticated signaling infrastructure across the network. Unfortunately, the current bandwidth to each home is very limited, typically at 64 kbps or less. To support fully interactive residential broadband applications, both telcos and cable networks must be upgraded to a switched broadband residential network.

Today's Residential Applications

Although today's residential networks do not support fully switched broadband applications,

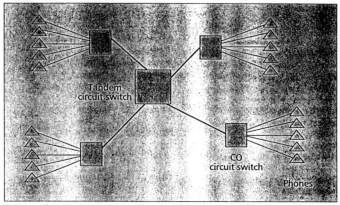

■ Figure 2. *The telephone network architecture.*

they do support various degrees of switching (interactiveness) and broadband capabilities. Today's telephony network supports a number of interactive applications such as telecommuting, on-line services, and Internet access (especially through the World Wide Web). However, these are all narrowband applications. The explosion of interests in these interactive applications have generated significant demand for broadband access to make applications more responsive.

Current cable networks also support a range of near-on-demand (NOD) applications. These NOD applications include both video based, such as impulse pay per view (IPPV) and near video on demand (NVOD), and image/data based such as broadcast carousel distribution of video games. NVOD provides an illusion of video on demand by broadcasting each movie over multiple channels at staggered start times (typically 10 to 30 minutes apart), so viewers can start watching the movie by waiting until the next available time when the movie begins on one of these channels. Viewers can also "pause" and "rewind/forward" by tuning to the corresponding channel. However, the large number of

To support
fully interactive
residential
broadband
applications,
a quality of
service based,
two-way
switched
broadband
residential
network
architecture is
required.

Attributes	Telephone network	Cable network	Switched broadband residential network
Transmission	Analog or digital (ISDN)	Analog	Digital and analog (for backward compatibility)
Information type	Voice, low quality video, narrowband data	Broadcast quality video	All information types
Connection types	Two-way point-to-point and multipoint-to-multipoint (by bridge)	One-way broadcast, not fully connected (islands of connectivity)	One-way or two-way; point-to-point, point-to-multipoint, multi-point-to-multipoint
Service	Switched	Broadcast	Switched, Multicast and Broadcast
Data rate	Low speed (at most on the order of 100kb/s)	If digitized, 10s Mb/s channel downstream	Bidirectional broadband 10s Mb/s downstream, symmetric bandwidth later

■ Table 2. *Comparison of traditional telephone and cable networks with the switched broadband residential network.*

channels that must be dedicated to NVOD to support a single movie makes it very bandwidth inefficient, as spectrum is expensive. One way to improve the bandwidth efficiency (especially in low viewership scenarios) is a video juke box model, whereby each channel originally dedicated to NVOD for the same movie is used only when viewers request the movie for that time period. The broadcast carousel model is useful for game distribution. It continuously broadcasts a set of games in the cyclical fashion, so the viewers can download the desired game to the local game machine by waiting (on the order of minutes) until the desired game broadcast on the network.

In general, NOD applications take advantage of the intrinsic sharing of information of the broadcast channel while giving viewers more choice for the start time (for video based applications) or the content (for image/data based applications). However, this incurs a waiting time for video or images to appear, and the choice remains limited. Ideally, we would like to have true video on demand (VOD) as viewers are unique in their interest and viewing habit. Note that VOD applications include not only movie on demand, but also TV on demand (TVOD), which allows individual programs in the past or future to be viewed on demand.

Switched Broadband Residential Network

To support fully interactive residential broadband applications, a *quality of service (QoS) based, two-way switched broadband* residential network architecture is required. A broadband network is required to support the high data rate, in addition to low bandwidth applications. A switched network is required to support independent connections to each viewer. A QoS-based network guarantees the performance of real-time delivery of both time-based information (such as video, audio, and animation) and non-time-based information (such as image, graphics and text). Ideally, the high bandwidth to the home should be symmetric in order to allow high bandwidth peer-to-peer communications. This will enable each home to be a source of multimedia information, without being limited to service providers as the information source. This will be important in the creation of a vibrant

residential broadband service market, as it will enable a large variety of sources of multimedia information from the general public. This could result in a similar, but potentially bigger, revolution than that of the desktop publishing industry.

Residential Broadband Networking Requirements

This section explores residential broadband applications requirements in greater detail.

What is an Application?

A communication application is defined as a task that requires communication of one or more information streams between two or more parties that are geographically separated. More specifically, an application can be characterized by the following main attributes [5].

Information Types — In general, the information to be communicated can be classified as time-based or non-time-based. Time-based information must be presented at specific instants to convey its meaning; i.e., time is an integral part of the information communicated or the information has a time component. Typical time-based types of information are video, audio, and animation. Non-time-based information includes images, graphics, and text. An application can include both time-based and non-time-based information. When an application involves multiple streams of information (possibly of different information types), synchronization among them is an important issue [6].

Delivery Requirements — An application can also be classified according to its information delivery requirements as a real-time or a non-real-time application. A real-time application is one that requires information delivery for immediate consumption. In contrast, non-real-time application information is stored (perhaps temporarily) at the receiving points for later consumption. The former requires sufficient bandwidth, while the latter requires sufficient storage (and potentially bandwidth as well if delivered at high speed). For example, a telephone conversation is considered a real-time application, while sending electronic mail is a non-real-time application. In the other words, users who communicate via a real-time application must be present at the same time, whereas those who communicate via a non-real-time application can participate at different times.

It is important to distinguish between the delivery requirement (real-time or non-real-time) of an application from the intrinsic time dependency of its information content (time-based or non-time-based). This is illustrated in Table 2. Video conferencing and image browsing are examples of real-time applications, while sending video clips and electronic mail are non-real-time applications. In the case of image browsing, although the image is non-time-based information, a maximum response time constraint is imposed to ensure an interactive response experience for the user; therefore, it is considered a real-time application (with non-time-based information). On the other hand, sending video clips is a non-real-time application because, even though the information content is time-based, the video clip can be treated as a single file transfer (similar to electronic mail), since it is not being displayed in real time during delivery. In general, the communications requirements for supporting an application depends on both the information type and the delivery requirement of the application. Since residential broadband applications encompass all combinations of information types and the delivery requirements, they must all be supported.

Symmetry of Connection — In general, a communication application is bidirectional, and bidirectional applications can be classified as either symmetric or asymmetric. A broadcast application is an extreme example of an asymmetric application that is one-way only, while telephony is a symmetric application.

Number of Parties — Depending on whether there are two or more parties involved, an application can be classified as point-to-point (two parties) or multipoint (more than two), respectively. Obviously, point-to-point applications require only point-to-point connections, while multipoint applications require multiparty connection types, such as point-to-multipoint, multipoint-to-point, or multipoint-to-multipoint connections. All of these must be supported in the residential broadband network. This will be discussed in more detail later.

Application Characterization

An application can be characterized by its traffic characteristics and the corresponding communication requirements. A communication application's traffic characteristics can be described as one or more sequence of packets, of arbitrary length, generated at a certain time and destined for one or more locations. Each packet has an associated set of communications requirements. Traffic characteristics, together with the corresponding communications requirements, determine the network resources (bandwidth and buffer) required to support this application.

Traffic Characteristics — The traffic characteristics of an application can be formally specified

	Real-time delivery	Non-real-time delivery
Time-based information	Video conferencing, telephony	Video clip transfer
Non-time-based information	Image browsing	Electronic mail

■ Table 2. *Example of applications with different information types and delivery requirements.*

by its traffic generation process. Since the traffic generation process (or traffic pattern) is basically a sequence of packets generated at arbitrary instants, each packet having an arbitrary length, it can be modeled as an on-off source. The traffic pattern can be characterized by two stochastic processes: a) the packet generation process (or packet arrival process); and b) packet length distribution [7].

Two important traffic patterns in residential broadband services are periodic and bursty traffic. If packet generation occurs at regular time intervals, it is a periodic traffic pattern. If these packet lengths are fixed in size, it is a constant bit rate (CBR) stream. Otherwise, it is a variable bit rate (VBR) stream. For example, compressed video streams (such as MPEG-2) are typically periodic traffic and can be CBR or VBR.

Bursty traffic is characterized by packets of arbitrary length generated at random times, separated by gaps of silence of random duration. Typically, the period of silence is long compared with packet generation periods, leading to the distinctive high peak to average bandwidth ratios. Image browsing is a bursty application because images are transferred on demand by the user, and such requests are unpredictable. Since this is a real-time application, performance guarantees (delay) are required.

In general, residential broadband applications consist of both periodic and bursty applications. The need to support both types of traffic with real-time requirements becomes the most challenging traffic management problem.

Communications Requirements — The key communications requirements of an application include bandwidth, delay, and error guarantees. The residential broadband network must support a minimum set of communications requirements to enable a large range of interactive multimedia applications. To support real-time (time-based and non-time-based) applications, the residential broadband network must provide bandwidth and QoS (delay and error) guarantees.

Bandwidth — The bandwidth requirements of an application (in each direction) are typically specified in terms of peak and average bandwidth. For CBR applications, the peak and average bandwidth are the same. To support broadcast quality movies, a CBR MPEG-2 compressed stream requires 3 to 4 Mb/s. The bandwidth requirements can increase to 6 or even 9 Mb/s for real-time compression of live sports events, due to the fast motion content. Since the amount of compressed information varies according to the content and instantaneous scene changes, compressed video is variable bit rate (VBR) in nature. The CBR MPEG-2 stream is created by traffic shaping, using a rate buffer and real-time adjustment of compression ratio (quantization level) to maintain the buffer fullness without overflow or underflow.

Real-time transfer of non-time-based information generates bursty traffic patterns, which are VBR applications. The peak bandwidth of such real-time applications very often exceeds that of real-time transfer of time-based information, such as real-time video. For real-time transfer of non-time-based information applications, there is an absolute delay constraint specified as part of the QoS requirements (usually about 100 ms end-to-end from the application level) to achieve the perception of instantaneous interaction. For image browsing applications, a full screen photo image of 3 Mbytes (1000 x 1000 x 24 b), after compression 300 Kbytes by JPEG compression [8]. This requires about 24 Mb/s link (peak) bandwidth to satisfy the response time requirements. However, this can be reduced with reduced image size, or high compression ratio, or relaxed response time to less than 10 Mb/s. Specifying the average bandwidth requirement for a bursty application is a challenge because it varies according to the duration for which the average is taken. Furthermore, the values obtained vary widely across different users (such as with image browsing), even for the same applications, because everyone has a unique usage pattern.

When residential broadband services are first deployed, each active subscriber may require about 10 Mb/s peak downstream bandwidth to support at least 1 MPEG-2 compressed stream that requires 4 to 6 Mb/s, plus additional bandwidth for downloading applications or graphics with acceptable latency (less than 100 ms). The minimum average bandwidth should be about 5 Mb/s to support at least 1 video stream, while the other applications may share the bandwidth among multiple users. In the upstream direction, a peak bandwidth of about 1-2 Mb/s should be available to satisfy the latency requirement for a variety of interactive applications. Of course, this 1 to 2 Mb/s bandwidth can be shared among multiple users. To support videotelephony, up to 384 kb/s sustained bandwidth should be available for the active user. Again, symmetric bandwidth of 10 Mb/s or higher should be available in the future to allow any user in the network to become an information source.

Delay — Absolute delay, or latency, is one of the key QoS performance parameters that must be satisfied by the residential broadband network. As mentioned above, to provide interactive response to viewers the response time between a user action and its effect should be less than 100 ms. To support network-based video games, a response time of 50 ms or less is required to support twitch actions. This puts an upper bound on the transmission times in each direction, which imposes a minimum upstream and downstream bandwidth requirement. Delay variation is another important QoS parameter. Real-time video probably requires the most demanding delay variation constraint to minimize the buffering requirement for end-to-end synchronization.

A New Class of Service

In general, to support residential broadband applications, three classes of service must be supported [5]:
- Best-effort delivery.
- Real-time delivery of time-based information.
- Real-time delivery of non-time-based information.

Although all three are important for residential broadband services, only the first two have been studied in detail. The first class is being addressed by the ATM Forum with the available bit rate (ABR) class of service. The second class is the CBR or VBR with timing requirements (bounds on delay variation). This can be supported by reserving peak bandwidth for each application over a QoS-based network. The third class of service includes image browsing, which is required for home shopping applications. This third class is probably the most challenging class of service to support because it is bursty and has an absolute delay requirement. Such unpredictability makes it very difficult to allocate bandwidth efficiently to support this class of service. Further research is required in this area.

ATM-to-the-Home for Residential Broadband Services

Since the adoption of ATM as the solution for B-ISDN in the late '80s, the focus on ATM has gone full circle. ATM was originally chosen by the telecommunications industry as the cornerstone of future public networking technologies. It was envisioned as the ultimate public networking technology to provide integrated services to a wide range of applications (especially those involving multimedia) for both residential and business services. In the early '90s, ATM was quickly adopted by the computer industry as an excellent local area network (LAN) solution to replace legacy LANs networks (such as ethernet and token ring) in supporting multimedia applications and the ever increasing bandwidth requirements of data applications as desktop computing power increases [9]. ATM LANs have become the key focus of the ATM Forum since its inception in late 1991. In 1994, ATM became important again for the public network operators deploying residential broadband services as it provides central office switching capability for residential services [10].

ATM-to-the-home (ATTH) provides an end-to-end pure ATM connectivity between headend or central office servers and intelligent home devices (such as PCs and set-top boxes). In other words, in an ATTH network, ATM terminates at the set-top box or the PC. ATTH architecture is being adopted by network operators deploying FTTC, FTTH, HFC, and ADSL [10]. In addition, the ATM Forum has just established a residential broadband subworking group to specify standard interfaces for the ATTH architecture for different residential access networks. Residential broadband services and applications have also been designed to support ATTH for different residential access networks [10].

There are also alternative approaches to

deploying residential broadband services. For example, in the case of the HFC access architecture [11] (an improvement of the cable TV network by replacing coaxial trunks by fibers, as shown in the following section), there is an MPEG-2-to-the-home hybrid network architecture approach using ATM protocols at the headend or central office only, and MPEG-2 Transport Stream (TS) packets over an HFC architecture between the headend or central office and the home devices. ATM cells are converted to MPEG-2 TS packets, which are 188 bytes with a payload of 184 bytes, at the headend or central office. Such a hybrid architecture is optimized for carrying MPEG-2 compressed video and audio, while carrying other information types is an afterthought and requires further study. As explained below, ATTH is a far superior architecture for supporting residential broadband applications for both technical and strategic reasons.

Technical Reasons

Since the technical advantages of ATM are well understood [9], ATM has been generally adopted as the switching technology to be deployed at the headend and central office for supporting residential broadband services. However, the advantages of deploying a pure ATM network between the headend/central office servers and the home devices are not well recognized. Next, this article discusses the important technical advantages of deploying the pure ATM solution (ATTH) for residential broadband services.

Guaranteed Performance — Since ATM is a connection-oriented protocol with signaling mechanisms for network resource reservation, ATM can guarantee end-to-end QoS and bandwidth. This is the key advantage of ATM because this is the fundamental requirement to support interactive multimedia applications. By deploying a pure ATM network solution, such performance guarantees can be achieved across the entire residential broadband network, all the way to the home devices. Each home device can specify and will have direct access to the ATM signaling protocols it requires to support each of its applications. Otherwise, if the above hybrid network model is used (i.e., ATM is terminated at the headend/central office), another performance guarantee model must be invented (and standardized) between the home devices and the headend/central office. Since ATM signaling protocol is not available to the home device in such a hybrid model, there is no standard way of communicating such requirements over the non-ATM network/link (such as an MPEG-2 TS link) from the home device to the headend/central office. Furthermore, the interoperability between the ATM and non-ATM models (such as QoS parameters mapping) needs to be designed and standardized, which will delay standardized solutions. ATTH prevents the nightmare of solving the interoperability of heterogeneous networks, yet provides a clean solution for guaranteeing QoS end-to-end between servers and home devices.

A Universal Residential Broadband Network Model — To create the biggest market for residential applications and services, it is essential that there is a universal residential broadband network model for developing those services. ATM provides the necessary layer of abstraction so that upper layer software can be residential access network independent; applications can use the same model for HFC, FTTC, FTTH, and ADSL, as all of them can be based on ATTH. Therefore, by designing an end-to-end ATM network such as ATTH, a universal residential broadband network model can be achieved, significantly reducing the cost of deployment of residential broadband services and applications across different network architectures.

Rich Signaling Capabilities — The rich signaling protocols of ATM makes it possible to support the different connection types required by many multimedia applications, such as point-to-multipoint, multipoint-to-point, and multipoint-to-multipoint connections (in addition to the basic point-to-point connection type). Since the ATTH model supports such rich signaling capabilities and connection types to all home devices, it enables a wide variety of residential broadband services. If, however, ATM is terminated at the headend/central office as specified in the MPEG-2-to-the-home architecture, then most of these connection types will be unavailable the home devices, thus tremendously limiting the number of residential services that can be deployed.

Enable Large Numbers of Applications — Providing performance guarantees and rich connection types gives ATTH the flexibility to support many different types of applications with diverse networking requirements. The ability to tailor the virtual connections for each application to the required bandwidth and QoS allows maximum flexibility to support a variety of different applications efficiently. This is extremely important to enable the residential broadband market because we need to support thousands of applications with diverse networking requirements on this platform. No one can predict which application will be the killer application. Since the ability to support thousands of applications means that, collectively, these applications can become a killer application, using ATTH is the best insurance policy for network operators deploying residential broadband services. In contrast, MPEG-2-to-the-home has been optimized for MPEG-2 compressed video and audio only; it is unclear that these applications alone can justify the investment for upgrading to such residential broadband networks.

Single Platform for all Applications — The flexibility of ATTH in supporting many different multimedia applications implies that a single platform can be used to support all residential broadband services and applications. This is an extremely important advantage of ATTH. Since the network architecture can remain the same as new services and applications are added to the platform, ATTH significantly reduces the incremental cost of deploying new residential services and applications.

Since ATM is a connection-oriented protocol with signaling mechanisms for network resource reservation, ATM can guarantee end-to-end QoS and bandwidth.

Many management capabilities already exist as part of the management plane of the ATM protocols, providing ATTH with standardized management protocols.

No Need for a Separate Level 1 Gateway — The function of a Level 1 gateway in the telco video dial tone paradigm is to provide connectivity through the Level 1 network and basic billing capability. It is unnecessary in the ATTH architecture because the ATM switch by definition is to provide connectivity to all connected parties, controlled by the ATM switch's switch controller (part of the ATM switch). Also, public ATM switches provide billing records of all connections, including durations and resources usage.

Bandwidth Efficiency — Since ATM is based on packet switching and asynchronous time division multiplexing, it is very efficient in multiplexing information in both upstream and downstream directions. Furthermore, the ABR service of ATM allows best effort traffic to fully utilize the slack left from guaranteed services. Hence, with ABR service, the ATTH architecture can achieve almost 100 percent network utilization in residential access networks. This is very important because access bandwidth is extremely precious for many access network architectures (which represent the last miles).

There has been a myth that ATTH is inefficient because of the 10 percent header overhead of ATM cells. However, if ATM is not used for the links to the home, the access network utilization cannot be 100 percent in the first place; such a packet network needs to reduce the load (and utilization) to below 80 percent to prevent overload (switch buffer overflow) [7]. Thus, contrary to the myth, ATTH can achieve a higher efficiency than the MPEG-2-to-the-home solution. Furthermore, the ATM header should be viewed within the context of its capabilities for providing QoS guarantees, flexibility for multiplexing, and rich connection types, rather than as overhead only.

Network Management — Since ATTH is a pure ATM network model, it significantly improves network manageability because it is not necessary to manage multiple networks with different networking technologies within the residential broadband network. This removes the interoperability problem between heterogeneous networks, where many standard management interfaces must be defined and interoperable. In addition, many management capabilities already exist as part of the management plane of the ATM protocols, providing ATTH with standardized management protocols.

Scalability — ATM switches have the highest switching capacity of any commercially available switches with standard interfaces. ATM switches running in the multi-gigabit range are commonplace today, and ATM switch capacity continues to grow to even higher capacity. The scalability to very high bandwidth is extremely important because the volume of information supported at the headend or central office for full scale deployment can easily be hundreds of Gb/s, due to the combination of multimedia applications bandwidth requirements and the large number of homes supported. Also, scalability of the link bandwidth is important for residential access

network architectures, such as FTTC, HFC, and ADSL, as their upstream and downstream transmission rates improve in the future. Since ATM is independent of the data rate of its underlying physical layer, ATTH supports all access network architectures independent of the data rate of those architectures and their future improvement.

Strategic Reasons

There are also a number of important strategic reasons for deploying ATTH for residential broadband networks. These are explained below.

Support More Services, Applications, and Revenue Streams — It has been recognized that the VOD application by itself cannot justify the billions of dollars of investment in various residential broadband networks being deployed worldwide [12]. To achieve the grand vision of the residential broadband market, thousands of applications must be enabled on these networks. ATTH provides bandwidth and QoS guarantees to support all interactive multimedia applications and provides a scaleable platform that can support as many applications as needed, while meeting the widely diverse networking requirements of these applications. Only with such a universal residential broadband networking platform can we support a large number of services and applications that will generate sufficient new revenue streams to justify the large investment.

Low Cost — With the large number of ATM vendors (over 100) already in the market and more going into the market, the ATM market is destined to become a commodity. ATM prices are already falling at a rapid rate; they have dropped by a factor of more than six within three years of first commercial introduction. It is extremely advantageous for network operators to ride the cost curve of ATM by deploying ATTH. The cost of ATM is already low enough for residential broadband deployment. Unfortunately, the cost of deploying ATM is probably the most misunderstood issue in the residential broadband industry. Many mistakenly believe that ATM is very expensive and that it will remain so for a long time. This is primarily because of the following misconceptions.

Myth #1: ATM Based Set-Top Boxes are Very Expensive — The worst cost impression of ATM-to-the-home probably comes from the most publicized residential broadband trial: the Time Warner full-service network trial in Orlando, Florida. Time Warner is deploying ATTH for their HFC network. Because their set-top boxes each costs more than US$5000, many who review the high costs assume the expense is due to the ATM components in the set-top box. In reality, the set-top boxes are unmodified SGI Indeo workstations. The high cost is *not* simply ATM in the set-top box.

Many think that because ATM adapters still cost hundreds of dollars, they will be expensive to put into the set-top box. However, if ATM is implemented in an integrated fashion with other components in the set-top box, its cost will not come close the cost of implementing ATM as an adapter. In fact, the cost of ATM components is negligible as compared to other set-top box components such as memory, CPUs, graphics processing, and MPEG-2 decoders.

Myth #2: The Technology is Too New — Many think that since ATM is such a new technology, the cost will remain high for many years. However, they fail to realize that ATM technology is unique in the large number of networking vendors, both existing and startups, that are pursuing this market because they believe ATM will be the most important networking technology for years to come. The ATM Forum has grown from four to more than 700 member companies in only three years, and is still growing at the same rate. In fact, since the introduction of ATM adapters on the market in 1992, the price of OC-3c adapters has dropped from $4500 to $695 (as of March 1995), a factor of six in less than three years! The trend is bound to continue, given the number of vendors and the availability of standards. ATM is destined to become a commodity market like ethernet.

Myth #3: ATM Switch Very Expensive — One of the biggest misconceptions about ATM prices is that of the ATM switch. This mainly arises from the huge discrepancy between the price of a public ATM switch and the price of a local ATM switch. Public ATM switches are those that are designed for the traditional telco market and meet the stringent fault tolerant capability and reliability requirements specified by Bellcore. Local ATM switches are those deployed for the LAN market; these do not need to meet the same Bellcore requirements, but are still reasonably reliable. For the same switching capacity, number of ports, and speed, the public ATM switch can be ten times more expensive than the local ATM switch! When people claim that ATM switches are expensive, they are referring to public ATM switches. Unfortunately, they fail to realize that public ATM switches are not necessary for residential broadband services; there is no need to provide lifeline services for entertainment applications, which will be the primary residential broadband applications (at least initially). As local ATM switches continue to drop in price and increase in functionality and reliability, this will encourage network operators to gradually adopt local ATM switches for residential broadband services. Also, it is very likely that local ATM switch vendors will build versions of their switches that are slightly more expensive but have increased reliability to meet the residential market requirements. In fact, an analogy of public versus local ATM switches is the market relationship between mainframe computers versus personal computers (PCs); the force of the high volume commodity of PCs has brought on the demise of the mainframe market and the same might happen to public ATM switches.

Myth #4: MPEG-2 TS-to-the-Home is Cheaper than ATM-to-the-Home — It is unclear that ATTH is more expensive than its alternatives, such as MPEG-2-to-the-home in the case of HFC architecture. It is possible that deploying MPEG-2-to-the-home can be more expensive both in the short and long term.

In the short term, supporting MPEG-2-to-the-home means that set-top boxes must terminate the 188 byte packets. This requires the set-top boxes to process the 188 byte packets, reassemble them from transport stream (TS), and convert them into PES format (the video and audio packetized elementary stream format). Moreover, by limiting the packet size of compressed video to only 188 bytes, software processing becomes unfeasible due to the resulting high interrupt frequency [13]. Furthermore, ATM-to-MPEG conversion is required if the headend supports ATM switching. Such conversion processes are proprietary and expensive because no standard exists and very few vendors support them. (Currently, the equipment for converting a single OC-3c MPEG-2 TS over ATM to 5 MPEG-2 TS streams at 27 Mb/s can cost easily more than $30,000, more than the cost of a complete 2.4 Gb/s local ATM switch with 16 OC-3c ports !) In contrast, in the ATTH architecture, MPEG-2 compressed video can be carried over AAL5 either by Program Stream packet format, which can be up to 64 Kbytes long, or k MPEG-2 TS packets (where k can be negotiated by signaling) [13], thus avoiding the above high interrupt frequency problem.

In the long term, MPEG-2-to-the-home creates a "future legacy" problem as operators realize the limitation of MPEG-2-to-the-home for supporting additional applications. The upgrade to ATM is going to be expensive, not because of ATM itself, but because of the cost of redeployment of new set-top boxes or set-top box interfaces and new headend equipment. Even if we just add ATM to other frequency channels in HFC for supporting newer applications, the new ATM set-top boxes for such applications will be more expensive due to the need for backward compatibility with MPEG-2 TS channels. Lastly, ATTH does not require a separate Level 1 Gateway while MPEG-2-to-the-home does.

Fundamentally, deploying a hybrid networking architecture like MPEG-2-to-the-home is more expensive because of the additional cost of managing multiple networking technologies, the need for (unnecessary) protocol conversions, and the development of standards for such conversions and the corresponding standards development delay. Furthermore, the intense competition in the ATM market is bound to make it more cost effective than the MPEG-2 - to-the-home architecture, which has far fewer vendors supporting it. Lastly, ATTH does not requires a separate Level 1 Gateway while MPEG-2-to-the-home does.

True Multivendor Support and Standard Interface — At an early stage of ATM standardization, it became widely recognized that, although ATM is the superior network architecture for the future, to make it successful in the market place multivendor support with true interoperability is essential. To avoid repeating ISDN's mistakes of non-interoperable products, ATM vendors quickly realized they needed an extensive interoperability agreement across all ATM

The intense competition in the ATM market is bound to make it more cost effective than the MPEG-2-to-the-home architecture, which has far fewer vendors supporting it.

interfaces in a rapid fashion. As a result, the ATM Forum was formed in late 1991 to expedite this process. The ATM Forum activities help tremendously in creating a multivendor ATM market and also help drive down the price of ATM to a commodity in a fast trajectory.

Furthermore, since the key basic interfaces for ATM such as UNI 3.1 [14] already exist, they can be used for the residential broadband market to expedite deployment. In contrast, if a hybrid networking architecture such as MPEG-2-to-the-home is employed, ATM to MPEG-2 conversion needs to be standardized, and it is not clear where and when this will occur. Since, in the cable industry, no standard network interfaces exist and they have been relying on proprietary technologies from few suppliers (which are intrinsically more expensive), creating standards for the cable industry becomes more critical. This is yet another reason for not using proprietary technologies such as MPEG-2-to-the-home.

Seamless Public and Private Network Architecture — ATM is the first high-speed network technology that has strong support across multiple industries. For the first time, both the public networking industry and the LAN industry have adopted a common networking technology — ATM — as the networking technology to support all future multimedia applications. In the public networking arena, ATM is the only networking technology being pursued for supporting broadband multimedia services. For private networking, ATM has been viewed as the premiere next-generation networking technology to deploy for campus backbones and to support multimedia applications in corporate networks. Hence, it is clear that ATM technologies will be pervasive across many different areas and will become *the* networking technology to invest in.

As the public network evolves to an ATM-based network in the backbone, access to public ATM services will become critical. There are already a number of telcos and IXCs that are providing direct ATM access to businesses. By using ATTH, residences with broadband access can take advantage of the public ATM services as they become available. Furthermore, we can assure a compatible public network architecture that will seamlessly connect residential broadband networks. We can provide end-to-end ATM connectivity between homes across the country and beyond; an end-to-end guaranteed QoS networking platform will appear. This is extremely important in supporting ATM end-to-end services across a wide area (beyond the residential broadband access networks). (This is actually the original vision behind adopting ATM for B-ISDN.) Moreover, by deploying ATTH, we can minimize the future risk of supporting alternative technologies that become islands of proprietary technologies (such as MPEG-2-to-the-home).

Future Proof — By deploying ATTH at the outset, we will put in place the networking technologies that are future proof. ATM is capable of supporting a wide range of applications and is data rate independent, so it will not be necessary to deploy alternative networking technologies as we add new services or transmission bandwidth to the home improves.

Broadband Residential Network Architectures

A Universal Model

To enable a residential broadband market with upwards of thousands of applications and services, there must be a large number of content and applications developers for this platform. Since it is very expensive for content developers to develop for multiple platforms, it is critical that they have a single model for content creation that works over the different network architectures being deployed. In other words, we need to design a universal model for residential broadband network architectures to abstract a single model for all content and applications developers. As discussed in the previous section, the universal model for residential network architecture should be based on an ATM-to-the-home (ATTH) network architecture.

The fundamental objective of the residential broadband network is to provide a communication network among service providers and home devices. The service providers typically provide their service (content and applications) using a collection of servers located in the headend, central office, a remote location, or the provider's premise. Currently, in the United States, the service providers can also be the cable network operators but not the telco network operators (except through a separately owned subsidiary). Home devices can be PCs, set-top boxes, and other intelligent devices. Note that although there is a debate over whether PCs or set-top boxes are the right home devices to support interactive residential services, it is clear that both are important because they serve different (but overlapping) classes of interactive applications. For example, PCs are more oriented to the individual due to usage distance from the user to the PC, whereas the set-top box is more family or group oriented. In the following discussion, the term set-top box is used to denote a generic intelligent home device; any occurrence of set-top box can be replaced by other intelligent home devices, such as the PC.

It is also very important to provide connectivity from residences to other services beyond the local service providers. These include access to the Internet, the PSTN, the emerging public ATM network, and the corporate networks. Since telephony (plain old telephony service, or POTS) remains as the core residential communication application, access to the PSTN is required in the universal model. Also, access to corporate networks is important for telecommuting.

To address the general problem of supporting residential broadband services, a functional model is required to understand all the networking requirements. Figure 3 shows a high level functional model for providing residential broadband services (including narrowband) over a universal residential broadband network model.

The universal model divides the network into three portions: private, public, and service provider networks. The private residential network refers to the in-home network connectivity. The set-top boxes can communicate either directly to the external public network or to a public network termination (NT) device or even a home network. NT allows multiple set-top boxes connected to the public residential network, while the home network provides direct communication between set-top boxes without going through the public network. If the set-top box connects directly to the external network, it can also be viewed as having a passive NT in between.

The public residential broadband network can be divided into two subnetworks: the residential access network (RAN) and the service distribution network (SDN), both of which belong to the network operator. The RAN provides broadband connectivity from each home to the headend or central office. The SDN provides connectivity for different service providers to all the homes through the RAN. The SDN is also responsible for providing connectivity to the Internet, PSTN, and emerging public ATM networks for both the residential customers and service providers. The term SDN is used to distinguish this network from a Level 1 network because a Level 1 network applies to telcos only, in the video dial tone model. Furthermore, the SDN is responsible for connectivity to entities other than service providers, and thus is a superset of the Level 1 network definition.

The service provider network (SPN) belongs to the individual service provider. The SPN is responsible for connecting the various servers of the service provider and connecting them to the SDN. In the simplest case, where the service provider has only a single server, there is no SPN and the server is connected directly to the SDN.

In the ATTH architecture, all networks between the service provider servers and the intelligent home devices are pure ATM networks. These ATM networks include the RAN, SDN, SPN, and home network. IP is supported over ATM at the endpoints (set-top boxes and servers) to provide connectivity to the Internet and other non-ATM external networks for these endpoints.

Residential Access Networks — Since the last mile to the residence is one of the most expensive components of residential broadband service deployment, each network operator chooses the RAN architectures that minimize the cost and risks according to the operator's driving economic factors, business models, and existing infrastructure. As a result, the RAN contains the largest variation among different residential broadband network architectures. Due to the cost of dedicating high bandwidth to every individual residence, a significant amount of design involves efficient sharing of the RAN. Deploying ATTH over various RAN architectures is discussed in a later section.

Service Distribution Networks — The SDN is responsible for interconnecting service providers

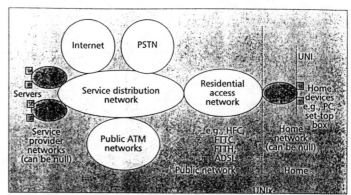

■ Figure 3. *Residential broadband network architecture model.*

to the RAN for providing services and applications to the residences. The SDN is a pure (public) ATM network. The SDN can be physically contained in a single headend or central office, or distributed across a metropolitan area connected to servers in different locations. The regional hub architecture proposed by CableLabs is an example of a distribution network connecting different headends to regional headends for better resource allocation. The interface between the SDN and the RAN should be a network-network interface (NNI) [14], because both the SDN and the RAN are part of the public ATM network. NNI allows resource allocation information to be communicated to set up an end-to-end ATM connection through the entire public residential network, which includes both SDN and RAN. On the other hand, the interface between the SDN and the Internet, PSTN, and SPN are public user-network interfaces (UNIs), because they are either non-ATM networks or do not belong to the public network.

Service Provider Network — The SPN is a private network that belongs to the service provider. The SPN is responsible for connecting all the servers of the service provider to the SDN (the public network), as well as providing internal communications among the servers of the service provider. For the ATTH architecture, the SPN is a pure ATM network. The interface between the SPN and the SDN should be a public UNI [14] because the SPN is similar to a traditional private ATM network, which operates independently of the public ATM network. (Since bandwidth allocation decisions in the SPN and SDN are independent, there is no need for an NNI interface between these two networks.)

Home Networks — In most current residential broadband network deployment, the set-top boxes are directly connected to the RAN. Unfortunately, this has the disadvantage of requiring different set-top boxes for different RAN architectures. The set-top boxes do not have any portability because UNI interfaces are different for different RAN architectures such as HFC, FTTC, FTTH, and ADSL. Due to a lack of standards in RAN design, even for a particular RAN architecture, the network interfaces to the RAN are different from different network vendors.

HFC is a modular architecture whereby the serving population is segmented into neighborhood areas, each of which is served by individual fiber trunks reaching the corresponding fiber node.

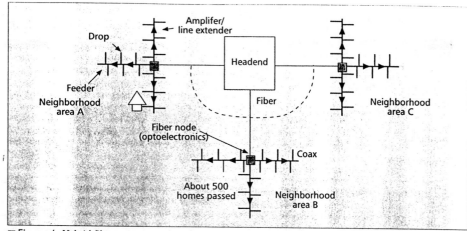

■ Figure 4. *Hybrid fiber-coax network architecture.*

Ideally, there should be a single UNI*x* for each type of RAN (*x* can be HFC, FTTC, FTTH, ADSL, and so forth) between the home network (can be a simple NT) and the RAN. Furthermore, between the home network and all intelligent home devices, there should be a standard interface (UNI), which can be defined for different speeds, such that any set-top box can be plugged into the home network through such a standard interface, independent of the RAN connecting the home network. This vision of a universal broadband home interface is similar to the RJ-11 universal interface today for POTS.

Standard Interfaces — To enable a large residential broadband market that can be as big, if not bigger, than today's PC market, the availability of networking equipment from a large number of vendors is critical. This can only be ensured by the availability of standard interfaces or interoperability agreements (such as the specifications from the ATM Forum). Hence, standard interfaces at the boundaries of SPN, SDN, RAN, and the home network are fundamental to supporting a multivendor environment for the residential broadband market. By adopting the ATTH architecture as the universal residential broadband network model, many of these interfaces can be defined immediately using existing standard ATM interfaces such as [14]. This expedites the development of standards in the residential broadband market, and thereby expedites its deployment.

Residential Access Network Architectures

Currently, one of the most active technical debates in the residential broadband deployment is the choice of RAN architectures. Since different RAN architectures have different intrinsic networking characteristics, they each dictate a set of possible applications that can be supported. These networking characteristics include upstream and downstream bandwidth for individual homes, the degree of switching (interactiveness), and dedicated versus shared bandwidth, error characteristics and reliability, power

issues, and others. The choice of one RAN architecture over another depends not only on technical merits, but also business models, and the types of applications the network operators intend to support in their residential broadband networks [4].

HFC — In the past few years, the HFC network architecture has emerged to become the cable network architecture for the '90s [11]. The HFC architecture consists of fiber trunks from the headend to individual neighborhoods, replacing coaxial trunks of traditional cable network. Each trunk terminates at a fiber node (Fig. 4). The main function of the fiber node is for opto-electronic conversion between fiber and coaxial cable. From the fiber node, multiple coaxial drops pass through the homes in the neighborhood (typically 500 homes), similar to traditional tree and branch cable architecture, except with shorter coaxial runs and hence with fewer amplifiers and lower noise. HFC is a modular architecture (similar to cellular) whereby the serving population is segmented into neighborhood areas, each of which is served by individual fiber trunks reaching the corresponding fiber node.

The spectrum allocation for the HFC architecture to support switched broadband services typically uses between 450 and 750 MHz for new interactive services in the downstream, while 50 to 450 MHz remains for standard analog broadcast services. However, it is up to network operators to choose the number of channels allocated to both analog and new digital interactive services, based on business reasons. Upgrades from 450 to 550 or even 750 MHz are being carried out in many cable plants across the United States to support these new services. At the same time, the return frequency from 5 to 40 MHz (or 30 MHz) is also being enabled during the upgrade process.

HFC is a passband transmission system [15]. The receiver must have a tuner that can tune to one of the fixed frequency bandwidth channels (6 MHz in the United States) between 50 and 750 MHz to receive any downstream signals (analog or digital). To support digital services over HFC, a digital modulation technique must be used to carry digital data across the channels. Two of the most popular digital modulation techniques for HFC are QAM [16] and VSB [17]. 64 QAM modulation carries about 27 Mb/s user data rate (after forward error correction, FEC) over a 6 MHz channel, while the emerging 256 QAM technology can support about 36 Mb/s of user data after FEC. The 16 VSB modulation supports about 38 Mb/s of user data rate, which is equivalent to the 256 QAM technology.

The HFC network, though broadcast in nature, can be upgraded to support fully switched broadband service by adding switching capability at the headend. To implement the ATTH architecture, an ATM switch interconnecting headend servers to the HFC cable plant can provide interactive services over the cable network. Each port on the ATM switch can be logically connected to a 6 MHz (in the United States) downchannel of the cable plant. To receive ATM cells, the set-top box (if connected directly to the RAN) must first tune to the right frequency channel before decoding the information. Each home device can set up its virtual channels (VCs) within its 6 MHz downchannel. In other words, each home device has a virtual link (carrying multiple VCs) between the home and the headend. This is equivalent to a point-to-point switched network; the only difference is that the link is virtual and has variable bandwidth. Each downchannel is shared by multiple home devices to increase efficiency. Each set-top box would receive its information by demultiplexing ATM cells based on VPI/VCI that has been preallocated for its communications. The return channel is used in a similar fashion to multiplex the return data from each home device, except a MAC protocol is required to manage bandwidth sharing in the upstream direction. Hence, standard ATM protocols must be enhanced to support the shared return channels and the passband architecture [4].

FTTC — Fiber-to-the-curb (FTTC) RANs (also known as switched digital video, or SDV) are baseband access networks [15]. FTTC networks run fibers from the central office all the way to the curbside of the houses they service (Fig. 5). Fibers are terminated at the optical network units (ONUs), which typically support between eight and 24 homes. If a passive optical network (PON) architecture is used, a fiber from the central office is split passively into multiple fibers to reach multiple ONUs to reduce laser cost [18]. From the ONU to each home, there can be both twisted pair and coaxial cable. Twisted pair is to support POTS, while coaxial cable is to support analog video services. The new digital interactive services can be supported on either twisted pair or coaxial cable. If analog services are not supported, only twisted pair is necessary to support telephony and digital interactive services.

Since FTTC is baseband, the multiplexing mechanism for distribution to different homes is by time division multiplexing (TDM). Hence, in addition to opto-electronic conversion, routing (or demultiplexing) is one of the key functions of the ONU; this can be accomplished using an ATM switch. The home devices demultiplex their information based on ATM cell headers.

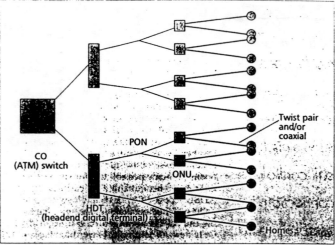

■ Figure 5. *Fiber-to-the-curb network architecture.*

The downstream bandwidth of an FTTC network can be as high as 51 Mb/s on coaxial cable or even on twisted pair, especially for short distances such as 500 ft.

If no PON architecture is used in the FTTC RAN, FTTC is a point-to-point switched network and implementing ATTH is trivial (using standard ATM protocols). If a PON is used, ATM protocols must be extended to support the shared nature of PON architecture [4].

FTTH — Fiber-to-the-home (FTTH) architecture is a point-to-point network topology being implemented by some telcos such as NTT [19] and Deutch Telecom [20]. However, initial deployment of FTTH may not be a truly point-to-point network because, again, a PON may be used to split each fiber from the central office to multiple fibers using a passive optical coupler. This reduces the cost of deployment by reducing the number of laser transceivers required for every home. Bi-directional communication is achieved by a MAC protocol that shares bandwidth on the PON among different homes served by these fiber drops [18]. The bandwidth on each fiber can be as high as OC-3c. Obviously, this gives the highest bandwidth in both directions of all the different access network types. Hence, the home can easily become the source of information and can provide services to other locations by attaching servers to the access network at the residence. Developing ATTH over FTTH is relatively straightforward because FTTH uses a point-to-point architecture. Again, standard ATM protocols must be enhanced to allow sharing of upstream transmission in the PON architecture [4].

ADSL — ADSL is a modem technology deployed over a standard POTS line to dramatically increase the data rate for supporting new applications. The original ADSL technology supports 1.5 Mb/s in the downstream direction and 64 kb/s in the upstream direction. It can carry an additional POTS simultaneously. However, this is not sufficient to support many interactive broadband applications because consumer quality MPEG-2 requires approximately 3 to 4 Mb/s for most content. Recently, ADSL has been improved to support 6 Mb/s in the downstream direction and 640 kb/s in the upstream direction (ADSL-2). However, the cost of deployment remains so high as to prevent many network operators from deploying this technology widely. As a result, the ADSL Forum was created last year to standardize this technology in order to quickly drive down the costs [21]. ADSL does, however, allow a telco to deploy a broadband access network in the shortest period of time (especially to remote areas), given the current installed base on twisted pair to the home. This opens up many possibilities for supporting fully interactive broadband applications. Since the ADSL access network technology is a point-to-point switched network architecture, implementing the ATTH architecture is straightforward. Only new ATM physical layer interfaces of the corresponding data rates need to be defined [4].

Signaling Requirements for Residential Broadband Services

There are two classes of signaling requirements for residential broadband services: functional and performance. To support a diverse range of residential broadband services and applications, a number of connection types must be supported by the signaling functions. In addition, to satisfy individual applications requirements and to provide scalability to support millions of subscribers in the residential broadband networks with guaranteed performance (even under heavy load), there are associated performance requirements for each signaling function.

Functional Requirements

ATM is a connection-oriented protocol. A virtual connection (VC) must be established before information transfer can occur. Originally, only a simple point-to-point connection was defined for ATM. Also, the concept of call is not distinguished from a connection. When an ATM call is made, it always refers to a single connection being established. To support residential broadband services, more sophisticated connection types and a generalized call model are required. These are discussed below.

Multi-Party Connection — The ITU-T has defined the following connection types, which are all important for residential broadband services.

Type 1: Bidirectional Point-to-Point — The type 1 connection is a bidirectional point-to-point connection between two parties. Bandwidth is independently specified in each direction. Asymmetric bandwidth can be supported, and unidirectional connection is the special case with zero bandwidth in one direction. Type 1 also specifies that the physical route taken by the connection in each direction must be identical. Type 1 is the fundamental connection type for ATM and, obviously, must be supported for residential broadband services.

Type 2: Unidirectional Point-to-Multipoint — The type 2 connection is a point-to-multipoint connection that involves three or more parties,

one of which is the root. This is a unidirectional connection for which the root is the only source, and multicasts its information over the type 2 connection to all the other parties of the connection (called leaves). The root is responsible for adding and dropping parties. The leaf parties can also drop from such a connection independently. It is up to the root to specify during the connection setup time whether it allows independent add from leaf parties (known as leaf initiated join), and whether the root should be notified of such actions. The type 2 connection is required to support multicast services, such as broadcast TV. The leaf initiated join mode allows viewers to independently join a particular TV channel multicast (i.e., tune to that channel).

Type 3: Unidirectional Multipoint-to-Point — The type 3 connection is a unidirectional connection between three or more parties with multiple sources and a single destination. This has the same logical configuration as type 2 connection, except the information flow is reversed, from the leaves back to the root.

Since the cells from different sources (leaves) arrive at the destination (root) carrying the same VPI/VCI, the root cannot reassemble the AAL PDU because the root will receive interleaved cells from different leaves. This cell interleaving problem is the main challenge for designing the signaling protocols to support the type 3 connection. There are two special cases, however, for which interleaving is not a problem; the first exception is when AAL 3/4 is used (which has MID field for demultiplexing), and the second is if only single cell messages are sent.

The type 3 connection is important for a number of residential broadband applications. One application is advertisement insertion. This requires merging of multiple ads (video clips) from potentially different servers. It is very useful to have a multipoint-to-point connection from all these servers to each viewer. The reason is that at any one instant, there is only one advertisement playing from the viewer's point-of-view, so the type 3 connection is the most efficient connection type for this application. Otherwise, if a separate point-to-point connection is set up from each server to the viewers, at any one time, only one of the connections is active and the rest are wasted.

Type 4: Bidirectional Multipoint-to-Multipoint — Type 4 is the bidirectional multipoint-to-multipoint connection that allows three or more parties to communicate with each other. The information sent by any party will be received by all other parties. This connection type faces the same challenge of cell interleaving as the type 3 connection, and hence can be solved similarly. The type 4 connection is important for supporting group communication, such as multi-user games and multiparty video calls.

Multiconnection Call — Originally, the concept of an ATM call was the same as that of an ATM connection [14]. Recently, ITU-T has extended the model of an ATM call such that a call can include multiple connections or even no connection [22]. As such, the concept of connections remains as before (i.e., a virtual connection). But a call between two users becomes an association that describes a set of connections between them. Of course, this can be easily extended to three or more users to become a multiparty/multiconnection call. Also, there can be multiple calls between two users.

By extending the call between two users to support multiple connections, multimedia applications can be supported more effectively. Since each media type of a multimedia communication application has its own communications requirements (bandwidth and QoS), it is desirable to carry each media type over a separate VC that satisfies its corresponding communications requirements. In addition, since these different connections belong to the same application, by defining a call that encompasses all these connections, management of this communication is simplified significantly. All these connections can be set up and torn down in parallel. Hence, this also results in performance improvements.

Since the call concept can also include multiple parties (three or more), it can support a very rich and flexible application paradigm. This is important for residential broadband service because many applications running on the set-top box require communication with multiple servers in the headend or central office. For example, it might be desirable to manage the collection of all connections that are set up as part of a particular application running on a set-top box. In this case, we can setup a call that includes all of these connections, and which may connect to more than one server at the headend or central office. In the telco environment, such a call can be billed to the service provider of that application, which in turn bills the subscriber of that set-top box for the application.

The concept of a call without a connection is also very useful. When a user makes a call to another user, it may or may not include a connection setup request. A user can set up a call without any connection. This is desirable because it allows prenegotiation of endpoint resources and determination of each other's capabilities without actually setting up the connection. Otherwise, if a connection setup is issued first, network resources could be held up temporarily, and the user could later discover that such a call cannot be completed because endpoint capabilities do not match, even though network resources are available.

Another advance feature supported by the multiconnection call model is the Common Routing Group (CRG) capability. The CRG capability is very important for routing multimedia calls, because different media types that are carried on different connections of the same call may need to be synchronized. For example, the audio and video portion of a movie must be synchronized. By assigning these related connections to the same CRG, they will be routed through the same physical path to minimize the differential cell transfer delay between them.

ATM Call versus DSM-CC Session — Recently, the MPEG standard committee began developing the digital stored media command and control (DSM-CC) protocol that supports a concept called the session. The goal of the DSM-CC session is to allow resource allocation across a het-erogeneous network architecture, especially one that includes a networking technology that does not support QoS and bandwidth allocation such as the MPEG-2-to-the-home architecture. The session concept attempts to define a higher layer association of resources across multiple networks. Although this solves the general problem of such heterogeneous networks such as MPEG-2-to-the-home, such a session concept is redundant in the case of a pure ATM network such as the ATTH architecture. The reason is that the ATM call model discussed above is already a superset of the functions provided by the DSM-CC concept. Furthermore, if the DSM-CC session is implemented over the ATTH architecture, a performance degradation will result because every connection setup has to go through the centralized DSM-CC controller that operates at a higher layer, external to the ATM network. On the other hand, the ATM call model operates at the same layer as the ATM switch call controller's connection establishment layer. Hence, the performance (call and connection setup time) is comparable to the simple connection setup time.

Performance Requirements

To support interactive services, there is a tight delay requirement on the end-to-end (between servers and set-top boxes) connection setup time. For viewers to perceive their actions as interactive, the response time (from the instant the viewer presses the remote to the appearance of the results on the screen) should be on the order of 100 ms. In a fully distributed operating system environment, many connections can be set up and torn down simultaneously to satisfy a user action on the screen (such as pressing a series of buttons). In general, a 10 ms end-to-end call setup time is required for a connection within the residential broadband network (within about 200 miles) across less than five ATM switches. From a call throughput point of view, about 300 calls per second should be achieved on a per OC-3c switch port basis. This assumes a conservative scenario with 30 set-top boxes sharing an OC-3c port through the access network, each requiring about a ten call/second peak calling rate.

Conclusion

*I*t has become clear that the VOD application by itself cannot justify the billions of dollars of investment in various residential broadband networks being deployed worldwide. To achieve the grand vision of the residential broadband market, thousands of applications must be enabled on these networks. Instead of constantly searching for the single killer application through market studies and speculative guesses, the best insurance policy is to build a platform of thousands of applications such that, collectively, these applications all become killer applications. This article presents a vision of a residential broadband network architecture based on an ATM-to-the-home architecture, which is not only the best technical solution available, but also the best strategic solution for deploying residential broadband services. It proposes a uni-

For viewers to perceive their actions as interactive, the response time (from the instant the viewer presses the remote to the appearance of the results on the screen) should be on the order of 100 ms.

versal residential model based on ATTH that allows content and applications be developed with the same abstraction. Finally, it discusses the signaling requirements that are critical to enable the vision of thousands of residential broadband services and applications.

References

[l] Electronic Industries Association.
[2] "Are PCs too powerful?" *Information Week*, Apr. 3, 1995.
[3] Jupiter 1995 Consumer On-line Services Report.
[4] T. Kwok, ATM: private, public and residential broadband networks, (Prentice Hall, to be published).
[5] T. Kwok, "Communications Requirements of Multimedia Applications: A preliminary study," *Proc. Int'l Conf. on Selected Topics in Wireless Commun.*, Vancouver, 1992, pp. 138-142.
[6] T. Little and A. Ghafoor, "Network Considerations for Distributed Multimedia Object Composition and Communication," *IEEE Network*, vol. 4, no. 4, Nov. 1990, pp. 32-49.
[7] T. Kwok, "Tandem Banyan Switching Fabric: A New High Performance Fast Packet Switch and its Performance Evaluation," Ph.D Dissertation, Stanford University, 1990.
[8] G. Wallace, "The JPEG still picture compression standard," *Commun. of the ACM*, vol. 34, no. 4, April 1991, pp. 30-44.
[9] T. Kwok, "Broadband ISDN to support Multimedia and Collaborative applications," *Proc. IEEE Compcon '92*, Feb. 1992, pp. 21-24.
[10] T. Kwok, " A Vision for Residential Broadband Services: ATM-to-the-home," *Proc. on Nara Int'l Symposium on Emerging Multimedia Community through ATM Networking*, Nara, Japan, May 24-26, 1995.
[11] J. Chiddix, J. Vaughan, and R. Wolfe, "The Use of Fiber Optics in Cable Communication Networks," *IEEE J. of Lightwave Technologies*, vol. 11, no. 1, Jan. 1993, pp. 154-166.
[12] T. Kwok, "A Vision for Residential Broadband Services: ATM-to-the-home," *Proc. IEEE Int'l Workshop on Community Networking '95*, Princeton, New Jersey, June 20-22, 1995.
[13] T. Kwok, "End-to-End Requirements for Supporting MPEG 2 over ATM Networks," ATM Forum Contribution 94-1109R2, Kyoto, Japan, Nov., 1994.
[14] The ATM Forum Technical Committee, User-Network Interface (UNI) Specification Version 3.1, Sept. 1994.
[15] J. R. Jones, "Baseband and Passband Transport Systems for Interactive Video Services," *IEEE Commun. Mag.*, vol. 32, no. 5, May 1994, pp. 90-101.
[16] B. Bauer, "Drop system and Component Performance: Emerging Requirements in a high bandwidth 64 QAM digital world," NCTA Technical Papers, 1993, pp. 244-270.
[17] R. Cita and R. Lee, "Practical Implementation of a 43 Mbit/sec (8bit/Hz) digital modem for cable television," NCTA Technical Papers, 1993, pp. 271-279.
[18] Y. Mochida, "Technologies for Local Access Fibering," *IEEE Commun. Mag.*, vol. 32, no. 2, Feb. 1994, pp. 64-73.
[19] T. Miki, "Toward the Service-Rich Era," *IEEE Commun. Mag.*, vol. 32, no. 2, Feb., 1994, pp. 34-39.
[20] W. Weippert, "The Evolution of the Access Network in Germany," *IEEE Commun. Mag.*, vol. 32, no. 2, Feb. 1994, pp. 50-55.
[21] P. Kyees, R. McConnell, and K. Sistanizadeh, "ADSL: A New Twisted-Pair Access to the Information Highway," *IEEE Commun. Mag.*, vol. 33, no. 4, April, 1995.
[22] ITU-T Draft Recommendation Q.298x.

Biography

TIM KWOK is the chief ATM architect for Microsoft, where he is responsible for developing Microsoft's ATM strategy. He architected Microsoft's ATM-to-the-Home vision to support the residential broadband services. This architecture is being deployed in Seattle, Richardson, and Japan for HFC, FTTC, and FTTH networks, respectively. Before the formation of the ATM Forum in 1991, he was instrumental in organizing the LATM group among Apple, Sun, Bellcore and Xerox PARC to pioneer ATM for LANs (while at Apple), and co-authored the landmark document "Network Compatible Local ATM" which became the basis of the first ATM Forum Specification (2.0). He has been the principal representative to the ATM Forum since its inception, actively particpating in its technical committee. He proposed the support of a new class of service (UBR) for LAN traffic in 1992, in addition to CBR or VBR. In 1995, he was elected to the Board of Directors of the ATM Forum and also serves as vice-president of Business Development Strategies. He was invited by Prentice Hall to author *ATM: Private, Public and Residential Broadband Networks*. He received a Ph.D. from Stanford University in 1990, for his invention of a high-performance ATM switch architecture. His e-mail address is: timkwok@microsoft.com.

Computer Networks and ISDN Systems 26 (1994) 1409–1424

COMPUTER
NETWORKS
and
ISDN SYSTEMS

ELSEVIER

Connectionless data service in an ATM-based customer premises network

Jean-Yves Le Boudec [a], Andreas Meier [a,*], Rainer Oechsle [b,†], Hong Linh Truong [a]

[a] *IBM Research Division, Zurich Research Laboratory, Säumerstrasse 4, CH-8803 Rüschlikon, Switzerland*
[b] *IBM European Networking Center, Vangerowstraße 18, D-69115 Heidelberg, Germany*

Accepted 27 July 1994

Abstract

We give an overview of methods that provide connectionless data service in a customer premises network based on ATM switches and ATM links. Under the assumption that a prospective user already has software for accessing a LAN in the usual connectionless mode, a connectionless data service is presented here which emulates traditional LAN access services. Several different methods are discussed.

Key words: ATM; Connectionless service

1. Introduction

The asynchronous transfer mode (ATM) was first introduced as a concept for public networks [1], but it is also becoming the target technology for many customer premises networks (CPNs) [2]. Most data traffic in existing CPNs is sent over local area networks (LANs), such as Token Rings and Ethernets; access to these networks is *connectionless*. However, ATM networks are inherently connection-oriented. Most networks which provide connection-oriented data services offer a connectionless data service as well. The latter requires a much simpler interaction between the

user of the service and the network to send messages to a peer. If the extensive existing software base is going to be reused in an ATM-based CPN, it is necessary to provide some software interface that emulates connectionless access. A number of methods have been suggested for providing this connectionless data service. The best known is the "B-ISDN connectionless data service" [3], which was originally designed for public service, but is suitable for the CPN as well. Other less known methods use radically different approaches [4]. This paper presents an overview of these methods and gives references for various techniques which provide connectionless data service in a CPN which is based on ATM switches.

1.1. ATM switch-based CPN

Our model is a customer premises network built on ATM switches and point-to-point links. Such a network is an alternative for shared-

---

† Also at: nowat Fachhochschule Rheinland–Pfalz, Abteilung Trier, Angewandte Informatik, Postfach 1826, D-54208 Trier, Germany.
* Corresponding author.

0169-7552/94/$07.00 © 1994 Elsevier Science B.V. All rights reserved
SSDI 0169-7552(93)E0056-K

medium LANs and WANs such as those discussed in Refs. [5–10]. An advantage of a network made of switches and point-to-point links is its aggregate bandwidth, which is considerably higher than the individual link bandwidths. But, some features that are inherently available in shared-medium networks require more elaborate solutions in switched networks. These features include, for example, broadcast, support for bursty sources, and provision of a connectionless data service. This paper does not evaluate the alternatives; rather, the goal is to review solutions for providing connectionless data service in a network with ATM switches and ATM point-to-point links.

1.2. What is connectionless data service?

The connectionless data service provided by our ATM CPN model emulates a LAN service. This allows a system connected to an ATM network to use its attachment as if it were connected to a LAN. But, in addition, it can access the native ATM services such as circuit transport or ATM connections.

Users of the connectionless data service are assumed in this paper to be identified by a unique identifier which has the format of a locally administered MAC address. This assumption is not essential to the schemes described below, but does facilitate their description. The connectionless data service allows the user to send and receive units of information (called hereafter *connectionless messages*) to and from other individual users of the service, and also to broadcast connectionless messages to all other users on the ATM network. For that purpose, a broadcast

MAC address is reserved. In addition to the strict emulation of a LAN service, it is also interesting to emulate directly such services as IEEE 802.2 logical link control (LLC), Sockets or OSI/TP4. This is not developed further in this overview.

The existence of a connectionless data service does not necessarily imply that the network operates in a connectionless mode, although that is usually the case. The same remark holds for the use of the broadcast MAC address. In most cases, LAN users send data to the broadcast MAC address in order to perform some *LAN signalling* function, such as translation of a higher layer address (e.g., an IP address, or a NetBIOS name) into an individual MAC address. The network may handle such frames directly without broadcasting them, using, for instance, directory service databases.

Of course, the connectionless data service co-exists with other, connection-oriented services. Also, users of the ATM connectionless data service can communicate with LAN users by means of bridges or routers. In that respect, the ATM CPN appears as one LAN. This aspect deserves to be discussed in a dedicated paper.

1.3. Connectionless data service in an ATM context

ATM is connection-oriented. It uses label addressing and requires a setup of the virtual path and virtual connection identifier (VPI/VCI) tables in switches before communication can occur. Typically, ATM connections are also associated with some form of bandwidth reservation, although ATM connections without bandwidth reservation are conceivable [11]. In addition, the label (VPI/VCI) used in ATM cell headers is

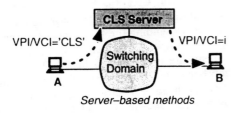

Server–based methods

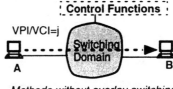

Methods without overlay switching

Fig. 1. Methods for supporting connectionless data service.

only 3 bytes long at the user–network interface, which makes it impossible to be used as a global destination identifier, at least in large networks. Therefore a direct, straightforward use of ATM is not possible, and more elaborate solutions are needed. In this paper, we list and classify the methods known to us.

These methods use a common set of functions in order to send and receive messages using ATM cells. The set of functions mainly include segmentation, reassembly and encapsulation. They are described in Section 2. Although alternatives for each of these do exist, the methods are essentially independent of the realization of the common functions.

In contrast, the methods for routing connectionless messages differ profoundly. There are two families of methods (Fig. 1):

• *Server-based methods*: these methods rely on an overlay network with non-ATM switching to transfer connectionless messages. This network consists of relays which are usually called *connectionless servers* and their interconnections. The ATM header (and in particular the label VPI/VCI) is used only to provide access to the connectionless servers, regardless of the addressing information contained in the message. Methods in this family vary in the nature of addressing information used by the servers to route the messages to the destination.

• *Methods without an overlay network*: these methods rely entirely on the ATM switches to transfer messages. Within this family, methods diverge in the way the VPI/VCI labels are handled by the network for routing the cells to the destination.

In the following we describe first the set of functions that are common to both families. Then each of the families is presented in a section of its own. Flow control aspects are gathered in Section 6.

2. ATM adaptation layer

Connectionless messages usually do not fit in one ATM cell, and have to be segmented. Segmentation and reassembly are specified in the CCITT *ATM Adaptation Layer* (AAL) [12]. Two competing solutions are being examined by CCITT: AAL 3/4 and AAL 5.

With both schemes, a message of any length is padded to match an integer number of cells and then segmented. The schemes differ in their error protection mechanism, in embedding control information, and how they support multiplexing. With AAL 3/4 [12], every segment carries a 10-bit *cyclic redundancy check* (CRC) that is checked before the entire message is reassembled (a wrong CRC causes the message to be aborted at the receiving or relaying point). Message integrity is further supported by a sequence number in every segment and a global message length in the last segment. AAL 3/4 allows the transmission of several messages interleaved on one ATM connection, by using the 10-bit *Message Identification* (MID) field. The different segments in one message have the same unique MID, and this MID cannot be used by other messages being sent concurrently on the same ATM connection (e.g., using the same VPI/VCI value). However the MID can be reused by subsequent messages, independent of whether the different messages are bound to the same destination. The MID is thus a local, temporary multiplexing assist, that is used solely for *gluing* the different segments of a message together. Message delineation is performed with the segment type field. The payload available per segment is 44 bytes (out of a 53-byte cell).

AAL 5 [13] attempts to relieve the large overhead of AAL3/4. It was originally designed to work without message interleaving, and thus saves the MID and associated fields. It also does away with the per-segment CRC and segment number, leaving the frame integrity function to a global, more powerful CRC (32 bits), and the message length in the last segment. Message delineation is provided by sending the last segment of the message as a *type 1* cell payload, whereas other segments are *type 0* cell payloads. The differentiation between the two types is supported by the ATM cell header. The overhead is reduced and leaves a full 48-byte payload for every segment except the last one. AAL 5 does not directly support message interleaving.

Unless otherwise stated, the connectionless data service is assumed hereafter to use AAL 3/4 or AAL 5 indiscriminantly.

2.1. AAL connections associated with ATM virtual path connections

With some of the methods described below, access to the connectionless service is supported by the use of a virtual path connection (VPC), over which all connectionless traffic is sent and received. The VPC is identified by a well-known VPI called 'CLS' in this paper. In such a case, the VCI is used as a multiplexing identifier to re-assemble interleaved messages sent over the VPC. There is not a connection for each active VCI within the VPC used for accessing the service (VPI = 'CLS'). Instead, there is one connection for the entire VPC. Thus, a reassembly machine is allocated to a given VCI only as long as a connectionless message is being reassembled with this VCI and released either at the end of the message or after a timeout due to the loss of the last cell. The number of active VCIs used at one station can be much larger than the number of messages it can reassemble concurrently.

2.2. Encapsulation and addressing

The CCITT connectionless data service assumes an ad-hoc network layer addressing using ISDN numbers (E.164 addresses) [3]. In the CPN, MAC addresses are used instead, as described earlier. If the connectionless data service also supports several message types (such as IP frames without MAC addresses), then some encapsulation information is needed before passing the message to the AAL. This can be done with a sub-network access point (SNAP) header as in the case of Frame Relay [14], or as in Ref. [3] with a protocol type identifier. This applies to all methods below.

3. Server-based methods

We describe in this section the methods based on an overlay network, or *servers*. All such methods have in common that the ATM is used merely to provide access to the servers. The servers are attached to switches as any terminal would be and they are accessed via ATM connections (see Fig. 1). Every user of the connectionless service

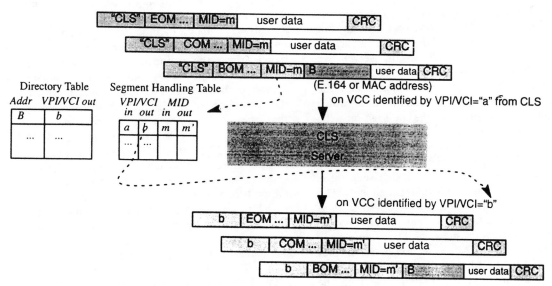

Fig. 2. Connectionless server operation for B-ISDN or SMDS (cut-through mode).

needs at least an ATM connection to the server, and there are ATM connections between servers.

3.1. Method of B-ISDN connectionless service and SMDS

We first consider the method used for the B-ISDN connectionless service and the switched multi-megabit data service (SMDS). Specifications of these two services have many similarities [3,15]; neither specifies how a network operates internally in order to provide the service. A description of possible operation is given in Ref. [16].

For the connectionless data transfer one or several ISDN numbers are allocated to each user of the B-ISDN or SMDS service. When a connectionless message is passed to the service, the destination and source E.164 addresses are added. Then the message is segmented; AAL 3/4 is used (AAL 5 is not excluded by CCITT but is not specified). The resulting cells are sent by the user over its well-known, pre-defined ATM connection to the server. The cells are transferred by the ATM switches to the server, with no processing of the cell payload, as is normal operation for ATM switches.

The server receives the cell payload with the indication of the ATM connection on which they arrived. The addressing information is always contained in the first cell, so the server can analyze it before receiving the entire message. The destination address (and possibly also the source address) is used to determine on which outgoing ATM connection the message must be sent next. For this routing decision, the structuring of the E.164 address is used. This is illustrated in Fig. 2 by the *Directory Table*.

In the *cut-through* mode, the first segment is sent on the outgoing connection immediately. The routing decision is stored (in the *Segment Handling Table* in the figure) and applied to all subsequent segments of the message. The segments are identified by the ATM connection on which they arrive and by the MID in the AAL 3/4 payload. The server interleaves several messages on the same outgoing ATM connection, and must then select a unique MID for every message, which is

also stored. When the last segment is received, or after a timeout if losses occurred, the routing decision and the outgoing MID are deleted. At the destination, messages are reassembled using the MID to distinguish segments of interleaved messages.

In a low-performance variant, the server reassembles entire messages before sending them out, thus eliminating the need for MID handling.

The main features of the methods are thus:
- routing of connectionless messages is performed by an overlay network of servers,
- determination of the outgoing connection is performed in every server on a message-by-message basis, using a mapping function from the address in the message to an outgoing ATM connection.

The method can be applied as such to the CPN, using E.164 addresses or not. Using E.164 addresses is not very appealing, given the large variety of addresses already in use. MAC addresses can be used, but then the route decision function performed in every server becomes complex unless the MAC address is structured. However, structuring the MAC removes some ease of use, in that the address of a terminal becomes dependent on the switching equipment to which it is connected.

This server-based method has the advantage of putting no specific requirement on the ATM switch, since the connectionless server can be developed independently and uses any standard access to the switch. The main concern with a direct application of the method to the CPN is that the performance and low cost of ATM switching is not fully utilized. Consider an ATM switch with 32 ports at 150 Mb/s; it is likely to cost no more than an equivalent FDDI concentrator [2], and has a total aggregate bit rate of 4.8 Gb/s. If one connectionless server is used on the switch to provide the connectionless data service, then it is not likely to approach such capabilities.

3.2. Servers with dynamic access

With the previous method, every terminal has a fixed ATM connection to a server. As a slight variation, it is possible to allow switched, dynamic access to one or more servers. An access procedure is then needed to connect the user dynamically to one server, which is triggered by the need to forward a connectionless message of a given type. As an application, this can be used to place protocol-dependent servers in various locations in the network: a user with IP communication needs to connect to one server performing IP routing, while a user with NetBIOS would connect to a 'MAC router' (as in the previous section). As another application, this allows load sharing based on the geographical position of the source or on the actual load on the servers. In all cases, some form of signalling is needed between user and network.

3.3. Source routing method

This method [17] is a variant that simplifies the server processing and allows more efficient server placement, as explained below. The source includes routing information in the message. Source routing is the basis of the high-speed network routing technique in Ref. [18], there called *Auto-matic Network Routing* (ANR). Here, it works as follows.

Every connectionless server has connections to the users it serves on one switch, and connections to other servers on other switches. Every such connection is identified at the connectionless server by a one-byte logical label, the *ANR label*. ANR labels have no global significance; they are meaningful for only one server. The server maintains a table that maps ANR labels to ATM connection identifications (VPI/VCIs). Such a table is relatively static, changing only as users move or as the network is reconfigured. Before sending a message to a destination, a source user must acquire knowledge of a route to that destination. A route is described first by a VPI/VCI identifying a connection that leads to a connectionless server, then by an *ANR field*, made up of a sequence of ANR labels that will be used by the servers. Consider Fig. 3. The route from the terminal on the left to the one on the right is made first of the VPI/VCI '*a*' that is used to reach the first connectionless server, then the ANR field '*e1 e2 e3*'. At the first connectionless

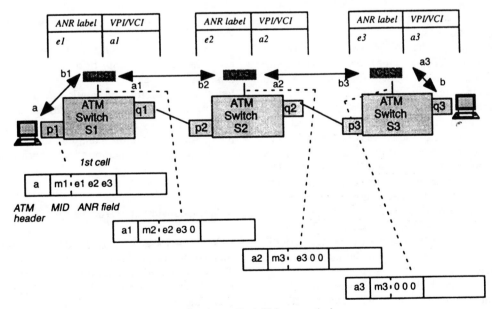

Fig. 3. Source routing method. CLS: connectionless server.

server, the first label ('*e1*') is used to determine the outgoing connection (in our example '*a1*'), the label is removed from the ANR field, and the cells are passed to the next connectionless server. The ANR field is padded in order to keep the length constant. As with the "B-ISDN or SMDS method", only the first segment in a message contains the routing information, and message interleaving can be performed with the MID function of AAL 3/4. Up to 250 connections may exist per server, and routes up to more than 40 hops can be defined.

The main issue is how sources determine the route. A route discovery procedure similar to that of the Token Ring can be used [19]. Sources send "route discovery" messages to discover a route to a destination. Route discovery messages are sent first to the serving server. This server then broadcasts them to all connectionless users it serves and to all other connectionless servers in the network, which in turn also broadcast them to their users. In relaying the route discovery messages, the servers accumulate the reverse route information, which is used by the destination to respond directly to the source, which is now informed of the route. The 'all route broadcast' method of the Token Ring is difficult to support, because the mechanisms for avoiding message looping do not fit well.

Alternatively, the ATM switches can also broadcast the ATM cells locally and provide some identification of the source port to assist the destination in reassembling the frame. In all cases, the connectionless servers maintain a spanning tree which they use to support broadcasting.

An alternative to the route determination procedure is to use a routing database, which is replicated in all switch control points [17]. The replicated databases contain access information (e.g., the MAC addresses present on the access ports) and network information (the global topology of connections between servers). The separate parts of the database must exchange periodic updates or confirmations, but the interval can be relatively long.

With this method, several servers can be used in parallel, since the first server can be selected as part of the route. A single source can thus use several servers for communication with different partners. It is thus possible to mitigate the performance drawback of the server-based method in that one server can be associated with every trunk. If ATM switch ports are a key resource, the server may even be integrated in the trunk adapter. With such a scenario, it is possible to approach the total switch bit rate for connectionless data services, a rate unattainable with the previous method.

3.4. Partial source routing method

A variant of the source routing method is described in Ref. [17]. It relieves the sources of the need to know about the network operating conditions for route discovery. For that purpose, the routing information consists of the identity of an ATM connection between the source and a server, the identity of a server connected to the destination, and the identity of an ATM connection between that destination server and the destination. The route between source and destination servers is not contained in the routing information; it is left to the servers to route messages from one server to another, as in an IP network. Route discovery by sources can be implemented again with broadcast discovery or directory services [20].

Compared to the full source routing method, this scheme allows more flexibility as it does not limit the number of hops due to the bounded length of the routing information field. Moreover, routing databases (if implemented) are simpler as they contain only local information. On the other hand, servers are more complex. Like the previous method, this one allows load sharing among servers.

4. Methods without overlay network

We now look at entirely different approaches that do not employ connectionless servers at all. The server-based methods described above merely provide access to an overlay network. However, there are reasons for providing the connectionless data service directly by the network of ATM switches, because in the CPN the setting is different than in public networks. Firstly, the number of addressable entities is considerably smaller. Therefore it is possible to use very short addresses (up to 3 bytes) to identify the various CPN equipment. This is done for instance in the switch-based CPN of Ref. [21], though in a non-ATM context. Such very short addresses can be carried in the ATM cell header. Secondly, cost and management issues are very critical, as the ATM technology is competing with a number of alternatives such as FDDI and its successors. Therefore, an integrated solution that avoids two sets of networking devices has definite advantages. Thirdly, the volume of connectionless traffic in the CPN is apt to be quite large and so it is important to dimension the components properly. If all the connectionless traffic flows cell-by-cell through a single connectionless server and twice through the switch, this dimensioning might be more difficult. Therefore approaches that avoid

points of congestion might prove to be more effective.

4.1. Direct ATM connectionless methods

We first begin with approaches where very short destination addresses are carried in the ATM cell header. Such a scheme is proposed in Ref. [22,23] where it is called "direct ATM" connectionless data service; a variant of which is described in Ref. [24]. To distinguish the two variants, we call the first one "direct ATM connectionless data service *with MID swapping on trunks*" and the second one "direct ATM connectionless data service *with VPC support*". We will summarize them both now.

Every cell has a self-contained destination address (called "domain address"), and is switched on this basis only. Within one domain, a user of the direct ATM connectionless service is uniquely identified by one domain address. A domain is an

Direct Connectionless with MID Swapping on Trunks

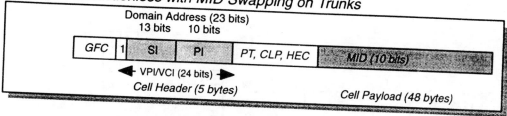

Direct Connectionless with VPC Support

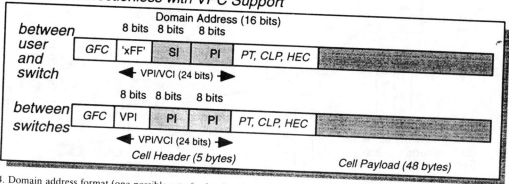

Fig. 4. Domain address format (one possible set of values) and cell format. The MID is present in the first case because AAL 3/4 is mandatory there. For the last cell format ("between switches"), the user–network interface (UNI) format of CCITT is assumed. If the network–network interface (NNI) format is used between switches in the CPN, then the generic flow control (GFC) field disappears and the VPI field is extended to 12 bits.

addressing space, i.e., either the entire CPN or part of it. The domain address is structured in two parts, one for the switch identifier (SI), the other for the port identifier (PI), as illustrated in Fig 4. It is used by ATM switches to route the cells. The management of the domain address values is performed within one domain by a directory service. Domain addresses are associated with switch ports, i.e., they correspond to physical locations. In contrast, other addresses such as MAC or IP addresses, SNA or NetBIOS names are associated with the system connected to the port or with applications running on this system, respectively.

4.1.1. Direct connectionless service with MID swapping on trunks

A connectionless message is placed into one or more ATM cells by the source AAL entity (AAL 3/4, as explained below). These cells are marked as connectionless cells. This is done for example by setting the first meaningful bit in the VPI/VCI to 1. The marking is used by the ATM switch to interpret the value in the VPI/VCI field as a

destination domain address. The value of the VPI/VCI field for the outgoing cell is unchanged, except on the switch that serves the destination, where it is set to the local input port value (Fig. 5). The reason for that is explained below. The switching operation is identical to the operation performed by an ATM node for a conventional ATM connection. This is why the method described here can be called "connectionless use of VPI/VCIs". The ATM switch may or may not use separate tables for both types of ATM cells. Implementations that take advantage of the structuring of the domain address in SI and PI reduce the size of swapping tables.

To use the direct ATM connectionless service, a user first needs to acquire a domain address. It can do so by registering with network control when it is activated; it can use the registration procedures already required for ISDN terminals [25]. The activation phase starts by establishing a point-to-point and selective broadcast signalling connection to the ATM network control. A user of the connectionless service uses this signalling connection to inform the directory service in the

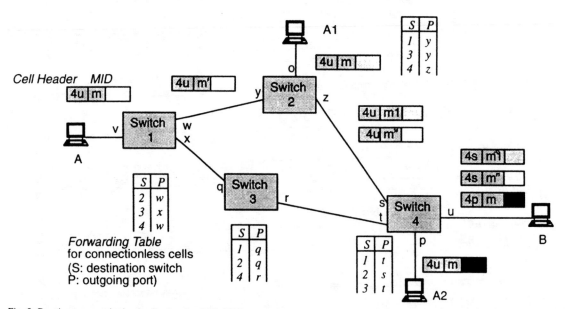

Fig. 5. Routing 'connectionless' cells showing VPI/VCI translation with the "direct connectionless service with MID swapping on trunks" method. *4u, 4s, 4p* are domain addresses, with switch identification equal to 4 and port identification equal to *u, s* or *p*. The figure shows cells sent by terminals *A, A1* and *A2* to terminal *B*.

network of its location and of the addresses it responds to, typically a MAC address. The directory service responds to the user with a domain address. Similarly, users become aware of target destination domain addresses by querying the directory service [22].

Destinations receive messages as sequences of possibly interleaved cells, since several sources may send to the same destination at the same time. The ATM header in the received cells carries the domain address of the local switch port on which they were sent. However, cells from various sources that arrive on the same input trunk will be received with the same VPI/VCI (in Fig. 5, cells from *A* and *A1* arrive at *B* with same VPI/VCI). Source identification is thus available only after a message has been reassembled.

For this method AAL 3/4 is well suited, since it allows message interleaving using MID. Every source generates an MID for every message. Sources that do not interleave messages can use any fixed value, the MID being unambiguous only on the source access link (thus for one domain address). The trunk adapters swap the MID field (in the cell payload) in order to guarantee frame integrity (in Fig. 5, trunk adapter *z* at switch 2

replaces MIDs *m* and *m'* by *m1* and *m''*). This is done on the fly, without reassembling the messages [16]. For both the user and the ATM switch only local information is used, and there is no need for a global management of the MID values. At the destination, messages are reassembled using both the VPI/VCI and the MID values as discriminators in the reassembly machine. Broadcasting is supported, assuming that the cell duplication is performed by the ATM switches.

Communication with users outside the domain and served by a B-ISDN connectionless service is provided by at least one access to the connectionless service for the entire CPN. Connectionless servers (possibly in the public domain) appear as a specific connectionless service user in the CPN. When the destinations are outside the CPN, the address resolution procedure returns the domain address of the connectionless server. Conversely, the connectionless server sends traffic to a CPN destination B using the VPI/VCI '*b*' where *b* is the domain address of B. The connectionless server need not be aware that a direct ATM connectionless service exists in the CPN, since the connectionless interpretation of VPI/VCIs is a matter for the CPN switches only. The only requirement is that the CPN can impose some

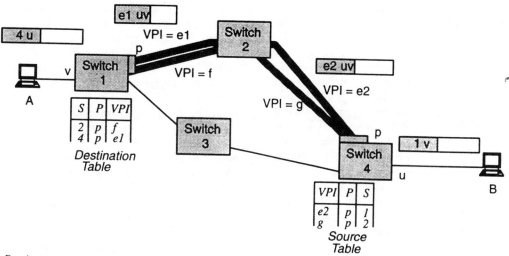

Fig. 6. Routing 'connectionless' cells showing VPI/VCI translation with the "direct connectionless data service with VPC support" method. The predefined VPI value (all 1s) is not shown at the access.

VPI/VCI values for the connection to the server. The same applies for communication between CPNs [4].

Note that the swapping of MIDs puts some adaptation layer functions into trunk adapters and increases memory requirements for swapping tables. This is avoided by the next method.

4.1.1. Direct connectionless service with VPC support

This alternative [24] allows sources to use either AAL 3/4 or AAL 5. If AAL 3/4 is used, then sources employ MIDs independently of each other while avoiding MID swapping. We will now describe this briefly.

As with the previous method, if both source and destination are on the same switch, then the value in the VPI/VCI field on the destination port contains the source domain address. The essence of the method is to use VPCs in order to extend that property to an entire domain. VPCs [16] differ from virtual channel connections in that part of the address in the cell header (the VCI) that is carried transparently. All switches are connected by means of VPCs in a full mesh. The VCI field is used to carry the PIs of both the source and the destination. Between user and switches, the VPI value in connectionless cells assumes a predefined value (all 1s, or 'xFF' for example, see Fig. 4). This is equivalent to establishing a permanent VPC between user and switch, reserved for this service ('access VPC'). The source switch terminates the access VPC and forwards cells to either the destination port (if it is on the same switch) or to the appropriate VPC to the destination switch (see Fig. 6). Between switches, the cells are switched as part of VPCs, and these VPCs are not different from any other VPC (used for services other than this connectionless data service). The same switches may be designed to perform both virtual channel switching and virtual path switching. In essence, the method can be viewed as providing a full mesh of predefined ATM connections, with rules for allocating VPI/VCIs based on a port and switch numbering plan.

At the destination switch, the VPC on which cells arrive is used to identify the source switch.

The resulting source domain address is put by the destination switch on the cells in the cell header before transmitting to the ultimate destination. At the destination the message is reassembled on the basis of the ATM cell header and possibly MID if AAL 3/4 is used. One global reassembly machine is needed, and there is no need for previous association of source and destination for that purpose, as explained above in Section 2. Broadcast is supported by having the access switch broadcasting cells to all ports, including to the inter-switch VPCs.

Compared to the previous one, this method puts further restrictions on the size of the domain address as illustrated in Fig. 4. It applies to smaller domains (250 ports per switch and 250 switches).

4.2. Connection-based methods

4.2.1. Emulation method

Bearing in mind that the goal is to provide connectionless *service* it is possible to use ATM virtual channel connections for that purpose. In this case, the connectionless service is provided by a convergence function that accepts connectionless messages and passes them to the appropriate ATM connections. The convergence function performs connection setup, maintenance and release as needed [26]. When a connectionless message is received for transmission, it is first checked whether an existing connection to the destination exists, and if not, such a connection is established. This assumes that a connection setup can be performed very quickly in the network.

4.2.2. Partial connection method

With straightforward emulation as described above, the convergence function hides the connection-oriented aspects of ATM to the user software, thus emulating connectionless access. The "partial connection" method goes one step further by relieving the equipment attached to the ATM switch from most of the connection control functions [27,28]. Users of the service implement a very limited set of functions, namely address resolution, cache management, and maintenance of the access to the service. Unlike the emulation method, the user of the service does not have to maintain a connection state machine for each of the partners it communicates with; only address information is stored. All partial connections use at the access the same VPC, identified by VPI ='CLS'. The protocol at the user–network interface (UNI) is illustrated in Fig. 7.

On the network side of the UNI, an *access agent* provides the necessary support. This agent is reachable via a special VCI, for example VCI 0. *SEARCH* messages originated by the user at the source trigger the setup of the partial connections. If a connection already exists between a given user pair, it is reused, even for different protocols. Here too, ATM labels (VPI/VCIs) are used for routing between network ports only, not for multiplexing different protocols. The access agent also monitors the activity of the connections, and releases them if resources are needed.

SEARCH messages are used by the user side to obtain a VCI value which is to be sent to a specific destination. The access agent returns this VCI value in the *FOUND* message.

As can be seen the VCIs are local to the access ports: they help the switches relay the cells to the destination. The meaning of the VCI in the partial connection method is the same as for a virtual channel. As for virtual channel connection, a partial connection is defined between users, but the main difference is that a partial connection terminates in the access switches and not in the end-stations.

Partial connections also vary from conventional virtual channel connections at the adaptation layer. There is not a connection for every active VCI within the VPC used for access (VPI ='CLS'), as explained in Section 2. The number of partial connections used at one station can be

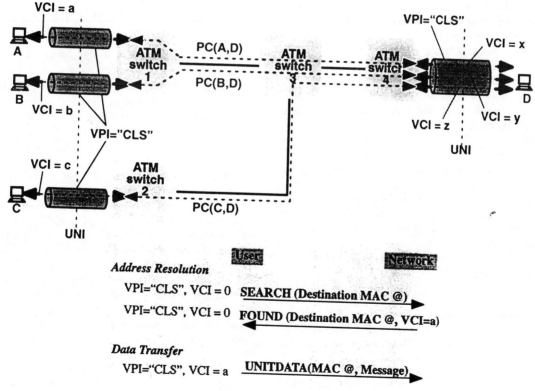

Fig. 7. Partial connection method.

much larger than the number of messages it can reassemble concurrently.

5. Hybrid methods

It can be shown that the protocol at the UNI can be specified in a common way for all methods described thus far. Indeed, the only difference between the methods is how the VPI/VCI value in the header of the ATM cells carrying the connectionless messages are interpreted by the ATM switches. In the server-based methods, they are used by the switches to identify the user–server and server–server connections. In the direct ATM connectionless methods, they contain the short address of the user at the destination. In the partial connection method, they identify the virtual channel connection along which the connectionless cells should be forwarded.

A common UNI could look like the one outlined in Fig. 7. For the address resolution it might also be necessary to have *SEARCH / FOUND* messages in the reverse direction. The *UNIT-DATA* message have to be valid in both directions in any case.

Since a common UNI is feasible, the various methods can be combined. For instance, a direct connectionless method can be used within one switch, while communication between switches requires servers or makes use of the partial connection method.

The evaluation of the benefits of each method is a subject of ongoing research. Criteria that have to be considered are, for example, performance, latency, load distribution, scalability, multicast support, and – of course – cost. A comparison of the approaches should include empirical results obtained from actual implementations, but they are rare.

6. Flow control aspects

6.1. Flow control on ATM connections supporting the connectionless service

A number of flow control problems have to be solved, depending on the method chosen for sup-porting connectionless service. In all methods, ATM connections are used. Therefore an important question is how bandwidth should be allocated to connections, since data traffic is typically very bursty. The problem in a switch-based environment is to meet two conflicting objectives:
1. Allocate to the data traffic as much of the available bandwidth as is reasonably possible. Available bandwidth is either unallocated bandwidth, or is allocated but actually unused.
2. Guarantee quality of service to other types of traffic. In particular, applications that require a fixed bit rate connection should not be disturbed by bursts of data traffic.

A simple way to satisfy objective 2 is to treat data traffic like any other source, and allocate (for instance) a fixed bandwidth to data connections. In general though, this wastes bandwidth, which may be disturbing even in a CPN where bandwidth is expected to be inexpensive. Conversely, peak rate allocation may result in every data connection receiving a fixed but very small bandwidth, not compatible with data application requirements.

If a fixed bandwidth is allocated, then the allocation tends to be inefficient as connectionless traffic is sporadic and highly bursty [29]. This may result in substantial network underutilization, and poor end-to-end performance. An alternative is to allow dynamic bandwidth usage and allocation. We identified three schemes that can be used.

Type 1. ATM connection with no reserved bandwidth and with backpressure: The ATM connections are allocated no bandwidth. The traffic with non-reserved bandwidth is given lowest priority by switches, which requires special buffers [11]. Buffer overflow is prevented by sending backpressure signals (one bit in the GFC field) that stop upstream traffic. This applies exclusively to the traffic with no reserved bandwidth; other traffic is never stopped by this mechanism. This type of mechanism has already been implemented, although not in an ATM context [21]. It offers a behavior similar to single-segment local area networks in that once a cell is accepted for transmission, it cannot be discarded by the network (except in the case of bit errors).

Type 2. ATM connections with feedback loop and excess traffic: This is an alternative method [30] for avoiding congestion that does not guarantee loss-free operation. Frame Relay uses the same basic mechanism. Every data connection is allocated two traffic rates, T_{nom} and T_{max}. The actual rate at which it is allowed to send depends on the feedback it gets from the network. This feedback is implicit, and is carried by means of the congestion experienced bit in the ATM cell header. Traffic in excess of T_{nom} (excess traffic) is marked with low loss priority (CLP bit set) which guarantees that other connection types are not affected. The network guarantees a minimal rate (possibly 0) at which resources are committed. The scheme allows automatic adjustment of traffic to network capacity. The loss priority is used to avoid degradations during the transient periods where congestion occurs but sources have not yet reacted. Unlike the case of Frame Relay, sources implement rate control and the feedback loop in the ATM layer, thus avoiding dependencies on end-to-end protocols.

If a connection sends only excess traffic, then it is possible to send this traffic as non-reserved bandwidth traffic, instead of using the CLP bit, and then to use the feedback mechanism as an alternative to the GFC backpressure protocol mentioned above. In contrast, if both excess and committed traffic are sent over one connection, then the excess traffic has to be sent with the CLP bit set over the same path, because cell sequence has to be guaranteed over an ATM connection.

Type 3. ATM connections with burstiness support and usage monitoring: ATM connections are allocated an amount of bandwidth that takes some allowed burstiness into account. The allocated bandwidth may be different for every link in a network, depending on the link characteristics (bit rate, buffer size) and the existing traffic. The usage of the connection is monitored at the network access point. Changes in the usage trigger a renegotiation of the allocated bandwidth, without involving signalling from the user side.

All three types place different characteristics and requirements on the hardware. Type 1 is simple to implement and has the advantage of loss-free operation. It requires that all switches implement: (i) separate queues for traffic with non-reserved bandwidth and other traffic, and (ii) a backpressure mechanism from the output ports to the input ports. Type 2 requires more complex connection management, and requires switches to handle loss priorities. Type 3 requires more complex functions at the access and interaction with the control plane to renegotiate allocated bandwidth (unlike types 2 and 1), and reacts slowly.

6.2. Application of flow control to the different connectionless methods

For direct ATM connectionless methods only types 1 and 2 are conceivable. An assessment of their respective advantages is a subject of current research.

For the partial connection method, all types are conceivable, although type 3 is probably not well suited because of its complexity and latency. For server-based methods, one should distinguish between access connections (to the servers) and inter-server connections. For access connections, all three types can apply, but types 1 or 2 are probably more appropriate. For inter-server connections, the traffic is probably more stable and types 2 or 3 can be used.

The server-based methods also need to control the flow within the connections to and from the server. Indeed, congestion can occur in servers because of simultaneous transmissions, even though the ATM connections are properly engineered and are not congested. This can be handled by simply discarding arriving messages, relying on end-to-end protocols to trigger a traffic decrease. Additionally, an overlay feedback mechanism can be used, such as the explicit congestion notifications used for Frame Relay. Note that in such a case, sources have to react to congestion indications both from the ATM layer and from connectionless servers.

Lastly, server-based methods need to implement flow control between servers, for instance with alternate routing to avoid focused overloads.

The applicability of various flow control schemes to specific connectionless methods is a subject of ongoing research.

7. Summary

We have presented a catalog of possible methods for providing connectionless data service in a CPN. We have shown that server-based methods are not the only possible methods, in spite of their merits. The direct ATM connectionless and the connection-oriented methods exploit the features of an ATM network to forward the connectionless messages end-to-end within ATM. All methods call for flow control support of ATM connections with bursty data traffic, for which we have presented a number of approaches. This topic needs more research until we can claim to know the solution. Especially the problem of how to estimate the required bandwidth is an interesting field for future activities.

Acknowledgment

This study was conducted in the context of RACE projects R1035 (CPN) and 2068 (LACE) with partial funding by the European Community. Organizations participating in this project are Alcatel SEL (Germany), Ericsson FATME (Italy), FUB (Italy), GMD (Germany), GPT (U.K.), IBM France (France) and the IBM Zurich Research Laboratory (Switzerland), INESC (Portugal), NOKIA (Finland), RNL (The Netherlands), Telenorma (Germany), Telia Research (Sweden), and Thomson (France). The views expressed in this paper represent only those of the authors.

The authors are grateful to Daniel A. Pitt for discussing and influencing some of the ideas described in this paper. Special thanks to all our colleagues at IBM and to the referees for their careful reading of the manuscript and their many constructive comments.

References

[1] CCITT Draft Recommendation I.150, B-ISDN asynchronous transfer mode functional characteristics, CCITT SG XVIII, TD 65, June 1992.

[2] L. Wirbel, ATM becomes part of the LANscape, *Electronic Engineering Times*, July 1992.

[3] CCITT Draft Recommendation I.364, Support of connectionless data services in a B-ISDN, Geneva, June 1992.

[4] J.-Y. Le Boudec, D.A. Pitt and H.L. Truong, A direct ATM connectionless service, IBM Research Report RZ 2259, 1992.

[5] M. Nassehi, Cyclic reservation multiple access, *Proc. 8th EFOC/LAN '90*, Munich, June 27–29, 1990.

[6] H.R. van As and W. Lemppenau, CRMA II: a Gbit/s MAC protocol for ring and bus networks with immediate access capability, *Proc. 9th EFOC/LAN '91*, London, June 19–21, 1991.

[7] P. Heinzmann, H.R. Müller, D.A. Pitt and H.R. Van As, Buffer-insertion cell-synchronized multiple access (BCMA) on a slotted ring, *2nd Int. Conf. on Local Communication Systems: LAN and PBX*, Palma, Spain, June 1991.

[8] I. Cidon and Y. Ofek, Metaring – A full-duplex ring with fairness and spatial reuse, *IEEE IN-FOCOM 90*, San Francisco, CA, June 1990, pp. 969–981.

[9] R.M. Falconer and J.L. Adams, Orwell: A protocol for an integrated services local network, *British Telecom Technol. J.* 3 (4) (1985) 27–35.

[10] K. Imai, T. Honda, H. Kasahara and T. Ito, ATMR: ring architecture for broadband networks, *IEEE GLOBE-COM 90*, San Diego, CA, December 1990, pp. 1734–1738.

[11] J. Cherbonnier and J.Y. Le Boudec, A GFC protocol for congestion avoidance in the ATM connectionless service, *Proc. EFOC/LAN '92*, Paris, France, June 1992, pp. 305–309.

[12] Draft Recommendation I.363, B-ISDN AAL specification, CCITT SG XVIII, June 1992.

[13] ANSI Committee T1 Contribution T1S1.5/91-449, AAL 5–A new high speed data transfer AAL, IBM et al. Dallas, TX, November 1991.

[14] T. Bradley and C. Brown, Multiprotocol interconnect over frame relay, RFC 1294, January 1992.

[15] Generic requirements in support of SMDS, Bellcore TA-TSY 000 772, October 1988.

[16] J.-Y. Le Boudec, The asynchronous transfer mode: A tutorial, *Comput. Networks ISDN Systems*, 24 (4) (1992) 279–309.

[17] J.-Y. Le Boudec, D. Pitt and H. Linh Truong, ATM connectionless service using computer networking methods, *Proc. Int. Conf. on Computer Communication*, Genova, Italy, Sept. 28–Oct. 2, 1992.

[18] I. Cidon and I. Gopal, PARIS: An approach to integrated high-speed private networks, *IJ-DACS* 1 (1988) 77–85.

[19] IEEE Unapproved Draft P802.5P-D2, Route determination entity for LLC, Addition to ISO 8802-2 ANSI/IEEE Std. 802.2, June 1992.

[20] R. Oechsle and H.L. Truong, Shortest path trees bridging for broadband LAN interconnection, *Proc. 10th EFOC/LAN '92*, Paris, France, June 92, pp. 287–292.

[21] M.D. Schroeder et al., Autonet: a high speed, self config-

uring local area network using point to point links, Digital Research Report No. 59, April 1990.

[22] J. Cherbonnier, J.-Y. Le Boudec and H.L. Truong, ATM direct connectionless service, *ICC'93*, Geneva, Switzerland, May 23–26, 1993, pp. 1859–1863.

[23] RACE Project 1035 (Customer Premises Network), Deliverable D17, Nature, scope and provision of connectionless service in the BCPN, Section 5, December 1991, pp. 55–69. Available from the Race Central Office, also from Ericsson-FATME, RACE Project 1035, Via Anagnina 203, 00040 Roma, Italy, Fax +39 6 7258 2370.

[24] J.-Y. Le Boudec, D.A. Pitt and H.L. Truong, Connectionless ATM network support using virtual path connections, RACE 2068 Contribution WP1/IBM/047.1, January 1992.

[25] CCITT Draft Recommendation I.311, B-ISDN general network aspects, TD 56 (XVIII), June 1992.

[26] M. De Prycker, Communications de données dans un réseau MTA, *Revue des Télécommunications* **62** (3/4) (1988) 333–337.

[27] J.Y. Le Boudec, R. Oechsle, D. Pitt and H.L. Truong, Connectionless ATM network using partial connections, RACE R2068 (LACE), Contribution A1.1/IBM/P/38.1, May 1992.

[28] J.Y. Le Boudec and H.L. Truong, Providing MAC services on an ATM Network with point-to-point links, *First Int. Symp. on Interworking*, Bern, Switzerland, November 1992.

[29] W.E. Leland and D.V. Wilson, High time-resolution measurement and analysis of LAN traffic: Implications for LAN interconnection, *IEEE INFOCOM 91*, Bal Harbour, FL, April 1991, pp. 1360–1366.

[30] S. Fuhrmann and J.-Y. Le Boudec, A congestion control framework for data services in the ATM CPN. RACE R2068 temporary document WP1/IBM/I/064.1, June 1992.

Jean-Yves Le Boudec was born in France in 1958. He graduated from "Ecole Normale Supérieure de Saint-Cloud" (Paris, France), where he obtained the "Agrégation" in Mathematics in 1980. He received his doctorate in 1984 from the University of Rennes, France. Then he was assistant professor at INSA/IRISA, Rennes. In 1987 and 1988 he was with Bell-Northern Research, Ottawa, Canada, as a Member of Scientific Staff in the Network and Product Traffic Design department. In 1988 he joined the IBM Zurich Research Laboratory at Rüschlikon, Switzerland, where he is now manager of the Customer Premises Network department. He is also managing editor of "Performance Evaluation." His interests are in the architecture and performance of communication systems.

Andreas Meier received the M.S. degree from the University of Erlangen, Germany, in 1990. In 1991 he joined the IBM Zurich Research Laboratory in Rüschlikon, Switzerland, where he is working towards his Ph.D. His interests include high-speed networking, interworking unit design and low-level networking support.

Rainer Oechsle received the M.S. degree from the University of Stuttgart, Germany, in 1984, and the Ph.D. degree from the University of Karlsruhe, Germany, in 1989, both in computer science. From 1984 to 1989 he was with the Institute of Operating Systems, University of Karlsruhe, where he worked in the field of network operating systems. In 1989 he joined the IBM European Networking Center in Heidelberg, Germany. From 1989 to 1992 he was at the IBM Zurich Research Laboratory in Rüschlikon, Switzerland, where he worked on LAN–LAN interconnection. His current work is in the area of communications for multimedia systems.

Hong Linh Truong received the M.S. degree in 1977 and the Ph.D. degree in 1981, both in Electrical Engineering from the University of Stuttgart, Germany. From 1977 to 1982 he was with the Institute of Switching and Data Techniques, University of Stuttgart, where he worked in the field of performance analysis of data communication networks. From 1982 to 1990 he was employed by SEL Alcatel, Stuttgart, where he led in the last years a group responsible for the definition and specification of signalling protocols in ISDNs and mobile networks. The results of his works were inputs to the specification of the ISDN D-channel protocol and the Signalling System No. 7 used in the German ISDN network. He joined the IBM Research Division in 1990 at the Zurich Research Laboratory, where he is currently working on architecture for broadband customer premises networks.

Voice over ATM: An Evaluation of Implementation Alternatives

David J. Wright, University of Ottawa

T his article analyzes alternatives for transport of voice over asynchronous transfer mode (ATM). It incorporates much of the ongoing work of the ATM Forum and the International Telecommunications Union (ITU), but does not restrict itself to standards and implementation agreements. In addition, it evaluates nonstandardized alternatives for ATM transport of voice traffic.

> The author identifies eight application scenarios for voice over ATM, and evaluates alternatives for implementing the required network functionality.

ATM Deployment

ATM is designed to transport all types of traffic, including motion video, still image, data, and voice. Adaptation types and quality of service (QoS) parameters have been designed to suit a broad range of user requirements for services involving multiple media. Initial deployment of ATM has not yet realized its full potential and has concentrated on motion video, still image, and high-bandwidth data applications, with a relatively small amount of voice traffic. There are three reasons for not using ATM for voice traffic today:

a) The high cost of early ATM interfaces precluded their use solely for voice traffic, which is more cost-effectively served by conventional 64 kb/s circuit-switched networks.

b) The diverse range of features available on conventional voice networks is not available on current ATM networks and involves costly software development to provide.

c) The standardization process for voice over ATM is not complete.

Commercial ATM deployment has been in two areas which are now described, indicating the major applications and the extent of current and future voice usage in a way that overcomes problems (a) and (b) above.

The Customer Premises Environment — First, in the customer premises ATM is cost-effective for applications requiring higher dedicated bandwidth than can be provided by shared media alternatives such as fiber distributed data interface (FDDI). ATM local area networks (LANs) are used for interconnecting lower-bandwidth LANs, computer visualization, computer-aided design, and computationally intensive distributed computing applications involving rapid exchange of information among several workstations, such as neural network analysis. These applications are essentially data only. ATM LANs are also successfully used for multiple access to motion video information.

The driver for voice in an ATM LAN environment is the introduction of multimedia workstations, for instance, for discussions between doctors and radiologists involving medical images. Another application involves videophone and data exchanges between stock brokers. In these cases the cost of the ATM interface is justified more by the multimedia application than by the voice component alone, thus overcoming problem (a) above. Also, in these applications software-intensive network features that are not currently implemented on ATM switches, such as call forwarding, are not required for initial deployment, thus overcoming problem (b).

Public Network Environment — The second area of ATM deployment is in the public network, both as a backbone technology and in the access network. In the network backbone, ATM is used to transport frame relay and switched multimegabit data service (SMDS) traffic and also to provide circuit emulation transport of DS1/E1 and DS3/E3. In the access network, ATM is used to multiplex a combination of traffic onto a single access line, including constant bit rate (CBR) circuits at voice speeds, variable bit rate (VBR) data applications, and multimegabit video traffic. Commercial access lines are currently operating on DS1/E1, DS3/E3, and STS-3c/STM-1 facilities. The network backbone may use ATM to transport voice traffic within DS1 circuit emulation, in which case the cost of the interface is shared among 24 voice calls, thus overcoming problem a above. Although individual voice calls require software-intensive network features such as call forwarding, multiple calls in a multiplex do not require that functionality, thus overcoming problem b.

Voice transport is therefore already possible over ATM, as long as the voice call is multiplexed with other voice or multimedia traffic and does not require that sophisticated call control features be provided by the ATM network.

This article analyzes the alternatives for more flexible provision of voice services over ATM in which the two above restrictions are removed. A broad range of applications for voice over ATM are identified in the next section. The third and fourth sections analyze the trade-offs between different ATM adaptation types and scenarios for echo canceller deployment.

Reprinted from IEEE Communications Magazine, May, 1996, pp. 72-80.

IEEE Communications Magazine • May 1996

APPLICATIONS OF VOICE OVER ATM

Voice over ATM refers to the transport of voice and voice-band data over ATM. In this context, "voice" refers to human speech, fax, and modem data. The term "speech" will be used in this article to distinguish human speech from the more broadly defined term "voice." "Voice over ATM" does not include high-quality audio coded at speeds greater than 64 kb/s. It includes:

* CBR using pulse code modulation (PCM), at 64 kb/s (G.711), adaptive differential PCM (ADPCM) at 64/40/32/24/16 kb/s (G.722, G.725, and G.726), 16 kb/s linear prediction (G.728), 1–8 kb/s voice in 20 ms packets for IS-54 and IS-95 wireless voice communications, fax modulation, and modem modulation.
* VBR using ADPCM with silence detection. When speech activity drops, voice samples are not generated or are generated with a small number of bits per sample [1]. It is also referred to as gap mode CBR and voice activity detection (VAD).

Key application areas requiring voice over ATM are as follows:

* ATM to the desktop — Including both multimedia applications and regular telephony applications.
* Distributed private branch exchange (PBX) — In which the PBX functionality is distributed around a campus in separate modules. ATM can be used to interconnect the modules.
* Broadband computer telephony integration (B-CTI) — In which the computing functionality is distributed to the broadband terminating equipment (B-TE) and the PBX functionality is also distributed into interconnected PBX modules.
* Cable company telephony service.
* Telephone company access network.
* Cellular company access network — On digital wireless interfaces the voice traffic is already packetized, using, for instance, IS-54 and IS-95, making it particularly suited for ATM transport on the wired portion of the cellular company network.
* Long distance terrestrial transport.
* ATM over satellite — To interconnect "islands" of terrestrial ATM deployment, and for intersatellite communications between low earth orbit satellites.

We now analyze alternative methods of providing voice over ATM capability. First, a comparison is made between the alternative ATM adaptation types and QoS requirements in the next section and then the following section analyzes the implications on the requirements for echo cancellers.

EVALUATION OF ADAPTATION ALTERNATIVES

SERVICE CLASSES

In order to provide a voice service over an ATM network, it is necessary to transport the voice plus associated signaling information. A summary of ITU service classes is given in Table 1, which also indicates the correspondence between service class and type of traffic requirement for voice over ATM.

Q.2931 ATM signaling for establishing voice and multimedia calls is naturally bursty data traffic and hence can use a VBR or available bit rate (ABR) service. Non-ATM signaling (e.g., Q.931 N-ISDN signaling) is carried in a 16 or 64 kb/s D channel. Since this is CBR, in order to transport it over an ATM network the appropriate service is CBR.

Class	Bit rate	End to end timing requirement	Voice service description
A	CBR	Yes	Single voice channel N x 64 Kb/s DSn, En Q.931 N-ISDN D-channel signaling
B	VBR	Yes	Single voice channel with silence detection
C	VBR	No	Q.2931 ATM signaling
Y	ABR	No	Q.2931 ATM signaling

ABR: Available bit rate. CBR: Constant bit rate; VBR: Variable bit rate; N-ISDN: Narrowband integrated services digital network

■ **Table 1.** *Service classes relevant to voice.*

The requirements of any service can be specified quantitatively in terms of the QoS factors listed in Table 2. Some ATM switch vendors allow users to program their own choices for each QoS factor, and all vendors have combinations of values preset for user selection.

ADAPTATION TYPES

The ATM adaptation layer (AAL) is divided into five different "types" which were originally designed to suit the requirements of the service classes described previously. However, there is nothing rigid about the assignment of AAL types to service classes. Any service class can be transported on any adaptation type as long as the performance is acceptable to the user. A summary description of the adaptation types is given in Table 3.

In order to evaluate the alternative adaptation types for voice, we analyze the three major contributions they make to voice transport: structuring of data, source clock recovery, and detection of cell loss/misinsertion.

STRUCTURING OF DATA

AAL1 offers both structured and unstructured data transfer, SDT and UDT. In SDT, user bytes are organized in blocks of length N, and a pointer in the seventh byte of an ATM cell indicates the start of a block of data. The sixth byte of the cell is taken up by AAL1 overhead. Since all blocks of data are the same length, pointers are required only in certain ATM cells, and current recommendations suggest a pointer every eight cells. The payloads of AAL1 cells using SDT are therefore either 46 or 47 bytes, with an average length of 46.875 bytes.

In UDT, the user data stream is segmented into 47-byte payloads for the AAL1 cells without regard for any structure in the user data or byte alignment between the user data and the ATM cell payload.

We now analyze the tradeoff between SDT and UDT, which takes into account the gain in networking efficiency, fault management, and the amount of processing and transmission overhead required.

Network Efficiency — Structured data transfer can be used, for instance, to transport N x 64 kb/s voice, and doing so can result in considerable network efficiency. Figure 1 illustrates a DS1 access line being used to provide a PBX user with a fractional T1 service (e.g., half T1). The user can set up a maximum of 12 calls and is tariffed accordingly, although

Accuracy
  Cell error ratio
  Cell loss ratio
  Cell misinsertion rate
  Severely errored cell block ratio

Delay
  Maximum cell transfer delay
  Peak-to-peak cell delay variation

■ **Table 2.** *Quality of service factors.*

AAL type	Overhead bytes per 48 byte ATM payload	Functionality
0	0	None
1/SDT	1.125	Cell sequence numbering to detect cell loss or misinsertion Optional forward error correction for delay-insensitive services Source clock recovery Transport of user data in blocks of constant length up to 93 bytes
1/UDT	1	Cell sequence numbering to detect cell loss or misinsertion Optional forward error correction for delay-insensitive services Source clock recovery Transport of a continuous stream of user information
2	?2?	At the time of writing, definition of AAL2 is in the course of specification in the ATM Forum and ITU Cell sequence numbering is proposed to detect cell loss or misinsertion Optional forward error correction for delay-insensitive services is proposed Timestamps are proposed to recover source clock
5	≥ 8*	Bit error control Segmentation and reassembly of user data units over 48 bytes

SDT: Structured data transfer
UDT: Unstructured data transfer
* For data units ≤ 80 bytes.

■ **Table 3.** *Functionality of ATM adaptation types.*

	Fault isolation	Networking efficiency gain	AAL1 transmission overhead bytes/ATM payload	Processing overhead
SDT	Yes	Yes	1.125	Yes
UDT	No	No	1*	Minimal
UDT/IWF	Yes	No	1*	Yes

*1.25 for DS1, including DS1 transmission overhead.

■ **Table 4.** *Alternative AAL1 options.*

	SDT	UDT
Single voice call, 64 kb/s	No	Yes
Single voice call, highly compressed	No	Yes
Single voice call with silence detection	No*	No*
N x 64 kb/s: 1 < N ≤ 93	Yes	No
DSn/En	Yes	Yes

*AAL0 or AAL2 can be used in this case

■ **Table 5.** *AAL1 structuring of voice services.*

there is capacity for 24. When the traffic is adapted into an ATM network, 12 x 64 kb/s SDT AAL1 can be used so that bandwidth is allocated more efficiently inside the ATM network than on the access line. In the network the ATM cell payloads are completely filled with voice samples, whereas on the access line there is only 50 percent utilization of the DS1 payload. Taking into account the ATM and DS1 overhead, the bandwidth utilization is 49.7 percent on the DS1 and 88.4 percent in the ATM network. When lower fractions of T1 are used on the access line, the ATM utilization remains constant.

The same procedure can be used at other interfaces between circuit-switched networks and ATM networks where the flexibility in choice of N allows ATM to provide more efficient transport than a network based on the highly granular DSn/En and STS-n/synchronous digital hierarchy (SDH)-n multiplexing hierarchies. Since multiple voice calls are multiplexed into a single ATM connection, the use of AAL1 SDT for N x 64 kb/s service is also referred to as the "composite cell" approach.

Fault Management and Associated Processing Overhead — A DS1 can be transported using SDT by terminating the DS1 and transferring the 24 bytes of data into a block of length N = 24 (Fig. 2). It can alternatively be transported using UDT, in which case the 24 bytes of data plus the one bit of DS1 overhead from consecu-tive DS1 frames are regarded as a continuous bitstream and segmented into 47-byte ATM payloads (Fig. 3).

With reference to Figs. 2 and 3, suppose a DS1 fault such as loss of signal (LOS) occurs on DS1 link A. In the case of SDT, the DS1 interface in ATM switch X detects the fault and can inform the network operations support center about where the fault has occurred. In the case of UDT, the DS1 is not terminated at switch X. The fault is not detected until DS1 equipment Z which identifies the fault as being located somewhere in links A, B, or C. The location of the fault is therefore not as precise with UDT as it is with SDT.

To get around this problem the ATM Forum recommends a third approach, which is to implement an interworking function (IWF) at the DS1/UDT interface (Fig. 4). The IWF detects upstream LOS and generates downstream a DS1 alarm indication signal carried in ATM cells. In this way the fault is identified as being in link A, and downstream DS1 equipment is informed of the LOS. The IWF provides additional functionality at the expense of additional processing. A standard IWF incorporates performance monitoring functionality in addition to the fault management just described, thus adding to the processing overhead.

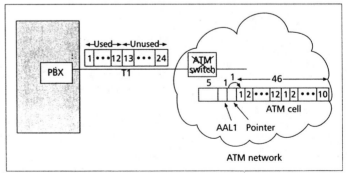

■ **Figure 1.** *N x 64 kb/s structured data transfer for fractional T1.*

Transmission Overhead — The amount of transmission overhead can be seen from Figs. 2 and 3. For both SDT and UDT there is 1 byte of AAL1 overhead in addition to the 5 bytes of ATM overhead. In the case of SDT, an additional byte is required every 8 cells for an average of 1.125 bytes of overhead. For DS1 using UDT an additional 2 bits of DS1 overhead is required every cell, for a total of 1.25 bytes. For CBR voice at ≤ 64 kb/s, there is no additional overhead using UDT.

The trade-off between SDT and UDT is summarized in Table 4, and their applicability to voice services is given in Table 5.

SOURCE CLOCK RECOVERY AND END TO END TIMING

Source clock recovery at the destination is an important function for voice, given the end-to-end timing requirement indicated in Table 1 and the need to synchronize source and destination DS*n* facilities for circuit emulation and transport of *N* x 64 kb/s voice. Methods for clock recovery can be divided into those that use adaptation overhead and those that do not.

The AAL1 and AAL2 overhead proposed at the ATM Forum for clock recovery is based on information derived from a network clock. In AAL2 a timestamp is proposed [2], and in AAL1 the residual part between source and network clocks is used (SRTS method: synchronous residual timestamp), resulting in less overhead than AAL2.

Methods of clock recovery that require no AAL overhead can be used with AAL0 and AAL5 as well as AAL1 and AAL2. If they are used with AAL1 or AAL2, the adaptation overhead is still present but not used for clock recovery.

- Timing can be obtained from an external source, for instance, from the legacy circuit-switched network or from global positioning satellite (GPS) transmissions. In the latter case, the capital cost of installation of GPS receiving equipment is incurred, and there is current discussion as to whether accuracy is sufficient.
- The "adaptive method" derives the clock from monitoring the stream of cells arriving at a buffer at the destination. A nominal clock at the destination is speeded up if the buffer starts to fill up and is slowed down if the buffer starts to empty. The adaptive method is accurate if the network introduces minimal cell delay variation during the transport of the ATM cells. It is incorporated in the ATM Forum implementation agreement for AAL1.
- The "immediate playout method" can be used in the case of VBR voice using silence detection. During silences, cells are either not sent or sent containing a highly compressed code representing the silence. The destination needs to know the length of those silence periods. If the network introduces minimal cell loss and minimal cell delay variation, VBR voice can be sent over AAL0 incurring zero overhead, with the voice samples being played out immediately upon receipt. More details on this

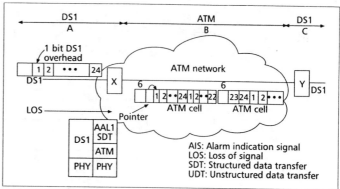

■ **Figure 2.** *Transporting a DS1 using AAL1 SDT.*

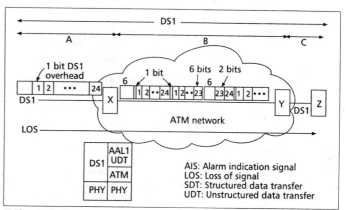

■ **Figure 3.** *Transporting a DS1 using AAL1 UDT.*

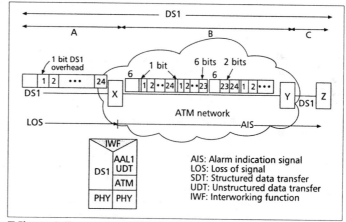

■ **Figure 4.** *Transporting a DS1 using AAL1 UDT with IWF.*

method can be found in a proposal to the ATM Forum [3].

Clock recovery using the SRTS, timestamp, or adaptive methods involves processing at the destination for *each* virtual circuit, because it is based on information in the stream of cells on each connection individually. Therefore, multiple local derived clocks need to be maintained at the destination. In the case of deriving clock from legacy circuit-switched networks or GPS transmissions, only one clock is required at the destination.

In order for the user to specify the complete characteristics

Method	Adaptation overhead required for clock recovery	AAL0	AAL1	AAL2	AAL5
Timestamp	Yes			VBR	
SRTS	Yes		CBR		
Adaptive*	No	CBR	CBR		CBR
Immediate playout*	No	VBR			VBR
Legacy network/GPS	No		CBR	CBR	CBR/Sig
None					Sig

* Requires low peak-to-peak cell delay variation
CBR — Constant bit rate voice, including single voice call, N x 64 kb/s, DSn/En; VBR — Variable bit rate voice coded with silence detection; Sig — Q.2931 ATM signaling

■ **Table 6.** *Source clock recovery options for CBR and VBR voice.*

of a voice connection at call establishment time, it is necessary to determine the AAL type and also the QoS, which includes parameters such as peak-to-peak cell delay variation (PCDV). AAL and QoS specifications are related in the adaptive and immediate playout methods. For instance, if the QoS specifies a low PCDV, AAL0 or AAL5 can be used. Otherwise, GPS, AAL1/SRTS, or AAL2/timestamp must be used to compensate for PCDV.

The options for clock recovery for voice connections are summarized in Table 6. In this table AAL5 is identified as a possible means of transporting voice; however, it has a high overhead for short data units (Table 3) and is therefore likely to be used to transport the following:

• Q.2931 signaling
• Voice traffic that is already packetized, such as wireless data for IS-54 and IS-95
• New voice traffic in situations where the user has already invested in AAL5 interfaces for data communications

DETECTION OF CELL LOSS AND MISINSERTION

Cell loss or misinsertion can be detected by the sequence numbering in AAL1 and AAL2, but not by AAL0 or AAL5. AAL5 detects bit errors only. A single cell loss affects 48 bytes of user data when AAL0 is used, 46 or 47 bytes when AAL1 is used, and approximately 46 bytes when AAL2 is used. Misinserted cells are discarded at the receiver.

If a cell loss is detected, the receiver may insert a replacement cell. For instance, the previous cell could be repeated or an interpolation made between the cells before and after the missing one. Because of the tight end-to-end delay requirements for voice, there is insufficient time to request a retransmission of missing cells. Forward error correction (FEC) is an option in AAL1 and is proposed as an option for AAL2 in the ATM Forum [2]. In AAL1, it can be used to recover up to 4 lost cells in a block of 124 cells or to correct up to 2 errored bytes out of 124. Assembling 124 cells and performing the error correction introduces a delay of approximately $47*8*124/64 = 728.5$ ms for a single 64 kb/s voice connection, which is unacceptable according to the delay requirements for voice calls specified in G.114, G.131, and G.126. We therefore conclude that FEC is inappropriate for voice unless multiplexing has already been performed on the individual voice calls. For instance, a DS1 emulation incurs a delay of approximately $728.5/24 = 30$ ms, and a DS3 incurs only $30/28 = 1$ ms delay as a result of performing FEC. A detailed analysis of FEC is given in [4, 5].

Suppose a cell is lost or misinserted and not detected, as in the case of AAL0. If the "adaptive" clock recovery method is used, the receiver clock will speed up or slow down to compensate for an undetected cell loss or misinsertion. When GPS/legacy network synchronization is used, a low cell delay variation can be specified in the QoS requirements so that a lost or misinserted cell can be detected immediately.

The maximum impact on voice quality is when 48 bytes of a single voice connection are lost: for 64 kb/s voice, 6 ms are lost. When N voice calls are multiplexed into a single ATM connection, a single cell loss results in a loss of between $23/(4N)$ and $6/N$ ms from each individual 64 kb/s voice call. The listener hardly notices a click on the line, approximately one 12-point character on a page of fax is corrupted, and for data modem traffic, higher-level protocols recover from the error.

The more compression is applied to speech, the longer the effect of cell loss (e.g., 24 ms for a single voice connection using 16 kb/s coding). Also, if encryption is used, recovering from cell loss or misinsertion can result in additional errors. The listener may therefore notice the effect of cell loss when a single highly compressed and/or encrypted voice call is carried over an ATM connection.

AAL5 provides bit error detection and is therefore suited to the transport of signaling traffic. It does not detect cell loss/misinsertion.

In summary, Table 7 analyzes the error control options provided by the different adaptation types as to whether they are acceptable, necessary, or unacceptable for different types of voice traffic.

CONCLUSION ON ADAPTATION ALTERNATIVES

This section has analyzed adaptation alternatives for any given voice service, taking into account three interrelated factors: data structuring, source clock recovery, and detection of cell loss or misinsertion. The discussion is summarized in Table 8, and the conclusion is as follows:

a) For a single voice channel at 64 kb/s, there are two options:
(a.1) AAL0 or AAL5 can be used with either adaptive clock recovery or GPS/legacy network timing if the QoS specifies a low cell delay variation.
(a.2) Alternatively, synchronization is available from the SRTS method, requiring AAL1/UDT, incurring 1 byte of overhead.
b) A compressed/encrypted single voice channel requires a QoS with an enhanced cell error ratio and cell loss ratio; otherwise, it is similar to a single 64 kb/s voice channel.
c) For a single voice channel with silence detection, there are two options:
(c.1) AAL0 or AAL5 with a QoS specifying low cell delay variation
(c.2) AAL2 for situations where cell delay variation is significant
d) N x 64 kb/s voice requires AAL1/SDT in order to maintain the structure information about which ATM payload byte corresponds to which 64 kb/s channel. This allows a gain in network efficiency by allocating ATM bandwidth according to the exact value of N required by the user.
e) DSn/En are most efficiently transported using AAL1/UDT with IWF as an option to provide improved fault management. FEC is an option to provide improved error control, allowing the user to specify a QoS with less stringent error ratio and cell loss/misinsertion rates.
f) Transport of ATM signaling for voice calls requires detection of bit errors, which can be obtained from

AAL5 without stringent cell error ratio QoS requirements.

In (a), (b), and (c), AAL5 is identified as an option for voice transport whenever AAL0 can be used, even though AAL5 has higher overhead than AAL0. Many ATM workstations have AAL5 adapters today for data applications. If those workstations require voice transport in the future, a low-cost option is to transport the voice over the current interface. Some AAL5 interfaces can be reconfigured to bypass the AAL5 convergence sublayer processing so that they default to AAL0, resulting in more efficient transport; but for those that cannot be reconfigured in this way, AAL5 is an economical option for voice. Cornell University uses AAL5 for voice over ATM.

It is important to note the interaction between AAL and QoS. Voice services require a combination of AAL and QoS in order to achieve the required performance. This is apparent in:
• The decision whether to compress and/or encrypt voice below 64 kb/s: (a) compared to (b)
• The use of silence detection: (c)
• The FEC option with circuit emulation: (e)
• The bit error rate requirements for signaling: (f)

The wide range of options available are not all standardized. At the time of writing, the ATM Forum has currently standardized (a.2), (d), and (e) without FEC. The other options above are available as proprietary implementations; for instance, MFS uses (c.2) with a proprietary version of AAL2 on Nortel's Passport ATM switch. It is to be noted that since AAL0 provides no functionality, it requires no standardization.

IMPLICATIONS FOR NETWORK OPERATORS

The implications of these conclusions for public network operators are that, in the medium term, they need to have the full range of QoS and AAL options available in order to satisfy their customers needs. In the short term a subset of features may be acceptable, for instance, allowing customers to specify only certain QoS parameters, but in the medium term the competitive nature of the telecommunications market is going to allow customers to demand the full range of flexibility identified in (a)–(f) above for voice transport. Moreover, carriers need to accept that some customers may choose to use AAL0, possibly with some of their own proprietary overhead in the cell payload, so the QoS specification that they impose on the network is correspondingly stringent. Customers may choose AAL0 because the interfaces are low-cost compared to AAL1 or because they have already sunk capital into AAL5 inter-

	AAL0 no error control	AAL1 seq #s	AAL1 Seq #s + FEC	AAL2 time stamp	AAL2 time stamp + FEC	AAL5 CRC for bit error detection
Single voice call, CBR, 64 kb/s	A	A	U			A
Single voice call, CBR, highly compressed and/or encrypted	E	E	U			E
Single voice call, VBR, with silence detection	A			A	U	A
N x 64 Kb/s	A	A	U*			
DS1/E1	U	A	A			
DS3/E3	U	A	A			
Signaling						N

* For low values of N
A — Acceptable. E — Enhanced QoS required for cell error ratio and cell loss/misinsertion rate. N — Necessary. U — Unacceptable. FEC: Forward Error Correction. CRC: Cyclical Redundancy Check.

■ **Table 7.** *Adaptation error control for voice.*

	AAL0	AAL1 SDT	AAL1 UDT	AAL2	AAL5
Overhead per 48 byte ATM payload	0	1.125	1	??? not standardized	≥ 8 for data units ≤ 80 bytes
Single voice channel at 64 Kb/s	Adaptive clock or GPS, with low PCDV		Adaptive clock, SRTS or GPS		Adaptive clock or GPS, with low PCDV
Single voice channel compressed and/or encrypted	Adaptive clock or GPS with low error ratio and PCDV		Adaptive clock, SRTS or GPS with low error ratio QoS		Adaptive clock or GPS with low error ratio and PCDV
Single voice channel with silence detection	Play out immediately if PCDV is low			Provides required time stamp if PCDV is significant	Play out immediately if PCDV is low
N x 64 Kb/s		Provides gain in network efficiency			
DSn/En				Minimal processing overhead. Improved fault management with IWF. FEC is an option.	
ATM Signaling					Provides required bit error detection

■ **Table 8.** *Evaluation of adaptation alternatives.*

	Delay (ms)		
	47 bytes, payload	20 bytes, partial fill	6 bytes, partial fill
Single speech channel: 64 Kb/s	5.875	2.5	0.75
Single speech channel: 16 Kb/s	23.5	10	3
Single speech channel with silence detection: 32 kb/s	11.75	5	1.5
6 x 64 kb/s	0.98	0.42	0.125
N x 64 kb/s	5.875/N	2.5/N	0.75/N
DS1	0.24	0.10	0.03

■ **Table 9.** *Cell assembly delay.*

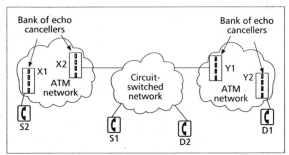

■ **Figure 5.** *Location of echo cancellers.*

faces for data applications which can be reconfigured to AAL0 but not to AAL1. This hardware cost saving on the customers part translates into tight QoS requirements from the network so that the tariffing of QoS becomes an important feature in the marketing of voice over ATM services.

EVALUATION OF METHODS FOR DEALING WITH DELAY

DELAY REQUIREMENTS FOR VOICE

The previous section analyzed alternative adaptation types for transporting voice over ATM and demonstrated the interrelationship between AAL and QoS. This section deals with end-to-end delay and involves a similar interaction between the QoS specification for ATM network delay and other methods of handling delay.

ITU-T recommendations G.114, G.131, and G.126 specify the average national network delay for speech traffic. If echo cancellers are used, the allowable delay depends on the degree of loss on the echo path and the subjective sensitivity of users to echo. In practice, a delay of about 15–30 ms is acceptable without echo cancellers. If they are used, international speech connections can have an average delay up to 150 ms and higher in certain circumstances. Data and fax communications are less sensitive to echo than human speech and do not require echo cancellers.

Echo cancellers constitute a considerable cost since they need to be included in *each* speech circuit. National circuit-switched voice networks are normally operated with echo cancellers only in exceptional circumstances. If ATM requires echo cancellers to transport speech, they must therefore be regarded as part of the cost of evolving the network to ATM.

In this section we first analyze how much delay is introduced by transporting different speech services over ATM. This is compared to the requirements of G.114, G.131, and G.126, and alternatives are evaluated for either deploying echo cancellers or using other methods to reduce delay.

DELAY INTRODUCED BY ATM

Delay is introduced by an ATM network in two ways. First, there is the delay introduced as cells traverse each switch. The hardware implementation of ATM switching equipment reduces switching delay to much less than 1 ms/switch, which is insignificant compared to the requirements of G.114, G.131, and G.126. Delay may be introduced in switch buffers due to other traffic,

	Delay (ms)		
	1	2	4
Single speech channel: 64 kb/s	16%	34%	67%
Single speech channel: 16 kb/s	4%	8%	16%
Single speech channel with silence detection: 32 kb/s	8%	16%	33%

■ **Table 10.** *Percentage of cell payload used to achieve a given cell assembly delay.*

and delay variation among cells on any given virtual circuit may be introduced by burstiness of other traffic. It is therefore necessary to specify a QoS at call setup, which includes low values for maximum cell transfer delay and peak-to-peak cell delay variation. Switch designers implement delay requirements by allocating priority levels to different traffic types to allow rapid scheduling of cells through buffers when necessary. Delay at network switch nodes can therefore be handled by QoS specification. The translation of QoS specification into ATM performance requirements is discussed in [6–8].

Second, delay is introduced during the assembly of speech traffic into ATM cells at the ATM network edge. For example, for 64 kb/s speech, 1-byte samples are generated every 125 µs. To fill a 47 byte ATM payload requires 47 x .125 = 5.875 ms. Table 9 shows the extent of delay corresponding to alternative speech services. The first column in Table 9 uses a figure of 47 bytes for the payload size, which is the median of the adaptation options identified in the previous section. The remaining columns in Table 9 deal with the case where ATM cells are only partially filled, and are discussed in detail later. The single speech channel services used in Table 9 use examples of coding at 16, 32, and 64 kb/s for illustrative purposes.

Table 9 shows that when six or more speech channels are multiplexed into full ATM cells for transport to a common destination, the cell assembly delay is less than 1 ms. This is small compared to the ITU requirements, and echo cancellers are not required in this case. It may be that fewer than 6 channels is also acceptable; for instance, 3 or 4 channels results in a delay of 2 ms and 1.5 ms, respectively.

However, assembling an entire ATM cell from a single speech channel introduces a delay of 6–23 ms, which is comparable with the network delay requirements of 15–30 ms in the absence of echo cancellers. One option for transport of single speech channels is therefore to deploy echo cancellers. Another option is to fill only part of the ATM payload with speech samples, thus reducing the delay. These two alternatives are now analyzed.

ECHO CANCELLER REQUIREMENTS

If single speech channels are carried in completely full ATM cells, echo cancellers are required at the interface of each speech circuit into the ATM network. Since delay is introduced when speech enters an ATM network but not when it leaves the network, the echo cancellers need only be unidirectional, sometimes called half echo cancellers.

Figure 5 illustrates an example network in which the destination phones D1 and D2 use two-wire interfaces to the network. The other interfaces are four-wire. When a call is set up from source S1 to destination D1, an echo canceller is allocated from the bank at Y1 for speech from S1 to D1 and from the bank at Y2 for speech from D1 to S1.

A single echo canceller on a speech circuit improves speech quality; however, multiple echo cancellers on the same circuit result in a degradation of speech quality. For speech from S2 to D1, one echo canceller is required from the bank at X1 but not from the bank at Y1.

Echo canceller bypass may also be required when a call is forwarded. In Fig. 5, for speech from S2 to D2 an echo canceller is allocated from the bank at X1. If D2 has forwarded the call to D1, an echo canceller would normally be allocated from the bank at Y1 when the forwarded leg of the call is established. However, it is important to take into account the fact that the first leg of the call, before forwarding, already has an echo canceller, so a second one is not allocated. Q.761 specifies the signaling requirements in this case for narrowband integrated services digital network (N-ISDN), and corresponding standards are required in the broadband case. Another case in which bypass arrangements can be used is for a fax or modem call, for which echo cancellation is not required.

Therefore, it is important for echo cancellers to be available on all speech circuits entering an ATM network, and also that they be bypassed in appropriate circumstances.

PARTIALLY FILLED ATM CELLS

At call establishment time, Q.2931 allows the user to optionally specify the number of bytes in an AAL1 cell that are filled with user data. Partial fill may also be incorporated in AAL2. It can also be used with AAL0 by agreement between the users at either end of the connection. A switch implementation of partial fill is given in [9]; performance issues are discussed in [10].

As seen in Table 9, acceptable delay levels can be reached without the use of echo cancellers for single speech circuits if ATM cells are only partially filled. This is at the expense of unused bandwidth, and would therefore only be done in situations where bandwidth is relatively inexpensive. It is a trade-off between the cost of bandwidth and the cost of echo cancellers.

Short-distance links in the customer premises and access networks are good candidates for the use of partially filled cells. Figure 6 illustrates the principle of using partial fill to bring speech traffic to the public network access switch where grooming takes place. Speech traffic for destinations on a common path through the ATM network backbone is aggregated onto an $N \times 64$ kb/s virtual circuit with composite cells using AAL1/SDT. On the destination access line the speech traffic can be converted back into partially filled cells with minimal cell assembly delay. Table 10 gives the percentage of the cell payload bandwidth used in order to achieve a given cell assembly delay.

CONCLUSION ON ALTERNATIVE METHODS OF HANDLING DELAY

Table 11 summarizes the conclusions of this section, which are as follows.

In ATM networks carrying bursty traffic, users can specify a speech QoS that has low values for maximum cell transfer delay and peak-to peak-cell delay variation to reduce the delay and delay variation introduced by buffers at network switching nodes.

	Single speech channel	Multiplex of ≥ 3–6 channels
Method 1 Specify QoS with low cell transfer delay and low peak-to-peak cell delay variation	Yes	Yes
Method 2 Use partially filled cells	Where bandwidth is relatively low-cost	Not necessary
Method 3 Install echo cancellers	Where bandwidth is relatively high-cost	Not necessary

■ **Table 11.** *Evaluation of methods of dealing with delay.*

Cell assembly delay at the network edge requires either echo cancellers or use of partially filled cells for single speech channels, but is not significant for multiplexes of approximately three to six or more channels. Partial fill results in unused bandwidth, which is a cost to be balanced against the alternative cost of echo cancellers. The customer premises and access networks are particularly suited to partial fill because of the relatively low cost of bandwidth in these areas.

IMPLICATIONS FOR NETWORK OPERATORS

The implications of these conclusions for public network operators is that provision of voice over ATM service implies a capital cost in addition to the cost of installing an ATM network. One strategy is to deploy echo cancellers in the regular circuit-switched voice network. In the short term the carrier achieves a competitive advantage by offering customers improved clarity on regular telephony services. In the medium term, the carrier already has the echo cancellers in place when they start to offer voice over ATM services.

CONCLUSIONS

This article has presented an evaluation of alternatives for transport of voice traffic across an ATM network. For single voice calls this involves evaluation of adaptation type, QoS, echo canceller deployment, and use of partially filled cells.

For a multiplex of at least three to six voice calls it involves evaluation of the structured data transport option in AAL1, interworking with DS*n*/E*n* for fault management and QoS.

These issues determine choices for network users plus implementation priorities for network operators, and are summarized in the sections entitled "Conclusions on Adaptation

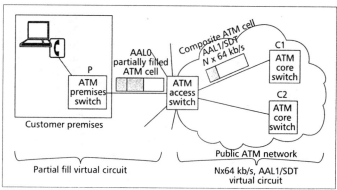

■ **Figure 6.** *Partial fill on access; composite cells on backbone.*

Time frame	Factor	Voice service
Short term	AAL1/SDT	n x 64 kb/s service to end users n x 64 kb/s transport on network backbone
	AAL1/UDT, DSn/En interworking	DSn/En circuit emulation
	Partially filled cells	
Medium term	Flexible QoS specification	Integration of multiplexed voice with bursty data traffic
	Echo canceller deployment	Single voice calls
	AAL2 standardization	Silence detection: improved bandwidth utilization

■ Table 12. *Rollout of factors determining voice transport over ATM.*

Alternatives" and "Conclusions on Alternative Methods of Handling Delay."

Table 12 indicates a rollout plan for the above factors and the resulting benefits in terms of voice services that can be offered.

REFERENCES

[1] K. Kondo and M. Ohno, "Packet Speech Transmission on ATM Networks Using a VBR Embedded ADPCM Scheme," *IEEE Trans. Commun.*, vol. 42, no. 2-4, Pt. 1, 1994, pp. 243–47.
[2] D. Beaumont "Further Clarification on an AAL Model for Real Time VBR Services," ATM Forum Contribution 95-0349, Apr. 1995.
[3] F. Faris *et al.*, "Basic Voice Call Transport over ATM with Optional Silence Removal and Voice Compression," ATM Forum Doc. # 95-1643, Dec. 1995.
[4] A. R. Kaye *et al.*, "FEC and Priority for VBR Video Distribution over ATM," *Canadian J. Elect. and Comp. Eng.*, vol. 19, no. 3, 1994, pp. 123–30.
[5] K. Kawahara *et al.*, "FEC in ATM Networks: An Analysis of Cell Loss Distribution in a Block," *Proc. IEE Infocom 1994*, vol. 3, pp. 1150–59.
[6] D. Seret and J. Jung, "Translation of Users QoS Parameters into ATM Performance Requirements," *Proc. IFIP Trans. C: Commun. Sys.*, no. C-24, 1994, pp. 51–64.
[7] C-S Li *et al.*, "Pseudo-Isochronous Cell Switching in ATM Networks," *Proc. IEEE Infocom*, vol. 2, 1994, pp. 428–37.
[8] J. Jung and A. Gravey, "QoS Management and Performance Monitoring in ATM Networks," *Proc. IEEE GLOBECOM*, vol. 2, 1993, pp. 708–12.
[9] I. Gard and L-G Petersen, "Supporting STM Traffic with ATM: A Switch Implementation," *Proc. Int'l. Switching Symp.*, 1995, pp. 62–66.
[10] Z. Tsai *et al.*, "Performance Analysis of Two Echo Control Designs in ATM Networks," *IEEE/ACM Trans. Networking*, vol. 2, no. 1, 1994, pp. 30–39.

BIOGRAPHY

DAVID J. WRIGHT specializes in broadband telecommunications and is the author of papers in that area which have appeared in *IEEE Network*, *IEEE JSAC*, *IEEE International Conference on Communications*, *IEEE Globecom*, and *IEEE Infocom*. He is also author of the book *Broadband: Business Services, Technologies and Strategic Impact*, published by Artech House. He graduated from Cambridge University, U.K., with a Ph.D. (engineering) and M.A. (mathematics), and is currently full professor at the University of Ottawa. His e-mail address is dwright@uottawa.ca.

MPEG-2 over ATM for Video Dial Tone Networks: Issues and Strategies

Market growth for PC multimedia and digital video owes largely to the rapid adoption of ISO compression standards by the industry. For VDT services, the MPEG-2 set of standards have clearly emerged as the preferred coding method for VDT networks. For point-to-point switched video or multimedia connections, ATM has emerged as the technology of choice for switching and transport.

Sudhir Dixit and Paul Skelly

mpending deregulation of the common carrier telecommunications industry, competitive pressures, and merging of computer, telecommunications and video technologies have catapulted the telco and cable TV service providers into designing and implementing Video Dial Tone (VDT) networks to offer digital video, voice, data, and multimedia services to residential users. Additionally, both information and network service providers believe that a common broadband access network will provide access to and eventually evolve into the Information Superhighway. In the near term, such an infrastructure is being created for new revenue generating services while enabling substantial cost savings on the operations side. Video server, MPEG-2, Asynchronous Transfer Mode (ATM), and digital transport technologies have matured to the extent that they enable us to build end-to-end digital VDT networks.

Market growth for PC multimedia and digital video owes largely to the rapid adoption of ISO compression standards by the industry, which include, e.g., JPEG, MPEG-1, and MPEG-2 (i.e., ISO/IEC 10918, 11172, 13818). Videoconferencing and video telephony have adopted the ITU-T H.320 standard, and standards bodies are working on the MPEG-4 standard for very low bit rate compression. For VDT services, the MPEG-2 set of standards have clearly emerged as the preferred coding method for VDT networks. For point-to-point switched video or multimedia connections, ATM has emerged as the technology of choice for switching and transport.

This article describes how compressed digital video is transported over a VDT network, what some of the issues are, and how they are being addressed by the industry. In the next section we describe a generic VDT reference architecture, and the delivery method of video and multime-

dia information over such a network. We then describe some of the major issues and problems of transporting MPEG-2 over a VDT network, and discuss their potential solutions. We then summarize and conclude the article.

VDT Reference Architecture

A VDT network needs to support a number of video services. In broadcast video service, the programs are broadcast, in analog or digital format, to all users. Its variations include basic TV, pay-per-view (PPV), and scheduled near video on demand (NVOD), with or without conditional access. Video on demand (VOD) service allows users to select programs or contents from a vast library of selections for personal viewing with a minimum of delay. The program material is almost invariably prestored in high-speed servers. The video source may be selected from any one of several libraries from different information providers. VOD is a switched point-to-point service, where ATM is used for switching and transmission between the server and the access network or the CPE. Video teleconferencing and video telephony services involve two or more subscribers connected over a single circuit or a multi-channel multi-point circuit with the ability to add and/or drop a single site at a time (or multiple sites one after another). At the present time, service providers are planning to offer the above bidirectional video and telephony (POTS) services over the existing circuit-switched network while sharing the same broadband access (loop) network with the VDT services.

A VDT reference architecture is shown in Fig. 1, which shows several of the underlying loop access technologies. Since this article focuses on the transport of the applications data, the control and OAM&P elements and networks are

SUDHIR DIXIT is responsible for architecting broadband video dial tone networks at NYNEX Science and Technology.

PAUL SKELLY is a member of technical staff at GTE Laboratories, Inc.

Reprinted from IEEE Network, Sept/Oct 1995, pp. 30-40.

not shown. The VDT network will carry MPEG-2 programming from the Video Information Provider (VIP), over ATM through the switching network, into the local loop access network, to the customer residence. The VIPs will typically be located close to a Hub Central Office (CO), or may even be located within the Hub CO. The digital programming originating at the VIP complex will be broadcast video-audio received from satellite transmissions, or precoded MPEG-2 Transport Streams (TSs) which can be played from a server for VOD, N-VOD, and other interactive services. Analog satellite television broadcasts may need to be encoded for transmission across the VDT network using real-time MPEG-2 encoders, depending on whether they are to be carried digitally across the switching network and the type of transmissions supported in the access network. The bit rates required per MPEG-2 program will fall within the range of 3 to 6 Mb/s for most programs, depending on content, desired program quality, and whether the program needs to be encoded in real time or can be encoded off-line. The MPEG-2 program streams are segmented into ATM cells in a network adaptation subsystem, and transmitted across the VIP interface, into the switching network, and over to the appropriate local CO (headend). The local CO passes the program streams from the switching network to the loop access network. At the customer premises, the digital programming is received by a set-top converter, which decodes the programming for presentation on the customer's television set. The network may use the same transport for delivering data as video and audio. All information components of a program can travel over the same or different physical and/or logical connection(s). When transported over separate physical or logical connections and if the program components have a timing relationship, they need to be synchronized at the receiving end station and presented as a single program. Due to technical and implementation reasons, all components of a single program are likely to follow the same logical and physical connection.

There are four major competing access network schemes: Hybrid Fiber-Coax (HFC), Fiber-to-the-Curb (FTTC), Asymmetric Digital Subscriber Line (ADSL), and Fiber-to-the-Home (FTTH) (Fig. 1). In the United States, HFC and FTTC access networks will dominate the initial VDT deployments. There is a certain amount of interest in ADSL around the world, but this technology can only offer limited bandwidth, typically 3 Mb/s, to the customer premises. FTTH deployment is not currently cost effective for VDT access networks.

HFC

HFC access networks provide approximately 750 MHz of RF analog bandwidth, which is broadcast from the HFC headend (MUX/MOD) over optical fiber to an optical-to-electrical (O/E) subsystem. The O/E converts the optical signal into an electrical one for transmission down coaxial cable to the customer premises. No switching or routing occurs between the HFC headend and the customer premises. The 750 MHz of analog

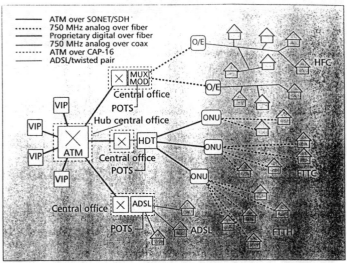

■ Figure 1. *A residential VDT transport architecture showing some of the commonly used access networks.*

bandwidth provides support for approximately 100 6-MHz analog video channels. It is up to the service provider to allocate the full spectrum of 750 MHz among various VDT services, and is, therefore, implementation dependent. Figure 2 shows an example allocation of the frequency spectrum. Conventional analog broadcasts which can be received by existing television sets will typically be carried on the channels between 50 and 550 MHz. The spectrum between 550 MHz and 750 MHz will typically carry the digital MPEG-2 programming and downstream telephony, which must be decoded with a set-top converter. The spectrum under 50 MHz will typically carry upstream telephony, and upstream and downstream data channels. Using QAM-64, QAM-256, or 16-VSB modulators, anywhere from 27 Mb/s to 38 Mb/s of digital payload can be carried on a single 6 MHz analog channel, providing capacity for approximately 6 to 10 MPEG-2 programs with bandwidths of at least 3.5 Mb/s. Current plans for HFC access network deployments support both ATM to the home and MPEG-2 to the home. In the latter case, the ATM network connections are terminated at the local CO, and MPEG-2 digital programs are multiplexed into multiprogram MPEG-2

TSs for transmission to the home. The digital bit-streams leaving the MUX/MOD can be split out to many O/Es, each broadcasting to as many as 500 homes. Therefore, the programming must be encrypted to ensure that only the subscriber (or subscribers for VOD, N-VOD, PPV, or premium broadcast services) who has paid for a particular program is able to decode and view it. This introduces the need for encryption and key management schemes. For more information on HFC, see [17, 18].

FTTC

FTTC access networks provide switched ATM connections into the customer premises. At the local CO, ATM connections are switched to a Broadband Host Digital Terminal (BHDT), which routes it to the appropriate ONU. The interface between the BHDT and ONU is typically a high-speed fiber-based interface, which can be either vendor-proprietary or standards-based. The ONU routes connections to the appropriate customer premises over a standard interface, such as ATM over CAP-16 at 51 Mb/s. An ONU might support 16 homes, and a BHDT might support as many as 130 ONUs. For more information on FTTC, see [19].

ADSL

Asymmetric Digital Subscriber Line(ADSL-1 and ADSL-3) is a technology for providing Plain Old Telephone Service (POTS) and high-bit rate digital information over existing copper loop plant. The digital transport is asymmetric, carrying 1.544 to 6.312 Mb/s video channel (combination of 1.544 and 3.1252 Mb/s signals) down to the customer premises. For control, 16 Kb/s or 64 Kb/s bidirectional channels are supported. POTS, ISDN, and 384 Kb/s (H0) services can also be supported. The actual transmission rate of an ADSL system depends on the system architecture, the distance from the central office or remote terminal, and the noise environment (including crosstalk from other copper-based digital transmission systems such as T-carrier systems, digital subscriber lines supporting Basic Rate ISDN, and high-bit-rate digital subscriber lines supporting DS1 service). The distances to which an ADSL system can deliver up to (over nonloaded loop plant) depends on the data rate, the crosstalk, the type of the system (ADSL-1 or ADSL-3), and the type of line encoding (CAP or DMT).

For ADSL-based access architectures, the ATM connections would most likely be terminated at the local central office (shown in Fig. 1) or a remote terminal (not shown in Fig. 1) and switched to an ADSL transmission system. From there, connections would be carried over copper twisted pair to the customer premises where it would be terminated and delivered to the customer's set-top box. An ADSL system in a central office would typically serve 20,000 homes. An ADSL system in a remote terminal operating over a Distribution Area (DA) would typically serve 500 homes, while an ADSL system in a remote terminal operating over a Carrier Service Area (CSA) would typically serve 2000 homes. For a detailed discussion of ADSL, see [1].

MPEG-2 Transport

MPEG-2 [2-4] has been embraced by the industry as the coding standard of choice for use in VDT services [5, 6, 15]. An MPEG-2 program is a collection of video, audio, and data components which are multiplexed together into a single bit stream for either transmission across a network or later playback from a storage device. The individual program components, called elementary streams, are packetized into large, variable size packets to make up Packetized Elementary Streams (PES). The MPEG-2 Systems Layer [2], provides the multiplexing and media synchronization functions necessary to combine the PES plus any additional Program Specific Information (PSI) Tables into a program, so that it can be properly decoded for playback. The MPEG-2 Systems Layer is also responsible for synchronizing MPEG-2 decoders to the MPEG-2 program source if necessary.

MPEG-2 was designed with a wide range of applications in mind, from playback from (relatively) lossless media like CD-ROM, to broadcast over digital networks. To meet the needs of the various applications, two standard interchange formats for communicating between encoders and decoders were defined: the Program Stream (PS) and the Transport Stream (TS). The PS, which is similar to the MPEG-1 System Stream, was designed for applications running on lossless systems and which do not have the need to multiplex multiple programs into a single bit stream. The PS is segmented into large, variable size packets. The TS was designed for applications running on systems which may introduce small amounts of data loss and/or where there is a need to multiplex several programs into a single bit stream. The TS is segmented into fixed size 188-byte packets, called Transport Packets (TPs), which help to contain the effects of data loss. PES, PS, and other TSs can be multiplexed into a new TS. The TS has been widely accepted in the industry for VDT applications.

The ideal connection between an MPEG-2 systems source multiplexer and an MPEG-2 receiver demultiplexer is a lossless, constant delay channel. Because MPEG-2 uses compression to reduce the amount of bandwidth required by the audio and video components of a program, the algorithm is susceptible to data loss. Data loss will cause "glitches" in the decoding process which will appear to the viewer as visual and audible impairments. These decoding glitches will last until the decoder receives the next update for the lost portion of the data. This can easily result in impairments that remain visible for long periods (e.g., one half-second), depending on the type of data lost. The constant delay requirement has a more subtle origin. The timing in MPEG-2 encoders and decoders are controlled by a 27 MHz System Clock Reference (SCR) which has a tolerance of plus or minus 30 parts per million (ppm). For transmission over a VDT network, it is important that the MPEG-2 program source and the MPEG-2 decoder be synchronized so that the decoder consumes information at the same rate that the source sends it. If the two are not synchronized, buffer overflows or underruns may occur in the decoder, resulting in unacceptable glitches in the decoded program. Even with a tolerance of 30 ppm in the SCR frequency, these overflows and underruns can occur within minutes of beginning to decode a new program. As a result, it is important that the decoder synchronize itself to the MPEG-2 program source. The MPEG-2 timing model assumes that there is a constant delay across the transmission channel (or storage device). This assumption is important because it allows the MPEG-2 decoder to synchronize itself to an MPEG-2 program source via time stamps called System Clock References (SCR) in the PS or Program Clock References (PCR) in the TS. A channel with a variable delay introduces phase errors in these time stamps, and complicates

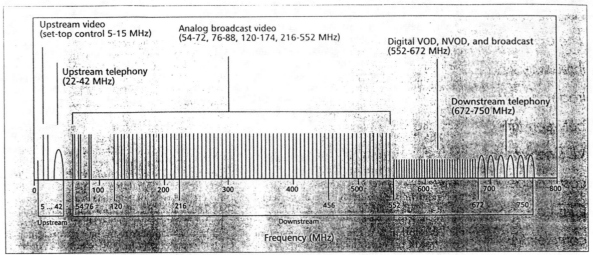

Upstream video
(set-top control 5-15 MHz)

Analog broadcast video
(54-72, 76-88, 120-174, 216-552 MHz)

Digital VOD, NVOD, and broadcast
(552-672 MHz)

Upstream telephony
(22-42 MHz)

Downstream telephony
(672-750 MHz)

Upstream Downstream

Frequency (MHz)

■ Figure 2. *An example allocation of frequency spectrum to VDT services.*

clock recovery and synchronization at the decoder.

ATM Protocols to Support VDT Applications

The ITU-T Recommendation H.310 specifies the broadband multimedia terminal recommendation for use over ATM networks, and includes a network adaptation protocol reference model [5, 6]. A simplified version of this model is shown in Fig. 3. Typically, an MPEG-2 subsystem outputs a 188-octet Transport Packet stream, which is then encapsulated into an ATM Adaptation Layer (AAL) packet. Standards organizations have defined four AAL formats [13]: AAL1, AAL2, AAL3/4, and AAL5. Except for AAL3/4, which is defined to support datagram services over pre-established connections, all are specified to support connection-oriented services. (For a more detailed discussion on AAL, see the section on AAL for MPEG-2 over ATM). An ATM cell consists of a 5-octet header which is made up of the routing, multiplexing, payload type, cell loss priority, and header error check fields. Typically, the ATM network concerns itself with the delivery of the ATM cells and operates at the ATM and physical layers. Layers above ATM (e.g., AAL, application) can be either terminated at the ATM User Network Interface (UNI) or the end-device (e.g., set-top). ATM cells are transported over an underlying physical medium (e.g., metallic, fiber) using a standard physical interface (e.g, DS3, OC-3c). On a DS3 ATM UNI interface, about 12 MPEG-2 channels of 3 Mb/s each, and on an OC-3c SONET ATM interface, about 45 MPEG-2 channels of 3 Mb/s each can be transported. Note that the MPEG-2 standard is scalable and can support bit rates of up to 15 Mb/s for Main profile/Main Level. Each video connection of desired bandwidth has a well defined route from the ATM UNI in the server to the destination UNI. The route is either preprovisioned on a Permanent Virtual Circuit (PVC) basis or established on-demand as a Switched Virtual Connection (SVC) basis. PVC connections are established at the time of service provisioning and can be changed as fast as the call manager will permit. SVC connections are made using Q.2931 signaling messages in a predesignated signaling VC. In architectures, where standard ATM UNI is not provided in the set-top, the connection from the server to the set-top consists of a series of connections, ATM and non-ATM, where a VDT Proxy Connection Management System sets up the individual connections based on resources available and coordinates the different connection segments.

Issues and Strategies of Transporting MPEG-2 over ATM

In both the interactive and broadcast digital video and multimedia applications, MPEG-2 TSs are transported over ATM. Although ATM products are being designed to meet service level end-to-end performance objectives, it is well known that the statistical nature of ATM technology results in cell delay variation and occasional cell loss. Therefore, a number of design and implementation issues must be addressed to ensure the quality of service (QoS) and inter-operability of equipment from different manufacturers [7, 8]. These include:

• Storage of information on the server, i.e., MPEG-2 storage format.
• Class of Service for ATM connections (CBR vs. VBR).
• MPEG-2 transport over ATM.
• Timing jitter at the ATM and AAL layers.
• Error recovery during the reassembly process (in the loop and in the CPE).
• Signaling and control.

From the end-to-end timing jitter and error recovery aspects, the third, fourth, and fifth issues are interrelated. Therefore, we will combine these issues into a single issue of choosing an AAL for MPEG-2 transport over ATM.

MPEG-2 Storage on Server

Content can be stored on the server in various formats. In the MPEG-2 Systems Layer paradigm a multimedia program can be made of audio, video, and data. These components can be stored as non-MPEG packet streams, PES streams, PSs, or TSs. Components of a multimedia content that need not be synchronized with each other can be stored as separate streams, e.g., PES. The PS and TS are the only multiplexing formats (producing a single stream) that define (and provide for) a common time base, which binds the PES streams of a multimedia content together for presentation at the correct time relative to each other. Therefore, a multimedia or video content can be stored as a PS or TS. As described earlier, the PS is designed with the assumption that the transport medium is error-free or the errors have been corrected, and the TS is designed for noisy environments where errors are likely, such as in the wide area network. Since the VDT networks involve transfer of information over long distances in a potentially lossy environment, the TS is more robust than the PS. While it is possible to store PSs, these will need to be converted to TSs requiring high speed and expensive real-time processing in the server-to-network interface. Another possibility is to store the content in ATM cell format. However, there is little point to this, since adapting TSs into ATM cells can be done readily by the AAL hardware, and the server may in fact need to correct the PCRs in the TS data as well as the information in the ATM cell header. Therefore, for VDT applications, the content is almost invariably stored in TS format.

Class of Service for ATM Connections (CBR Vs. VBR)

ATM was standardized to support both Constant Bit Rate (CBR) and Variable Bit Rate (VBR) services over a single network. VBR services enable bursty traffic to be statistically multiplexed, thus increasing network utilization. This has resulted in several ATM switch manufacturers designing switching platforms to support multiple quality of service (QoS) classes and priorities for CBR and VBR connections. Independent of the type of AAL used, whether a CBR or VBR service is used depends on how resource allocation, service segregation, and QoS are implemented in the switching platform. While VBR class of service could be used to transport MPEG-2 over ATM there are potential problems in several areas:
- Management of bandwidth resources in the distribution loop,
- Ability to limit the cell or MPEG packet delay jitter at the input to the set-top which impacts timing recovery and video playback.
- Ability to limit Program Clock Reference (PCR) or cell jitter at the server-ATM switch interface.
- Jitter introduced due to the AAL and MPEG-2 Transport Packet reassembly.

Therefore, at the present time, the CBR class of service is the preferred choice for many VDT service providers.

AAL for MPEG-2 over ATM

The issue of how to transport MPEG-2 data over ATM has been a topic of discussion in the industry for an extended period of time. The focus of this debate is on what additional functionalities beyond ATM need to be provided by the network to meet the needs of VDT applications.

As described earlier, the ideal channel for transporting MPEG-2 programs is a lossless one which introduces a constant delay. However, it is well known that ATM networks by themselves do not provide connections which meet those requirements. By adding an AAL with facilities for error correction and delay variation removal, we could meet the data loss and delay variation requirements reasonably well at the expense of additional complexity in the network. Such an ideal channel is not really required in order to deliver high quality video services over ATM. With extra processing capability in encoders and decoders, high quality MPEG-2 applications can still run over ATM networks that introduce data loss and delay variation. Alternatively, we could forgo the additional complexity in the CPE for a lower quality video service. Thus, there is a three-way trade-off between the VDT network cost/complexity, CPE cost/complexity, and the quality of the video service itself. The question that must be answered is: How much impairment, in the form of delay variation and data loss, can MPEG-2 applications sustain without having to drastically increase the cost of the CPE? Given the trade-off between network cost, CPE cost, and the quality of the VDT service, the challenge is to develop a cost effective transport network that still delivers a high quality video service to its subscribers. We will now discuss the data loss and delay variation service requirements in more detail, and then investigate the alternatives for adapting ATM networks for VDT services.

ATM Network Impairments

Effects of Data Loss

The principal two types of errors which will cause data loss in the ATM portion of a VDT network are random bit errors and ATM cell loss. Bit errors occur at the physical transmission layer, while cell loss occurs due to:
- Congestion in ATM multiplexers or buffers.
- Data corruption in cell header.

Once errored data arrives at the decoder, a decoding error will occur. The decoder may be able to mask the effects of this error. If not, the viewer will see or hear some type of error event, or "glitch," in the decoded program. The trend in industry right now is to attempt to model the QoS at the video application layer in terms of a perceivable Error Event Rate (EER). Typical acceptable error event rates range from one event per 15 minutes to one event per half hour [9, 10]. However, exact definition of acceptable EER for a VDT service will be up to the service provider.

Before physical layer bit errors or ATM layer cell losses can affect the application, they must

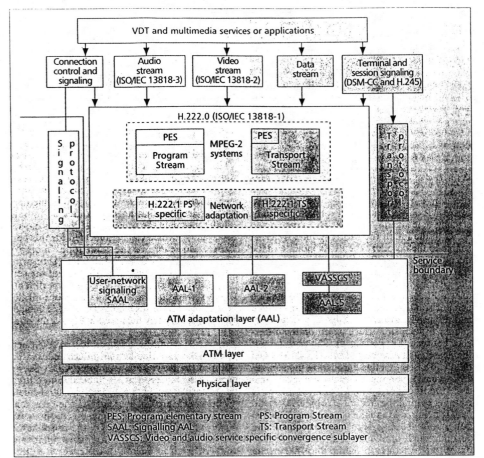

■ Figure 3. *Protocol stack to support MPEG-2 over ATM.*

pass through an AAL. The effect of these types of errors on a VDT application depends on the behavior of the AAL used for the network connection. If the AAL supports forward error correction (FEC), application data may never be lost. If the AAL supports error detection, it may discard the entire AAL Protocol Data Unit (AAL PDU) if an error is found. This is the case with AAL5. Discarding the entire AAL PDU could actually amplify the effect of the network error if the AAL PDUs used are large. If the AAL does not support any form of error detection or correction, the errors will be passed on to the application as they occur, as would be done by a "null" AAL. In delay-sensitive isochronous (e.g., video-audio) applications, lost cells and resulting AAL PDUs cannot be recovered since retransmission is not possible as an option. On the other hand, FEC probably will not be practical in VDT networks for correcting cell losses because of its complexity. Furthermore, its effectiveness is called into question when we consider the possibility that cell losses occur in bursts during congestion periods, since cell loss bursts will most likely overwhelm any FEC scheme.

Regarding bit error correction, the prevailing view in the industry is that the physical layer segments should be responsible for maintaining the integrity of the bit stream to the requirements of the VDT service. Given this, we still need to assume that the cells delivered to the ATM layer may contain occasional bit errors. The issue now becomes whether error detection is sufficient or if FEC is needed. This depends on the specific bit rate of the MPEG-2 compressed stream, the bit error rate (BER) of the physical medium, and the rate to which we would like to limit the "glitches" detected by the viewer. For example, the long-term SONET end-to-end BER objective is typically 10^{-10}, although it can be much lower. Carried over such a physical connection, a 3 Mb/s MPEG-2 bit stream would experience an error, on the average, every 50 to 60 minutes assuming only single bit errors occur. At higher MPEG-2 bit rates and over networks with higher BER, such errors would occur much more frequently. With a BER of 10^{-10}, most of the errors would land on encoded data, as opposed to the more critical tables needed to decode the data, and the resulting glitches that appear would be minor. For example, if a single block on the screen changed color for a single frame period, or even a large fraction of a second, it is unlikely that this would bother the viewer. However, if an error detection scheme in the AAL discarded an entire PDU every time a bit error was detected, much more data would be lost (assuming the PDU is much larger than a bit, as is the case for

560

AAL5), and the resulting decoder glitches would be more severe. In this case, error detection at the AAL could make the end-to-end performance at the application layer worse! A typical BER target for VDT networks being planned is less than 10^{-10}. At this rate, data loss due to bit errors are infrequent enough that error detection at the AAL can be used to detect errors in the ATM data stream caused by cell loss without causing serious performance degradation at the application layer.

Effects of Delay Variation (Jitter)

As mentioned above, for VDT applications MPEG-2 decoders need to be synchronized with the source of the program they are decoding. System clock synchronization is accomplished by sending time stamps, called PCRs in the TS and SCRs in the PS, in the MPEG-2 data from the source to the decoder. The PCRs indicate to the decoder what time its system clock should be read at the instant the time stamp is received at the systems level demultiplexer. The decoder uses a Phase Locked Loop (PLL) to make a comparison between the state of its own clock and the newly arrived PCR and adjusts the frequency of its system clock based on the difference between the two (Fig. 4). The error term is the phase difference between the local clock and the PCR-based timeline encoded in the MPEG-2 program. When the phase difference is positive, the decoder system clock reference is running behind the MPEG-2 source clock and data is being held in memory for an additional delay before being decoded. Therefore, the decoder needs to allocate more memory space for holding encoded program data. When the phase difference is negative, the decoder system clock is running ahead of the MPEG-2 source clock and data is being decoded early. To compensate for this case, the decoder must impose a delay before beginning to decode an incoming program, which also requires it to allocate more memory for holding data before it is decoded. Therefore, we see that this phase error term places requirements on the amount of buffer space that is required in the decoder. In general, the PLL will introduce a non-zero phase error between the two time lines once it has reached a steady state and acquired the remote clock.

The system clock reference recovered at the MPEG-2 decoder must be very stable, since besides being used for controlling timing in the decoder, it is used to derive the timing for the analog video signal (e.g., NTSC, PAL, or SECAM), that is ultimately output to the viewer's television set. For example, the Systems part of the ISO/ITU document specifies a long-term rate of change of the system clock frequency of 75×10^{-3} Hz/s. The stability requirements for the various components of these analog video signals are very stringent, particularly for the color subcarrier. Frequency shifts in the color subcarrier will lead to noticeable color distortion in the video image presented on the television screen.

Ideally, there is a constant delay between the MPEG-2 data source and the decoder, and the PCR values arriving at the decoder are all consistent. However, this will not be the case in ATM-based video network systems. Delay varia-

tion between the MPEG-2 data source and the decoder complicates the clock synchronization problem because it effectively introduces noise, or jitter, to the PCR values received at the decoder. If the jitter is passed on to the system clock reference, it will not provide a sufficiently stable time reference. As a result, the PLL must perform additional filtering in order to correctly estimate the remote system clock frequency. The additional filtering slows the PLL's responsiveness and increases the amount of time it requires to estimate the remote system clock frequency. This in turn affects the maximum phase error introduced by the PLL between the PCR-based time line and the local system clock reference, and therefore increases the amount of memory in the decoder that must be allocated to hold undecoded data. To some extent, there is memory available which can be allocated for this purpose. However, if the additional memory requirement causes a set-top manufacturer to need to add memory chips, the cost of the set-top will jump significantly. Early experiments have shown that PCR delay variations on the order of a few milliseconds are easily manageable by a properly designed MPEG-2 decoder [11, 12].

AALs can both remove end-to-end ATM network delay variation and introduce delay variation of their own. For example, AAL1 uses a smoothing buffer in order to be able to output data smoothly so as to appear as though the data is being delivered in a circuit-switched environment. This smoothing buffer removes network delay variation by design. On the other hand, AAL5 hardware actually introduces significant delay variation because of the way it builds PDUs for transport across the ATM network. This is mainly due to the variable size of the SDU that AAL5 supports and the data validity checks that are performed on the CPCS-PDU. Regardless of how a PDU is sent across the network, the AAL5 hardware at the terminating end of the connection will collect all of it before performing its PDU length and CRC checks and delivering the data to the application layer and, in the case of the MPEG-2 decoder, into the system demultiplexer. The rate at which data will be transferred between the AAL5 hardware and the system demultiplexer will typically be much faster than the average bit rate of the program being carried. Therefore, the data at the beginning of the AAL5 PDU will be delayed for a longer period across the network than the data at the end of the AAL5 PDU. If the PDU is large, this difference will be non-negligible. For example, for a PDU size of 20 cells and a program rate of 6 Mb/s, it takes an average of approximately 1.2 ms for a complete AAL5 PDU to arrive at the ATM connection termination point. If the PDU is transferred to the decoder at a rate of 50 Mb/s (a conservative estimate), it will be transferred in 150 μs. This means that the bits at the front of the PDU will be delayed over a millisecond more than the bits at the end of the PDU, assuming the rate of transfer between the AAL5 hardware and the MPEG-2 system decoder is much larger than the average program rate. For most MPEG-2 data, this type of delay variation does not have any adverse effects on the decoder. However, for the PCR values, this delay variation is very significant.

Whereas the delay variation can be handled at the decoder to some extent, it must be limited across the network to a range which is manageable by the set top. There are two approaches which can be used to reduce the delay variation across the network. The first is to dimension the various network elements so that they are underutilized, resulting in little network congestion and therefore smaller amounts of delay variation. The second approach is to provide additional functionality in the AAL which dynamically buffers data in order to provide a constant network delay to the application layer.

In practice, there are three options available for adapting MPEG-2 to ATM for VDT services: AAL1, AAL2, and AAL5. AAL1 has been defined to provide circuit emulation services over ATM networks. AAL2 is a place holder for an AAL which provides real-time services for VBR applications. AAL5 was defined for carrying variable bit rate data services, and by itself does not have any special functions provided for real-time applications.

AAL1 — AAL1 was designed to provide support for circuit emulation services across ATM networks. It provides for constant delay across network connections, and has support for FEC. As such, it provides the services required for an ideal network connection carrying CBR MPEG-2 traffic. However, AAL1 also has a few shortcomings with respect to MPEG-2. The first is that it only supports CBR connections. This is not a problem in the short term, since the initial VDT deployments will use CBR MPEG-2 programming. However, service providers will want to support the use of VBR MPEG-2 programming in their networks in the future in order to improve performance and reduce costs. The second shortcoming is that AAL1 hardware was not widely available for incorporation into the VDT network equipment as of early 1995. Furthermore, using AAL1 will require the end equipment to support two AALs, since AAL5 is already required to support nonisochronous data and signaling.

AAL2 — The functionality for AAL2 has not yet been defined, and therefore it is not a viable option for any of the VDT deployments being planned. If it is ever defined, AAL2 could eventually become the solution of choice for supporting VDT services on ATM networks. However, this will depend on how well the definition of AAL2 functionality takes into account the economic and performance considerations of VDT applications.

AAL5 — The AAL5 functionality with respect to VDT can be divided into two layers: the video-audio service specific convergence sublayer (VASSCS) and the common part sublayer (CPAAL5) (Fig. 3). Much of the debate in the standards bodies and industry forums over AAL5 has focused on whether a VASSCS is necessary and, if so, what error correction and timing recovery functionality it should have. In theory,

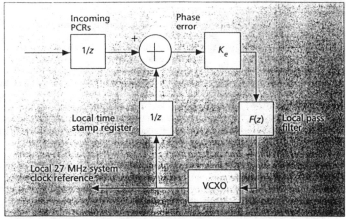

■ Figure 4. *Block diagram of a phase locked loop (PLL) used to recover an MPEG-2 system clock reference from PCR values embedded in a Transport Stream. Phase errors in the PCR values are filtered to an extent by the PLL, but some noise (in the form of frequency fluctuations) will occur in the recovered system clock.*

it would be possible to use this sublayer to provide constant delay across the network connection, as well as introduce error detection or correction. The VASSCS could be designed to support CBR as well as VBR MPEG-2 traffic, and more generally to support other nonMPEG video-audio services that do not have all the functionality of the MPEG-2 Systems layer. Therefore, one disadvantage of including a VASSCS is that the additional functionality it provides would be redundant with functionality provided at the MPEG-2 systems sublayer. This makes it unclear whether the increased cost and complexity of the additional hardware would justify itself in overall end-to-end cost savings. In the end, a concensus has emerged that the services provided by CPAAL5 will be sufficient for MPEG-2 transport (at least for constant bit rate programming).

The advantages of AAL5 over alternate solutions are as follows:

• Equipment adapting MPEG-2 to ATM will already support AAL5, since it will be used to carry the Q.2931 signaling messages required to support SVCs. Both the computer and telecommunications industries strongly support AAL5, which is a particularly important consideration with respect to MPEG-2, since it will eventually be used in a wide variety of environments. AAL5 hardware is available now, and this approach does not require support of any other AALs which may or may not have been standardized (e.g., AAL2).

• With the adoption of the "null" CS for this proposal, no further hardware support will be required of the network, and the standards bodies do not need to define further network functionality. (A "null" CS will be a VASSCS without any functionality.)

• In theory, the same solution should work for VBR MPEG-2 transport. However, it should be kept in mind that introducing large amounts of VBR traffic to a VDT network will most likely increase the network impairments experienced by the traffic carried. It may be that in this case,

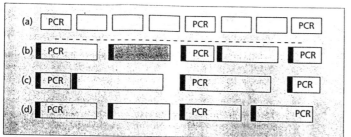

■ Figure 5. *AAL5 encapsulation of MPEG-2 transport packets; a) original Transport Stream — transport packets carrying a PCR are marked as such (note that in reality, PCR values are transmitted infrequently up to once every 100 ms); b) PCR-aware packing of transport packets into AAL5 PDUs with a maximum PDU size of two transport packets; c) PCR-aware packing of transport packets into AAL5 PDUs with a maximum PDU size of three transport packets; d) PCR-unaware packing of transport packets into AAL5 PDUs with a maximum PDU size of two transport packets.*

AAL5 will not be able to provide sufficient QoS for VBR VDT services. The challenge that network providers will face is how to control, manage, and operate a large network whose traffic can be nondeterministic yet requiring that stringent and bounded performance criteria be met.

This approach also has the following disadvantages:

• CPAAL5 does not have facilities for FEC. However, error correction, particularly cell error correction, is expensive at the AAL. As described earlier, it makes more sense to deliver sufficiently low bit error rates for MPEG applications using appropriate error correction at the physical layer, and to dimension the ATM network appropriately for the intended applications to control the cell loss rates.

• Although the AAL5 Receiver Process (as it is currently defined) can indicate to the management plane what types of errors it detects, it does not pass the user payload of "damaged" AAL5 PDUs up to the application layer [13]. Therefore, in the event that the AAL5 Receiver Process detects any bit errors or cell losses, one or more TS packets will be lost, preempting the MPEG-2 decoder's ability to do error management and recovery. However, recent deliberations at the ATM Forum have concluded that passing of the corrupted CPCS-PDUs (to the higher layer with appropriate primitives between CPAAL5 and MCPAAL5 entities) that pass the Length field check is highly desirable, and must be supported as an option. Moreover, those CPCS-PDUs that fail the above test are discarded in the reassembly process with appropriate primitives between CPAAL5 and MCPAAL5 entities. The above agreement leaves it up to the decoder to decide whether or not to use the errored CPCS-PDU with or without error concealment.

• Depending on how MPEG-2 TS is encapsulated into AAL5 PDUs, AAL5 can potentially introduce large amounts of delay variation across the network connection, and therefore introduce large phase errors into the PCRs used for system clock recovery. In particular, some video server and set-top decoder manufacturers would like to use large fixed-size AAL5 PDUs, allowing them to improve the performance of their systems

without incurring significant costs. However, as described above, large fixed-size AAL5 PDUs will introduce significant delay variation for their payload.

It is important to remember that using AAL5 for MPEG-2 transport does not by itself put constraints on the QoS delivered by the network to the application. The performance delivered by AAL5 in VDT networks must be carefully controlled through proper network provisioning and dimensioning so that it is acceptable for VDT services.

Status of Standards and Industry Implementation Agreements

At present, the ATM Forum has been most active in defining how ATM will be adapted to VDT services. The Phase 1 ATM Forum Implementation Agreement (IA) for Audio-visual Multimedia Services (AMS) under development by the Service Aspects and Applications Sub-Working Group (SAA SWG) is limited in scope to VOD services. However, many equipment manufacturers will follow the implementation described in this document for the other VDT services as well. The ATM Forum agreement is scheduled to be completed in December 1995, and will be publicly available to the industry some time in early 1996. (Note that the AMS: Video on Demand Implementation Agreement 1.0 [6] is a draft document that is yet to be approved both by the SAA SWG and the whole Forum membership).

The draft ATM Forum IA specifies the use of AAL5 to support carrying MPEG-2 Single Program Transport Streams (SPTS) over ATM. In November 1994 in Kyoto, the SAA SWG had voted to adopt a "PCR-aware" scheme for encapsulating MPEG-2 TS packets into AAL5 PDUs. However, at its most recent meeting in August 1995 in Toronto, when the straw ballot was taken, the SWG decided to reopen the TS packing issue. The Group decided to study an alternate scheme (in addition to the one that was agreed to in November 1994) that can be termed a "PCR-unaware" scheme. A decision on which proposal (or variation) to adopt is planned to be reached at the next meeting of the Forum in October 1995 in Hawaii. (Note that the current IA [6] specifies only the "PCR-aware" scheme. This document is being updated to reflect the decisions and the agreements reached at the Forum's most recent meeting in Toronto. The new version of the document is scheduled for a second straw ballot in October 1995. For the latest on the status of the resolution of the MPEG-2 TS packing issue, the reader is strongly advised to check with the ATM Forum.)

"PCR-Aware" Proposal
As shown in Fig. 5, the PCR-aware packing scheme encapsulates *N* MPEG-2 SPTS packets into fixed-size AAL5 PDUs, with the exception that, if a TS packet is carrying a PCR, it must be the last TS packet in the PDU. However, the very last AAL5 PDU from the TS can have fewer than *N* non-PCR packets. The default PDU size is eight cells, which is large enough to carry two

TS packets, and must be supported by all implementations. The PDU size can be negotiated through either network provisioning for PVCs or signaling for SVCs.

While this scheme increases the cost of equipment on the transmitting side, it should help to control costs on the receiving end. This is because the delay variation (packetization jitter) introduced by AAL5 convergence sub-layer is minimized at the source, resulting in potentially smaller dejittering buffer and less complex timing recovery circuitry at the receiver. Since there are many more receivers than transmitters in a VDT network, this additional complexity in the transmitter seemed justified to the ATM Forum membership. Note that the requirements of the PCR-aware encapsulation scheme can be met in many different ways, and therefore exact implementations will be up to the equipment manufacturers.

"PCR-Unaware" Proposal

The PCR-unaware packing scheme encapsulates 'N' MPEG-2 TS packets into fixed size AAL5 PDUs without regard to where the PCRs occur in the TS (Fig. 5). However, the very last AAL5 PDU from the TS can have fewer than N Transport Packets. The default PDU size is eight cells, which is large enough to carry two TS packets, and must be supported by all implementations. The PDU size can be negotiated through either network provisioning for PVCs or signaling for SVCs.

While this proposal will simplify the transmitter design at the source, the receiver will need to absorb higher levels of PCR jitter, especially in the case of $N > 2$, resulting in potentially more complex MPEG-2 receivers. At the present time, the issue of where to keep the complexity (at the server or the set-top box) is a highly debatable one in the industry. Furthermore, a satisfactory resolution of the above issue is hindered due to the lack of reliable and in-depth (and exhaustive) experimental results on performance and cost trade-offs of the various packing proposals.

According to a recent implementation agreement at the ATM Forum [6] passing of the corrupted CPCS-PDUs (to the higher layer with appropriate primitives between CPAAL5 and MCPAAL5 entities) that pass the Length field check is highly desirable, and must be supported as an option. Moreover, those CPCS-PDUs that fail the above test are discarded in the reassembly process with appropriate primitives between CPAAL5 and MCPAAL5 entities. The above agreement leaves it up to the decoder to decide whether or not to use the errored CPCS-PDU with or without error concealment.

Signaling and Control

At the present time, Q.2931 supports the capability to request and negotiate upstream and downstream QoS and bandwidth requirements, class of service (CBR or VBR), and the CPCS-SDU size. Other signaling parameters that need to be supported include the H.222.1 profile and the content and session correlation ID [6]. This work is in progress at the ATM Forum and the ITU.

A multimedia session is defined as an association between two or more users, providing capability to group together the resources needed for an instance of a service [14]. User-to-Network and User-to-User control and operations specific primitives are provided in a set of protocols being specified in the Digital Storage Media Command and Control (DSM-CC) document [14]. The Annex F of the document provides details and examples of the association between session and ATM connection management and control, and the resources that are requested both at the session and the connection layers.

For VOD sessions, the time it takes to set up and tear down a point-to-point connection or session between information source(s) and the end-user impacts the service response time. Until SVC capability (based on ITU-TS Q.2931) becomes available on the ATM switches and the associated termination devices, the on-demand connections through the switch would continue to be made on a fast-PVC basis. Some performance parameters for the call set-up are connection set-up time and the number of connections a switch's connection manager can make per unit of time at busy hour. Both SNMP- and OSI/CMISE-based protocol stacks in the call or connection manager are being optimized by reducing overhead. At the same time, high-speed processors are being implemented to improve the performance. Furthermore, in addition to supporting first-party call control, most ATM switch manufacturers and system designers will support third-party session and call control. For interactive applications, once the session and the associated connections have been set up, the response time to any user initiated commands should be comparable to that in a local environment using a multimedia PC or workstation.

Summary and Conclusions

The technology needed to transport digital video and multimedia over the emerging video dial tone networks is now on the horizon. MPEG-2 video and audio coding standards and the MPEG-2 Systems Recommendation for multiplexing video, audio, and data into single or multiple streams suitable for storage or transmission are being adopted by the industry. At the systems layer, the TS is the widely preferred multiplexing and packetization technique and, for transmission and switching, ATM has emerged as the technology of choice for digital broadcast and interactive applications. H.310 is a multimedia terminal protocol stack for adapting multimedia and VDT applications and services over ATM, and has been adopted by the ITU and the ATM Forum. For the past two years, major issues of PCR recovery, type of AAL to use, and error recovery have been the subjects of intense debate and discussion in the industry and standards organizations. To meet immediate interoperability requirements, a strong consensus has emerged in the industry to carry TS over CPAAL5 with a null VASSCS. Currently, H.222.1 (Fig. 3) has not been defined, and therefore, will not be implemented in early deployments. PCR jitter removal and recovery will rely on the MPEG-2 layer with the expectation that the delay jitter at the ATM layer will be con-

The requirements of the PCR-aware encapsulation scheme can be met in many different ways, and therefore exact implementations will be up to the equipment manufacturers.

strained within a specified upper bound. On error recovery, it would be up to the physical layer to ensure bit-stream integrity, and in the event of any bit or cell errors where the CRC fails but the Length field check passes, it is highly desirable to pass the reassembled AAL5 SDU to the MPEG layer along with the error indication. This will provide the decoder the option to ignore or use the errored Transport Packet(s) with or without error concealment. On TS packing, there continues to be intense debate in the industry on standardizing a packing scheme to encapsulate MPEG-2 TS in CPAAL5 PDU. In the future, other service classes (e.g., VBR) and AAL(s) may be defined or supported. In view of the intense efforts (and interest shown) by the industry to arrive at solutions to interoperability issues, it is clear that we will see the maturing of the VDT technology sooner than later; and, this would mean its rapid deployment to realize digital video, multimedia, and related services for everyone.

Acknowledgments

The ideas presented in this article were developed through extensive interaction with our colleagues at NYNEX, Bellcore, and the ATM Forum. Readers are encouraged to review the contributions to the ATM Forum Service Aspects & Applications (SAA) Sub-Working Group for detailed discussions on many of these issues. Another good source of information is the ATM Forum's tutorial on MPEG-2 over ATM available through the Ambassador Program.

References

[1] W. Y. Chen and D. L. Waring, "Applicability of ADSL to Support Video Dial Tone in the Copper Loop," *IEEE Commun. Mag.*, vol. 32, no. 5, May 1994, pp. 102-108.

[2] Information Technology -Generic Coding of Moving Pictures and Associated Audio, Part 1: Systems, Recommendation ITU H.222.0, ISO/IEC 13818-1.

[3] Information Technology — Generic Coding of Moving Pictures and Associated Audio, Part 2: Video, Recommendation H.262, ISO/IEC 13818-2.

[4] Information Technology — Generic Coding of Moving Pictures and Associated Audio, Part 3: Audio, ISO/IEC 13818-3.

[5] ITU-T Study Group 15 Experts Group for Video Coding and Systems in ATM and Other Network Environments, "Network Adaptation for the Broadband Audiovisual Communication Systems and Terminals," TD.22 (Kamifukuoka) with Annexes 1 and 2, Jan. 27, 1995.

[6] S. Wright, ed., "SAA Audio-visual Multimedia Service (AMS) Implementation Agreement, Version 1.0," ATM Forum Technical Committee Draft, Contribution No. 95-0012R5.

[7] S. Dixit, " AAL, Timing Recovery and Error Detection/Correction for MPEG over ATM, "ATM Forum Contribution 94-0100, Jan. 1994.

[8] S. Dixit, "Role of ATM in Digital Broadband Video Dial Tone Networks," *Proc. of 1st Tech. Conf. on Telecommunications R&D in Massachusetts*, vol. VI, Oct. 1994, pp. 39-49.

[9] R. Hilton and R. Prodan, "CBR MPEG-2 Transport over ATM," ATM Forum Contribution 94-0691, July, 1994.

[10] M. Schwartz and D. Beaumont, "Quality of Service Requirements for Audio-Visual Multimedia Services," ATM Forum Contribution 94-0640, July, 1994.

[11] M. Perkins and P. Skelly, "A Hardware MPEG Clock Recovery Experiment in the Presence of ATM Jitter," ATM Forum Contribution 94-0434, May 1994.

[12] M. Perkins et al., "Packing of MPEG-2 Transport Packets into AAL5 PDUs," ATM Forum Contribution 94-1146, Nov. 1994.

[13] "Asynchronous Transfer Mode (ATM) and ATM Adaptation Layer (AAL) Protocols," Bellcore GR-1113-CORE, Issue 1, Release 1, July 1994.

[14] Information Technology -Generic Coding of Moving Pictures and Associated Audio, Part 6: MPEG-2 Digital Storage Media Command and Control (Committee Draft), ISO/IEC 13818-6, May 1995.

[15] M.-T. Sun, "MPEG-2 Systems and the Transport over ATM," Circuits and Systems Tutorial, IEEE ISCAS '94, C. Toumazou, Editor, pp. 139-146.

[16] S. Dixit and A. Kumar, "Proposals for Carrying CBR MPEG-2 Transport Streams Over ATM for Interactive and Broadcast Video-Audio Services," ATM Forum Contribution 94-1124, Nov. 1994.

[17] D. Large, "Creating a Network for Interactivity," *IEEE Spectrum*, vol. 32, no. 4, April 1995, pp. 58-63.

[18] S. Dixit, "A Look at the Video Dial Tone Network," *IEEE Spectrum*, vol. 32, no. 4, April 1995, pp. 64-65.

[19] Special issue on Fiber-Optic Subscriber Loops, *IEEE Commun. Mag.*, vol. 32, no. 2, Feb. 1994.

Biographies

SUDHIR S. DIXIT [SM '94] received a B.E. in electrical engineering from Maulana Azad College of Technology, Bhopal University, an M.E. in electronics engineering from Birla Institute of Technology and Science, a Ph.D. in electronics and telecommunications engineering from the University of Strathclyde, and an M.B.A. from the Florida Institute of Technology. He has held various engineering and management positions with Standard Telecommunication Laboratories (now BNR Europe Ltd), Harris Corporation, Motorola Codex, Wang Laboratories, and most recently GTE Laboratories, before joining NYNEX Science and Technology, Framingham, Massachusetts, in 1991. He is currently responsible for architecting broadband VDT networks, and specializes in such areas as ATM, multimedia compression and communication, loop architectures, traffic management and control, and session and signaling protocols. His other areas of interest and involvement are in wide area network services (e.g., Frame Relay, Cell Relay, SMDS) over ATM backbone network. Prior to joining NYNEX, he worked on several projects that led to work on modeling and analysis of packet switched (ATM) networks, congestion control, video compression, document imaging, image restoration, image analysis & synthesis, data modems, and VLSI design. He has published more than 30 technical papers, has been granted four U.S. patents, and represents NYNEX at the ATM Forum. His e-mail address is: dixit@nynexst.com.

PAUL SKELLY received a B.S. in engineering from Cornell University in 1989, and M.S. and Ph.D degrees in electrical engineering from Columbia University in 1991 and 1994, respectively. After graduating, he worked at Bellcore as a member of technical staff on real-time video transport problems. Since April 1995 he has been a member of technical staff at GTE Laboratories, where he is responsible for doing performance analysis and developing engineering tools for SS7 networks as well as broadband video systems. His e-mail address is: pauls@gte.com.

Building Networks for the Wide and Local Areas Using Asynchronous Transfer Mode Switches and Synchronous Optical Network Technology

John H. Naegle, Steven A. Gossage, Nicholas Testi, Michael O. Vahle, and Joseph H. Maestas

Abstract— Sandia National Laboratories is using a set of evolving technologies to develop a standards-based approach to wide- and local-area networking, which offers the potential of gigabit speeds. In particular, asynchronous transfer mode (ATM) switches and synchronous optical network (SONET) technologies were used to build a supercomputing network between its California and New Mexico sites and now is being deployed in the local-area environment. The progress of these endeavors and the lessons learned are discussed in this paper.

I. INTRODUCTION

SANDIA National Laboratories is a multiprogram research and development facility operated for the United States Department of Energy (DOE) by Martin Marietta. It employs more than 8500 people, with headquarters in Albuquerque, NM, and a major site in Livermore, CA. During four decades of existence, its mission has expanded from its original focus on nuclear weapons research and development to include research on advanced military technologies, energy programs, arms verification and control technology, and applied research in numerous scientific fields' [1].

To support these mission areas, Sandia has deployed large supercomputers and developed associated data networks to support its many research efforts. A few years ago, many of Sandia's researchers began focusing outward on partnerships with industry, academia, and other government agencies in a major effort to support technology transfer and economic competitive initiatives encouraged by the DOE. To support the historical mission and its evolving outward focus, Sandia was faced with providing supercomputer facilities in two environments, open and secure.

To avoid duplicating both environments at both of its sites, Sandia elected to consolidate supercomputing at its New Mexico site. A group of customers was gathered to define current and future speed, reliability, and extensibility requirements for both the network and the supercomputers. At a high level the network requirements can be summarized as:

- The network had to be compatible with existing networks and provide secure, remote access equivalent to what was available locally.

- The network had to be extensible to partners throughout the country.
- The network had to match the performance the users thought they would be able to achieve in their local environment; that is, sustain at least four concurrent 6 Mb/s data transfers between Albuquerque and Livermore.
- The network technology had to be scalable to gigabit per second speeds.
- The network had to be highly reliable.
- The technology had to hold the promise of being useful in both the local and wide areas to avoid the long term need of supporting and maintaining multiple technologies.

A design group was assigned to identify and evaluate the available and evolving network and communications technologies to meet the identified requirements. After evaluating several different technologies, the design team selected asynchronous transfer mode (ATM) switches and synchronous optical network (SONET) technology as the most promising to meet the set of identified requirements. A six-prong strategy was adopted to embody the promise of the technology. It consisted of

- building a SONET infrastructure at Sandia,
- developing an ATM testbed to study the performance and capability of the technology,
- deploying the technology as part of the supercomputer consolidation,
- deploying ATM in the local-area environment to high end customers and using conferences and national forums to demonstrate the capabilities of the technology,
- participating in national standards bodies and research networks focusing on ATM [2], [3],
- focus on enabling and exploring areas like security, encryption, and high performance interfaces.

The remainder of this paper details Sandia's early experiences with implementing this strategy. In particular, the reasons for choosing SONET and ATM are discussed, Sandia's envisioned network architecture is described, the supercomputer network that was built between Livermore, CA, and Albuquerque, NM, is presented, and early experiences with ATM in the local-area environment are detailed along with an experiment conducted in association with the Supercomputing '93 conference in Portland, OR. The areas of advanced study are in their infancy and will be discussed in later publications.

Manuscript received March 11, 1994; revised September 7, 1994. This work was performed at Sandia National Laboratories and was supported in part by the U.S. Department of Energy under Contract DE-AC04-94AL85000.
The authors are with Sandia National Laboratories, Albuquerque, NM 87185 USA.
IEEE Log Number 9407072.

Reprinted from IEEE Journal on Selected Areas in Communications, Vol. 12, No. 4, May 1995, pp. 662-671.

II. WHY SONET AND ATM?

Before launching on a program to deploy ATM and SONET, Sandia compared many high performance networking technologies [4]. It is not within the scope of this paper to fully discuss all of those comparisons so we will focus on the major features of SONET and ATM that are important to Sandia. Because the Albuquerque campus more closely resembles the metropolitan area network (MAN) model than it does a local-area network (LAN), the integration of traditional telecommunications technologies (DS1 and DS3) with the LAN technologies had been going on for some time in order to overcome the loss budget and distance limitations of LAN technologies. The best early fit of the "telco" technologies with the LAN technologies came about when we were able to interconnect distributed routers over DS3 (internal) links multiplexed at optical carrier (OC) 3 rates. The SONET transport network provided these key benefits:

1) very high reliability through ring and alternate routing topologies, one-to-one protection, and automatic switch over; a standard defined from OC-3 (155 Mb/s) through OC-48 (2.488 Gb/s)—a much wider range than any competing LAN transport technology;
2) very efficient utilization of optical fiber conductors (only four fibers required in any protected link);
3) very high bandwidth capacity available in a scalable, modular fashion; bandwidth increases through increases in modulation rates instead of in the number of conductors required;
4) standard for both national and international telecommunications networks to further enhance interoperability in a heterogeneous environment and to improve the seamless interconnection of local- and wide-area environments;
5) support for interfaces to all types of information — voice, video, and data;
6) essentially unlimited loss budget and distance range; and
7) integrated operations, administrations, management, and provisioning support.

We first focused on ATM switches as a means to interconnect distributed LAN's and to overcome the bottleneck of interconnecting LAN's with shared-media technologies. ATM offers the following advantages for LAN and wide-area network (WAN) interconnection or LAN fabric implementation:

1) low latency;
2) high bandwidth, capacity, and scalability;
3) support for multiple data rates;
4) insulation/isolation of independent networks; and
5) transparency to application or data type.

At Sandia, ATM brought not only a new integrating technology but also introduced switching to our LAN/WAN picture which had been dominated by essentially point-to-point links. Switching allowed pairwise connections between hosts and networks to utilize the full bandwidth of their respective ports instead of some portion of a shared-media network. Because ATM supports access at many different data rates, one host-to-host circuit could be operated at DS3 rates while another operated at OC-3 concatenated (OC-3c) rates without

any conflict. Each network end point can use the amount of bandwidth needed and not be required to operate at a higher (or lower) rate than meets their application. In shared-media networks with N nodes, each node is required to operate at the same transmission rate and yet only share 1/Nth of the total bandwidth depending on other traffic in the network. A sixteen port ATM switch operating at 155 Mb/s per port supplies about 2.5 Gb/s of networking capacity where each workstation can utilize up to 155 Mb/s (full duplex) in independent, pairwise links. In comparison, on a fiber distributed data interface (FDDI) network with sixteen simultaneous transfers operating, each pair of workstations would only obtain about 8.25 Mb/s, a very small fraction of the top bandwidth the host was required to have in order to be a member of the network. Adding ATM switching multiplied the number of simultaneous, independent LAN interconnections that could occur at full host interface throughput in our network. By changing from shared media interconnection to switching, more scalable bandwidth was added in a very cost effective way. The cost per Mb/s of bandwidth delivered through interconnecting networks with ATM switches is approximately three to thirteen times lower than interconnecting with routers, especially when considering multiple ports each with a bandwidth of greater than 100 Mb/s. Although switches and routers are not equivalent devices, this difference in bandwidth cost suggests that switches are a much more economical way to interconnect networks when extra routing functionalities are not required.

ATM technology offers the potential to scale beyond shared media technologies as illustrated by Fig. 1. There has been a great deal of speculation concerning the key applications that will be necessary to make ATM the networking technology of choice. Much of the speculation has pointed to multimedia and other video applications as the main drivers to bring the ATM technology to the LAN environment. Sandia and other National Laboratories have pioneered the visualization of complex data [5] in order to analyze and understand fundamental processes at work. For this type of analysis, data, and high resolution video are coupled together and passed through high performance networks to researchers. In 1987, Winkler and his colleagues at Los Alamos National Laboratory created a state-of-the-art numerical analysis laboratory where problems in fluid dynamics could be simulated and visualized. In their visualizations, they were able to create a sustained data rate of 60 Mb/s for images of 512×512 (pixels) with 8 bits per color at 30 frames/s. Due to the innovative nature of the experiments, many parts of the network that supported a maximum burst rate of 80 Mb/s were proprietary [6]. In contrast, today pairs of workstations connected by standard OC-3c (155 Mb/s) circuits through an ATM switch can sustain 71 Mb/s of application data throughput (memory to memory) in a low cost desktop environment that could well be extended to the wide area. Further tests indicated that the full SONET payload of over 149 Mb/s was available. The proprietary state-of-the-art visualization network of seven years ago can now be implemented with the standard ATM and SONET technologies.

ATM and SONET technologies have the capability to deliver the operational and performance goals noted above.

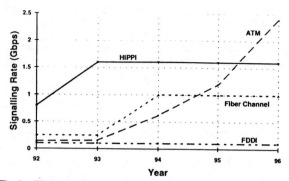

Fig. 1. Workstation/host network access rates.

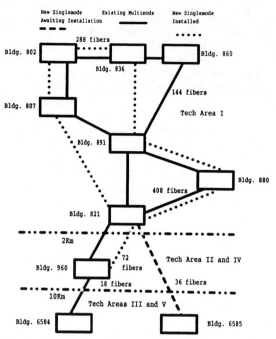

Fig. 2. Optical fiber interbuilding trunks.

Early adoption of these technologies will enable Sandia to bypass intermediate networking approaches to deliver higher performance at lower cost and avoid the cost of pervasive shared media networking implementation and replacement. ATM technology treats all information (voice, data, video) as cells and thus provides a single virtual networking technology that can be connected via a single, standard, physical transport technology (SONET) over copper or fiber in both LAN and WAN applications. SONET physical layer transport offers critical advantages to Sandia in the areas of network integration (all information types in a single network), seamless WAN/LAN (same technologies in both environments), scalable and variable data rates (51 Mb/s–2.5 Gb/s), large capacity at low cost for delivered bandwidth, efficient use of cable plant, distance insensitivity, and high reliability. Also, a single set of networking technologies will be more cost efficient and easier to maintain or extend than the multiplicity of technologies currently employed. The ability of ATM/SONET to support a variety of data rates in a single cohesive network with heretofore unrealized capacity (2.5–80 Gb/s) provides unprecedented opportunities for network applications and evolution as client requirements evolve.

III. Sandia's SONET Infrastructure

Sandia National Laboratories operates two sites separated by 1100 m. One site is in Livermore, CA and the other is in Albuquerque, NM. Both Laboratories have been involved in the deployment of optical fiber cables since the early 1980's. More recently, both Laboratories have begun aggressive installation of optical fiber (multimode and single mode) to the desktop in order to keep pace with the increasing demand for additional bandwidth by a variety of applications. The standard desktop distribution will provide four multimode (FDDI specification) fibers, four single-mode fibers, and three each, four pair unshielded twisted pair (UTP) copper (Class V) connections. The copper will be terminated with RJ45 connectors while the optical fibers will be terminated with the ST connector [7]. The physical size differences between the two campuses led to the selection of two different networking architectures. In Livermore, a more compact site with a smaller customer population (approximately ten subnets) and a rich fiber environment, the collapsed backbone topology was selected relying on the fiber optic interrepeater link (FOIRL) standard to link distributed

smart Ethernet hubs to a central site router that was in turn connected to high performance resources through a FDDI ring. In Albuquerque, customer LAN's were typically located 2–3 km (wire distance) from the central computing center with significant customer populations up to 10 km away and there were more than 300 individual networks to be served. See Fig. 2. Because more networks with wider distribution had to be served in Albuquerque, a distributed router network was implemented. Early deployment of SONET is already benefiting the production router network by providing a highly reliable, flexible interconnection infrastructure.

Customer requirements for reliable, high performance, private links accelerated the SONET deployment and positioned the transport network for the evolution to the delivery of ATM at OC-3c rates to the Massively Parallel Computing Research Laboratory (MPCRL) for an early customer trial. The MPCRL was also the first customer for the delivery of DS3 over OC-3 in 1991 [8]. Fig. 3 shows the scope of the SONET implementation at Sandia. In Livermore, SONET OC-3 multiplexers are used to deliver SMDS over DS3 to four individual FDDI rings. In Albuquerque, the OC-3 SONET backbone is used to provide DS3 to 11 buildings and to bring DS3 to the US West point of presence where DS3 and OC-3c are available through an external OC-48 connection. In addition, the OC-3 backbone distributes DS3 throughout the central computing facility. OC-3c and DS3 are also provided internally to three locations through an OC-12 backbone that will support two additional connections by the end of 1994. In Livermore, the external link will be upgraded to OC-12 by the end of this year.

The key enabler for our SONET backbones is an extensive inter and intrabuilding optical fiber cable plant. In

TABLE I
POWER DELIVER BANDWIDTH OVER LONG DISTANCES

Interface Standard	Maximum Unrepeated Distance (km)	Fiber Type	Power*
Ethernet	5	Multimode	0.05
FDDI	2	Multimode, Single mode	.2
	20		2
SONET OC-3	20	Single mode	3.1
HiPPI	20	Single mode	22
SONET OC-48	40	Single mode	100

*Power = Bandwidth in Gbps * Distance in Km

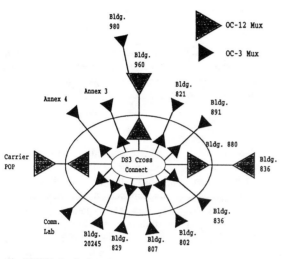

Fig. 3.   SONET distribution of DS3 at Sandia.

Livermore, the interbuilding cable facility consists typically of 48 multimode fibers and 12 single-mode fibers. The first intrabuilding distribution included 144 multimode (50 μm) fibers but that has given way to a 144 single-mode fiber trunk. The design decision to utilize a multiplexed, independent transport demarcation network based on SONET simplified the design of the optical fiber backbone and clarified the performance requirements of the media. The choice of single mode exclusively for the interbuilding cable plant versus multimode or some combination of the two media types was carefully considered. Use of the single-mode-based SONET LAN transport network decoupled interbuilding transport performance requirements from the primarily multimode based intrabuilding networks. None of the LAN technologies could meet the bandwidth requirements or the distance/attenuation challenges of the Albuquerque campus. See Table I. By selecting an independent physical transport network of SONET multiplexers that was well-matched to even more challenging optical fiber environments, we were able to install and provision high bandwidth, high-reliability channels with a standard facility.

IV. SUPERCOMPUTER CONSOLIDATION NETWORK

The long haul environment represented by the Supercomputing Consolidation Project presented some unique networking problems, including high delay, protocol tuning, and reliability. Several different technologies for the end equipment were considered, ranging from bridges/routers to switch gear. A design using ATM switches with switched multimegabit data service (SMDS) as the access method from the legacy LAN environment was selected. SMDS was the first cell-based technology for connectionless LAN interconnection and provided a migration route to an all ATM network. Sandia was an early adopter of the cell based SMDS service. Frequently, there is debate over the deployment of SMDS versus "pure ATM." At the time that the consolidation of the supercomputer networks was required (1991) the only mature cell based technology/service was SMDS. In addition, there were no direct switch or router interfaces available to accomplish the interconnection of legacy LAN's. SMDS also provided several features that we exploited to achieve our security requirements. Switch-to-switch communications are done on encrypted DS3 (44.736 Mb/s) trunks.

Our implementation strategy was to simulate the proposed intersite link in the laboratory using ATM switches, routers, DSU's, and an error/delay simulator built in house. The testbed was used to investigate the feasibility and validate the performance of the consolidation design. This configuration reflects the model of production supercomputing at Sandia, in which distributed transmission control protocol/ Internet protocol (TCP/IP) LAN's (Ethernets and FDDI rings) are routed onto central FDDI rings which house the central compute, file store, and visualization services.

Network performance was measured using the new test TCP (NTTCP) code, a client/server application which sends raw data from host to host over a standard TCP socket using the full TCP guaranteed delivery mechanisms. In order to test the maximum TCP/IP throughput of a network, NTTCP sends data from host memory to host memory so the transfer is not constrained by disk-speed limitations. When used in a short-distance LAN environment, this is a maximum throughput test used to determine how fast bits can be sent through the computer bus, software drivers, hardware interfaces, and network interconnections. In the presence of long delays in the network, NTTCP tests the efficiency of the acknowledgment methodology used by TCP. Because of the large bursts (up to 64 Kbyte) of data it produces in the network, NTTCP also tests for limitations in network buffers and flow control mechanisms. We used NTTCP extensively in our SMDS

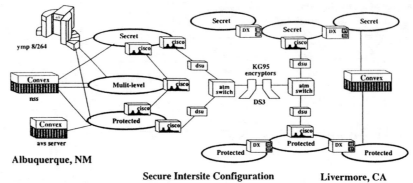

Fig. 4. Sandia's Supercomputer Consolidation Production Network.

testbed to tune the equipment and the TCP/IP protocol to give the best possible performance in the WAN environment. In this high delay environment (30 ms round-trip), we are able to sustain 29 Mb/s of throughput using two workstations and the NTTCP metric code. For an in depth discussion of the supercomputer consolidation network design and performance, see reference [9].

The production version of this network utilizing two DS3 lines between New Mexico and California, one for secure and the other for restricted communications, has been in production since May 1992. Availability of the network has been approximately 98% [10]. Fig. 4 shows the configuration of the secure network. Based on the performance and availability metrics, the design has exceeded the requirements in the requirements document. Upgrades to the network will involve moving from the DS3 links to SONET links, depending on cost and availability. We will also migrate to a switch with much greater backplane capacity which can also provide direct ATM connectivity as opposed to using SMDS as the access method.

V. DEVELOPING AN ATM TESTBED FOR THE LAN/WAN ENVIRONMENT

We are now using the Supercomputer Consolidation testbed to evaluate ATM without SMDS as the basis of the next generation networking technology at Sandia. In the process, the testbed has gone through several evolutions of technology ranging from telco class ATM switches utilizing SMDS to small work-group ATM switches for TCP/IP LAN's.

Initial efforts involved several site visits to vendors that were either testing or selling ATM switch gear and workstation interface cards. At that time, there were surprisingly few switches that could be acquired because most of the vendors were still designing or prototyping their equipment. The testbed is now a highly heterogeneous environment in terms of both switch platforms and workstations. Switches from AT&T, Fore Systems, Newbridge, and SynOptics were included in testbed experiments. Workstations from SUN, SGI, and DEC were used. Fig. 5 shows the different configurations that have been tested. Areas of investigation that will be discussed in this paper include interoperability, performance and protocol tuning, IP routing, switch/multiplexer configurations, and applications. We are also pursuing several other areas

of research including security and encryption, supercomputer interfaces, flow control, alternative and lightweight protocols, AAL 1 and 2 use, and network management. Our work in these areas will be discussed in future papers.

A. Interoperability

We have found it prudent to carefully verify claims of interoperability and performance of all new equipment. Even after a standard has been published, it takes some time for all of the interpretations to be reconciled and for truly plug-and-play equipment to become available. As can be expected from a rapidly evolving standard such as ATM, we have dealt in the testbed with interoperability issues that ranged from the physical SONET level all the way up to the application layer.

1) Physical: There are several physical interfaces defined in the ATM Forum UNI 3.0 standard; 100 Mb/s transparent asynchronous xmitter-receiver interface (TAXI), SONET OC-3c, DS-3, and 155 Mb/s FiberChannel [11]. Several early ATM vendors used 140 Mb/s TAXI although it is not defined in the ATM Forum standard. Our early switches had various combinations of all of these interfaces.

Our goal was to have one common OC-3c interface since we have deployed SONET in our communications infrastructure. Although all of the switch vendors did eventually supply SONET interfaces, only TAXI interfaces are still available from the host interface vendors. We found that the TAXI interfaces interoperated well, but interoperability was unfortunately not guaranteed with the current SONET interfaces. There are a few major issues that must further be considered; the two different "flavors" of SONET, the wealth of available physical mediums for SONET, and clocking issues.

SONET, as defined by the American National Standards Institute (ANSI), is actually a subset of the International Telephone and Telegraph Consultative Committee's (CCITT) synchronous digital hierarchy (SDH) standard [12]. The SDH standard used most everywhere but North America is a subset (also called SDH) defined by the European Telecommunications Standards Institute (ETSI). Although both of these standards derive from the CCITT standard, SONET and ETSI SDH use different values in the pointer field of the frame overhead bits [11]. Therefore, interfaces using the two standards will not talk directly to each other. Knowing that ATM

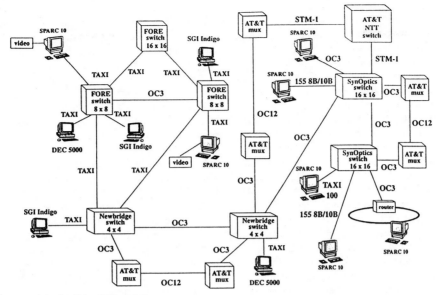

Fig. 5.   Configurations tested in Sandia's ATM testbed.

will be a big market both in North America and elsewhere, most vendors designed their 155 Mb/s interfaces to software select either synchronous transmission mode 1 (STM1) for SDH or OC-3c for SONET. Since ATM switches move generic 53-byte ATM cells from an input port to an output port, the switch effectively decouples interfaces such that different types of physical layer interfaces can effectively communicate. Our multiplexer equipment was also able to convert between OC-3c and STM1 since the rate is exactly the same and only the header pointer values had to be changed. Therefore, we were, able to build one large network with all of our testbed switches even though we had both STM1 and OC-3c as integral parts of the network.

Currently, the only physical media defined in the CCITT SDH standard is single mode (SM) optical fiber [13]. The UNI 3.0 specification references the ANSI T1E1.2/93-020R1 standard which defines a multimode (MM) physical interface for OC-3c. Although there is some debate about the completeness of the MM standard [14], several of the switch vendors provided MM optical drivers for their interfaces. The standardization of MM interfaces is attractive since their lower cost and performance is better suited to the LAN environment than the more expensive and higher performance SM optics. Since some vendors only offer SM interfaces while others provide only MM, we were forced to deal with interconnecting SM and MM interfaces. The SM interfaces transmit at much higher power than the MM receivers can handle. Also, we have experienced coupling alignment problems if we attempted to interconnect MM and SM cables. Since it is a common practice to run a SM cable from an internal SM transmitter to the device faceplate coupler ("pigtail"), we always used SM cables with attenuators to connect SM transmitters to MM receivers. If we use SM cable to connect to the MM transmitters, the mismatch in core size causes unacceptable coupling loss. We are, therefore, forced to use MM cable to go from the MM

transmitters to the SM receivers. This mixed use of SM and MM cable for a single ATM connection is obviously not an acceptable wiring practice for production networks, but it will work until all of the vendors provide both SM and MM optical interfaces.

Clocking on the SDH interfaces was the last physical layer issue that must be considered when building SDH ATM networks. Each SDH interface is capable of three basic clocking modes: master, loop, and external. In the master mode, each interface generates its own clock for transmitting and regenerates the clock from its input signal for receiving. In loop mode, the receiver interface regenerates the clock from its received signal and uses that clock both for transmitting and receiving. In external mode, clocking is taken directly from an external source. These modes allows for distribution of a very accurate central clocking source which will reduce jitter and therefore potential cell loss. Since-SONET clocking modes result in asymmetric interface configurations, careful network design and implementation is crucial. Two connected interfaces should either be externally clocked from the same source, or one of the interfaces should be a slave (loop mode) and the other in master mode. A mismatch in clocking could result in clock slippage, which could cause cell loss.

We were very hampered in our efforts to find out what was happening on our network since we did not have an ATM analyzer. Although we did get all of our switches and hosts to interoperate, an analyzer would have sped the process and given us much more knowledge about our network performance. We use several very capable tools to debug our Ethernet and FDDI networks, and we would like comparable tools to be available for our ATM production networks.

2) ATM Cells: All of our switches could correctly route cells generated by any of the other switches or host interfaces. We did find one significant difference between the way our North American switches and our European switch dealt with "idle" cells. ATM interfaces that use synchronous cell time slots, such as SONET and 8B/10B must continuously transmit valid cells in order to maintain synchronization. When there is no valid data for an interface to send, a special cell with a valid header but no valid data must be generated and transmitted. This cell is then discarded at the physical layer of the receiver interface. This special cell is called an "idle" cell in the European switch and an "unassigned" cell in other switches. Since the headers of these cells are different, it causes each switch to think that the other switch is sending it a constant stream of valid data cells. Instead of discarding these empty cells at the physical layer, the cells pass up to the higher layer where they are discarded only after no valid entry in the routing table for their virtual channel is found. This extra table lookup processing time can significantly affect the performance of and cause cell loss in the interface. Since those switches that were designed for either European or American deployment could be set to use either the "idle" or "unassigned" format, this is not a serious problem, but care must be taken to be consistent when building an ATM connection so both interfaces are using the same format.

3) ATM Signaling: Although Permanent Virtual Circuits (PVC's) interoperated very well among the switches, maintenance of a PVC network was very difficult. Completely interconnecting all of the 10 hosts on our testbed required 45 PVC's and 90 host configuration entries. The number of entries required in the switches varied with the network configuration since each PVC had to be set up in each switch in the path between the two hosts. Assuming an average of three switches between each host pair, 270 switch-routing entries were required! Even with the aid of well-documented spread-sheets and network maps, we found it impractical to keep more that a few hosts correctly communicating over PVC's at any given time. The required number of PVC's for a fully interconnected network grows quadratically with the number of hosts. PVC's may be manageable in very static networks, but in the dynamic environment of production computer LAN's that average over 30 hosts, PVC's are impractical. Since the ATM Forum has finalized the switched virtual circuit (SVC) standard, which will allow the network to automatically set up connections, in the UNI 3.0 specification, a heterogeneous network should have SVC capability in the near future.

4) IP Transport and Applications: We did not have to worry about the transport level interoperability since all of the crucial computers in our network were using host cards and software drivers from a single vendor. To show that interoperability could be achieved at this level also, we introduced one machine into the network using a prerelease host interface and driver from a second vendor. We found two major problems.

We first had to make sure that the two vendor's host cards were using the same ATM adaptation layer (AAL). AAL3/4 and AAL5 are both suited for transporting bursty TCP/IP data over an ATM network. Although AAL3/4 was the first to be implemented, AAL5 was designed specifically to be more lightweight and efficient in carrying bursty network type traffic. Although most of the early release host interfaces can support either AAL, they do not default to a common one. Therefore, care must be taken to assure an AAL is chosen and the interfaces configured consistently throughout the network since the two AAL's are not compatible.

The second issue was encapsulation of the IP packets just before the AAL5 segmentation. The Request For Comment (RFC) 1483 standard for IP encapsulation over ATM was not available when our early interface drivers were written. The proprietary method that was used is not compatible with the RFC. Using special backward compatibility options, we were able to get the two vendors' interfaces to talk to each other. This gave us a truly multivendor environment for all pieces of the ATM network. As all vendors move to the AAL5 and RFC 1483 standards, interoperability at this level should be assured.

We have demonstrated interoperability of the major protocols on top of IP: TCP, UDP, and ICMP. We have also demonstrated many of the major applications that use these protocols: Telnet, FTP, AVS, SNMP, NFS, workstation video conferencing, and X-windows. IP is the only protocol that we know of that can currently be transported over a host ATM interface. This is currently not a problem for us since our high performance workstations use exclusively IP. The other common protocols such as IPX, AppleTalk, DecNet, XNS, and others must be supported before we can move this technology from our top 20% high-end customer base to the rest of our production networks.

B. Performance and Protocol Tuning of ATM in the LAN Environment

The first experiments in the testbed were merely to quantify workstation performance using TAXI 140 Mb/s interfaces. These tests were done for Sparc, SGI and DEC workstations and used back-to-back TAXI connections with no switch in the circuit. All performance was measured using the NTTCP metric code.

Performance from these first generation cards was below FDDI, in the 20-30 Mb/s range, depending on workstation type. A major factor in the performance of these workstations/cards is the segmentation and reassembly (SAR) function required to break IP packets into cells and reassemble cells into IP packets. First generation cards used the workstation CPU and software to perform the SAR function and consequently the process was both time consuming and CPU intensive. Second generation cards moved the SAR function to the board itself. This decreased the load on the CPU and sped up the SAR process considerably. Second generation cards from several vendors are currently available only for Sparc stations, and throughput ranged from 55-75 Mb/s, depending on the interface vendor.

The next step was to connect the workstations to a switch and repeat the tests. This allowed us to quantify the effect of the switch latency on network throughput. Using the Sparc pair as an example, the addition of a switch into the circuit had no measurable affect on the throughput. We then increased the complexity of these tests by measuring concurrent session throughputs, using two sources to one sink and also independent pairs of workstations. This allowed us to quantify the behavior of the switch under a larger aggregate load. The configuration for these tests can be seen in Fig. 5. The two sources to one sink configuration showed that the maximum throughput achieved in the single session test was evenly split between the two source workstations. The tests using independent workstation pairs showed that each pair was able to achieve the same throughputs as the single session tests. This indicates that there was no contention for switch resources at this low load level.

We were also interested in the performance of workstations using multiple switch hops, as this relates directly to our communications model. Fig. 5 shows two scenarios in which a pair of workstations communicates over double and triple switch hops. The results of these tests showed that the additional latency present from additional switches did not measurably affect the throughputs.

C. IP Routing in the ATM LAN

Initial tests with the ATM LAN switches did not required IP routing functionality because all devices were assigned addresses in the same subnet. Since our network model involves many different subnets running on legacy LAN technologies, the IP routing function is required. Fig. 5 also shows the configuration of the testbed used to investigate the functionality and performance of IP routers and ATM switches. We have tested IP routers that connect FDDI rings to ATM switches using native OC-3c router interfaces. These native interfaces can communicate directly through switches to ATM attached hosts. Preliminary results indicate that these interfaces do not affect throughput performance of the first generation ATM interfaces. More extensive tests will be performed to determine the performance, functionality, and latency of legacy LAN to ATM routers.

D. Wide-Area Deployment Using ATM Switches and SONET Multiplexers

Since the Sandia environment comprises several remote areas (greater than 10 km apart), the wide-area deployment of ATM switches is of particular interest. All the testbed switches were configured with SONET OC-3c interfaces to provide wide-area connectivity. Since our communications design relies heavily on SONET multiplexers, we were also interested in how well they communicated with switches. We also tested the STM1 framing scheme in the two switches and the multiplexers that supported the standard. Fig. 5 also shows the various multiplexer/switch configuration schemes successfully tested.

VI. SUPERCOMPUTING '93 ATM NETWORK

The first outside demonstration of the knowledge and experience we have gained from our testbed was presented at the Supercomputing '93 conference. The annual IEEE sponsored Supercomputing (SC) conference is a showcase for supercomputer systems and applications. The high-speed networks used in the supercomputing environment are an integral part of the conference. The conference includes both technical presentations and exhibits where vendors and users demonstrate products and applications. Every major network-ing technology such as ATM/SONET, HIPPI, Fiber Channel, and FDDI are represented in the exhibits.

As major users of supercomputer systems, the National Laboratories have been very active participants in the SC conferences. Sandia has participated in the conferences to focus and provide a target for our activities. For the SC '93 conference held in Portland, OR, Sandia was involved in several state-of-the-art network demonstrations [15]. For the purpose of this paper, we will only discuss our demonstration of a heterogeneous ATM network that extended our ATM testbed to Portland using a full OC-3c link. Fig. 6 shows the configuration of our SC '93 ATM network. Creating such a heterogeneous, high-speed network attests to the power of standardization and the rapid pace of the ATM Forum. We used several different applications with different network requirements to demonstrate the effectiveness of a long-haul OC-3c ATM network. The applications and the network performance will be discussed.

A. Applications

We demonstrated several different video applications, the most demanding being IP-based video conferencing using a large (640 × 480 pixels) video displayed at about 12 frames/s. Many of the current IP-based video conferencing products use only quarter size (160 × 120 pixels) video at about 6–10 frames/s. Hardware JPEG compression and decompression was used to achieve this tremendous improvement in picture quality. The sustained bandwidth in each direction was between 3 and 4.5 Mb/s, depending on how much activity there was in the field of view.

A second, less demanding video application was a video classroom. A standard VHS video recorder was attached to a computer in Albuquerque. A previously recorded math class was JPEG compressed and sent in real time to a remote computer in Portland. The receiving station, which was roughly a 5 Mips processor, did software decompression to display the image. The image was again full size NTSC, but the host could only decompress at a rate of 8 frames/s. Although this was an effective demonstration of the potential of cost-effective IP based video classrooms, we felt that the frame rate needs to increase before such a product reaches acceptable performance to be popular.

Our last video demonstration was similar to the classroom idea except that we prerecorded the tape onto a disk file in JPEG format. Our 20 min of tape showing a Sandia sponsored rocket launch required about 80 Mbytes of storage on the disk. In order to display the file in real time in Portland, we exercised the standard NFS protocol by mounting, over the OC-3c intersite link, the disk that contained the video file. There was no difference in the video display between a local disk and the disk mounted 2000 m away.

We used a Sandia-developed model of the human knee in conjunction with the AVS software to demonstrate the effectiveness of X-windows over our wide-area ATM network. This application was demonstrated by logging on to the Albuquerque compute server from Portland and X-windowing the AVS display back to Portland.

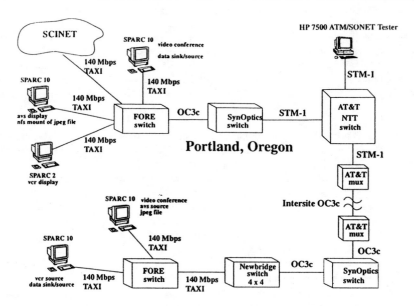

Fig. 6. Sandia's Supercomputing '93 ATM Network.

B. Network Performance

We set up the exact network configuration of the show network in our local testbed in order to determine the "best" performance for each application. Since delay and error simulators for OC-3c did not exist at the time, we could not simulate the true network characteristics before the show. When we did get the intersite link, we found that the round trip delay time was roughly 34 ms and the bit error rate (BER) was better than 10^{-12}.

Our local NTTCP test resulted in approximately 51 Mb/s throughput from host to host. Using the 34 ms of delay in the intersite connection and our 51 Mb/s throughput, the delay-bandwidth product was roughly 1.7 Mbytes. This means that the transmitting host could send 1.7 Mbytes of data before an acknowledgment could be received back from the receiving host. We could not keep the transmission pipe full since the operating system was limited to a TCP window size of 51 kbytes. Therefore, our maximum measured throughput for a single session across the link was 8.5 Mb/s. This agrees quite well with our modeling of the TCP acknowledgment scheme [16] [17]. Since 8.5 Mb/s is a small fraction of the roughly 133 Mb/s (149 Mb/s SONET payload minus 10% ATM header overhead) of user available bandwidth on an OC-3c line, we performed several tests to show that the link could share the bandwidth effectively. We tested two concurrent TCP sessions and verified that the aggregate throughput was exactly the same as the sum of each independent session. We also used UDP to fill the OC-3c line with roughly 60 Mb/s and verified that a single concurrent NTTCP session was not affected.

Since the video applications used UDP, which does not use an acknowledgment scheme, to transport their data, they were not affected at all by the intersite delay. We noticed that even in the local environment, there was about 500 ms of delay

between the receiving and transmitting displays. We assume this was due to software processing and compression delays. Since the extra 34 ms of network delay was small compared to the 500 ms of processing time, the intersite link did not affect the performance of the video applications.

It was also impossible to tell the difference between the local X-window display of the knee model and shipping the X-window display across the OC-3c link. Not only was there more than enough network bandwidth, but also the mouse picks and other interactive functions did not have any appreciable degradation in performance. There is no easy way to measure response time of mouse picks, but the subjective look and feel of the interface was indistinguishable from LAN performance.

When all of our applications were running, we sustained a load of about 14 Mb/s on the network. This was obviously not enough load to cause any problems for an OC-3c ATM network. To determine the effect of network congestion, we applied an ATM cell generator capable of loading the network to any specific level. As we increased the network load with the generator, the extra load did not affect our applications until we reached an aggregate throughput of about 100 Mb/s on the OC-3c link. At that point, our NTTCP throughput went to less than 1 Mb/s and we started to get several TCP retransmissions per second. The video also became unusable since the screen started to freeze regularly. We found that due to the lack of flow control in the available ATM equipment, we were overloading an output buffer on one of the switches. Sandia has performed in-depth simulations of various proposed ATM flow-control mechanism [18]. The simulations indicate that cell loss due to network congestion seriously degrades IP performance, but there are flow control mechanisms that are very effective in minimizing cell loss. We have presented our work at the ATM Forum and we will continue our efforts to standardize effective flow control mechanisms for the LAN and WAN environments.

VII. CUSTOMER TRIALS OF ATM/SONET AT SANDIA

There has been a great deal of discussion concerning the evolution of ATM into the computer networking environment. Early adopters are wondering whether to start the introduction at the desktop and then move up into the backbone or to reverse that process. There are also the attendant architectural design questions [19], [20]. Sandia has decided to utilize ATM to the desktop for a tightly integrated group of high performance customers as a trial where current applications can outstrip FDDI. We are building two separate customer trials of "pure" ATM networks.

Sandia's first deployment of ATM in a pseudo-production LAN follows the star topology of the single-mode fiber trunk. Connections from the remote switches to the central switch are accomplished using OC-3c interfaces on the switches and SONET multiplexing equipment. Local connections to desktop high performance workstations are made with multimode fiber and TAXI 140 Mb/s interfaces. Our second customer trial features OC-3c interfaces directly to the desktop workstation and private OC-3c network-network interfaces (NNI's). This trial will also heavily exercise our legacy to ATM LAN routers.

Proprietary SVC signaling is currently used in these networks in order to minimize management since research networks are reconfigured quite frequently for specific experiments. The main purpose of these networks is to introduce high end applications, including interactive simulation codes and the visualization of results, to the ATM LAN technology. These early customer trials will provide valuable feedback concerning the transparency of the ATM technology, real and perceived benefits, effectiveness of widespread hardware-assisted desktop video conferencing, suitability for high traffic client/server networks, and insight into the maintenance and operational aspects of reasonably sized local ATM networks.

VIII. SUMMARY

The Supercomputer Consolidation Project and the SC'93 ATM network established real world tests of the emerging technologies in the Regional Bell Operating Company (RBOC)/interexchange carrier (IEC) environment. The carriers have demonstrated their technical ability to provide high-speed (155 Mb/s) national networks. Our work has demonstrated the effectiveness of multimedia as well as traditional applications using end-to-end ATM networking. We have had good success operating heterogeneous ATM networks as long as the network is engineered to mitigate the effects of congestion. Although the need for tuning the TCP/IP window parameters has been well documented in technical journals, more education is needed to help application programmers and end users understand and adapt to the high-speed, long-distance networking environment. Our experience indicates that ATM/SONET technologies will be able to support our production and supercomputer networks in both the local and wide area. The emerging SONET backbone at Sandia is already delivering high quality, high availability service to the

Laboratory. The SONET network transport is reliable, flexible, and critical to our extension of ATM throughout the campus.

Our goal is to distribute voice/data/video to any location within Sandia (NM or CA) at whatever data rate required (i.e., from Kb/s through Gb/s) over an infrastructure that utilizes copper and glass (physical media), SONET physical layer transport, and ATM switching as the fundamental networking technology. This network will provide a seamless integration of WAN and LAN by using scalable, reliable, adaptable, and maintainable technologies.

REFERENCES

[1] "Visiting Sandia National Laboratories," pamphlet, Jan. 1992.
[2] P. Bernier, "NIIT lunches first application," *Telephony*, vol. 225, no. 21, p. 3, Nov. 22, 1993.
[3] "AT&T announces operation of hi-speed ATM research network over fully optical links," *ATM Newslett.*, vol. 2, no. 9, pp. 4–6, Sept. 1993.
[4] S. A. Gossage, "Delivery of very high bandwidth with ATM switches and SONET," *SAND92-1295*, Nov. 1992.
[5] C. J. Pavalakos, L. A. Schoof, and J. F. Mareda, "A distributed visualization environment for engineering sciences," *SAND92-0778C*, Dec. 1992.
[6] K. A. Winkler *et al.*, "A numerical laboratory," *Physics Today*, vol. 40, no. 10, pp. 23–37, Oct. 1987.
[7] R. L. Adams, "Intra-building telecommunications cabling standards for Sandia National Laboratories, New Mexico," *SAND93-0002*, Aug. 1993.
[8] C. F. Diegert, "Gigabit-per-second networking at supercomputing '91," *MPCRL Res. Bull.*, vol. 2, no. 1, pp. 1–4, Mar. 1992.
[9] J. H. Naegle, N. Testi, and S. A. Gossage, "Developing an ATM network at Sandia National Laboratories," *Telecommun.*, vol. 28, no. 2, pp. 21–23, Feb. 1994.
[10] J. P. Brenkosh, internal Sandia communication.
[11] ATM Forum, *ATM User-Network Interface Specification 3.0*. Englewood Cliffs, NJ: Prentice-Hall, 1993.
[12] M. Sexton and A. Reid, *Transmission Networking: SONET and the Synchronous Digital Hierarchy*. Boston, MA: Artech, 1992.
[13] S. Miller, I. Kaminow, *Optical Fiber Telecommunications II*. Boston, MA: Academic, 1988.
[14] Edward S. Chang, "ATM forum contribution 94-0147," Mar. 1994.
[15] S. A. Gossage and M. O. Vahle, "Sandia's research network for supercomputing '93: A demonstration of advanced technologies for building high-performance networks," *SAND93-3807*, Dec. 1993.
[16] J. Eldridge, "Modeling data throughput on communication networks," *SAND93-0817*, Nov. 1993.
[17] H. Y. Chen, J. A. Hutchins, and N. Testi, "TCP performance analysis for wide area networks," *SAND93-8243*, Aug. 1993.
[18] H. Y. Chen *et. al.*, "ATM Forum 94–0119 simulation results of TCP over ATM," Jan. 1994.
[19] J. McQuillan, "ATM: Bottom up or top down?," *Bus. Commun. Rev.*, vol. 23, no. 5, pp. 10–11, May 1993.
[20] P. J. Sevcik, "Arguments and architectures for ATM," *Bus. Commun. Rev.*, vol. 23, no. 10, pp. 14–21, Oct. 1993.

John H. Naegle received the B.S. and M.S. degrees in electrical and computer engineering at Brigham Young University, Provo, UT, in 1987 and 1988, respectively. He is working toward the Ph.D. degree at the University of New Mexico, Albuquerque.

For the last six years, he has been with the Advanced Networking Integration group at Sandia National Laboratories, Albuquerque, NM. During this time, he has worked with the latest technologies used for Sandia's corporate computer networks. His research has focused on developing and deploying the next generation of ATM/SONET networks.

Steven A. Gossage received the B.S. and M.S. degrees in electrical engineering from the University of Kansas, Lawrence, in 1974 and 1977, respectively.

He is a Senior Member of the Technical Staff at Sandia National Laboratories, Albuquerque, NM, where he is a Member of the Advanced Networking Department. He is the Project Leader for the team that is creating an ATM-network testbed to examine ATM performance versus other technologies in the Sandia campus and wide-area environment. Prior to working with SMDS and ATM network design, he was responsible for the development of high-performance optical-fiber interbuilding and intrabuilding cable-distribution systems and the preliminary design of a private SONET-based data and video transport network.

Michael O. Vahle received the B.S. and M.S. degrees in mathematics from the University of Missouri at Rolla.

He is currently a Manager of the Advanced Networking Group at Sandia National Laboratories, Albuquerque, NM, which is looking at high-speed communications and networking technologies.

Mr. Vahle is a member of Phi Kappa Phi, the Mathematical Association of America, and Kappa Mu Epsilon.

Nicholas Testi received the M.A. degree in anthropology/archaeology from the State University of New York, Albany, in 1980, and the M.S. degree in computer science from Utah State University, Logan, in 1985.

He is currently a Senior Member of Technical Staff in the Advanced Networking Department at Sandia National Laboratories, Albuquerque, NM. He has several years' experience in designing and maintaining production supercomputing networks and is currently engaged in designing the next-generation ATM/SONET network at Sandia.

Joseph H. Maestas received the B.S. degree from New Mexico State University, Las Cruces, and the M.S. degree from the University of New Mexico, Albuquerque, in 1984 and 1993, respectively, both in electrical engineering.

He is with Sandia National Laboratories, Albuquerque, NM, in the Advanced Networking Group, where he is currently involved with a team of engineers in developing scalable ATM encryption technologies. He also leads the SONET Deployment project at the Livermore and Albuquerque sites. He was granted a U.S. patent in 1990 for the development of Crypto Synchronization Recovery by Measuring Randomness of Decrypted Data.

ATM Signaling Transport Network Architectures and Analysis

As public carriers plan to offer new broadband services and consolidate different types of services into a single ATM network platform, the identification of an appropriate target broadband signaling transport network architecture is necessary to ensure smooth and cost-effective signaling network evolution.

Tsong-Ho Wu, Noriaki Yoshikai, and Hiroyuki Fujii

s public carriers plan to offer new broadband services and consolidate different types of services into a single ATM network platform, how to evolve today's SS7 signaling networks to accommodate future broadband signaling needs becomes an important issue, especially many public carriers plan to offer switched broadband services in 1995-96. The identification of an appropriate target broadband signaling transport network architecture is necessary to ensure smooth and cost-effective signaling network evolution.

Two major aspects in evolving requirements from today's signaling networks to future broadband signaling networks are:
- The evolution of the signaling user parts
- The evolution of signaling transport in the broadband environment

The evolution of signaling user parts (i.e., broadband integrated services user part—B-ISUP) has made significant progress in the past few years, while work on broadband signaling transport in the ATM environment has just been started in the standards organizations — e.g., International Telecommunications Union — Telecommunications sector (ITU-T) Recommendations I.311 and Q.2010) [1, 2] — and the telecommunications industry. The technical aspects of broadband signaling transport that need to be addressed include signaling transport architectures and protocols. These architectures and protocols may be used in the ATM environment to provide reliable signaling transport, while making efficient use of the ATM broadband capabilities in support of new and vastly expanded signaling applications. To economically use the ATM transport capability, services and control/signaling messages are carried by the same physical network, as depicted in Fig. 1 [1]. In Fig. 1, both the ATM control/signaling and service connections are carried in the same physical network, but are logically separated from each other by using different virtual channels (VCs)

or virtual paths (VPs). The potential benefits of using an ATM VP transport network to carry the signaling/control messages include possible simplification of the existing signaling transport protocols, shorter control and signaling message delays, and reliability enhancement via the possible self-healing capability at the VP level [1].

A number of suggestions have been made for possible broadband signaling transport architectures, ranging from the retention of signal transfer points (STPs) to the adoption of a fully distributed signaling transport architecture supporting the associated signaling mode only. The purpose of this article is to describe these architecture alternatives and discuss their qualitative and quantitative tradeoffs. Note that this article focuses on public networks only. The signaling network architecture and routing used in private or enterprise networks may be different from those used in public networks. Please refer to [15] for details on private network signaling and routing.

This article is organized as follows. The following section summarizes previous work that may suggest possible limitations of today's SS7 networks in supporting new services. The third section describes three alternatives of ATM-based signaling transport network architectures, and the fourth section discusses high-level qualitative tradeoffs among the three architecture alternatives. Some preliminary economic and availability results are briefly discussed in the fifth section, and concluding remarks are given in the sixth section.

Potential Limitations of SS7 Network Capabilities

In this section, we briefly review previous results that may suggest potential limitations of today's SS7 network capability in supporting new services. Figure 2 depicts an architecture model used in today's SS7 networks. The SS7 architecture is composed of three major components: a

TSONG-HO WU is a director with the Network Control Research Department at Bellcore.

Reprinted from IEEE Communications Magazine, Dec. 1995, pp. 90-99..

service switching point (SSP), signal transfer point (STP), and service control point (SCP). All nodes in the network that have common channel signaling (CCS) capability are SSPs that are interconnected by signaling links. Nodes that serve as intermediate signaling message transport switches are called STPs. SCPs are the SSPs that provide database access to support transaction-based services. Signaling links are the transmission facilities that convey the signaling messages between two SSPs.

The STP is engineered on a paired basis to enhance its reliability. The SS7 network is physically separated from the plain old telephony service (POTS) transport network, since the SS7 network is a packet-switched network, while the POTS network is a circuit-switched network. The associated signaling mode is referred to as point-to-point signaling transport, while the quasi-associated mode is that the SSP pair and the SSP-SCP pair communications must be through the STP. Although the SS7 network architecture allows for supporting both the associated and quasi-associated signaling modes, today's SS7 networks in the United States implement the quasi-associated mode only due to economic considerations. However, as will be shown later, these design assumptions, used to optimize the SS7 network in early 1980, may not fully apply to the new ATM network environment (e.g., the service and signaling messages may be carried on the same physical ATM network with overlay end-to-end connections).

A number of studies regarding the impact on today's signaling networks due to the introduction of new services have been conducted and reported in [3, 14]. Reference [14] identifies the enhancements required to meet the signaling requirements of network services, intelligent network, mobility management, mobility services, broadband and multimedia. These studies evaluated the signaling network capacity and delay impacts due to the penetration of PCS and advanced intelligent network (AIN) services. The results in [3] have suggested, from a delay

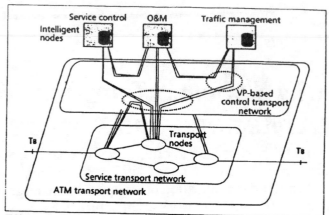

■ **Figure 1.** *ATM service and control transport network (ITU-T Rec.I.311)*

perspective, that use of today's 56 kb/s links may lead to unacceptable network response times, particularly for services requiring long network paths and extensive user-network or SCP-SCP interactions. Higher-speed signaling links are needed to alleviate this signaling delay performance concern. For example, as shown in Fig. 3 [3], the total network response time improves by about 30 percent when 56 kb/s links are replaced by 1.5 Mb/s links under the same load and network configuration. The results also suggested that a significant increase in the speed of SCP A-links would be needed, and the number of SCPs also increases significantly due to the capacity limitation of the incoming SCP A-linksets (which therefore limits the traffic entering the SCP). These potential limitations would eventually result in increased network complexity and cost due to additional investments in new SCP, reconfiguration of network components (nodes and links) and additional resources needed to maintain and administer the network [3].

At the moment this report is being written, there is no impact analysis for broadband services on the SS7 network capacity. However, it is expected that the network capacity requirement for broadband signaling will be much higher than its narrowband counterpart due to its more

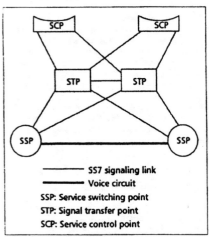

■ **Figure 2.** *The architecture model for today's SS7 networks.*

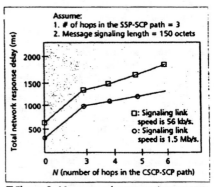

■ **Figure 3.** *Mean network response times vs. number of hops in the SCP-SCP path [3].*

The impacts of ATM technology on signaling transport are still an open issue, which depends on services and the implementation time frame.

intelligent nature and the need to support both point-to-point and point-to-multipoint connections. It has also been suggested that existing SS7 network physical interfaces may not be able to support stringent end-to-end signaling time goals (20 ms–100 ms) which are advocated by potential users of the broadband switched virtual connection (SVC) services.

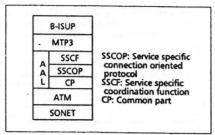

■ Figure 4. *Part of the NNI signaling protocol*

There are several approaches that have been proposed in [3] to alleviate potential limitations of today's SS7 networks. The ATM signaling network platform may be better suited to accommodate signaling traffic growth and stringent delay requirement due to its flexible bandwidth management (i.e., bandwidth on demand) and connection establishment. In the next section, some potential long-term broadband signaling transport network architectures based on the ATM transport platform are discussed.

ATM-Based Signaling Transport Network Architectures

The design impacts of ATM technology on signaling transport are still an ongoing study issue, which depends on services and the implementation time frame being considered in the broadband network evolution plan. These design

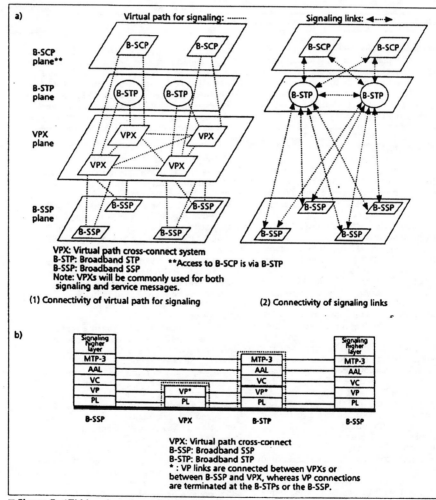

■ Figure 5. *ATM-based quasi-associated signaling transport architecture: a) an example of ATM-based quasi-associated signaling transport; b) protocol stacks of network elements involved in signaling transport.*

	Broadband Signaling Transfer Mode		
	Quasi-associated mode	**Associated mode**	**Hybrid of associated/quasi-associated mode**
Network configuration	Signaling messages between two SSPs are transported via B-STPs (Use B-STPs) Signaling and service messages are carried via physically separated networks One-to-one replacement of today's dedicated copper data transport.	Signaling messages between two SSPs are transported without higher-layer termination (No B-STPs) Both signaling and service messages are carried in the same physical network, but logically separated	No B-STPs for associated mode Use B-STPs for quasi-associated mode Same physical network for associated mode. Separate physical network for quasi-associated mode.
Signaling message routing	Network layer routing (MTP-3) ATM layer routing (without MTP-3 functions in ATM switches)	Network layer routing (e.g., MTP-3)	Network layer routing or ATM layer routing for associated mode Network layer routing for quasi-associated mode
Database access	B-SSP - B-STP - B-SCP	B-SSP - B-SCP Database management distributed/centralized	B-SSP - B-SCP (for associated mode) B-SSP - B-STP - B-SCP (for quasi-associated mode)

■ **Table 1.** *A class of ATM signaling transport architectures.*

impacts include a possible simplified MTP-3 protocol, a new SCP planning strategy, a distributed signaling transport feature, and new signaling engineering rules needed to best utilize ATM technology to provide reliable and flexible broadband signaling transport. Technically, services supported by the target broadband signaling transport architecture should include all types of services (e.g., today's POTS, PCS and high-speed data services) which will be provided by the service provider. In reality, the target broadband signaling transport network architecture may evolve from an architecture that is used initially for a particular broadband service whose signaling requirements dominate other types of services (e.g., video dial tone).

Part of the network-network interface (NNI) signaling protocol stack that has been recommended in ITU-T Rec. Q.2010 [2] in December 1993 and in ATM-Forum [13] is shown in Fig. 4. This signaling protocol stack indicates that ATM-based signaling transport should support both the associated mode and the quasi-associated mode, if applicable. However, the actual implementation of this signaling protocol stack for ATM-based signaling transport networks depends on the individual signaling network evolution plan, services that will be supported and their implementation time frame.

The signaling protocol stack described in Fig. 4 can be implemented in three different ways that form a class of ATM-based signaling transport architectures, as shown in Table 1. These possible architectures are classified based on the signaling message routing principle:
• The quasi-associated mode only
• The associated mode only
• A hybrid of the quasi-associated and associated modes.

For the first and third architecture options, the MTP-1 and MTP-2 functions residing within today's STP will be replaced by ATM and ATM adaptation layer (AAL) functions in the ATM-based signaling transport network. To differentiate broadband signaling network components from today's SS7 network components, the B-STP, the B-SSP and the B-SCP used in Table 1 are defined as an ATM-based STP, SSP and SCP, respectively, which implements the signaling transport protocol stack as described in Fig. 4. The details are described in the following subsections.

Quasi-Associated Mode Only

Figure 5a depicts an example of the quasi-associated signaling transport architecture, and an example of the protocol stacks of network elements involved in the signaling transport path is depicted in Fig. 5b. This architecture follows today's SS7 network concept with enhanced STP and SCP capabilities for broadband signaling needs. In this architecture, B-SSPs communicate with each other, and the B-SSP communicates with the B-SCP through the B-STP, as today's SS7 networks do. Note that in this architecture, the B-STP is an ATM-based switching system with an MTP-3 controller which supports signaling traffic only.

The quasi-associated signaling transport architecture uses ATM transport as a one-to-one replacement of today's dedicated copper data transport. This architecture requires a significant capacity upgrade of today's SS7 components. Due to economic and reliability considerations, two or more B-SCPs are needed to accommodate requirements of both the narrowband and broadband network intelligence (see "Potential Limitations of SS7 Network Capabilities"). The increased number of B-SCPs means that more A-links between the B-STP and the B-SCP are needed, which eventually could make the signaling transport network difficult to grow to a large-scale network from both the economics and operations perspectives.

It is noted that the ATM transport structure shown in Fig. 5 is implemented at the VP level.

This transport structure for supporting SVC services is usually referred to as a "virtual central office" (CO) or "large switch" structure that brings the remote customer traffic to larger ATM switches in some strategic locations for switching and processing through high-speed transport systems such as synchronous optical network (SONET) digital cross-connect systems (DCSs) or ATM virtual path cross-connect systems (VPXs). This "virtual CO" transport structure has been implemented by some local exchange carriers (LECs) who use less expensive SONET transport equipment to support switched voice services. Alternately, the ATM transport structure for supporting SVCs may be implemented at the VC level, which is usually referred to as a "traditional" or "small switch" structure. This "small switch" transport structure brings the switch to the customers by deploying smaller ATM switches closer to the customer sites. The use of the "small switch" or "big switch" structure depends on the network size, traffic patterns and volumes, costs, and reliability and performance requirements. In this article, the broadband signaling transport network architectures discussed are based on the "virtual CO" (or "big switch") transport structure. Thus, throughout this article, unless otherwise speci-

fied, the transport structure is referred to as the "virtual CO" or "big switch" structure that is implemented at the VP level.

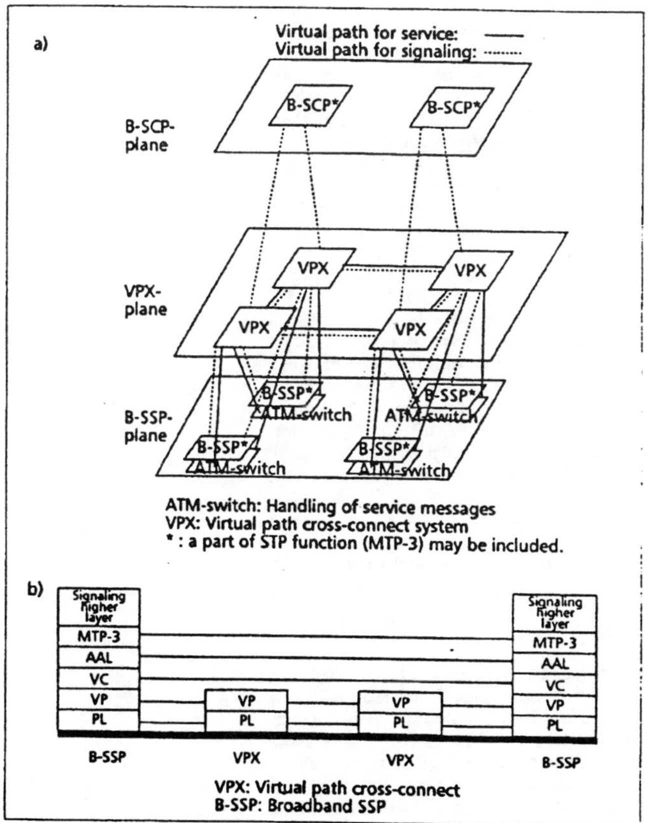

Associated Mode Only

Figure 6 depicts an example of the associated signaling transport architecture. In this figure. messages related to a particular signaling relation between two adjacent B-SSPs are conveyed over a link set, directly interconnecting those B-SSPs by virtual paths. This architecture essentially distributes the STP function into each signaling node, and signaling message routing is performed on a distributed basis. For the associated mode, the B-SSP may include "network layer routing (e.g., MTP-3)" or "ATM layer routing." The option of network layer routing has been used in Europe and proposed by most major organizations. This option does not use B-STP, but implements the "simplified" MTP-3 in each ATM switch. This supports management functions such as changeover of signaling traffic from a failed signaling link to an alternate signaling link. The approach may be a natural choice from the signaling evolution perspective. Another option is to use ATM layer routing. which is primarily taken from the network integration perspective. Whether network layer routing or ATM layer routing should be used remains to be determined.

In the associated mode architecture. each ATM signaling node can directly access the B-SCPs, which may be placed in a centralized or distributed manner. Note that the example in Fig. 6 only shows a centralized SCP placement configuration with protection (i.e.. duplication). As discussed previously, the existing SS7 network may require more than two SCPs and more physical connectivities between STPs and SCPs to support new services (e.g., PCS and AIN) requiring access to SCP. This could impose a potential limitation for SS7 network growth. This potential network scalability limitation in existing SS7 networks may be alleviated when ATM-based signaling transport is introduced. By partitioning and replicating the database one can meet the high throughput and reliability that will be required of the B-SCPs in a cost-effective manner. This distributed B-SCP placement scenario can be more cost-effective in the ATM-based signaling transport network than its SS7 counterpart because fewer signaling links for B-SCP access are required and because of its flexible signaling bandwidth allocation. One example of the distributed database architecture and its performance analysis in the integrated signaling and control ATM network can be found in [9]. Note, however, that the reliability requirement for the associated signaling transport network architecture is still an open issue.

The following paragraphs describe rerouting functions in the associated mode. Since the signaling VC is usually a permanent or semi-permanent ATM connection, the normal rerouting can be predetermined or dynamic [5]. The signaling rerouting issue here is how to reroute signaling messages when the network component fails or becomes congested. In the case of the associated mode, there is no separate signaling network. This means MTP-3 can be greatly sim-

■ **Figure 6.** *ATM-based associated signaling transport; a) an example of ATM-based associated signaling transport; b) protocol stacks of network elements involved in signaling transport.*

plified, as mentioned in [13]. For the rerouting protocol, we may use the existing or "simplified" MTP-3 protocol and management procedures (with some modifications if needed). However, it is also possible to use other routing protocols that may take advantage of the ATM layer rerouting capability. In this case, one possible rerouting protocol is to use the ATM VP self-healing [5–7] or protection switching protocol [8] to reroute both signaling messages as well as service data in the same process but with different restoration or rerouting priorities under network stress conditions. This approach is particularly attractive since signaling messages, control messages, and service data can be carried on the same physical network, but are logically separated by different VPs with varied performance requirements that can be easily accommodated by ATM VP restoration techniques.

Table 2 summarizes a comparison between rerouting at the network layer and at the ATM VP level. Both network-layer rerouting and VP path restoration are similar in the sense that they are autonomous rerouting mechanisms triggered by failure indication messages (e.g., AIS) or some other control messages [8]. The major difference between the MTP-3 and VP rerouting mechanisms is that MTP-3 rerouting is used for failure recovery only and is performed in the connectionless manner, whereas VP rerouting may be able to handle both failure and congestion situations in the connection-oriented manner.

For the signaling transport application, it is crucial to completely restore signaling messages as quickly as the technology allows in the network failure situation. There are three possible rerouting schemes: rerouting at the network layer only, VP self-healing only, or a hybrid of rerouting at the network layer and VP self-healing. The last rerouting scheme requires a coordination capability of layer management across the physical layer (i.e., SONET layer), the VP level at the ATM layer, the VC level at the ATM layer, and the network layer. The timing for triggering rerouting in this multilayer structure is crucial for ensuring qualities of both services and signaling traffic. Currently, the waiting time requirement to initiate changeover at the network layer in existing SS7 networks is 146 ms in the case of a signaling link failure [4]. However, whether this timing requirement is still applicable to ATM-based signaling transport remains to be determined. Note that rerouting against network failures can be performed at four possible transport layers: SONET line/path, ATM VP, ATM VC, and the network layer. The rerouting function at the network layer is performed by broadband signaling points, such as the B-SSP or the B-STP. For ATM rerouting, all rerouting schemes against network failures currently proposed by both industry and academies are at the ATM VP level due to its operations simplicity. According to [1], VCs are connected in a point-to-point manner in the SS7 network and are accommodated by some VPs terminated in the same network element. In the extreme case, one VP may be constructed by a single VC. As VP routing is carried out between two VP termination points, VC routing is considered as VP routing, if this VP only accommodates one VC.

	MTP-3 rerouting	VP-restoration (path restoration)
Functional layer	Network layer	ATM VP layer
Handling object	Signaling messages	Virtual path
Routing information	Signaling link selection/ Originating point code/ Destination point	Virtual path identifier
Network element	STP-SSP	VP cross-connect/SSP
How to decide alternate link	Preplanned	Preplanned or dynamic rerouting
Role of rerouting	Restoration against link failure/node failure	Restoration against link/ node failure and possible rerouting for congestion control
Trigger signal	Alarms from level-2 Changeover message	VP-AIS/VP-FERF or other protection switching messages
Priority control	Yes	Yes
Changeback function	Yes	Yes

■ **Table 2.** *A comparison between rerouting schemes.*

Hybrid Signaling Transport

This architecture supports both the quasi-associated mode (through B-STPs) and the associated mode in the same ATM control transport network. This hybrid signaling transport architecture uses an architecture similar to the existing SS7 network, except that point-to-point signaling links are also supported. If the signaling messages use the associated mode, the provision of point-to-point signaling links may provide flexible and direct linking connectivity to access B-SCPs. The hybrid signaling transport architecture has been studied in ITU-T [1]. A rationale of using the hybrid network architecture is that the associated mode transport will be used most of the time, while the B-STPs may be used in situations where the traffic volume is low between two signaling points or between the B-SSP and B-SCP [1]. The concept of using B-STPs is based on the basic understanding of today's SS7 network design (i.e., the direct point-to-point dedicated data link is not economical when the traffic volume on that link is low). If this design philosophy is still applicable in new ATM network environment, the hybrid architecture may be an attractive option for broadband signaling network.

Analysis

This section compares the alternative signaling transport architectures described previously based on three criteria: economics, performance, evolvability and scalability. The analysis discussed here is a high-level, qualitative preliminary analysis. Some preliminary study results on architecture comparisons will be discussed in the next section.

Economics and Performance Criteria

The criteria of economics and performance are

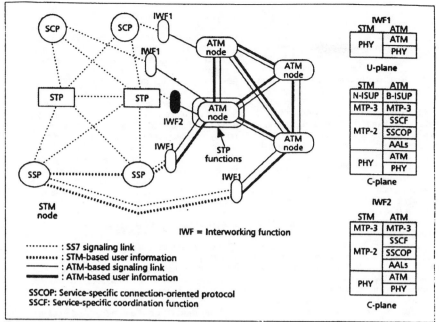

■ **Figure 7.** *Interworking between the ATM-based signaling transport network and SS7 network.*

to evaluate which architecture may best utilize the inherent ATM technology potential to support both the narrowband and broadband signaling requirements. Thus, it is likely a more long-term solution. The best architecture for this criterion may not necessarily be the best architecture when other factors, such as network evolvability, are considered. However, it is important to study this criterion since the best technology-oriented architecture may be preferable if it has an acceptable capital gap compared with other architecture alternatives. Thus, the analysis using this criterion serves as a base model for further architecture comparisons.

The primary benefit of the quasi-associated architecture is that it can reuse most of the operations systems designed for today's SS7 networks. This architecture simply uses ATM signaling links as a one-to-one replacement of today's dedicated copper signaling link. However, the B-STP may require a significant capacity upgrade, and the engineering rules should also be re-examined due to the expected increase in signaling volumes and different performance and reliability requirements for broadband services. This significant capacity upgrade requirement could make the B-STP very difficult or expensive to build or could result in a totally new system which may not be upgradable from the existing STP. This results in a higher cost for operations and maintenance compared with other alternatives.

Conceptually, the quasi-associated architecture may not be economical from the operations or equipment costs points of view when compared with the associated signaling transport architecture that can support both signaling and services in the same physical network. This is because any two signaling points in ATM networks have already carried ATM connections for

services, and the cost of adding additional signaling connections on the same connection paths would be minimal (compared with the stand-alone B-STP). In particular, the bandwidth requirement for these signaling channels is relatively small when compared with broadband services (e.g., video). It is especially true when the ATM broadband network is designed to support video dial tone services. Thus, the questions that should be answered for supporting the quasi-associated architecture include:

- Can the stand-alone B-STP system and operations costs justify the costs of concentrating low-volume signaling pair traffic?
- Could the use of the B-STP improve any aspect of signaling performance, compared with the case of no B-STPs?

These two questions require detailed quantitative study, and the result may vary from one network to another. We will discuss some ongoing research work for these quantitative studies later.

To realize the associated signaling transport architecture, many control and management mechanisms need to be redesigned and redeveloped. Due to the significant capital and longer development cycle required to implement a distributed associated broadband signaling transport architecture, a detailed analysis should be performed to explore and quantify potential strengths in terms of operations and transport economics over its quasi-associated counterpart. The fifth section shows the preliminary economics and availability analysis for these architectures.

Evolvability Criterion

To realize the target cost-effective signaling transport networks, the interworking between today's SS7 networks and the broadband signaling networks is a critical issue from the viewpoint of evolvability. If the quasi-associated signaling network becomes a target transport architecture, it will easily interwork with today's SS7 networks. This is because the quasi-associated network architecture can easily evolve from today's SS7 network by upgrading its current STP to an ATM-based B-STP and supporting existing POTS and some other new services.

On the other hand, the associated signaling network architecture may not be as easy to evolve from today's SS7 networks as the quasi-associated signaling network is. In that case, however, the associated broadband signaling transport network may interwork with today's SS7 networks as shown in Fig. 7. Note that this figure is only described for NNI signaling. The interworking scenario using interworking function #1 (IWF#1) has been specified in ITU-T Rec. I.580 [12]. In this case, IWF#1 shall translate both today's and broadband signaling messages. For instance, the IWF#1 translates between B-ISUP and N-ISUP messages. This covers the generation, termination, and protocol conversion of signaling messages. The interworking scenario using IWF#2 in the figure may be an option for network migration, but is not yet specified in the current version of ITU-T Rec. I.580. This interworking configuration would allow the signaling transport network to support broadband services first and then integrate voice services later when economics (operations and transport costs) can be justified.

The following is one possible scenario to evolve from today's networks using the associated mode. POTS can still be carried through the STP-like structure (which can later be upgraded to ATM-based STPs if the economics can be justified; this corresponds with the hybrid architecture as described previously), while other services may be carried through the new associated mode. This service mapping strategy would minimize the change of existing STPs for POTS, while taking advantage of ATM network flexibility and economical connectivity to support new services requiring direct access to service modules (e.g., B-SCPs). For POTS, this architecture avoids the expensive capacity upgrade for existing SS7 system components (e.g., STP) and reduces operations and maintenance costs due to a possible use of a single ATM network management and operations system. For PCS and AIN, this architecture offers a flexible and fast scheme to directly access B-SCPs and AIN service modules. Also, the flexible ATM connectivity may allow this architecture to easily accommodate the message volume increase, and to implement the distributed B-SCP architecture when the capacity of the SCP in today's SS7 network becomes exhausted. Thus, from the evolution perspective, the interworking architecture with today's SS7 networks will be used to support POTS and new broadband services.

Scalability Criterion
As mentioned earlier, PCS and other new services, including broadband services, would certainly exhaust today's SCPs if the centralized SCP placement strategy remains unchanged.

Thus, the only economical and flexible way to accommodate new database access needs for these broadband services is to distribute the SCP functions throughout the network. In that case, if the B-STP is used (e.g., for the hybrid signaling transport architecture) more A-links that physically connect the B-STP to the SCP are needed, which would make the quasi-associated signaling transport network architecture relatively difficult to grow to a large signaling transport network when comparing its associated signaling transport counterpart, since the latter does not require physical connectivity from B-STPs to B-SCPs. However, the quasi-associated signaling network may more easily accommodate the addition of new B-SSPs than its associated mode counterpart from a link design perspective due to its hierarchical link design structure.

Preliminary Results

To better understand the tradeoffs among the two possible target broadband signaling transport architectures described previously (i.e., associated mode vs. quasi-associated mode), detailed quantitative analyses in terms of economics and performance are needed. These analyses depend on the services and network being considered. The following summarizes some ongoing activities and progress for the signaling transport architecture alternative analysis.

As mentioned earlier, the economic analysis for signaling transport architecture alternatives depends on the service(s) and the network under consideration. Some results of economic and reliability analyses for POTS over ATM-based services on a large Nippon Telephone and Telegraph (NTT) long-distance network have been reported in [11] and are summarized in Fig. 8 (cost analysis) and Fig. 9 (reliability analysis). The Type-1 and Type-2 architectures shown in both Figs. 8 and 9 are with and without STPs, respectively. For architectures without STPs, there are three options considered: the one-route option (i.e., each SSP pair uses one VP route), the four-route option (each SSP pair uses four disjoint VP routes), and the option of the VPX having the copy function. The model network includes 63 SSP switching nodes accommodating 84 SSP units, 20 STP nodes accommodating 34 STPs, and 20 SCP nodes. In general, if the STP is used, the VP can carry signals efficiently, which results in a smaller VP capacity being needed, but at the expense of expensive STPs being needed. Because the STP-unit cost is higher than the transmission cost (fiber, VPX, etc.) in this study, the Type-2 architecture without the STP-unit is quite economical. This cost evaluation does not include the operation costs of STP-units. It is expected that a network without STPs may require lower operation costs than one having STPs. Note that since this study considered the signaling transport part only, the hardware cost of the SSP is small compared with the STP or the VPX. Thus, the costs of SSPs are assumed to be negligible here.

As also shown in Fig. 8, in the Type-2 architecture the one-route model is more economical. However, since there is no alternative route under failure conditions, the one-route model is

Special servers are necessary to manage VP/VC connections. Intelligent operation using ATM technology is expected to meet this requirement.

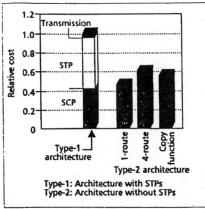

■ Figure 8. *A result of cost evaluatiohn reported in [11].*

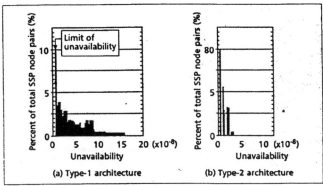

■ Figure 9. *A reliability analysis result in [11].*

less reliable than the four-route model. Using the copy function at the VPX may further decrease the transmission cost to about 78 percent. In this evaluation, since the copy function is assumed to be a mandatory function of the VPX, the cost of the copy function was included in the VPX cost model.

Figure 9 depicts unavailability distribution histograms of SSP node pairs. The horizontal axis indicates unavailability and the vertical one indicates the number of SSP node pairs. The model structures and assumptions used in Fig. 9 are the same as those used in Fig. 8. In this analysis, there are about 1900 SSP node pairs in the network model. As shown in Fig. 9a, for the Type-1 architecture the average unavailability of the SSP node pair is 3.3×10^{-8}, and the worst one is 1.5×10^{-7}. In this case, the unavailability of STP nodes is the major reason for higher SSP node pair unavailability, where the mated STP node structure has a minimum SSP node pair unavailability. For the four-route model of the Type-2 architecture (Fig. 9b), the average SSP node pair unavailability is 2.5×10^{-9}, and the worst is 3.3×10^{-8}. More than 80% of SSP node pairs have unavailability under 1.0×10^{-9}. The SSP node pair unavailability for the four-route model of the Type-2 architecture is much smaller than that for the Type-1 architecture due to

the absence of STP nodes in the former. On the other hand, for the one-route model of the Type-2 architecture the average SSP node pair unavailability is 3.5×10^{-4}, with the worst being 1.0×10^{-3} (not shown in the figure), which is much worse than the other two architectures. This result, along with the result shown in Fig. 8, implies that the four-route model of the Type-2 architecture may provide better SSP node pair availability with a moderate cost investment when compared with the other two architecture alternatives.

Summary

We have reviewed some possible target broadband signaling transport network architectures that could be used to support both today's services and future broadband services. Some preliminary, qualitative analysis is also discussed to provide some high-level technical insight for understanding the difference of alternative signaling transport network architectures. Detailed quantitative work is needed to study network-dependent economic and performance issues.

Acknowledgments

The authors would like to thank Carol Adams, who prepared some figures in this article, and Nim K. Cheung, Joe E. Berthold, Richard Cardwell, Gary A. Hayward and George H. Dobrowski for their valuable comments on the first draft.

References

[1] ITU-T Recommendation I.311, "B-ISDN General Network Aspects," Geneva, Switzerland, Jan. 1993.
[2] ITU-T Draft Recommendation Q.2010, "Broadband Integrated Service Digital Network Overview Signaling Capability," Geneva, Switzerland, Dec. 1993.
[3] Special Report, "Alternatives for Signaling Link Evolution," Bellcore SR-NWT-002897, issue 1, Feb. 1994.
[4] Bellcore Technical Reference TR-TSY-000082, "Signaling Transfer Point (STP) Generic Requirements," Issue 4, Dec. 1992.
[5] T.-H. Wu, *Fiber Network Services Survivability*, [Artech House, May 1992].
[6] R. Kawamura, K. Sato, and I. Tokizawa, "High-Speed Self-Healing Techniques Utilizing Virtual Paths," *Proc. 5th Int'l. Network Planning Symp.*, Kobe, Japan, May 1992.
[7] N. Yoshikai and T.-H. Wu, "Control Protocol and Its Performance Analysis for Distributed ATM Virtual Path Self-Healing Networks," *IEEE JSAC*, Aug. 1994, pp. 1020–30.
[8] Y. Fujita, T-H Wu, and H. Fowler, "ATM VP Protection Switching and Applications," in *Proc. ISS '95*, Apr. 1995.
[9] L. Demounem and H. Arai, "A Performance Evaluation of an Integrated Control & OAM information Transport Network with Distributed Database Architecture", *IEICE*, vol. E-75-B, no. 12, 1992, pp. 1315–26.
[10] Bellcore Technical Advisory, "LATA Switching Systems Generic Requirements — Common Channel Signaling," TA-NWT-000606, issue 2, Mar. 1993.
[11] N. Yoshikai et al., "Proposal of ATM Based Signaling Transport Network Architectures," Conf. Rec., 7th Joint Japan and Korea Tech. Conf. (JC-CNSS), Taejon, Korea, July 1994.
[12] ITU-T Draft Recommendation I.580, "General Arrangements for Interworking between B-ISDN and 64 Kbps Based ISDN," Mar. 1994.
[13] ATM-Forum Draft B-ICI Specification Document, Version 2/0, Apr. 10–14, 1995.
[14] J. Luetchford, N. Yoshikai, and T.-H. Wu, "Network Common Channel Signalling Evolution", in *Proc. ISS '95*, vol. 2, pp. 234–38, Apr. 1995.
[15] ATM-Forum 94-0471R12, "PNNI Draft Specification," ATM Forum, Oct. 1995.

Biography

TSONG-HO WU [SM '92] received the B.S. in mathematics from the National Taiwan University in 1976, and M.S. and Ph.D degrees in operations research from the State University of New York at Stony Brook in 1981 and 1983, respectively. He has been with the Network Control Research Department at Bellcore, Red Bank, New Jersey, since 1986, where he is a director responsible for broadband fiber network design, survivable network architectures, emerging technology applications for SONET and ATM virtual path-based networks, ATM-based control and signaling transport for video dial tone services, and PCS mobility management. From 1983 to 1986 he was with United Telecommunications, Inc. (now Sprint) in its data communications division as a senior research scientist, where he was responsible for project management and research for planning and designing a new advanced nationwide packet-switched data network. From 1978 to 1979 he taught at the Department of Mathematics of National Taiwan University. His current research interests include broadband ATM/SONET transport and control network architectures and their applications to signaling for broadband video services and PCS mobility management.

NORIAKI YOSHIKAI (M '88) received the B.S. and M.S. degrees in electronics engineering from Kumamoto University,

Kumamoto, Japan, in 1977 and 1979, respectively, and the Ph.D. degree in electrical engineering from the Tokyo Institute of Technology, Tokyo, Japan, in 1988. He joined Yokosuka Electrical Communications Laboratories, Nippon Telegraph and Telephone Corporation, Kanagawa, Japan, in 1979, and was engaged in research on line terminal equipment for high-speed digital transmission systems. Since 1987 he has been doing research in the area of ATM network architecture at NTT Telecommunication Network Laboratories, with special interest in the interworking of B-ISDN with another network. From 1992 to 1993 he was a visting scientist at Bell Communications Research. He iscurrently a senior research engineer in the NTT Telecommunications Network Laboratories Groups. Dr. Yoshikai is a member of the Institute of Electronics, Information and Communications Engineers (IEICE) of Japan.

HIROYUKI FUJII received the B.S. and M.S. degrees in electronic engineering from Osaka University, Osaka, Japan, in 1987 and 1989, respectively. He joined the Telecommunication Networks Laboratories, Nippon Telegraph and Telephone Corporation, Tokyo, Japan, in 1989, and has been engaged in research in the area of ATM network architecture, especially network reliability. Since 1993 he has been doing research related to ATM-based signaling network architectures. He is currently a research engineer in the Network Architecture Laboratory at NTT. Mr. Fujii is a mmber of the IEICE of Japan.

INTERNATIONAL JOURNAL OF SATELLITE COMMUNICATIONS, VOL. 12, 211–222 (1994)

ASYNCHRONOUS TRANSFER MODE (ATM) OPERATION VIA SATELLITE: ISSUES, CHALLENGES AND RESOLUTIONS

D. M. CHITRE, D. S. GOKHALE, T. HENDERSON, J. L. LUNSFORD AND N. MATHEWS

COMSAT Laboratories, 22300 Comsat Drive, Clarksburg, MD 20871, U.S.A.

SUMMARY

Key issues regarding the operation of the broadband integrated services digital network (BISDN) via satellite are presented herein. The specific issues, challenges, and their resolutions are detailed. In particular, the impact of error characteristics and propagation delay on the operation of BISDN via satellite is discussed. Solutions are presented for removing adverse effects and providing high-quality service to users of BISDN via satellite.

KEY WORDS   ATM   BISDN

1. INTRODUCTION

The basic transport mechanism that has been defined[1] for the broadband integrated services digital network (BISDN) era is asynchronous transfer mode (ATM), which uses fixed-size data units known as cells. The ATM cell format is made up of 53 bytes; 48 of these contain data and five contain overhead. The data bytes correspond to the ATM adaptation layer (AAL) and the overhead bytes define the ATM cell header, which includes cell routeing information and an error detection/correction mechanism to protect routeing information. The AAL also includes an error detection mechanism to mitigate transmission errors in the AAL data.

In principle, ATM cells may be transported using any digital transmission format. However, the recently approved synchronous digital hierarchy (SDH) and plesiochronous digital hierarchy (PDH) signal formats are of interest from the viewpoint of national and international standardization. An important feature in SDH transmission is the inclusion of pointer bytes, which are used to indicate the location of the first byte in the payload of the SDH frame and also to avoid slips and their associated data loss due to slight phase or frequency variations between the SDH payload and the frame. ATM cell transmission via SDH further incorporates a cell delineation mechanism for the acquisition and synchronization of ATM cells on the receive side of the network.

Transmission considerations and performance criteria for both ATM and its carriage in the SDH and PDH frames are currently based on the assumption that transmission bit errors are randomly distributed. This assumption is generally valid for most terrestrial microwave and fibre-optic-based transmission systems. However, owing to the necessity of including channel coding in the satellite channel

to reduce the receive earth-station size and thereby minimize ground segment cost, transmission bit errors in a satellite channel environment are likely to occur in bursts. The bursty nature of transmission errors requires careful evaluation of transmission performance of both the SDH/PDH transport signals and the ATM cells contained within them.

ATM is a connection-oriented transport technology designed to provide a wide variety of services. ATM networks can achieve bandwidth efficiency through statistical multiplexing of cells from different connections, each of which may have widely differing traffic characteristics. ATM networks must manage traffic in such a way as to maximize bandwidth utilization while minimizing the proability of losses due to congestion. If higher loads are supported by an ATM network, a small probability exists that the instantaneous load on the network will exceed the capacity. In such cases, some mechanisms (such as feedback) are needed to limit the spread and duration of the congestion so that the connection quality of service (QOS) is not degraded.

In the satellite case, relatively large propagation delays can significantly increase the latency of feedback mechanisms. The result is that unless a robust feedback mechanism is designed, the mechanism may become ineffective at a certain point.

Finally, problems regarding reliable data transport via an ATM satellite link are considered. Error correction for reliable data transfer is generally performed through coding or a retransmission protocol. For data connections using ATM, existing protocols such as the transmission control protocol (TCP) can be encapsulated into ATM cells. However, this approach is limited by two factors, scalability and error robustness, which are encountered in the high-speed or stressed (high-error-rate) environment. Another option is to use the service specific connec-

CCC 0737–2884/94/030211–11

Received February 1994

tion oriented protocol (SSCOP), which has been standardized for BISDN signalling, but which is also applicable to high-speed data transfer.

2. IMPACT OF TRANSMISSION ERROR CHARACTERISTICS

The burst errors on a coded satellite link affect the operation of both ATM and AAL protocols and their transportation in the SDH/PDH frames.

2.1. *ATM layer considerations*

ATM cell performance parameters include cell acquisition time, cell in-synch time and cell discard probability. ATM performance is dependent upon the transmission channel bit error ratio (BER) and also on the nature of transmission bit errors. In the case of a satellite transmission channel, ATM cell performance parameters can only be quantified if the nature of transmission bit errors is first characterized. Here, bit errors are likely to occur in bursts due to the presence of encoding and decoding. The major performance objective for BISDN links is specified in terms of acceptable ATM cell discard probability (defined as the ratio of the number of ATM cells that are discarded because of uncorrectable errors to the total number of cells received). The stringent performance requirements being defined are driven by the characteristics of optical fibre, which can provide for BERs that are better than 10^{-10}. Moreover, the single bit correcting ATM header error correction (HEC) code is capable of correcting most errors encountered, given the random distribution of errors, over fibre links.

Satellite links that operate at such high rates (BISDN at 155 Mb/s, as well as the 45 Mb/s) employ error correction schemes for providing acceptable link BER (10^{-7} or better). The burst error characteristics generated as a result of using these error correction schemes have been studied extensively. The burst errors cannot be corrected by the ATM HEC since it is capable of correcting only single-bit errors. The ATM cell discard probability over such links is therefore orders of magnitude higher than over links with random errors.

To make ATM service feasible over satellites at the same quality level as fibre, COMSAT has developed a proprietary ATM link enhancement (ALE) technique that is capable of providing significant improvements in cell discard probability. The ALE incorporates a selective interleaving technique which does not impose additional overheads, allowing it to be transparently introduced into the satellite transmission link. The selective interleaving also takes into account the constraints imposed by the error detection and correction mode of operation specified in International Telecommunications Union (ITU-T) Recommendation I.432.[2] Hardware that implements the ALE functionality can be trans-parently introduced into a satellite transmission path. The ALE, which includes an interleaver and deinterleaver module, is inserted in the transmit and receive data path between the ATM switch and the satellite modem.

Figure 1 shows the improvement in the ATM cell discard probability when ALE is used to transport ATM over a 45 Mb/s intermediate data rate (IDR) satellite link. A comparison between the curves labelled 'no interleaving' and 'full bit interleaving' clearly shows that the ATM cell discard probability is considerably degraded when transmission is through a satellite system that introduces burst errors. In particular, there is a high probability that an ATM cell header will be in error by two or more bits every time it encounters an error burst. The single-bit error correction capability of the FEC in the ATM cell header is ineffective in this situation, and the ATM cell is likely to be discarded every time its header encounters an error burst.

Full bit interleaving of ATM cell headers, on the other hand, tends to distribute or 'spread' the bit errors among ATM cell headers after deinterleaving on the receive side. The probability of an ATM cell header being in error by two or more bits is considerably reduced, and cell headers having single-bit errors will be corrected by the cyclic code in the header.

The ALE was tested both in the laboratory and over the satellite to calibrate the ALE performance versus expected performance. Testing was performed using an HP ATM analyser as the cell source. The ALE was successfully demonstrated to reduce ATM cell loss significantly on a satellite link.

As described earlier, the HEC in the ATM cell header is capable of correcting single bit errors. Cell discard (or cell loss) occurs when multibit errors are present in the header. This probability will increase as a function of BER, and is also dependent on the burst error statistics. Cell synchronization will also fail due to framing errors in the physical layer. The burst error characteristics associated with convolutionally coded satellite links can significantly increase the cell discard probability.

The analytical model burst error generation in the 45 Mb/s IDR system was used to compute the ATM cell discard probability as a function of BER, and the results obtained are illustrated by the curves labelled 'no interleaving' in Figure 1. Note that Figure 1 is relevant to the case where the receiver is in the 'correction mode' only (it attempts to correct every errored cell header).

For comparison, the ATM cell discard probability was computed assuming that transmission bit errors are randomly distributed, as opposed to occurring in bursts as in the IDR system. This situation would result if the ATM cell headers were fully bit-interleaved prior to transmission so that the errored bits within an ATM cell header after deinterleaving on the receive side are distributed into different headers. The appropriate curve labelled 'full bit

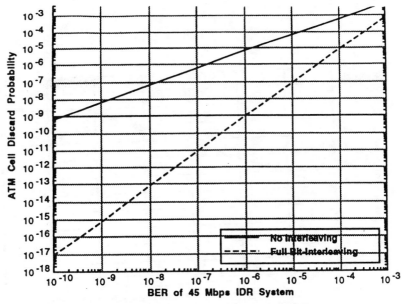

Figure 1. Computed ATM cell discard probability

interleaving' in Figure 1 shows the results obtained when this is the case.

A comparison between the curves labelled 'no interleaving' and 'full bit interleaving' in the Figure clearly shows that the ATM cell discard probability with the receiver in the 'correction mode' only is considerably degraded when transmission is through a satellite system that introduced burst errors. In particular, there is a high probability that an ATM cell header will be in error by two or more bits every time it is 'hit' by an error-burst. The single-bit error-correction capability of the FEC in the ATM cell header is ineffective in this situation, and the ATM cell is highly likely to be discarded every time its header is hit by an error-burst.

Full bit interleaving of ATM cell headers, on the other hand, tends to 'distribute' or 'spread' the bit errors between ATM cell headers after de-interleaving on the receive side. The probability of an ATM cell header being in error by two or more bits is reduced. Further, errored cell headers having single-bit errors are more likely, and these can be corrected by the cyclic code in the cell header. Satellite experiments were conducted without and with the ALE. In both cases, testing was performed to confirm the expected results for ATM cell discard in the case of no interleaving.

Results of the COMSAT ALE employing bit interleaving of the ATM cell header are plotted in Figure 2. There is very good agreement with the predicted results at a BER less than or equal to 10^{-5}. Owing to the steep slope of the performance of the ALE, it was difficult to obtain a significant number of points to verify the analytical results below an IDR BER of 10^{-5}. This is because at BERs less than 10^{-5}, the cell discard probability

(according to predicted results) is below 10^{-7}, and it was not possible during the limited experiment time to run trials to obtain a sufficient sample size. A number of samples were collected with a link BER between 10^{-6} and 10^{-8}. A high percentage of these samples exhibited zero HEC errors, whereas a few of these samples registered one or more HEC errors. Further testing is required (testing over several days with a stable BER source) to verify points on the predicted curve below a BER of 10^{-5}.

2.2. AAL considerations

The AAL's main function is to map the service requirements of a user application to the services provided by the ATM network layer. If performs this function by means of specific protocols. One common function of these protocols is to format the user data into ATM cell payloads. Other functions vary with the service needs of the user and include a transfer of timing from the source to the destination, error detection and error correction. AAL protocols generally operate end-to-end. This greatly simplifies the processing requirements in an ATM network, in that the switches route cells at the ATM layer independent of the AAL protocol of a connection.

The AAL is functionally divided into a common part and a service-specific part. The common part protocols are just above the ATM layer and provide for segmentation and reassembly of user data. The service-specific protocols, if needed, lie above the common part.

There are four classes of common part protocols, for which three AAL protocols are currently standardized. In principle, there are many possibilities of service-specific AALs; to date, standardization

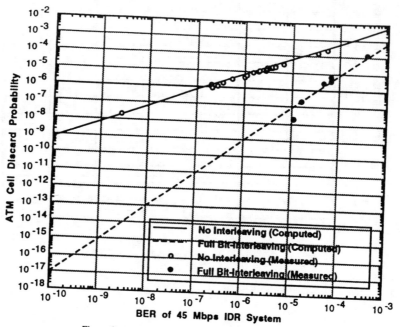

Figure 2. ATM cell discard probability vs. BER with ALE

is nearing completion on two such protocols. The protocols discussed herein regarding performance in a satellite environment include AAL type 1 (constant bit rate services), AAL type 3/4 and AAL type 5 (variable bit rate services), and SSCOP (variable bit rate services with error correction).

2.2.1. *AAL common part protocols.*

AAL types 1, 3/4 and 5 employ some type of cyclic code for error detection. These codes, like the ATM HEC, are sensitive to burst errors, which may occur on a satellite forward error correction (FEC)-coded channel. It is important to determine the probability of a satellite burst error passing undetected through the code and corrupting either the protocol mechanism or the data integrity.

2.2.1.1. AAL type 1

AAL type 1 provides for the transfer of user data with a constant source bit rate and delivery with the same bit rate. The service also provides for the transfer of timing and structure information between the source and the destination. Therefore, AAL type 1 can be used to transfer constant bit rate voice and video over ATM.

The layer functions provided by AAL type 1 are segmentation and reassembly of user information, handling of cell delay variation and cell payload assembly delay, handling of lost and misinserted cells, source data structure and clock frequency recovery, and handling of bit errors with possible corrective action. Satellite error characteristics have an impact on the operation of this protocol. AAL

type 1 performance requirements have not been specified. However, excessive numbers of lost cells and errored cells will affect the performance of the protocol, and certain levels of errors in the user data may degrade the data service.

AAL type 1 employs a 3-bit cyclic redundancy check (CRC) and a parity check on the segmentation and reassembly (SAR) header. This protects the four-bit sequence number (SN) field, which contains a three-bit sequence number and a one-bit change-of-status indicator (CSI) field. The error protection works analogously to the ATM HEC, in that it supports two modes, correction and detection. Fifteen of the 255 possible error bursts, all with a weight of four or more, will pass the CRC and parity check undetected.

The consequence of an undetected error at the SAR layer is that the convergence sublayer will determine that continuity has not been preserved, and that a loss condition exists. Depending on the performance objectives, dummy information may be generated to maintain the alignment of framing bit patterns. An artificial loss condition will be induced for eight AAL payloads by an undetected error on the sequence number, resulting in the insertion of the equivalent dummy data. This would affect the synchronization mechanism of the receiving user, for example, causing a loss of frame synchronization. Performance requirements are not available to assess the impact of such an event. Whether such an undetected error would significantly affect the AAL service would depend on the capability of the user, and the specific implementation of the protocol. In most cases, it would probably cause a synchronization error. The solution for the above problem again is to interleave the first byte of the AAL type 1 payload.

2.2.1.2. AAL type 3/4

AAL type 3/4 provides for the transfer of user data with a variable source bit rate. The layer services provided by AAL type 3/4 are segmentation and reassembly of user information, message mode or streaming mode communications, error detection and handling, multiplexing/demultiplexing abort, and buffer allocation. AAL type 3/4 performance requirements have not been specified. However, burst errors introduced by FEC and scrambling on the satellite channel will increase the probability of an undetected error, thereby resulting in the delivery of corrupted data to the user.

AAL type 3/4 employs a 10-bit CRC at the SAR level. For 10-bit polynomials, this code is particularly strong: it detects all single, double and triple errors (any length bursts with weights lower than 4), and all combinations or two burst errors of length two or less. It also detects all single bursts of length 10 or less, 99.8 per cent of the bursts of length 11, and 99.9 per cent of longer bursts.

The performance of AAL type 3/4 in the IDR system has been evaluated analytically. An analysis of the dominant bursts on the IDR channel showed that one of the bursts was, in fact, a CRC-10 syndrome. The effect of this syndrome is that the undetected error rate is only an order of magnitude smaller than the detected error rate.

The probability of undetected errors can be greatly reduced if full byte interleaving is performed on the ATM cell payload. This distributes the burst error into two AAL payloads. The net result is that, on average, the detected error rate, and hence the AAL payload discard rate, doubles. However, the undetected error rate, which could result in corrupted data, drops by several orders of magnitude.

2.2.1.3. AAL type 5

AAL type 5 provides for the transfer of user data with a variable source bit rate. AAL type 5 offers a service very similar to that of AAL type 3/4. Satellite impairments to the operation of this protocol have not been identified.

AAL type 5 employs a 32-bit CRC, which is a much stronger polynomial for error detection. All burst errors of length 32 or less are detected, and the error detection capabilities for longer bursts are much stronger than AAL type 3/4. In addition, the CRC is backed up by a length-check field which detects the loss or gain of cells in an AAL type 5 payload, even when the CRC confirms such an errored payload as valid. It is unlikely that undetected errors would occur on a general FEC-coded satellite channel.

2.3. *Physical layer*

The impact of burst errors on the operation of ATM carried by a DS3 (44.745 Mbs) signal is addressed in this subsection.

2.3.1. *DS3 performance.*
The DS3 signal is partitioned into multiframes (M-frames) of 4760 bits each. The M-frames are divided into seven M-subframes having 680 bits each. Each subframe is further divided into eight blocks of 85 bits each, with 84 of the 85 bits available for information (the overhead is therefore 1.2 per cent). Figure 3 illustrates the DS3 signal format. Two functions of the protocol—framing and parity checking—could be affected by burst errors.

2.3.1.1. Framing

DS3 framing is implementation-dependent. However, the DS3 framing mechanism was expected to be tolerant of burst errors because of the separation of framing (F) bits by 168 information bits and a C bit, and the separation of multiframe (M) bits by 679 bits. A single burst error should not encounter more than one or two framing or control bits.

The out-of-frame state is declared when three F-bit errors are observed out of either 8 or 16 consecutive F bits. Out-of-frame is also declared when one or more M-bit errors are detected in three of four consecutive M-frames. At these thresholds, framing errors should not cause a problem.

2.3.1.2. Parity checking

Parity is computed over the 4704 information bits of the M-frame, and the results are inserted into the P-bit position of the subsequent frame. The C-bit channel in DS3 enhances the accuracy of the parity check, since three bits are available for majority decision. The C-bit parity is an accurate approximation of the number of errors occurring on the DS3 channel, for a random error channel. However, parity checks do not accurately indicate the number of errors for a burst error channel. Therefore parity checking is not expected to reflect burst error occurrences accurately.

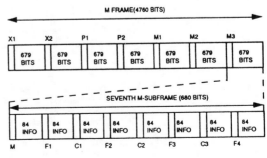

Figure 3. DS3 signal format

2.3.2. *PLCP performance.* The physical layer convergence protocol (PLCP) for DS3 systems is specified in IEEE Standard 802.6. The frame format consists of 12 rows by 57 octets, with the last octet containing a trailer of either 13 or 14 'nibbles'. (A nibble is 4 bits.) The frame repeats every 125 μs and is asynchronously mapped into the DS3 payload. Twelve ATM cells and 12 octets of path overhead are contained in each frame. Figure 4 illustrates the PLCP format.

The path overhead octets for framing, cycle/stuff counter, and bit interleaved parity (BIP)-8 can be affected by transmission errors, as described below.

2.3.2.1. Framing

Framing is based on the A1 and A2 bytes in the PLCP frame. The state machine can be in one of four states: in-frame (INF3), out-of-frame (OOF1a), out-of-frame-jam (OOF_J1b), and loss-of'frame (LOF2). After the PLCP has acquired a frame, any transition to a state other than INF3 results in loss of the PLCP payload for more than one payload slot. Therefore, to avoid cell loss, it is important to maintain the INF3 state.

The IEEE standard specifies that if consecutive A1 and A2 octets are in error, the OOF1a state is entered, and a jam signal is generated on the bus. The INF3 state cannot be re-entered until two valid consecutive A1 and A2 octet pairs, with valid path overhead indicator (POI) octets, are found. Depending on the implementation (some implementations will not lift the jam signal until the beginning of the next frame), between 2 and 14 ATM cells will be lost for every transition to the OOF1a state, depending on the relative location of the error in the frame. The OOF1a state will be entered whenever a burst error overlaps the A1 and A2 bytes.

The implication of the PLCP framing state machine is that any single burst error that overlaps the A1 and A2 octets of the PLCP frame can cause implementations that strictly adhere to the IEEE standard to go into the OOFa1 state. Even under an immediate error recovery scenario, between 2 and 14 ATM cells may be lost due to such an event.

2.3.2.2. Cycle/stuff counter

Framing errors may also occur due to errors on the C1 cycle/stuff byte. The C1 code works for the frame cycle are separated by a Hamming distance of 4. The stuff/no-stuff code words are separated by a distance of 8. The tolerance of this code to errors is implementation-dependent. However, burst errors on this byte with a weight of four or more will cause errors in the trailer length estimation which may cause framing errors.

2.3.2.3. Bit interleaved parity (BIP)-8

BIP-8 is an 8-bit interleaved parity code using even parity. This code provides for eight separate, even parity codes covering the corresponding bit of each octet in the 12 × 54 structure (12 rows consisting of an ATM cell plus one octet of path overhead). Parity counts are available for error

PLCP Framing		POI	POH	PLCP Payload	
A1	A2	P11	Z6	First ATM Cell	
A1	A2	P10	Z5	ATM cell	
A1	A2	P09	Z4	ATM cell	
A1	A2	P08	Z3	ATM cell	
A1	A2	P07	Z2	ATM cell	
A1	A2	P06	Z1	ATM cell	
A1	A2	P05	X	ATM cell	
A1	A2	P04	B1	ATM cell	
A1	A2	P03	G1	ATM cell	
A1	A2	P02	X	ATM cell	
A1	A2	P01	X	ATM cell	
A1	A2	P00	C1	Twelfth ATM Cell	Trailer
1 byte	1 byte	1 byte	1 byte	53 bytes	13 or 14 nibbles

```
A1, A2  =  PLCP framing bytes
POI     =  Path Overhead Indicator
POH     =  Path Overhead
Z1 - Z6 =  Reserved byte (for future use)
X       =  Unassigned byte (ignored by receiver)
B1      =  BIP-8 (Bit Interleaved Parity-8) byte
G1      =  PLCP Path Status byte
C1      =  Cycle/Stuff Counter byte
```

Figure 4. PLCP frame format for ATM

should account for the possibility of errored BIP-8 code bytes.

Parity checks are most accurate for random bit errors. If a burst is longer than 8 bits, it may actually corrupt an even number of bits in the parity count. Usually, BIP-8 errors will indicate the presence of burst errors, but no granularity information can be obtained from the count.

2.3.2.4. Summary

The PLCP protocol is not designed to function well in a burst error environment. Despite the ample framing overhead available, the framing algorithm goes into the out-of-frame state upon a single burst error overlapping the A1 and A2 bytes. In addition, a burst error corrupting the C1 byte may cause implementations to go into a loss-of-frame state. Finally, the BIP-8 counter does not accurately detect burst errors. However, by using the COMSAT ALE, it is possible to maintain PLCP framing in a burst error environment.

3. IMPACT OF SATELLITE DELAY ON ATM

With ATM via satellite, relatively large propagation delays can significantly increase the latency of feedback mechanisms essential for congestion control. The result is that, unless a robust feedback mechanism is designed, the ATM mechanism may become ineffective at a certain point. The second area where satellite delay plays an important role is concerned with reliable data transport via an ATM satellite link. Error correction for reliable data transfer is generally performed through coding or a retransmission protocol. For data connections using ATM, existing protocols such as TCP can be encapsulated into ATM cells, but this approach is limited by two factors scalability and error robustness, which are encountered in the high-speed, or stressed (high-error-rate), environment. Another option is to use the SSCOP, which has been standardized for BISDN signalling, but which is also applicable to high-speed data transfer. Its principal function is to ensure data delivery, using error recovery procedures if necessary, for high-bandwidth/delay connections. If offers an efficient error recovery mechanism, network delay insensitivity and flow control, and is suitable for high-speed implementations.

The performance of retransmission protocols depends on the bandwith and delay of connections, as well as the underlying error rate. It is expected that SSCOP will be more resilient to degraded broadband environments that other protocols.

3.1. *ATM traffic and congestion control*

ATM networks are designed to multiplex traffic of many different types, requiring different QOS and different network capacities, on a single back-constant bit rate services (such as digital circuit emulation) and cells from data services will be intermixed. When a connection is made, a 'traffic contract' is established between the user and the network. This contract stipulates the required network performance, and bounds the statistics of the traffic that the user may submit to the network. The network is expected to deliver the user's compliant traffic at the performance (QOS) level specified.

For many types of ATM traffic, transfer capacity needs will vary with time. On a large scale, traffic from different sources that varies over time should smooth out. However, it is possible that coincident peaks from many users may arise intermittently. The possibility of this increases as the average network load approaches capacity. Such traffic patterns, or other fault conditions in the network, may give rise to congestion. Congestion is defined as a state in which the network is not able to meet the required QOS for already established connections and/or for new connection requests.

In order to avoid congestion, a set of traffic control and congestion control procedures has been established for ATM. Traffic control refers to the set of actions taken by the network to avoid congested conditions. Congestion control refers to the set of actions taken by the network to minimize the intensity, spread and duration of congestion. A robust set of traffic and congestion control procedures is necessary to maintain high network efficiency. The relationship between such procedures and a satellite environment is the subject of this subsection.

3.1.1. *Currently defined traffic and congestion controls.* ATM networks are in the initial stages of definition and deployment, and traffic control for these networks has been simplified. Nevertheless, several groups (ITU, American National Standards Institute [ANSI], and ATM Forum) have produced initial specifications and recommendations for traffic and congestion control.[3]

In the near term, ATM network designers and operators will avoid congestion by ensuring adequate capacity to support all connections. Aside from faults in the network, congestion can only occur in this case if the network permits more traffic into it than it can handle. In current fibre-based networks, ATM represents such a growth in capacity that traffic levels are not expected to stress the network. Therefore, the emphasis within current specifications has been to define traffic controls that prevent troublesome connections from being established. For example, only one traffic descriptor, the peak cell rate, is required in current specifications. Upon connection set-up, a peak cell rate is specified for the connection, and during the lifetime of the connection, the edge of the network will monitor the connection's rate and accordingly discard or lower the priority of any traffic that exceeds the peak rate specified. Therefore, a network can easily decide if it can support a new connection request by comparing the network capacity along the connection with the sum of the peak rates of the current traffic and the new connection for each link of the connection. In this manner, congestion can generally be avoided.

However, in the long term networks will be challenged to use their capacity more efficiently, and more elaborate traffic and congestion controls for ATM will be needed. For satellite networks, the need is already present, since satellite links are bandwidth-limited compared to optical-fibre links. Therefore, additional procedures are needed in order to use the statistical multiplexing capabilities of ATM fully.

3.1.2. *Traffic controls and network efficiency.*
Some services, such as circuit emulation, are well-defined in terms of bandwidth, but require a high QOS in terms of acceptable loss, delay, and jitter (delay variation). Other services, such as variable-bit-rate video, are not as well defined in terms of bandwidth but still require a high QOS. Some services, such as data, can be very unpredictable in terms of bandwidth but are less demanding of QOS, particularly in terms of delay and jitter. In a network where all types of services compete for the same bandwidth, the most efficient network will be one that can maintain the high QOS for constant-bit-rate or timing-dependent variable-bit-rate services while transporting as much data as possible.

Many possibilities exist for supporting a heavier traffic load within the network, and a number of such procedures can be classified as 'preventive controls'. One possibility is to require sources to define their traffic flows more precisely so that the capacity demands can be accurately predicted. This approach helps somewhat, but some sources, such as data, inherently have trouble characterizing their traffic patterns in advance. Another possibility is for the network to perform traffic shaping on the flow to change its statistics, although the ability of the network to perform traffic shaping is limited to procedures that maintain the established QOS of the connection. Therefore, there is some limit to the effectiveness of preventive traffic controls, although they should be implemented to the extent possible.

Another technique which may be widely used is priority. Cells of a particular virtual channel have a cell loss priority (CLP), which allows for two different priorities. The user can establish a QOS for two different flows on a connection: those cells with CLP = 0 (high priority) and cells with CLP = 1 (low priority). If congestion occurs, the network will attempt to discard cells with CLP = 1 before it discards cells with CLP = 0. An example of a traffic source which may be able to exploit this type of service is variable-bit-rate video, in which the user can separate the traffic into high- and low-priority information. In addition, a traffic policer may have the option of changing the CLP of non-compliant cells from CLP = 0 to CLP = 1 instead of simply discarding the cell. This mechanism, called 'cell tagging', would allow the network to attempt to deliver non-compliant data if possible. However, this mechanism may not be advantageous for ensuring data delivery, in which retransmissions of lost data are necessary. In fact, the reliance on priority as a mechanism for allowing increased network loads may be more of a problem for satellite connections, because losses due to congestion cause retransmissions and, typically, degradation in the protocol throughput for links with long propagation delay.

In summary, the preventive traffic controls currently defined are somewhat useful, but are not adequate to allow efficient ATM networking. In order to achieve maximum efficiency in a statistical multiplexing environment, a certain probability of congestion must be tolerated, or feedback must be used to anticipate congestion and to slow down users. If congestion can be quickly alleviated, loss of data can be avoided. Congestion control procedures should be designed to accomplish this as the current specified congestion control procedures discussed below are inadequate to perform this task.

3.1.3. *Reactive congestion controls.*
As stated above, currently defined congestion control functions are scant. Congestion controls must operate on a very short time scale in order to be successful, since at broadband rates, finite-sized queues may quickly overrun during congested conditions. In general, two mechanisms are discussed: cell discard and feedback. As they are currently defined, however, both mechanisms may present problems to networks that incorporate satellites due to propagation delays.

Selective cell discard allows a congested network element to selectively discard cells that are identified as belonging to a non-compliant ATM connection and/or those cells with the CLP set to 1. This action preserves, as long as possible, CLP = 0 flows. For example, the strategy may be to let the user submit CLP = 1 traffic as 'best effort' traffic, which can be easily dropped by the network if necessary. Although this approach can be rather simple from a control standpoint, it does have drawbacks in some environments. The dropping of data on an assured connection will lead to retransmissions, which may be efficient if selective retransmission is used, but which will on average delay the delivery of a substantial number of packets in the satellite case. Furthermore, it will be difficult to guarantee a relatively good QOS for CLP = 1 flows if a substantial probability of discard exists.

The other frequently discussed mechanism is feedback. The goal of feedback is to provide the traffic sources causing congestion with information about the congestion event so that the sources can take appropriate action to temporarily reduce the traffic load. Two main mechanisms are needed to accomplish this goal:

1. The network element must incorporate a mechanism to determine when it is congested.
2. A mechanism is needed to convey such information back to the source.

Typically, the first mechanism has not been subject to standardization, since such mechanisms are implementation-dependent. However, some type of semantics is needed for such a mechanism so that responders (traffic terminals) can properly interpret the message.

Currently, one mechanism (explicit forward congestion indication [EFCI] for conveying congestion notification back to the source has been partially defined. This indication is the basic mechanism of what is known as forward explicit congestion notification (FECN). EFCI is carried through the use of a payload-type coding in the ATM cell header. If a network element determines that it is 'congested', it may set the EFCI bit in the ATM header on each cell of particular virtual paths or virtual channels contributing to, or causing, the congestion. (Note: If a particular queue is congested, all virtual paths or virtual channels through the queue may have the EFCI set). At the destination end system, this indication is sent to the higher protocol layer, which is instructed to notify its peer protocol entity to reduce its traffic load. The higher layer might need to filter the indications before reacting to them, depending on how the EFCI is set by the switch.

As currently defined, EFCI is inadequate for effective reaction congestion control. First, no semantics have been specified for EFCI; as a result, an end system receiving this notification cannot be sure of the true state of congestion in the network. Secondly, no current user protocol can make use of this indication, although some types of future protocols (such as SSCOP within the AAL) may incorporate this function. Thirdly, EFCI is unenforceable; no mechanism exists for the ATM layer to act on this indication and regulate the flow. Finally, and most critical for satellites, EFCI, and any other type of FECN mechanism, necessarily incurs at least a one-way propagation delay in notifying the source. Therefore, the effectiveness of various detection and reaction algorithms is limited by propagation delay.

For these reasons, COMSAT and other organizations have been advocating a faster mechanism, called backward explicit congestion notification (BECN). In the proposed BECN scheme, a congested network element would send a notification in the reverse direction of the congested path. This notification could be either a performance-management type cell or another new type of cell. A network element, if it determined that it was congested, would send a cell on the reverse path. The destination end system could act upon this notification by directing the source to reduce its traffic rate, and by enforcing the rate reduction at the ingress to the ATM network.

The effectiveness of BECN could be significantly better than FECN if satellite links are involved and if users can respond quickly to notification. However, for a robust algorithm, network configurations must be considered in that the congestion occurs on the destination side of a satellite link or other long propagation delay trunk. The comparative utility of FECN and BECN will vary, depending on the network configuration and the source traffic characteristics. If a worst-case environment for BECN must be designed, FECN may perform comparably and may be simpler to implement. Satellite ATM networks require a high degree of network efficiency with resulting minimal cell loss, and the control algorithms to achieve this efficiency must be relatively delay-insensitive. Currently, however, traffic management specifications do not adequately address the problem.

3.2. AAL service-specific part protocols

The service specific convergence sublayer (SSCS) is one component of the AAL. Its function is to provide a convergence between the services of the common part AAL protocol (such as AAL type 5) and the service requirements of a user protocol (such as MTP-3 for network node interface signalling). The SSCS may be null if the user is able to directly use the service of the common part AAL or ATM protocols.

For connections that require error recovery (from lost or errored ATM cells) a particular SSCS has been defined, initially for signalling use, and ultimately for user applications. This SSCS is functionally divided into a unique SSCOP, and a service specific co-ordination function (SSCF) which varies depending on the user. The SSCOP is principally concerned with providing assured data delivery, whereas the SSCF provides convergence between the SSCOP and the AAL user. The design strategy has been to develop a common high-performance protocol (SSCOP) that can run on all protocol stacks, and to define convergence functions with no peer-to-peer protocol in order to adapt the SSCOP service to the needs of a particular user.

The SSCOP's principal function is to provide assured delivery of PDUs that were submitted to the SSCOP, using error recovery procedures if necessary. In the past, error recovery (or automatic repeat request [ARQ]) protocols have exhibited poor performance over satellite links. However, SSCOP has been developed to operate well in a wide variety of environments, including satellite networks.

The following SSCOP protocol features are beneficial in a high-speed, high-delay environment such as BISDN:

Selective retransmissions. SSCOP provides assured delivery service to its user. If missing data are detected at the receiver, retransmission of the data is requested. SSCOP uses a very efficient selective retransmission mechanism that prevents unnecessary retransmissions.

Window size. The window size of a protocol is the number of outstanding data units that are permitted for a connection. In an error recovery protocol, the data units are numbered sequentially to allow a receiver to detect missing units. Typically, the data unit is a variable-length frame of data, although it can be measured in other units (e.g. TCP sequences octets of data). At most, the window size is bounded by the numbering space allotted to the sequence numbers. For example, if the sequence number if N bits long, the window is constrained to be no longer than $(2^N - 1)$ data units long.

The window size is set based on the minimum of the range of the possible window size and the receiver's buffer availability. If the window is small, a protocol transmitter may be forced to suspend data transmission until acknowledgements for outstanding frames arrive. To ensure that the sequence number space is sufficiently large for future growth, a 24-bit modulus and a sliding window credit mechanism based on units of SSCOP frames were selected. The modulus is large enough to accommodate gigabit-per-second connections with multiple satellite hops.

Flow control. The SSCOP receiver manages the rate of data exchange. It grants the transmitter a credit value which represents the number of frames that the receiver is willing to accept. The credit value sent periodically by the receiver allows for dynamic window size control and flexible management of local buffer resources. In addition, a rate-based flow control mechanism can be used in conjunction with window size control for better performance. This is an area for future study within the protocol.

High speed implementation. The transmitter and receiver state machines are decoupled and provide for parallel implementation. The use of timers is minimized to benefit the satellite environment, where timers have often been set to inappropriate default values. Optimization of a protocol for a high-speed environment has the effect of optimizing it for a high-delay environment as well.

Network delay insensitivity. In summary, the protocol has been designed to be insensitive to variations in the round-trip delay for a connection, and to provide speedy recovery of lost data. The receiver notifies the transmitter immediately upon detection of missing data, and new data transmission can continue during error recovery.

3.3. *High speed data over a satellite ATM link*

High-speed data (e.g. LAN interconnection, host to host), will be one of the major applications used over ATM networks. At multi-megabit per second rates, the performance of a widely used transport protocol, namely, transmission control protocol (TCP), is suboptimal when operating over satellite links. There are primarily two factors that result in the poor performance — the inadequate window size, and the acknowledgement and the retransmission scheme for error recovery.

The window size of a protocol is the number of outstanding data units that are permitted for a connection. In an error recovery protocol, the data units are sequentially numbered to allow a receiver to detect missing data units. Typically the data unit is a variable length frame of data, although it can be measured in other units (e.g. TCP sequences octets of data). At most, the window size is bounded by the numbering space allotted to the sequence numbers. For example, if the sequence number is N bits long, the window is constrained to be no longer than $(2^N - 1)$ data units long. The default value for the TCP window size is 16 Kbyte, which severely restricts the throughput efficiency over a satellite link. Newer extensions to protocols (e.g. the window scaling option in TCP-RFC 1323) have made it possible for better operation at higher satellite links speed, but very few equipment vendors have incorporated these modifications.

The majority of link and transport layer protocols (e.g. HDLC, TCP) implement error recovery procedures, which result in unacceptable performance when operating over links that have a large bandwidth-delay product. The primary reason for the poor performancce is the retransmission of a large number of packets even if a single packet was lost due to error or some other reason such as congestion. The inefficiency associated with these protocols increases as the bandwidth–delay product (and correspondingly the window size required to fill the round-trip delay) increases. Given the high-speed ATM links (e.g. 45 Mb/s), even link BERs of 10^{-7} can significantly degrade the throughput efficiency of these protocols.

However, the service specific connection oriented protocol (SSCOP) protocol, specified by ITU-TS as Draft Recommendation Q.SAAL.2, has been defined for reliable end-to-end delivery of data in the ATM enviornment and is designed to compensate for the satellite delay. It features a large (24 bit) sequence space and incorporates a selective repeat protocol for error recovery. The window size can be set to a size much larger than needed for the satellite case. Therefore, it is expected that SSCOP would provide close to optimal performance even in the satellite environment. SSCOP provides assured delivery service to its user. If missing data is detected at the receiver, that data is requested to be retransmitted from the transmitter. SSCOP uses a very efficient selective retransmission mechanism that prevents any unnecessary retransmissions.

4. DISCUSSION

BISDN can function satisfactorily over satellite links despite some major differences in their characteristics compared to fibre links. The COMSAT ALE can significantly improve performance in two areas: maintaining physical layer framing in a burst error environment, and reducing the ATM cell loss probability by several orders of magnitude. The general concept of the ALE—interleaving ATM cells to distribute burst errors into single-bit errors in cells—can be extended to the ATM cell payload to remove adverse burst error impact on AAL protocols.

Satellite networks have additional strengths. A major distinguishing feature of satellite communications networks is their ability to obtain variable bandwidth on demand. This is typically achieved via a demand-assigned multiple-access method. This capability, coupled with the fundamental characteristics of ATM networks as virtual networks that statistically multiplex traffic as demand arises, can be exploited to provide ATM via satellite in a resource- and cost-efficient manner.

REFERENCES

1. 'Broadband aspects of ISDN', *ITU-T Recommendation I.121*, December 1988.
2. 'B-ISDN user-network interface - physical layer specification', *ITU-T Recommendation I.432*, March 1993.
3. 'Traffic control and congestion in B-ISDN', *ITU-T Recommendation I.371*, March 1993

Author's biographies:

Dattakumar M. Chitre received his B.Sc. from the University of Bombay, India; an M.A. in mathematics from the University of Cambridge, U.K.; and a Ph.D. in physics from the University of Maryland. He is currently an Associate Executive Director of the Network Technology Division at COMSAT Laboratories. He has been involved in research and development activities in ISDN, VSAT networks, data communications and network systems and architectures. Prior to his current positions, Dr. Chitre was a Principal Scientist in the Network Technology Division at COMSAT Laboratories.

Dr. Chitre joined COMSAT Laboratories in 1980. He has made major contributions to the analysis and architecture of data communication, ISDN, and BISDN via satellite. Dr. Chitre directs and participates in the international and national standards activities in ISDN, BISDN, and data communication as they apply to satellite communication. He was Chairman of the Working Group on Protocols and Network Timing Function of the CCIR/CCITT Joint Ad Hoc Group on ISDN/Satellite Matters during 1990–1992. Currently, he is the Chairman of the Working Group on New Technologies in the ITU Intersector Coordinating Group (ICG) on Satellite Matters. Dr. Chitre was a programme manager during 1990 and 1991 on a contract from INTELSAT on systems studies on satellite communications systems architectures for ISDN and broadband ISDN systems. Currently, he is the technical manager of the DoD Contract on ATM via satellite demonstration and the programme manager for the INTELSAT contract on analysis and top-level specification of INTELSAT ISDN subnetworks and SDH compatible transport network.

Dilip Gokhale is department manager for ISDN/Data Communications in the Network Technology Division of COMSAT Laboratories. His responsibilities include managing the implementation of next generation telecommunication systems for fixed and mobile satellite systems. Current projects include the development of a high data rate gateway switch that provides for the interconnection of Inmarsat B mobile users with ISDN services provided by interexchange carriers, and the development of an IBS overlay system to provide bandwidth on demand capability over the INTELSAT satellites. Mr. Gokhale managed the software development and conducting of experiments for an 'Asynchronous Transfer Mode (ATM) via Satellite' project under contract to the U.S. Department of Defense. Mr. Gokhale was the project manager for conducting studies, and developing the specifications of the North American real time packet data system via the AMSC/TMI satellites. Other projects that he has worked on in the past include the development of a satellite efficient X.75 protocol converter, a higher performance LAN-WAN router platform, and a packet VSAT network. Mr. Gokhale joined COMSAT Laboratories in 1984, after completing an M.S. in Electrical Engineering, at the New Jersey Institute of Technology, Newark, NJ.

Thomas R. Henderson received the B.S. and M.S. degrees in electrical engineering from Stanford University in 1990 and 1991, respectively. Since 1991 he has been a Member of the Technical Staff in the Network Technology Division at COMSAT Laboratories. He has contributed to a number of study projects for advanced satellite network architectures, including BISDN and integrated video architectures. More recently, he has performed simulation, analysis, and experiments of ATM performance via satellite links. He is currently involved in the design of satellite architectures and signalling for the integration of the INTELSAT network into ISDN. In addition, he has represented COMSAT at various telecommunications standards organizations, including ITU-T Study Groups 11 and 13, ANSI Subcommittee T1S1, and the ATM Forum. he has authored over 50 technical contributions concerning NISDN and BISDN protocol development, and is currently serving as vice-chair of the AAL Sub-Working Group of T1S1, convener of an ITU-T Study Group 13 question concerning the use of satellites in the ISDN, and editor of a new ISDN signalling recommendation in ITU-T Study Group 11.

John A. Lunsford received a B.S.E.E. from the University of Maryland in 1973 and an M.S.E.E. from the University of Pennsylvania in 1980. From 1973 to 1980 Mr. Lunsford worked on advanced radar signal processing equipment development projects for the RCA Missile and Surface Radar Division (MSRD) including the AEGIS Advanced Radar Signal Processor for the U.S. Navy's AEGIS shipboard radar system. He joined COMSAT Laboratories in 1980 where he participated in a number of TDMA system specification and equipment development efforts including the system specifications for the INTELSAT TDMA/DSI system. From 1985 to 1989 Mr. Lunsford worked as an independent contractor for INTELSAT where he made major contributions to the SSTDMA system design and specification, as well as the specifications for the INTELSAT Operation Center TDMA Facility, Satellite Control Center, and SSTDMA burst time plan generation software system. In addition, he held a principal role in the implementation, installation, testing, and documentation of all elements of the SSTDMA system.

Mr. Lunsford rejoined COMSAT Laboratories in 1990

as manager of the Network Systems department in the Network Technology Division where he led an engineering team performing research and development in the areas of on-board processing, ISDN, TDMA, network control, and system architectures for advanced satellite communications systems. He is currently manager of the Network Engineering department where he is responsible for hardware development for various satellite communications projects.

Neville A. Mathews was born in Visakhapatnam, India, on 17 April 1943, and received the Ph.D. degree in Electronics from the University of Southampton, England, in 1967. He worked for fifteen years in various industrial and academic institutions in England, and undertook research in solid state devices, microwave propagation, microwave integrated circuits, and digital communications systems. From 1982 to 1987 he was with INTELSAT, Washington, DC, USA, where he worked on the analysis and design of various analog and digital satellite transmission systems. He joined COMSAT Laboratories, Clarksburg, MD, USA, in 1988 and worked in both the Communications Technology and Network Technology Divisions. He left COMSAT in January 1994 to become an independent Consultant on satellite communications and networking issues.

IEEE JOURNAL ON SELECTED AREAS IN COMMUNICATIONS, VOL. 12, NO. 8, OCTOBER 1992

ATM-Based Transport Architecture for Multiservices Wireless Personal Communication Networks

Dipankar Raychaudhuri, *Senior Member, IEEE*, and Newman D. Wilson, *Member, IEEE*

Abstract—This paper presents an ATM-based transport architecture for next-generation multiservices personal communication networks (PCN). Such "multimedia capable" integrated services wireless networks are motivated by an anticipated demand for wireless extensions to future broadband networks. An ATM compatible wireless network concept capable of supporting a mix of broadband ISDN services including constant bit-rate (CBR), variable bit-rate (VBR), and packet data transport is explored from an architectural viewpoint. The proposed system uses a hierarchical ATM switching network for interconnection of PCN microcells, each of which is serviced by high-speed, shared-access radio links based on ATM-compatible cell relay principles. Design issues related to the physical (modulation), media access control (MAC), and data-link layers of the ATM-based radio link are discussed, and preliminary technical approaches are identified in each case. An example multiservice dynamic reservation (MDR) TDMA media access protocol is then considered in further detail, and simulation results are presented for an example voice/data scenario with a proportion of time-critical (i.e., multimedia) packet data. Time-of-expiry (TOE) based queue service disciplines are also investigated as a mechanism for improving the quality-of-service (QoS) in this scenario.

I. Introduction

WIRELESS personal communication networks (PCN[1]) based on new digital technologies have emerged as an important field of activity in telecommunications [8], [15], [9], [14], [32], [33]. This surge of R&D and commercial interest is based on the timely convergence of several factors including: proliferation of tetherless personal computing, entertainment, and communication devices; liberalization of spectrum allocation procedures for both public personal communication system (PCS) and private wireless local-area network (LAN) applications; advances in digital signal processing and radio modem technologies; improvements in cost/size/power consumption characteristics of digital electronics; etc. Although initial PCS proposals have generally focused on near-term voice applications, it is recognized that these systems will be required to evolve towards supporting a wider range of telecommunications applications involving packet data, video, and multimedia. At the same time, wireless local-area networks, which were initially designed for conventional data, face a growing requirement to support computer applica-

Manuscript received February 15, 1994.

D. Raychaudhuri is with NEC USA, C&C Research Laboratories, Princeton, NJ 08540 USA.

N. Wilson is with the David Sarnoff Research Center, Princeton, NJ 08543 USA.

IEEE Log Number 9403388.

[1] The term "next-generation PCN" is used here in a broad sense to include both public PCS systems such as UMTS/FPLMTS [6], and private wireless local-area networks of the future.

tions incorporating image and/or video transfer. Thus, the demand for multimedia-capable multiservice wireless networks is driven by parallel trends towards integration of voice, video, image, and data in both telecommunication and computing environments.

Next-generation PCN's will be required to co-exist with fiber-optic based broadband communication networks, which should become far more ubiquitous during this decade. These broadband systems (such as B-ISDN/ATM [5] and ATM LAN [12]) will offer constant bit-rate (CBR), variable bit-rate (VBR), and packet transport services designed to support a range of voice, data, video, and multimedia applications. In order to avoid a serious mismatch between future wireline and wireless networks, it is now timely to begin consideration of broadband wireless systems with similar service capabilities [2], [29], [20]. Personal communication networks introduced into the future multimedia application scenario should provide new service features such as high-speed transmission, flexible bandwidth allocation, VBR/CBR/packet modes, quality-of-service (QoS) selection, etc. Clearly, implementation of these broadband features on the wireless medium is a more difficult technical challenge than for fiber, but it is important to aim at system designs which provide qualitatively similar attributes even if quantitative equivalence with the fiber network is not feasible.

Based on the above considerations, we propose that an ATM cell-relay paradigm be adopted as the basis for next-generation wireless transport architectures. The proposed PCN system uses a hierarchical ATM switching network for interconnection of PCN microcells, each of which is serviced by high-speed, shared-access radio links based on ATM-compatible cell relay principles. In this approach, an ATM cell serves as the basic unit for protocol processing and switching in both wired and wireless portions of the network. The overall transport architecture is based on the ATM protocol stack, with appropriate extensions added where necessary to support new mobility functions and wireless channel specific requirements. In particular, the wireless segment of the network will require additional medium access control (MAC) and data-link layers for channel sharing and error control on the radio links. If properly designed, these wireless channel specific layers should be able to provide a degree of transparency for a useful subset of broadband/ATM services. Of course, physical limitations of the radio channel are likely to impose some transmission speed and quality-of-service constraints. Nevertheless, the availability of qualitatively equivalent ATM service classes in a seamless manner would provide significant

Reprinted from IEEE Journal on Selected Areas in Communications, Vol. 12, No. 8, Oct. 1992, pp. 1401-1414.

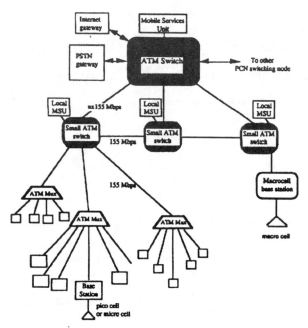

Fig. 3. Typical organization of ATM-based backbone switching network.

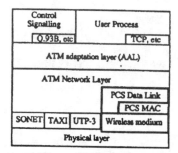

Fig. 4. Relation of wireless network (PCN) protocol layers and ATM.

type) ATM switches, small (LAN type) ATM switches, and ATM multiplexors, respectively.

B. Protocol Layering

The multiservices PCN system should follow a protocol layering that is harmonized with the ATM protocol stack. The approach that will be presented here is to add new wireless channel specific physical, medium access control and data-link layers below the ATM network layer as shown in Fig. 4. This means that regular ATM network layer and control services such as call set-up, VCI/VPI addressing, cell prioritization, and flow control indication will continue to be used for mobile services. Of course, the baseline ATM network and signaling protocol will have to be augmented to support specific mobility related functions such as address registration (roaming), broadcasting, handoff, QoS renegotiation in response to channel impairments, etc. It is possible that some of these additional network layer/signaling functions could later be incorporated into an extended ATM standard that covers the wireless physical layer option. Alternative ATM adaptation layer (AAL) protocols may also be considered for customized support of wireless applications.

In the following sections, we discuss issues related to design of the wireless medium specific layers (i.e., physical layer, medium access control, and data-link) outlined in bold in Fig. 4.

C. Physical Layer

Selection of a modulation method and set of bit-rates for macro/micro/pico cell operation is a basic design issue for next generation PCN. The actual bit-rates to be used will depend upon the balance between service requirements and signal quality/bandwidth/power constraints. From the service requirements summarized in Table I, it is observed that with the exception of HDTV, most other anticipated applications can be supported with a wireless transmission bit-rate in the range of 5–10 Mb/s. Thus, a reasonable level of ATM service could be provided on a wireless channel of say 8 Mb/s, a bit-rate that can readily be achieved in picocellular environments with existing modem technology and may also prove to be feasible in microcells using a combination of antenna and modulation enhancements. Note that the use of a transmission bit-rate below the nominal B-ISDN specification of 155.5 Mb/s for wireless ATM access is similar in spirit to several current ATM Forum proposals [36] which aim to standardize a lower bit-rate (e.g., 25/50 Mb/s) for twisted-pair copper access. It is possible that as bit-rate limitations of PCS and LAN pico/micro/macro cell scenarios become clearer, a well chosen set of wireless channel access speeds could be incorporated into applicable ATM standards.

As for the digital cellular systems now under consideration, future PCS may employ either narrow-band or spread spectrum modulation approaches. There is considerable controversy among experts in the field regarding the relative merits of spread spectrum (CDMA) and narrow-band (TDMA) for PCN; see for example [10] and [16], and further work will be required to settle the issue definitively. The preferred technique may actually vary with the specific PCN application scenario to be addressed, so that it is likely that both TDMA and CDMA solutions will co-exist for some time to come.

Spread Spectrum: Spread spectrum techniques provide significant signal quality advantages in the presence of interference and multipath typical of the radio medium [7], [38]. In addition, spread spectrum CDMA (code division multiple access) provides an efficient integrated solution for frequency reuse and multiple access, and can typically achieve a net bandwidth efficiency 2–4 times that of comparable narrowband approaches [13], [42], [43]. However, a major weakness of CDMA for multiservice PCN is that for a given system bandwidth, spectrum spreading limits the peak user data rate to a relatively low value. For example, even with 50 MHz bandwidth and a spreading factor of 512, user data rate is limited to just ∼100 kb/s. This problem could be ameliorated via multiple code transmissions per user or multirate CDMA operation [44]; further research will be required to demonstrate the viability of either approach. Spread spectrum implementation issues such as dynamic power control (to avoid near-far effects), code synchronization, and VLSI power consumption need to be addressed as well.

Narrow Band: On the narrow-band side, the baseline approach is to use conventional QPSK, MSK or QAM modulation at the higher speeds considered sustainable in the microcell and picocell environment. In general, adaptive equalization should be avoided [3] at the mobile unit in order to limit cost and power consumption. Since implementation of QPSK or QAM is relatively well understood, the main open issue for narrow band is to determine the sustainable bit-rates and corresponding availability statistics for given transmission system assumptions. Based on reported results to date [37], [18], [40], [41], it is likely that achieving reasonable signal availability levels (e.g., 99–99.5%) at high bit-rates (~2–10 Mb/s) will require the use of antenna diversity, sectorization, beam steering or other advanced physical level techniques. Overall, it appears that with good physical level design, it should be possible for macro (5–10 km), micro (~0.5 km), and pico (100 m) cells to support unequalized QAM/QPSK baud rates of the order of 0.1–0.25 Msym/s, 0.5–1.5 Msym/s, and 2–4 Msym/s (these numbers may vary, depending on specific usage scenarios). In that case, a pico-cellular system may be able to provide between 8 and 16 Mb/s with 16-QAM.[2] Wireless bit rates in this range are sufficient to accommodate many of the target broadband services listed in Table I. Of course, much further design and field trial work is required to establish the viability of these relatively high narrow-band bit-rates over a range of practical micro and pico cell scenarios.

An alternative more "scalable" narrow-band modulation approach is based on coherent orthogonal frequency division multiplexing (COFDM) of multiple($N \gg 1$) QAM carriers (each of relatively narrow bandwidth less than the coherence bandwidth of the radio medium). This approach is currently being used for digital audio broadcast (DAB) in Europe [1], and is also under consideration for digital HDTV. Using this technique, bit-rates up to the 155.5 Mb/s nominal ATM speed could potentially be achieved (for example with 256 parallel carriers each of approximately 0.6 Mb/s). The OFDM approach is distinguished from a bank of separate QAM modems in that FFT techniques can be employed at the encoder and decoder for direct modulation and demodulation of the transmitted signal [39]. This modulation method is relatively impervious to multipath interference and (in full duplex mode) can be set up to avoid specular interferers or fine-structure channel impairments in an adaptive manner. Observe also that OFDM permits any subset of transmitters to compatibly operate at a peak bit-rate lower than the nominal channel speed, thus providing a useful mechanism for supporting a range of remote units with peak power constraints. Open problem areas in OFDM include amplifier linearity requirements and VLSI power consumption.

[2]For the 2 Msym/8 Mbps pico-cellular scenario, per channel bandwidth is of the order of 2.5 MHz. Thus the mimimum (duplex) system bandwidth requirement may be expected to be of the order of 20–30 MHz depending on the frequency reuse methods applied. Public systems with multiple 8 Mb/s carriers per pico/micro cell may typically require bandwidth allocations in the region of 50–100 MHz. In principle, such frequency allocations should be feasible even for multiple service operators, assuming that some consolidation of currently occupied bands is possible.

D. Media Access Control (MAC)

A major technical issue related to multiservices PCN design is the selection of a suitable channel sharing/media access control (MAC) technique at the data-link layer (for inbound remote-to-base transmissions). The MAC technique used in PCN will have a significant impact on user performance, system capacity, and remote terminal complexity, and is therefore an important design parameter. As discussed in Section II, next-generation PCN will be required to handle a more diverse mix of traffic types, including connection-oriented constant bit-rate (CBR) and variable bit-rate (VBR), as well as connectionless interactive packet data and burst (file transfer) data. Thus the adopted MAC approach must provide mechanisms to deal with each of these B-ISDN type services at reasonable quantitative quality-of-service (QoS) levels. Of course, it is recognized that shared-media access characteristic of wireless will lead to poorer quantitative performance than that achievable in switched ATM. The design challenge is to identify a wireless "multimedia capable" MAC approach that provides a sufficient degree of transparency for many ATM applications.

CDMA: The class of MAC protocols in a wireless system depends strongly on the physical level definition. When spread spectrum modulation is used, CDMA is the de-facto mode of operation unless a relatively low bandwidth efficiency can be accepted [24], [35]. Although it suffers from a low maximum bit-rate limit, CDMA can be operated in a "resource shared" packet mode that is quite efficient for the multiservices scenario. Specifically, in packet CDMA [25], [23] each terminal transmits (using a suitably selected CDMA code) without any coordination with other stations whenever it has data to send. CBR, VBR, and packet data modes required in a multiservice system are readily supported, subject of course to the maximum (despread) data rate of R b/s per subscriber. For example, any CBR service of $R_c \leq R$ can be accommodated by a periodic transmission of fixed length transport packets with duty cycle $\alpha = (R_c/R)$, as shown in Fig. 5. If a block-oriented error correction technique is used, each packet will consist of one or more independently decodable data blocks. Similarly, VBR can optionally be implemented via periodic transmission of variable length transport packets, as shown. Data services are supported by random access transmission of variable length transport packets (which are retransmitted with random delay unless acknowledged within a suitable time-out interval, as illustrated in Fig. 5).

In contrast to narrow-band systems (where medium access level traffic congestion is manifested in the form of blocking and/or delay), contention for channel capacity in random access packet CDMA results in increasing bit/packet error rate due to multiuser interference. In general, packet CDMA systems exhibit good performance (i.e., low error rate) right up to the capacity limit region, followed by a fairly rapid decrease in throughput as a function of offered load. The performance threshold can be particularly steep when strong forward error correction coding is used. Stable operation in the capacity region requires the use of appropriate retransmission control procedures similar to those used in narrow-band random access

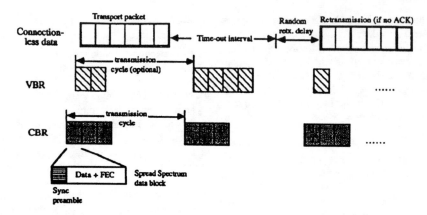

Fig. 5. Alternative transmission modes in packet CDMA.

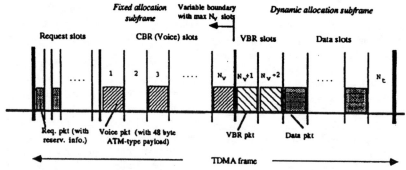

Fig. 6. Multiservice dynamic reservation (MDR) TDMA frame format.

systems [26]–[28]. Overall, performance results from earlier studies [43] show that packet CDMA can achieve good traffic multiplexing efficiency and performance for CBR, VBR, and low-speed interactive data services. However, as mentioned earlier, implementation of higher speed services ∼1 Mb/s or more remains an open issue for the CDMA approach.

Dynamic TDMA: When narrow-band modulation is used at the physical level, some form of TDMA-based medium access control is typical for PCS systems supporting isochronous CBR traffic [4], [19]. When multiservice VBR and packet data requirements are also taken into account, static TDMA approaches must be extended to provide dynamic resource allocation. Such integrated demand assigned TDMA protocols were previously developed for satellite network scenarios, (e.g., CPODA in [11]), [17], and many of the principles can be carried over to the PCS application. A notable early proposal for integration of voice and data in the wireless scenario is the packet reservation multiple access (PRMA) protocol proposed in [21]. More recently, other variations of dynamic TDMA have also been proposed for multiservices PCS [42], [43]. The overall MAC design problem is to provide sharing of isochronous, VBR, and packet data services with high channel utilization while maintaining a reasonable QoS level on each.

A fairly general MAC framework for CBR, VBR, and packet data can be realized with the multiservices dynamic

reservation (MDR) TDMA channel format outlined in Fig. 6. The TDMA frame is subdivided into N_r request slots and N_t message slots. Each message slot provides for transmission of a packet or ATM-like "cell" with data payload of 48 bytes (or a submultiple $48/n$ bytes, where appropriate) together with PCN protocol headers. Request slots are comparatively short and are used for initial access in slotted ALOHA (contention) mode. Of the N_t message slots, a maximum of $N_v < N_t$ slots in each frame can be assigned for CBR voice traffic. VBR and packet data messages are dynamically assigned one or more 48 byte slots in the TDMA interval following the last allocated voice slot in a frame. Long data messages (bursts) which cannot be accommodated in a single frame may be segmented and rate controlled for transmission in multiple frames.

The basic channel access scheme follows a combination of circuit mode reservation of slots over multiple TDMA frames for CBR voice calls, along with dynamic assignment of remaining capacity for VBR or packet data traffic. For VBR, allocation will be based on a suitable statistical multiplexing algorithm in which available capacity is prorated among demands based on usage parameter control (UPC) values declared during call establishment. For packet data, the default mode of operation is first-come-first-served (FCFS), although "fair queueing" and/or burst (e.g., file transfer) servicing policies may also be applied. Alternatively, a more advanced

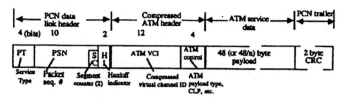

Fig. 7. Example PCN data-link packet format.

time-of-expiry (TOE) based queue service scheme, [30], [22], may be used to expedite real-time packet traffic. Specifically, in the TOE approach, request packets contain an indication of the expiry time of the data to be transmitted (an appropriately large value of expiry time is used for non-real time traffic). The demand assignment controller then makes allocations on the basis of smallest expiry time first, rather than FCFS. This TOE queue service approach is expected to provide useful reductions in packet loss (expiry) rate for real-time data in mixed time-critical/noncritical traffic scenarios.

E. Data-Link Layer

As shown in Fig. 4, the wireless medium will generally require a custom data-link layer protocol that interfaces with the ATM transport layer in a relatively transparent manner. This layer is required to insulate the ATM-type service from wireless medium specific problems caused by high error rate at the physical level and/or delay/blocking at the medium access control level. At the same time, it is desirable to keep the additional PCN data-link functionality to a minimum in order to limit the amount of gateway processing required at the base stations (which are required to be small and inexpensive for use in micro and pico cells).

As indicated in Fig. 2, the baseline approach for maximum ATM compatibility is to define a PCN data-link packet as a 53 byte ATM cell encapsulated by an additional PCN header. However, depending on the achievable channel speed, the type of low-speed applications (e.g., 8 kb/s voice codec, e-mail messaging, etc.) to be supported, and the relative importance of high wireless channel efficiency, it may be necessary to compromise on this requirement and use PCN data-link packets with payloads that are integer submultiples of an ATM cell (e.g., 16 or 24 bytes). In addition, in order to avoid high protocol header overheads, it may be appropriate to compress essential ATM header information into an abbreviated network layer header and then add a wireless medium-specific data-link header. An example of ATM header compression is to use 2-bytes containing 12-bit VCI (virtual channel identifier) and 4 bit control (payload type, cell loss priority, etc.), as illustrated in Fig. 7. The reduced VCI space should be acceptable for the more limited addressing requirements of a single wireless channel, and can be expanded to standard ATM form at the base station interface.

A complete definition of the PCN data-link header is not presented here, since several issues are currently under study. As shown in Fig. 7, functions of the PCN data-link layer may include:

TABLE II
SUMMARY OF PARAMETERS USED FOR MDR-TDMA SYSTEM SIMULATION

item	symbol	value
TDMA channel speed (Kbps)	R	1920
TDMA frame length (msec)	T	12
Request slots per TDMA frame (slots/frame)	N_r	20
Voice/data slot size (bytes)	*	53 (48 payload)
Arrival rate of new voice calls (calls/sec/user)	λ_v	0.0005
Arrival rate of new data messages (msg/sec/user)	λ_d	0.1
Average length of a voice call (min)	T_c	3
Voice data rate (Kbps)	Rv	32
Maximum (fixed) voice call set up time (sec)	W_{vmax}	5
Average request retransmission delay (sec)	T_{drx}	0.01
Average length of data messages (Kb)	L	5.12
Expiration time for time-critical, non-critical messages (msec)	T_{e1}, T_{e2}	50, 1000
ratio of time-critical to the total message traffic (%)	α	25

Service Type Definition: A suitable field (e.g., 4 bits) in the PCN header may be provided to indicate whether a packet is of type supervisory/control, CBR, VBR, data, burst, etc. This simplifies base station protocol processing and resource allocation, enabling segregation and prioritization of data types without reference to VC-level call setup information.

Error Control: For each service type, the PCN data-link layer should provide an appropriate error control mechanism to protect against the relatively poor physical level characteristics of the wireless medium. In general, this is achieved using a PCN packet sequence number field (e.g., 10 bits) in the header along with a standard 2-byte CRC frame check sequence trailer. For connectionless data classes, a conventional HDLC-type error recovery protocol will be executed per VC, preferably on a selective reject basis to maintain efficiency at the relatively high bit-rates under consideration. It is recognized that severe channel impairments may not be recoverable at the data-link layer, and will require transport level detection and recovery on application protocol data units (PDU's). For connection-oriented CBR and VBR, the nominal error control mode is to detect and filter out erroneously received ATM cells before they can enter the low error rate fixed network. Alternatively, if some buffering delay can be tolerated, the PCN data-link layer may optionally attempt time-constrained retransmission within a permissible sequence number window (this option would be selected at call setup).

Segmentation and Reassembly: In the baseline case with PCN packet = ATM cell, no additional segmentation is required in the wireless data-link. However, when system design considerations dictate the use of smaller PCN cells (e.g., 16 or 24 byte), a limited amount of segmentation and

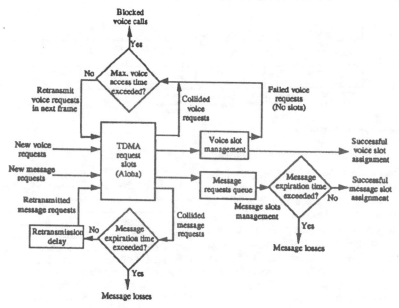

Fig. 8. Summary of simulated MDR-TDMA protocol logic.

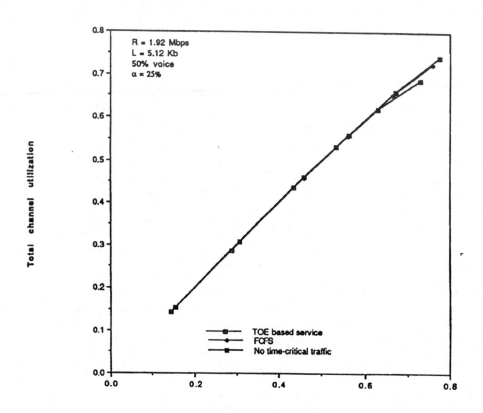

Fig. 9. TDMA channel utilization versus offered traffic.

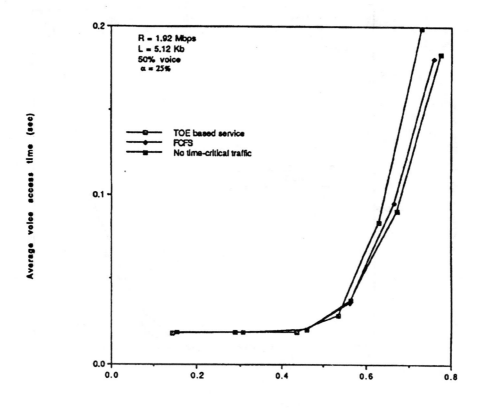

Fig. 10. Voice call access delay versus offered load.

reassembly function will be required. This can be achieved with a segment counter that uses, for example, the two least significant bits of the error control sequence (PSN) number. The PCN SAR function may thus be implemented as a subset of the error control function outlined above.

Handoff Support: Handoff from one base station to another is an important characteristic of mobile wireless scenarios. In future PCN systems with frequent movement of mobile units between micro/pico cells, "soft" handoff without data loss is an important feature required for service transparency. The packet switching approach for PCN transport under consideration here provides an opportunity for better implementation of handoff, since specific support features may be added at appropriate PCN protocol layers. For example, the data-link layer may contain a 2-bit field that indicates the last and first data-link packets before and after handoff. In conjunction with appropriate control signaling support, this data-link feature helps to seam together service data streams received at two different base stations, as required for soft handoff.

V. NUMERICAL EXAMPLE: MDR TDMA

In this section, we provide some additional detail on the medium access control (MAC) protocol design problem for the narrow-band TDMA approach discussed earlier. Numerical performance results are given for a specific multiservices

dynamic reservation (MDR) TDMA protocol operating in a mixed voice/data environment [43]. The simulation example under consideration is based on a channel speed of approximately 2 Mb/s, corresponding to a potential microcellular scenario with unequalized 16-QAM. The channel is shared by constant bit-rate (CBR) voice users operating at 32 kb/s and packet data users transmitting in "available bit-rate (ABR)" mode with long file/image transfer messages averaging 5.12 kb. Particular attention is given to the problem of supporting real-time data associated with multimedia applications, and a time-of-expiry (TOE) based scheduling policy is investigated [30] as a possible means for improving the real-time data traffic handling capability. The performance results presented in this section are based on a discrete event simulation model outlined below.

Source Traffic Model: The population of users accessing the inbound channel (from remote to base station) in each cell is assumed to be divided into two sets of users: one set of U_v voice (CBR) users and a second set of U_d packet data (ABR) users. An idle voice user generates new voice calls at the rate of λ_v (calls/sec/user) and an idle data user generates new messages at the rate of λ_d (messages/sec/user), both with exponential inter-arrival time. A user with a new (call or message) arrival is considered to be busy until the (call or message) transmission is completed or a time-out

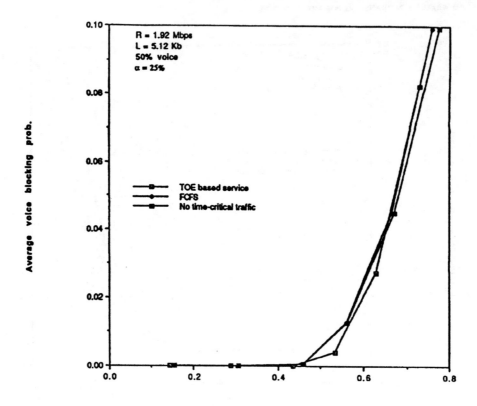

Fig. 11. Voice call blocking versus offered load.

occurs. No new arrivals are generated by the busy user until the current transmission is complete or time-out occurs, and the user becomes idle again. A voice call originates a continuous bit stream at a constant rate of R_v kb/s/call, with an average (exponential) holding time of T_c s.

A data user will generate packets from a specified message length distribution; for the present study exponential messages with mean duration L (kb) are assumed. The data users are further subdivided into two groups, with αU_d users generating real-time (time-critical) messages having an expiration time constraint, T_{e1} (s) and the remaining $(1-\alpha)U_d$ users generating the non-time-critical traffic (having a comparatively large expiration time, T_{e2} s). As an example of the time-critical data, variable bit-rate teleconferencing codecs, e.g., [45], produce data packets that are approximately exponential (or gamma distributed) in size, and may typically tolerate network delays in the region of 50–250 ms depending on the rate buffering parameters used.

Performance Measures: In the TDMA system, a voice caller quits if a voice assignment is not made within a certain waiting time W_{vmax}, and becomes idle. The voice call is then said to have experienced blocking. The voice call blocking probability (P_B) and mean access delay W_v, in obtaining a voice channel assignment are the two traffic dependent performance measures for voice calls.

For data, the average message transmission delay (D_m), i.e., elapsed time between a message arrival and completion of its successful transmission is the customary measure of performance. Note that an HDLC-type protocol is assumed for data applications, so that messages that are not positively acknowledged within a pre-selected acknowledgment time-out interval are retransmitted. In addition to data delay, an important measure of performance for real-time data is the packet loss probability (denoted as PL_c and PL_{nc} for time-critical and noncritical data, respectively) that measures the fraction of packets that fail to reach the destination before the expiry time. This packet loss rate relates directly to the delivered application quality; for example, in VBR video applications, a packet loss rate of 10^{-3} or lower may be required to maintain reasonable decoded image quality [34].

Simulation Model: The MDR-TDMA protocol model implemented for this study is an accurate discrete event simulation of the protocol with the source traffic assumptions described earlier. The key internal variables of the program include: the number of ready voice and data users with time-critical/noncritical messages, the number of unacknowledged voice and data messages accessing the slotted ALOHA request channel, the number of active voice circuits, the number of active data users, the global demand assignment queue status, etc. In addition to these global variables, an activity record

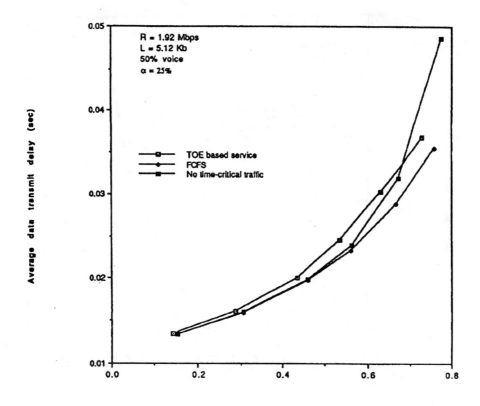

Fig. 12. Data transmission delay versus offered load.

for each voice or data transaction is maintained in order to compute user-level performance measures. These variables are updated once per frame, depending on the voice/data arrival, request collision, voice assignment/completion or blocking, and data message assignment or "time-out" events that are simulated. A summary of the simulated MDR-TDMA protocol logic is shown in Fig. 8.

The program was allowed to run for a relatively long duration on the channel (i.e., hours), and appropriate statistics (e.g., message delay, packet loss rate, voice blocking probability, channel throughput, etc.) were logged after allowing sufficient time to reach a steady state. The baseline parameters used for evaluation of MDR-TDMA are summarized in Table II.

As mentioned earlier, the above set of baseline parameters corresponds to a 1.92 Mb/s microcellular scenario with 32 kb/s voice users and high-speed file/image transfer data users. Note also that the TDMA frame parameters were selected to ensure relatively light loading on the contention request channels. Thus, the main component of message delay for data traffic is generally the queue service time rather than request delay. Also, the maximum number of TDMA message slots that may be used for CBR traffic was set equal to the ratio of the offered voice traffic to total offered traffic. This selection is based on our previous results [42], indicating that such a constraint provides a good balance between voice blocking probability and data delay.

Performance Results: The numerical results presented here are aimed mainly at evaluation of channel throughput versus voice and data quality-of-service (QoS), with and without TOE queue service algorithm for time-critical packets. Fig. 9 shows curves of channel utilization (S) versus offered channel load (G) for three scenarios: i) no time-critical traffic; ii) time critical traffic with FCFS queue service; and iii) time-critical traffic with TOE queue service. All these results are based on channel speed $R = 1.92$ Mb/s, average data message length = 5.12 kb, 50% voice traffic, and ratio of time-critical traffic $\alpha = 0.25$. As expected, the S versus G curves are fairly linear, tapering off as the useful capacity limit of about 60–70% is reached. There is no significant difference in S versus G behavior when different queue service algorithms are employed, with small variations due to slightly different packet loss rates at high load. Corresponding voice call access delay versus G curves are shown in Fig. 10, and it is observed that voice call delay remains acceptably low except in the $S \geq 0.6$ region, with only small differences due to the queue service policy. This is to be expected, since the impact of TOE on request packets is indirect, via inhibition of data terminals waiting for reservation. Curves of voice blocking probability (VBP) versus offered load are also shown in Fig. 11, and it is observed here that the important blocking probability parameter rises steeply in the peak capacity region. For example, if VBP= 1% is desired, channel utilization

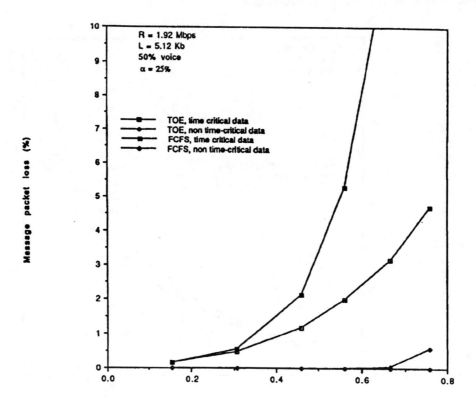

Fig. 13.   Message loss for time-critical and noncritical data traffic.

(throughput) in the region of 55–60% may be achievable at the nominal operating point. As in Figs. 9 and 10, time-critical traffic and TOE processing has little impact on the voice blocking performance.

Fig. 12 shows the average data delay (for both time-critical and noncritical traffic) and packet loss probabilities (PL_c and PL_{nc}) as functions of offered channel load, G. From Fig. 12 it is observed that TOE results in slightly higher average delay than the nominal FCFS policy, a typical effect in priority queueing systems. Note also that at high offered load, the curve for the case without time-critical traffic exhibits a sharper increase than those with some fraction of real-time traffic. This is due to the fact that queueing delays are reduced by departure of expiring time-critical packets in the TOE and FCFS cases. Also, since the packet loss rates due to expiry are generally higher for the FCFS case, data queueing delays are correspondingly lower under congested conditions. In terms of actual values, it is observed from Fig. 12 that average delays in the range of 20–30 ms are experienced by data messages in the nominal operating region with $G \sim 50$–60%.

Fig. 13 shows the effect of TOE processing on the packet loss (expiration) rate of time-critical messages. In this example, 25% of the simulated packet data traffic has a real-time delivery deadline of 50 ms, while the remaining 75% is less time-critical data with an expiration time of 1 s.

It is observed that as channel load levels increase, TOE provides a noticeable improvement over FCFS processing for real-time traffic, while slightly degrading the performance for the non-time-critical service (as expected in a priority queueing system). In particular, for the nominal operating region with channel load between 0.5–0.6, TOE processing typically reduces the packet loss rate of time-critical data by a factor of 3. Such a gain may be quite useful for time-sensitive personal multimedia applications, since it reduces the burden of packet loss handling (concealment) that must be borne by the application. The gain from TOE scheduling is readily obtained with only a modest impact on hardware and software complexity at the base station. Of course, some type of message time-stamping must be incorporated in the reservation control packet, requiring accurate time-clock distribution to remote units. There is also a minor overhead penalty associated with the bits required to transmit the time stamp over the channel.

Since the results in Fig. 13 apply to a specific set of channel and traffic parameters, additional simulations were performed to determine the generality of the above conclusions regarding TOE performance. Alternative channel speeds of 240 and 480 kb/s (with TDMA frame size of 48 ms), along with low bit-rate 8 kb/s voice (CBR) and 5.12 kb packet data messages were considered. For these cases with lower channel speed (and

TABLE III
PACKET LOSS RATE ($PL_c\%$) FOR TIME-CRITICAL
TRAFFIC (AT OPERATING POINT WITH VBP $\sim$ 1%)

Case (TDMA speed; Average data length)	% Voice	Norm Chan. Util.	$\alpha = 10\%$		$\alpha = 25\%$		$\alpha = 40\%$	
			FCFS	TOE	FCFS	TOE	FCFS	TOE
240 Kbps;5.12 Kb	75%	−0.51	20.7	15.7	19.5	15.9	18.7	16.3
	50%	−0.46	7.78	3.79	7.36	4.16	6.93	4.57
480 Kbps;5.12 Kb	75%	−0.62	24.1	7.03	21.0	8.32	19.0	9.81
	50%	−0.60	6.76	0.48	5.89	0.65	5.33	0.90

hence poorer QoS), a larger real-time delivery deadline of 250 ms was also assumed. Table III shows packet loss rates for time-critical data (PL_c) at a few different values of channel speed (R), real-time traffic ratio (α), % voice traffic. Note that in each case, the operating channel load was selected to meet a constraint of voice blocking probability (VBP) $\leq$ 1%. From the results in the table, it is observed that TOE generally helps to improve the packet loss rate for time critical traffic. This is particularly true when the ratio of time-critical data (α) is small, since the prioritization mechanism is more effective in such a scenario. In some cases, it is observed that the improvements in time critical cell loss rate PL_c approach an order of magnitude. Of course, these improvements for time critical data need to be balanced against other performance criteria such as average and peak delay for non-time-critical traffic. In general our results show that a reasonable balance between these disparate performance measures can be obtained when TOE queue scheduling is applied to the MDR-TDMA system.

Overall, this simulation study of MDR-TDMA indicates that demand assigned protocols of this type are a viable candidate for multiservices PCN. The general framework readily supports a mix of CBR, VBR, and packet (ABR) data, and a variety of call admission and processing algorithms (including TOE considered here) may be used for QoS-based support of these services. The actual QoS values achieved on the wireless network segment will, of course, depend on various factors including traffic mix, channel utilization level, bit-rate, and TDMA frame parameters. For the specific 1.92 Mb/s case considered here, voice blocking probabilities $\leq$ 1% and average data delay $\leq$ 25 ms are obtained at channel utilizations in the region of 55–60%. These QoS levels may be acceptable for many near-term nomadic multimedia applications, and may be further improved by operating at lower channel efficiency. More significant improvements in QoS and/or channel efficiency may be expected as transmission bit-rates are increased to the 8–16 Mbps (or higher) that may later prove to be feasible in micro and picocellular environments.

VI. CONCLUDING REMARKS

This paper has presented a discussion of multiservices traffic support issues in next-generation PCN systems. An ATM compatible wireless transport architecture was outlined, and key design issues were identified at the physical, media access control, and data-link layers. We believe that such integrated ATM-type wireless networks will play an important role in broadband communications networks of the future, and that it

is timely to start considering technology selection and system design issues. An example dynamic TDMA based media access control protocol (with optional time-of-expiry service scheduling for real-time traffic support) has been described, and performance issues related to multimedia traffic have been investigated for an example scenario.

Overall, the exploratory research summarized here leads us to conclude that the general concept of an ATM compatible multiservices wireless network with CBR, VBR, and data services is feasible, albeit with certain bit-rate and performance limitations imposed by the radio medium. Of course, much further work remains before the viability of such systems can be conclusively demonstrated. Ongoing research and development efforts in high-speed modulation, multiservice MAC (for which preliminary results were presented here), and higher layer protocols will determine the degree of transparency relative to B-ISDN/ATM that can be achieved in practice.

REFERENCES

[1] M. Alard and R. Lassalle, "Principles of modulation and channel coding for digital broadcasting for mobile receivers," *EBU-UHF Satellite and Broadcasting*, pp. 47–69. Also, *EBU Review—Technical No. 224*, Aug. 1987.
[2] H. Armbuster and B. Marchent, "Advanced terminal and personal mobility: A challenge for ATM concepts and switching," in *Proc. ISS'92*, vol. 1, pp. B.1.1.
[3] B. Baccetti et al., "Full digital adaptive equalization in 64-QAM radio systems," *IEEE J. Select. Areas Commun.*, vol. SAC-5, no. 3, pp. 466–475, April 1987.
[4] Special Issue on Mobile Communications, *British Telecom Tech. J.*, vol. 8, no. 1, Jan. 1990.
[5] CCITT Recommendation I.212, "Broadband aspects of ISDN," CCITT IXth Plenary Assembly, Melbourne, Australia, vol. 3, fasc. III.7, 1988.
[6] S. Chia, "Universal mobile telecommunication system," *IEEE Commun. Mag.*, pp. 54–62, June 1991.
[7] G. R. Cooper and R. W. Nettleton, "Cellular mobile technology: The great multiplier," *IEEE Spectrum*, vol. 20, no. 6, pp. 30–37, June 1983.
[8] D. C. Cox, "Universal portable radio communications," *Proc. IEEE*, pp. 436–477, Apr. 1987.
[9] _____, "Personal communications—A viewpoint," *IEEE Commun. Mag.*, pp. 8–20, Nov. 1990.
[10] _____, "Wireless network access for personal communications," *IEEE Commun. Mag.*, pp. 96–115, Dec. 1992.
[11] G. Falk et al., "Integration of voice and data in the wideband packet satellite network," *IEEE J. Select. Areas Commun.*, vol. SAC-1, no. 6, pp. 1076–1083, Dec. 1983.
[12] Fore Systems, "ASX-110 and ASX-120 self-contained ATM switches" Product Literature, 1992.
[13] K. S. Gilhousen et al., "On the capacity of a cellular CDMA system," *IEEE Trans. Veh. Technol.*, vol. 40, May 1991.
[14] D. J. Goodman, "Cellular packet communications," *IEEE Trans. Commun.*, pp. 1272–1280, Aug. 1990.
[15] _____, "Trends in cellular and cordless communications," *IEEE Commun. Mag.*, vol. 29, no. 6, pp. 31–40, June 1991.
[16] D. J. Goodman, G. P. Pollini, and K. S. Meier-Hellstern, "Network control for wireless communications," *IEEE Commun. Mag.*, pp. 116–125, Dec. 1992.
[17] J. G. Gruber and N. Le, "Performance requirements for integrated voice/data networks," *IEEE J. Select. Areas Commun.*, vol SAC-1, no. 6, pp. 981–1005, Dec. 1983.
[18] L. Greenstein et al., "Microcells in personal communication systems," *IEEE Commun. Mag.*, pp. 76–88, Dec. 1992.
[19] Electronic Industries Association, "Dual mode subscriber equipment—Network equipment compatibility specification," *Interim Standard 54*, Dec. 1989.
[20] P. Mermelstein et al., "Integrated services on wireless multiple access networks," in *Proc. ICC'93*, pp. 863–867.
[21] S. Nanda, D. J. Goodman, and U. Timor, "Performance of PRMA: A packet voice protocol for cellular systems," *IEEE Trans. Veh. Technol.*, vol. 40, no. 3, pp. 584–598, Aug. 1991.

[22] S. Panwar, D. Towsley, and J. Wolf, "Optimal scheduling policies for a class of queues with customer deadlines to the beginning of service," J. ACM, pp. 832–844, Oct. 1988.

[23] A. Polydoros and J. Silvester, "Slotted random access spread-spectrum networks: An analytical framework," J. Select. Areas Commun., pp. 989–1002, July 1987.

[24] M. B. Pursley, "Performance evaluation of phase coded spread spectrum multiple access communication—Part 1: System analysis," IEEE Trans. Commun., pp. 795–799, Aug 1977.

[25] D. Raychaudhuri, "Performance analysis of random-access packet-switched code division multiple access systems," IEEE Trans. Commun., pp. 895–901, June 1981.

[26] S. S. Rappaport and S. Bose, "Demand assigned multiple access systems using collision type request channels: Stability and delay considerations," Proc. IEE, vol. 128, no. 1, Jan. 1981.

[27] K. Joseph and D. Raychaudhuri, "Stability analysis of asynchronous random access CDMA systems," in Proc. IEEE Global Commun. Conf., Dec 1986, pp. 48.1.1–7.

[28] D. Raychaudhuri, "Stability, throughput and delay of asynchronous selective reject ALOHA," IEEE Trans. Commun., pp. 767–772, July 1987.

[29] D. Raychaudhuri and N. Wilson, "Multimedia personal communication networks: System design issues," in Proc. 3rd Workshop Third Generation Wireless Information Networks, Rutgers University, Apr. 1992, pp. 259–288 (in Wireless Communications J. M. Holtzman and D. J. Goodman, Eds. Kluwer Academic, 1993, pp. 289–304).

[30] ——, "Multi-media transport in next-generation personal communication networks," in Proc. Int. Conf. Commun., May 1993, pp. 858–862.

[31] D. L. Schilling, R. L. Pickholtz, and L. B. Milstein, "Spread spectrum goes commercial," IEEE Spectrum, pp. 40–45, Aug. 1990.

[32] R. Steele, "The cellular environment of lightweight hand-held portables," IEEE Commun. Mag., pp. 20–29, July 1989.

[33] R. Steele, "Deploying personal communication networks," IEEE Commun. Mag., pp. 12–15, Sept. 1990.

[34] H. Sun, J. Zdepski, and D. Raychaudhuri "Error concealment for MPEG video over ATM," CCITT ISO-IEC/JTC1/SC2/WG11, MPEG92 AVC-308, July 1992.

[35] J. T. Taylor and J. K. Omura, "Spread spectrum technology: A solution to the personal communications services frequency allocation dilemma," IEEE Commun. Mag., vol. 29, no. 2, pp. 48–51, Feb. 1991.

[36] UTP-3 PHY Subworking Group, "ITU TSS SGXIII/WP3 discussion on sub-rate broadband service," ATM Forum, 1993.

[37] R. Valenzuela, "Performance of quadrature amplitude modulation for indoor radio communications," IEEE Trans. Commun., vol. COM-35, no. 11, pp. 1236–38, Nov. 1987.

[38] A. J. Viterbi "Wireless digital communication: A view based on three lessons learned," IEEE Commun. Mag., vol. 29, no. 9, pp. 33–36, Sept. 1991.

[39] S. B. Weinstein and P. M. Ebert, "Data transmission by frequency-division multiplexing using discrete Fourier transform," IEEE Trans. Commun. Technol., vol. COM-10, no. 5, pp. 628–34, Oct. 1971.

[40] W. T. Webb, "QAM: The modulation scheme for future mobile radio communications?" Electron. and Commun. Eng. J., pp. 167–176, Aug. 1992.

[41] W. T. Webb, "Modulation methods for PCNs," IEEE Commun. Mag., pp. 90–95, Dec. 1992.

[42] N. Wilson, R. Ganesh, K. Joseph, and D. Raychaudhuri, "CDMA vs. dynamic TDMA for access control in an integrated voice/data PCN," in Proc. 1st Int. Conf. Universal Personal Commun., Sept. 1992, pp. 267–272.

[43] N. Wilson, R. Ganesh, K. Joseph, and D. Raychaudhuri, "Packet CDMA versus dynamic TDMA for multiple access in an integrated voice/data PCN," IEEE J. Select. Areas Commun., vol. 11, no. 6, pp. 870–884, Aug. 1993.

[44] R. Wyrwas, M. J. Miller, R. Anjaria, and W. Zhang, "Multiple access options for multi-media wireless systems," in Proc. 3rd Workshop Third Generation Wireless Information Networks Rutgers University, Apr. 1992, pp. 289–294.

[45] J. Zdepski, K. Joseph, D. Raychaudhuri, and D. Daut, "Prioritized packet transport of VBR H.261 format compressed video on a CSMA/CD LAN," in Proc. Third Int. Workshop Packet Video, Morristown, NJ, Mar. 1990.

Dipankar Raychaudhuri (S'78–M'79–SM'87) received the B.Tech. (Honors) degree in electronics and electrical communication engineering from the Indian Institute of Technology, Kharagpur, India, in 1976, and the M.S. and Ph.D. degrees in electrical engineering from the State University of New York at Stony Brook in 1978 and 1979, respectively.

From 1979 to 1992 he was with the David Sarnoff Research Center (formerly RCA Laboratories), Princeton, NJ, as Member of Technical Staff (1979–1987), Senior Member of Technical Staff (1988–1989), and Head of Broadband Communications Research (1990–1992). At Sarnoff he has worked on a range of R&D topics including: very small aperture terminal (VSAT) based satellite networks, direct broadcast satellite (DBS), packet video, digital HDTV, multimedia communication, and wireless data networks. During the period 1990–1992, he led the project team responsible for system design and specification of the "Advanced Digital HDTV" prototype tested by the U.S. FCC in 1992. Since January 1993 he has been with NEC USA, C&C Research Laboratories, Princeton, NJ, where he is currently Department Head, Systems Architecture, with current research focus on high-speed ATM networks and wireless personal communication systems. He has authored approximately 60 technical papers and 8 U.S. patents (1 pending).

Dr. Raychaudhuri is a Technical Editor for the IEEE TRANSACTIONS ON NETWORKING and the IEEE COMMUNICATIONS MAGAZINE. He is an active participant in IEEE Communications Society activities, and was Chairman of the Data Communication Systems Committee during 1990–1991. He was the recipient of RCA Laboratories Outstanding Achievement Awards in 1981, 1984, and 1986, and the David Sarnoff Research Center Team Award in 1992.

Newman D. Wilson (S'83–M'87) received the B.Tech. degree from I.I.T., Madras, India and the M.S. and Ph.D. degrees in electrical engineering from the State University of New York, Stony Brook in 1982 and 1986, respectively.

He joined the David Sarnoff Research Center, Princeton, NJ, in 1986 and has worked on various communications and video compression related projects. his current research interests include multiple access, wireless/PCN, digital video, multimedia and ATM communications.

An Architecture and Methodology for Mobile-Executed Handoff in Cellular ATM Networks

Anthony S. Acampora, *Fellow, IEEE*, and Mahmoud Naghshineh, *Student Member, IEEE*

Abstract—An architecture is presented for a high-speed cellular radio access network based on ATM transport technology. Central to this approach is a new concept known as the virtual connection tree which avoids the need to involve the network call processor for every cell handoff attempt. Such an approach can readily support a very high rate of handoffs, thereby enabling use of physically small radio cells to provide very high system capacity, but may occasionally cause the volume of traffic to be handled by one cell site to exceed that cell site's capacity. A simple analytical methodology is developed which can be used for admission control, the purpose of which is to limit the number of in-progress calls such that two new quality of service metrics (overload probability and average time in overload) can be kept suitably low. Finally, a general framework is presented for overall system organization and signaling.

I. INTRODUCTION

THE FIELD of modern telecommunication is rapidly being redefined by events surrounding two emerging concepts: broadband networks and personal communication services. Broadband networks [1]–[4] are characterized by packet-based transport, bandwidth-upon-demand, and multimedia traffic integration. All types of telecommunication traffic (voice, data, image, video) are carried by a broadband network in a common fixed-length packet format, and the only distinction between low rate and high rate connections is the frequency with which such fixed-length packets are generated. Network resources are statistically shared among users and are actively consumed only when packets are actually generated. Personal communication services are based upon the notions of tetherless access and networks that support connections between people or between people and places, rather than merely supporting connections between places [5]–[10]. Implicit here is the ability of the network to locate and communicate with a called person wherever that called person may be (as contrasted with today's network which interconnects specific fixed ports regardless of whether or not the called person is in the vicinity of the called fixed port), and the ability of the network to hand-off connections among network ports in response to user mobility. Also, central to the notion of personal communication service (PCS) are specific network services customized to the unique needs of a given user (e.g., filtering and forwarding of electronic mail).

Manuscript received February 15, 1994.
A. S. Acampora is with the Department of Electrical Engineering and the Center for Telecommunications Research, Columbia University, New York, NY 10027.
M. Naghshineh is with IBM T. J. Watson Research Center, Yorktown Heights, NY, 10598 USA.
IEEE Log Number 9403385.

In this paper, we present a model for a ubiquitous telecommunication network which merges these two concepts. This model is based upon 1) a broadband wired infrastructure supporting Asynchronous Transfer Mode (ATM) packet transport; 2) a system of radio base stations, each connected on one side to the wired infrastructure and each supporting an on-demand packet access shared radio channel serving all users within the vicinity or "cell" surrounding the base station; and 3) portable communication units which transform user generated signals into ATM cells which are transferred to/from the base station over the shared radio channels. As will be explained, this model generalizes upon and exploits the concept of the ATM virtual connection in such a way as to accommodate a very high rate of connection handoff among base stations. This, in turn, allows the use of geographically small radio cells, a high degree of spatial frequency reuse, and the establishment of a high capacity environment as required to support bandwidth-intensive tetherless multimedia services.

Specifically, we shall address and resolve the following issues. In today's wired ATM environment, the user-network interface is a fixed port which remains stationary throughout the connection life time. At the connection setup time, a call processor establishes a path or a network route based on the connection traffic characteristics such that no network node or transmission link is overburdened and the quality of service guaranteed to other existing calls is maintained [11]–[15]. However, in a personal communication network, mobility or changing channel quality causes the users' access point to the wired network to change constantly, and a mobile user's call must be rerouted each time that the connection is handed over to a new base station. Thus, in principle, a mobile connection must be re-established (new setup procedure) each time it is handed over to a new base station. As a result, the network call processor may need to become involved many times during a mobile connection's life time. As personal wireless communication systems move toward smaller sized cells in order to accommodate more users or to provide higher capacity (greater frequency reuse over the same geographical region), the conventional procedures for call setup and control would fail due to the frequency of the handoffs, and the network call processor would become a bottleneck (this problem has been discussed in [8] where a Metropolitan Area Network based solution was provided). Our proposed solution to this problem is based on a new concept known as the *virtual connection tree*. In a distributed fashion, connections of mobile users who remain within a geographical area called the *neighboring mobile access region* may be handed over to any base station

Reprinted from IEEE Journal on Selected Areas in Communications, Vol. 12, No. 8, Oct. 1994, pp. 1365-1375.

without involving the network call processor. In general, if the neighboring mobile access region is large, most mobile users would remain within this area (which is covered by a virtual connection tree) for the duration of a connection, although a large number of handover events may occur as mobiles roam throughout this area and/or propagation effects cause a change in the channel quality between a mobile and its current base station. At the time that a mobile connection is admitted to a virtual connection tree, a collection of virtual circuits numbers (VCN) are assigned to the call. Each of these virtual connection numbers defines a path between the root of a connection tree (part of the wired network) and a distinct base station within the neighboring mobile access region. A given mobile selects its base station from among those in its connection tree merely by transmitting ATM cells with the appropriate VCN. In this way, an ATM cell associated with a given tetherless connection will eventually flow through the root of the connection tree and, from there, to its destination by means of a fixed wired path if the connection is to a hard-wired network port or to a root of another connection tree if the connection is to another mobile user. At the root of the tree, the currently used VCN is translated to that which is needed to switch the ATM cells along the appropriate wired path.

Similarly, in the reverse direction, the VCN of an ATM cell appearing at the root of a connection tree is appropriately translated such that the ATM cell flows over the correct branch of the tree, eventually arriving at the base station currently serving the receiving mobile. The most recent ATM cell sent by the mobile and appearing at the root of the tree identifies the currently serving base station and serves to update the VCN translation table for cells flowing from the tree root to the mobile. Although, for each direction, a set of VCN's is assigned for each connection in a connection tree, only one in each direction is actually in use per connection at any given time, namely that which is selected by the mobile station as evidenced by the VCN number appearing in the ATM cell header. Thus, creation of a virtual connection tree and assignment of a set of VCN's for each connection wastes neither radio channel capacity nor wired link capacity. Also, the call processor is involved only at connection setup time, but is totally uninvolved in processing handovers within a connection tree, which are handled *entirely* by the handed-off mobile itself in a totally distributed fashion.[1]

The call processor becomes involved only in handovers to different connection trees and, since the geographical area served by a given connection tree may include many base stations and become quite large, the frequency of call processor involvement remains low and any potential handover problems which might have resulted from the use of small radio cells is avoided. In effect, use of the virtual connection tree combines the capacity advantage of a microcellular approach with the call-processing handover infrequency of a macrocellular approach.

Since mobile users are free to hand-off from one base station to another within the virtual connection tree, overload

---

[1] This reduction in call processing is, however, partially offset by the need to initialize an entire tree, rather than merely one virtual path. We believe that this additional burden will prove to be negligible.

may occur if the number of in-progress calls through a given base station should temporarily exceed the base station's call capacity. One way to avoid this is by limiting the number of simultaneous calls in an entire connection tree to a value not in excess of a single base station's call capacity, but such an approach would be unacceptably wasteful of radio link capacity. Another possibility, which we do not consider here but which is the subject of an on-going research project, is to drop any handed-off call that causes base station overloading. Rather, we propose to exploit the statistical nature of the mobile environment and admit a larger number of mobile connections such that an overload condition is possible but not very likely (base station capacity $\leq$ number of calls admitted to the connection tree $<$ total capacity of all base stations within the tree). When an overload condition occurs, the quality of service (ATM cell loss or delay) enjoyed by connections currently using the overloaded base station is temporarily degraded. We refer to this situation as the *overload state* and use the *probability of being in an overload state* as well as *the average time duration of the overload state* as two new quality of service metrics to be managed in the mobile environment by means of connection tree admission control.

Assuming that each mobile is equally-likely to be found within any radio cell in its connection tree and that time spent by a given mobile within any radio cell is an exponentially distributed random variable, we provide closed form expressions for the maximum number of mobile connections that can be admitted to a connection tree such that a specified quality of the newly defined service metrics is guaranteed. For example, consider a simple virtual connection tree connecting 8 base stations, each with a call capacity of 130 mobile connections. Under these conditions, 860 mobile connections can be admitted to the virtual connection tree (out of a total capacity of 1040 calls) while maintaining an overload probability of 1%. Also, under these conditions, the average time spent in the overload state is 3% of the mean time spent within a radio cell.

Section II of this paper contains a detailed description of the connection tree approach. Implementation is discussed in Section III, and admission control is the subject of the Section IV where we compute the probability of overload and mean time spent in the overload state. Some numerical results are presented in Section V. Finally, in Section VI, we provide a general framework for overall radio system organization and signaling.

II. VIRTUAL CONNECTION TREE ARCHITECTURE

A virtual connection tree is a collection of cellular base stations and wired network switching nodes and links. The root of the tree is a fixed switching node of the wired network and the leaves of the tree are mobile access points or base stations. For each mobile connection, the connection tree provides a set of Virtual Connection Numbers (in each direction), each associated with a path from the root to one leaf. To complete a mobile connection, a fixed virtual connection is created for that connection from the tree's root node back to either a wired network port (if the connection is to a fixed port) or to the root

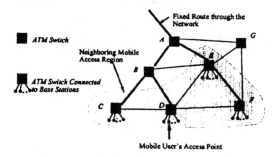

Fig. 1. A virtual connection tree.

of some other connection tree (if the connection is to another mobile user).

Fig. 1 illustrates a virtual connection tree in an ATM network that supports mobile cellular radio connections. We refer to the base station which is currently communicating with a given mobile user as that *mobile user's access point*. Also, we call all base stations which belong to the same virtual connection tree the *neighboring mobile access points*. In Fig. 1, connection tree links are shown as thick lines and other links of the network are shown as narrow lines. Each square box appearing in Fig. 1 is an ATM switch. At the time that a mobile connection is admitted to a connection tree, the call setup procedure is executed in two steps. First, the fixed portion of the virtual connection is established between the root of the tree and the appropriate fixed point of the wired network (the fixed user terminus or the root of a destination tree, as described above). This fixed portion is maintained as long as the mobile stays within the connection tree. Second, within the connection tree, two sets of connection numbers are assigned to that mobile connection (one in each direction) with one member of each set used to define a path from the root to one of the leaves, and the routing tables of the switches within the connection tree are appropriately updated to include the new connection numbers. At any given time, only the two VC connections (one in each direction) between the access point chosen by the mobile and the root of the virtual connection tree are actually in use as a result of the mobile's decision to choose that access point as evidenced by the connection number included in its ATM cell headers. (The virtual connection tree is similar to a point-to-multipoint connection, except that only one path of the tree is in use at any given time.)

When a mobile user already admitted to a virtual connection tree wishes to hand-off to another base station in the same virtual connection tree, it simply begins to transmit ATM cells with the connection number assigned for use between itself and the new base station. Using the pre-established path between the new base station at the root of the tree, that mobile's ATM cells will flow to the root, across the fixed portion of the network, and to their ultimate destination. In this way, the call processor is not involved in the handover. In the reverse direction, the first ATM cell to arrive at the root from a given mobile connection which bears a new connection number is properly interpreted (in hardware) as evidence of a handover. Using its knowledge of the connection number assigned for

that mobile connection from the root of the tree to the new mobile access point, the routing table at the root switch is appropriately updated so that ATM cells flowing from the root to that mobile receive the connection number appropriate to the deliverance of those cells to that new mobile access point. Details of this procedure will be described later.

Note that collision avoidance on the radio link is the responsibility of the Medium Access Protocol (MAP), a lower level of support which provides a service to ATM cells. Several possible MAP's might be envisioned; in particular, the modified polling scheme described in [16] provides high utilization efficiency of the radio channel and would suffice. Lower level procedures such as the MAP are outside the scope of this paper, which is concerned exclusively with admission control and handoff procedures for ATM connections. Nonetheless, in Section V, we shall present a framework which provides for a possible signaling scheme enabling a mobile to decide, on the basis of physical level channel measurements, when a handover is to be executed and to choose the new mobile access point.

Whenever the mobile connection reaches the boundary of a connection tree, it seeks admission to a new connection tree. We refer to this procedure as the *virtual connection tree handoff*. At this point, the network call processor must again become involved. However, since the geographical coverage of a virtual connection tree is large compared to the size of the radio cells which comprise the tree, the rate of connection tree handover is assumed to be acceptably low and manageable by the call processor. To prevent the connection of a mobile situated at the boundary of two connection trees from oscillating between the two, connection trees would overlap in space (i.e., some base stations might belong to two trees) such that, as a mobile approaches the geographical boundaries of its current tree, it hands over to the new tree and appears in the new tree safely within the new tree's interior. Thus it is highly unlikely that the connection will immediately seek to again handover to yet another tree.

III. IMPLEMENTATION

Transport in an ATM network is accomplished by means of the virtual connection field contained within each ATM cell and by means of lookup tables contained within the switching and multiplexing equipment. A route consists of a sequence of links, each of which connects two switching and/or multiplexing units. At call setup time, the lookup tables along the route chosen by a newly established virtual connection are supplied with connection number and link information such that each ATM cell associated with that new virtual connection is carried along the appropriate set of links. Although the route or path of a fixed-point connection remains the same over the entire lifetime of a connection, the actual connection number (contained within the ATM cell header) may change along different links. Thus, a particular virtual connection is defined by a sequence of connection numbers and links.

At each switching or multiplexing unit, the virtual connection number (VCN_{in}) and incoming port ($Port_{in}$) of an arriving ATM cell are used as indexes in the lookup table (or routing table) to uniquely identify the outgoing port ($Port_{out}$) and the virtual connection number associated with the next link (VCN_{out}). Thus, at each switching or multiplexing point, the tuple (VCN_{in}, $PORT_{in}$, VCN_{out}, $PORT_{out}$) uniquely defines a virtual connection. Each lookup table contains such tuples for all the virtual connections that it supports. At call setup time, a route through the network is selected, and a new tuple is added to the lookup table of each intermediate switching point such that an end-to-end virtual connection is established.

Since the access point of a mobile connection changes continuously, new routes must continually be established, without requiring intervention of the computationally intensive call processor. This is accomplished by means of the virtual connection tree. At call setup time, the routes from each access point to the head end are established (i.e., the lookup tables of all switching and multiplexing units are initialized), thereby allowing mobile-initiated ATM cells to flow from any access point to the head end of the tree and, from there, along a fixed route to either their fixed-point termination or to the root of another tree. In the reverse direction (ATM cells flowing from the root to one of the access points), the entry for each virtual connection contained in the lookup table of the switch at the root of the tree consists of a list of tuples (VCN_{in}, $Port_{in}$, VCN_{out}^{i}, $Port_{out}^{i}$), $i = 1, \cdots , N$, where N is the number of access points in the tree. Each i defines the route from the root to one of the access points. For a given mobile connection, the route chosen by the lookup table at the root of the tree corresponds to that leading to the access point from which the most recent ATM cell originating at that mobile has been received. Note that this procedure requires that each mobile connection consists of two mobile half duplex connections, one in each direction, and that the bandwidths of the two half-duplex connections need not be the same. What is mandatory is that the two half-duplex connections involve the same access point and the same root; operation of the system requires two half-duplex virtual connection trees, one to carry information in each direction, both originating from the same root and both covering the same set of access points.

The process of locating the current access point of a mobile connection and selecting the appropriate route for cells flowing from the root of the tree to that access point is performed by a special piece of real-time equipment which we call the VCN monitor/translator. This equipment is needed only within the switch situated at the root of a connection tree. Once the current access point has been identified (i.e., once that one particular route out of the N established at the call setup time which leads to the current access point has been selected), the cells flow along that route by means of conventional lookup tables contained in the intermediate switches. While roaming within the area covered by a connection tree, all ATM cells originating from (destined to) a mobile user's terminal flow through the same outgoing (incoming) root switch port located at the root of the connection tree. Each pair of root ports has a VCN monitor/translator as illustrated in Fig. 2, which shows the root switch and the special VCN monitor/translator equipment needed at the root ports. An ATM cell arriving from

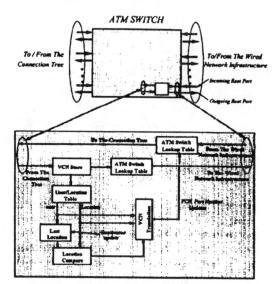

Fig. 2.   An ATM switch supporting mobile connections.

the connection tree is always transferred to the outgoing root port where its VCN is translated to that needed to transport the cell along its fixed route. The stored VCN of an ATM cell arriving from the connection tree is also used by the *User/Location* table to identify the mobile user and its current location or base station. This table, which is updated whenever a new mobile connection enters the connection tree (and also whenever an existing mobile connection exits the connection tree) associates with every VCN a unique mobile user and location (or base station). After the mobile user associated with a newly arriving cell has been identified, its last location is read from the *Last Location* table. (To each mobile user in the virtual connection tree, this table associates a base station, or location, from which the mobile sent its last ATM cell; as shown, this last location table is continually updated, as needed, by current user location data.) Once the current and last location of the mobile user have been identified, they are compared to see if there has been a handover, in which case the mobile user and location information is used to find the appropriate VCN from the switch port to the connection tree. The Port ID and the VCN corresponding to the new location are then stored (or enabled) in the ATM switch lookup table at the incoming root port to appropriately route ATM cells received from the fixed route in the wired network to the current location of the mobile. No updating to the ATM switch lookup table is performed unless an actual handoff has taken place.

Mobile connection rerouting in a virtual connection tree is illustrated in Fig. 3. Here, the ATM switch at the root of the connection tree is represented by A. Ports 1 and 2 of A are connection tree ports, and root ports 3 (incoming root port) and 4 (outgoing root port) are equipped with a VCN monitor/translator. Shown in the diagram are the VCN's associated with a single mobile connection which may terminate in either mobile access points C or D. Suppose that the mobile connection is initially established in base station C.

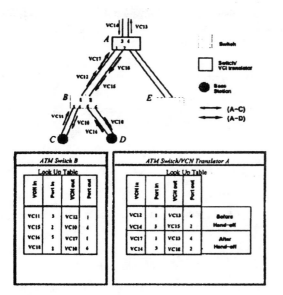

Fig. 3. An example of mobile connection rerouting.

Then, its ATM cells arrive at port 3 of switch B bearing $VC11$, and are switched to port 1 where the connection number is translated to $VC12$. These cells next arrive at port 1 of root switch A where the VCN monitor/translator concludes that the mobile is located with the area served by base station C. The ATM cells are then switched to port 4 and their connection number is translated to $VC13$. In the reverse direction (from the root to the mobile), cells arriving at port 3 of the root switch A bear connection number $VC14$, and are switched to port 2 with their connection number translated to $VC15$ such that, at switch B, they arrive at port 2, are switched to port 4, and arrive at base station C bearing connection number $VC10$. Upon handing off to base station D, the mobile begins to send ATM cells bearing connection number $VC16$. These appear at port 5 of switch B, their connection number is translated to $VC17$, and they exit on port 1. Upon arriving at root switch A, the VCN monitor/translator concludes that a handoff to base station D has occurred; the ATM cells are switched to port 4 where their connection number is translated to $VC13$ such that they exit on port 4 and follow the same fixed path as before the handoff, and the ATM switch lookup table is modified such that subsequent ATM cells arriving at port 3 bearing connection number $VC14$ are switched to port 2 and their connection number translated to $VC18$. At switch B, ATM cells arriving at port 2 bearing connection number $VC18$ are switched to port 6 and their connection number is translated to $VC10$, thereby completing the connection to the mobile through base station D with ATM cells bearing the same connection number as was borne prior to the handoff.

IV. ADMISSION CONTROL

For a mobile connection, the call admission function is invoked to manage two sets of network resources. First, the call must be admitted to a fixed portion of its route (from the root of virtual connection tree to the fixed point or to the root of the connection tree corresponding to the other end of the connection). This can be done by any of several means (see [13]–[15], [17], [18] for example), in such a way that the quality of service enjoyed by other connections sharing any common link of the fixed route is not unacceptably degraded; if this cannot be done, the request for connection must be rejected. Second, the mobile connection must be admitted to the appropriate virtual connection tree, each of which we view as a single collective resource of the mobile network. Admission control of mobile connections to a virtual connection tree is mandatory since, once admitted, mobile users can freely hand-off to any base station within the virtual connection tree, and, as a result, overload or congestion may occur at any given base station if too large a number of mobile users simultaneously seek access through the same limited-capacity base station (we would expect that the capacity-constrained cellular channel is usually the bottleneck, rather than the bandwidth-abundant wired infrastructure links). Note that, as mentioned in the Introduction, the current study precludes the use of call dropping as an overload avoiding strategy; call dropping is another manageable quality-of-service metric which will be treated in a subsequent paper. Since base station overload may cause ATM cell loss and delay, the purpose of connection tree admission control is to limit the number of connections concurrently established through the tree such that adequate ATM cell-level Quality-of-Service objectives are met.

In the following, we introduce and study two new metrics namely the base station overload probability and the expected time spent in overload, the service qualities of which must be managed by connection tree admission control such that other cell-level QOS objectives can be achieved with a prescribed confidence level.

A. Our Model

We consider a connection tree for which the cellular radio links are the major bottlenecks. Assuming that we admit at most N mobile connections to a virtual connection tree and that each of them is equally likely to be in communication with any particular test base station within the connection tree, then the probability that there are i connections established with the test base station, P_i, is simply given by the binomial distribution,

$$P_i = \binom{N}{i}\left(\frac{1}{B}\right)^i\left(\frac{B-1}{B}\right)^{N-i}$$
$$= \binom{N}{i}\left(\frac{1}{B-1}\right)^i\left(\frac{B-1}{B}\right)^N \quad (1)$$

where B is the number of base stations in the connection tree and $1/B$ is the probability that a given mobile is communicating with the test base station.

If a base station can support up to m connections without violating the ATM cell-level QOS criteria (whatever they may be for the type of mobile service being supported), then its overload probability $P_{O,m}$ is given by

$$P_{O,m} = \sum_{i=m+1}^{N} P_i = \left(\frac{B-1}{B}\right)^N \sum_{i=m+1}^{N} \binom{N}{i}\left(\frac{1}{B-1}\right)^i. \quad (2)$$

Although the assumption that any user is equally likely to be found within any radio cell of its connection tree may seem to be somewhat artificial, it may, nonetheless, be at least partially rationalized as a result of the user's mobility, the user's freedom to choose any cell site based on radio channel parameters, the user's ability to communicate with any base station (not necessarily the geographically closest) offering adequate channel quality, and the uncertainty and randomness of the multipath and shadow fading environments. Models based on refinements to this assumptions are readily envisioned, but their study is beyond the scope of this present paper.

We further assume that, when a handoff occurs, the new cell site is equally-likely to be any of the remaining $B-1$ cell sites within the connection tree, and that when a mobile hands-off from its current base station, the number of base stations that it visits (or hand-offs to) prior to returning to that then-current base station is a geometrically distributed random variable:

$$P(\text{number of visited base stations} = k)$$
$$= p(1-p)^{k-1}, \qquad k = 1, 2, \cdots \quad (3)$$

where $p = 1/(B-1)$. Finally, we assume that, upon newly entering a given cell site, the time spent by a mobile user in communication with that cell site's base station is an exponentially distributed random variable with mean value T_{in} (this assumption is particularly appropriate in a microcell/picocell environment, see [19]); note that T_{in} is simply the mean time between handoff events for any given mobile. These assumptions imply that, after handing out of a given cell site, the time spent by a mobile before returning to that particular cell site is also exponentially distributed with mean value $T_{out} = (1/p)T_{in} = (B-1)T_{in}$; we will now use these observations to find an expression for the average time that any particular base station spends in overload.

From the above, the number of mobile connections, i, communicating to any given base station can be modeled by a birth-death process with birth rate $\lambda_i = (N-i)/T_{out}$, and the death rate $\mu_i = i/T_{in}$ ($N \geq i \geq 0$), where N is the maximum number of connections admitted to a virtual connection tree. To calculate the expected base station overload period θ, we can now use the approach outlined in [20]. Let γ_i be the mean first passage time from state i to the state $i-1$, that is, the expected time from when a base station leaves state i (with i current mobile connections) until it first arrives in state $i-1$ (with $i-1$ current mobile connections); note that a base station may leave state i by virtue of having an additional mobile handed in, and may experience several other hand-ins and hand-outs before arriving in state $i-1$. For a finite state birth-death process,

$$\gamma_i = (1 + \lambda_i \gamma_{i+1})/\mu_i, \qquad 1 \leq i < N \quad (4)$$
$$\gamma_N = 1/\mu_N. \quad (5)$$

and since the mean overload period θ is simply the mean first passage time from state $m+1$ to m, we can find it recursively from (4) and (5) above. The result is

$$\theta = \frac{1}{(m+1)\mu} + \sum_{i=m+2}^{N} \frac{1}{i\,\mu} \prod_{k=m+1}^{i-1} \frac{(N-k)\,\lambda}{k\,\mu} \quad (6)$$

where $\lambda = 1/T_{out}$ and $\mu = 1/T_{in}$. Finally, substituting $1/T_{in}$ for μ and $1/(B-1)$ for λ/μ, we obtain

$$\theta = T_{in}\left[\frac{1}{m+1} + \sum_{i=m+2}^{N} \frac{1}{i}\left(\frac{1}{B-1}\right)^{i-m-1} \prod_{k=m+1}^{i-1} \frac{N-k}{k}\right] \quad (7)$$

As shown in Appendix A, we can further relate the expected overload period to the overload probability:

$$\theta = T_{in}\left(\frac{B-1}{N-m} \cdot \frac{P_{O,m}}{P_{in}}\right). \quad (8)$$

Equation (8) is useful when seeking to limit the number of calls admitted to the connection tree such that both an overload probability QOS metric and a mean time in overload QOS metric are simultaneously met.

V. DISCUSSION AND NUMERICAL RESULTS

In this section, we apply the model and analysis of Section IV to numerically find the new quality-of-service metrics (overload probability and expected overload period) for selected values of virtual connection tree parameters (total number of admitted calls, number of connections supported by each base station, and number of base stations in the connection tree). Shown in Fig. 4 is the overload probability ($P_{o,m}$) as a function of the number of connections (N) admitted to a connection tree with 4, 8, or 16 base stations (B), assuming that each base station has adequate capacity to handle $m = 50$ connections. Also, plotted in Fig. 4 is an approximation for the number of connections which can be admitted such that a given overload probability is maintained, as described in Appendix B. We note that the approximation is accurate and may safely be used by admission controller, as opposed to "inverting" (2) to find N as a function of $P_{o,m}$ or storing the exact curves of Fig. 4 in graphical form.

From the curves of Fig. 4, we see, for example, that for a system in which each base station can support 50 connections, a total of 530 connections can be admitted to a tree containing 16 base stations (such a tree would have a total capacity of $16 \times 50 = 800$ connections) while maintaining an overload probability of 1×10^{-3}.

The other new quality-of-service metric is the expected overload period (θ) which is plotted in Fig. 5 normalized by the mean time spent by a mobile in any cell site T_{in}, as a function of N for connection trees of size 4, 8, and 16 base stations, each capable of supporting 50 connections. We note, for example, that 600 connections can be admitted to a tree containing 16 base stations, each capable of supporting 50 connections, such that the average time spent in overload is 6% of the mean-time-to handoff for any given mobile.

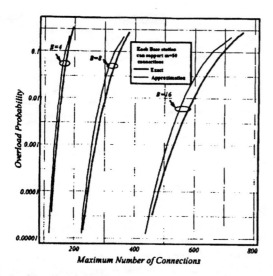

Fig. 4. Connection admissibility based upon guaranteed overload probability.

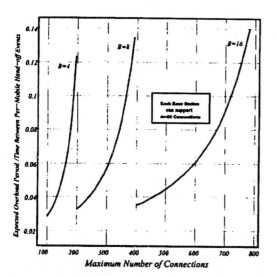

Fig. 5. Connection admissibility based on guaranteed mean overload period.

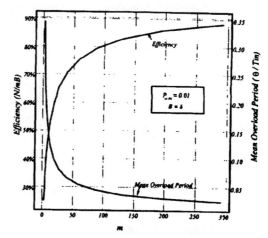

Fig. 6. Virtual Connection Tree utilization efficiency and mean overload period for trees containing eight base stations and overload probability equal to 1%.

One important measure of performance is the utilization efficiency of virtual connection tree resources when a certain quality of service (such as overload probability) is guaranteed by the call admission controller. Here, we define utilization efficiency ρ, as the number of calls, N, which may be admitted to the connection tree subject to some quality of service guarantee, normalized by the "raw" capacity of a tree containing B base stations, each capable of handling m connections:

$$\rho = \frac{N}{Bm} \qquad (9)$$

This is plotted in Fig. 6 as a function of m for a connection tree containing $B = 8$ base stations and a guaranteed overload probability of 1%. Also, plotted in Fig. 6 is the expected overload period (normalized by the mean time between handoff events for any mobile) for the same number of tree

base stations and guaranteed service quality. We note that as the capacity per base station increases, the connection tree utilization efficiency improves and the mean overload period diminishes,[2] implying that for large m, the instantaneous connection load is approximately balanced among the base stations. For a fixed wireless bandwidth, these results suggest that utilization efficiency diminishes as the bandwidth required for each connection increases.

Shown in Fig. 7 is the utilization efficiency as a function of overload probability for connection trees containing 4, 8, and 16 base stations. We note that, for a given overload probability, the utilization efficiency of a virtual connection tree decreases as the number of its base stations increases, suggesting a tradeoff between the size of a connection tree (larger is more desirable) and its utilization efficiency (higher is more desirable).

A. Comparison to a Dynamic Model

In Appendix C, we find the steady state probability (P_i^*) of having i connections established with any base station in a connection tree for a dynamic homogeneous system. This model takes new call arrivals, call completions, and call handoff into account. We note that, under heavy traffic conditions

$$\lim_{(\lambda/\mu)\to\infty} P_i^* = \lim_{(\lambda/\mu)\to\infty} (\lambda/\mu)^i/i! \frac{\sum_{k=0}^{N-i}[(B-1)\lambda/\mu]^k/k!}{\sum_{k=0}^{N}(B\lambda/m\mu)^k/k!}$$

$$= \frac{(B-1)^{N-i}/[i!(N-i)!](\lambda/\mu)^N}{(B\lambda/\mu)^N/N!}$$

$$= \binom{N}{i}\left(\frac{1}{B-1}\right)^i\left(\frac{B-1}{B}\right)^N = P_i. \qquad (10)$$

Equation (10) shows that, as the load on the system increases, the dynamic model produces the same results as predicted by the simple model of Section IV-A.

---

[2] This is simply the effect of trunking efficiency.

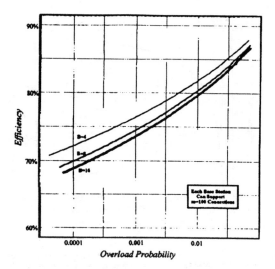

Fig. 7. Virtual Connection Tree utilization efficiency for given overload probability for different connection tree sizes.

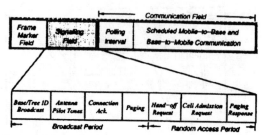

Fig. 8. Overall framework for operation of the Virtual Connection Tree.

VI. SYSTEM FRAMEWORK

A possible framework for operation of the virtual connection tree concept appears in Fig. 8, which shows a timing diagram for the various signals involved. Each transmission frame is divided into three sections: the frame marker field, the signaling field, and the communication field. All transmission frames are of equal length, and their boundaries are delimited by the frame marker fields. Time-duplexed transmission is used, i.e., the same channel is time shared for base-to-mobile and mobile-to-base communications. The modified polling media access scheme described in [16] is used within the communication field, whereby each base station regularly polls each mobile for which it is currently responsible, to obtain from each information on instantaneous communication needs. Replies to the polling also provide information needed to adequately equalize the channel to each mobile, thereby maintaining low link outage. The base station then schedules transmission time for mobile-to-base and base-to-mobile communication. Permission to transmit is sequentially conferred to each mobile by means of a permission token. In [16], this scheme was shown to produce high radio LAN access utilization efficiency (> 80%) over a wide range of operating conditions. The communication field is used concurrently by all radio cells in the connection tree, with the various base stations managing the communication flow for their mobiles. The frame marker and signaling fields are used sequentially in sequential frames by the radio cells in the connection tree. The signaling field of the transmission frame is used primarily to admit a given mobile to the polling sequence of a given base station. The frame marker field is a unique word periodically (and sequentially) broadcast from the base stations and is used by the mobiles to establish a basic time reference for start-of-frame. All mobiles which are in either an active state of communication or in a standby state available to accept calls maintain continuous frame marker synchronization. Upon powering up, a mobile will lock onto the frame marker

broadcast from one of the base stations, thereby establishing its basic timing reference.

The signaling field is subdivided into a broadcast period (base-to-mobile) and a random access period (mobile-to-base), neither of which contain any communication signals. The first segment of the broadcast field is used to uniquely identify the cell site associated with that frame, as indicated by the base station-ID, and the connection tree to which that base station belongs. This is followed by pilot tones transmitted by the various antenna elements of that base station's array (we assume the use of an adaptive array to equalize the delay distortion introduced by the multipath propagation environment; an equivalent set of pilot signals would be transmitted during this segment if a transversal equalizer were used). These pilot signals broadcast in successive frames (with only one base station sending its pilots in each frame) are processed by each mobile in the connection tree to determine those base stations to which a satisfactory channel can be established. By continuously monitoring these pilot signals, each mobile can decide when it wishes to initiate a handoff (when the channel to its current base station becomes unusable as a result of user mobility and/or changing propagation environment), and to which base station it wishes to handoff (the one to which the strongest channel can be established, any one chosen randomly from the list of those to which a satisfactory channel can be established, etc.).

Moving now to the Random Access period of the signaling field (we shall return later to the broadcast period), a mobile can request to join a given base station's polling sequence by signaling its request during the handoff request segment of the frame associated with that base station (remember that the frame marker and signaling fields of each frame is associated with one and only one base station). Since the handoff request field is randomly accessed (Aloha, Aloha with capture, etc.) successful receipt is acknowledged by the base station during the connection acknowledgment of some later frame's signaling field broadcast period.

A mobile can also request the establishment of a new virtual connection tree (a request which must be processed by the connection tree's admission controller) by randomly accessing the Call Admission Request segment of the desired base station's signaling field; successful receipt of request and decision to admit are in the connection acknowledgment field of some later frame. Finally, a call may be placed to a given user by means of the paging segment of the signaling field, with the called mobile's ID being successively broadcast by all base stations in the connection tree. When the mobile hears its page, it replies with a paging response in the signaling field of a frame associated with a base station to which a satisfactory channel can be established. Since the paging response is randomly accessed, paging continues until a paging response is produced or a time-out interval elapses (the mobile may not be located within that connection tree, or the mobile may not be in standby mode).

VII. CONCLUSION

We see that the virtual connection tree concept provides a useful means for allowing mobile controlled handoff in a packet (ATM) access microcell/picocell environment. Use of this approach permits the enormous capacity advantages of microcell/picocell to be enjoyed (relative to macrocells), without requiring the intervention/involvement of the call controller each time a handoff event occurs. In essence, the capacity gain of a microcell/picocell system is enjoyed, along with the infrequency of handoff initiated call controller involvement expected from a macrocellular system. The approach involves some risk of temporarily overloading a given cell site, and appropriate quality-of-service criteria must be maintained. Two possible quality-of-service metrics which can readily be managed by connection tree admission control are the probability of cell overload and the mean time spent in overload. For reasonable connection tree parameters, we have shown that, in accordance with these criteria, satisfactory service quality can be maintained at very slight cost as measured by overall utilization efficiency, that is, the call controller must limit the number of allowable connections admitted to the tree to a value slightly lower than inherent capacity of the tree.

Future work on the virtual connection tree concept will address issues such as nonuniform probability of finding any mobile in any connection tree cell site, choosing handoff cell site on the basis of both channel quality and current traffic load in acceptable new cell sites, and use of call dropping to reduce overload occurrence and duration. If call dropping is involved, it becomes yet another quality-of-service metric which must be managed. Computation of call dropping probability and management of call dropping probability by means of admission control represent interesting and challenging extensions of this work.

APPENDIX A

In this Appendix, we relate the expected overload period to the overload probability. Starting with (7),

$$\theta = T_{in}\left(\frac{1}{m+1} + \sum_{i=m+2}^{N} \frac{1}{i}\left(\frac{1}{B-1}\right)^{i-m-1} \prod_{k=m+1}^{i-1} \frac{N-k}{k} \right) \tag{A.1}$$

we expand the product term to yield

$$\prod_{k=m+1}^{i-1} \frac{N-k}{k}$$

$$= \frac{[N-(m+1)][N-(m+2)]\cdots[N-(i-1)]}{(m+1)(m+2)\cdots(i-1)} \tag{A.2}$$

$$= \frac{[N-(m+1)]\cdots[N-(i-1)][N-i]\cdots 1}{1\cdots m(m+1)(m+2)(m+3)\cdots(i-1)}\frac{m!}{(N-i)!} \tag{A.3}$$

$$= \frac{(N-(m+1))!m!}{(i-1)!(N-i)!} = \frac{N!/(i!(N-i)!)}{N!/(N-m)!m!)}\frac{i}{N-m} \tag{A.4}$$

$$= \frac{i\binom{N}{i}}{(N-m)\binom{N}{m}}. \tag{A.5}$$

Substituting (A.5) into (7), we obtain

$$\theta = T_{in}\left(\frac{1}{m+1} + \sum_{i=m+2}^{N} \frac{1}{i}\left(\frac{1}{B-1}\right)^{i-m-1} \frac{i\binom{N}{i}}{(N-m)\binom{N}{m}} \right) \tag{A.6}$$

$$\Rightarrow \theta = T_{in}\left(\frac{1}{m+1} + \frac{(B-1)^{m+1}}{(N-m)\binom{N}{m}}\sum_{i=m+2}^{N}\binom{N}{i}\left(\frac{1}{B-1}\right)^{i} \right), \tag{A.7}$$

or, from (2),

$$\theta = T_{in}\left(\frac{1}{m+1} + \frac{(B-1)^{m+1}}{(N-m)\binom{N}{m}}\left(\frac{B}{B-1}\right)^{N} P_{O,m+1} \right) \tag{A.8}$$

$$= T_{in}\left(\frac{1}{m+1} + \frac{B-1}{N-m}\cdot\frac{P_{O,m+1}}{P_m} \right) \tag{A.9}$$

$$= T_{in}\left(\frac{1}{m+1} + \frac{B-1}{N-m}\cdot\frac{P_{O,m}-P_{m+1}}{P_m} \right) \tag{A.10}$$

Finally, again applying Equation (2), we obtain the following expression for the mean time in overload:

$$\theta = T_{in}\left(\frac{B-1}{N-m}\cdot\frac{P_{O,m}}{P_m} \right). \tag{A.11}$$

APPENDIX B

In this Appendix, we obtain an approximate expression for the number of calls admissible to a connection tree subject to prescribed probability of overload. We note from (2) that $P_{O,m}$ is the tail of a binomial distribution, which we approximate as Gaussian [21] of appropriate mean and variance:

$$P_{O,m} \simeq 1 - G\left(\frac{mB-N}{\sqrt{N(B-1)}} \right) \simeq \frac{1}{\sqrt{4\pi}}e^{\frac{-B(m-N/B)^2}{2N(1-1/B)}} \tag{B.1}$$

where

$$G(x) = \int_{-\infty}^{x}\frac{1}{\sqrt{2\pi}}e^{-t^2/2}. \tag{B.2}$$

Solving for N, in terms of $P_{o.m}$, we obtain

$$N \simeq mB - \ln(\sqrt{4\pi}P_{O,m})(B-1) - \frac{}{}$$
$$\sqrt{\left(\ln(\sqrt{4\pi}P_{O,m})(B-1)\right)^2 - 2mB\ln(\sqrt{4\pi}P_{O,m})(B-1)}$$

(B.3)

Finally, we can approximate the utilization efficiency as

$$\rho = N/mB \simeq 1 - \frac{\ln(\sqrt{4\pi}P_{O,m})(B-1)}{mB} - \frac{1}{mB}$$
$$\cdot \sqrt{\left(\ln(\sqrt{4\pi}P_{O,m})(B-1)\right)^2 - 2mB\ln(\sqrt{4\pi}P_{O,m})(B-1)}$$

(B.4)

APPENDIX C

In this Appendix, we consider a dynamic model which incorporates arrival, handoff, and departure of calls in a connection tree which is subject to call admission control. Let us consider a homogeneous system in which the new call arrivals are Poisson with rate λ per radio cell, the call duration is exponentially distributed with mean $1/\mu$, and the time a call spends with any base station before handing-off to another is exponentially distributed. We assume that a call visits any adjacent cell with equal probability after a handoff event.[3] In accordance with the model of Section IV-A, a base station can support up to m connections, and if the number of calls visiting a base station is greater than m, then that base station is considered to be in an overload state. This model is similar to an open queueing network of M/M/∞ queues in which the steady state distribution has a known product form

$$\pi(\underline{n}) = \pi(n_1, n_2, \cdots, n_B) = \pi(0) \prod_{i=1}^{B} \pi_i(n_i), \quad \text{(C.1)}$$

where $\pi(0)$ is the normalization constant, $\pi_i(n_i) = (\lambda/\mu)^{n_i}/n_i!$ and n_i denotes the number of mobile connections within base station i. Now, if we perform call admission control and limit the number of calls admitted to a virtual connection tree with B base stations to a value not greater than N, then the state-space of the system is a truncation of the state-space of the above open queueing network and has an equilibrium distribution $\pi_A(\underline{n})$ of the form [22]

$$\pi_A(\underline{n}) = \frac{\pi(\underline{n})}{\sum_{\underline{k} \in A} \pi(\underline{k})}, \quad \underline{n} \in A, \quad \text{(C.2)}$$

where A is the truncated state space containing all $(n_1, n_2, \cdots, n_B)$ such that $\sum_{i=1}^{B} n_i \leq N$ for $i = 1, 2, \cdots, B$, and $\pi(\underline{n})$ is given by (C.1).

We define A_k to be a subspace of A containing all $(n_1, n_2, \cdots, n_B)$ such that $\sum_{i=1}^{B} n_i = k$ with $n_i \leq k$ for all i. Moreover, let us define $A_{k,i}$ to be a subspace of the state space A_k containing all $(n_1, n_2, \cdots, n_B)$ such that $n_1 = i$. Since we consider a homogenous model, all base stations have

[3]This model can be easily extended to incorporate different rates in a nonhomogeneous system. In addition, we assume that the handoff process out of a connection tree is statistically identical to the process of handoffs into a connection tree.

the same state probability distribution. Thus, from (C.2), if we define P_i^* as the probability of having i mobiles in any cell, then

$$P_i^* = \frac{[(\lambda/\mu)^i/i!] \sum_{k=0}^{N-i} \sum_{\underline{n} \in A_{k,i}} (\lambda/\mu)^{n_2 + \cdots + n_B}/(n_2! \cdots n_B!)}{\sum_{k=0}^{N} \sum_{\underline{n} \in A_k} (\lambda/\mu)^{n_1 + n_2 + \cdots + n_B}/(n_1! n_2! \cdots n_B!)}$$

(C.3)

$$= \frac{[(\lambda/\mu)^i/i!] \sum_{k=0}^{N-i} (\lambda/\mu)^k/k! \sum_{\underline{n} \in A_{k,i}} k!/(n_2! \cdots n_B!)}{\sum_{k=0}^{N} (\lambda/\mu)^k/k! \sum_{\underline{n} \in A_k} k!/(n_1! n_2! \cdots n_B!)}$$

(C.4)

Since $(x_1 + \cdots + x_t)^n$ is equal to the sum of $[n!/(n_1! \cdots n_t!)]x_1^{n_1} \cdots x_t^{n_t}$ for all values of n_i such that $\sum_{i=1}^{t} n_i = n$ where $0 \leq n_i \leq n$, we have the following simplification for the probability of having i mobiles in any given cell:

$$P_i^* = [(\lambda/\mu)^i/i!] \frac{\sum_{k=0}^{N-i} [(B-1)(\lambda/\mu)]^k/k!}{\sum_{k=0}^{N} (B\lambda/\mu)^k/k!}$$

(C.5)

REFERENCES

[1] J.-Y. Le Boudec, "The asynchronous transfer mode: A tutorial," *Comput. Networks and ISDN Syst.*, vol. 24, 1992.
[2] M. De Prycker, "ATM switching on demand," *IEEE Network Mag.*, vol. 6, no. 2, Mar. 1992.
[3] S. Minzer, "BISDN and ATM," *IEEE Commun. Mag.*, Sept. 1989.
[4] *Int. J. Digital and Cabled Syst.*, Special Issue on Asynchronous Transfer Mode, vol. 1, no. 4, 1988.
[5] D. Cox, "Personal communications—A view point," *IEEE Commun. Mag.*, Nov. 1990.
[6] ——, "Wireless network access for personal communications," *IEEE Commun. Mag.*, Dec. 1992.
[7] ——, "A radio system proposal for widespread low-power tetherless communications," *IEEE Trans. Commun.*, vol. 39, no. 2 Feb. 1991.
[8] D. Goodman, "Cellular packet communications," *IEEE Trans. Commun.*, vol. 38, no. 8, Aug. 1990.
[9] ——, "Trends in cellular and cordless communications," *IEEE Commun. Mag.*, Feb. 1991.
[10] I. Ross, "Wireless network directions," *IEEE Commun. Mag.*, June 1991.
[11] A. E. Eckberg, "B-ISDN/ATM traffic and congestion control," *IEEE Network Mag.*, Sept. 1992.
[12] J. Filipiak, "M-Architecture: A structural model of traffic management and control in broadband ISDNs," *IEEE Commun. Mag.*, May 1989.
[13] G. Gallasi, G. Rigolio, and L. Verri, "Resource management and dimensioning in ATM networks," *IEEE Network Mag.*, May 1990.
[14] D. Hong, and T. Suda, "Congestion control and prevention in ATM networks," *IEEE Network Mag.*, July 1991.
[15] J. Y. Hui, "Resource allocation for broadband networks," *IEEE J. Select. Areas Commun.*, vol. 6, no. 9, Dec. 1988.
[16] Z. Zhang and A. Acampora, "Performance of a modified polling strategy for broadband wireless LANs in a harsh fading environment," in *Proc. GLOBECOM'91*.
[17] R. Guerin, H. Ahmadi, and M. Naghshineh, "Equivalent capacity and its applications to bandwidth allocation in high-speed networks," *IEEE J. Select. Areas Commun.*, Sept. 1991.
[18] K. Sohraby, "On the theory of ON-OFF sources with applications in high-speed networks," in *Proc. INFOCOM '93*.
[19] R. Guerin, "Channel occupancy time distribution in a cellular radio system," *IEEE Trans. Veh. Technol.*, vol. VT-36, no. 3, Aug. 1987.
[20] D. Heyman and M. Sobel, *Stochastic Models in Operations Research*, Vol. I. New York: McGraw-Hill, 1982.
[21] A. Papoulis, *Probability, Random Variables, and Stochastic Processes*. New York: McGraw-Hill, 1991.
[22] F. P. Kelly, *Reversibility and Stochastic Networks*. New York: Wiley, 1979.

Anthony S. Acampora (S'68–M'75–SM'86–F'88) received the Ph.D. degree in electrical engineering from the Polytechnic Institute of Brooklyn.

He is a Professor Electrical Engineering at Columbia University and Director of the Center for Telecommunications Research, a national engineering research center. He joined the faculty at Columbia in 1988 following a 20-year career at AT&T Bell Laboratories, most of which was spent in basic research where his interests included radio and satellite communications, local and metropolitan area networks, packet switching, wireless access systems, and lightwave networks. His most recent position at Bell Labs was Director of the Transmission Technology Laboratory where he was responsible for a wide range of projects, including broadband networks, image communications, and digital signal processing. At Columbia, he is involved in research and education programs concerning broadband networks, wireless access networks, network management, optical networks, and multimedia applications. Many of these projects enjoy active industrial participation and involve cross-disciplinary research teams to develop new system approaches, analytical methodologies, VLSI circuitry, lightwave devices, and telecommunications software. He is a former member of the IEEE Communications Society Board of Governors. He has published over 140 papers, holds 24 patents, and has authored a recently completed textbook entitled *An Introduction to Broadband Networks: Mans, ATM, B-ISDN, Self-Routing Switches, Optical Networks, and Network Control for Voice, Data, Image, and HDTV Telecommunications.* He sits on numerous telecommunications advisory committees and frequently serves as a consultant to government and industry.

Mahmoud Naghshineh (S'87) received the Vordiplom degree in electrical engineering from RWTH Aachen, Germany, in 1985, and the B.S. (computer engineering) and M.S. (electrical engineering) degrees from Polytechnic University in 1988 and 1991, respectively.

Currently, he is a doctoral candidate at Columbia University's Department of Electrical Engineering in New York City. He joined IBM in 1988. Currently, he is working in the communication networks department of the IBM Thomas J. Watson Research Center, Hawthorne, NY. In the past, he has worked on the design, analysis, and control of high-speed packet switched networks, as well as network design tools. Currently, he is with the wireless networks architecture and analysis group. His research interests are in the area of design of network protocols for wireless/mobile computing and communications, media access protocols for PCN, design and control of high-speed microcellular networks, as well as mobile ATM.